Salomon Fritz Forkel

2020

D1657655

HARDPRESS.NET

ISBN: 9781313489423

Published by:
HardPress Publishing
8345 NW 66TH ST #2561
MIAMI FL 33166-2626

Email: info@hardpress.net
Web: http://www.hardpress.net

CORNELL
UNIVERSITY
LIBRARY

Cornell University Library
PK 231.M13

Vedic grammar /

3 1924 023 050 325

WIE DU KANNST SO WOLLE 1872

GRUNDRISS DER INDO-ARISCHEN PHILOLOGIE UND ALTERTUMSKUNDE
(ENCYCLOPEDIA OF INDO-ARYAN RESEARCH)
BEGRÜNDET VON G. BÜHLER, FORTGESETZT VON F. KIELHORN,
HERAUSGEGEBEN VON H. LÜDERS UND J. WACKERNAGEL.
I. BAND, 4. HEFT.

VEDIC GRAMMAR

BY

A. A. MACDONELL.

STRASSBURG
VERLAG VON KARL J. TRÜBNER
1910.

The printing was commenced in May, 1907, and afterwards delayed by the death of the editor Prof. Kielhorn.

GRUNDRISS DER INDO-ARISCHEN PHILOLOGIE UND ALTERTUMSKUNDE
(ENCYCLOPEDIA OF INDO-ARYAN RESEARCH)
BEGRÜNDET VON G. BÜHLER, FORTGESETZT VON F. KIELHORN.
I. BAND, 4. HEFT.

VEDIC GRAMMAR

BY
A. A. MACDONELL.

INTRODUCTION.

1. General Scope of this Work.—Vedic grammar has never till now been treated separately and as a whole. Both in India and in the West the subject has hitherto been handled only in connexion with Classical Sanskrit. Hundreds of Pāṇini's Sūtras deal with the language of the Vedas; but the account they give of it is anything but comprehensive. In the West, BENFEY was the first, more than half a century ago (1852), to combine a description of the linguistic peculiarities of the Vedas with an account of the traditional matter of Pāṇini; but as Vedic studies were at that time still in their infancy, only the Sāmaveda[1] and about one-fourth of the Ṛgveda[2] having as yet been published, the Vedic material utilized in his large grammar[3] was necessarily very limited in extent. In WHITNEY's work[4] the language of the Vedas, which is much more fully represented, is treated in its historical connexion with Classical Sanskrit. Partly for this reason, his work does not supply a definite account of the grammar of the Saṃhitās as compared with that of the later phases of the language; thus what is peculiar to the Brāhmaṇas or to a particular Saṃhitā is often not apparent. Professor WACKERNAGEL's grammar[5], which when finished will present the ancient language of India more completely than any other work on the subject, deals with the combined Vedic and post-Vedic material from the point of view of Comparative Philology. Different sections or individual points of Vedic grammar have been the subject of separately published treatises or of special articles scattered in various Oriental and philological journals or other works of a miscellaneous character. It is advisable that all this as well as additional material[6] should now be brought together so as to afford a general survey of the subject.

In view of the prominent position occupied by the Indo-Aryan branch in Comparative Philology and of the fact that the language of the Vedas

1 Edited by BENFEY, with German translation and glossary, Leipzig 1848.

2 Vol. I edited by MAX MÜLLER, London 1849, vol. VI 1875; 2nd ed. London 1890—92; edited by AUFRECHT, Berlin 1861 and 1863 (vols. VI and VII of Indische Studien), 2nd ed. Bonn 1877.

3 Vollständige Grammatik der Sanskritsprache, Leipzig 1852.

4 A Sanskrit Grammar, Leipzig 1879; 3rd ed. 1896.

5 Altindische Grammatik von JACOB WACKERNAGEL, I. Lautlehre, Göttingen 1896; II, 1. Einleitung zur Wortlehre. Nominalkomposition, 1905. (Cp. BARTHOLOMAE, Beiträge zur altindischen Grammatik, ZDMG. 50, 674—735).

6 Such additional material is supplied in this work from collections made for me by my pupils Prof. H. C. NORMAN (Benares) from the Vājasaneyi Saṃhitā, and Mr. A. B. KEITH from the Taittirīya Saṃhitā, the Mantras in the Aitareya Āraṇyaka, and the Khilas of the Ṛgveda.

represents the foundation of the subsequent strata, it seems important for the sake of clearness and definiteness that the earliest phase should be treated as a whole independently of later developments. The present work will therefore deal with the grammar of only the Mantra portions of the Saṃhitās; that is to say, it will embrace the whole of the Ṛgveda, the Atharvaveda[1], the Sāmaveda[2], and the Vājasaneyi Saṃhitā[3], but will exclude those portions of the Taittirīya Saṃhitā[4], the Maitrāyaṇī Saṃhitā[5] and the Kāṭhaka[6] which have the character of Brāhmaṇas[7]. Reference will also be made to Mantra material not found in the canonical texts of the Saṃhitās, that is, to the Khilas[8] of the Ṛgveda and the occasional Mantras of this type occurring in the Brāhmaṇas[9] and Sūtras. As the linguistic material of the Ṛgveda is more ancient, extensive and authentic than that of the other Saṃhitās, all of which borrow largely from that text[10], it is taken as the basis of the present work. Hence all forms stated without comment belong to the Ṛgveda, though they may occur in other Saṃhitās as well. From the other Vedas, such matter only is added as occurs in their independent parts or, if borrowed from the Ṛgveda, appears in an altered form, the source being in such cases indicated by an abbreviation in parentheses (as VS., TS., AV.). The addition of the abbreviation 'RV.' means that the form in question occurs in the Ṛgveda only.

2. Verbal Authenticity of the Texts[11].—In dealing with the linguistic material of the Saṃhitās the question of the authenticity of the forms which it embraces is of great importance. What guarantees then do we possess that the original form of the texts handed down by tradition has not in the course of ages undergone modification and modernization in respect to vocabulary, phonetics, and grammatical forms? This question must first be applied to the Ṛgveda, the oldest of the Saṃhitās, which forms the very foundation of Vedic tradition. The evidence of the Sarvānukramaṇī[12], which states the number of stanzas, the metre, and the deity for every hymn of the RV., shows that in general extent, form, and matter, this Saṃhitā was in the Sūtra period the same as now. The Prātiśākhya[13] demonstrates that its phonetic character was also the same. Yāska's commentary[14] proves that,

1 Edited (Saṃhitā text only) by ROTH and WHITNEY, Berlin 1856 (Index Verborum in JAOS., vol. XII); translated by WHITNEY (Books I—XIX), with a critical and exegetical commentary, Cambridge, Mass., 1905 (vols. VII and VIII of the Harvard Oriental Series); also edited by SHANKAR P. PANDIT (both Saṃhitā and Pada text), Bombay 1895—99.

2 Besides BENFEY's edition also that of SATYAVRATA SĀMAŚRAMĪ, 5 vols., Calcutta 1874—78 (Bibliotheca Indica).

3 Edited by WEBER, with the commentary of Mahīdhara, London and Berlin 1852.

4 Edited by WEBER (vols. XI and XII of Indische Studien), Berlin 1871—72.

5 Edited by L. v. SCHROEDER, Leipzig 1881—86.

6 Edited by L. v. SCHROEDER, vol. I (books I—XVIII), Leipzig 1900.

7 Cp. OLDENBERG, Die Hymnen des Ṛigveda, Band I (Prolegomena), Berlin 1888, p. 294 ff.

8 See AUFRECHT, Die Hymnen des Ṛigveda[2], vol. II, 672—88; MAX MÜLLER, Ṛgveda[2], vol. IV, 519—41; cp. MACDONELL, Bṛhaddevatā, vol. I, introduction, § 15 (Cambridge, Mass., 1904); SCHEFTELOWITZ, Die Apokryphen des Ṛgveda (edition of the Khilas), Breslau 1906 (cp. OLDENBERG, Göttingische Gelehrte Anzeigen 1907, 210—41).

9 Cp. OLDENBERG, op. cit., 359 ff.; AUFRECHT, Das Aitareya Brāhmaṇa, Bonn 1879, p. 420 f.

10 Cp. OLDENBERG, op. cit., chapter III; MACDONELL, History of Sanskrit Literature, 181 and 186.

11 Cp. OLDENBERG, op. cit., chapter III (271—369) Der Ṛiktext und der Text der jüngeren Saṃhitās und der Brāhmaṇas; LUDWIG, Ueber die Kritik des Ṛgveda-Textes, Abhandlungen d. k. böhm. Gesellschaft der Wissenschaften, Prag 1889.

12 Edited by A. A. MACDONELL, Oxford 1886.

13 The Ṛgveda Prātiśākhya, edited with German translation by MAX MÜLLER, Leipzig 1856—69; edited with UVAṬA's commentary, Benares Sanskrit Series 1894.

14 Yāska's Nirukta, edited by ROTH, Göttingen 1852; edited by SATYAVRATA SĀMAŚRAMĪ, 4 vols. (II—IV with the commentary

as regards the limited number of stanzas explained by him, his text was verbally identical with ours. The frequent statements of the Brāhmaṇas concerning the number of verses contained in a hymn or liturgical group agree with the extant text of the Ṛgveda. The explanatory discussions of the Brāhmaṇas further indicate that the text of the Ṛgveda must have been regarded as immutably fixed by that time. Thus the Śatapatha Brāhmaṇa, while speaking of the possibility of varying some of the formulas of the Yajurveda, rejects as impossible the notion of changing the text of a certain verse of the Ṛgveda as proposed by some teachers[1].

Probably soon after the completion of the actual Brāhmaṇas the hymns of the Ṛgveda were fixed in the phonetic form of the Saṃhitā text; and after no long interval, in order to guard that text from the possibility of any change or loss, the Pada text was constituted by Śākalya, whom the Āraṇyakas or appendixes to the Brāhmaṇas, the Nirukta, and the Ṛgveda Prātiśākhya presuppose[2]. By this analysis of the Saṃhitā text, its every word, stated in a separate form as unaffected by the rules of euphonic combination, has come down to us without change for about 2,500 years.

The Saṃhitā text itself, however, only represented the close of a long period in which the hymns, as originally composed by the seers, were handed down by oral tradition. For the condition of the text even in this earlier period we possess a large body of evidence corresponding to that of Mss. for other literary monuments. It was then that the text of the other Vedas, each of which borrowed extensively from the Ṛgveda, was constituted. With each of them came into being a new and separate tradition in which the borrowed matter furnishes a body of various readings for the Ṛgveda. The comparison of these variants, about 1200 in number, has shown that the text of the Ṛgveda already existed, with comparatively few exceptions, in its present form when the text of the other Vedas was established. The number of instances is infinitely small in which the Ṛgveda exhibits corruptions not appearing in the others. We have thus good reason for believing that the fixity of the text and the verbal integrity of the Ṛgveda go several centuries further back than the date at which the Saṃhitā text came into existence. As handed down exclusively by oral tradition, the text could hardly have been preserved in perfectly authentic form from the time of the composers themselves; and research has shown that there are some undeniable corruptions in detail attributable to this earliest period. But apart from these, the Saṃhitā text, when the original metre has been restored by the removal of phonetic combinations which did not prevail in the time of the poets themselves, nearly always contains the very words, as represented by the Pada text, actually used by the seers. The modernization of the ancient text appearing in the Saṃhitā form is only partial and is inconsistently applied. It has preserved the smallest minutiae of detail most liable to corruption and the slightest differences in the matter of accent and alternative forms which might have been removed with the greatest ease. We are thus justified in assuming that the accents and grammatical forms of the Ṛgveda, when divested of the euphonic rules applied in the Saṃhitā text, have come down to us, in the vast majority of cases, as they were uttered by the poets themselves.

Though the tradition of nearly all the later Saṃhitās has in a general way been guarded by Anukramaṇīs, Prātiśākhyas, and Pada texts, its value is clearly inferior to that of the Ṛgveda. This is only natural in the case

of DURGA), Calcutta 1882—91 (Bibliotheca Indica).

[1] See OLDENBERG, op. cit., 352.
[2] See OLDENBERG, op. cit., 380 f.

of collections in which the matter was largely borrowed and arbitrarily cut up into groups of verses or into single verses solely with a view to meet new liturgical wants. Representing a later linguistic stage, these collections start from a modernized text in the material borrowed from the Ṛgveda, as is unmistakable when that material is compared with the original passages. The text of the Sāmaveda is almost entirely secondary, containing only seventy-five stanzas not derived from the Ṛgveda. Its variants are due in part to inferiority of tradition and in part to arbitrary alterations made for the purpose of adapting verses removed from their context to new ritual uses[1]. An indication that the tradition of the Yajur and Atharva Vedas is less trustworthy than that of the Ṛgveda is the great metrical irregularity which is characteristic of those texts[2]. Of all these the Vājasaneyi Saṃhitā is the best preserved, being not only guarded by an Anukramaṇī, a Prātiśākhya, and a Pada text, but partially incorporated in the Śatapatha Brāhmaṇa, where the first 18 books are quoted word for word besides being commented on. The Taittirīya Saṃhitā has also been carefully handed down, being protected by an Anukramaṇī, a Prātiśākhya, and a good Pada text[3]. The Maitrāyaṇī Saṃhitā is not so well authenticated, having no Prātiśākhya and only an inferior Pada text, of which but a single somewhat incorrect Ms. is known[4]. Least trustworthy of all is the tradition of the Kāṭhaka which lacks both a Prātiśākhya and a Pada text. Moreover only one complete Ms. of this Saṃhitā is known[5]. As that Ms. is unaccented, it has only been possible to mark the accent in small portions of that part of the text which has as yet been published (Books I—XVIII). As, however, the texts of the Black Yajurveda often agree even verbally, and the Maitrāyaṇī Saṃhitā is closely connected with the Kāṭhaka, the readings of the latter can to some extent be checked by those of the cognate Saṃhitās.

The inferiority of tradition in the Atharvaveda was increased by the lateness of its recognition as a canonical text. It contains many corrupt and uncertain forms, especially in Book XIX, which is a later addition[6]. The text is guarded by Anukramaṇīs, a Prātiśākhya, and a Padapāṭha[7]. The latter, however, contains serious errors both in regard to accentuation and the division of compound verbal forms, as well as in other respects. The Padapāṭha of Book XIX, which is different in origin from that of the earlier books[8], is full of grave blunders[9]. The critical and exegetical notes contained in WHITNEY's Translation of the Atharvaveda accordingly furnish important aid in estimating the value of the readings in the Śaunakīya recension of the Atharvaveda. The Paippalāda recension is known in only a single corrupt Ms., which has been reproduced in facsimile by Professors GARBE and BLOOMFIELD[10]. About one-eighth or one-ninth of this recension is original, being found neither in the Śaunakīya text of the Atharvaveda nor in any other known collection of Mantras[11]. The various readings of this recension, in the

1 On the Padapāṭha of the Sāmaveda see BENFEY's edition of that Saṃhitā, p. LVII—LXIV.

2 See WHITNEY's Introduction to the Atharvaveda, p. CXXVII; BLOOMFIELD, The Atharvaveda, Grundriss II, 1 B, § 1.

3 Cp. WEBER's edition p. VIII f., and Indische Studien 13, 1—114 (Ueber den Padapāṭha der Taittirīya-Saṃhitā).

4 See L. v. SCHROEDER's edition, Introduction, p. XXXVI f.

5 Cp. L. v. SCHROEDER's Introduction to his edition, § 1.

6 See LANMAN's Introduction to Book XIX in WHITNEY's Translation of the Atharvaveda.

7 See LANMAN's Introduction to WHITNEY's Translation, p. LXIX—LXXIV.

8 The Padapāṭha of the Atharvaveda has been edited in full by SHANKAR P. PANDIT in his Atharvaveda.

9 Cp. BLOOMFIELD, The Atharvaveda p. 16.

10 The Kashmirian Atharva-Veda, Baltimore 1901.

11 BLOOMFIELD, The Atharvaveda p. 15;

material common to both recensions, are given in the critical notes of WHITNEY's Translation. The variations range from slight differences to complete change of sense, and exact textual agreement between parallel stanzas is comparatively rare[1]. The text of this recension has not yet been critically edited except Book I[2].

I. PHONOLOGY.

Ṛgveda Prātiśākhya, ed. with German translation by MAX MÜLLER, Leipzig 1856—69; with UVAṬA's Commentary, Benares Sanskrit Series, 1894. — Atharvaveda Prātiśākhya, ed. WHITNEY, JAOS. vols. VII and X. — Taittirīya Prātiśākhya, ed. WHITNEY, JAOS. vol. IX, 1871. — Vājasaneyi Prātiśākhya, ed. WEBER, IS. vol. IV, 1858; with UVAṬA's Commentary, Benares Sanskrit Series, 1888. — Ṛiktantravyākaraṇa (= Prātiśākhya of the SV.), ed. and transl. by BURNELL, Mangalore 1879.

BENFEY, Vollständige Grammatik p. 1—70. — WHITNEY, Sanskrit Grammar p. 1—87. — WACKERNAGEL, Altindische Grammatik. I. Lautlehre (very full bibliography).

3. **Ancient Pronunciation.** — Evidence throwing light on the phonetic character of the language of the Saṃhitās is furnished not only by the pronunciation of its sounds by the Brahmans of to-day, who still recite those texts, but also by the transcription of Sanskrit words in foreign languages, particularly Greek, in ancient times; by the summary information contained in the works of the old Sanskrit grammarians, Pāṇini and his successors; and more especially by the detailed statements of the Prātiśākhyas and the Śikṣās. From these sources we derive a sufficiently exact knowledge of the pronunciation prevailing about 500 B. C. This pronunciation, however, need not necessarily have coincided in every particular with that of the Saṃhitās, which date from many centuries earlier. Nevertheless, judging by the internal evidence supplied by the phonetic changes and analogical formations occurring in the language of the texts themselves and by the external evidence of comparative philology, we are justified in concluding that the pronunciation, with the possible exception of a very few doubtful points, was practically the same.

4. **The Sounds of the Vedic Language.** — There are altogether 52 sounds, 13 of which are vocalic and 39 consonantal. They are the following:

A. Vocalic sounds.

1. Nine simple vowels: *a ā i ī u ū ṛ ṝ ḷ*.
2. Four diphthongs: *e o*[3] *ai au*[4].

B. Consonantal sounds.

1. Twenty-two mutes, divided into five classes, each of which has its class nasal, making a group of twenty-seven:
   a) five gutturals: *k kh g gh ṅ*,
   b) five palatals: *c ch j jh ñ*,
   c) seven cerebrals: *ṭ ṭh ḍ* and *ḷ*[5] *ḍh* and *ḷh*[5] *ṇ*,
   d) five dentals: *t th d dh n*,
   e) five labials: *p ph b bh m*.

---

cp. WHITNEY's Translation of the Atharvaveda p. 1013—23.

[1] On the readings of the Paippalāda recension, see LANMAN's Introduction p. LXXIX—LXXXIX.

[2] The Kashmirian AtharvaVeda, Book One. Edited with critical notes by LEROY CARR BARRET, in JAOS. 26, 197—295.

[3] These are really simple long vowels, being diphthongs only in origin (= *ăi, ău*).

[4] Pronounced *āi, āu* (see WHITNEY on APr. I. 40 and TPr. II. 29), but derived from diphthongs with a long first element.

[5] These sounds take the place of *ḍ ḍh* respectively between vowels; e. g. *īḷe* (but *īḍya*), *mīḷhúṣe* (but *mīḍhvā́n*).

2. Four semivowels: *y r l v*.
3. Three sibilants: *ś* (palatal), *ṣ* (cerebral), *s* (dental).
4. One aspiration: *h*.
5. One pure nasal: *ṃ* (*ṁ*) called Anusvāra ('after-sound').
6. Three voiceless spirants: *ḥ* (Visarjanīya), *ẖ* (Jihvāmūlīya), *ḫ* (Upadhmānīya).

5. Losses, changes, additions.—In order that the phonetic status of the Vedic language may be understood historically, the losses, changes, and additions which have taken place in it as compared with earlier linguistic stages, must be pointed out.

a. It has **lost** the IE. 1) short vowels *ĕ ŏ* and *ə*; 2) long vowels *ē ō*; 3) diphthongs *ĕi ŏi, ĕu ŏu; āi ēi ōi, āu ēu ōu*; 4) sonant nasals; 5) voiced spirant *z*.

b. It has **replaced** a number of IE. sounds by others: 1) the short vowels *ĕ ŏ* by *ă*, *ə* by *ĭ*; 2) the long vowels *ē ō* by *ā*; 3) the diphthongs *ĕi ŏi* by *ē*, *ĕu ŏu* by *ō*; also *ăz ĕz ŏz* by *ē ō*; 4) *ṝ* by *īr* (*ūr*), *ḷ* by *ṛ*; 5) *āi ēi ōi* by *ăi*, *āu ēu ōu* by *ău*; 6) *ṛ*, when followed by a nasal, has become *ṝ*; 7) gutturals (velars) have, under certain conditions, become palatals[1]; 8) a palatal mute has become the palatal spirant *ś*[2].

c. It has **added** the whole series of eight cerebrals (including the spirant *ṣ*).

The above innovations are specifically Indian, excepting (1) the loss of the vowels *ĕ̄ ŏ̄ ə*, together with the diphthongs formed with them; (2) the loss of the sonant nasals; and (3) the addition of the spirants *ś* and *ṣ*. These the Avesta shares with the Vedas.

1. The simple vowels.

6. The vowel *a*.—This is by far the commonest vowel, being much more than twice as frequent as *ā*; while these two *a*-vowels combined occur as often as all the rest (including diphthongs) taken together[3]. According to the modern Indian pronunciation, *a* has the sound of a very short close neutral vowel like the English *u* in *but*. That such was its character as early as the time of Pāṇini appears from his last Sūtra, according to which *a* is not the short sound corresponding to *ā*. To the same effect are the statements of the Prātiśākhyas[4], which describe *a* as a 'close' (*saṃvṛta*) sound. This pronunciation is borne out by the reproduction of Indian words in Greek, where the vowel, though usually represented by *a*, appears as *ĕ* or *ŏ* also; on the other hand, the frequent reproduction of the Greek *a* by the Indian *ā* indicates that, to the Indian ear, that vowel was both longer and had more distinctively the sound of *a*. Similarly, Hindus of the present day make the observation that the English pronunciation of *ă* in Sanskrit words sounds long (*dīrgha*) to them. As the ancient Iranian languages have the normal *ă* throughout, the close pronunciation must be an Indian innovation. But whether it already prevailed in the period when the Saṃhitās were composed is uncertain. The fact, however, that in the RV. the metre hardly ever admits of the *ă* being elided after *e* or *o*, though the written text drops it in about 75 per cent of its occurrences, seems to indicate that when the hymns of the RV. were composed, the pronunciation of *ă* was still open, but that at

---

1 Cp. BRUGMANN, Kurze vergleichende Grammatik der indogermanischen Sprachen 1902, I, 244.

2 Op. cit. 233.

3 Cp. WHITNEY, 22 and 75.

4 APr. I. 36; VPr. I. 72.

the time when the Saṃhitā text was constituted, the close pronunciation was already becoming general.

a. Though *a* ordinarily represents IE. *ă ĕ ŏ*[1], it also often replaces an original sonant nasal[2] representing the reduced form of the unaccented Vedic syllables *a*+nasal: 1) *an* in derivative and inflexional syllables; e. g. *sat-á* beside the stem *sánt-* 'being'; *júhv-ati* 'they sacrifice' (suffix otherwise *-anti*); 2) *a*+nasal in radical syllables; e. g. *ta-tá-* 'stretched': √*tan-*; *ga-tá-* 'gone': √*gam-*; *das-má-* 'wondrous': √*daṃs-*; stem *pathí-* 'path', beside *pánthā-*; 3) in words as shown by comparative philology; e. g. *śatá-m* 'hundred' (Lat. *centum*), *dáśa* 'ten' (Lat. *decem*)[3].

Very rarely *a* is a Prakritic representative of *r̥*, as in *vi-kaṭa-*[4] 'monstrous', beside *vi-kr̥ta-* 'deformed'.

7. The vowel ā. — This sound represents both a simple long vowel[5] and a contraction; e. g. *á-sthā-t* 'he has stood'; *ā́sam* 'I was' (= *á-as-am*), *bhárāti* 'may he bear' (= *bhára-a-ti*).

a. Like *a*, the long vowel *ā* frequently corresponds to or is derived from a syllable containing a nasal; e. g. *khā-tá-* 'dug': √*khan-*; *ā-tmán-* 'soul': *an-* 'breathe'. In very rare instances the nasal is retained in the RV.: *jíghāṃsati* 'desires to strike': √*han-*; *śrāntá-* 'wearied': √*śram-*; *dhvāntá-* 'dark': √*dhvan-*; there are six or eight more instances in the later Saṃhitās[6]. Here the reappearance of the nasal in a weak radical syllable is an innovation due to the influence of other forms with nasals[7].

8. The vowel i. — This sound in the first place is an original vowel; e. g. *div-í* 'in heaven'. It also frequently represents the low grade of *e* and *ya* both in roots[8] and suffixes; e. g. *vid-má* 'we know', beside *véd-a* 'I know'; *náv-iṣṭha-* 'newest', beside *náv-yas-* 'newer'. It further appears as the low grade of *ā* in roots containing that vowel: e. g. *sídhyati* 'succeeds', beside *sādhati*; *śiṣṭá-* 'taught', beside *śā́sti* 'teaches'; especially when the vowel is final, as in *sthi-tá-* 'stood': √*sthā-*. From the latter use it came to assume the function of a 'connecting' vowel; e. g. *jan-i-tŕ̥-* 'begetter': √*jan-*; after heavy syllables also in the ending *-ire* of 3 pl. pf. mid. *vavand-iré* (beside *nunudré*). In *śithirá-* 'loose' *i* would be a Prakritic representative of *r̥*, if the word is derived from √*śrath-*[9].

9. The vowel ī. — This sound is an original vowel, e. g. in *jīvá-* 'living'[10]. It also often represents the low grade of *yā* both in roots and suffixes; e. g. *jī-tá-* (AV.), 'overcome': √*jyā-*; *aś-ī-máhi* 'we would attain', beside *aś-yā́m* 'I would attain'. It further seems to represent the low grade of both radical and suffixal *ā*; but this can probably in all instances be explained as either a low grade of *ai* or a later substitution for *i*; e. g. *gī-tha-* (AV.) beside *gā-thá-* 'song', is from the root *gai-*; *adī-mahi* (VS.) and *dī-ṣva* (VS.), from √2 *dā-* and √3 *dā-*, occur beside forms in *i* from the three roots *dā-* which have *i* only in the RV.; *hīná-* 'forsaken', from √*hā-*, occurs once in RV. x beside forms with *i* only in RV. I—IX. A similar explanation probably applies to the *-nī-* of the ninth class of verbs beside *-nā-*, e. g. *gr̥bhṇī-* : *gr̥bhṇā-*[11].

---

[1] Cp. Brugmann, KG. 92, 104, 116.
[2] Cp. Brugmann 184.
[3] See Wackernagel I, 7 (p. 7—10).
[4] Cp. Wackernagel I, 146.
[5] It represents IE. *ā ē ō*: cp. Brugmann, KG. 98, 110, 122. It also appears for IE. *ŏ* before single consonants: cp. Wackernagel I, 10.
[6] See below, past passive participles 574, 2 a.
[7] See Wackernagel I, 13.
[8] This term will be retained in the present work in its conventional sense (cp. Brugmann, KG. 365), and 'roots' will be quoted in the usually low grade form in which they appear in Sanskrit grammar. The term 'base' will be used to designate the phonetic unit which is the starting point of vowel gradation (cp. Brugmann, KG. 211). Thus *bhāva-* or *bhavi-* is a 'base', *bhū-* is a 'root'.
[9] Cp. Wackernagel I, 16 (p. 19, note).
[10] Cp. Brugmann, KG. 73.
[11] See Wackernagel I, 18.

10. The vowel *u*. — This sound is an original vowel; e. g. *úpa* 'up to'; *duhitṛ́-* 'daughter'; *mádhu-* 'sweetness'. It also represents the low grade of *o* or *va* both in roots and suffixes; e. g. *yugá-* m. n. 'yoke', beside *yóga-* m. 'yoking'; *suptá-* (AV.) 'asleep' : *svápna-* m. 'sleep'; *kṛṇu-* : *kṛṇó-* present base of *kṛ-* 'make'.

11. The vowel *ū*. — This sound is an original vowel; e. g. *bhrū-* 'brow'; *śū́ra-* 'hero'. It is also the low grade for *avi*, *au*, *vā*; e. g. *bhū́-t* 'has become' : *bhavi-syáti* 'will become'; *dhūtá-*'shaken' : *dhautárī-*, f. 'shaking'; *sūd-* 'sweeten' : *svād-* 'enjoy'.

12. The vowel *ṛ*. — The vowel *ṛ*[1] is at the present day usually pronounced as *ri*; and that this pronunciation is old is shown by the confusion of the two sounds in inscriptions and Mss., as well as by the reproduction of *ṛ* by *ri* in the Tibetan script[2]. But *ṛ* was originally pronounced as vocalic *r*. The Prātiśākhyas of the RV., VS., AV.[3] describe it as containing an *r*, which according to the RPr. is in the middle. According to the commentator on the VPr. this medial *r* constitutes one-half of the sound, the first and last quarter being *ă*[4]. This agrees with *ərə*, the equivalent of *ṛ* in the Avesta.

Except in the acc. and gen. plur. of *ṛ*-stems (where *ṝ* is written), the long vowel is in the RV. represented by the sign for *ṛ*: always in forms of the verb *mṛḍ-*[5] 'be gracious', in the past participles *tṛḷhá-* 'crushed', *dṛḷhá-* 'firm', in the gen. *nṛṇā́m*, and in the one occurrence of the gen. *tisṛṇā́m*[6]. In the later Saṃhitās, the vowel in these instances was pronounced short[7]; and it was doubtless for this reason that *ṛ* came to be erroneously written for *ṝ* in the text of the RV.

13. The vowel *ṝ*[8]. — This long vowel, according to RPr. and APr.[9], contains an *r* in its first half only. It appears only in the acc. and gen. plur. masc. fem. of *ṛ*-stems; e. g. *pitṝ́n*, *mātṝ́s*; *pitṝṇā́m*, *svásṝṇām*. Thus the *ṝ* was written only where *a- i- u*-stems showed analogous forms with *ā ī ū*; and prosodical evidence proves that, in the RV., *ṝ* is required even in the two genitives in which *ṛ* is written (*nṛṇā́m* and *tisṛṇā́m*)[10]. In the TS., however, all these genitives plur. have *ṛ*[11] (that is, *pitṛṇā́m* as well as *nṛṇā́m*, *tisṛṇā́m*).

14. The vowel *ḷ*. — This sound, though pronounced as *lri* at the present day, was originally a vocalic *l*. Its description in the Prātiśākhyas[12] is analogous to that of *ṛ*. It is found only in a few forms or derivatives of the verb *kḷp-* 'be in order' : *cākḷpré*, 3 pl. perf.; *ciklpāti*, 3 sing. aor. subj.; *kḷ́pti-* (VS.) 'arrangement'. In the RV. *ṛ* appears beside it in *kṛ́p-* 'form'[13].

2. The diphthongs.

15. The diphthongs *e* and *o*. — At the present day these sounds are pronounced in India as long monophthongs like *ē* and *ō* in most European

[1] In several instances *ṛ* appears to represent an IE. *l* sound. Cp. WACKERNAGEL I, p. 33.

[2] See WACKERNAGEL I, 28.

[3] RPr. VIII. 14; VPr. IV. 145; APr. I. 37, 71.

[4] Cp. BENFEY, Vedica und Verwandtes I, 18.

[5] Except possibly RV. VII. 56[17] where the vowel is metrically short; cp. op. cit. I, 6; ARNOLD, Vedic Metre, p. 143.

[6] RV. V. 69[2].

[7] In the AV. the vowel is still metrically long in some of these instances: OLDENBERG, Prolegomena 477.

[8] The *ṝ* of the gen. pl. is an Indian innovation; cp. 5, b 6 and 17. On the other hand, IE. *ṝ-* is represented by *īr* and (after labials) *ūr*; e. g. from *kṝ-* 'commemorate', *kīr-ti-* 'fame'; *pṝ-* 'fill' : *pūr-tá-*, n. 'reward'; as low grade of *rā* in *dīrgh-á-* 'long', beside *drā́gh-īyas-* 'longer'. Cp. WACKERNAGEL I, 22.

[9] RPr. XIII. 14; APr. I. 38.

[10] See above, 5, b 6.

[11] Cp. BENFEY, Vedica und Verwandtes I, 3.

[12] RPr. XIII. 14; VPr. IV. 145.

[13] Cp. WACKERNAGEL I, 31.

languages. That they already had this character at the time of the Prātiśākhyas[1] and of Pāṇini's successors Kātyāyana[2] and Patañjali[3], appears from the accounts given by those authorities, who at the same time recognize these two sounds to be in many instances the result of the euphonic combination (*saṃdhi*, Sandhi) of *a*+*i* and *a*+*u* respectively. This evidence is borne out by the reproduction of Indian words by the Greeks[4] and of Greek words by the Indians[5] from about 300 B. C. onwards.

a. These two sounds as a rule represent earlier diphthongs of which the second element was *i* or *u* respectively. 1. This is most evidently so when they are produced in Sandhi by the coalescence of *ă* with *ĭ* and *ŭ*. As the result of such a combination they are explicable only on the assumption of an earlier pronunciation of these sounds as the genuine diphthongs *ăi* and *ău*. — 2. They are further based on prehistoric contractions within words in declension and conjugation; e. g. loc. sing. of *áśva-* 'horse': *áśve* (cp. *nāv-í-* 'in the ship'); nom. acc. du. neut. of *padá-* 'step': *padé* (cp. *vácas-ī* 'two words'); 3. sing. pot. mid. *bháveta* 'should become' (cp. *ās-īta* 'would sit'); *maghón-* weak stem (= *magha-un*) of *maghávan-* 'bountiful'; *á-voc-at* 3. sing. aor. of *vac-* 'speak' (= *á-va-uc-at*)[6]. — 3. These two sounds also represent the high grade corresponding to the weak grade vowels *i* and *u*; e. g. *sécati* 'pours', beside *sik-tá-* 'poured'; *bhoj-am*, beside *bhúj-am*, aor. of *bhuj-* 'enjoy'[7].

b. 1. In a small number of words *e*[10] represents Indo-Iranian *az* (still preserved in the Avesta) before *d dh* and *h* (= *dh*): *dehí* 'give', and *dhehí* 'set' (Av. *dazdi*); *e-dhi* 'be', beside *ás-ti*; *néd-īyas-* 'very near', *néd-iṣṭha-* 'nearest' (Av. *nazdyo, nazdišta-*); *medhá-* 'insight' (Av. *mazdā*); *miyédha-* 'meat-juice' (Av. *myazda-*); *vedhás-* 'adorer' (Av. *vazdah-*); *sed-*[8] weak perf. of *sad-* 'sit' (Av. *hazd-* for Indo-Iranian *sazd-*)[9]. — 2. Similarly *o*[10] represents *az* in stems ending in *-as* before the *bh* of case-endings, e. g. from *dvéṣ-as-* n. 'hatred', inst. pl. *dvéṣo-bhis*; and before secondary suffixes beginning with *y* or *v*: *aṃho-yú-* 'distressing' (but *apas-yú-* 'active'); *duvo-yú-* 'wishing to give' (beside *duvas-yú-*); *sáho-van-* (AV.) 'mighty', beside *sáhas-vant-* (RV.). In derivatives of *ṣáṣ-* 'six', and of *vah-* 'carry', *o* represents *az* before *d* or *dh*, which it cerebralizes: *ṣó-ḍaśa* (VS.) 'sixteen'; *ṣo-ḍhá* 'six-fold'; *vó-ḍhum* 'to carry'.

16. The diphthongs *ai* and *au*. — These sounds are pronounced at the present day in India as diphthongs in which the first element is short. Even at the time of the Prātiśākhyas they had the value of *ăi* and *ău*[11]. But that they are the etymological representatives of *āi* and *āu* is shown by their becoming *āy* and *āv* respectively before vowels both in Sandhi[12] and within words; e. g. *gáv-as* 'kine', beside *gáu-s* 'cow'[13]. That such was their original value is also indicated by the fact that in Sandhi *a* contracts with *e*[14] to *ai*, and with *o* to *au*[15].

17. Lengthening of vowels. — 1. Before *n*, vowels are lengthened only (except *ṛ* in the gen. pl.) in the acc. pl. in *-ān, -īn, -ūn, -ṝn*[16], where the long vowel is doubtless pre-Indian[17].

2. Before suffixal *y*, *i* and *u* are phonetically lengthened: a) as finals of roots; e. g. *kṣī-yate* 'is destroyed' (√*kṣi-*); *sū-yáte* 'is pressed' (√*su-*); *śrū-yás* 'may he hear' (√*śru-*); b) as finals of nouns in denominatives formed with *-yá* and their derivatives; e. g. *janī-yánt-* 'desiring a wife' (*jáni-*); *valgū-*

1 See WHITNEY on APr. I. 40.
2 Vārttika on Pāṇini VIII. 2, 106.
3 Comment on Vārttika 1 and 3 on Pāṇini I. 1, 48.
4 Thus *Kekaya-*, name of a people, becomes *Κήκεοι*; *Goṇḍa-* name of a people, *Γόνδαλοι*.
5 Thus *κάμηλος* becomes *kramela-ka-*; *ὥρα* becomes *horā*.
6 Cp. WACKERNAGEL I, 33 b.
7 Op. cit. I, 33 c, d, e.
8 On this base see below on the Perfect, 483 a, 2.
9 Cp. WACKERNAGEL I, 34 a.
10 These *e* and *o* are not distinguished in pronunciation from the monophthongs representing the diphthongs *ăi* and *ău*.
11 See WHITNEY on APr. I. 40 and TPr. II. 29.
12 See below 73.
13 Cp. WACKERNAGEL I, 36.
14 That is, originally *ă* + (*e* =) *ăi* became *āi*.
15 That is, originally *ă* + (*o* =) *ău* became *āu*.
16 For original *a i u ṛ* + *ns*.
17 As the *s* which caused the length by position had already for the most part disappeared in the Vedic language.

yáti 'treats kindly' (*valgú-*); *gātū-yáti* 'desires free course' (*gātú-*; but also *gātu-yáti*) [1] The AV.[2] has a few exceptions: *arāti-yáti* 'is hostile'; *jani-yáti* as well as *janī-yáti*[3]; **c)** *i* in the suffix *-ī-ya* and in the comparative suffix *-īyas*.

3. Before *r*, if radical, *i* and *u* seem to be lengthened when a consonant follows; e. g. *gīr-bhís* beside *gír-as* (*gír-* 'song of praise'); *pūr-ṣú* beside *púr-as* (*púr-* 'fort'), but *īr* and *ūr* here represent IE. *r̥̄*[4]. In a few instances this is extended by analogy to words in which the *r* is not radical: *āśír* 'blessing' (*āśís-*); *sajúr* 'together' (√*juṣ-*)[5].

4. Before *v*, the vowels *a i u* are lengthened: **a)** in some instances the augment: *āvidhyat* 'he wounded' (√*vyadh-*)[6]; **b)** once before the primary suffix *-vāṃs* of the perfect participle: *jigī-vā́ṃs-* 'having conquered' (√*ji-*); **c)** often before the secondary suffixes *-van*, *-vana*, *-vant*, *-vala*, *-vin*; e. g. *r̥tá-van-* 'observing order'; *kā́rṣī-vaṇa-* (AV.) 'ploughman'; *yā́-vant-* 'how great'; *śvā́sī-vant-* (RV[1].) 'snorting' (√*śvas-*); *-kr̥ṣī-vala-* 'ploughman'; *dvayā-vín-* 'dishonest'; **d)** often before the second member of a compound; e. g. *gūrtá-vasu-* 'whose treasures are welcome'[7].

5. Before IIr. *z* and *ẓ*, when followed by one or more consonants, vowels are lengthened by way of compensation for the loss of the *z* or *ẓ*[8]; **a)** *ā* (= *aẓ*) in *tā́ḍhi* 'hew' (√*takṣ-*); *bāḍhá-* 'firm' (√*baṃh-*); *sā́ḍhr-* 'conquering', *á-ṣāḍha-* 'invincible' (√*sah-*); **b)** *ī* = *iẓ* in *īḍ-* 'adore' (√*yaj-* 'sacrifice', or √*iṣ-* 'wish'); *nīḍá-* 'nest'; *pīḍ-* 'press'; *mīḍhá-* 'reward'; *mīḍhvā́ṃs-* 'bounteous'; *rīḍhá-* 'licked' (√*rih-*); *vīḍú-* 'swift'; *sī́dati* (= *sizdati*) 'sits'; *hīḍ-* 'be angry' (cp. *hiṃs-* 'injure'). **c)** *ū* = *uẓ* in *ūḍhá-* 'borne' (√*vah-*); *gūḍhá-* 'concealed' (√*guh-*)[9].

6. Vowels also appear lengthened under conditions other than those enumerated above (1–5).

a. Final *a i u* are very frequently lengthened in the Saṃhitās before a single consonant owing to rhythmical predilections; from this use the lengthening of the vowels is extended to syllables which are reduplicative or precede suffixes[10].

b. For metrical reasons the length is in a few words shifted to another syllable. Thus *didīhi* often appears instead of the regular *dīdihi*; and in *virā-ṣā́ṭ* 'ruling men', *virā-*[11] stands for *vīra-*. A similar explanation perhaps applies to *carā́tha-* 'moving', beside *carátha-*; and *mā́hīna-* 'gladsome', beside *mā́hina-*.

c. The long vowel beside the short in the same stem appears in some instances to be due to vowel gradation; as in *tvát-pitāras* (TS.) 'having thee as a father', beside *pitáras*; *pr̥thu-jā́ghana-* 'broad-hipped', beside *jaghána-*

---

1 Before this *-yá*, the final of *a*-stems is sometimes lengthened, but probably not phonetically; see below 6 d.

2 See WHITNEY on APr. III. 18.

3 No lengthening takes place in the optative present of verbs of the 5th or 8th class, e. g. *śr̥ṇu-yāma* (*śru-* 'hear'); nor in adverbs formed with *-yā* from *u*-stems; e. g. *āśu-yā́* 'swiftly'; *amu-yā́* 'thus'.

4 See above on *r̥̄*, p. 8, note 8.

5 Cp. WACKERNAGEL I, 23. When *ir* stands for suffixal *-is*, it remains unchanged; e. g. *havírbhis* 'with oblations' (*hav-is-*), *krivír-dat-ī* 'saw-toothed'; *-ur*, with genuine *u*, remains short in *urvárā-* 'field', *urvī́-* 'wide', *urviyā́* 'widely' (*uru-* 'wide'), *urv-ā́śī-* 'desire', *dur-* (for *dus-*) e. g. in *dur-gá-* 'hard to traverse'.

6 The lengthening of the augment in *āyunak*, *āyukta* (√*yuj-*) and *āriṇak*, *āraik* (√*ric-*), follows this analogy.

7 The lengthening here probably started from that in Sandhi: cp. WACKERNAGEL I, 42.

8 This appears to be the only kind of compensatory lengthening in the Vedic language. Cp. 17, 1.

9 On *e* and *o* for *az aẓ*, see above, 15, a, b, and cp. WACKERNAGEL I, 40.

10 See WACKERNAGEL I, 43.

11 Metrical shortening of a long syllable

'hip'; *ānu-ṣák* 'in continuous order', beside *ánu-* 'along' as first member of a compound.

d. The lengthening of the vowel in a certain number of instances appears to be due to analogy; thus the denominatives in *-āyá* beside *-ayá* from *a*-stems (e. g. *ṛtāyá-* 'observe order', beside *ṛtayá-*)[1], seem to follow the model of those in *-īyáti* and *-ūyáti*, which would account for the fluctuation in quantity. *Tīkṣṇá-* 'sharp' (beside *tigmá-* : *tij-* 'be sharp') and *hálīkṣṇa-* (TS.) beside *halíkṣṇa-* (VS.), a kind of animal, appear to owe their *ī* to the influence of desideratives which in several instances have *ī* (partly for older *i*) before *kṣ*. The reason for the *ū* in *tūṣṇím* 'silently' (*tuṣ-* 'become quiet'), and in *sūmná-* (VS.), otherwise *sumná-* 'favour', is, however, obscure.

18. Loss of vowels.—Vowels are very rarely dropped in the language of the Saṃhitās. **Medial** loss is almost entirely restricted[2] to the isolated disappearance of *u* before *v* and *m*. That vowel is dropped at the end of the first member of a compound in *anvartitá* (RV[1].) 'wooer' (= *anu-vartitá*); *ánvartiṣye* (AV.) 'I shall follow'[3]; *cār-vadana-* (AV. Paipp.) 'of lovely aspect' (= *cāru-vadana-*) and *cār-vāc-* (AV. Paipp.) 'speaking pleasantly'[4]. The only example of the loss of *ă* in this position seems to be *til-piñja-* (AV[1].) a kind of plant, beside *tila-piñjī-* (AV[1].). The vowel *u* is further dropped before the *m* of the 1 pers. pl. pres. ending of the 5th (*-nu-*) class, when the *u* is preceded by only one consonant, in *kṛṇ-mahe* and *kṛṇ-mási* (AV.)[5] 'we do'.

Initial vowels also occasionally disappear. The only vowel that is lost with any frequency is *ă*, which is dropped in Sandhi after *e* and *o*, according to the evidence of metre, in about one per cent of its occurrences in the RV. and about twenty per cent in the AV. and the metrical portions of the YV.[6] In a few words its disappearance is prehistoric: in *ví-* 'bird'[7] (Lat. *avi-*), possibly in *ní-* 'in' (Greek ἐνί)[8], in *pīḍ-* 'press'[9], *bhi-ṣáj-*[10] 'healer'. *ā* is lost in *tmán-*, beside *ā-tmán-*, but the reason has not been satisfactorily explained[11]. In *va* 'like', beside *iva*, the loss of *i* is probably only apparent: cp. *vā* 'like' (Lat. *vĕ* 'or')[12]. Initial *u* seems to be lost, if the reading is not corrupt, in *śmasi* (RV. II. 31[6]) beside *uśmási* 'we desire' (√*vaś-*).

19. Contraction.—Long vowels and diphthongs are often the result of contraction in Sandhi[13]. They have frequently a similar origin in the interior of words[14].

a. Contractions of *a* with a vowel or diphthong are the following:

1. *ā* often stands for *a* + *a*, *ā* + *a*, or *a* + *ā*; e. g. *áj-at*, augmented imperfect (= *á-aj-at*); *ád-a*, red. perf. (= *a-ád-a*); *bhárāti*, pres. subj. (= *bhára-ati*); *ukthá*[15], inst. sing. (= *ukthá-a*); *áśvās* 'mares', nom. pl. (= *áśvā-as*); *dáti*, aor. subj. (= *dá-ati*); *devám*, gen. pl. (= *devá-ām*).

2. *e* stands for *a* + *ĭ* and *ā* + *ī*; e. g. *áśve*, loc. sing. (= *áśva-i*); *padé*,

(at the end of a triṣṭubh-line), without interchange of quantity, appears in *sirásu*, loc. plur. of *sīrá-* 'stream'.

1 See below, Denominatives, 563, a.

2 Apart from the syncopation of *ă* in low grade syllables: cp. 25, A 1.

3 Cp. BÖHTLINGK, ZDMG. 39, 533; 44, 492 f.; cp. OLDENBERG 324.

4 See BÖHTLINGK's Lexicon s. v. Perhaps also in *jāmbila-* (MS.) 'knee-pan', if = *jānu-vila-*.

5 Cp. DELBRÜCK, AIV. 174; v. NEGELEIN, Zur Sprachgeschichte des Veda 60 (*ṛ*-Wurzeln).

6 Cp. WACKERNAGEL I, p. 324; OLDENBERG, ZDMG. 44, 321 ff. (Der Abhinihita Sandhi im Ṛgveda).

7 Cp. 25, A 1; WACKERNAGEL I, 71.

8 Cp. SCHMIDT, KZ. 26, 24; WACKERNAGEL 2[1], p. 73.

9 Op. cit. 2[1], p. 71 (bottom).

10 Op. cit. 2[1], p. 72 (bottom).

11 Op. cit. 1, p. 61 (top).

12 Cp. op. cit. I, 53 c, note; ARNOLD, Vedic Metre, 129 (p. 78).

13 See below 69, 70.

14 See above 15, a 2.

15 The original inst. ending *-a* under the influence of this contracted form became *-ā*; cp. WACKERNAGEL I, p. 102, mid.

nom. acc. du. neut. (= *padá-ī*); *bhándves*, opt. pres. (= *bháva-īs*); *yamé* 'twin sisters', nom. acc. du. fem. (= *yamā́-ī*).

3. *o* stands for *a* + *u*; e. g. *ávocam*, aor. of *vac-* 'speak' (= *áva-uc-am*).

4. *ai* stands for *ă* + *e* and, in augmented forms, *a* + *ī*; e. g. *tásmai* 'to him', dat. sing. masc. (= *tásma-e*); *devyái*, dat. sing. fem. (= *devyā́-e*); *áicchat*, 3. sing. impf. (= *á-icchat*); *áirata*, 3. pl. impf. (= *á-īrata*) 'set in motion'.

5. *au* stands for *a* + *ŭ* in augmented forms; e. g. *áucchat*, 3. sing. impf. of *vas-* 'shine' (= *á-ucchat*); *auhat*, 3. sing. impf. of *ūh-* 'remove' (= *a-ūh-at*).

b. **Contractions of *i*** with *i* or *ā* are the following:

1. *ī* stands for *i* + *i* in the nom. acc. pl. neut. of *i*-stems; e. g. *trī́* 'three' (= *trí-i*).

2. *ī* stands for *i* + *i* in weak forms of the perfect, when the reduplicative vowel is immediately followed by *i* (either original or reduced from *ya*); e. g. *īṣ-úr* (= *i-iṣ-úr* from *iṣ-* 'speed'); *īj-é* (= *i-ij-é* from *yaj-* 'sacrifice').

3. *ī* stands for *i* + *ā* in the inst. sing. fem. and the nom. acc. du. masc. fem. of stems in *-i*; e. g. *matī́* (= *matí-ā*) 'by thought'; *pátī* 'the two lords' (= *páti-ā*, cp. *ṛtvíj-ā*), *śúc-ī*, du. fem. 'the two bright ones' (= *śúci-ā*).

4. *ī* stands for *i* + *ā* in compounds of *dvi-* 'two', *ní* 'down', *práti* 'against', with the low grade of *áp-* 'water': *dvīp-á-* 'island'; *nīp-á-* 'low-lying' (K.)[1]; *pratīpám* 'against the stream'[2].

5. *ī* stands for *i* + *ā* when reduplicative *i* is followed by the low grade form of a root beginning with *ā*: *ī́psa-ti* (AV.), desiderative of *āp-* 'obtain' (= *í-ip-sa-*)[3]. A similar contraction takes place when initial radical *a* is long by position, in *ī́kṣ-ate* 'sees' (cp. *ákṣ-i* 'eye') and *īṅkh-áyati* 'swings' (cp. *pari-aṅkháyāte* 'may he embrace'). In *ī́j-ate* 'drives', beside *áj-ati* 'drives', the contraction to *ī* of *i* + *ă* is perhaps due to analogy[4].

c. **Contractions of *u*** with *u* or *ā* are the following:

1. *ū* stands for *u* + *u* in weak forms of the perfect when the reduplicative vowel is immediately followed by *u* (either original or reduced from *va*); e. g. *ūc-e*, 3 sing. mid. (= *u-uc-e*) from *uc-* 'like'; *ūc-úr* (= *u-uc-úr*) from *vac-* 'speak'.

2. *ū* stands for *u* + *ā* in the compound formed with *ánu* 'along' and the low grade of *áp-* 'water': *anūp-á-*[4] 'pond'.

3. *ū* stands for *u* + *ā* in the nom. acc. du. masc. fem. of *u*-stems; e. g. *bāhū́* 'the two arms' (= *bāhú-ā*).

4. *ū* seems to stand for *u* + *i* in the nom. acc. pl. neuter of *u*-stems; e. g. *vásū* (= *vásu-i*), from *vásu-* 'good'; but the vowel may possibly be lengthened by analogy[5], for the Pada text always has *ŭ*.

20. **Hiatus.** — a. In the **written** text of the Saṃhitās, hiatus is, as a rule, tolerated in diphthongs only, vowels being otherwise separated by consonants. It nevertheless appears:

1. in Sandhi, when a final *s y* or *v* has been dropped before a following vowel; when final *ī ū e* of dual endings are followed by vowels; when *a* remains after final *e* and *o*; and in some other instances[6];

2. in compounds, when the final *s* of the first member has disappeared before a vowel; e. g. *dyo-agra-* 'iron-pointed' (*áyas-* 'iron'); *pura-etṛ́-* 'leader' (*purás* 'before'); and when, by a Prakritism, *y* is lost in *prá-uga-* 'fore-part of the shaft' (= *prá-yuga-*);

---

[1] Cp. *nī́p-ya-* (VS.), 'lying at the bottom'.

[2] Cp. *ánīka-* and *prátīka-* 'face'.

[3] Cp. Samprasāraṇa *ī* and *ū* for *yā* and *vā*.

[4] Cp. WACKERNAGEL I, 90 c, p. 104.

[5] That is, of the *a* and *i* stems; e. g. *bhadrā́*, *trī́*.

[6] See below, Sandhi 69—73.

3. in the simple word *titaü-*[1] 'sieve' (probably from *taṃs-* 'shake'), by a loss of *s*, due most likely to borrowing from an Iranian dialect (where medial *s* would have become *h*, which then disappeared).

b. 1. Though **not written**, hiatus is common elsewhere also in the Saṃhitās[2]. The evidence of metre shows that *y* and *v* must often be pronounced as *i* and *u*, and that a long vowel or a diphthong has frequently the value of two vowels. When the long vowel or diphthong is the result of contraction, the two original vowels must often be restored, within a word as well as in Sandhi. Thus *pā́nti* 'they protect', may have to be read as *pā̊-anti* (= *pā́-anti*)[3], *ā́ñjan* 'they anointed' as *á-añjan*; *jyéṣṭha-* 'mightiest' as *jyá-iṣṭha-* (= *jyā́-iṣṭha-* from *jyā-* 'be mighty'); *áicchas* as *á-icchas* 'thou didst wish'; *aurṇos* as *a-ūrṇos* 'thou didst open'[4].

2. Hiatus is further produced by distraction of long vowels[5] which, as the metre shows, are in the Ṛgveda often to be pronounced as two short vowels. This distraction was doubtless originally due partly to a slurred accentuation which practically divided a syllable into two halves, and partly to the resolution of etymological contraction. From such instances distraction spread to long vowels in which it was not historically justified. It appears most often in *ā*, especially in the gen. pl. in *-ām*, also in the abl. sing. in *-āt*, the nom. acc. pl. in *-ās*, *-āsas* of *a*-stems, in the acc. sing. in *-ām* of such words as *abjā́m* 'born in the water'; and in many individual words[6]. Distraction is further found in the diphthongs of words in which it is not etymologically justified; as in the genitives *vés* 'of a bird', *gós* 'of a cow', in *tredhā́* 'threefold', *nétṛ-* 'leader', *rékṇas-* 'property', *śréṇi-* 'row'; and in other words[7].

21. Svarabhakti. — When a consonant is in conjunction with *r* or a nasal, a very short vocalic sound tends to be developed between them, and the evidence of metre shows that a vowel must often be pronounced between them. It is the general view of the Prātiśākhyas[8] that when an *r* precedes another consonant a vowel is sounded after it; according to some of them this also takes place after *l* or even after any voiced consonant. They call it *svarabhakti* or 'vowel-part', which they describe as equal to $^1/_8$, $^1/_4$, or $^1/_2$ mora in length and generally as equivalent to *a* or *e* (probably = *ĕ*) in sound.

a. The metre of the RV. shows that an additional syllable is frequently required in words in which *r* either precedes or follows[9] another consonant; e. g. *darśatá-* 'worthy to be seen' (quadrisyllabic); *índra-*[10], name of a god (very often trisyllabic); *prá* 'forth' (dissyllabic)[11].

---

1 Cp. WACKERNAGEL I, 37 b, note.

2 See OLDENBERG, Prolegomena 434 ff.: 'Hiatus und Contraction'; ARNOLD, Vedic Metre, chapter IV, p. 70 ff. (Sandhi), chapter V, p. 81 ff. (Syllabic Restoration).

3 As a rule, one vowel (including *e* and *o*) is shortened before another: see OLDENBERG, op. cit., 465 ff.; 447 ff.

4 WACKERNAGEL I, 46 b.

5 See OLDENBERG, op. cit., 163 ff. (Vocale mit zweisilbiger Geltung).

6 See WACKERNAGEL I, 44. This is a very old phenomenon, as it is found in the Avesta in the gen. pl. and in other forms: OLDENBERG 181; WACKERNAGEL I, p. 50.

7 WACKERNAGEL I, 46. This distraction of diphthongs is also pre-Vedic, parallels being found in the Avesta. Its use gradually decreases in the RV. and is lacking in the later Saṃhitās, doubtless owing to the disappearance of slurred accentuation: WACKERNAGEL I, 47.

8 RPr. VI. 13 f., VPr. IV. 16; TPr. XXI. 15 f.; APr. I. 101 ff.

9 The vowel which has to be restored in the gen. loc. du. termination *-tros*, which must always be read as a dissyllable, is not to be explained as Svarabhakti, since *-taros* is the original ending.

10 Cp. OLDENBERG, ZDMG. 60, 711—745 (Die Messung von *índra*, *rudrá* u. a.).

11 There seem to be a few instances of a Svarabhakti vowel being actually written: *tarásantī*, beside *tras-* 'tremble'; the secondary derivative *śvaitárīm*, beside *śvitrá-* (AV.) 'white'; *púruṣa-* and *pū́ruṣa-* 'man', probably for **pūrṣa-* (WACKERNAGEL I, 51, cp. 52). The initial vowel of *uloká-*, which is commoner than *loká-* 'world', has not yet been satisfactorily explained; cp. op. cit. I, 52 d.

b. When a consonant is followed by *ñ*, *n*, or *m*, the same parasitic vowel often appears; e. g. *yajñá-* (= *yaj^a^ná-*) 'sacrifice'; *gnā́-* (= *g^a^nā́-*) 'woman'. It is, however, here frequent only as representing the second syllable after the caesura in triṣṭubh and jagatī verses; it rarely occurs at the beginning of such verses, and never at the end[1].

VOWEL GRADATION.

I. The Guṇa series: *e o ar*.

22. **A. Low grade:** ***i u ṛ***.—In the same root or stem the simple vowels *i u ṛ ḷ* are found to interchange[2] with the respective high grade forms *e o ar al*[3] called Guṇa ('secondary form'?) by the native grammarians, according to the conditions under which the formative elements are attached. Beside these appear, but much less frequently, the long grade forms *ai au ār* called Vṛddhi ('increase') by the same authorities. The latter regarded the simple vowels as the fundamental grade, which, from the Indian point of view, these vowels often evidently represent: thus from *ūrṇavā́bhi-* (ŚB.) 'spider', we have the derivative formation *aurṇavābhá-* 'sprung from a spider'[4]. Comparative grammar has, however, shown that in such forms we have only a secondary application of an old habit of gradation derived from the IE. period, and that Guṇa[5] represents the normal stage from which the low grade form, with reduced or altogether lacking vowel[6], arose in less accented syllables. This theory alone can satisfactorily explain the parallel treatment of Guṇa gradation (*e o ar* beside *i u ṛ*) and Samprasāraṇa gradation (*ya va ra* beside *i u ṛ*), as in *diṣ-ṭá-*, *di-déś-a* (*diś-* 'point out') and *iṣ-ṭá-*, *iyáj-a* (*yaj-* 'sacrifice'). In other words, *i u ṛ* can easily be explained as reduced forms of both Guṇa and Samprasāraṇa syllables (as ending or beginning with *i u ṛ*), while the divergent 'strengthening' of *i u ṛ*, under the same conditions, to *e o ar* or *ya va ra* cannot be accounted for[7].

The interchange of Guṇa and simple vowel is generally accompanied by a shift of accent: Guṇa appears in the syllable which bears the accent, but is replaced by the simple vowel when the accent is transferred to the following syllable. This shows itself most clearly in inflexional forms; e. g. *é-mi* 'I go', but *i-más* 'we go'; *āp-nó-mi* (AV.) 'I obtain', but *āp-nu-más* 'we obtain'; *várdhāya*, but *vṛdhā́ya* 'to further'. Hence it is highly probable that change of accent was the cause of the gradation[8].

a. **Long grade or Vṛddhi:** ***ai, au, ār***.—Vṛddhi is far more restricted in use than Guṇa, and as it nearly always appears where Guṇa is to be expected, it may be regarded as a lengthened variety of it[9] dating back to the IE. period.

---

1 See OLDENBERG, Prolegomena, 374, note.

2 This interchange was already noticed by Yāska; see Nirukta x. 17.

3 The only root in which the gradation *al* : *ḷ* is found is *kḷp-*, cp. 14. It is employed in word-formation much in the same way as in verbal and nominal inflexion.

4 See below a, 3 and cp. 25 B 2; WACKERNAGEL I, 55, p. 62, note (top).

5 Both *a* and *ā* represent the Guṇa or normal stage in the gradation of the *a*-vowels in many roots: see 24; WACKERNAGEL I, 55 b.

6 The vowel sometimes disappears in the low grade of the *a*-series ('Schwundstufe') see 24.

7 Cp. WACKERNAGEL I, 55.

8 Occasional exceptions, such as *vṛ́ka-* 'wolf', are capable of explanation: cp. WACKERNAGEL I, 57.

9 'Dehnstufe'; cp. WACKERNAGEL I, 61.

It is to be found 1) in strong forms of a few monosyllabic substantives, in the nom. sing. of *sákhi-* 'friend' and of stems in *-r*, and in the loc. sing. of stems in *i* and *u*: *su-hárd-* 'good-hearted' (from *hṛ́d-* 'heart'), *dyáu-s* 'heaven' (from *dyú-*), *gáu-s* 'cow' (from *gó-*); *sákhā*[1], *pitā́*[2]; *agnā́*[3] (from *agní-* 'fire'), *aktáu* (from *aktú-* 'night'); 2) before the primary nominal suffixes *-a*, *-i*, *-ti*, *-tna*, *-man*, *-vana*; e. g. *spārh-á-* 'desirable' (√*spṛh-*); *hárd-i-* 'heart' (from *hṛ́d-*); *kārṣ-i-* (VS.) 'drawing' (√*kṛṣ-*); *śráuṣ-ṭī* 'obedient' (√*śruṣ-*); *cyau-tná-* 'stimulating' (√*cyu-*); *bhárman-* 'board' (√*bhṛ-*); *kārṣ-ī-vaṇa-* (AV.) 'ploughman'; 3) in secondary nominal derivation, generally to form patronymics or adjectives expressive of connexion or relation[4]; e. g. *gairikṣitá-* 'descended from *giri-kṣít*'; *auśijá-* 'son of *Uśíj*'; *śrautrá-* 'relating to the ear' (*śrótra-*); *hairaṇyá-* 'golden' (*híraṇya-* 'gold'); 4) in the singular pres. of a few verbs of the second class and in the active *s*-aorist of roots ending in vowels: *kṣṇáu-mi* 'I sharpen' (√*kṣṇu-*); *mārṣ-ṭi*[5] 'he wipes' (√*mṛj-*); *yáu-mi* (AV.) 'I unite' (√*yu-*); *a-jai-ṣam* 'I have conquered' (√*ji-*); *yáu-s*, 2 sing. 'ward off' (√*yu-*); *a-bhār-ṣam* 'I have borne' (√*bhṛ-*).

B. Low grade: *ī ū ṝ*.—The same Guṇa and Vṛddhi forms as a rule correspond to these long vowels as to their short forms *i u ṛ*. Thus *bhī-* 'fear': *bi-bháy-a* and *bi-bhāy-a*; *hū-* 'call': *ju-háv-a*; *tṝ-* 'cross': *ta-tār-a*, beside *tir-áte* and *-tīr-ṇa-* (just like *śri-* 'resort': *śi-śrāy-a*; *śru-* 'hear': *śu-śrāv-a*; *kṛ-* 'do': *ca-kār-a*). Before consonants the roots *prī-* 'love', *vī-* 'desire', *vī-* 'impel', *śī-* 'lie', *nī-* 'lead', *bhī-* 'fear', have Guṇa forms in *e*, the last two also Vṛddhi forms in *ai*; but roots in *ū* and *ṝ* have *avi*[6] and *ari* as Guṇa, *āvi* and *āri* as Vṛddhi, respectively; e. g. *pū-* 'purify', aor. *pavi-ṣṭa* and *apāviṣur*; *kṝ-* 'scatter', aor. subj. *kāri-ṣat*[7].

a. *ī* and *ū* instead of Guṇa. In a few verbs and some other words *ī* and *ū* are the old weak grade vowels (almost invariably medial) of *e* and *o*, the length of which has been preserved by the accent shifting to them (while when not thus protected they have been shortened to *ĭ* and *ŭ*), and which as thus accented, sometimes appear instead of the Guṇa vowels. Thus *ī* is found in *rī́ṣ-ant-* 'injuring' (= **rīṣ-ánt-*), beside *reṣa-*, the low grade form of the radical syllable otherwise becoming *riṣ-*[8]. Similary *gū́hati* 'hides' appears beside *góh-a-* 'hiding-place', the root being also shortened in *guh-yáte*, etc.; *dūṣ-áyati* 'spoils', beside *doṣ-ā́-* and *doṣás-* (AV.) 'evening', also *dúṣ-ṭi-* (AV.) 'destruction'; *ū́h-ati* 'removes', beside *óh-a-* 'gift'; *nū́* 'now', *nū́-tana-* 'new', *nū-nám* 'now', beside *náva-* 'new', also *nú* 'now' (never at the beginning of a sentence); *mū́s-* 'mouse', beside *móṣatha* 'ye rob', also *muṣitá-* 'stolen'; *yū́pa-* 'post', beside *yuyópa* 'has infringed', also *yupitá-* (AV.) 'smoothed'; *stū́-pa-* 'tuft', beside *sto-ká-* 'drop', also *stu-pá-* (VS.) 'tuft'[9].

b. In a few roots ending in *v*[10], the radical vowel *ī* represents the low

---

1 With loss of the final element, which however, remains in datives like *tásmai*, probably because the diphthong was here pronounced with a slurred accent: cp. WACKERNAGEL 1, 93.

2 With loss of *r*, the preceding vowel having compensatory IE. lengthening (cp. WACKERNAGEL 1, 61 c). In a few instances, the Vṛddhi of the nom. sing. spread to other cases (cp. 25 B b 1); e. g. *tā́r-as*, nom. pl., from old nom. sing. **stār* (beside *stṛ́-bhis*).

3 Also *agnáu*, like the *u*-stems.

4 See below 191.

5 From the present the *ār* spread to other forms, e. g. perf. *mamārja* (AV.).

6 They have *o* in the intensive reduplication only; e. g. *soṣū-* : √*sū-*.

7 Cp. WACKERNAGEL 1, 76.

8 The accentuation of *ī*, the low grade of *yā́*, is probably to be explained similarly in feminines like *naptī́-s* (masc. *nápāt-*); shortened to *nápti* in voc.; cp. 19 b 3 and 29.

9 The accentuation of *ū*, the low grade of *vā́* is probably to be explained similarly in feminines like *kadrū́-s* (TS. B.) 'brown' (masc. *kádru-m*, TS. B.); shortened to *u* in voc., e. g. *bábhru*; cp. WACKERNAGEL 1, 82.

10 That is, the original form would have been *īṷ-* or *i̯ū-* according as a vowel or a consonant followed.

grade, but early began to supplant *e*; thus from *dīv-* 'play', beside *didéva* (AV.), *dév-ana-* 'game of dice', occur *dī́v-yati*, *dīv-é* and *dīv-í* dat. and loc. of *dī́v-* 'game of dice'; from *srīv-* 'fail', beside *śrevayánt-*, *srīvayati* (AV.); but from *mīv-* 'push', only *mī́v-ati* etc.; from *sīv-* 'sew', only *sī́v-yati* etc. It is a peculiarity of these roots that *īv* appears before vowels and *y* only, becoming *yū* or *ū* before other consonants; thus *dyū-tá-* (AV.) 'play'; *-mū-ta-* 'impelled', *mū-rá-* 'dull', *mū́-tra-* (AV. VS.) 'urine'; *syū-tá-* 'fastened', *sū-cí-* 'needle', *sū́-tra-* (AV.) 'thread'; *srū́-* 'lead ball'[1].

II. The Samprasāraṇa[2] series.

a. Gradation of *ya va ra*.

23. Low grade: *i u ṛ*[3].—In place of the accented syllables *ya va ra* (corresponding to the Guṇa vowels *e o ar*) appear the low grade vowels *i u ṛ*[4] when the accent shifts to the following syllable in some fourteen roots, viz. *yaj-* 'sacrifice', *vyac-* 'extend', *vyadh-* 'pierce', *vac-* 'speak', *vad-* 'speak', *vap-* 'strew', *vaś-* 'be eager', *vas-* 'dwell', *vas-* 'shine', *vah-* 'carry'; *svap-* 'sleep', *grabh-* and *grah-* 'seize', *pracch-* (properly *praś-*) 'ask', *vraśc-* 'hew'; e. g. *iṣ-ṭá-* : *yáṣ-ṭave*; *uś-mási* : *váṣ-ṭi*; *suṣup-vā́ṃs-* : *suṣvā́pa*.

a. Besides these, a good many other roots, in occasional verbal forms or nominal derivatives, show the same gradation in the radical syllable.

1. *i* appears in *mimikṣúr* : *mimyákṣa* perf. of √*myakṣ-*; *vithurá-* 'wavering', *vithuryáti* 'wavers', beside *vyáth-ate* 'wavers'.

2. *u* in *úkṣant-* 'growing' : *vavákṣa* 'has grown'; *śuṣ-ánt-* : *śvas-iti* 'breathes'; *ju-hur-as* : *hvár-ati* 'is crooked'; *ur-ú-* 'broad': comp. *vár-īyas-*, superl. *vár-iṣṭha-*; *dúr-* : *dvā́r-* 'door'; *dhún-i-* 'resounding' : *dhvan-í-* (AV.) 'sound'.

3. *ṛ* in *kṛpate* 'laments': aor. *akrapiṣṭa*; *gṛnatti* (AV.) : *grath-itá-* 'tied'; *-śṛth-ita-* : *śrath-nāti* 'becomes loose'; *ṛj-ú-* 'straight' : *ráj-iṣṭha-* 'straightest'; *ṛbh-ú-* 'adroit' : *rábh-ate* 'grasps'; *dṛh-ya* 'be firm' (impv.) : *drah-yát* 'firmly'; *pṛth-ú-* 'broad' : *práth-ati* 'spreads out'; *bhṛm-á-* 'error' : *bhram-á-* 'whirling flame'; *á-ni-bhṛṣ-ṭa-* 'undefeated': *bhraś-at* aor., *bhraṣ-ṭá-* (AV.) 'fallen'; *mṛd-ú-* 'soft': *mrada* 'soften' (impv.), *ū́rṇa-mradas-* 'soft as wool'; *sṛ́k-van-* : *srák-va-* 'corner of the mouth'.

b. This gradation also appears in the stems of a few nouns and in certain nominal suffixes: *dyú-bhis* : *dyáv-i* loc., *dyáu-s* nom. 'heaven'; *śún-* : *śvá-*, *śvā́n-* 'dog'; *yū́n-* (= *yú-un-*) : *yúva-*, *yúvān-* 'youth'; *catúr-* : *catvā́r-* 'four'; the superlative and comparative suffixes *-iṣ-ṭha* and *-yas*; the perf. part. suffix *-uṣ* : *-vat*, *-vāṃs*[5].

b. Gradation of *yā vā rā*.

24. Low grade: *ī ū ī̆r*.—Corresponding to the reduction of the short syllables *ya va ra* to the short vowels *i u ṛ*, the long syllables *yā vā rā* appear as *ī ū ī̆r* (= IE. *ṝ*).

[1] The etymology of this word is, however, doubtful. Cp. WACKERNAGEL I, 81.

[2] In the terminology of the native grammarians Samprasāraṇa ('distraction') designates the change of the semi-vowel only to the corresponding vowel (but see also Paṇini VI. 1, 108). Here we use the word to express the reduction of the entire syllables *ya va ra* to the corresponding vowels *i u ṛ*.

[3] Though *ṛ* seems invariably to have resulted from the reduction of Guṇa or Samprasāraṇa syllables, there is no reason to suppose that every *i* and *u* has a similar origin. On the contrary, it is more likely that IE. *i* and *u* have been preserved by the side of the reduced vowels and that the Guṇa grade has in many instances been subsequently added to original *i* and *u*. Cp. PEDERSEN, IF. 2, 323, note.

[4] This reduction goes back to the IE. pretonic syncope of *ĕ ŏ*: cp. WACKERNAGEL I, 62 (p. 69, mid.). — On the two forms of the roots cp. also Nirukta II. 2 and Mahābhāṣya I, 112.

[5] See WACKERNAGEL I, 63.

a. *ī* is found thus both in radical and suffixal syllables: 1. in *jī-tá-* (AV.) *jī-yáte* (AV.) and *jí-yate*: *-jyā́-* 'might', *jyā́-yas-* 'stronger', *jí-jyā-sant-* 'desiring to overcome'; 2. in the fem. suffix *-ī*: *kan-ī-nā́m* (for *kanī-nā́m*) from *kan-yā̀-* 'girl'; in nom. acc., e. g. *devī́*, *devī́m*, *devī́s*, beside *-yā-* in dat. abl. gen. loc. sing. *devyái* (= *devyā́-e*), *devyā́s* (= *devyā́-as*), *devyā́m* (= *devyā́-am*); 3. in the optative, either before or after the accented syllable, beside *-yā-*; e. g. *bruv-ī-tá* and *bháret* (= *bhára-ī-t*), but *i-yā́-t*.

b. *ū* is found: 1. in forms of *sūd-* 'put in order' (= 'make palatable'), e. g. *sú-ṣūd-ati*, *sūd-áyati*, *saṃ-sūd-á-* (TS.) 'gum', beside forms and derivatives of *svād-* 'enjoy', 'taste', e. g. *svā́da-te*, *svāttá-*, *svād-ú-* 'sweet'; 2. in fem. nouns in *-ū* beside *-vā* in dat. abl. gen. loc. sing.; e. g. *śvaśrū́-* 'mother-in-law', dat. *śvaśr-vái* (AV., = *śvaśr-vā́-e*), gen. *śvaśr-vā́s* (AV., = *śvaśr-vā́-as*), loc. *śvaśr-vā́m* (= *śvaśr-vā́-am*).

c. *īr* (= *r̥̄*) is found in *dīrgh-á-* 'long', beside *drā́gh-īyas-* 'longer', *drā́gh-iṣṭha-* 'longest', *drāgh-mán-* 'length'.

III. The ă-series.

a. Gradation of *a*.

25. **A. Low grade: *a* or -.** — Many roots and formatives have *a* in the Guṇa or normal stage. The reduction of *r̥* from *ar* or *ra* indicates that in low grade syllables this *a* would normally disappear. As a rule, however, it remains[1], doubtless because its loss would in most cases have led to unpronounceable or obscure forms[2]. At the same time, the syncope takes place in a considerable number of instances:

1. **in verbal forms:** *ad-* 'eat': *d-ánt-* (= old pres. part.) 'tooth'; *as-* 'be': *s-ánti*, *s-yā́t*, *s-ánt-*, beside *ás-ti* 'is'; *gam-* 'go': *ja-gm-úr*; *ghas-* 'eat': *a-kṣ-an*, 3. pl. impf., *g-dha* (= *ghs-ta*), 3. sing. impf. mid., *ja-kṣ-īyā́t*, perf. opt., beside *ghas-a-t* 'may he eat'; *pat-* 'fall': *pa-pt-ima*, *pa-pt-úr*, *pa-pt-ivā́ṃs-*, perf., *a-pa-pt-at*, aor., beside *pát-anti*; *pad-* 'go': *pí-bd-a-māna-*, red. pres. part., *pi-bd-aná-* 'standing firm', beside *pád-yate* 'goes'; *bhas-* 'chew': *ba-ps-ati*, 3 pl. pres., *bá-ps-at-*, pres. part., beside *bhás-a-t* 'may he chew'; *sac-* 'follow': *sá-śc-ati*, 3. pl. red. pres., *sa-śc-ata*, 3. pl. impf. mid., *sa-śc-iré*, 3. pl. perf. mid., beside *sác-ante* 'they accompany'; *sad-* 'sit': *sī́d-ati* (= *si-zd-ati*), 3. sing. pres., *sed-úr* (= *sa-zd-úr*), 3. pl. perf., beside *á-sad-at* 'he sat'; *han-* strike': *ghn-ánti*, 3. pl. pres., beside *hán-ti* 3. sing.

2. **in nominal derivatives:** *ghas-* 'eat': *a-g-dhā́d-* (TS.) 'eating what is uneaten' (= *a-ghs-ta-ad-*), *sá-g-dhi* (VS.) 'joint meal' (= *sa-ghs-ti-*); *bhas-* 'chew': *á-ps-u-* 'foodless'; *pad-* 'walk': *upa-bd-á-*, *upa-bd-í-* 'noise' (lit. 'tread'); *tur-íya-* 'fourth' (= **ktur-iya-*): *catúr-* 'four'; *napt-í-* 'granddaughter': *nápāt-* 'grandson'.

3. **in suffixes:** *-s-* for *-as-* in *bhī-ṣ-ā́*, inst. sing.: *bhiy-ás-ā* 'through fear'; *śīr-ṣ-án-*: *śír-as-* 'head'; *-s* for *-as* in the abl. gen. sing. ending of stems in *i u o*: e. g. *agné-s*, *viṣṇo-s*, *gó-s*.

B. Long grade: *ā*. — The Vr̥ddhi corresponding to the *a* which represents the Guṇa stage is *ā*. It appears:

a. in the root:

1. in primary nominal derivation: thus *pā́d-* 'foot': *pad-*, *bd-* 'walk'; *rā́j-*

[1] See WACKERNAGEL I, 70.

[2] When *a* is followed by *n* or *m*, the syllables *an* and *am*, if preceded by a consonant, usually lose the nasal before mutes; e. g. *han-* strike': *ha-thás* 2. du. pres.; *gam-* 'go': *ga-tá-*; *dyu-mánt-*, inst. sing. *dyu-mát-ā*; *nā́-man-*, inst. pl. *nā́ma-bhis*. The *a* in such low grade syllables is generally regarded as historically representing the sonant nasal *n̥*: cp. WACKERNAGEL I, 66.

'king' : *raj-*, *ṛj-* 'direct'; *vā́c-* 'voice' : *vac-*, *uc-* 'speak'; *kṣā́s*, nom., *kṣā́m*, acc., 'earth' : *kṣam-*, *kṣm-*; *nā́bh-* 'well' : *nábh-as*, *abh-rá-* (*abh-* = *ṇbh-*) 'cloud'. Also before primary suffixes: *ā́p-as* : *áp-as* 'work'; *vā́s-as* 'garment' : *vas-*, *uṣ-* 'wear'; *vā́h-as* 'offering' : *vah-*, *uh-* 'convey'; *vā́s-tu* 'abode' : *vas-*, *uṣ-* 'dwell'. Perhaps also *pā́th-as* 'place' : *path-* 'path'[1].

2. in secondary nominal derivation; e. g. *kāṇvá-* 'descended from Kaṇva'; *vāpuṣ-á-* 'marvellous' : *váp-us-* 'marvel'.

3. in the active of the *s*-aorist: thus *a-cchānt-s-ur* : *chand-*, *chad-* (= *chṇd-*) 'appear'; *a-yāṃ-s-am*, 1. sing. : *yam-*, *ya-* (= *yṃ-*) 'stretch'; *sāk-ṣ-āma*, also mid. *sāk-ṣ-i*, *sāk-ṣ-ate* : *sah-* 'overcome'[2].

b. in the suffix of nominal stems:

1. in the nom. sing. masc. of stems in *-mant* and *-vant*, and throughout the strong cases of stems in *-an*, of *mahát-* 'great', and of *nápāt-* 'grandson': thus *dyu-mā́n* 'brilliant' : *dyu-mánt-*, *dyu-mát-* (= *-mṇt-*); *re-vā́n* 'rich' : *re-vánt-*, *re-vát-* (= *vṇt-*)[3]; *rā́j-ā*, acc. *rā́j-ān-am* 'king' : *rā́j-an-*, *rā́j-ñ-*, *rā́j-a-* (= *rāj-ṇ-*); *mah-ā́n*, acc. *mah-ā́nt-am*; *nápāt*, acc. *nápāt-am*.

2. in the nom. acc. pl. neuter of stems in *-an* and *-as* and of one in *-ant*; thus *nā́mā*[4] 'names' : *nā́man*, *nā́ma-* (= *nā́mṇ-*); *mánāṃs-i* 'minds' : *mán-as*; *sā́nt-i* : *s-ánt-* 'being'.

c. in *ānu-* as first member of a compound in *ānu-ṣák* and *ānūkám* 'continuously' : otherwise *anu-*.

b. Gradation of *ā*.

26. Low grade: *i*. — The vowel *ā* is not always the long grade vowel: in a number of roots it represents Guṇa. The low grade of this *ā* is normally *i*; it sometimes, however, appears as *ī*, owing to analogy[5], and, especially with a secondary accent, as *a*. Thus *sthi-tá-* : *sthā́-s* 'thou hast stood'; *dhi-tá-* : *dá-dhā-ti* 'places'; *pu-nī-hí* : *pu-nā́-ti*, from *pū-* 'purify'; *gáh-ana-* 'depth', *gáh-vara-* (AV.) 'hiding-place' : *gā́h-ate* 'plunges'.

a. The low grade **vowel disappears**: 1. in roots ending in *ā* before vowel terminations; in the weak forms of the reduplicated present base of *dā-* 'give' and *dhā-* 'put', before all terminations; and in the weak form of the suffix *-nā-* in the ninth class before vowel terminations; thus in the perf. of *dā-*: *dad-áthur*, *dad-atur*; *dad-á*, *dad-úr*; *dad-é*; in the pres. of *dhā-*: *dadh-mási*; beside *pu-nā́-ti* 'he purifies', *pu-n-ánti* 'they purify'. Similarly from *hā-* 'forsake' occurs, in the opt. pres., the form *jah-yāt* (AV.).

2. in the final member of compounds formed with the perf. part. passive of *dā-* 'give', and *dā-* 'cut', or with a substantive in *-ti-* from *dā-* 'give': *devá-tta-*, a name ('given by the gods'); *áva-tta-* (VS.) 'cut off'; *párī-tta-* (VS.) 'given up'; *á-pratī-tta-* (AV.) 'not given back'; *bhága-tti-* 'gift of fortune'; *maghá-tti-* 'gift of presents'; *vásu-tti-* 'gift of wealth' (beside *vásu-dhiti-* 'bestowal of wealth' : *dhā-*). Also in *agní-dh-*[6] 'fire-placer', a kind of priest[7].

---

1 Cp. Aufrecht, BB. 14, 33; Wackernagel 1, 72 (p. 79, bottom).

2 Op. cit. 1, 72 b δ (p. 80).

3 The long vowel in these nominatives is to be accounted for by IE. compensatory lengthening (*-mān* = *mant-s*, etc.); in the following examples it has spread from the nominative to other cases.

4 Such neuter plurals were in origin probably feminine singular collectives: cp. Brugmann, KG. 481; Wackernagel 1, 73 and 95.

5 That is, under the influence of *ī* as low grade of *ai* which before consonants appears as *ā*, as in *gī-tá-* beside *gā-thá-*, from *gai-* 'sing', pres. *gā́y-ati*; cp. 27 a.

6 Cp. *agni-dhā́na-* 'fire-place'; in VS. *agnī́dh-* appears instead, as if 'fire-kindler' (from *idh-* 'kindle').

7 For a few other examples (which are doubtful) of the loss of the low grade vowel in the final member of compounds, see Wackernagel 1, p. 82 (mid.).

IV. The *ai* and *au* series.

a. Gradation of *ai*.

27. Low grade: *ī*. — As the final of roots and in suffixes *ī* is graded with *ai* (as with *yā*[1]), which appears as *āy-* before vowels and as *ā-* before consonants[2]. The roots in which this gradation is found are stated by the Indian grammarians in five different forms. They are:

a. 1. roots given with *-ai-* (because their present base appears as *-āy-a*): *gai-* 'sing': *gī-tá-*, *gī-yá-māna-*, beside *gấy-ati* 'sings', *-gấy-as* 'song', and *gā-s-i*, 1. sing. aor. mid., *gā-thá-* 'song'; *pyai-* 'swell': *pī-ná-*, beside *pyấy-ate*; *śrai-* 'boil': *śrī-ṇā-ti*, *śrī-tá-*, beside *śrấy-ati*, *śrā-tá-*. — 2. with *-āy-*: *cāy-* 'observe': *cikī-hi* (AV.), beside *cấy-amāna-*, *cāy-ú-* 'respectful'. — 3. with *-e-*: *dhe-* 'suck': *dhī-tá-*, beside *dhấy-as* 'drink', *dhāy-ú-* 'thirsty', and *dhấ-tave* 'to suck', *dhā-rú-* (AV.) 'sucking'. — 4. with *-ā-*: *pā-* 'drink': *pī-tá-*, *pī-tí-* 'drink', beside *pāy-áyati*, caus., *pāy-ána-* 'causing to drink', and *á-pā-t*, aor., *pấ-tave*; *rā-* 'give': *ra-rī-thās*, 2. sing. injv., beside *rāy-ấ* 'with wealth', and *rấ-sva*, impv., *rấ-m*, acc. — 5. with *-ī-*: *nī-* 'lead': *nī-tá-*, beside *nāy-á-* 'leader', and *-nā-thá-* (AV.) 'help'; *pī-* 'revile': *pī́-yati*, *pī-ya-tnú-* and *pī-y-ú-* 'reviler', beside *pāy-ú-* (VS.) 'anus'; *prī-* 'love': *prī-ṇā́-ti*, *prī-tá-*, beside *prấy-as-e*[3]; *śī-*[4] 'lie'; *-śī́-van-* 'lying', beside *a-śāy-ata*, 3. sing.[5]

b. This gradation also occurs in the final of dissyllabic **bases**: thus *grabhī-ṣṭa*, *a-grabhī-t*, *gṛbhī-tá-*, beside *gṛbhāy-áti* 'seizes'[6]; and in the base of the ninth class: *gṛbhṇī-ta*, 2. pl., beside *gṛbhṇā́-ti*.

c. It is also found in the **suffixes** *-ethe -ete* and *-ethām -etām* of the 2. 3. du. mid. of the *a*-conjugation, which can only be explained as containing *īthe īte* and *īthām ītām*, with weak grade *ī* corresponding to the accented *ā* of *ấthe ấte* and *ấthām ấtām* of the non-thematic conjugation (and parallel to the *-ī-* of the optative beside *-yā-*[7]).

b. Gradation of *au*.

28. Low grade: *ū*. — As the final of roots *ū* is graded with *au* (parallel with *vā*[8]), much in the same way as *ī* with *ai*, appearing as *āv* before vowels, *ā* before consonants[9]; but the certain examples are few. Thus *dhū-nó-ti* 'shakes', *dhū́-ti-* 'shaker', *dhū-má-* 'smoke', beside *dhấv-ati* 'runs', *dhấ-rā-* 'stream'; *dhū-tá-* 'washed', beside *dhấv-ati* 'washes'. But here *au* appears before consonants as well as *ā*; thus *dhau-tárī-* 'shaking', beside *dhū-* 'shake'; and *dhau-tí-* 'spring', *dhau-tá-* (SV.), beside *dhấv-ati* 'washes'. Similarly *gấ-m*

[1] See above 24.

[2] *ai* appears only in the *s*-aor., as *nai-ṣ-ṭa*, 2. pl., *nī-* 'lead', owing to the analogy of forms like *á-jai-ṣ-ma*, from *ji-* 'conquer'.

[3] Occurs RV. IV. 21⁷ (Pp. *prá áyase* (and is explained by BÖHTLINGK (pw.) as = *práyase*.

[4] Perhaps also in *śī-* 'fall': *śī́yate* (AV.), beside *śātá-yati* 'cuts off', which may be a denominative from **śā-tá-* 'fallen'. Cp. WHITNEY, Roots, under √*śat-* and √1 *śī-*; WACKERNAGEL I, 79 a δ (p. 88).

[5] In some of the above roots *e* appears instead of *ā* before consonants; e. g. *cé-ru-* 'devout', beside *cāy-ú-*; *pe-rú-* 'causing to drink', beside *pāy-ána-*; *dhe-nú-* 'milch cow', *dhé-nā-* id.; *śé-ṣe*, beside *a-śāy-ata*; *ne-tṛ́-*, beside *nāy-á-*; *ste-ná-* 'thief', beside *stāy-ú-* (VS.) id., and *stāy-ánt-* (AV.) 'furtive'; *sénā-* missile', beside *sấy-aka-*. It is, perhaps, due to this *e* that *ay-* sometimes appears instead of *āy-* in some of the above verbs; as *práy-as-* 'enjoyment', from √*prī-*; *ray-í-* 'wealth', from √*rā-*; *śáy-e*, 3. sing., from *śī-* 'lie'.

[6] Cp. WACKERNAGEL I, 79 b (p. 89).

[7] Op. cit. I, 79 c (p. 89).

[8] See above 24 b.

[9] Similarly in the RV. the *-au* of duals and of *aṣṭáu* 'eight' normally appears as *āv* before vowels and *ā* before consonants in Sandhi. The nominatives in *ā* of *-ṛ* stems and *-an* stems, e. g. *mātấ*, *śvấ* 'dog', are probably due originally to the loss of the final *r* and *n* before consonants in the sentence, then becoming the regular form everywhere. Conversely *aṣṭáu* has become the only independent form in the AV., *aṣṭā-* appearing only as first member of a compound. Cp. WACKERNAGEL I, 94, 95.

and *gā́-s,* acc., beside *gā́v-as,* nom. pl., but *gáu-s,* nom. sing., 'cow'; and *dyā́-m,* acc. sing., beside *dyā́v-as,* nom. pl., but *dyáu-s,* nom. sing., 'heaven'.

V. Secondary shortening of ī ū ṝ.

29. Low grade: *i u ṛ.* — Owing to the shift of the accent from its normal position in a word to its beginning, the low grade vowels *ī ū īr ūr* (= *ṝ*) are often further shortened to *i u ṛ* in compounds and reduplicated forms. A pre-tonic syllable thus acquires a post-tonic position, where the force of the accent is weakest. It is the same cause which shortens final weak grade *ī* and *ū* in the vocative singular; e. g. *dévi,* nom. *devī́; śváśru,* nom. *śvaśrū́s*[1]. This shortening often appears in:

a. compounds[2]:

1. those in which the final member is derived with *-ta-* and *-ti-*, the accent being regularly thrown back on the first member[3]: thus *á-ni-śi-ta-* 'restless', *ní-śi-tā-* (TS. B.) 'night', from *śī* 'lie'; *prá-si-ti-* 'onset', beside *sā́y-aka-* 'missile'[4]; *sú-ṣu-ti-* 'easy birth', beside *sū́ti-kā-* (AV.) 'lying-in woman'; *á-stṛ-ta-* 'unconquered', *á-ni-ṣṭṛ-ta-* 'not overthrown', beside *stīr-ṇá-*, from *stṝ-* 'strew'[5]; *ā́-huti-* 'invocation', otherwise *-hū-ti-* in *sá-hūti-* 'joint invocation', *devá-hūti-* 'invocation of the gods', and other compounds.

2. those in which the final member is a root in *ī*[6] or *ū* with or without the suffix *-t;* e. g. *dhī-jú-* 'thought inspiring', beside *jū́-* 'hastening', *jū-tá-* 'impelled'; very often *-bhu-*, beside *bhū-*, as in *á-pra-bhu-* 'powerless', *vi-bhú-* 'mighty'; *ni-yú-t-* 'team', beside *yū-* 'unite' (as in *yū-thá-* 'herd').

3. those in which the final member is formed with other suffixes; thus *madhyán-di-na-* 'midday', *su-dí-na-* 'bright', beside *dī-* 'shine'; *su-ṣu-mánt-* 'very stimulating', beside *sū-tá-* 'impelled'; also in *tuvi-gr-á-* and *tuvi-gr-í-* 'much devouring', beside *saṃ-gir-á-* (AV.) 'devouring', as *r* here = *ṛ*[7].

4. some Bahuvrīhis (in which the first member is normally accented)[8]; thus *bṛhád-ri-*[9] 'possessing much wealth' (*rái-*); *try-udh-án-* 'having three udders', beside *ū́dh-an-* 'udder'.

b. reduplicated forms[10] in which accentuation of the reduplicative syllable, especially in the third class and one form of the aorist, counteracts the normal accent of the verb; thus from *dī-* 'shine', are formed *dī-di-hi,* 2. sing. impv., *dī-di-vā́ṃs-*, perf. part., *dī́-di-vi-* 'shining', beside *dī-paya-* (causative)

---

[1] Cp. 23.

[2] The application of this shortening process becomes obscured, on the one hand because the phonetically shortened vowel has found its way into accented final members of compounds as being characteristic of the end of a compound; while, on the other hand, *ī ū īr ūr* (= *ṝ*) for the most part have remained unchanged, even when the accent has shifted, because of the influence of the uncompounded word; e. g. *sú-sūta-* 'well-begotten', *prá-sūta-* 'impelled'; *ā́-kūti-* 'intention'; *ṛtá-dhīti-* 'truly adored'; *prá-tūrti-* 'onset'.

[3] That this is the cause of the shortening is shown by the fact that the *ī* of the inst. sing. of derivatives in *-ti* appears as *ĭ* only when such words are compounded: e. g. *prá-yukti* 'with the team'. Cp. WACKERNAGEL I, 84.

[4] Cp. 27, note 5.

[5] The secondarily shortened form of the past part. *stṛ-ta-* is not found as an independent word in the RV.; it first appears in later texts.

[6] An example of the shortening of *ī* is perhaps *adhi-kṣi-t-* 'ruler', *kṣī-* being according to J. SCHMIDT, Pluralbildung 419, the original weak form of the root; cp. WACKERNAGEL I, 83 b.

[7] Cp. KRETSCHMER, KZ. 31, 397; WACKERNAGEL I, 83 c.

[8] See accentuation of compounds, 90.

[9] Occurring only in the dat. sing. *bṛhád-raye,* beside *rāy-é,* dat. of *rái-* 'wealth'.

[10] On the shortening of the radical syllable in some verbs of the fifth and the ninth classes, *ji-nó-ṣi,* beside *jī-rá-* 'lively', *du-no-ti* 'burns', beside *dū-ná-* (AV.); *ju-nā́-ti* 'impels', beside *jū-tá-*; *pu-nā́-ti* 'purifies', beside *pū-tá-*, see WACKERNAGEL I, 85, note (bottom).

'kindle'; from *dhī-* 'think', *dī-dhi-ma*, 1. pl. perf., *dí-dhi-ti-* 'devotion', beside *dhī-tí-* 'thought'; from *kṝ-* 'commemorate', *cár-kṛ-ṣe*, intv., *car-kṛ-tí-* 'praise', beside *kīr-tí-* 'praise'; from *pṝ-* fill', *pi-pṛ-tám*, 3. du., beside *pūr-ṇá-* and *pūr-tá-*. Such shortening often occurs in red. aor., e. g. *bī-bhiṣ-a-thās*, 2. sing. mid., beside *vi-bhī́ṣ-aṇa-* 'terrifying'. It is also found in a few nouns; e. g. *śí-śi-ra-* (AV.) 'coolness', beside *śī-tá-* 'cold'; *tū-tu-má-* beside *tū́-ya-* 'strong'[1].

The Consonants.

30. Doubling of consonants.—All consonants, except *r h ḷ*, Anusvāra, and Visarjanīya, can be doubled, and the distinction between double and single consonants is known to the Prātiśākhyas as well as to Pāṇini. Aspirates are, however, nearly always written double by giving the first in the unaspirated form. A double consonant[2] is pronounced by the organs of speech dwelling longer on it than on the single sound. Within words[3] a double consonant appears:

1. as the result of the contact of the same consonants or the assimilation[4] of different ones; e. g. *cit-tá-* 'perceived' (= *cit-ta-*); *uc-cá-* 'high' (= *ud-ca-*); *bhet-tṛ́-* 'breaker' (= *bhed-tṛ-*); *án-na-* 'food' (= *ad-na-*).

2. in a few onomatopoetic words: *akhkhalī-kṛ́tyā* 'shouting'; *ciccikā́-* a kind of bird; *kukkuṭá-* (VS.) 'cock'; *tittiri-* (VS.) and *tittirí-* (TS. B.) 'quail'; *pippakā-* (VS.) a kind of bird.

3. in the case of the palatal aspirate, which regularly appears as *cch* between vowels (though often written as *ch* in the Mss.), for it always makes the preceding vowel long by position and is derived from an original conjunct consonant[5]. Some forms of *khid-* 'press down', are doubled after a vowel in the TS. (*akkhidat*, *á-kkhidra-*; *ā-kkhidaté*, *pari-kkhidaté*). In the TS.[6] *bh* appears doubled in *pári bbhuja*. In a school of the White Yajurveda initial *v* was regularly doubled[7].

4. when final *n* is doubled after a short vowel if followed by any vowel sound[8].

a. In the Mss., when double consonants are preceded or followed by another consonant[9], one of them is frequently dropped, because in such consonantal groups there was no difference in pronunciation between single and double consonants. Hence the VPr. (VI. 27) prescribes a single *t* in *kṣattrá-* 'dominion' (= *kṣad-tra-*), and in *sattrá-* 'sacrificial session' (= *sad-tra-*). Such shortening is further presupposed by the analysis of the Pada texts in *hṛ(d)-dyotáḥ* (AV. I. 22[1]) and *hṛ(d)-dyótanaḥ* (AV. V. 20[12]) as *hṛ-dyotáḥ* and *hṛ-dyótanaḥ*; in *tá(d)dyā́m* (AV. IV. 19[6]) as *tát yā́m* (instead of *tát dyā́m*); and in *upástha-*, which appears in the RV. Pada as *upá-stha-* instead of *upás-stha-*, if GRASSMANN's suggestion is right[10]. In some instances this reduction is IE., as in *satrá-* (IE. *setlo-*)[11].

---

[1] On variations in cognate forms between *i u ṛ* and *ī ū ṝ* in some other words see WACKERNAGEL I, 86.

[2] Sometimes a single *s* represents the double sound, as in *ási* 'thou art' (= *as-si*); *apásu* (RV. VIII. 4[14]), loc. pl. of *apás-* 'active'; *áṃhasu* (AV.), loc. pl. of *áṃhas-* 'distress'; *jó-ṣi* 'thou shalt taste' (*juṣ-*); probably also in *ghó-ṣi* (from *ghuṣ-* 'sound'), in *uṣ-ás*, gen. sing., acc. pl. of *uṣ-*, weak stem of *uṣ-ás-* 'dawn' (for **uṣṣ-as*), possibly in *usṛ-* 'dawn' (for **uss-ṛ-*). As the single *s* in such forms is shown by cognate languages also, it seems here to be pre-Vedic, and the double *ss* in forms like *rájas-su*, loc. pl., is probably an Indian innovation. The change of *ṣṣ* to *kṣ*, as in *dvikṣat* (AV.) = **dviṣ-ṣat*, aor. of *dviṣ-* 'hate', is also an Indian innovation.

[3] On double consonants in Sandhi, see below 77.

[4] The evidence of the Avestan form *vərəδka-* shows that the double consonant in *vṛkká-* (AV. VS.) 'kidney' is due to assimilation.

[5] See below 40; WACKERNAGEL I, 133.

[6] See TPr. XIV. 8.

[7] See WEBER, Abh. d. Berliner Ak. d. Wiss. 1871, p. 83 f.

[8] See below 46; cp. WACKERNAGEL I, 279 a.

[9] Cp. ROTH in ZDMG. 48, 102 f.

[10] See his Lexicon, s. v. *upástha-*.

[11] See WACKERNAGEL I, 98 b, note.

Mutes.

31. **Modes of articulation.**—There are 20 mutes (or 22 counting *ḷ ḷh* among the cerebrals), which comprise a tenuis, an aspirate tenuis, a media, and an aspirate media in each of the five groups of gutturals, palatals, cerebrals, dentals, and labials (4). These four modes of articulation are initially and medially liable to but little variation except when they come into contact with other mutes or with following sibilants.

1. The **tenues** regularly represent IE. tenues; e. g. *cakrá-* 'wheel', Gk. *κύκλο-ς*; *pitṛ́-* 'father', Gk. *πατήρ*, Lat. *pater*.

2. The **mediae** regularly represent IE. mediae; e. g. *gácchati*, Gk. *βάσκει*; *rā́j-* 'king', Lat. *rēg-*; *mád-ati* 'is drunk', Lat. *mad-et*. There are a few instances in which a media appears in place of an older tenuis: *gulphá-* (AV.): *kulphá-* 'ancle'; *árbhaga-* 'youthful': *arbhaká-* 'little'; *túj-* : *túc-*, *toká-* 'offspring'; *án-ava-pṛgṇa-* 'undivided': *pṛc-* 'mix'; *giriká-* (MS.) : *kiriká-* (VS.)[1] a kind of demon. These examples may be due to popular dialects, in which tenues largely became mediae[2]. In a few derivatives the media *g* appears instead of *k* before the *n m v* of suffixes owing to the influence of Sandhi: e. g. *vag-nú-* 'sound', from *vac-* 'speak', but *rék-ṇas-* 'wealth', from *ric-*; *śag-má-* 'helpful', from *śak-*, but *ruk-má-* 'gold', from *ruc-* 'shine'; *vāg-vín-* (AV.) 'eloquent', from *vā́k* 'speech', but *tak-vá-* 'swift', from *tak-* 'hasten'.

3. The evidence of cognate languages shows that the Vedic **aspirate tenuis** in a large number of instances is original, and it is highly probable that it is the regular representative of IE. aspirate tenuis. The following are examples in which mutes of this character are inherited[3]:

a. *khan-* 'dig'; *khā́-* 'spring'; *khā́d-ati* 'chews'; *nakhá-* 'nail'; *makhá-* 'lively'; *múkha-* 'mouth'; *śaṅkhá-* (AV.) 'shell'; *sákhi-* 'companion'.

b. *ch* = IE. *sḱh*, e. g. in *chid-* 'split'; = IE. *sḱ* in inchoative *gácchati* 'goes', *ucchá́ti* 'shines'.

c. *ṭh* = *th* in *ṣaṣ-ṭhá-* (VS. AV.) 'sixth'; *ṣṭhīv-ati* (AV.) 'spits'.

d. *th*[4] in *átha* 'then'; *athari-* 'tip'; *átharvan-* 'fire-priest'; *ártha-* 'use'; *granth-* 'knot'; *path-* 'way'; *pṛth-ú-* 'broad'; *práth-as* 'breadth'; *próthat-* 'snorting'; *math-* 'stir'; *mith-* 'alternate'; *yá-thā* 'as'; *rátha-* 'car'; *vyathate* 'wavers'; *śnath-* 'pierce'. Further in the various suffixes *-tha*: forming primary nouns; e. g. *uk-thá-* 'praise', *gā-thá-* f. *gā-thā́-* 'song'; as *-atha* in *śvas-átha-* 'hissing'; forming ordinals: *catur-thá-* (AV.) 'fourth'; *saptá-tha-* 'seventh'; forming 2. sing. perf.: *dadā-tha* 'thou gavest', *vét-tha* 'thou knowest'; forming 2. pl. pres.: *bhava-tha* 'ye are'; also in *-thās* of 2. sing. mid., e. g. *a-sthi-thās* 'thou hast stood'.

e. *ph* in *phála-* 'fruit'; *phā́la-* 'ploughshare'; *sphar-* and *sphur-* 'jerk'; *sphā(y)-* 'grow fat'.

4. The **aspirate media**, which represents the same IE. sound, is a media combined with *h*. This is proved by the express statements of the Prātiśākhyas[5]; by the fact that *ḷh* = *ḍh* is written with the separate letters *ḷ* and *h*; and by the change of *h* following a media to an aspirate media (as *tád dhí* for *tád hí*).

a. In two or three words an aspirate media interchanges with an aspirate tenuis: *nā́dhamāna-* 'praying', *nādhitá-* 'distressed', beside *nāthitá-* 'distressed' (where *th* is probably due to the influence of *-nāthá-* 'help'); *ádha* and *átha* 'then'[6]; *niṣaṅgádhi-* (VS.) and *niṣaṅgáthi-* (TS.) 'scabbard'.

---

[1] For some doubtful instances of media representing IE. tenuis, see Wackernagel I, 100 b, p. 117, note.

[2] l. c.

[3] Op. cit. 101.

[4] A complete list of Vedic and Sanskrit words containing *th* in his article 'Die ursprachliche tenuis aspirata dentalis im arischen, griechischen und lateinischen' by Zubaty in KZ. 31, 1—9.

[5] RPr. xiii. 2. 5; TPr. ii. 9.

[6] There seem to have been a few IE. doublets of this kind: see Wackernagel I, 103.

32. Loss of aspiration. — Aspiration is lost when there is another aspirate in the same syllable or at the beginning of the next in roots[1]. Hence

a. initial aspiration is lost: 1. in the reduplicative syllable: e. g. *ja-ghán-a* (*han-*, *ghan-* 'strike'); *ca-cchand-a* (*chand-* 'please'); *da-dhā́-ti* (*dhā-* 'put'); *par-phar-at* (*phar-* 'scatter'?). But when the reduplication consists of two syllables, the rule does not apply; e. g. *gháni-ghan-at*, intv. part. of *han-* (beside *jáṅ-ghn-at*), *ghanā-ghan-á-* 'fond of striking'; *bhári-bhr-at*, intv. part. of *bhṛ-* 'bear'. Loss of aspiration, however, began, even in the RV.[2], to spread from monosyllabic to dissyllabic reduplication; thus *ā-pánī-phaṇ-at*, intv. part. of *phaṇ-* 'bound'. — **2.** in the following words, according to the evidence of cognate languages: *kumbhá-* 'pot'[3]; *gadh-* 'attach'; *gábhas-ti-* 'arm'; *guh-* 'conceal'; *gṛdh-* 'be greedy'; *gṛhá-* 'house'; *grabh-* 'seize'; *jáṃhas* 'gait'; *jáṅghā-* 'leg'; *jaghána-* 'buttock'; *dabh-* 'harm'; *dah-* 'burn'; *dih-* 'besmear'; *duh-* 'milk'; *duhitṛ́-* 'daughter'; *drahyát* 'strongly'; *druh-* 'injure'; *bandh-* 'bind'; *babhrú-* 'brown'; *bādh-* 'distress'; *bāhú-* 'arm'; *budh-* 'awake'; *budhná-* 'bottom'; *bṛh-* 'be great'. It is probable also in *dagh-* 'reach': *baṃh-* 'be firm'; *badhirá-* 'deaf'; *bahú-*, *bahulá-* 'much'; *bradhná-* 'pale red'; *bráhman-* 'devotion'.

b. Final aspiration is often **lost**[4]. **1.** When this occurs before suffixal *s*, orignal initial aspiration is lost in some cases; thus from *guh-* 'hide', desid. 3. du. *ju-guk-ṣa-tas*; *gṛdh-* 'be eager': *gṛtsá-* 'dexterous'; *dabh-* 'harm': desid. *díp-sa-ti*, *dip-sú-* 'intending to hurt'; *dah-* 'burn': impv. *dak-ṣi*, aor. part. *dákṣat-*, *dákṣu-* and *dakṣús-* 'flaming'; *duh-* 'milk': aor. *a-dukṣat*, *dukṣás*, etc., des. part. *dúdukṣan*[5]; *bhas-* 'chew': *bap-sati*, part. *báps-at-*; *ghas-* 'eat': *jak-ṣīyā́t*, perf. opt.; *has-* 'laugh': part. *jákṣ-at-*; also in the word *drap-sá-* 'drop'[6].

But in some of the above and in analogous forms with *s*, the original initial aspirate remains; thus from *guh-*, aor. *aghukṣat*; *dah-*: *dhákṣi*, part. *dhákṣat-*, fut. part. *dhakṣyán*; *duh-*: aor. *ádhukṣat*, *dhukṣán*, etc. 2. impv. *dhuk-ṣva*; *bādh-* 'distress': *bī-bhat-sú-* 'loathing'; *budh-* 'awake': aor. *á-bhut-s-i*.

2. When the loss of final radical aspiration is due to any other cause than suffixal *s*, the original initial aspirate regularly remains; thus from *dah-*, aor. *a-dhāk*; *budh-* 'waken': nom. *-bhut* 'waking'; *dhā-* 'put': *dhat*[7], 3. sing., *dhat-thas*, *á-dhat-tam*, etc.; and in the latter verb always before *s* also: *dhat-se*, *dhat-sva*, desid. *dhit-sati*.

c. On the other hand, there is no loss of aspiration in the root if an aspirate follows which belongs to a suffix or second member of a compound; e. g. *vibhú-bhis* 'with the Vibhus'; *proth-átha-* 'snorting'; *dhéṣṭha-* 'giving most' (*dhā-iṣṭha-*); *ahi-hán-* 'serpent-slaying'; *garbha-dhí-* 'breeding-place'. The only exceptions[8] are the two imperatives *bo-dhí* 'be' (for **bho-dhi*[9] instead of **bhū-dhi*) and *ja-hí* (for **jha-hi*) from *han-* 'strike'[10].

---

1 Except when the second aspirate belongs to a suffix or second member of a compound, see below c.

2 Later this became the rule.

3 Initial aspiration has perhaps been lost also in *śákhā-* 'branch', and in the roots *stigh-* 'mount', and *stambh-* 'make firm'. Cp. WACKERNAGEL I, 105 a.

4 This may also be the case in the roots *bhuj-* 'bend', *chid-* 'split', *chad-* 'cover', *dhraj-* 'sweep': op. cit I, 105 b, note.

5 These forms from *dah-* and *duh-* almost always appear in the Pada text with *dh*, doubtless because from the time of the Brāhmaṇas this initial aspiration had become the rule; cp. BENFEY, GGA. 1873, p. 18 f.

6 IE. *dhrebh-* 'coagulate'.

7 For *dhadh-t*.

8 Forms like *bud-dha-* for *budh-ta* can hardly be regarded as exceptions since the aspiration is assumed by the suffix instead of reappearing in the initial of the root.

9 Here *bho-* is a Prakritic contraction for *bhava-*.

10 Also *vidátha-* 'feast', if correctly derived from *vidh-* 'worship'; on this word see MAX MÜLLER, SBE. 32, 350; FOY, KZ. 34, 226; BLOOMFIELD, JAOS. 19, 2, 12 ff.; GELDNER, ZDMG. 52, 730—61; WACKERNAGEL I, 108. A few more uncertain examples might be exceptions: *garda-bhá-* 'ass'

d. There are a few cognate words in which an aspirate is found beside the corresponding media or tenuis: *máj-man-* 'greatness' : *máh-* 'great'; *vi-ṣpuliṅga-ká-* 'scattering sparks' : *sphur-áti* 'darts'[1].

e. In a few isolated words a media seems, according to the evidence of cognate languages, to stand for an IE. aspirate: *gmá-* 'earth', gen. *gmás*; *jmá-* 'earth', gen. *jmás*, inst. *jmá*; *dvár-*, *dur-*[2] 'door'; *majján-* marrow'.

33. **Aspirates in contact with other mutes.** — Of two mutes in juxtaposition (of which both must be voiced or both voiceless[3]), the second only can be aspirated. In such case either

1. the second represents an original aspirate, the first an aspirate or not: e. g. *dhat-thás* = **dhadh-thás* (*dhā-* 'put'); *ran(d)-dhi* = **randh-dhi* (*randh-* 'make subject'), *uk-thá-* 'song' = *uk-thá-* (*vac-* 'speak'); *vét-tha* = **véd-tha* (*vid-* 'know'); *śag-dhí* 'help' = **śak-dhí* (*śak-* 'be strong'); or

2. the first represents an aspirate media[4], the second a dental tenuis[5] which assumes the mode of articulation of the first; e. g. *dág-dhṛ-* 'one who burns' (acc.) = **dágh-tṛ-* (*dah-* 'burn'); *-vid-dha-* 'pierced' = **vidh-ta-* (*vyadh-*); *-lab-dha-* 'taken' = **labh-ta-* (*labh-*). An intervening sibilant (*z* = *s*) did not prevent the same result: *jag-dhá-*, *jag-dhváya*, *jag-dhvá* (AV.), *a-g-dha* (TS.) from *ghas-* 'eat', *gdh* representing *gzdh-* for *gzh-t-* from *gh(a)s-t-*.

a. When the first is *h* representing an old palatal aspirate (= *ẓh*, IE. *ĝh*)[6], it disappears after cerebralizing the dental and lengthening the preceding vowel; e. g. *ūḍhá-* = **uẓ-dhá-* for *uẓh-tá-* from *vah-tá-*[7].

b. In a few instances the *t* does not become *dh* owing to the influence of cognate forms: thus *dhaktam* (instead of **dagdham* = **dhagh-tám*) according to 2. 3. sing. *dhak* (= **dhagh-t*) from *dagh-* 'reach'; *dhat-tám* etc. (instead of **dad-dham* for **dhadh-tam*) according to 3. sing. *dhat* (= **dhadh-t*), 2. sing. mid. *dhát-se*, etc. (= **dhádh-se*)[8].

The Five Classes of Mutes.

34. **The gutturals.** — These mutes, by the Indian phoneticians called *kaṇṭhya* ('produced from the throat'), are minutely described in the Prātiśākhyas as formed at the 'root of the tongue' (*jihvā-mūla*) and at the 'root of the jaw' (*hanu-mūla*)[9]. They are therefore velar[10] sounds and, as the evidence

(if from *gṛdh-* 'be greedy'), *bárjaha-* 'udder' (if from *bṛh-* 'be great'), *sabar-dúgha-*, *sabar-dhú-*, *sabar-dhúk*, epithet of cows (if *sabar-* = Gk. ἄφαρ: BARTHOLOMAE, BB. 15, 18): cp. WACKERNAGEL I, 108, note, 217 b; ZDMG. 43, 667 f.; 46, 292 (*bárjaha-*).

1 A few doubtful examples discussed by WACKERNAGEL I, p. 129 bottom.

2 Op. cit. I, 109, note (mid.); according to BLOOMFIELD, Album Kern, p. 193 f., the media is due to the influence of the numeral *dva-* 'two'.

3 This was often due to assimilation, the mode of the articulation of the second generally prevailing; e. g. *át-ti* = **ad-ti* (*ad-* 'eat'); *vét-tha* = **véd-tha*; *śag-dhí* = **śak-dhí*; the articulation of the first prevails in 33, 2.

4 An aspirate tenuis loses its aspiration in these circumstances; thus *gṛṇatti* (AV.) for **gṛnath-ti*, if this form is derived from *grath-* 'tie'.

5 There seems to be no example of any other tenuis in contact with a preceding aspirate media within a word, but the result would probably have been the same. There is no example of *th* becoming voiced in this combination; it remains in *dhat-thás* (= **dadh-thás*).

6 See below 58.

7 According to this rule *úṣ-ṭra-* 'buffalo', could not be derived from *vah-* 'carry' (as in that case it would have become *úḍhra-*): cp. WACKERNAGEL I, 111 b, note.

8 Before sibilants, all aspirates as well as mediae become tenues; but according to TPr. XIV. 12, APr. II. 6 (cp. RPr. VI. 15) a tenuis in such a position may be pronounced as an aspirate; see WACKERNAGEL I, 113.

9 See APr. I. 20 and WHITNEY's note.

10 That is, pronounced with the velum or soft palate.

of cognate languages shows, derived from IE. velars[1]. Gutturals are found interchanging to some extent with sounds of the four other classes.

1. Under certain conditions they **interchange with** the new **palatals** (*c j h*) which are derived from them[2]; with the old palatal *ś*[3] (also old *j* and *h*) only when followed by *s* (which then becomes *ṣ*)[4]. Between this *kṣ* = *ś-s* and *kṣ* = *k-s* it is possible to distinguish by the aid of Iranian, where the two are represented by different sounds[5]; and the original value of the *k* can thus be determined even in words in which no form without the sibilant occurs. This evidence shows that, in the following words, *kṣ* represents[6].

a. *ś-s*: *ákṣi-* 'eye'; *ṛ́kṣa-* 'bear'; *kákṣa-* 'armpit'; *kukṣí-* 'belly'; *kṣi-* 'dwell'; *kṣúdh-* 'hunger'; *cakṣ-* 'see'; *takṣ-* 'fashion'; *dákṣiṇa-* 'right'; *pákṣman-* (VS.) 'eyelash'; *makṣú* 'quickly'; *rakṣ-* (AV.) 'injure'; *rákṣ-as-* 'injury';

b. *k-s*: *kṣatrá-* 'dominion'; *kṣáp-* 'night'; *kṣi-* 'rule'; *kṣip-* 'throw'; *kṣīrá-* 'milk'; *kṣud-* 'shake', *kṣód-as-* 'rush of water', *kṣudrá-* 'small' (VS.), n. 'minute particle'; *kṣúbh-* 'swift motion'; *tvakṣ-* 'be strong'; *vṛkṣá-* 'tree'.

2. In a few instances ***k*** stands for a medial ***t***: in *vṛkkáu* (AV.) 'kidneys', for **vṛtkáu*[7]; *pṛkṣú* (SV.) = *pṛtsú* 'in battles'. In these two forms the substitution is due to Prakritic influence; this is probably also the case in *skambh-* beside *stambh-* 'prop'[8]. The guttural only seems to stand for a dental in *ásiknī-* beside *ásita-* 'black', *páliknī-* beside *palitá-* 'grey', and *hárikṇikā-* (AV.) beside *hárita-* 'yellow', as there is no etymological connexion between *-knī-* and *-ta-*[9].

3. In a few words a **guttural interchanges with a labial** medially: *kakárdu-* beside *kaparda-* 'braid of hair'; *kulīkā* (VS.) : *pulīkā* (MS.) a kind of bird; *kulīkáya-* (TS.) : *pulīkáya-* (MS.), *kulīpáya-* (VS.) : *purīkáya*[10] (AV.) a kind of aquatic animal; *nicuṅkuṇá-* (TS.) : *nicumpuṇá-* 'flood'; and in the TS. (B.) *triṣṭúgbhis* and *anuṣṭúgbhyas* occur beside *triṣṭúb-bhis* and *anuṣṭúbbhyas*[11].

4. In a few verbal forms from three roots ***k*** stands for ***ṣ*** before suffixal *s*[12], though this *k* never made its way into the loc. pl. (where only *-ṣ-ṣu-* or *-ḥ-ṣu*, *-ṭ-su* occur). The only example in the RV. is *piṇak* (for *piṇak-ṣ*) 2. sing. impf. of *pinaṣ-ṭi* (*piṣ-* 'crush'). In the AV. occur *dvik-ṣ-at*, *dvik-ṣ-ata*, aor. of *dviṣ-* 'hate'; *śiślikṣate*, *-śiślikṣu-*, desid. of *śliṣ-* 'embrace'. Other possible examples from the RV. are *-ṛkṣará-* 'thorn' (if from *ṛṣ-* 'prick'); *rírikṣa-ti* and *rírikṣú-*, desid. (if from *riṣ-* 'injure'); *vivekṣi* (if from *viṣ-* 'work')[13].

35. The palatals.—These are pronounced in India at the present day as a close combination of a *t*-sound followed by a palatal spirant *ś*. The evidence of the Greek reproduction of Indian words[14] points in the same

[1] That is, the *q*-sounds; some, however, are derived from IE. labio-velars or *q*ᵘ-sounds; see BRUGMANN, KG. 1, 244 and 254; WACKERNAGEL 1, 115.

[2] See BRUGMANN, op. cit. 244.

[3] Op. cit. 233.

[4] See below 56.

[5] That is, *ś-s* by *š* and *k-s* by *hš*; thus *vakṣi*, from *vaś-* = *vaši*; *vaksyā-mi*, from *vak-* (for *vac-*) = *vahšyā*.

[6] The two components of *kṣ* cannot yet have coalesced when *ṣ* dropped out between two mutes in *ábhakta*, for *abhak-ṣ-ta* (aor. of *bhaj-*), and *ataṣṭa* for *atak-ṣ-ta-* from *takṣ-* (Av. *taš-*) 'fashion'; otherwise the two different original sounds could not have been kept apart in these two forms.

[7] See above 30, note 4.

[8] Cp. WACKERNAGEL 1, p. 136, note (top).

[9] Cp. J. SCHMIDT, Pluralbildung 398.

[10] See ZDMG. 33, 193.

[11] See WEBER, IS. 8, 40. 54; 13, 109.

[12] This probably started from the parallelism of the 3. sing. of roots in *ṣ* and *ś*: thus *dveṣ-ṭi* from √*dviṣ-*, and *vaṣ-ṭi* from √*vaś-*; then the 2. sing. *dvek-ṣi* for *dveṣ-ṣi*, followed *vak-ṣi*.

[13] The relation of the *k* in *dadhṛ́k* 'firmly', to *dadhṛṣá-*, *dadhṛṣ-váṇi-* 'bold', is uncertain. Cp. WACKERNAGEL 1, 118, note (end).

[14] Thus τζάνδανον = *candana-* 'sandalwood'; Τιαστάνης = *caṣṭana-*, N.; Παζάλαι = *pañcāla-*, N. of a people; Σανδρόκυπτος = *candragupta-*, N.; 'Οζήνη = *ujjayinī-* (Prakrit

direction. It is therefore likely that they were thus pronounced in Vedic times[1]. Prosodically, however, they have the value of a single consonant (excepting *ch*[2]). They date from the Indo-Iranian period only; but in order to understand their place in the Vedic language, especially in relation to the gutturals, we must go back to their ultimate origin. The evidence of comparative grammar shows that **two** distinct **series of palatals,** the later and the earlier, must be distinguished. This evidence alone can explain how the same Vedic palatal sound (*j* or *h*) is, under certain conditions, treated differently.

36. The **new palatals** (*c, j, h*) are derived from gutturals (velars), being interchangeable, in most roots and formatives, with gutturals, and being in most cognate languages represented by the same sounds as represent original gutturals. Thus from the root *śuc-* 'shine' come verbal forms such as *śócati*, beside the nominal derivatives *śóka-*, *śúkvan-*, *śukrá-*, *śuklá-* (AV.); from *yuj-* 'yoke', *yuje* 1. sing. mid., etc., beside *yugá-*, *yóga-*, *yuktá-*, *yúgvan-*; from *druh-* 'injure', *dudróha*, 3. sing. perf., etc., beside *druhyú-*, a name, and *drógha-* 'deceitful'.

The (Indo-Iranian) change from gutturals to palatals was regularly produced before the palatal sounds *i ī y*[3]; e. g. *cittá-* 'noticed', beside *kéta-* 'will', from *cit-* 'perceive'; *ójīyas-* 'stronger', beside *ugrá-* 'strong'; *druhyú-* beside *drógha-*. This change invariably takes place in Iranian, while the exceptions in Vedic appear only before vowels which were not originally palatal.

a. **Gutturals** thus appear **instead of palatals** before *ir* (*il*) and *īr* (= IE. *ṛr-* and *ṝ*)[4], which were not yet pronounced with an *i*-sound in the Indo-Iranian period[5]: thus *áṅgiras-*, a name; *girí-*[6] 'mountain'; *kiráti*, 3. sing., *kiráṇa-* 'dust', from *kṝ-* 'scatter'; *carkirāma*, *carkiran*, *kīrtí-* 'fame', from *kṝ-* 'commemorate'; *gír-* 'lauding', from *gṝ-* 'praise'; *giráti* (AV.), 3. sing., *-gila-* (AV.) 'devouring', from *gṝ-* 'swallow'. Before *i* (= IE. *ə*)[7] *k* appears in *ok-i-vāṃs-*, part. from *uc-* 'be pleased', and *g* in *tigitá-*[8] 'sharp', beside *tejate*, *téjas-* 'brilliance', and other derivatives, from *tij-* 'be sharp'.

Otherwise a guttural followed by a palatal vowel is due to the influence of cognate forms. This is the case

1. in the **initial of roots** *α*) in *gī-*, the weak stem of *gai-* 'sing', beside *gāy-*, *gā-*; *β*) in reduplicated forms with *cik-*, *jig-*, due to forms like *cikáya*, *jigáya-* (where the guttural is in accordance with phonetic law) and to the frequency of palatal reduplication of guttural initial; thus perf. *ciky-ur*, part. *cíky-at-*, desid. *cikīṣate*, impv. *cikīhi* (AV.), from *ci-* 'perceive'; intv. *cékit-*, *cikit-*, desid. *cikits-*, from *cit-* 'perceive'; perf. *jigy-ur*, desid. *jigīṣate*, *jigyú-* 'victorious',

ujjenī), N. of a city; Διαμοῦνα = *yamunā-*, N. of a river. Cp. WACKERNAGEL I, 119.

1 Cp. WHITNEY on APr. I. 21.

2 Cp. above 30, 3; 31, 3 b; and below 40.

3 The sphere of the palatals has been extended by analogy at the expense of the gutturals and *vice versâ*. The aspirate guttural *kh* appears where the other gutturals are replaced by palatals; thus before the *y* in *khyā-* 'see' (but *jyā-*) 'overpower'; before the thematic *a* of the present: *ríkhati* 'sits' (but *dahati*); before the *-ayati* of the Causative: *īṅkhayati* 'swings' (but *arcáyati*); and notably in *sákhi-* 'friend': dat. *sákhye*, pl. *sákhibyas* (IIr. *sachi-*): cp. WACKERNAGEL I, 121 (p. 140, top). The palatal aspirate in fact never represents a guttural aspirate, but only an IE. palatal, or sibilant and palatal.

4 Cp. WACKERNAGEL I, 24. 25.

5 Cp. WACKERNAGEL I, 123 a *α*.

6 In Av. *gairi-*.

7 This sound had probably not yet become a pure palatal in IIr.

8 Otherwise the palatal regularly appears before this *i* in perfect forms; e. g. *saściré* (*sac-* 'accompany'); *bhejiré* (*bhaj-* 'divide'); *uvócitha*, *ūciṣe* (*uc-* 'be pleased'); *dudóhitha* (*duh-* 'milk').

from *jí-* 'conquer'; γ) in the pronominal forms *kís, kím, kī́m, kíyat, kívant-, kī́dṛś-*, beside the enclitic *cid*, because owing to the influence of the frequent forms *ká-s, ká-d*, etc., *k* appeared to be characteristic of the interrogative pronoun[1].

2. in the final of roots in which guttural forms predominate, before the *y* of the optative and the gerund; thus *dagh-yās*, from *dagh-* 'reach'; *śak-yām*, from *śak-* 'be able'; *sagh-yāsam* (TS.), from *sagh-* 'be equal to'. It also appears very often before the suffixes *-i, -ī, -in, -ya* forming derivatives from nouns the last consonant of which is a guttural: e. g. *plā́yogi-* 'descendant of Playoga'; *vṛk-ī́-* 'she-wolf' (*vṛka-*); *śak-ín-* 'powerful' (*śáka-*); *śṛṅg-ín-* 'horned' (*śṛ́ṅga-*); *upa-vāk-yà-* 'to be praised' (beside *upavā́cya-*) from *upavāká-* 'praise'. Similarly *drā́gh-īyas-* 'longer', *drā́gh-iṣṭha-* 'longest' (beside *dīrghá-* 'long', *drāgh-mán-* 'length'); *sphig-ī́-* 'buttock', with *g* from the nom. *sphik* of *sphij-*, which occurs in the post-Vedic language only.

3. in a certain number of abnormal words, almost invariably at the beginning:

α) words which may be suspected of foreign origin owing to meaning or phonetic form: *kiṃśuká-, kiyámbu-* plant names; *kimī́din-, kíkaṭa-, kirā́ta-* (VS.), *śva-kiṣkín-* (AV.) names of foreigners or demons; *kī́ja-* a kind of utensil; *kílbiṣa-* 'guilt' (contains the rare letter *b*), *kīstá-* 'singer' (*st* instead of *ṣṭ*); β) onomatopoetic words: *kikidīví-* 'blue jay'; *kikirá-kṛ-* 'tear to tatters'; *kikkiṭā́* (TS.) an interjection; γ) some words of doubtful origin: *kíkasā-* 'vertebra'; *kīnā́ra-* 'ploughman' (?); *kīnā́śa-* 'ploughman'; *kīlā́la-* 'sweet draught'; *kirmirá-* (VS.) 'variegated'; *kiśorá-* (AV.) 'foal'; *kiṣmī́la-* (AV. Paipp.) a kind of disease.

37. **New palatals as radical initials.** — a. Before *a, ā*, and diphthongs, both palatals and gutturals are very frequent in Vedic and Iranian. Comparative grammar shows that the palatals occur before a vowel or diphthong representing IE. *ĕ ē* or a diphthong beginning with *ĕ ē*[2]; but gutturals before IE. *a o* or sonant nasal. According to this evidence the palatal has come into being in the following words: *ca* 'and'; *cakrá-* 'wheel'; *catvā́ras* 'four'; *caramá-* 'last'; *carú-* 'pot'; *cā́ru-* 'agreeable'; *páñca* 'five'; *jaṭhára-* 'belly'; *jánī-, -jā́ni-* 'woman'; *jāmí-* 'akin'; *háras-* 'flame'.

On the other hand, the original guttural has remained in *kakúd-* 'peak'; *kákṣa-* 'armpit'; *kārú-* 'poet'; *kéta-* 'will'; *gáus* 'cow'; *gharmá-* 'hot'; *ghorá-* 'terrible'; and in the roots *kās-* (AV.) 'cough'; *gadh-* 'clasp'; *gā-* 'go'; *gāh-* 'plunge'; *gai-* 'sing'[3].

b. Among the roots with *ŭ ṛ̆ ḷ* as low grade vowels, the only one in which the regular phonetic interchange of palatal and guttural takes place, is *jar-* : *gṝ-* 'call'; *g* appearing before *ṛ ir ar* (= IE. *ŏr*), *j* before *ar* (= IE. *ĕr*) preceding the thematic -*a*- of the present or the suffix -*tṛ*-; thus *gṛ-ṇā́ti, gír-, -gará-* (VS.), beside *járate, jarā́dhyai, jaritṛ́-*. In other roots either the guttural or the palatal appears throughout; mostly the guttural, because the forms with *ŭ ṛ̆ ḷ* and *o ar al* (= IE. *ŏṵ ŏr ŏl*), which required the guttural, were more numerous than those with *o ar al* (= IE. *ĕṵ ĕr ĕl*); thus from *kṛ-* 'do', *ákar* aor. 'has done', *kartṛ́-* 'agent', *kárman-* 'action', retain the guttural, though the palatal would be phonetic (as *ar* here = IE. *er*), through the influence of forms with *kṛ-* and of *káraṇa-* 'deed' (where *ar* = IE. *ŏr*).

---

[1] Cp. WACKERNAGEL I, 128 a (p. 150, bottom).
[2] Cp. Italian and the Balto-Slavic languages which palatalize before *e* as well as *i*.

[3] In the IE. vowel gradation of these roots only *ā̆* and *ō̆* appear. In other roots in the IE. vowel gradation of which *ĕ* is found, an initial palatal would be expected

On the other hand, the palatal appears in *cud-*[1], *códati* 'impel'; *ścut-*, *ścotati* 'drip', because here forms with *u*, which required a guttural, were rare; in *car-*, *carati* 'move', where the palatal is almost invariably phonetic in RV. (but AV. has *cacāra*); in *cṛt-* 'bind', the palatal has fixed itself in spite of many forms with *ṛ*; while beside *harṣate* 'rejoices', *hárṣant-*, part., both *h* and *gh* occur in weak forms: *hṛṣitá-*, *ghṛ́ṣu-* 'lively', *ghṛ́ṣvi-* 'gladdening'.

c. Among **roots in -*an* and *am***, survivals of the regular interchange are found in *kan-* 'be pleased', and *han-* 'strike'. The former has the palatal (= IE. *kĕ-*) in the aor. *caniṣṭam*, in the superl. *cániṣṭha-*, and in *cánas-* 'favour', but otherwise the guttural. In *han-*, *h* appears before *an* (= IE. *en*) and, by analogy, also before *an* = *ṇn* and *a* = *ṇ*; but *gh* before *n* and *ă* = IE. *ŏ*; thus *hán-ti*, inf. *hán-tave*; *han-mas*, *han-yā́ma*; *ha-thás*, *-ha-tá*, and with *j* in impv. *jahí* (= **jhahi*), but perf. *jaghā́na*, and *ghaná-* 'striker', *ghanāghaná-* 'found of striking'. In the intv. *jaṅghan-*, *gh* stands for *h* before *a* = IE. *ĕ* owing to the influence of the weak stem *jaṅghn-*. In *gam-* 'go', *ga-* = *gṃ-* (e. g. in *gácchati*, *ga-tá-*) has led to the use of *gam-* = **jam-*, as in *gám-anti*[2].

d. In the remaining **verbs**, that is, those **with *a*** (25) or ***e*** (22) as high grade vowel, there appears chiefly the palatal throughout; thus *cakṣ-*: *cacákṣa* (for **cakákṣa*). The phonetic guttural is, however, preserved in some forms of the three verbs *ci-* 'observe' (perf. *cikā́ya*); *cit-* 'observe' (perf. *cikéta*; *kéta-* 'will'; *ketú-*[3] 'appearance'); and *ji-* 'conquer' (perf. *jigā́ya*; *gáya-* 'household'). A guttural not phonetically justified appears before *a* (= IE. *ĕ*) only in *ghas-* 'eat' (aor. *ághas*, subj. *ghas-a-t*) and in *gal-* 'drop' (*galgalīti* VS.).

e. In **reduplicative syllables** containing *a* of roots having initial guttural or palatal, the **palatal** always appears in the perfect, pluperfect, or reduplicated aorist; thus *kṛ-* 'make' : *cakā́ra*; *khād-* 'chew' : *cakhā́da*; *gam-* 'go' : *jagā́ma*; *ghas-* 'eat' : *jaghā́sa*; *cakṣ-* 'see' : *cacákṣa*; pluperf. of *kṛ-* : *acakrat*; red. aor. of *jas-* 'be exhausted' : *jajas-tám*. The palatal is here historically phonetic, as the IE. reduplicative vowel was *ĕ*.

In the intensive, however, the palatal is **invariable only when** the reduplication is **monosyllabic**[4]; e. g. *kram-* 'stride' : *caṅ-kramata*; *gṛ-* : *jā-gṛ-* 'awake'; *han-* 'strike' : *jaṅ-ghanti*. But when the reduplication is dissyllabic, the guttural[5] predominates; thus *kṛ-*, part. *kári-kr-at-*; *krand-* 'roar' : *káni-kra(n)d-*; *gam-* 'go' : *gani-gan-*, *gani-gm-*; *han-* 'strike' : *ghani-ghn-* (cp. *ghanāghaná-*); *skand-* 'leap' : both *káni-ṣkand-* and *cani-ṣkadat* subj.

38. New palatals as radical finals. a. Verbal forms. — Before the thematic verbal endings (including those of the *a*-aorist and the reduplicated aorist) the final of roots regularly appears as a palatal which, though phonetic[6] only in about the same degree as the guttural, has prevailed. Gutturals are

---

in certain forms; but few traces of this remain, as the forms of each verb have been normalized.

1 If *kútsa-* N. is derived from *cud-*, and *carṣaṇí-* 'active', from *kṛ-*, the initial consonant has not been affected by the normalizing influence of the roots, because these words have been isolated.

2 The correct phonetic interchange appears in *jáṅgahe* 'kicks', and *jáṃhas-* 'course', if these forms are connected, as BR. think. WHITNEY, Roots, however, considers the former an intensive of *gāh-* 'plunge'.

3 Beside *céru-* 'devout', *keru-* appears in the compound *máhi-keru-* 'very devout'; cp. WACKERNAGEL 2[1], p. 101 (43 b).

4 In the post-Vedic language, the palatal is invariable even in dissyllabic reduplication.

5 But if the initial of the root is a palatal, the reduplicative consonant is of course always a palatal; thus *cand-* 'shine' : *cániścad-*; *car-* 'move' : *carācará-*; *cal-* 'move' : *calācalá-* 'ever moving'. Cp. 32 a.

6 Phonetically we should have **pákāmi* (IE. *ŏ*), *pác-asi* and *pác-ati* (IE. *ĕ*).

rare at the end of the root, appearing only[1] in *śak-* 'be able'; 2. sing. *śak-as*; *sagh-* 'be equal to': 3. sing. *sagh-at*; *dagh-* 'reach' : *dagh-at* (TS.); in these roots the guttural prevails throughout owing to the influence of the present stem *śak-nu-*, *sagh-nu-*[2]. Even in the non-thematic presents and in the perfect the palatal carried the day, though phonetic in still fewer forms; thus the guttural alone would be historically justified in the forms *yunájā*, *yuñje*; *yuyója*[3]. The palatal further regularly appears before the causative[4] suffix *-áya-*, where it is phonetic (= IE. *éi̯e*); e. g. *arc-áya-ti* from *arc-* 'praise'[5].

b. As shown by the appearance, in cognate forms, of a guttural before other consonants than *s*, the final of the following verbs is a new palatal: *añj-* 'anoint'; *ej-* 'stir'; *tij-* 'sharpen'; *tuj-* 'beat'; *tyaj-* 'forsake'; *nij-* 'wash'; *bhaj-* 'divide'; *bhañj-* 'break'; *bhuj-* 'bend'; *yuj-* 'yoke'; *rañj-* 'colour'; *ruj-* 'break'; *vij-* 'shoot up'; *vṛj-* 'turn'; *śiñj-* 'sound'; *sañj-* 'attach'; *svañj-* 'embrace'; also in the noun *sráj-* 'garland'.

c. Apart from being the result of the Sandhi of *d* + *j*, *jj* is shown by the evidence of cognate languages to be derived from a sibilant + guttural (= IE. *zg*) and thus to belong to the series of new palatals in *majján-* 'marrow'; *rájju-* 'rope'; *bhṛjjáti* 'roasts'; *majjati* 'dives', from which is derived *madgú-* (VS.) 'diver' (a bird).

d. Nominal derivatives. 1. Before the suffix *-a*, the final of the root is mostly guttural, because the *a* in nearly all the cases of the noun represents IE. *ŏ*. The rule in the RV. is that the guttural appears before both unaccented *-a* and accented *-á*, but the palatal before accented *-á* only[6]; e. g. *abhi-droh-á-*, *druh-ā́-* 'injury' : *drógh-a-* 'injuring'; *bhoj-á-* 'liberal' : *bhóg-a-* 'enjoyment'; *a-yuj-á-* 'companionless'; *yóg-a-* 'yoking'; *ruj-á-* 'breaking' : *róg-a-* (AV.) 'disease'; *vevij-á-* 'swift' : *vég-a-* (AV.) 'speed'; *śuc-á-* 'bright' : *śók-a-* 'flame'; *ruc-á-* (VS.) and *roc-á-* (AV.) 'shining' : *rók-a-* and *rok-á-* 'light'[7].

2. Before the suffix *-as*, the palatal generally appears, as it is for the most part phonetically required; e. g. *ój-as-* 'force' : *ug-rá-* 'mighty'. The guttural, however, prevailed in *áṅk-as-* 'bend'; *ā́g-as-* 'offence'; *-ny-ogh-as-* 'streaming'; *bhárg-as-* 'brilliance'; as there were no corresponding verbs with palatal beside these words; it also prevailed in *ók-as-* 'ease' and *ny-òkas-* 'comfortable', as well as *-śok-as-* 'flaming', though there are such verbs (*uc-* 'be pleased', and *śuc-* 'shine').

3. Before other suffixes beginning with *a*, the final of the root is generally palatal; thus before *-ana* (= IE. *-eno-*), *vac-anà-* 'speaking'; *téj-ana-* 'act of sharpening'; *maṃh-ána-* 'gift'[8]; before *-ant*, *-āna* (under the influence of

---

1 Apart from roots ending in *kh*, see 35, note 3.

2 In *ni-mégha-māna-* 'drenching oneself', the *gh* seems to be phonetic (as *-amāna* = *-ŏmenŏ*). In *válgate* (AV.) 'springs', the guttural is perhaps due to the preceding *l*, as neither *lj* nor *lc* is ever found to occur.

3 This normalization of the palatal is probably Indo-Iranian, see J. SCHMIDT, KZ. 25, 104.

4 The denominatives in *-ayá-* (IE. *ei̯é* and *oi̯é*) follow the noun from which they are derived; e. g. from *aghá-* 'evil', *aghāyáti* 'wishes to injure'.

5 The causative *iṅgáyati* of *éjati* 'stirs' is probably due to an old present base **inag-*, *iṅg-* formed according to the 7th class; the phonetic form *-iñjayati* is found in the BAU. VI. 4, 23.

6 The fluctuation of words in *-a-* probably arose from some cases in oxytones having had IE. *ĕ*, others *ŏ*; hence in some words the palatal prevailed throughout, in others the guttural. The agent-nouns, being mostly oxytone, show a preference for the palatal, which originally appeared in oxytones only. Cp. WACKERNAGEL I, 128 a (p. 150, note, end).

7 A palatal before an unaccented *-a* first appears in *dóh-a-* (RV. x. 122), otherwise *dógha-* 'milking'; *móh-a-* (AV.) 'delusion', beside *mógh-a-* 'vain'; *krúñc-a-* (VS.) 'curlew', is probably only an extension of *krúñc-* (VS.)

8 The *gh* of *jaghána-* 'buttock', is phonetic (Gk. κοχώνη).

verbal forms), e. g. *dúh-āna-* and *duduh-āná*[1]; before *-ata* (= IE. *-ĕtŏ*), e. g. *pac-atá-* 'cooked'[2]; before *-an* in *majj-án-* 'marrow'[3].

4. Nouns formed without suffix (including infinitives and gerunds) have the palatal of the corresponding verb; e. g. *pṛ́c-as,* nom. pl. 'food'; *ā-pṛ́c-as* and *ā-pṛ́c-e* 'to satisfy'; *tuj-áye* 'to procreate'. A guttural of course appears where the verb has a guttural only; e. g. *pra-táṅk-am* (AV.) 'gliding' (*tak-*'run').

5. The suffix *-ka* is treated analogously to the final guttural of roots[4]. The guttural regularly appears except when the suffix, being attached to unaccented prepositions, is itself accented; thus *asmā́-ka-* 'our'; *yuṣmā́-ka-* 'your'; *ápā-ka-* 'coming from afar'; *abhī́-ka-* 'collision'; and even with the suffix accented in locatives such as *upā-ké*, *upā-káyos* 'in the vicinity' and in the abl. *parā-kā́t* 'from a distance'; but *uc-cā́* and *uc-cáis* 'above'; *parā-cáis* 'aside'; *paś-cā́* and *paś-cā́t* 'behind'; *prā-cáis* 'forwards'.

39. **Irregular palatalization.**—Before *ŭ ṛ* and consonants (except *y*), the gutturals were not originally palatalized. Hence roots which regularly have palatals before *a* and diphthongs, usually retain the guttural before *u ṛ* and consonants. Thus from *ric-* 'leave', are formed, *rék-u-* 'empty', *rék-ṇ-as-* 'property', perf. part. *ririk-vā́ṃs-*; 3. sing. pres. *riṇák-ti,* 2. sing. perf. mid. *ririk-ṣe* (but opt. *riric-yāt*); *ug-rá-* 'mighty', beside *ój-as-* 'strength'; *ghn-* beside *han-* 'strike'). Nevertheless palatals appear by analogy before *u*, *ṛ*, *n*, *m*, *r*, *v*:

a. initially: 1. in the roots *ścut-* 'drip', *cṛt-* 'bind', *hṛṣ-* 'rejoice', in which the unphonetic palatal before the low grade vowel[5] is due to the phonetic palatal before the high grade vowels *o* (= IE. *ĕu̯*) and *ar* (= IE. *ĕr*).

2. in the reduplicative syllables *cu-*[6] and *ju-* of the perfect and aorist (in RV. occurring only in *cyu-* 'shake', *gup-* 'guard', *gur-* 'praise') for older **ca- *ja-* (*a* = *ĕ*, the IE. reduplicative vowel).

b. finally: 1. in verbal inflexion, the palatal which appears before *a* and diphthongs always appears also before *u*, and nearly always before *m* and *r* (instead of the phonetic guttural); thus *sisic-ur* beside *siṣic-atur*, *sisic-e*, from *sic-* 'pour'; *bubhuj-máhe* beside *bhunáj-āmahe*, from *bhuj-* 'enjoy'; *añj-mas* beside *añj-ánti*, *anáj-an* from *añj-* 'anoint'; *riric-ré* beside *riric-é*, from *ric-* 'leave'; *á-yuj-ran*, *yuyuj-ré* beside *yuyuj-é*, from *yuj-* 'yoke'; *duh-ré*, *duh-rate*, *duduh-ré*, *duh-rā́m* and *duh-ratām* (AV.) beside *duh-é*, from *duh-* 'milk'.

The guttural, however, regularly remains before the *-nu* of the 5th class: *śak-nu-* 'be able', *sagh-nu-* 'be equal to', spreading thence to other forms[7]. Phonetic *k* remains before *m* in *vívak-mi* from *vac-* 'speak'; and before *r* in *vāvak-re* beside *vac-yáte*, *váñc-ati* (AV. VS.) from *vañc-* 'move crookedly'.

2. in nominal derivation the guttural as a rule remains[8]: e. g. *rug-ṇá-* 'broken', from *ruj-* 'break'; *ruk-má-* 'brilliant', from *ruc-* 'shine'; *śuk-rá-*, *śuk-lá-* (AV.) 'bright', from *śuc-* 'shine'; *pak-vá-* 'ripe', from *pac-* 'cook'. The perf. part. for the most part follows this rule: e. g. *ru-ruk-vā́ṃs-*, from *ruc-* 'shine';

1 Strictly phonetic (but rarer) is *dúgh-āna-* 'milking'; also *vāgh-át-* (IE. *-n̥t-*) 'institutor of a sacrifice'.

2 The *k* in *sik-atā-* (AV. VS.) 'sand', is phonetic (IE. *-n̥ta-*).

3 Beside *yák-ṛt* (AV.) 'liver', and *śák-ṛt* 'dung', the *k* is found in the stems *yak-an-*, *śak-an-*, but only in weak forms before *n* or *a* (= *n̥*): *yak-nás*, *yak-nā́* (VS.); *śak-nā́* (VS.); *śak-nás* (AV.); *śáka-bhis* (TS.)

4 See above 38 d, 1; WACKERNAGEL I, 129.

5 The phonetic guttural, however, appears in *ghṛṣ-ú-* 'lively', *ghṛ́ṣvi-* 'gladdening'; while on the other hand the palatal appears unphonetically before *u* in the intv. part. *car-cūryá-māṇa-* from *car-* 'move'.

6 Otherwise *cu-* occurs only in the onomatopoetic *ni-cumpuṇá-* 'swell' — and in a few words suggestive of foreign origin: *cúmuri-*, N. of a demon; *cu-puṇīkā-*, N. of a *kṛttikā* (TS.).

7 Also *dagh-nu-* 'reach', in a Brāhmaṇa passage of the Kaṭhaka, and *stigh-nu-* 'mount', in a similar one of the TS.

8 COLLITZ, BB. 3, 230 f.; J. SCHMIDT, KZ. 25, 70 f.

vi-vik-váṃs-, from *vic-* 'divide'; *ok-i-váṃs-* (36 a), from *uc-* 'find pleasure' (but dat. sing. *ūc-úṣ-e*).

The following are, however, exceptions: *ój-man-* 'might'[1]; *bhuj-mán-* 'fruitful'; *múh-ur* 'suddenly'; *druh-ú-* (AV.) 'injurer'; *yāc-ñyá-* (AV.) 'request'.

40. The old palatals (*ch, j, ś, h*). — **The aspirate *ch*.** This sound is, in pronunciation, the aspirate of *c*[2] and is therefore represented in reduplication by *c*. But in origin *ch* has nothing to do with *c*. The fact that after a mute it takes the place of *ś* in Sandhi shows that it is allied to *ś*. In fact, unlike *j* and *h*, it belongs exclusively to the old series of palatals; for it does not interchange with a guttural *kh*[3]. In the Avesta *ch* is regularly represented by *s* and in cognate European languages by a conjunct consonant beginning with *s* and standing for IE. *sk̑h* (that is, *s* + palatal mute aspirate); e. g. *chid-* 'cut off', Gk. σχιδ-. This in Indo-Iranian probably became *śś́h*, which differentiated into Avestic *s* and Vedic *ch*. In the inchoative suffix *-cha* (*gácchati*, Gk. βάσκω) this palatal aspirate seems to represent IE. *sk̑*, a conclusion which is supported by the old inchoative verb *rapśate* 'is full' = *rap(s)śate*, where after the *s* has been dropped between two consonants[4], *ś* = IE. *k̑* remained. Thus *ch* represents a double sound and metrically lengthens a preceding short vowel. Hence the RPr. (VI. 1) prescribes the doubling of *ch* (that is *c-ch*) between vowels. Though the Vedic Mss. almost invariably write *ch*[5] and AUFRECHT's edition of the RV. and V. SCHROEDER's edition of the MS.[6] follow this practice, the spelling *cch* is to be preferred.

a. In *śākhā-* 'branch', the initial *ś* probably stands for *ch* owing to the law by which two aspirates in the same syllable are avoided[7].

b. In a few instances *ch* is a Prakritic representative of *kṣ* and *ps*: *-ṛcchárā-* (AV.) beside *ṛkṣálā-* (VS.)[8], part of an animal's leg; *kṛcchrá-* 'distress', perhaps for **kṛpsrá-*, and allied to *kṛpate* 'laments', and *kṛpáṇa-* 'misery'[9].

41. The old palatal *j*. — This *j* is the media of *ś* (while as a new palatal it is the media of *c*). It is recognizable as an old palatal by the following indications:

1. when there are parallel forms with *ṣ* before *t*, *th*, or a cerebral appears either as final or before mutes; e. g. beside *yáj-ati* 'sacrifices', *yáṣ-ṭṛ-* 'sacrificer', *iṣ-ṭá-* 'sacrificed', *a-yāṭ* 'has sacrificed'; similarly in the roots *bhrāj-* 'shine'; *mṛj-* 'wipe off'; *rāj-* 'rule'; *rej-* 'tremble'(?); *vraj-* 'wander'; *sṛj-* 'send forth'; possibly also in *bhrajj-* 'roast'[10].

2. when in the form in question or in cognate forms, sounds follow which do not palatalize gutturals[11], that is, *u ṛ n m r v*; such are: *áj-ra-* 'plain'; *áj-ma(n)-* 'course'; *árjuna-* 'white', *ṛj-rá-* 'reddish'; *ṛj-ú-* 'straight', *ṛ́j-īyas-*

---

1 Under the influence of *ój-īyas-* 'stronger' and *ój-iṣṭha-* 'strongest', such nouns in *-man* being often closely connected with comparatives and superlatives.

2 In the Kāṭhaka *ch* is spelt *śch*, which is probably only a provincial assibilation, and not the survival of an older sound; cp. J. SCHMIDT, KZ. 27, 332.

3 *mūrkhá-* 'dull', occurring in a B. passage of the TS., is probably a new formation analogous to *śoká-* (AV.) from *śócati*. Some scholars hold that there is an etymological connection between *chand-* 'appear', *chand-as-* 'song', and *skándati* 'leaps'; between *chid-* 'cut off' and *khid-* 'press'; between *chā-* (AV.) 'cut off' and *khā-* (*khan-*) 'dig'. Cp. WACKERNAGEL I, 131, note, bottom.

4 Cp. above p. 25 note 6; cp. here *cch* = *t* + *ś* in Sandhi and *ducchúnā-* for **dus-śunā-* 'misfortune'.

5 Except those of the Kāṭhaka, which write *śch* (cp. note 2).

6 Also ROTH's ed. of the Nirukta and MACDONELL's ed. of the Bṛhaddevatā; cp. AUFRECHT, RV², p. VI.

7 Cp. 32.

8 On AV. Ms. spelling *ch* for *kṣ* in two or three words, see WHITNEY, JAOS. 12, 92. 175.

9 On the origin of *ch*, cp. BRUGMANN, KG. 240; on the sound as a whole, WACKERNAGEL I, 133 f.

10 But cp. 38 c, and WACKERNAGEL I, 139.

11 Apart of course from the exceptions due to analogy: see 39.

'straighter', *ráj--iṣṭha-* 'straightest'; *jā́nu-* 'knee' beside *jñu-*; *jṛmbh-* 'yawn'[1]; *jñā-* 'know'; *jmā́-*, gen. *jm-ás* 'earth'; *jri-* 'go'; *-jvārá-* 'suffering'; *paj-rá-* 'fat'; *maj-mán-* 'greatness'; *váj-ra-* 'thunderbolt'; *juráti, jū́ryati, jujur-vā́ṃs-, jūr-ṇá-*, from *jṝ-* 'grow old'.

3. when in inflexional forms, in which roots with a new palatal show a guttural, the *j* remains; e. g. *jajā́na* from *jan-* 'beget'; *jajāsa* (AV.) from *jas-* 'be exhausted'; *jujóṣa* from *juṣ-* 'like'; *jujur-vā́ṃs-, jajā́ra* (AV.), from *jṝ-* 'grow old'[2].

4. when *j* is the reduplication of an old palatal *j* or *h*; e. g. *jajā́na, jajā́ra* (AV.), *juhóti*.

5. when it is shown to be an old palatal by the evidence of the cognate languages; thus in *ajá-* 'he-goat', *ajā́-* 'goat'; *ajina-* (AV.) 'skin'; *ū́rj-* 'nourishment'; *jáṃhas-* 'course'; *jáṅghā-* 'leg'; *jambh-* 'chew up'; *jā́mātṛ-* 'son-in-law'; *dhraj-* 'sweep'; *bhiṣaj-* 'heal'; *rajatá-* 'silvery'; *vā́ja-* 'swiftness'; *ṛjipyá-* 'going straight'.

a. It is **uncertain** whether *j* represents an old or a new palatal in the following words:

1. because the comparative evidence is conflicting: *vi-jā́man-* 'related'; *jū-* 'hasten'; *jyā-, jināti* 'overpower'[3].

2. because the Vedic and comparative evidence is insufficient: *ubj-* 'coerce'; *kūj-* (AV.) 'hum'; *jā́ñjat-ī-*, pres. part., of uncertain meaning (ἅ. λ.); *járate* 'approaches'; *jéhamāna-* 'panting'; *jihmá-* 'transverse'; *dhváj-, dhvajá-* 'banner'; *paj-* 'be rigid' (in *ápa ... pāpaje* 'started back'); *-pūjana-* 'honouring'; *bajá-* a kind of plant; *bīja-* 'seed'; *múñja-* 'sedge'.

b. Irregular *j*.—1. As the two kinds of *j* were indistinguishable in pronunciation, a guttural sometimes intruded among the old palatals owing to the analogy of the new palatals; thus from *bhiṣaj-* 'heal', *bhiṣák-tama-*, spv., *bhiṣák-ti*, 3. sing. pres., *a-bhiṣṇak*, 3. sing. impf. (like *anak-ti* from *añj-* 'anoint'); from *mṛj-* 'wipe': *ni-mṛg-ra-* 'attached', *apā-mārgá-* (AV.) a kind of plant, *vi-mṛ́g-varī-* (AV.) 'cleanly'; from *sṛj-* 'discharge', *asṛg-ram, asṛgran, ásasṛgram, sasṛgmáhe* (SV.) beside *sasṛjmáhe*; from *jṝ-* 'grow old', *jāgāra* (AV.) beside *jajā́ra* (AV.).

2. The guttural beside the palatal may be due to IE. dialectic variety in *gnā́-* 'woman' beside *jan-* 'beget'; *gm-ás* beside *jm-ás* 'of the earth'; *bhárgas-* 'splendour', *bhṛ́gu-* a name, beside *bhrāj-* 'shine'.

3. In *jyótis-* 'light', *jy* seems, by an old Prakritism, to represent *dy*, as the word is probably derived from *dyut-* 'shine'.

4. The media aspirate *jh*[4] occurs only in one form, *jájhjhat-ī-* (RV.[1]), a pres. part. probably meaning 'laughing' as an epithet of lightning (a metaphor connected with lightning elsewhere also in the RV.); it appears to be derived, by an old Prakritism, from *has-* 'laugh': *jhjh* probably for *jjh*[5] here = IE. *ĝzh*, which otherwise would become *kṣ-*, as in *jákṣ-at-*, part., 'laughing'.

42. **The cerebrals.**—The designation given to these sounds by the native phoneticians[6], *mūrdhanya* 'produced in the head', indicates that they were pronounced at the highest point in the mouth nearest the (upper part

---

[1] In which only forms with *ṛ* occur; cp., however, HÜBSCHMANN, KZ. 23, 393.

[2] The only instance of a new palatal (*c j h* = *k g gh*) before *ū̆r* (= IE. *ṝ*) is *carcūryá-māṇa-* (RV. x). For some more or less doubtful examples of old palatal *j*, see WACKERNAGEL I, 137 b note.

[3] Op. cit. I, 137 e, note.

[4] The other two old palatals *ś* and *h* will be dealt with below in their alphabetical order: 54, 58.

[5] The Kashmir Ms. of the RV. reads *jájjhatīr* for *jájhjhatīr* (V. 52[6]): SCHEFTELOWITZ, WZKM. 21, 86.

[6] See RPr. I. 19; APr. I. 32; TPr. II. 37.

of the) head. They are described by the Prātiśākhyas as pronounced by turning the tip of the tongue up to the roof of the mouth and bending it backwards. They were therefore pronounced farther back in the mouth than the palatals. This is also their pronunciation at the present day in India. An indication that it was such even in Vedic times is the fact that *ḍ* is sometimes found in the later Saṃhitās interchanging, between vowels, with *l*[1] (which itself interchanges with *r*), and that in the RV. itself *ḍ ḍh* become *ḷ ḷh* between vowels. It is also to be noted that the Greeks reproduced *ḍ* not only with δ, but also with ρ[2]. The cerebrals, however, were a specifically Indian product, being unknown in the Indo-Iranian period[3]. They are still rare in the RV., where they occur medially and finally only. According to most scholars, they are due to aboriginal, especially Dravidian, influence[4]. As a rule, they have arisen immediately after *ṣ* or an *r* sound from dentals. But before consonants and finally they may represent the old palatals *j ś h*.

a. The voiceless cerebrals *ṭ ṭh* take the place of the dentals *t th* **after *ṣ*** (= *s*, *ś* or *j*); e. g. *vṛṣ-ṭi-* 'rain' (suffix *-ti*); *duṣ-ṭára-* 'invincible' (= *dus-tára-*); *nákiṣ ṭe* (= *nákis te*); *váṣ-ṭi* 'wishes' (= *váś-ti*); *mṛṣ-ṭá-* 'cleansed' (= *mṛj-tá-*)[5]. Similarly the voiced cerebrals *ḍ ḍh* take the place of the dentals *d dh* **after **ẓ*** (= *s* or old palatal *j*, *h*), which has disappeared[6]; e. g. *nīḍá-* 'nest' (= IE. *nizdó-*); *dū-ḍhī́-* 'ill-disposed' (= *dus-dhī́-*); *īḍ-é* 'I worship' (**iẓ-ḍ-* = *ij-d-* for *yaj-d-*); *dṛḍhá-* 'firm' (= *dṛh-tá-*). The preceding voiced sibilant **ẓ* (= *ś* and *ṣ*) has (instead of disappearing) itself become *ḍ* in *didiḍ-ḍhi* (from *diś-* 'show') and *viviḍ-ḍhi* (from *viṣ-* 'be active')[7].

α. When the dental here was immediately followed by an *r* sound, the cerebralization seems originally to have been stopped. Hence *dṛdhrá-* (= *dṛh-tra-*), beside *dṛḍhá-* (= *dṛh-ta-*) 'firm'; and though *ṣṭr* occurs several times in the RV.[8], the *r* seems to have been dropped in pronunciation, as the only stems ending in *-ṣṭra-* which show a case-form with *n*, do not cerebralize it: *úṣṭrānām* and *rāṣṭrā́nām*, as if no *r* preceded. In TS. I. 2. 5², *r* is actually dropped after *ṣṭ* in *tváṣṭīmatī-* 'accompanied by Tvaṣṭrī'.

b. In several instances a cerebral appears by an evident **Prakritism**, in place of a dental originally preceded by an *r* (or *l*) sound; thus *ví-kaṭa-* 'monstrous', beside *kṛ-tá-* 'made'; *kāṭá-* 'depth', beside *kartá-*[9] 'pit'; *avaṭá-* (SV. VS.) 'pit', beside *avár*[10] 'down'[11]; and as shown by comparative evidence, *káṭuka-* 'sharp'; *kūḍayati* 'singes'; *kévaṭa-* 'pit'; *jáḍhu-* 'dull'; *kūṭá-* (AV. TS.) 'hornless'. In the following words, though cognate languages show *l*[12], the cerebral is similarly based on Indian *ṛ* or *r*[13] + dental: *kū́ṭa-* 'frontal bone'; *jaṭhára-* 'belly'; *taḍít-* 'contiguous', *tā́ḍa-* (AV.) 'blow'; *píṇḍa-* 'lump'; *kā́ṇḍa-* (AV.) 'piece'[14].

c. Cerebrals have in some instances supplanted dentals owing to the

---

[1] Cp. VPr. IV. 143; v. BRADKE, KZ. 28, 298.

[2] See WACKERNAGEL I, 143, note.

[3] Op. cit. I, 144.

[4] Ibid., note.

[5] Cp. above 41, 1.

[6] Cp. above 17, 5.

[7] See WACKERNAGEL I, 145 a, note (end). Cp. 42 d (p. 34) end.

[8] In *rāṣṭrá-* 'dominion', *úṣṭra-* 'buffalo', *deṣṭrī́-* 'Directress'; *dáṃṣṭra-* 'tooth'; *ṣṭṛ-* in *á-ni-ṣṭṛta-* 'not shaken off', *tváṣṭṛ-mant-* 'accompanied by Tvaṣṭṛ'; *ṇḍṛ* in *kuṇḍṛ-ṇā́cī-* 'house-lizard' (?).

[9] WACKERNAGEL I, 146 a.

[10] Cp. BARTHOLOMAE, IF. 3, 179.

[11] Perhaps also *reṇúka-kāṭa-* 'stirring dust', if from *kṛt-* 'cut'; but see BARTHOLOMAE, IF. 3, 180 f.

[12] IE. *l* by rhotacism became *r* in IIr.

[13] MS. II. 47 has the reading *jinva rāváṭ* for that of TS. II. 4. 7¹ *jinvár āvṛ́t* and K. XI. 9 *jinva rāvat*. Cp. below p. 70, note 4.

[14] The cerebral could be similarly accounted for in *kúṭa-* (RV¹.) 'house' (?), if it is related to *kula-(pa-)* 'family', and *kulā́ya-* (AV.) 'nest'. In *daṇḍá-* 'staff' if identical with Gk. δένδρον (J. SCHMIDT, KZ. 25, 52, note 1) we seem to have an instance of a cerebral for a dental + following *r*, but such a change seems not to be in accordance with the phonetic laws of either Vedic (cp. *dṛdhrá-*, above a, α) or Prakrit. On two other examples of this supposed change, *āṇḍá-*

analogy of similar words with phonetic cerebral. In *paḍbhís* 'with feet', and perhaps *páḍ-gṛbhi-*, N., it is due to *paḍbhís*, inst. pl. of both *páś-* 'look', and of *páś-* 'cord', and to *páḍbīśa-*, *páḍvīśa* (VS.) 'fetter', which is derived from *páś-* 'cord'[1]. *Vásaṭ* and *śráuṣaṭ*, sacrificial calls, probably for *vákṣat* and **śróṣat* (3. sing. aor. subj. of *vah-* 'convey', and *śru-* 'hear'), seem to owe their cerebral to the influence of the sacrificial call *vā́ṭ* (VS.), *váṭ* (TS.), 3. sing. aor. of √*vah-*. The *ḍ* of *puroḍā́ś-* 'sacrificial cake' (from *dāś-* 'worship'), is perhaps due to *dū-ḍā́ś-* 'impious' (for *duẓ-dāś-*)[2].

d. In a few instances a cerebral *ṭ* or *ḍ* appears **in place** of the cerebral sibilant *ṣ*. The phonetic representative of the latter before *bh* would be *ḍ* (parallel to *d* for IE. *z* before *bh*)[3], where it appears in *vipruḍ-bhis* (VS.) 'with drops'. From here the cerebral spread to the nom. sing., where it appears in *vi-prúṭ* (AV.) 'drop', from *pruṣ-* 'sprinkle', and in *edhamāna-dvíṭ* 'hating the arrogant' (from *dviṣ-* 'hate').

The cerebral *ḍ* also appears before the *-dhi* of the 2. sing. impv. for *ṣ* in *aviḍḍhi* (= *avi-ṣ-dhi*) aor. of *av-* 'favour', and in *viviḍḍhi* (= *viviṣ-dhi*), red. aor. of *viṣ-* 'be active'. The phonetic form here would be **īḍh* (= *iẓ-dh*)[4], instead of which *iḍḍh* appears under the influence, perhaps, of the cognate verbal forms with the short vowel (*aviṣṭu*, *aviṣṭám* etc.).

43. **Cerebrals** in many instances **represent the old palatals** *j ś h*. They are found thus:

a. **as final**: 1. in nom. sing. m. f.: *bhrā́ṭ* 'lustre' (*bhrā́j-*); *rā́ṭ* 'ruler' (*rā́j-*); *vipā́ṭ*, N. of a river (*vipā́ś-*); *víṭ* 'settlement' (*víś-*), *spáṭ* 'spying' (*spáś-*); *ṣā́ṭ* 'overcoming' (*sáh-*); *-vā́ṭ* 'conducting' (*-vāh-*), *paṣṭhavā́ṭ* (VS.), *-vā́t* (TS.). The guttural *k* would have been phonetic in this case, as the nom. sing. originally ended in *s*[5], and even the old palatals became *k* before *s*; the cerebral must here therefore be due to the influence of forms in which it was phonetic.

2. in nom. acc. *ṣáṭ*, from *ṣáṣ-* 'six'. As *k* might have been expected (IE. *sveks*), the cerebral is doubtless due to forms containing *ṣaṣ-*, as *ṣaṣṭí-* 'sixty', *ṣaṣṭhá-* (AV. VS.) 'sixth'.

3. in the first member of a compound, where the final of the nom. sing. appears, in *ṣáṭ-* 'six', and *páḍ-* (from *páś-* 'cord', in *páḍ-bīśa-*).

4. in 2. 3. sing. aor. for the radical palatal after the endings have been dropped: thus *á-bhrāṭ* (*bhrāj-* 'shine'); *yāṭ* (*yaj-* 'sacrifice'); *rāṭ* (*rāj-* 'shine'); *naṭ*, *ā́-naṭ* (*naś-* 'reach'); *á-prāṭ* (*praś-* 'ask' in *praś-ná-* 'question'); *á-vāṭ* (*vah-* 'convey'). Here *ṭ* is phonetic in the 3. pers. only, standing for *ṣ-ṭ* (= IE. *k̂-t*). It has been transferred to the 2. sing., where *k* would be phonetic (standing

'egg', and *maṇḍū́ka-* 'frog', see WACKERNAGEL 1, 147, note.

1 Op. cit. 1, 148 a (p. 172, top).

2 The form *vy-ávāṭ* in MS. III. 49 (B.) beside *vy-àvāt*, AV. VIII. 1[21], from *vi-vas-* 'shine forth', is probably due to the influence of *a-vāṭ*, aor. of √*vah-*; but cp. BARTHOLOMAE, Studien 1, 24, note. On the cerebral in *avaṭá-* (SV. VS.), beside *avatá-*, *naḍá-* 'reed', beside *nadá-*, and in *kīṭá-* (AV.), *markáṭa-* (VS.) cp. WACKERNAGEL 1, 148 b, note.

3 See below 44 a, 3.

4 Cp. above 17, 5.

5 This phonetic *k* for an old palatal is preserved in the nominatives *-dṛ́k* 'seeing' (*dṛś-*), *-spṛ́k* 'touching' (*spṛś-*), *spṛ́k* 'desiring' (*spṛh-*), *an-ák* 'eyeless' (*-akṣ-* : *aś-* 'penetrate'); *ṛtvík* 'sacrificer' (√*yaj-*); *ū́rk* (VS.) 'nourishment' (*ū́rj-*); *dik* (AV.) 'region' (*diś-*). For *-dṛ́k*, the later Saṃhitās have *-dṛ́ṅ* also. In the n. nom. the m. f. form appears: *-dṛ́k*, *-spṛk*; but as there was no *s* here, it must be assumed that the cerebral was originally used in these neuter forms. In *bhiṣáj-* 'healer', the *k* has spread from the nom. to other cases, where it is not phonetic (cp. WACKERNAGEL 1, 138). The original value of the palatal in *uśíj-* 'desiring', *uṣṇíh-* (AV. VS.), a kind of metre, which have *k* in the nom. is uncertain. The *k* in the nom. *nák* 'night' is probably not based on an old palatal *ś* (cp. WACKERNAGEL 1, 149 a α, note).

for *k-ṣ* = IE. *k̂s*). The reverse transference of *k* to the 3. sing. has taken place in *prá ṇak* beside *á-naṭ* (*naś-* 'reach') and in *á-srāk* (from *sṛj-* 'discharge').

b. before consonant suffixes:

1. the phonetic cerebral appears before case-endings beginning with *bh* in *paḍ-bhis*, from *páś-* 'look' and 'cord'; *viḍ-bhis* from *viś-* 'settlement'; *saráḍ-bhyas* 'for the bees' (probably from **saráh-*); *ṣaḍ-bhis*[1]. In *anaḍúd-bhyas* (AV.), from *anaḍ-váh-* 'bull', *d* appears for *ḍ* by dissimilation; while the guttural of the nom. instead of the phonetic *ḍ* appears in *susaṃdṛ́g-bhis* (from *dṛś-* 'see') 'fair to see' and in *dig-bhyás* (AV.) from *diś-* 'region'.

2. before the *-su* of the loc. pl. *k* is phonetic, and appears in *vik-ṣú*, from *viś-*, in spite of the unphonetic *ṭ* of the nom. *viṭ*. But owing to the influence of the other cases the unphonetic cerebral (in the form of *t* dissimilated for *ṭ*) appears in *anaḍút-su*.

3. before the *dhi* of the 2. sing. impv. the cerebral is phonetic in *didiḍḍhi*, from *diś-*[2]; also in *ẓ* (= *ṣ*), which after cerebralizing the *dh* is dropped, leaving a compensating length, in *tāḍhi* from *takṣ-* 'hew' (= IE. *teĝzdhi*); also in *ṣo-ḍhā́* 'sixfold' (for *ṣaṣ-dhā* : *aṣ-*, like *as-*, becoming *o* before a voiced mute)[3].

c. The cerebrals in the following words have **not** been satisfactorily **explained:** *āghāṭi-* and *ā-ghāṭá-* (AV.) 'striker', beside *-ā-ghāta-* (VS.); *āṇḍá-* 'egg'; *iṭánt-* (x. 171[1]) 'wandering'(?), *kúṭa-* 'house'(?); *kū́ṭa-* 'frontal bone'; *kṛ́pīṭa-* 'fuel'(?); *maṇḍū́ka-* 'frog'; *iṭa-* (AV.) 'reed'; *varā́ṭa-* (VS.), *lalā́ṭa-* (AV.) 'forehead'. Some others, mostly containing *b*, may be suspected of non-Aryan origin: *báṭ*, *baḍā́*, interjections; *baṭū́rin-* 'broad'(?), *bíriṭa-* 'troop'(?); *bekanā́ṭa-* 'usurer'; *āḍámbara-* (VS). 'drum'; *khaḍgá-* (VS. MS.) 'rhinoceros'; *cāṇḍālá-* (VS.) 'outcast'; *markáṭa-* (VS.) 'ape'.

44. **The dentals.**—The dentals are at the present day pronounced as interdentals in India, but according to the Prātiśākhyas[4] they were post-dental, being produced at the root of the teeth (*dantamūla*). They represent IE. dentals, corresponding to similar sounds in the cognate languages. When two IE. dentals met, there seems to have been a tendency to change the first to a sibilant[5]. A survival of this appears in some Vedic combinations of *d* or *dh* with *dh*, which point to an earlier *zdh*, viz. in *de-hí*, beside *dad-dhí* 'give'; *dhe-hi* (for **dhadh-dhi*) 'put'; *kiye-dhā́* 'containing much', in all of which examples *e* is based on IIr. *az*[6].

a. Change of *s* to *t*. The dental sibilant as the final of roots or nominal stems becomes *t*[7]:

1. **before** the *s* of verbal suffixes (future, aorist, desiderative) in the three verbs *vas-* 'dwell', *vas-* 'shine', and *ghas-* 'eat'[8]: thus *avātsīs* (AV.) 'thou hast dwelt'; *vát-syati* (MS.) 'will shine'; *jíghat-sati* (AV.) 'desires to eat', and *jighat-sú-* (AV.) 'hungry'.

---

1 From this phonetic change of *ṣ* to *ḍ* before *bh* is to be explained the stem *iḍ-* 'refreshment', beside *iṣ-* (which occurs before vowel endings only): *iḍ-bhis* etc. would have led to the formation of *iḍ-ā́*, etc. (inst. sing.), which then gave rise to *iḍ-ā-* as an extension of *iḍ-*; cp. also *iḍáyata* (RV. I. 191[6] MM., *iḷáyata*, AUFRECHT) : *iḷáyati* (AV.) 'be quiet'.

2 It is not phonetic in *aviḍḍhi* and *viviḍḍhi* (see above, 42 d). Cp. WACKERNAGEL I, 149 c (end).

3 The cerebral which in this paragraph represents (except before *s*) the old palatals, is based on an IIr. *sh-* sound *š ž* (as shown by the Avesta having *š ž* in the corresponding forms). This sibilant, Indian *ṣ*, first became the cerebral mute *ḍ* before the *bh*-suffixes (as dental *s* became dental *d*) when it first spread to the nom., and lastly to the loc. pl.

4 See RPr. I. 19; TPr. II. 38.

5 For example, Gk. ϝοῖσθα, Av. *voistā*, beside *vét-tha* 'thou knowest'. Cp. WACKERNAGEL I, 152 b.

6 Loc. cit., also note.

7 See discussion of attempted explanations in WACKERNAGEL I, 153, note.

8 All the other roots in *s* add the suffix with connecting vowel *i*.

2. before the *t* of the 3. sing. of a past tense: thus *vy-àvāt* (AV.) 'has shone forth', from *vi-vas-*. This is, however, probably not a phonetic change, but is rather due to the influence of the 3. sing. of other preterites with *-t*; **á-vās-t* having thus, instead of **á-vās*, become *á-vāt*[1].

3. before case-terminations beginning with *bh*, and when final (in nom. acc. sing. neut.), in the perf. part. and in four other words: thus *jāgr̥-vád-bhis*, inst. pl., 'having awakened', *tatan-vát*, acc. n., 'having stretched'; *uṣád-bhis*, from *uṣás-* 'dawn'; *mād-bhís*, *mād-bhyás* (AV.), from *mā́s-* 'month'; *svá-tavad-bhyas* (VS.), from *svá-tavas-* 'self-strong'. The change of *s* to *t* began before the *bh* endings (like that of *ṣ* to *ṭ* or *ḍ*)[2] and was extended to the nom. acc. sing. neut. in the RV., but not till later before the *-su* of the loc. pl.[3]

a. Allied to the change of final *s* of roots and stems to *t*, is the apparent change of the medial dental sibilant to *d* in *madgú-* (VS.) 'diver', from *majj-* 'dive' (*jj* = IE. *zg*)[4].

β. The substitution of dentals for other mutes is extremely rare. In consequence of dissimilation, a dental replaces a cerebral in *anaḍútsu* and *anaḍúdbhyas* (AV.), from *anaḍvā́h-* 'bull'; in *dr̥dhrá-* 'firm', beside *dr̥ḍhá-*[5]; in *paṣṭhavā́t* (TS.) 'four year old bull', beside *paṣṭhavā́ṭ* (VS.).

A dental seems to take the place of a labial in *ad-bhís*, *ad-bhyás*, beside *ap-* 'water': but this is probably due to the analogy of **nadbhís*, *nadbhyás*, beside *nápāt-* 'grandson'[6].

45. The labials. — These sounds as a rule represent IE. labials; e. g. *pitŕ̥-*, Gk. πατήρ; *bhára* 'bear', Gk. φέρε. But owing to the great rarity of IE. *b*, there are very few Vedic examples of inherited *b*; e. g. *rambate* 'hangs down', Lat. *lābī* 'glide'[7].

a. The number of words containing *b* has been greatly **increased by new formations.** **1.** Thus *b* replaces *p* or *bh* before other voiced mutes: e. g. *pi-bd-aná-* 'firm', beside *pad-á-* 'place'; *rab-dhá-*, beside *rabhante* 'they take'. — **2.** It is the regular substitute for *bh* in reduplicative syllables or when initial aspiration is lost owing to a following aspirate; e. g. *ba-bhū́va* from *bhū-* 'be', *bāhú-* 'arm', *bandh-* 'bind'[8]. — **3.** In a few examples it takes the place of or interchanges with *v*[9]; thus *páḍbīśa-* (RV.), beside *páḍvīśa-* (VS.); *bāṇá-* beside *vāṇá-* 'arrow'; *-balśa-* (AV.) beside *-valśa-* 'twig'; *bāṇá-* (AV.) 'music' beside *vāṇá-*; *-blīna-* (AV.) 'crushed', beside *vlīna-* (B.)[10]. — **4.** It further occurs in some new onomatopoetic words; *budbudá-* 'bubble'; *bál* (AV.) interj. 'dash!'; *bata* interj. 'alas!' and *batá-* 'weakling'. — **5.** In one instance *b* seems to stand for *m* before *r*, in *brū-* 'speak', for **mrū-*[11], originally appearing most likely after a pause or after a final consonant[12].

b. In many words the **origin of *b* is obscure.** Most of these probably come from a foreign source: **1.** owing to their meaning: *arbudá-* and *árbuda-*, *balbūthá-*, *śámbara-*, *sŕ̥binda-*, names of foes of Indra and of the Aryans; *br̥bú-*, a proper name; *bajá-* (AV.), *bálbaja-* (AV.), *bilvá-* (AV.), names of plants; *bákura-* and *bākurá-*, a musical instrument. — **2.** owing to their phonetic form: *kilbiṣa-* 'sin'; *bísa-* 'root-fibre'; *busá-* 'vapour'; *báṭ* and *baḍā́*, interjections;

---

1 Cp. WACKERNAGEL I, 154.

2 See 42 d (p. 34).

3 Cp. WACKERNAGEL I, 155 a, note.

4 Op. cit. I, 155 b, note.

5 See 42 a α (p. 33).

6 The name *in-d-ra* and *nánān-dr̥-* 'husband's sister', are explained by some scholars as containing a Prakritic *d*. See WACKERNAGEL I, 157, note.

7 On some words (*sabar-*, *batá-*, *bála-*, *balbūthá-*) in which *b* is regarded as IE. by different scholars, see WACKERNAGEL I, 158 b, note.

8 See above 32 a, 1, 2.

9 There is some confusion between forms of *br̥h-* 'be great', and *vr̥h-* 'tear'.

10 On some doubtful or wrong explanations of *b* for *v* (*ni-br̥h-* 'crush', *bála-*, *bálbaja-*, *báṭ*, *śabála-*, *śámba-*), see WACKERNAGEL I, 161, note.

11 Cp. Gk. βροτός for *μροτός.

12 See WACKERNAGEL I, 159.

baṇḍá- (AV.) 'crippled'; *bársva-* (VS.) 'socket'; *baṣkáya-* 'yearling'; *báṣkiha-* (VS.) 'decrepit'; *bíla-* 'cave', *bílma-* 'chip'; *bíriṭa-* 'troop' (?); *bekanā́ṭa-* 'usurer'. — 3. for both reasons: *ilī́bisa-* and *bṛ́saya-*, names of demons; *alā́bu-* (AV.) 'bottle gourd'. — 4. Other words which if not of foreign origin, are as yet insufficiently explained: *bárjaha-* 'udder'; *bastá-* 'he-goat'; *básri* 'quickly'; *-bāra-* 'aperture'; *bī́ja-* 'seed'; *bundá-* 'arrow'; *bṛbád-uktha-*, an epithet of Indra; *chúbuka-* 'chin'; *śabála-* 'brindled'; *śámba-*, a weapon of Indra; *balā́sa-* (VS. AV.), a disease; *bleṣka-* (K.) 'noose'.[1]

46. **The nasals.** — There are five nasals corresponding, in regard to place of articulation, to the five classes of mutes. Each of them can only appear before a mute of its own class[2]. Before sibilants and *h* the nasals do not appear[3]; before *l* only *m* is found; *ñ* does not appear finally any more than the palatal mutes.

a. The **guttural** nasal *ṅ* regularly appears before gutturals: e. g. *aṅká-* 'hook'; *aṅkháya-* 'embrace'; *áṅga-* 'limb'; *jáṅghā-* 'leg'. Before other consonants or as a final, it appears only when a following *k* or *g* has been dropped, as in stems ending with *-ñc-* or *-ñj-* and in those compounded with *-dṛ́ś-*; e. g. *pratyáṅ*, nom. sing. of *pratyáñc-* 'facing'; *yuṅdhi* (= *yuñj-dhi*), 2. sing. impv. of *yuj-* 'join'; *kī-dṛ́ṅ*, nom. sing. of *kī-dṛ́ś-* 'of what kind?'.

b. The **palatal** nasal *ñ* is found only before and after *c* or *j*, and before *ch*; e. g. *váñcati* (AV.) 'wavers'; *yajñá-* 'sacrifice'; *vāñchantu* 'let them desire'.

c. The **labial** nasal *m* as a rule represents IE. *m*; e. g. *mātṛ́-* 'mother', Lat. *māter*; *nā́man-* 'name', Lat. *nōmen*. It is by far the most common labial sound[4], its frequency being greater than that of the four labial mutes taken together[5]. By some scholars *m* is regarded as representing an original *n* or *v* in certain instances[6].

d. The **dental** nasal *n* as a rule represents IE. *n*; e. g. *ná* 'not', Lat. *-nĕ*; *mánas-* 'mind', Gk. *μένος*. It is the commonest of the nasals, being more frequent than *m*, and about three times as frequent as the other three taken together[7]. The dental nasal also appears instead of dental mutes and of the labial nasal.

α. It appears **in place of** ***d*** before the nominal suffix *-na*, and of *t*, as well as *d*, before the *m* of secondary suffixes; e. g. *án-na-* 'food' (*ad-* 'eat'); *chin-ná-* 'cut off' (*chid-*); *vidyún-mant-* 'gleaming' (*vidyút-* 'lightning'); *mṛ́n-maya-* 'earthen' (*mṛ́d-* VS. 'earth'). This substitution is in imitation of Sandhi, as *dn tm dm* otherwise occur within words; e. g. *udnā́* (from *udán-* 'water'), *ātmán-* 'breath', *vid-má* 'we know'.

β. dental *n* regularly appears **in place of** ***m***: 1. before *t*; e. g. from *yam-* 'restrain': *yan-túr-* and *yan-tṛ́-* 'guide', *yan-trá-* 'rein'; from *śram-* 'exert oneself': *śrāntá-* 'wearied'; 2. before suffixal *m* or *v*; e. g. from *gam-* 'go': *á-gan-ma*, *gan-vahi*, *jagan-vā́ṃs-*[8]; 3. when radically final, originally followed by suffixal *s* or *t*; e. g. from *gam-* 'go', *á-gan*, 2. 3. sing. aor. (= *á-gam-s*, *á-gam-t*); from *yam-* 'restrain', *a-yān*, 3. sing. aor. (= *a-yām-s-t*); from *dám-* 'house', gen. (*pátir*) *dán*[9]

[1] Op. cit. I, 162.

[2] Excepting in a few instances when a mute has been dropped, as in *yuṅdhi* = *yuṅgdhi* (see a).

[3] Excepting in a few instances *ṅ* or *n* before the *-su* of the loc. pl.

[4] Excluding the semivowel *v*.

[5] Cp. WHITNEY 50 and 75.

[6] Cp. WACKERNAGEL I, 177, note.

[7] WHITNEY 75.

[8] This change of *m* to *n* may be due to the influence of the cognate forms in which *m* phonetically becomes *n* when final (below 3).

[9] On this explanation of *dán* (denied by PISCHEL, VS. 2, 307 ff.) see especially BARTHOLOMAE, IF. 8, in 'Arica' 229—249; also RICHTER, KZ. 36, 111—123, on *dám-pati-*.

'of the house' (= *dam-s*). Here the change of *m* to *n* was evidently due (as in 1) to the dental *s* or *t* which originally followed[1].

47. **The cerebral *ṇ*.**—This nasal, like the cerebral mutes, is an Indian innovation. It is for the most part the result of a regular phonetic development, but is also in a number of words due to Prakritic influence.

A. Besides regularly appearing before cerebral mutes, e. g. in *daṇḍá-* 'staff', the cerebral *ṇ* phonetically takes the place of dental *n* after *ṛ r ṣ*[2], either immediately preceding, e. g. *nṛṇā́m* 'of men', *várṇa-* 'colour', *uṣṇá-* 'hot'; or when only vowels[3], guttural or labial mutes[4] or nasals, *y v* or *h*, intervene; e. g. *kṛpáṇa-* 'misery'; *krámaṇa-* 'step'; *kṣóbhaṇa-* 'exciting'. This rule is followed throughout within a word even when a *ṣ* which it contains is produced by Sandhi[5]; thus not only *tṛpṇóti* (*tṛp-* 'be satisfied') and *gṛbhṇā́ti* (*gṛbh-* 'seize'), but also *u ṣuvāṇáḥ* (for *suvānáḥ*, IX. 107[8]). In *su-ṣumná-* 'very gracious' (where the *ṣ* is produced by internal Sandhi), the dental *n* remains probably owing to the influence of the simple word *sumná-*.

a. The cerebralization of dental *n* takes place almost as regularly **in verbs** compounded with the prepositions *prá* 'before', *párā* 'away', *pári* 'round', *nir* (for *nis*) 'out'; as well as in nominal derivatives of these combinations. But the *r* does not cerebralize *n* when there is tmesis or any other preposition but *ā* intervenes[6]. The cerebralization takes place:

1. **in the initial of roots**; e. g. *práṇak* (*naś-* 'reach'); *parāṇúde* (*nud-* 'thrust); *pra-ṇetṛ́-* 'guide' (*nī-* 'lead'). But *n* remains if *ṛ* or *kṣ* follows; hence *prā́nṛtyat* (AV.) from *nṛt-* 'dance', and *pári nakṣati* 'encompasses' (*nakṣ-* 'reach'). The cerebralization is also absent, without this dissimilating cause[7], in *abhí prá nonu-* (SV.) beside *abhí prá ṇonu-* 'shout towards', and in *prá-nabh-*[8] (AV.) 'burst'.

2. **medially or finally** in the roots *hnu-* 'hide', *an-* 'breathe', *han-* 'strike' (though not in forms with *ghn*); thus *pári-hṇutā* (AV.) 'denied'; *prā́ṇiti* 'breathes'; *nír haṇyāt* (AV.), but *abhi-pra-ghnánti*.

3. **in suffixal *n*** the cerebralization fluctuates: it always takes place in the *n* of the 1. sing. subj., e. g. *nír gamāṇi*; not always in the pres. base of *hi-* 'impel'; e. g. *prá hiṇomi*, etc., but *pari-hinómi*[9]; never in that of *mināti* 'diminishes' or of *minóti* 'establishes'; it is also absent in *yáju ṣkannám* (X. 181[3])[10]; but *-tṛṇṇa-* (VS.), from *tṛd-* 'pierce'.

b. In nominal compounds cerebralization takes place less regularly when there is *ṛ r* or *ṣ* in the first member, and *n* in the second:

1. **an initial *n*** is here nearly always cerebralized in the RV.: e. g. *dur-ṇā́man-* 'ill-named'; *prá-ṇapāt-* 'great-grandson'; also *dur-ṇā́śa-* (AV.) 'un-

[1] The dental *n* may stand for *l* in *carma-mná-* 'tanner' (cp. *cármāṇi mlātā́ni*): BR. According to BENFEY, it is used to fill the hiatus in declension, e. g. *kavi-n-ā*; and in the perf. red. syllable *ān-*, e. g. in *ānṛcúr*; cp. WACKERNAGEL I, 175 c, note.

[2] The cerebral mutes and nasal not only do not cerebralize a *n* separated from them by a vowel, but even stop the influence of a preceding *ṛ r ṣ*; thus in reduplication only the first *n* is cerebralized; e. g. *pra-ṇinā́ya* (*nī-* 'lead'); cp. *maṇinā* inst. of *maṇi-* 'pearl' (B. b.). This arises from a disinclination to pronounce cerebral mutes and nasals in successive syllables.

[3] On the absence of cerebralization in *úṣṭrānām* and *rāṣṭrānā́m*, see above 42 a, *α*.

[4] In some instances where the mute immediately precedes the *n*, the cerebralization does not take place; e. g. *vṛtra-ghné*; *kṣepnú-* 'springing'.

[5] In one curious instance, *sám ... piṇák* (beside *pinaṣṭi*, from *piṣ-* 'crush'), the cerebral lost at the end of a syllable bas transferred its cerebral character to the beginning of the syllable.

[6] The preposition *ni* following another containing *r* is mostly cerebralized.

[7] Cp. above 42 a, *α*.

[8] Cp. *tri-nā́bhi-* 'three-naved', and *vṛ́ṣa-nābhi-* 'strong-naved'.

[9] Cp. VPr. III. 87; APr. III. 88; IV. 95; TPr. XIII. 12.

[10] Cp. WACKERNAGEL I, 167 b *ε*.

attainable', *dur-ṇihita-* (AV.) 'ill-preserved'; but (because a *ṛ r* or *ṣ* follows) not in *-nṛmṇa-* 'manhood', *-niṣṭhá-* 'eminent'; *-niṣṣídh-* 'gift'; *-nirṇíj-* 'adornment'; nor (owing to the intervening *gh* and *m*) in *dīrghá-nītha-*, N., *yuṣmá-nīta-* 'led by you'. The cerebralization is further absent, without any preventing cause, in *akṣā-náh-* 'tied to the axle' (beside *parī-ṇáh-* 'enclosure'); *tri-nāká-* 'third heaven'; *tri-nā́bhi-* 'three-naved', and *vṛ́ṣa-nābhi-* 'great-naved'; *púnar-nava-* 'renewing itself' (but AV. *púnar-ṇava-*); *dur-niyántu-* 'hard to restrain'.

2. it is less frequent **medially**; e. g. *pūrvāhṇá-* forenoon'; *aparāhṇá-* (AV.) 'afternoon'; *nṛ-vā́haṇa-* 'conveying men'; *pra-vā́haṇa-* (VS.) 'carrying off'; *purīṣa-vā́haṇa-* (VS.) beside *purīṣa-vā́hana-* (TS. K.) 'removing rubbish'; *nṛ-máṇas-* 'kind to men', *vṛ́ṣa-maṇas-* 'manly-spirited', but *ṛ́ṣi-manas-* 'of far-seeing mind'; *dru-ghaṇá-* 'wooden club', but *vṛtra-ghné*, dat., 'Vṛtra-slaying'; *su-ṣumná-*[1] 'very gracious'; *su-pra-pāṇá-* 'good drinking place'; *nṛ-pā́ṇa-* 'giving drink to men'; but *pari-pā́na-* 'drink', *pari-pā́na-* (AV.) 'protection'; *pary-uhyamāṇa-* (VS.) beside *pary-uhyamāna-*(√*vah-*).

c. Even **in a** closely connected **following word** cerebralization may take place after *ṛ r ṣ* in the preceding one.

1. This is frequently the case with initial *n*, most usually in *nas* 'us', rarely in other monosyllables such as *nú* 'now', *ná* 'like'[2]; e. g. *sahó ṣú ṇaḥ* (VIII. 7³²). Initial *ṇ* occasionally appears thus in other words also; e. g. *pári ṇetā́ .. viśat* (IX. 103⁴); *śṛ́ṅga-vṛṣo ṇapāt* (SV., *napāt*, RV.); *asthūrí ṇau* (VS., *no* RV. TS.); (*gómad*) *ū ṣú ṇāsatyā* (VS.) *prá ṇā́māni* (TS.); *púnar ṇayāmasi* (AV.); *suhā́r ṇaḥ* (MS.) = *suhārd naḥ*; *vā́r ṇā́ma* (TS. v. 6. 1³).

2. Medial *ṇ* also occurs thus, most often in the enclitic pronoun *ena-* 'this'; e. g. *índra . eṇam*. It occasionally appears in accented words also after final *r*: *gór ohéṇa* (I. 180⁵); *nír éṇasaḥ* (AV.); *nṛ́bhir yemāṇáḥ* (SV., *yemānáḥ*, RV.); *paṇíbhir vīyámāṇaḥ* (TS.)[3]. A final *n* is treated as medial and cerebralized thus in *tṛ́ṇ imā́n* (MS.) and *akṣā́ṇ áva* (MS.).

B. In a number of words *ṇ* has a **Prakritic origin.**

a. It is **due to a preceding** *ṛ* **or** *r* which has been replaced by *a i u* or has disappeared through assimilation. This is indicated to be the case by the appearance beside them of cognate words containing *r* or *l* sounds: **1.** in Vedic itself: thus *āṇí-* 'pin of the axle'; *kāṇá-* 'one-eyed', beside *karṇá-*[4] 'crop-eared' (MS.); *káṇa-* (AV.) 'particle' : *kalā́-* 'small part'; *jañjaṇā-bhávan* 'glittering' : *jū́rṇi-* 'glow' (*-jaṇ-* probably = *jṛṇ-* from old pres. **jṛṇāti*); *púṇya-* 'auspicious' : *pṝ-* 'fill'; *phaṇ-* 'bound' (= **phṛṇ-*, **pharṇ-*) cp. *parpharat* 'may he scatter'; *dhā́ṇikā-* 'cunnus' : *dhā́rakā-* (VS.), id.—**2.** in allied languages: *gaṇá-* 'crowd'; *paṇ-* (VS.) 'purchase'; *vaṇíj-* 'merchant'[5]; *áṇu-* 'minute'; *kúṇāru-* 'having a withered arm'; *pāṇí-* 'hand'; *sthāṇú-* 'stump'[6].

b. Owing to the predilection for cerebrals in Prakrit, which substituted *ṇ* for *n* throughout between vowels, **even without** the influence of **neighbouring cerebrals,** one or two words with such *ṇ* seem to have made their way into Vedic: *maṇí-* 'pearl' (Lat. *monile*); *amṇáḥ* (MS.) 'at once' : *amnáḥ* (AV.), id.[7].

c. The exact **explanation** of the *ṇ* in the following words (some of which may be of foreign origin) is **uncertain**: *káṇva-*, N.; *kalyā́ṇa-* 'fair';

[1] See above 47 A (end).

[2] Cp. BENFEY, Göttinger Abhandlungen 20, 14.

[3] *agnér ávena* (I. 128⁵), Pp. *agnéḥ | ávena*, is probably wrong for *agnéḥ | ravéṇa*. On the other hand, for *máno rúhāṇā* (I. 32⁸), Pp. *mánaḥ | rúhāṇāḥ*, the reading should perhaps be *mánor úhāṇā*. Cp. LANMAN, Sanskrit Reader, note on this passage.

[4] See WACKERNAGEL I, 172 a (p. 192, mid.).

[5] See FRÖHDE, BB. 16, 209.

[6] Cp. WACKERNAGEL I, 172 d, note, 173, note.

[7] On a few doubtful instances, op. cit. I, 173, note.

kāṇuká-, of doubtful meaning; *nicumpuṇá-*, of doubtful meaning; *niṇík* 'secretly', *niṇyá-*[1] 'inner'; *paṇí-*, a kind of demon; *bāṇá-* 'arrow'; *vāṇá-* 'udder', 'arrow', 'music'; *vā́ṇī-* 'music'; *vā́ṇīcī-*, a kind of musical instrument; *śóṇa-* 'red'; *ū́gaṇa-* (SV. VS.), of doubtful meaning; *kúṇapa-* (AV.) 'corpse'; *guṇá-* 'division' (AV.); *cupuṇīkā-* (TS.), N.; *nicaṅkuṇá-* (TS.) and *nicuṅkuṇá-* (TS.), of doubtful meaning; *veṇú-* (AV.) 'reed'; *śáṇu-* (AV.) 'hemp'[2].

48. The semivowels.—The semivowels *y, r, l, v* have the peculiarity that each has a vowel corresponding to it, viz. *i ṛ ḷ u* respectively. They are called *anta(ḥ)sthā* in the Prātiśākhyas[3], the term doubtless meaning 'intermediate', that is, standing midway between vowels and consonants.

a. ***y* and *v*** regularly represent the final *i* and *u* of diphthongs before vowels, *e* and *ai* becoming *ay* and *āy*, *o* and *au av* and *āv*. But while *y* and *v* are regularly written for *i* and *u* before vowels, they were **often pronounced** as *iy* and *uv*. This is shown by the fact that:

1. *iy* and *uv* are frequently written, beside *y* and *v*, in the inflexion of *ī*- and *ū*-stems. Thus from *dhī́-* 'thought', there are several compounds, in some of which the stem is written with *iy* before vowels, as *itthā́dhiy-* 'very devout', in others with *y*, as *ādhy-* 'longing'. Similarly *-jū-* 'hastening', regularly appears as *-juv-*; but *-pū-* 'purifying', *-śū-* 'swelling', *-sū-* 'bringing forth', always as *-pv-*, *-śv-*, *-sv-*[4]. In the same way, the suffix *-ya* is often written *-iya*; e. g. *ágr-iya-* 'first', beside *ágr-ya-* (VS.); *ṛ́tv-iya-* and *ṛ́tv-ya-* 'regular'; *urv-iyā́* and *urv-yā́* (VS. TS.) 'widely'. This spelling is characteristic of the TS. Here *iy* is generally written where more than one consonant precede, almost invariably so in the inflexion of stems in *i* and *ī*; e. g. *indrāgniy-ós* 'of Indra and Agni', *lakṣmiyā́* 'by Lakṣmī'; very often also in the suffix *-ya*; e. g. *áśv-iya-* beside *áśv-ya-* (RV.) 'relating to horses'[5]. Similarly *uv* appears here for *v* in *súvar-* and *suvargá-* 'heaven', beside *svàr* (RV.) and *svargá-* (RV.); in the inflexion of *tanū́-* 'body', in some forms of *vāyú-* 'wind', *bāhú-* 'arm', *ūrú-* 'thigh'[6]. In the SV. and MS.[7] there are two or three other examples of *iy* and *uv* for *y* and *v*[8].

2. according to metrical evidence, *y* and *v* (though written as pronounced in classical Sanskrit) have a syllabic value in a large number of examples in the Vedic hymns[9]. This was recognized to be the case by the Prātiśākhyas[10].

3. *r* appears instead of *ṛ* before the suffix *-ya*; e. g. in *pítr-ya-* 'paternal', from *pitṛ́-* 'father'.

4. *ay āy ey* appear before the suffix *-ya*[11]; e. g. *saha-śéy-yāya*, dat., 'for lying together'. Here *yy* is always to be read as *y-iy* in the RV. (except in Book x and *dakṣā́yya-* in I. 129[2])[12].

---

1 Perhaps from **nirnaya-*, see Benfey, GGA. 1858, p. 1627.

2 On these words see Wackernagel I, 174 b and 173 d, note.

3 RPr. I. 2; VPr. IV. 101; also Nirukta II. 2. Cp. Whitney on APr. I. 30.

4 Cp. Wackernagel I, 181 a, note.

5 Several other examples, loc. cit.

6 Cp. Whitney on TPr. II. 25.

7 See Wackernagel I, 181 a, note (p. 201, mid.).

8 On the other hand there are some isolated instances of *y* and *v* in the Vedas as compared with *iy* and *uv* in classical Sanskrit; see Wackernagel I, p. 201, bottom.

9 In certain words and formatives *y* and *v* are regularly consonantal: in the relative *yá-*; the present suffix *-ya*; the comp. suffix *-yas*; the gen. ending *-sya*, and the fut. suffix *-sya*; the initial *v* of suffixes; the *nv-* of the 5th class; in *áśva-* 'horse' and *tváṣṭṛ-*, N. On the other hand the syllabic pronunciation is sometimes used artificially by the poets, as is apparent from the isolation of such occurrences. In some individual words the written *iy* and *uv* have to be pronounced as consonantal *y* and *v*: always in *suvāná-*. pres. part. of *su-* 'press'; occasionally in *bhiyás-* 'fear', *hiyāná-* 'impelled'. Cp. Wackernagel I, 181 b, note, bottom.

10 RPr. VIII. 22; XVII. 14.

11 See Grassmann, Wb. 1711, columns 4 and 5.

12 Wackernagel I, 181 c γ.

That this syllabic pronunciation was not simply *i* and *u* (with hiatus), but *iy* and *uv*, is rendered probable not only by the spelling *iy uv* beside *y v*, but by the consideration that *y* and *v* are respectively the natural transition from *i* and *u* to a following dissimilar vowel.

b. In the RV. *y* and *v* are pronounced **with a syllabic value** under the following conditions:

1. almost invariably after a group of consonants and generally after a single consonant if preceded by a long vowel. Thus the ending *-bhyas* and the suffix *-tya* are regularly pronounced as dissyllables after a long vowel, but as monosyllables after a short vowel. Hence, too, *v* is pronounced as well as written in the forms *davidhv-át, suṣv-ati, suṣv-āṇá-, juhv-é, júhv-ati*[1].

2. after a single initial consonant at the beginning of a verse, or, within a verse, if the preceding syllable is heavy, in some half dozen words. Thus *tyá-* 'that', and *tvám* 'thou' are nearly always pronounced as they are written after a short vowel, but *tiyá-* and *tuvám* at the beginning of a Pāda or after a long vowel. The *y* is pronounced as *iy* in *jyā́-* and *jyākā́-* 'bowstring' only at the beginning of a verse or after a long vowel, in *jyā́yas-* 'mightier' only after a long vowel. Finally *tva-* 'many', must generally be read as *tuva-* after a long vowel, but almost invariably *tva-* after a short vowel.

3. in the inflexion of the nouns in *ī* (nom. sing. *-ī-s*) and *ū*[2], where the stem has (with only six exceptions) to be pronounced with *iy* and *uv*.[3]

Thus the transition from *iy* and *uv* to *y* and *v* began in the RV., the traditional text writing for the *iy* and *uv* which was pronounced by the poets of that Veda, sometimes *iy* and *uv*, sometimes *y* and *v*.

49. The semivowel *y*.—This semivowel, when not derived from *i* before other vowels (48 a) within Vedic itself, is based either on IE. *i̯* (= Gk. spiritus asper) or voiced palatal spirant (= Gk. ζ)[4]; e. g. *yá-s* 'who' (ὅ-ς); *yaj-* 'sacrifice' (ἅγ-ιος); *yudh-* 'fight' (ὑσ-μίνη); but *yáva-* 'corn' (ζειά); *yas-* 'boil' (ζέω); *yuj-* 'yoke' (ζυγ-); *yūṣán-* 'broth' (ζύ-μη). It is probably due to this difference of origin that *yas-* 'boil' and *yam-* 'restrain', reduplicate with *ya-* in the perfect, but *yaj-* 'sacrifice', with *i-*.

a. This semivowel sometimes appears **without etymological justification:** 1. after roots in *-ā* before vowel suffixes; e. g. *dā-y-i*, 3. sing. aor. (*dā́-* 'give'), *á-dhā-y-i* (*dhā-* 'put'), *á-jñā-y-i* (*jñā-* 'know'); *upa-sthā́-y-am*, abs. 'approaching'; *ṛṣabha-dā-y-in-* (AV.) 'bestowing bulls'. This is probably due to the influence of roots in *-ai* (27 a), which have *ā-* before consonants, but *āy-* before vowels; e. g. *pai-* 'drink' : *pā́-tave, á-pāy-i, pāy-ána-*.—2. owing to the influence of closely allied words or formations, in: *yū-y-ám* 'you' (for **yūṣam*, Av. *yūžem*, cp. *yuṣ-má-*, stem of other cases)[5] because of *vay-ám* 'we'; *bhū́-y-iṣṭha-* 'most' because of *bhū́-yas-* 'more'; *bhávey-am*, 1. sing. opt. (for **bhávayam*) because of *bháves, bhávet*, etc.

b. very rarely in the later Saṃhitās after palatals: *tiraścyè* (AV. XV. 3[5]) var. lect. for *tiraścé*, dat., 'transverse'; *śnyáptra-* (TS. I. 2. 13[3]) : *śnáptra-* (VS.) 'corner of the mouth'.

c. interchanging (after the manner of Prakrit) occasionally with *v*[6] in

---

[1] On *vyūrṇv-án, vy-ūrṇv-atī́-* beside *aporṇuv-ántas*, see WACKERNAGEL I, 182 a α, note.

[2] See below 375, 382 a.

[3] For various explanations of this see WACKERNAGEL I. 182 a γ, note (p. 205).

[4] See BRUGMANN, KG. I, 302.

[5] Cp. WACKERNAGEL I, 86 c; 187, note.

[6] In *khyā-* 'tell', *y* seems at first sight to be interchanged with the *ś* of *kśā-*, which occurs in the K. and the MS. (cp. v. SCHROEDER's ed., I, p. XLIII, 7); but the two verbs, though synonymous, have probably a different origin. Cp. WACKERNAGEL I, 188 c, note.

the Saṃhitās of the YV.; e. g. *ātatāyín-* (VS.) beside *ātatāvín-* (TS.) 'having one's bow drawn'[1].

50. The semivowel *v*.— This sound was, at the time of the Prātiśākhyas[2], a voiced labio-dental spirant like the English *v* or the German *w*. Within Vedic it is very frequently derived from *u*[3]. It seems otherwise always to be based on IE. *u̯*; there is no evidence that it is ever derived from an IE. spirant *v* which was not interchangeable with *u*[4].

a. This semivowel is sometimes found interchanging with *b*[5], with *y*[6], and according to some scholars, with *m*[7].

b. In two roots in which *v* is followed by *ṛ*, an interchange of sonantal and consonantal pronunciation, together with metathesis takes place, *vṛ* becoming *ru*: hence from *dhvṛ-* 'bend' are derived both *-dhvṛ-t-* and *-dhrú-*, *-dhrú-t-*, *dhrú-ti-*; from *hvṛ-* 'go crooked', *-hvṛ-t-*, *-hvṛ-ta-*, *-hvṛ-ti-* and *hru-ṇā-ti*, 3. sing., *hrú-t-*, *-hru-ta-*. The root *rudh-* 'grow', may be a similar variation of *vṛdh-* 'grow'[8].

51. The semivowel *r*.— The liquid sound *r* must originally have been a cerebral, as is shown by its phonetic effect on a following dental *n* (47 A). By the time of the Prātiśākhyas[9], it was, however, pronounced in other phonetic positions also. Being the consonantal sound corresponding to *ṛ* before vowels (like *y v* to *i u*), it is in that position correspondingly graded with *ăr*; e. g. *á-kr-an*, *á-kr-ata*, beside *á-kṛ-thās* : *á-kar-am*, aor. of *kṛ-* 'do'; *dr-ú-* : *dắr-u-* 'wood'.

a. ***r* generally corresponds to *r*** in the cognate languages, but not infrequently to *l* also; and where these languages agree in having *l*, the latter may in these instances be assumed to be the original sound. As old Iranian here invariably has *r*, there seems to have been a tendency to rhotacism in the Indo-Iranian period[10]. Words in which Vedic *r* thus **represents IE. *l*** are the following:

1. **initially**: *rakṣ-* 'protect'; *ragh-ú-* 'swift'; *raṃhate* 'speeds'; *rabh-* 'grasp'; *ramb-* 'hang down'; *rā-* 'bark'; *ric-* 'leave', *rip-* 'smear'; *rih-* 'lick'; *ruc-* 'shine', *ruj-* 'break'; *rudh-* and *ruh-* 'grow'.

2. **medially**: *áṅgāra-* 'coal'; *ajirá-* 'agile'; *aratní-* 'elbow'; *arh-* 'be worthy'; *iyárti* 'sets in motion'; *īr-* 'set in motion'; *ū́rṇā-* 'wool'; *ūrmí-* 'wave'; *garútmant-*, a celestial bird; *gardabhá-* 'ass'; *gárbha-* 'womb'; *cakrá-* 'wheel'; *car-* 'move'; *caramá-* 'last'; *cirá-* 'long'; *chardís-* 'protection'; *dhārú-* (AV.) 'sucking'; *paraśú-* 'axe'; *píparti* 'fills'; *púr-* 'fort'; *purú-* 'much'; *prath-* 'spread out'; *-prú-t-* 'swimming', *-pruta-* part. 'floating', *pravate* 'waves'; *márdhati* 'neglects'; *-marśana-* (AV.) 'touching'; *mūrdhán-* 'head'; *vará-* 'suitor', and various forms of *vṛ-* 'choose'; *várcas-* 'light'; *śaraṇá-* 'protecting'; *śárman-* 'protection'; *śárkara-* 'gravel'; *śíśira-* (AV.) 'cold season'; *śri-* 'lean'; *śru-* 'hear'; *śróṇi-* 'buttock'; *sar-* in forms of *sṛ-* 'run', and *sarirá-* (VS.) 'flood'; *sarpís-* 'clarified butter'; *sahásra-* 'thousand'; *svàr-* 'heaven'; *sū́rya-* 'sun'; *harít-* and *hárita-* 'yellow'; *híraṇya-* 'gold'; *hrādúni-* 'hail'[11].

---

1 Cp. BENFEY, GGA. 1852, 114 f.; WEBER, IS. 2, 28; WACKERNAGEL I, 188 c.

2 See WHITNEY on APr. I. 26.

3 See above 48 a.

4 Cp. WACKERNAGEL I, 196; BRUGMANN, KG. I, 148 and 155.

5 See 45 a, 3.

6 49 c.

7 46 c.

8 For some other possible instances see WACKERNAGEL I, 184 b, note.

9 See WHITNEY on APr. I. 20, 28.

10 It seems as if the Vedic relation of *r* to *l* could only be accounted for by assuming a mixture of dialects; one dialect having preserved the IE. distinction of *r* and *l*; in another IE. *l* becoming *r* (the Vedic dialect); in a third *r* becoming *l* throughout (the later *Māgadhī*). See BRUGMANN, KG. I, 175, note.

11 See WACKERNAGEL I, 189.

b. *r* appears in place of phonetic *ḍ* (= *ẓ*, IIr. *ž*)[1] as final of stems in *-is* and *-us*, before endings which begin with *bh-*; e. g. *havír-bhis* and *vápur-bhis*. This substitution is due to the influence of Sandhi, where *is*, *us* would become *ir*, *ur*. *r* also takes the place of *ḍ* in *írā-* beside *íḍā-* 'refreshing draught'. In *urubjá-* 'wide open' *r* apparently takes the place of dental *d* (= **ud-ubjá-*), perhaps under the influence of the numerous compounds beginning with *uru-* 'wide', e. g. *uru-jrí-* 'wide-striding'[2].

c. Metathesis of *r* takes place when *ăr* would be followed by *ṣ* or *h* + consonant. Under these conditions it appears to be phonetic, being due to the Svarabhakti after *r* being twice as great before *h* and sibilants as before other consonants[3]: when a vowel followed the sibilant or *h* (e. g. *darśatá-*)[4], the Svarabhakti was pronounced; but if a consonant followed, *ră* took the place of *ăr* + double Svarabhakti. This metathesis appears in forms of *dṛś-* 'see' and *sṛj-* 'send forth': *dráṣṭum* (AV.), *draṣṭṛ́-* (AV.) 'one who sees'; *sáṃ-sraṣṭṛ-* 'one who engages in battle', 2. sing. aor. *srās* (= **srāk*)[5]; also in *práṣ-ṭi-* 'side-horse', beside *párś-u-* and *pṛṣṭí-* 'rib'; moreover in *brahmán-* 'priest', *bráhman-* 'devotion', beside *barhís-* 'sacrificial litter' (from *bṛh-* or *barh-* 'make big'); perhaps also *drahyát* 'strongly' (*dṛh-* 'be firm'). The same metathesis occurs, being, however, very rare and fluctuating, before *kṣ-*: thus *tuvi-mrakṣá-* 'injuring greatly', *mrakṣa-kṛ́tvan-* 'rubbing to pieces' (from *mṛj-* 'wipe', or *mṛś-* 'stroke'), but *tā́rkṣya-*, N.[6].

52. The semivowel *l*. — The liquid sound *l* is the semivowel corresponding to the vowel *ḷ* (which however occurs only in some half dozen perfect and aorist forms of the root *kḷp-* 'be adapted'). It is pronounced at the present day in India as an interdental; but it must have had a post-dental sound at the time of the Prātiśākhyas[7], by which it is described as being pronounced in the same position as the dentals[8].

a. It represents IE. *l*[9] and, in a few instances, IE. *r*. It is rarer in Vedic than in any cognate language except old Iranian (where it does not occur at all)[10]. It is much rarer than *r*, which is seven times as frequent[11]. The gradual increase of *l*, chiefly at the cost of *r*, but partly also owing to the appearance of new words, is unmistakable. Thus in the tenth Book of the RV. appear the verbs *mluc-* and *labh-*, and the nouns *lóman-*, *lohitá-*, but in the earlier books only *mruc-* 'sink', *rabh-* 'seize', *róman-* 'hair', *rohitá-* 'red'; similarly *daśāṅgulá-* 'length of ten fingers', *hlā́daka-* and *hlā́dikā-vant-* 'refreshing', beside *sv-aṅguri-* 'fair-fingered', *hradá-* 'pond'. Moreover, while in the oldest parts of the RV. *l* occurs[12] in a few words only, it is eight times as common in the latest parts. Again, in the AV. it is seven times as common as in the RV.[13]; thus for *rap-* 'chatter', *rikh-* 'scratch', *a-śrīrá-* 'ugly', appear in the AV. *lap-*, *likh-* (also VS.), *aślīlá-*. The various texts

---

1 Cp. above p. 35, note 3.

2 On a supposed parasitic *r* in *chardís-* 'fence', *yájatra-* 'adorable', *vibhṛtra-* 'to be borne hither and thither', see Wackernagel 1, 189, note γ.

3 According to the APr. I. 101.

4 Cp. above 21 a.

5 Cp. v. Negelein, Zur Sprachgeschichte des Veda 83, note 7.

6 On the interchange of *ră* and *ar* in *raj-* 'colour', *rajatá-* 'silvery', *rāj-* 'shine', and *árjuna-* 'bright'; *bhrāj-* 'shine', and *bhárgas-* 'brilliance'; *bhrā́tṛ-* 'brother', and *bhártṛ-* 'husband'; see Wackernagel 1, 190 e, note (end). In *vrajá-* 'fold', *vratá-* 'ordinance', *sráj-* 'wreath', *ra-* does not stand for *ar*, Wackernagel 1, 190 d, note.

7 Cp. Pischel, BB. 3, 264. An indication that it was not a cerebral is the fact that *lṣ* never occurs (while *rṣ* is common).

8 See 44.

9 Which, however, is largely represented by *r* also: cp. 51 a.

10 Loc. cit.

11 See Whitney, JAOS. 11, p. xl ff.

12 See Arnold, 'L in the Rigveda', in Festgruss an Rudolf von Roth, 1893, p. 145—148; Historical Vedic Grammar, JAOS. 18, 2, p. 258f.; Vedic Metre p. 37, 3.

13 Cp. Wackernagel 1, 191 c.

of the YV. also show an increased number of words with *l* as compared with the RV.; thus *babhluśá-* (VS.) 'brownish' beside *babhrú-* 'brown'; *kúlāla-* (VS.) 'potter' beside *carú-* 'pot'. The MS. has a special predilection for *l*[1]; thus *pulītát* 'pericardium' beside *purītát* (AV. VS.). The SV. has *pāṃsulá-* 'dusty', for *pāṃsurá-* in the corresponding passage of the RV.

In a certain number of words **r interchanges with l** in the same period: thus *purú-* and *pulú-* 'much'; *miśrá-* and *-miśla-* 'mixed'; *jargur-* and *jalgul-*, intv. of *gṝ-* 'swallow'; in the AV.: *-girá-* and *-gilá-* 'swallowing', *kṣudrá-* and *kṣullaká-* (= **kṣudla-ka*) 'small', *tiryà-* and *tilá-* 'sesamum'.

The above considerations render it probable that the Vedic dialect was descended from an Indo-Iranian one in which rhotacism had removed every *l*. But since the oldest parts of the RV. contain some words with IE. *l*, and in its later parts as well as in the other Saṃhitās *l* predominantly interchanges with *r* representing IE. *l*, there must have been another Vedic dialect in which IE. *r* and *l* were kept distinct; from the latter *l* must have found its way into the literary language to an increasing extent[2].

b. **In the oldest** parts of the **RV.** there are **no verbal forms** which **preserve IE. l**, and only a few nouns, viz. (*u*)*loká-* 'free space', *ślóka-* 'call', and *-miśla-* 'mixed'. A few other words containing *l* have no IE. cognates and may therefore be of foreign origin: *níla-* 'dark-coloured', *jálāṣa-* 'healing', *tílvila-* 'fertile', and the denominative *tilvilāyáte*.

In the **latest** parts of the **RV. l represents IE. l** in: 1. **verbal forms** and primary derivatives: *lebhire*, *lebhāná-*, *labdhá-*, from *labh-* 'grasp', *layantām*, from *lī-* 'cling'; *alipsata*, aor. of *lip-* 'anoint'; *lobháyantī-* part. from *lubh-* 'desire'; *calā-calá-*, *-cācalí-* 'swaying' (also *puṃś-calí-* 'whore', AV. VS.), from *cal-* 'move'; *plávate*, *plavá-* 'boat', from *plu-* 'swim'.

2. the following **nouns**: *logá-* 'clod'; *úlūka-* 'owl'; *ulká-* 'meteor'; *úlba-* 'membrane'; *kaláśa-* 'jar'; *kalá-* 'small portion'; *kāla-* 'time'; *kalyāṇa-* 'fair'; *kúla-* 'family'; *gáldā-* 'trickling' (VS. *gal-* 'drop'); *palitá-* 'grey'; *pulu-* (in compounds) 'much'; *phalgvà-* 'weakly'; *bála-* 'strength'[3]; *balí-* 'tax'; *mála-* 'dirty garment'; *salilá-* 'surging'; *hlādaka-* and *hlādikāvant-* 'refreshing'; also words with the suffix *-la*[4], especially with diminutive sense; e.g. *vṛṣa-lá-* 'little man', *śiśū-la-* 'little child'[5].

a. In the later Saṃhitās *l* represents IE. *l* in the following words: *-kulva-* (VS.) 'bald'; *klóman-* (AV. VS.) 'lung'; *gláhana-* (AV.) 'dicing'; *gláu-* (AV. VS.) 'excrescence'; *tulá-* (VS.) 'balance'; *palāva-* (AV.) 'chaff'; *pula-stí-* (VS.) 'smooth-haired'; *plīhán-* (AV. VS.) 'spleen'; *phalgú-* (VS.) 'reddish'; *laghú-* (AV.) 'light'; *lap-* (AV.) 'prate' (= *rap-* RV.).

c. On the other hand, **l** to some extent **represents IE. r** also[6].

1. In the RV. this value of *l* is rare and occurs only in the neighbourhood of labial sounds (*u*, *o*, *p*, *m*, *v*): *ulūkhala-* 'mortar' beside *urú-* 'broad'; *jalgul-*, intv. of *gṝ-* 'swallow'; *plúṣi-*, a kind of insect, beside *pruṣ-* 'squirt'; *klóśa-* 'call' beside *króśant-* 'calling', *krośaná-* 'crying'; *-lohitá-* 'red', *lodhá-*, a kind of red animal, beside *rohít-*, *rohitá-* 'red'; *lopāśá-* 'jackal', *lup-* (AV.) 'break', beside *rup-* 'break'; *úpala-* 'upper millstone' beside *upári* 'above'; *jálpi-* 'muttering'; *píppala-* 'berry'; *mlā-* 'fade' beside *mṛ-* 'die'; *valá-* 'cave' beside *várate* 'encloses'.

2. In the later Saṃhitās the use of this *l* = IE. *r* extends further than in the RV.; thus *álam* (AV.) 'enough' : *áram*; *liś-* (VS.) 'tear' : *riś-*; *-luñcá-* (VS.)

1 L. v. SCHROEDER, ZDMG. 33, 196.

2 See WACKERNAGEL 1, 192 b, and cp. above p. 42, note 10.

3 Cp. above p. 36, note 10.

4 See ARNOLD, Festgruss an Roth 147.

5 See WACKERNAGEL 1, p. 218.

6 Cp. above 51 a.

'tearing out'; *babhluśá-* (VS.) 'brownish' : *babhrú-* 'brown'; *sthūlá-* (AV. VS.) 'gross' : *sthūrá-*[1].

3. In a few instances *l* represents IE. *r* by dissimilation; thus *álarṣi álarti*, intv. of *ṛ-* 'go' (= *arar-*); *prá tilāmi* (VS.) = *prá tirāmi* 'I promote'[2].

d. In the later Saṃhitās *l* occasionally **appears in place of** phonetic *ḍ*[3] between vowels; and that this change could easily arise, is shown by the fact that *ḷ* regularly appears instead of *ḍ* between vowels[4]. This substitution is regularly found in the Kaṇva recension of the VS.; e. g. *íle* = *íḍe* (RV. *íḷe*); *áṣālhā* = *áṣāḍhā* (RV. *áṣāḷhā*). Other instances are *iláyati* (AV.) 'stands still', for **iḍáyati* (RV. *iḷayati*)[5] from *íḍ-* 'refreshment'; *ilā-* (MS.) 'refreshment', byform of *íḍā-* (RV. *íḷā-*); *mīl-* (AV.) 'close the eyes'[6], connected with *miṣ-* 'wink'.

In the later Saṃhitās *l* is also found for *ḍ* between vowels when the final of a word (like *ḷ* in RV.): thus *turāṣāl áyuktāsaḥ* (VS.) for *turāṣāṭ* 'overpowering quickly'; *phál íti* (AV.) for *pháṭ* (AV.); probably also in *śál íti* (AV.) and *bál íti* (AV. TS.), cp. RV. *báḷ itthá*.

e. In at least one word *l* stands **for dental** *d*: *kṣulla-ká-* (AV.) 'small', for **kṣudlá-*, byform of *kṣudrá-* (VS.) 'small'.

f. Sometimes *l* has an independent Indian origin in **onomatopoetic** words; thus *alalā-bhávant-* 'sounding cheerfully'.

g. On the other hand there are many words in which a **foreign origin** may be suspected; such are, besides those already mentioned in 45 b, the following: *kaulitará-*, N.; *álina-* and *bhalānás-*, names of tribes; *líbuja-* 'creeper'; *lavaṇá-* (AV.) 'salt'.

53. **The sibilants.**—The three sibilants, the palatal *ś*, the cerebral *ṣ*, and the dental *s*, are all voiceless. Even apart from the regular phonetic change of *ś* or *s* to *ṣ*, and of *s* to *ś*, both the palatal and the dental are further liable, in many words and forms, to be substituted for each of the other two.

a. **Assimilation** of *s* is liable to occur

1. **initially,** when *ś* or *ṣ* appear at the end of the same or the beginning of the next syllable. This is the case in *śváśura-* 'father-in-law'; *śvaśrū́-* 'mother-in-law'; *śmáśru-* and *-śmaśāru-* 'beard'; *śáśvant-* 'ever-recurring'; in *ṣáṣ-* 'six' (Lat. *sex*), and its various derivatives, *ṣaṣ-ṭí-* 'sixty', *ṣoḍhā́* (= **ṣaẓ-dhā*) 'sixfold', and others[7].

2. initially *s* **in the RV.** almost invariably **becomes** *ṣ* in *sah-* 'overcoming', when the final *h* (= IIr. *ž*), with or without a following dental, becomes cerebral: nom. sing. *ṣā́ṭ* 'victorious', and the compounds *janā-ṣā́ṭ*, *turā-ṣā́ṭ*, *purā-ṣā́ṭ*, *pṛtanā-ṣā́ṭ*, *vīrā-ṣā́ṭ*, *vṛthā-ṣā́ṭ*, *ṛtā-ṣā́ṭ* (VS.), *viśvā-ṣā́ṭ* (TS. AV.); also *á-ṣāḍha-* 'invincible'. The only exceptions are *sā́ḍhā*, nom. sing. of *sā́ḍhṛ-* 'conqueror', and the perf. part. pass. *sāḍhá-* (AV.)[8]. The *ṣ* of the nom. has been transferred to forms with *-săh-*, when compounded with *pṛtanā-*, though

---

[1] In B. passages of the TS. and MS. are found intv. forms of *lī* 'sway': *álelāyat*, pf. *lelā́ya*, also the adv. *leláyā* 'quiveringly'. In similar passages the prepositions *prá* and *párā* are affected: *pleṅkhá-* (TS.) = *preṅkhá-* 'swing'; *plā́kṣārayan* (MS. III. 10²) 'they caused to flow' (√*kṣar-*), *palā-y-ata* (TS.) 'fled' (*parā-i-*). Some uncertain or wrong explanations of *alātṛṇá-* 'miserly', *uloká-* 'wide space', *gal-* 'drop', with *l* = IE. *r*, are discussed by WACKERNAGEL I, p. 221, top.

[2] See WACKERNAGEL I, 193 b, note.

[3] See above 51 b.

[4] See above p. 5, note 5.

[5] According to BÖHTLINGK, *iḷáyati* is wrong for *iláyati*. Cp. above p. 35, note 1.

[6] A form with the original *ḍ* is found in *mīḍam* (K.) 'in a low tone'.

[7] Cp. WACKERNAGEL I, 197 a, note.

[8] A B. passage of the MS. has *sāḍhyái* (I. 83).

there is no phonetic justification for the cerebral (as the *s* is preceded by *ā*): thus *pṛtanā-ṣāham*, gen. *pṛtanā-ṣáhas*, *pṛtanā-ṣáhya-* 'victory in battle', but *pṛtanā-sáham* (SV.). When compounded with *dyumnā-*, *dhanvā-*, *rathā-*, *vibhvā-*, *sadā-*, the phonetic form *-sāh-* remains[1].

3. **Medial s** has been assimilated to initial *ś* in *śaśá-* 'hare' (IE. *k̑asó-*[2]).

b. **Without assimilation**[3], *s* or *ṣ* has been **changed to ś**, mostly under the influence of allied words, in the following: *kéśa-* 'hair' : *késara-* (AV. VS.); *śákṛt*[4] 'excrement'; *śubh-* 'adorn' (probably owing to *śudh-* 'purify'); *śúṣka-* 'dry' (IIr. *suṣka-*), *śúṣyati* 'dries'; *śru-* 'flow', *śrávas-* 'stream' : *sru-*, *srávas-*; *śvas-*, *śuṣ-* 'breathe'; *śvātra-*, *śvātrya-* 'dainty' : *svad-* 'taste'[5]; *pyāśiṣīmahi* (AV.) : *pyāsiṣīmahi* (VS.), aor. (534) of *pyā-* 'swell'; *ośiṣṭha-hán-* (VS. TS.) 'striking very swiftly' beside *osiṣṭha-dāvan-* (TS.) 'giving very rapidly' (from *oṣám* 'quickly', lit. 'burningly'), owing to *āśiṣṭha-* 'very swift'; *kóśa-* 'receptacle' (in the later language often also *koṣa-*); *kūśmá-* (VS.) beside *kūṣmá-* (MS.), a kind of demon; *ruśatī-* (AV.) 'angry', beside *ruṣ-* 'be angry', probably owing to *rúśant-* 'shining'.

a. On the other hand, *s* occasionally appears in the later Saṃhitās, chiefly AV., for *ś*: thus *asyate* (AV. v. 19[2]) : *aś-* 'eat'; *vāsī-* (AV.) 'pointed knife': *vāśī-*; *sáru-* (AV.) 'arrow': *śáru-*; *arus-srāṇa-* (AV.), a kind of wound preparation: *śrā-* 'boil'; *saspiñjara-* (TS.) 'ruddy like young grass', owing to *sasá-* 'grass', for *śaṣ-piñjara-* (VS. MS.) = *śaṣ[pa]-piñjara-*[6].

54. **The palatal ś.**—This sibilant is a palatal both in origin (= IIr. *ś*), as indicated by cognate languages, and in employment, as its combination with other consonants shows. Thus it represents an old palatal in *śatám* 'a hundred', *áśva-* 'horse', *śván-* 'dog', *śru-* 'hear'[7]. In external Sandhi it regularly appears before voiceless palatal mutes, e. g. *indraś ca*. At the present day the pronunciation of *ś* in India varies between a *sh* sound (not always distinguished from *ṣ*) and a *s* sound followed by *y*. It is to some extent confused with the other two sibilants even in the Saṃhitās, but it is to be noted that here it interchanges much oftener with *s* than with *ṣ*[8].

The aspirate of *ś* is *ch*[9]; its media is represented by *j* and when aspirated by *h*. These four form the old palatals (IIr. *ś*, *śh*, *ź*, *źh*), representing IE. *k̑ k̑h g̑ g̑h*. The exact phonetic character of the latter is doubtful, but it is probable that they were dialectically pronounced in two ways, either as mutes (guttural[10] or palatal) or as spirants, the *centum* languages later following the former, the *satem* languages the latter[11].

a. In external Sandhi **ś** regularly appears **for s before the palatals** *c*, *ch*, *ś*[12]. It also stands for *s* internally in *paścā́t* and *paścā́tāt* 'behind'[13], and in *vṛścáti* 'hews' beside *-vraská-* 'lopping'.

b. **Before s** the palatal sibilant when medial is regularly **replaced by k**, and sometimes also when final; e. g. *dṛ́k-ṣase* and *-dṛk*, from *dṛś-* 'see'. Otherwise *ś* very rarely interchanges with *k* or *c*; thus *rúśant-* 'brilliant', beside *ruc-* 'shine'; perhaps *kárṇa-* 'ear' : *śru-* 'hear'[14]. There are also a few words

[1] WACKERNAGEL I, 197 b.
[2] See, however, op. cit. I, 197 c, note.
[3] For *ś* and *ṣ* are strictly distinguished in the RV.; cp. op. cit. I, 197 d *α*, note (end).
[4] Cp., however, op. cit. I, 197 d *α*.
[5] Op. cit. p. 226, top.
[6] See op. cit., p. 226 *β*; and below 64, I a.
[7] On the relation of *ś* to the corresponding sounds in cognate languages, see WACKERNAGEL I, 200 a; BRUGMANN, KG. I, 233.
[8] See above 53, 3.
[9] Cp. above 40.
[10] The fact that *ś* before *s* regularly becomes *k* and sometimes also when final, seems to favour the assumption of the guttural pronunciation.
[11] Cp. WACKERNAGEL I, 200 b.
[12] See below, Sandhi, 78.
[13] Cp. Av. *paskāt̰* and *pasca*.
[14] For some words in which such an assumption is doubtful or wrong, see WACKERNAGEL I, 201 a.

with *ś* to which *k* corresponds in the *satem* languages; such are *kruś-* 'cry'; *áśman-* 'stone'[1].

55. The dental *s*.—This sound as a rule represents IE. dental *s*; e. g. *sa* 'he', Gothic *sa*; *áśva-s* 'horse', Lat. *equo-s*; *ásti*, Gk. ἔστι. In the combinations *ts* and *ps*, when they stand for etymological *dhs* and *bhs*, the *s* represents IE. *zh*; as in *gṛ́tsa-* 'adroit' (from *gṛdh-* 'be eager') and *dípsa-*, 'wish to injure' (from *dabh-* 'injure'), where the final aspirate of the root would have been thrown forward on the suffix, as in *bud-dhá-* from √*budh-*, and *-rab-dha-*, from √*rabh-*[2].

The dental *s* is in Sandhi frequently changed to the palatal *ś*[3], and still more frequently to the cerebral *ṣ*[4].

56. The cerebral *ṣ*. — The cerebral sibilant is altogether of a secondary nature, since it always represents either an original palatal or an original dental sibilant.

The cerebral *ṣ* stands for a palatal **before cerebral tenues** (themselves produced by this *ṣ* from dental tenues) in the following two ways:

a. for the palatal *ś* (= IIr. *ś*) and *j* (= IIr. *ź*); e. g. *naṣ-ṭá-*, from *naś-* 'be lost'; *mṛṣ-ṭa*, 3. sing. mid., from *mṛj-* 'wipe'; *pṛṣ-ṭá-* 'asked', *práṣ-ṭum* 'to ask', from *praś-* 'ask' in *praś-ná-* 'question' (present stem *pṛcchá-*[5] with inchoative suffix *-chá*). In some instances it is shown by the evidence of cognate words to represent *ś*; thus *aṣṭáu* 'eight' beside *aśītí-* 'eighty'; *pṛṣṭí-* 'rib', *práṣṭi-* 'side-horse', beside *párśu-* 'rib'; *áṣṭrā-* 'goad', beside *aśáni-* 'thunderbolt'; possibly also *apāṣṭhá-*[6] 'barb', beside *áśman-* 'bolt'.

b. for the combination *kṣ*, which in origin is *ś* + *s*[7]; e. g. *cáṣ-ṭe*, *a-caṣṭa*, from *cakṣ-*[8] 'see'; *a-taṣ-ṭa*, *taṣ-ṭá-*, *táṣ-ṭṛ-*[9], beside *takṣ-* 'hew'; *nír-aṣ-ṭa-* 'emasculated' beside *nír-akṣ-ṇu-hi* (AV.) 'emasculate'; also aorist forms like *á-yaṣ-ṭa*, 3. sing. mid. from *yaj-* 'sacrifice', beside 3. sing. subj. *yákṣ-at*; *á-sṛṣ-ṭa*, 3. sing. mid., beside *á-sṛkṣ-ata*, 3. pl. mid. from *sṛj-* 'emit'. As in all these instances *kṣ* = *ś* + *s* or *j* (= *ź*) + *s*[10], loss of *s* before *t* must here be assumed, the remaining *ś* or *j* combining with the following *t* as usual to *ṣṭ*[11]. A similar origin of *ṣ* is indicated by the evidence of cognate languages in *ṣaṣ-ṭhá-* (AV.) 'sixth', where the final *s* has been dropped (as in Gk. ἕκ-τος), while retained in Lat. *sex-tus*; also in *ṣaṣ-ṭí-* 'sixty', *ṣoḍhā́* 'sixfold', *ṣoḍaśá-* (AV.) 'sixteenth'. It has possibly the same origin in *aṣṭhīvánt-* 'knee'[12].

57. The cerebral *ṣ* stands **for dental *s* after vowels** other than *a* or *ā*, **and** after the consonants *k*, *r*, *s*.

1. Medially this change regularly[13] takes place, both when the *s* is **radical** — e. g. *tí-ṣṭhati*, from *sthā-* 'stand'; *su-ṣup-ur*, 3. pl. perf. from *svap-*

---

[1] This seems to point to fluctuation in the IE. pronunciation; cp. WACKERNAGEL I, 201 b.

[2] See WACKERNAGEL I, 210.

[3] Cp. above 54 a, and below 78, 2.

[4] See below 56.

[5] Cp. 40.

[6] Cp. WACKERNAGEL I, 202 b; and below p. 48, note γ.

[7] Cp. op. cit. I, 116 b.

[8] Cp. Av. *caśman-*.

[9] On the origin of *tváṣṭṛ-* = **tvarṣṭṛ-*, see WACKERNAGEL I, 202 c, note.

[10] Though *kṣ* is regularly based on a palatal or a guttural + *s* in the Vedic language, there are some words of IE. origin in which the *ṣ* appears to represent not *s* but a dental spirant tenuis (*þ*) or media (*dh*). In a few words, *kṣip-*, *kṣu-*, *kṣubh-*, *kṣurá-*, the sibilant comes first in the cognate languages: see WACKERNAGEL I, 209.

[11] Similarly, when *kṣ* = guttural + *s* is followed by *t*, the *s* disappears and the guttural combines with the *t*; thus from *ghas-* 'eat', *-gdha-* (= *ghz-ta-*); from *jakṣ-* 'eat', *jagdhá-* (= *jaghz-ta-*), *jagdhvā́ya* (= *jaghz-tvā́ya*); from *bhaj-* 'share', aor. *á-bhak-ta* (= *abhaj-s-ta*), beside *á-bhak-ṣ-i*.

[12] Cp. BARTHOLOMAE, Studien zur indogermanischen Sprachgeschichte 2, 103.

[13] The change does not take place in some forms of the perfect of *sic-* 'pour': *sisice* (III. 32[15]), *sisicur* (II. 24[4]), beside *siṣicatur*.

'sleep'; *uṣ-āṇá-*, part., from *vas-* 'wear'; *ṛṣa-bhá-* 'bull'; *ukṣán-* 'ox'; *varṣá-* 'rain' — and when the *s* is **suffixal**; as in the superlative suffix *-iṣṭha*; in the loc. pl. suffix *-su*, e. g. *agní-ṣu*, *aktú-ṣu*, *nṛ́-ṣu*, *vik-ṣú*, *gīr-ṣú*, *haviṣ-ṣu*; in the *s*-suffix of the aorist, e. g. *yák-ṣ-at*, from *yaj-* 'sacrifice'.

The change is phonetic **even when Anusvāra intervenes** between *ĭ ŭ ṝ* and *s*; e. g. *piṃṣánti* from *piṣ-* 'crush'; *havī́ṃṣi* 'offerings' from *havís-*; *cákṣūṃṣi* 'eyes' from *cákṣus-*. The *s*, however, remains in forms of *hiṃs-* 'injure', *niṃs-* 'kiss', and *puṃs-* 'man', being probably transferred from the strong forms *hinásti*, *púmāṃsam*, etc.

a. The *s*, however, remains when immediately followed by *r* or *ṛ*, owing to a distaste for a succession of cerebrals [1]; e. g. *tisrás*, *tisṛ́bhis*, *tisṝṇā́m*, f. of *tri-* 'three'; *usrás* gen., *usri* and *usrā́m*, loc. (beside *uṣar*, voc.), *usrá-* 'matutinal'; *usrá-* 'bull'; *sarīsṛpá-* 'creeping'. Owing to the influence of forms with *sr*, the *s* further remains in the syllable *sar*, instead of *ṣar*, as in *sisarṣi*, *sisarti* (beside *sisrate*, *sisrat-*, *sarsré* etc.). In *késara-* (AV. VS.) 'hair', the retention may be due to the *r* having originally followed the *s* immediately [2]. The *s* also remains unchanged in the combinations *stir*, *stūr*, *spar*, *spṛ*, *sphūr*; e. g. *tistiré*, from *stṝ-* 'strew'; *pispṛśas*, from *spṛś-* 'touch' [3]. It remains in the second of three successive syllables in which *s-ṣ-ṣ* would be expected; thus *yāsisīṣṭhās*, beside *ayāsiṣam*, from *yā-* 'go'; *sisakṣi*, beside *siṣakti*, from *sac-* 'follow'.

β. Words in which *s* otherwise follows *r* or any vowel but *ă*, must be of foreign origin; such as *bisa-* 'root fibre'; *busá-* 'vapour'; *bṛ́saya-*, a demon; *ṛbīsa-* 'cleft'; *kīstá-* 'praiser'; *bársvá-* (VS.) 'socket'; *kusū́la-* (AV.), a kind of demon; *músala-* (AV.) 'pestle' (for *músra-*?); *sī́sa-* (AV. VS.) 'lead' [4].

γ. The cerebral *ṣ* is sometimes found even after *ă*, representing an early Prakritic change in which *aṣ* is based on *ṛṣ* and *āṣ* on *arṣ* [5]. Instances of this are *kaṣati* (AV.) 'scratches'; *paṣṭhavā́h-* (VS. TS.) 'young bull' (lit. 'carrying on the back') and *paṣṭhauhī́-* [6] 'young cow', beside *pṛṣṭhá-* 'back'; *pāṣyà-* [7] 'stone'; *bhaṣá-* [8] (VS.) 'barking' [9]. There are besides several unexplained instances, doubtless due to foreign influence or origin; such are *áṣatara-* 'more accessible'; *kaváṣa-*, N.; *cā́ṣa-* 'blue jay'; *caṣā́la-* 'knob'; *jáláṣa-* 'remedy'; *baṣkáya-* 'yearling'; *baṣkiha-* (VS.) 'decrepit'; *mā́ṣa-* 'bean' (AV. VS.); *śáṣpa-* (VS.) 'young grass' [10].

2. Initially [11] the change regularly takes place, in the RV.:

a. in verbal compounds after prepositions ending in *i* or *u*, and in nominal derivatives from such compound verbs; also after the preposition *nis* 'out'; e. g. *ní ṣīda* (x. 98^{4}); *ánu ṣṭuvanti* (VIII. 3^{8}); *niḥ-ṣáhamāṇaḥ* (I. 127^{3}).

a. But (as when it is medial) the *s* remains unchanged when followed by *ṛ* (even when *t* or *p* intervenes) or *r* (even though *a* intervene, with an additional *m* or *v* in the roots *smar-* and *svar-*); e. g. *vi sṛja* 'let flow', *vi-sṛṣṭi-* 'creation'; *vi stṛṇītā́m* 'let him extend'; *ni-spṛ́śe* 'to caress' (but *á-ni-ṣṭṛta-* 'unchecked'); *pári-sruta-* 'flowed round'; *vi-sargá-* 'end', *vi-sárjana-* 'extension' (owing to the influence of the forms with *sṛ* from *sṛj-*); *vi-sarmán-* 'dissolving', *vi-sārá-* 'extent', and even *ví sasre* (owing to the influence of forms with *sṛ* from *sṛ-* 'flow'); *práti smarethām* 'may ye two remember' ($\sqrt{}$*smṛ-*); *abhi-svárantí* 'praise', *abhi-svár-* 'invocation', *abhi-svaré*, loc., 'behind', *abhi-svartṛ́-* 'invoker'. But *st sp sph* are changed according to the general rule, when *ăr ir ur* follow; e. g. *práti ṣphura* 'repel'. In roots which contain no *r*, the initial *s* rarely remains; thus in forms of *as-* 'be': *abhí santi*, *pári santu*, *pári santi* (beside *pári ṣanti*), *abhí syāma* (beside *abhi-ṣyāma*); and owing to dislike of repeated *ṣ*: *anu-séṣidhat* (*sidh-* 'drive off'); *ánu-spaṣṭa-* 'noticed' (*spaś-* 'see'); *pári sani-ṣvaṇat* (*svan-* 'sound').

---

[1] Cp. above 42 a, *α* and p. 38, note 2.

[2] See WACKERNAGEL 1, 50.

[3] The combination *ṣr* is found only where *sr* would be quite isolated amid cognate forms with *ṣ*; thus *ajuṣ-ran*, from *juṣ-* 'be satisfied', since all the other very numerous forms of this verb have *ṣ*.

[4] See WACKERNAGEL 1, 203 e, note.

[5] Sometimes representing also IE. *ḷs* and *ls*; cp. WACKERNAGEL 1, 208 b *α*.

[6] Cp. BARTHOLOMAE, KZ. 29, 579; WINDISCH, KZ. 27, 169.

[7] Cp. FORTUNATOV, BB. 6, 217; J. SCHMIDT, KZ. 32, 387.

[8] FORTUNATOV, l. c.

[9] On doubtful instances like *kā́ṣṭhā-* 'goal', *aṣṭhīvántau* 'knees', *apāṣṭhá-* 'barb', cp. WACKERNAGEL 1, 208 b *α*, note; b *β*, note.

[10] Cp. WACKERNAGEL 1, 208 b *β*.

[11] Finally, *ṣ* stands for *s* in the first

β. In the later Saṃhitās initial *s* is similarly changed to *ṣ*; but its retention is in some instances somewhat less restricted; thus *abhí sphūrjati* (AV.) 'sounds towards'; *ádhi skanda* (AV.) and *abhi-skándam*[1], beside *pari-ṣkandá-* (AV., VS.), from *skand-* 'leap'; *prati-spāśana-* (AV.) 'lying in wait', *prati-spaśá-* (TS.) 'spying'; *ánu sthana* (TS. v. 6. 1[3]), from *as-* 'be'; owing to the following *ṣ* also in *abhi siṣyade* (AV.) from *syand-* 'run'.

γ. The divergence between the later Saṃhitās and the RV. is much greater when the augment intervenes between a preposition ending in *i* and the initial *s* of a root. In the RV. the *s* regularly remains unchanged (as *ny-ásīdat, vy-ásthāt,* etc.) except in *pary áṣasvajat* 'embraced' (under the influence of *pári ṣasvaje*). In the other Saṃhitās, however, the *s* here regularly becomes *ṣ*; thus *abhy-áṣiñcan* (TS.), *abhy-áṣicyanta* (AV.) from *sic-* 'sprinkle'; *vy-àṣahanta* (AV.)[2], from *sah-* 'overcome'; *ádhy-aṣṭhām* (AV.), *ádhy-aṣṭhāt* (AV.), *abhy-àṣṭhām* (AV.) from *sthā-* 'stand'. In the root *ṣṭhīv-* 'spit', which first occurs in the AV., the initial *s* has been displaced by *ṣ* throughout. The form *praty áṣṭhīvan* indicates the transition which led to the change.

Similarly when a reduplicative syllable containing *ă* intervenes between a preposition ending in *i* and an initial radical *s*, the latter always remains unchanged in the RV.; thus *pári ṣasvaje*; *ni-ṣasáttha* (VIII. 48[9]); *ati-tasthúu* (x. 60[3]); but the AV. has *vi-taṣṭhiré*, *vi taṣṭhe* (owing to *vi tiṣṭhate, vi-ṣṭhita-*), but also *ádhi tasthúr*.

b. Initially in the second member of other than verbal compounds *ṣ* is more common than *s* when preceded by vowels other than *ă*. But *s* even in the RV. the is not infrequently retained; not only when *ṛ* or *r* follows as in *hṛdi-spṛ́ś-* 'touching the heart', *su-sártu-*, N., *ṛṣi-svará-* 'sung by seers', but also when there is no such cause to prevent the change; thus *gó-sakhi-* beside *gó-ṣakhi-* 'possessing cattle'; *go-sáni-* (AV. VS.) beside *go-ṣáṇi-* 'winning cattle'; *rayi-sthā́na-* beside *rayi-ṣṭhā́na-* (AV.) 'possessing wealth'; *tri-saptá-* beside *tri-ṣaptá-* (AV.) 'twenty-one'; *sú-samiddha-* beside *sú-ṣamiddha-* (SV.) 'well-kindled'; *āpāke-stha-* (AV.) 'standing in the oven' beside *-ṣṭha-* in other compounds after *-e-*; *pṛthivī-sád-* (VS.) beside *pṛthivī-ṣád-* (AV.) 'seated on the earth'; *sú-samṛddha-* (AV.) 'quite perfect'. After *r* the *s* becomes *ṣ* in *svar-ṣā́-* 'light-winning', *svàr-ṣāti-* 'obtainment of light'; after *k*, probably only in *ṛ́k-ṣama-* (TS.) 'resembling a *ṛc*', beside *ṛ́k-sama-* (VS.).

α. In Avyayībhāvas *ṣ* seems to appear in the RV. only; thus *anu-ṣvadhám* 'according to wish'; *anu-ṣatyám* 'according to truth'; *anu-ṣvā́pam* 'sleepily'.

β. In some compounds *ṣ* appears where it is not phonetically justifiable, owing to the influence of cognate words; thus *upa-ṣṭút*, adv., 'at one's call' (because of the frequency of *-ṣṭu-* after *i* and *u*), beside *úpa-stut-* 'invocation'; *sa-ṣṭúbh-* (TS.), a metre, owing to *anu-ṣṭubh-*, *tri-ṣṭúbh-*; *savya-ṣṭhā́-* (AV.), owing to compounds in *-e-ṣṭha-*.

γ. In Āmreḍita compounds, however, the *s* regularly remains unchanged because of the desire to leave the repeated word unaltered; thus *suté-sute* and *somé-some* 'at every Soma draught'; also in *stuhí stuhí* 'praise on'[3].

3. **Initially in external Sandhi** *s* frequently becomes *ṣ* after a final *i* and *u* in the RV. This change chiefly takes place in monosyllabic pronouns and particles, such as *sá(s)*, *sā́*, *syá(s)*, *sīm*, *sma*, *svid*, and particularly *sú*. It also appears in verbal forms like *stha sthas sthana, santu, syām, syāma* (from *as-* 'be'); *sīdati, satsat, satsi* (from *sad-* 'sit'); *siñca, siñcata* (from *sic-* 'pour'); *stavāma, stave, stuhi* (from *stu-* 'praise'); in participles like *sán, satás* (from *as-* 'be'); *sī́dan* (from *sad* 'sit'); *suvānás* (*su-* 'press'); *sitám* (*si-* 'bind'); *stutás* (*stu-* 'praise'); *skannám* (*skand-* 'leap'). In other words the change

member of the compound and often in external Sandhi; see below 78.

1 Cp. APr. II. 104.

2 Cp. WHITNEY's Translation of the AV. I, p. LXIV (mid.).

3 This is not treated as an Āmreḍita compound in the Padapāṭha (VIII. 13[0]): *stuhi | stuhi | it |*; but *pibā-piba* (II. 11[11]) is analyzed as *piba-piba | it |*.

rarely takes place; e. g. *ánu rājati ṣṭúp* (IX. 96^{18}); *trī ṣadhásthā* (III. 56^{5}); *níḥ ṣadhásthāt*[1] (V. 31^{9}); *nū́ ṣṭhirám* (I. 64^{15}); *ádhi ṣṇúnā* (IX. 97^{16}).

The *ṣ* usually follows short words such as *u*, *tū́*, *nū́*, *sū́*, *hí*, and occurs where there is a close syntactical connection of two words; e. g. *rájaḥsu ṣīdan* (VII. 34^{16}); *vámsu ṣīdati* (IX. 57^{3}); *diví ṣán* (VI. 2^{6}); *diví ṣantu* (V. 2^{10}); *ṛcchánti ṣma* (X. 102^{6}). In no word, however, even when these conditions are fulfilled, is the change of initial *s* to *ṣ* invariably made.

a. In the later Saṃhitās, apart from passages adopted from the RV. this form of external Sandhi is very rare except in the combination *ū ṣú*. Examples are *ád u ṣṭenám* (AV. IV. 3^{4}); *máhi ṣád dyumán námaḥ* (TS. III. 2. 8^{2})[2].

58. The breathing *h*.—The sound *h* is, at the present day, pronounced as a breathing in India, and this was its character at the period when Greek and Indian words were interchanged, as is shown e. g. by ὥρα being reproduced by *hōrā*. It is already recognised as a breathing by the TPr. (II. 9), which identifies it with the second element of voiced aspirates (*g-h*, *d-h*, *b-h*). This is borne out by the spelling ळ्ह *ḷ-h* (= *ḍh*) beside ळ *ḷ* (= *ḍ*). The TPr. further (II. 47) assigns to it, on the authority of some, the same place of articulation as the following vowel, this being still characteristic of the pronunciation of *h* at the present day in India[3]. The breathing is, moreover, stated by the Prātiśākhyas[4] to have been voiced. This pronunciation is proved by the evidence of the Saṃhitās themselves; for *h* is here often derived from a voiced aspirate, e. g. *hitá-* from *dhā-* 'put'; it is occasionally replaced by a voiced aspirate, e. g. *jaghána* from *han-* 'strike'; and in Sandhi initial *h* after a final mute regularly becomes a voiced aspirate, e. g. *tád dhí* for *tád hí*. It is in fact clear that whatever its origin (even when = IIr. *źh*)[5], *h* was always pronounced as a voiced breathing in the Saṃhitās.

As *h* cannot be final owing to its phonetic character[6], it is represented in that position by sounds connected with its origin[7]. It appears in combination with voiced sounds only; being preceded only by vowels, Anusvāra, or the semivowels *r* and *l*[8] (in Sandhi also by the nasals *ṅ* and *n*), and followed only by vowels, the nasals *ṇ*, *n*, *m*, or the semivowels *y*, *r*, *l*, *v*.

The breathing *h* as a rule represents a voiced aspirate, regularly a palatal aspirate, occasionally the dental *dh* and the labial *bh*. It usually represents a new palatal (= IIr. *jh*, Av. *j*[9]), appearing beside *gh*, e. g. *druhyú-* : *drógha-*, as *j* beside *g*, e. g. *ójīyas* : *ugrá-*. But in many words it also stands (like *j* for *ź*) for the old palatal *źh*, the voiced aspirate of *ś*, being recognizable as such in the same way as *j*[10].

1 a. *h* represents the palatalization (= IIr. *jh*) **of *gh*** when, in cognate forms, *gh* (or *g*) is found before other sounds than *s*; e. g. *hán-ti* 'strikes' : *ghn-ánti*, *jaghána*; *árhati* 'is worthy' : *arghá-* 'price'; *ṛh-ánt-* 'weak' : *ragh-ú-* 'light'; *jáṃh-as-* 'gait' : *jáṅghā-* 'leg'; *dáhati* 'burns' : *dag-dhá-* 'burnt'; *dóhate* 'milks' : *dúghāna-* 'milking', *dug-dhá-* 'milked'; *dudróha* 'have injured' : *drug-dhá-* 'injured', *drógha-* 'injurious'; *máṃhate* 'presents' : *maghá-* 'gift'; *míh-* 'mist' :

---

1 *iḥ* and *uḥ* produce the same effect as simple *i* and *u*, as they were originally pronounced as *iṣ* and *uṣ* (cp. Sandhi, p. 71, e 2); e. g. *agní(ṣ) ṣṭave*; *yáju(ṣ) ṣkannám*.

2 Cp. WACKERNAGEL I. 207 b.

3 Cp. WHITNEY on APr. I. 13 and TPr. II. 47.

4 See RPr. I. 12; XII. 2; APr. I. 13.

5 See below 1 b.

6 See below, Sandhi, 66.

7 Ibid. b 6, δ.

8 The combination *lh* is rare; it is found in *upa-valh-* (VS.) 'test by riddles'; *vihálha-* (AV.), of unknown meaning; and in the Kāṇva recension of the VS. as representing *ḍh*.

9 Cp. 36. This *h* being related to *gh* as *j* is to *g*, it must represent IE. *gh*. This survives, with loss of the aspiration, in *jahí* (= IIr. *jha-dhi*), 2. sing. impv. of *han-* 'strike'.

10 Cp. 41.

meghá- 'cloud'; *múhyati* 'is perplexed' : *mugdhá-* 'gone astray', *mógha-* 'vain'; *ráṃhi-* 'speed' : *raghú-* 'swift'; *háras-* and *gharmá-* 'heat'; *harmye-ṣṭhā́-* and *gharmye-ṣṭhā-* 'dwelling in the house'; *hṛṣitá-* 'glad' : *ghṛ́ṣu-* 'joyful', *ghṛ́ṣvi-* 'gladdening'. In *áhi-* 'serpent' and *duhitṛ́-* 'daughter' the guttural origin of *h* is shown by cognate languages[1].

b. *h* represents the old palatal aspirate (= IIr. *ẑh*):

α. when, either as a final or before *t*, it is replaced by a cerebral (like the old palatals *ś* and *j* = IIr. *ẑ*); e. g. *vah-* 'carry' : *á-vāṭ*, 3. sing. aor. *guh-* 'conceal' : *gūḍhá-*[2] 'concealed'; *tṛháti* 'crushes' : *tṛḍhá-*[3]; *dṛ́ṃhati* 'makes; firm', *dṛhyati* 'is firm' : *dṛḍhá-* 'firm'; *bahú-* 'abundant' : *bāḍhá-* 'aloud'; *mih-* 'make water' : *méḍhra-* (AV.) 'penis'; *riháti* 'licks' : *réḍhi* 'licks', *rīḍha-* 'licked'; *váhati* 'carries' : *vóḍhum* 'to carry', *ūḍhá-* 'carried'; *sáhate* 'overcomes' : *sā́ḍhṛ-* 'victor'.

β. when it is followed by sounds which do not palatalize gutturals[4], before which *dh* and *bh* do not become *h*, and before which the other old palatals *ś* and *j* (= *ẑ*) appear; thus *áṃhas-* and *aṃhatí-* 'distress' because of *aṃhú-* 'narrow'; *áhan-* 'day', because of *áhnām*, g. pl., and *pūrvāhṇá-* 'forenoon' (not *ghn* as in *ghnanti* from *han-*); *jéhamāna-*[5] 'panting', because of *jihmá-* 'oblique'; *bāhú-* 'arm'; *bráhman-* n. 'devotion', *brahmán-* 'one who prays'; *rāhú-* (AV.), demon of eclipse; *yahvá-*, *yahvánt-* 'ever young', because of *yahú-*, id. This applies to all words beginning with *hū-*, *hṛ-*, *hn-*, *hr-*, *hv-*; e. g. *hu-* 'pour'; *hṛd-* and *hṛ́daya-* 'heart'; *-hraya-* 'ashamed'; *-hvā-*, *hū-* 'call'; *hvṛ-* 'be crooked'.

γ. when the 'satem' languages have a corresponding voiced spirant (*z* or *ž*)[6]; thus *ahám* 'I'; *ehá-* (AV.) 'desirous'; *garhate* 'complains of'; *dih-* 'besmear'; *plīhán-* (AV. VS.) 'spleen'; *barhís-* 'sacrificial straw'; *mah-* 'great'; *varāhá-* 'boar'; *sahásra-* 'thousand'; *siṃhá-* 'lion'; *spṛh-* 'desire'; *haṃsá-* 'goose'; *hánu-* 'jaw'; *hi-* 'impel'; *hemán-* 'zeal', *hetí-* 'weapon'; *háya-* 'steed'; *hári-* and *hárita-* 'tawny'; *háryati* 'likes'; *hásta-* 'hand'; *hā-* 'forsake'; *hāyaná-* (AV.) 'year'; *hí* 'for'; *himá-* 'cold'; *hiraṇya-* 'gold'; *hirā́-* (AV. VS.) 'vein'; *hiṃs-* 'injure'; *héṣas-* 'wound'; *hṛ-* 'take'; *hyás* 'yesterday'[7].

δ. *h* according to the evidence of cognate languages, represents other palatals in some words. Thus in *hṛ́d-* 'heart', *ś* = IE. *k̂* would be expected; and *j* = IE. *ĝ* in *ahám* 'I', *mahánt-* 'great', *hánu-* 'jaw', *hásta-* 'hand', *hvā-*, *hū-* 'call'. These irregularities are probably due to IE. dialectic variations[8].

2. *h* also represents *dh* and *bh* not infrequently, and *ḍh* at least once.

a. It takes the place of *dh* in four or five roots (with nominal derivatives) and in a few nominal and verbal suffixes. Thus it appears initially in *hitá-*, *-hiti-*, beside *-dhita-*, *dhiti-*, from *dhā-* 'put'. Medially it is found in *gā́hate* 'plunges' (with the derivatives *gāhá-* 'depth', *gáhana-* 'deep', *dur-gáha-* 'impassable place') beside *gādhá-* 'ford'; *róhati* 'rises', 'grows' (with the derivatives *rúh-* 'growth', *róhaṇa-* 'means of ascending', *róhas-* 'elevation') beside *ródhati* 'grows' (with the derivatives *vī-rúdh-* 'creeper', *-ródha-* 'growing', *ródhas-* 'bank', *ā-ródhana-* 'ascent'); derivatives of **rudh-* 'be red' : *rohít-*, *róhita-*,

1 Cp. WACKERNAGEL I, 214 b.

2 That is for **guẓḍhá* (through *guẑh-tá-* for *gugh-tá-*), the cerebral *ẓ* disappearing but leaving the vowel long.

3 Cp. 12 and 17, 5.

4 See above 41, 2.

5 See WHITNEY, Roots, under *jeh*; and cp. 41 a, 2.

6 This includes several examples given under *α* and *β*.

7 Perhaps also in *has-* 'laugh' and *hā-* 'go', as these verbs have no forms with *gh*; also *nah-* 'bind' in spite of *nad-dhá-*. In several words the origin of the *h* is uncertain, e. g. *jáṅgahe* 'struggles', as the evidence is doubtful.

8 See WACKERNAGEL I, 216 b; for a few doubtful examples, ibid. 216 a, note.

-lohitá- 'red', beside *lodhá-* 'reddish animal', *rudhirá-* (AV.) 'red'; also *rauhiṇá-* beside *rudhikrā́-*, names of demons; the evidence of cognate languages further shows that *h* represents *dh* in *gṛhá-* 'house'[1].

h moreover represents *dh* in the adverbial suffix *-ha* in *viśvá-ha* beside *viśvá-dha* 'always'; in *sahá* 'together', beside *sadha-* in compounds; in *ihá* 'here', as shown by the Prakrit *idha*; and doubtless also in *sama-ha* 'somehow', though there is no direct evidence. The evidence of cognate languages, moreover, shows that in the endings of the 1. du. *-vahe, -vahi, -vahai* and the 1. pl. *-mahe, -mahi, -mahai* *h* represents *dh* (cp. Gk. -μεθα, etc.)[2].

b. *h* takes the place of ***bh*** in the verb *grah-*, *gṛh-* 'seize' (with its derivatives *gráha-* 'ladleful', *grā́hi-* 'demoness', *grāhyà-* 'to be grasped', *gṛhá-* 'servant', *hasta-gṛ́hya* 'having take the hand') beside *grabh-*, *gṛbh-* (with the derivatives *grábha-* 'taking possession of', *grābhá-* 'handful'); and in the nouns *kakuhá-* 'high', beside *kakúbh-* 'height', *kakubhá-* (VS. TS.) 'high', m. (AV.) a kind of demon; *bali-hṛ́t-* 'paying tax' (beside *bhṛ-* 'bear'); probably *bárjaha-* 'udder' (?), if formed with suffix *-ha* = *-bha* (in *ṛṣa-bhá-*, etc.)[3].

c. *h* takes the place of *ḍh* in *bárbṛhi*, 2. sing. impv. of the intv. *bárbṛh-* of the root *bṛh-* 'make strong', for **barbṛḍhi* (= **barbṛẓḍhi*, with the cerebral dropped after lengthening the preceding *ṛ* in pronunciation)[4].

d. The rule is that *h* appears for *ḍh, dh, bh,* only between vowels[5], the first of which is unaccented; e. g. *ihá, kakuhá-, gṛhá- bárjaha-, bali-hṛ́t- rauhiṇá-, sahá.* Similarly in *grabh-* 'seize', *h* alone appears after unaccented *ṛ* in RV. I—IX[6]; while on the other hand, in the 2. sing. impv. of graded roots, *-dhi* regularly appears after strong and therefore originally accented vowels; e. g. *bodhí* (from *bhū-* 'be'), *yòdhi* (from *yu-* 'yoke'), *yuyodhí* (from *yu-* 'separate'); *śiśādhi*, but *śiśīhi* (*śā-* 'sharpen'). Again, in *rudh-* 'rise', the unaccented form of the root is regularly *ruh-*, while when it is accented, forms such as *ródhati* appear beside *róhati*, and in nominal derivatives *dh* predominates in accented radical syllables, the RV. having *ródha-* and *ā-ródhana-* only, but the AV. *róha-* and *āróhaṇa-*[7].

α. At the same time *dh* and *bh* remain in a good many instances after an unaccented vowel; thus in the 2. sing. impv. *kṛdhi, gadhi, śrudhí, śṛṇudhí*; in *adhás* 'below', *adhamá-* 'lowest', *abhí* 'towards'; *ṛbhú-* 'deft'; *mīḍhá-* 'reward'; *medhā́-* 'wisdom'; *vidháti* 'adores'; *vidhú-* 'solitary'; *vidhávā-* 'widow'; *vadhū́-* 'bride'; *sādhú-* 'right'; *rudhirá-* (AV.) 'red'; derivatives formed with *-dhi-*, *-bhá-*, etc.[8] The retention of the *dh* and *bh* here is partly to be explained as an archaism, and partly as due to borrowing from a dialect in which these aspirates did not become *h*, and the existence of which is indicated by the Prakrit form *idha* beside the Vedic *ihá* 'here'. The guttural aspirate media is probably to be similarly explained in *meghá-* 'cloud' and *aghá-* 'sinful'.

---

1 Cp. Wackernagel I, 217 a.

2 The *h* in the perf. *ā́ha, āhúr*, may represent *dh*; not, however, in *náhyati* 'binds', in spite of *naddhá-*; *nah-* rather stands for IIr. *nažh-* (cp. Lat. *necto*); the pp. instead of **nāḍhá-*, became *naddhá-* through the influence of *baddhá-* from *bandh-* 'bind'. Cp. Wackernagel I, 217 a, note, where several other wrong explanations of *h* = *dh* are discussed.

3 Some erroneous etymologies in which *h* is explained as = *bh* are discussed in Wackernagel I, 217 b, note.

4 Cp. 12 and 17, 5.

5 It appears initially in *hitá-* = *-dhita-*, but originally it was doubtless preceded in this position by a final vowel. That *h* appears, though a vowel does not follow, in *gṛhṇātu* (IV. 57) and *hasta-gṛ́hya*, is due to other forms of *grabh-* in which *h* is followed by a vowel.

6 In RV. X, however, *gráha-* and *grā́hi-* occur; cp. above, 2 b.

7 Exceptions like *róhita-*, *viśváha* and inflected forms such as *gā́hate*, are due to normalization.

8 Where the RV. fluctuates between *h* and *dh bh* (above 2, a, b), *h* appears throughout in the later Saṃhitās; thus always *-hi*, after vowels in imperatives except *edhi* 'be'; thus for *śṛṇudhí* (RV. VIII. 84[3]), SV. has *śṛṇuhí*. But a new *h* of this kind hardly occurs. Cp. Wackernagel I, 219 a.

3. **The various origins** of *h* led to some **confusion** in the groups of forms belonging to roots which contain *h*.

a. roots in which *h* represents an original guttural (IIr. *jh*) show some forms which would presuppose an old palatal (IIr. *źh*). Thus from *muh-* 'be confused', phonetic derivatives of which are *mugdhá-*, *mógha-*, are formed *mūḍhá-* (AV.) 'bewildered' and *múhur* 'suddenly'.

b. roots in which *h* represents an old palatal (IIr. *źh*) show forms with a guttural before vowels and dentals; thus from *dih-* 'besmear' is formed *digdhá-* (AV.) 'owing to the influence of *dah-* 'burn', and *duh-* 'milk'. Similarly, from **saráh-* 'bee', beside *saráḍbhyas*, is formed *sāraghá-* (AV. VS.) 'derived from the bee'[1].

c. the root *ruh-*, though = *rudh-* 'ascend', is treated as if the *h* represented (as in *vah-*) an old palatal (IIr. *źh*); hence aor. *árukṣat*, des. *rúrukṣati*, pp. *-rūḍha-* (AV.), ger. *rūḍhvá* (AV.).

59. **The cerebral *ḷ*.** — This sound, as distinguished from the ordinary dental *l*, is a cerebral *ḷ*[2]. It appears in our (*Śākala*) recension of the RV. as a substitute, between vowels, for the cerebral *ḍ* and, with the appended sign for *h*, for the cerebral aspirate *ḍh*[3]; e. g. *íḷā-* 'refreshment'; *á-ṣāḷha-* 'invincible'. It also appears in Sandhi when final before an initial vowel; e. g. *turāṣáḷ abhíbhūtyojāḥ* (III. 43[4]). In the written Saṃhitā text, however, it does not appear if followed by a semivowel which must be pronounced as a vowel; e. g. *vīḍv-àṅga-* 'firm-limbed', to be pronounced as *vīḷú-aṅga-* and analysed thus by the Padapāṭha. In one passage of the RV. the readings fluctuate between *ḷ* and *l* in *nīḷavat* or *nīlavat* (VII. 97[6])[4].

60. **Anusvāra and Anunāsika.** — Anusvāra, 'after-sound', is a pure nasal sound which differs from the five class nasals; for it appears after vowels only, and its proper use is not before mutes, but before sibilants or *h* (which have no class nasal). But it resembled the class nasals in being pronounced, according to the Prātiśākhyas of the RV. and the VS.[5], after the vowel. The vowel itself might, however, be nasalized, forming a single combined sound. The Prātiśākhya of the AV.[6], recognizes this nasal vowel, called Anunāsika, 'accompanied by a nasal', alone, ignoring Anusvāra, which with the preceding vowel represents two distinct successive sounds. WHITNEY[7], however, denies the existence of any distinction between Anunāsika and Anusvāra. In any case, the Vedic Mss. have only the one sign ँ (placed either above or after the vowel) for both[8], employing the simple dot ं where neither Anusvāra nor Anunāsika is allowable. The latter sign is used in the TS. for final *m* before *y v*, and in both the TS. and MS. before mutes instead of the class nasal[9], a practice arising from carelessness or the desire to save trouble. There is thus no ground for the prevalent opinion that ँ represents Anunāsika and ं Anusvāra[10]. Throughout the present work *m* with a dot (*ṃ*) will be used for both, except if they appear before a vowel, when *m* with the older sign (*m̐*) will be employed.

---

1 The root *sagh-* 'take upon oneself', has no connexion with *sah-* 'overcome'; nor *vāghát-* 'institutor of a sacrifice', with *vah-* 'convey'. The relation of *gó-nyoghas-* 'streaming among milk', to *vah-* is uncertain; cp. WACKERNAGEL I, 220 b, note.

2 Cp. above 42.

3 This practice is followed by the Mss. of secondary texts of the RV.

4 Cp. BENFEY, Gött. Abhandl. 19, 138, note. See also WHITNEY on APr. I. 29.

5 See RPr. XIII. 13; VS. I. 74 f., 147 f.

6 See WHITNEY on APr. I. 11.

7 On TPr. II. 30; JAOS. 10, LXXXVI f.

8 Cp. WHITNEY on TPr. II. 30.

9 In the MS. also when *-aṃ* is written for *-ān*.

10 See WHITNEY, JAOS. 7, 92, note.

Anusvāra and Anunāsika are commonest when final. As in that position they belong to the sphere of Sandhi, the conditions under which they then appear, will be stated below[1]. **Medially** Anusvāra and Anunāsika are found under the following conditions:

a. regularly before sibilants and *h*; e. g. *vaṃśá-* 'reed'; *havíṃṣi* 'offerings'; *māṃsá-* 'flesh'; *siṃhá-* 'lion'. This is generally recognized as the sphere of Anusvāra, except by the APr.[2]; but *māṃścatú-* 'light yellow', is stated[3] to have Anunāsika, while *puṃścalī́-* (AV. VS.) is said to have both Anunāsika and Anusvāra[4]. The Anusvāra usually appears before *s*, and all forms with *ṃs* are shown to be based on original *ns* or *ms* by the evidence of cognate forms corroborated by that of allied languages[5]; thus *máṃsate*, 3. sing. subj. aor. of *man-* 'think'; *jíghāṃsati*, des. from *han-* 'strike'; *piṃśánti* beside *pinásṭi*, from *piṣ-* 'crush'; the neuter plurals in *-āṃsi*, *-īṃṣi*, *-ūṃṣi* from stems in *-as*, *-is*, *-us*, with nasal after the analogy of *-ānti*, nom. acc. pl. from neuters in *-nt*; stems in *-yāṃs*, *-vāṃs* beside nom. sing. in *-yān*, *-vān*; *kraṃsyáte* (AV.) from *kram-* 'stride'. When Anusvāra appears before *ś* and *h* derived from an IE. palatal or guttural, it represents the corresponding class nasal. The reduction of these old nasals to Anusvāra is probably IIr. after long vowels (*ām̊*, *-īṃr*, *-ūṃr*); probably later after short vowels, for it does not appear in forms like *áhan* (for *áhans*), though *s* was not dropped after *an* in the IIr. period; but the *s* must have been dropped early in the Indian period, before *-ans* became *-aṃs*[6]. Anusvāra before *h* (= Av. *ŋj*) must have arisen in the Indian period.

b. before any consonant in the intensive reduplicative syllable, the final of which is treated like that of the prior member of a compound; e. g. *náṃnamīti* (v. 83[5])[7] from *nam-* 'bend'.

c. before any consonant which is the initial of secondary suffixes; thus from *śam-* 'blessing', is formed *śaṃ-yú-* 'beneficent'; *śáṃ-tāti-* or *śánt.āti-* 'blessing'.

61. Voiceless Spirants.— **a.** The sound called **Visarjanīya**[8] in the Prātiśākhyas[9], must in their time have been pronounced as a voiceless breathing, since they describe it as an *ūṣman*, the common term for breathings and sibilants. This conclusion is borne out by the fact that, in the RPr., Jihvāmūlīya and Upadhmānīya, the sounds which are most nearly related to and may be replaced by Visarjanīya, are regarded as forming the second half of the voiceless aspirates *kh* and *ph* respectively, just as *h* forms the second half of the voiced aspirates *gh*, *bh*, etc. At the present day Visarjanīya is still pronounced in India as a voiceless breathing, which is, however, followed by a weak echo of the preceding vowel. According to the TPr.[10], Visarjanīya has the same place of articulation as the end of the preceding vowel. The proper function of this sound is to represent final *s* and *r* in pausā; it may, however, also appear before certain voiceless initial sounds, viz. *k*, *kh*, *p*, *ph*, and the sibilants (occasionally also in compounds)[11].

b. Beside and instead of Visarjanīya, the Prātiśākhyas recognise two voiceless breathings as appropriate before initial voiceless gutturals (*k*, *kh*)[12]

1 See below, Sandhi, 75.
2 APr. I. 67; II. 33f.
3 Cp. RPr. IV. 35.
4 Cp. VPr. IV. 7f.
5 Cp. Wackernagel I, 224 a.
6 Loc. cit.; cp. Brugmann, KG. 354, 17.
7 In Aufrecht's edition printed *nánnamīti.*
8 The term *visarga* is not found in the Prātiśākhyas (nor in Pāṇini).
9 RPr. I. 5 etc., VPr. I. 41 etc.; APr. I. 5 etc.; TPr. I. 12 etc.
10 See Whitney on TPr. II. 48.
11 See below, Sandhi, 78, 79.
12 See RPr. I. 8; VPr. III. 11 etc.

and labials (*p*, *ph*)[1] respectively. The former (*ẖ*) called **Jihvāmūlīya**, or sound 'formed at the root of the tongue', is the guttural spirant χ; the latter (*ḫ*), called **Upadhmānīya**, or 'on-breathing', is the bilabial spirant *f*[2]. In Mss. they are regularly employed in the Kaśmirian Śāradā character.

62. Loss of Consonants.— Consonants have been lost almost exclusively when they have been in conjunction with others. The loss of a single consonant which is not in conjunction with another is restricted to the disappearance of ***v*** **before *u***, and much more rarely of ***y*** **before *i***. The *v* thus disappears finally in the Sandhi of *ăv* before *u* in the RV. and VS.[3] Initially, *v* is lost before *ŭr* derived from a *ṛ* vowel; thus in *úraṇa-* and *úrā-* 'sheep'; *úras-* 'breast'; *ur-āṇá-*, mid. part. (*vṛ-* 'choose'); *ū́rj-* 'vigour'; *ū́rṇā-* 'wool'; *ūrṇóti* 'covers' (*vṛ-* 'cover'); *ūrdhvá-* 'high'; *ūrmí-* 'wave'. Such loss of *v* before *ŭr* also occurs after an initial consonant in *tūrtá-* 'quick' (= IIr. *tvṝtá-*); *dhū́rvati*, *ádhūrṣata*, *dhūrtí-*, from *dhvṛ-* 'cause to fall'; *hū́rya-*, *juhūr-thās*; *juhur*, from *hvṛ-* 'go crookedly'[4]. Before simple *u* the *v* has disappeared at the beginning of the reduplicative syllable *u-* (= **vu-* for original *va-*), in *u-vā́c-a* from *vac-* 'speak'; *u-vā́sa* from *vas-* 'shine'; *u-vā́h-a* from *vah-* 'convey'.

Similarly initial *y* has disappeared from the reduplicative syllable *i-* = **yi-* in the desiderative *í-yak-ṣati*, *í-yak-ṣamāṇa-*, from *yaj-* 'sacrifice'[5].

1. When a **group of consonants** is **final**, the last element or elements are regularly lost (the first only, as a rule, remaining) in pausā and in Sandhi[6].

2. When a **group of consonants** is **initial**, the first element is frequently lost. The only certain example of an initial mute having disappeared seems to be *tur-ī́ya-* 'fourth', from **ktur-*, the low grade form of *catúr-* 'four', because the Vedic language did not tolerate initial conjunct mutes[7]. An **initial sibilant** is, however, **often lost** before a mute or nasal. This loss was originally[8] doubtless caused by the group being preceded by a final consonant. There are a few survivals of this in the Vedas; thus *cit kámbhanena* (x. 111[5]), otherwise *skámbhana-* 'support'; and the roots *stambh-* 'support', and *sthā-* 'stand', lose there *s* after *ud-*; e. g. *út-thita-*, *út-tabhita-*. On the other hand the sibilant is preserved after a final vowel, in compounds or in Sandhi, in *á-skṛdhoyu-* 'uncurtailed', beside *kṛdhú-* 'shortened'; *ścandrá-* 'brilliant', in *áśva-ścandra-* 'brilliant with horses'[9], *ádhi ścandrám* (VIII. 65[11]), also in the intens. pres. part. *cáni-ścad-at* 'shining brightly', otherwise *candrá-* 'shining', and only *candrá-mas-* 'moon'. In derivatives from four other roots, forms with and without the sibilant[10] are used indiscriminately, without regard to the preceding

---

1 See VPr. I. 41.

2 Cp. EBEL, KZ. 13, 277 f.

3 See below, Sandhi, 73.

4 The *v* has either remained or been restored before such *ŭr* and *ūr* in *hotṛ-vū́rya-* 'election of the invoker'; in the opt. *vurīta*, from *vṛ-* 'choose'; and in the 3. pl. perfect *babhū-vúr*, *jūhu-vur*, *suṣu-vur*, *tuṣṭu-vúr*.

5 The evidence of cognate languages seems to point to the loss of initial *d* in *áśru-* 'tear' (Lat. *dacruma*, Gk. δάκρυ). It is, however, probable that there were two different but synonymous IE. words *aḱru* and *daḱru*. On some doubtful etymologies based on loss of initial consonants, see WACKERNAGEL I, 228 c, note.

6 See below, Sandhi, 65.

7 There are some words in which an initial mute seems to have been lost in the IE. period; thus *t* in *śatám* 'hundred' (= IE. *tk̂ṇtóm*); *d* perhaps in *viṃśatí-* 'twenty' and *vi-* 'between'; *l* perhaps in *yákṛt-* 'liver'. An initial mute seems to have been lost before a sibilant (originally perhaps after a final consonant) in *stána-* 'breast', *svid-* 'sweat'; *ṣaṣ-* 'six' (KZ. 31, 415 ff.).

8 Dissimilation may also have played some part in the loss of the sibilant in the reduplicative syllable of roots with initial *sk*(*h*) *st*(*h*), *sp*(*h*), as *caskánda*, *tíṣṭhāmi*, *paspárśa*.

9 See GRASSMANN's Wörterbuch sub verbo *ścandrá-*.

10 The verb *kṛ-* 'do', after *pári* and *sam*, shows an initial *s*; e. g. *pariṣkṛṇvanti*, *pári-*

sound; from *stan-* 'thunder', *stanayitnú-*, beside *tanayitnú-* 'thunder', *tanyatú-* (also AV.) 'thunder', *tanyú-* 'thundering', *tanyati* 'resounds'; *stená-* 'thief', *stāy-ánt-* (AV.) 'stealing', *stāyú-* (VS.) 'thief', *stéya-* 'theft', beside *tāyú-* 'thief'; *stṛ́-*, beside *tṛ́-* 'star'; *spáś-* 'spy' and *spaś-* 'see' in verbal forms *á-spaṣ-ta* aor., *paspaś-* perf., *spāśáyati* caus., *-spaṣṭa-* part., 'seen', beside *páśyati* 'sees'[1].

The loss of initial *s* may be inferred in the following words from the evidence of cognate languages in which it has been preserved: *tij-* 'sharpen'; *tuj-* 'strike'; *tud-* 'beat'; *narmá-* (VS.) 'jest'; *nṛt-* 'dance'; *parṇá-* 'wing'; *piká-* (VS.) 'Indian cuckoo'; *plīhán-* (VS. AV.) 'spleen'; *phéna-* 'foam'; *mṛd-* 'crush', *mṛdú-* (VS.) 'soft'; *vip-* 'tremble'; *śupti-* 'shoulder'.

A few examples occur of the **loss of the semivowels *y* or *v***[2] as the last element of an initial consonant group. Thus *y* disappears in derivatives of roots in *īv* formed with suffixes beginning with consonats: *-mūta-* 'moved', *mū-rá-* 'impetuous', *mú-tra-* (AV. VS.) 'urine', from *mīv-* 'push'; *sūcí-* 'needle', *sū-ná-* 'plaited basket', *sú-tra-* (AV.) 'thread', beside *syú-man-* 'thong', *syū-tá-* 'sewn', from *sīv-* 'sew'. Loss of *v* seems to have taken place in *śiti-* 'white' (only at the beginning of compounds), beside *śvit-* 'be bright', *śvity-áñc-* 'brilliant', *śvitrá-* (AV.) 'white', *śvítrya-*, perhaps 'white'; and, on the evidence of the Avesta, in *kṣip-* 'throw' (Av. *hšiw*), *ṣáṣ-* (Av. *ḫšvaš*).

3. When the **group is medial**, the loss usually taken takes place between single consonants. a. The **sibilants** *s* and *ṣ* thus regularly disappear between mutes; e. g. *á-bhak-ta*, 3. sing. aor., for **ábhak-s-ta* beside *á-bhak-ṣ-i*, from *bhaj-*, 'share'; *caṣ-ṭe* for *cakṣ-ṭe* (= original **caś-s-te*)[3]. Similarly *a-gdha-* (TS.) 'uneaten', for **a-ghs-ta-*, from *ghas-* 'eat'[4].

b. The **dental** *t* has disappeared between a sibilant and *c* in *paś-cá* and *paś-cā́t* 'behind' (= IE. *post-qé*, *post-qḗt*); and between *p* and *s* in **nap-su* which must have been the loc. pl. (AV. *nafšu*), from **napt-*, 'weak stem of *nápāt-*, beside the dat. *nád-bhyas* 'to the grandsons', for *napt-bhyas*, where on the other hand the *p* has been dropped.

c. A **mute** may disappear between a nasal and a mute; e. g. *paṅtí-* for *paṅktí-*, *yundhí* for *yuṅgdhí*. This spelling is common in Vedic Mss.; it is prescribed in APr. II. 20, and, as regards the mediae, in VPr. VI. 30.

4. The only example of the **loss of an initial**[5] mute **in a medial group** of consonants seems to be that of *b* before *dbh* in *nádbhyas* for **nabdbhyas* from *napt-* for *nápāt-*. The semivowel *r* seems to be lost before a consonant when another *r* follows in *cakr-dt* (Pp. *cakrán*) and *cakr-iyās*[6] for **carkr-* beside *carkar-mi*, from *kṛ-* 'commemorate'; and, on the evidence of the Avesta, in *tváṣṭṛ-* (cp. *þwarəs* 'cut', *þwaršta-* 'created'),

ṣkṛta-, *sám-skṛta-*; also after *nis* in *nir askṛta* (Pp. *akṛta*), perhaps owing to Sandhi forms with *ṣk* such as *niṣkuru* (AV.). There can be little doubt that the *s* here was not original but was due to analogy; cp. WACKERNAGEL I, 230 *a*, *β*, note.

1 WACKERNAGEL I, 230 a *γ*, note, discusses several uncertain or erroneous etymologies based on loss of initial *s* (including *maryās* interpreted as 2. sing. opt. of *smṛ-*). The evidence of Prakṛit seems to point to the loss of initial *s* in *śépa-* 'tail', *krīḍ-* 'leap', *kruś-* 'cry', *paraśú-* 'axe', *paruṣá-* 'knotty'; cp. WACKERNAGEL I, 230 b.

2 On the possible loss of *r* in *bhañj-* (Lat. *frango*) and of *k* in *savyá-* (Lat. *scaevus*), see WACKERNAGEL I, 232 c, note.

3 See above 56, b.

4 On *ápnas-* 'property', *dámpati-* 'lord of the house', see WACKERNAGEL I, 233 c, note.

5 The guttural mute only seems to be lost when *kṣ* + *t* becomes *ṣṭ*: see above, 56, 6. The loss of *m* in the inst. sing. *-nā* of nouns in *-man* is only a seeming one; for *dānā́*, *prāthinā́*, *preṇā́*, *bhūnā́*, *mahinā́*, *variṇā́* (TS.) appear beside the stems *dā́man-* etc., because some of them had a stem in *-n* without *m*, so that *-nā* seemed an alternative from of *-mnā*: see BENFEY, GGA. 1846, 702. 880; Göttinger Abhandlungen 19, 234; BLOOMFIELD, JAOS. 17, 3; cp. IF. 8, Anzeiger, p. 17.

6 But see GELDNER, VS. I, 279.

probably starting from forms like *tváṣṭrā* (AV.) in which the *r* immediately followed[1]

But the **loss of a spirant** (IIr. *s*, *z*, *ž*, *žh*) at the beginning of a medial group is common.

a. The **sibilant** *s*[2] has thus been lost before *k* followed by a consonant in *vavṛktam*, *vṛkṇá-*, *vṛktví*, *vṛkṣi* (TS.), from *vraśc-* 'lop' (cp. *-vraská-*).

b. The voiced form (IIr. *z*) of dental *s* has disappeared[3] before voiced dentals, without leaving any trace, in the roots *ās-* 'sit', and *śās-* 'order'; thus *ā-dhvam*, *śaśā-dhi*. But when *ă* preceded the *z*, the disappearance of the sibilant is indicated by *e* taking the place of *az* before *d*, *dh*, *h* (= *dh*); thus *e-dhí*, from *as-* 'be'; *sed-*[4], perfect stem of *sad-* 'sit' (for *sazd-*, like *saśc-* from *sac-*). This *e* also replaces *az* with loss of the sibilant in *de-hí* 'give'; *dhe-hí* 'put'; *kiye-dhā́-* 'containing much'; *néd-īyas-* and *néd-iṣṭha-* 'very much'; *ped-ú-*[5] N.; *medati* 'is fat'; *medhā́-* and *medhás-* 'wisdom'; *médha-* 'juice'[6].

c. When a vowel other than *ă* preceded, the *z* was cerebralized (like *s* before a voiceless dental) and disappeared after cerebralizing the following dental and lengthening the preceding vowel; thus *a-sto-ḍhvam*[7] (= *á-stoẓ-ḍhvam* for *a-stos-dhvam*) 2. pl. aor., beside *a-sto-ṣ-ṭa*, 3. sing., from *stu-* 'praise'. Thus also are to be explained *nīḍá-* 'nest' (= *niẓḍa-* for *ni-sd-a-*); *pīḍ-* 'press' (= *piẓḍ-* for *pi-sd-* or *piṣ-d-*); *mīḍhá-* 'reward' (Gk. μισθός); *vīḍ-ú-* 'strong', *vīḍáyati* 'is strong' (from *viṣ-* 'work' + *-d*)[8]; *hīḍ-*[9] 'be angry', and its Guṇa forms, e. g. *héḍ-as-* 'anger'; *mṛḍáti* 'be gracious', *mṛḍīká-* 'gracious' (for *mṛẓ-ḍ-* from *mṛṣ-* 'forget') with vowel pronounced long (12), *á-reḍ-ant-* (TS.) 'not deceiving' (= *a-reẓḍ-ant-*), from *riṣ-* 'injure'.

d. Similarly the **old voiced palatal spirant** (IIr. *ź*) disappeared after cerebralizing a following *d* or *dh* and lengthening the preceding vowel; thus *tā-ḍhi* for **taź-ḍhi* (= *tak-ṣ-dhi*) from *takṣ-* 'fashion'; *ṣo-ḍhā́* for **ṣaṣ-dhā́* (= *sak-ṣ-dhā*), beside *ṣaṣ-ṭhá-* (AV.) 'sixth'. A similar loss is to be assumed in *īḍ-* 'praise' (= *iź-ḍ* for *yaj-* + *d*)[10].

e. This loss is specially frequent in the case of the old voiced palatal aspirated spirant (IIr. *źh*) represented by *h*, which was dropped after cerebralizing and aspirating a followed *t* and lengthening the preceding vowel; thus *bāḍhá-*

[1] In a few forms of the AV. the semi-vowel *y* seems to be lost at the *end* of the medial group *kṣy*: *mekṣāmi*, *yokṣe*, *vidhakṣán*, *sākṣe*. But these forms may be due to errors in the MSS.

[2] In *ch* = IE. *ŝkh*, the original *s* was lost in a pre-Indian period.

[3] Before voiced mutes other than dentals, *z* became *d*, as in *madgú-* (44, 3 a) 'diver'; similarly *ẓ* became *ḍ*, as in *paḍbhis*, from *páś-* 'look' or 'cord'; and in *vi-prúḍ-bhis* from *viprúṣ-* 'drop'.

[4] The loss of the voiced sibilant (*z*) must be older than the original text of the RV., as the *e* of *sed-* has been transferred to other stems which contain no sibilant, as in *bhej-iré*, from *bhaj-* 'divide'. Similarly the vowel of *hīḍ-*, though derived from *iẓ*, is regarded as a primitive *ī* in the form *ájīhiḍat* (AV.): cp. WACKERNAGEL I, p. 272 (mid.).

[5] Cp. BARTHOLOMAE, KZ. 27, 361. On *edh-* 'thrive', *miyédha-* 'broth', *vedhás-* 'virtuous', see WACKERNAGEL I, 237 c.

[6] In stems in *-as* before case terminations beginning with *bh*, and before secondary suffixes beginning with *m*, *y* or *v*, the sibilant is lost (instead of becoming *d* in the former circumstances, or remaining in the latter) owing to the influence of Sandhi; e. g. *dvéṣo-bhis* from *dvéṣ-as-* 'hate'. An original sibilant has perhaps been lost in *mahiṣá-*, *sāhvāṃs-*, *jāhuṣá*, *hrādúni-*, *jas-* 'be exhausted'; cp. WACKERNAGEL I, 237 a β, note.

[7] The origin of *kroḍá-* (AV. VS.) 'breast' (Av. *hraoždra-* 'hard') and of many words with *ḍ* or *ḍh* preceded by a long vowel, and with no collateral forms containing a sibilant, is obscure.

[8] Cp. HÜBSCHMANN, KZ. 24, 408. In *sīda-* (= *sizda-*) from *sad-* 'sit', the *d* has been retained owing to the influence of other forms of the verb *sad-*. See, however, ROZWADOWSKI, BB. 21, 147, and cp. ZDMG. 48, 519.

[9] *Piṇḍa-* perhaps stands for **pinẓḍa-*, from *piṣ-* 'crush; cp. WACKERNAGEL I, 146, d.

[10] On *krīḍ-*, cp. WACKERNAGEL I, 238 b, note; PISCHEL, BB. 23, 253 ff. On *īḍ-*, cp. OLDENBERG, SBE. 30, 2.

'strong', *nī-bīḍha-* 'dense' (= *baẓḍhá-* for *bah-tá-*) from *baṃh-* 'be strong'; *sā́ḍhṛ-* 'conqueror', *á-ṣāḍha-* 'invincible', from *sah-*; *rīḍhá-* (= *riẓḍhá-*), from *rih-* 'lick'; *ūḍhá-* (= *uẓḍhá-*) from *vah-* 'carry'; *gūḍhá-* 'concealed', from *guh-* 'hide'; *tṛḍhá-*, *tṛḍhvā* (AV.), from *tṛh-* 'crush'; *dṛḍhá-* 'firm', from *dṛh-* 'be strong'. Here *e* also appears for *aẓ* in *tṛnéḍhu* (AV.) from *tṛh-* (= *tṛnaẓḍhu*); and *o* in *voḍhám* (= *vaẓḍham*), 2. du. aor. of *vah-* 'carry'. We also find *e* as Guṇa of *i* in *méḍhra-* (AV.), from *mih-* 'mingere' (= *meẓḍhra-*).

63. **Metathesis.**—Apart from the few examples of *ra* before *ṣ* and *h* (51 c), there are probably no certain instances of metathesis in the RV.[1]. In the later Saṃhitās, however, a few other forms of metathesis are to be found. Thus *-valh-* seems to be a transposition of *hval-* 'go deviously' in *upa-valh-* (VS.) 'propound a riddle to'[2]. In *valmīka-* (VS.) 'anthill', *m* appears transposed beside *vamrī́-* and *vamrá-* 'ant', *vamra-ká-* 'little ant'. Metathesis of quantity occurs in *ās-thas* for **as-thās*, 2. sing. mid. aor. of *as-* 'throw'. This is analogous to the shortening, in the RV., of the radical vowel of *dā-* 'give', in the forms *ā́dam, ā́das, ā́dat,* where the verb is compounded with the verbal prefix *ā*[3], while otherwise the forms *dām, dās, dāt* alone appear.

64. **Syllable.**—The notion of the syllable is already known to the late hymns of the Ṛgveda, though the word (*a-kṣára-*) is there generally used as an adjective meaning 'imperishable'. Thus *akṣáreṇa mimate saptá vā́ṇīḥ* means 'with the syllable they measure the seven metres'. The vowel being according to the Prātiśākhyas[4] the essential element of the syllable, the word *akṣara-*[5] is used by them in the sense of 'vowel' also. Initially, a vowel, or a consonant and the following vowel form a syllable. Medially, a simple consonant begins a syllable, e. g. *ta-pas*; when there is a group of consonants, the last begins the syllable, e. g. *tap-ta-*, and if the last is a sibilant or semivowel, the penultimate also belongs to the following syllable[6], e. g. *astām-psīt, an-tya-*. A final consonant in pausā belongs to the preceding vowel, e. g. *i-dam*.

By the process called **haplology** one of two identical or similar syllables in juxtaposition is dropped. Syllable is here to be taken in the sense not only of a consonant with a following vowel, but of a vowel with a following consonant.

1. The first of the two syllables is dropped within a word in *tuvī-rá[va]vān* 'roaring mightily'[7], beside *tuvī-ráva-*; *madh[ya]yā́* 'in the middle', from *mádhya-* (like *āsa-yā́*, *nakta-yā́*); *vṛ́[ta]thā* 'at will', from *vṛtá-* 'willed' (like *ṛtu-thā́* 'according to *ṛtu-*'); *svapatyái* for *svapat[yā́]yai*, dat. sing. f. of *sv-apatyá-* 'having good offspring'; perhaps also *yós*, beside *yáyos*, gen. loc. du. of *yá-*[8]. Examples of a vowel with following consonant being dropped are: *ir[adh]ádhyai*, inf. of *iradh-* 'seek to win'; *cak[an]anta, r[an]anta, v[an]anta*[9]; perhaps *sád[as]as-páti-* beside *sádasas-páti-* 'lord of the seat'[10].

a. The final syllable of the first member of a compound is sometimes dropped in this way; thus *śé[va]-vāra-* 'treasury'; *śé[va]-vṛdha-* 'dear'; *madúgha-* (AV.),

[1] Perhaps *stoká-* 'drop', may stand for **skotá-*, from *ścut-* 'drip-, under the influence of *stúkā-* 'tuft'.

[2] Cp. WACKERNAGEL I, 212 b, note, and 239 b.

[3] These forms are not resolved in the Pada text, i. e. they are treated as if they did not contain the verbal prefix *ā́*.

[4] RPr. XVIII. 17; VPr. I, 99.

[5] Though known to Kātyāyana and Patañjali as well as to the Prātiśākhyas, *akṣara-* as the designation of syllable is not found in Pāṇini.

[6] See TPr. XXI. 7, 9. On the division of syllables cp. further RPr. I. 15; VPr. I. 100ff.; APr. I. 55ff.; TPr. XXI. 1ff.; and WHITNEY on TPr. XXI. 5.

[7] Cp. BARTHOLOMAE, KZ. 29, 527, 562.

[8] Cp., however, *en-os* for *ena-yos*.

[9] See KZ. 20, 70f.

[10] See BLOOMFIELD, JAOS. 16, XXXV.

N. of a plant yielding honey, beside *madhu-dúgha-* 'shedding sweetness'; *śaṣ[pa]-piñjara-* (VS.) 'tawny like young grass' [1].

2. The second syllable is dropped in the datives *páuṃsyā[ya]*, *ratnadhéyā[ya]*, *sakhyá[ya]*, and *abhikhyá* beside *abhikhyā́ya*; also in *vṛkát[āt]i-* 'destruction', beside *vṛkátāt-* and *devá-tāti-*; and at the beginning of the second member of a compound in *śīrṣa-[sa]ktí-* (AV.) 'headache' [2].

a. A following syllable is sometimes dropped in spite of a different one intervening; thus in the dative *maryā́dā[ya]* 'boundary'; and somewhat peculiarly in *ā́varīv[ar]ur*, 3. pl. impf. beside the 3. sing. *á varīvar* and 3. sing. pres. *á varīvarti*.

II. EUPHONIC COMBINATION (SANDHI).

BENFEY, Vollständige Grammatik p. 21—70. — WHITNEY, Sanskrit Grammar p. 34—87. — WACKERNAGEL, Altindische Grammatik 1, 301—343. — ARNOLD, Vedic Metre p. 70—80.

65. The nature of Vedic Sandhi.—The sentence is naturally the unit of speech which forms an unbroken chain of syllables euphonically combined. It is, however, strictly so only in the prose portion of the AV. [3] and the prose Mantras of the YV. As the great bulk of the Vedas is metrical, the RV. and the SV. being entirely so, the editors of the Saṃhitā text treat the hemistich (consisting generally of two Pādas or verses) [4] as the euphonic unit, applying the rules of Sandhi with special stringency between the Pādas or metrical units which form the hemistich. The evidence of metre, however, shows that, in the original form of the text, Sandhi at the end of an internal Pāda is all but unknown [5]. The verse, therefore, is the true euphonic unit [6]. The final of a word appears either at the end of this unit in pausā (*avasāne*) [7], or within it as modified by contact with a following initial. The form which the final of a word assumes in pausā, being regarded as the normal ending, is generally the basis of the modification appearing within the verse. It will therefore conduce to clearness if the rules relating to absolute finals are first stated.

66. Finals in pausā.—**a. Vowels** [8] in this position undergo no change other than occasional nasalization.

1. In all the Saṃhitās *ă ĭ ŭ* [9] are frequently **nasalized** when prolated; e. g. *vindatī3ṃ* | = *vindati* (x. 146[1]); *babhūvā3ṃ* | = *babhūva* (AV. x. 2[28]); *viveśā3ṃ* | = *viveśa* (VS. XXIII. 49); *mamā́3ṃ* | = *mamá* (TS. VII. 4[20]).

2. In the Saṃhitā text of the RV. there survive, at the end of a verse within a hemistich, from the period when such end also was accounted a pause, several instances of **nasalized** *ā̆*, preserved to avoid hiatus and con-

[1] This explanation is doubtful in *ulokā́-* for *u[lu]loká-* (cp. BRUGMANN, Grundriss 1, 624, p. 471); *śuṣmayá-* (TS.) for *śuṣmamáya-*; *bhīmalá-* (VS.) 'terrible', for *bhīmamala-*; improbable in *rujā́nās* for *rujāná-nās*, 'with broken nose' (BLOOMFIELD, JAOS. 16, XXXIV).

[2] Cp. WHITNEY, Translation of AV. I, 123.

[3] See BLOOMFIELD, The Atharvaveda, in this Encyclopedia, § 1 (beginning) and note 1.

[4] In the Gāyatrī metre, in which there are three Pādas, the third alone constitutes the second hemistich; in the Paṅkti, which has five Pādas, the last three constitute the second hemistich.

[5] The only probable exception is RV. IX. 113, 7 c d; cp. ARNOLD, Vedic Metre 119.

[6] The sentence within a Pāda, as well as the Pāda itself, is the unit of accent; cp. below, 83.

[7] Cp. RPr. I. 3; VI. 5; X. 5; XI. 30.

[8] Final *ṝ* never occurs in the RV., its place being supplied by *ur* as nom. acc. s. n. e. g. *sthātúr* 'standing' (cp. WACKERNAGEL, KZ. 25, 287 f.); but the TS. already has *janayitṝ́* and *bhartṝ́* (B?), WACKERNAGEL 1, 259 a, note.

[9] The vowels *ī* and *ū*, when dual terminations (pragṛhya), cannot be nasalized.

traction. Thus *ă* appears as *aṁ̊* before *e* and *o*; e. g. *ghanénaṁ̊'ékaś* (I. 33[4]); *ā* appears *āṁ̊* before *e o ṛ*; e. g. *yāṁ̊'ṛṇaṃcayé* (V. 30[14]); while the prepositions *ā́* 'near', and *sácā* 'together', are nasalized before any vowel; e. g. *sácāṁ̊'udyán*. The vowel *ā* once appears as *ăṁ̊* before *ṛ* in *vipanyáṁ̊'ṛtásya* (IV. 1[12]), following the regular rule that unnasalized *ā* is shortened before *ṛ* in the RV.

b. Consonants are liable to change of mode of articulation and, to some extent, of place of articulation.

1. Final **mutes**, whether tenuis, media, or aspirate, are without distinction **represented by** the corresponding **tenuis**; e. g. *dūrā́t* (III. 59[3]) = *dūrā́d* 'from afar'; *uṣar-bhút* (I. 65[9]) = *uṣar-búdh* 'waking at dawn'.

2. The **palatals** *c* and *j* revert to the original guttural, becoming *k*; thus *arvā́k* (I. 118[2]) = *arvā́c* 'coming hither'; *su-yúk* = *su-yúj* 'well yoked'. The old palatal *j*, however, becomes *ṭ*, e. g. *rā́ṭ* (I. 121[3]), m. f. 'king', 'queen', = *rā́j*; in *ṛtvík*, however, it becomes the guttural, = *ṛtvíj* 'priest' (from *yaj-* 'sacrifice')[3].

3. The ritual exclamations *váṣaṭ* (X. 115[9]) and *śráuṣaṭ* (I. 139[1]), which are probably modified forms of the 3. sing. aor. subj. of *vah-* 'carry', and *śru-* 'hear'[4], have ***ṭ* for *t*** owing to the analogy of the exclamations *vā́ṭ* (VS.), *váṭ* (TS.), 3. sing. aor. of √*vah-*[5].

4. The **nasals** occurring as finals, *ṅ*, *n*, *m*[6], remain **unchanged**. Of these, *n* and *m* are very common; but *ṅ* is found very rarely and only secondarily after the loss of a following *k* (representing an original palatal; e. g. *prā́ṅ* for **prā́ṅk*, from *prā́ñc-*). Probably no instance of final *ṇ* can be found in Vedic Mantras. The palatal *ñ* never occurs, since final palatals become guttural (b, 2).

a. In the rare instances in which a **radical *m*** becomes final after dropping a following *-t* or *-s*, it appears as *n* owing to the influence of the dental; thus *dán* (= **dam-s*) 'of the house' (*dam-*)[7]; *á-kran* (= **á-kram-t*), 3. sing. aor. of *kram-* 'stride'; *á-gan* (= **a-gam-s*, **a-gam-t*), 2. 3. sing. aor., *a-jagan* (= **ajagam-t*), 3. sing. plup., *aganīgan* (VS.), 3. sing. intv. of *gam-* 'go'; *á-yān* (= **a-yam-s-t*), 3. sing. aor. of *yam-* 'reach'[8].

5. The **semivowels** *y v l*[9] do not occur as finals. *r* is represented by Visarga; thus *púnar* 'again', is written *púnaḥ*[10].

6. The **sibilants** and ***h*** are all changed when final.

α. The **dental *s***, which is by far the commonest of final sibilants, becomes Visarga; e. g. *ketús* is written *ketúḥ* (III. 61[3]).

β. The **cerebral *ṣ***, which is very rare as a final, becomes cerebral *ṭ* in *ṣáṭ* 'six', for *ṣáṣ*; *-dvíṭ* 'hating', for *-dviṣ*; *vi-prúṭ* (AV.) 'sprinkling',

---

1 The ritual interjection *óm* (VS.) may be due to the nasalization of an original *o* prolated (cp. RPr. XV. 3). Thus the JUB. I. 24. 3 ff., mentions the pronunciations *o* as well as *om*, both of which it rejects in favour of *oṃ*.

2 Cp. RPr. I. 13; WHITNEY on APr. I. 43.

3 Cp. WACKERNAGEL I, 149 a *α*.

4 Cp. above 42 c (p. 34).

5 Loc. cit.

6 Final *m* is often incorrectly written as Anusvāra in Mss. (as conversely in Prakrit Mss. *ṃ* is often written as *m* under Sanskrit influence: cp. PISCHEL, Grammatik der Prakrit-Sprachen, in this Encyclopedia, 339, 348), and their example is sometimes followed in printed editions.

7 In the K. also occurs the form *a-ṇān* = **-nām-s-t*, from *nam-* 'bend'. The ŚB. has *praśān* 'painless', = **pra-śam-s*.

8 See 46 d, *β*.

9 Final *l* is spoken of as occurring rarely (WACKERNAGEL I, 260 c), or as very rare (WHITNEY 144), but I have been unable to find a single example in the Vedas (or even in post-Vedic Sanskrit). But though no etymologically final *l* seems to occur either in pausā or in Sandhi, it is found as a substitute for *ḍ* in two or three words in the later Saṃhitās (see above 52 d, p. 45).

10 When *ḥ* stands for etymological *r*, this is indicated by an added *iti* in the Padapāṭha; e. g. *púnar íti* (X. 85[18]).

for *vi-prúṣ*. These are the only examples occurring in the RV. and AV. In the only two examples in which *ṣ* occurs in the RV. as a final in the compound form *kṣ*, it is dropped: *anák* 'eyeless', from *an-ákṣ-*; *á-myak*, 3. sing. aor. of *myakṣ-* 'be situated' (?).

γ. The palatal **ś becomes** either ***k*** or ***ṭ***[1]; e. g. *-dṛk* for *dṛś-* (III. 61[9]); *vipāṭ*, N. of a river, for *vipāś-*.

δ. According as it is guttural or palatal in origin, ***h* become *k*** or ***ṭ***; thus *á-dhok*, 3. sing. impf. of *duh-* 'milk'; but *á-vāṭ*, 3. sing. aor. of *vah-* 'carry'.

c. The rule is, that only a **single consonant** may be final. Hence all but the first of a group of consonants are dropped; e. g. *ábhavan* for **ábhavant*; *tā́n* for **tā́ns*; *tudán* for *tudánts*; *prā́ṅ* for **prā́ṅks* (= **prā́ñcs*); *acchān* for **achantst*, 3. sing. aor. of *chand-* 'be pleasing'.

α. *k ṭ* or *t*, when they follow an *r* and belong to the root, are allowed to remain; e. g. *várk*, 2. 3. sing. aor. of *vṛj-* 'bend'; *ū́rk* (VS.), nom. of *ū́rj-* 'strength'; *á-mārṭ*, 3. sing. impf. of *mṛj-* 'wipe'; *á-vart*, 3. sing. aor. of *vṛt-* 'turn'; *suhā́rt* (AV.), nom. of *suhā́rd-* 'friend'. The only instance of a suffix remaining after *r* is *dar-t*, 3 sing. aor. of *dṛ-* 'cleave', used also for 2. sing. beside *á-daḥ* = *á-dar* (for **á-dars*).

β. Some half-dozen instances have been noted, in the Saṃhitās, in which a suffixal *s* or *t* seems to have been retained instead of the preceding consonant; but they are probably all to be explained as due to analogical influence. They are:

1. the nominatives *sadha-mā́s* (beside *sadha-mā́d*) 'companion of the feast'; *ava-yā́s* 'sacrificial share', and *puro-ḍā́s* (acc. *puroḍā́śam*) 'sacrificial cake'. *Sadha-mā́s* may be due to the influence of nom. with phonetic *s* like *-mās* 'moon', beside inst. pl. *mād-bhis* (44 a 3). *Ava-yā́s*, in the only passage in which it occurs in the RV., has to be read as quadrisyllabic (also in AV.), i. e. as *ava-yā́jaḥ*, and is probably to be explained as a contraction which retains the living *-s* of the nom. (and not the prehistoric *s* of **-yāj-s*). *Puro-ḍā́s* (from *dāś-* 'worship'), occurring only twice in the RV., may be due to the influence of a frequent nom. like *draviṇo-dās* 'wealth-giver'. That the prehistoric nom. *-s* should in these three forms have survived in the linguistic consciousness of the Vedic poets, and as such have ousted the preceding consonant, which in all other analogous nominatives alone remains, is hardly conceivable[2]. The only reasonable explanation is to assume the analogical influence of the nom. *-s* which was in living use after vowels.

2. The four verbal preterite forms (*a-yās* (for **a-yāj-s*) beside *a-yāṭ*, 2. sing. aor. of *yaj-* 'sacrifice'; *srās* (AV.) = **a-srāj-s*, 2. sing. aor. of *sṛj-* 'emit'; *a-bhanas* (AV.) = **a-bhanak-s*, 2. sing. impf. of *bhañj-* 'break'; and *a-srat* (VS.) = **a-sras-t*, 3. sing. aor. of *sras-* 'fall') are the beginnings of the tendency (of which there are several other examples in the Brāhmaṇas)[3], to normalize the terminations, so as to have *-s* in 2. sing. and *-t* in 3. sing. This tendency is extended in the RV. from the *s* and *t* of 2. 3. sing. even to 1. sing. in the forms *a-kramīm* (beside *a-kramiṣam*) owing to *a-kram-īs*, *a-kram-īt*; and *vam* (for *var-am*) owing to 2. sing. *vaḥ* (for *var*), aor. of *vṛ-* 'cover'.

67. Rules of Sandhi.—The body of euphonic rules by which final consonants are assimilated to following initials and hiatus is avoided between final and initial vowels is called Sandhi in the Prātiśākhyas[4]. The editors of the Saṃhitā of the RV. have greatly obscured the true condition of the text with which they dealt by applying to it rules of euphonic combination which did not prevail at the time when the text was composed. Thus though the Sandhi between the verses of a hemistich is (excepting a few survivals from the older form of the text)[5] applied with greater stringency than elsewhere, the metre clearly shows that the end of the first verse of a hemistich constitutes a pause as much as the end of the last. Within the verse, moreover, Sandhi is, according to metrical evidence, not applied where the caesura occurs; *ná*, when it means 'like' (as opposed to *ná* 'not'), is never contracted with any following vowel, nor *ā́d* 'then' with a preceding *a*[6]; *ĭ* and *ŭ* before

[1] Cp. 43 a.

[2] Cp. WHITNEY 146 a; BLOOMFIELD, AJP. 3, 28 ff.; BARTHOLOMAE, KZ. 29, 578 ff.

[3] Cp. WHITNEY 555 a.

[4] RPr. II. 2. 7. 13; VII. 1; VPr. III. 2; APr. IV. 414.

[5] E. g. *manīṣā́* | *agníḥ* (I. 70[1]).

[6] In these instances there is a pause in

dissimilar initial vowels are hardly ever changed to the corresponding semivowels[1], and often remain uncontracted even before similar vowels[2]; the elision of *a* after *e o* is rare[3]; contraction is commonly avoided by the final vowel of monosyllabic words, and by an initial vowel followed by conjunct consonants[4]. Nevertheless, it may be said in a general way that the poets of the RV. show a tendency to avoid the meeting of vowels[5]. The divergences between the apparent and the real Sandhi which appear in the RV., decrease in the later Vedas, while the application of particular rules of Sandhi becomes more uniform[6].

a. External Sandhi, or that which applies between words in the sentence, is to a considerable extent identical with internal Sandhi, or that which applies within words. The most striking difference is, that in the latter consonants remain unchanged before verbal and nominal terminations beginning with vowels, semivowels, or nasals[7]. External Sandhi is on the whole followed in the formation of compounds, the divergences from it in the latter being merely survivals of an earlier stage of external Sandhi due to the closer connexion between members of a compound that renders them less liable than separate words to be affected by modifications of phonetic laws.

External Sandhi is to a considerable extent affected by the law of finals in pausā. Under that influence it avoids final aspirates and palatals. There are, however, in the treatment of final *n r*, and *s*, certain survivals which do not agree with the corresponding forms in pausā.

b. There are certain **duplicate forms** which were originally due to divergent euphonic conditions. Thus the tendency was to employ the dual ending *ā* before consonants, but *au* before vowels. Similarly, the word *sádā* 'always', was used before consonants, but *sádam* before vowels[8].

68. Lengthening of final vowels.—Final vowels as a rule remain unchanged before consonants. But *ă ĭ ŭ* are very frequently lengthened[9] before a single initial consonant[10] both in the metrical portion of the Saṃhitās and in the prose formulas of the Yajurveda; e. g. *śrudhī́ hávam* 'hear (our) call'. This practice includes examples in which the consonant is followed by a written *y* or *v*, to be pronounced, however, as *i* or *u*; e. g. *ádhā hy àgne* (IV. 10^{2a}) = *ádhā hí agne; abhī́ ṣv àryáḥ* (X. 59^{3a}) = *abhī́ ṣú aryáḥ*. The lengthening here appears to have arisen from an ancient rhythmic tendency of the language to pronounce long, between two short syllables, a final short vowel which was liable to be lengthened elsewhere as well[11]; this tendency being utilized by the poets of the Saṃhitās where metrical exigencies required a long syllable. Thus *ádha* 'then', appears as *ádhā* when a short syllable follows. Similarly *tú* 'but' generally becomes *tū́* before a short syllable; and *sú* 'well' nearly always becomes *sū́* between short syllables[12].

---

the sense; cp. OLDENBERG, Prolegomena 443, note 2; ARNOLD 122.

1 ARNOLD 125.

2 Op. cit. 124.

3 Op. cit. 127.

4 Thus *mā́psavaḥ* (IV. 47^d) must be read *mā́ ápsavaḥ*, but *mā́duvaḥ* (for *mā́ áduvaḥ*) remains (ibid.).

5 Cp. OLDENBERG 434 f.

6 Cp. BARTHOLOMAE in KZ. 29, 37, p. 511 f.

7 Thus *śakat, á-śaknuvan, śakra-, śákvan-* (from *śak-* 'be able'), in all which forms *g* would be required by external Sandhi.

8 Cp. WACKERNAGEL I, 309, bottom.

9 The Padapāṭha in these instances regularly gives the original unlengthened vowel.

10 Except in compounds, this lengthening disappears in the later language; there are, however, several survivals in the Brāhmaṇas; see AUFRECHT, Aitareya Brāhmaṇa 427; and cp. WACKERNAGEL I, 264 b.

11 This tendency survived in the post-Vedic language in compounds, in words (which followed the analogy of compounds) before suffixes beginning with consonants, and in reduplicative syllables.

12 Cp. WACKERNAGEL I, 266 b.

a. The short vowel regularly remains unchanged at the end of a verse[1] (even within a hemistich); and often before the caesura of a Triṣṭubh or Jagatī Pāda (even in terminations otherwise liable to be lengthened)[2].

b. The final vowel is not lengthened in 1. vocatives (except *vṛṣabhā* VIII. 45[38], and *hariyojanā* I. 61[16]); 2. datives in *-āya*; 3. nom. plur. neuter in *-i*; 4. verbal forms ending in *-i* and *-u* (excepting imperatives in *-dhi* and the 3. sing. *rákṣati* II. 26[4])[3]; 5. the prepositions *úpa*[4] and *ápa* (except *ápā vṛdhi* VII. 27[2]).

c. In some instances final vowels appear to be lengthened before vowels[5] or two consonants[6].

69. Contraction of similar vowels.—When a final *ă ĭ* or *ŭ*[7] is followed by corresponding initial *ă ĭ* or *ŭ*, contraction resulting in the long form of the respective vowel regularly takes place; e. g. *ihā́sti* = *ihá asti*; *índrā́* = *índra ā́*; *tvāgne* = *tvā agne*; *vī́dám* (VI. 9[9]) = *ví idám*;

a. The contraction of *ā* + *a* and of *ŭ* + *ŭ* occasionally does not take place even in the written text of the RV. both at the end of and within a Pāda; thus *manīṣā́* | *agníḥ* (I. 70[1]); *manīṣā́ abhí* (I. 101[7]); *pūṣā́ ásuraḥ* (V. 51[11]), *pūṣā́ abhi-* (VI. 50[5]), *pūṣā́ aviṣṭu* (X. 26[1 d]); *vīḷū́ utá* (I. 39[2]); *sú ūrdhvá(ḥ)* (VI. 24[9]); *sú ūtíbhiḥ* (I. 112[1–23]); the compound *suūtáyaḥ* (VIII. 47[1–18])[8].

b. On the other hand, in many instances where the contraction is written, the original vowels have to be restored in pronunciation with hiatus[9]. The restored initial in these instances is long by nature or position, and the preceding final if long must be shortened in pronunciation[10]; e. g. *cāsā́t* (I. 27[3]) = *ca āsā́t*; *cārcata* (I. 155[1]) = *ca arcata*; *mā́péḥ* = *mā́ āpéḥ*; *mā́psávaḥ* = *mā́ apsávaḥ*; *mṛḷatī́dṛ́śe* (IV. 57[1]) = *mṛḷati īdṛ́śe*; *yántíndavaḥ* (IV. 47[2]) = *yánti índavaḥ*; *bhavantūkṣáṇaḥ* (VI. 16[47]) = *bhavantu ukṣáṇaḥ*. After monosyllables, the hiatus is regular in the case of the written contractions *ī* and *ū*, especially when the monosyllables are *ví* and *hí*; e. g. *vī́ndra* (X. 32[2]) = *ví indra*; *hī́ndra* (I. 102[5]) = *hí indra*[11].

c. Duals in *ā ī ū* are regularly uncombined. Such *ī* and *ū* are usually written with hiatus in the Saṃhitā text; the dual *ā* always appears before *u*[12], but at the end of internal Pādas invariably coalesces in the written text.

70. Contraction of *ă* with dissimilar vowels.—1. When final *ă* is followed by *ĭ ŭ*, contraction takes place resulting in *e o*[13] respectively; e. g. *pitéva* = *pitā́ iva*; *ém* = *ā́ īm*; *óbhā* = *ā́ ubhā́*. When *ă* is followed by *ṛ*, contraction is never written in the RV. and VS.[14], but the metre shows that the combination is sometimes pronounced as *ar*, as is the case in the compound *saptarṣáyaḥ* 'the seven seers'[15].

---

1 Apparent exceptions are due to erroneous metrical division of Pādas by the editors of the Saṃhitās, or to mechanical repetition of formulas originally used in a different position in the verse. Thus *śrudhī* | *hávam* (I. 25[19]) appears in imitation of *śrudhī́ hávam* which is frequent at the beginning of a verse (II. 11[1], etc.). Cp. OLDENBERG 420 f.

2 See ZUBATY, Der Quantitätswechsel im Auslaute vedischer Wörter, Vienna Or. Journal 2, 315.

3 See ZUBATY, op. cit. 3, 89.

4 See OLDENBERG 399.

5 Op. cit. 60.

6 Cp. WACKERNAGEL I. 265 b, note.

7 There is no example of contracted *ṛ* in the Saṃhitās, as *ṛ ṛ* never meet; and in the RV. final *ṛ* never occurs (cp. above, p. 59, note [8]).

8 Cp. BENFEY, SV. XXXII f.; ROTH, Litteratur 67 f.

9 *ná* 'like', is never combined in pronunciation, see above 67; cp. ARNOLD 120.

10 Long vowels being regularly shortened before vowels; see OLDENBERG 465 f.

11 Cp. ARNOLD 124.

12 Op. cit. 120. Before other vowels, *āv*, the Sandhi form of *au*, the alternative dual ending, appears.

13 Because the long monophthongs *ē* and *ō* represent IE. *ăi* and *ău*.

14 The MS. does not contract either, but on the contrary often lengthens *ă* to *ā*, even where the metre requires contraction. Cp. WACKERNAGEL I, 267 a α, note.

15 See GRASSMANN, Wörterbuch p. VII.

a. In the RV. *ǎ+i* is once contracted to *ai-* in *práiṣayúr* (I. 120[5]) = *prá iṣayúḥ* (Pp.)[1]; in the SV. *ā+i* is once contracted to *ai-* in *áindra* = *ā́ indra* (I. 2. 1. 45); and in the AV. and VS. the preposition *ā* contracts with *ṛ* to *ār* in *ārti-* = *ā-ṛ́ti-* 'suffering', and *ā́rchatu* = *ā́-ṛcchatu*[2]. The last three instances are perhaps survivals of an older contraction. That *ā* is not otherwise contracted with *ĭ ŭ ṛ* to *ai au ār*, is doubtless to be accounted for by the previous shortening of *ā* in hiatus[3].

b. Occasionally *ǎ* followed by *i* remains uncontracted in the written text of the RV.; thus *jyā́ iyám* (VI. 75[3]); *píbā imám* (VIII. 17[1]); *raṇayā ihá* (VIII. 34[11])[4]. When *ā* is followed by *ṛ*, it is either shortened[5] or nasalized; e. g. *tátha ṛ-túḥ* for *táthā ṛ-*; *kadā́ṁ ṛtacid* (V. 39) = *kadā́ ṛ-*; *vibhvāṁ ṛbhúr* (IV. 33[3])[6] = *vibhvā ṛ-*; *vipanyā́ṁ*[7] | *ṛtásya* (IV. 1[12]) = *vipanyā́ ṛtásya*.

c. On the other hand, in many instances where the contraction *e* or *o* is written, the original simple vowels must be restored with hiatus; e. g. *éndrāgnī* (I. 108[4]) = *ā́ indrāgnī*; *subhágoṣā́ḥ* (I. 48[7]) = *subhágā uṣā́ḥ*[8].

2. Final *ǎ* contracts with a following *e* or *ai* to *ai*; and with *o* or *au* to *au*; e. g. *áibhiḥ* for *ā́ ebhiḥ*. But though the contraction is written, the original vowels must sometimes be restored; e. g. *áiṣu* (I. 61[16]) must be read *ā́ eṣu*.

a. Final *ǎ*, instead of being contracted with *e* and *o*, is in a few instances elided before those diphthongs; thus *tatār' evéd* (VII. 33[3]) = *tatāra evéd*; *iv' étayaḥ* (X. 91[4]) = *iva étayaḥ*; *aśvin' evét* (VII. 99) = *aśvinā | evét*; *yáth' ohiṣe* (VIII. 53) = *yáthā oh ṣe*; *úp' eṣatu* = *úpa eṣatu*[9]. An example of a compound with this elision seems to be *dáśoṇi-*[10] = *dáśa-oṇi-* 'having ten aids'.

b. Final *ǎ*, instead of being contracted with *e* is, in a few instances, nasalized before that diphthong; thus *aminantaṁ évaiḥ*[11] (I. 79[2]) for *-a é-*; *śāśadānāṁ éṣi* (I. 123[10]) for *-ā é-*; *upásthāṁ* | *ékā* (I. 35[6]) for *-ā é-*.

3. When *ǎ* remains after a final *y* or *s* has been dropped, it does not as a rule contract with the following vowel. Nevertheless such contraction is not infrequent in the Saṃhitās. In some instances it is actually written; thus *sártavā́jáu* (III. 32[6]) = Pp. *sártavái ājáu*; *vā́sáu* (V. 17[3]) = Pp. *vái asáu*; and the compound *rā́jeṣitam* (VIII. 46[28]) = Pp. *rā́jaḥ-iṣitam*; in the later Saṃhitās are found *kṛ́tyéti* (AV. X. 1[15]) = Pp. *kṛ́tyaḥ íti*; *pívopavasānanām* (VS. XXI. 43) = Pp. *pívaḥ-upavasanānām*[12].

In other instances the contraction, though not written, is required by the metre; thus *ta indra* (VII. 21[9]), Pp. *te indra*, must be read as *tendra*; *pṛthivyā́ antárikṣāt* (AV. IX. 1[9]), Pp. *pṛthivyā́ḥ*, as *pṛthivyā́ntárikṣāt*[13]; *goṣṭhá úpa* (AV. IX. 4[23]), Pp. *goṣṭhé úpa*, as *goṣṭhópa*.

a. There appear to be several other instances of such written contraction, which are however otherwise explained by the Padapāṭha; thus *rāyótá* (X. 93[10]) = *rāyé utá*,

1 Several instances of this contraction occur in B and later.

2 The TS. extends this contraction to prepositions ending in *a*: *úpārchati, avā́rchati*; see WHITNEY, APr. III. 47 f., TPr. III. 9 f. In the post-Vedic language this contraction was extended to all prepositions ending in *ǎ*.

3 Cp. BENFEY, GGA. 1846, p. 822.

4 The Pp. explains *píbā* and *raṇayā* as imperatives (*piba, raṇaya*); but the *ā* here may represent *-ās* of the subjunctive (cp. WACKERNAGEL I, p. 311 mid.). Occasionally *ǎ* remain uncontracted because the editors regarded them as representing *aḥ-e*, or *āḥ*, as in *ranta ityā́* (VII. 36[3]) *jmayā́ átra* (VII. 39[3]). Cp. RPr. II. 28 f.; BENFEY, SV. XXX f.; WACKERNAGEL I, 267 a β.

5 See p. 63, note 10; *ā* is shortened before *ṛ* in the AB.; see AUFRECHT's ed. 427.

6 *vibhvāṁ* occurs thus three times; see LANMAN 529.

7 In opposition to the Mss. MAX MÜLLER, RV[2]. reads *vipanyā́ṃ ṛtásya* because Sāyaṇa appears to favour that reading.

8 See ARNOLD, Vedic Metre 123.

9 This is a precursor of the post-Vedic rule by which the *ǎ* of a preposition before initial *e* and *o* of verbs (except *eti* etc. and *edhate* etc.) is elided.

10 Though the AV. has *páñcaudana-* = *páñca odana-* the elision of *a* before *-odana-* often takes place in the Sūtras and later.

11 The old hiatus is here treated as it would be at the end of an internal Pāda. The TS. (III. 1, 11[5]) retains the hiatus in the same verse without nasalization; cp. OLDENBERG 469 ff.

12 See WACKERNAGEL I, 268 b.

13 In the Paippalāda recension this contraction is actually written.

Pp. *rāyā́ utá*; *bhū́myopári* (X. 75[3]) = *bhū́myāḥ upári*, Pp. *bhū́myā upári*[1]. In a few of these the contraction must be removed as contrary to metre; thus *uṣa yāti* (III. 61[4]), Pp. *uṣáḥ yāti*, which means 'Dawn goes', should be read as *uṣá ā́ yāti*, as the sense requires 'Dawn comes', and the metre requires an additional syllable; *abhiṣṭipā́si* (II. 20[2]), Pp. *-pā́ asi*, should be read as *abhiṣṭipā́(ḥ) asi*; *vṛṣabhéva* (VI. 46[4]), Pp. *vṛṣabhā́ iva*[2], as *vṛṣabhā́(ḥ) iva*.

b. In a very few instances a final *m* is dropped after *a*, which then combines with a following vowel. This contraction is actually written in *durgáhaitát* (IV. 18[2]) for *durgáham etát* (but Pp. *durgáhā etát*)[3], and *sávanedám* (TS. I. 4. 44[2]) for *sávanam idám* (Pp. *sávanā idám*). Occasionally this contraction though not written is required by the metre; thus *rāṣṭrám ihá* (AV.) must be read *rāṣṭréhá*.

71. Final *ĭ* and *ŭ* before dissimilar vowels.—1. The final vowels *ĭ* and *ŭ*[4] before dissimilar initial vowels and before diphthongs are in the Saṃhitās **regularly written as *y* and *v***[5] respectively; e. g. ***práty āyam*** (I. 11[6]) = ***práti āyam***; *ā́ tv étā* (I. 5[1]) = *ā́ tú étā*; ***jánitry ajījanat*** (X. 134[1]) = ***jánitrī ajījanat***. The evidence of the metre, however, shows that this *y* or *v* nearly always has the syllabic value of *i* or *u*[6]; e. g. *vy ùṣā́ḥ* (I. 92[4]) must be read as *ví uṣā́ḥ*: ***vidátheṣv añján*** (I. 92[5]) as ***vidátheṣu añján***.

a. The final of disyllabic prepositions must, however, frequently be pronounced as a semivowel, especially before augmented forms; e. g. *adhyásthāḥ* (I. 49[2]); *ánv acāriṣam* (I. 23[23]); also *ánv ihi* (X. 53[6])[7].

b. In all the Saṃhitās the particle *u* following a consonant is written as *v* and pronounced as *u* before a vowel; e. g. *ávéd v indra* (I. 28[1])[8]; but the long form of the same particle occasionally remains unchanged in the RV. even after a consonant; e. g. *úd ū ayāṃ* (VI. 71[5]); *tám ū akṛṇvan* (X. 88[10]).

c. In RV. I—IX there are other instances of monosyllabic and disyllabic words at the end of which *y* and *v* are pronounced; but the only example of a trisyllabic word in which this occurs is *sī́vyatu* in *sī́vyatv ápaḥ* (II. 32[4]). In RV. X there are a few further examples; e. g. *devéṣv ádhi* (X. 121[8])[9].

d. The semivowel is regular in the compounds *ṛtv-ij-*, *gávy-ūti-*[10], *sv-ā́hā*, and *sv-id*[11].

2. Unchangeable *ī* and *ū*. a. The **dual** *ī* and *ū* never change to *y* or *v*; nor is the former ever prosodically shortened, though the latter sometimes is; e. g. *hárī* (⏑ –) *ṛtásya*; but *sādhū́* (– ⏑) *asmai* (II. 27[15]). The dual *ī* may remain even before *i*; e. g. *hárī iva*, *hárī indra*, *akṣī́ iva*; but the contraction is written in ***upadhī́va***, ***pradhī́va***, ***dámpatīva***, ***viśpátīva***, ***nṛpátīva*** (AV.), ***ródasīmé*** (VII. 90[3]) = ***ródasī imé*** 'these two worlds'. There are also several passages in which the contraction, though not written, must be read[12].

b. The rare **locatives** in *ī* and *ū*[13] (from stems in *ĭ* and *ŭ*) are regularly written unchanged in the Saṃhitā text of the RV., except *védy asyám* (II. 3[4]),

---

[1] Cp. WACKERNAGEL I, 268 a.

[2] In instances in which contraction with *iva* seems to take place, the existence of a byform *va* has to be taken into consideration; cp. GRASSMANN, Wörterbuch, column 221; WACKERNAGEL I, 268 a, note.

[3] Cp. DELBRÜCK, Verbum 67, end.

[4] In the RV. *ṛ* is never final, and I doubt whether any example can be quoted from the other Saṃhitās in which it is followed by an initial vowel.

[5] The Sandhi which changes a vowel to the semivowel is called *kṣaipra* 'gliding', in the Prātiśākhyas; cp. RPr. II. 8; III. 7; VII. 5.

[6] The long vowel being regularly shortened; cp. OLDENBERG 465.

[7] WACKERNAGEL I, 271 b; OLDENBERG 438, note, ZDMG. 44, 326 note; ARNOLD, Vedic Metre 125.

[8] The TS. has *uv* for *v*. Elsewhere also *iy* and *uv* are sometimes written for *i* and *u*; e. g. *suv-itá-* = *su-itá-* 'accessible'; hence the pronunciation may have been *iy*, *uv*; cp. WACKERNAGEL I, 270 c, 271 a.

[9] See ARNOLD, Vedic Metre 125.

[10] If the analysis of BR., *gávi-ūti-*, is correct; the Pp. divides *gó- yūti-*.

[11] See ARNOLD, Vedic Metre 125.

[12] Cp. WACKERNAGEL I, 270 b, note. Here we have probably not contracted forms with *iva*, but the dual *ī* + *va*, the byform of *iva*.

[13] The vowels which regularly remain unchanged are called *pragṛhya*, 'separated', by the native phoneticians; see RPr. I. 16 etc.; VPr. I. 92 etc.; APr. I. 73 etc. They are indicated as such in the Pp. by an appended *iti*. The particle *u* is indicated as *pragṛhya* in the Pp. of RV. and AV. by its nasalized form *ūṃ* (nasalization being employed to avoid hiatus: see above 66, 1).

where, however, the vowel must be pronounced (⏓ ⏑ – –). The vowels here (unlike the dual *ī*) seem always to be treated as prosodically short[1].

c. The final *ī* of **other cases** also occasionally remains unchanged; thus the nominatives *pṛthivī́*, *pṛthujráyī*, *samrā́jñī* and the instrumental *suśámī* sometimes retain their *ī*, and the inst. *ūtī́* frequently does so[2].

72. **Final e and o.—1. a. Before a.** The diphthongs *e* and *o* remain unchanged before an initial *a*. This *a* is often not written in the Saṃhitās[3], being dropped in about three-fourths of its occurrences in the RV. and in about two-thirds in the AV.[4]; but the evidence of metre shows that, in 99 instances out of 100 in the RV., and in about 80 in the AV. and the metrical parts of the YV., it is, whether written or not, to be read, and at the same time shortens the preceding diphthong to *ĕ* or *ŏ*[5]. In *víśve devā́so aptúraḥ* (I. 3[8]) the *a* is both written and pronounced; in *sūnávé* | *'gne* (I. 1[9]) it must be restored: *sūnáve* | *ágne*[6]. The exceptional treatment of *e* in *stótava ambyàm* (VIII. 72[5]), for *stótave ambyàm*, indicates that the Sandhi of *e* and *o* before *a* was originally the same as before other vowels[7]. But their unchanged form, as before consonants, gained the day, because the short close *ă*, when coming immediately after them in their character of monophthongs, would have a natural tendency to disappear and thus leave a consonant to follow.

b. **Before other vowels.** The diphthongs *e* and *o* before any vowels but *ă* would naturally become *ay* and *av*, as being originally = *ăi* and *ău*, and as having the form of *ay* and *av* within a word. But *ay* regularly drops the *y*; e. g. *agna ihá* (I. 22[10]); *av* on the other hand generally retains the *v*, dropping it before *ŭ*[8]; e. g. *vā́yav ā́ yāhi* (I. 2[1]); but *vā́ya ukthébhir* (I. 2[2]).

2. **Unchangeable e. a.** The *e* of the **dual nom. acc.** f. n. of *a*-stems, e. g. *úbhe* 'both', is regularly uncontracted (*pragṛhya*), because it consists of *a* + the dual *ī*[9].

b. Under the influence of this nominal dual *e*, the **verbal dual** *e*[10] of the 2. 3. present and perfect middle, e. g. *váhethe* 'ye two bring', *bruvāte* 'they two speak', *āś-āthe* 'ye two have obtained', come to be uncontractable, though the *e* is nearly always prosodically shortened; e. g. *yuñjāthe apáḥ* (I. 151[4]); but *parimamnā́thĕ asmā́n* (VII. 93[6]).

c. The *e* of the **locative** *tvé* 'in thee', is uncontractable. Under its influence the other pronominal forms *asmé* 'us', and *yuṣmé* 'you', are also always treated as *pragṛhya* by the Saṃhitā as well as the Padapāṭha; it is,

---

1 Cp. OLDENBERG 456, note; WACKERNAGEL I, 270 b.

2 Cp. op. cit. I, 270 b, note. Such forms, in which the absence of contraction is only occasional, are not indicated by *iti* in the Pp.

3 This form of Sandhi is in the Prātiśākhyas called *abhinihita* 'elided'; RPr. II. 13 etc.; VPr. I. 114, 125; APr. III. 54; TPr. II. 8.

4 See WHITNEY 135 c.

5 Cp. OLDENBERG 435 f., 453 ff., ZDMG. 44, 331 ff.; WACKERNAGEL I, p. 324.

6 The few instances (70 out of 4500) of the elision of *a* in the RV. are the forerunners of the invariable practice of post-Vedic Sandhi.

7 Internally the original Sandhi of the compound *gó-agra-* must have been *gáv-agra-*; cp. WACKERNAGEL I, p. 325, note.

8 There are a few survivals of *ay*; e. g. *táy ā́* (MS. I. 1[1]) = *tá ā́* (TS.); cp. TPr. X. 23; OLDENBERG 447 ff. In the MS., the K., and Mantras occurring in the Mānavasūtras, unaccented *a* for *e* before an accented initial vowel is lengthened; e. g. *ā́ dadhā iti*.

9 See above 71, 2. A dual *e* once appears contracted in *dhiṣṇyemé* (VII. 72[3]), which, however, should probably be read uncontracted as *dhiṣṇye imé*. The *-eva* which occurs several times (I. 186[4] etc) and looks like a contraction of the dual *e* with *iva*, in reality probably stands for the dual *e* + *va*, the byform of *iva*; cp. WACKERNAGEL I, p. 317, note, top.

10 There was originally no difference between this dual *e* and any other *e* in middle forms, such as that of the dual *-vahe*, the singular *-te*, and the plural *-ante*.

however, doubtful whether they were so treated in the original text of the RV.[1].

3. **Unchangeable *o*.** a. When *o* is the result of combining the final *ă* of particles **with *u*** (which itself is often unchangeable)[2], it is *pragṛhya*; thus *ó* (= *á u*), *átho* (= *átha u*), *utó* (= *utá u*), *mó* (= *mā́ u*).

b. Following this analogy, the **vocative** in *o* of *u*-stems is sometimes treated as *pragṛhya* in the Saṃhitā of the TS.; e. g. *pito ā́* (TS. v. 7. 2[4]). It is regularly so treated in the Padapāṭhas of the RV., AV., VS., TS. (but not SV.). Thus in *vā́yav ā́* (I. 2[1]), *vā́ya ukthébhir* (I. 2[2]), *vā́yo táva* (I. 2[3]) the vocative is equally given in the Padapāṭha as *vā́yo íti*.

73. **The diphthongs *ai* and *au*.**—The diphthongs *ai* and *au* are treated throughout in the same way as *e* and *o* before vowels other than *a*. Thus *ai* is regularly written *ā* (having dropped the *y* of *āy*); e. g. *tásmā akṣí* (I. 116[16]); *tásmā índrāya* (I. 4[9]). On the other hand, *au* is generally written *āv*, but always *ā* before *ŭ* in the RV. and VS.; e. g. *tā́v ā́* (I. 2[5]); *tā́v indrāgnī* (I. 108[3]); but *sujihvā́ úpa* (I. 13[8]). In the AV. *ā* appears before *u* in *pā́dā ucyete* (AV. XIX. 6[5]). In the MS. *ā* appears before other vowels also[3].

74. **Euphonic combination of consonants.** — The Sandhi of final consonants, generally speaking, starts from the form which they assume in pausā. Thus an aspirate first loses its aspiration; the palatal *c* becomes *k*; *j ś h* become *k* or *ṭ*[4]; and of a group of consonants the first alone remains. Final *n* is, however, to a great extent differently treated from what it is in pausā; and the Sandhi of *s* and *r* is, for the most part, based not on *ḥ*, their form in pausā, but on the original letter.

A final consonant is assimilated[5] in quality[6] to the following initial, becoming voiceless before a voiceless consonant, and voiced before a voiced sound[7]; e. g. *tát satyám* (I. 1[5]) for *tád*; *yát tvā* (I. 15[10]) for *yád*; *havyavā́ḍ juhvā̀syaḥ* (I. 12[6]), through *-vā́ṭ* for *-vā́h*; *gámad vā́jebhiḥ* (I. 5[3]) for *gámat*; *arvā́g rā́dhaḥ* (I. 9[5]) for *arvā́c* through *arvā́k*.

a. A final media before a nasal may become the nasal of its own class. There seems to be no certain instance of this in the RV.; *cakrán ná* (X. 95[12. 13]), however, probably stands for *cakrát ná*, though the Pp. has *cakrán ná*. This assimilation is regular in some compounds; e. g. *ṣáṇ-ṇavati-* '96' for *ṣáṭ-navati-*. From here it penetrated into internal Sandhi; e. g. *ṣaṇ-ṇā́m*.

b. Assimilation not only in quality, but also largely in the place of articulation occurs in the Sandhi of final *m*, of the final dentals[8] *t n s*, and of final *r* (under the influence of *s*).

75. **Euphonic combination of final *m*. — 1. Before vowels,** final *m* remains unchanged; e. g. *agním īḷe* (I. 1[1]). In a very few instances, however, the *m* is dropped, and the vowels then contract. This Sandhi is mostly indicated by the metre only: it is very rarely written[9], as in *durgáhaitát*

1 Cp. OLDENBERG 455, note.

2 Cp. above 71, 1 b.

3 See GARBE, GGA. 1882, 117 f.; WACKERNAGEL I, 274; OLDENBERG, ZDMG. 60, 755—758 (Duale auf *-ā* und *-au*).

4 Some compounds, however, preserve survivals of an earlier phase of Sandhi; e. g. *viś-páti-* 'lord of the house'; *viśpálā-* N., not *viṭ-*; *nabh-rā́j-* (MS.) 'cloud-king', not *nab-rā́j-*. Cp. L. v. SCHROEDER, ed. of MS. 1, p. XVI.

5 Final *ṭ* before vowels becomes *ḷ* in the RV., not *ḍ* as later; e. g. *báḷ itthā́*, for *báṭ*.

6 Within a word a voiced consonant is not necessary before vowels, semivowels, and nasals.

7 Some scholars think that the 3. sing. impv., e. g. *bhávatu* represents *bhavat u* for original *bhavad u*, the *t* being retained owing to the influence of the innumerable forms of the 3. sing. with *-t*, *-ti*, *-te*, etc. (cp. WACKERNAGEL I, 276 b); but this is doubtful; DELBRÜCK, Altindische Syntax 517 ff., thinks it may originally have been *bháva* + *tú* (particle); cp. IF. 18, 71.

8 An example of a final guttural becoming a dental before a dental occurs in TS. I. 2. 7[1], where *samyát te* stands for *samyák te*. There are a few other examples in B. passages of the TS.; see WACKERNAGEL I, 277 b.

9 See above 70, 3 b.

(IV. 18[2]) for *durgáham etát*, and it is never analysed by the Padapāṭha in this way. It may perhaps have started from the analogy of the doublet *túbhya* beside *túbhyam* 'to thee'[1].

2. **Before mutes**, final *m* is regularly assimilated[2], becoming the corresponding nasal, and before *n* similarly becoming *n*. The Mss. and printed texts, however, represent this assimilated *m* by the Anusvāra sign; e. g. *bhadráṃ kariṣyási* (I. 1[6]) for *bhadráṅ kariṣyási*; *bhadráṃ no* (X. 20[1]) for *bhadrán no*. This actual change of *m* to *n* before dentals led to some errors in the Pada text; e. g. *yán ni-pā́si* (IV. 11[6]), analysed as *yát* instead of *yám*; *ávi-venan tám* (IV. 24[6]), analysed as *ávi-venan* instead of *ávi-venam* (cp. IV. 25[3]).

3. **Before r ś ṣ s and h**[3], final *m* becomes Anusvāra (*ṃ*); e. g. *hótāraṃ ratnadhā́tamam* (I. 1[1]); *várdhamānaṃ své* (I. 1[9]); *mitráṃ huve* (I. 2[7]). From its original use before sibilants and *h*, Anusvāra came to be employed before the semivowel also[4]. A compound like *sam-rā́j-* 'overlord' shows that *m* originally remained unchanged in Sandhi before *r*.

4. **Before y l v**, final *m* is assimilated as nasalized *y̐ l̐ v̐*. The TPr.[6], however, allows Anusvāra beside these, while the APr. even requires Anunāsika before *y* and *v*; and the printed texts regularly use Anusvāra; e. g. *sáṃ yudhí* (I. 8[3]); *yajñáṃ vàṣṭu* (I. 30[10]). Forms like *yamyámāna-* 'extended' and *ápamlukta-* 'concealed' show that final *m* originally remained unchanged in Sandhi before *y* and *l*[5]; and forms like *jaganvā́n*, from *gam-* 'go', point to its having at one time become *n* before *v* in Sandhi.

76. **Euphonic combination of final t.** — 1. Before *l*, final *t*[6] becomes fully assimilated as *l*; e. g. *áṅgāl lómnaḥ* (X. 163[6]) for *áṅgāt lómnaḥ*.

2. Before palatals (including *ś*)[7] final *t*[1] becomes palatal[8]; e. g. *tác cákṣuḥ* (VII. 66[16]) for *tád cákṣuḥ*; *rohíc chyāvā́* (I. 100[16]) for *rohít śyāvā́*; and in a compound *yātayáj-jana-* 'marshalling men', for *yātayát-jana-*.

77. **Euphonic combination of final n. — 1. Before vowels.** Final *n*[9], a. if preceded by a short vowel, is doubled[10]; e. g. *áhann áhim* (II. 11[5]) for *áhan*. The final *n* is here chiefly based on original *ns* or *nt*. Though it is always written double[11], the evidence of metre shows that this rule was only partially applied in the RV.[12].

b. If preceded by a long vowel, it becomes within[13] a Pāda in the RV. *m̐* after *ā*[14], but *m̐r* after *ī ū ṝ*[15]; e. g. *sárgām̐ iva*, for *sárgān*; *paridhī́m̐r áti*, for *paridhī́n*; *abhī́śūm̐r iva*, for *abhī́śūn*; *nṝ́m̐r abhí*, for *nṝ́n*. This Sandhi was caused by the *n* having originally been followed by *s*[16]; e. g. *vṛ́kān* originally

1 Cp. WACKERNAGEL I, 283 a, note.

2 Op. cit. I, 283, b α.

3 Op. cit. I, 283 d.

4 In the post-Vedic language Anusvāra came to be allowed before mutes and nasals also.

5 Cp. WACKERNAGEL I, 283 c.

6 Representing *th d dh* also, if they occur.

7 In the MS. *t* anomalously becomes *ñ*, instead of *c*, before *ś*; see L. v. SCHROEDER, ZDMG. 33, 185; ed. of MS. I, p. XXIX. On the aspiration of *ś* in this Sandhi, see below 80 a.

8 Final dentals never come into contact with initial cerebrals in the Saṃhitās.

9 This rule applies to final guttural *ṅ* also; e. g. *kīdṛ́ṅṅ i-* (X. 108[3]), cp. LANMAN 490; *híṅṅ akṛṇot* (I. 164[28]) for *híṅ a-*.

10 The compound *vṛṣaṇ-aśvá-* 'having stallions as steeds', forms an exception.

11 For various explanations of this doubling, see WACKERNAGEL I, 279 a (p. 330).

12 Cp. OLDENBERG 424 f., 429 ff.

13 At the end of a Pāda, *-ān -īn -ūn* remain unchanged (as being in pausā) before a vowel. For passages in which *-ān* is unchanged within a Pāda, see below and OLDENBERG 428.

14 In the MS. and K., *-ām̐* is shortened to *-am̐*; e. g. *asmám̐ aśnotu* for *asmā́n*. Cp. v. SCHROEDER, ed. of the MS. I, p. XXIX.

15 *ṝn* becomes *ṝm̐r* only once (V. 54[15]), remaining unchanged elsewhere because two *r* sounds are avoided in the same syllable (see below 79).

16 For examples of this Sandhi applied to nominatives in *-ān*, see LANMAN 506 A, note (*mahā́n*), 512 (*-vān*), 514 (*-yān*), 517 (*-mān*); for accusatives, 346.

**vṛkans*[1]; *mahā́n* for **mahā́nts*; *á-yān*, 3. sing. aor. for **á-yān-st* (1. sing. *á-yāṃsam*)[2]. The *n* became Anusvāra (or Anunāsika) before this *s*, which was treated in exactly the same way as when it followed an unnasalized vowel (*ās* becoming *ā*, but *īs*, *ūs*, *ṝs* becoming *īr*, *ūr*, *ṝr*).

a. The *ān* of the 3. pl. subjunctive (originally *ānt*), however, remains unchanged before vowels within a Pāda, obviously owing to the *-t* which at one time followed. There happen to be only five occurrences of this form under the conditions required: *ā́ vahān āśú* (I. 84^{18}); *ghóṣān úttarā* (III. 33^{8}); *sphurā́n ṛjipyám* (VI. 67^{11}); *gácchān íd* (VIII. 79^{5}); *gacchān úttarā* (X. 10^{10}) 3.

2. Before consonants. Final *n* remains unchanged before all gutturals and labials (including *m*), as well as before voiced dentals (including *n*). It is, however, liable to be changed before the following sounds:

a. Before *p*, final *n*, when etymologically = *ns*, sometimes becomes *ṃḥ*; thus *nṝ́ṃḥ pāhi* (VIII. 84^{3})[4]; *nṝ́ṃḥ pā́tram* (I. 121^{1}).

b. Before all palatals that occur it becomes palatal *ñ*; e. g. *ūrdhvā́ñ carā́thāya* (I. 36^{14}) for *ūrdhvā́n*; *tā́ñ juṣethām* (V. 51^{6}) for *tā́n*; *vajriñ chnathihi* (I. 63^{5}) for *vajrin śnathihi*[5]; *devā́ñ chlókaḥ* (X. 12^{5}) for *devā́n ślókaḥ*.

Before *c*, however, the palatal **sibilant** is sometimes inserted[6] in the RV., the *n* then becoming Anusvāra. This insertion occurs **only when** the sibilant is **etymologically justified** (that is, in the nom. sing. and acc. pl. masc.) almost exclusively (though not invariably) before *ca* and *cid*; thus *anuyājā́ṃś ca* (X. 51^{8}), *amenā́ṃś cid* (V. 31^{2})[7]. In the other Saṃhitās the inserted sibilant becomes commoner, occurring even where it is not etymologically justified (that is, in the 3. pl. impf., and the voc. and loc. of *n*-stems)[8].

c. Before dental *t*[9], final *n* usually remains; but the dental sibilant is sometimes inserted in the RV., the *n* then becoming Anusvāra. This insertion, however, occurs in the RV. only when it is etymologically justified; it is commoner in the other Saṃhitās[10], where it appears even when not etymologically justified.

d. Before *y r v h*, final *n* as a rule remains unchanged; but *-ān*, *-īn*, *-ūn* sometimes become *-ām̐*[11], *-īm̐r*, *-ūm̐r*, as before vowels; e. g. *-annām̐ rayivṝ́dhaḥ* (VII. 91^{3}) for *-annān*; *dadvā́m̐ vā* (X. 132^{3}) for *dadvā́n*; *paṇī́m̐r hatam* (I. 184^{2}) for *paṇī́n*; *dásyūm̐r yónau* (I. 63^{4}) for *dásyūn*.

e. Before *l*, final *n* always becomes nasalized *l̐*[12]; e. g. *jigīvā́l̐ lakṣám* (II. 12^{4}).

f. Before the dental sibilant, final *n* remains; but a transitional *t*[13] may be inserted; e. g. *ahant sáhasā* (I. 80^{10}) 'he slew with might'; *tā́n sám* may also be written *tā́nt sám*[14]. In the former example the *t* is organic; from such survivals it spread to cases where it was not justified. A similar insertion may take place before *ś*; that is, *vajrin śnathihi* may become *vajriñ śnathihi* or *vajriñ chnathihi* (through *vajriñc śnathihi* for *vajrint śnathihi*)[15].

---

1 Cp. Cretic λύκονς.

2 In all the other Saṃhitās the pause forms *-ān -īn -ūn -ṝn* predominate. In the post-Vedic language they became the only allowable forms.

3 Cp. OLDENBERG 428.

4 The MS. (II. 13^{11}) has *nṝ́m̐ṣ pāhi*.

5 For examples of nominatives with this Sandhi, see LANMAN 506 A, note, 512 (top), 517.

6 Op. cit., 506 A, note, and 514.

7 Op. cit., 512.

8 There are no examples of the inserted sibilant before *ch* in the Saṃhitās. In the post-Vedic language a sibilant is invariably inserted after *n* before all voiceless palatals, cerebrals, and dentals.

9 Neither *th* nor *ṭ ṭh* occur in the Saṃhitās after final *n*.

10 Cp. LANMAN 516 A, note.

11 For *dadhanvā́m̐ yáḥ* of the RV. (IX. 107^{1}) and SV., the VS. (XIX. 2) has *dadhanvā́ yáḥ*.

12 As *m* does before *l*; see above 75, 4.

13 Before *s* a transitional *k* may similarly be inserted after a final *ṅ*; e. g. *pratyáṅ sá* may also be written *pratyáṅk sá*.

14 See LANMAN 506 A, note, and 346.

15 Cp. WACKERNAGEL I, 282, note.

78. Euphonic combination of final *s*. — 1. Before voiced sounds. a. Final *s* after all vowels except *ă̄*, assumes its voiced form *r* before all vowels and voiced consonants[1]; e. g. *ṛ́ṣibhir ī́dyo* (I. 1^{2}) for *ṛ́ṣibhis; agnír hótā* (I. 1^{5}) for *agnís; paribhū́r ási* (I. 1^{4}) for *paribhū́s; nū́tanair utá* (I. 1^{2}) for *nū́tanais*.

The *s* doubtless became *r* through an older transitional voiced cerebral *ẓ*[2], as is shown by the Avesta, e. g. in *dužita-* = *dur-ita-*[3].

b. Final *s* **after *ă̄*** must originally have become *z* before voiced sounds. But *āz* drops the sibilant before vowels and voiced consonants, while *az* drops it before vowels except *a*[4], but becomes *o*[5] before voiced consonants[6] and *a*; thus *sutā́ imé* (I. 3^{4}) for *sutā́s; víśvā ví* (I. 3^{12}), for *víśvās; khya á* for *khyas* (I. 4^{3}); *no áti* (I. 4^{3}) for *nas; índavo vām* (I. 2^{1}) for *índavas*.

2. Before voiceless consonants. a. Before **the palatals *c, ch, ś*** final *s* becomes the palatal sibilant *ś*[7]; e. g. *devā́ś cakṛmá* (X. 37^{12}).

b. Before the dental *t*[9], final *s* following *ă̄* always remains; e. g. *yás te* (I. 4^{4}); *médhirās téṣām* (I. 11^{7}). After *ĭ̄ ŭ̄*[10], it remains as a rule; e. g. *áṇvībhis tánā* (I. 3^{4}). But *s* becomes *ṣ*, which cerebralizes the following *t* to *ṭ*: *α.* regularly in compounds[11] in all the Saṃhitās; e. g. *dúṣ-ṭara-* 'insuperable' for *dús-tara-* (but *rajas-túr-* 'traversing the air'); *β.* often in external Sandhi in the RV. This occurs chiefly, and in the independent passages of the other Saṃhitās[12] only, before pronouns; e. g. *agníṣ ṭe; krátuṣ ṭám;* otherwise it occurs occasionally only in the RV.; thus *niṣ-ṭatakṣúr* (X. 31^{7}); *gobhíṣ ṭarema* (X. 42^{10}); *nákiṣ ṭanū́ṣu* (VIII. 20^{12})[13].

c. Before *k kh p ph*, final *s* as a rule becomes Visarjanīya (its pause

---

1 When final *s* becomes *r* before *r*, it is treated like an original *r*, being dropped after lengthening the preceding vowel.

2 This *ẓ* would be the voiced cerebral corresponding to the voiceless *ṣ* which appears before voiceless consonants (e. g. in *duṣkha-*).

3 This *ẓ* would account for the Sandhi of some Vedic compounds formed with *dus-* 'ill': *dū-ḍábha-, dū-ḍáś-, dū-ḍhí-, dū-ṇáśa-, dū-ṇā́śa-*, beside *dur-niyántu-*. It may possibly also account for the forms *svádhitīva* (V. 8^{7}), for *svádhitiẓ va* (Pp. *svádhitir-iva*), and *urv iva* (IX. 96^{15}), where the metre requires *urū́ va* (Pp. *urú-iva*); the cerebral being dropped after lengthening the preceding vowel.

4 In the MS. unaccented *-a* for *-as* is lengthened before an accented vowel; e. g. *látā indraḥ*. In TS. II. 4. 7^{1} *ar* for *a* in *jinvár āvṛ́t* is merely a bad reading (MS. II. 4^{7} *jinva rāvát*); cp. above p. 33, note 13.

5 In the compound *ánar-viś-* (I. 121^{7}) 'having a wain as his abode', *ar* instead of *o* (cp. *ánas-vant-* 'possessed of a wain)' is perhaps due to the influence of *vanar-*, beside *vanas-* and *vana-*. On a still more anomalous compound of the same word, *anaḍ-vā́h-* 'drawer of a cart', 'bull', cp. WACKERNAGEL 1, p. 339, top. The vowel *ā* appears instead of *o* in *pracetā | rā́jan* (I. 24^{14}) 'O wise king' (*praceto rā́jan* in the same verse, TS. I. 5. 113), probably owing to the voc. *pracetaḥ*, as it would have been pronounced at the end of a Pāda in the original text, having been misunderstood as a voc. in *-tar* (from a stem in *-tṛ*), which would become *-tā* before *r*.

6 The starting point of this Sandhi was probably the treatment of *az* before voiced dentals, where the sibilant was dropped and the preceding vowel lengthened to *e* or *o*. The latter finally carried the day, *e* surviving only in *sū́re duhitā́* (I. 34^{5}); cp. BARTHOLOMAE, BB. 15, 1 f.; WACKERNAGEL 1, p. 338.

7 *Só cit* does not stand for *sáḥ cit*, but for *sá u cit*.

8 If initial cerebral mutes had existed in the Saṃhitās, final *s* would doubtless have become the cerebral sibilant *ṣ* before them.

9 No example of initial *th* occurs in the Saṃhitās; but the internal Sandhi of *sthā-* 'stand', in *ti-ṣṭhati* (for *ti-stha-ti*) shows that initial *th* would have been treated in the same way as *t*.

10 Final *ṛs* never occurs; *ṝs*, occurring only once in the RV., remains unchanged in *mātṝ́s trī́n* (I. 164^{10}).

11 The only exception in the RV. is *cátus-triṃśat* 'thirty-four', doubtless due to the avoidance of the combination *ṣṭr*.

12 The TS. also has *niṣ ṭap-* 'heat'. On the usage of the SV., see BENFEY, SV. p. XLIII; on that of the AV., see WHITNEY, APr. II. 84.

13 Owing to the far more numerous occurrences of *ă̄s* before *t*, combined with the disinclination to change the following initial, the retention of *s* after *ĭ̄ ŭ̄* gradually gained ground and finally prevailed in the post-Vedic language, even in compounds.

form), or Jihvāmūlīya (*ẖ*) before the gutturals and Upadhmānīya (*ḫ*) before the labials; e. g. *índraḥ páñca* (I. 7[9]). But *ăs* remains and *ĭs ŭs ṝs* become *ĭṣ ŭṣ ṝṣ*[1]: *a.* regularly in **compounds** in all the Saṃhitās; e. g. *paras-pā́-* 'far-protecting'; *haviṣ-pā́-* 'drinking the offering'; *duṣ-kṛ́t-* 'evil-doing'; *duṣ-pád-* 'evil-footed'. The general rule, however, applies in the following compounds: *puráḥ-prasravaṇa-* 'streaming forth'; *chándaḥ-pakṣa-* (AV.) 'borne on the wings of desire'; *śréyaḥ-keta-* (AV.) 'striving after superiority'; *sadyaḥ-krī́-* (AV.) 'bought on the same day'; *bahiḥ-paridhí* (TS.) 'outside the enclosure'; *itáḥ-pradāna-* (TS.) 'offering from hence (= this world)'.

The repeated (or *āmreḍita*) compounds also follow the general rule, doubtless from a desire to change the repeated word as little as possible; thus *pū́rvaḥ-pūrvo* 'each first'; *paráḥ-paraḥ* 'always without' (AV.); *páruṣaḥ-paruṣas* (VS.) 'from every knot'; *púruṣaḥ-puruṣo* (TS.) 'every man'; *páruḥ-paruḥ* (TS.) 'joint by joint', but *páruṣ-parur* also in RV. AV. TS.

β. Often in **external Sandhi** in the RV.[2]; e. g. *divás pári* (X. 45[1]) 'from the sky'; *pátnīvatas kṛdhi* (I. 14[7]) 'make them possessed of wives'; *dyáuṣ pitā́* (IV. 1[10]) 'Father Heaven'.

d. **Before mutes immediately followed by *s* or *ṣ*,** final *s* regularly becomes Visarjanīya; e. g. *śatákratuḥ tsárat* (VIII. 1[11]); *ubhayataḥ-kṣṇúr* (TS.) 'two-edged'. Occasionally the sibilant disappears, as in *ádha kṣárantīr* (VII. 34[2])[3].

e. 1. **Before a simple sibilant** final *s* is either assimilated or becomes Visarjanīya; e. g. *vaś śivátamo* or *vaḥ śivátamo* (X. 9[1]); *dévīṣ ṣaḷ* or *dévīḥ ṣaḷ* (X. 128[5]); *nas sapátnā* or *naḥ sapátnā* (X. 128[9]). Assimilation is undoubtedly the original Sandhi[4] and is required by some of the Prātiśākhyas[5]; but the Mss. usually employ Visarjanīya, and European editions regularly follow this practice[6].

a. The sibilant disappears in the compounds *barhi-ṣád-* 'sitting on the sacrificial litter'; *dyáu-saṃśita-* (AV.) 'sky-sharpened'; and, after lengthening the preceding *a*, *ayā-śayā́ rajā-śayā́ harā-śayā́* (TS. I. 2. 11[2] = MS. I. 27) for *ayaś-*, *rajaś-*, *haraś-*.

2. Before a sibilant immediately followed by a voiceless mute, a **final sibilant is dropped**; e. g. *mandíbhi stómebhir* (I. 9[3]) for *mandíbhis*; *mitha-spṛ́dhyā* (I. 166[9]) for *mithas-*; *du-ṣṭuti-* 'ill praise' for *duṣ-*[7]. The omission is required by the Prātiśākhyas of the RV., VS., TS., and is the practice of all the Mss. of the MS.

3. Before a sibilant immediately followed by a nasal or semivowel, a final **sibilant is optionally dropped**; thus *kṛta śrávaḥ* (VI. 58[3]), beside which (though the Pp. reads *kṛta*) the MS. reads *kṛtaḥ śrávaḥ*[8]; *ni-svarám* (VII. 1[7]) for *nis-svarám* 'noiseless' (Pp., however, *ni-svarám*).

79. **Euphonic combination of final *r*.** — As *ḥ* is the pause form of both *r* and *s*, a certain amount of mutual contamination appears in their Sandhi; *r*, however, suffers much more in this respect than *s*. Since both *s* and *r* when preceded by *ĭ ŭ* have the same natural Sandhi, it is in a few

1 This treatment of final *s* before voiceless gutturals and labials, which is parallel to that before *t*, was doubtless the original from of sentence Sandhi.

2 *adó pito* (I. 187[7]) is probably only an apparent exception, as *adó* = *áda u*, not *ádas* (Pp. *adáḥ*); the Paippalāda recension of the AV., however, has *ádaṣ pito*, for *adás*.

3 Though the Pp. reads *ádha*, the PB. in quoting the verse has *ádhaḥ*; see OLDENBERG 369, note 1.

4 Cp. WHITNEY on APr. II. 40.

5 Cp. WACKERNAGEL I, p. 342, top.

6 In *párītó ṣiñcata* (X. 107[1]), *itó* probably = *itá u* (Pp. *pári itáḥ*).

7 The omission was doubtless due to the fact that it made no difference to the pronunciation. Hence probably the wrong analysis of *iṣastút* by the Pp. as *iṣaḥ-stút*, instead of *iṣa-stút*, as in *iṣá-vant-* (cp. BR.).

8 Cp. BOLLENSEN, ZDMG. 45, 24; PISCHEL, Vedische Studien I, 13.

instances uncertain which was the original sound. Thus it is somewhat doubtful whether the *-uḥ* of the abl. gen. sing. of *ṛ*-stems and of the 3. pl. act. of past tenses represents original *us* or *ur*. In the verbal form, the *r* in the corresponding middle termination of the perfect, *-re*, seems to decide in favour of *ur*[1].

1. a. **Before vowels and voiced consonants** (except *r* itself) *r* remains not only when preceded by *ĭ ŭ*[2], but by *ă* also[3]; e. g. *gír | iṣá* (I. 117[1]); *pūr devatrā* (VII. 52[1]); *prātár agníḥ* (V. 18[1]); *púnar naḥ* (X. 57[5]); *svàr druhó* (II. 35[6])[4].

b. **Before *r*, *r* disappears,** after lengthening a preceding vowel; e. g. *púnā rūpáṇi* (AV. I. 24[4]). In a few instances, however, *o* appears instead of *ā* (= *ar*), under the influence of *-aḥ* as the pause form of neuters in *-as*; thus *ū́dho romaśám* (VIII. 31[9]), for *ū́dhā*; and the compound *aho-rātrá-* 'day and night', for *ahā-*.

2. **Before voiceless consonants** final *r* is as a rule treated like *s*.

a. **Before the gutturals *k kh* and the labials *p ph*,** it becomes *ḥ* under the influence of the pause form; e. g. *púnaḥ kaléḥ* (X. 39[8]); *púnaḥ pátnīm* (X. 85[39]); *púnaḥ-punar* (I. 92[10]). But that the *r* originally remained before these consonants is shown by its survival in the compounds *pūr-pati-*, *svàr-pati-*, *vār-kāryá-*, *ahár-pati-* (VS.). But even here the pause form was gradually introduced; e. g. *svàḥ-pati-* (SV.); it supplanted the *r* of *antár* throughout; e. g. *antaḥ-péya-* 'drinking up'; *antaḥ-kośá-* (AV.) 'inside of a store-room'; *antaḥ-parśavyá-* (VS.) 'flesh between the ribs'; *antaḥ-pātrá-* (AV.) 'interior of a vessel'; and because the pause form of *r* and *s* was identical, the Sandhi of *s* came to be applied here even in the RV.; thus *ántas-patha-* 'being on the way' (for *ántar-*); *cátuṣ-kaparda-* 'having four braids', *cátuṣ-pād-* 'four-footed' (for *cátur-*).

b. **Before the palatals *c ch*,** final *r* invariably (like *s*) becomes the palatal sibilant *ś*; e. g. *pū́ś ca* (I. 189[2]) for *pū́r ca*. This applies almost always even in compounds; e. g. *cátuś-catvāriṃśat* (VS.) 'forty-four'. There are only two examples of the *r* being retained even here: *svàr-cakṣas-* 'brilliant as light', *svàr-canas-* 'lovely as light'.

c. **Before dental *t*,** final *r* is without exception treated like *s*; e. g. *gīs tribarhíṣi* (I. 181[8]) for *gír*; *cátus-triṃśat* 'thirty-four' for *cátur-*. The retention of *r* before *t* in *āvar támaḥ* (I. 92[4]) is only apparently an exception, as this really stands for *āvart támaḥ*[5].

d. **Before sibilants,** final *r* appears in its pause form as Visarjanīya in sentence Sandhi, e. g. *púnaḥ sám* (II. 38[4]). In compounds, however, it

1 Cp. WACKERNAGEL I, 284 note (p. 335).

2 A list of root-stems in *-ir* and *-ur* will be found in GRASSMANN's Wörterbuch 1693—1694, columns 3—4.

3 *r* is original in *dvā́r-* 'door'; *vā́r-* 'protector'; *vā́r-* 'water'; *áhar-* 'day'; *uṣár-* 'dawn'; *ū́dhar-* 'udder'; *vádhar-* 'weapon'; *vanar-* 'wood'; *svàr-* 'light'; *antár* 'within'; *avár* 'down'; *púnar* 'again'; *prātár* 'early'; the voc. of *ṛ*-stems, e. g. *bhrātar*; the 2. 3. sing. of past tenses from roots in *-ṛ*, e. g. *āvar*, from *vṛ-* 'cover'.

4 *áha evá* (VI. 48[7]) for *áhar evá* is due to *áhaḥ*, the pause form of *áhar*, being treated like that of a neuter in *-as*, *áhas*. In *akṣā indur* (IX. 98[3]) for *akṣār indur* (Pp. *akṣār*), the editors of the Saṃhitā misunderstood *akṣāḥ*, as the form would originally have been pronounced at the end of an internal Pāda. *ū́dho* for *ū́dhar*, which appears before *u* and *m*, is due to the influence of neuters in *as*, the pause form of which, *-aḥ*, would be the same as of those in *-ar*. The form *avó*, for *avár* 'down', which appears before *d* (*avó diváḥ* V. 40[6], etc.; but before *m*, *avár maháḥ*, I. 133[6]), is due to the influence of *páro diváḥ* and *páro divā́* (for *páras*), cp. RPr. I. 32. *āvo* before *a*, *d*, *m*, explained by BENFEY (SV. XL and 176) as standing for *āvar* is probably from *vas-* 'shine' (cp. WACKERNAGEL I, p. 335, top).

5 Cp. above 62, 1.

frequently remains; thus *vanar-sád-* and *vanar-ṣád-* 'sitting in the wood'; *dhūr-ṣád-* 'being on the yoke'; *svar-ṣā́-* 'winning light'; *svàr-ṣāti-* 'acquisition of light'; *dhūr-ṣāh-* (VS.) 'bearing the yoke'. This indicates that it originally remained before sibilants in sentence Sandhi also.

80. Initial aspiration. — The palatal sibilant *ś* and the breathing *h*, when initial, may under certain conditions be changed to aspirates.

a. After a final *c*, initial *ś* may become, and in practice always does become, *ch*; e. g. *yác chaknávāma* (x. 2[3]) for *yád śaknávāma*. The same change occasionally takes place after *ṭ*; thus *vipāṭ chutudrī́* (III. 33[1]), for *śutudrī́*; *turāṣā́ṭ chuṣmī́* (v. 40[4]) for *śuṣmī́*.

b. After a final voiced mute, initial *h* may be and usually is changed to the aspirate of that mute; e. g. *tád dhí* (I. 126[2]) for *tád hí*; *sī́dad dhótā* (x. 12[1]) for *sī́dad* (= *sīdat*) *hótā*; *ávāḍ ḍhavyā́ni* (x. 16[12]) for *havyā́ni*.

81. Sandhi of compounds[1]. — The euphonic combination at the junction of the members of compounds is on the whole subject to the rules prevailing in external Sandhi or between words in a sentence. Thus the evidence of metre shows that contracted vowels are often even in compounds to be read with hiatus, when the initial vowel of the second member is in a heavy syllable; e. g. *yuktá-aśva-* 'having yoked horses', *devá-iddha-* 'kindled by the gods', *áccha-ukti-* 'invitation'. Many archaisms of Sandhi are, however, preserved in compounds which have either disappeared from or are obsolescent in the sentence.

1. An **earlier stage** of Sandhi has been **preserved** by compounds alone in the following instances:

a. Several old phonetic combinations appear in single words: *dvi-bárha-jman-* 'having a double course' for *dvi-bárhaj-jman-* (= **dvi-bárhad-* from *bárh-as*, with *-ad* for *-as* before the voiced palatal)[2]; *barhi-ṣád-* 'sitting on the sacrificial litter' (from *barhís-* for *barhiṣ-ṣád-*); *viś-páti-* 'lord of the house' and *viś-pátnī-* 'mistress of the house' (with *ś* retained instead of *ṭ*)[3], *sam-rā́j-* 'sovereign ruler' (with *m* preserved before *r*)[4].

b. In a group of compounds with *dus-* 'ill' as first member, the combinations *dū-ḍ* = *duẓ-d* and *dū-ṇ* = *duẓ-n* appear instead of *dur-d* and *dur-ṇ*: *dū-ḍábha-* 'hard to deceive', *dū-ḍhī́-* 'malevolent', *dū-ṇáśa-* 'hard to attain', *dū-ṇā́śa-* 'hard to attain' and 'hard to destroy', *dū-ḍā́ś-* (AV.) 'not worshipping'. But *dur-*, the form which would be required by external Sandhi, is already commoner in the RV.; e. g. *dur-dṛ́śīka-* 'looking bad', *dur-dhár-ī-tu-* 'hard to restrain', *dur-ṇā́man-* 'having a bad name', *dur-ṇáśa-* (AV.) 'hard to attain'.

c. Final *r* in the first member is **preserved** in the RV. before voiceless sounds[5]; thus *vār-kāryá-* 'producing water', *svàr-cakṣas-* 'brilliant as light', *pū́r-pati-* 'lord of the stronghold', *svàr-pati-* 'lord of heaven', *dhūr-ṣád-*[6] 'being on the yoke'.

d. Radical stems ending in ***-ir*** and ***-ur*** mostly **lengthen their vowel** before consonants (as within words), e. g. *dhūr-ṣád-* 'being on the yoke', *dhūr-ṣāh-* (VS.) 'bearing the yoke', *pū́r-pati-* 'lord of the stronghold', *pūr-bhíd-* 'breaking down forts', *pūr-bhídya-* n. 'destruction of forts', *pūr-yā́ṇa-*[7] 'leading to the fort'.

---

[1] See BENFEY, Göttingische Abhandlungen 15, 105 ff.; WACKERNAGEL 2[1], 125—139.

[2] Cp. above 44 a, 3.

[3] Later *viṭ-pati-* (TB. II. 5. 7[4]), and even in the RV. *páḍ-bīśa-* 'fetter' from *paś-* 'bind'.

[4] Otherwise Anusvāra, as in *saṃ-rā́jantam*.

[5] While in external Sandhi it would become Visarjanīya or a sibilant.

[6] External Sandhi gradually encroaches here in the later Saṃhitās, as in *svàḥ-pati-* (SV.). On *punaḥ-* for *punar-* in *punaḥ-sará-*, *ántas-* for *ántar-* in *ántas-patha-*, and *antaḥ-* in *antaḥ-péya-* see WACKERNAGEL 2[1], 126 γ, note, and above 79, 2 a.

[7] But *gir* retains the short vowel in *gir-vaṇas-* 'fond of praise', *gir-vāhas-* 'praised in

e. As first member of a compound ***dyu-*** 'heaven' appears as ***div-*** before vowels[1] (while *yu* would in external Sandhi become *yv*), as *dív-iṣṭi-* 'striving for heaven', *div-ít-* 'going to heaven'.

2. Compounds in the Saṃhitās preserve many euphonic archaisms which, while still existing in external Sandhi, disappear from the sentence in later periods of the language though still partially surviving in compounds.

a. A final consonant disappears before the same consonant when the latter is the initial of a group: *upá(s)-stha-* 'lap', *ná(k)-kṣatra-* 'star', *hṛ(d)-dyotá-* (AV.), an internal disease, *hṛ(d)-dyótana* (AV.) 'breaking the heart'[2].

b. A final **sibilant disappears** before a mute followed by a sibilant, as in *divá-kṣa-* 'heavenly' ('ruling over heaven', *div-ás*, gen.)[3].

c. A **sibilant as initial** of the second member is **retained**; thus *ścandra-* 'bright' in *puru-ścandrá-* 'much-shining' and many other compounds, but almost invariably *candrá-* as an independent word[4].

d. A **final *s*** in the first member **or an initial *s*** in the second is **cerebralized**; e. g. *duṣ-ṭára-* 'invincible', *niṣ-ṭákvarī-* (AV.) 'running away', *duṣ-ṣvápnya-* 'evil dream'.

e. An original ***n*** in the second member **is cerebralized** after a *ṛ r ṣ* with the necessary phonetic restrictions (47) **α.** In derivatives from verbs compounded with prepositions containing *r*, initial, medial, or final *n* of the root is almost invariably cerebralized in the Saṃhitās; thus *nir-ṇíj-* 'bright garment', *pari-hṇuta-* (AV.) 'denied' ($\sqrt{}$*hnu-*), *parī-ṇáh-* 'enclosure', *pary-ā-ṇaddha-* (AV.) 'tied up', *pra-ṇī-* and *pra-ṇetṛ́-* 'leader', *prá-ṇīti-* 'guidance', *prāṇá-* 'breath', *prā́ṇana-* and *prāṇátha-* (VS.) 'respiration' (*an-* 'breathe'). The cerebralization appears even in suffixes, as *pra-yā́ṇa-* 'advance'[5].

β. In other compounds *ṇ* greatly predominates when the second member is a verbal noun; e. g. *grāma-ṇī́-* 'chief of a village', *dur-gā́ṇi* 'dangers'; *nṛ-pā́ṇa-* 'giving drink to men', *pitṛ-yā́ṇa-* 'trodden by the fathers', *pūr-yā́ṇa-* (AV.) 'leading to the fort', *rakṣo-hán-* 'demon-slaying', *vṛtra-háṇ-* 'Vṛtra-slaying'. The **cerebralization fluctuates** in *-yāvan*: thus *prātar-yā́vaṇ-* 'going out early', *vṛ́ṣa-pra-yāvaṇ-* 'going with stallions', but *puro-yā́van-* 'going in front', *śubhra-yāvan-* 'going in a radiant chariot'; also in *purīṣa-vā́haṇa-* (VS.) and *purīṣa-vā́hana-* (TS. K.) 'removing rubbish'. **Cerebralization never takes place in *-ghn-***, the weak form of *-han-* 'killing'; nor in *akṣā-náh-* 'tied to the axle', *kravya-vā́hana-*[6] 'conveying corpses', *carma-mná-* 'tanner', *yuṣmā́-nīta-* 'led by you'.

γ. The cerebralization takes place somewhat less regularly when the second member is an ordinary (non-verbal) noun; e. g. *urū-ṇasá-* 'broad-nosed', *tri-ṇavá-* (VS.) 'consisting of three times nine parts', *tri-ṇāman-* (AV.)[7] 'having three names', *dru-ghaṇá-* 'mallet', *nṛ-máṇas-* 'friendly to men', *purú-ṇāman-* 'many-named', *pūrvāhṇá-* 'forenoon', *prá-ṇapāt-* 'great-grandson'. There is

---

song'. The long vowel in *án-āśīr-dā-* 'not fulfilling expectation', *āśī́r-dā́-* and *āśī́r-dāyā́-* 'fulfilment of a benediction' is due to analogy, as *ā-śis-* is derived from the root *śās-*.

1 *dyu-* remains before consonants: *dyu-kṣá-*, *dyu-gá-t-*, *dyú-bhakta-*.

2 Also in external Sandhi *'tá dyā́m* (AV. IV. 19[6]) for *tád dyā́m*.

3 Also in external Sandhi *ádha kṣárantīr* (VII. 34[2]), cp. above 78, 2 d.

4 Divergence from external Sandhi is sometimes not archaic but due to innovation; as *go-* 'cow' instead of *gav-* before vowels, e. g. *gó-agra-* 'headed by cows'; cp. WACKERNAGEL 2[1], p. 129 e. Another kind of innovation in compounds is due to haplology; cp. WACKERNAGEL 1, 241 a β; 2[1], p. 128 bottom.

5 There are a few exceptions: *pari-pā́na-* 'drink', *pary-uhyámāna-* 'being led home' ($\sqrt{}$*vah-*), *prá-pīna-* (VS.) 'distended'.

6 Like *havya-vā́hana-* 'conveying oblations'.

7 The later Saṃhitās always have *ṇ* after *tri-*, while the RV. always has *n*; as *tri-*

fluctuation when *dus-* 'ill' assumes the later Sandhi form of *dur-*, as *dur-ṇā́man-* 'having a bad name', *dur-haṇu-* 'having ugly jaws', but *dur-niyántu-* 'hard to restrain'[1]; also in *vārdhra-ṇasá-* (TS.) 'rhinoceros' and *vārdhrī-nasá-* (VS.) 'having streaks on the nose'; *śrī-maṇas-* (TS.) and *śrī-manas-* (VS.) 'well-disposed'.

But *n* often **remains** in this type of compound: initially in *kṛpá-nīḷa-* 'whose home is splendour', *candrá-nirṇij-* 'having a brilliant garment', *varṣá-nirṇij-* 'clothed with rain', *tveṣá-nṛmṇa-* 'of brilliant power', *dīrghá-nītha-*, N. of a man, *púnar-nava-* 'again renewed', *babhrú-nīkaśa-* (VS.) 'looking brownish', *vṛ́ṣa-nābhi-* 'having a mighty nave'; medially in *ṛ́ṣi-manas-*[2] 'inspired', *indrāgnī́* 'Indra and Agni', *kṣatra-váni-* (AV.) 'addicted to military rule', *bráhma-vani-* (VS.) 'well disposed to the priesthood', *cátur-anīka-* 'four-faced', *try-anīká-* 'three-faced', *jyótir-anīka-*[3] 'having a shining face', *citrá-bhānu-* 'having bright lustre', *dhruvá-yoni-* (VS.) 'having a fixed abode', *pra-mánas-* (AV.) 'careful', *hári-manyu-sāyaka-*[4] (RV. x) 'stimulating the mettle of the bays'.

f. The **final vowel** of the first member is often **lengthened**. This frequently occurs before *v-*; e. g. *anná-vṛdh-* 'prospering by food', *pratī-vartá-* (AV.) 'returning into itself', *prā-vṛ́ṣ-*[5] 'rainy season'. It is often **due to** the **rhythmical tendency** (which also prevails in the sentence) to lengthen a vowel before a single consonant between two short syllables; e. g. *ahī-śúva-*, N. of a demon (from *ahi-*), *urū-ṇasá-* 'broad-nosed', *ṛtā-ṣáh-* (VS.) 'maintaining the sacred law', *pavī-nasá-* (AV.) 'having a nose like a spearhead', *naghā-riṣá-*[6] (AV.) N. of a plant', *rathā-sáh-* 'able to draw the car'. Lengthening of a vowel between other than two short syllables is less common, being probably due to imitation of compounds in which the long vowel is produced by the normal rhythm; e. g. *dhanvā-sáh-* 'skilled in archery' and *vibhvā-sáh-* 'overcoming the rich' like *rathā-sáh-*; *sahásrā-magha-* 'having a thousand gifts' like *śatá-magha-* 'having a hundred gifts'. The interchange of short and long is entirely regulated by the rhythmic principle in *sană-* 'of old' and almost entirely in *tuvĭ-* 'much'; e. g. *sanā-júr-* 'long since aged' and *sána-śruta-* 'famous of old', *tuvī-maghá-* 'very rich' and *tuvi-bādhá-* 'killing many'[7]. The final vowel of prepositions is particularly often lengthened in the later Saṃhitās without reference to rhythm, especially before nouns ending in *-a* with long radical vowel, e. g. *nī-vid-* (AV.) 'liturgical invitation', *abhī-moda-múd-* (AV.) 'excessively joyful', *nī-nāhá-* (AV.) 'girth', *pratī-bodhá-* (AV.) 'vigilance', *vī-barhá-* (AV.) 'scattering'. Sometimes the final vowel is left unlengthened between two short syllables; e. g. *rayi-páti-* 'lord of wealth', *ghṛta-duh-as* (voc. pl.) 'yielding ghee'[8].

g. On the other hand, **final *ā* and *ī*** of the first member are often **shortened** before a group of consonants or a long syllable; e. g. *amīva-cā́tana-* (AV.) 'driving away disease' and *amīva-hán-* 'destroying disease' (*ámīvā-*); *ū́rṇa-mradas-* 'soft as wool' (*ū́rṇā-*) and **ūrṇa-vābhi-* 'spinning wool', 'spider', in the patronymic *aurṇavābhá-*; *kakṣya-prā́-* 'filling out the girth' (*kakṣyā̀-*);

nāká- 'third heaven', *tri-nā́bhi-* 'having three naves'.

1 The AV. here always has the cerebral, as *dur-ṇihita-* 'badly kept'.

2 But *nṛ-máṇas-* 'friendly to men' and *vṛ́ṣa-maṇas-* 'manly-spirited'.

3 But *purv-aṇīka-* 'having many faces'.

4 But *vṛ́ṣa-maṇyu-* (RV. I) 'vigorous-minded'.

5 Cp. WACKERNAGEL 1, 42.

6 Beside *nagha-mārá-* (AV.) N. of a plant.

7 Cp. also *prā-sáh-* and *pra-sáh-* 'victorious'. The long vowel in the former is probably historic, = IE. *prō*.

8 The vowel is originally long, in *aṣṭá-* 'eight', probably also in *acchā-* 'to' and *viśvā-* 'all', and may be differently explained in *ā́-deva-* 'hostile to the gods', *ā́-rupita-* (IV. 5[7]) meaning, and *ā́-sat-*; see WACKERNAGEL 2[1], p. 131, note.

sena-jit- (VS.) 'vanquishing armies' (*sénā-*); *gáuri-vīti-* N. of a seer (from *gaurī-*), *pṛthivi-ṣṭhā-* 'standing on the earth'; even before a short syllable in *pṛthivi-ṣád-* (AV.) and *pṛthivi-ṣád-* (VS.) 'sitting on the earth' (*pṛthivī-*), *sárasvati-kṛta-* (VS.) 'made by Sarasvatī'[1].

82. **Extension of external to internal Sandhi.** — The rules of sentence Sandhi as applied between members of a compound are often found to affect the internal form of words.

a. **Nominal** (chiefly secondary) **suffixes** with initial consonants are frequently treated like the second member of a compound; e. g. beside *duvas-yú-* 'worshipping', appears *duvo-yú-*[2]. This influence extends even to radical finals before primary suffixes; e. g. *án-na-* 'food' for *ád-na-*; *ṣaṇ-ṇām* for *ṣaṭ-nām*, from *ṣáṣ-* 'six'; *námo-bhis*, from *námas-* 'obeisance', with *o* for *ad* (as in *uṣád-bhis* from *uṣás-* 'dawn')[3]; *haviḥ-ṣu*[4] for *haviṣ-ṣu*, from *havís-* 'oblation'; *jigī-vāṃs-* for *jigi-vāṃs-* 'having conquered', with radical final lengthened as in sentence Sandhi.

b. **In the verb** the influence of sentence Sandhi is seen in reduplicated forms. Thus parallel with the lengthening of final syllables in the sentence, the final radical vowel is made long before the ending *-hi* in *didīhi* beside the more usual *dīdihi*, from *dī-* 'shine'. The rhythmical lengthening in the reduplicated aorist is probably due to a similar influence.

III. ACCENT.

ROTH, Nirukta LVII—LXXII: Ueber die Elemente des indischen Accentes nach den Prâtiçâkhja Sûtren. — BENFEY, Vollständige Grammatik p. 9—13. — WHITNEY, 'On the nature and designation of the accent in Sanskrit', Transactions of the American Philological Association, 1869—70; Oriental and Linguistic Studies 2, 318 ff.; Sanskrit Grammar3, p. 28—33; see also General Index, s. v. 'Accent'. — HAUG, Ueber das Wesen und den Werth des wedischen Accents, München 1873 (cp. WEBER, Indische Streifen 3, 335 ff.; WHITNEY, JAOS. 10, IX ff., CIII f.). — WACKERNAGEL, Altindische Grammatik 1, 243 ff. — Cp. also HIRT, Der indogermanische Akzent, Strassburg 1895, and Akzentstudien in IF. VI—IX; BRUGMANN, Kurze vergleichende Grammatik 1 (Strassburg 1902), p. 52—66.

Besides the Prātiśākhyas several other native authorities refer to the accent. Pāṇini and his commentators give an account of it; all the Sūtras of Pāṇini relating to accentuation are collected in a chapter of the Siddhānta-kaumudī called *vaidika-svara-prakriyā* 'section on the Vedic accent'. The accent is further dealt with in the Bhāṣikasūtra, in the Pratijñāsūtra, in the Śikṣās, and as regards the position of the accent in individual words, in the Uṇādisūtras and especially in the Phiṭsūtras.

83. **General character of the Vedic accent.** — In Vedic literature sacred texts only, primarily all the Saṃhitās[5] have been handed down in an accented form. Of all other sacred texts, only those to which a special importance was attached, have preserved the accent. These are the Taittirīya Brāhmaṇa (together with its Āraṇyaka) and the Śatapatha Brāhmaṇa (including the Bṛhadāraṇyaka Upaniṣad). There is, however, evidence to show that the Pañcaviṃśa Brāhmaṇa[6] and other Brāhmaṇas were at one time accented[7].

1 On the relation of this shortening to the lengthening in the same position, and its probable explanation, see WACKERNAGEL 2[1], p. 135 (56 g).

2 Hence the Padapāṭha treats a nominal stem which takes a suffix with initial consonant like the first member of a compound, separating it from the suffix by Avagraha; e. g. *duvaḥ-syúḥ* for *duvoyúḥ*; *adri-vaḥ* for *adrivaḥ*, voc., 'armed with a bolt'; *ūtí-bhiḥ* for *ūtíbhis* 'with aids'.

3 See above 44 a, 3.

4 See 57, 1.

5 The Mss. of the Kāṭhaka are so defective as regards accentuation that L. v. SCHROEDER found it possible to print parts only of his edition of the text (vol. 1, 1900) with accents.

6 WEBER, Indische Studien 10, 421; cp. MAX MÜLLER, ASL. 348; BURNELL, Sāmavidhāna Brāhmaṇa p. VI. The Mantra parts of the Aitareya Āraṇyaka are accented (KEITH's ed. p. 10).

7 The Suparṇādhyāya, an artificially archaic

The Sūtras, though not themselves accented, occasionally accent the Mantras which they quote.

The **Vedic accent**, like that of ancient Greece, was of an essentially **musical** nature. This is indicated by the fact that the accent exercises no influence on the rhythm of versification. The phoneticians of the Prātiśākhyas, in describing it, speak only of its pitch, which is also indicated by the name of the chief tone, *ud-ātta* 'raised', 'high'[1]. But that the Vedic accent was accompanied by some stress[2], is shown by certain phonetic changes which cannot otherwise be explained[3].

In the Vedic accent **three degrees of pitch** may be distinguished: the high, properly represented by the *udātta*, the middle by the *svarita* ('sounded'), and the low by the *an-udātta* ('not raised'). That the **Udātta originally** denoted the **highest pitch** in the oldest form of the Vedic language, is shown by the evidence of Comparative Philology, and especially of Greek which, as far as its peculiar laws of accent will admit, has the acute on the same syllable as in the Vedic language has the Udātta (e. g. Διϝός : *divás*; ἑπτά : *saptá*; ὀκτώ : *aṣṭáu*). This conclusion is also supported by the method of marking the Udātta in the Sāmaveda, the Maitrāyaṇī Saṃhitā, and the Kāṭhaka. In the Ṛgveda, however, the Udātta has a middle pitch, lower than that of the Svarita, as is shown both by the way in which it is marked and by the account given of it in the Prātiśākhyas. This must be an innovation, though an old one.

The **Svarita** is a **falling accent** of a dependent nature, marking the transition from an accented to a toneless syllable. It regularly follows an Udātta, to the rise of which its fall corresponds in pitch. It assumes an independent appearance when the preceding Udātta is lost in consequence of the vowel that bears the Udātta being changed to a semivowel in Sandhi. It is described in Pāṇini I. 2[31][4] as a combination of Udātta and Anudātta, which means that it falls from the high pitch of the acute to the low pitch of unaccented syllables. According to the RV. Prātiśākhya and the TS. Prātiśākhya, however, the first part of the Svarita sounds higher than the Udātta. This means that, instead of falling immediately from the high pitch of the preceding Udātta, it first rises somewhat before falling to low pitch[5]. It would thus have something of the nature of a circumflex in the RV.; only the rise in pitch above the highest level of the Udātta is but slight (corresponding to the initial rise of the Udātta from Anudāttatara to Anudātta level), while the fall corresponds to the total rise of the Udātta[6]. The **low tone** of the syllables preceding an accented syllable (with Udātta or Svarita) is called ***an-udātta*** 'not raised' in the Prātiśākhyas[7]. When it follows a Svarita it is called the ***pracaya***[8] (*svara*), or 'accumulated pitch' (as several such unaccented syllables often occur in succession) which continues at the low level reached by the preceding Svarita till the syllable immediately

poem composed in the style of the Vedic hymns, is also accented, but with many mistakes; see GRUBE's edition in Indische Studien, vol. XIV.

[1] Cp. HAUG, op. cit. 19.

[2] The Vedic accent, like the Greek, was, after the beginning of our era, changed to a stress accent which, however, unlike the modern Greek stress accent, did not remain on the original syllable, but is regulated by the quantity of the last two or three syllables, much as in Latin; cp. HAUG 99, end.

[3] See WACKERNAGEL I, 218 and cp. OSTHOFF, Morphologische Untersuchungen 4, 73.

[4] In agreement with VPr. I. 126; APr. I. 17; cp. HAUG 73.

[5] See OLDENBERG, Prolegomena 483 f.

[6] According to Pāṇini's account the Svarita does not rise above Udātta pitch before falling; see OLDENBERG, loc. cit.

[7] See RPr. III. 1; cp. HAUG 91.

[8] HAUG 92 f.

preceding the next accent[1]. The latter syllable, called *sanna-tara* 'lower' or *anudātta-tara*[2] 'more lowered', sinks somewhat below this monotone.

84. Methods of marking the accent.—The accent is marked in the Vedic texts in four different ways.

1. The **system of the Ṛgveda** is followed also by the Atharvaveda[3], the Taittirīya Saṃhitā (along with its Brāhmaṇa) and, with only slight deviations in the treatment of the Svarita, by the Vājasaneyi Saṃhitā. This system is peculiar in not marking the principal accent at all. The explanation is doubtless to be found in the fact that the pitch of the Udātta is in the RV. intermediate between that of the other two tones. Hence the preceding **Anudātta,** as having low pitch, is marked by a horizontal stroke **below** the syllable, while the following **Svarita,** as rising to a higher pitch, is marked by a vertical stroke **above** the syllable[4]; e.g. अग्निना *agninā* = *agninā́*. The presence of successive Udāttas at the beginning of a hemistich is recognizable by the absence of all marks till the Svarita which follows the last of them, or the Anudātta which follows the last of them and precedes the next accented syllable; thus तावा यातम् *tāv ā yātam* = *tā́v ā́ yātam*; *tavet tat satyam* = *tā́vét tát satyám*. On the other hand, all the unaccented syllables at the beginning of a hemistich are marked; e. g. वैश्वानरम् = *vaiśvānaram* = *vaiśvānarám*. But all the syllables following a Svarita remain unmarked till the one immediately preceding the next Udātta or Svarita; e. g. इमं मे गङ्गे यमुने सरस्वति शुतुद्रि *imaṃ me gaṅge yamune sarasvati śutudri* = *imáṃ me gaṅge yamune sarasvati śútudri*[5].

a. The hemistich being treated as the unit with regard to accentuation[6], the marking of the Anudātta and of the Svarita is not limited to the word containing the Udātta which those accents precede and follow respectively[7]. Hence the final syllable of one word may be marked with an Anudātta as preceding an Udātta of the next initial syllable; or the initial syllable of one word may be marked with the Svarita following the Udātta at the end of the preceding word; e. g. पूर्वेभिर्ऋषिभिर् *pūrvebhir ṛṣibhir* = *pū́rvebhir ṛ́ṣibhir*; यज्ञमध्वरम् *yajñam adhvaram* = *yajñám adhvarám*. But if an initial syllable after a final Udātta precedes an accented syllable, it loses the enclitic Svarita and must be marked as Anudātta; e. g. देवमृत्विजम् *devam ṛtvijam* = *devám ṛtvijam*.

b. If an independent Svarita[8] precedes an Udātta, it is marked with the numeral १ (1) when its vowel is short, and with ३ (3) when it is long, the figures receiving both the sign of the Svarita and that of the Anudātta[9] which precedes an Udātta; e.g. अप्स्व१न्तर् = *apsv àntár*; रायो३वनिः = *rāyò 'vániḥ*. The phenomenon is described by the phoneticians with the words *kampa*

---

[1] See OLDENBERG, Prolegomena 485, end.

[2] *Sanna-tara*, APr. 1. 43; *anudātta-tara* in Kāśikā vṛtti on Pāṇini 1. 2, 40.

[3] The Mss. of the AV., however, show considerable variations; see WHITNEY'S Translation p. CXXI ff.

[4] In the Kashmir Ms. of the RV. the Udātta and the independent Svarita only are marked, the former by a vertical stroke above the accented syllable, the latter by a hook (ᴗ) above the accented syllable; see SCHEFTELOWITZ, Die Apokryphen des Ṛgveda 48 ff.

[5] Cp. HAUG, op. cit. 92 f.

[6] From the point of view of the sentence accent the Pāda is the unit; thus a verb or vocative is always accented at its beginning.

[7] In the Padapāṭha, on the other hand, each word receives its natural accent only, so that where the one text has a Svarita, the other may have an Anudātta; e. g. in I. 1[3] the Saṃhitā has *rayim àśnavat*, the Pada *rayim aśnavat* (the latter word being unaccented has the Anudātta marked under each syllable).

[8] Examples of independent Svarita are *svàr* for *súar*; *kvà* for *kúa*; *vīryàṃ* for *vīriam*. 'Independent' Svarita in the above rule is intended to include that which results from change to a semivowel (*kṣaipra*), from contraction (*praśliṣṭa*) and from elision of *a* (*abhinihita*).

[9] The long vowel before the ३ receives the Anudātta stroke as well.

'quaver', *vikampita*, and the verb *pra-kamp-*. In the TS. it appears only when the second syllable as well as the first has the Svarita, and the figure 2, as well as 1 and 3, is here used.

2. In the **system of the Maitrāyaṇī Saṃhitā**[1] and of the **Kāṭhaka**[2], the **Udātta** is marked by a vertical stroke **above** (which seems to indicate that this accent was here pronounced with the highest pitch); e. g. अग्निना = *agninā*. The two Saṃhitās, however, diverge in their method of indicating the Svarita. The MS. marks the independent Svarita by a curve below the accented syllable, e. g. वीर्यम् *vīryàm*; but the dependent Svarita by a horizontal stroke in the middle or three vertical strokes above the accented syllable. The Kāṭhaka, on the other hand, marks the independent Svarita by a curve below (if an unaccented syllable follows), e. g. वीर्यं बध्नाति *vīryàṃ badhnāti*; or by a hook below (if an accented syllable follows) e. g. वीर्यं व्याचष्टे *vīryàṃ vyắcaṣṭe*; but the dependent Svarita by a dot below the accented syllable[3]. Both these Saṃhitās mark the Anudāttatara in the ordinary way by a stroke below the syllable. In L. v. SCHROEDER's editions, however, the Udātta and the independent Svarita only are marked. When the text of any of the Saṃhitās is transliterated in Roman characters, it is the regular practice to omit any indication of the dependent Svarita and of the Anudātta as unnecessary.

3. In the **system of the Sāmaveda**, the figures 1 2 3 are written above the accented syllables to represent three degrees of pitch. Here 1 always stands for the highest pitch (Udātta), and 3 always for the lowest (Anudātta), and 2 generally for the middle pitch (Svarita); e. g.
3 1 2
barhiṣi = RV. *barhiṣi* (*barhíṣi*). But 2 also represents the Udātta when the latter is not followed by a Svarita (that is when the Udātta syllable is final in the hemistich or when an Anudāttatara preceding another accented
3 2 3 2 3 2 3 1 2
syllable follows); e. g. *girā* = RV. *girā* (*girā́*); *yajñānāṃ hotā viśveṣāṃ* = RV. *yajñānāṃ hotā viśveṣām* (*yajñā́nāṃ hótā viśveṣām*). If there are two successive Udāttas, the second is not marked, but 2 r is written over the
3 1 2r
following Svarita; e. g. *dviṣo martyasya* = RV. *dviṣo martyàsya* (*dviṣó mártyasya*). If in such case there is no room for 2 r, the first Udātta has 2 u written over
3 2u 3 1 2
it instead; e. g. *eṣa sya pītaye* = RV. *eṣa sya pītaye* (*eṣá syá pītáye*). The independent Svarita (as well as the dependent one which follows two successive Udāttas) is marked with 2 r; and the Anudātta which precedes it, with 3 k;
3k 2r
e. g. *tanvā*. Syllables which follow a Svarita and in which the pitch remains
3 1 2 3 1 2
unchanged, are left unmarked; e. g. *dūtaṃ vṛṇīmahe hotāram* = RV. *dūtaṃ vṛṇīmahe hotāram* (*dūtáṃ vṛṇīmahe hótāram*)[4].

4. Though the Brāhmaṇas do not come within the scope of this work, the **system** of accentuation in the **Śatapatha Brāhmaṇa** cannot be passed over here, as it must be treated in connexion with the other systems of the Vedic period. It is historically important as forming a transition to the post-Vedic period, when the accent assumed a different character[5]. The system of the ŚB. in various respects differs considerably from the three described above.

---

1 See HAUG 27—32; L. v. SCHROEDER, Introduction to his edition 1, p. XXIX—XXXIV; ZDMG. 33, 186 ff.

2 Cp. L. v. SCHROEDER, Introduction to his edition, 2, p. X—XI.

3 On some peculiarities of the VS. in marking the Svarita, see HAUG 32—35.

4 For further details see HAUG 35—42.

5 Cp. LEUMANN, KZ. 31, 50 (mid.).

a. Its chief peculiarity is that it **marks only** the main accent, **the Udātta.** This is done by means of a horizontal stroke **below** the accented syllable; e. g. पु॒रुषः *púruṣaḥ*. If there are two or more successive Udāttas, only the last is marked; e. g. *agnir hi vai dhūr a̱tha* = *agnír hí vái dhúr átha*. When, however, an Udātta is thrown back as the result of Sandhi, an immediately preceding Udātta is also marked; e. g. *so 'gni̱m e̱vābhī̱kṣamāṇaḥ* = *só 'gním évābhíkṣamāṇaḥ*, where *évābhí-* stands for *evàbhí-* = *evá abhí-*. Two successive syllables are also sometimes marked when a compound receives a secondary Udātta; e. g. *spṛhaya̱d-va̱rṇaḥ*, for *spṛhayád-varṇaḥ*.

b. An **independent Svarita** is thrown back on the preceding syllable in the form of an Udātta; e. g. *manu̱ṣye̱ṣu*, that is, *manúṣyeṣu* for *manuṣyèṣu*. The Svarita resulting from change to a semivowel (*kṣaipra*), from contraction (*praśliṣṭa*), or elision of *a* (*abhinihita*), is similarly treated; e. g. *katha̱ṃ nv ima̱m*, that is, *katháṃ nv imám* for *katháṃ nv ìmám*; *e̱vaita̱d*, that is, *évaitád* from *evá etád*; *te̱ 'rcantaḥ*, that is, *té 'rcantaḥ* for *té àrcantaḥ*.

When, however, the prepositions *á* and *prá*, and final *á* in the first member of a compound, combine with an unaccented vowel, the contracted syllable retains the Udātta; e. g. *éhi* (= *á ihi*); *práha* (= *prá āha*); *citróti-* (= *citrá-ūti-*) 'bestowing wondrous gifts'.

c. Before a pause an **accented syllable may lose its Udātta** or receive a reduced accent marked with three dots, if the initial syllable after the pause has an Udātta or independent Svarita; e. g. *sa̱ bhāga̱ḥ* | *sa̱ṃsthite*, for *sá bhāgáḥ* | *sáṃsthite*. The penultimate syllable may also be thus reduced; e. g. *juho̱ti* || *a̱tha*, for *juhóti* || *átha*. This may occur even when the following initial syllable is unaccented; e. g. *na̱psu* || *apa̱*, for *nápsu* || *apá*.

d. Reduplicated forms or long compounds accented on the first syllable or prior member, sometimes receive a **secondary accent** near the end of the word; e. g. *ba̱lbalī̱ti*, that is *bálbalíti* for *bálbalīti*; *e̱ka-catvāriṃśa̱t*, that is, *éka-catvāriṃśát* for *éka-catvāriṃśat*. Sometimes, in such case, the primary accent itself is lost; e. g. *eka-saptatíḥ* beside *éka-saptatiḥ*. Somewhat analogous to this double accentuation of compounds is the frequent accentuation of both verbal prefix and verb at the same time; e. g. *abhí gopayéd* (cp. 109). Finally, the accent occasionally appears on a syllable different from that on which it usually rests. The irregularities mentioned here (d) are much commoner in Books X—XIII than in the earlier Books; they are commonest of all in XIV[1].

85. Normal accentuation of words.—As a general rule, every Vedic word is both accented and has one main accent only. The Udātta is the only main accent in the original text of the Ṛgveda. It is generally found on the syllable which, according to the evidence of Comparative Philology[2], bore it in the Indo-European period[3]. Sometimes, however, the Udātta is secondary, being a substitute for the independent Svarita (itself the result of an original Udātta). Thus there is already a tendency in the RV. to change a final Svarita into a final Udātta: the vocative *dyàus* (= *díaus*) 'O Heaven', appears as *dyáus* (VIII. 89[12]); *aryà-* (= *aría-*) 'kind', occurring only once (I. 123[1]), otherwise and very frequently appears as *aryá-*; thus, too, *śvā́n-* 'dog', was probably at one time *śvàn-* for *śúan-* (Gk. κύων), which would explain the

[1] For further details, see HAUG, 43—48; LEUMANN, Die accentuation des Çatapatha-Brāhmaṇa, KZ. 31, 22—51; cp. also WACKERNAGEL I, 252; Bhāṣikavṛtti, ed. by KIELHORN IS. 10, 397 ff.

[2] Cp. BRUGMANN, KG. 45, 1.

[3] Under the influence of analogy the Vedic Udātta shifted, in a few instances, to other syllables in the Brāhmaṇas and in Pāṇini's system; thus *saptá*, ŚB. and C. *sápta*, *aṣṭáu*, C. *áṣṭau*; AV. VS. ŚB. *tilá-* 'sesamum', C. *tíla-*; *sī́dati* 'sit', C. also *sīdáti*; AV. *gáhvara-* 'deep', C. *gahvará-*.

abnormal accentuation *śúnas* etc. instead of the regular accentuation **śunás* etc. prevailing in monosyllabic stems (93). Or the final Svarita is thrown back as an Udātta on the preceding syllable: thus *mítrya-* 'friendly', beside *mitryà-*[1].

In some Vedic words, however, the only accent which is written is the 'independent' Svarita, by the native phoneticians called the 'genuine' (*jātya*)[2] or also the 'invariable' (*nitya*). Always following a *y* or *v*, it is, however, just as much due to a preceding Udātta (lost by the change of *ī* and *ŭ* to *y* and *v*), as the dependent Svarita is; e. g. *kvà* (= *kúà*) 'where?'; *svàr* (= *súàr*, TS. *súvar*) 'light'; *rathyàm* (= *rathíàm*, from *rathī́-* 'charioteer'); *tanvàm* (= *tanúàm* from *tanū́-*'body'); *ok-yà-* (= *ok-íà-*) 'belonging to home'; *vasav-yà-* (= *vasav-íà-*) 'wealthy'. In reading the RV. the original vowel with its Udātta must be restored except in a very few late passages[3].

a. Double accent. Contrary to the general rule that a word has a single accent only, a certain class of infinitives and a special type of compounds have a double accent[4]. The infinitives in *-tavai*, of which more than a dozen examples occur, accent both the first and the last syllable; e. g. *é-tavái* 'to go', *ápa-bhartavái* 'to take away'. The Udātta on the final syllable is probably to be explained as a secondary accent like that of the ŚB. in intensives and compounds (*bálbalīti*, *éka-catvāriṃśát*, cp. 84, 4 d), where an accent at the beginning of a word is counterbalanced by another at the end.

A good many compounds of a syntactical type, in which both members are duals in form or in which the first member is nearly always a genitive in form, accent both members; e. g. *mitrá-váruṇā* 'Mitra and Varuṇa', *bṛ́has-páti-* 'Lord of prayer'[5].

b. Lack of accent. Contrary to the general rule that every word is accented, some words never have an accent, while others lose their accent under special conditions.

1. The following are **invariably enclitic**:

α. **pronouns**: *tva-* 'another'; *sama-* 'some'; *ena-* 'he', 'she'[6]; *me*, D. G., 'of or to me'; *mā*, A., 'me'; *nau*, du. A. D. G., 'us two', etc.; *nas*, A. D. G., 'us', etc.; *te*, D. G., 'of or to thee'; *tvā*, A., 'thee'; *vām*, A. D. G., 'ye two', etc.; *vas*, A. D. G., 'you', etc.; *īm*, *sīm* 'him', 'her', 'it', 'them', etc.; *kis* 'some one' in *ná-kis*, *mā́-kis* 'no one'; *kīm* in *ā́-kīm* 'from', *ná-kīm*, *mā́-kīm* 'never'.

β. **particles**: *ca* 'and'; *u* 'on the other hand'; *vā* 'or'; *iva* 'like', 'as it were'; *kam* 'indeed' (after *nú*, *sú*, *hí*); *gha*, *ha* 'just' (emphasizing); *cid* 'at all'; *bhala* 'indeed'; *sama-ha* 'somehow'; *sma* 'just', 'indeed' (almost invariably with the present tense); *svid* 'probably'.

2. The following classes of forms or individual words are subject to **loss of accent** according to their position or function in the sentence:

α. **vocatives**, unless beginning the sentence or Pāda.

β. **finite verbs**, in principal clauses, unless beginning the sentence or Pāda.

γ. all oblique cases formed from the demonstrative **pronoun** *a-*, when used merely to replace a preceding substantive, and not occurring at the beginning of a sentence or Pāda; e. g. *asya jánimāni* 'his (i. e. Agni's) births' (but *asyā́ uṣásaḥ* 'of that Dawn').

---

[1] Cp. the accentuation of the ŚB., 84, 4 b. In Pāṇini's system of accentuation this tendency went still further; thus V. *vīryà-* (= *vīría-*), becomes in C. *vī́rya-*; and the gerundive in *-tavyà* (= *-tavía*) appears in C. as *-távya* also.

[2] RPr. III. 4, VPr. I. 111 f.; cp. HAUG 75.

[3] Cp. BENFEY, Gött. Abhandlungen 27, 31 ff.

[4] In the Brāhmaṇas also the particle *vā́vá*.

[5] See below, on the accentuation of compounds, 91.

[6] The A. sing. f. occurs once (VIII. 6[19]) accented at the beginning of a Pāda as *enā́m*.

δ. *yáthā* 'as', when used in the sense of *iva* 'like', 'as it were', at the end of a Pāda; e. g. *tāyávo yathā* (I. 50²) 'like thieves'.

ε. *ná* 'not', when followed by *hí* 'for'[1], the two particles being treated as one word; e. g. *nahí tvā . . . invataḥ* (I. 10⁸) 'for the two do not restrain thee'; similarly when combined with the particle *nú* 'now' : *na-nú* 'certainly not'.

1. Accentuation of Nominal Stems.

86. A. In **primary derivation** no general law for the accentuation of nominal suffixes can be stated; but there is a tendency, when *-a, -ana, -as, -an, -man* are added, to accent the root in action nouns, and the suffix in agent nouns; and in nouns formed with *-as* and *-man* difference of gender is to some extent accompanied by difference of accent.

1. **Root stems** when reduplicated or compounded with prepositions as a rule retain the accent on the radical syllable; e. g. *juhū́-* 'tongue' and 'ladle', *yavī-yúdh-* 'eager to fight'; *pra-ṇení-* 'guiding constantly'. In stems formed with intensive reduplication, however, the reduplicative syllable is sometimes accented; thus *jógū-* 'singing aloud', *vánīvan-* 'desiring', *dáridra-* (VS.) 'roving'. The prefix is accented in *áva-sā-* 'deliverance', *úpa-stu-t-* 'invocation', *pári-jri-* 'running round'[2].

2. When the **suffix** ***-a*** is added, the root is accented in action nouns, but the suffix in agent nouns; e. g. *véd-a-* 'knowledge', *śiśnáth-a-* 'perforation'; but *cod-á-* 'instigator', *cacar-á-* 'moveable'[3]. When there is a verbal prefix, the final syllable is as a rule accented; e. g. *saṃ-gam-á-* m. 'coming together'. In a few of these compounds, however, the root is accented, as *ut-pā́t-a-* (AV.) 'portent', *ā-śréṣ-a-* (AV.) 'plague'; and in some others (mostly agent nouns) the prefix: *ā́-bhag-a-* 'sharing', *práti-veś-a-* 'neighbour', *vy-òṣ-a-* (AV.) 'burning', *sáṃ-kāś-a-* (AV.) 'appearance'.

3. The **suffix** ***-ata*** is always accented on the final syllable; e. g. *darś-atá-* 'visible', *pac-atá-* 'cooked', *yaj-atá-* 'to be adored'.

4. Of the participial **suffixes** ***-at*** **and** ***-ant*** the former is never accented when the sense is verbal; e. g. *dád-at-* 'giving', *dā́ś-at-* 'worshipping'. A few old participles, however, which have become substantives, have shifted the accent to the suffix: *vah-át-* 'stream', *vegh-át-* (AV. VS.) 'barren cow', *vāgh-át-* 'sacrificer', *srav-át-* 'stream', *saśc-át-* 'pursuer'. The suffix ***-ant*** is accented in the present participle of the second (450) and sixth (429) classes and of the denominative (562), e. g. *ad-ánt-*, *tud-ánt-*, *aghāy-ánt-*; in the future (537), e. g. *dāsy-ánt-* (AV.); in the root aorist, e. g. *bhid-ánt-* and sometimes in the *a*-aorist, e. g. *vṛdh-ánt-*; also in the old present participles which have become adjectives, *ṛh-ánt-* 'weak', *bṛh-ánt-* 'great', and (with lengthened vowel) *mah-ā́nt-* 'great'.

5. The **suffix** ***-an*** is generally accented; e. g. *ukṣ-án-* m. 'bull', *ud-án-* n. 'water'. The radical syllable is, however, not infrequently accented; e. g. *rā́j-an-* m. 'king', *ū́dh-an-* n. 'udder'.

6. Stems formed with ***-ana*** predominantly accent the root; e. g. *kár-aṇa-* n. 'act', *cód-ana-* (AV.) 'impelling'. The final syllable is, however, accented fairly often; e. g. *kar-aṇá-* 'active', *kroś-aná-* 'yelling', *kṣay-aṇá-* (VS.) 'habitable', *tvar-aṇá-* (AV.) 'hastening', *roc-aná-* 'shining' (AV.), n. 'light', *svap-aná-* (VS.) 'sleepy'. The penultimate is also accented in several words: the substantives

[1] The ŚB., however, accents both particles; cp. LEUMANN, KZ. 31, 22.

[2] Cp. WHITNEY 1147 g.

[3] Cp. WHITNEY 1148; LINDNER p. 34.

kir-áṇa- m. 'dust', *kṛp-áṇa-* n. 'misery' (but *kṛp-aṇá-* 'miserable' AV.), *daṃs-ána-* n. 'great deed', *vṛj-ána-* n. 'enclosure', *veṣ-áṇa-* n. 'service'; and the adjectives *tur-áṇa-* 'hastening', *doh-ána-* 'milking', *bhand-ána-* (VS. TS.) 'rejoicing', *man-ána-* 'considerate', *mand-ána-* 'joyful', *sakṣ-áṇa-* 'overcoming'. When the stem is compounded with a verbal prefix, the root is nearly always accented; e. g. *saṃ-gámana-* 'gathering together'; but the final syllable is accented in *vi-cakṣaṇá-* 'conspicuous', *upari-śayaná-* (AV.) 'couch'.

7. The suffix **-anā**, whether forming the feminine of adjectives in *-ana* or f. action nouns, is always accented either on the penultimate or the final syllable; e. g. *tur-áṇā-* 'speeding', *spand-anā́-* (AV.) 'kicking'; *arh-áṇā-* 'merit', *jar-aṇā́-* 'old age'. The word *pṛ́t-anā-* 'fight' is irregularly accented on the radical syllable.

8. The suffix **-ani** is always accented, either on the final or the penultimate syllable; e. g. *dyot-aní-* 'brilliance'; *aś-áni-* 'missile'.

9. The suffix **-anī** being the feminine form of action and agent nouns in *-ana*, is similarly accented; e. g. *péś-anī-* (AV.) 'beautiful' (*péś-ana-*). The accent is, however, sometimes shifted to the final syllable; e. g. *tap-anī́-* 'heat' (*táp-ana-*).

10. Stems formed with the suffix **-as** accent the root if they are action nouns, but the suffix if they are agent nouns; e. g. *áp-as-* n. 'work', but *ap-ás-* 'active'. There are also some masc. substantives with the accent on the suffix; e. g. *rakṣ-ás-* m. beside *rákṣ-as-* n. 'demon'.

11. The suffix **-ā**, forming action nouns from roots and secondary conjugation stems, is invariably[1] accented; e. g. *nind-ā́-* (AV.) 'blame'; *jigīṣ-ā́-* 'desire to win'; *gamay-ā́-* (AV[1].) 'causing to go'; *aśvay-ā́-* 'desire for horses'.

12. The suffix **-āna**, forming middle participles, is normally accented on the final syllable; e. g. *ad-āná-* 'eating'. Reduplicated stems, however, regularly accent the first syllable; e. g. *dád-āna-* 'giving', *jóhuv-āna-* 'invoking'. A few others accent the root; e. g. *cít-āna-* (AV[1].) 'shining', *dyút-āna-* (RV[1].) 'beaming' (beside the usual *dyut-āná-*)[2]. There are also a few adjectives and substantives ending in *-āna* in which the primary character of the suffix or the derivation of the word is doubtful. These also accent the first syllable; e. g. *vásav-āna-* 'possessing wealth', *párś-āna-* m. 'abyss'[3].

13. No general rule can be stated regarding the suffix **-i**, either the suffix or the root being accented with about equal frequency; e. g. *āj-í-* 'race', *grā́h-i-* 'seizure'. Action nouns used as infinitives, however, regularly accent the suffix; e. g. *dṛś-áye* 'to see'. Reduplicated derivatives tend to accent the initial syllable; e. g. *cákr-i-* 'active'; while stems compounded with a preposition usually accent the final syllable; e. g. *parā-dad-í-* 'delivering over'.

14. Stems formed with the superlative suffix **-iṣṭha** regularly accent the root; e. g. *yáj-iṣṭha-* 'sacrificing best'. The only exceptions are *jyeṣṭhá-* when meaning 'eldest' (but *jyéṣṭha-* 'greatest') and *kan-iṣṭhá-* 'youngest' (but *kán-iṣṭha-* 'smallest', TS. B). When the stem is compounded with a preposition the latter is accented; e. g. *ā́-gam-iṣṭha-* 'coming best'.

15. The suffix **-is** is nearly always accented; e. g. *arc-ís-* 'flame'. The exceptions are *ám-is-* 'raw flesh', *jyót-is-* 'light', and *vyáth-is-* 'course'(?).

16. The few action and agent nouns formed with the suffix **-ī**, are accented either on the root or the suffix; e. g. *deh-ī́-* 'rampart', *śác-ī-* 'power'.

[1] If *jáṅghā-* 'leg' is formed with this suffix, it is the only exception.

[2] See Lindner p. 54, top.

[3] See below, Nominal stem formation, under *-āna-* (130).

17. Stems formed with the comparative **suffix** ***-īyāṃs*** invariably accent the root; e. g. *jáv-īyāṃs-* 'swifter'. When the stem is compounded with a preposition the latter is accented; e. g. *práti-cyav-īyāṃs-* 'pressing closer against'.

18. The **suffix** ***-u*** is usually accented; e. g. *ur-ú-* 'wide', *pād-ú-* m. 'foot'. The radical syllable is, however, not infrequently accented; e.g. *ták-u-* 'speeding', *ás-u-* m. 'life'. The suffix is regularly accented in adjectives formed from desiderative, causative, and denominative stems; e. g. *dips-ú-* 'wishing to harm', *bhāvay-ú-* 'cherishing', *aghāy-ú-* 'malignant'.

19. Substantives formed with the **suffix** ***-us*** regularly accent the root (excepting *jan-ús-* 'birth'); e. g. *dhán-us-* 'bow'. But a few adjectives which are never used as substantives accent the suffix; e. g. *jay-ús-* 'victorious', but *táp-us-* both 'hot' and 'heat'.

20. The **suffix** ***-ū*** forming independent feminine substantives is regularly accented; as *cam-ú-* 'dish', *vadh-ú-* 'bride'.

21. When the **suffix** ***-ta*** forms past passive participles it is invariably accented; e. g. *jā-tá-* 'born', *rakṣ-i-tá-* 'protected'. But a few ordinary nouns formed with this suffix accent the radical syllable: *é-ta-* 'variegated'; m.: *gár-ta-* 'car-seat', *már-ta-* 'mortal', *vā́-ta-* 'wind', *hás-ta-* 'hand'; n.: *ás-ta-* 'home', *nák-ta-* 'night'.

22. Stems formed with the **suffix** ***-tar*** generally accent the root when the meaning is participial, but the suffix when it is purely nominal; e. g. *dā́-tar-* 'giving' (with acc.), but *dā-tár-* 'giver'.

23. Stems formed with the **suffix** ***-ti*** accent the root more frequently than the suffix; e. g. *íṣ-ṭi-* 'offering', *kṣí-ti-* (AV.) 'destruction', *dhú-ti-* m. 'shaker', but *iṣ-ṭí-* 'desire', *kṣi-tí-* 'abode', *jñā-tí-* m. 'relative', *rā-tí-* 'gift'. Reduplicated derivatives seem to have accented either the first syllable or the suffix; e. g. *dī́dhi-ti-* 'devotion' and *carkṛ-tí-* 'fame'. When these stems are compounded with prepositions, the latter are nearly always accented; e. g. *ā́-hu-ti-* 'offering'; the only exceptions are *ā-sak-tí-* 'pursuit', *ā-su-tí-* 'brew' and 'enlivening', and *abhi-ṣ-ṭí-* m. 'helper' beside *abhí-ṣ-ṭi-* f. 'help'.

24. Derivatives formed with the **suffix** ***-tu***, with some half dozen exceptions, accent the root (invariably when they are used as infinitives); e. g. *tán-tu-* 'thread', but *ak-tú-* 'ray'.

25. The **suffix** ***-tnu*** is always accented; e. g. *ha-tnú-* 'deadly', *jígha-tnú-* 'harming'.

26. Derivatives formed with the **suffix** ***-tra*** generally accent the root; e. g. *mán-tra-* 'prayer', but *kṣa-trá-* 'dominion'.

27. **Gerundives** formed with the **suffix** ***-tva*** regularly accent the root; e. g. *kár-tva-* 'to be made', *vák-tva-* 'to be said', *bháv-i-tva-* 'future'.

28. Derivatives formed with the **suffix** ***-tha*** generally accent the latter; e. g. *uk-thá-* n. 'saying'. Sometimes, however, the root is accented; e. g. *ár-tha-* 'goal'. When the suffix is added with the connecting vowel *-a-*, the latter is generally accented; e. g. *uc-á-tha-* n. 'praise'.

29. The **suffix** ***-na*** when forming past passive participles is invariably accented; e. g. *bhin-ná-* 'split'. When forming ordinary nouns, whether adjectives or masc. substantives, it is usually accented; e. g. *ṛ-ṇá-* 'guilty', *ghṛ-ṇá-* m. 'heat'; but a few masculines accent the root, as *kár-ṇa-* 'ear', *vár-ṇa-* 'colour', *svápa-na-* 'sleep'. Neuters (except *śu-ná-* 'welfare') and feminines (*-nā*) accent the root; e. g. *án-na-*[1] 'food', *tṛ́-ṇa-* 'grass', *tṛ́ṣ-ṇā-* 'thirst'.

[1] Originally a past participle of *ad-* 'eat'.

30. Derivatives formed with **-ni** accent either the root or the suffix; e. g. *yó-ni-* m. 'receptacle', but *ag-ní-* m. 'fire'.

31. The suffix **-nu** is almost invariably accented; e. g. *vag-nú-* 'sound'. An exception is *víṣ-ṇu-*[1], N. of god.

32. Derivatives formed with the suffix **-ma** accent the suffix more than twice as often as the root; e. g. *tig-má-* 'sharp', *ghar-má-* 'heat', *dhū-má-* 'smoke', but *ú-ma-* 'friend', *só-ma-* 'Soma'.

33. Derivatives formed with **-man** regularly accent the root in neuter substantives; e. g. *kár-man-* 'action', *ján-man-* 'birth', *nā́-man-* 'name'. There are, however, several masculine agent nouns which accent the suffix; e. g. *dar-mán-* 'breaker'. In several instances the accent varies in the same word according to the gender and meaning; e. g. *bráh-man-* n. 'prayer', *brah-mán-* m. 'one who prays'; *sád-man-* n. 'seat', *sad-mán-* m. 'sitter'. These stems when compounded with prepositions nearly always accent the latter; e.g. *prá-bharman-* n. 'presentation'.

34. The participial suffix **-māna** is never accented except in the anomalous perfect participle *sasṛ-māṇá-* (RV[1].) = *sasr-āṇá-* 'speeding'. The accent of these derivatives is regularly on the same syllable as in the tense-stem to which the suffix is added; e. g. *yája-māna-* 'sacrificing', *icchá-māna-* 'desiring', *idhyá-māna-* 'being kindled', *yakṣyá-māṇa-* 'about to sacrifice'.

35. Gerundives formed with the suffix **-ya** invariably accent the root; e. g. *háv-ya-* 'to be invoked'.

36. The suffix **-ra** is usually accented; e. g. *ak-rá-* m. 'banner', *rud-rá-*, m. N. of a god, *abh-rá-* n. 'cloud'. The root is, however, accented in a good many words; e. g. *gṛ́dh-ra-* 'greedy', *áj-ra-* m. 'field', *índ-ra-*, N. of a god, *ág-ra-* n. 'point'.

37. Derivatives formed with the suffix **-ri** accent the root oftener than the suffix; e. g. *bhú-ri-* 'abundant', but also *sū-rí-* m. 'patron'.

38. Derivatives formed with the suffix **-va** accent the suffix rather oftener than the root; e. g. *ṛk-vá-* 'praising', but also *ṛ́bh-va-* 'skilful'.

39. The root is regularly accented in derivatives formed with the suffix **-van**; e. g. *kṛ́-t-van-* 'active', *pát-van-* 'flying', *yáj-van-* 'sacrificing'. This is the case even when the stem is compounded with a preposition; e. g. *vi-mṛ́g-van-* (AV.) 'cleansing'.

40. The suffixes **-vana**, **-vanu**, **-vani** are always accented, the first two on the final, the last on the initial syllable; e. g. *vag-vaná-* 'talkative', *vag-vanú-* m. 'noise', *bhur-váṇi-* 'restless'.

41. Derivatives formed with the suffix **-vara** chiefly accent the final syllable when they are masc. nouns, but the root when they are neuter substantives; e. g. *i-t-vará-* 'going', *īś-vará-* (AV.) 'able', but *kár-vara-* n. 'deed', *gáh-vara-* (AV.) n. 'thicket'. The suffix appears with *l* instead of *r* in the adjective *vid-valá-* 'cunning'.

42. The suffix **-vāṃs** of the perfect participle is always accented, even in the reduced form *-us* appearing in the weak cases; e. g. *cakṛ-vā́ṃs-* and *cakr-úṣ-* 'having made'.

43. Derivatives formed with the suffix **-vi** from the simple root accent the radical syllable, but the first syllable of the reduplicated root; thus *ghṛ́ṣ-vi-* 'lively', but *jā́gṛ-vi-* 'watchful'.

[1] This word may, however, be differently derived; possibly *vi-ṣṇu-* 'der in die Weite strebende', according to UHLENBECK, Kurzgefasstes etymologisches Wörterbuch der altindischen Sprache, Amsterdam 1898; cp. BLOOMFIELD, AJPh. 17, 427 f., 'crossing the back (of the world)'.

44. Derivatives formed with the **suffix** ***-sa*** sometimes accent the root, sometimes the suffix; e. g. *gṛ́t-sa-* 'adroit', *út-sa-* m. 'fountain', but *pṛk-ṣá-* 'dappled', *ghraṃ-sá-* m. 'sun's heat'.

45. The **suffix** ***-snu*** is always accented; e. g. *ji-ṣṇú-* 'victorious', *vṛdh-a-snú-* 'joyful', *car-i-ṣṇú-* 'wandering', *ni-ṣat-snú-* 'sitting down', *tāpay-i-ṣṇú-* 'tormenting', *abhi-śocay-i-ṣṇú-* (AV.) 'causing torments'.

B. In **secondary derivation** five groups of stems may be distinguished with regard to accentuation: **a.** those which accent the suffix, being formed with *-āyaná*, *-ā́yī*, *-ā́yya*, *-ín*, *-iya*, *-ī́na*, *-ī́ya*, *-ení*, *-énya*, *-tá*, *-tav-yà*, *-tvá*, *-tvá-tā*, *-tvaná*, *-má*, *-máya*, *-mín*, *-mná*, *-yín*, *-vá*, *-vát*, *-valá*, *-vín*; **b.** those in which the suffix is not accented, being formed with *-taya*, *-tara*, *-tā*, *-tāt*, *-tāti*, *-tya*, *-vya*; **c.** those in which only the first syllable is accented, being formed with *-i* and *-nī*; **d.** those in which either the first or the last syllable is accented, being formed by means of Vṛddhi with the suffixes *-eya*, *-a* or *-na* (the last two also without Vṛddhi); **e.** those in which the accent is sometimes on the suffix, and sometimes on one or other syllable of the primitive stem, being formed with the suffixes *-ā*, *-āni*, *-ima*, *-ī*, *-ka*, *-tana* or *-tna*, *-tama*, *-tha*, *-bha*, *-mant*, *-ya*, *-ra*, *-la*, *-van*, *-vant*, *-vaya*, *-śa*. The following is a detailed account of the accent in derivatives formed with the above secondary suffixes in their alphabetical order.

1. **Stems** formed with the **suffix** ***-a*** and **Vṛddhi** of the first syllable from primitive stems ending in *-a* are predominantly accented on the final syllable. This is, however, mostly the case when the primitive is accented on any syllable other than the last; e. g. *āmitrá-* 'hostile' from *amítra-* 'foe', *nārāśaṃsá-* 'belonging to Nárā-śáṃsa', *śaucadrathá-*, patronymic from *śucád-ratha-* 'having a shining car', *pāvamāná-* 'relating to the clear-flowing (*pávamāna-*) Soma'. In several instances, however, the primitive stem is also oxytone, e. g. *kauśiká-* 'belonging to Kuśiká'. On the other hand, stems formed with Vṛddhi sometimes accent the first syllable, when the primitive is otherwise accented; e. g. *mā́dhyaṃdina-* 'belonging to midday' (*madhyáṃ-dina-*), *sáubhaga-* n. 'luck' from *su-bhága-* 'lucky', *vā́dhryaśva-* 'descendant of Vadhryaśvá'. The derivative *dáivodāsa-* 'belonging to Divodāsa' is, however, formed from a stem similarly accented (*dívo-dāsa-*).

A similar rule prevails in the accentuation of stems derived from other primitives by means of the **suffix** ***-a*** **and Vṛddhi** of the first syllable; e. g. *āyas-á-* 'made of metal' (*áyas-*), *saumanas-á-* 'benevolence' from *su-mánas-* 'well-disposed'; also sometimes from stems similarly accented, as *paidv-á-* 'belonging to Pedú'. On the other hand, the first syllable is accented in derivatives from primitives mostly accented on the last; e. g. *pā́rthiva-* 'earthly' from *pṛthivī́-* 'earth', *mā́ghona-* 'belonging to the bountiful one' (*maghávan-*); but sometimes also from stems similarly accented, as *nā́huṣ-a-* 'neighbouring' from *náhus-* 'neighbour'. The accentuation is similar when the secondary *-a* is added without Vṛddhi; e. g. *paruṣ-á-* 'knotty' from *párus-* 'knot', but *hárit-a-* 'fallow' from *harít-*.

2. The **suffix** ***-ā*** forming feminines to masculines in *-a* retains the accent on the same syllable as in the masculine; e. g. *priyā́-* beside *priyá-* 'dear'.

3. **Stems** formed with the somewhat rare **suffix** ***-ānī*** accent one of the last three syllables; e. g. *indrā́ṇī-* 'wife of Índra', *mudgalā́nī-* 'wife of Múdgala', *purukútsānī-* 'wife of Purukútsa', *uśī́nárāṇī-* 'queen of the Uśī́naras'.

4. The only example of the patronymic **suffix** ***-āyana*** in the RV. *kāṇv-āyana-* 'descendant of Kaṇva' is unaccented (occurring in the voc. only); the final syllable seems to have been accented judging by *dākṣ-āyaṇá-*

(VS. AV.) 'son of Dakṣa', and the fem. *rāmāyaṇī-* (AV.) 'daughter of the Black one'. The derivative *ukṣaṇyáyana-*, N. of a man, is unique both in accentuation and absence of Vṛddhi.

5. The **suffix** ***-āyī*** occurs accented on the first syllable only in *agn-áyī-* 'wife of Agní'; *vṛṣākap-āyī-* (RV[1].) 'wife of Vṛṣákapi', occurring in the voc. only, is unaccented.

6. The **suffix** ***-āyya-*** forming gerundival adjectives is always accented on its first syllable; e. g. *pan-áyya-* 'to be admired'.

7. Derivatives formed with the **suffix** ***-i*** and Vṛddhi, being almost exclusively patronymics, always accent the first syllable; thus *ágniveś-i-* 'son of Agniveśa', *páurukuts-i-* 'descendant of Purukútsa', *prátardan-i-* 'descendant of Pratardana', *práhrād-i-* (AV.) 'son of Prahrāda', *sáṃvaraṇ-i-* 'descendant of Saṃváraṇa'. Similarly formed and accented is *sárath-i-* 'charioteer' (from *sa-rátha-m* 'on the same chariot'). Two other words, formed without Vṛddhi, take the secondary *-i*: *tápuṣ-i-* 'burning' (*tápus-* 'heat') and, accented on the final syllable, *śucant-í-*, N. of a man.

8. The very frequent **suffix** ***-in*** forming possessive adjectives is always accented; e. g. *aśv-ín-* 'possessing horses', *dhan-ín-* 'wealthy'; *manīṣ-ín-* 'wise'; *abhimāt-ín-* 'insidious'. The adjective *śāk-ín-* 'powerful' occurs once accented on the first syllable: *śā́k-ī* (I. 51[8]); the accentuation of this form and of the two nominatives (each occurring once) *ír-ī* 'violent' and *sár-ī* 'speeding' is perhaps due to error.

9. The accentuation of the **suffix** ***-ima***, which is attached to three stems in *-tra-* and to one in *-ra*, varies: *khanítr-ima-* 'made by digging', *kṛtr-íma-* 'artificial', *pūtr-íma-* (AV.) 'purified'; *agr-imá-* 'foremost'.

10. The **suffix** ***-iya*** is regularly accented either on its first or its second syllable; e. g. *abhr-íya-* and *abhr-iyá-* 'derived from the clouds' (*abhrá-*), *kṣatr-íya-* 'having authority' (*kṣatrá-*), *amitr-íya-* 'inimical' (*amítra-* 'foe'); *agr-iyá-* 'foremost', *indr-iyá-* 'belonging to Indra'. The only exceptions are *ṛ́tv-iya-* (AV.) 'being in season' (*ṛtú-*), beside *ṛtv-íya-*, and *śrótr-iya-* (AV.) 'learned' (*śrótra-* 'learning').

11. Derivatives with the feminine **suffix** ***-ī*** commonly accent the same syllable as the corresponding masculines (except oxytones); e. g. *bhávant-ī-* 'being', m. *bhávant-*. But the feminine in *-ī* from masculines in *-a* that are not accented on the final syllable usually accents the *-ī* (and follows the radical *ī-* declension); e. g. *rath-ī́-* 'charioteer' (m. f.) from *rátha-* 'chariot'. The *-ī* is also accented when it forms the fem. of masc. oxytones in *-u*, e. g. *pṛthv-ī́-* 'broad' (*pṛth-ú-*); in *-ant*, e. g. *uśat-ī́-* 'desiring' (*uś-ánt-*); in *-tár*, e. g. *avitr-ī́-* 'protectress' (*avi-tár-*); in *-añc* taking Samprasāraṇa, e. g. *pratīc-ī́-* 'facing' (*praty-áñc-*). The fem. in *-ī* from masc. oxytones in *-a* sometimes retains the accent on the suffix, e. g. *devī́-* 'goddess' (*devá-* 'god'), but more usually throws it back on the first syllable, e. g. *áruṣ-ī-* 'ruddy' (*aruṣá-*).

12. The **suffix** ***-īna*** is generally accented on its first syllable, rarely on its last; e. g. *apāc-ī́na-* 'western', *saṃvatsar-ī́ṇa-* 'annual'; *pratīc-īná-* 'turned towards'. The suffix is unaccented only in *mā́k-īna-* (RV[1].) 'mine'.

13. The **suffix** ***-īya*** is always accented on its first syllable; e. g. *ārjīk-ī́ya-* a kind of Soma vessel, *āhavan-ī́ya-* (AV.) 'sacrificial fire', *gṛhamedh-ī́ya-* 'relating to the domestic sacrifice', *parvat-ī́ya-* (AV.) 'mountainous'. Similarly in the ordinals *dvit-ī́ya-* 'second', *tṛt-ī́ya-* 'third', *tur-ī́ya-* 'fourth'.

14. The **suffix** ***-ena*** is accented on the final in its only occurrence in the feminine form *sāmidh-enī́-* 'relating to fuel' (*samídh-*).

15. The **suffix** ***-enya***, nearly always forming gerundives, regularly accents

its first syllable; e. g. *dṛś-énya-* 'worthy to be seen'. The only exception is *vár-eṇya-* 'desirable'. Similarly accented are the ordinary adjectives *vīr-éṇya-* 'manly' (*vīrá-*) and *kīrt-énya-* 'famous' (*kīrtí-* 'fame').

16. Derivatives formed with the **suffix** ***-eya*** and Vṛddhi accent the final syllable when they have a patronymic sense, but otherwise the first; e. g. *ārṣ-eyá-* 'descendant of a seer' (*ṛ́ṣi-*), but *páuruṣ-eya-* 'relating to man' (*púruṣa-*). The analogy of the gerundive from roots ending in *-ā*, which is formed with *-eya* (e. g. *déya-* 'to be given'), is followed by *didṛkṣ-éya-* 'worth seeing' (*didṛkṣā́-*) and *sabh-éya-* 'fit for an assembly' (*sabhā́-*).

17. Derivatives formed with ***-ka*** are variously accented. Those which have a diminutive sense regularly accent the suffix; e. g. *arbha-ká-* 'small', *kanīna-ká-*[1] 'youth', *kumāra-ká-* 'little boy'. Otherwise the accent sometimes remains on the same syllable as in the primitive; e. g. *ánta-ka-* 'making an end' (*ánta-*), *yuṣmā́-ka-* 'your' (*yuṣmá-*); or it shifts to the suffix, e. g. *anya-ká-* 'other' (*anyá-*), *sana-ká-* 'old' (*sána-*); or to the first syllable, e. g. *rū́pa-ka-* (AV.) 'having an assumed form' (*rūpá-* 'form').

18. The rare **suffix** ***-ta*** is regularly accented: *eka-tá-* (VS.) 'First', *dvi-tá-* 'Second', *tri-tá-* 'Third' as Proper Names, *ava-tá-* 'well', *muhūr-tá-* 'moment'.

19. Derivatives formed with the **suffix** ***-tana*** or its syncopated form ***-tna*** are variously accented: *nū́-tana-* and *nū́-tna-* 'present', *sanā-tána-* (AV.) and *saná-tna-* (AV.) 'lasting', *pra-tná-* 'ancient'.

20. The **suffix** ***-tama*** when forming superlatives is hardly ever accented[2], the primitive nearly always retaining its original accent; e. g. *tavás-tama-*[3] 'very strong'. But when it forms ordinals the final syllable is accented; e. g. *śata-tamá-* 'hundredth'.

21. A few adjectives formed with ***-taya*** from numerals meaning 'consisting of so many parts', accent the primitive: *cátuṣ-ṭaya-* (AV.) 'fourfold', *dáśa-taya-* 'tenfold'.

22. The **suffix** ***-tara*** forming comparatives is hardly ever accented, the primitive retaining its original accent; e. g. *rathī́-tara-* 'better car-fighter'. An exception is *vṛtra-tára-* 'a worse Vṛtra'.

23. Derivatives formed with ***-tā*** regularly accentuate the syllable preceding the suffix; e. g. *a-gó-tā-* 'want of cows', *devá-tā-* 'divinity', *puruṣá-tā-* 'human nature'. The only exception is *a-vīra-tā-* 'want of sons'.

24. Derivatives formed with ***-tāti*** and ***-tāt*** have the same accentuation as those formed with *-tā*; e. g. *a-riṣṭá-tāti-* 'security', *devá-tāti-* 'divinity', *śáṃ-tāti-* 'good fortune'. The accent is exceptional in *ásta-tāti-* 'home' and *dákṣa-tāti-* (AV.) 'cleverness'.

25. The **suffix** ***-tya***, forming nouns from particles, is never accented: *ápa-tya-* n. 'offspring', *amā́-tya-* 'companion', *āvíṣ-ṭya-* 'manifest', *ní-tya-* 'own', *níṣ-ṭya-* 'foreign', *sánu-tya-* 'secret'. When attached to the substantive *ap-* 'water' it is, however, accented: *ap-tyá-* and *āp-tyá-* 'watery'.

26. The **suffix** ***-tva*** is invariably accented; e. g. *amṛta-tvá-* 'immortality', *pati-tvá-* 'matrimony'.

27. The very rare **suffix** ***-tva-tā*** is accented on its first syllable: *iṣita-tvátā-* 'excitement', *puruṣa-tvátā-* 'human nature'.

28. The **suffix** ***-tvana*** is always accented on its final syllable; e. g. *kavi-tvaná-* 'wisdom', *pati-tvaná-* 'matrimony', *sakhi-tvaná-* 'friendship'.

---

[1] Accented *kanī́naka-* in the VS. The fem. in the RV. is *kanīnakā́-* but in the AV[1]. *kanī́nikā-*.

[2] Except *puru-táma-* 'very many' and *ut-tamá-* 'highest', *śaśvat-tamá-* 'most frequent' (with the ordinal accent).

[3] It is shifted in *mṛḍayát-tama-* 'showing great compassion' (*mṛḍáyat-*). Cp. below 89.

29. The suffix **-tha**, forming ordinals from a few numerals and adjectives of a cognate sense from pronominal stems, is nearly always accented: thus *catur-thá-* (AV.) 'fourth', *ṣaṣ-ṭhá-* (AV. VS.) 'sixth', *kati-thá-* 'the how-maniest'; but *saptá-tha-* 'seventh'.

30. The rare derivatives formed with the **suffix -na** are accented either on the first or the last syllable: *stráí-ṇa-* 'feminine' (*strí-* 'woman'), *víṣu-ṇa-* 'various'; but *purā-ṇá-*[1] 'ancient', *samā-ná-* 'like'.

31. With the **suffix -bha**[2] are formed the names of a few animals with one exception accented on the final syllable: *ṛṣa-bhá-* and *vṛṣa-bhá-* 'bull', *garda-bhá-* 'ass', *śara-bhá-* (AV. VS.) 'fabulous eight-legged animal', *rása-bha-* 'ass'. This suffix also occurs once in the adjective *sthūla-bhá-* (AV.) 'big'.

32. The **suffix -ma** is regularly accented, whether forming superlatives; e. g. *adha-má-* 'lowest', *madhya-má-* 'middle-most', or ordinals; e. g. *aṣṭa-má-* 'eighth'. An exception is *ánta-ma-*[3] 'next'.

33. Derivatives formed with the **suffix -mant** retain the accent of the primitive, unless the latter is oxytone, when the accent in the great majority of instances (about three-fourths) is thrown forward on the suffix; e. g. *óṣadhī-mant-* (AV.) 'rich in herbs', *aśáni-mant-* 'bearing the thunderbolt'; but *agni-mánt-* 'having fire' (*agní-*).

34. The **suffix -maya** is always accented on the first syllable; e. g. *ayas-máya-* 'made of metal', *go-máya-* 'consisting of cows', *śaka-máya-* 'arising from excrement'.

35. The **suffix -min** is accented (like *-in*) in the only two derivatives formed with it: *iṣ-mín-* 'impetuous', and *ṛg-mín-* 'jubilant with praise' (*ṛ́c-*).

36. The rare **suffix -mna** is always accented: *dyu-mná-* 'brightness', *nṛ-mṇá-* 'manliness', *ni-mná-* 'depth', *su-mná-* 'welfare'.

37. Derivatives formed with the **suffix -ya and Vṛddhi** accent the initial or the final syllable with the same shift as appears in those formed with *-a*: the initial, when the primitive is accented on the final (or sometimes a medial) syllable, but the final, when the primitive is accented on the initial (or sometimes a medial syllable); e. g. *dáiv-ya-* 'divine' (*devá-* 'god'), *ā́rtvij-ya-* 'office of priest' (*ṛtvíj-*), *gā́rhapat-ya-* 'position of a householder' (*gṛhá-pati-*); but *ādit-yá-* 'son of Aditi', *prājāpat-yá-* (AV.) 'relating to Prajā́pati'. In a very few instances the accent remains unchanged, as *ā́dhipat-ya-* 'lordship' (*ádhi-pati-* 'lord'), *páuṃs-ya-* 'manliness' (*púṃs-* 'man'), *váiś-ya-* 'man of the third caste' (*víś-* 'settler'), *śráiṣṭh-ya-* (AV.) 'superiority' (*śréṣṭha-* 'best'); while in several instances it shifts from the final syllable to the suffix (instead of to the initial syllable); e. g. *kāv-yá-* 'descendant of Kaví' (but *kā́v-ya-* 'endowed with the qualities of a sage', *kaví-*).

a. In derivatives formed **without Vṛddhi** the accentuation is to some extent similar; thus a final accent shifts to the first syllable; e. g. in *pítr-ya-* 'belonging to the fathers' (*pitṛ́-*), *prátijan-ya-* 'adverse' (*prati-janá-* 'adversary' AV.); or from the first to the last; e. g. *grām-yá-* 'belonging to the village' (*grā́ma-*); or it remains on the first syllable; e. g. *áv-ya-* 'belonging to sheep' (*ávi-*), *gáv-ya-* 'derived from cows' (*gó-*); or it shifts from the final syllable to the suffix (instead of the first syllable); e. g. *kav-yá-* 'wise' (*kaví-*). But here the accent may also remain on or be shifted to a medial syllable; e. g. *svarā́j-ya-* 'autocracy' (*svarā́j-* 'sovereign'), *viśvádev-ya-* 'belonging to all gods' (*viśvá-deva-*); *hiraṇyá-ya-* 'golden' (*híraṇya-* 'gold'), *avyá-ya-* 'derived from sheep' (beside *ávya-ya-*), *gavyá-ya-* 'derived from cows' (beside *gávya-*).

[1] Cp. BB. 28, 318, bottom. [2] Cp. PRELLWITZ, BB. 22, 74—114, on animal names in *-bha*.
[3] But *antamébhiḥ* (I. 165⁵).

But a peculiarity of the derivatives formed without Vṛddhi is that the majority of them have the Svarita accent on the suffix; e. g. *rājan-yà-* 'belonging to the royal class' (*rā́jan-*); *doṣaṇ-yà-* 'relating to the arm' (*doṣán-*); *vāyav-yà-* 'belonging to Wind' (*vāyú-*); *-dundubh-yà-* (VS.) 'relating to a drum' (*dundubhí*); *budhn-yà-* 'belonging to the bottom' (*budhná-*). The suffix thus accented also appears in the gerundive in **-tav-yà-** (twice found in the AV.) formed from an infinitive stem in *-tu* (585, 4).

38. The rare suffix **-yin** is (like *-in*) always accented: *ātatā-yín-* (VS.) 'having one's bow drawn', *dhanvā-yín-* (VS.) 'bearing a bow', *marā-yín-*, N. of a man, *sṛkā-yín-* (VS.) 'having a spear', *svadhā-yín-* (VS.) 'owning the Svadhā'.

39. Derivatives formed with **-ra** having a comparative sense (chiefly from prepositions) accent the initial syllable: *ádha-ra-* 'lower', *ápa-ra-* 'later', *áva-ra-* 'lower', *úpa-ra-* 'lower', *ánta-ra-*[1] 'near' (*ánta-* 'end'). Other nouns formed with the suffix are chiefly accented on the final syllable; e. g. *a-śrī-rá-* 'ugly', *dhūm-rá-* (VS.) 'dusky' (*dhūmá-* 'smoke'), *pāṃsu-rá-* 'dusty, *rath-i-rá-* 'riding in a chariot'; but sometimes otherwise; thus *ā́gnīdh-ra-* 'belonging to the fire-kindler' (*agnī́dh-*), *médh-i-ra-* 'wise', *karmā́-ra-* 'smith'.

40. Derivatives formed with **-la** nearly always accent the suffix; e. g. *a-ślī-lá-* (AV.) 'ugly', *jīva-lá-* (AV.) 'lively', *bahu-lá-*[1] 'abundant', *madhu-lá-* 'sweet'; but *tílvi-la-* 'fertile', *śéva-la-* (AV.) 'slimy', *śiśú-la-* 'little child'.

41. The suffix **-va** is regularly accented: *arṇa-vá-* 'billowy', *keśa-vá-* (AV.) 'hairy', *añji-vá-* (AV.) 'slippery', *śanti-vá-* (AV.) 'friendly', *śraddhi-vá-* 'credible'.

42. The fem. substantives formed from adverbs or prepositions with the suffix **-vat** always accent the final syllable: *arvā-vát-* 'proximity', *ā-vát-* (AV.) 'proximity', *ud-vát-* 'height', *ni-vát-* 'depth', *parā-vát-* 'distance', *pra-vát-* 'height', *saṃ-vát-* 'region'.

43. Derivatives formed with the suffix **-van** may have the accent on any syllable; e. g. *áthar-van,* 'fire-priest', *índhan-van-* 'possessed of fuel', *ṛ́ghā-van-* 'violent'; *ṛtá-van-* 'regular', *maghá-van-* 'bountiful'; *arātī-ván-* 'hostile', *śruṣṭī-ván-* 'obedient'.

44. Derivatives formed with **-vant** generally retain the original accent except in oxytone stems (if not ending in *a* or *ā*), which as a rule throw it on the suffix; e. g. *kéśa-vant-* 'hairy', *putrá-vant-* (VS.) 'having a son', *prajā́-vant-* 'having offspring', *dyā́vāpṛthivī́-vant-* 'connected with heaven and earth'; but *agni-vánt-* 'having fire' (*agní-*), *āsan-vánt* (AV.) 'having a mouth'. The accent is anomalously shifted in *kṛśanā́-vant-* 'decorated with pearls' (*kṛ́śana-*) and *viṣū-vánt-* 'central' (*víṣu-*) 'in both directions'.

45. The very rare derivatives formed with the suffix **-vaya** accent either the suffix or the primitive: *dru-váya-* (AV.) 'wooden dish' and *cátur-vaya-* 'fourfold'.

46. Derivatives formed with the rare suffix **-vala** accent their final syllable: *kṛṣī-valá-* 'peasant', *naḍ-valā́-* (VS.) 'reed bed'.

47. The suffix **-vin** is always accented; e. g. *namas-vín-* 'reverential', *yaśas-vín-* (AV.) 'beautiful', *medhā-vín-* (AV.) 'wise', *dhṛṣad-vín-* 'bold'.

48. The very rare names of relationship formed with the suffix **-vya** accent the first syllable: *bhrā́tṛ-vya-* (AV.) 'nephew'.

49. A few adjectives and substantives formed with the suffix **-śa** accent either the final or, less often, the first or second syllable: *arva-śá-* or

[1] This word may, however, be derived from *antár-* 'within', with BR. and WHITNEY 1209 i.

árva-śa- 'hasting', *eta-śá-* or *éta-śa-* 'variegated', *babhlu-śá-* (VS. MS.) 'brownish', *roma-śá-* 'hairy', *yuva-śá-* 'youthful', *aṅku-śá-* 'hook', *turvá-śa-*, N. of a man. Perhaps also *káśma-śa-* (AV.) 'stupefaction' (?), and *kalá-śa-* 'jar'.

2. Accentuation of Compounds.

AUFRECHT, De accentu compositorum Sanscriticorum, Bonn 1847. — GARBE, KZ. 23, 470 f. — REUTER, Die altindischen nominalcomposita, ihrer betonung nach untersucht, KZ. 31, 157—232; 485—612. — WACKERNAGEL, Altindische Grammatik 2[1], p. 40—43, etc.

87. The rule as to the accentuation of compounds, stated in the most general way, is that iteratives, possessives, and governing compounds place the accent on the first member; determinatives and regularly formed copulatives (with one accent) on the last member and to a large extent on its final syllable. Speaking generally the accent of a compound is that of one of its members. But some words always change their accent when compounded; thus *víśva-* 'all' regularly becomes *viśvá-*, and in the later Saṃhitās *sárva-* 'all' sometimes becomes *sarvá-*. Other words when compounded change their accent in certain combinations only; thus some paroxytones become oxytone, as *pū́rva-* 'prior' in *pūrvá-citti-* 'foreboding', *pūrvá-pīti-* 'precedence in drinking', *pūrvá-hūti-* 'first invocation'; *néma-* 'one' in *nemá-dhiti-* 'separation'; *médha-* 'sacrifice' in *medhá-pati-* 'lord of sacrifice', and *medhá-sāti-* 'receiving the oblation'; *vṛ́ṣan-* in *vṛṣā́-kapi-*, N. of a monkey; on the other hand some oxytones throw back the accent, as *khādí-* 'bracelet' in *khā́di-hasta-* 'having hands adorned with bracelets'; *grīvā́-* 'neck' in *tuvi-grī́va-* 'powerful-necked'; *vīrá-* 'hero' in *puru-vī́ra-* 'possessed of many men' and *su-vī́ra-* 'heroic'; *dhūmá-* 'smoke' in *śaka-dhū́ma-* (AV.) 'smoke of cowdung'.

An adjective compound may shift the accent from one member to the other if it becomes a substantive or a Proper Name; thus *a-kṣára-* 'imperishable', *á-kṣarā-* 'speech'; *sú-kṛta-* 'well done', *su-kṛtá-* n. 'good deed'; *á-rāya-* 'niggardly', *a-rā́ya-*, N. of a demon.

88. In **iteratives**, which may consist of repeated nouns, pronouns, adverbs, prepositions, or particles, the first member alone is accented, the two words being separated by Avagraha in the Pada text, like the members of other compounds. Examples are: *áhar-ahar jāyate māsí-māsi* (x. 52[3]) 'day after day he is born, month after month'; *yád-yad yā́mi tád ā́ bhara* (VIII. 61[6]) 'bring to me whatever I ask'; *yáthā-yathā matáyaḥ sánti nṛṇā́m* (x. 111[1]) 'as are the desires of men in each case'; *adyā́dyā śváḥ-śva índra trā́sva paré ca naḥ* (VIII. 61[17]) 'on each to-day, on each to-morrow protect us, Indra, and in the future'. The prepositions which appear as iteratives are *úpa, párā, prá, sám*; e. g. *prá-pra pūṣṇás tuvijātásya śasyate mahitvám* (I. 138[1]) 'forth and again the greatness of the mighty Pūṣan is praised'[1]. The only verbal iterative occurring is *píba-piba* (II. 11[11])[2] 'drink again and again'.

89. **Governing compounds** always accent the first member when it is a verbal noun[3], as *trasá-dasyu-* 'terrifying the foe', N. of a man. When the first member is a present or aorist participle, its final syllable is invariably accented, whatever the original accentuation may have been, e. g. *vidád-vasu-* 'winning wealth', *tarád-dveṣas-* 'overcoming (*tárat-*) foes'.

1 In a few instances the repeated words are not treated as a compound and are both accented, as *nū́ nú* 'now, now', *ihéhá* (AV.) 'here, here', *sáṃ sám* (AV.).

2 Otherwise a repeated verbal form is not treated as an iterative, e. g. *stuhí stuhí* (VIII. 13[30]).

3 Except *śikṣā-nará-* 'helping men'.

a. When the first member is a preposition, the accentuation is much the same as in possessives: either the first member is accented on its proper syllable, as *abhí-dyu-* 'directed to heaven'; or the last member on the final syllable, but only when it ends in the compositional suffix *-a*, or when as a simple word it is not accented on the final syllable; e. g. *adhas-pad-á-* 'being under the feet', *anu-kāmá-* 'according to wish' (*kā́ma-*). The accentuation of *api-prā́ṇa-* (f. *-ī-*) 'accompanying the breath' is quite exceptional.

90. A. Possessive compounds (Bahuvrīhis) normally accent the first member on the same syllable as the simple word, e. g. *rā́ja-putra-* 'having kings as sons' (but *rāja-putrá-* 'son of a king'). Other examples are: *án-abhimlāta-varṇa-* 'whose colour is not dimmed', *iddhā́gni-* 'whose fire is kindled', *índra-jyeṣṭha-* 'having Indra as chief', *índra-sakhi-* 'having Indra as a friend', *ghṛtá-pṛṣṭha-* 'butter-backed', *rúśad-vatsa-* 'having a bright calf', *sahásra-pad-* 'thousand-footed'[1]. Similarly when the first member is a preposition, an ordinary adverb, or *sahá-* and (chiefly in the later Vedas) *sa-* in the sense of 'accompanied by'; e. g. *nír-hasta-* (AV.) 'handless', *prá-mahas-* 'having pre-eminent might', *ví-grīva-* 'wrynecked', *viśváto-mukha-* 'facing in all directions', *sahá-vatsa-* 'accompanied by her calf', *sá-kāma-* ('accompanied by' =) 'fulfilling desires' (VS.), *sá-cetas-* 'intelligent'[2].

a. The original accent of the first member is sometimes changed. 1. The adjective *víśva-* 'all' always, and (owing to its influence) *sárva-* 'all' sometimes in the later Saṃhitās, shift their accent to the final syllable; e. g. *viśvá-peśas-* 'having all adornment', *sarvá-janman-*[3] (AV.), *sarvá-śuddha-vāla-* (VS.) 'having a completely white tail', *sarvā́yus-* (VS.) 'having all life'[4]. — 2. Present participles in several instances shift the accent to their final syllable; e. g. *krandád-iṣṭi-* 'having roaring (*krándat-*) speed', *dravád-aśva-* 'having swift (*drávat-*)[5] steeds'. Other participles with this shift of accent are *arcát-* and *bhandát-* 'shining', *rapśát-* 'swelling', *svanát-* 'resounding'. — 3. There are also a few miscellaneous examples of shift of accent in the first member: *abhiṣṭi-dyumna-* 'abounding in aid', *jyotí-ratha-* 'whose car is light' (*jyótis-*), *dadṛśāná-pavi-* 'whose felly is visible' (*dádṛśāna-*), *avákolba-* (AV.) 'surrounded with Avakā plants' (*ávakā-*); *cátur-aṅga-* 'four-membered' (*catúr-*), *khā́di-hasta-* 'having hands adorned with bracelets' (*khādí-*).

B. About one eighth of the total number of Bahuvrīhis accent the second member, and in the majority of instances on the final syllable.

a. This accentuation is common when the first member is a dissyllabic adjective ending in *i* or *u*. It is invariable in the RV. after the very frequent *purú-* 'much' and the less frequent *kṛdhú-* 'shortened', *bahú-* 'much', *śíti-* 'white'; e. g. *puru-putrá-* 'having many sons', *puru-vā́ra-* 'having many treasures', *kṛdhu-kárṇa-* 'having short ears', *bahv-anná-*[6] 'having much food' (*ánna-*), *śiti-pád-* 'white-footed'. Examples of this accentuation after other adjectives ending in *i* and *u* are: *āśu-héṣas-* 'having swift steeds', *uru-kṣáya-* 'having a wide abode', *ṛju-krátu-* 'whose works are right', *tuvi-dyumná-* 'having great glory', *tṛṣu-cyávas-* 'moving greedily', *pṛthu-pákṣas-* 'broad-flanked', *vibhu-krátu-* 'having great strength', *vīḷu-pāṇí-* 'strong-hoofed', *hiri-śiprá-* 'golden-cheeked'[7]. In the later Saṃhitās there is an increasing tendency to follow

---

[1] When another adjective or an adverb precedes the first member, it has the accent; e. g. *éka-śiti-pad-* (VS. TS.) 'having one foot white'; cp. WACKERNAGEL 2[1], p. 291.

[2] There are, however, a few exceptions in which the final member is accented, as *vi-śikhá-* 'hairless' (but *vi-śikha-* AV.), *puro-rathá-* 'whose car is foremost', *sa-práthas-* 'extensive', *sāṅgá-* (AV.) 'together with the limbs'.

[3] This is the only example (occurring beside *viśvá-janman-*) of this shift of accent in *sárva-* in the AV., where *sárva-* as first member is common.

[4] *sárva-* shows this shift of accent in the RV. in the adverb *sarvá-tas* 'from all sides' and in the derivative *sarvá-tāti-* 'totality'.

[5] Here the accent may be affected by that of the adverb *dravát* 'swiftly'.

[6] After *bahu-* the final syllable is always accented, even in the later Saṃhitās.

[7] Both accentuations occur in *pṛthu-budhná-* and *pṛthú-budhna-* 'broad-based'.

the general rule; e. g. *purú-ṇāman-* (AV.) 'many-named', *śíti-kakud-* 'having a white hump', and *śíti-bhasad-* 'having white buttocks' (TS. v. 6. 14[1]).

b. Bahuvrīhis beginning with *dvi-* and *tri-* generally accent the second member; e. g. *dvi-pád-* 'two-footed', *dvi-dhā́ra-* 'forming two streams', *tri-tántu-* 'having three webs', *tri-nā́bhi-* 'having three naves', *tri-vandhurá-* 'three-seated'[1]. The only exceptions to this rule in the RV. are *dví-śavas-* 'having twofold might', *try-àmbaka-* 'having three mothers' and *try-ā̀śir-* 'having three products of milk'. The later Saṃhitās accent *dví-* and *trí-* in new Bahuvrīhis as often as not. In a few possessives beginning with other numerals the second member is accented on the last syllable, e. g. *catur-akṣá-* 'four-eyed'[2].

c. Possessives beginning with the negative prefix *a-* or *an-* almost invariably accent the final syllable irrespectively of the original accent of the second member (doubtless in order to distinguish them clearly from determinatives); e. g. *a-dánt-* 'toothless', *a-phalá-* 'unfruitful' (*phála-*), *a-balá-* 'not possessing strength' (*bála-*). A very few accent the penultimate; *a-bhrā́tṛ-*[3] (AV.) 'brotherless', *a-vī́ra-* 'childless', *a-śéṣas-* 'without offspring'. On the other hand a good many (though only a small proportion of the whole) accent the prefix (like determinatives), especially when the second member is a noun formed with the suffix *-ti*; e. g.[4] *á-gu-* 'kineless', *á-jñās-* 'kinless', *á-dyu-* 'not burning', *án-āpi-* 'kinless', *á-prajas-* (AV.) 'childless', *á-mṛtyu-* 'deathless', *á-hri-* 'bold', *á-kṣiti-* 'imperishable'[5].

d. Possessives beginning with *dus-*[6] 'ill' or *su-* 'well' regularly accent the second member, usually on the original syllable; e. g. *dur-mánman-* 'ill disposed', *su-bhága-* 'well endowed'. There is, however, a tendency to throw the accent forward on the final syllable; e. g. *sv-aṅgurí-* 'fair-fingered' (*aṅgúri-*), *su-phalá-* (AV.) 'fruitful', *su-bandhú-* (AV.)[7] 'closely related'[8]. On the other hand, the accent is in a few instances shifted from the final to the penultimate syllable, as *su-vī́ra-* 'rich in heroes' (*vīrá-*), and *su-gándhi-* 'sweet-smelling' beside *su-gandhí-* (from *gandhá-* 'smell')[9].

91. Determinatives as a rule accent **the last member**, and prevailingly on the final syllable.

A. 1. In the descriptive type, that is, those in which a substantive is described by an adjective or an appositional substantive (Karmadhāraya) and those in which a verbal noun is described by an adverbial word, the accent is on the final syllable; e. g. *kṛṣṇa-śakuná-* (AV.) 'black bird', *mahā-dhaná-* 'great spoil', *ajñāta-yakṣmá-* 'unknown disease', *yāvayat-sakhá-* 'a protecting friend', *rāja-yakṣmá-* ('king' =) 'royal disease'[10], *sūrya-śvít-* 'sun-bright'; *pura-etṛ́-* 'going before', *prathama-já-* 'first-born', *prātar-yúj-*[11] 'early yoked', *svayam-bhú-* 'self-existent', *duṣ-kṛ́t-* 'acting wickedly', *su-pra-túr-*[12] 'victorious', *a-ghārín-* (AV.) 'not anointing', *a-cít-* 'senseless', *a-jarayú-*[13] 'not aging', *a-júr-* 'unaging'.

1 But *aṣṭā́-vandhura-* 'having eight car-seats'.

2 Cp. WHITNEY 1300 c.

3 But in the RV. with the usual accentuation *a-bhrātṛ́-*.

4 For many other examples see WACKERNAGEL 2[1], 114 note (p. 293).

5 The only possessive of this kind in which the second member ends in *-ti* and accents the final syllable seems to be *a-gavyūtí-* 'pastureless'.

6 The only exception in the case of *dus-* is *dúr-āśir-* 'ill-mixed'.

7 The RV. retains the original accent, *su-phála-*, *su-bándhu-*.

8 For other examples see WACKERNAGEL 2[1], p. 294, bottom.

9 Op. cit. 2[1], p. 295 γ, note.

10 Exceptions, when the first member is a noun, are all compounds formed with *viśva-* 'all', as *viśvá-mānuṣa-* 'every man', also *madhyáṃ-dina-* 'midday', *vṛṣā́-kapi-* 'male ape', in all of which the original accent of the first member is shifted.

11 *ádhri-gu-* 'irresistible' and *sadhá-stha-* 'standing together', are exceptions.

12 *sv-ā́-vṛj-* 'easy to acquire' is an exception.

13 But *á-maviṣṇu-* 'immoveable'.

a-yoddhṛ́- 'not fighting', *a-rājín-* 'not shining', *a-pra-mṛṣ-yá-*[1] 'indestructible', *a-budh-yá-* 'not to be wakened', *an-aty-ud-yá-* (AV.) 'unspeakable', *an-ādhṛṣ-yá-* 'unassailable', *an-āmayi-tnú-* 'not making ill'.

a. When, however, the second member ends in *-van*, *-man* or *-i*, or has the form of a gerundive used as a neuter substantive, the penultimate (radical) syllable is accented; e. g. *raghu-pátvan-* 'swift-flying', *puro-yā́van-*[2] 'going in front'; *su-tárman-* 'crossing well', *vīḷu-pátman-* 'flying mightily', *raghu-yā́man-* 'going swiftly', *su-váhman-* 'driving well', *dur-gṛ́bhi-* 'hard to hold', *ṛju-váni* 'striving forward', *tuvi-ṣváṇi-* 'roaring mightily', *pūrva-pā́yya-* and *pūrva-péya-* n. 'precedence in drinking', *saha-śéyya-* n. 'act of lying together', *amutra-bhū́ya-*[3] (VS.) n. 'state of being in the other world'.

2. The **first member** is, however, **accented** under certain conditions. **a.** It is generally accented if it is an adverbial word and the last member is a past participle in *-ta* or *-na*[4] or a verbal noun in *-ti*; e. g. *dáṃsu-jūta-* 'speeding wondrously', *dúr-hita-* 'faring ill', *sána-śruta-*[5] 'famed from of old'; *puró-hiti-* 'priestly ministration', *sadhá-stuti-* 'joint praise'.—**b. The privative particle** *a-* or *an-* when compounded with a participle[6], adjective, or substantive is **nearly always accented**; e. g. *án-adant-*[7] 'not eating', *á-ditsant-* 'not wishing to give', *á-manyamāna-* 'not thinking', *á-hiṃsāna-* 'not injuring', *á-vidvāṃs-* 'not knowing', *á-kṛta-*[8] 'not done'; *á-kr-a-*[9] 'inactive', *á-suṣv-i-* 'not pressing Soma', *á-tandra-* 'unwearied', *á-kumāra-*[10] 'not a child'; *á-citti-* 'thoughtlessness'. The particle is regularly accented when it negatives a compound; e. g. *á-duṣ-kṛt-* 'not doing ill', *án-aśva-dā-* 'not giving a horse', *á-paścād-daghvan-* 'not remaining behind'; *á-punar-dīyamāna-*[11] (AV.) 'not being given back', *án-agni-dagdha-* 'not burnt with fire', *án-abhi-śasta-*[12] 'blameless'.

B. 1. Dependent determinatives as a rule **accent the second member** and that mostly on the last syllable, even if the simple word is not an oxytone.

a. When the second member is a root[13], a verbal noun in *-a*, an ordinary substantive (without verbal sense), or an adjective ending in *-in*[14], the final

---

1 This is the regular accent of the gerundive with the negative prefix, which is, however, accented in some half dozen instances: *á-gohya-*, *á-jeṣya-*, *á-dabhya-*, *á-nedya-*, *á-yabhya-* (AV.) and *á ghnya-* beside *a-ghnyá-*. Two of these compounds in the AV. retain the Svarita of the simple gerundive: *an-ativyādhyà-* and *an-ādharṣyà-*.

2 *satyá-madvan-* 'truly rejoicing' is an exception.

3 *sadhá-stutya-* n. 'joint praise', is an exception.

4 Here the adverb is treated like a preposition compounded with a past participle.

5 There are a good many exceptions in which the original accent of the past participle remains on the final syllable; e. g. *tuvi-jātá-* 'mightily born', *duṣ-kṛtá-* 'ill done', *su-jātá-* (beside *sú-jāta-*). This is the regular accentuation when the first member is *puru-*; e. g. *puru-ṣṭutá-* 'much praised'.

6 Not, however, when the second member is a gerundive, a root, or a noun with verbal meaning ending in *-yu*, *-tnu*, *-snu*, *-in*, *-tṛ-*; see examples above (A 1).

7 But *a-saścánt-* beside *á-saścant-* 'not ceasing', *a-codánt-* (v. 44[2]) and as substantives *a-rundhat-ī́-* (AV.) a name, and *a-járant-ī-* (VS.) 'unaging'.

8 Exceptions are *a-citta-*, *a-dṛ́ṣṭa-*, *a-mṛ́ta-*, *a-yúta-* n. 'myriad' but (AV.) *á-yuta-* 'undisturbed', *a-tū́rta-* (beside *á-tūrta-*), *a-bhinná-* (AV.) beside *á-bhinna-*.

9 There are also some verbal derivatives in *-a* which accent the second member; e. g. *a-kṣár-a-* 'imperishable', *a-jár-a* 'unaging', *a-dábh-a-* 'not-deceiving', *a-tṛp-á-* 'dissatisfied', *a-vadh-á-* 'inviolable', *a-vṛdh-á-* 'not furthering', *an-āvrask-á* (AV.) 'not falling off'; cp. WHITNEY 1283—88.

10 There are also several ordinary nouns which are accented as second member; e. g. *a-citrá-* 'colourless', *a-mitra-* 'enemy', *-a-vī́ra-* 'unmanly'.

11 But *a-ni-pádyamāna-* (AV.) 'not going to rest' where RV. has *á-ni-padyamāna*.

12 But *an-ā-śastá-* (RV[1].) 'not praised', *a-pra-śastá-* beside *á-pra-śasta-* 'not praised'.

13 There are a few exceptions when derivation from a root is not clear, as in *óṣa-dhi-* 'plant'; otherwise *-dhi* from *dhā-* 'put' is regularly accented; e. g. *iṣu-dhí* 'quiver'.

14 This suffix being invariably accented in the simple word (86 B. 8).

syllable is regularly accented; e. g. *gotra-bhíd-* 'opening the cowpens', *ghṛtā-vṛ́dh-* 'delighting in ghee', *divi-spṛ́ś-* 'touching the sky', *pataṃ-gá-* 'going by flight', 'flying', *varuṇa-dhrú-t-* 'deceiving Varuṇa'; *agnim-indh-á-*[1] 'fire-kindling', *hasta-grābh-á-* 'hand-grasping', *puraṃ-dar-á-* 'fort-destroying'; *uda-meghá-* 'shower of water', *go-śaphá-* (VS.) 'cow's hoof', *jīva-loká-* 'world of the living', *indra-senā́-* 'Indra's missile' (*sénā-*), *kṛṣṇājiná-* (AV. TS.) 'hide (*ajína-*) of the black antelope', *deva-kośá-*[2] (AV.) 'cask (*kóśa-*) of the gods', *deva-māná-*[3] 'abode (*mā́na-*) of the gods'; *uktha-śaṃs-ín-* 'uttering praise', *bhadra-vād-ín-* 'uttering auspicious cries'.

a. The word *páti-* 'lord' follows this rule in only a few compounds occurring in the later Saṃhitās; thus in the AV.: *apsarā-patí-* 'lord of the Apsarases', *vrāja-patí-* 'lord of a troop' (*vrājá-pati-*, RV.); in the VS.: *aṃhasas-patí-* 'lord of perplexity', *upa-patí-* 'paramour', *edidhiṣuḥ-patí-* 'husband of a younger sister', *nadī-patí-* 'lord of rivers'; in the MS.: *ahar-patí-* 'lord of day', *cit-patí-* 'lord of thought', *vāk-patí-* 'lord of speech'. In a few determinatives *páti-* retains its own accent as second member, as *nṛ-páti-* 'lord of men', *rayi-páti-* 'lord of wealth', *viś-páti-* 'lord of the tribe', also the f. in *vasu-pátnī-* 'mistress of wealth', *viś-pátnī-*[4] 'mistress of the tribe'; in the VS. *ahar-páti-*, *cit-páti-*, *vāk-páti-*; in the AV. *ṛtu-páti-* 'lord of proper seasons', *paśu-páti-* 'lord of animals' (VS.), *puṣṭi-páti-* 'lord of welfare', *bhūta-páti-* 'lord of beings', *stha-páti-*[5] 'governor'. In compounds with *páti-*, however, the first member is usually accented, there being 22 cases in the RV., besides 10 with *patnī-*; e. g. *gṛhá-pati-* 'lord of the house', *gó-pati-* 'lord of kine', *páśu-pati-* 'lord of creatures', *medhá-pati-*[6] 'lord of animal sacrifice' (*médha-*), *vásu-pati-* 'lord of wealth', *vā́ja-pati-* 'lord of booty', *svàr-pati-*[7] 'lord of light'; *gṛhá-patnī-* 'mistress of the house', *devá-patnī-* 'wife of a god', *vā́ja-patnī-* 'queen of booty'. In the AV., of 15 new masculines ending in *-pati-* more than half accent the first member as do all the 8 new ones ending in *patnī-*; e. g. *átithi-pati-* 'entertainer of a guest'. In the other Saṃhitās also occur: *kṣatrá-pati-* (VS.) 'lord of dominions', *bhúva-pati-* (VS.) 'lord of the atmosphere', *bhúvana-pati-* (VS. TS.) 'lord of beings', *bhū́-pati-* (TS.) 'lord of the world', *saṃveśá-pati-* (VS.) 'lord of rest', *viṣṇu-patnī-* (VS. TS.) 'Viṣṇu's wife'[8].

b. Determinatives which have as their second member verbal nouns in *-ana*[9], adjectives in *-i* and *-van*, as well as action nouns in *-ya*, regularly accent the radical syllable of the second member; e. g. *deva-mā́d-ana-* 'exhilarating the gods', *keśa-várdh-ana-*[10] 'causing the hair to grow'; *pathi-rákṣ-i-* 'protecting the road'; *soma-pā́-van-* 'somadrinking', *talpa-śī́-van-* 'lying on the couch', *prātar-í-t-van-*[11] 'coming early'; *ahi-hát-ya-* 'slaughter of the dragon', *deva-hū́-ya-* 'invocation of the gods', *mantra-śrú-t-ya-* n. 'listening to counsel', *vṛtra-tū́r-ya-*[12] 'conquest of Vṛtra'.

2. Dependent determinatives, however, which have as their second member past passive participles in *-ta* and *-na* or action nouns in *-ti* accent

---

[1] *dúgha-* retains its original accent, as *madhu-dúgha-* 'yielding mead', *kāma-dúgha-* (AV. VS.) 'yielding desires'. A few others have the original accent of the first member: *marúd-vṛdha-* 'delighting in the Maruts', *divi-cara-* (AV.) 'moving in the sky', *suti-kara-* 'active at the Soma offering'. Cp. WHITNEY 1278.

[2] A few accent the penultimate syllable of the final member with shift of the original accent, as *go-dhū́ma-* (VS.) 'wheat', *śaka-dhū́ma-* (AV.), *yama-rā́jya-* (AV. VS.) 'Yama's sway' (*rājyá-*); cp. WACKERNAGEL 2[1], p. 268, top, note.

[3] But *deva-yā́na-* 'going to the gods'.

[4] Also the Karmadhāraya *sa-pátnī-* 'cowife' and the Bahuvrīhi *su-pátnī-* 'having a good husband'.

[5] Cp. BLOOMFIELD, SBE. 42, 319.

[6] In K. *médha-pati-*.

[7] *svá-pati-* 'one's own lord' is a Karmadhāraya; as a Bahuvrīhi it is accented *sva-patí-* (AV.) 'having an own consort'.

[8] On doubly accented compounds with *-pati-* see below (3).

[9] Just as when such nouns are compounded with prepositions.

[10] The very few apparent exceptions to this rule are due to these words losing their verbal character; e. g. *yama-sādaná-* (AV.) 'Yama's realm'.

[11] In *mātarí-śvan-* and *mātarí-bhvan-* the suffix is probably *-an*; here the original accent of the first member (if it is the loc. *mātári*) has shifted, perhaps owing to the influence of words like *prātar-í-tvan-*.

[12] An exception is *sadhá-stu-t-ya-* 'joint praise'. A few feminines in *-yā́*, which are closely allied to these neuters in *-ya*, retain their accent on the final syllable, as *deva-*

the first member (like a preposition); e. g. *indra-prasūta-* 'incited by Indra', *devá-hita-* 'ordained by the gods', *hásta-yata-* 'guided by the hand'[1]; *devá-hūti-*[2] 'invocation of the gods', *dhána-sāti-*[3] 'winning of wealth'.

3. **Double accentuation.** A certain number of determinative compounds, syntactical in origin, which have a genitive case-form in the first member, and nearly always *-páti-* in the second, are doubly accented. Such are *bṛ́has-páti-* and *bráhmaṇas-páti-*[4] 'lord of prayer', *gnā́s-páti-* 'husband of a divine woman' (with the anomalous fem. *gnā́s-pátnī-* 'divine wife'), *jā́s-páti-*[5] 'head of a family'. The compound *sádas-páti-* 'lord of the seat' (*sádas-*) probably stands by haplology for **sádasas-páti-*, but *vána-s-páti-*[6] 'lord of the wood' perhaps, and *rátha-s-páti-* 'lord of the car' (*rátha-*) probably, owe their *s* to the analogy of *bṛ́has-páti-*[7]. Though without case-ending in the first member, *śácī-páti-* 'lord of might' follows the analogy of the above compounds. Other doubly accented compounds with case-form in the first member but not ending in *-pati-* are *śúnaḥ-śépa-* 'Dog's tail', N. of a man; *dásyave-vṛ́ka-* 'Wolf to the Dasyu', N. of a man; *apā́ṃ-nápāt-* 'son of waters', the analogy of which is followed by *tánū-nápāt-* 'son of himself' (*tanū́-*) though it is without case-ending in the first member; *nárā-śáṃsa-*[8] 'Praise of men' (for **nárāṃ-śáṃsa-*), the analogy of which is followed by *nṛ́-śáṃsa-*. The name *nábhā-nédiṣṭha-* seems to contain an old locative in the first member, while the uninflected stem appears in *ā́s-pātra-* (TS. II. 5. 9[3]) 'vessel for the mouth'.

92. 1. The **regular** class of **copulatives**, which have only one accent, places the acute on the **final syllable**[9] irrespective of the accent of the uncompounded word. In the plural occur: *ajāváyaḥ* m. 'goats and sheep', *ukthārkā́* n. 'praises and songs', *ahorātrā́ṇi* 'days and nights'; in the dual: *ṛk-sāmé* n. 'song and chant', *satyānṛté* n. 'truth and untruth', *sāśanānaśané* n. 'what eats and does not eat'; in the singular: *nīlalohitám* n. 'blue and red'[10], *iṣṭā-pūrtám*[11] n. 'what is sacrificed and presented', *keśa-śmaśrú-* (AV.) n. 'hair and beard', *añjanābhyañjanám* (AV.) n. 'salve and ointment', *kaśipu-barhaṇám* (AV.) n. 'mat and pillow', *kṛtākṛtám* (AV.) n. 'what is done and undone', *cittākūtám* (AV.) n. 'thought and desire', *bhadra-pāpám* (AV.) 'good and evil', *bhūta-bhavyám* (AV.) n. 'past and future', n. pl. *priyāpriyā́ṇi* (AV.) 'things

---

yaj-yā́- 'worship of the gods', beside *deva-yáj-ya-*, *jāta-vid-yā́-* 'knowledge of things', *muṣṭi-hat yā́-* 'hand to hand fight'.

1 There are, however, a good many exceptions in which the final syllable is accented (as in prepositional determinatives), e. g. *agni-taptá-* 'glowing with fire', *agni-dagdhá-* 'burnt by fire'.

2 The original accent of the first member is shifted in *nemá-dhiti-* 'putting opposite' 'fight', *vaná-dhiti-* 'layer of wood', *medhá-sāti-* 'receiving of the oblation'.

3 When the verbal sense is lost in the second member, the general rule of final accentuation applies; e. g. *deva-sumati-* 'favour of the gods', *deva-heti-* (AV.) 'weapon of the gods'. This analogy is followed by *sarva-jyāní-* (AV.) 'loss of one's all'.

4 Though *bráhmaṇas-páti-* is not treated as a compound in the Pada text, it is so treated in the Dvandva *indrā-brahmaṇaspatī* (II. 24[12]).

5 Thus accented in Book VII, but *jā́s-pati*, in Book I. The latter is the only Tatpuruṣa in the RV. in which double accentuation does not take place when *-páti-* is preceded by *s*. The only other instance in the RV. of a Tatpuruṣa with case-ending in the first member and yet singly accented is *divo-dāsa-*, N. of a king. Elsewhere occur *apsu-yogá-* (AV.) 'connecting power in water', *aṃhasas-patí-* (VS.), perhaps *mātúr-bhrātrá-* (MS. I. 6[12]) 'mother's brother' (the Mss. read *mātur-bhrātrá-*).

6 In *vánas-páti-* the first member may be the gen. sing. of *van-* 'wood' (gen. pl. *vanā́m*); but in *rátha-s-páti-* the *s* must be inorganic; cp. Garbe, KZ. 23, 490; Richter, IF. 19, 17; Bartholomae, BB. 15, 15 note[1]; Wackernagel 2[1], p. 247.

7 The only new instance of double accentuation of a compound with *-páti-* after the RV. seems to be *nṛ́ṃs-páti-* (MS.); cp. Wackernagel 2[1], p. 248 d.

8 Cp. Foy, JAOS. 16, CLXXII–IV.

9 The two or three exceptions which occur in the AV. and VS. are doubtless due to wrong readings.

10 The adjectives being used as substantives.

11 In the VS. used in the dual also.

agreeable and disagreeable'; and as adjectives *tāmra-dhūmrá-* (AV.) 'tawny and dark', *dakṣiṇa-savyá-* (AV.) 'right and left', *saptamāṣṭamá-* (AV.) 'seventh and eighth'.

a. The very few **adverbial copulatives** which occur **accent** the first **member**: *áhar-divi* 'day by day', *sāyám-prātar* (AV.) 'at even and at morn'.

2. The class of **Devatā-dvandvas**, each member of which is dual in form, and which in the RV. is about thrice as frequent as the regular class, retains the **accent** of simple words in **each member** of the compound[1]: thus *agnā́-víṣṇū* (AV.), *agnī́-ṣómā*, *índrā-pūṣáṇā*, *índrā-bṛ́haspátī*[2], *índrā-váruṇā*, *índrā-víṣṇū*, *índrā-sómā*, *uṣā́sā-náktā* 'Dawn and Night', *dyā́vā-kṣā́mā* 'heaven and earth', *dyā́vā-pṛthiví*, *dyā́vā-bhū́mī*, *náktoṣā́sā*, *párjanyā-vā́tā*, *pṛthiví-dyā́vā*, *mitrā́-váruṇā*, *sū́ryā-mā́sā*. A few others are formed in the same way from substantives which are not the names of deities: *krátū-dákṣau* (VS.) 'understanding and will', *turváśā-yádū* (IV. 30[17]) 'Turvaśa and Yadu', *dhúnī-cúmurī* 'Dhuni and Cumuri', *mātárā-pitárā* (IV. 6[7]) 'mother and father'.

a. A certain number of these compounds have been assimilated to the regular class of copulatives by giving up the accent of the first member: *indrāgnī́*, *indrā-pūṣáṇā*, *somā-pūṣáṇā*, *vātā-parjanyā́*, *sūryā-candramásā*, *bhavā-rudráu* (AV.), *bhavā-śarváu* (AV.)[3]; one has been completely assimilated by giving up also the dual form in the first member: *indra-vāyū́*.

a. There occurs once a secondary adjective copulative accented on both members, being formed from an adverbial Dvandva: *áhar-divá-* (VS.) 'daily' (*áhar-divi* 'day by day').

3. Accent in Declension.

93. The vocative, when accented at all (85, 2) invariably has the acute on the first syllable; e. g. *pítar*, N. *pitā́* 'father'; *déva*, N. *devá-s* 'god'. The regularly accented vocative of *dyú-* (*dyáv-*) 'heaven' is *dyàu-s*[4], that is *díaus*, but the nominative form *dyáus* is also used in its stead.

a. Otherwise, in the *a*-declension (f. *-ā*) the accent always remains on the same syllable; e. g. N. *devá-s*, G. *devá-sya*, pl. *devā́-nām*. This rule is also followed by monosyllabic pronominal stems in *-a*; e. g. from *ma-*: I. *máy-ā* 'by me', D. *má-hyam*, L. *máy-i*; from *tá-* 'that', G. sing. *tá-sya*, pl. G. *té-ṣām*, I. *tā́-bhis*[5].

a. An exception to this rule is formed by the plural cardinal stems ending in *-a*. They regularly accent that vowel before endings with initial consonant, and throw the acute on the ending of the genitive; e. g. *páñca* 'five': I. *pañcá-bhis*, G. *pañcānā́m*; *aṣṭá* 'eight', however, shifts the accent to the endings generally, thus I. *aṣṭā-bhís*, D. *aṣṭā-bhyás* (TS.).

94. When the final syllable of the stem is accented, the acute (except in the *ā́*-declension) is liable to shift to the endings in the weak cases.

1. This is the rule in monosyllabic stems; e. g. *náu-* 'ship': A. *nā́v-am*, but I. *nāv-ā́*, pl. I. *nau-bhís*, L. *nau-ṣú*; *dánt-* m. 'tooth': I. *dat-ā́*, pl. A. *dat-ás*[6], I. *dad-bhís*.

[1] The double accent is retained even in the derivatives *mitrā́-váruṇa-vant-* 'accompanied by Mitra and Varuṇa', and *dyā́vā-pṛthivī́-vant-* (AV.) 'accompanied by heaven and earth'.

[2] Retaining the double accent of the second member.

[3] In the AV. the number of Devatā-dvandvas is only about half that in the RV. (though the total number of Dvandvas is more than double); about one-half of these, again, have only one accent, which as in the regular class is on the final syllable.

[4] Retaining the nom. *-s*, instead of **diau* (Gk. Ζεῦ).

[5] An exception is the pronoun *a-* 'this', which is treated like a monosyllabic stem, e. g. G. *a-syá*, pl. m. *e-ṣā́m*, f. *ā-sā́m*; a few times, however, the accentuation *á-smai*, *á-sya*, *ā́-bhis* occurs; cp. Whitney 502 b.

[6] The accusative plural is treated as a weak case and accented on the ending in

a. Exceptions to this rule are the rare monosyllabic stems in *-ā*, which retain the accent on the stem; e. g. *gnā́-* 'woman': pl. I. *gnā́-bhis*, L. *gnā́-su*. Individual exceptions are *gó-* 'cow', *dyó-* 'sky'; e. g. I. *gáv-ā*, pl. G. *gáv-ām*, I. *gó-bhis*; L. *dyáv-i*, pl. I. *dyú-bhis*. Similarly *nṛ́-* 'man': D. *nár-e*, pl. I. *nṛ́-bhis*, L. *nṛ́-ṣu*, but G. *nar-ā́m* and *nṛ-ṇā́m*; *kṣám-* 'earth'; L. *kṣám-i*; *tán-* 'succession: I. *tán-ā* (and *tan-ā́*), D. *tán-e*; *rán-* 'joy': *ráṇ-e*, pl. L. *rám-su*; *ván-* 'wood': pl. L. *vám-su* (but G. *van-ā́m*); *víp-* 'rod': G. *víp-as*; *stṛ́-* 'star': pl. I. *stṛ́-bhis*; *svàr-* 'light': G. *sū́r-as* (but D. *sūr-é*); also the infinitives *bā́dh-e* 'to press', *vā́h-e* 'to convey'. In some words the irregular accentuation is due to their having originally been dissyllables; such are *drú-* 'wood', *snú-* 'summit', *śván-* 'dog', *yū́n-* weak stem of *yúvan-* 'young'; e. g. I. *drú-ṇā*; pl. L. *snú-ṣu*; I. *śún-ā*, pl. *śvá-bhis*; I. *yū́n-ā* [1].

2. When the accented vowel of the final syllable in polysyllabic stems disappears either by syncope or by changing to a semivowel, the acute is thrown on endings with initial vowel in the weak cases; thus from *mahimán-* 'greatness', I. *mahimn-ā́*; from *mūrdhán-* 'head', D. *mūrdhn-é*; from *agní-* 'fire', G. du. *agny-ós*; from *dhenú-* 'cow', I. sing. *dhenv-ā́*; from *vadhū́-* 'bride', D. *vadhv-ái* (AV.); from *pitṛ́-* 'father', I. *pitr-ā́*.

a. Polysyllabic stems in *-í*, *-ú*, *-ṛ́*, and in the RV. usually those in *-ī*, throw the acute on the ending of the G. pl. also, even though the vowel retains its syllabic character in this case; e. g. *agnī-nā́m*, *dhenū-nā́m*, *dātṝ-ṇā́m*; *bahvī-nā́m* [2]

3. Present participles in *-át* and *-ánt* throw the acute on the endings with initial vowel in the weak cases; e. g. from *tud-ánt-* 'striking': I. sing. *tud-at-ā́* (but *tud-ád-bhis*). This rule is also followed by the old participles *mah-át-* 'great' and *bṛh-át* 'large', e. g. *mahat-ā́* (but *mahád-bhis*) [3].

4. In the RV. derivatives formed with accented *-añc* throw the acute on endings with initial vowel in the weak cases when contraction to *ī* and *ū* appears in the final syllable; thus from *praty-áñc-* 'turned towards', I. sing. *pratīc-ā́* (but L. pl. *pratyák-ṣu*); from *anv-áñc-* 'following'; G. *anūc-ás* (but from *prā́ñc-* L. sing. *prā́c-i*). The other Saṃhitās, however, generally retain the accent on the stem [4].

4. Verbal Accent.

95. As regards **personal endings**, those of the singular active in all tenses and moods are always unaccented except the 2. imperative *-dhí* or *-hí*. Others may be accented; if dissyllabic, they have the acute on the first syllable, as *-ánti*, *-máhi*.

When the tense stem ends in *-a* in the present, in the future, in the unaugmented imperfect and aorist, and throughout the subjunctive, the accent is never on the ending, as it remains on the same syllable of the stem throughout.

96. All tenses formed with the **augment** invariably accent the latter, if the verb is accented at all (85, 2 β); e. g. impf. *á-bhara-t*, plupf. *á-jagan*, aor. *á-bhū-t*, conditional *á-bhariṣya-t*. If the augment is dropped, the accentuation is as follows. In the **imperfect** the acute is on the same syllable as in the present; e. g. *bhára-t*, pres. *bhára-ti*. The **pluperfect**, if regularly

hardly more than one third of the stems occurring; see Whitney 390 a; cp. Lanman 494, 499, 504 top, 505.

1 When a monosyllable becomes the final member of a compound, it loses its monosyllabic accent; e. g. *su-dhī́-* 'wise', G. pl. *su-dhīnām*. On the other hand *préṣ-* 'pressing on' though a compound (*pra-iṣ-*) is accented like monosyllables in the I. sing. *preṣ-ā́*.

2 This regularly takes place in the G. of the plural cardinals in *-a*: as *páñca* 'five', *pañcā-nā́m*, *dáśa* 'ten', *daśā-nā́m*.

3 The accent is, however, not shifted in the old participle *vāghát-* m. 'worshipper'; nor in the two forms *a-codát-e* 'not urging' (from *cód-ant-*) and *rathirāyát-ām* 'speeding'; cp. Lanman p. 505—6 (top).

4 Thus the f. stem *pratīc-ī-* (AV.), but RV. *pratīc-ī́-* (once in the A. *pratīcī́m*).

formed, accents the root, as 3. sing. *cākán* (√*kan*-), 3. sing. *rārán* (√*ran*-), 1. sing. *cikétam* (√*cit*-); when formed with thematic *-a*, it accents that vowel, as 3. pl. *cakṛpá-nta*. The aorist if formed with *-sa*, accents that syllable, e. g. 3. pl. *dhuk-ṣá-n, dhuk-ṣá-nta* (from *duh*- 'milk'); if formed with *-s*, it accents the root, as may be inferred from 1. sing. *váṃ-s-i* (from *van*- 'win'), the only accented example occurring; if formed with *-iṣ*-, it accents the root, e. g. 1. sing. *śáṃs-iṣ-am*[1]. If formed from the root, it accents the radical vowel in the singular active, but the endings elsewhere, as 3. sing. *várk* (√*vṛj*-), but 2. sing. mid. *nut-thā́s* (√*nud*-). If formed from the root with thematic *-a*, it usually follows the analogy of the present *á*-class, e. g. *ruhá-m, bhujá-t, vidá-t, budhá-nta*; in several instances, however, it accents the root, as *ára-nta* (*ṛ*- 'go'); *sára-t* (*sṛ*- 'flow'); *sáda-tam* (*sad*- 'sit'); *sána-t* (*san*- 'gain') but opt. *sanéma*; *vóca-t* (*vac*- 'speak') but opt. *vocéyam*. The reduplicated aorist usually accents the reduplicative syllable, as 2. sing. *dídharas, nínaśas*, 3. sing. *píparat, síṣvap, jíjanat*, pl. *jíjanan*; but sometimes the root, as 2. sing. *śiśráthas*, 3. sing. *pīpárat, śiśnáthat*. Passive aorists accent the root, e. g. *dhā́-y-i, śrā́v-i, véd-i, ján-i, pā́d-i, sā́d-i*.

97. Present system. — 1. Throughout the present system of the *a*-conjugation the accent remains on the same syllable of the stem in all moods; on the radical syllable in verbs of the first and fourth classes; e. g. *bháva-ti* from *bhū*- 'be', *náh-ya-ti* from *nah*- 'bind'; on the thematic *-a* in the sixth class; e. g. *tudá-ti* from *tud*- 'strike'.

2. In the second or graded conjugation, the singular indicative active, the whole of the subjunctive, and the 3. sing. imperative active[2] accent the stem, while all other forms accent the endings[3]. In the strong forms the radical syllable is accented in the second class; generally the reduplicative syllable, but sometimes the root, in the third class; the suffix in the fifth, eighth, seventh, and ninth; e. g. 3. sing. ind. *ás-ti*, subj. *ás-a-t*, impv. *ás-tu*, from *as*- 'be', 2nd cl.; 3. sing. ind. *bí-bhar-ti* from *bhṛ*- 'bear', 3rd cl.; 3. sing. ind. *kṛ-ṇó-ti*, subj. *kṛ-ṇáv-a-t*, 2. pl. impv. *kṛ-ṇó-ta*, and *kṛ-ṇó-tana* from *kṛ*- 'make', 5th cl.; 3. sing. subj. *man-áv-a-te* from *man*- 'think', 8th cl.; 1. sing. ind. *yu-ná-j-mi*, 3. sing. subj. *yu-ná-j-a-t* from *yuj*- 'join', 7th cl.; 3. sing. ind. *gṛbh-ṇā́-ti*, 2. sing. subj. *gṛbh-ṇā́-s* from *grabh*- 'seize', 9th cl.; but 2. sing. impv. *ad-dhí*, 3. pl. opt. *ad-yúr* from *ad*- 'eat', 2nd cl.; 1. pl. ind. *bi-bhṛ-mási*; 1. sing. ind. mid. *kṛ-ṇv-é*, 2. sing. impv. *kṛ-ṇu-hí*; 1. pl. opt. *van-u-yā́ma*, 3. pl. impv. *van-v-ántu* from *van*- 'win', 8th cl.; 3. sing. mid. *yuṅk-té*, 2. sing. impv. mid. *yuṅk-ṣvá*; 1. pl. ind. *gṛ-ṇī-mási*, 2. sing. impv. *gṛ-ṇī-hí* from *gṛ*- 'praise', 9th cl.

a. **Irregularities.** In the second or root class, several verbs accent the radical syllable throughout[4]: *śī*- 'lie' does so besides taking Guṇa; e. g. 1. sing. *śáy-e*, 2. sing. *śé-ṣe* etc.[5] Occasional accentuation of the root in weak forms appears in 2. sing. impv. *ján-i-ṣva*[6] (√*jan*-), *mát-sva* (√*mad*-), *yák-ṣva* (√*yaj*-), *sák-ṣva* and *sā́k-ṣva* (√*sah*-), *ṛ́dh-a-t*, subj. (*ṛdh*- 'thrive'), 3. pl. impv. *sváp-antu* (AV.) and *śvás-antu* (AV.)[7]. A few roots of the third class accent the root instead of the reduplicative syllable in the strong forms. These are *ci*- 'note', *mad*- 'exhilarate', *yu*- 'separate', *hu*- 'sacrifice'; e. g. 2. sing. *ci-ké-ṣi* (AV.); 3. sing. subj. *ma-mád-a-t*, 3. sing. impv. *ma-mát-tu*; 3. sing. subj. *yu-yáv-a-t*, 2. pl. impv. *yu-yó-tana*; 3. sing. *ju-hó-ti*. Occasional forms thus accented are 2. sing. *iy-ár-ṣi* (RV[1].) from

1 Of the *siṣ*-aorist no accented forms occur.

2 The 2. pl. impv. active often accents the stem, which is then strong, as *é-ta*, *é-tana* from *i*- 'go'; this is sometimes also the case with the 2. du. in *-tam*.

3 The final syllable of the ending of the 3. pl. middle is regularly accented in several verbs, as *ri-haté, duh-até*; see WHITNEY 613, 685, 699; DELBRÜCK, Verbum 73.

4 These are *ās*- 'sit', *īḍ*- 'praise', *īr*- 'set in motion', *īś*- 'rule', *cakṣ*- 'see', *takṣ*- 'fashion', *trā*- 'protect', *niṃs*- 'kiss', *vas*- 'clothe', *sū*- 'bring forth'.

5 See WHITNEY 628 and 629.

6 Op. cit. 631 a.

7 Op. cit. 630.

ṛ- 'go', 2. sing. mid. *dhát-se* from *dhā-* 'put', and *bi-bhár-ti* (RV[1]. AV[2].) beside the usual *bi-bhar-ti*. Both types, when the ending begins with a vowel, throw the accent back on the reduplicative syllable; e. g. 3. pl. *júhv-ati* and *bíbhr-ati*, but 2. pl. *juhu-thá* and *bibhṛ-thá*. The subjunctive here, as usual, follows the accentuation of the strong indicative; its stem from the same two roots would be *juháv-a-* and *bíbhar-a-*. In the optative middle the accent is thrown back on the reduplicative syllable because the modal affix begins with a vowel; e. g. 1. sing. *dádh-īya* etc. beside 1. sing. act. *dadh-yā́m* etc.[1] The RV., however, once has *dadhī-tá* beside *dádhī-ta* (3 times). In the imperative, endings with initial consonant are accented in the weak forms, otherwise the reduplicative syllable; e. g. 2. sing. *de-hi*, 2. du. *dat-tám*, but 3. mid. pl. *jíhatām*. The strong 3. sing. impv. act. follows the strong ind., e. g. *dádhātu*, *pipartu*; the 2. pl. is often strong; e. g. *juhóta*, *dádhāta*. The participle regularly accents the reduplicative syllable; e. g. *júhv-at*, *júhv-āna*, except only *pipāná-* (*pā-* 'drink'). — In the seventh class the root *hiṃs-* 'injure' (originally perhaps a desiderative of *han-* 'strike') accents the radical syllable in weak forms, as 3. sing. *híṃs-te*, pl. *híṃs-anti*, part. *híṃs-āna-*. — In the fifth and eighth classes the RV. has several instances of irregular accentuation of the final syllable in the 3. pl. mid.: *kṛ-ṇv-até*, *vṛ-ṇv-até*, *spṛ-ṇv-até*; *tan-v-até*, *man-v-até*. — In the ninth class the irregular accentuation of the 3. pl. mid. occurs in *pu-n-a-té* and *ri-ṇ-até* (*ri-* 'flow'). The ending *-āna*, which is here added in the 2. sing. impv. act. to a few roots with final consonant, is accented on the last syllable: *gṛh-āṇá*, *badh-āná* (AV.), *stabh-āná* (AV.).

98. The perfect. — The singular indicative active and the whole subjunctive[2] accent the radical syllable; all other forms of the indicative, as well as the whole imperative and optative accent the endings; e. g. ind. 3. sing. *cakár-a*, pl. *cakr-úr*, 1. pl. mid. *cakṛ-máhe*; subj. sing. 2. *papráth-a-s*, *pipráy-a-s*; 3. *jabhár-a-t*, *pipráy-a-t*, *mumóc-a-t*; *dadhárṣ-a-ti*, *vavárt-a-ti*; pl. 1. *cākán-āma*, *śūśáv-āma*, 3. *papráth-a-n*; opt. sing. 1. *vavṛt-yā́m*, 2. *śuśrū-yā́s*, 3. *tutuj-yā́t*; du. 2. *śuśrū-yā́tam*; pl. 3. *vavṛj-yúr*; mid. sing. 2. *vāvṛdh-ī-thā́s*, 3. *śiśrī-tá* (*śri-* 'resort'); impv. sing. 2. *piprī-hí*, *mumug-dhí* (√*muc-*), du. 2. *jajas-tám*; mid. sing. 2. *dadhi-ṣvá*[3]. The participle, both active and middle, accents the suffix; e. g. *cakṛ-vā́ṃs-*; *cakr-āṇá-*.

99. The aorist. — The accentuation of the unaugmented forms of the indicative has already been stated (96). With regard to that of the moods, the following notes may be added.

1. The **root aorist** accents the radical syllable in the **subjunctive**; e. g. sing. 2. *kár-a-s*, 3. *kár-a-t*, du. 3. *śráv-a-tas*, pl. 3. *gám-a-nti*, mid. sing. 3. *bhój-a-te*; in the **injunctive**, the radical syllable in the singular, but the ending elsewhere; e. g. sing. 1. *nám-s-i*, pl. 3. *dabh-úr*, mid. sing. 2. *mṛ-thā́s*; in the **optative**, the endings throughout; e. g. act. sing. 1. *aś-yā́m*, 2. *bhū-yā́s*, mid. pl. 1. *aś-īmáhi*; in the **imperative**, the root in the 3. sing. act., but the ending elsewhere; e. g. sing. 3. *śró-tu*, but 2. *kṛ-dhí*, du. 2. *ga-tám*, pl. 2. *bhū-tá*[4], mid. sing. 2. *kṛ-ṣvá*; in the **participle**, the suffix is accented in the active, e. g. *bhid-ánt-*, and generally in the middle, e. g. *budh-āná-*, but in several instances the root; e. g. *dyút-āna-*.

2. In the ***a*-aorist** the accentuation follows that of the unaugmented indicative; thus the subjunctive sing. 3. *vidā́t*; the injunctive sing. 1. *dárśa-m ruhá-m*, 3. *rúha-t*, *vidá-t*, *sána-t*, pl. 3. *vidá-nta*; optative, sing. 1. *vidéyam*, *sanéyam*, pl. 1. *śakéma*, *sanéma* and *sánema*; the imperative, sing. 2. *sána*, *sára*, du. 2. *ruhá-tam*, *sáda-tam*, pl. 2. *khyá-ta*. The participle usually accents the thematic *-a*, but sometimes the root; e. g. *tṛpá-nt-*, but *sáda-nt-*; *guhá-māna-*, but *dása-māna-*.

---

[1] Cp. WHITNEY 645 a, 668 a, 669.

[2] When the primary endings are added, the reduplicative syllable is almost always accented; e. g. *jújoṣasi*; some others, which take secondary endings, but do not strengthen the root, also accent the reduplicative syllable, as *dádhṛṣanta*; see below 490.

[3] A few forms accent and strengthen the radical syllable, du. 2. *mumóc-a-tam*, pl. 2. *mumóc-a-ta*, mid. sing. 2. *pipráy-a-sva*.

[4] But the root is strong and accented in several forms, *kár-ta* etc., of the 2. pl. imperative.

3. In the **reduplicated aorist** the only accented form in the subjunctive seems to be *vócati*; in the injunctive, either the reduplicative syllable or the root is accented; e. g. sing. 2. *nínaś-as*, *śiśráthas*, 3. *píparat* and *pīpárat*; in the optative, the thematic vowel or the ending; e. g. pl. 1. *vocéma*, *cucyuv-ī-máhi*; in the imperative, the thematic vowel or the ending; e. g. du. 2. *jigṛ-tám*, pl. *jigṛ-tá*, *suṣūdá-ta* (AV.).

4. The **s-aorist** accents the root in the subjunctive; e. g. *dár-ṣ-a-t* (*dṛ-* 'split'), *yák-ṣ-a-t* (*yaj-* 'sacrifice'), du. 2. *pár-ṣ-a-thas* (*pṛ-* 'take across'); the root in the injunctive as far as can be judged from the extremely few accented forms, as mid. sing. 1. *váṃ-s-i* (*van-* 'win'); the ending[1] in the optative, as mid. sing. 1. *bhak-ṣ-ī-yá* (√*bhaj-*), pl. *dhuk-ṣ-ī-máhi* (*duh-* 'milk'); in the imperative no accented forms occur; the participle accents the root in the active, as *dák-ṣ-ant-* (*dah-* 'burn'), but in the irregularly formed middle[2] nearly always the suffix, as *arc-a-s-āná-*, but *óh-a-s-āna-* (527).

5. The **iṣ-aorist** accents the root in the subjunctive; e. g. sing. 3. *bódh-iṣ-a-t*; the root in the injunctive, e. g. sing. 2. *máth-īs*, but once the ending in pl. 3. *tār-iṣ-úr* (AV.); the ending in the optative; e. g. sing. 1. *edh-iṣ-īyá* (AV.); the ending in the imperative; e. g. sing. 2. *av-iḍ-ḍhí*, du. 2. *av-iṣ-ṭám*.

6. In the **siṣ-aorist** no accented forms occur except one in the imperative, where the ending has the acute, du. 2. *yā-siṣ-ṭám*.

7. The **sa-aorist** accents that syllable in the injunctive, as pl. 3. *dhuk-ṣá-nta* (but once sing. 3. *dhúk-ṣa-ta*), and in the imperative, as sing. 2. *dhuk-ṣá-sva* (√*duh-*). No subjunctive or optative forms occur.

100. The future.—The accent in all forms of this tense remains on the suffix *-syá-* or *-i-ṣyá*; e. g. sing. 3. *e-ṣyá-ti* (AV.) 'he will go' (√*i-*); sing. 1. *stav-i-ṣyā́mi* 'I shall praise' (√*stu-*), 3. *kar-i-ṣyáti* 'he will do' (√*kṛ-*); participle *kar-i-ṣyánt-* 'about to do'.

101. Secondary conjugations.—All these, except the active form of the intensive, accent the same syllable of the stem throughout. They are the causative, the denominative, the passive, the secondary form of the intensive, and the desiderative, the stem of all of which ends in *-a*. The **causative** accents the penultimate syllable of the stem; e. g. *krodh-áya-* 'enrage'.—The **passive**, the **secondary** form of the **intensive**, and the **denominative**, accent the suffix *-yá*; e. g. *pan-yá-te* 'is admired'; *rerih-yá-te* 'licks repeatedly'; *gopā-yánti* 'they protect'. A certain number of unmistakable denominatives, however, have the causative accent; e. g. *mantrá-ya-te* 'takes counsel'.—The **desiderative** accents the reduplicative syllable; e. g. *píprī-ṣa-ti*.—The **primary** form of the **intensive** agrees in accentuation with the third or reduplicating class of verbs, that is, it accents the reduplicative syllable in the strong forms, but the endings with initial consonant in the weak forms of the indicative active; e. g. sing. 3. *jóhav-ī-ti*, du. 3. *jar-bhṛ-tás*, pl. 3. *vár-vṛt-ati*. In the middle indicative, however, the reduplicative syllable is more often accented than not; e. g. *té-tik-te* and *nenik-té*. In the subjunctive the reduplicative syllable is regularly accented; e. g. sing. 3. *jáṅghan-a-t*, but once the root in sing. 1. *jaṅghán-āni*; mid. pl. 3. *jáṅghan-anta*, but once the ending in du. 3. *tantas-áite*. No accented form of the optative occurs. In the imperative the ending is accented; e. g. sing. 2. *jāgṛ-hí*, *car-kṛ-tā́t*. In the participle, both active and middle, the reduplicative syllable is regularly accented; e. g. *cékit-at-*, *cékit-āna-*; there are, however, two exceptions in the middle: *badbadh-āná-* and *marmṛj-āná-* (548 a).

[1] Once the root is accented in the irregular form du. 2. *trā́-s-ī-thām*.

[2] The root is accented in two middle participles irregularly formed with *-māna*. *hā́-s-a-māna-* and *dhí-ṣ-a-māṇa-*.

5. Accent of nominal verb forms.

102. The accentuation of **participles** formed from tense and conjugation stems has already been stated. When these are **compounded with prepositions**, they retain their accents; thus the present and perfect participles of *apa-gám-* 'go away' would be *apa-gácchant-, apa-gácchamāna-; apa-jaganvā́ṃs-, apa-jagmānā́-.* The preposition is, however, not infrequently found separated from the participle by another word or is placed after it, when it is treated as independent and accented, e. g. *prá śmáśru dódhuvat* (x. 23[1]) 'shaking his beard'; *ápa dṛḷhā́ni dárdrat* (vi. 17[5]) 'bursting strongholds asunder'; *ā́ ca párā ca pathíbhiś cárantam* (i. 164[31]) 'wandering hither and thither on (his) paths', *mádhu bíbhrata úpa* (i. 166[2]) 'bringing sweetness near'; *tanvánta ā́ rájaḥ* (iv. 45[2]) 'extending through the air'. The preposition is occasionally found independently accented immediately before the participle, as *abhí dákṣat* (ii. 4[7]) 'burning around'; *ví vidvā́n* (i. 189[7]) 'distinguishing' (probably in distinction from *vividvā́n,* perfect participle of *vid-* 'find').

a. When there are **two prepositions**, either both are compounded and unaccented, as *vi-pra-yántaḥ* (ix. 22[5]) 'advancing', *pary-ā-vívṛtsan* (vii. 63[2]) 'turning round'; or one is compounded and the other independent and accented, as *abhí ā-cárantīḥ* (viii. 96[15]) 'approaching'; *ava-sṛjánn úpa tmánā* (i. 142[11]) 'bestowing indeed'; *prá vayā́m uj-jíhānāḥ* (v. 1[1]) 'flying up to a branch'.

b. **Participles in *-tar*** generally accent the root, as *kár-tar* 'making', but when compounded the suffix. But *ní-cetar-* 'observing' occurs beside *ni-cetár-* 'observer'.

103. The **past passive participle** regularly accents the suffix; e. g. *ga-tá-* 'gone', *pat-i-tá-* (AV.) 'fallen', *chin-ná-* 'cut off' (√*chid-*). But when this participle is **compounded** with prepositions, the latter are as a rule accented. In several instances, however, the accent of the simple participle is retained, as *apa-krī-tá-* (AV.) 'bought', *ni-ci-tá-* 'seen', *niṣ-kṛ-tá-* 'prepared', *ni-ṣat-tá-* 'seated', *ni-vā-tá-* (AV.) 'uninjured', *pra-jah-i-tá-* 'given up' (from *jah-*, a secondary form of *hā-* 'leave'), *pra-śas-tá-* 'celebrated', *saṃ-skṛ-tá-* 'prepared' (beside *sáṃ-skṛ-ta-*), *saṃ-hi-tá-* (VS.) 'variegated'[1]. The preposition may be separated from the participle by another word, as *pári soma siktáḥ* (ix. 97[15]) 'poured, O Soma, around'. When there are **two prepositions,** the first remains unaccented, as *apā́-vṛktāḥ* (viii. 80[8]) 'removed' (*apa-ā́-*), *sam-ā́-kṛ-tam* (x. 84[7]) 'accumulated'; or it may be separated and independently accented, as *prá yát samudrá ā́-hitaḥ* (ix. 64[19]) 'when despatched forth to the ocean'; *pári góbhir ā́-vṛtam* (ix. 86[27]) 'encompassed round by streams of milk'.

104. Of the **gerundives,** those in *-ya* (or *-t-ya*) and *-tva* accent the root; e. g. *cákṣ-ya-* 'to be seen', *śrú-t-ya-* 'to be heard', *car-kṛ́-t-ya-* 'to be praised', *vák-tva-* 'to be said'; those in *-āyya, -enya, -anīya* (AV.) accent the penultimate; e. g. *pan-ā́yya-* 'to be admired', *īkṣ-éṇya-* 'worthy to be seen', while those in *-tavya* accent the final syllable, as *jan-i-tavyà-* (AV.) 'to be born'[2]. When compounded with prepositions[3], gerundives nearly always leave the accent unchanged; e. g. *pari-cákṣ-ya-* 'to be despised'; with Svarita on the final syllable in the RV. only *ā-kāy-yà-* 'desirable' and *upa-vāk-yà-*

[1] Such compounds are also thus accented when turned into substantives, as *niṣ-kṛ-tá-* n. 'rendezvous', *upa-stutá-*, N. of a man.

[2] The gerundives in *-anīya* and *-tavya* only begin to appear in the AV., where two examples of each occur (581 a, b).

[3] The preposition is here always inseparable.

'to be addressed'; *abhy-ā-yaṃs-énya-* 'allowing oneself to be drawn near'; *ā-mantr-aṇíya-* (AV.) 'to be addressed'.

105. Infinitives are as a rule accented like ordinary nominal cases formed from the same stems.

a. The **dative** infinitive from root stems accents the ending; e. g. *dṛś-é* 'to see', but when compounded, the root; e. g. *sam-ídh-e* 'to kindle', *abhi-pra-cákṣ-e* (I. 113[6]) 'to see'. Those formed from stems in *-as* generally accent that suffix, but sometimes the radical syllable; e. g. *car-ás-e* 'to fare', but *cákṣ-as-e* 'to see'. Those formed from stems in *-i* and *-ti* accent the suffix; e. g. *dṛś-áy-e* 'to see', *pī-táy-e* 'to drink'. Those from stems in *-tu* accent the root, as *bhár-tav-e;* also those from stems in *-tavā*, but with a secondary accent on the final syllable, as *gán-tavái.* When these two forms are compounded with prepositions, the latter are accented; e. g. *prá-vantave*[1] 'to win', *ápa-bhartavái* 'to be taken away', the latter retaining its final accent as well. When there are two prepositions, the first may be independent and accented as well; e. g. *ví prá-sartave* (VIII. 67[12]) 'to spread'. Infinitives formed with *-dhyai* generally accent the preceding *a* of the verbal stem, but sometimes the root; e. g. *iyá-dhyai* 'to go', but *gáma-dhyai* 'to go'. Those formed from stems in *-man* accent the root; e. g. *dá-man-e* 'to give', except *vid-mán-e* 'to know'; from stems in *-van* there are *dā-ván-e* 'to give', *tur-váṇ-e* 'to excel', but *dhū́r-vaṇ-e* 'to injure' (√*dhvṛ-*)[2].

b. The **accusative** infinitive if formed from a radical stem accents the root even when compounded with a preposition; e. g. *śúbh-am* 'to shine', *ā-sád-am* 'to sit down'; if formed from a stem in *-tu*, it accents the root in a simple stem, but the preposition in a compounded stem; e. g. *dā́-tum* 'to give', *prá-bhar-tum* 'to present', *ánu prá-voḷhum* 'to advance'[3].

c. The **ablative-genitive** infinitive, if formed from radical stems, which here occur only in combination with prepositions, accents the root; e. g. *ava-pád-as* '(from) falling down'; if formed from a stem in *-tu*, the root in a simple stem, but the preposition in a compound stem; e. g. *gán-tos* 'going', *ní-dhā-tos* 'putting down'.

d. The **locative** infinitive if formed from radical stems accents the ending in the simple form, but the root in the compounded form; e. g. *budh-í* 'at the waking', but *saṃ-dṛ́ś-i* 'on seeing'. The one locative infinitive formed from a stem in *-tar*, and those from stems in *-san* accent the suffix; e. g. *dhar-tár-i* 'to bestow', *ne-ṣáṇ-i* 'to lead'.

106. Uncompounded **gerunds** formed with *-tvī, -tvā, tvāya* accent the suffix, while the compounded gerunds[4] formed with *-yā́* or *-tyā́* accent the root; e. g. *ga-tví* 'having gone', *bhū-tvā́* 'having become', *ga-tvā́ya* 'having gone'; *saṃ-gṛ́bh-yā* 'gathering', *upa-śrú-tya* (AV.) 'having overheard'.

107. Case-forms used as **adverbs** frequently show a shift of accent. This appears oftenest in the accusative neuter. Thus *drav-át* 'quickly', but *dráv-ant-* 'running', probably also *drah-yát*[5] 'stoutly'; *aparám* 'later', but *áparam* as neuter adjective; *ā-vyuṣ-ám* (AV.) 'till dawn'[6]; and the adverbs in *-vát*, as *aṅgiras-vát* 'like Aṅgiras', *manuṣ-vát* 'as Manus did', *purāṇa-vát,*

[1] The infinitive from stems in *-tu* in all its cases accents the preposition; e. g. *sáṃ-hartum* 'to collect', *ápi-dhātave* 'to cover up', *áva-gantos* 'of descending'.

[2] A preposition is occasionally uncompounded with or separated from the infinitive, when both are accented, as *prá dāváne* (IV. 32[9]; V. 65[3]); *prá dāśúṣe dā́tave* (IV. 20[11]).

[3] When there are two prepositions, the first is independent and therefore also accented.

[4] The preposition is here always inseparable.

[5] Which seems to be formed from an irregular present participle of *dṛh-* 'be firm'.

[6] The ordinary A. of *vy-úṣ-* 'dawn' would be *vyúṣ-am.*

pūrva-vát, *pratna-vát* 'as of old', which are accusative neuters of the adjective suffix *-vant*[1] (unaccented); and some adverbs from the comparative in *-tara*, *ut-tarám* (AV.) 'higher', but *út-tara-* as adjective; similarly *ava-tarám*, *paras-tarám* and *parā-tarám* 'farther away', *vi-tarám* 'more widely'[2] *saṃ-tarám* (AV.) 'still farther'. Similarly the instrumental *dívā* 'by day', but *divā́* 'through heaven'; and the dative *aparā́ya* 'for the future', but *áparāya* 'to the later'; and the ablatives *apākā́t* 'from afar' (*ápāka-* 'far'), *amā́t* 'from near' (*áma-* AV. 'this'), *sanā́t* 'from of old' (*sána-* 'old')[3].

6. Accent in Sandhi.

108. 1. When two vowels combine so as to form a long vowel or diphthong, the latter has the Udātta if either or both of the original vowels had it[4]; e. g. *nudasvā́tha* for *nudasva átha*; *távét* for *táva ít*; *kvét* for *kvà ít*[5]; *ágāt* for *ā́ agāt*; *pitéva* for *pitā́ iva*, *śató* for *śatā́ u*; *nā́ntaras* (VI. 63[2]) for *ná ántaras*.

The contraction of *í* + *i* is, however, accented *ī̀*,[6] the (dependent) Svarita having here (in *í ì*) ousted the preceding Udātta[7]; e. g. *divī̀va* (RV. AV.) for *diví ìva*. This is the *praśliṣṭa*, 'contracted', Svarita of the Prātiśākhyas[8].

2. When *ī́* and *ū́* with Udātta are changend to *y* and *v*, a following unaccented vowel receives the Svarita; e. g. *vy ànaṭ* for *ví anaṭ*.

The uncontracted form with Udātta must, however, almost invariably be read in the RV. This is the *kṣaipra*[9] Svarita of the Prātiśākhyas[8]. Here the enclitic Svarita assumes the appearance of an independent accent.

3. When *á* is elided, it throws back its Udātta on unaccented *e* or *o*; e. g. *sūnávé 'gne* for *sūnáve ágne*; *vó 'vasaḥ* for *vo ávasaḥ*. But when unaccented *a* is elided, it changes a preceding Udātta to Svarita; e. g. *sò 'dhamáḥ* for *só adhamáḥ*. This is the *abhinihita* Svarita of the Prātiśākhyas[8]. Here also the enclitic Svarita (in *ó à*) has ousted the preceding Udātta (as in *divī̀va*)[10].

7. The Sentence Accent.

HASKELL, Vocative-Accent in the Veda, JAOS. 11, 57. — BÖHTLINGK, ein erster Versuch über den Accent im Sanskrit (Mémoires de l'Académie imp. de St. Pétersbourg 1843) p. 38 ff. — WHITNEY, JAOS. 5, 193 ff., 387 ff. — AUREL MAYR, Beiträge aus dem Rigveda zur Accentuirung des verbum finitum (Sitzungsberichte der phil.-hist. Classe der kaiserlichen Akademie der Wissenschaften, Wien 1871, p. 219 ff.). — WEBER, IS. 13, 70ff. — BÖHTLINGK, Sanskrit-Chrestomathie[2] p. 356. — WHITNEY, Sanskrit Grammar 591 ff. — DELBRÜCK, Altindische Syntax (Halle 1888) 21—29. — OLDENBERG, Die Verbalenklisis im Ṛgveda, ZDMG. 60, 707—740.

109. **The vocative.** — a. The vocative, which whether it consist of a single word or a compound expression, is invariably accented on the first syllable, retains its accent only at the beginning of a sentence or Pāda[11];

1 Cp. WHITNEY 1107 a.
2 See op. cit. 1119.
3 Cp. op. cit. 1114 a.
4 Cp. BENFEY, Vollständige Grammatik 64.
5 But when a Svarita is followed by an unaccented syllable, it of course remains; e. g. *kvèyatha* for *kvà iyatha* (VIII. 17).
6 Except in the Taittirīya texts which follow the general rule (*divī́va*).
7 This also takes place in *sū́dgātā́* (TS.) for *sú-udgātā́* 'a good Udgātṛ' (TS. VII. 8[1]: B.).
8 Cp. HAUG 75.
9 So called because 'uttered with a quick' (*kṣipra-*) pronunciation, the semivowel replacing the vowel.
10 Cp. WACKERNAGEL I, 251, b α; BRUGMANN, KG. 45, 2.
11 This applies to the second as well as the first Pāda of a hemistich (as some of the above examples show), thus indicating the independent character of these Pādas, which is obscured by the way in which the redactors of the Saṃhitās apply the rules of Sandhi and mark the dependent Svarita.

that is to say, when, having the full force of the case, it occupies the most emphatic position; e. g. *ágne sūpāyanó bhava* (I. 1⁹ᵇ) 'O Agni, be easy of access'; *ū́rjo napāt sahasāvan* (x. 115⁸ᵃ) 'O mighty son of strength'; *hótar yaviṣṭha sukrato* (IV. 4¹¹ᵈ) 'O most youthful, skilful priest'. This rule also applies to doubly accented dual compounds, as *mítrāvaruṇa* (I. 15⁶ᵇ) 'O Mitra and Varuṇa' (N. *mitrā́-váruṇā*).

a. Two or more vocatives at the beginning of a Pāda are all accented; e. g. *ádite, mítra, váruṇa* (II. 27¹⁴ᵃ); *ū́rjo napād, bhádraśoce* (VIII. 71³ᵇ) 'O son of strength, O propitiously bright one'[1].

b. The vocative, when it does not begin the sentence, loses its accent, being unemphatic as referring only incidentally to a person already invoked; e. g. *ṛténa mitrāvaruṇāv ṛtāvṛdhāv ṛtaspṛśā* (I. 2⁸) 'through Law, O Mitra and Varuṇa, lovers and cherishers of Law'; *úpa tvā‿agne divé-dive, dóṣā-vastar dhiyā́ vayám | . . . émasi* (I. 1⁷) 'to thee, O Agni, day by day, O illuminer of darkness, with prayer we come'; *ā́ rājānā*[2] *maha ṛtasya gopā* (VII. 64²) 'hither (come), O ye two sovereign guardians of great order'; *yád, indra brahmaṇas-pate, abhidrohám cárāmasi* (x. 164⁴)[3] 'if, O Indra, O Brahmaṇaspati, we commit an offence'[4].

a. The vocative, whether at the beginning of or within a sentence, not being regarded as part of it, does not interfere with the normal accentuation of the sentence. Hence a verb at the beginning of a sentence, following a vocative, is accented as the first word of the sentence; while a verb within a sentence, following a vocative, remains unaccented; e. g. *dévā, jī́vata* (AV. XIX. 70¹) 'O gods, live'; *asmé ū ṣú, vṛṣaṇā, mādayethām* (I. 184²) 'beside us, ye two heroes, enjoy yourselves'.

110. The verb.—A. The finite verb **in a principal sentence** is unaccented except when it is the first word; e. g. *agním īḷe puróhitam* (I. 1¹) 'I praise Agni, the domestic priest'; but *ī́ḷe agníṃ vipaścítam* (III. 27²) 'I praise Agni the wise'. This rule and its exception must, however, be understood with the following restrictions:

1. A sentence is regarded as capable of having only one verb. Hence all other verbs syntactically connected with the subject of the first, are accented as beginning new sentences (a subject or object coming between two such verbs being generally counted to the first); e. g. *téṣām pāhi, śrudhī́ hávam* (I. 2¹) 'drink of them, hear our call'; *asmábhyaṃ jeṣi yótsi ca* (I. 132⁴) 'conquer and fight for us'; *tarádṇir ij jayati, kṣéti, púṣyati* (VII. 32⁹) 'the energetic man conquers, rules, thrives'; *jahí prajā́ṃ náyasva ca* (AV. I. 8³) 'slay the progeny and bring (it) hither'.

2. The verb, though not beginning a sentence, receives the accent if it coincides with the beginning of a Pāda (which is treated as the beginning of a new sentence); e. g. *átha te ántamānām | vidyā́ma sumatīnā́m* (I. 4³).

3. Since a vocative (or vocatives) at the beginning of a sentence is treated as extraneous to it, the verb which immediately follows it becomes the first word of the sentence and is accordingly accented; e. g. *ágne, juṣásva*

---

[1] Here *bhádraśoce* is treated as an independent vocative; it would lose its accent if intended to form a compound expression with *ū́rjo napāt* = 'O propitously bright son of strength', as is the case in *hótar yaviṣṭha sukrato*.

[2] When the first word of a compound vocative is an adjective (not a genitive), it retains its accent within a Pāda; thus *víśve devāsaḥ* 'O All-gods', would appear within a Pāda as well as at the beginning.

[3] This is an example of two distinct vocatives. The preceding example may contain two also, as the accent of two as well as of one vocative would be lost within a Pāda; but if *rājānā* stood at the beginning of a Pāda, the accentuation would be *rā́jānā máha ṛtasya gopā*, supposing two vocatives were intended.

[4] The very rare exceptions to the rules given above (*a*, *b*) are doubtless due to errors on the part of the editors or of tradition.

no havíḥ (III. 28[1]) 'O Agni, enjoy our sacrifice'. Thus the following sentence of six words contains three accented verbs as well as three accented vocatives: *índra, jíva, sū́rya, jíva, dévā, jívata* (AV. XIX. 70[1]) 'O Indra, live; O Sūrya, live; O gods, live'.

4. There are some instances in the RV. of the verb when emphatic, even though not placed at the beginning of the sentence, being accented before the particle *íd*, and even before *caná*[1]; e. g. *ádha smā no maghavañ carkṛtā́d íd* (I. 104[5]) 'then be mindful of us, bounteous one'; *ná, devā, bhasáthaś caná* (VI. 59[4]) '(him) O gods, ye two never consume'[2].

B. The accent always rests on the verb of a **subordinate clause** (which is almost invariably introduced by the relative *ya-* and its derivatives, or contains the particles *ca* and *céd* 'if', *néd* 'lest', *hí* 'for', *kuvíd* 'whether'); e. g. *yáṃ yajñám paribhū́r ási* (I. 1[4]) 'what offering thou protectest'; *gṛhā́n gaccha gṛhapátnī yáthā‿ásaḥ* (X. 85[26]) 'go to the house, that thou be lady of the house'; *índraś ca mṛḷáyāti no, ná naḥ paścā́d aghám naśat* (II. 41[11]) 'if Indra be gracious to us, no hurt will thereafter reach us'; *ví céd ucchánty, aśvinā, uṣā́saḥ, prá vāṃ bráhmāṇi kārávo bharante* (VII. 72[4]) 'when the dawns shine forth, O Aśvins, the singers offer their prayers to you'; *mā́ cirám tanuthā ápaḥ, nét tvā . . tápāti sū́ro arcíṣā* (V. 79[9]) 'do not lông delay thy work, lest the sun burn thee with his beam'; *tváṃ hí baladā́ ási* (III. 53[18]) 'for thou art a giver of strength'; *tám, indra, mádam ā́ gahi, kuvín*[3] *nv àsya tṛpṇávaḥ* (III. 42[2]) 'come to this gladdening drink, O Indra, (to see) whether thou mayst enjoy it'.

1. When the first of two clauses, though in form a principal one, is **virtually subordinate** in sense (being equivalent to one introduced by 'if' or 'when'), its verb is occassionally accented; e. g. *sám áśvaparṇāś cáranti no náro, 'smā́kam, indra, rathíno jayantu* (VI. 47[31]) 'when our men winged with steeds come together, may the car-fighters of our side, O Indra, win the victory'.

2. Similarly, but much more frequently, the verb of the first of two clauses which are **antithetical** in sense, is accented[4]. The occurrence of correlative words like *anyá-anyá, éka-éka, vā-vā, ca-ca*, often makes the antithesis obvious; e. g. *prá-pra‿anyé yánti, páry anyá āsate* (III. 9[3]) '(while) some go on and on, others sit about'; *sáṃ ca‿idhásva‿agne, prá ca bodhaya‿enam* (VS. XXVII. 2) 'both be kindled, O Agni, and waken this man's knowledge': *úd vā siñcádhvam úpa vā pṛṇadhvam* (VII. 16[11]) 'either pour out or fill up'. If the verb of both clauses is the same, it usually appears (as is natural in the circumstances) in the first only; e. g. *dvipā́c ca sárvaṃ no rákṣa, cátuṣpād yác ca naḥ svám* (AV. VI. 107[1]) 'protect both every biped of ours and whatever quadruped is our own'.

3. The second clause, on the other hand, accents the verb if it contains an **imperative** (with a final sense), and follows a clause with an imperative of *i-, gam-* or *yā-* 'go'; e. g. *éta, dhíyaṃ kṛṇávāma* (V. 45[6]) 'come, let us (= that we may) make prayer'; *tū́yam ā́ gahi, káṇveṣu sácā píba* (VIII. 4[3]) 'come quickly, beside the Kaṇvas drink thy fill'.

III. **Verbal prepositions.—A.** The preposition, which generally precedes, but sometimes follows the verb, being often separated from it by other words,

[1] Cp. DELBRÜCK 23, 3, 4; 26, 2; WHITNEY 598a. In the ŚB. *hánta* regularly accents the verb.

[2] Cp. GRASSMANN, Wb. under *íd* and *caná*.

[3] There are only two passages in the RV. (V. 3[10], 36[3]) in which *kuvíd* does not accent the verb; cp. GRASSMANN, sub verbo; DELBRÜCK 550, end.

[4] This accentuation is more strictly applied in B. than in V., and among the Saṃhitās least strictly in the RV.; cp. WHITNEY 597 a.

is regularly accented in principal sentences; e. g. *ā́ gamat* (I. 1⁵) 'may he come'; *jáyema sáṃ yudhí spṛ́dhaḥ* (I. 8³) 'may we conquer our foes in fight'; *gávām ápa vrajáṃ vṛdhi* (I. 10⁷) 'unclose the stable of the kine'; *gámad vā́jebhir ā́ sá naḥ* (I. 5³) 'may he come to us with booty'.

a. When there are **two prepositions**, both are accented in the RV., being treated as separate words; e. g. *úpa prá yāhi* (I. 82⁶) 'come forth'; *pári spáśo ní ṣedire* (I. 25¹³) 'the spies have sat down around'; *úpa práyobhir ā́ gatam* (I. 2⁴) 'come hither with refreshments'; *ágne, ví paśya bṛhatā́ abhí rāyā́* (III. 23²) 'O Agni, look forth towards (us) with ample wealth'.

a. When *ā́* immediately follows another preposition (unless it ends in *i*), it alone is accented, both being compounded with the verb; e. g. *upā́gahi*¹ (I. 91¹⁰) 'come hither'; *samā́kṛṇoṣi jīvā́se* (X. 25⁶) 'thou fittest (them) for living'. The general rule, however, is followed if the preposition preceding *ā́* ends in *i*; e. g. *práty ā́ tanuṣva* (IV. 4⁴) 'draw (thy bow) against (them)'². In the only passage in which it has been noted in combination with another preposition preceding it, *áva* is treated like *ā́: upā́vasṛja* (X. 110¹⁰) 'pour out'³.

B. The preposition **in subordinate clauses** is generally compounded with the verb, when it is regularly unaccented; e. g. *yád .. niṣī́dathaḥ*⁴ (VIII. 9²¹) 'when ye two sit down'. It is, however, often separated from the verb, and is then accented as well as the verb. In this case it is commonly the first word of a Pāda, but occasionally comes after the verb; e. g. *ví yó mamé rájasī* (I. 160⁴) 'who measured out the two regions'; *yás tastámbha sáhasā ví jmó ántān* (IV. 50¹) 'who with might propped earth's ends asunder'. Occasionally the preposition is separate and accented even when immediately preceding the verb; e. g. *yá āhutim pári véda námobhiḥ* (VI. 1⁹) 'who fully knows the offering with devotion'.

a. When there are **two prepositions**, either both are unaccented and compounded with the verb, or the first only is separate and accented; e. g. *yūyáṃ hí, devīr, ṛtayúgbhir áśvaiḥ pariprayāthá* (IV. 51⁵) 'for ye, O goddesses, proceed around with steeds yoked by eternal order'; *sáṃ yám āyánti dhenávaḥ* (V. 6²) 'to whom the cows come together', *yátra abhí saṃnávāmahe* (VIII. 69⁵) 'where we to (him) together shout'. A very rare example of two independent prepositions in a dependent sentence is *prá yát stotā́ ... úpa gīrbhír íḷe* (III. 52⁵) 'when the praiser pours forth laudation to (him) with songs'.

IV. NOMINAL STEM FORMATION.

GRASSMANN, Wörterbuch zum Rig-veda 1687—1738 (list of nominal stems according to alphabetical order of the final letter). — LINDNER, Altindische Nominalbildung. Nach den Saṃhitās dargestellt. Jena 1878. — WHITNEY, Sanskrit Grammar 1136—1245; Roots, Verb-forms, and Primary Derivatives, 1885.

112. The bare root, both verbal and pronominal, is often used as a declinable stem. But much more generally the stem in declension is formed by means of suffixes. These are of two kinds: **primary**, or

---

¹ There seems to be an exception in *átaś cid, indra, ṇa upā́ yāhi* (VIII. 92¹⁰) 'thence, O Indra, come to us', but *úpa* here coming at the end of a Pāda, is used adnominally with *naḥ*.

² The treatment of two prepositions is on the whole the same in the AV. (cp. WHITNEY, APr. 185 ff.) and the TS. (cp. WEBER, IS. 13, 62 ff.); but the TS. treats some other prepositions like *ā́*, and the MS.

goes much further, apparently making accentuation of the second preposition the rule; cp. DELBRÜCK p. 48.

³ Cp. DELBRÜCK p. 47, end.

⁴ It is not clear why the Pada text analyses forms like *ny ásīdat* (I. 143¹), *ny ástaḥ* (VII. 18¹¹), *vy ásthāt* (II. 4⁷) as *ni ásīdat, ni ástaḥ, vi ásthāt*. There are about thirty instances of this; cp. WHITNEY 1084 a.

those that are added directly to roots; **secondary**, or those that are added to stems already derivative (pronominal stems being also accounted as such). The distinction between these two kinds is, however, not absolute. Suffixes containing a secondary element sometimes have the appearance and application of primary suffixes (as *-anīya* = *-an-īya*). Less frequently primary suffixes come to be used as secondary ones; thus the participial suffixes are added not only to the root, but also to primary and secondary conjugation stems as well as to tense stems. These nominal suffixes are sometimes added by means of what looks like and may conveniently be called a connecting vowel, though it may not be so in origin. Primary suffixes are also added to roots compounded with verbal prefixes[1].

I. Primary Nominal Derivation.

113. As regards form, the root when used without suffix usually remains unchanged in respect to its vowel[2]; it is then, however, liable to modification in two ways: always adding the determinative *-t* if it ends in *-i, u*, or *-ṛ*, and occasionally appearing in a reduplicated form. But before primary suffixes the root usually appears in a strong form: either with Guṇa of medial or final vowels, as *véd-a-* 'knowledge' from √*vid-*, *sár-aṇa-* 'running' from √*sṛ-*; or with Vṛddhi of final *-i, -u, -ṛ* and lengthening of medial *a*, as *kār-á-* 'making' from √*kṛ-*, *grābh-á-* 'seizer', from √*grabh-*.

a. As regards **meaning**, there are two classes of **primary derivatives**: the one expressing abstract **action nouns** (with an infinitival character), the other concrete **agent nouns** (with a participial character) used as adjectives or substantives. Other senses are only modifications of these two; as that of the passive participle, which expresses an agent who becomes the recipient of an action. The primary suffixes forming action nouns can also nearly all be used to form agent nouns; and many of those properly forming agent nouns may also form action nouns. Those which properly form **action nouns** are: *-a, -an, -ana, -anā, -ani, -anī, -as, -ā, -i, -is, -ī, -īka, -us, -tas, -ti, -tu, -tna, -tha, -thu, -nas, -ni, -nu, -pa, -ma, -man, -mi, -yu, -van, -sas.* Those which properly form **agent nouns** are: *-aka, -at* or *-ant, -ata, -anīya, -asi, -āku, -āna, -in, -iṣṭha, -īyāṃs, -u, -uka, -ū, -ūka, -ka, -ta, -tar, -tnu, -tra, -tri, -tva, -thi, -na, -māna, -min, -ya, -ra, -ri, -ru, -la, -li, -lu, -va, -vana, -vani, -vanu, -vara, -vas, -vāṃs, -vi, -sa, -sani, -saru, -sna, -snu.*

Root stems.

114. These stems are used both as action nouns (often in the function of infinitives) and as agent nouns, either substantives or adjectives.

1. Examples of the simple root form are: *dyút-* f. 'splendour', *nṛ́t-* (AV.) f. 'gesticulation', *búdh-* f. 'awaking'; *dā́-* 'giver', *bhíd-* f. 'destroyer', *yúj-* m. 'companion', *spáś-* m. 'spy'; *máh-* 'great', *vṛ́dh-* 'strengthening'.—**2.** With root determinative *-t*: *mí-t-* f. 'pillar', *stú-t-* f. 'praise'.—**3.** With reduplicated root: *cikít-* 'wise' (*cit-* 'observe'), *juhū́-* f. 'sacrificial spoon' (*hu-* 'offer'), *juhū́-* 'tongue' (*hū-* 'call'), *dadṛ́h-*[3] 'hearty' (*dṛh-* 'be firm'), *didyú-* m. 'missile', *didyú-t-* f. 'missile', 'lightning', *sasyád-* f. 'running stream' (*syand-* 'run')[4] and with intensive

[1] Those chiefly thus used are approximately in the order of their frequency: *-a, -ana, -ti, -tar* and *-tra, -in, -ya, -van* and *-man, -i, -u, -as*; cp. WHITNEY 1141 c.

[2] That is, the root appears in the weak form, in which it is usually stated.

[3] In *dadhṛ́k* adv. 'heartily'.

[4] Perhaps also *gáṅgā-* f. 'Ganges' if

reduplication: *jógū-* 'singing aloud' (*gu-* 'sound'), *pra-ṇenī́-* 'guiding constantly' (*nī-* 'lead'), *yaviyúdh-* 'warlike' (*yudh-* 'fight'), *vánīvan-* 'desiring', *a-sūsū́-* (AV.) 'barren' ('not bringing forth'). *dáridra-* (VS.) 'roving' (*drā-* 'run') is a transfer to the radical *a*-stems[1].

-*a*: action and agent.

115. A vast number of derivatives is formed with this suffix, before which the root is generally strengthened, but sometimes remains unchanged or is reduplicated. Those formed with Guṇa are more than twice as numerous as all the rest taken together. Medial *a* generally remains unchanged.

1. Examples of derivatives with **Guṇa** are the following **action nouns:** *áy-a-* m. 'course' (*i-* 'go') *háv-a-* m. 'invocation' (*hū-* 'call'), *tár-a-* m. 'crossing' (*tṝ-* 'cross'); *véd-a-* 'knowledge' (*vid-* 'know'), *jóṣ-a-* 'enjoyment' (*juṣ-* 'enjoy'), *sárg-a-* 'emission' (*sṛj-* 'send forth'); **agent nouns:** *plav-á-* m. 'boat' (*plu-* 'float'), *megh-á-* m. 'cloud' (*mih-* 'discharge water'), *cod-á-* 'instigator' (*cud-* 'incite'). With medial *a*: *grábh-a-* m. 'seizure' (*grabh-* 'seize'), *śrám-a-* m. 'weariness' (*śram-* 'be weary').

a. In several words thus formed the meaning varies according as the root is accented or the suffix, the word in the former case being nearly always an abstract substantive, in the latter regularly an adjective or an agent noun; thus *árdh-a-* m. 'side', *ardh-á-* 'half'; *éṣ-a-* m. 'speed', *eṣ-á-* 'speeding'; *cód-a-* m. 'goad', *cod-á-* m. 'instigator'; *vár-a-* m. 'choice', *var-á-* m. ('chooser') 'suitor', *śā́s-a-* m. 'command', *śās-á-* m. 'commander', *śók-a-* m. 'glow', *śok-á-* (AV.) 'glowing'.

2. **Vṛddhi** of final vowels and lengthening of *a*[2]: action nouns are *dāv-á-* (AV.) 'fire' (*du-* 'burn'), *tār-á-* (VS.) 'crossing' (*tṝ-* 'cross'), *bhāg-á-* 'share' (*bhaj-* 'divide'); agent nouns are *nāy-á-* 'leader' (*nī-* 'lead'), *jār-á-* 'lover', *grābh-á-* 'seizer'.

3. Several derivatives are formed from the **weak** form of the **root**, the suffix being accented[3]; thus *priy-á-* 'dear' (*prī-* 'please'), *sruv-á-* m. 'spoon' (*sru-* 'flow'), *vr-á-*[4] m. 'troop' (*vṛ-* 'surround'), *tur-á-* 'rapid' (*tṝ-* 'cross'); *yug-á-* n. 'yoke', *śuc-á-* 'bright', *kṛś-á-* 'lean'[5].

a. Several derivatives of this type, which occur almost exclusively at the end of compounds, are made from various tense stems; e. g. *-ā-saj-a-* 'stopping', *-tud-á-* (AV.) 'impelling', *-paś-ya-* 'seeing', *-inv-á-* 'urging', *-pṛ-ṇá-* 'bestowing', *-indh-á-* 'kindling', *-bruv-á-* (AV.) 'saying', *-pib-á-* (AV.) 'drinking', *-ej-ayá-* 'exciting'[6]; *je-ṣ-á-* m. 'attainment' (aor. stem of *ji-* 'conquer'), *neṣá-* m. 'guidance' (aor. stem of *nī-* 'lead').

4. A considerable number of derivates are formed from the reduplicated root; thus *cacar-á-* 'movable', *dadhṛṣ-á-* 'bold', *vavr-á-* m. 'hiding' (*vṛ-* 'cover'), *śiśay-á-* 'strengthening' (*śi-* 'sharpen'), *śiśnáth-a-* 'perforation' (*śnath-* 'pierce'). *sasr-á-* 'flowing' (√*sṛ-*). They are more usually formed directly from the intensive stem or from stems analogously reduplicated; e. g. *cākṣm-á-* 'gracious' (*kṣam-* 'forbear'), *rerih-á-* (AV.) 'continually licking' (*rih-* 'lick), *-rorud-á-* (AV.) 'shedding tears' (*rud-* 'weep'), *vevij-á* 'quick' (*vij-* 'dart'); *carā-car-á* 'far-extending', *calā-cal-á-* 'unsteady', *pani-ṣpad-á-* (AV.) 'palpitating' (√*spand-*), *marī-mṛś-á-* (AV.) 'groping' (*mṛś-* 'feel'), *mali-mluc-á-* (AV.) 'moving about in

from *gā-* 'go'; *śíśu-* m. 'child', if from *śū-* 'grow'.

[1] *jágat-* 'going', 'living', is an old participle present of the reduplicated stem of *gā-* 'go'; Whitney, however, thinks (1147 e) that it is made from the reduplicated form *jaga-* (= *ja-gam-*) with the root determinative *-t*.

[2] In these words the suffix is almost invariably accented; *kā́m-a-* 'desire' is accented on the root as differentiated from *kām-á-* 'desiring'; similarly *śā́k-a-* 'help' and *śāk-á-* 'helpful'.

[3] See Lindner p. 33.

[4] According to Grassmann, f. *vrā́-*.

[5] Some of the derivatives of this type are transitions from the root stems to the *a*-declension, especially at the end of compounds.

[6] See below, Determinative Compounds, 272.

the dark', a kind of demon (*mluc-* 'set', of the sun), *varī-vṛt-á-* (AV.) 'rolling' (*vṛt-* 'turn'), *sani-ṣyad-á-* (AV.) 'running' (√*syand-*), *sani-sras-á-* (AV.) 'decrepit' (*sraṃs-* 'fall'), *sarī-sṛp-á-* 'crawling' (√*sṛp-*).

a. The suffix *-a* is by far the most frequent one used in forming derivatives from the root with a verbal prefix, being nearly always accented whether the noun expresses an action or an agent; e. g. *anu-kar-á-* (AV.) 'assistance', *abhi-droh-á-* 'enmity', *ud-ān-á-* (VS.) m. 'breathing upwards', *ni-meṣ-á-* (VS.) 'wink', *praty-ā-śrāv-á-* 'response', *sam-gam-á-* 'assembly'; *ati-yāj-á-* 'sacrificing excessively', 'over-pious'. *adhi-caṅkram-á-* (AV.) 'climbing over', *ā-dardir-á-* 'crushing', *ut-tud-á-* (AV.) 'rousing', *pari-car-á-* (AV. VS.) 'wandering', *vi-bodh-á-* 'wakeful', *sam-gir-á-* (AV.) 'swallowing', *sam-jay-á-* 'victorious'[1].

b. There are many words which have the appearance of ending in this suffix, though the root cannot be found elsewhere. They include several nouns of plants and animals. Examples are *ukhá-*[2] (AV.) 'caldron', *kroḍá-* (VS. AV.) 'breast', *khilá-* (AV.) 'waste land', *nakhá-* 'nail', *pakṣá-* 'wing', *vaṃśá-* 'reed'[3].

-a-ka : agent.

116. This suffix, which consists of the primary *-a* with the secondary *-ka* added, is in a few words used as a primary suffix forming agent nouns only: *abhi-krós-aka-* (VS.) 'reviler', *pī́y-aka-* (AV.) 'abuser', a class of demon, *vádh-aka-* (AV.), a kind of reed ('destructive'), *sā́y-aka-* n. 'missile' (√*si-*); also *pāv-aká-* 'purifying', 'bright', which though always written thus is invariably to be pronounced *pavāká-*[4].

-ata : agent.

117. In a few adjectives the primary suffix *-a* with *-tá* added is attached to the strong form of the root, chiefly with the sense of the gerundive: *darś-atá-* 'visible', *pac-atá-* 'cooked', *bhar-atá-* 'to be tended', *yaj-atá-* 'to be adored', *raj-atá-*[5] 'silvery', *hary-atá-*[6] 'desirable'.

-at and -ant : agent.

118. The suffixes *-at* and *-ant* are almost restricted to the formation of active **participles**. The former appears chiefly in the formation of present participles of the reduplicating class, as *dád-at-* 'giving'; also in *dáś-at-* 'worshipping', *śā́s-at-* 'instructing', and the aorist participle *dákṣ-at-* and *dhákṣ-at-* from *dah-* 'burn'. There are besides a few substantives originally participles, which have shifted their accent, formed with *-at*: *vah-át-* f. 'stream', *vegh-át-* (AV. VS.) f. 'barren cow', *vāgh-át-* m. 'sacrificer', *srav-át-* f. 'stream', *saśc-át-* m. 'pursuer'[7]. The suffix *-ant* is used to form the active participle of present stems (excepting those of the reduplicating class), of future stems, and aorist stems. Some of these have become independent adjectives: *ṛh-ánt-* 'weak', *pṛ́ṣ-ant-* 'spotted', *bṛh-ánt-* 'great', *mah-ánt-*[8] 'great', *rúś-ant-* 'brilliant'; also the substantive *d-ánt-* m. 'tooth'[9]. *dvay-ant-* in *á-dvay-ant-* (RV[1].) 'not double-tongued' has the appearance of a participle of a denominative stem from *dvi-* 'two'. With the same suffix are formed the two pronominal stems *í-y-ant-* 'so great' ('making this', *í-*) and *kí-y-ant-* 'how great?' ('making what?' *kí-*).

an- : action and agent.

119. Few words are formed with this suffix, and in some of them the root is doubtful.

---

1 Cp. LINDNER p. 35.
2 Also in *ukha-cchid-* (RV[1].) 'fragile as a pot', f. *ukhā́-*.
3 Cp. LINDNER p. 33, bottom.
4 *-āka-* also appears in the Proper Name *nabh-āka-*.
5 Probably from the root *raj-* 'colour'.
6 Formed from the denominative stem of *hári-* 'bright'.
7 See below, Participial stems in *-at*, 311 A.
8 With lengthened vowel in the strong cases.
9 See below, Participles in *-ant*, 313.

The only **action nouns** are the following neuters: *mah-án-*[1] 'greatness', *rāj-án-* (RV[1].) 'guidance', *gámbh-an-* (VS[1].) 'depth'. The infinitives in *-ṣ-áṇ-i* (588c) are, however, probably locatives of action nouns formed with *-an* from aorist stems.

Agent nouns are: *ukṣ-án-* m. 'ox', *cákṣ-an-* (AV.) n. 'eye', *tákṣ-an-* m. 'carpenter', *pūṣ-án-* m., N. of a god, *plīh-án-* (VS. AV.) m. 'spleen', *majj-án-* m. 'marrow', *mūrdh-án-* m. 'head', *rāj-an-* m. 'king', *vṛ́ṣ-an-* adj. 'virile', m. 'bull', *ságh-an-* (TS. III. 2. 1[1]) 'vulture'.

a. There are also several words formed with *-an* the root and original meaning of which are mostly doubtful: 1. *yú-v-an-* m. 'youth', *yóṣ-an-* f. 'maiden', *śv-án-* m. 'dog'; 2. defective neuter nouns; *akṣ-án-* 'eye', *ás-an-* 'blood', *asth-án-* 'bone', *áh-an-* 'day', *ās-án-* 'face', *ud-án-*[2] 'water', *ū́dh-an-* udder', *dadh-án-* 'sour milk', *doṣ-án-* (AV.) 'arm', *yak-án-* 'liver', *śák-an-* (AV. VS.) 'dung', *sakth-án-* 'thigh'; 3. stems occurring at the end ot compounds only: *-gm-an-* and *-jm-án-* (also used independently) 'course', *-dī́v-an-*[3] 'playing'; *-bhv-an-*[4] 'being', *-śv-an-*[5] 'growing' (?)[6].

-ana : action and agent.

120. With the suffix *-ana* are formed a large number of derivatives with both types of meaning. The root generally shows Guṇa, sometimes Vṛddhi, occasionally no change, rarely a weakened vowel. These derivatives very often appear with a preposition, such verbal compounds coming next in frequency to those formed with the suffix *-a*.

1. With **Guṇa** are formed neuter **action nouns**; e. g. *kár-aṇa-* 'deed', *cáy-ana-* (AV.) 'piling', *dév-ana-* 'play', *bhój-ana-* 'enjoyment', *várdh-ana-* 'increase', *véd-ana-* 'possession', *háv-ana-* 'invocation', *adhi-vi-kárt-ana-* 'cutting off'; also **agent nouns**; e. g. the adjectives *kar-aṇá-* 'active', *cét-ana-* 'visible', *cód-ana-* (AV.)[7] 'impelling', *vi-móc-ana-* 'releasing'; from a duplicated (intensive) stem: *jāgar-aṇá-* (VS.) 'waking' (√*gṛ-*).

2. With **Vṛddhi**[8] **or lengthened** medial *a* are formed neuter **action nouns**, sometimes with a concrete sense; e. g. *ut-pā́r-aṇa-* (AV.) 'transporting', *upa-vā́s-ana-* (AV.) 'clothing', 'dress', *pra-vā́c-ana-* 'proclamation', *sā́d-ana-* 'seat'; also **agent nouns**; e. g. *saṃ-srā́v-aṇa-* (AV.) 'flowing together'; *-cā́t-ana-* 'driving away', *mā́d-ana-* 'gladdening', *-vā́h-ana-* 'conveying', *-spā́ś-ana-*[9] (AV.) 'spying'; *svā́d-ana-* m. 'sweetener'.

3. With **unchanged vowel** (final *-ā* and medial *a*) are formed neuter **action nouns**; e. g. *dā́na-* 'giving', *ud-yā́na-* (AV.) 'going out', *ni-dhā́na-* 'receptacle', *rákṣ-aṇa-* 'protection', *sád-ana-* 'seat', *ava-pra-bhráṃś-ana-*[10] (AV. XIX. 39[8]) 'slipping down', *prā́ṇ-ana-* 'breathing' (√*an-*); anomalously formed directly from a preposition, *sám-ana-* 'meeting'; also **agent nouns**; e. g. *táp-ana-* 'burning', *ā-krám-aṇa-* (VS.) 'stepping upon', *saṃ-gám-ana-* 'assembling'.

4. With **weak vowel** are formed very few derivatives: either neuter **action nouns** partly with concrete meaning: *kṛp-áṇa-* 'misery', *pṛ́ś-ana-* 'tenderness', *bhúv-ana-* 'being', *vṛj-ána-* and (once) *vṛ́j-ana-* 'enclosure', *-súv-ana-* (AV.) 'procreation'; or **agent nouns**: *kṛp-aṇá-* (AV.) 'miserable', *tur-áṇa-*

---

1 Used in the instrumental only.

2 From *ud-* 'be wet'.

3 From *dīv-* 'play' in *prati-dī́v-an-* 'adversary at play'.

4 From *bhū-* 'be' in *vi-bhvan-* and *vi-bhván-* 'far-reaching'.

5 In the Proper Names *mātari-śv-an-* and *ṛji-śv-an-*, cp. Wackernagel 2[1], p. 125, bottom, and above, p. 95, n. 11.

6 *-kāman-* in *ni-kāman-* 'desirous' is a transition form for the *a*-stem *ni-kāma-*.

7 In the RV. only as final member of compounds, *ṛṣi-códana-* etc.

8 In this type the only vowel appearing in the radical syllable is *ā*.

9 In *prati-spā́śana-* (AV. VIII. 5[11]).

10 See Whitney's note on *nāvaprabhráṃśana-* in his translation of AV. XIX. 39[8] and Weber's erroneous interpretation of this as 'descent of the ship'.

'speeding'; m. *úr-aṇa-* 'ram' (*vṛ-* 'cover'), *kir-áṇa-* m. 'dust' ('scattering'), *vṛ́ṣ-aṇa-* (VS.) 'testicle'.

-*anā* : action and agent.

121. With this suffix (accented on the first or the last syllable) are formed some feminine **action nouns** (like the neuters in *-ana*) which sometimes have a concrete meaning: *as-anā́-* 'missile', *jar-aṇā́-* 'old age', *dyot-anā́-* 'brilliance', *man-anā́-* 'devotion', *rodh-anā́-* ('obstruction') 'dam', *śvet-anā́-* 'daybreak', *has-anā́-* 'laughter'. *kap-anā́-* 'caterpillar' and *raś-anā́-* 'rein' have the appearance of being formed with this suffix, though the radical parts are not found in independent use. Accented on the penultimate syllable: *arh-áṇā-* 'merit', *jar-áṇā-* 'dry wood' (?), *barh-áṇā-* 'might', *bhand-ánā-* 'brilliance', *maṃh-ánā-* 'readiness', *meh-ánā-* 'abundance', *vakṣ-áṇā-* 'belly', *vadh-ánā-* 'slaughter', *van-ánā-* 'desire'. The formation of *yoṣ-áṇā-* (RV[1].), usually *yóṣ-aṇā-*, 'woman' is obscure[1]. With the suffix *-anā-* is also formed (though irregularly accented on the radical syllable) *pṛ́t-anā-*[2] 'fight' from a root not found in independent use[3]. The suffix *-anā* also forms feminine **agent nouns** (adjectives) corresponding to masculines in accented *-ana-*; thus *tur-áṇā-*[4] 'speeding', *tvar-aṇā́-* (AV.) 'hasting', *spand-anā́-* (AV.) 'kicking'.

a. Derivatives in *-ana* with verbal prefixes, if compounded with other words, form their f. in *-anā-*; thus *an-apa-vāc-anā́-* (AV.) 'not to be ordered away', *sūpa-vañc-anā́-* and *sūpa-sarp-aṇā́-*[5] (AV.) 'easy of approach', *ṣáḍ-vi-dhānā-* 'forming an order (*vi-dhā́na-*) of six'.

-*ani* : action and agent.

122. This suffix, accented either on the first or the last syllable, is added to either the strong or the weak form of the root.

1. It forms feminine **action nouns**, sometimes with concrete sense; thus *aś-áni-* 'missile', *iṣ-áṇi-* 'impulse', *kṣip-aṇí-* 'blow', *dyot-aní-* 'brilliance', *dham-áni-* 'piping', *vart-aní-* 'track', *śar-áṇi-* 'injury'; also *jaraṇi-* 'noise' (?) in the compound *jaraṇi-prā́-* 'moving with noise' (?).

2. It forms **agent nouns**, both m. f. substantives and adjectives; thus *ar-áṇi-* f. 'fire-stick', *cakṣ-áṇi-* m. 'enlightener', *car-áṇi-* 'movable', 'active', *tar-áṇi-* 'swift', *dhvas-áni-* 'sprinkling', *vakṣ-áṇi-* m. 'strengthener'; also in the compounds *án-arś-ani-*, N. of a demon, *ā́j-ani-* (AV.) f. 'stick for driving' (*ā-aj-*) and *udani-mát-* 'abounding in waves' (*ud-ani-* 'undulating' from *ud-* 'be wet').

a. From the reduplicated root: *papt-ani-* (*pat-* 'fly') in *su-papt-aní-* f. 'swift flight'. From aorist stems: *carṣ-aṇí-* 'active' (*car-* 'move'), f. pl. 'men', *parṣ-áṇi-* 'crossing' (*pṛ-* 'cross'), *sakṣ-áṇi-* 'overcoming' (√*sah-*). From desiderative stems: *rurukṣ-áṇi-* 'willing to destroy' (*ruj-* 'break'), *siṣās-áni-* 'eager to win' (√*sā-*), *ā-śuśukṣ-áṇi-* 'gleaming forth' (*śuc-* 'shine').

-*anī* : action and agent.

123. This suffix is the feminine form corresponding to the action and agent nouns formed with *-ana* from the strengthened or unreduced root[6], with or without verbal prefix; thus *-códani-*[7] 'urging' (*códana-*), *péś-anī-* (AV.) 'well-formed' (*péś-ana-*), *prókṣ-aṇī-* (VS. AV.) f. 'sprinkling water', *pra-jñā́nī-*

---

1 Other stems with the same meaning are: *yóṣ-an-*, *yóṣ-ā-*, *yóṣ-it-*. The root is probably *yu-* 'unite'.

2 The suffix *-anā* never otherwise occurs when the root is accented.

3 Only as a nominal stem *pṛ́t-* 'fight'.

4 This is the only example of such accentuation.

5 That is, *su-upa-vañc-anā́-* and *su-upa-sarp-aṇā́-*.

6 See *-ana*, 120, 1—3.

7 In *brahma-códanī-* 'stimulating devotion'.

(AV.) 'easily known', *spár-aṇī-* (AV.) 'preserving'; *abhi-ṣáv-aṇī-* (AV.) 'pressing implement', *vi-dhár-aṇī-* (AV.) 'preserving'.

a. In some (partly obscure) words the accent here shifts from the radical vowel to the final of the suffix: *arṣ-aṇí-* (AV.) 'piercing pain', *cet-aní-* (AV.) 'visible' (*cét-ana-*), *tap-aní-* 'heat' (*táp-ana-* 'burning'), *ted-aní-* (AV. VS.) 'blood', *pṛś-aní-* 'tender' (*pṛ́ś-ana-* 'tenderness'), *vṛj-aní-* 'enclosure' (*vṛj-ána-* and *vṛ́j-ana-*).

-an-īya : gerundive.

124. This is a new compositive suffix beginning to be attached directly to the root in the formation of the gerundive. It is based on the primary suffix *-ana* of neuter action nouns extended with the secondary adjective suffix *-īya*. There are two examples in the AV.: *upa-jīv-anī́ya-* 'to be subsisted on', and *ā-mantr-aṇī́ya-* 'to be addressed'.

-ar : agent.

125. This suffix is found in a very few words: *uṣ-ár-* f. 'dawn', *dev-ár-* m. 'husband's brother', *ná-nānd-ar-* f. 'husband's sister'[1].

-as : action and agent.

126. This suffix forms a large class of neuter action nouns (which sometimes acquire a concrete sense) accented on the root, and a small class of agent nouns (mostly adjectives) accented on the suffix. Some words belong to one class or the other according to the accent. The root generally takes Guṇa, and medial *a* is sometimes lengthened, while the vowel is reduced in a few instances.

1. Examples of **action nouns** are: **with Guṇa,** *práy-as-* 'pleasure' (√*prī-*), *śráv-as-* 'fame' (√*śru-*), *kár-as-* 'deed' (√*kṛ-*), *cét-as-* 'brilliance' (√*cit-*), *téj-as-* 'splendour' (√*tij-*), *dóh-as-* 'milking' (√*duh-*)[2]. **With medial *a*** unchanged: *áv-as-* 'aid', *táp-as-* 'heat', *práth-as-* 'breadth', *vác-as-* 'speech'; and with partially or wholly concrete meaning, *cákṣ-as-* 'lustre', 'eye', *mán-as-* 'thought', 'mind', *sár-as-* 'lake'. **With lengthened *a*:** *-vāc-as-*[3], *vā́s-as-* 'covering', 'garment', *vā́h-as-* 'offering', *-svād-as-* 'flavour' in *prá-svādas-* 'agreeable'; and from roots not in independent use: *pā́j-as-* 'brilliance' and *pā́th-as-*[4] 'path'. **With reduced vowel:** *úr-as-* 'breast', *jú́v-as-* 'speed' (beside *jáv-as-*), *mṛ́dh-as-* 'contempt', *śír-as-* 'head'; also *vip-as-* 'inspiration' in the compounds *vipaś-cit-* 'inspired' and *vipo-dhā́-* 'bestowing inspiration'; *iras-* 'anger' in the denominative *iras-yá-* 'be angry'; *hur-as-* 'deceit' in *huraś-cit-* 'plotting mischief'. Perhaps also the adverbs (with shift of accent) *tir-ás* 'across' and *mith-ás* 'mutually'.

a. To roots ending in *-ā* the suffix is added direct in *bhā́s-*[5] n. 'light' (*bhā-* 'shine') and *-dās-*[5] 'giving'[6] (√*dā-*). *jñā́s-* 'kinsman' and *mā́s-* 'moon' are probably also formed with the suffix *-as*, but being masculines were most likely agent nouns in origin: *mā-ás-* = 'measurer' (*mā-* 'measure'). The suffix seems to be added with an intervening *y* in *-hā́y-as* 'agility'[7] if it is derived from *hā-* 'leave'[8], while in *dhā́y-as-* n. 'enjoyment' and *-gā́y-as-* 'song'[9] the *y* probably belongs to the root[10].

---

1 *svásar-* 'sister' in probably an old compound in which *-sar* represents a root; cp. BRUGMANN, Grundriss 2, 8, note.

2 The word *héṣ-as-* 'missile' is perhaps formed from the aorist stem of *hi-* 'impel'.

3 In *vi-vācas-* (AV.) 'speaking variously' and *sá-vācas-* (AV.) 'speaking similarly'.

4 According to OLDENBERG, ZDMG. 54, 607 this word means 'home' and is perhaps formed with a suffix *-thas* from *pā-* 'protect'; according to SIEG, Gurupūjākaumudī 97, it means 'food', and is derived from *pā-* 'drink'.

5 Often to be read as dissyllables, *bhaas-* and *daas-*.

6 In *-das-* 'giving' and *-dhas-* 'placing' an *-as* has been formed probably by a misunderstanding of the N. sing. *-dā-s* and *-dhā-s*.

7 In *vi-hāyas-* 'vigorous' and *sárva-hāyas-* (AV.) 'having all strength'.

8 But it may be a derivative of *hi-* 'impel'.

9 From *dhe-* 'suck' and *gai-* 'sing'; cp. above 27 a.

10 In *pī́-v-as-* n. 'fat' (*pī-* 'swell') the *v* may

2. **Agent nouns** in *-ás*, mostly adjectives, correspond in several instances to action nouns accented on the root. These are *ap-ás-* 'active' (*áp-as-* 'work'), *tar-ás-* (VS[1].) 'quick' (*tár-as-* 'quickness'), *tyaj-ás-* m. 'descendant' (*tyáj-as-* 'abandonment'), *duv-ás-* 'stirring' (*dúv-as-* 'worship'), *mah-ás-* 'great' (*máh-as-* 'greatness'). The derivative *tav-ás-* occurs both as an adjective 'strong' and without change of accent[1] as a m. substantive 'strength'. A few others have no corresponding action noun: *toś-ás-* 'bestowing', *dhvar-ás-* 'deceiving', *yaj-ás-* 'offering', *vedh-ás-* 'worshipper', *veś-ás-* (AV.) 'neighbour'; and from a denominative stem *mṛgay-ás-* (AV[1].) 'wild animal'[2].

a. There are a few substantives accented on the suffix and seemingly never neuter, which are allied to the neuter action nouns in meaning, some being abstract, others concrete in sense. The change of accent may be due to change of gender[3]. Thus *rakṣ-ás-* m. occurs beside *rákṣ-as-* n. both meaning 'demon'. There also occur *jar-ás-* m. 'old age', *bhiy-ás-* m. 'fear', *tveṣ-ás-*[4] 'impulse', *hav-ás-* 'invocation'; *uṣ-ás-* f. 'dawn' may have been an agent noun originally; *doṣ-ás-* (AV[1].) f. (?) beside *doṣ-ā́-* 'night' may be due to parallelism with *uṣ-ás-*. The stem *upás-* 'lap' (the gender of which is uncertain, as it occurs only in the locative singular) may have been formed under the influence of *upá-stha-*[5] m. 'lap'.

a. A few Proper Names are formed with the suffix *-as*; thus *nodh-ás-*; *arcanā́nas-* is a compound of *ánas-* 'wain', possibly also *bhalānás-*. *ap-sarás-*[6] f. 'nymph' is perhaps a compound ('moving in the waters'). *áṅgiras-*, a name of Agni, has the appearance of being formed with this suffix, but the *-s* is perhaps secondary[7].

-así: action and agent.

127. This suffix, which is an extension of *-as* with *-i*, forms a couple of action nouns with concrete sense, and a few agent nouns: *dhāsí-* m. 'drink' (*dhe-* 'suck') and *dhāsí-* f. 'abode'; *at-así-* m. 'beggar', *dharṇ-así-* 'strong', *sān-así-* 'victorious'.

-ā: action.

128. By far the greatest proportion of words in *-ā* consists of secondary feminine adjectives corresponding to masculines and neuters in *-a*.

There is, however, also a considerable number of feminine action nouns of an independent character, formed by adding *-ā́* sometimes to the root, but usually to secondary conjugation stems (desiderative, causative, denominative). Thus *īś-ā́-* (AV.) 'dominion', *nind-ā́-* (AV.) 'blame'; *jigīṣ-ā́-* 'desire to win', *bhikṣ-ā́-* (AV.) 'begging', *vīrts-ā́-*[8] 'desire to frustrate'; *gamay-ā́-*[9] (AV[1].) 'causing to go'; *aśvay-ā́-* 'desire for horses', *apasy-ā́-* 'activity', *uruṣy-ā́-* 'readiness to help', *jīvanasy-ā́-* (TS. II. 3. 10[2.3]) 'desire of life', *sukratūy-ā́-* 'skill'.

a. This suffix has the appearance of being added to a reduplicated stem in *jáṅgh-ā-*[10] 'leg' and *jihv-ā́-* 'tongue'; it may also be contained in the very obscure word *sūṣā́-*[11] (AV[1].).

---

have been inserted owing to the influence of *pī́-van-* adj. 'fat'.

1 WHITNEY 1152, 2 e, erroneously, *távas-* 'strength'.

2 The suffix is probably contained in *ā-han-ás-* 'wanton', but the derivation is obscure, Cp. FRÖHDE, BB. 21, 321—330.

3 The dative infinitives from stems in *-as* are sometimes accented on the root, but usually on the suffix (105 a). This may indicate a difference of gender, the former being neuter, the latter masculine.

4 As *tveṣ-ás-* and *hav-ás-* occur in the I. sing. only, the gender is uncertain, but owing to the accent it is probably masc.

5 According to GRASSMANN, however, *upástha-* probably = *upás-stha-*; cp. 81, 2 *α*.

6 See MACDONELL, Vedic Mythology 47, note 3; but cp. PISCHEL, VS. 3, 197.

7 Cp. BRUGMANN, Grundriss 2, p. 188.

8 From *vi-īrtsa-* desiderative of *ṛdh-* 'prosper'.

9 The causative stem used in the formation of the periphrastic perfect.

10 Cp. BRUGMANN, Grundriss 2, p. 106, top.

11 See WHITNEY's note on AV. I, 11[3].

-*āku* : agent.

129. This very rare suffix seems to have been limited to the formation of agent nouns. It appears in *mṛḍay-ā́ku-* 'gracious' (formed from a causative stem), *pṛ́d-āku-* (AV. VS.)[1] 'adder', *íkṣv-āku-*, N. of a man.

-*āna* : agent.

130. This suffix forms a middle participle[2] from the present (455, 461, 467, 473, 479), the perfect (493) and (in the form of *-s-āna*) from the aorist tense stem[3] (527). It also appears in the formation of a few adjectives and substantives, a preceding *u* always taking Guṇa. Such adjectives are: *tákav-āna-* 'speeding' (beside *ták-u-* and *ták-va-*), *bhṛ́gav-āṇa-* 'beaming' (beside *bhṛ́gu-* m.), *vásav-āna-* 'possessing wealth' (*vásu-*), *ūrdhva-s-āná-* 'being erect' (formed like an aorist participle from *ūrdhvá-* 'upright').

There are also the Proper Names *ápnav-āna-*, *cyáv-āna-*, *pṛ́thav-āna-*; also *cyávat-āna-* which looks as if formed by adding *-āna* to the active present participle stem of *cyu-* 'fall'. Of doubtful derivation are the substantives *párś-āna-* m. 'abyss' and *rujā́nā-*[4] f. 'river' (I. 32[6]).

-*i* : action and agent.

131. With this suffix are formed numerous feminine action nouns, agent nouns (adjectives and masculine substantives), and a few neuters of obscure etymology[5].

The root appears in various forms: sometimes with Guṇa, Vṛddhi or lengthened *a*, generally with unchanged or weak vowel, often reduplicated. Before the suffix a final radical palatal regularly appears (not the original guttural). In many of these derivatives the root is not traceable elsewhere. The accent is so fluctuating that no general rule can be stated. The meaning is often greatly specialised.

1. Examples of **action nouns** are: **with Guṇa,** *róp-i* (AV.) 'pain', *śoc-í* (AV.) 'heat'; with **lengthened** ***a*****:** *āj-í-* m. f. 'race', *grā́h-i-* 'seizure', *dhrā́j-i-* 'course'; with **unchanged vowel:** *san-í-* 'gain'; with **weak vowel:** *tvíṣ-i-* 'brilliance', *kṛṣ-í-* 'tillage', *rúc-i-* (AV.) 'brightness'.

2. Examples of **agent nouns** are: **with Guṇa,** *ar-í-* 'devout', *arc-í-* m. 'beam'; **with Vṛddhi,** *kā́rṣ-i* (VS.) 'drawing'; **with lengthened vowel** *-jāni-*[6] f. 'wife', *śā́r-i-* f. 'arrow' (RV[1].), a kind of bird (VS. TS.), *dū́ṣ-i-* (AV.) 'poisonous matter'; also in a few words of obscure etymology, *drāp-í-* m. 'mantle', *nā́bh-i-* f. 'navel', *pāṇ-í-* m. 'hand', *rāś-í-* m. 'heap'; with **unchanged vowel:** *krīḍ-í-* 'playing', *granth-í-* m. 'knot', *máh-i-* 'great'; with **weak vowel:** *śúc-i-* 'bright', *gṛ́bh-i-* (AV.) 'container', *bhṛ́m-i-* 'lively' (beside *bhṛm-í-* f. 'lively motion'). From the **reduplicated root,** which nearly always has a weak or reduced radical vowel, are formed with ordinary reduplicative vowel: *cíkit-i-*[7] (SV.) 'understanding', *cákr-i-* 'active', *jághr-i-* 'sprinkling about' (*ghṛ-*), *pápr-i-* 'bestowing abundantly', *babhr-í-* 'carrying', *vavr-í-* m. 'covering', *sásr-i-* 'speeding', *súṣv-i-* 'pressing'; *yúyudh-i-* 'warlike', *vívic-i-* 'appropriating' (√*vyac-*);

[1] It occurs in the RV. only as the first member of a compound in *pṛ́dāku-sānu-* 'having a surface like that of a snake'.

[2] See Lindner p. 53—55.

[3] *āpnāna-* seems to be an irregular present participle of *āp-* 'obtain' formed from the stem *āp-nā-* instead of *āp-nu-*.

[4] For this word occurring in the form of *rujā́nās* see p. 59, note 1.

[5] See Grassmann, Wörterbuch 1718 f.; Lindner p. 55—58.

[6] At the end of compounds beside the independent *jáni-*.

[7] Various reading for the *cikit-ú-* of the RV.

jágm-i- 'hastening' (*gam-* 'go'), *jághn-i-* 'striking' (√*han-*), *sásn-i-* 'winning'; *jágur-i-* 'conducting' (√*gṝ-*), *tátur-i-* 'victorious' (√*tṝ-*), *pápur-i-* and *pipur-i-* (SV.) 'bestowing abundantly' (√*pṝ-*) beside *pápr-i*; with lengthened or **strong reduplicative vowel:** *tấtṛp-i-* 'gladdening', *dấdhṛṣ-i-* 'bold', *vấvah-i-* 'driving swiftly', *sāsah-í-* 'victorious'; *tū́tuj-i-* 'speeding', *tūtuj-í-* m. 'stimulator', *yū́yuv-i-* 'driving away', *yū́yudh-i-* 'warlike'; *jarbhár-i-* 'nourishing' (√*bhṛ-*)[1]. The **weak reduplicated** present **stem** appears in *dad-í-* 'giving' and *dádh-i-* 'bestowing'; from similar stems (appearing in the perfect) are formed *pap-í* 'drinking' (√*pā-*) and *yay-í* 'speeding' (√*yā-*).

a. There are only about half a dozen **neuters** formed with the suffix *-i*, nearly all being obscure in origin. They are *ákṣ-i-* 'eye', *ásth-i-* (AV. VS.) 'bone', *dádh-i-* 'sour milk', *śám-i-* 'toil' (*śam-* 'work'); and with Vṛddhi *hā́rd-i-* 'heart'.

b. The root is sometimes **compounded** with **verbal prefixes** in these derivatives, the suffix being then usually accented; thus *ā-ján-i-* f. 'birth', *vi-vavr-i-* m. 'opening', *saṃ-tan-í-* f. 'harmony', 'music', *ā-yaj-í-* 'bringing near by offerings', *ā-múr-i-* m. 'destroyer', *ni-jaghn-í-* 'striking down', *parā-dad-í-* 'delivering over', *vi-ṣāsah-í-* 'victorious', *vy-ānaś-í-*[2] 'pervading'.

c. From *dhā-* 'put' is derived the **stem** *-dhi-* which is used in forming many m. compounds; e. g. *antar-dhí-* (AV.) 'concealment', *ud-dhí-* (AV.), part of a car, *ni-dhí-* 'treasure', *pari-dhí-* 'fence'. From *sthā-* 'stand' is similarly formed *-sthi-* in *prati-ṣṭhí-* f. 'resistance'. There is here some doubt as to whether we have a reduced form of the root (as in *dhi-ta-*) or displacement of the radical vowel by the very frequent suffix *-i*. The latter alternative is perhaps the more probable owing to the almost invariable accentuation of the *i* and the occurrence of a stem like *prati-ṣṭhí-* 'resistance' beside *prati-ṣṭhā́-* 'standpoint'.

-in : agent.

132. The very frequent secondary suffix *-in* seems sometimes to have the value of a primary suffix, exclusively, however, at the end of compounds; thus *-ād-in-* 'eating', *-eṣ-ín-* (AV.) 'seeking', *-tod-ín-* 'piercing', *á-nām-in-* 'unbending', *-vyādh-in-* (AV.) 'piercing'; from a present stem *-aś-nuv-in-* (VS.) 'reaching'; from an aorist stem *-sakṣ-ín-*[3] overpowering (√*sah-*); from a reduplicated stem *-yay-in-* 'going'[4].

-iṣṭha : agent.

133. With this suffix attached to the root is formed the superlative with an adjectival sense. The root is regularly accented[5], *ĭ* and *ŭ* taking Guṇa, while *a* remains unchanged, though in two or three instances it is strengthened with a nasal. Roots in *-ā* combine that vowel with the initial *-i* of the suffix to *e*, which, however, is usually to be read as two syllables. About fifty superlatives formed with this suffix occur in the Saṃhitās. Examples are: *náy-iṣṭha-* 'leading in the best manner' (*nī-* 'lead'), *jáv-iṣṭha-* 'quickest' (*jū-* 'speed'), *véd-iṣṭha-* 'procuring most' (*vid-* 'find'), *śóc-iṣṭha-* 'most brilliant' (*śuc-* 'shine'); *yáj-iṣṭha-* 'sacrificing best'; *báṃh-iṣṭha-* 'most abundant' (*baṃh-*

[1] The words *bámbhār-i-* (VS.) m., a soma-guarding genius, *karkar-í-* f. 'lute', *dundubh-í-* m. 'drum' may be onomatopoetic in origin.

[2] From the perfect stem *ān-aś-* of *aś-* 'attain'.

[3] In *pra-sakṣ-ín-* 'victorious'.

[4] In *ni-yay-ín-* 'passing over'. Cp. LINDNER p. 59; WHITNEY 1183 a.

[5] Except two or three times *jyeṣṭhá-* and *kan-iṣṭhá-* (see above p. 83, 14); and when the superlative is compounded with a prefix, which then has the accent.

'make firm'), *mámh-iṣṭha-* 'most liberal' (*mah-* 'be great'); *jyéṣṭha-* 'greatest' and *jyeṣṭhá-* 'eldest' (*jyā-* 'overpower'), *dhéṣṭha-* 'bestowing the most' (√*dhā-*), *yéṣṭha-* 'going fastest' (√*yā-*).

a. In many instances these superlatives attach themselves in meaning to derivative adjectives, being formed from the root which the latter contain; thus *oṣ-iṣṭha-*[1] (TS. I. 6. 12[3]) beside *óṣa-m* 'quickly', *bárh-iṣṭha-* 'greatest' beside *bṛh-ánt-* 'great', *vár-iṣṭha-* 'choicest' (*vṛ-* 'choose') beside *vár-a-* 'choice', *sádh-iṣṭha-* 'straightest' beside *sādh-ú-* 'straight'. In a few cases the suffix is added to the derivative form of the root which appears in the adjective; thus *ā́ś-iṣṭha-* (AV[1].) 'swiftest' beside *āś-ú-* (from *aś-* 'reach'); and in *náv-iṣṭha-* 'newest' the suffix is attached to the radical element in *náv-a-*[2] 'new' (and not directly to the root from which that word may be derived).

b. In some cases the root is compounded with a verbal prefix or other indeclinable; thus *ā́-gam-iṣṭha-* 'coming best', *á-śram-iṣṭha-* 'never tiring', *śám-bhav-iṣṭha-*[3] 'most beneficial'.

a. There are some irregularities in the formation of this superlative. Thus *bhū-* retains its vowel unchanged, adding the suffix with an intervening *-y*: *bhū́-y-iṣṭha-*[4] 'greatest'; the roots *prī-* and *śrī-* are treated as if they ended in *-ā*: *préṣṭha-* 'dearest', *śréṣṭha-* 'most glorious'; *pár-ṣ-iṣṭha-* 'taking across best' is made from an aorist stem of *pṛ-* 'cross'. The abnormal accentuation of *jyeṣṭhá-* 'eldest' is doubtless intended to differentiate its meaning from *jyéṣṭha-* 'greatest'. The use of *kan-iṣṭhá-* 'youngest' is parallel to that of the former[5].

-is : action.

134. This suffix forms a dozen neuter action nouns, mostly used in a concrete sense. Though the root takes Guṇa, the suffix is accented except in three instances. The words thus formed are: *arc-ís-* 'flame', *ā́m-is-*[6] 'raw flesh', *krav-ís-* 'raw flesh', *chad-ís-* 'cover', *chard-ís-* 'protection', *jyót-is-* 'light', *barh-ís-* 'straw', *roc-ís-* 'light', *vart-ís-* 'track', *vyáth-is-* 'course' (?), *śoc-ís-* 'flame', *sarp-ís-* 'melted butter', *hav-ís-* 'oblation'.

a. Besides these *av-is-* appears for *av-as-* 'aid' and *mah-is-* for *máh-as-* 'greatness' in a few derivatives: *aviṣ-yánt-* 'helping readily', *aviṣ-yá-* 'desire', *aviṣ-yú-* 'desirous'; *máhiṣ-vant-* 'great'; and with inorganic *-s* *túvi-s-* 'might', *śuci-s-* 'flame', *su-rabhi-s-* 'fragrant' for *tuvi-*, *śuci-*, *surabhi-* in a few derivatives: *túviṣ-mant-* 'mighty', *śuciṣ-mant-* (only voc.) 'brilliant', *surabhiṣ-ṭama-* 'very fragrant'.

-ī: action and agent.

135. This suffix, besides its secondary use in the formation of feminines, chiefly adjectives, from m. and n. stems in *-a*, *-i*, *-u*, *-ṛ*, as well as various consonant stems (201), seems to be primary in forming a few independent feminine action and agent nouns. Such are *deh-ī́-* 'rampart', *nad-ī́-* 'stream', *nānd-ī́-* 'joy', *péṣ-ī-* (RV[1].) 'swaddling clothes' (?), *veś-ī́-* 'needle', *śác-ī-* 'power', *śám-ī-* and *śím-ī-* 'work'; seemingly from an aorist stem (√*vah-*) *vakṣ-ī́-* (RV[1].) 'flame'. There are also about a dozen masculines: *ah-ī́-* 'serpent', *upāv-ī́-* (VS.) 'encouraging', *dakṣ-ī-* (RV[1].)[7] 'flaming', *prāv-ī́-* 'attentive', *duṣ-prāv-ī́-*

[1] In the compound *oṣiṣṭha-dā́van-* 'giving immediately'.

[2] Probably from a demonstrative root *nu-* which appears in *nú* 'now', *nū-tana-* 'present'.

[3] This superlative is formed under the influence of the positive *śam-bhú-* as the independent superlative of *bhū-* is *bhū́-y-iṣṭha-*.

[4] The regular form *bhav-iṣṭha-* occurs in combination with *śam-*.

[5] *kán-iṣṭha-* 'smallest' appears in books V and VI of the TS.

[6] This word, which occurs in the L. sing. form *ā́miṣ-i* only, is given as m. in BR., pw., and GRASSMANN, but why it should not be like all the rest a neuter, is not clear.

[7] Only voc. *dakṣi*, Pada *dhakṣi-*, I. 141[8]. Cp. p. 119, note 5.

'unfriendly', *su-prāv-í-* 'very attentive', *rath-í-* 'charioteer', *á-rath-ī-* 'not a charioteer'; and the Proper Names *nám-ī-* and *pṛ́th-ī-*[1].

-*īka* : action and agent.

136. This suffix forms a few neuter substantives and some adjectives: thus *án-īka-* n. 'face', *dṛ́ś-īka-* n. 'aspect', *mṛḍ-īká-* n. 'grace', *ā́-śar-īka-* (AV.) n. 'rheumatic pains'; *-ṛj-īka-*[2] 'beaming', *dṛ́bh-īka-* m., N. of a demon, *vṛdh-īká-* m. 'increaser', *ví-śar-īka-* (AV.) m., a kind of disease; from a reduplicated stem: *par-phar-íka-* m. 'filler'.

-*īyāṃs* : agent.

137. This suffix is used in forming comparatives, being added to the root in the same way as the superlative suffix *-iṣṭha* (133). At least 40 of these derivatives[3] occur in the Saṃhitās. Examples are: *jáv-īyāṃs-* 'quicker', *máṃh-īyāṃs-* 'more liberal', *yáj-īyāṃs-* 'sacrificing better', *téj-īyāṃs-* 'sharper', *véd-īyāṃs-* 'procuring more', *yódh-īyāṃs-* 'fighting better', *préyāṃs-*[4] 'dearer' (√*prī-*), *śréyāṃs-*[5] (√*śrī-*) 'more splendid', *-stheyāṃs-* 'lasting' (√*sthā-*). Connected in sense with the corresponding positive are *áṇ-īyāṃs-* (AV.) 'smaller', beside *aṇu-* 'minute', *śáś-īyāṃs-* 'more frequent', beside *śáś-vant-* 'constant'; and from a derivative form of the root *tíkṣṇ-īyāṃs-* (AV.)[5] 'sharper', beside *tīkṣṇá-* 'sharp' (*tij-* 'be sharp').

a. Beside the usual form in *-īyāṃs-* there appear some half dozen comparatives made with a **shorter form** of the suffix **-*yāṃs***: *táv-yāṃs-* beside *táv-īyāṃs-* 'stronger', *náv-yāṃs-* beside *náv-īyāṃs-* 'new', *pán-yāṃs-* beside *pán-īyāṃs-* 'more wonderful', *bhū́-yāṃs-*[6] '(becoming) more', 'greater', beside *bháv-īyāṃs-* 'more plentiful', *rábh-yāṃs-* beside *rábh-īyāṃs-* (VS.) 'more violent', *sáh-yāṃs-* beside *sáh-īyāṃs-* 'stronger'; *jyá-yāṃs-* 'greater', 'older', and *sán-yāṃs-* 'older' (*sána-* 'old') appear without an alternative form beside them.

b. With **verbal prefixes or particles**: *vi-kled-īyāṃs-* (AV.) 'moistening more', *pári-ṣvaj-īyāṃs-* (AV.) 'clasping more firmly', *práti-cyav-īyāṃs-* 'pressing closer against'; *á-stheyāṃs-* 'not enduring'.

-*u* : agent.

138. This suffix forms a considerable number of agent nouns, both adjectives and substantives. The latter are chiefly masculines, but there are also several feminines and neuters. The suffix is usually accented. The root is generally weak, but sometimes shows Vṛddhi, least often Guṇa; it also occasionally appears in a reduplicated form. Medial *a* usually remains unchanged, but is sometimes lengthened; occasionally it is nasalized or appears as *e*. Final *-ā* adds an intervening *y*, but is occasionally dropped. Gutturals only (not palatals) appear before this suffix.

1. Examples of **adjectives** are: *ur-ú-* 'wide', *ṛj-ú-* 'straight', *pṛth-ú-* 'broad', *mṛd-ú-* (VS.) 'soft', *vidh-ú-* 'solitary'; *jāy-ú-* 'conquering' (√*ji-*), *dār-ú-* 'splitting' (√*dṛ-*); *śay-ú-* 'lying' (√*śī-*), *cikit-ú-* 'shining' (√*cit-*), *jigy-ú-* 'victorious', *siṣṇ-u-* 'ready to give' (√*san-*)[7]; *tak-ú-* 'swift', *tan-ú-* 'thin',

[1] See below 375 B; LINDNER p. 80; WHITNEY 355 b.

[2] As final member of a few compounds, as *bhā́-ṛjīka-* 'light-shedding'.

[3] See LINDNER p. 155; WHITNEY 466—470.

[4] The roots *prī-* and *śrī-* being treated as ending in *-ā*: *prā́-īyāṃs-* and *śrā́-īyāṃs-* as in the superlative.

[5] In the TS. *pā́p-īyāṃs-* is formed directly from the adjective stem *pāpá-*, the radical element of which is uncertain.

[6] With the radical vowel unchanged as in the superlative.

[7] Some other words have the appearance of being reduplicated: *babhr-ú-* 'brown', *a-rár-u-* 'hostile' (*rā-* 'give'); *malimlu-* (VS.) seems to be a mutilated form of *malimlucá-* (AV.) 'robber'.

táp-u- 'hot', *āś-ú-* 'swift' (*aś-* 'reach'); *aṃh-ú-* 'narrow'; *cér-u-* 'active' (*car-* 'move'); *dhā-y-ú-*[1] 'thirsty', *pā-y-ú-* 'protecting'; *y-ú-* 'going' (√*yā-*)[2]; *réku-* 'empty' (√*ric-*).

2. Examples of **substantives** are: m. *gṛh-ú-* 'beggar', *rip-ú-* 'cheat'; *pípr-u-*, N. of a demon; *ás-u-* 'life', *mán-u-* 'man', *pād-ú-* 'foot', *bāh-ú-* 'arm', *aṃś-ú-* 'filament', *vā-y-ú-* 'wind'; f. *íṣ-u-* (also m.) 'arrow', *síndh-u-* (also m.) 'river', *dhán-u-* 'sandbank', *párś-u-* 'rib', *hán-u-* 'jaw'; n. *áy-u* 'life', *ján-u-* 'knee', *tál-u-* (VS.) 'palate', *tráp-u-* (AV. VS.) 'tin', *dár-u-* (also m.) 'wood', *sán-u* (also m.) 'summit'; with syncope, *kṣ-ú-* 'food' (*ghas-* 'eat'); with reduplication, *tí-ta-ü-* 'sieve'.

a. In a few of these derivatives the root appears with a **prefix**: *upā-y-ú-* (TS. I. I. I[1]) 'approaching', *ni-cer-ú-* 'gliding', *pra-may-ú-* (AV.) 'liable to destruction', *pari-tatn-ú-* (AV.) 'surrounding', *sáṃ-vas-u-* 'dwelling together'; *abhīś-ú-*[3] m. 'rein', *vi-klínd-u-* (AV.) m. a kind of disease.

139. There is besides a large class of **agent nouns** formed **with -*u*** not directly from the root but from tense or secondary conjugation stems.

1. From **present stems** are formed: *tany-ú-* 'thundering' (*tanya-ti* 'roars'), *bhind-ú-* m. 'destroyer' (*bhind-ánti* 'they split'), *-vind-ú-*[4] 'finding' (*vindá-ti* 'finds'); from an aorist stem *dákṣ-u-*[5] and *dhákṣ-u-* 'burning'.

2. From **desiderative stems** are formed *i-yakṣ-ú-* 'desirous of sacrificing' (√*yaj-*), *cikits-ú-* (AV.) 'cunning' (√*cit-*), *jigīṣ-ú* 'desirous of winning' (√*ji-*), *jíghats-u-* (AV.) 'greedy' (*ghas-* 'eat'), *titikṣ-ú-* (AV.) 'patient', *dits-ú-* 'ready to give' (√*dā-*), *didṛ́kṣ-u-*[6] (VII. 86[3]) 'eager to see' (√*dṛś-*), *didhiṣ-ú-* 'wishing to obtain' (√*dhā-*), *dips-ú-* 'wishing to harm' (√*dabh-*), *ninits-ú-* 'wishing to revile', *bībhats-ú-* 'feeling disgust' (√*bādh-*), *mimikṣ-ú-* 'mingling' (√*miś-*), *mumukṣ-ú-* 'desiring release' (√*muc-*), *ririkṣ-ú-* 'wishing to damage' (√*riṣ-*), *vivakṣ-ú-* (AV.) 'calling aloud' (√*vac-*), *siṣās-ú-* (AV.) 'eager to win' (√*sā-*).

3. From **causative stems** are formed: *dhāray-ú-* 'streaming', *bhājay-ú-* 'liberal', *bhāvay-ú-* 'cherishing', *maṃhay-ú-* 'liberal', *manday-ú-* 'joyous', *śramay-ú-* 'exhausting oneself'; from a causative denominative *mṛgay-ú-* (AV.VS.) m. 'hunter'.

4. By far the commonest are the derivatives from regular **denominatives**, of which nearly 80 occur in the RV., and at least half a dozen additional cases in the AV. About 35 of these words are formed from denominative stems in actual use[7]; thus *aghāy-ú-* 'malignant', *arātīy-ú-* (AV.) 'hostile', *vasūy-ú-* 'desiring wealth', *caraṇy-ú-* 'mobile', *manasy-ú-* 'desirous'. A few are formed from pronouns, as *ahaṃy-ú-* 'selfish', *asmay-ú-* 'favouring us', *kiṃy-ú-* 'desiring what?', *tvāy-ú-* 'loving thee', *yuvay-ú-* and *yuvāy-ú-* 'desiring you two', *svay-ú-* 'left to oneself'. In the absence of an accompanying denominative, there is the appearance of a secondary suffix *-yu* (with the sense of 'desiring' or some more general adjectival meaning) attached directly to nouns. Thus there are derivatives in the RV. in which the *-as* of noun stems is changed to *-o*, as if the suffix were actually *-yu*: *aṃho-yú-* 'threatening', *duvo-yú-* 'honouring' beside *duvas-yú-*, and *á-skṛdho-yu-* 'not niggardly'.

-*uka* : agent.

140. This suffix probably consists of the primary *-u* extended with the secondary *-ka*. It is very rare in the Saṃhitās. There is no certain example

---

[1] Here the *y* really belongs to the root *dhe-* 'suck'.

[2] Also in the reduplicated form *yáy-u-* (VS.) 'swift'; the final-*ā* seems also to be dropped in *ā-kh-ú-* 'mole' (*khā-* 'dig') and in *su-ṣṭh-ú* '(standing) well' (*sthā-* 'stand').

[3] Probably from *abhi*+*īś-* 'rule'.

[4] In *go-vindú-* 'searching for milk'.

[5] The Pada text has *dhákṣ-u-*. Cp. p. 117, note 7.

[6] With irregular accent.

[7] See the list in LINDNER p. 63.

in the RV., but *sān-uká-* (RV[1].) 'desirous of prey' (√*san-*) and the Proper Name *per-uká-* (RV[1].) may be instances. In the AV. occur *ghā́t-uka-* 'killing', *vi-kas-uka-* 'bursting', *sáṃ-kas-uka-* 'crumbling up', *á-pra-māy-uka-* 'not dying suddenly'. In the TS. occurs *vas-uká-*, but the meaning and derivation are doubtful.

-us : action and agent.

141. This suffix forms **neuter action nouns** which have mostly a concrete sense, and **masculine agent nouns**, altogether less than 20 in number. All the substantives except one are accented on the root, which generally takes Guṇa, but in one instance Vṛddhi. Those adjectives which also appear as substantives have the same accentuation; but those stems which are used solely as adjectives accent the suffix.

1. The neuter substantives are: *ár-us-* (AV.) 'wound', *ā́y-us-* 'life', *cákṣ-us-* 'light', *táp-us-* 'heat', *tár-us-* 'battle', *dhán-us-* 'bow', *pár-us-* 'knot', *yáj-us-* 'worship', *váp-us-* 'marvel', *śā́s-us-* 'command'; with accent on the suffix: *jan-ús-* 'birth' (also m.).

2. The masculine substantives are: *náh-us-* 'neighbour', *mán-us-* 'man'; **adjectives** identical in form with neuter substantives are: *cákṣ-us-* 'seeing', *táp-us-* 'glowing', *váp-us-* 'wondrous'; adjectives without corresponding substantives are: *jay-ús-* 'victorious', *van-ús-* 'eager', *vid-ús-*[1] 'heedful'; also *dakṣ-ús-* 'flaming' from the aorist stem.

-ū : feminine substantives.

142. This rare suffix chiefly forms feminines corresponding to masculines and neuters in *-u*[2]. Independent feminine substantives are: *cam-ū́-* 'dish', *tan-ū́-* 'body', *vadh-ū́-* 'bride'; perhaps *pan-ū́-*[3] 'admiration'. There are also the compounds *puṃś-cal-ū́-* (VS.) 'courtesan', *pra-jan-ū́-* (AV.) 'organ of generation'.

-ūka : intensive adjectives.

143. This suffix is merely the lengthened form of *-uka* used in forming a few derivatives from the reduplicated intensive stem. It appears in *jāgar-ū́ka-* 'wakeful', *dandaś-ū́ka-* (VS.) 'mordacious', *salal-ū́ka-* (RV[1].) 'wandering aimlessly'.

-ka : agent.

144. This is a very common secondary suffix, but very rarely appears in a primary character. It is thus used in *át-ka-* m. 'garment', *su-mé-ka-* 'firmly fixed' (*mi-* 'fix'), *śúṣ-ka-* 'dry', *śló-ka-* m. 'call' (*śru-* 'hear'), *sto-ká-* m. 'drop'. In *vṛ́śc-i-ka-* m. 'scorpion' the suffix is added with connecting *-i-*. The feminine form of the suffix appears in *stú-kā-* 'flake', *rā-kā́-*, N. of a goddess.

-ta : agent.

145. This suffix is employed almost exclusively to form past participles[4], chiefly with passive, sometimes with intransitive meaning. Its more general and original sense is, however, preserved in some words used as adjectives or as substantives with concrete meaning; thus *tṛṣ-ṭá-* 'rough', *dṛḍhá-* 'firm', *śī-tá-* 'cold', *vāvā́-ta-*[5] 'dear'; m. *dū-tá-* 'messenger', *sū-tá-* (AV. VS.) 'charioteer',

---

1 With weak root; the only instance of medial vowel other than ă in the radical syllable.

2 See below, derivative *-ū* stems, 384.

3 The stem may be *pan-ú-*, as the only form occurring is the I. sing. *panvā́*.

4 See below, Past passive participles, 572, and the lists in LINDNER p. 70f.

5 From a reduplicated form of *vā-* 'win', and with unusual accent.

kīstá-[1] 'singer', *bastá-*[1] 'he-goat'; **n.** *ṛ-tá-* 'right', *ghṛ-tá-* 'ghee', *jā-tá-* 'kind', *dyū-tá-* (AV.) 'gambling', *nṛt-tá-* (AV.) 'dance', *pūr-tá-* 'reward', *vra-tá-*[2] 'ordinance'; with accented and strong radical syllable: *é-ta-* 'variegated'; **m.** *gár-ta-* 'car-seat', *már-ta-* 'mortal', *vā́-ta-* 'wind', *hás-ta-* 'hand'; **n.** *ás-ta-* 'home', *nák-ta-* 'night'.

a. In many past participles the suffix is added **with connecting** ***-i-***, as *rakṣ-i-tá-* 'protected'. Some of these are used as n. substantives; thus *jīv-i-tá-* 'life', *car-i-tá-* 'behaviour'. Several words thus formed appear as adjectives only; thus *tig-i-tá-*[3] 'sharp', *pal-i-tá-* 'grey'; also some other names of colours with strong and accented radical syllable: *ás-i-ta-* 'black', *róh-i-ta-* 'red', *lóh-i-ta-* (AV.) 'red', *hár-i-ta-* 'yellow'; *śye-tá-* 'white' is perhaps anomalously formed with *-ita-* from *śyā-*[4] 'freeze'[5].

-tar : agent.

146. The agent nouns formed with this very frequent suffix[6] are often used participially, governing an accusative. The root is generally accented when they have this verbal force, but the suffix, when they are purely nominal (86 A 22). The root regularly has Guṇa, *a* and *ā* remaining unchanged; thus *né-tar-* 'leader' (√*nī-*), *hó-tar-* 'priest' (√*hu-*), *kar-tár-* 'doer' (√*kṛ-*), *bhet-tár-* 'breaker' (√*bhid-*), *yok-tár-* 'yoker' (√*yuj-*); *yaṣ-ṭár-* 'sacrificer' (√*yaj-*), *dā-tár-* 'giver'[7]. With weak root: *uṣ-ṭár-* m. 'ploughing bull'[8].

a. Less commonly the suffix is added to the root **with connecting** ***-i-***: regularly when the root ends in more than one consonant[9], as *vand-i-tár-* 'praiser', but also often when it ends in a single consonant and sometimes when it ends in a vowel, as *cod-i-tár-* 'instigator', *sav-i-tár-* 'stimulator' (√*sū-*).

b. The suffix is combined **with** ***-ī-*** instead of *-i-* in *grábh-ī-tar-* (AV.) 'seizer', *prati-grah-ī-tár-* (AV.) 'receiver', *saṃ-grah-ī-tár-* (VS.) 'charioteer', *pra-tar-ī-tár-* 'prolonger', *ā-mar-ī-tár-* 'destroyer'; **with** ***-u-*** in *tár-u-tar-* 'winning' and *tar-u-tár-* 'conqueror', *dhán-u-tar-* 'running swiftly', *sán-u-tar-* 'winning'; **with** ***-ū-*** in *var-ū-tár-* 'protector'; **with** ***-o-*** in *man-ó-tar-*[10] and *man-o-tár-* 'inventor'.

c. These derivatives are very frequently compounded with **prepositions**[11]; e. g. *pura-e-tár-* 'leader', *apa-bhar-tár-* 'taking away', *prāv-i-tár-* 'protector' (*av-* 'favour'), *pra-sav-ī-tár-* 'vivifier'.

d. They are very rarely formed from secondary conjugation or from tense stems, as *coday-i-tár-* 'stimulator'[12], *bodhay-i-tár-* 'awakener', *né-ṣ-ṭar-*[13], a kind of priest. From the reduplicated root is formed *vāvā́-tar-* 'adherent'.

e. Several **names of relationship** appear to be formed with this suffix. Being all very old words, the radical syllable is obscure in meaning or irregular in form. They are *jā́-mā-tar-* 'son-in-law', *duh-i-tár-* 'daughter', *náp-tar-* 'grandson', *pi-tár-* 'father', *bhrā́-tar-* 'brother', *mā-tár-* 'mother'.

---

[1] These two words are of doubtful origin.

[2] If derived from *vṛ-* 'choose' with anomalous form of radical syllable; but according to Whitney (1176 b) it is to be explained as *vrat-á-* formed from *vṛt-* 'turn' like *vraj-á-* from √*vṛj-*.

[3] With anomalous guttural before *-i-*.

[4] Originally perhaps 'rimy', cp. *śī-tá-* 'cold'.

[5] The f. of these adjectives of colour is formed from other stems: *énī-*, *ásiknī-*, *páliknī-*, *róhiṇī-*, *lóhinī-* (AV.), *śyénī-*, *háriṇī-*.

[6] See the lists in Lindner p. 72—75.

[7] *-tur* appear, instead of *-tar* in *yan-túr-* beside *yan-tár-* 'guide' and in *sthā-túr-* beside *sthā-tár-* 'stationary'.

[8] The f. of these words is formed with *-ī* from the weak stem, i. e. in *-trī*.

[9] Except *daṃṣ-ṭár-* (AV.) 'biter'.

[10] Connected with the present stem *manu-te* etc. of *man-* 'think'.

[11] See Lindner p. 73 f.

[12] In the f. *coday-i-tr-ī́-*.

[13] From the aorist stem of *nī-* 'lead'.

-tas : action.

147. This suffix is identical in meaning with *-as*, being used to form neuter action nouns which have acquired a concrete meaning. It is very rare, occurring only in *ré-tas-* 'semen' (*ri-* 'flow') and *sró-tas-* 'stream', 'current' (*sru-* 'flow').

-ti : action and agent.

148. This suffix is used to form a large number of feminine action nouns; it also appears in a few agent nouns employed either as adjectives or masculine substantives[1]. The root generally has the same weak form as appears before the *-ta* of the past passive participle[2]; it is, however, more often accented than the suffix. In a few words the suffix is added with the connecting vowels *-a-*, *-i-* or *-ī-*.

1. **Action nouns.** With **accent on the suffix** are formed e. g. *iṣ-ṭí-* 'desire' (*iṣ-* 'seek'), *ū-tí-* 'aid' (√*av-*), *kīr-tí-* 'praise' (*kṛ-* 'commemorate'), *dhau-tí-* 'stream' (*dhāv-* 'flow'), *pī-tí-* 'draught' (*pā-* 'drink'), *pūr-tí-* 'reward' (*pṛ-* 'fill'), *bhak-tí-* 'distribution' (*bhaj-* 'divide'), *ma-tí-* 'thought' (*man-* 'think'), *rā-tí-* 'gift' (*rā-* 'give'), *rī-tí-* 'flow' (*ri-* 'flow'), *viṣ-ṭí-* 'work' (*viṣ-* 'be active'), *stu-tí-* 'praise'; from the **reduplicated root**: *carkṛ-tí-* 'praise' (*kṛ-* 'commemorate'); with **connecting *-a-***[3]: *aṃh-a-tí-* 'distress', *dṛś-a-tí-* 'appearance', *mith-a-tí-* 'conflict', *vas-a-tí-* 'abode'. With **accent on the root** are formed e. g. *íṣ-ṭi-* 'offering' (√*yaj-*), *gá-ti-* 'motion' (√*gam-*), *dí-ti-* 'liberality' (*dā-* 'give'), *vṛ́d-dhi-* 'increase' (√*vṛdh-*), *śán-ti-* (AV. VS.) 'repose' (√*śam-*); from the **reduplicated root** *dídhi-ti-* 'devotion' (*dhī-* 'think')[4]; with **connecting *-a-***: *ám-a-ti-*[5] 'indigence' (*am-* 'be afflicted').

a. The derivative *di-ti-* 'giving' when used as the final member of a compound is reduced to *-tti-*: *bhága-tti-*, *maghá-tti-*, *vásu-tti-*; above 26 a 2.

2. **Agent nouns.** These are rare, amounting to hardly 20 in number. **Accented on the suffix**: *jñā-tí-* m. 'relative', *pat-tí-* m. (AV. VS.) 'pedestrian', *rā-tí-* 'willing to give'; with connecting *-a-*: *ar-a-tí-* m. 'servant', *khal-a-tí-* (VS.) 'bald', and with accent on the connecting vowel *vṛk-á-ti-* m. 'murderer'. **Accented on the root**: m. *dhú-ti-* 'shaker', *pá-ti-* 'master', *múṣ-ṭi-* 'fist', *sáp-ti-* 'steed'; adjectives: *dhṛ́ṣ-ṭi-* (VS.) 'bold', *pú-ti-* (AV.) 'putrid', *váṣ-ṭi-* 'eager'; and from the reduplicated root *jígar-ti-* m. 'swallower'; with connecting vowels: *ám-a-ti-* 'poor', *rám-a-ti-* (AV. TS.) 'liking to stay', *ṛ́j-ī-ti-* 'glowing', *turv-ī́-ti-*, N. of a man (*turv-* = *tur-*, *tṛ-* 'overcome'), *dabh-ī́-ti-*[6], N. of a man'[7], *snéh-a-ti-* 'carnage' and *snīh-i-ti-* (SV.).

a. These derivatives are often compounded with **prepositions**[8], which are almost always accented; thus *ánu-ma-ti-* 'assent', *abhíti-* 'attack' (*abhi-iti-*), *ā́-hu-ti-* 'offering', *nír-ṛ-ti-* 'dissolution', *vy-ā́p-ti-* (AV.) 'attainment', *sáṃ-ga-ti-* 'coming together', *abhí-mā-ti-* 'insidious' (*man-* 'think')[9]; with suffix accented, only *ā-sak-tí-* 'pursuit', *ā-su-tí-* 'brew' (√*su-*) and 'enlivening' (√*sū-*); also *abhi-ṣ-ṭí-* m. 'helper' beside *abhí-ṣ-ṭi-* f. 'help'.

---

1 See the list in GRASSMANN, Wörterbuch 1719—21; LINDNER p. 76—79.

2 The roots *tan-* 'stretch', *ram-* 'rest', *han-* 'strike' may retain the nasal: *tán-ti-* f. 'cord', *rán-ti-* 'enjoyment' (AV. VS. TS.) beside *rá-ti-* (VS.), *á-han-ti-* (VS[1].) beside *á-ha-ti-* 'uninjured condition'.

3 The *-a-* here often, if not always, belongs to a verbal stem.

4 Roots which have the connecting *-i-* in the past participle, do not take it here: *gúp-ti-* (AV.) 'protection' beside *gup-i-tá-*, *prá-dṛp-ti-* 'arrogance' beside *á-dṛp-i-ta-* 'not infatuated' (also *á-dṛp-ta-*). These are, however, the only two examples.

5 But with the connecting *-a-* accented: *am-á-ti-* 'lustre', *ram-á-ti-* (AV.) 'haunt', *vrat-á-ti-* 'creeper'.

6 This word may be a compound (**dabhi-iti-*).

7 *yayā́ti-*, N. of a man, is according to BR. and GRASSMANN derived from *yat-* 'stretch'.

8 See LINDNER p. 77 f.

9 Compounded with a noun: *kā́ma-kā-ti-* 'requiring the fulfilment of a wish'.

b. The suffix is added to a secondary stem in *ján-aya-ti-* (VS.) f. 'generation'; it seems to have a secondary character in *yúva-ti-* f. 'maiden', adj. 'young'. It is secondary in *pakṣa-ti* (VS.) 'root of the wing'; in the numerals *viṃśa-ti-* '20', *ṣaṣ-ṭi-* '60', and others; in *paṅk-ti-* f. 'set of five'; in the pronominal words *ká-ti* 'how many?', *tá-ti* (AV.) 'so many', *yá-ti* 'as many as'; and in *addhā-ti-* m. 'sage', formed from the adverb *ad-dhā́* 'truly'.

-*tu* : action and agent.

149. The great majority of the words derived with this suffix are infinitives appearing in the form of the dative, ablative-genitive, and accusative cases. Besides these, there are a few action nouns used independently, and still fewer agent nouns. The root is usually accented[1] and takes Guṇa; but the suffix is accented in some half dozen instances, in two or three of which the radical syllable is weakened. The gender is usually masculine, but a few feminines and neuters also occur.

1. **Accented on the root:** m. *ó-tu-* 'weft' (*vā-* 'weave'), *krá-tu-* 'capacity' (*kṛ-* 'make'), *tán-tu-* 'thread', *-dhā́-tu-*[2] 'element', *sák-tu-* 'groats' (√*sañj-*), *sé-tu-* 'bond' (*si-* 'bind'), *só-tu-* 'libation' (*su-* 'press'), *dhā́-tu-* adj. 'drinkable' (*dhe-* 'suck'); m. *mán-tu-* 'adviser'; f. *vás-tu-* 'morning' (*vas-* 'shine'), *sū́-tu-*[3] (AV.) 'birth'; n. *dā́-tu-* 'division' (*dā-* 'divide'), *vā́s-tu-*[4] 'abode' (*vas-* 'dwell').

2. **Accented on the suffix:** m. *ak-tú-* 'ray' (*añj-* 'anoint'), *gā-tú-* 'way' (*gā-* 'go') and 'song' (*gā-* 'sing'), *jan-tú-* 'creature', *he-tú-* 'cause' (*hi-* 'impel'); with weak radical vowel: *ṛ-tú-* 'season', *pi-tú-* 'drink' (*pī-* 'swell')[5].

a. The suffix is attached in a few instances (as in some infinitives) with **connecting** -*ī*-: *dur-dhár-ī-tu-* 'irresistible', *su-háv-ī-tu-* 'to be successfully invoked', *tur-phár-ī-tu-*[6].

b. The suffix appears in a few instances to be attached to a present or a secondary **conjugational stem:** *edha-tú-* m. 'welfare' (*édha-te* 'thrives'), *tapya-tú-* adj. 'glowing' (*tapyá-te* 'is heated'), *vaha-tú-* m. 'wedding' (*váha-ti* 'conveys'), *siṣāsá-tu-*[7] 'desirous of obtaining'; *jīvā́-tú-* f. 'life' (*jīva-ti-* 'lives').

c. Derivatives formed with *-tu* are in several instances compounded with the particles *dus-* and *su-*: *dur-dhár-ī-tu-* and *dur-dhár-tu-* 'irresistible', *dur-vár-tu-* 'difficult to ward off', *duṣ-ṭár-ī-tu-* 'unconquerable', *su-yán-tu-* 'guiding well', *su-śró-tu-* 'hearing willingly', *su-hán-tu-* 'easy to slay'; also with a pronoun in *sváitu-* 'going one's own (*sva-*) gait' (*etu-*).

-*tna* : action and agent.

150. This suffix is very rare, occurring only in *cyau-tná-* n. 'concussion', adj. 'animating' (*cyu-* 'stir') and in *rá-tna-* n. 'gift' (*rā-* 'give').

-*tnu* : agent.

151. This suffix, which is always accented, forms more than a dozen adjectives and a few substantives. It is added to the root either directly or more commonly with the connecting vowel *-a-* (which probably belongs to the present stem) or *-i-* (which is almost exclusively used with causative stems).

1. **Attached directly** to the root: *kṛ-tnú-* 'active', *dar-tnú-* m. 'breaker', *ha-tnú-* 'deadly' (√*han-*); with reduplication: *jiga-tnú-* 'hastening' (*gam-* 'go'), *jigha-tnú-* 'harming' (*han-* 'strike').

2. With **connecting -a-**: *kav-a-tnú-*[8] 'miserly', *pīy-a-tnú-* 'reviling' (*pī́ya-ti*

---

[1] The infinitives always accent the root (105).

[2] Only in the compounds *tri-dhā́tu-* 'threefold' and *saptá-dhātu-* 'sevenfold'.

[3] Without Guṇa.

[4] With lengthened *a*.

[5] *kṛ́tv-as* 'times' is probably an acc. pl. of a stem *kṛ́-tu-* 'making'. Cp. BB. 25, 294.

[6] The derivation of this word is uncertain and its meaning is obscure. [Cp. Mahābhāṣya Vol. I, p. 363, l. 25.]

[7] From the desiderative stem of *sā-* 'obtain'.

[8] Cp. WHITNEY, Roots, under *kū-* 'design'.

'abuses'), *meh-a-tnú-*, N. of a river (*méha-ti*), *ā-ruj-a-tnú-* 'breaking' (*rujá-ti* 'breaks').

3. With **connecting -*i*-**: *drav-i-tnú-* 'running' (*dru-* 'run'); from causative stems: *tanay-i-tnú-* 'thundering', *drāvay-i-tnú-* 'hasting' (*dru-* 'run'), *poṣay-i-tnú-* 'causing to thrive' (√*puṣ-*), *māday-i-tnú-* 'intoxicating' (√*mad-*), *sūday-i-tnú-* 'causing sweetness to flow' (√*sūd-*), *stanay-i-tnú-* m. 'thunder' (√*stan-*); *an-āmay-i-tnú-* 'not making ill', 'curative' (√*am-*).

-*tra* : agent.

152. This suffix was doubtless originally formed by a secondary *-a* added to *-tṛ* (the weak form of *tar-*). But having early attained an independent character, it came to be largely employed as a primary suffix. It is used to form some half dozen adjectives[1] and about 60 substantives, the latter being neuters except about a dozen (partly masc. and partly fem.)[2]. The substantives generally express the means or instrument by which the action of the verb is performed, sometimes the place where it is performed. The root is generally accented and has Guṇa; but it is sometimes unaccented and has a weak vowel. The suffix is generally added directly to the root, but in about a dozen instances with a connecting vowel.

1. **Attached directly to the root: adjectives:** *jái-tra-*[3] 'victorious', *śvā-trá-*[4] 'invigorating'; with reduplication: *johū́-tra-* 'calling aloud' (√*hū-*).

m. *a-trá-*[5] 'eater', *úṣ-ṭra-*[6] 'buffalo', *dáṃṣ-ṭra-* 'tusk' (*daṃś-* 'bite'), *mán-tra-* 'prayer'; with weak (etymologically doubtful) root: *pu-trá-* 'son', *mi-trá-*[7] 'friend', *vṛ-trá-*[8] 'foe'.

f. *áṣ-ṭrā-* 'goad' (*aś-* 'reach'), *nāṣ-ṭrā́-* (AV. VS.) 'destroyer' (√*naś-*), *mā́-trā-* 'measure', *hó-trā-* 'sacrifice'.

n. With **accent on the root:** *á-tra-*[9] 'food', *kár-tra-* (AV.) 'spell', *kṣé-tra-* 'field', *kṣṇó-tra-* 'whetstone', *gā́-tra-* 'limb', *jñā́-tra-* (VS.) 'intellectual faculty', *tán-tra-* 'warp', *dā́-tra-*[10] 'gift', *dā-tra-* 'knife', *dhár-tra-* 'support' (VS. TS.), *pát-tra-* (VS.)[11] 'wing', *pā́-tra-* 'cup', (*pā-* 'drink'), *péṣ-ṭra-* (AV.) 'bone', *mū́-tra-* (AV.) 'urine', *méḍhra-* (AV.) 'penis', *yók-tra-* 'rope', *vár-tra-* (AV.) 'dam', *vás-tra-* 'garment', *śró-tra-* 'ear', *sū́-tra-* (AV.) 'thread' (*sīv-* 'sew').

With **accent on the suffix** and often with an abstract meaning: *as-trá-* (AV.) 'missile', *kṣa-trá-*[12] 'dominion', *dā-trá-* 'share', *deṣ-ṭrá-* 'indication' (√*diś-*), *ne-trá-* (AV.) 'guidance', *rāṣ-ṭrá-* 'dominion', *śas-trá-* (VS.) 'invocation', *śās-trá-* 'command', *sat-trá-* 'sacrificial session', *sto-trá-* 'praise', *sthā-trá-* 'station', *ho-trá-* 'sacrifice'.

2. With **connecting vowel -*a*-:** *ám-a-tra-* 'violent', *yáj-a-tra-* 'adorable'; *kṛnt-á-tra-* 'shred', *gāy-a-trá-* 'song', *pát-a-tra-* 'wing', *vádh-a-tra-* 'deadly weapon', f. *var-a-trā́-* 'strap'; with **-*i*-:** *khan-í-tra-* 'shovel', *car-í-tra-* 'foot', *jan-í-tra-* 'birthplace', *pav-í-tra-* 'sieve', *bhar-í-tra-* 'arm', *bhav-í-tra-* 'world', *san-í-tra-* 'gift'; with **-*u*-:** *tár-u-tra-*[13] 'overcoming'.

---

1 These have mostly masc. forms, some neuter; the only one which has fem. forms is *yájatra-* 'deserving adoration'.

2 Six or seven masculines and five feminines.

3 With exceptional Vṛddhi of the radical syllable.

4 From *śvā-* = *śū-* 'swell'.

5 For *at-trá-* from *ad-* 'eat'. Cp. p. 125, note 1.

6 With weak root though accented.

7 Occurs in the RV. as a n. when it means 'friendship'.

8 Occurs also as a n. in the RV. when plural.

9 For *át-tra-* from *ad-* 'eat'.

10 Probably for *dát-tra-* from the present-stem of *dā-* 'give'.

11 Only at the end of a compound in the RV.

12 *nakṣatra-* 'asterism' is perhaps a compound. Cp. above 81, 2 a.

13 Cp. *tar-u-tár-* 'victor'.

-tri : agent.

153. This very rare suffix occurs in only three or four derivatives: *á-tri-*[1] 'devouring', *śá-tri-* m., N. of a man[2]; with connecting *-a* in *arc-á-tri-* 'roaring'; also in the f. form with *ī* in *rá-trī-*[3] 'night'.

-tru : agent.

154. This suffix is found only in *śátru-* 'enemy' for **śát-tru-*, perhaps from *śad-* 'prevail'.

-tva : agent.

155. This suffix probably arose by the addition of the secondary suffix *-a* to action nouns in *-tu*, which turned them into adjectives used in a gerundive sense. It occurs in about a dozen such derivatives which are almost restricted to the RV.; e. g. *kár-tva-* 'to be made'[4].

-tha : action.

156. This suffix is almost exclusively used to form action nouns (some of which have acquired a concrete meaning) in all genders[5]. The root generally appears in a weak form, as the suffix is mostly accented. The suffix is attached to the root either directly or more commonly with a connecting vowel[6].

1. **Attached directly to the root:** m. *ár-tha-*[7] 'goal', *gā-thá-* 'song', *pak-thá-*, N. of a man, *bhṛ-thá-* 'offering', *rá-tha-*[8] 'car', *há-tha-*[9] 'slaughter'; in composition with prepositions: *sam-i-thá-* 'conflict', *nir-ṛ-thá-* 'destruction', *saṃ-ga-thá-* 'union' (*gam-* 'go'), *ud-gī-thá-*[10] (AV.) 'singing of chants'; in composition with nouns: *putra-kṛ-thá-* 'procreation of sons', *dīrgha-yā-thá-* 'long course', *go-pī-thá-*[11] 'protection' (*pā-* 'protect') and 'draught' (*pā-* 'drink') of milk'.—f. *kā́ṣ-thā-* 'course', *gā́-thā-* 'song', *nī́-thā-* 'trick'.—n. *uk-thá-* 'saying' (√*vac-*), *tīr-thá-* 'ford' (*tṝ-* 'cross'), *nī-thá-* 'song', *yū-thá-*[12] 'herd', *rik-thá-* 'inheritance'[13].

2. **With connecting vowel *-á-*:** *ay-á-tha-* n. 'foot', *uc-á-tha-* n. 'praise' (√*vac-*), *car-á-tha-* n. 'mobility', *tveṣ-á-tha-* m. 'fury', *proth-á-tha-* n. 'snorting', *yaj-á-tha-*[14] 'worship', *rav-á-tha-* m. 'roar', *vakṣ-á-tha-* m. 'growth', *vid-á-tha-*[15] n. 'assembly', *śap-á-tha-* m. 'curse', *śay-á-tha-* n. 'lair', *śvas-á-tha-* m. 'snorting', *sac-á-tha-* m. 'aid', *stan-á-tha-* m. 'thunder', *stav-á-tha-* m. 'praise', *srav-á-tha-* m. or n. 'flow'; with prefix: *ā-vas-a-thá-* (AV.) 'abode', *pra-vas-a-thá-* n. 'absence', *prāṇ-á-tha-*[16] (VS.) 'respiration'.

a. **With *-ū*:** *jár-ū-tha-*, m. a kind of demon ('wearing out', *jṛ-*), *vár-ū-tha-* n. 'protection'; **with *-u*:** *mat-ú-tha-*[17] m. 'sage'.

[1] For *át-tri-* from *ad-* 'eat'. Cp. p. 124, note 5.
[2] For *śat-tri-* from *śat-* 'cut in pieces'.
[3] In AV. *rā́-tri-* also.
[4] See below, Future Passive Participles, 581.
[5] The fem. form of the suffix is *-thā*.
[6] This vowel for the most part belongs in reality to a present stem.
[7] With accented strong root.
[8] The root is uncertain.
[9] With root accented though weakened by loss of nasal (*han-* 'slay').
[10] With *gā-* 'sing' weakened to *gī-*.
[11] Both *pā-* 'protect' and *pā-* 'drink' are weakened to *pī-*. Cp. above 27.
[12] The root in this word is uncertain.
[13] *pṛṣṭhá-* 'back' probably contains the root *sthā-* 'stand', = **pra-sthá-* 'prominent'.
[14] The gender is uncertain, as the word occurs in the dat. sing. only.
[15] Probably from *vidh-* 'worship': OLDENBERG, ZDMG. 54, 608—611; cp. above p. 23, note 10.
[16] When there is a prefix the accent is thrown on the suffix; but *prāṇ-* (= *pra-an-*) is treated like a root.
[17] Perhaps from *man-* with double suffix (*-tu*, *-tha*).

-thi : agent.

157. As far as can be judged from the very few examples occurring, this suffix was used to form agent nouns. It is attached with or without a connecting vowel. The derivation of all the words which seem to be formed with this suffix is doubtful: *át-i-thi-* m. 'guest' (if from *at-* 'wander'); *ud-ār-a-thí-* adj. 'rising'; *me-thí-* (AV.) m. 'pillar' (*mi-* 'fix'). The neuters *ásthi-* (AV. VS., beside *asth-án-*) 'bone' and *sákthi-* (beside *sakth-án-*) may be formed with the suffix *-i*.

-thu : action.

158. This very rare suffix, which is not found in the RV., appears only with the connecting vowel *-a-* (which in reality belongs to a present stem), forming masculine action nouns: *ej-á-thu-* (AV.) 'trembling', *vep-á-thu-* 'quivering', *stan-á-thu-* (AV.) 'roar'.

-na : action and agent.

159. This suffix is in the first place used, like *-ta*, to form past passive participles[1]; e. g. *bhin-ná-* from *bhid-* 'split'; but, unlike *-ta*, it is never added to the root with a connecting vowel or to a secondary conjugation stem.

It is further employed to form a number of adjectives and masculine substantives, mostly accented on the suffix. It also forms a few feminine (*-nā*) and neuter substantives, all but one of the latter being accented on the root. The substantives have partly an abstract and partly a concrete meaning. A medial vowel never takes Guṇa, but a final vowel nearly always does.

1. The **adjectives** (f. *-ā*) are: *áś-ná-* 'voracious', *uṣ-ṇá-* 'hot', *ū-ná-* 'deficient', *ṛ-ṇá-* 'guilty', *kṛṣ-ṇá-* 'black', *kṣo-ṇá-* 'immovable' (?), *nag-ná-* 'naked', *bradh-ná-* 'pale red', *śó-ṇa-* 'red', *śro-ṇá-* and *ślo-ṇá-* (AV.) 'lame', *ślakṣ-ṇá-* (AV.) 'slippery', *śvit-na-* 'white', *syo-ná-* 'agreeable'; compounded: *an-āmṛ-ṇá-* 'inviolable', *á-rūkṣ-ṇa-* (AV.) 'tender', *sadā-pṛ-ṇá-* 'always munificent'.

2. **Substantives** are: **m.** *ghṛ-ṇá-* 'heat', *budh-ná-* 'bottom', *bhrū-ṇá-* 'embryo', *yaj-ñá-* 'sacrifice', *śye-ná-* 'eagle', *ste-ná-* 'thief'; *sam-praś-ná-* 'question'; accented on root: *áś-na-* 'stone', *kár-ṇa-* 'ear', *vár-ṇa-* 'colour', *śúṣ-ṇa-*, N. of a demon, *svá́p-na-* 'sleep'. — **n.** *tṛ́-ṇa-* 'grass', *dhá-na-*[2] 'booty', *par-ṇá-* 'wing', *vas-ná-* 'price', *śíś-na-* 'penis', *śu-ná-* 'welfare', *śú-na-* 'want', *rí-na-* 'property'. — **f.** *tṛ́ṣ-ṇā-* 'thirst', *dhé-nā-* 'milch cow', *sé-nā-* 'missile', *sthū́-ṇā-* 'post'.

-nas : action.

160. This suffix, which has the same meaning as *-as* and *-tas*, is used in forming a few action nouns which have mostly acquired a concrete sense. These are *áp-nas-* n. 'possession', *ár-ṇas-* n. 'flood', *-bhar-ṇas-*[3] 'bearing' (?), *rék-ṇas-* n. 'property left by bequest' (*ric-* 'leave'). With connecting vowel: *dráv-i-ṇas-* n. 'movable property' (*dru-* 'run'), *pár-ī-ṇas-* m. 'abundance' (*pṝ-* 'fill'). It also appears in the agent noun *dám-ū-nas-* adj. 'domestic', m. 'friend of the house' (*dam-*).

-ni : action and agent.

161. This not very frequent suffix is employed to form m. and f. action nouns as well as agent nouns (adjectives and substantives). Either the radical vowel or the suffix may be accented; and the root in several instances takes Guṇa. The feminines have rarely an abstract sense, having generally acquired a concrete meaning.

---

[1] For a list of these see below 576.
[2] Probably from *dhā-* 'place'.
[3] In *sahásra-bharṇas-* 'thousandfold'.

1. The **feminines** are: *jūr-ṇí-* 'heat', *-jyā-ni-*[1] (AV.) 'injury', *me-ní-* 'missile', *śré-ṇi-* 'line', *śró-ṇi-* 'hip', *sṛ́-ṇi-* and *sṛ-ṇí-* 'sickle'; **masculines** are: *ghṛ́-ṇi-*[2] 'heat', *yó-ni-* 'receptacle'.

2. **Agent nouns**, adjectives and m. substantives, are: *ag-ní-* m. 'fire', *jū́r-ṇi-* 'singeing', *tū́r-ṇi-* 'speeding', *dhar-ṇí-* m. 'supporter', *pṛ́ś-ni-* 'speckled', *pre-ṇí-* 'loving' (√*prī-*), *bhū́r-ṇi-* 'excited', *váh-ni-* m. 'draught animal', *vṛ́ṣ-ṇi-* and *vṛṣ-ṇí-* 'virile', m. 'ram'.

a. The suffix occurs with a connecting *-u-* in *hrād-ú-ni-* f. (?) 'hail'[3].

-nu : action and agent.

162. With this suffix is formed a small number of action and agent nouns of all genders, but mostly masculine. The action nouns often have a concrete meaning. As the suffix is almost invariably accented, the radical vowel, with one exception, never shows Guṇa. This suffix, like *-tu*, is sometimes preceded by *-a* (which really belongs to present stems).

1. The **substantives** occurring are: *kṣep-nú-* m. 'jerk' (x. 51[6]), *dā́-nu-*[4] m. f. 'demon', f. 'dew', n. 'drop', *dhe-nú-* f. 'cow', *bhā-nú-* m. 'light', *vag-nú-* m. 'sound', *víṣ-ṇu-*[5] m., N. of a god, *sū-nú-* m. 'son', *sthā-ṇú-*[6] m. 'pillar'; with connecting *-a-*: *krand-a-nú-* m. 'roaring', *kṣip-a-ṇú-* m. 'missile', *nad-a-nú-* m. 'roaring', *nabh-a-nú-*[7] m. 'fountain'[8].

2. **Adjectives** are: *gṛdh-nú-* 'hasty', *dhṛṣ-ṇú-* 'bold'; with connecting *-a-*: the compound *vi-bhañj-a-nú-* 'breaking to pieces'.

-pa : concrete substantives.

163. A few words are formed with this suffix, but the origin of all of them is more or less obscure[9]. These are: *púṣ-pa-* n. 'flower', *stu-pá-*[10] (VS.) m. 'tuft', *stú-pa-*[10] m. 'top-knot'; perhaps also *tál-pa-* m. 'couch', *śáṣ-pa-* (VS.) n. 'blade of grass', *śíl-pa* (VS.) n. 'ornament', *śū́r-pa-* (AV.) 'winnowing basket'; possibly *apū-pá-* m. 'cake', *úla-pa-* m. 'shrub', *kúṇa-pa-* (AV.) n. 'corpse'[11].

-ma : action and agent.

164. This suffix forms a considerable number of action nouns (almost exclusively masculine) as well as agent nouns, both adjectives and substantives. Only a single neuter and one or two feminine substantives occur. The suffix is accented more than twice as often as the root. The vowel *ṛ* always takes Guṇa in the radical syllable; on the other hand, initial or medial *i* and *u* never take Guṇa; when final they only do so if the root is accented. Several of these derivatives in *-ma* appear beside others in *-man*; some at least are transfers from the latter; thus *dhár-man-* 'ordinance' alone is found in the RV., while *dhár-ma-* appears beside it in the later Saṃhitās.

1. **Accented on the suffix: adjectives**: e. g. *jih-má-* 'oblique', *tig-má-* 'sharp', *das-má-* 'wondrous', *bhī-má-* 'terrible', *śag-má-* mighty'; with reduplication,

[1] In *sarva-jyāni-* (AV.) 'complete loss of property'.

[2] Beside *ghṛ-ṇá-* m. and *ghṛ-ṇā-* f.

[3] This suffix is in several words preceded by *-a-*, much in the same way as *-ti*; but as *-ani* has assumed a more independent character it is treated above (122) as a separate suffix.

[4] With irregular accent.

[5] Perhaps originally an adjective **viṣ-ṇú-*, with shift of accent on becoming a Proper Name. But cp. p. 85, note 1.

[6] The origin of the cerebral *ṇ* here is obscure.

[7] Also *nabh-anū́-* f.

[8] The Proper Name *kṛś-ánu-* is perhaps similarly formed, but with long *-ā-*.

[9] Cp. LINDNER p. 69; LIDEN, IF. 18, 496.

[10] Probably from a root *stu-* 'drip'; see WHITNEY, Roots.

[11] *yū́pa-* m. 'sacrificial post' is probably derived from *yup-* 'obstruct'.

tūtu-má- 'powerful'; **substantives: m.** *aj-má-* 'course', *idh-má-* 'fuel', *ghar-má-* 'heat', *dar-má-* 'breaker', *dhū-má-* 'smoke', *nar-má-* (VS.) 'jest', *ruk-má-* 'ornament', *hi-má-* 'cold'.

2. **Accented on the root: substantives: m.** e. g. *ú-ma-* 'friend' (*av-* 'favour'), *é-ma-* (VS.) 'course', *dhár-ma-* (AV. VS. TS.) 'ordinance', *bhá-ma-* 'brightness', *sár-ma-* 'flow', *só-ma-* 'Soma' (√*su-*), *stó-ma-* 'praise' (√*stu-*), *hó-ma-* 'offering'; f. *hí-mā-* 'winter'; n. *bíl-ma-* 'chip'.

a. The suffix seems to be added once with connecting *-a-* (which really belongs to a present stem) in the f. *sar-á-mā-* 'the fleet one', N. of a goddess.

-man: action and agent.

165. This suffix forms a large number of derivatives [1], which are almost exclusively action nouns. The great majority of these are neuters accented on the root, but there are also a good many masculines accented on the suffix. Besides these occur a few agent nouns, mostly accented on the suffix, both adjectives and masculine substantives, all of them, except *brah-mán-* 'priest', of rare occurrence. The same word in several instances varies in meaning according to the accent and gender [2]; e. g. *dhár-man-* n. ordinance', m. *dhar-mán-* 'ordainer'. The **root** in these derivatives usually takes Guṇa; in a few instances it has Vṛddhi or lengthens *a*; sometimes it is weak. The suffix is often added with the connecting vowels *-i-* or *-ī-*. The derivatives are occasionally compounded with prepositions, which are then nearly always accented.

1. Examples of **action nouns** are: n. *ád-man-* 'food', *é-man-* 'course', *kár-man-* 'action', *kárṣ-man-* 'goal', *ján-man-* 'birth', *trá-man-* 'protection', *dá-man-* 'gift' (*dā-* 'give') and 'bond' (*dā-* 'tie'), *ná-man-* 'name', *pát-man-* 'flight', *bráh-man-* 'devotion', *bhár-man-* 'table', *bhú-man-* 'world', *vák-man-* 'invocation', *várt-man-* 'course', *véś-man-* 'dwelling', *śák-man-* 'power', *śás-man-* 'praise', *śák-man-* 'power', *hó-man-* 'sacrifice' (√*hu-*) and 'invocation' (√*hū-*); with **connecting** *-i-*: *ján-i-man-* 'birth', *vár-i-man-* 'expanse' (beside *var-i-mán-* m.); with **connecting** *-ī-*: *dár-ī-man-* 'destruction', *dhár-ī-man-* 'ordinance', *pár-ī-man-* [3] 'abundance', *bhár-ī-man-* 'maintenance', *vár-ī-man-* 'expanse', *sár-ī-man-* 'course', *sáv-ī-man-* 'impulse' [4], *háv-ī-man-* 'invocation'.— m. *ūṣ-mán-* (AV. VS.) 'heat', *o-mán-* 'favour', *je-mán-* (VS. TS.) 'superiority', *drāgh-mán-* (VS.) 'length' (beside *drāgh-i-mán-*), *pāp-mán-* (AV.) 'wickedness', *bhū-mán-* 'abundance', *vid-mán-* 'knowledge', *svād-mán-* 'sweetness', *he-mán-* 'impulse'; with **connecting** *-i-*: *jar-i-mán-* 'old age', *prath-i-mán-* 'breath', *mah-i-mán-* 'greatness', *var-i-mán-*, *varṣ-i-mán-* (VS.) 'height' (beside *várṣ-man-* and *varṣ-mán-*), *har-i-mán-* 'yellowness'.

2. **Agent nouns accented on the suffix** are: *dar-mán-* 'breaker' *dā-mán-* 'giver', *dhar-mán-* 'supporter', *brah-mán-* 'one who prays', *bhuj-mán-* 'fertile', *vad-mán-* 'speaker', *sad-mán-* 'sitter', *so-mán-* 'Somapresser'; **accented on the root**: *áś-man-* 'stone', *ó-man-* 'friend', *jé-man-* 'superior', *bhás-man-* 'chewing' [5].

a. The following words are according to difference of accent neuter action nouns or masculine agent nouns *dá-man-* 'gift' and *dā-mán-* 'giver'; *dhár-man-* 'ordinance' and *dhar-mán-* 'ordainer'; *bráh-man-* 'worship' and *brah-mán-* 'priest'; *sád-man-* 'seat' and *sad-mán-* 'sitter'.

---

1 For lists of these see Grassmann, Wörterbuch 1730 f.; Lindner p. 91—93.

2 Somewhat in the same way as the derivatives in *-as* (126).

3 Also with anomalous *-e-*: *pár-e-man-* (SV[1].).

4 Also *stár-ī-man-* 'spreading' used in the loc. as an infinitive.

5 In a compound also *svādu-kṣád-man-* 'having sweet food'.

b. In a few words difference of gender and accent is not accompanied by difference of meaning: *várṣ-man-* n. and *varṣ-mán-* m. both mean 'height'; *svā́d-man-* n. and *svād-mán-* m. 'sweetness'; *vár-i-man-* n. and *var-i-mán-* m. 'expanse'.

c. In a few instances difference of accent is accompanied by a reversal of the usual distinction of meaning: *jé-man-* 'victorious', *je-mán-* (VS. TS.) 'superiority'; *ó-man-* m. 'friend', *o-mán-* m. 'favour'.

d. A few derivatives in *-man* both action and agent nouns are compounded with prepositions: *ví-gā-man-* n. 'step', *prá-bhar-man-* n. 'presentation', *prá-yā-man-* n. 'departure', *ví-dhar-man-* m. 'maintainer', *ví-pat-man-*[1] 'flying through', *ánu-vart-man-* (AV.) 'following after', *vi-sar-mán-*[2] m. 'flowing asunder'.

-māna : agent.

166. This suffix is used to form the present[3], future, and aorist middle participle and the present passive participle[4]. It is always preceded by *a* except in the anomalous perfect participle *sasṛ-māṇá-* (= *sasr-āṇá-*) 'speeding'.

-mi and *-mī* : action and agent.

167. The suffix *-mi* is used to form a few adjectives and masculine substantives; it also forms (generally in the form of *-mī*) a few feminine substantives with a concrete meaning: *ūr-mí-* m. 'wave' (√*vṛ-*), *-kūr-mi-* 'action' in *tuvi-kūr-mi-* 'working mightily', *jā-mí-* 'related', 'kinsman'; *bhū́-mi-* and *bhū́-mī-* f. 'earth', *lakṣ-mí-* f. 'sign', *sūr-mí-* f. 'tube'; probably also *raś-mí-* m. 'ray' and the adj. *krudh-mi-*[5] (RV[1].) 'irascible'.

-min : agent.

168. A few adjectives have the appearance of being formed with a suffix *-min*. They are *iṣ-mín-* 'impetuous', *bhā-mín-* 'shining', *śuṣ-mín-* 'roaring'. They may, however, be explained as secondary derivatives made with the suffix *-in*, like *dhūm-ín-* from *dhūmá-* 'smoke'.

-ya : gerundive.

169. This suffix is used to form a large number of future participles passive[6]. It probably has a primary character in other derivatives besides these; but it is so difficult to distinguish them from those which are secondary, that it is preferable to treat all but gerundives under secondary *-ya* (228).

-yu : action and agent.

170. This suffix forms a few action and agent nouns. The root remains unchanged, while the accent varies. Action nouns are: *man-yú-* m. 'anger', *mṛt-yú-* m. 'death'. Agent nouns are: *dás-yu-* m. 'enemy', *druh-yú-*, N. of a man ('hostile'), *śím-yu-* 'enemy'; *bhuj-yú-* both adj. 'wealthy' and m. as N. of a man. Adjectives only are: *yáj-yu-* 'pious', *śundh-yú-* 'pure', *sáh-yu-* 'strong'.

-ra : agent.

171. A large number of derivatives are formed with this suffix[7], which is usually accented, the root consequently almost always appearing with a weak vowel. These words are mostly adjectives, but a few substantives occur in all genders. The suffix is frequently added with the connecting vowels *-a-*, *-i-*, *-ī-*, *-u-*.

1 Or as a Bahuvrīhi 'having the flight of a bird' (*ví-*).

2 With unusual accent on the suffix instead of on the preposition.

3 In the *a*-conjugation.

4 See below under those tenses, 427, 435, 442, 447; 512, 538; and cp. Delbrück, Verbum 226; Lindner 72.

5 The only form occurring *krudhmí*, N. pl. n. might, however, come from *krudh-min-*.

6 See below, Future participles passive, 578; cp. Delbrück, Verbum 230; Lindner 76, p. 96—99.

7 See Lindner 78, p. 100—102; Whitney 1188.

1. Of derivatives **accented on the suffix** there are more than 60 **adjectives**; e. g. *ak-rá-* 'swift', *ug-rá-* 'mighty', *cit-rá-* 'bright', *tu-rá-* 'strong', *mū-rá-* 'stupid', *śak-rá-* 'mighty', *śuk-rá-* 'bright', *hiṃs-rá-* 'injurious', **Substantives** are: m. *us-rá-* 'bull', *kṣu-rá-* 'razor', *mṛdh-rá-* 'foe', *rud-rá-*, N. of a god, *vam-rá-* 'ant', *vī-rá-*'man', *śūd-rá-* 'man of the fourth caste'; n. *abh-rá-* 'cloud', *kṛcch-rá-* 'distress', *krū-rá-* (AV. VS.) 'wound', *kṣī-rá-* 'milk', *khid-rá-* 'weight', *rip-rá-* 'defilement', *sī-rá-* 'plough'; f. *hi-rā-* (AV. VS.) 'vein'.

a. With **connecting vowel** *-a-*: *drav-a-rá-* 'running', *pat-a-rá-* 'flying', *ny-oc-a-rá-* (AV.) 'suiting'[1]; n. *gambh-a-rá-* 'depth', *tas-a-rá-* 'shuttle'[2]; **with** *i*: *aj-i-rá-* 'swift', *iṣ-i-rá-* 'lively', *dhvas-i-rá-* 'stirring up', *badh-i-rá-* 'deaf', *mad-i-rá-* 'pleasing', *rudh-i-rá-* (AV.) 'red', *sphi-rá-* 'fat'; m. *khad-i-rá-*, a kind of tree; n. *sar-i-rá-* (VS.) 'wave'; **with** *ī*: *gabh-ī-rá-* and *gambh-ī-rá-* 'deep'; **with** *u*: *aṃh-u-rá-* 'narrow', *vith-u-rá-* 'tottering'.

2. Of stems **accented on the root** the only **adjectives** are: *gṛ́dh-ra-* 'greedy', *túm-ra-* 'stout', *dhī́-ra-* 'wise', *víp-ra-* 'inspired'; **substantives** are: m. *áj-ra-* 'field', *índ-ra-*, N. of a god, *váj-ra-* 'thunderbolt', *várdh-ra-* (AV.) 'girth', *śū́-ra-* 'hero'; n. *ág-ra-* 'point', *rándh-ra-* 'hollow', *śvábh-ra-* 'pit'; f. *dhā́-rā-* 'stream', *śíp-rā-* 'jaw', *sú-rā-* 'intoxicating liquor'.

a. With **connecting vowel** *-i-*: *stháv-i-ra-* 'firm'; m. *áṅg-i-ra-*, N. of a seer, *ás-i-ra-* 'missile'; **with** *-ī-*: *śáv-ī-ra-* 'mighty'; n. *śár-ī-ra-* 'body'; **with** *-u-*: m. *ás-u-ra-* 'spirit', *bák-u-ra-* 'trumpet'.

α. A few of these derivatives are compounded with prepositions: *ni-ci-rá-* 'attentive', *ni-mṛg-ra-* 'attached'; m. *ā-kha-rá-* 'lair', *sam-ud-rá-* 'sea'.

-ri: agent.

172. This suffix forms adjectives as well as m. and f. substantives. It is sometimes added with connecting *-u-*. The root is more frequently accented than the suffix.

1. **Adjectives** are: *bhū́-ri-* 'abundant', *vádh-ri-* 'emasculated', *śubh-ri-* 'beautiful'; with **connecting** *-u-*: *jás-u-ri-* 'exhausted', *dā́ś-u-ri-* 'pious', *sáh-u-ri-* 'mighty'.

2. **Substantives** are: m. *áṅgh-ri-* (VS.) 'foot', *jī-rí-* 'flowing water', *sū-rí-* 'patron'; f. *ábh-ri-* (AV. VS.) 'hoe', *áś-ri-* 'edge', *ús-ri-* 'dawn', *váṅk-ri-* 'rib'; with **connecting** *-u-*: *aṅg-ú-ri-* 'finger'; *-rī* occurs in *tand-rī́-* (AV.) 'weariness'.

-ru: agent.

173. This rare suffix forms adjectives and a very few neuter substantives. It is added either directly to the root or with a preceding *-a-*, *-ā-*, or *-e-*. Either the root or the suffix may be accented.

1. **Adjectives** are: *cā́-ru-* 'dear', *dhā-rú-* (AV.) 'sucking', *pé-ru-* 'causing to swell' (*pī-*), *bhī-rú-* 'timid'; *ar-á-ru-* 'hostile', *pat-á-ru-* 'flying'; *jáb-ā-ru-*[3] (RV[1].) 'speeding', *pīy-ā-ru-* 'reviling', *vand-ā́-ru-* 'praising', *śar-ā́-ru-* 'injurious'; *mad-e-rú-* 'intoxicating', *san-é-ru-*[4] 'obtaining'.

2. **Substantives** are: n. *áś-ru-* 'tear', *śmáś-ru-* 'beard'.

-la: agent.

174. This rare suffix, a later form of *-ra*, is equivalent in sense and use to the latter, sometimes also interchanging with it. It forms adjectives and a

[1] *bhārvará-* (of doubtful meaning) is probably a secondary formation, and *vāsará-* 'matutinal' seems to be derived from *vasar-* 'morning'.

[2] Also *-ṛkṣará-* 'thorn' m. in *an-ṛkṣará-* 'thornless'.

[3] Perhaps for **jáv-ā-ru-* from *jū-* 'speed'.

[4] The suffix is secondary in *mitré-ru-* 'ally'.

few masculine and neuter substantives. The radical syllable is accented in two or three substantives only. The suffix is added either directly to the root or with the connecting vowels *-a-*, *-i-*, *-u-*.

Derivatives thus formed are: *-pā-lá-* (VS.) m. 'guardian' in *aja-pālá-* (VS.) 'goat-herd', *śuk-lá-* (AV.) n. 'white colour' (beside *śuk-rá-* 'white'), *sthū-lá-* (AV.) 'thick' (beside *sthū-rá-*); **with connecting -a-**: *tṛp-á-la-* 'joyous', *bhṛm-a-lá-* (AV.) 'torpid', *mús-a-la-* (AV.) m. 'pestle', *śab-á-la-* 'mottled', *śám-a-la-* (AV.) n. 'defilement'; **with -i-**: *án-i-la-* m. 'wind', *trd-i-lá-* 'porous', *sal-i-lá-* 'surging' (beside *sar-i-rá-* VS. 'flood'); **with -u-**: *taṇḍ-u-lá-* (AV.) m. 'grain', *śak-u-lá-* (AV. VS.) m., a kind of fish.

-li and -lu : agent.

175. The suffix *-li* occurs only once as the equivalent of *-ri* in *aṅg-ú-li-* (VS[1].) f. 'finger' (beside *aṅg-ú-ri-*). Similarly *-lu* occurs only once as the equivalent of *-ru* in *patayā-lú-* (AV[1].) 'flying', formed from the conjugation stem *patáya-* (from *pat-* 'fly').

-va : agent.

176. This suffix forms about 20 adjectives and seven or eight substantives, mostly masculines with a concrete meaning. With one or two exceptions it is added directly to the root. The accent is rather oftener on the suffix than on the radical syllable. The root hardly ever appears in a strengthened form.

1. **Accented on the suffix** are the **adjectives**: *ūrdh-vá-* 'upright', *ṛk-vá-* 'praising', *ṛṣ-vá-* 'lofty', *tak-vá-* 'swift', *dhru-vá-* 'fixed', *pak-vá-* 'ripe', *mal-vá-* (AV.) 'foolish', *yah-vá-* 'swift', *raṇ-vá-* 'joyful', *viś-vá-*[1] 'all', *śik-vá-* (AV.) 'deft', *śyā-vá-* 'dark brown', *hras-vá-* (VS.) 'short'; the **substantives**: **m.** *ūr-vá-* 'stall', *śar-vá-* (AV. VS.), N. of a god, *sru-vá-* 'ladle'; f. *pruṣ-vā́-* (AV.) 'rime'; *vidh-á-vā-*[2] 'widow'.

2. **Accented on the root** are: *ṛ́bh-va-* 'skilful', *é-va-* 'quick', m. 'course', *pī́-va-* 'fat', *pū́r-va-* 'preceding', *vák-va-* 'twisting', *víś-va-* 'all', *sár-va-* 'all'; **m.** *áś-va-* 'horse', *khál-va-* (AV. VS.), a kind of grain, *srák-va-* 'corner of the mouth'; f. *ám-ī-vā-* 'disease'[3].

a. A few such derivatives occur only compounded with prefixes: *á-khar-va-* 'not shortened', *áti-kulva-* (VS.) 'too bald', *vi-bhā́-va-* 'brilliant'.

-van : agent.

177. This suffix is used almost exclusively to form agent nouns[4], both adjectives and substantives, which are mostly masculine, but sometimes neuter. Though the root is regularly accented[5], it almost invariably appears in its unstrengthened form. If it ends in a short vowel *-t-* is added before the suffix. The feminine of these words is regularly formed with *-varī* (179 a).

Examples of **adjectives** are: *ṛ́k-van-* 'praising', *kṛ́-t-van-* 'active', *drúh-van-* 'injurious', *pát-van-* 'flying', *pī́-van-* 'fat', *yáj-van-* 'sacrificing', *rā́-van-* (VS.)

1 Cp. BRUGMANN, Grundriss 2, p. 126.

2 Cp. ROTH, KZ. 19, 223; BRUGMANN, Grundriss 2, p. 126.

3 Also n. *úlba-* 'caul' if this stands for **úlva-* from *vṛ-* 'cover'.

4 The only action nouns are the few which in the active are employed as infinitives; cp. WHITNEY 1169 e.

5 The only exceptions are two words formed with the connecting vowel *-i-*, *mūṣ-i-ván-* 'robber', *san-i-t-van-* 'bestower', and two others from the reduplicated root, *rárā-van-* 'liberal', *cikit-ván-* 'wise'.

'bestowing', *śák-van-* (VS.) 'able', *sú-t-van-* 'pressing Soma'; **substantives: m.** *ádh-van-* 'road', *ár-van-* 'steed', *grá-van-* 'stone'; **n.** *túg-van-* 'ford', *dhán-van-* 'bow' and 'desert', *pár-van-* 'joint', *snā́-van-*[1] (AV. VS.) 'sinew'.

a. Several derivatives with *-van* are compounded with prepositions; thus *ati-ṣkád-van-* (VS.) 'transgressing', *upa-hás-van-* 'mocking', *vi-vás-van-* 'shining forth', *vi-mṛ́g-van-* (AV.) 'cleansing', *sam-bhṛ́-t-van-* (AV.) 'accumulating'[2].

-vana, -vani, -vanu : agent.

178. These rare suffixes are doubtless secondary forms of *-van*. They are all three accented: *-vana* and *-vanu* on the final, *-vani* on the first syllable. With ***-vana*** are formed: *vag-vaná-* 'talkative', *sat-vaná-*, m. 'warrior' (beside *sát-van-*), and from the reduplicated root *śuśuk-vaná-* 'shining' (√*śuc-*). The suffix ***-vani*** seems to be preferred for derivatives from the reduplicated root; thus besides *tur-váṇi-* 'overcoming', *bhur-váṇi-* 'restless', occur *jujur-váṇi-* 'praising', *tutur-váṇi-* 'desiring to gain', *dadhṛṣ-váṇi-* 'daring', *śuśuk-váni-* 'shining' (√*śuc-*); the obscure word *arhariṣváṇi-* 'exultant' seems to be derived with this suffix from an irregularly reduplicated form of *hṛṣ-* 'be excited'. With ***-vanu*** is formed only *vag-vanú-* m. 'noise'.

-vara, -vala : action and agent.

179. This suffix makes a few masculine nouns (f. *-ī*) chiefly accented on the final syllable of the suffix, and a very few neuter substantives accented on the root. The **masculines** are: *i-t-vará-* 'going', *īś-vará-* (AV.) 'able', *phár-vara-* 'sower', *vyadh-vará-* (AV.) 'piercing'[3] (√*vyadh-*). **Neuter substantives** are: *kár-vara-* 'deed', *gáh-vara-* (AV.) 'thicket'. There are also two **feminines** which have the appearance of being derived with this suffix, *ur-várā-* 'field' and *ur-várī-* (AV.) 'filament', but their origin is uncertain. This suffix appears **with *l*** instead of *r* in *vid-valá-* 'cunning'.

a. The f. of this suffix, *-varī*, is used as the f. of adjectives in *-van*, with which it corresponds in accent and treatment of the radical syllable. There are about 25 of these feminines in the RV.; e. g. *yáj-varī-* 'pious', *sṛ́-t-varī-* 'speeding'[4].

-vas : action and agent.

180. This very rare suffix forms only the neuter subtantive *vár-i-vas-* 'wide space' (beside *vár-i-man-*) and the adjectives *ṛ́bh-vas-* 'skilful' (beside *ṛ́bh-va-* and *ṛ́bh-van-*) and *śík-vas-* 'skilful' (beside *śík-van-*). The vocative *khid-vas* (VI. 22⁴) 'oppressing' is probably from a perfect participle *khid-vā́ṃs-*[5] formed without reduplication, not from a stem *khid-vas-*.

-vāṃs : agent.

181. This suffix is used to form a large number of **perfect participles** active, being added with or without the connecting vowel *-i-*; e. g. *cakṛ-vā́ṃs-* 'having done', *īy-i-vā́ṃs-* 'having gone'; sometimes without reduplication; e. g. *vid-vā́ṃs-* 'knowing'[6]. This suffix, which is always accented, is in the weak cases reduced to *-ús-* before vowels[7].

---

[1] On two or three doubtful derivatives with this suffix see WHITNEY 1169 b.

[2] Several others are compounded with nouns; see LINDNER p. 107.

[3] According to the Pada text *vi-adhvará-*.

[4] See WHITNEY 1171 b; for such feminines occurring in the AV. see his Index Verborum 375.

[5] Cp. pw.; in BR. the stem is given as *khid-van-*. According to WHITNEY 1173 b, it is derived from √*khād-*.

[6] For the forms occurring see below 492.

[7] See Declension, *-vāṃs* stems, 347.

-vi : agent.

182. This rare suffix is used to form some half dozen adjectives and one f. substantive, partly from the simple root (which is accented), partly from the reduplicated root (of which the reduplicative syllable is accented). The **adjectives** are: *ghṛ́ṣ-vi-* 'lively', *jír-vi-*[1] (AV.) 'aged', *dhrú-vi-* 'firm'; *jā́gṛ-vi-* 'watchful', *dā́-dhṛ-vi-* 'sustaining', *dī́-di-vi-* 'shining'[2]; f. *dár-vi-*[3] 'ladle'.

-vit : agent.

183. This suffix, which is perhaps an extension of *-vi* with *-t*, occurs in the single form *cikit-vít* (RV^1.) 'deliberately'.

-sa : agent.

184. This suffix is used to form about two dozen adjectives and substantives of all genders. It is added to the root with or without the connecting vowels *-ĭ-* or *-ŭ-*. The accent is sometimes on the suffix, sometimes on the root, which is usually unstrengthened. Many of these derivatives are of obscure origin.

The **suffix** is **added direct** in: *gṛ́t-sa-* 'adroit', *-dṛ́k-ṣa-*[4] (VS.), *pṛk-ṣá-* 'dappled' (√*pṛc-*); *út-sa-* m. 'fountain', *kút-sa-*, N. of a man, *ghraṃ-sá-* m. 'sun's heat', *drap-sá-* m. 'drop', *ruk-ṣá-* m. 'tree'; *bhī-ṣā́-*[5] f. 'fear'.

a. The suffix is added **with a connecting vowel** (*-ĭ-*, *-ŭ-*) in: *tav-i-ṣá-*[6] 'strong', *bhar-i-ṣá-* 'rapacious', *mah-i-ṣá-* 'mighty'[7]; *ṛj-ī-ṣá-* 'rushing', *ṛbī́-sa-*[8] n. 'chasm', *púr-ī-ṣa-* n. 'rubbish'; *man-ī-ṣā́-* f. 'devotion'; *ar-u-ṣá-*[9] 'red', *aś-úṣ-a-* 'voracious', *tár-u-ṣa-* m. 'overcomer', *púr-u-ṣa-* m. 'man', *mán-u-ṣa-* 'man'; *áṅg-ū-ṣá-* m. 'hymn', *pīy-ū́-ṣa-* n. 'biestings'.

-sani : agent.

185. This suffix is found only in the derivatives *car-ṣaṇí-* 'active', f. pl. 'people', and *par-ṣáṇi-* 'carrying across' (*pṛ-* 'cross').

-sara : agent.

186. This suffix appears only in *mat-sará-* 'intoxicating' (√*mad-*) and perhaps in *sap-sará-* (I. 168^9) 'inspiring awe'(?) if derived from *sap-* 'do homage'.

-sas : action.

187. This suffix seems to be contained in *váp-sas-* (RV^1.) 'beauty'(?)[10], and possibly in *tár-ū-ṣas-* (RV.) 'superior' (√*tṛ-*).

-sna : agent.

188. This suffix (perhaps syncopated for *-sana*) forms some half dozen adjectives and m. or n. substantives: *tīk-ṣṇá-* 'sharp' (√*tij*), *de-ṣṇá-*[11] n. 'gift'

---

[1] From *jṛ-* 'age'; see Whitney's note on AV. xiv. 1^{21}. The RV. has *jív-ri-*.

[2] The derivation of *pra-pharví-* (RV^1.) is uncertain.

[3] In VS. *dárvī-* in the vocative *darvi*.

[4] In *ī-dṛ́k-ṣa-* (VS.) 'looking like this' 'such' (from *dṛś-* 'see').

[5] Only in the I. s. *bhīṣā́* which is a contraction for *bhiyasā*.

[6] The f. is *táviṣī-*.

[7] The f. is *máhiṣī-*.

[8] The absence of cerebralization in the *s*, together with the *b*, makes the origin of this word quite uncertain; it is most probably borrowed.

[9] The f. is *áruṣī-*.

[10] This is Sāyaṇa's interpretation of the word.

[11] Generally to be read trisyllabically as *da-iṣṇá-*.

(*dā-* 'give'), *ślak-ṣṇá-* (AV.) 'smooth'; with connecting *-a-*: *kar-á-sna-* m. 'fore-arm', *mát-a-sna-*, n. 'lung', *vadh-a-sná-* n. 'deadly weapon'.

-snu : agent.

189. This suffix, which is always accented, forms adjectives, being added with or without a connecting vowel to the simple root, or more usually with connecting *-i-* to the causative stem.

1. **From the simple root**: *ji-ṣṇú-* 'victorious', *daṅk-ṣṇú-* (VS.) 'biting' (√*daṃś-*), *ni-ṣat-snú-* 'sitting down'; *vadh-a-snú-* 'murderous', *vṛdh-a-snú-* 'joyous'; *car-i-ṣṇú-* 'wandering', *á-maviṣṇu-*[1] (x. 94^{11}) 'immovable (√*mū-* = *mīv-*).

2. **From the causative stem**: *tāpay-i-ṣṇú-* 'tormenting', *namay-iṣṇú-* 'bending', *patay-i-ṣṇú-* 'flying', *pāray-i-ṣṇú-* 'saving', *poṣay-i-ṣṇú-* (AV.) 'causing to thrive', *māday-i-ṣṇú-* 'intoxicating', *abhi-śocay-i-ṣṇu-* (AV.) 'causing torments'.

II. Secondary Nominal Derivation.

Lindner, Altindische Nominalbildung p. 114—52. — Whitney, Sanskrit Grammar p. 454—80.

190. Secondary nominal stems are those derived from stems already ending in a suffix. They, however, include derivatives from pronominal roots, as *i-tara-* 'other', and exceptionally from indeclinable words or case-forms, as *antár-vant-* 'pregnant' (*antár* 'within'), *máma-ka-* 'belonging to me' (*máma* 'of me)'. The stem to which secondary suffixes are added is subject to certain changes. Thus final *-a* and *-i* vowels are regularly dropped before suffixes beginning with a vowel or *y*, while final *-u* generally takes Guṇa; thus *aśv-ín-* 'possessing horses' (*áśva-*), *khād-ín-* 'adorned with rings' (*khādí-*), *vāyav-yà-* 'relating to the wind' (*vāyú-*). Again, the *n* or the *a* of stems ending in *-an* is occasionally lost, e. g. *vṛṣa-tvá-* 'manly power', *vṛ́ṣṇ-ya-* 'manly' (but *vṛ́ṣaṇ-vant-* 'drawn by stallions'); while stems in *-ant* regularly appear in the weak form of *-at*, e. g. *váivasvat-a-* 'son of Vivásvant'. The commonest change is, however, the strengthening of the initial syllable with **Vṛddhi**[2], e. g. *āmitrá-* 'hostile' (*a-mitra-* 'enemy'), *pā́rthiv-a-* 'relating to the earth' (*pṛthiví-*), *maitrāvaruṇá-* 'derived from Mitrā́-váruṇa', *sáubhaga-* 'luck' (*su-bhága-* 'lucky').

As regards **meaning**, the great majority of secondary suffixes form adjectives with the general sense of 'relating to' or 'connected with'. In several, however, the meaning has become specific. Thus the suffixes *-āyana*, *-i*, *-eya*, form patronymics or metronymics; *-in*, *-mant*, *-vant* express possession; *-tama* and *-tara* imply degrees of comparison; *-tā* and *-tva* form abstract substantives. The masculines and feminines of adjectives are frequently used as appellatives, while the neuter is commonly employed as a substantive expressing the attributive sense of the adjective as an abstraction.

a. The **secondary suffixes** are in their alphabetical order the following: *-a*, *-ā*, *-ānī*, *āyana*, *āyī*, *āyya*, *-i*, *-in*, *-ima*, *-iya*, *-ī*, *-īna*, *-īya*, *-enī*, *-enya*, *-eya*, *-eyya*, *-ka*, *-ta*, *-tana* and *-tna*, *-tama*, *-taya*, *-tara*, *-tavya*, *-tā*, *-tāt*, *-tāti*, *-tya*, *-tva*, *-tvatā*, *-tvana*, *-tha*, *-na*, *-nī*, *-bha*, *-ma*, *-mant*, *-maya*, *-min*, *-mna*, *-ya*, *-yin*, *-ra*, *-la*, *-va*, *-vat*, *-van*, *-vant*, *-vaya*, *-vala*, *-vin*, *-vya*, *-śa*.

---

[1] Thus derived in pw.; in BR. emended to *á-mariṣṇu-* 'immortal'; in Grassmann explained as *áma-viṣṇu-* 'mit Ungestüm andringend'.

[2] Strengthening with Guṇa is, on the other hand, extremely rare in secondary derivation, as *devá-* 'divine' (*dív-* 'heaven'), *dróṇa-* 'wooden vessel' (*drú-* 'wood'), *bheṣaj-á-* 'medicine' (*bhiṣáj-* 'healing'); cp. 191 a α.

191. With the **suffix** *-a* is formed a very large number of derivatives which are primarily adjectives expressing the sense of relation to or connexion with the primitive word; in the m. and f. they are, however, often used as appellatives, and in the neuter as abstracts. The first syllable of the primitive word, whether it is simple or compound is in the great majority of instances strengthened **with Vṛddhi**; e. g. *mấrut-a-* 'relating to the Maruts' (*marút-*), *mấghon-a-* n. 'bountifulness' (*maghávan-* 'bountiful')[1], *dāśarājñ-á-* 'battle of the ten kings' (*daśa-rājan-*)[2]; *jaítr-a-* 'victorious' (*jé-tṛ-* 'conqueror'), *tvāṣṭr-á-* 'belonging to Tvaṣṭṛ'; *mānav-á-* 'belonging to man' (*mánu-*), *tấnv-a-*[3] 'belonging to the body' (*tanú-*); *sārasvat-á-* 'coming from the Sarasvatī', *aindrāgn-á-* (AV. VS. TS.) 'belonging to Indra and Agni' (*indrāgnī́*); *yāmun-á-* (AV.) 'coming from the Yamunā'; *vấdhryaśv-a-*[4] 'descended from Vadhryaśvá', *vaiśvadev-á-* (AV. VS.) 'sacred to all the gods' (*viśvá-deva-*).

a. A comparatively small number of derivatives add the suffix **without** taking **Vṛddhi**. These are probably to a considerable extent due to transfers from other declensions to the *a*-declension. Such are *tamas-á-* (AV.) 'dark-coloured', *paruṣ-á-* 'knotty' (*párus-* 'knot'), *hemant-á-* 'winter'; *ápāk-a-* 'distant' (*ápāñc-* 'behind'); *hotr-á-* 'office of priest' (*hótṛ-*); *sakhy-á-* 'friendship' (*sákhi-* 'friend').

a. With Guṇa are formed *tray-á-* 'threefold' (*tri-* 'three'), *dvay-á-* 'twofold' (*dvi-* 'two'), *náv-a-* 'new' (*nú-* 'now'); *dev-á-* 'divine' (*div-* 'heaven'), *bheṣaj-á-* 'medicine' (*bhiṣáj-* 'healer').

192. The **suffix** *-ā* is used in a very large number of stems to form the feminine of adjectives which in the masculine and neuter end in *-a*. Thus *náv-ā-* f., *náva-* m. n. 'new'; *priy-ā́-* f., *priyá-* m. n. 'dear'; *gat-ā́-* f., *gatá-* m. n. 'gone'.

193. The **suffix** *-ānī*[5] is used to form the feminine from stems in *-a*, designating the wife of the corresponding male being, or expressing a feminine personification: *araṇy-ānī́-* 'Forest Nymph' (*áraṇya-* 'forest'), *indr-ānī́-* 'wife of Indra', *uśīnár-ānī-* 'Queen of the Uśīnaras', *ūrj-ā́nī-* 'Strength' (personified), *purukúts-ānī-* 'wife of Purukutsa', *mudgal-ā́nī-* 'wife of Mudgala', *varuṇ-ānī́-* 'Varuṇa's wife'.

194. The **suffix** *-āyana-* forms a few patronymics **with Vṛddhi** in the first syllable: *ānty-āyaná-* (VS. TS.) 'descendant of Āntya', *āmuṣy-āyaṇá-* (AV.) 'descendant of so and so' (*amúṣya-* gen. of *adás*), *kāṇv-āyana-* 'descendant of Kaṇva', *dākṣ-āyaṇá-* (VS. AV.) 'descendant of Dakṣa'; also the f. *rām-āyaṇī́-* (AV.) 'daughter of the Black One' (*rāmá-*). The derivative *ukṣaṇ-áyana-*, N. of a man, being formed without Vṛddhi is perhaps not meant for a patronymic.

195. The **suffix** *-áyī* occurs perhaps only twice, forming the feminine from two masculine stems in *-i* and designating the wife of the corresponding male: *agn-āyī-* 'wife of Agni' and *vṛṣākap-āyī-* (only voc.) 'wife of Vṛṣākapi'.

196. The **suffix** *-āyya* forms gerundives[6]; e. g. *śrav-ā́yya-* 'glorious' (*śru-* 'hear'). There are also a few other derivatives similarly formed, which are used as ordinary adjectives or as neuter abstracts; thus *nṛ-pā́yya-* 'guarding

---

[1] Formed from the weakest stem *maghón-*.

[2] With syncope of the vowel of the suffix.

[3] Without Guṇa of the *ū*; similar exceptions in *pārśv-á-* 'side' (*párśu-* 'rib'), *paidv-á-* 'belonging to Pedu', *mā́dhv-a-* 'full of sweetness' (*mádhu-*), *yā́dv-a-* 'belonging to Yadu'.

[4] It is natural to suppose that the suffix *-a* is added to stems in *-a* as to others (the final vowel of the primitive disappearing before it) and not that derivation by Vṛddhi alone takes place here; cp. Whitney 1208 i.

[5] Cp. Leumann, KZ. 32, 294 ff.

[6] These are probably formed from dative infinitives in *-ai* + *-ya*; cp. Brugmann, Grundriss 2, p. 1422; cp. also IF. 12, 2.

men', *bahu-pā́yya-* 'protecting many'; *pūrva-pā́yya-* 'first drink', *mahay-ā́yya-* 'enjoyment', *kuṇḍa-pā́yya-* and *puru-mā́yya-* as Proper Names; also formed from nouns, *ras-ā́yya-* 'tasteful' (*rása-* 'sap') and *uttam-ā́yya-* n. 'summit' (*uttamá-* 'highest')[1].

197. The **suffix** *-i* forms a few patronymics from nouns in *-a* **with Vṛddhi** in the initial syllable: *ā́gniveś-i-* 'descendant of Agniveśa', *pā́urukuts-i-* 'son of Purukutsa', *prā́tardan-i-* 'descendant of Pratardana', *prā́hrād-i-* (AV.) 'son of Prahrāda, *sā́ṃvaraṇ-i-* 'descendant of Saṃvaraṇa'. Similarly formed, but with the sense of an ordinary substantive, is *sā́rath-i-* 'charioteer' (from *sa-rátha-m* 'on the same chariot'). Two other words add a secondary *-i* without Vṛddhi or patronymic sense: *tápuṣ-i-* 'burning' and *śucant-í-*, N. of a man (seemingly an extension of the participle *śuc-ánt-* 'shining')

198. Hundreds of adjectives are formed with the **suffix** *-in* from stems in *-a*, but very rarely from stems with any other final; e. g. *ark-ín-* 'praising' (*arká-* 'praise'), *manīṣ-ín-* 'wise' (*manī-ṣā́-* 'wisdom'), *arc-ín-* 'radiant' (*arcí-* 'beam'), *śatagv-ín-* 'consisting of hundreds' (**śata-gva-*), *varm-ín-* 'clad in armour' (*várman-*), *śvan-ín-* (VS.) 'keeping dogs' (*śván-*). With loss of final *-as*: *ret-ín-* 'abounding in seed' (*rétas-*) and perhaps in the Proper Name *varc-ín-* (*várc-as-* 'power'); with loss of *-ya*: *hiraṇ-ín-* 'adorned with gold' (*híraṇ-ya-*).

199. The **suffix** *-ima* is very rare, being employed to form adjectives from the stems in *-tra* and from one in *-ra*: *kṛtr-íma-* 'artificial', *khanítr-ima-* 'made by digging', *pūtr-íma-* (AV.) 'purified'; *agr-imá-* 'foremost' (*ág-ra-* 'front').

200. The **suffix** *-iya* is employed to form some 20 adjectives (from stems in *-a*). It is only a modified form of *-ya* which is added for facility of pronunciation after two or more consonants, the last of which is generally *r*, rarely *n*, *m* or *v*; e. g. *abhr-iyá-* 'derived from the clouds' (*abhrá-*), *samudr-íya-* 'belonging to the sea' (*samudrá*)-, *indr-iyá-* 'belonging to Indra'; *kṛṣṇ-iyá-*, N. of a man (*kṛṣṇá-* 'black'); *ṛgm-íya* 'praiseworthy'; *aśv-iyá-* 'consisting of horses', 'troop'.

201. The **suffix** *-ī* is employed in a very large number of derivatives to form the feminine of masculine stems; often from stems in *-a*[2]; e. g. *áruṣ-ī-* 'ruddy' (*aruṣá-*), *dev-ī́-* 'goddess' (*devá-*); or in *-u*; e. g. *pṛthv-ī́-* 'broad' (*pṛth-ú-*); or from stems formed with suffixes ending in consonants, as participles in *-at* or *-ant*, e. g. *píprat-ī-* ,'protecting' (*pṛ-* 'take across'), *ad-at-ī́-* 'eating' (*ad-ánt-*), *mád-ant-ī* 'rejoicing' or in *-vā́ṃs-*, e. g. *jagm-úṣ-ī-* 'having gone'; comparatives in *-īyāṃs-*, e. g. *náv-īyas-ī-* 'new'; stems in *-tar*, e. g. *avitr-ī́-* 'protectress'; in *-mant*, e. g. *dhenu-mát-ī-* 'abounding in nourishment'; in *-vant*, e. g. *áma-vat-ī-* 'impetuous'; in *-an*, e. g. *sóma-rājñ-ī-* 'having Soma as king'; in *-in*, e. g. *arkíṇ-ī-* 'radiant'; in *-añc*, e. g. *arvā́c-ī-* 'hitherward'; in compounds of *-han* 'slaying', e. g. *a-pati-ghn-ī-* 'not killing a husband', of *-dṛś-* 'look', as *su-dṛ́ś-ī-* 'well-looking', and of *-pád* 'foot', as *a-pád-ī-* 'footless'.

202. The **suffix** *-īna* forms more than a dozen adjectives from the weak stems of derivatives in *-añc-*, expressing direction without change of meaning; e. g. *arvāc-ína-* and *arvāc-īná-* 'turned towards' (*arvā́ñc-* 'hitherward'). It also forms six or seven adjectives from other words, expressing the general sense of relation; e. g. *añjas-ína-* 'straightforward' (*añjasa-* 'straight'), *viśvajan-ína-* (AV.) 'containing all kinds of people'.

---

[1] See Whitney 1218 a.

[2] This is regularly the case in stems formed with Vṛddhi in the initial syllable; e. g. *mā́nuṣ-a-* 'human', f. *mā́nuṣ-ī-*.

203. The suffix ***-īya*** forms fewer than a dozen general adjectives, of which only two occur in the RV.; e. g. *ārjīk-íya-*, designation of a Soma vessel, *gṛha-medh-íya-* 'relating to the domestic sacrifice'; *āhav-an-íya-* (AV.) 'sacrificial fire', *parvat-íya-* (AV.) 'mountainous'. This suffix also appears in the three ordinals *dvit-íya-* 'second', *tṛt-íya-* 'third', *tur-íya-* 'fourth'.

204. The suffix ***-ena*** with Vṛddhi of the initial syllable, occurs only once, forming a general adjective, in its feminine form *sāmidh-ení-* 'relating to fuel' (*samídh-*).

205. The suffix ***-enya*** was doubtless originally formed by the addition of *-ya* to derivatives made with *-na*, but it nearly always has a primary value as forming gerundives; e. g. *dṛś-énya-* 'worthy to be seen'. It appears, however, also in the two ordinary adjectives *kīrt-énya-* 'famous' (*kīrtí-* 'fame') and *vīr-éṇya-* 'manly' (*vīrá-* 'hero').

206. The suffix ***-eya***, with Vṛddhi of the initial syllable, is employed to form fewer than a dozen adjectives of a patronymic or metronymic value and some half dozen adjectives of a general character, the latter occasionally appearing in the neuter as abstract substantives; e. g. *ārṣ-eyá-* 'descended from a seer' (*ṛ́ṣi-*), *ādit-eyá-* 'son of Aditi'; *páuruṣ-eya-* 'relating to man' (*púruṣa-*), *máun-eya-* 'position of a sage' (*múni-*). Two words with this suffix are formed without initial Vṛddhi, following the analogy of gerundives from roots ending in *ā* like *déya-* 'to be given' (*dā-* 'give'): *didṛkṣ-éya-* 'worth seeing' (as from *didṛk-ṣā-* 'desire to see') and *sabh-éya-* 'fit for an assembly' (*sabhā́-*).

207. The very rare suffix ***-eyya*** forms adjectives with a gerundive sense in *stuṣ-éyya-*[1] 'praise-worthy', and *śapath-eyyà-* (AV.) 'worthy of cursing'. It also forms an ordinary adjective used as a neuter substantive, *sahaś-éyya-* n. 'lying together' (*śī-* 'lie)'.

208. The suffix ***-ka*** was probably used originally to form adjectives expressive of connexion, but it has become so attenuated in meaning as often to be added to substantives or adjectives without changing the sense; while on the other hand it has become specialized as a suffix forming diminutives. **1.** Examples of its **significant use** are: *ánta-ka-* 'making an end' (*ánta-*), *rūpa-ka-* (AV.) 'having an assumed form' (*rūpá-* 'form'); *asmā́-ka-* 'our' (*asmá-* 'us'), *máma-ka-* 'my' (*máma* 'of me'); *ánti-ka-* 'near' (*ánti* 'before'). **2.** The suffix appears **without changing the meaning** in e. g. *dūra-ká-* 'distant' (*dūrá-* 'far'), *vamra-ká-* 'ant' (*vamrá-* 'ant'), *sarva-ká-* (AV.) 'all' (*sárva-*), and in the fem. form of *-kā* in: *avi-kā́-* 'ewe' (*ávi-* 'sheep'), *iṣu-kā́-* (AV.) 'arrow' (*íṣu-*), *dhénu-kā-* (AV.) 'cow' (*dhenú-*). **3.** The **diminutive sense** appears in e. g. *arbha-ká-* 'small', *kumāra-ká-* 'little boy', *pāda-ká-* 'little foot', *putra-ká-* 'little son'[2]. Sometimes a contemptuous meaning is conveyed at the same time, as in *anya-ká-* 'other' (*anyá-*), *ála-ka-m* 'in vain' (*ála-m* 'enough')[3].

a. **With Vṛddhi** in the first syllable is formed *māma-ká-*[4] 'belonging to me' (*máma*); and with connecting *-i-*: *vā́rṣ-i-ka-* (AV. VS.) 'belonging to the rains' (*varṣá-*), *vā́sant-i-ka-* 'belonging to the spring' (*vasantá-*), and in the fem. *kairāt-ikā́-* (AV.) 'relating to the Kirātas'.

209. The rare secondary suffix ***-ta*** has an ordinal sense in *eka-tá-* (VS.)

---

[1] This gerundive is probably based on the infinitive *stuṣé* 'to praise'; cp. BRUGMANN, Grundriss 2, p. 1422 (5).

[2] The feminine of some of these diminutives is formed with *-ikā*: *iyatt-ikā-* 'so small', *kumār-ikā́-* (AV.) 'little girl', *khárv-ikā-* (AV.) 'mutilated', *śakunt-ikā́-* 'little bird', *śīt-ikā-* 'cool' (AV. *śītá-* 'cold').

[3] Cp. WHITNEY 521.

[4] Beside the more normal *máma-ka-*.

'First', *dvi-tá-* 'Second', *tri-tá-* 'Third' as Proper Names. It also appears in *ava-tá-* 'well' and *muhūr-tá-* 'moment'.

210. With the suffix **-tana** and its syncopated form *-tna* are made, from adverbs or prepositions, a very few adjectives with a temporal sense: *nú-tana-* and *nú-tna-* 'present' (*nú* 'now'), *sanā-tána-* (AV.) and *saná-tna-* (AV.) 'eternal' (*sánā* 'from of old'), *pra-tná-* 'ancient' (*prá* 'before').

211. The suffix **-tama** has two uses. It is employed to form superlatives from nominal stems and from the preposition *úd*; e. g. *puru-táma-* 'very many', *mádhumat-tama-* 'very sweet', *rathī́-tama-*[1] 'best charioteer'; *ut-tamá-*[2] 'highest'. It is also used to form ordinals; e. g. *śata-tamá-* 'hundredth'.

212. With the suffix **-taya** are formed only two adjectives from numerals in the sense of 'consisting of so many parts': *cátuṣ-ṭaya-* (AV.) 'fourfold' and *dáśa-taya-* 'tenfold'.

213. The suffix **-tara** is regularly used to form comparatives from adjectives, substantives, or the preposition *úd*; e. g. *tavás-tara-* 'stronger', *rathī́-tara-* 'better charioteer', *vṛtra-tára-* 'worse Vṛtra'; *út-tara-* 'higher'. It also forms the ordinary adjective *dívā-tara-* (RV[1].) 'diurnal' (*dívā* 'by day'), and a few substantives in which the meaning of the suffix is somewhat obscure: *aśva-tára-*[3] (AV.) 'mule' (f. *-ī*), *vatsa-tará-*[4] 'weaned calf'[5] (f. *-ī*).

214. The suffix **-tav-ya**, probably originating from the predicative use of dative infinitives in *-tav-e* and beginning to be used in a gerundive sense, appears only twice in the AV.: *jan-i-tav-yà-* 'to be born' and *hiṃs-i-tav-yà-* 'to be injured'.

215. The suffix **-tā** forms, from adjectives and substantives, some two dozen abstract nouns expressing the sense conveyed by the English suffixes *-ness* and *-ship*; e. g. *bandhú-tā-* 'relationship', *vasú-tā-* 'wealthiness'; *agó-tā-* 'lack of cattle', *devá-tā-* 'divinity', *puruṣá-tā-* 'human nature'; *janá-tā-* (AV.) has acquired the concrete sense of 'mankind'[6]. Exceptional formation appears in *mamá-tā-* 'selfishness' and *tré-tā-*[7] (VS. TS.) 'triad'. This suffix is probably contained in *sū-nṛ́-tā-*[8] 'gladness' also.

a. The suffixes **-tāti** and **-tāt** are related to *-tā* and have the same sense. With the former are made about a dozen abstract substantives; e. g. *a-riṣṭá-tāti-* 'security', *gṛbhītá-tāti-* 'the being seized', *jyeṣṭhá-tāti-* 'superiority', *devá-tāti-* 'divinity', *vasú-tāti-* 'wealth', *sarvá-tāti-* 'completeness'. The two substantives *śáṃ-tāti-* 'good fortune' and *satyá-tāti-* 'truth' also appear as adjectives meaning respectively 'beneficent' and 'truthful'. The suffix *-tāt*, which seems to be an abbreviation of *-tāti* and occurs only in the RV., is employed to form four or five abstract substantives: *upará-tāt-* 'proximity', *devá-tāt-* 'divine service', *vṛká-tāt-* 'wolfishness', *sarvá-tāt-* 'completeness'.

216. The suffix **-tya** forms some half dozen adjectives and substantives from prepositions and adverbs. These are *ápa-tya-* n. 'offspring', *amā́-tya-* 'companion' (*amā́* 'at home'), *āvíṣ-ṭya-* 'manifest' (*āvís* 'openly'), *níṣ-ṭya-* 'foreign' (*nís* 'out'), *sánu-tya-* 'secret'[9]. This suffix is also added to

1 Also in the Proper Name *gó-tama-*.

2 The superlatives *túvi-ṣ-ṭama-* 'strongest' and *surabhí-ṣ-ṭama-* 'most fragrant' insert a sibilant before the suffix.

3 Perhaps 'more (like a) horse' (than an ass).

4 Probably 'more than a calf'.

5 In *ratham-tará-*, designation of a kind of Sāman, in which the case ending of the acc. remains, the second part is doubtless the verbal *-tara* 'speeding' (*tṛ-* 'cross'). *kārotará-* 'filter' and *kaulitará-*, designation of Śambara, are probably formed with *-a* and Vṛddhi.

6 Like 'humanity' in English.

7 Also in *tret-ín-ī-* (RV.) 'the threefold flame of three fires'.

8 Though it appears also as a neuter *sū-nṛ́ta-* 'gladness' and as an adjective 'joyful'.

9 Cp. *sanu-tár* 'aside'.

the substantive *āp-* 'water' to form the two adjectives *ap-tyá-* and *āp-tyá-* 'watery'.

217. With the **suffix *-tva*** are formed more than thirty abstract substantives with the same sense as those in *-tā*; e. g. *amṛta-tvá-* 'immortality', *aham-uttara-tvá-* (AV.) 'assertion of superiority', *bhrātṛ-tvá-* 'brotherhood', *maghavat-tvá-* 'liberality', *rakṣas-tvá-* 'sorcery'. The final syllable of the primitive is lengthened in *an-āgās-tvá-* 'sinlessness'; while it is shortened in *sadhani-tvá-*[1] 'companionship'. Owing to the influence of the nominative, *s* is inserted before the suffix in *su-prajā-s-tvá-* 'possession of many children' and with initial Vṛddhi in *sauprajā-s-tvá-*[2] (AV[1].) 'possession of good offspring'.

a. The two suffixes *-tā* and *-tva*, identical in meaning, are pleonastically combined in the form of ***-tva-tā-*** in the two derivatives *iṣita-tvátā-* 'excitement', and *puruṣa-tvátā-* 'human nature'.

218. The **suffix *-tvana***, an extension of *-tva* with *-na*, appears in the formation of some eight neuter abstracts occurring almost exclusively in the RV. These are *kavi-tvaná-* 'wisdom', *jani-tvaná-* 'state of a wife'; *pati-tvaná-* 'matrimony', *martya-tvaná-* 'the ways of man', *mahi-tvaná-* 'greatness', *vasu-tvaná-* 'wealth', *vṛṣa-tvaná-* 'manliness', *sakhi-tvaná-* 'friendship'. All of these except *martya-tvaná-* have beside them the corresponding abstracts formed with *-tva*[3].

219. The **suffix *-tha*** forms a few ordinals from cardinals, and adjectives from pronominal stems with a general numerical sense. Thus *catur-thá* (AV.) 'fourth', *ṣaṣ-ṭhá-* (AV. VS.) 'sixth', *saptá-tha-* 'seventh'; *kati-thá-* 'the how manieth?'.

220. The rare secondary **suffix *-na*** appears in one adjective derived with initial Vṛddhi from a substantive, *strái-ṇa-* 'feminine' (*strī́-* 'woman), and in three adjectives derived from adverbs without any internal change: *purā-ṇá-* 'ancient (*purā́* 'before'), *víṣu-ṇa-* 'various' (*víṣu-* 'apart'), *samā-ná-* 'like' (*samá-* 'equal').

221. The **suffix *-nī*** is used to form the feminine of *páti-* 'lord' and *paruṣ-á-* 'knotty', as well as of several adjectives in *-ta* denoting colours. Thus *pát-nī-* 'mistress', *páruṣ-ṇī-*, as N. of a river. The suffix is substituted for *-ta* in *é-nī-* 'variegated' (*é-ta-*), *róhi-ṇī-* 'red cow' (*róhi-ta-* 'red'), *śyé-nī-* 'white cow' (*śye-tá-* 'white'), *hári-ṇī-* 'fallow' (*hári-ta-*). In a few such words *-nī* is substituted for the final *a*, while *k* takes the place of the *t*[4]: *ásik-nī-* 'black' (*ási-ta-*), *pálik-nī-* 'grey' (*pali-tá-*), *hárik-ṇī-* in the diminutive form *hárikn-ikā-* (AV.) 'yellowish' (*hári-ta-* 'fallow').

222. The **suffix *-bha*** forms half a dozen derivatives, all names of animals except one adjective[5]: *ṛṣa-bhá-* and *vṛṣa-bhá-* 'bull', *garda-bhá-* and *rā́sa-bha-*[6] 'ass', *śara-bhá-* (AV. VS.) 'fabulous eightlegged animal'. The one adjective is *sthūla-bhá-* (AV[1].) beside *sthūlá-* 'big'.

223. The **suffix *-ma*** forms some eight superlatives, partly from prepositions, and the ordinals from the cardinals for 'five' and 'seven', 'eight', 'nine', 'ten'. The former are: *adha-má-* 'lowest', *apa-má-* 'farthest', *ava-má-* 'lowest',

---

1 From *sadha-nī́-* ('one who leads with him') 'companion', which is, however, analysed in the Pada text as *sa-dhanī́-*.

2 *saubhaga-tvá-* 'happiness' is formed from *sáubhaga-* 'welfare' = 'condition of welfare', not from *su-bhága-* 'lucky', from which is formed *subhaga-tvá-* 'welfare'.

3 Cp. LINDNER 26 and 28.

4 See BRUGMANN, Morphologische Untersuchungen 2, p. 198, and Grundriss 2, p. 315.

5 See BRUGMANN, Grundriss 2, p. 203; cp. p. 89, note 2.

6 Formed, with Vṛddhi and accented on the initial syllable, from *ras-* 'roar', 'bray' etc.

upa-má- 'highest', *ánta-ma-*[1] 'nearest', *cara-má-* 'last', *para-má-* 'remotest', *madhya-má-* 'middlemost'. The ordinals are: *pañca-má-* (AV. VS.) 'fifth', *sapta-má-* (VS.) 'seventh', *aṣṭa-má-* 'eighth', *nava-má-* 'ninth', *daśa-má-* 'tenth'.

224. The **suffix** ***-mant*** forms in the Saṃhitās between 80 and 90 possessive adjectives, like the parallel suffix *-vant*[2], with which it is to some extent interchangeable. Unlike *-vant*, however, it never forms derivatives from stems ending in *-ă* except *káṇva-mant-* (RV[1].) 'prepared by the Kaṇvas' and *yáva-mant-* 'rich in barley'. Examples are: *aśáni-mant-* 'possessing the thunderbolt', *óṣadhi-mant-* (AV.) 'rich in herbs', *krátu-mant-* 'having power', *vadhū-mant-* 'drawn by mares'(?), *hótṛ-mant-* 'provided with a sacrificer', *gó-mant-* 'rich in kine', *virúk-mant-* 'gleaming', *garút-mant-* 'winged'(?), *kakúd-mant-*[3] 'provided with a hump', *cákṣuṣ-mant-* 'possessed of eyes', *vidyún-mant-*[4] 'containing lightning'.

a. A final *-i* is sometimes lengthened: *tviṣī-mant-* 'vehement' (*tviṣi-* 'vehemence'), *dhrájī-mant-* 'gliding' (*dhráji-* = *dhrā́ji-* 'gliding motion'), *hirī-mant-* 'tawny-horsed' (*hiri-* = *hári-* 'bay steed'); *-ī-* is inserted in *jyótiṣ-ī-mant-* (AV.)[5] 'full of light' (beside *jyótiṣ-mant-*), and *s* in *śuci-ṣ-mant-*[6] 'shining'. In the derivative *suṣu-mánt-* (RV[1].) 'very stimulating' the suffix seems to have primary value[7]. The adverb *āśu-mát* (AV[1]), formed from the neuter of this suffix, seems to follow the analogy of adverbs in *-vat* from derivatives in *-vant*.

225. The **suffix** ***-maya*** (f. *-ī*) forms fewer than a dozen adjectives with the sense of 'consisting of', 'derived from', 'abounding in'. The suffix *-as* remains unchanged before the *m*, but *d* is assimilated as in external Sandhi. Derivatives thus formed are: *ayas-máya-* 'made of metal', *aśman-máya-* 'made of stone', *kim-máya-* 'consisting of what?', *go-máya-* 'consisting of cattle', *nabhas-máya-* 'vaporous', *manas-máya-* 'spiritual', *mṛn-máya-* 'made of clay' (*mṛd-*), *śaka-máya-* 'arising from dung', *sū-máya-*[8] 'well-fashioned'.

226. The suffix ***-min*** was most probably due to the derivatives in *-in* from nouns in *-ma*, like *dhūm-ín-* 'smoking' (*dhūmá-* 'smoke') which are fairly common. It has an independent character, however, in *iṣ-mín-* 'impetuous' and *ṛg-mín-*[9] 'jubilant with praise' (*ṛ́c-*).

227. The rare **suffix** ***-mna*** forms a few neuter abstracts from nouns or particles. It seems to be an extension with *-a* of *-man* syncopated like *-tna* for *-tana*. The derivatives formed with it are: *dyu-mná-* 'brightness' (*dyú-* 'sky'), *nṛ-mṇá-* 'manliness' (*nṛ́-* 'man'), *ni-mná-* 'depth' (*ní* 'down'), *su-mná-* 'welfare' (*su-* 'well').

228. The very common **suffix** ***-ya***[10] forms a large number of adjectives of relation, including a good many patronymics, and abstract substantives. It is pronounced *-ia* nearly four times as often as *-ya*. The feminine is usually *-yā*, both in adjectives and abstract substantives; but in the former it is sometimes *-ī*, as *ár-ī-* and *ár-yā-* 'Āryan', *dáiv-ī-*[11] and *dáiv-yā-* 'divine'.

a. All the **patronymics** besides a good many general adjectives, and most of the **abstract substantives** are formed with **initial Vṛddhi**; e. g. *ādit-yá-* 'Son of Aditi', *sāhadev-yá-* 'descendant of Sahadeva'; *gráiv-ya-* (AV.) 'relating to the neck' (*grīvā́-*), *dáiv-ya-* 'divine' (*devá-* 'god'), *prājāpat-yá-* (AV.)

---

[1] Once (I. 165[5]) *anta-má-*; cp. p. 89, note 3.

[2] Which is, however, about three times as common.

[3] The VS. has *kakún-mant-* as in external Sandhi.

[4] With assimilated *t* as in external Sandhi.

[5] Following the analogy of *táviṣī-mant-* 'strong',

[6] Occurring only once in the vocative *śuciṣ-mas.*

[7] The word is analysed in the Pada text as *suṣu-mán.*

[8] This derivative seems to preserve the originally nominal character of this suffix.

[9] In this derivative the original guttural appears, though it has become sonant as in external Sandhi.

[10] See WHITNEY 1210—1213 (p. 459—466) and LINDNER 36 (p. 138—144).

[11] These are evident instances of the reduction of unaccented *yā* to *ī*; cp. 24 a.

'relating to Prajāpati'; *ā́dhipat-ya-* 'lordship' (*ádhi-pati-* 'lord'), *jā́narāj-ya-* (VS.) 'kingship' (*jana-rā́jan-* 'king of the people'), *vaimanas-yá-* (AV.) 'dejection' (*ví-manas-*), *sā́ṃgrāmajit-ya-* (AV.) 'victory in battle' (*saṃgrāma-jít-* AV.) 'conquering in battle'), *sáuvaśv-ya-*[1] 'wealth in horses' (*sv-áśva-*).

b. Derivatives formed **without Vṛddhi** are mostly **ordinary adjectives**, being about four times as numerous as those formed with Vṛddhi. They are made from stems with all kinds of finals. The following are examples: *áśv-ya-* 'relating to horses' (*áśva-*); *urvar-yà-* (VS.) 'belonging to cultivated land' (*urvárā-*); *áv-ya-* 'belonging to sheep' (*ávi-*); *vāyav-yà-*[2] 'belonging to wind' (*vāyú-*); *nár-ya-* 'manly' (*nṛ́-* 'man'); *pítr-ya-* 'belonging to the fathers' (*pitṛ́-*); *gáv-ya-* 'derived from cows' (*gó-*); *nāv-yà-* (AV.) 'navigable' (*náu-* 'boat'), *svarā́j-ya-* 'autocracy' (*sva-rā́j-* 'sovereign'); *karmaṇ-yà-* 'skilful in work' (*kárman-*), *vṛ́ṣṇ-ya-*[3] 'virile' (*vṛ́ṣan-* 'male'); *sat-yá-*[4] 'true' (*sánt-*), *prāc-yà-* (AV.) 'eastern' (*prā́ñc-*); *āyuṣ-yà-* (VS. AV.) 'length of life' (*ā́yus-*).

α. The final *-a* is retained before the suffix in *hiraṇyá-ya-* 'made of gold' (*hiraṇya-*), while *-an* is dropped before it in *aryam-yà-* 'intimate' (*arya-mán-* 'companion'). The suffix is added pleonastically in *avyá-ya-* and *ávya-ya-* 'belonging to sheep' (beside *áv-ya-*) and *gavyá-ya-* 'derived from cows' (beside *gáv-ya-*); also in forming a few possessive compounds, as *su-hást-ya-* 'skilful-handed' (beside *su-hásta-*)[5]. It is also used in forming a few governing compounds, as *ádhi-gart-ya-* 'being on the driver's seat' (*gárta-*), *abhi-nabh-yá-m*, adv. 'near the clouds' (*nábhas-*)[6].

β. In some adjectives and substantives, the suffix has a primary appearance; e. g. *púṣ-ya-* 'flower', *yúj-ya-* 'related', *mádh-ya-* 'middle', *már-ya-* 'young man', *sū́r-ya-* 'sun', f. *sūr-yā́-*[7] (*svàr-* 'light').

γ. Though as a gerundive suffix *-ya* must be regarded as primary, it is manifestly secondary in certain adjectives which have a gerundive sense; thus *a-vi-mok-yá-* (AV.) 'not to be loosened', *pari-varg-yà-*[8] (AV.) 'to be avoided'.

δ. Akin to the gerundives are a few abstract feminines in *-yā*; e. g. *kṛ-t-yā́-* 'action', 'enchantment', *vid-yā́-*[9] (AV.) 'knowledge', *deva-yaj-yā́-* 'worship of the gods'.

229. The rare **suffix *-yin***, like *-in*, forms a few possessive adjectives, all of which except one occur in the VS. They are *ātatā-yín-* (VS.) 'having one's bow drawn' (*ā́-tata-*), *dhanvā-yín-* (VS.) 'bearing a bow' (*dhánvan-*), *marā-yín-*[10] (RV[1].), N. of a man, *sṛka-yín-* (VS.) 'having a spear' (*sṛká-*), *svadhā-yín-*[11] (VS.) 'owning the Svadhā'.

230. The **suffix *-ra*** forms four superlatives from prepositions and about a dozen ordinary nouns, most of which are adjectives. The **superlatives** are *ádha-ra-* 'lower', *ápa-ra-* 'later', *áva-ra-* 'lower', *úpa-ra-*[12] 'lower'. The **ordinary adjectives** formed with the suffix have the sense of 'belonging to' or 'connected with'. It is usually added direct; e.g. *dhūm-rá-* 'grey' (*dhūmá-* 'smoke'), *aśrī-rá-* 'ugly', *pāṃsu-rá-* 'dusty' (*pāṃsú-* 'dust', AV.), and with initial Vṛddhi *ā́gnīdh-ra-* 'belonging to the fire-kindler' (*agnídh-*). It is added with connecting *i* in *medh-i-rá-* 'wise' (*medhā́-* 'wisdom') and *rath-i-rá-* 'riding in a car'. It also occurs in a few **substantives**, some of which are of

---

[1] As if from *suvaśva-*; like *vaiyaśv-á-* 'descendant of Vyaśva'; cp. WHITNEY 1204 b, c.

[2] With Guṇa of final *-u* as usual before secondary suffixes (190); *prāśav-yà-* 'to be partaken of' (*pra-aś-*) and *ūrjav-yà-* 'rich in nourishment' (*ū́rj-*) are formed without any primitives *prāśu-* and *ūrju-*.

[3] With syncope in the suffix of the primitive; cp. 190.

[4] From the weak stem of the primitive; cp. 190.

[5] Cp. WHITNEY 1212 c.

[6] Cp. WHITNEY 1212 m.

[7] Cp. WHITNEY 1213 e; and Roots, under *svar-* 'sound'.

[8] Here the guttural shows that these words are derived from nominal stems *-moka-* and *-varga-*.

[9] In the RV. only in the compound *jātá-vidyā-* 'knowledge of creatures'.

[10] Perhaps meaning 'brilliant' or, according to Sāyaṇa, 'destroying' enemies.

[11] The TS. IV. 4. 114 has *svadhā-vín-*.

[12] For *ánta-ra* cp. above p. 90, 39 and note 1.

doubtful etymology: *karmá-ra-*[1] 'smith', *muṣka-rá-* (AV.), a kind of small animal[2], *śámbara-*[3], N. of a demon, *śáṅkurá-* (AV.) 'penis', *sahás-ra-* 'thousand'.

231. The **suffix *-la*** forms about a dozen **adjectives** with the same meaning as those formed with *-ra*, with which it sometimes interchanges and of which it is generally a later form. Examples are: *aślī-lá-* (AV.) 'ugly', *kapi-lá-* 'brown', *jīva-lá-* (AV.) 'lively', *tilvi-la-* 'fertile', *bahu-lá-* 'abundant', *madhu-lá-* 'sweet', *śéva-la-* (AV.) 'shiny'. This suffix also forms two or three **diminutives**: *vṛṣa-lá-* 'little man', *śiśú-la-* 'little child', and the fem. *śalāka-lā́-* (AV.) 'small splint'.

232. The **suffix *-va*** forms a few **adjectives**: *arṇa-vá-* 'billowy', *keśa-vá-* (AV.) 'hairy', *añji-vá-* (AV.) 'slippery', *śanti-vá-* (AV.) 'friendly', *śraddhi-vá-* 'credible'.

233. The **suffix *-vat*** forms seven feminine **abstract substantives**, with a local sense, from adverbs or prepositions: *arvā-vát-*[4] 'proximity', *ā-vát-* (AV.) 'proximity', *ud-vát-* 'height', *ni-vát-* 'depth', *parā-vát-* 'distance', *pra-vát-* 'height', *saṃ-vát-* 'region'.

234. With the **suffix *-van***, before which *-a* and *-i* may be lengthened, are formed some twenty derivatives, nearly all adjectives with the sense of 'possessing' or 'connected with'. The **adjectives** are: *amatī-ván-* 'indigent', *arātī-ván-* 'hostile', *ṛ́ghā-van-* 'impetuous', *ṛṇā-ván-* 'indebted', *dhitā́-van-*[5] 'rich in gifts', *dhí-van-* (AV.) 'clever', *maghá-van-* 'bountiful', *śruṣṭī-ván-* 'obedient', *satyā́-van-*[6] (AV.) 'truthful', *samád-van-* 'warlike', *svadhā́-van-*, f. *-varī-*[7] 'faithful', *hā́rd-van-* (VS.) 'hearty'; also the feminines *sumnā-várī-* 'bringing favour', *sūnṛ́tā-varī-* 'joyous'. Somewhat anomalously formed are *índhan-van-* 'possessed of fuel' (*indhana-*), *sahā-van-*[8] and *sáho-van-*[9] (AV.) 'mighty'. There are also the **substantives** *átharvan-* m. 'fire-priest', *muṣī-ván-* m. 'robber', and *saní-t-van-*[10] 'reward'.

235. The **suffix *-vant*** forms, from nominal stems of every kind, possessive adjectives numbering at least 250 in the Saṃhitās. A final vowel is often lengthened before the suffix, most frequently *-a*, but very rarely *-u*. Examples are: *kéśa-vant-* 'hairy', *áśvā-vant-* 'possessed of horses' (beside *áśva-vant-*); *prajā́-vant-* 'having progeny'; *sákhi-vant-* 'having friends', *śáktī-vant-* 'mighty' (*śákti-* 'might'); *dyā́vā-pṛthiví-vant-*[11] (AV.) 'connected with heaven and earth'; *viṣṇu-vant-* 'accompanied by Viṣṇu', *viṣū-vánt-* 'dividing' (*víṣu-* 'apart'); *hárit-vant-* 'gold-coloured'; *āsan-vánt-* (AV.) 'having a mouth', *róman-vant-* and *lóma-vant-* (AV.) 'hairy', *śīrṣaṇ-vánt-* (AV.) 'having a head'; *kakúbh-vant-* (MS. I. 11[1]) 'having a peak'; *svàr-vant-* 'splendid'; *páyas-vant-* 'containing milk', *nas-vánt-* (AV.) 'having a nose'. With external Sandhi: *pṛ́ṣad-vant-* 'variegated'[12].

a. Some of these derivatives, especially if formed from pronominal stems, have the meaning of 'resembling' instead of 'possessing'; thus *mā́-vant-* 'like me', *í-vant-* 'so great', *kí-vant-* 'how far?', *indras-vant-*[13] 'like Indra', *níla-vant-*

1 *śévāra-* 'treasury' probably stands by haplology for *śéva-vāra-*.

2 The word occurs in TS. v. (B) as an adjective meaning 'having testicles'.

3 Probably a foreign word.

4 From *arva-* 'hither' contained in *arvā́ñc-* 'hitherward' and some other derivatives.

5 The Pada text has *dhitá-van-*.

6 The Pada text has *satyá-van-*.

7 The fem. of the secondary *-van* being formed like that of the primary *-van*; see 177 and cp. 179 a.

8 The Pada text has *sahá-van-*.

9 The only instance of external Sandhi with this suffix.

10 With *-t* interposed, as after short radical vowel preceding primary *-van*; e. g. *kṛ́-t-van-*.

11 Retaining the double accent of the primitive.

12 In a few derivatives *-vant* has the appearance of a primary suffix: *vivás-vant-* or *vi-vasvant-* 'shining', *ár-vant-* 'swift', *yah-vánt-* 'speeding'.

13 With the *s* of the nominative.

'blackish', *nṛ-vánt-* 'manly'. From this sense is derived the use of the **neuter** acc. as an **adverb of comparison**, e.g. *manuṣ-vát* 'like Manus', 'as Manus did'.

236. The very rare **suffix *-vaya***, probably a noun in origin, seems to be found only in one numeral adjective, *cátur-vaya-* 'fourfold', and one substantive, *dru-váya-* (AV.) 'wooden dish'.

237. The **suffix *-vala*** (cp. 179) seems to be used in the formation of secondary derivatives only in *kṛṣī-valá-* 'peasant' (*kṛṣí-* 'tillage') and in the fem. *naḍ-valā́-* (VS.) 'reed-bed'.

238. The **suffix *-vin*** is used in forming nearly twenty possessive adjectives from stems ending in *-a* (which is lengthened), *-ā*[1], *-as*; thus *ubhayā-vín-* 'partaking of both' (*ubháya-*), *aṣṭrā-vín-* 'obedient to the goad', *yaśas-vín-* (AV.) 'beautiful'. To the analogy of the derivatives from stems in *-as* is due the insertion of *s* in *śata-s-vín-* 'possessing a hundred'. The only derivatives from stems ending in any consonant other than *s* are *dhṛṣad-vín-* 'bold' (*dhṛṣát-*) and *vāg-vín-* (AV.) 'eloquent' (*vā́c-* 'speech'), both formed as in external Sandhi.

239. The only derivative of the **suffix *-vya*** forming names of relationship which occur in the Saṃhitās seems to be *bhrā́tṛ-vya-* (father's) 'brother's son'[2].

240. The **suffix *-śa*** forms eight or nine adjectives or substantives without in most instances changing the original meaning. The **adjectives** are *éta-śa-* 'variegated', *babhlu-śá-* (VS.) 'brownish', *yuva-śá-* 'youthful', and with possessive sense *roma-śá-* 'hairy'. The **substantives** are *aṅku-śa-* m. 'hook', *káśma-śa-* (AV.) m. or n. 'stupefaction'(?), *kalá-śa-* m. 'jar', *turvá-śa-*, N. of a man, *lopā-śá-*[3] m. 'jackal'.

V. COMPOUNDS.

BENFEY, Vollständige Grammatik p. 245—282. — WHITNEY, Sanskrit Grammar 1246—1316. — REUTER, Die altindischen nominalcomposita, ihrer betonung nach untersucht, KZ. 31, 157—232; 485—612. — WACKERNAGEL, Altindische Grammatik, 2[1], Nominalkomposition, 1905: cp. BARTHOLOMAE, IF. 20, 162—172 (Anzeiger).

241. Form of compounds. — The Vedic language has inherited from the Indo-European speech the power of combining words into a compound treated like a simple word as regards accent, inflexion, and construction. Both in the frequency and the length of compounds the Vedic language resembles that of Homer. In the RV. and the AV. no compounds of more than three independent members occur; and those which consist of three members are rare, such as *ádabdha-vrata-pramati-* 'superior-minded owing to unbroken observances', *pūrva-kāma-kṛ́tvan-* 'fulfilling former wishes', *mithó-avadya-pa-* 'mutually warding off want', *hári-manyu-sāyaka-* 'stimulating the mettle of the bays'.

The **two characteristic features** of a compound are **unity of accent** and use of the **uninflected stem in the first member** (or members). There are, however, exceptions to both these rules. The Sandhi between the two numbers is occasionally different from that between words in a sentence. Occasionally also tmesis of a compound occurs[4]. Generally speaking a

1 The doubtful word *vy-aśnuv-in-* (VS[1].) seems to add *-in* to the present stem with interposed euphonic *-v-*.

2 *pitṛ-vya-* 'father's brother', 'uncle', occurs in the later language.

3 Cp. GUSTAV MEYER, IF. 1, 328.

4 Frequently in dual compounds, as *dyā́vā ha kṣā́mā* 'heaven and earth'; occasionally in others also, as *śúnaś cic chépam* for *śúnaḥ-śépam*; *nárā vā śáṃsam* for *nárā-śáṃsam*; *saptá me saptá* for *saptá-sapta me*.

compound assumes a modified and single meaning as compared with the same words used in juxtaposition in a sentence; e. g. *kṛṣṇa-śakuní-* (AV.) 'raven', while *kṛṣṇáḥ śakúniḥ* would mean 'black bird'. Compounding must take place when a derivative has to be formed from the two words; as *kṣáitrapat-ya-* 'property' beside *kṣétrasya páti-* 'lord of the field'. Sometimes, however, the case-ending remains while the compound accent is used, as *rāyas-poṣa-dā́-* 'bestowing abundance of wealth', beside *rāyás póṣa-* 'abundance of wealth'. There is a tendency to compounding when the first of two syntactical words is indeclinable. Thus beside *śáṃ yós* 'happiness and welfare' also appears *śaṃ-yós* (I. 34[6]); and analogously the indeclinable form or stem of a word takes the place of the case[1]. Sometimes compounds are formed by the coalescence of inflected words occurring side by side in a sentence. Thus *viśvā́hā* (TS.) 'all days' beside *áhā víśvā* (RV.) has become *viśvā́ha* 'daily' with a single accent. Occasionally, when two compounds have the same final member, the latter is used only once, as *mitrótá*[2] *médhyātithim* (I. 36[7]) for *mitrā́tithim utá médhyātithim*; *patayán mandayát-sakham* (I. 4[7]) for *patayát-sakham mandayát-sakham.* Sometimes one of the members of a compound governs a case[3] outside the compound, as *árvato māṃsa-bhikṣā́m* (I. 162[12]) 'begging for the flesh of the steed'; in some instances pleonastically, as *gaṇā́nāṃ gaṇá-patim* (II. 23[1]) 'troop-leader of troops'. A case-form may agree with the first member of a compound when that member has the form or even only the sense of that case, as *rāyás-kāmo viśvápsnyasya* (VII. 42[6]) 'desirous of wealth of all forms'; or a case-form may agree with the second member, while coordinated in sense with the first, as *mahā-dhané . . árbhe* (I. 7[5]) 'in great booty (and) in small'.

a. The **gender of compounds** is, in Copulatives (Dvandvas) and Determinatives (Tatpuruṣas) ending in substantives, that of the last member[4]; but collective compounds are regularly neuter[5]. Compounds ending in adjectives, possessives, and governing compounds have the gender of the substantives with which they agree or which they represent. The **number** in Determinatives is that of the last member. In Copulatives of the older types it is dual or plural according to the total number meant by the combination, while it is singular (and neuter) in the later type. Collective compounds (whether copulatives or possessives) are singular. Compounds ending in adjectives, possessives, and governing compounds, have the number of the substantive with which they agree or which they represent.

A. The First Member of Compounds.

242. **Its form.** — The first member of nominal compounds may consist of nouns (including numerals and pronouns) or indeclinables suitable for qualifying nouns. Exceptionally an inflected form appears in this position qualifying the second member in dependent determinatives and possessives. This is mainly due to words frequently in juxtaposition becoming permanently joined; thus beside the two independent words *jā́s pátiḥ* (VII. 38[6]) 'lord of the family'

1 Thus for *viṣṇoḥ kráma-* (AV. TS.) 'step of Viṣṇu' there appears in a B. passage of the TS. (V. 2. 1[1]) the compound *viṣṇu-kramá-*.

2 The Pada text reads *mitrā́ utá.*

3 This seems to be almost restricted to the genitive in the Saṃhitās, but many examples of other cases (acc., inst., dat., abl.) occur in the later language.

4 In a few Dvandvas the gender of the first member prevails (265, notes 1 and 2); and a few Determinatives change the gender of the final member, as *patnī-śā́la-* (VS.) n. (*śā́lā-*) 'shed for the wives (of sacrificers)' and *agra-jihvá-* (VS.) n. 'tip of the tongue' (*jihvā́-*).

5 Both Dvandvas (266) and Bahuvrīhis (290).

we find the compound *jā́s-patim* (I. 185[8])[1]. But it partly also arises from a desire to express the syntactical relation of the words in the compound even without antecedent juxtaposition; as in the verbal determinatives *dhanaṃ-jayá-* 'winning booty', *apsu-ṣád-* 'dwelling in waters'; or in possessives like *rāyás-kāma-* 'desirous of wealth'. Such case-endings show a tendency to encroach beyond their legitimate sphere; thus the frequency of the ending *-as* before *-pati-*, e. g. *vāc-ás-páti-* 'lord of speech', led to its becoming the general genitive sign before that word, as in *rátha-s-páti-* 'lord of the car' (*rátha-*). Similarly, according to *apsu-kṣí-t-* 'dwelling in the waters' was formed *apsu-jí-t-* beside *ab-jí-t-* 'winning waters', where the locative is not appropriate. Ordinarily the first member appears only in its stem form. As the stem cannot express **number** it may mean either the singular or the plural. That it often indicates the plural is shown by expressions like *narā́ṃ* or *jánānāṃ nṛ-pā́tṛ́-* 'man-guardian of men' or 'people'. The plural sense is also evident in compounds like *devá-kṛta-* 'made by the gods', *vīrá-jāta-* 'produced by men', *nṛ-páti-* 'lord of men'. In personal pronouns and cardinals the number is of course inherent in the stem itself.

a. The **gender** is expressed in the first member only in as far as feminine words retain their f. stem when coordinated in copulatives or dependent on the final member in the sense of a case in determinatives; e. g. *patnī-śā́la-* (VS.) 'shed for wives'. The f. suffix *-ā* is, however, often shortened to *a*[2], as in *amīva-hán-* 'destroying suffering', *amīva-cā́tana-* 'dispelling suffering' (*ámīvā-*). But when a feminine adjective as first member agrees attributively with a feminine in the last member, it appears in the masculine stem-form[3]; e. g. *práyata-dakṣiṇa-* 'one by whom a sacrificial fee (*dákṣiṇā-*) has been presented'[4].

243. If the **stem** is liable to gradation, that form is used which occurs in the **weak** cases. Thus in the **vowel stems** *-i, -u, -ṛ*, appear; e. g. *páti-juṣṭa-* 'dear to a husband', *vasu-víd-* 'finding wealth', *pitṛ-yajñá-* 'sacrifice to the manes'. Similarly *dyu-* (*diu-*) 'heaven' appears before consonants, as *dyu-kṣá-* 'dwelling in heaven', *dyú-bhakta-* 'presented by heaven', but *div-* before vowels, as *div-ít-* 'going to heaven', *dív-iṣṭi-* 'prayer'. The two stems *dā́ru-* 'wood' and *áp-* 'water' are reduced to *dru-* and *ap-*: *dru-padá-* 'wooden pillar', *dru-ṣád-* 'sitting on the tree'; *ap-túr-* 'overcoming the waters', *ab-jā́-* 'derived from waters'. The stem *púmāṃs-* 'man' appears in the weak form *puṃs-* in *puṃś-calí-* (VS. AV.) and *puṃś-calū́-* (VS.) 'courtezan' ('running after men').

a. Stems in *-an* have *-a* not only before consonants[5], but also before vowels[6] and *y, v*[7]; e. g. *rāja-putrá-* 'king's son', *ukṣā́nna-* 'devouring bulls' (*ukṣán-*), *áśmāsya-* 'whose mouth is a rock' (*áśman-*), *bráhmeddha-* 'kindled with devotion' (*bráhman-*), *brahmaudaná-* (AV.) 'boiled rice (*odaná-*) for Brāhmans' (*brahmán-*). Exceptions, however, are *nemann-íṣ-* 'following the lead', *vṛṣaṇ-aśvá-* 'drawn by stallions', *vṛ́ṣaṇ-vasu-* 'having great wealth'[8].

b. Stems in *-in* seem to follow the same analogy, dropping the *-n* before consonants; thus *śā́ci-gu-* (only voc.) 'having strong cattle' and *śā́ci-pūjana-* (only voc.) 'worshipping the strong'[9].

1 The compounding of such forms probably often started from vocatives like *sahasas putra* treated as a unit in regard to accent.

2 This, however, seems to be due to metrical influence.

3 An exception in *urvy-ūtí-* 'giving wide aid', where the f. stem *urvī́-* appears instead of the m. *urú-*.

4 In *bṛhác-chandas-* (AV.) 'having Bṛhatī as metre' and *jágac-chandas-* (AV. VS.) 'having Jagatī as metre', the first members doubtless represent neuter names of the metres.

5 As in *rā́ja-bhis* etc.

6 Unlike *rā́j-ñ-e* etc.

7 Not *-an* as in *rājan-yà-*, *udan-vánt-*.

8 In *āsánn-iṣu-* 'having arrows in his mouth' the first member is a locative.

9 Cp. WACKERNAGEL 2[1], p. 54 β, note.

c. Occasionally the **weak grade stem** used as first member does not occur as an independent word; thus *kṣá-pávant-* and *kṣa-pávant-* 'earth-protector' from *kṣám-* 'earth'; *jñu-bádh-* 'bending the knee' from *jánu-* 'knee'; *man-dhātṛ́-* 'devout man' from *mán-as-* 'mind' (through **manz-*), *sát-pati-* 'lord of the abode', probably from *sád-as-* 'abode' (through **sats-*).

204. When in the inflexion of a word two or more **collateral stems** (not differing in gradation only) are used, the one which appears in weak cases is mostly employed as first member in compounds. 1. Even though the stem *ās-yà-* 'mouth' is inflected throughout, the alternative stems of weak cases ***ās-*** and ***āsan-*** are preferred: *ā-daghná-* 'reaching to the mouth', *āsánn-iṣu-*[1] 'having arrows in his mouth'. 2. ***udán-***[2] 'water' is preferred to *uda-ká-*[3]: *uda-grābhá-* m. 'holding water', *uda-pū́-* (AV.) 'purified by water', *uda-meghá-* 'water-shower'; *uda-ká-* appears only in *udákātman-*[4] (AV.) 'having water for its chief substance'. 3. Of the three stems *pánthān-*, ***pathí-***, *páth-*, only the middle one, which appears before consonant endings, is used: *pathi-kṛ́t-* 'path-making', *pathi-rákṣi-* 'protecting roads'. 4. ***śákan-***[5] is preferred to *śákṛt-* 'dung': *śaka-dhū́ma-* (AV.) 'dung-smoke', *śaka-piṇḍá-* (VS.) 'lump of dung', *śáka-pūta-* ('purified by dung'), N. of a seer. 5. ***śīrṣán-*** is preferred to *śíras-* 'head': *śīrṣa-kapālá-* (AV.) 'skull', *śīrṣa-bhidya-* (AV.) n. 'head-splitting', *śīrṣā-mayá-* (AV.) m. 'disease (*āmaya-*) of the head'. 6. There is **fluctuation** between *pád-* and *páda-* 'foot', *māṃs-*[6] and *māṃsá-* 'flesh', *hṛ́d-* and *hṛ́daya-* 'heart': *pad-ghoṣá-*[7] (AV.) 'sound of footsteps', but *pāda-gṛ́hya*, ger. 'seizing by the foot'; *māṃs-pácana-* 'used for cooking flesh', but *māṃsa-bhikṣā-* 'begging for flesh', *hṛd-rogá-* 'heart-disease', but *hṛdayā-vídh-* 'wounding the heart'[8].

245. **Alternative adjective stems** sometimes appear in the first member of compounds. Thus in the RV. *mahi-* interchanges with *mahā-*[9] 'great' in Karmadhārayas and Bahuvrīhis, as *máhi-kṣatra* 'owning great sway', but *mahā-dhaná-* 'great booty', *mahā́-manas-* 'great-minded'[10]. A few stems in *-i* appear instead of or interchanging with others in *-ra*: *ṛji-* in *ṛji-pyá-* and the Proper Names *ṛjí-śvan-*[11] beside *ṛjrá-* 'quick' in *ṛjrā́śva-* ('having quick horses'), N. of a man; **dabhí-* in *dabhīti-* (for **dabhi-iti-*) 'injurer', beside *dabhrá-* 'small' in *dabhrá-cetas-* 'of little wit'; *śviti-* in *śvity-áñc-*[12] 'bright', beside *śvitrá-* (AV.) 'white'; *saci-* in *saci-víd-* 'belonging together', beside *á-sk-ra-*[13] 'united'; perhaps also *-kravi-* for **kruvi-* in *á-kravi-hasta-* 'not having bloody hands', beside *krū-rá-*[14] (AV.) 'bloody'.

a. A few adjective stems in *-i* used as first member neither occur as uncompounded adjectives nor have corresponding adjective stems in *-ra*: *tuvi-jātá-* 'mightily born', *tuvi-grī́va-* 'strong-necked', *tuvy-ójas-* 'very strong'; *gabhi-ṣák* (AV.) 'deep down'.

---

1 See above p. 145, note 8.
2 Inst. sing. *udā́*, pl. *udá-bhis*.
3 Nom. *n* acc. *udakám*.
4 With irregular accent; cp. WACKERNAGEL 2[1], p. 56, note.
5 Inst. *śáka-bhis* (TS.), nom. acc. *śákṛt*.
6 Beside *vaná-* 'wood' (which is fully inflected and appears in *vaná-dhiti-* 'layer of wood'), the stem *van-* (gen. *van-ā́m*, loc. *vaṃ-sú*) is perhaps used in *váṃ-saga-* 'bull', *van-dhúra-* 'car-seat', and *van-ád-* 'devouring wood' (?).
7 Perhaps in *páḍ-gṛbhi-*, N. of a man or demon, if *paḍ-* = *pad-*, cp. WACKERNAGEL 1, 148 a.
8 On the other hand, of the alternative stems *ásṛj-* and *asán-* 'blood', only the nom. acc. form is used; e. g. *asṛk-pávan-* (AV.) 'drinking blood', *ásṛṅ-mukha-* (AV.) 'bloody-faced'.
9 *mahā-* being the m., *mahi-* the n. nom. acc. stem, beside the weak dat. *mah-é* etc.
10 The AV. has the stem *mahát-* in the Karmadhāraya *mahat-kāṇḍá-*, 'great section'.
11 Perhaps also in *ṛ́jīti-* (= *ṛji-iti-*), cp. WACKERNAGEL 2[1], p. 59.
12 Cp. *śiti-pā́d-* 'white-footed', *śiti-pṛ́ṣṭha-* 'white-backed'.
13 From *sac-* 'be attached' with syncope.
14 Cp. WACKERNAGEL 2[1], p. 59.

246. Extension of the stem sometimes takes place in the first member. The commonest addition is *-a* owing to the frequency of that ending: *dur-a-dabhná-* (AV.) 'eluding doors', *aśvín-a-kṛta-* (VS.) 'done by the Aśvins'; *viśaujas-*[1] (VS.) 'ruling the people'; *ṣaḍ-a-rcá-*[2] (AV.) 'collection of six verses'. An *a*-stem becomes one in *-as* in *yakṣmo-dhā́-* (AV.) 'seat of a disease' (*yákṣma-*). An extension with *-d* appears in *śatád-vasu-*[3] 'having a hundred (*śatá-*) treasures', and in *án-atid-bhuta-*[4] 'unsurpassed'.

a. **Shortening of the stem** sometimes takes place by the dropping of a final *t* or *s* (preceded by *a*) or of the vowel *-a*; thus *pṛṣodará-* (TS. v. 6. 14[1]) 'having a spotted (*pṛṣat-*) belly' (*udára-*); *apna-rā́j-* 'ruling over riches' (*ápnas-*); *bhar-iṣá-*[5] (IV. 40[2]) 'desiring booty' (*bhára-*); *til-piñja-* (AV.) 'barren sesamum' (*tilá-*); *sas-piñjara-* (TS. IV. 5. 2[1]) 'reddish like grass' (*sasá-*), may also be an example, but it is more probably a modification of *śaṣ-piñjara-* (VS. XVI. 17) by haplology for **śaṣpa-piñjara-*.

247. Adverbs often occur as first member of compounds. In several instances a nominal stem in *-a* represents an adverbial case (acc., inst., abl., loc.) formed from that stem; thus *nítya-vatsa-* 'having a calf continually' (*nítyam*); *satya-yáj-* 'sacrificing truly' (*satyám*), *samantá-śiti-bāhu-* (VS.) 'whose forefeet are white all round' (*samantám*); *sana-jā́-* 'born of old' (= *sanā́* or *sanā́t*); *upākā́-cakṣas-* 'visible from near at hand' (*upāké* 'near'). Occasionally a nominal stem which has no separate existence is abstracted from the adverb; thus *ará-manas-* 'ready-minded' (from *áram* 'ready'), *ará-mati-* 'suitable prayer', *abhyardha-yájvan-* 'offering apart' (*abhyardhás*). A cardinal is sometimes thus used instead of its adverb: *try-àruṣa-* 'reddish in three places' (*trí-s*), *dvi-já-* (AV.) 'born twice' (*dví-s*).

248. The **case-ending** is also **preserved** in several instances; thus *araṃ-kṛ́t-* 'preparing', *sākam-úkṣ-* 'sprinkling together', *sākaṃ-yúj-* 'joined together' (*sākám*), *sāyam-bhavá-* (AV.) 'becoming evening'; *paścā-doṣá-* (VS.) 'late evening'. Adverbs that are neither case-forms nor look like them regularly remain unchanged; thus *akṣṇayā-drúh-*[6] 'injuring wrongly'; *itthā́-dhī-* 'truly devout'; *idā-vatsará-* (VS. AV.) 'the present year', a particular kind of year; *púnar-nava-* 'renewing itself', *punar-bhū́-* 'arising again'; *viśváto-dhī-* 'observing in all directions', *víṣu-rūpa-* 'coloured variously' (*viṣu-*), *viṣū-vṛ́t-* 'rolling in various directions'. A nasal is added in *makṣu-ṃ-gamá-* 'approaching quickly' (*makṣū́*).

249. Prepositions frequently occur as the first member of a compound. 1. Owing to their originally adverbial character they may **qualify ordinary adjectives or substantives** like adverbs; thus *áti-kṛṣṇa-* (VS.) 'excessively dark', *ví-mahī-* 'very great'; *prá-napāt-* 'great grandson', *ví-vāc-* 'opposing shout'; and in Bahuvrīhis: *prā-śṛṅgá-* (VS.) 'having prominent horns', *vy-àṃsa-* 'having shoulders wide apart'.

2. Owing to their constant connexion with verbs they are very common **before verbal nouns**; e. g. *úpa-ṣṭu-t-* and *úpa-stuti-* 'invocation'; *puró-hita-* 'domestic priest'.

3. Owing to their frequent connexion with cases, they also appear in a **governing sense**; e. g. *ádhi-gart-ya-* 'being on the car-seat', *anu-pathá-* 'following the path'.

---

[1] For *viśa-ojas-* like (AV. VS.) *satyáujas-* (= *satya-ojas-*) instead of *viḍ-ojas-*.

[2] Like *pañcarcá-* = *pañca-ṛca*.

[3] Influenced by the analogy of *pañcāśád-* '50' etc., and *vidád-vasu-*, etc.

[4] Due to a confusion of **ati-bhuta-* = *ati-bhūta-* 'surpassed' and *ádbhuta-* 'marvellous'.

[5] According to the analogy of *gav-iṣá-* 'desiring cows'.

[6] *akṣṇa-yā́van-* 'going across' stands by haplology for **akṣṇayā-yā́van-*. Cp. WACKERNAGEL 2[1], p. 128 d.

a. Prepositions as first member sometimes appear in a shortened form; thus *bhi-* = *abhi*[1] in *bhi-ṣáj-*[2]: 'healer'; *o-* = *ava* in *o-gaṇá-* ('away from the crowd') 'isolated', 'wretched', and in *o-paśá-* 'top-knot' ('that which is tied down', from *paś-* 'fasten'). On the other hand, *ánu* several times appears lengthened to *ānu-*: thus *an-ānu-kṛtyá-* 'inimitable', *an-ānu-dá-* 'not giving way', *án-ānu-diṣṭa-* 'unsolicited', *án-ānu-bhūti-* 'disobedient', *ānu-ṣák* 'in constant succession'.

250. ***Sam* and *sa-*.** — The preposition *sám* is of very common occurrence as first member. This is its form **invariably before vowels**, and when accented originally always before consonants. Its unaccented form *sa-* (= *sṃ-*) should phonetically always appear before consonants. But the proper use of *sám-* and *sa-* before consonants has begun to be confused.

a. In **determinatives** (1) when the final member is a verbal noun ***sam-*** always appears before a vowel, as *sam-aṅká-* (AV.) 'hook' (from *añc-* 'bend'), *sam-ídh-* 'fuel'; and *sám-* if accented predominates[3] before consonants, being phonetic; e. g. *sáṃ-gati-* f. 'coming together', *sáṃ-dhātṛ-* 'one who puts together', *sám-pṛkta-* 'mixed'. *sá-*, however, also occurs in *sá-gdhi-* (VS. MS.) f. 'eating together', *sá-cyuti-* (MS. II. 7[12]) 'falling together', *sá-pīti-* (VS. MS.) f. 'drinking together', *sá-hūti-* f. 'joint invocation'.

(2.) ***sa-*** is preserved **before accented verbal nouns** formed from the simple root with or without *-t*, or with the suffixes *-a*, *-ana*, *-van*, *-in*; thus *sa-cít-* 'thinking', *sa-bádh-* (TS. III. 2. 12[4]) 'oppressed', *sa-yúj-* 'united', *sa-vṛ́dh-* 'increasing together', *sa-ṣṭúbh-* (TS. IV. 3. 12[2]), a kind of metre. *sa-syád-* 'streaming together'[4]; *sa-kṣí-t-* 'dwelling together', *sa-srú-t-* 'streaming'[5]; *sa-gm-á-* (VS.) 'coming to terms', *sa-jóṣa-* 'unanimous', *sa-mádana-* 'conflict'[6]; *sa-yā́-van-* 'going along with', *sa-yúg-van-* 'united with', *sa-sthā́-van-* 'standing together', *sa-jí-t-van-* 'victorious'; *sa-vās-ín-* (AV.) 'dwelling together'[7].

(3.) Before ordinary adjectives ***sam-*** appears in *sáṃ-vasu-* 'fellow-dweller', *sám-miśla-* 'commingling', *sám-priya-* (VS.) 'loving one another', and even when unaccented before ordinary substantives in *saṃ-vatsará-* 'year', *saṃ-grāmá-* (AV.) 'assembly', but *sa-pátnī-* 'co-wife'.

b. In **Bahuvrīhis** when the meaning is (1.) **'together'** (as in the verbal use of the preposition) ***sam-*** appears, as *sáṃ-hanu-* (AV.) 'striking the jaws together', *saṃ-gavá-* m. '(time when the) cows (are driven) together', and (as usual before vowels) *sam-udrá-* m. 'sea'. But when the meaning is (2) **'united with'**, 'accompanied by' what is expressed by the final member, ***sa-*** is almost exclusively used (and nearly always even accented)[8], as *sá-cetas-* 'accompanied by intelligence', 'rational'; ***sam-*** occurs here only in *sáṃ-sahasra-* 'accompanied by a thousand', and in *sám-patnī-* (AV.) 'accompanied by her husband'[9]. In this sense ***sam-*** still appears before vowels in *sám-agra-* and *sam-agrá-* (AV.) ('including the top'), 'complete', *sám-aṅga-* (AV.) 'accompanied by all limbs'[10], 'complete', *sám-āśir-* 'accompanied by mixture', 'mixed'; but even here *sa-* once in the RV. takes the place of *sam-* in the compound *sā́śana-* (x. 90[4])

[1] The initial *a-* of some other prepositions is lost in the later language: *pi-* = *ápi* (ŚB.); *dhi-* = *ádhi* and *va-* = *áva* are post-Vedic.

[2] See Wackernagel 2[1], p. 72 e, and cp. Brugmann, KZ. 25, 214, note.

[3] *sam-* occurs more than three times as often as *sa-* before consonants, doubtless owing to the parallel use of *sam-* with verbs.

[4] But also *saṃ-gír-* 'assenting', *saṃ-yát-* 'contiguous'.

[5] But also *saṃ-jí-t-* 'conqueror', *saṃ-há-t-* 'layer'.

[6] But also *saṃ-gamá-* 'coming together', *saṃ-cárana-* 'suitable for walking on'.

[7] With verbal nouns otherwise formed, as with *-tra* or *-na* only *sam-* occurs, as *saṃ-hotrá-* 'joint sacrifice', *sam-praśná-* 'interrogation'.

[8] With the usual Bahuvrīhi accent on the first member.

[9] In order to distinguish this sense from that of *sa-pátnī-* 'co-wife'.

[10] Cp. also the adv. *sam-antá-m* (AV.) 'including the ends', 'completely'.

'provided with food' (*áśana-*), 'eating', and becomes common in the later Saṃhitās; e. g. *sáṅga-* (AV.) 'accompanied by the limbs' (*áṅga-*), *sántardeśa-* (AV.) 'accompanied by the intermediate quarters' (*antar-deśá-*). — When the meaning is (3.) **'in common'**, 'same', 'identical'[1] ***sa-***[2] is very common before consonants, as *sá-keta-* 'having the same intention', *sá-lakṣman-* 'having the same characteristics'; while *sam-* appears only in *saṃ-śiśvarī-* 'having a calf in common', *sám-manas-* (AV.) 'being of the same mind', unanimous', *sám-mātṛ-* 'having the same mother'. In this sense *sam-* alone appears (as usual) before vowels: *sám-anta-* 'contiguous' ('having the same boundary'), *sám-okas-* 'having a common abode', 'living together'.

251. **Particles,** which for the most part have no independent existence, frequently appear as first member of compounds.

1. The **negative particle,** the form of which in the sentence is *na*, almost invariably appears in composition as ***a-***[3] before consonants, and invariably as ***an-*** before vowels. It completely reverses the meaning of the final member; thus *mitrá-* 'friend', *a-mitra-* 'enemy', *śastí-* 'praise', *á-śasti-* 'curse'[4]. As participles, infinitives, and gerunds are nominal forms, they may be compounded with the privative particle: thus *á-bibhyat-* 'not fearing', *á-budhya-māna-* 'not waking', *á-dāsyant-* (AV.) 'not about to give', *á-vidvāṃs-* 'not knowing'[5]. The syntactical form of the particle is very rare: *na-murá-* (AV^{1}.) 'non-dying' (?)[6]. Perhaps also in *ná-pāt-* 'grandson', if it originally meant 'un-protected'[7].

2. ***su-*** 'well', 'very', except in the RV. very seldom used independently[8], and ***dus-*** 'ill', 'hardly', which occurs as a prefix only, appear as first member in determinatives and possessives; e. g. *su-kára-* 'easy to be done', *sú-kṛta-* 'well-done', *su-dā́-* 'giving willingly', *su-vasaná-* 'fair raiment', *su-varṇá-* 'fair-coloured', *sv-áśva-* 'having excellent horses'; *dū-ḍāś-* (AV.) 'not-worshipping', 'irreligious', *duś-cyavaná-* 'difficult to be felled', *dur-vásas-* 'having bad clothing', 'ill-clad'; *dur-áhā* (AV^{1}.) 'wail!' is formed as an antithesis to *sv-áhā* 'hail!'.

3. There are a few prefixes beginning with *k-* which seem to be etymologically connected with the **interrogative,** and express depreciation, badness, or difficulty: ***ku-***[9] in *ku-cará-* 'wandering about', *ku-nakhín-* (AV.) 'having diseased nails', *ku-namnamá-* 'hard to bend', *kú-yava-* (VS.) 'bringing bad harvest'[10]; ***kad-*** in *kat-payá-* 'swelling horribly'; ***kim-*** in *kiṃ-śilá-* (VS. TS. MS.) (land) 'having small stones', *kim-puruṣá-*, a kind of mythical being ('somewhat like a man'); a collateral form ***kavā-*** perhaps in *kavārí-* 'stingy', *kavā-sakhá-* 'selfish'[11].

4. The particles ***-id*** and ***-cid*** make their way into the first member of compounds in the company of pronominal words to which they may he

---

[1] *samāna-* is also used in this sense: as *samāná-bandhu-* 'having the same relatives'.

[2] *sa-* has the sense of 'one' in *sāhná-* (AV.) 'lasting one day', *sa-kṛ́t* 'once', *sa-dívas* and *sa-dyás* 'on one and the same day'.

[3] This is the low-grade form (= *ṇ-*) of *ná-*.

[4] It frequently reverses the pregnant sense of the final member, as *vi-śastṛ́-* '(good) dissector', *a-viśastṛ́-* 'bad dissector'.

[5] See KNAUER, Ueber die betonung der composita mit *a* privativum im Sanskrit, KZ. 27, 1—68; examples from the later Saṃhitās in DELBRÜCK, Altindische Syntax p. 540 f., Syntaktische Forschungen 2, p. 530 f.

[6] *ná-puṃsa-ka-* 'neuter' also occurs in MS. and ŚB.

[7] See LEUMANN, Festgruss an Böhtlingk, p. 77 f. For a few other doubtful compounds with *na-* see WACKERNAGEL 2^{1}, p. 78, note.

[8] *sú* occurs as an independent particle about 250 times (but never at the beginning of a sentence) in the RV., rarely in the later Saṃhitās: only 14 times in AV.

[9] Often in adverbs such as *kú-tas* 'whence', *kú-tra* 'where'.

[10] On a few doubtful compounds with *ku-*, see WACKERNAGEL 2^{1}, p. 83, note.

[11] Also in *kávā-tiryañc-* (TS.) 'directed somewhat across'.

appended; thus *tad-íd-artha-* 'directed to that particular object'; *kā-cit-kará-* 'effecting all manner of things'; *kū-cid-arthín-* 'striving to get anywhere', *kuha-cid-víd-* 'wherever being'.

5. A few **interjectional** or **onomatopoetic words** are compounded with *-kāra-* and *-kṛti-* 'making' = 'sound', 'utterance', or *-kartṛ-* 'maker', to express the actual phonetic sound of those words: thus *vaṣaṭ-kārá-* (AV. VS.) 'the interjection *vaṣaṭ*', *svadhā-kārá-* 'pronouncing (the benediction) *sva-dhā́*', *svā́hā-kṛti-* 'consecration with the call *svā́hā*', *hiṅ-kartṛ́-* (TS.) 'one who utters the sound *hiṅ*', *hiṅ-kārá-* (VS.) 'the sound *hiṅ*'. In *has-kartṛ́-* 'enlivener', *has-kārá-* 'laughter', *hás-kṛti-* 'loud merriment', the first member represents either an interjection connected with the verb *has-* 'laugh', or a reduced form of **hasas-* 'laughter' (like *sát-pati-* for *sádas-pati-* through **sáts-pati-*).

B. The Last Member of Compounds.

252. **Its form.** — Practically all nouns may appear in this position. But many verbal nouns, especially participles, if used in their primary sense, are found exclusively after indeclinables which are capable of being combined with the corresponding verbs. Some stems also occur as final members though not used independently; such are verbal nouns formed from the simple root with or without an added determinative *-t*; also derivatives like *-janīna-* (AV.) 'belonging to the people (*jána-*) of —'.

a. **Change of ending.** — When the gender of the final member is changed, the *-ā* of feminine words, even though radical, becomes *-a* in masculine or neuter compounds; thus *priyosriyá-* 'fond of cows' (*usríyā-*); *an-avasá-* 'restless' (from *ava-sā́-* 'rest'), *a-śraddhá-* 'unbelieving' (from *śrad-dhā́-* 'belief'), *ṛtá-jya-* 'well-strung' (from *jyā́-* 'bowstring'). Even *-ī* in a few instances becomes *-a*; thus *ati-rātrá-* 'performed overnight' and *aho-rātrá-* 'day and night' (*rā́trī-*); *api-śarvaré* 'early in the morning' and *ati-śarvaré* or *ati-sarvaréṣu* (AV.) 'late at night' (*śárvarī-*).

On the other hand m. and n. stems in *-a* regularly end in *-ā* in the feminine, as *cittá-garbhā-* 'having evident offspring' (*gárbha-* m.); and *páti-* 'husband' in f. possessives substitutes *-patnī-*; thus *éka-patnī-* (AV.) 'having a single husband', *dāsá-patnī-* 'having demons as lords', *sa-pátnī-* 'having one husband in common', *sám-patnī-* (AV.) and *sahá-patnī-* (AV.) 'having her husband with her', *su-pátnī-* 'having a good husband'; also in the determinative *vīrá-patnī-* 'wife of a hero'.

253. **Alternative stems.** — When in the inflexion of a word alternative stems are used, only one of these, and as a rule the older one, appears as final member of possessive compounds: thus *dánt-* 'tooth' (not *dánta-*) in *śatá-dant-* (AV.) 'hundred-toothed', *śúci-dant-* 'bright-toothed'; *pád-* 'foot' (not *pā́da-*): *a-pā́d-* 'footless', *uttāná-pad-* 'whose feet are extended', *éka-pad-*[1] 'one-footed'; *nás-* 'nose' (not *nā́sā-*) in *ṛjū-nas-*[2] 'straight-nosed', N. of a man[3]; *ū́dhan-* 'udder' (not *ū́dhar-*) in *an-ūdhán-*[4] 'udderless', *rapśád-ūdhan-* 'having a distended udder', f. *á-cchidrodhn-ī-* 'having an intact udder'; *dhánvan-* 'bow' (not *dhánus-*) in *abalá-dhanvan-* (AV.) 'having a weak bow', *ávatata-dhanvan-* (VS.) 'having an unstrung bow', *kṣiprá-dhanvan-* 'having a swift bow', *śatá-*

[1] The AV., however, has the nom. sing. *éka-pāda-ḥ*.

[2] According to BLOOMFIELD also in *rujā́nās*, for *rujāná-nās* 'broken-nosed'; see p. 59, note 1.

[3] According to WACKERNAGEL 2[1], p. 92 (top), *a-nāsiká-* occurs in TS. (VII. 5. 12[1].

[4] Cp. WACKERNAGEL 2[1], p. 93, note.

dhanvan- (VS.) 'having a hundred bows'[1]; *śīrṣán-* 'head' (not *śíras-*) in *a-śīrṣán-* 'headless', *tri-śīrṣán-* 'three-headed'[2], f. *rúru-śīrṣn-ī-* 'having the head of a Ruru antelope'[3]; *hṛ́d-* 'heart' (not *hṛ́daya-*) in its long-grade form *-hārd-* in *dur-hárd-* (AV.) 'ill-disposed' and *su-hárd-* 'good-hearted'.

a. Sometimes an alternative stem is used which has not been preserved as an independent word; thus *-jñu-* 'knee' (weak form of *jánu-*) in *asitá-jñu-* (AV.) 'dark-kneed', *mitá-jñu-* 'firm-kneed'[4]; an old stem *-medhas-* in *su-medhás-* 'wise' and *puru-médhas-* (SV.) 'wise' beside the regular compounds in *-medha-* (from *medhá-* 'wisdom') such as *puru-médha-* 'having much wisdom'; *-tvacas-*[5] 'skin' in *sū́rya-tvacas-* (AV. VS.) 'having a skin bright as the sun' and *híraṇya-tvacas-* (AV.) 'having a golden skin', beside *tvac-* in *sū́rya-tvac-* and *híraṇya-tvac-*.

254. **Transfer stems.** — Some four stems appear in certain forms changed to stems in *-as* from a misunderstanding of the nom. *-s* in *-ā-s* (as in *su-prajā́-s*); thus from *prajā́-* 'offspring', *á-prajas-* (AV.) 'having no offspring', and *su-prajás-*[6] 'having good offspring', *íḍa-prajas-*[7] (MS. I. 5[3]) 'descendant of Iḍā'; from *kṣā-* 'dwell', *divá-kṣas-* 'living in heaven'; from *dā-* 'give', *draviṇo-dás-* 'bestowing wealth'; from *dhā-* 'put', *vayo-dhás-* (AV. VS.) 'bestowing strength' and *varco-dhás-* (AV.) 'bestowing vigour'. On the other hand, by the loss of final *-s* or *-t* a few consonant stems are transformed to *a*-stems; thus beside *án-āgas-* 'guiltless' appears *án-āga-*, and beside *puru-dáṃsas-* 'abounding in wondrous deeds', *puru-dáṃsa-*; *ūrv-aṣṭhīvá-* (VS.)[8], n. du. 'thigh and knee', beside *aṣṭhī-vánt-* m. du. 'knees ('bony')'; *ubhayā́-da-*[9] (AV.) 'having teeth in both (jaws)', beside *ubhayā́-dat-*.

255. **Vowel gradation in final member.** — a. 1. The low grade **vowel** of the roots *dā-* 'give' and *dā-* 'cut' **disappears** when the past participles **dita-* 'given'[10] and *dita-* 'cut' and the action noun **diti-* 'giving' become unaccented final members in a compound: thus *dva-tta-* (VS.) 'cut off', *devá-tta-* 'given by the gods', *vy-ā́-tta-* (AV. VS.) 'opened', *párī-tta-* (VS.) 'given up'[11], *á-pratī-tta-* (AV.) 'not given back'; *bhága-tti-* 'gift of fortune', *maghá-tti-* 'giving of presents', *vásu-tti-* 'granting of wealth'[12]. Unreduced forms, however, occur in *tvā́-dāta-* and *tvā́-datta-* 'given by thee' and in *havyá-dāti-* 'sacrificial gift'[13].

2. The vowels *ī* and *ū* in the radical syllable of the final member is in a few instances **reduced** to *i* and *u*; thus *try-udhán-* 'having three udders' (*ū́dhan-*), *dhī-jú-* 'inspiring the mind' (*jū-* 'impel'), *su-ṣirá-* 'having a good channel', 'hollow' (*sīrā́-* 'stream'), *sú-ṣuti-* 'easy birth' (*sū-tí-* TB.), *ā́-huti-* 'invocation' (otherwise *sá-hūti-* 'joint invocation', etc.). Derivative *-ī* is reduced to *-i* in *á-ni-bhṛṣṭa-taviṣi-* 'having unabated power' (*táviṣ-ī-*).

1 The determinative *indra-dhanús-* 'Indra's bow', occurs in the AV.

2 The AV. however has *pṛthú-śiras-* 'broad-headed'.

3 From *ásthan-* (beside *ásthi-*, AV.) occur both *an-asthán-* and *an-asthá-* 'boneless'.

4 Other reduced stems are *sá-gdhi-* (VS.) 'joint meal' (√*ghas-*), *nīḍá-* 'nest' (*ni*+√*sad-*). *upa-bd-i-* 'noise' (*upa*+√*pad-*) *ā́-sk-ra-* 'united' (√*sac-*); perhaps *pari-ṃśá-* 'best part of' (*áṃśa-* 'part').

5 Also in the derivative *tvacas-yà-* (AV.) 'being in the skin'.

6 Under the influence of this new stem is formed *su-prajās-tvá-* 'possession of good offspring' (for **su-prajā-tva-*).

7 In K. *iḍā-prajas-* (IS. 3, 463) with the *ā* of *iḍā-* unshortened.

8 Formed by dropping the *-t* of the weak stem *aṣṭhī-vát-*.

9 Formed by dropping the *-t* of the weak stem *-dat-*.

10 This phonetic form has otherwise been ousted by the anomalous participle *dat-tá-* made from the weak present stem *dad-*.

11 The participle *prá-tta-* 'given up' also occurs in TS. II. 2. 8[4] (B).

12 *prá-tti-* 'gift' also occurs in TS. V. 4. 7[2] (B) and *nir-áva-tti* 'distribution of shares' in K.

13 The *ā* of *sā́man-* 'chant' is perhaps reduced to *a* in *ṛ́k-sama-* (VS.), *ṛ́k-ṣama-* (TS.), and *ṛ́cī-ṣama-*; cp. WACKERNAGEL 2[1], 43 f., note.

3. The *o* of *gó-* 'cow' is **reduced** to *-u* in *púṣṭi-gu-* 'rearing cows', N. of a man, and *su-gú-* 'having fine cows'. The *-ai* of *rái-* 'wealth', is reduced to *-i* in *bṛhád-ri-*[1] 'having abundant wealth'; perhaps also in *ṛdhád-ri-*[2], N. of a man.

4. Final *-i* **and** *-u* of the first member combine with the low grade form of *ā* of *áp-* 'water' in the last member to *ī* and *ū*, in *dvīp-á-*[3] 'island' (*dvi-āp-*), *pratīp-á-m* 'against' (*prati-*) 'the stream', *anūp-á-* 'pond' (*anu-āp-*).

b. On the other hand, **radical *a*** in several instances appears **lengthened** to *ā*[4]. This occurs in several possessive compounds of *jáni-* 'wife': *bhadra-jāni-* 'having a beautiful wife' (only voc.), *yúva-jāni-* 'having a young wife', *vittá-jāni-* 'having found a wife', 'married', and with shifted accent *dvi-jāni-* 'having two wives' and *a-jāni-* (AV.) 'having no wife'. A similar lengthening appears in *pṛthu-jāghana-* (only voc. f.) 'broad-hipped'; *sahá-jānuṣa-* 'with offspring' (*janús-*); *ni-pādá-* 'low ground' (*padá-*); *tvát-pitāras* (TS. I. 5. 10²), N. pl. 'having thee as father'; *su-vā́cas-* 'having good speech', 'very eloquent', *sá-vācas-*[5] (AV.) 'employing similar speech', *ví-vācas-* (AV.) 'speaking in various ways' (*vácas-*), *viśvá-śārada-* (AV.) 'occurring every autumn' (*śarád-*) 'annual', *śatá-śārada-* 'lasting a hundred autumns'[6].

256. Adjectival suffixes. — Adjective compounds not infrequently add certain suffixes to mark their adjectival character more clearly. These suffixes are ***-ka, -i, -ya, -a, -in***.

1. The suffix ***-ka***[7] is thus used in only two somewhat obscure compounds in the RV. *trí-kadru-ka-* (only pl.), a designation of certain soma vessels (*kadrú-*) and *try-àmba-ka-* 'having three mothers' (*amba* voc.); in the AV. occur *ví-manyu-ka-* 'free from anger' and *sahá-kaṇṭhi-kā-* f. 'with the throat' (*kaṇṭhá-*, B.)[8].

2. In the final member of a few **Bahuvrīhis**, the suffix ***-i*** sometimes takes the place of *-a*; thus *práty-ardhi-* 'to whom the half (*árdha-*) belongs'; *ā́ñjana-gandh-i-* 'having a smell (*gandhá-*) of ointment', *dhūmá-gandhi-* 'smelling of smoke', *su-gándhi-* or *su-gandhí* 'sweet-smelling'; *kṛṣṭá-rādhi-* (AV.) 'attaining success (*rā́dha-*) in agriculture'.

3. The suffix ***-ya*** is frequently added **in Bahuvrīhis**; thus *anyódar-ya-* 'born from another womb' (*udára-*), *dáśa-mās-ya-*[9] 'ten months old', *dīrgha-jihv-yà-* 'long-tongued'[10], *mádhu-hast-ya-* 'honey-handed', *mayū́ra-śep-ya-* 'peacock-tailed'[11], *viśvá-jan-ya-* 'belonging to all men', *viśvá-dev-ya-* 'relating to all gods', *viśvāṅg-yà-* (AV.) 'being in all limbs', *sá-garbh-ya-* (VS.) 'born from the same

---

1 In the dative *bṛhádraye*; cp. BB. 25, 250.

2 In the anomalous gen. sing. *ṛdhád-rayas*.

3 Also *nīp-a-* 'low-lying' (*ni-āp-* 'into which the water flows down') in K.

4 For a phonetic explanation of this phenomenon see WACKERNAGEL 2¹, 43 (p. 100); and cp. 1, 68.

5 There is a various reading *sú-vācasas* in AV. VII. 12², on which see WHITNEY's note.

6 On *vi-hāyas-* 'of extensive power', *sárva-hāyas-* (AV.) 'having all vigour', *su-rāmá-* 'delighting', *su-yāmá-* 'guiding well', see WACKERNAGEL 2¹, p. 101 (middle).

7 This suffix, which is never accented, is probably identical with that which forms adjectives, as *ánta-ka-* 'ending' from *ánta-* 'end'.

8 In the YV. several examples occur; WACKERNAGEL 2¹, p. 102, quotes from the TS. *a-karṇá-ka-* 'earless', *a-dantá-ka-* 'toothless', *a-pādá-ka-* 'footless', *an-akṣi-ka-* 'eyeless', *an-asthi-ka-* 'boneless', *a-tvák-ka-* 'skinless', *sā́śīr-ka-* 'accompanied by a blessing', *an-āśīr-ka-* 'lacking a blessing'; from the MS. *a-cchandás-ka-* 'metreless', *an-ástha-ka-* 'boneless'.

9 Also *ṣaṇ-māsya-* 'six months old', and *sapta-māsya-* 'seven months old' in K.

10 Also in TS. some compounds formed with *-deva-tyà-* 'having — for a deity' (*devátā-*); *nānā-viś-yá-* (MS.) 'consisting of various villages'.

11 Also *vi-śiśn-ya-* (K.) 'tailless'.

womb', *sa-dhan-yà-* 'accompanied by gifts', *sá-yūth-ya-* (VS.) 'belonging to the same herd', *su-hást-ya-* 'fair-handed' (beside *su-hásta-*), *hiraṇya-keś-ya-* 'golden-maned' (beside *hiraṇya-keśa-*)[1].

The suffix **-ya** is also common **in governing compounds** with prepositions as first member; thus *ádhi-gart-ya-* 'being on the car-seat', *antaḥ-parśav-yá-* (VS.) and *antaḥ-pārśv-yá-* (VS.) 'being between the ribs', *ánv-āntr-ya-* (AV.) 'being in the entrails', *api-kakṣ-yà-* 'situated near the arm-pit', *úpa-tṛṇ-ya-* (AV.) 'being in the grass', *úpa-mās-ya-* (AV.) 'occurring every month', *pári-rath-ya-* (AV.)[2] 'being around the car', n. part of the car. It also appears in the adverbially used governing compounds *abhi-nabh-yá-m* 'near the clouds' and *ud-āp-yà-m* (AV.) 'upstream'.

4. The final member of **Bahuvrīhis** is very frequently **extended by** the suffix **-a**. In the RV. there are at least fifteen such stems; thus *akṣ-* 'eye' in *an-akṣ-á-*'eyeless', *ádhy-akṣ-a-*'eye-witness', *catur-akṣ-á-* 'four-eyed', *bhūry-akṣ-á-* 'many-eyed', *sahasrākṣ-á-* 'thousand-eyed', *hiraṇyākṣ-á-* 'golden-eyed', *áktākṣ-a-* (AV.) 'whose eyes are anointed', *án-āktākṣ-a-*[3] (AV.) 'whose eyes are not anointed', *dhūmākṣá-* (AV.) 'smoke-eyed', *paryastākṣ-á-* (AV.) 'with eyes cast about', *sanisrasākṣ-á-* (AV.) 'having constantly falling eyes', *hary-akṣ-á-* (VS.) 'yellow-eyed'; **asth-*[4] 'bone' in *an-asth-á-* 'boneless' beside *an-asthán-*; **udar-* 'water' in *an-udr-á-* 'waterless'; *gó-* 'cow' in *su-gáv-a-* 'having fine cows', *saṃ-gav-á-* 'time when cows come together', and in *atithi-gv-á-*, a name, *éta-gv-a-* 'variegated', *dáśa-gva-*, N. of a mythical group, *náva-gv-a-*[5], N. of a mythical group; *janus-* in *sahá-jānuṣ-a-* 'with offspring'; *div-* 'heaven' in *bṛhád-div-a-* and *bṛhad-div-á-*, N. of a seer, *su-div-á-* (AV.) 'bright day'; *dur-* 'door' in *śatá-dur-a-* 'having a hundred doors'; *dhur-* 'yoke' in *su-dhúr-a-* 'going well under the yoke' (beside *su-dhúr-*), *sá-dhur-a-* (AV.) 'harnessed to the same yoke'; *nas-* 'nose' in *urū-ṇas-á-* 'broad-nosed', *pavī-nas-á-* (AV.) 'having a nose like a spear-head', *vārdhrī-nas-á-* (VS.) 'rhinoceros'; *mṛ́dh-* in *vi-mṛdh-á-*[6] (AV.) 'warding off foes' (beside *vi-mṛ́dh-*, VS.); *rái-* 'wealth' in *á-rāy-a-* 'not liberal'; *vástu-* 'dwelling' in *náva-vāstv-a-* 'having nine abodes'; *śarád-* 'autumn' in *śatá-śārad-a-* 'lasting a hundred autumns'; *āp-* 'water' in *dvīp-á-* 'island'[7].

In the later Saṃhitās several other final members extended with *-a* occur: *áhan-* 'day' in *sāhn-á-* (AV.) 'lasting a day'; *ṛ́c-* 'verse' in *eka-rc-á-* (AV.) 'consisting of one verse'; *kṣám-* 'earth' in *su-kṣm-á-* (VS.) 'consisting of good earth'; *netṛ́-* 'leader' in *agní-netr-a-* (VS. TS.)[8] 'having Agni as leader': *path-* 'road', in *vi-path-á-* (AV.), a kind of chariot ('fit for untrodden paths'); *pád-* 'foot' in *á-bd-a-* (VS.) 'year'; **vatas-* 'year' in *tri-vats-á-* (VS.) 'three years old'; *saṃ-dṛ́ś-* 'aspect' in *mádhu-saṃdṛś-a-* (AV.) 'sweet-looking'.

a. The final member is also sometimes **extended with -a after a governing preposition**; thus *ánu-path-a-* 'going along the road', *ántas-path-a-* 'being on the road', *anūp-á-* 'tank' ('lying along the water'), *upānas-á-* 'being on the car' (*-ánas-*), *paró-kṣ-a-* (AV.) 'away from the eye' (*akṣ-*), *puro-gav-á-* 'leader' ('preceding the cows').

---

1 *áśva-budh-ya-* 'based on horses' is probably for **áśva-budhn-ya-* (from *budhná-* 'bottom') beside *áśva-budhna-* 'borne by horses'.

2 The accent of these words in *-ya* is usually the same as it would be without the suffix; for a few exceptions, see WACKERNAGEL 2[1], 47 d (p. 108).

3 The Mss. (AV. XX. 128[6]) read *anāktákṣa-*.

4 See WACKERNAGEL 2[1], p. 108 (bottom).

5 See BLOOMFIELD, AJPh. 17, 422 ff.

6 Also the f. *vi-mṛdh-á-* (TS. II. 4. 2[1] B).

7 On a few doubtful instances see WACKERNAGEL 2[1], p. 109 (bottom).

8 In TS. I. 8. 7[1] = VS. IX. 35, 36 several other names of deities compounded with *-netr-a-* occur.

b. A similar extension with *-a* occurs **in collectives** which are allied to Bahuvrīhis: thus *try-āyuṣ-á-* (VS.) 'threefold lifetime', *dvi-rāj-á-* (AV.) 'battle of two kings', *ṣaḍ-ṛc-á-* 'aggregate of six stanzas', *sam-udr-á-* 'collection of waters' (**udar-*), 'sea', *sa-vidyut-á-* (AV.) 'thunderstorm' ('accompanied by lightning'). Akin to these are compounds in which the first member expresses a part of the last (with change of gender); thus *ardha-rc-á-* (AV. VS.) m. 'half-stanza', *aparāhṇ-á-* (AV.) m. 'afternoon', *ny-áhn-a-* (AV.) 'decline of day', *pūrvāhṇ-á-* 'forenoon', *prá-pad-a-* 'tip of the foot'. There are further some neuter determinatives which probably had originally a collective sense; thus, with change of gender, *tri-div-á-* 'third heaven', *su-div-á-* (AV.) 'fine day'; *á-path-a-* (AV.) 'pathlessness', *su-páth-a-* 'good path'. From neuter stems in *-as*, *devainas-á-* (AV.) 'curse of the gods', *manuṣyainas-á-* (AV.) 'sin (*énas-*) of men'; *brahma-varcas-á-* (AV. VS.) 'divine power', *hasti-varcas-á-* (AV.) 'vigour of an elephant', *brāhmaṇa-varcas-á-* (AV.) 'dignity of a Brahman'.

c. The ending ***-a*** frequently **takes the place of *-an*** [1] in the final member of Bahuvrīhis, collectives, and Karmadhārayas; thus *deva-karmá-* 'doing divine work', *viśvá-karma-* 'performing all work', *vīrá-karma-* 'performing manly work', *priyá-dhāma-* 'occupying desirable places', *chando-nāma-* (VS.) 'named metre', 'metrical', *ví-parva-* 'jointless', *dvi-vṛṣá-* [2] (AV.) 'having two bulls', *añji-sakthá-* (VS.) 'having coloured thighs', *ut-sakthá-* (VS.) 'lifting up the thighs', *lomaśá-saktha-* (VS.) 'having hairy thighs' [3], *ṛk-sāmá-* 'the Ṛc verses and the Sāmans', *ṣaḍ-ahá-* (AV.) m. 'period of six days'; *bhadrāhá-* (AV.) n. 'auspicious day', *eka-vṛṣá-* (AV.) 'only bull', *mahā-vṛṣá-* (AV.) 'great bull'.

d. The suffix ***-a* takes the place of *-i*** in *kavā-sakhá-* 'having a niggard for a friend' (*sákhi-*), in *mandayát-sakha-* 'gladdening his friend', and in *daśāṅgulá-* 'length of ten fingers' (*aṅgúli-*).

5. **In Bahuvrīhis** the suffix ***-in*** is sometimes pleonastically **added**; thus *ku-nakh-ín-* (AV.) 'having bad nails', *mahā-hast-ín-* 'having large hands', *yaśo-bhag-ín-* (VS.) 'rich in glory', *sa-rath-ín-* (VS.) 'riding on the same chariot'.

257. **Classification of Compounds.**—The Indian grammarians divided compounds into three main classes according to their syntactical relations: 1) **copulatives,** or those in which the members are coordinated, called *dvandva-* [4] ('couple'); 2) **determinatives,** or those in which the first member determines the second, called *tat-puruṣa-* ('his man') [5]; 3) those which are **dependent** on another word, called *bahu-vrīhi-* [6]. The latter are usually regarded as compounds of the determinative class transmuted to adjectives, which would thus have a secondary character. They are often called **'possessives'** since their meaning can usually be rendered by 'possessing', as *bahv-anná-* 'possessing much food'. To these may be added three other groups in order to treat Vedic compounds exhaustively: 4) **governing compounds,** or those in which the first member governs the last in sense; e. g. *kṣayád-vīra-* 'ruling men'; 5) a certain remnant of **irregular combinations** which are best dealt with together; 6) **iteratives,** or repeated words which are treated as compounds in the Saṃhitās inasmuch as they have only one accent and a special meaning when thus combined; in these the second member is called *āmreḍita-* 'repeated' by the Indian grammarians.

1 This *-a* probably started in stems ending in *-man*, representing **-mn-a-*; see WACKERNAGEL 2[1], p. 118 c.

2 *-vṛṣa-* for *-vṛ́ṣan-* occurs in the AV. after other numerals also.

3 For some doubtful examples see WACKERNAGEL 2[1], p. 116.

4 The word first occurs in a B. passage of the TS. (1. 6. 9[4]) in the form of *dvandvāni* 'couples', and in the AB.

5 An example used as the name of the class.

6 'Having much rice', an example used as the name of the class.

1. Iteratives.

COLLITZ, Transactions of the Oriental Congress of Berlin 2[2], 287 ff. — DELBRÜCK, Vergleichende Syntax, Dritter Theil (1900), p. 141—153: Iterativcomposita. — WACKERNAGEL 2[1], p. 142—148.

258. The repetition of an inflected form with loss of accent in the second word is very frequent in the RV. Such repetitions are treated in the Pada texts as compounds the members being separated by the Avagraha. The word thus repeated is **generally a substantive** and iteration is expressed chiefly in regard to time or distribution in regard to space; e. g. *áhar-ahar*, *divé-dive*, *dyávi-dyavi* 'every day'; *gṛhé-gṛhe*, *dáme-dame*, *viśé-viśe* 'in every house'; *diśó-diśaḥ* (AV.) 'from every quarter'. Substantives are also thus repeated to express frequency or constant succession in other matters: *śátroḥ-śatroḥ* 'of every foe'; *ánnam-annam* (AV.) 'food in perpetuity'; *agním-agniṃ vaḥ samídhā duvasyata* (VI. 15[6]) 'worship Agni again and again with your fuel', *yajñásya-yajñasya* 'of every sacrifice' (X. 1[5]), *áṅgād-aṅgāt* 'from every limb' (X. 163[6]), *párvaṇi-parvaṇi* 'in every joint' (X. 163[6]). **Adjectives** repeated in this way are **less common**; e. g. *pányam-panyam* .. *á dhāvata* .. *sómam* (VIII. 2[25]) 'cleanse Soma who is again and again to be praised'; *prácīm-prācīm pradíśam* (AV. XII. 3[7]) 'each forward (eastern) direction'; *úttarām-uttarāṃ sámām* (AV. XII. 1[33]) 'each following year', 'year after year'[2].

a. The repeated word was originally used in the singular only. But the plural meaning of this repetition led to the beginnings of plural forms, as *ékam-ekā śatá daduḥ* (V. 52[17]) 'they have given a hundred each' (lit. 'hundreds, each one'). But a word thus iterated seems never to be in the plural except in agreement with a plural.

b. The frequency of *-e* as locative of *a*-stems led to the occasional use of the dative in consonant stems; *div-é-div-e* (for **div-i-div-i*) and *viś-é-viś-e* (for **viś-i-viś-i*).

c. The transition from iteratives to regular compounds, which appears in B., began with numerals. Thus the *éka-ekaḥ* of the RV. (III. 29[15]) appears in the ŚB. as *ékaika-*; and from the *dvá-dvā* of the RV. (VIII. 68[14]) we come to the adverbial *dvan-dvám* 'in pairs' in the MS., and finally to *dvandvá-* 'pair' in the TS. (B).

d. Adjective compounds in which a word is repeated for emphasis are unconnected with iteratives, differing from them both in sense and accent; thus *mahā-mahá-* 'mightily great'; *eṣaiṣí-* f. of **eṣaiṣá-* (= *eṣa-eṣá-*) 'very speedy'[3]. Whether *carā-cará-* and *calā-calá-* 'moveable' belong to this group is somewhat uncertain.

2. Copulative Compounds.

REUTER, Die altindischen nominalcomposita, KZ. 31, 172—87: I. Copulative composita. — DELBRÜCK, Altindische Syntax 31. — RICHTER, Die unechten Nominalkomposita des Altindischen und Altiranischen: IF. 9, 23 ff. — WHITNEY, Sanskrit Grammar 1252—61. — WACKERNAGEL 2[1], 62—74 (p. 149—173).

259. **Classification of Dvandvas.**—This class consists of compounds consisting of two substantives, far less commonly adjectives, the syntactical relation of which in the sentence is the same and which may be regarded as connected in sense by 'and'. The successive stages in the development of this class can be closely traced from the beginning in the Saṃhitās. 1. First we have in the RV. the most numerous group (about three-fourths

1 A vocative repeated to express emphasis is not treated in the same way: in *áraṇyāny áraṇyāni* (X. 146[1]) both vocatives are accented, the second being as emphatic as the first.

2 The only repetition of a verbal form in this way is *píba-piba* (II. 11[11]) 'drink again and again'; cp. above 88.

3 According to GELDNER, VS. 2, 15 the form *eṣaiṣyā́* (RV[1].) is the inst. sing. of *eṣaiṣí-* f. of **eṣaiṣá-*; but according to BR. and GRASSMANN it is neut. pl. of *eṣaiṣyà-* (= *eṣa-eṣyà-*) 'to be striven for with desire', 'desirable'.

of all the Dvandvas) in which the compound consists of two co-ordinated nouns in the dual, each with its own accent. **2.** The first member assumes an unchangeable form. **3.** Only one accent remains and is restricted to the last syllable of the final member. **4.** The first member assumes (but quite rarely in the RV.) the form of the stem. **5.** The formation, becoming more general, can assume plural endings (but the RV. has only a few examples in the last book). **6.** In the later Saṃhitās this type becomes quite general, forming a single category with the dual Dvandvas. **7.** The final stage (of which the examples are few) is that of Dvandvas which are neuter singulars of a collective character.

260. In the commonest and earliest type of the old Dvandvas **each member is dual** in form and has a separate accent. This type seems to have originated from two grammatical practices frequent in the Vedas: **(a)** the juxtaposition of two coordinate words without *ca*; e. g. *bhū́mano diváś pári* (IX. 73^{5}) 'away from earth and heaven', *krátuṃ dákṣam* (VIII. 42^{3}) 'understanding and will'; **(b)** the use of the elliptic dual[1] which puts one of a pair in the dual to express both, as *dyā́vā* 'heaven and earth'. This origin is probable because the dual Dvandvas are found alternating with one or both of these usages; thus *mitrā́-váruṇā* 'Mitra and Varuṇa' appears beside both *mitrā́* alone and *mitró váruṇaḥ* (or *mitró váruṇaś ca* and *mitráś ca váruṇas ca*); *mātárā-pitárā* 'mother and father' beside *mātárā* or *pitárā* and *pitré mātré* and other cases, the VS. (IX. 19) having pleonastically even *pitárā-mātárā ca* meaning 'father and mother'. The transition from the syntactical collocation *divás .. pṛthivyā́s* (VI. 30^{1}) to a dual compound is seen in *divás-pṛthivyós* 'of heaven and earth' (occurring four times in the RV.) where the second word is put in the dual to show clearly that an associated couple is meant. In the RV. the two duals of the compound are often separated; e. g. *dyā́vā ha kṣā́mā* (X. 12^{1}) 'heaven and earth'; *dyā́vā yajñáiḥ pṛthivī́* (VII. 53^{1}); *índrā no átra váruṇā* (IV. 41^{1})[2]; *ā́ náktā barhíḥ sadatām uṣā́sā* (VII. 42^{5}) 'let Night and Dawn seat themselves upon the litter'; *índrā nú pūṣáṇā* (VI. 57^{1}) 'Indra and Pūṣan'; *índrā nv àgnī́* (VI. 59^{3}) 'Indra and Agni', *índrā yo agnī́* (VI. 60^{1})[3]; *cákṣur máhi mitráyor ā́m̐ éti priyáṃ váruṇayoḥ* (VI. 51^{1}) 'the great, dear eye of Mitra and Varuṇa comes'. In two or three examples of tmesis the dual ending appears in the first member only, while the singular remains in the second; thus *mitrā́ ... váruṇaḥ* (VIII. 25^{2}) and *índrā yó vāṃ varuṇa*[4] (VI. 68^{5}) 'O Indra and Varuṇa'. Generally, however, the two duals are in immediate juxtaposition, as *índrā-bṛ́haspátī* 'Indra and Bṛhaspati'; *dyā́vā-pṛthivī́* 'Heaven and Earth'; *agnī́-ṣómā* 'Agni and Soma'; gen. *mitráyor-váruṇayoḥ*[5] 'of Mitra and Varuṇa'.

The characteristic final vowel of the first member is *-ā*[6], as *uṣā́sā-náktā* (or *náktoṣā́sā*); hence it even ousts *-ī* as in *ágnā-viṣṇū* (AV.) 'O Agni and Viṣṇu'. Beside this *-ā* there sometimes appears *a* in the vocative, both in tmesis, as in *mítra rājānā varuṇā* (V. 62^{3}) 'O kings Mitra and Varuṇa' (voc. of *rā́jānā mitrā́-váruṇā*, III. 56^{7}; X. 64^{5}); and when the members are joined, as

---

1 Cp. WACKERNAGEL, KZ. 23, 302 ff., REUTER, KZ. 31, 176 ff., DELBRÜCK, Altindische Syntax 58 (p. 98), Vergleichende Syntax, Erster Theil 41 (p. 137 f.).

2 In each of the first 6 stanzas of IV. 41 *índrā* and *váruṇā* are separated by one or two words of two or three syllables.

3 Also *víṣṇū agan váruṇā* 'Viṣṇu and Varuṇa' in a Mantra in TB. II. 8. 4^{5}.

4 The Pada text here reads *váruṇā*; cp. *índrā kó vāṃ varuṇā* (IV. 41^{1}).

5 Double duals in *-bhyām* do not appear to occur.

6 The ending *-au* or *-āv* never occurs in the first member.

in *párjanya-vātā* (VI. 49[6]), voc. of *parjánya-vātā* (VI. 50[12]), and always in *índra-vāyū*[1] 'O Indra and Vayu'. The ending *-ī* appears in the first member in *agnī-ṣómau* 'Agni and Soma'; and *-ū* in *krátū-dákṣau* (VS.)[2].

261. These coordinate duals having early come to be regarded as a unit, the commonest ending of the **first member**, that of the nom. acc., came to be retained **unaltered** in other cases and in derivatives[3]. Thus arose the forms *mitrā́-váruṇābhyām*; *mitrā́-váruṇayos* beside *mitráyor-váruṇayos*, *índrā-váruṇayos*; in the AV. *dyā́vā-pṛthivī́bhyām* and *dyā́vā-pṛthivyós* (instead of the *divás-pṛthivyós* of the RV.).

262. In a minority of instances, but comparatively oftener in the later Saṃhitās than in the RV., the **first member loses its accent** and only the last syllable of the final member (irrespectively of its original accent) has the acute[4]; thus *indrā-pūṣṇós* (beside *indrā-pūṣáṇā*); *somā-pūṣábhyām*; *bhavā-rudráu* (AV.) 'Bhava and Rudra', *bhavā-śarváu* (AV.) 'Bhava and Śarva'[5]; *vātā-parjanyā́* 'Vāta and Parjanya' (*parjánya-*); *sūryā-candramásā* 'sun and moon' (*candrá-mas-*).

a. In the later Saṃhitās there are a few examples in which the nom. sing. of stems in *-tṛ* has, doubtless owing to identity in form of the final vowel with the Vedic dual ending *-ā*, become fixed in the first member: *pitā-putráu* (AV.) 'father and son'; *neṣṭā-potṛ́bhyām* (TS. I. 8. 18[1]) 'to the Neṣṭṛ and the Potṛ'[6]. They doubtless started from syntactically coordinated nominatives (like *divás-pṛthivyós* beside *divás pṛthivyā́s*, VI. 47[27])[7].

263. Dvandvas with a single accent having established themselves, the **stem form** began to encroach **in the first member**. The only two examples from RV. I.—IX, are *indra-vāyū́* (the transition being facilitated by the more frequent occurrence of the vocative *índra-vāyū*) and *satyānṛté*[8] (VII. 49[3]) 'truth and untruth'. Two additional neuters occurs in book X: *sāśanānaśané* 'what eats (*sa-aśana-*) and does not eat' (*an-aśana-*); and *ṛk-sāmábhyām* 'with hymns and chant'. In the later Saṃhitās this becomes the prevailing type regularly followed in new formations; *prastotṛ-pratihartṛ́bhyām* (TS. I. 8. 18[1]) 'to the Prastotṛ and Pratihartṛ'; *krátū-dákṣau* (VS.); *dakṣa-kratū́* (TS.), *śūdrāryáu* (VS.) 'a Śūdra and an Ārya'[9].

264. The stem form having established itself in the first member, the compounding of Dvandvas became freer, and not only neuters but **feminines** began to be admitted, as *dīkṣā-tapás-os* (VS.) 'consecration and austerity'. Here, too, the final syllable of the compound has the acute; the svarita of the original word is, however, retained in *brahma-rājanyàu* (VS. XXVI. 2; AV. XI. 32[8]) 'a Brahman and a warrior'.

265. Dvandvas with **plural ending** are on the whole later than those with dual ending. They would first have been used to express the plural sense of the pair in question, thus *ṣáḷ āhur dyā́vā-pṛthivī́ḥ* (VIII. 9[16]) 'they speak of six heaven-and-earths'; *aho-rātrā́ṇi* = 'pairs of day-and-night'.

1 This Dvandva always has *u* even in the nom. *indra-vāyū́*.

2 The dual notion is sometimes emphasized by the addition of *ubháu* 'both', as *ubhā́ mitrā́-váruṇā*; *sūryā-candramásāv ubhā́* (AV.).

3 Like *jeder-manns* for *jedes-manns* in German. BARTHOLOMAE, IF. 20, 168 (Anzeiger) regards these Dvandvas as abbreviations by dropping the common ending in the first member.

4 This accentuation is probably due to the influence of collective compounds which are nearly allied to Dvandvas. *Indrāgnī́*, *indrāgnī́bhyām*, *indrāgnyós* and *agnīndrā́bhyām* are examples which may contain the stem form in the first member (263).

5 WACKERNAGEL 2[1], p. 153, also quotes *somā-rudráyos* (TS.), *uṣṇihā-kakúbhau* (MS.).

6 On *tvaṣṭī-varūtrī* see WACKERNAGEL 2[1], 64 (p. 154).

7 The three divisions of Dvandvas treated above include masculines and feminines only. Neuters of similar type first appear in the Sūtras, as *idhmā-barhiṣī* 'fuel and litter'.

8 This is the earliest example of a neuter Dvandva.

9 WACKERNAGEL 2[1], p. 155, gives some further examples from B. portions of the later Saṃhitās.

A transition to the use of plural Dvandvas, that is, of pairs of groups, is made by *indrā-marutas* 'O Indra and Maruts', where the dual notion is made up of a singular on the one hand and a group on the other. The older type of such plural Dvandvas (which express two coordinated plurals, the first member retaining its accent and the archaic ending *-ā*, like the *-ā* of dual Dvandvas) is represented by *áṅgā-párūṃṣi* 'limbs and joints' occurring in a B. passage of the TS. (II. 5. 6[1]). Examples of the later type with one accent are *ukthā-śastrā́ṇi* (VS. XIX. 28) 'recitations and praises', *ukthā-madā́ni* (AV.) 'recitations and rejoicings', and probably *ukthārkā́* (VI. 34[1]) 'recitations and hymns'[1]. The latest type of these plural Dvandvas (like that of the duals) has the stem form in the first as well as the acute on the last syllable of the final member. The only examples of this type in the RV. occur in book X: *aho-rātrā́ṇi*[2] 'days and nights', *ajāváyas* 'goats and sheep', *dhana-bhakṣéṣu* 'in riches and enjoyments'. In the later Saṃhitās this type becomes quite general, forming a single category with the duals; e. g. *deva-manuṣyā́s* (AV. VIII. 10[9]), *bhadra-pāpā́s* (AV.) 'the good and the bad', *priyāpriyā́ṇi* (AV.) 'pleasant and unpleasant things'[3].

a. The expression *ámṛta mártyānām* (I. 26[9]) appears to be an abridgment for *amṛ́tānām mártyānām* 'of immortals (and) mortals', amounting almost to a plural Dvandva (= *amṛta-martyā́nām*)[4].

266. A few Dvandvas appear in the Saṃhitās with a **singular** ending, these being **neuter** only. The older type in which a dual or plural has been turned into a singular at the end, only in order to express a collective meaning, is represented in the RV. by *iṣṭā-pūrtám*[5] 'what has been offered or given', originally a pl. n. in both members (**iṣṭā́-pūrtā́*) which has become a singular to emphasize its collective character[6]. Both owing to the lack of an early type of neuter Dvandvas and because of the desire to express a collective sense, nearly all the neuter Dvandvas of the later kind are singular. In most instances both members are neuter; e. g. *kṛtākṛtá-m* (AV.) 'what has been done and not done', *cittākūtá-m* (AV.) 'thought and intention' (*ā́kūta-*), *bhūta-bhavyá-m* (AV.) 'the past and the future', *samiṣṭa-yajús* (VS.) 'sacrifice and sacrificial formula'; *bhadra-pāpásya* (AV.) 'of good and evil', *añjanābhyañjana-m* (AV.) 'unction and inunction' (*abhyañjana-*), *kaśipūpabarhaṇá-m* (AV.) 'mat and pillow'.

a. In a few instances the first member is a masculine or feminine: *keśa-śmaśrú* (AV.) 'hair and beard', *iṣv-āyudhé* (loc. sing.) 'arrows and weapons' (AV.).

267. Adjectives also occur **as Dvandvas**, but they are of rare occurrence. Three types may be distinguished.

1. Adjectives of **colour** expressing a mixture: e. g. *nīla-lohitá-* 'dark-blue and red' = 'dark red'; *tāmra-dhūmrá-* (AV.) 'red and black' = 'dark red'; *aruṇá-babhru-* (VS.) 'ruddy and yellow', *dhūmrá-rohita-* (VS.) 'grey and red'[7].

---

1 Probably = *ukthā́-arkā́*, not *uktha-arkā́*, the gender of the first member having prevailed over that of the last.

2 The gender of the first member here prevails over that of the second.

3 Some other examples from B. passages of the Saṃhitās in WACKERNAGEL 2[1], p. 157. The oldest example of a Dvandva consisting of three members is *prāṇāpānodānéṣu* (TS. VII. 3. 3[1]) 'in the outward, the downward and the upward airs', where the plural results from the addition of three individual things (not three groups).

4 Cp. WACKERNAGEL 2[1], p. 157.

5 See WINDISCH in Festgruss an Böhtlingk, p. 115 ff.

6 WACKERNAGEL (2[1], 68) quotes *idhmā́-barhís* from the MS., 'fuel and litter', which with its double accent as well as dual ending in the first member represents a still earlier type.

7 Except in these colour adjectives in the VS., the accentuation of the adjective Dvandvas is the same as that of neuter substantive Dvandvas, that is, the last syllable of the final member has the acute.

2. Adjectives expressing a **contrast**; e. g. *utkūla-nikūlá* (VS.) 'going uphill and downhill'.

3. Adjectives used with dual or plural substantives to express that **each is an attribute** of one unit of the kind; e. g. *padbhyā́ṃ dakṣiṇa-savyā́bhyām* (AV. XII. 1[28]) 'with the right foot and the left'; or with the substantive to be supplied, *saptamāṣṭamā́bhyāṃ svā́hā* (AV.) 'hail to the seventh and the eighth (Aṅgirasa)'; *aghaśaṃsa-duḥśaṃsā́bhyām* (AV.) 'by those plotting evil and those plotting ill'; *sāhnātirātráu* (AV.) 'terminating with a day (*sa-ahna-*) and exceeding a day' (*ati-rātrá-*).

268. As regards the **order of the members** in a Dvandva, the rule seems to be that the more important or the shorter word comes first; thus *dyā́vā-kṣā́mā, dyā́vā-bhū́mī, dyā́vā-pṛthivī́*[1] 'heaven and earth'; *sū́ryā-mā́sā* and *sūryā-candramásā* 'sun and moon'; *índrā-váruṇā* 'Indra and Varuṇa'; *ulūkhala-musalé* (AV.) 'mortar and pestle'. *Indrā-* regularly comes first in the RV. and the later Saṃhitās in some dozen Dvandvas[2]; e. g. *indrāgnī́*; otherwise *agnī-* always precedes; *sóma-* comes after *indrā-* and *agnī-*, but before *pūṣan-* and *rudra-*. The longer word comes first, perhaps, as the more important, in *parjányā-vā́tā*[3] 'Parjanya and Vāta' and in *turváśa-yádū* 'Turvaśa and Yadu'. This can hardly be the reason in *sambādha-tandryàs* (AV.) 'oppressions and weariness'. The shorter word comes first in *mitrā́-váruṇā*, though Varuṇa is the more important of the two[4]; in *ṛk-sāmā́bhyām* the shorter word is at the same time the more important.

3. Determinative Compounds.

269. Classification.—The large class of determinative compounds in which the first member determines or limits the sense of the last, is best divided into **two main groups.** In the one, the final member is a verbal noun which governs the first member in meaning, and often even in form, as a verb governs its case. In the other, the final member is an ordinary noun (either adjective or substantive), the relation of which to the first member is a purely nominal one.

a. Verbal Noun as final member.

270. The final member is often a **verbal noun** either **not occurring as a simple word** or at least not belonging to a type used as simple words: either the **bare root**[5] or a verbal derivative formed with the **suffixes** ***-a, -ana, -i, -in, -man, -van.*** These nouns limited to use as final members are **agent nouns**; e. g. *havir-ád-* 'eating the oblation', *sam-ídh-* 'flaming', *jyotiṣ-kṛ́-t-* 'producing light', *abhi-hrú-t-* 'causing injury', *go-ghn-á-* 'cow-slaying', *ā-kar-á-* 'scattering'; *amitra-dámbh-ana-* 'injuring enemies', *tuvi-gr-í-* 'devouring much', *uru-cákr-i-* 'doing large work'; *bhadra-vād-ín-* 'uttering an auspicious cry'; *āśu-hé-man-* 'swiftly speeding', *bhūri-dā́-van-*[6] 'giving much'.— Occasionally agent-nouns limited to use as final members are formed with other suffixes: *prati-dī́v-an-* 'adversary at play', *ví-bhv-an-* 'far-reaching' and *vi-bhv-án-* 'skilful'; *pra-py-asá-* (AV.) 'swelling', *sva-bhy-asá-* (AV.) 'spontaneously frightened';

---

1 This form occurs 79 times in the RV. and *pṛthivī-dyā́vā* only once.

2 Otherwise only *agnīndrā́bhyām* (VS.) 'Agni and Indra'. Cp. the list of dual divinities in Vedic Mythology, Grundriss III, 1 A, p. 126.

3 Once also *vātā-parjanyā́*.

4 Cp. WACKERNAGEL 2[1], p. 168 (middle).

5 Appearing in its weakest form or, if ending in a short vowel, with determinative *-t*.

6 *-mant* and *-vant* occasionally appear as variations for *-man* and *-van*, as *vi-rúkmant-* 'shining'; *prāṇa-dá-vant-* (AV.) 'life-giving' (cp. WHITNEY on AV. IV. 35[5]); see REUTER, KZ. 31, 560 f.

duḥ-śás-u- 'malignant', *vi-bhind-ú-* 'splitting', *pra-yíy-u-* 'used for driving', *go-vind-ú-* 'seeking cows', *pari-tatn-ú-* (AV.) 'encompassing', *puṃś-cal-ū́-* (VS.) 'prostitute'; *pīva-sphā-ká-*[1] (AV[1].) 'abounding in fat', *ni-há-kā-* 'whirlwind'; *vi-bhañj-anú-* 'shattering'; *pra-cet-úna-* 'affording a wide prospect'; *div-i-tmant-* 'going to heaven'; *tuvi-kūrm-í(n)-* 'stirring mightily'; *vāsaḥ-palpūl-ī́-* (VS.) 'washing clothes'.

a. The meaning of these agent-nouns restricted in use as final members is chiefly active. But in those of them which consist of the bare root (with or without the determinative *-t*) it is often intransitive; e. g. *namo-vṛ́dh-* 'growing by adoration'; it is not infrequently passive, as *mano-yúj-* 'yoked at will', *su-yúj-* 'well-yoked'; *yāma-hū́-* 'called by entreaties', *indra-pā́-tama-* 'most eagerly drunk by Indra', *tīvra-sú-t-* 'pressed from the fermenting mass', *hṛdaya-vidh-* 'pierced to the heart'[2] (AV.). The passive meaning also appears in one derivative formed with *-a*: *pari-mar-á-* (TS.) 'died around' = 'around whom people die'. Final members formed with *-a*, *-ana*, *(i)-tu* when compounded with *su-* or *dus-* also have a passive (gerundive) meaning expressive of the ease or difficulty with which the verbal action is performed; e. g. *su-kár-a-* 'easy to be done', *su-mán-tu-* 'easily recognisable', *su-ved-aná-* 'easily acquired'; *dur-āp-aná-* 'hard to attain'; *dur-ni-yán-tu-* 'hard to restrain', *dur-dhár-ī-tu-* 'irresistible', *dū-ḍábha-* 'hard to deceive'; also an isolated derivative with *-i*, *dur-gṛ́bh-i-* 'hard to catch', and one with *-na*, *su-śrú-ṇa-* 'easily heard' (beside *su-śrú-t-* 'hearing easily').

271. A certain number of **verbal nouns** restricted to employment as final members which are formed **from the simple root** (with or without determinative *-t*) or **with the suffixes *-a*, *-ana*, *-tha*** are **nouns of action**; e.g. *śrad-dhā́-* 'belief', *āśīr-dā́-* (VS. TS.) 'fulfilment of wishes', *úpa-stu-t-* 'invocation', *pari-pád-* 'snare', *saṃ-nám-* (AV.) 'affection'; *kṣudhā-mār-á-* (AV.) 'death by hunger', *pāpa-vād-á-* (AV.) 'evil cry'; *deva-héḍ-ana-* 'offence against the gods', *baddhaka-móc-ana-* (AV.) 'release of a prisoner'; *go-pī-thá-* 'drink of milk', *putra-kṛ-thá-* 'procreation of sons', *sam-i-thá-* 'conflict'. *kāma-pr-á-* is both a noun of action, 'fulfilment of desires' (AV.) and an agent-noun, 'fulfilling desires' (RV.)[3].

a. A class of secondary nouns of action is here formed by adding the **suffixes *-ya* and *-yā́*** to agent nouns formed from the simple root (with or without *-t*). These are abstracts (neuter and feminine respectively); e. g. *havir-ád-ya-* 'enjoyment of the oblation'; *pūrva-pā́y-ya-* and *pūrva-pé-ya-* 'precedence in drinking' (*pūrva-pā́-* 'drinking first'), *nṛ-pā́y-ya-* 'protection of men', *bahu-pā́y-ya-* 'protection of many', 'large hall', *deva-yáj-ya-* n. and *-yaj-yā́-* f. 'adoration of the gods' (*deva-yáj-* 'adoring the gods', VS.), *nṛ-ṣā́h-ya-* 'overcoming of men' (*nṛ-ṣā́h-* 'overcoming men'), *rāja-sū́-ya-* (AV.) 'royal consecration' (*rāja-sū́-* 'creating a king', VS.), *madhyama-sthéy-ya-* 'standing in the middle' (*madhyama-sthā́-* adj., VS.); *su-kṛt-yā́-* 'righteousness' (*su-kṛ́-t-* 'righteous').

272. The **close verbal connexion** of these final members **with the roots** from which they are derived, shows itself formally. Thus they retain the palatal of the verb where the guttural would otherwise appear[4]. Again, agent nouns of this kind are formed from almost every kind of present stem. The following are examples of such nouns **from present stems** of: **1.** the **first class**: *cakram-ā-sajá-* 'stopping[5] the wheel'; **2.** the **sixth class**: *ut-tudá-* (AV.) 'instigator' (*tudá-ti*), *saṃ-girá-* (AV.) 'swallowing' (*sáṃ girāmi*). **3.** stems with ***-cha***: *go-vyacchá-* (VS.) 'cow-tormentor' (from a lost present stem **vyaccha-*)

---

1 For *pīvas-sphāká-*; the Mss. read *pībasphāká-m* (Pada *pībaḥ-phākám*): see Whitney on AV. IV. 73.

2 But 'heart-piercing' (RV.).

3 Isolated examples of nouns of action formed with other suffixes are *su-papt-ani-* 'good flight', *saṃ-śreṣ-iṇá-* (AV.) 'conflict'(?).

4 See Wackernagel 2[1], 76. Exceptions to this would be *tuvi-kūrmi-(n)-* and *divā-kará-* (AV.) 'sun', if these words are derived from *car-* 'fare'.

5 From *ā́ sajāmi* 'I attach'.

4. the **fourth class or passive with** ***-ya***: *akṛṣṭa-pacyá-*[1] (AV. VS. TS.) 'ripening in unploughed ground', *a-paśyá-* 'not seeing', *ugram-paśyá-* (AV.) 'fierce-looking', *mām-paśyá-* (AV.) 'looking at me', *adhi-paśya-* (AV. Paipp.) 'superintendent', *punar-manyá-* 'remembering' (*mánya-te* 'thinks'), *á-riṣaṇya-* 'not failing' (*riṣaṇyá-ti*), *bála-vi-jñāyá-* 'recognized by his strength', *a-vi-dasyá-* 'not ceasing' (*ví dasyanti* 'they cease'), *a-vi-driyá-* 'not bursting' (*dṛ-* 'split'). 5. stems with ***-aya***: *vācam-īṅkhayá-* 'stirring the voice', *samudram-īṅkhaya-* (only voc.) 'stirring the vat' (*īṅkháya-nti* 'they shake'), *viśvam-ejaya-* (only voc.) 'exciting all' (*ejáya-ti* 'sets in motion)', *ati-pārayá-* 'putting across'. 6. the **fifth (*-nu*) and ninth (*-nā*) classes**: *viśvam-invá-* 'all-urging' (*inó-ti*, *inv-a-ti* 'urges'), *dhiyaṃ-jinvá-* 'stirring devotion' and *viśva-jinvā* (voc. du.) 'all-quickening' (*jínv-a-ti* 'stirs'), *ā-daghná-* 'reaching to the mouth'[2] (*dagh-nu-yāt* 'may reach', K.), *dura-dabhná-* (AV.) 'eluding doors' = 'not to be kept by bars and bolts' (*dabhnuv-anti* 'they deceive'), *dānu-pinvá-* 'swelling with drops' (*pinv-āná-* 'swelling'), *sadā-pṛṇá-* 'always giving' (*pṛṇá-ti* 'fills', 'bestows'), *a-miná-*[3] (beside *á-minant-*) 'undiminishing' (*minā́-ti* 'diminishes'), *pra-mṛṇá-* 'destroying' (*pra-mṛṇánt-* 'crushing', *prá mṛṇa* 'destroy'), *a-sinvá-*[4] (beside *á-sinvant-*) 'insatiable', *a-sunv-á-* 'not pressing Soma' (beside *á-sunv-ant-*). 7. the **sixth and seventh classes**: *agnim-indhá-* 'fire-kindling' (*indh-áte* 'they kindle'), *pra-kṛntá-* (TS. IV. 5. 3[1]) and *vi-kṛntá-* (VS.) 'cutting to pieces' (*kṛntá-ti* 'cuts'), *bhūmi-dṛṃhá-* (AV.) 'firmly fixed on the ground' (*dṛ́ṃha-ta* 'make firm'), *ni-limpá-* (AV.) a kind of supernatural being (*ní limpāmi* 'I besmear', AV.). 8. the **root class**: *vrātya-bruvá-* (AV.) 'calling himself a Vrātya' (*bruv-ánti* 'they say'). 9. the **reduplicating class**: *anu-jighrá-* (AV.) 'snuffing at' (*jíghrantī* 'smelling'), *sam-pibá-* (AV.) 'swallowing down' (*sám pibāmi*, AV.)[5].

a. In a few instances verbal nouns which are final members of compounds in the RV. or the later Saṃhitās subsequently appear as independent words. Thus *jāta-vidyā́-* 'knowledge of things', *vidyā́-* (AV. TS.) 'knowledge'[6]. On the other hand, verbal nouns derived from roots without suffix, which in the RV. appear both as independent words and as final members of compounds, often survive in the later Saṃhitās in their compound form only; such are *túr-* 'racing', *dā́-* 'giver', *sū́-* m. 'begetter', f. 'mother', *sthā́-* 'standing'. As a rule verbal nouns which occur independently have the same general meaning as when they form the final member of a compound. But those formed without any suffix generally, and those formed with *-a* occasionally, have the sense of agent nouns at the end of compounds, but of action nouns or of designations of things conceived as feminine, when they are used independently. Thus *gṛ́bh-* f. 'act of seizing', *jīva-gṛ́bh-* adj. 'seizing alive'; *vid-ā́* 'with knowledge', *hotrā-víd-* adj. 'knowing the oblation', *yúdh-* f. 'fight', *pra-yúdh-* adj. 'assailing'; *bhar-á-* (AV.) 'act of carrying', *puṣṭim-bhará-* 'bringing prosperity'. Sometimes the simple word has the meaning of an agent noun as well as of an action noun; e. g. *dṛ́ś-* adj. 'seeing' and f. 'act of seeing'; *bhúj-* adj. 'enjoying' and f. 'enjoyment'; *stúbh-* adj. 'shouting' and f. 'shout'; but at the end of a compound these three words express the agent only. Similarly *grābh-á-* m. 'seizer' (AV.) and 'grasp', but *grāva-grābh-á-* 'handling the Soma stones'[7].

273. **Independent verbal nouns.** — Several kinds of verbal nouns which are also capable of independent use occur as final member of compounds. Among these the only ones of frequent occurrence are those in *-ta* which are adjectives (often used as substantives) and the corresponding abstract

[1] WACKERNAGEL 2[1], p. 179 (bottom), refutes the view that this *-ya* is identical with that of the gerundive.

[2] *-daghna-* forms the last member of several other compounds in the later Saṃhitās. See WACKERNAGEL 2[1], p. 181.

[3] Cp. WACKERNAGEL 2[1], p. 181, note.

[4] From a lost root **si-nó-ti* 'satisfies'.

[5] There is also a transition form (leading to the later *-dada-*) in *āyur-dád-am* (AV.) acc. f. 'life-giving' (beside *āyur-dā́-*, AV. VS. TS.): *dád-ati* 'they give'.

[6] For examples of verbal nouns which assume an independent character in the later language, see WACKERNAGEL 2[1], 77 a.

[7] On the origin of these verbal compounds and the relation of the final member to the independent word, see WACKERNAGEL 2[1], 78 b and note (p. 186 f.).

substantives in *-ti*; e. g. *puró-hita-* adj. 'placed in front', m. 'domestic priest'; *puró-hiti-* f. 'domestic priesthood'.

1. **Agent nouns.** Those which are formed with *-aka* and *-snu* are compounded with prepositions only: *abhi-krόś-aka-* (VS.) 'one who cries out', *vi-lā́y-aka-* (VS.) 'melter'; *abhi-śocayi-ṣṇú-* (AV.) 'causing heat', *ni-ṣat-snú-* 'sitting firmly'. Agent nouns in *-tṛ* may be compounded with adverbs, as *pura-etṛ́-* 'going before', *puraḥ-sthātṛ́-* 'standing at the head', and rarely with substantives, as *nṛ-pātṛ́-* 'protecting men', *man-dhātṛ́-*[1] 'applying (his) mind', 'thoughtful man'. Agent nouns formed with *-u* from secondary present stems are in a few instances compounded with substantives: *gir-vanasy-ú-* 'fond of hymns', *deva-pīy-ú-* (AV. VS.) 'hating the gods', *rāṣṭra-dips-ú-* (AV.) 'wishing to injure the country'.

2. **Action nouns.** A few action nouns formed with *-ā* from adjectives in *-u* derived from secondary verbal stems, begin in late passages of the RV. to appear in composition with a substantive: *māṃsa-bhikṣ-ā́-* (I. 162^{12}) 'request for flesh', *śraddhā-manasy-ā́-* 'faithful intent' (X. 113^{9}); *sajāta-vanasy-ā́-* (TS. II. 6. 6^{7}) 'desire to rule over relatives'. Much more common are the abstracts in *-ti* (corresponding to adjectives in *-ta*), which may be compounded with indeclinables or nouns (adjective or substantive)[2]; e. g. *án-ūti-* 'no help', *á-śasti-* 'curse', *nír-ṛti-* 'dissolution', *sá-hūti-* 'joint invocation', *su-ūtí-* 'good aid'; *sóma-pīti-* 'drinking of Soma', *sóma-suti-* 'pressing of Soma'. Some of these are becoming or have become agent nouns; thus *jarád-aṣṭi-* 'attaining great age' as well as 'attainment of old age'; *vásu-dhiti-* 'bestowing wealth' as well as 'bestowal of wealth'; but *vásu-nīti-* (AV.) only 'bringing wealth'. Others, even in the RV., approximate to the type of the non-verbal determinatives, as *ásu-nīti-* 'world of spirits', *ṛjú-nīti-* 'right guidance', *devá-hiti-* 'divine ordinance', *námo-vṛkti-* 'cleansing for adoration', *pūrvá-citti-* 'foreboding': these can, however, be understood as abstracts to corresponding compounds in *-ta*[3].

3. **Gerundives.** The gerundives formed with ***-ya*** are ordinarily compounded with adverbial prepositions, as *puro-'nuvākyā̀-* (sc. *ṛ́c-* AV.) '(verse) to be repeated beforehand'. In the later Saṃhitās a noun here sometimes appears as first member: *nīvi-bhāryà-* (AV.) 'to be worn in a skirt', *prathama-vāsyà-* (AV.) 'worn formerly'. The Proper Names *kuṇḍa-pā́yya-*, *puru-māyyà*, *vṛṣṭi-hávya-*, if they are formed with the gerundive suffix *-ya*, would be examples from the RV.[4]. — Gerundives formed with ***-anīya*** and ***-enya***[5] are compounded with prepositions and *a(n)-* only: *ā-mantraṇīya-* (AV.) 'to be asked'; *saṃ-caréṇya-* 'suitable for walking on', *a-dviṣeṇyá-* 'not malevolent'. — Gerundives in ***-tva*** are not compounded at all except with *a(n)-*.

4. **Participles.** Besides prepositions and *a(n)-*, only indeclinable words occurring in connexion with verbs are found compounded with participles (exclusive of the past passive participle): thus *alalā-bhávant-* 'murmuring' (waters) and *jañjanā-bhávant-* 'crackling' (flame), *astaṃ-yánt-* (AV.) 'setting' and *astam-eṣyánt-* (AV.) 'about to set', *á-punar-dīyamāna-* (AV.) 'not being given back', *āviṣ-kṛṇvāná-* 'making visible', *dúr-vidvāṃs-* 'ill-disposed, *sú-vidvāṃs-* 'knowing well'.

---

1 From *manas-* through **manz-dhātṛ́-*.

2 The verbal force is strongest when the preceding substantive has the sense of an object.

3 As *devá-hiti-* 'act of ordaining by the gods' beside *devá-hita-* 'ordained by the gods'.

4 The compounds *amā-vāsyā̀-* (AV.) sc. *rā́trī-* 'night of the new moon', *eka-vādyā́-* (AV.) 'uttering a single sound', a kind of spectre, and *vār-kāryā́-* (I. 88^{4}) are obscure in their formation.

5 A few gerundives in *-tavya* begin to be compounded with prepositions or particles in the B. portion of the TS. and MS.: *pra-vastavyàm* (TS.) 'one should go on a journey'; *a-bhartavyá-* (MS.) 'not to be borne', *sv-ètavyam* (TS.) 'easy to go'.

a. By far the commonest verbal nouns occurring as final member are the **past participles in *-ta***, which are compounded with nouns as well as prepositions and other indeclinables. The meaning is mostly passive. It is, however, sometimes active, but in the RV. almost exclusively when a preposition precedes, as *úd-ita-* 'risen'; when a noun precedes, only in *sárga-takta-* 'speeding with a rush' and *sárga-pratakta-* 'darting forth with a rush'. In the AV. a noun appears also in *uda-plutá-* 'swimming in the water'; occasionally even transitively governing the first member in sense: *kṛtá-dviṣṭa-* (AV.) 'hating what has been done' (by another)[1].

b. The **past participle in *-na*** is less frequent and occurs in the RV. only compounded with prepositions, *a(n)-* and *su-*; e. g. *pári-cchinna-* 'lopped around'; *á-bhinna-* 'not split'; *sú-pūrṇa-* 'quite full'. But it is found a few times in the later Saṃhitās with a preceding substantive: *agní-nunna-* (SV.) 'driven away by fire', *reṣmá-cchinna-* (AV.) 'rent by a storm'; and with active (transitive) sense *gara-gīrṇá-* (AV.) 'having swallowed poison'.

5. There are besides some **verbal adjectives in *-ra*** or (after a vowel) ***-tra*, *-la*** and ***-ma***, the first of which occurs compounded with nouns as well as prepositions: *á-sk-ra-* 'united'[2], *ní-mṛg-ra-* 'attached to', *tanú-śubh-ra-* 'shining in body', *hári-ścand-ra-* 'shining yellow'; *ví-bhṛ-tra-* 'to be borne about in various directions'; *á-miś-la-*, *ní-miś-la-*, *sám-miś-la-* 'commingling'; *áva-kṣā-ma-* (AV.) 'emaciated', *úc-chuṣ-ma-* (TS. I. 6. 2[2]) 'hissing upwards', *ní-śuṣ-ma-* (TS. I. 6. 2[2]) 'hissing downwards'.

6. **Comparatives and superlatives in *-īyāṃs*** and ***-iṣṭha*** having originally been verbal adjectives are found in composition with prepositions and *śám-* when they still retain their verbal meaning: *úd-yamīyāṃs-* 'raising excessively', *pári-ṣvajīyāṃs-* (AV.) 'clasping more firmly', *práti-cyavīyāṃs-* 'pressing closer against', *ví-kledīyāṃs-* (AV.) 'moistening more'; *á-gamiṣṭha-* 'coming quickly', *śám-bhaviṣṭha-* 'most beneficial'.

First member in verbal determinatives.

274. a. **Prepositions.** At the beginning of **determinatives** prepositions are employed in accordance with their use in verbal forms; e. g. *pra-ṇí-* and *prá-ṇīti-* 'furtherance', *pra-ṇetṛ́-* 'leader', *prá-ṇīta-* 'furthered', *pra-ṇení-* 'guiding constantly'. Even in the many instances in which the corresponding verbal combination has not been preserved, it may be assumed to have existed; e. g. in *abhi-pra-múr-* 'crushing' and *abhi-pra-bhaṅgín-* 'breaking'. Occasionally, however, the preposition has a meaning which otherwise occurs only before non-verbal nouns; e. g. *ati-yājá-* 'sacrificing excessively'[3]. A preposition belonging to the second member is once prefixed to the first in *saṃ-dhanā-ji-t* (AV.) 'accumulating (= *saṃ-ji-t-*) 'wealth'.

b. **Adverbs.** Various kinds of adverbs occur in this position, as *puro-yávan-* 'going before', *akṣṇayā-drúh-* 'injuring wrongly'; *amutra-bhúya-* (AV. VS.) 'state of being there' (i. e. in the other world). The privative *a(n)-* though belonging in sense to the final member always precedes the first; e. g. *án-agni-dagdha-* 'not burnt by fire'; *á-paścād-daghvan-* 'not remaining behind'; *á-dāra-sṛ-t* (AV.) 'not falling into a crack'.

c. **Nouns.** The first member, when a noun, expresses various relations to the last.

[1] Cp. WACKERNAGEL 2[1], p. 195; but also WHITNEY on AV. VII. 113[1].

[2] From *sac-* 'be associated'.

[3] In TS. II. 5. 4[4] (B.) *ati-yaj-* means 'to pass over in sacrificing'.

It expresses: 1. the **object**, which is the prevailing meaning when the final member is an agent noun or an action noun; e. g. *ab-jí-t-* 'winning waters', *aśva-hayá-* 'urging on steeds', *nṛ-pāti-* 'protecting men', *vája-sāti-* 'act of winning booty', *vṛtra-hátya-* n. 'act of slaying Vṛtra'[1]. When the final member is a verbal noun formed from *kṛ-* 'make', the first member does not necessarily express the product, but may mean the material with which the activity is concerned; thus *hiraṇya-kārá-* (VS.) is not 'gold-maker' but 'worker in gold', 'goldsmith'.

2. the **agent** when the last member has a passive sense; e. g. *indra-pá-tama-* 'most drunk by Indra', *sóma-śita-* 'excited by Soma'; occasionally also when the final member is an action noun, as *devá-hiti-* 'ordinance of the gods', *parṇa-śadá-* (AV. VS.) 'fall of leaves', *mitra-túrya-* (AV.) 'victory of friends'.

3. the **instrument**, the **source**, or the **locality** when the final member is an agent noun or a past passive participle; e. g. *ádri-dugdha-*[2] 'milked with stones', *aritra-páraṇa-* 'crossing with oars'; *gó-jāta-* 'produced from kine', *tīvra-sú-t-* 'pressed from the fermenting mass'; *uda-plutá-* (AV.) 'swimming in the water', *áhar-jāta-* (AV.) 'born in the day', *puru-bhú-* 'being in many places', *bandhu-kṣí-t-* 'dwelling among relatives', *pṛśni-ni-preṣita-*[3] 'sent down to earth'.

4. in an **appositionally nominative sense**, that as or like which the action of the final member is performed; e. g. *íśāna-kṛ́-t-* 'acting as a ruler', *pūrva-pá-* 'drinking first', *vāmá-jāta-* 'born as one dear' = 'dear by nature'; *dhāra-vāká-* 'sounding like streams', *śyená-jūta-* 'speeding like an eagle'.

5. in the sense of a **predicative nominative** before a past participle, or a **predicative accusative** before an agent noun expressive of 'saying'; e. g. *bhakṣám-kṛta-* (TS.) 'enjoyed', *stóma-taṣṭa-* 'fashioned as a hymn of praise'; *vrātya-bruvá-* (AV.) 'calling oneself a Vrātya'.

6. **adverbially the manner** in which an action is done, sometimes by means of a substantive, more often by means of an adjective; e. g. *ṛtv-íj-* 'sacrificing at the proper time', that is, 'regularly', *sárga-takta-* 'speeding with a rush'; *āśu-pátvan-* 'flying swiftly', *dhruva-kṣí-t-* (VS.) 'dwelling securely', *satya-yáj-* 'sacrificing truly'; with a numeral in *dvi-já-* (AV.) 'twice-born'.

275. Before a verbal noun a nominal **first member** very often appears **with a case-ending**[4], generally with that which the corresponding verb would govern in a sentence. The accusative is here the commonest case, the locative coming next, while the other cases are rarer. A singular case-ending (the acc. or inst.) may here indicate a plural sense; e. g. *áśvam-iṣṭi-* 'seeking horses', *puraṃ-dará-* 'destroyer of forts', *śúneṣita-* 'driven by dogs' (*śúnā-*). Plural (acc.) endings sometimes occur, but dual endings are never found in these compounds.

The **accusative** case-ending is very common, generally expressing the object of a transitive verb, as *dhanaṃ-jayá-* 'winning booty'. But it also expresses other senses, as that of the cognate accusative; e. g. *śubhaṃ-yá-(van)-* 'moving in brilliance'; or of an adverbial accusative, e. g. *ugram-paśyá-*[5]

1 WACKERNAGEL 2[1], p. 198, quotes *loka-jít-aṃ svargám* (AV. IV. 34[8]) as showing that the first member was felt to have an accusative sense = 'winning the heavenly world' (*svargáṃ lokám*); but the Paipp. Ms. has the reading *svargyam*, which WHITNEY regards as better, translating 'world-conquering, heaven-going'.

2 When the first member is a part of the body it expresses the sense of 'with reference to', as *bāhú-jūta-* 'quick with the arms'.

3 The local sense here is that of the accusative of the goal.

4 Cp. LINDNER, Nominalbildung p. 28.

5 Occasionally the *-m* is inorganic, as in *makṣum-gamá-* and *āśum-gá-* (AV.) 'going swiftly'. In *pataṃ-gá-* 'bird', *patam-* probably

(AV.) 'looking fiercely'; or of a predicative accusative, e. g. *ayakṣmaṃ-kárạṇa-* (AV.) 'producing health', *śṛtaṃ-kartṛ́-* (TS. III. 1. 4[4]) 'making cooked'[1]. The acc. pl. occurs in *kā-cit-kará-* 'doing all manner of things', *páśva-iṣṭi-*[2] 'desiring kine', *vipaś-cít-* 'understanding eloquence', *vipo-dhā́-* 'granting eloquence', *huraś-cít-*[3] 'intending evil'[4].

a. The accusative form is commonest before agent nouns ending in *-a* or *-i* which begin with a single consonant and the first syllable of which is short; that is, the *-m* here appears in a syllable in which rhythmic lengthening would be allowed[5]. This **accusative form** is the regular rule in the RV. **when** the stem of the **first member** ends in **-a**, being found before *-kara-* 'making', *-caya-* 'collecting', *-jaya-* 'conquering', *-tara-* 'overcoming', *-dara-* 'cleaving', *-bhara-* 'bearing', *-ruja-* 'breaking', *-sani-* 'winning', *-saha-* 'overwhelming'; e. g. *abhayaṃ-kará-* 'procuring security'. The only exceptions to this rule in the RV. are *aśva-hayá-* 'urging on steeds', *śukra-dúgha-* 'emitting clear fluid'. In the RV. the **ending** ***-im*** also occurs in *puṣṭim-bhará-* 'bringing prosperity' and *harim-bhará-*[6] 'bearing the yellow-coloured (bolt)'; and ***-um*** inorganically in *makṣuṃ-gamá-* 'going quickly'. In the later Saṃhitās also occur *iram-madá-* (VS.) 'rejoicing in the draught', *dūraṃ-gamá-* (VS.) 'going far', *devaṃ-gamá-* (TS.) 'going to the gods', *yudhiṃ-gamá-* (AV.) 'going to battle', *viśvam-bhará-* (AV.) 'all-sustaining', *śakam-bhará-*[7] (AV.) 'bearing ordure'[8].

b. The accusative form in ***-am*** is not uncommon **before** a final member with **initial vowel** (coalescence of the two vowels being thus avoided); e. g. *cakram-āsajá-* 'obstructing the wheel', *viśvam-invá-* 'all-moving', *áśvam-iṣṭi-* 'desiring horses', *vācam-īṅkhayá-* 'word-moving', *samudram-īṅkhaya-* (only voc.) 'stirring the vat', *viśvam-ejayá-* 'all-exciting'; in ***-im***: *agnim-indhá-* 'fire-kindler'; in ***-ām***: *tvā́m-āhuti-* (TS.) 'offering oblations to thee'.

c. The accusative form is common when the **final member** is formed from a **present stem**, owing to the close connexion of such verbal nouns with the verb; e. g. *dhiyaṃ-jinvá-* 'exciting meditation', *ugram-paśyá-* (AV.) 'looking fiercely', *mām-paśyá-* (AV.) 'looking at me'.

d. Apart from the conditions stated above (**a, b, c**) the accusative case-ending rarely occurs in the first member of verbal determinatives; e. g. *vanaṃ-kárạṇa-*, a particular part of the body; *dhiyaṃ-dhā́-* 'devout', *śubhaṃ-yā́-(van)-* 'moving in brilliance'[9].

a. In the great majority of instances the first member, if it has the accusative case-form, ends in *-am*, mostly from stems in *-a*, but also from monosyllabic consonant stems (*pur-am-* etc.)[10], and from one stem in *-ī* (*dhiy-am-*). Otherwise there are three or

---

represents IE. *petn-*; while in *púraṃ-dhi-* 'fertile woman' and *vṛ́ṣan-dhi-* 'bold', the origin of the nasal is doubtful; cp. WACKERNAGEL 2[1], p. 202.

[1] In B. this predicative accusative sometimes comes to have the value of a predicative nominative when compounded with a gerundive or a derivative of *bhū-*, as *śṛtaṃ-kṛ́tya-* (TS.) 'to be made cooked', *nagnam-bhā́vuka-* (TS.) 'becoming naked'.

[2] *paśvás* acc. pl.

[3] Here *huras-* might be a genitive as √*cit-* governs that case as well as the acc.

[4] *puro-hā́* 'destroying forts' may contain an acc.; also *iṣa-stút-* 'praise of prosperity', which the Pada analyses as *iṣaḥ-stút-*.

[5] How much the use of these forms is dependent on rhythm is seen in the alternation of *ṛṇaṃ-cayá-* and *ṛṇa-cít-* 'paying a debt', *khajaṃ-kará-* and *khaja-kṛ́t-* 'causing the din of battle', *dhanaṃ-jayá-* and *dhana-jí-t-* 'winning booty', *janaṃ-sahá-* 'overcoming beings' and *vrāta-sāhá-* 'conquering crowds'.

[6] Beside *kavi-vṛdhá-* 'prospering the wise'.

[7] Here the acc. of an *a*-stem is substituted for *śakán-*.

[8] The compound *narā́ṃ-dhiṣa-* (VS.) is of doubtful meaning and irregular accent.

[9] For several other examples occurring in Brāhmaṇa passages of the later Saṃhitās see WACKERNAGEL 2[1], p. 207 d, e.

[10] In *hṛd-am-sáni-* 'winning the heart' the neuter *hṛd-* is treated as if it were a masc. or fem.

four in *-im* (*agnim-* etc.), one in *-um* (*makṣum-*), and two pronominal accusatives in *-ām* (*mām-*, *tvām-*). Polysyllabic consonant stems never have the accusative case-ending in the first member[1].

276. The **locative case-ending** is in the RV. almost limited to employment before agent-nouns formed from the **simple root** with or without determinative *-t*: *agre-gá-* 'going before', *agre-gú-* (VS.) 'moving forwards', *agre-ṇí-* (VS.) 'leader', *agre-pā́-* 'drinking first', *agre-pú-* (VS.) 'drinking first', *aṅge-ṣṭhā́-*[2] (AV.) 'situated in a member of the body', *ṛte-jā́-*[3] 'produced at the sacrifice', *kṛcchre-śrí-t-* 'running into danger', *gahvare-ṣṭhá-* (VS.) 'being at the bottom', *divi-kṣí-t-* 'dwelling in heaven', *divi-yáj-* 'worshipping in heaven', *divi-śrí-t-* (AV.) 'sojourning in heaven', *divi-ṣád-* (AV.) 'sitting in heaven', *dūre-dṛ́ś-* 'visible afar', *doṣaṇi-śríṣ-* (AV.) 'leaning on the arm', *rathe-śúbh-* 'flying along in a car', *rathe-ṣṭhā́-* 'standing in a car', *vane-rā́j-* 'shining in a wood', *vane-ṣáh-* 'prevailing in woods', *sute-gṛ́bh-* 'taking hold of the Soma', *hṛdi-spṛ́ś-* 'touching the heart'[4].

2. The RV. has only two examples of a locative before an agent noun formed with the suffix *-a*: *divi-kṣayá-* 'dwelling in heaven', *vahye-śayá-* 'resting in a litter'[5]. There are several others in the later Saṃhitās: *agre-vadhá-* (VS.) 'killing what is in front', *talpe-śayá-* (AV.) 'resting on a couch', *divi-cará-* (AV.) 'faring in heaven', *divi-ṣṭambhá-* (AV.) 'supported on the sky', *dūre-vadhá-* (VS.) 'far-striking', *harā-śayá-*[6] (MS. I. 2[7]) 'resting in gold'. In the AV. also occurs an example of the locative before an agent noun formed with *-in*: *parame-ṣṭh-ín-* 'standing in the highest (place)'.

3. The **locative plural** is much rarer than the singular in the first member: *apsu-kṣí-t-* 'dwelling in the waters', *apsu-jā́-* 'born in the waters', *apsu-jí-t-* 'vanquishing in the waters', *apsu-ṣád-* 'dwelling in the waters', *apsu-vā́h-* (SV.) 'driving in water', *apsú-saṃśita-* (AV.) 'excited in the waters', *goṣu-yúdh-* 'fighting in (= for) kine', *pṛtsu-túr-* 'conquering in battles', *bhareṣu-jā́-* 'produced in fights', *hṛtsv-ás-* 'piercing to the heart'.

a. In these locative compounds the second member is most commonly *-stha-* or *-sthā-* in the RV., while the first member is most usually *agre-*, *dū́re-* or *vane-*. The locative in *-e* is the predominant one, even displacing *-i* in *pathe-ṣṭhā́-* 'standing on the road' beside *pathi-ṣṭhā́-* (AV.).

277. The **instrumental** case-ending occurs several times in the first member of verbal determinatives: *kṣamā-cará-* (VS.) 'being in the ground', *girā-vṛ́dh-* 'rejoicing in song', *dhiyā-júr-* 'aging in devotion', *yuvā́-datta-* 'given by you two', *yuvā́-nīta-* 'led by you two', *yuṣmā́-datta-* 'given by you', *yuṣmā́-nīta-* 'led by you', *śúneṣita-* 'driven by dogs' (*śúnā*). When the stem of the first member ends in *-a* there is some doubt whether *-ā* here represents the instrumental ending or lengthening of the vowel[7]; thus *śaphā-rúj-* may mean 'breaking with the hoof' or 'hoof-breaker'; and in *yuvā-yúj-* 'yoked by you two' the vowel may be simply lengthened. In *divā-kará-* (AV.) 'sun' the first member is an old instrumental used adverbially[8].

a. The examples of the **ablative** case-ending are rare: *dakṣiṇāt-sád-*

[1] *śakan-* substitutes the acc. of an *a*-stem; above p. 165, note 7.

[2] There are several other locatives compounded with *-ṣṭhā-*.

[3] There are several other locatives compounded with *-jā́-*.

[4] In *nare-ṣṭhā́-* (RV[1].), an epithet of the car, the first member may be a locative (Sāyaṇa), but it may also be a dative of *nṛ́-* (BR., Grassmann), 'serving for a man to stand on'.

[5] In *sutè-kara-* 'active in (offering) Soma', the accent shows that the final member has an adjectival, not a verbal sense. In the name *mātari-śvan-* the first member is interpreted in RV. III. 29[11] as a locative; cp. Richter, IF. 9, 247, note; Macdonell, Grundriss III. I A, p. 72 (middle).

[6] In VS. V. 8 *hari-śayá-*; *harā-* here is the locative of *hári-*.

[7] Cp. Wackernagel 2[1], 56.

[8] See Wackernagel 2[1], 213 a, note.

(MS. II. 6[3]) 'sitting in the south'; *divo-já-* 'produced from heaven', *divo-dúh-* (SV.) 'milking from the sky', *divo-rúc-* 'shining from the sky'.

b. The ending of the **genitive** would naturally appear only before derivatives from verbs governing the genitive. There seem to be no certain examples: *divá-kṣas-* 'ruling over the sky' (*divás*) however seems probable[1].

b. 1. Ordinary Adjective as final member.

278. Ordinary adjectives which are not of a verbal character may appear as final member of determinatives much in the same way as past participles in *-ta* and *-na* (273, 4). But adjectives ending in *-u* are almost exclusively compounded with the privative *a(n)-* and prepositions; e. g. *an-āśú-* 'not swift', *án-ṛju-* 'dishonest', *á-dāśu-* 'impious', *á-bhīru-* 'not terrible'; *prāśú-* 'very (*prá*) swift' (*āśú-*). The only final members otherwise compounded are *-vasu-* 'rich' in *vibhā́-vasu-* 'radiant' and other compounds, and *-raghu-* 'swift', in *máde-raghu-* 'quick in exhilaration'.

a. The **first member** may be a **substantive** in the relation of a case to the last; e. g. *tanū́-śubhra-* 'shining in body', *yajñá-dhīra-* 'versed in sacrifice', *vakmarā́ja-satya-* 'faithful to the ordainers of hymns', *viśvá-śambhū-* 'salutary for all'. The relation is sometimes expressed by the case-ending: the **locative** in *gávi-ṣṭhira-* (AV.) 'strong in kine (*gávi*)' as a name, *máde-raghu-* 'quick in exhilaration', *suté-kara-* 'active in (offering) Soma', *sumná-āpi-* 'united in affection (*sumné*)'; **instrumental**[2] in *dhiyā́-vasu-* 'rich in devotion', *vidmanā́pas-* 'working (*apás-*) with wisdom (*vidmánā*)'. The first member may also appositionally express a comparison as representing a type: *śúka-babhru-* (VS.) 'reddish like a parrot'[3].

b. The first member may be an **adjective** qualifying the final member in an adverbial sense; thus *aprāmi-satya* (voc.) 'eternally true', *ūrdhvá-pṛśni-*[4] (VS.) 'spotted above', *try-àruṣa-* 'reddish in three (parts of the body)', *mahā-nagnī́-*[5] (AV.) 'courtezan' ('very naked'), *mahā́-mahi-vrata-* 'ruling very mightily', *mahā́-vaṭūrin-* 'very broad', *viśvá-ścandra-* 'all-glittering'[6].

c. Adverbs and particles often appear as first member; e. g. *an-āśú-* 'not swift', *anyáta-enī-* (VS.) 'variegated on one side (*anyátas*)', *evā́ra-* 'quite (*evá*) ready (*ára-*)', *duḥ-śéva-* 'unfavourable', *púnar-nava-* 'renewing itself', *sató-mahānt-* 'equally (*sa-tás*) great', *sató-bṛhatī-* (VS.) 'the equally great' (a metre), *satyám-ugra-* 'truly mighty', *sú-priya-* (AV.) 'very dear'.

d. Several **prepositions** appear as first member, mostly with their original adverbial meaning; e. g. *áti-kṛṣṇa-*[7] (VS.) 'very dark'; *ā́-miśla-tama-* 'mixing very readily'[8]; *upottamá-* (AV.) 'penultimate'; *ní-dhruvi-* ('fixed down') 'persevering', *níṣ-kevalya-* (VS.) 'belonging exclusively'; *prāśú-* 'very swift', *pra-*

---

[1] But it has also been otherwise explained; cp. WACKERNAGEL 2[1], p. 213 c, note; who also quotes *á-kasya-vid-* 'knowing nothing' from the MS.

[2] The word *jātū́-ṣṭhira-* probably contains an old instrumental = 'naturally solid'; in *nā́bhā-nédiṣṭha-* 'nearest in kin' as a name, the first member though looking like a locative, probably represents an IIr. stem *nabhā-*; cp. RICHTER, IF. 9, 209. The compounds *ṛcī-ṣama-*, an epithet of Indra, and *ghāsé-ajra-* (VS.) are Bahuvrīhis.

[3] A transition to this compound use appears in *máno jáviṣṭham* (RV. VI. 9[5]) 'very swift as thought'.

[4] Here the adjectival stem is used for the adv. *ūrdhvám*.

[5] From this is formed the m. *mahā-nagná-* (AV.) 'paramour'.

[6] The meaning of *sādhv-aryá-* 'truly faithful'(?), which occurs only once, is doubtful; cp. WACKERNAGEL 2[1], p. 237 (top).

[7] *ati* in the sense of 'very' does not occur in the RV., but in the later Saṃhitās it is the commonest of the prepositions compounded with adjectives.

[8] 'Very slightly mixed', GELDNER, VS. 3, 181. — *ā́-tura-* 'suffering' is obscure in origin.

śardha- (voc.) 'bold'; *vi-mahī-* 'very great', *vi-ṣama-* (VS.) 'uneven', *vi-sadṛśa-* 'dissimilar', *vy-ènī-* 'variously tinted' (dawn); *sáṃ-vasu-* 'dwelling together', *sám-priya-* (VS.) 'mutually dear'.

b. 2. Ordinary Substantive as final member.

279. Determinatives with ordinary non-verbal substantives as their final member[1] are not common in the earliest period of the language. In the first nine books of the RV., except the frequent compounds in *-pati-* and *-patnī-*, there are not many more than three dozen examples[2]; the tenth book has quite two dozen more, and the AV. seven dozen more.

The **first member** is frequently a **substantive** also. Its relation to the final member seems to be limited to the **genitive sense** in the Saṃhitās. This genitive sense appears when the final member is a word expressive of relationship, or *-pati-* 'husband' or 'lord'; e. g. *rāja-putrá-* 'king's son', *mṛtyu-bándhu-* 'companion of death', *viś-páti-* 'lord of the tribe'. It sometimes expresses the material, as *dru-padá-* 'post of wood', *hiraṇya-rathá-* 'car of gold' or 'car full of gold'. In *deva-kilbiṣá-* 'offence against the gods' we have an example of an objective genitive. There seems to be no instance in the RV. of a Proper Name appearing as the first member of a determinative in the genitive sense[3] except in *indra-sená-* (x. 102[2]) 'Indra's missile'[4], which compound is itself perhaps a Proper Name[5]. In *camasā́dhvaryu-* (AV.) 'the priest of the cups', the first member expresses quite a general genitive sense of relation = 'the priest who is concerned with the cups'.

280. As in determinatives with verbal noun as final member, the **case-ending** may appear **in the first member**. But it is less common here, and owing to the purely nominal character of the final member, is almost restricted to the **genitive**. The ending of this case is very common **before *-pati-*** 'lord' or 'husband': *aṃhas-as-pati-* (VS.) 'lord of distress', N. of an intercalary month, *gnā́-s-páti-*[6] 'husband of a divine woman', *jā́-s-páti-* 'lord of the family', *bṛ́h-as-páti-*[7] and *bráhmaṇ-as-páti-* 'lord of devotion', *mánas-as-páti-* 'lord of mental power', *ván-as-páti-*[8] 'lord of the wood', 'tree', *vāc-ás-páti-* 'lord of speech', *vā́stoṣ-páti-* 'lord of the dwelling', *śubh-ás-páti-* 'lord of splendour', *sádas-as-páti-*[9] 'lord of the sacrificial seat'. According to the analogy of these compounds which end in *-s-pati-*, were also formed from *a*-stems *ṛta-s-pati-* (only voc.) 'lord of pious works' and *rátha-s-páti-* 'lord of the car'. The word *dám-pati-* may stand for **dám-s-pati-*[10] 'lord of the house' (*dám-*, the gen. pl. of which, *dam-ā́m*, occurs).

---

1 Bahuvrīhis with ordinary substantives as final member were common from the beginning; hence combinations which appear as Bahuvrīhis in the older period, are often only found later as Tatpuruṣas, the latter being thus occasionally affected by the formal peculiarities of Bahuvrīhis.

2 See WACKERNAGEL 2[1], p. 241 (97 note).

3 If this compound is a Proper Name, it is the only instance with the stem-form in the first member; but the genitive case-ending appears in the first member of a few determinative Proper Names; see below, 280 a.

4 'Indra's missile' (BR.), 'Indra's army' (GRASSMANN).

5 This is the opinion of GELDNER, VS. 2, 1, and of DELBRÜCK, Vergl. Syntax 3, p. 202.

6 An anomalous f. *gnā́s-pátnī-* was formed from this word after the etymology had been forgotten, as conversely the m. *sapátna-* 'rival' was formed from *sa-pátnī-* 'co-wife'.

7 **bṛ́h-* here is synonymous with *bráhman-*, *bráhmaṇas-páti-* being a parallel and explanatory formation. On *bṛ́has-páti-* and cognate compounds see OTTO STRAUSS, Bṛhaspati im Veda (Leipzig 1905), p. 14—17.

8 *van-* 'wood' appears also in the pl. G. *van-ā́m*, L. *váṃ-su*.

9 It is unnecessary to assume the existence of a stem *sad-* to explain *sádas-páti-* and *sát-pati-* since the stem *sadas-* occurs; nor is *rādh-* necessary to explain *rādhas-pati-* (only voc.) as *rā́dhas-* is frequent.

10 PISCHEL, VS. 2, 93 ff., 307 ff., rejects any connexion between *dámpati-* and *dám-* 'house'. Cp. WACKERNAGEL 2[1], p. 249 e, note.

α. These compounds in *-páti-* are treated by the Pada text in three different ways: 1. *gnā́spáti-*, *bṛ́haspáti-*, *vánaspáti-*, *viśpáti-* (and *viśpátnī-*) appear as simple words; 2. *gnā́ḥ-pátnī-*, *jā́ḥ-páti-*, *sácī-páti-*, *ṛta-pate* (voc.), *rādhas-pate* (voc.), and those with a single accent (except *viśpáti-*) as compounds separated by the Avagraha sign; 3. all other doubly accented compounds (e. g. *bráhmaṇas-páti-*) as two separate words; even *ráthas-pátis* is written *ráthaḥ* | *pátiḥ* | as if *ráthaḥ* were a nom. sing.[1]

a. Otherwise the **genitive ending** appears only two or three times in the RV. **in Proper Names**: *dívo-dāsa-* 'Servant of heaven' (?), *śúnaḥ-śépa-*[2] 'Dog's tail', and (with gen. pl.) *nárā-śáṃsa-* (for **nárāṃ-śáṃsa-*)[3] 'Praise of men', an epithet of Agni. The VS. has also *rāyas-poṣa-* 'increase of wealth' in *rāyas-poṣa-dā́-* 'bestowing increase of wealth' and *rāyas-poṣa-váni-* 'procuring increase of wealth'.

b. Other case-endings are very rare in such determinatives. The **locative** appears in *svapne-duṣvapnyá-* (AV.) 'evil dreaming in sleep'[4]; the **instrumental** in *vācā́-stena-* 'thief by speech', 'one who makes mischief by his words'; the **dative** in *dasyave-vṛka-* (voc.) 'Wolf to the Dasyu', N. of a man; and possibly *dásyave sáhaḥ* (I. 36^{18}) may be meant as a name with double accent.

281. In a few instances the first member is a **substantive used appositionally** to express sex or composite nature: *puruṣa-mṛgá-* (VS.) 'male antelope'; *úlūka-yātu-* 'owl demon' (= demon in form of an owl), *śuśulū́ka-yātu-* 'owlet demon'; *puruṣa-vyāghrá-* 'man-tiger', a kind of demon, *vṛṣā́-kapi-* 'man-ape'.

282. An **adjective** may appear **as first member** determining the sense of the following substantive. This type, which is called **Karmadhāraya** by the Indian grammarians, is uncommon in the Saṃhitās. Among the oldest are *candrá-mās-*[5] '(bright) moon'[6] and *pūrṇá-mās-a-* (TS. III. 4. 4^{1}) 'full moon'. Besides these occur *eka-vīrá-* 'unique hero', *kṛṣṇa-śakuní-* (AV.) 'raven'[7], *nava-jvārá-* 'new pain', *mahā-grāmá-* 'great host', *mahā-dhaná-* 'great booty', *mahā-vīrá-* 'great hero'[8], *sapta-ṛṣáyas* 'the Seven Seers', N. of a group of ancient sages (beside the separate words *saptá ṛ́ṣayaḥ* and *ṛ́ṣayaḥ saptá* in Books I—IX), *sapta-gṛdhrā́ḥ* (AV^{1}.) 'the seven vultures'[9].

a. A variety of Karmadhāraya is that in which the first member expresses a part of the last: *adhara-kaṇṭhá-* (VS.) 'lower part of the neck', *ardha-devá-*[10] 'demi-god', *ardha-māsá-* (AV. VS.) 'half-month', *madhyáṃ-dina-* 'midday'; also with change of gender: *agra-jihvá-* (VS.) n. 'tip of the tongue (*jihvā́-*)'; with the suffix *-a*: *ardha-rc-á-* (AV. VS.) 'hemistich', *pūrvāhṇ-á-* 'forenoon'[11].

283. **Prepositions** frequently occur **as first member**, all except *prá* in their ordinary adverbial senses. Those which are thus used in the RV.

---

[1] See WACKERNAGEL 2^{1}, p. 241 (97 a *α*, note).

[2] This name occurs once with tmesis, *śúnaś cic chépam* (V. 2^{7}).

[3] Cp. *narā́ṃ ná śáṃsa-* (I. 173^{9} etc.) and *śáṃso narā́m* (VI. 24^{2}); see WACKERNAGEL 2^{1}, p. 248 d, note.

[4] *hradé-cakṣus* 'mirrored in the lake' is regarded by GELDNER (VS. I, 173) as a Tatpuruṣa = 'eye in the lake'. For one or two doubtful examples of locative pl. see WACKERNAGEL 2^{1}, p. 249 (bottom).

[5] That this is a very old combination is shown by the fact that *mā́s-* 'moon' occurs almost exclusively in compounds (*sū́ryā-mā́sā* and *pūrṇá-mās*, SB.), only two or three times alone (though often in the sense of 'month'), and is therefore obsolescent in the RV.

[6] In the later Saṃhitās *candrá-* comes to mean 'moon' as an abbreviation of *candrá-mās-*.

[7] With change of meaning from 'black bird'.

[8] In K. appears the dative *viśva-devāya*, the expression *víśve devā́ḥ* having become a Karmadhāraya.

[9] Translated by WHITNEY (AV. VIII. 9^{18}) as a Bahuvrīhi, 'seven-vultured'.

[10] *ardhá-* 'half' is here used in a figurative sense.

[11] *pitā-mahá-* (AV. TS. VS.) and *tatā-mahá-* (AV.) 'grandfather' and *prá-pitāmaha-* (VS. TS.) and *pra-tatāmaha-* (AV^{1}.) 'great grandfather' (only voc.) are probably not Karmadhārayas, but formed in imitation of *mahā-mahá-* which appeared to be a gradation of *mahā́nt-*; cp. WACKERNAGEL 2^{1}, p. 255, note.

are *ádhi* 'over', *ní* 'down', *pári* 'around', *prá* 'forward'[1], 'front part of'[2], 'extreme' (of high degree), 'great' (in names of relationship), *práti* 'against', *ví* 'asunder'[3], *sám* 'together' (also *sa-* in the same sense); and in the later Saṃhitās, *antár* 'between', *ápa* 'away', *ā́* 'at hand', *úd* 'up', *úpa* 'beside', *úpari* 'above'. The following are examples in the alphabetical order of the prepositions: *ádhi-pati* (AV. VS.) 'over-lord', *ádhi-patnī-* (AV. VS.) 'sovereign lady', *ádhi-bhojana-* 'additional gift', *adhi-rājá-* 'supreme king'; *antar-deśá-* (AV.) 'intermediate region', *antaḥ-pātrá-* (AV.) 'inner (= interior of the) vessel'; *ápa-rūpa-* (AV.)[4] 'absence of form', 'deformity'; *ā́-pati-* (VS. MS. I. 2[7]) 'the lord here'; **ut-sūrya-* 'sunrise' in *otsūryám* (AV.) 'till sunrise' (*ā-utsūryám*); *upa-patí-* (VS.) 'paramour' (lit. 'sub-husband'); *upari-śayaná-* (AV.) 'elevated couch'; *ni-dhána-* (AV.) 'conclusion', *ní-pakṣati-* (VS.) 'second rib', *ni-pādá-* 'low ground', *ny-áhna-*[5] (AV.) 'close of day'; *pári-pati-* 'lord (of all) around', *pari-vatsará-* 'full year'; *pra-gāthá-* (VS.) 'fore-song', a kind of stanza, *pra-díś-* 'region' and (AV.) 'intermediate quarter', *pra-dhána-* 'prize of battle', *prādhvaná-* ('forward course', *ádhvan-*) 'bed of a river', *prā́rtha-* (AV.) 'preparation', 'implement'; *prá-pada-*[6] 'tip of the foot', *prá-uga-* 'forepart of the shafts (of a chariot)'[7]; *prá-ṇapāt-* 'great-grandson', *pra-tatāmaha-* (AV[1].) and *prá-pitāmaha-* (VS. TS.) 'great-grandfather'; *pra-dív-* (AV.) 'third (or fifth) heaven', *prá-patha-* 'distant path', *prá-maganda-* 'arch-usurer', *prá-vīra-* 'great hero', *prā́yus-* (MS. I. 5[4]) 'long life' (*ā́yus*); *prati-janá-* (AV.) 'adversary', *prati-dī́van-* 'adversary at play'; *vi-díś-* (VS.) 'intermediate region', *ví-madhya-* 'middle', *ví-manyu-* 'longing'[8], *ví-vāc-* 'opposing shout', 'contest', *vy-ódana-* (RV[1].) 'different food'[9]; *sa-pátnī-* 'co-wife', *saṃ-grāmá-* (AV.) 'assembly', 'encounter', *sam-anīká-* 'battle-array'[10], *sam-bándhu-* 'akin', *saṃ-vatsará-*[11] 'full year'.

284. **Other indeclinables** sometimes occur **as first member**, but very rarely in the RV. They include a few adverbs and the particles *a(n)-*, *dus-*, *su-*, *kim-*, *ku-*: *paścā-doṣá-* (VS.) 'late evening', *puró-agni-* (VS.) 'fire in front'; *a-mítra-* 'enemy', *á-hotṛ-* (AV.) 'incompetent Hotṛ'; *duc-chúnā-* 'calamity'[12]; *sú-brāhmaṇa-* (AV.) 'good Brāhman', *sú-bheṣaja-* (AV. TS.) 'good remedy', *su-vasaná-*[13] 'fair garment'; *kim-puruṣá-* (VS.) a kind of mythical being, *kú-śara-* (RV[1].), a kind of reed.

4. Bahuvrīhi Compounds.

285. The term **Bahuvrīhi**, employed by the Indian grammarians to designate this type, is perhaps the most convenient name for these **secondary adjective compounds**, as it represents their general character both in form and meaning. For the final member is practically always a substantive, and the relation of the first member to the last is mostly attributive

1 Without perceptibly changing the meaning of the final member.

2 This and the following meanings do not occur in the combination of *prá* with verbs.

3 Expressing separation, extension, derivation.

4 In *apa-kāmá-* 'aversion' the final member is a verbal noun. There seem to be no certain instances of this kind of compound with *ápi*: cp. WACKERNAGEL 2[1], p. 259 β, note.

5 In *ny-arthá-* 'destruction' the second member is a verbal noun. On the relation of *ny-àrbuda-* (AV. VS.) and *ny-àrbudi-* (AV.) to *árbuda-* and *árbudi-*, see WACKERNAGEL 2[1], p. 260 (top).

6 Once *prá-pad-* in AV.

7 Probably for *prá-yuga-*.

8 From *manyú-* 'zeal'.

9 This is Sāyaṇa's explanation (*vividhe 'nne*) of the word in VIII. 52[9].

10 From *ánīka-* 'front'.

11 *sám* in this compound expresses completeness.

12 Cp. *śunám* 'with success'. On the Sandhi see p. 31, note 4.

13 Though *vasana-* has a concrete sense here, the compound may have arisen when the word had a verbal meaning.

(Karmadhāraya), less commonly dependent (Tatpuruṣa), and very rarely coordinative (Dvandva). The best name otherwise is **'possessive'**[1], as this is their meaning in the vast majority of instances. In a few examples, however, the more general sense of 'connected with' (which may usually be expressed more specifically) is required to explain the relation between the substantive and the Bahuvrīhi which agrees with it; thus *áśva-pṛṣṭha-* 'borne on horse-back', *devá-psaras-* 'affording enjoyment for the gods', *parjánya-retas-* 'sprung from the seed of Parjanya', *viśvá-kṛṣṭi-* 'dwelling with all peoples', *viśvā́-nara-*[2] 'belonging to or existing among all men', *vīrá-pastya-* 'belonging to the abode of a hero', *śatá-śārada-* 'lasting a hundred autumns', *śū́ra-vīra-* (AV.) 'characterized by heroic men' = 'making men heroic' (amulet).

286. Attributive Bahuvrīhis. — The commonest form of Bahuvrīhi is that in which an **attributive noun** is the **first member**. It is most frequently an **adjective**, as *ugrá-bāhu-* 'powerful-armed', *urvy-ū́ti-*[3] 'giving wide aid', *jīvá-putra-* 'having living sons', *śukrá-varṇa-* 'bright-coloured'[4]. The first member is also often a **past passive participle** in *-ta* or *-na*, the action expressed by which is usually performed by the person denoted by the substantive with which the Bahuvrīhi agrees; e. g. *práyata-dakṣiṇa-* 'he by whom the sacrificial fee has been presented', *rātá-havis-* 'who offers an oblation'[5]. The action is, however, not infrequently supposed to be performed by others, always in the case of *hata-* 'slain'; e. g. *hatá-vṛṣṇ-ī-* 'whose husband has been slain', *hatá-mātṛ-* 'whose mother has been slain'. Both senses appear in *rātá-havya-* 'he by whom' and 'to whom offerings have been made'. An outside agent is sometimes expressed by an additional member at the beginning of the compound, as *jīvá-pīta-sarga-* 'whose streams have been drunk by the living'[6]. A present participle occasionally occurs as first member; e. g. *ā-yád-vasu-* (AV.) and *saṃ-yád-vasu-* (AV.) 'to whom wealth comes', *bhrā́jad-ṛṣṭi-* 'having glittering spears', *rúśad-vatsa-* 'having a shining calf', *śucád-ratha-* 'having a brilliant car'[7]; also a perfect-participle in *dadṛś-āná-pavi-* 'whose felly is visible', *yuyujāná-sapti-* 'whose steeds are yoked'.

a. The first member is further often a **substantive** used predicatively; e. g. *áśva-parṇa-* 'horse-winged' = 'whose wings are horses' (car); *índra-śatru-* ,whose foe is Indra'; *tad-íd-artha-*[8] 'having just that as an aim', *dróṇāhāva-* ,whose pail (*āhāvá-*) is a trough', *śiśná-deva-* 'whose god is a phallus', *sū́rodaka-* (AV.) 'whose water is spirit' (*súrā-*). The final member is here sometimes a comparative or superlative (including *pára-*) used substantively: *avaras-pará-*[9] (VS.) 'in which the lower is higher' = 'topsy-turvy'[10], *ásthi-bhūyāṃs-* (AV.) 'having bone as its chief part' = 'chiefly bone', *índra-jyeṣṭha-* 'having Indra as chief', 'of whom Indra is chief', *yamá-śreṣṭha-* (AV.) 'of whom Yama is best', *sóma-śreṣṭha-* (AV.) 'of which Soma is best'.

---

1 For other names see WACKERNAGEL 2[1], p. 273 (107 a, note).

2 For several other examples formed with *viśvá-* see WHITNEY 1294 b.

3 Cp. p. 145, note 3.

4 Cp. WHITNEY 1298.

5 The sense is thus identical with verbal determinatives or verbally governing compounds such as *vājam-bhará-* and *bharád-vāja-* 'bearing booty'. In *vīti-hotra-* 'having an invitation sacrifice' = 'inviting to sacrifice', a stem in *-ti* is used almost like a past participle in *-ta*; cp. *vītá-havya-* as a name.

6 Cp. WHITNEY 1299 a.

7 Cp. WHITNEY 1299 b.

8 Here a pronoun appears instead of a substantive in the first member.

9 Here the first member retains the *-s* of the nom. surviving from the use of the two words in syntactical juxtaposition; the first member also is used substantively in this compound.

10 On *eka-pará-* (said of dice) see now LÜDERS, Das Würfelspiel im alten Indien (Abh. d. K. Ges. der Wiss. zu Göttingen 9, 2) p. 64.

A **comparison** is sometimes **implied** between the first substantive and the second: *varṣā́jya* (AV.) 'whose rain is like butter', *vṛkṣá-keśa-* 'tree-haired' = 'whose trees are like hair' = 'wooded' (mountain).

The first member further sometimes expresses the **material** of which the second consists; e. g. *rajatá-nābhi-* (VS.) 'whose naval is (made of) silver'; *hiraṇya-nemi-* 'whose fellies are (made of) gold'; or something closely connected with and characteristic of it, as *niyúd-ratha-* 'whose car is (drawn by) a team'.

287. Dependent Bahuvrīhis. — The first member is dependent on the last in the sense of a **case-relation,** the case-ending being sometimes retained.

a. It has often a **genitive** sense[1], as *páti-kāma-* (AV.) 'having desire for a husband'; with genitive ending, *rāyás-kāma-* 'having a desire of wealth'. Here the first member often implies a comparison (when it never has the case-ending): *agní-tejas-* (AV.) 'having the brightness of fire', 'fire-bright', *ṛ́kṣa-grīva-* (AV.) 'having the neck of a bear' (demons), *gó-vapus-* 'having the form of a cow', *jñātí-mukha-* (AV.) 'having the face of (= like) relatives', *máno-javas-* 'having the swiftness of thought' = 'swift as thought', *mayū́ra-roman-* 'having the plumes of peacocks' (Indra's steeds).

b. In a few instances it has the sense of, and then always the ending of, the **instrumental:** *á-giraukas-* 'not to be kept at rest (*ókas-*) by a song (*girā́*)', *krátvā-magha-* 'constituting a reward (gained) by intelligence', *bhāsā́-ketu-* 'recognisable by light'[2].

c. The **locative** sense is more frequent, being often accompanied by the case-ending: *āsánn-iṣu-* 'having arrows in his mouth', *diví-yoni-* 'having origin in heaven'; also several formed with *dūre-* 'in the distance', as *dūré-anta-* 'ending in the distance', *dūré-gavyūti-* (AV.) 'whose sphere is far away'[3].

There are further examples in which the last member has the locative sense when it is a part of the body and what is expressed by the first member appears in or on it: *aśru-mukhī́-* (AV.) 'having tears on her face', 'tear-faced', *kīlā́lodhn-ī-* (AV.) 'having sweet drink in her udder', *ghṛtá-pṛṣṭha-* 'butter-backed', *pā́tra-hasta-* (AV.) 'having a hand in which is a vessel', *maṇi-grīvá-* 'having pearls on the neck', *mádhu-jihva-* 'having a tongue on which is honey', *vájra-bāhu-* 'having an arm on which is a bolt'.

288. Coordinate Bahuvrīhis. — No example is found in the RV. and hardly any in the other Saṃhitās of the first and last members of Bahuvrīhis being coordinated in sense. The VS. has *stóma-pṛṣṭha-* 'containing Stomas and Pṛṣṭhas'; also *áhar-divá-* (xxxviii. 12) 'daily', which is a kind of Dvandva Bahuvrīhi, being formed from the adverb *áhar-divi* 'day by day'. The form *somendrá-* 'belonging to Soma and Indra', occurs only in B. passages of later Saṃhitās (TS. MS. K.).

289. Indeclinables as first member. — In a number of Bahuvrīhis the first member is not a noun, but an indeclinable word, either a preposition or an adverb.

a. Prepositions are common as first member of Bahuvrīhis, expressing the local position of the final member in relation to the substantive with which the Bahuvrīhi agrees. Some sixteen prepositions are thus used, the most frequent being *vi* which occurs as often in the RV. as all the rest put together. They are *áti* 'beyond', *ádhi* 'on', *antár* 'within', *ápa* 'away', *abhí*

1 An accusative in sense and form appears in *tvā́ṃ-kāma-* 'having a desire for thee'.

2 The compound *vidmanā́pas-* 'working with skill' (*vidmánā*) is probably a determinative formed with the adj. *apás-* 'working', not a Bahuvrīhi with *ápas-* 'work'; cp. 278 a and 91 B.

3 On a few doubtful instances of such locative compounds see Wackernagel 2[1], p. 278 (bottom).

'around' and 'toward', *áva* 'down', 'away', *ā́* 'near', *úd* 'upward', *úpa* 'near', *ní* 'down', *nís* 'away', *pári* 'around', *prá* 'in front', 'very', *práti* 'against', *ví* 'apart', *sám* 'together'. Of these *úpa* is used thus in the RV. only, while *antár, áva, ní* appear in the later Saṃhitās only. The following are examples of compounds thus formed in the alphabetical order of the prepositions: *áty-ūrmi-* 'overflowing', *áti-cchandas-* (VS.) 'having redundant metres' (verse); *ádhi-nirṇij-* 'having a garment on', *ádhy-akṣa-* 'having an eye on', 'overseer'; *antar-dāvá-* (AV.) 'having fire within'; *ápodaka-* 'waterless', *apa-rtú-* (AV.) 'unseasonable'; *abhí-vīra-* and *abhí-satvan-* 'having heroes around', *abhí-rūpa-* (AV.) 'beautiful', *abhi-ṣeṇá-* 'directing arrows'; *ava-keśá-* (AV.) 'having hair hanging down', *áva-toka-* (AV. VS.) 'miscarrying'; *ā́-deva-* 'having the gods near', 'devoted to the gods', *ā́-manas-* (AV. TS.) 'kindly disposed'; *út-saktha-* (VS.) 'having the thighs raised', *úd-ojas-* 'highly powerful'; *upa-manyú-* 'having zeal at hand', 'zealous', *úpā-vasu-* 'bringing riches near'; *ní-manyu-* (AV.) 'whose anger has subsided', *ní-vakṣas-* (TS. v. 6. 23[1]) 'having a sunken breast', *ni-kūlá-* (VS.) 'going down hill', *ni-kilbiṣá-* 'deliverance from sin' ('that in which sin has subsided'); *nír-jarāyu-* (AV.) 'having cast its skin', *nír-māya-* 'powerless', *nír-hasta-* (AV.) 'handless'; *pari-mará-* (TS. v. 6. 21[1]) 'having death around' = 'round whom people have died', *pari-manyú-* 'very angry'; *prā-śṛṅgá-* (VS. TS.) 'having prominent horns', *prá-tvakṣas-* 'very energetic'; *prá-maṇas-* (AV.) 'very thoughtful'; *práti-rūpa-* 'having a corresponding form', 'like', *prati-vartmán-* (AV.) 'having an opposite course', *práti-veśa-* 'neighbour' ('living opposite'); ***ví* = 'apart'**: *vi-karṇá-* (AV.) 'having ears far apart', *ví-śākha-* (AV.) 'branched', *vy-àṃsa-* 'having the shoulders apart', 'broad-shouldered'; **= 'extensive'**: *ví-manas-* 'wide-minded', 'sagacious', *ví-hāyas-* 'of extensive power'; **= 'divided'**: *vy-adhvá-* (AV.) 'having a divided course' = 'being midway between zenith and earth'; **= 'various'**: *vy-àilaba-* (AV.) 'making all kinds of noises'; **= 'divergent'**: *ví-pathi-* 'following wrong paths', *ví-vrata-* 'refractory'; **= 'distorted'**: *vi-grīva-* 'having a twisted neck', *vy-àṅga-* (AV.) 'having distorted limbs'; **= 'different'**: *ví-rūpa-* 'having a different form', *ví-vācas-* (AV.) 'speaking differently'; **= 'devoid of', 'less'**: *ví-māya-* 'devoid of magic', *vy-ènas-* 'guiltless'; *sám-hanu-* (AV.) 'striking the jaws together'.

b. Adverbs with a local meaning, which are akin to prepositions, also frequently appear as first member of Bahuvrīhis, being generally speaking equivalent in sense to predicative adjectives. Examples of such Bahuvrīhis in the alphabetical order of the adverbs are the following: *adhás* 'below' : *adhó-varcas-* (AV.) 'powerful below'; *ánti* 'near' : *ánti-mitra-* (VS.) 'having friends at hand', *ánti-sumna-* (AV.) 'having benevolence at hand', *ánty-ūti-* 'having aid at hand'; *avás* 'down' : *avó-deva-* 'attracting the gods down'; *āré* 'afar' : *āré-agha-* 'having evil far-removed', *āré-śatru-* (AV.) 'whose foes are far away'; *itás* 'hence' : *itá-ūti-* 'helping from hence'; *ihá* 'here' : *ihéha-mātṛ-* 'whose mothers are, the one here, the other there'; *ihá-kratu-* (AV.) 'whose will is hitherward', *ihá-citta-* (AV.) 'whose thought is hitherward'; *ṛ́dhak* 'apart' : *ṛ́dhaṅ-mantra-* (AV[1].) 'having a special sacred text'[1]; *kuhayā́* 'where?' : *kuhayā-kṛti-* (only voc.) 'where active?'; *dakṣiṇa-tás* 'on the right' : *dakṣiṇatás-kaparda-* 'having a coil of hair on the right'; *nīcā́* 'downward' : *nīcā́-vayas-* 'whose strength is low'; *purás* 'in front' : *puro-rathá-* 'whose car is in front', *puro-vasu-* (TS. III. 2. 5[1]) 'preceded by wealth' (only voc.); *prācā́* 'forward' : *prācā́-jihva-* 'moving the tongue forward', *prācā-manyu-* (only voc.) 'striving forward'.

1 According to WHITNEY on AV. V. 1[1]; BR., pw. 'lacking speech'; LUDWIG 'of distinguished meditations'.

a. Bahuvrīhis are also formed with a few adverbs of another kind as first member: *itthā́-dhī-* 'having such thought', 'devout', *nā́nā-sūrya-* 'illuminated by various suns', *púnar-magha-* (AV. TS.) 'repeatedly offering oblations', *purudhā́-pratīka-* 'having various aspects', *sadyá-ūti-* 'helping at once'[1]. There are also several formed with *sahá-*, *sumád-*, *smád-*[2] 'together with', as *sahá-gopa-* 'having the cowherds with them', *sahá-puruṣa-* (AV.) 'accompanied by the men', *sumáj-jāni-* 'accompanied by his wife', *sumád-gu-* (AV.) 'accompanied by the cows', *smád-abhīśu-* 'provided with reins', *smád-iṣṭa-* 'having an errand', *smád-ūdhan-* 'provided with an udder'.

c. Certain **particles** frequently appear as the first member of Bahuvrīhis. These are the privative *a-* or *an-*, *ku-*[3] expressing depreciation, *dus-* 'ill', *su-* 'well'; e. g. *a-pád-* 'footless', *a-sapatná-* 'having no rivals', *an-udaká-* 'having no water', 'waterless'; *kú-yava-* 'causing a bad harvest', *duṣ-pád-* 'ill-footed'; *su-parṇá-* 'having beautiful wings'.

290. Bahuvrīhis are very frequently used as m. (sometimes f.) **substantives** in the sense of **Proper Names**, in many instances without the adjectival sense occurring at all; thus *bṛhád-uktha-* m., as the N. of a seer and adj. 'having great praise'; *bṛhád-diva-* m., N. of a seer (*bṛhad-divā́-* f., N. of a goddess) and adj. 'dwelling in high heaven'; but *priyá-medha-* m. ('to whom sacrifice is dear') and *vāmá-deva-* m. ('to whom the gods are dear') only as the names of seers.

a. Bahuvrīhis are further not infrequently used as **neuter substantives** with an **abstract** and a **collective sense**, especially when the first member is the privative particle *a-* or *an-* and *sárva-* 'all'; e. g. *a-śatrú-* 'free from foes', n. (AV.) 'freedom from foes', *a-sapatná-* 'having no rivals', n. (AV.) 'peace', *a-sambādhá-* (AV.) n. 'non-confinement', *a-skambhaná-* (AV.) n. 'lack of support', *an-apatyá-* 'childless' (AV.), n. 'childlessness', *an-amitrá-* (AV.) 'foeless', n. (AV. VS.) 'freedom from foes'; *sarva-rathá-* 'the whole line of chariots', *sarva-vedasá-* (AV. TS.) 'whole property'; *ni-kilbiṣá-* n. 'deliverance from sin', *pitṛ-bandhú-* (AV.) 'paternal kinship', *mātṛ-bandhú-* (AV.) 'maternal kinship', *rikta-kumbhá-*[4] (AV[1].) 'empty-handedness', *su-mṛgá-* (AV.) 'good hunting'[5].

b. A special category of Bahuvrīhis used as substantives are those in which the **first member** is a **numeral** from *dvi-* 'two' upwards[6]. They express a collection or aggregate and are singular neuter[7] except those formed with *-ahá-* 'day', which are singular masc.; e. g. *tri-yugá-* n. 'period of three lives', *tri-yojaná-* (AV.) n. 'distance of three Yojanas', *try-udāyá-* n. 'threefold approach to the altar', *daśāṅgulá-* n. 'length of ten fingers', *daśāntaruṣyá-* n. 'distance of ten stations', *dvi-rājá-* (AV.) n. 'battle of two kings', *pañca-yojaná-* (AV.) n. 'distance of five Yojanas', *ṣaḍ-ahá-*(AV. TS.) m. 'series of six days'. These numeral collectives always end in accented *-á*[8].

291. Origin of Bahuvrīhis.—Considering that Bahuvrīhis, which are adjectives, are far commoner than the corresponding determinatives, which are substantives, it cannot be assumed that the former always passed through

1 The Bahuvrīhi compound *āvír-ṛjīka-* is of uncertain meaning; see Wackernagel 2[1], p. 287 (middle).

2 Compounds formed with these three words might also be explained as belonging to the 'governing' class.

3 Also the cognate *kim-* in *kiṃ-śilá-* (VS. TS.) (land) 'having small stones'.

4 See Whitney's note on AV. xix. 8[4].

5 Accentuation of the final syllable (as in the cognate singular Dvandvas) prevails in these n. Bahuvrīhis; exceptions are *á-bhaya-*, n. 'safety' (adj. 'free from danger'), and *vi-hṛdaya-* (AV.) 'lack of courage'.

6 These are called Dvigu by the Hindu grammarians, and are classed by them as a subdivision of Tatpuruṣas.

7 A few numeral collectives are determinatives used in the pl. and the original gender: *saptarṣáyas* 'the seven seers', *sapta-gṛdhrā́s* 'seven vultures' (AV.); *tri-kadru-ka-* pl. 'three soma-vessels' (from *kadrū́-* f.).

8 With the suffix *-ya* is formed *sahasrāhṇ-yá-* n. (AV.) 'a thousand days' journey'.

the process of transmutation from the latter. They must in the vast majority of instances have been formed directly and independently in conformity with the type of these secondary adjectives which had come down from the IIr. period[1]. WACKERNAGEL (2[1], 112) adopts the view that the origin of Bahuvrīhis is not to be explained by transmutation from determinatives, but from the predicative or appositional use of groups of words characterizing a substantive[2]. This use he exemplifies by the following quotations from the RV.: *urúḥ kákṣo ná gāṅgyáḥ* (VI. 45[31]) 'like the broad shoulder dwelling on the Ganges', that is, for **urú-kakṣaḥ* 'Broad-shoulder' as a Proper Name; *sá jāyase sáho mahát* (V. 11[6]) 'thou art born a great power' (= **mahā́-sahāḥ* 'one having great power'); *tvácaṃ kṛṣṇā́m arandhayat* (I. 130[8]) 'he delivered over the black skin' (that is, 'those having a black skin', 'the black-skins'); *drógħāya cid vácasa ā́navāya* (VI. 62[9]) 'to Ānava, deceitful speech', that is, 'who utters deceitful speech'[3]; and *narā́m .. śáṃsaḥ* (II. 34[6]) 'praise of men' as representing an earlier stage than *nárā-śáṃsa-* 'receiving the praises of men' as a Bahuvrīhi. Appositional Bahuvrīhis, he thinks, similarly arose from explanatory clauses, as *índra-jyeṣṭhā devā́ḥ* 'the gods having Indra as their mightiest' from *devā́ḥ índro jyéṣṭhaḥ* 'the gods — Indra their mightiest'. The first step here would have been assimilation in case and number to the main substantive, involving change to a compound (with stem-form and single accent), followed by assimilation in gender. The change to the Bahuvrīhi had already become the rule in the pre-Vedic period.

5. Governing Compounds.

292. In a considerable number of compounds the first member governs the last in sense, being either a preposition (prepositional adverb) or a verbal noun. These compounds being adjectives are allied to Bahuvrīhis.

1. In the **prepositional** group the first member is a preposition or adverb capable of governing a case. There are about twenty examples in the RV. In some instances they seem to have arisen from the corresponding syntactical combination, as *ádhi-ratha-* n. 'wagon-load' from *ádhi ráthe* (X. 64[12]) 'on the wagon'. In other instances they seem to have originated from the corresponding adverb; thus the adjective in *pra-dív-ā ketúnā* (V. 60[8]) 'with long-existing light' has been changed from the adverb *pra-dívas* 'from of old' to agree with a substantive in the instrumental. The ending of the second member has been preserved for the most part only when it was *-a*; otherwise the suffix *-a* or *-ya* is generally added. Like Bahuvrīhis, compounds of this type may become neuter substantives; thus *upānas-á-* 'being on the wagon', n. (AV.) 'space in a wagon'.

a. All prepositions which govern cases (except *áva*) as well as *prá* (though it never governs a case), besides several adverbs capable of being used with a case, are employed as first member in these compounds[4]. The following are examples of prepositional governing compounds: *ati-mātrá-* (AV.) 'beyond measure', *ati-rātrá-* 'lasting overnight', *áty-aṃhas-* (VS.) 'beyond the reach of distress', *áty-avi-* 'running over the wool'; *ádhi-gart-ya-* 'being on the car-seat', *adhi-gav-á-* (AV.) 'derived from cows'; *adhas-pad-á-* 'being

---

1 Cp. BRUGMANN, Grundriss 2, p. 88; IF. 18, 63 ff.

2 On substantives used instead of adjectives cp. BRUGMANN, Grundriss 2, p. 89.

3 Cp. *drogha-vā́c-* 'uttering deceitful speech'.

4 This type of governing compound is similar in form to the prepositional Bahuvrīhis; the meaning, however, is quite different, as in the latter the preposition does not govern the following member, but refers adverbially to the substantive with which the Bahuvrīhi agrees.

under the feet', *adho-akṣá-* 'remaining below the axle'; *ánu-path-a-* and *ánu-vartman-* (AV. VS.) 'along the road', *anu-kāmá-* 'according to wish', *ánu-vrata-* 'obedient'; *ántas-path-a-* 'being within the path'; *api-prāṇa-* 'being on (= accompanying) the breath', *api-śarvará-* 'bordering on night' (*śárvarī-*); *abhí-dyu-* 'directed to heaven', *abhí-rāṣṭra-* 'overcoming dominion'; *ā-jaras-á-*[1] 'reaching to old age', *á-pathi-* and *ā-pathí-* 'being on the way', *á-bhaga-* 'taking part in', 'participator'; *upa-kakṣá-* 'reaching to the shoulder', *upānas-á-* 'being on a wagon', *úpa-tṛṇ-ya-* (AV.) 'lurking in the grass', *úpa-mās-ya-* (AV.) 'occurring every month'; *upári-budhna-* 'raised above the ground', *upári-martya-* 'being above men'; *ūrdhvá-nabhas-* (VS.) 'being above the clouds', *ūrdhvá-barhis-* (VS.) 'being above the litter'; *tiró-ahn-ya-* ('being beyond a day' =) 'belonging to the day before yesterday'; *pari-panth-ín-*[2] ('lying around the path') 'adversary', *pari-hastá-* (AV.) ('put round the hand') 'hand-amulet'; *paró-mātra-* ('being beyond measure') 'excessive', *paró-kṣ-a-* (AV.) ('lying beyond the eye') 'invisible'; *puro-gav-á-* ('going before the cows') 'leader'; *prati-kāmyà-* (AV.) 'being in accordance with desire'; *śaṃ-gayá-* 'blessing the household'.

2. In **verbal governing compounds** the first member is either an agent noun or an action noun governing the last member as an object. The abnormal position of the verbal form before the object in this class is probably to be explained by the first member having originally been an imperative, which usually has this position. These compounds are an old formation, two types going back to the Indo-European period, and one to the Indo-Iranian. They are adjectives, but the final member never adds a compositional suffix except in *śikṣā-nar-á-* 'helping men'. Three types are to be distinguished.

a. The **first member** consists of a **present stem** or the root, which probably represents an imperative[3]; of this type there are few examples: *trasá-dasyu-* m., N. of a man ('terrify the foe'), *radā-vasu-*[4] (only voc.) 'dispensing wealth', *śikṣā-nará-*[4] 'helping men', *sthā-raśman-*[5] 'loosening bridles'[6].

b. Examples of the second type are more numerous. Here the **first member ends in** *-át*, but the participle, being formed from present stems in *-a*, *-á* or *-aya*, which appears in these compounds, in a few instances does not occur in independent use. This type, which is almost entirely restricted to the RV., is also Iranian. It seems to have taken the place of the older one (a), which owing to its form was apt to be confused with Bahuvrīhis though differing from them in meaning. The form which they assumed was probably aided by the analogy of Bahuvrīhis with a present participle as their first member, like *śucád-ratha-* 'having a brilliant car', which are formed from intransitive verbs, while those in the governing compounds are of course transitive. Examples of this type are the following: *ṛdhád-ray-*[7] ('increasing wealth') m., N. of a man, and *ṛdhád-vāra-*[7] 'increasing goods', *kṣayád-vīra*[8] 'ruling men', *codayán-mati-*[9] 'stimulating devotion', *jamád-*[10]

---

[1] Occurs only in the dative as an adverb meaning 'up to old age'.

[2] Formed with the suffix *-in* which is not properly attached to compounds; cp. WACKERNAGEL 2[1], 53 (p. 121 bottom).

[3] See BRUGMANN, IF. 18, 76; DELBRÜCK, Vergleichende Syntax 3, 174; JACOBI, Compositum und Nebensatz (1897), 46—82; WACKERNAGEL 2[1], p. 315.

[4] Rhythmically lengthened for *rada-*, *śikṣa-*.

[5] The Pada has *sthāḥ-raśman-*. The meaning is doubtful; it may be a simple Bahuvrīhi, 'having firm bridles' (GRASSMANN).

[6] *kṛpá-nīḍa-* would be another example if it means 'arranging his abode', but the meaning of the first member is doubtful.

[7] *ṛdhát-* is an aorist participle of *ṛdh-* 'increase'.

[8] From *kṣáyati* 'rules'.

[9] From *codáyati* 'urges'.

[10] *jamát-* a palatalized form from *gam-* 'go'.

agni- ('going to Agni'), N. of man, *tarád-dveṣas-*[1] 'overcoming foes', *drāvayát-sakha-*[2] 'speeding the comrade', *dhārayát-kavi-* 'supporting the wise' and *dhārayát-kṣiti-*[3] 'supporting men', *bharád-vāja-* ('carrying off the prize') m., N. of a man, and *ā-bharád-vasu-*[4] 'bringing wealth', *maṃhayád-rayi-*[5] 'lavishing wealth', *mandád-vīra-*[6] 'gladdening men', **vidád-aśva-*[7] 'possessing steeds', *vidád-vasu-*[8] 'winning wealth', *śrāvayát-pati-* 'making his lord famous', and *śrāvayát-sakhi-*[9] 'making his friend famous', *sanád-rayi-* 'bestowing possessions' and *sanád-vāja-*[10] 'bestowing booty', *sādád-yoni-*[11] 'sitting in one's place', *spṛhayád-varṇa-*[12] 'striving after lustre'. Two such governing compounds are once combined in such a way that the final member common to both is dropped in the first: *patayán mandayát-sakham* (I. 4[7]) 'causing his friend to fly (*patáya-*) and to be glad' (*mandáya-*)[13].

c. In the third type, which goes back to the Indo-European period[14], the first member is a noun of action variously accented. There are some half-dozen examples in the RV.: *dáti-vāra-* 'giving treasures', *púṣṭi-gu-* ('rearing kine') m., N. of a man, *rīty-āp-*[15] 'causing waters to flow', *vītí-rādhas-* 'enjoying the oblation', *vītí-hotra-* 'enjoying the sacrifice', *vṛṣṭí-dyāv-* 'causing the sky to rain'[16].

6. Syntactical Compounds.

293. There are some irregular formations in which words not in coordinate, attributive, dependent or governing relation are compounded owing to constant juxtaposition in the sentence.

1. The **relative word** *yát* (abl.) 'in so far as' is compounded with a superlative in RV. III. 53[21]: *ūtíbhiḥ ... yāc-chreṣṭhábhiḥ*[17] 'with the best possible aids', lit. 'with aids in so far as (they are) the best'. The adverb *yād-rādhyàm* (II. 38[8]) 'as quickly as possible', lit. 'in so far as possible', is analogous.

2. The **initial words** of a text begin to be compounded in the later Saṃhitās as a designation of that text; thus *ye-yajāmahá-* (VS.) in the nom. pl. m. means the text beginning with the words *yé yájāmahe*[18].

3. Phrases, almost always consisting of two words, used in connexion with certain actions are compounded; thus *aham-uttará-*[19] (AV.) 'dispute for precedence', from the phrase used by each disputant *ahám úttaraḥ* 'I (am) higher'; *mama-satyéṣu* 'in disputes as to ownership', in which every one says *máma satyám* '(it is) certainly mine'; *mām-paśyá-* (AV.) as the name of a plant used by a woman to secure the love of a man with the words *mám paśya* 'look at me'[20]. Similarly in connexion with persons, as *kuvít-sa-* 'some

[1] From *tára-ti* 'overcomes'.
[2] From *drāváya-* causative of *dru-* 'run'.
[3] From *dhāráya-* causative of *dhṛ-* 'support'.
[4] From *bhára-ti* 'bears'.
[5] From *maṃháya-* causative of *maṃh-* 'be great'.
[6] From *mánda-ti* 'gladdens'. The SV. has the wrong variant *vandád-vīra-*.
[7] To be inferred from the patronymic *váidadaśvi-*.
[8] From *vidá-ti* 'finds'.
[9] From *śrāváya-* causative of *śru-* 'hear'.
[10] From *sána-ti* or *saná-ti* 'wins'.
[11] Lengthened for *sadád-* from *sáda-ti* 'sits'.
[12] From *spṛhaya-ti* 'desires'.
[13] On the doubtful examples *arcád-dhūma-*, *kṛtád-vasū*, *pratád-vasū*, *bhuvad vásuḥ* (VIII. 19[37]), *vṛṣad-añji-* (voc.) see WACKERNAGEL 2[1], p. 319 note.
[14] See WACKERNAGEL 2[1], p. 320 (bottom).
[15] This is the only example recognized by BR. as belonging to this type; GRASSMANN explains them all as Bahuvrīhis.
[16] BRUGMANN, IF. 18, 70 f., explains these compounds as having originated in imperatives, while JACOBI, Compositum und Nebensatz p. 64 f., thinks the first member represents an original 3. pers. sing.
[17] In AV. VII. 31[1] *yāvac-chreṣṭhábhis* is a corrupt variant. Compounds formed with *yāvat-* do not otherwise occur till the Sūtras.
[18] In the TS. also occurs *idám-madhu-* m. as a designation of the text *idám evá sāraghám mádhu*. This kind of compound becomes common in the ancillary literature when particular hymns are referred to.
[19] Used in the locative only.
[20] One or two doubtful examples are discussed by WACKERNAGEL 2[1], p. 327 (top).

one' from the phrase *kuvít sá* 'is it he?'. This type is more commonly based on phrases used by people about themselves; thus *áhaṃ-sana*[1] (voc.) 'rapacious', that is, one who says *ahám saneyam* (*dhánāni*) 'may I obtain (wealth)'; *aham-pūrvá-* 'eager to be first', that is, one who says *ahám pūrvaḥ* (*syām*) 'I (should be) first'; *kiṃ-tvá-* (VS.) 'asking garrulously' that is, one who continually says 'what (are) you (doing)?'.

VI. DECLENSION.

BENFEY, Vollständige Grammatik 707—780. — WHITNEY, Grammar 261—526.

294. **General character.** — Declension means the inflexion of nominal stems by means of endings which express the various relations represented by what are called cases. The stems belonging to the sphere of declension are most conveniently divided, owing to difference of meaning, form, and use, into **nouns, pronouns,** and **numerals.** Pronouns have to be treated separately because they have certain peculiarities of inflexion, besides to some extent lacking the distinction of gender. Numerals again show other peculiarities of form as well as partial lack of gender. Nouns are divided into substantives as names of things and adjectives as names of attributes. But as no definite line of demarcation can be drawn between substantive and adjective in any of the classes of declension in the Vedic language, these two categories are nowhere treated separately in the present work.

I. Nouns.

LANMAN, Noun-inflection in the Veda, JAOS. vol. X (1880), p. 325—600.

295. Owing to considerable divergencies of inflexion, nominal stems are best grouped in the **two main divisions** of **consonant and vowel** declension. Stems ending in semivowels form a transition from the former to the latter. The stems contained in the two main classes have further to be sub-divided, owing to difference of derivation and, in part, consequent variety of inflexion, into **radical** and **derivative** stems.

a. Like other Aryan tongues, the Vedic language distinguishes in declension the **three genders,** masculine, feminine, and neuter. It also distinguishes **three numbers,** the singular, dual, and plural, the dual being in full and regular use[2].

b. There are **eight cases:** nominative, vocative, accusative, instrumental, dative, ablative, genitive, locative, all in regular and unrestricted use. The same ending, however, is to a limited extent employed to express the sense of two and sometimes of three cases. Thus the eight cases of the dual have among them only three endings; in the plural the single ending *-bhyas* does duty for both dative and ablative; while in the singular the same ending *-as* appears for both ablative and genitive in all but the *a*-declension.

c. The **normal endings** of cases are the following:

Singular: nom. m. f. *-s*, n. none; voc. of all genders, none; acc. m. f. *-am*, n. none; inst. *-ā*, dat. *-e*, abl. gen. *-as*, loc. *-i*.

Dual: nom. voc. acc. m. f. *-ā*, *-au*, n. *-ī*, inst. dat. abl. *-bhyām*, gen. loc. *-os*.

Plural: nom. voc. acc. m. f. *-as*, neut. *-i*; inst. *-bhis*, dat. abl. *-bhyas*, gen. *-ām*, loc. *-su*.

---

[1] RV. VIII. 61[9]; cp. *ahám sánā* V. 75[2].

[2] But while the employment of the dual is generally strict, the plural is often used instead of the dual of natural pairs in the 'hieratic' parts of the RV.; see BLOOMFIELD, Johns Hopkins University Circular for 1905, p. 18 f., OLIPHANT, ibid. p. 22—31.

d. A distinction is often made in the stem between **strong** (or full) **and weak** (or reduced) **case-forms.** It appears in its full development only in derivative consonant stems, affecting the suffixes *-añc*[1]; *-an, -man, -van*; *-ant, -mant, -vant*; *-tar*; *-yāṃs*; *-vāṃs*. The strong form of the stem appears in the **masculine** nom. voc.[2] acc. singular and dual, and in the nom. voc. plural; and in the **neuter** nom. voc. acc. plural only. The weak form of the stem appears in the remaining cases. But in the first four and in the last of the above suffixes the weak stem which appears before endings with initial consonant is further weakened before endings with initial vowel.

e. The way in which the **normal** endings are attached to the strong and the weak stem with accompanying shift of accent, may be illustrated by the **inflexion** of the stem *ad-ánt-* 'eating' in the **masc.**:

Singular: N. *ad-án.* V. *ád-an.* A. *ad-ántam.* I. *ad-at-á.* D. *ad-at-é.* Ab. G. *ad-at-ás.* L. *ad-at-í.*

Dual: N. A. *ad-ánt-ā, -au.* V. *ád-ant-ā, -au.* I. D. Ab. *ad-ád-bhyām.* G. L. *ad-at-ós.*

Plural: N. *ad-ánt-as.* V. *ád-ant-as.* A. *ad-at-ás.* I. *ad-ád-bhis.* D. Ab. *ad-ád-bhyas.* G. *ad-at-ám.* L. *ad-át-su.*

The **neuter** differs only in the N. A. V. of all numbers: Sing.: N. A. *ad-át*; V. *ád-at.* Du.: N. A. *ad-at-ī́.* Pl.: N. A. *ad-ánt-i.*

A. Consonant Stems.

296. Among these stems there are none ending in gutturals[3] and only two ending in the cerebral *ḍ*. Those which end in the labials *p, bh, m* are fairly numerous. The majority end in dentals, the only class of consonants in which every sound contained in the group (*t, th, d, dh, n*) is represented. Of the semivowels, *y* is represented by one stem, *v* by three stems, and *r* by a large number of stems. There are many stems ending in the sibilants *ś, ṣ, s*, and several in the breathing *h* as representative of both a new and an old palatal.

1. Palatal Stems.

297. 1. Radical stems in -c. — All **uncompounded stems** (being of course monosyllabic) are, with very few isolated exceptions, **feminine substantives.** The exceptions are: *tvác-* 'skin', otherwise f., occurs twice in the L. sing. *tvací* as a m.; *árc-*, in its only occurrence, I. sing. *arc-á*, is a m. adj. in the sense of 'shining'; and *krúñc-*, 'curlew' (VS.) is a m. substantive.

Compounds, as being **adjectives,** are often m.; but excepting those formed with *añc-* the only n. is *ā-pṛ́k* (from *pṛc-* 'mix'), used adverbially. Compounds ending in *-añc*[4] regularly distinguish **strong and weak forms.** This distinction elsewhere appears to a limited extent only in compounds ending in the three roots *vyac-* 'extend', *vac-* 'speak', *sac-* 'accompany': the first by nasalization in *uru-vyáñcam*[5] 'far-extending', the other two by lengthening the radical vowel in several compounds.

[1] Though in origin a radical element, *-añc* is practically a suffix; cp. 298.

[2] The voc. sing., however, generally assumes a somewhat shortened form owing to the accent invariably shifting to the initial syllable in this case.

[3] The gutturals as finals of nominal stems having become the new palatals *c, j*[2] and *h*[2] (as distinguished from the old palatals *j*[1] and *h*[1]).

[4] These compounds formed with the root *añc-* will, owing to the peculiar changes which the stem undergoes, be treated apart from other words ending in radical *c*.

[5] Through the influence of compounds formed with *-añc*, like *praty-áñcam*.

Inflexion.

The forms actually occurring, if made from *vā́c-* f. 'speech', would be the following:

Sing.: N. V. *vā́k.* A. *vā́cam.* I. *vācā́.* D. *vācé.* Ab. G. *vācás.* L. *vācí.* — **Dual:** N. A. V. *vā́cā* and *vā́cau.* I. *vāgbhyā́m* (VS.). — **Plur.:** N. V. *vā́cas.* A. *vā́cas* and *vācás.* I. *vāgbhís.* D. *vāgbhyás* (VS). Ab. *vāgbhyás* (AV.). G. *vācā́m.*

a. The forms actually occurring are:

Sing. N. f. *ṛ́k* (AV.) 'stanza', *tvák* 'skin', *vā́k* 'speech', *śúk* (AV. VS.) 'flame', *srúk* 'ladle'; *ni-mrúk* (AV.) 'sunset', *puruṣa-vā́k* (VS. XXIV. 33) 'human-voiced', *puro-rúk* (TS. VII. 3. 13[1]) 'forward light', *saṃ-vā́k* (VS. IX. 12) 'argument'. — **m.** *krúṅ* (VS. XIX. 43) 'curlew'; *anṛta-vā́k* (AV.) 'speaking untruth', *upa-pṛ́k* 'adhering to', *tri-śúk* (VS. XXXVIII. 22) 'having triple light', *yatá-sruk* 'extending the ladle', *sū́rya-tvak* (AV.) 'having a covering (bright) as the sun', *hiraṇya-tvak* 'coated with gold'.

A. f. *ṛ́cam, tvácam, rúcam* (VS. TS.) 'lustre', *vā́cam, śúcam* (AV.), *sícam* 'hem', *srúcam* (AV.); *ā-sícam* 'oblation', *vi-múcam* 'unyoking', *sū́rya-tvacam.* — **m.** *aṃho-múcam* 'delivering from distress', *ádrogha-vācam* 'free from treacherous speech', *kúya-vācam* 'speaking ill', *tanū-rúcam* 'brilliant in person', *dhánarcam* 'shining (*ṛcam*) with booty', *puro-rúcam* 'shining in front', *madhu-pṛ́cam* 'dispensing sweetness', *mṛdhrá-vācam* 'speaking injuriously', *su-rúcam* 'shining brightly', *su-vā́cam* 'very eloquent', *sū́rya-tvacam* (Kh. IV. 6[3]). With **strengthened stem:** *uru-vyáñcam*; *satya-vā́cam* 'truth-speaking'; *apatya-sā́cam* 'accompanied with offspring', *abhi-ṣā́cam* 'accompanying', *droṇa-sā́cam* 'clinging to the trough', *dhāma-sā́cam* 'keeping his place', *rāti-ṣā́cam* 'bestowing gifts'. — **n.** (adv.) *ā-pṛ́k* 'in a mixed manner'.

I. f. *ṛcā́, tvacā́, mṛcā́* 'injury', *rucā́, vācā́, śucā́, sicā́, srucā́*; *puro-rúcā* (VS. XX. 36) 'forward light', *su-rúcā.* — **m.** *arcā́* 'shining'; *uru-vyácā, sū́rya-tvacā.*

D. f. *ṛcé* (VS. XIII. 39), *tucé* 'offspring', *tvacé* (AV.), *rucé, vācé* (VS. XXII. 23), *śucé* (VS. XXXIX. 12); *uru-vyáce* (AV.). — **m.** *aṃho-múce* (TS. I. 6. 12[3]), *údyata-sruce* 'extending the ladle', *yatá-sruce, viśva-śúce* 'all-enlightening'.

Ab. f. *tvacás, srucás* (AV. VS.); *ni-mrúcas.*

G. f. *ṛcás, tvacás, vācás*; *vi-mucas* (*napāt,* V.). — **m.** *puru-rúcas* 'shining brightly', *su-rúcas.*

L. f. *tvací, vācí, srucí*; *ā-túci* 'evening', *ud-ṛ́ci* 'end', *ni-mrúci, vi-vāci* 'crying aloud'. — **m.** *tvací* 'skin' (IX. 69[3], 101[16]).

V. m. *ákṛtta-ruk* 'possessing unimpaired lustre' (X. 84[4]).

Du. N. A. V. f. *vā́cau, sícau*; *ghṛta-pṛ́cā* 'sprinkling fatness', *tanū-rúcā.* — With **strengthened stem:** *satya-vā́cā.* — **m.** *krúñcau* (VS. XXX. 6); *tanū-rúcā, yatá-srucā, su-vā́cā*; *sam-pṛ́cau* (VS. IX. 4) 'united'.

I. m. *ati-rúgbhyām* (VS. XXV. 3) 'fetlocks'.

Pl. N. f. *ṛ́cas, pṛ́cas* 'food', *rúcas, vā́cas, sícas* (AV.), *srúcas*[1]; *ā-pṛ́cas* 'filling' (VIII. 40[9])[2], *divo-rúcas* 'shining from heaven', *ni-mrúcas* (AV. VS.), *vi-múcas* (AV.), **V.** *bhadra-vācas* 'speaking auspiciously'. — **m.** *dudhrá-vācas* 'speaking confusedly', *yatá-srucas, vasu-rúcas* 'bright as the Vasus', *vi-pṛ́cas* (VS. XIX. 11) 'parted', *ví-vācas, saṃ-sícas* (AV.) 'shedding together', *saṃ-pṛ́cas* (VS. XIX. 11), *su-rúcas, su-vā́cas, sūktá-vācas* 'uttering good speech', **V.** *sūrya-tvacas.* — With **strengthened stem:** *abhi-ṣā́cas, áyajña-sācas* 'not performing sacrifice', *drogha-vā́cas* 'speaking maliciously', **V.** *nṛ-ṣācas* 'befriending men',

---

1 AV. once (XIX. 42[2]) with wrong accent *srucás.*

2 According to BR., infinitive of *á-pṛc-* 'satiate oneself'.

raṇya-vā́cas 'speaking agreeably', *rayi-ṣā́cas* 'possessing wealth', *rāti-ṣā́cas*, *satya-vā́cas*, *smád-rāti-ṣācas* 'attended by liberal men', *hari-ṣā́cas* 'occupied with the tawny (Soma)'.

A. f. *rúcas*, *vā́cas* and (once) *vācás*, *śúcas* (AV.), *sícas* (AV.), *srúcas* and (once) *srucás* (AV.); *dur-vácas* (AV.) 'having a bad voice', *mṛdhrá-vācas*, *su-rúcas*. — **m.** *an-ṛ́cas* 'hymnless', *a-rúcas* 'lustreless', *mṛdhrá-vācas*, *vádhri-vācas* 'talking idly', *ví-vācas*.

I. f. *ṛgbhís*. — **D. f.** *srugbhyás* (VS. II. 1). — **Ab. f.** *ṛgbhyás* (AV.) — **G. f.** *ṛcā́m*, *tvacā́m* (AV.); *madhu-pṛ́cām* (AV.).

298. Stems in -*añc*. A considerable number of compounds is formed by adding as final member the root *añc-* 'bend', which almost assumes the character of a suffix[1] expressing the meaning of '-ward'; e. g. *prā́ñc-* (= *prá-añc-*) 'for-ward'. **Strong and weak forms** are regularly distinguished, the nasal which appears in the former being always lost in the latter. If *-añc* is preceded by a word ending in *i* or *u*, the syllables *ya* and *va* thus produced are further weakened to *ī* and *ū* before vowel endings, and if bearing the accent, shift it to those endings[2]; e. g. Sing. A. m. *pratyáñcam*, N. n. *pratyák*, G. *pratīcás*.

In these compounds *-añc* is added to words ending in 1. *ă*, with which it coalesces: *adharā́ñc-* 'tending downward' (*ádhara-*)[3], *ápāñc-* 'backward' (*ápa*), *arvā́ñc-* 'hitherward' (*arvá-*), *ávāñc-* 'downward' (*áva*), *asmatrā́ñc-* 'turned toward us', *ghṛtā́ñc-*[4] 'filled with ghee' (*ghṛtá-*), *devā́ñc-* 'directed toward the gods' (*devá-*), *párāñc-* 'turned away' (*párā*), *prā́ñc-* 'forward' (*prá*), *viśvā́ñc-* 'universal' (*viśva-*)[5], *satrā́ñc-* 'going together' (*satrā́*)[6]. 2. *-i*: *akudhryàñc-*[7] 'going nowhere' (*aku-dhri-*), *asmadryàñc-* 'turned towards us' (*asmad-ri-*)[7], *údañc-*[8] 'turned upward' (*úd*), *kadryáñc-*[7] (turned towards what' (*kád-*), *tiryáñc-* 'going across' (*tiri-*)[9], *dadhyáñc-* 'sprinkling curds' (*dádhi-*), *devadryàñc-*[7] 'turned towards the gods' (*devá-*), *nyáñc-* 'turned down' (*ní*), *pratyáñc-* 'turned towards' (*práti*), *madryàñc-*[7] 'turned towards me' (*mad-rí-*), *viṣvadryàñc-* 'going everywhere' (*viṣu-a-drí-*), *śvityáñc-* 'whitish' (*śvit-i-*), *sadhryàñc-*[7] 'coming together' (*sa-dhrī́-* 'the same goal'), *samyáñc-* 'going together' (*sam-i-*). 3. *-u*: *anvā́ñc-* 'going after' (*ánu*), *ṛjvā́ñc-* 'moving straight forward' (*ṛjú-*), *viṣvañc-* 'going in all directions' (*víṣu-*), *svā́ñc-* 'going well' (*sú*). The two feminines *purūc-ī́-* 'abundant' and *urūc-ī́-* 'far-reaching' presuppose similar stems (**puru-áñc-* and **uru-áñc-*).

Inflexion.

299. These stems are inflected in the m. and n. only, as they form a f. in *-ī* from the weak or contracted stem, e. g. *prā́ñc-*, f. *prā́c-ī-*; *pratyáñc-*, f. *pratīc-ī́-*. The only cases occurring in the pl. are the N. A. and in the du. the N. A. and L.

The forms actually found, if made from *pratyáñc-*, would be as follows: **Sing.** N. m. *pratyáṅ*, n. *pratyák*. A. m. *pratyáñcam*. I. *pratīcā́*. D. *pratīcé*. Ab. G. *pratīcás*. L. *pratīcí*. — **Du.** N. A. m. *pratyáñcā*, *pratyáñcau* (AV.), n. *pratīcī́*. L. m. *pratīcós*. — **Pl.** N. m. *pratyáñcas*. A. m. *pratīcás* and *pratī́cas* (AV.).

a. The forms actually occurring are the following:

Sing. N. m. *adharā́ṅ* (AV.), *ápāṅ*, *arvā́ṅ*, *ávāṅ* (TS. III. 2. 5[3]), *údaṅ* (AV.),

---

1 Cp. WHITNEY 407; LINDNER, Nominalbildung, Addenda p. 167, prefers to treat *-añc* as a suffix.

2 The accent is similarly shifted to the suffix *-ī* with which the f. of these stems is formed (cp. 86 B 11, p. 87)). This rule of accentuation applies to the RV. only, not to the later Saṃhitās; cp. A. pl. below (p. 182).

3 With shifted accent.

4 In this and some other of these compounds only the weak unnasalized form of the stem occurs.

5 With shift of accent.

6 The f. *narāc-ī́-* (AV.), N. of a plant, is doubtless based on a similar stem formed from *nára-* 'man', with shift of accent.

7 The suffix *-ri-* in these compounds perhaps spread from *sadhrī́-añc-* (the *dh* also to *akudhryāñc-*), while the *d* of *deva-dryàñc-* and *viṣvadryàñc-* may be due to the pronominal forms *mád-* and *asmád-*.

8 The weak stem *udīc-* being formed as if from **úd-i-añc-*.

9 *tiri-* appearing instead of *tirás-* 'across' from which the weak stem *tiráśc-* (= *tirás-ac-*) is formed.

tiryáṅ (AV.), *dadhyáṅ*[1], *nyàṅ*, *párāṅ* (AV.), *pratyáṅ*[2], *práṅ*, *víṣvaṅ*, *sadhryàṅ* (AV.), *su-práṅ*. — n. Nearly all the following forms are used adverbially: *akudhryàk*, *adharák* (AV.), *ápāk*, *árvāk* and *arvák* (AV.), *asmadryàk*, *údak*, *tiryák* (AV.), *nyàk*, *párāk* (AV.), *pratyák*, *prák*, *madryàk*, *víṣvak*, *viṣvadryàk*, *sadhryàk*, *samyák*[3].

A. m. *adharáñcam* (AV.), *anváñcam* (AV.), *ápāñcam* (AV.), *arváñcam*, *údañcam*, *tiryáñcam* (VS. x. 8), *nyàñcam*, *párāñcam* (AV.), *pratyáñcam*, *práñcam*, *madryàñcam*, *víṣvañcam*, *samyáñcam*, *sváñcam*.

I. m. *arvácā*. — n. *devadrícā*, *satrácā*; used **adverbially** with shifted accent: *tiraścā́*, *nīcā́*, *prācā́*[4].

D. m. *dadhīcé*, *śvitīcé*. — **Ab. m.** *pratīcás*. — **G. m.** *dadhīcás*, *viṣvácas*[5]. — **L. m.** *práci*.

Du. N. A. m. *ápāñcau* (AV.), *arváñcā* and *arváñcau* (AV.), *víṣvañcau* (AV.), *sadhryàñcā*, *samyáñcā* and *samyáñcau* (AV. VS.). — **n.** *pratīcī́*, *samīcī́* (VS. I. 31, TS. IV. 1. 3[2]). — **L. m.** *viṣūcos*.

Pl. N. m. *adharáñcas* (AV.), *ápāñcas* (AV.), *arváñcas*[6], *asmatráñcas*, *asmadryàñcas*, *údañcas*, *ṛjváñcas*, *tiryáñcas* (AV.), *párāñcas*, *pratyáñcas*, *práñcas*, *víṣvañcas*, *śvityáñcas*[7], *sadhryàñcas*, *samyáñcas*, *sváñcas*.

A. m. *adharácas*, *anūcás* and *anúcas* (AV.), *ápācas*, *arvácas*, *ávācas*, *údīcas*, *nī́cas* (AV.), *párācas*, *pratīcás* and *pratī́cas* (AV.), *prácas*, *víṣūcas*, *satrácas*.

300. **Radical stem in *-ch*.** — Only one stem ending in *ch*, which occurs in a single form as a noun, has been found. This is made from the root *pṛcch-* 'ask', in the compound N. du. m. *bandhu-pṛ́cch-ā* 'asking after kinsmen'. The D. and A. of the same stem also appear as infinitives in the forms *pṛcché* 'to ask', *sam-pṛ́cche* 'to greet'; *vi-pṛ́ccham* and *sam-pṛ́ccham* 'to ask'.

301. **Stems in radical *-j*.** — These stems are inflected in all three genders alike. The neuter would of course differ in N. A. V. dual and plural, but these forms do not occur. When **uncompounded** these **stems** are **f. substantives** except *yúj-* and *rā́j-*, which appear as m. also; *bhrā́j-*, which occurs as a m. adj. as well as a f. substantive; *áj-*, which is found once (AV.)[8], and *víj-* twice as a m. only. Neuter cases occur from *bhā́j-*, *yúj-*, *rā́j-* and *vṛj-* as final members of adj. compounds, but no distinctively neuter forms (N. A. V. du. pl.) are met with even here.

The only stem showing traces of the distinction of **strong and weak** cases is ***yúj-***, which has the nasalized form *yúñj-* beside the unaltered stem in the N. A. sing. and du.

In the **N. sing.** the *j*, when derived from a guttural, appears as *k*, but when it represents an old palatal, it becomes the cerebral *ṭ* except in *ṛtv-íj*[9] 'priest'; but before the *-su* of the L. pl. both alike[10] become *k*.

---

1 On the doubling of the *ṅ* before vowels, see LANMAN 456.

2 *pratyáṅk-* before *s-* in TS. I. 8. 21[1].

3 The forms *tvadrík*, *madrík* and *madryadrík*, *yuvadrík*, 'towards thee, — me, — you', are doubtless shortened forms of *-dryák*, which pronunciation is favoured by the metre in some instances: LANMAN 456 (bottom).

4 *prācā́* is probably used adverbially in III. 31[5] also. As an adj. the form, being a compound, would be accented *prácā*.

5 N. of a demon, formed with *-añc*, from *viṣva-*, an extension of *viṣu-*, as in *viṣva-dryàñc-*.

6 The weak form *arvácas* seems to be used for *arváñcas* in VII. 48[1].

7 A transition form, N. m. *śvitīcáyas* (x. 46[7]) = *śvityáñcas*, is made from an *i-* stem *śvitīci-* based on the regular f. *śvitīcī́-*.

8 In AV. XIX. 50[5], where the reading *ájam* is somewhat doubtful; see WHITNEY's note.

9 Which is derived from *yaj-* 'sacrifice': *ṛtu-ij-* 'sacrificing in due season'.

10 See above 34, 1.

Inflexion.

302. Sing. N. 1. with *-k*: m. *yúṅ*[1] (VS. x. 25) 'associate'; *a-bhúk* 'not having enjoyed', *ardha-bhā́k* (AV.) 'sharer', *ṛta-yúk* 'duly harnessed', *ṛtv-ík* 'priest', *ghṛtá-nirṇik* 'having a garment of fat', *candrá-nirṇik* 'having a brilliant garment', *parā-vṛ́k* 'outcast', *bhi-ṣák*[2] 'healing', *śatá-bhiṣak* (AV.) 'requiring a hundred physicians', *saṃ-vṛ́k* 'overpowering', *sa-yúk* 'companion', *híraṇya-srak* (AV.) 'having a golden garland'. — **f.** *ū́rk* (VS. IV. 10) 'vigour', *nir-ṇík*[3] 'bright garment', *híraṇya-nirṇik*. — **n.** N. A. *sv-ā́-vṛk* 'easily acquired', *su-yúk* 'well-joined' (adv.).

2. with *-ṭ*: m. *bhrā́ṭ*[4] 'shining', *rā́ṭ* 'king'; *eka-rā́ṭ* 'monarch', *jana-rā́ṭ* (VS. v. 24) 'lord of men', *vane-rā́ṭ* 'shining in a wood', *vi-bhrā́ṭ* 'resplendent', *vi-rā́ṭ* 'ruling far and wide', *viśva-bhrā́ṭ* 'all-illuminating', *satra-rā́ṭ* (VS. v. 2) 'king of a Soma sacrifice', *sam-rā́ṭ* 'universal ruler', *sarva-rā́ṭ* (VS. v. 24) 'ruler of all', *sva-rā́ṭ* 'self-ruler'. — With anomalous loss of the final of the root and retention of the **N. *-s***: *áva-yās*[5] (I. 162[5]), a priest who offers the share of the oblation (*ava-yā́j-*). — **f.** *rā́ṭ* 'mistress'; *vi-rā́ṭ*. — With anomalous loss of the final of the root (*yaj-*) and retention of the **N. *-s***: *ava-yā́s*[6] 'share of the sacrificial oblation' (I. 173[12]).

A. m. *ájam* (AV.) 'driver', *yúñjam*[7], *yújam*; *ṛtv-íjam*, *jyeṣṭha-rā́jam* 'sovereign', *tri-bhújam* (AV.) 'threefold', *deva-yā́jam* (VS. I. 17) 'sacrificing to the gods', *parā-vṛ́jam*, *púṣkara-srajam* (VS. II. 33) 'wearing a lotus wreath', *pūrva-bhā́jam* 'first sharer', *pṛtanā́jam* 'rushing (*-ájam*) to battle', *prathama-bhā́jam* 'receiving the first share', *prātar-yújam* 'yoking early', *bhi-ṣájam* (VS. XXVIII. 9), *yuvā-yújam* 'yoked by both of you', *ratha-yújam* 'yoking to a chariot', *vi-rā́jam*, *śaphā-rújam* 'destroying with hoofs', *satya-yā́jam* 'worshipping truly', *sam-rā́jam*, *sa-yújam*, *su-tyájam* 'easily letting loose', *su-yā́jam* 'worshipping well', *su-yújam* 'well-yoked', *su-srájam* (AV.) 'wearing a beautiful garland', *sva-rā́jam*, *sva-vṛ́jam* 'appropriating to oneself'. — **f.** *ū́rjam*, *tújam* 'offspring', *bhújam* 'enjoyment, *bhrā́jam* (VS. IV. 17) 'splendour', *srájam* 'garland'; *upa-spíjam*[8] (x. 88[18]) 'emulation', *nir-ṇíjam*, *pari-vṛ́jam* 'avoiding', *pra-yújam* (VS. XI. 66) 'impulse', *mano-yújam* 'yoked by thought', *vi-rā́jam*, *sahásra-nirṇijam* 'having a thousand adornments', *sva-rā́jam* (AV.).

I. m. *yujā́*; *bhi-ṣájā* (VS. AV.), *mano-yújā*, *vaco-yújā* 'yoked by a mere word', *sa-yújā* (AV.), *sahásra-nirṇijā*, *su-yájā* (VS. TS.) 'good sacrifice', *su-yújā*. — **f.** *ūrjā́*, *tujā́*, *bhrājā́* 'lustre'; *nir-ṇíjā*, *mano-yújā* (AV.), *vi-rā́jā*. — **n.** *śvātra-bhā́jā* 'strengthening'.

D. m. *yujé* (AV.); *mṛtá-bhraje*[9] (AV.) 'whose virility is dead', *rakṣo-yúje* 'associated with demons', *vi-rā́je* (VS. AV.), *sam-rā́je*, *sva-rā́je*[10]. — **f.** *ūrjé*, *tujé*[11], *bhujé*; *nir-ṇíje*. — **Ab. m.** *yujás*; *vi-rā́jas*. — **f.** *nir-ṇíjas*.

G. m. *sam-rā́jas*, *sva-rā́jas*. — **f.** *ūrjás*, *bhrajás*[12] (AV.) 'virility', *yujás*; *pra-yújas* 'team', *ratna-bhā́jas* 'dispensing gifts', *vi-rā́jas* (AV.) — **n.** *sva-rā́jas*.

---

[1] For *yúṅk*; cp. VPr. IV. 104.

[2] Probably 'one who conjures', cp. in the later language, *abhi-ṣajati* 'utters an imprecation'; cp. BRUGMANN, Grundriss 2, p. 8, bottom; UHLENBECK, Etymologisches Wörterbuch, rejects this etymology in favour of a derivation connected with Av. *-biš* 'healing'.

[3] From *nir-ṇij-* 'wash out'.

[4] There is also the transition form *bhrājá-s* (IX. 170[3]).

[5] See LANMAN 463.

[6] See above 66 c β (p. 61).

[7] Strong form (301).

[8] According to Sāyaṇa, used adverbially in the sense of 'emulously'.

[9] *-bhraj-* is probably a reduced form of *bhrāj-*: cp. the later meaning of *téjas-* 'lustre'.

[10] There is also the transfer form *bhrājáya* (VS. VIII. 40) 'for the bright one'.

[11] There is also the transfer form *tujáye* (v. 46[7]) from *tuj-i-*.

[12] Probably a reduced form of *bhrā́j-* 'lustre'. Cp. WHITNEY on AV. VII. 90[2].

L. m. *áśva-nirṇiji* 'adorned with horses'. — f. *saṃ-sṛ́ji* 'collision'.

V. m. *ghṛ́ta-nirṇik, sam-rāṭ.*

Du. N. A. V. m. *yúñjā*[1], *yújā*; *ṛtv-ijā, tanū-tyájā* 'risking one's life', *puru-bhujā* (V.) 'enjoying much', *púṣkara-srajā, prātar-yújā, brahma-yújā* 'harnessed by prayer', *bhi-ṣájā, mano-yújā* (VS. AV.), *vaco-yújā, sam-rā́jā, sa-yújā, sākaṃ-yújā* 'joined together', *su-yújā*; *anū-vṛ́jau* (AV.) a part of the body near the ribs, *apna-rā́jau* 'ruling over wealth' (*apna-* = *apnas*), *bhi-ṣajau* (V.), *sam-rā́jau, sa-yújau* (AV.), *su-yújau* (AV.). — f. *aśva-yújau* (AV.) 'harnessing horses'.

D. m. *bhi-ṣágbhyām* (AV.). — G. m. *sam-rā́jos.*

Pl. N. m. *yújas*; *ā-yújas* (AV.) 'joining on', *ṛtv-ijas*, V. *ṛtv-ijas* (AV.), *kṛtá-dhvajas* 'furnished with banners', *giri-bhrájas*[2] 'glittering on the mountains', *ghṛtá-nirṇijas, tanū-tyájas, divi-yájas* 'worshipping in heaven', *dur-yújas* 'difficult to be yoked', *niḥ-sṛ́jas* 'pouring out', *pitu-bhā́jas* 'enjoying food', *pūrva-bhā́jas, pṛtanā́jas* (*-ajas*), *pra-yújas* (AV.), *brahma-yújas, bhi-ṣájas, mano-yújas, mitra-yújas* 'joined in friendship', *ratha-yújas, varṣá-nirṇijas* 'clothed with rain', *vāma-bhā́jas* 'partaking of goods', *viśva-sṛ́jas* (AV.) 'all-creating', *sam-rā́jas*, V. *sam-rājas, su-yújas, sva-yújas* 'allies', *sva-rā́jas, hárita-srajas* (AV.) 'wearing yellow garlands'. — f. *ū́rjas, tújas, bhújas*; *abhi-yújas* 'assailants', *go-bhā́jas* 'bestowing cows', *nir-ṇíjas, pṛkṣá-prayajas* 'in which oblations begin to be offered', *pra-yújas, vi-rā́jas* (VS. XVII. 3), *stanā-bhújas*[3] 'enjoying the udder', *sv-ā-yújas* 'easy to yoke'.

A. m. *víjas* 'stakes' (at play); *ádhi-nirṇijas* 'covered over', *aśva-yújas, catur-yújas* 'yoked as (a team of) four', *śaphā-rújas, sa-yújas, su-yújas.* — f. *tújas, bhújas, srájas*; *abhi-yújas.*

I. m. *aruṇa-yúgbhis* 'furnished with ruddy (rays)', *ṛta-yúgbhis, vi-yúgbhis*[4] (AV.), *su-yúgbhis, sva-yúgbhis.*

D. f. *pra-yúgbhyas* (VS. XXX. 8) 'impulses'. — Ab. m. *bhi-ṣágbhyas* (AV.) — G. m. *ṛtv-íjām, bhi-ṣájām.* — f. *ūrjā́m, bhujā́m*; *nir-majām*[5]. — L. f. *srakṣú*; *pra-yákṣu* (AV.) 'offerings'[6].

303. **Stems in derivative *-j*.** — There are seven m. and f. adjectives or substantives formed with the suffixes *-aj* and *-ij*: *á-svapnaj-* 'sleepless', *tṛṣṇáj-* 'thirsty', *dhṛṣáj-* 'bold', *sanáj-* 'old'; *uś-íj* 'desiring', *bhur-íj-* f. 'arm', *vaṇ-íj-* m. 'trader'. There is also the n. *ásṛj-*[7] 'blood', which is of obscure etymology, but the *-j* of which is probably a reduced suffix. The forms occurring are the following:

Sing. N. m. *uśík, vaṇík.* — n. *ásṛk.* — A. m. *uśíjam, tṛṣṇájam, vaṇíjam* (AV.) — I. *uśíjā* (VS. XV. 6) 'ghee'. — D. m. *tṛṣṇáje, vaṇíje.* — G. m. *uśíjas.*

Du. N. f. *sanájā.* — G. f. *bhuríjos.* — L. f. *bhuríjos.*

Pl. N. m. *uśíjas, tṛṣṇájas, á-tṛṣṇajas, dhṛṣájas, á-svapnajas.* — f. *uśíjas.* — A. m. *uśíjas.* — I. m. *uśígbhis.* — D. m. *uśígbhyas.* — G. *uśíjām.*

2. Cerebral Stems.

304. There is only one doubtful derivative stem in *-ṭ, raghaṭ-*, which occurs in the single form *raghátas* (AV. VIII. 7^{24}), possibly a mistake for *raghávas*[8] 'swift'.

---

[1] Strong form (301).

[2] Occurring once (x. 68^{1}), *bhraj-* being a reduced form of *bhrāj-*; cp. D. m. *mṛtá-bhraje*, G. f. *bhrajás* (AV.); cp. p. 183, notes 9 and 12.

[3] The Pada text reads *stana-bhújas.*

[4] See Whitney's note on AV. VII. 4^{1}.

[5] A word of doubtful derivation and meaning, occurring only once (VIII. 4^{20}).

[6] The corresponding form is *pra-yátsu* in TS. IV. 1. 8^{1} and VS. XXVII. 14.

[7] Cp. Brugmann, Grundriss 2, p. 559, 560.

[8] See Lanman 466, and Whitney, note on AV. VIII. 7^{24}.

There are besides only two radical stems ending in -*ḍ*, *íḍ-*[1] 'praise', and *íḍ-*[2] 'refreshment'. Of the former occurs only the sing. I. *īḍā́*; of the latter only the sing. I. *iḍā́* and the G. *iḍás*[3].

3. Dental Stems.

305. Stems ending in all the dental mutes as well as the nasal are of frequent occurrence except those in *-th*. There are radical stems ending in each of the dentals, but no derivative stems in *-th* or *-dh*. The distinction of strong and weak appears with slight exceptions only in the derivative stems in *-ant* and *-an*.

306. **Stems in radical -*t*.** — The only four monosyllabic stems occurring are feminine substantives: *dyút-* 'splendour', *nṛ́t-* 'dancing', *pṛ́t-* 'battle', *vṛ́t-*[4] 'hostile array'. There are also two reduplicated stems, which are primarily adjectives: *cikít-* 'knowing' (√*cit-*) and *didyút-* 'shining'. The rest are compounds, used mostly in the masculine or feminine. Neuter cases occur from only four of them: *akṣi-pát-* 'falling into the eye', *án-apā-vṛt-* 'not turning away', *tri-vṛ́t-* 'three-fold', *saṃ-yát-*[5] 'continuous'.

Inflexion.

The forms occurring would, if made from *tri-vṛ́t-*, be as follows:

Sing. N. m. f. *tri-vṛ́t* (also **n.**). — **A. m. f.** *tri-vṛ́tam.* — **I. m. f.** *tri-vṛ́tā* (also **n.**). — **D. m. f.** *tri-vṛ́te.* — **Ab. G. m. f.** *tri-vṛ́tas.* — **L. n.** *tri-vṛ́ti* (AV.).

Du. N. A. m. f. *tri-vṛ́tā, tri-vṛ́tau.* — **L. f.** *tri-vṛ́tos.*

Pl. N. A. m. f. *tri-vṛ́tas.* — **I. n.** *tri-vṛ́dbhis* (AV.). — **G. m. f.** *tri-vṛ́tām.* — **L. f.** *tri-vṛ́tsu.* — **V. m. f.** *trí-vṛtas.*

The forms actually ocurring are the following:

Sing. N. m. *anā-vṛ́t* 'not returning', *ábandhu-kṛt*[6] (AV.) 'not cutting off kin', *eka-vṛ́t* (AV.) 'one-fold', 'simple', *cikít* 'knowing', *tri-vṛ́t* (VS. x. 10) 'triple', *pra-vṛ́t* (VS. xv. 9), *manaś-cít* 'thinking in the mind', *mūla-kṛ́t* (AV.) 'cutting roots', *vipaś-cít* 'inspired', *vi-vṛ́t* (VS. xv. 9), *viṣū-vṛ́t* 'rolling in various directions', *sa-vṛ́t* (VS. xv. 9), *su-vṛ́t* 'turning well'. — **f.** *cít* (VS. iv. 19) 'thought'; *apa-cít* (AV.) a noxious insect, *didyút* 'shining', *vi-dyút* 'flashing'. — **n.** *eka-vṛ́t* (AV.), *tri-vṛ́t*: as adv. *akṣi-pát* 'a little' and *ánapā-vṛt* 'unremittingly'.

A. m. *a-cítam* 'unthinking', *eka-vṛ́tam* (AV.), *ghṛta-ścútam* 'sprinkling ghee', *tri-vṛ́tam*, *duś-cítam* (AV.) 'thinking evil', *madhu-ścútam* 'distilling sweetness', *vipaś-cítam*, *viṣū-vṛ́tam*, *su-vṛ́tam*, *huraś-cítam* 'plotting deceit'. — **f.** *dyútam*, *vṛ́tam*; *ā-vṛ́tam* 'turning home', *ghṛta-ścútam*, *vi-cṛ́tam* 'loosening', *vi-dyútam*, *vipaś-cítam*, *saṃ-yátam*, *saṃ-vṛ́tam* (AV.) 'approach', *saṃ-cṛ́tam* 'union'.

I. m. *tri-vṛ́tā*, *vipaś-cítā* (VS. iv. 32), *su-vṛ́tā*. — **f.** *dyutā́*, *vṛtā́*; *ā-cítā* 'attention', *ghṛta-ścútā*, *tri-vṛ́tā*, *pra-cátā* 'with concealment' (adv.), *vi-dyútā*. — **n.** *saṃ-yátā*, *tri-vṛ́tā* (AV.).

D. m. *a-cite*, *tri-vṛ́te* (VS. xv. 9), *pra-vṛ́te* (VS. xv. 9), *vipaś-cíte*, *vi-vṛ́te* (VS. xv. 9), *sa-vṛ́te* (VS. xv. 9), *su-dyúte*. — **f.** *vi-dyúte*.

Ab. m. *tri-vṛ́tas* (VS. xiii. 54), *vi-dyútas*[7]. — **f.** *didyútas*.

---

[1] Cp. above 17, 5.

[2] Derived from *íṣ-* 'refreshment' which is of very frequent occurrence; cp. above p. 35, note 1.

[3] This form is regarded by GRASSMANN in one passage (VII. 47[1]) as an A. pl.: cp. LANMAN 466.

[4] *vṛ́t-* occurs once in the dual as a fem. adjective.

[5] From *yat-* 'unite'.

[6] From *kṛt-* 'cut'; but it may be 'not relative-making' (*kṛ-t*); see WHITNEY's note on AV. IV. 19[1].

[7] The Ab. *didyót* (TS. I. 8. 14[1]) and *vidyót* (VS. XX. 2) are probably irregular formations due to parallelism; cp. LANMAN 468.

G. m. *tri-vṛ́tas, vipaś-citas, sa-citas* 'wise', *su-dyútas* 'shining beautifully'. — **f.** *vi-dyútas.* — **L. n.** *tri-vṛ́ti* (AV.).

Du. N. A. V. m. *vipaś-citā* (V.), *iṣu-kṛ́tā*[1] (I. 184[3]). — **f.** *vṛ́tau; ā-vṛ́tā, madhu-ścútā, vi-cṛ́tau* (AV.). — **L. f.** *vi-cṛ́tos* (AV.).

Pl. N. m. *ā-vṛ́tas, ṛṣṭi-vidyutas* 'glittering with spears', *eka-vṛ́tas* (AV.), *ghṛta-ścútas, duś-citas* (AV.), *vi-dyútas, vipaś-citas, saṃ-yátas, sūrya-śvitas* 'bright as the sun', *svá-vidyutas* 'self-lightning', *hrādunī-vṛ́tas* 'bringing hail'. — **V.** *ṛṣṭi-vidyutas, vi-dyutas.* — **N. f.** *apa-citas* (AV.), *ā-vṛ́tas* (AV.), *upā-vṛ́tas* (VS. AV.) 'return', *ghṛta-ścútas, ghṛta-ścyútas* (VS. XVII. 3), *madhu-ścútas, madhu-ścyútas* (VS. XVII. 3), *vi-dyútas, saṃ-yátas.* — **V.** *ápa-citas* (AV.).

A. m. *a-citas, a-dyútas* 'lacking brightness', *ghṛta-ścútas, vipaś-citas, huraś-citas.* — **f.** *nṛ́tas* (AV.), *vṛ́tas; tri-vṛ́tas* (AV.), *dakṣiṇā-vṛ́tas, didyútas, purū-vṛ́tas* (AV.) 'moving in various ways', *madhu-ścútas, vi-dyútas, viṣū-vṛ́tas* (AV)., *saṃ-yátas, saṃ-vṛ́tas* (AV.).

I. n. *tri-vṛ́dbhis* (AV.). — **G. m.** *vipaś-citām.* — **f.** *apa-citām* (AV.), *vi-dyútām* (AV.). — **L. f.** *pṛtsú*[2].

307. **Stems in determinative** *-t.* — Derivative nominal stems are formed from nearly thirty roots ending in the short vowels *i, u* and *ṛ* by means of the suffix *-t*[3]. The roots adding it are *i-* 'go', *kṛ-* 'make', *kṣi-* 'dwell', *gu-* 'sound', *ci-* 'pile', 'note', *cyu-* 'move', *ji-* 'conquer', *dhṛ-* 'hold', *dhvṛ-* 'injure', *pi-* 'swell', *pru-* 'flow', *bhṛ-* 'bear', *mi-* 'fix', *yu-* 'join' and 'separate', *ri-* 'flow', *vṛ-* 'cover', *śri-* 'resort', *śru-* 'hear', *su-* 'press', *sṛ-* 'flow', *stu-* 'praise', *spṛ-* 'win', *sru-* 'flow', *hu-* 'sacrifice', *hṛ-* 'take', *hvṛ-* or *hru-* 'be crooked'. Two other roots, *gam-* 'go', and *han-* 'strike', are modified so as to end in short *a* (representing the sonant nasal) before adding the suffix: *-gá-t* and *há-t.*

These stems are mostly m. and f. Neuter cases are very rare, occurring from five or six stems only. The inflexion is exactly the same as that of the stems in radical *-t.*

Inflexion.

308. **Sing. N. m. with** *-kṛ́t*: *anukāma-kṛ́t* 'acting according to desire', *abhiṣṭi-kṛ́t* 'giving help', *āji-kṛ́t* 'instituting a contest', *īśāna-kṛ́t* 'acting as a lord', *ṛṣi-kṛ́t* 'making into a seer', *khaja-kṛ́t* 'causing the din of battle', *jyotiṣ-kṛ́t* 'causing light', *tanū-kṛ́t* 'preserving life', *pathi-kṛ́t* 'path-making', *puru-kṛ́t* 'doing much', *pūrva-kṛ́t* (VS. XX. 36) 'active from of old', *bhadra-kṛ́t* 'bestowing blessings', *uloka-kṛ́t* 'procuring free space', *vayas-kṛ́t* 'creating youthful vigour', *varivo-kṛ́t* 'bestowing freedom', *vijeṣa-kṛ́t* 'procuring victory', *su-kṛ́t* 'acting well', *steya-kṛ́t* 'committing theft', *syona-kṛ́t* 'causing comfort', *sviṣṭa-kṛ́t* (VS. II. 9) 'offering right sacrifice'; **with** *-jít*: *apsu-jít* 'conquering in the waters', *ab-jít* 'winning waters', *abhimāti-jít* (VS. XXVII. 3) 'conquering foes', *aśva-jít* 'winning horses', *ṛta-jít* (VS. XVII. 83) 'winner of right', *go-jít* 'winning kine', *dhana-jít* 'winning booty', *raṇya-jít* 'winning in battle', *ratha-jít* 'winning chariots', *viśva-jít* 'all-conquering', *saṃsṛṣṭa-jít* 'conquering combatants', *satya-jít* (VS. XVII. 83) 'winner of truth', *satrā-jít* 'wholly victorious', *samarya-jít* 'winning battles', *sahasra-jít* 'conquering a thousand', *sena-jít* (VS. XV. 19) 'conquering armies', *svar-jít* 'winning heaven', *hiraṇya-jít* 'winning gold'; **with other roots:** *acyuta-kṣít* (VS. V. 13) 'dwelling immovably'; *acyuta-cyút* 'shaking what is firm'; *á-dāra-sṛt* (AV.) 'not falling into a crack'; *ā-kṣít* 'dwelling'; *ṛṇa-cít* 'avenging guilt', *ṛta-cít* 'observing sacred order';

[1] *iṣu-kṛ́teva* here may, however, be a D. sing. for *iṣukṛ́te va*; see LANMAN 468.

[2] With double ending once (I. 129[4]) *pṛtsú-ṣu.*

[3] This suffix *-t* partakes of the character of a root determinative, as roots in *-i -u -ṛ* are hardly ever used without it as nominal stems.

kilbiṣa-spṛ́t 'removing sin'; *kṣatra-bhṛ́t* (VS. XXVII. 7) 'holder of sway'; *carṣaṇī-dhṛ́t* 'preserving men'; *dīrgha-śrút* 'heard afar', *deva-śrút* (VS. XXXVII. 18) 'heard by the gods'; *dhana-spṛ́t* 'winning booty'; *dhruva-kṣít* (VS. V. 13) 'dwelling firmly'; *pari-hrút* 'overthrowing'; *pūta-bhṛ́t* (VS. XVIII. 21) a kind of soma vessel; *bhāra-bhṛ́t* 'bearing a load'; *mada-cyút* 'reeling with excitement'; *madhu-ṣút* 'emitting sweetness'; *yakṣa-bhṛ́t* 'supporting pursuers' (?), *vajra-bhṛ́t* 'wielding a thunderbolt'; *vāja-sṛ́t* 'running for a prize'; *sapatna-kṣít* (VS. I. 29) 'destroying rivals'; *suparṇa-cít* (VS. XXVII. 45) 'heaped up like the bird Suparṇa'; *soma-sút* 'pressing Soma'; *sva-sṛ́t* 'going one's own way'; *havana-śrút* 'hearing invocations'. — f. *upa-bhṛ́t* (VS. II. 6) 'sacrificial ladle'; *upa-mít* 'prop'; *ṛta-cít*; *pari-srút* (VS. XIX. 15) 'fermented liquor'; *praśasta-kṛ́t* 'bestowing praise'. — **N. A. n.** *viśva-jít*; *dīrgha-śrút*, *nava-gát* (AV. TS.) 'first-bearing', *purītát*[1] (VS. XXXIX. 9) 'pericardium'; as adverbs: *upa-ṣṭút* 'invoked', *dyu-gát* 'going to heaven', *sa-kṛ́t* ('one-making') 'once'.

A. m. *adhi-kṣítam* 'ruler', *adhvara-kṛ́tam* (VS. I. 24) 'performing sacrifice', *arṇo-vṛ́tam* 'enclosing the waters', *uktha-bhṛ́tam* 'offering verses', *uda-prútam* 'swimming in water', *ṛṇa-cyútam* 'inciting to (fulfil) obligations', *carṣaṇī-dhṛ́tam*, *tīvra-sútam* 'pressing pungent (juice)', *tṛṣu-cyútam* 'moving greedily', *dīrgha-śrútam*, *duṣ-kṛ́tam* 'acting wickedly', *dveṣo-yútam* 'removing hostility', *dhana-jítam* (VS. XI. 8), *dhana-spṛ́tam*, *nadī-vṛ́tam* 'stream-obstructing', *pari-srútam* 'flowing around', *prātar-jítam* 'conquering early', *mada-cyútam*, *mithū-kṛ́tam* 'fallen into trouble', *vayas-kṛ́tam* (VS. III. 18), *vāja-jítam* (VS. II. 7) 'winning spoil', *śravo-jítam* 'winning renown', *sam-jítam* 'conqueror', *satya-dhvṛ́tam* 'perverting truth', *satrā-jítam* (VS. XI. 8), *sahas-kṛ́tam* (VS. III. 18) 'bestowing strength', *sāma-bhṛ́tam* 'bringing chants', *su-kṛ́tam*, *svar-jítam*, *sviṣṭa-kṛ́tam* (VS. XXI. 47), *havana-śrútam*, *haviṣ-kṛ́tam* 'preparing the oblation'. — f. *araṃ-kṛ́tam* 'making ready', *upa-prútam* 'flowing near', *deva-śrútam*, *ni-yútam* 'team', *pari-srútam*.

I. m. *abhi-jítā* (VS. XV. 7) 'victorious', *upari-prútā* (VS. VII. 3) 'falling from above', *carṣaṇī-dhṛ́tā*, *brahma-kṛ́tā* 'offering prayers', *soma-sútā*. — f. *ni-yútā*, *pari-srútā* (VS. XIX. 83), *pari-hvṛ́tā*[2] (VIII. 47[6]) 'deceiving'.

D. m. *araṃ-kṛ́te*, *duṣ-kṛ́te*, *dharma-kṛ́te* 'establishing order', *brahma-kṛ́te*, *su-kṛ́te*; *ab-jíte*, *aśva-jíte*, *urvarā-jíte* 'winning fertile fields', *go-jíte*, *dhana-jíte*, *nṛ-jíte* 'conquering men', *viśva-jíte*, *satrā-jíte*, *svar-jíte*; *giri-kṣíte* 'dwelling in mountains', *parvata-cyúte* 'shaking mountains', *soma-bhṛ́te* (VS. V. 1) 'bringing Soma'.

Ab. m. *pari-srútas* (VS. XIX. 75) 'foaming', *brahma-kṛ́tas*, *sarva-hútas* 'offered completely'. — f. *abhi-hrútas* 'injurious'.

G. m. *carṣaṇī-dhṛ́tas*, *vāja-jítas* (VS. IX. 13), *vīrya-kṛ́tas* (VS. X. 25) 'doing mighty deeds', *saṃ-jítas*, *su-kṛ́tas*, *haviṣ-kṛ́tas*. — f. *iṣa-stútas*[3], *deva-stútas* 'praising the gods', *pari-srútas* (AV.).

L. m. *mada-cyúti*, *go-jíti*, *vasu-jíti* (AV.) 'winning goods', *saṃ-dhanā-jíti*[4] (AV.) 'winning booty together'.

V. m. *acyuta-cyut*, *uru-kṛt* 'making wide', *ṛta-cit*, *khaja-kṛt*, *puru-kṛt*, *raṇa-kṛt* 'causing joy', *vandana-śrut* 'listening to praise', *vāja-jit* (VS. II. 7), *sahasra-jit*, *hávis-kṛt* (VS I. 15). — f. *upa-bhṛt* (AV.), *rā́ṣṭra-bhṛt* (AV.) 'bearing sway'.

---

1 The second part of the word may be derived from *tan-* 'stretch' like *-ga-t-* from *gam-* 'go'.

2 With anomalous accent; but the form may be L. of *pari-hvṛti-*, the normal accent of which would be *pári-hvṛti-*; see LANMAN 502 (bottom).

3 *iṣa-* = *iṣ-* 'refreshment', BR.; but the Pada text reads *iṣaḥ-stútas*, and GRASSMANN regards *iṣa* = *iṣaḥ* (before *st-*) as G. of *iṣ-*.

4 Instead of **dhana-saṃ-jíti*.

Du. N. A. V. m. *go-jítā, divi-kṣítā* 'dwelling in the sky', *pari-kṣítā* 'dwelling around', *mada-cyútā, su-śrútā* 'hearing well', *havana-śrútā*, V. *páthi-kṛtā* (AV.); *á-duṣ-kṛtau, kṛṣṇa-prútau* 'moving in darkness', *sa-kṛ́tau* (AV.) 'acting at once', *sa-kṣítau* 'dwelling together', *su-kṛ́tau* (AV.), *bhadra-kṛ́tau* (AV.), *su-śrútau* (AV.). — **f.** *ugra-jítau* (AV.) 'fierce-conquering' (name of an Apsaras). — **G. f.** *su-kṛ́tos, pari-kṣítos.*

Pl. N. V. m. *cítas* (VS. I. 18) 'heaping up', *hrútas* 'stumbling-blocks'; **with** ***-kṛ́t***: *araṃ-kṛ́tas, íśāna-kṛ́tas, karma-kṛ́tas* (VS. III. 47) 'skilful in work', *dudhra-kṛ́tas* 'boisterous', *duṣ-kṛ́tas, dhānyā-kṛ́tas*[1] 'preparing grain', *brahma-kṛ́tas, yajña-niṣ-kṛ́tas* 'preparing the sacrifice', *vayas-kṛ́tas, su-kṛ́tas, haviṣ-kṛ́tas*; **with** ***-cyút***: *dhanva-cyútas* 'shaking the ground', *dhruva-cyútas* 'shaking the immovable', *parvata-cyútas, mada-cyútas*; **with** ***-kṣít***: *apsu-kṣítas* 'dwelling in the waters', *upa-kṣítas* 'dwelling near', *vraja-kṣítas* (VS. x. 4) 'resting in their station', *sa-kṣítas*; **with other roots**: *adhva-gátas* (AV.) 'travellers', *arthétas*[2] (VS. x. 3) 'swift', *uda-prútas, ūrdhva-cítas* (VS. I. 18) 'piling up', *kṛcchre-śrítas* 'undergoing danger', *grāma-jítas* 'conquering troops', *carṣaṇī-dhṛ́tas, jana-bhṛ́tas* (VS. x. 4) 'supporting people', *divi-śrítas* (AV.) 'going to heaven', *deva-śrútas* (VS. VI. 30), *dveṣo-yútas, ni-gútas* 'enemies', *pari-cítas* (VS. XII. 46) 'piling up around', *pitu-bhṛ́tas* 'bringing food', *pūrva-cítas* (VS. XXVII. 4) 'piling up first', *mano-dhṛ́tas* 'intelligent', V. *vāja-jitas* (VS. IX. 9), *vi-cítas* (VS. IV. 24) 'sifting', *viśva-bhṛ́tas* (VS. x. 4) 'all-nourishing', *satya-śrútas* 'hearing the truth', *satrā-jítas, su-kṛ́tas* (VS. XXXIII. 16), *su-śrútas, soma-sútas, sva-sṛ́tas, havana-śrútas.* — **f.** *mítas* 'posts', *stútas* 'praises'; *uda-prútas, ni-yútas, pari-srútas, pitu-bhṛ́tas, saṃ-hátas* 'layers', *sa-srútas* 'streaming'. — **N. A. n.** *dīrgha-śrút* 'far-renowned' appears to be used as a n. pl. in agreement with *vratá* (VIII. 25[17])[3].

A. m. *hrútas* and *hrutás*[4] (AV.); *a-pítas* 'not swelling', *go-jítas, jyotiṣ-kṛ́tas, duṣ-kṛ́tas, ni-gútas, mada-cyútas, su-kṛ́tas.* — **f.** *rítas* 'flowing'; *úpa-stutas* 'invocations', *dīrgha-śrútas, ni-yútas, bali-hṛ́tas* 'paying tribute', *varuṇa-dhrútas* 'deceiving Varuṇa', *vi-sṛ́tas* 'flowing asunder', *sa-srútas.*

I. m. *soma-súdbhis.* — **f.** *antarikṣa-prúdbhis* 'floating over the atmosphere', *ni-yúdbhis.*

D. m. *iṣu-kṛ́dbhyas* (VS. XVI. 46) 'arrow-makers', *dhanuṣ-kṛ́dbhyas* (VS. XVI. 46) 'bow-makers', *pathi-kṛ́dbhyas, bandhu-kṣídbhyas* 'dwelling among kinsmen'. — **Ab. n.** *tanū-kṛ́dbhyas.*

G. m. *agni-hotra-hútām* (AV.) 'offering the oblation to Agni', *iṣu-bhṛ́tām* (AV.) 'archers', *mantra-kṛ́tām* 'composers of hymns', *su-kṛ́tām.* — **f.** *abhi-hrútām, upa-cítām* (VS. XII. 97) a kind of disease, *upa-mítām* (AV.), *ni-yútām, pari-mítām* (AV.) 'rafters', *prati-mítām* (AV.) 'props', *ratha-jítām* (AV.).

L. m. *su-kṛ́tsu.*

Derivative Stems in *-vat*, *-tāt*, *-it*, *-ut* and secondary *-t*.

309. The following stems are formed with the suffix (1) ***-vat***[5]: *arvā-vát-* f. 'proximity', *ā-vát-* (AV.) f. 'proximity', *ud-vát-* f. 'height', *ni-vát-* f. 'depth', *parā-vát-* f. 'distance', *pra-vát-* f. 'height', *saṃ-vát-* f. 'region'; (2) ***-tāt***[6]: *upará-tāt-* f. 'vicinity', *devá-tāt-* f. 'divine service', *vṛká-tāt-* f. 'wolfishness', *satyá-tāt-* f. 'reality', *sarvá-tāt-* f. 'totality'; (3) ***-it***: *taḍ-ít-* f. 'contiguous', *div-ít-*[7]

---

[1] *dhānya-kṛ́tas* in the Pada text.

[2] That is, 'going (*i-t*) to the goal' (*ártha-*).

[3] See LANMAN 503 (bottom), and 474 on the N. A. pl. n.

[4] With irregular accent.

[5] See above, secondary nominal derivation, 233.

[6] Cp. above 215 a.

[7] In this word the suffix *-it* probably consists of the root *i-* 'go' with the primary (determinative) *-t* (307).

'going to the sky', *yoṣ-ít-* f. 'young woman', *roh-ít-* f. 'red mare', *sar-ít-* f. 'stream', *har-ít-* f. 'fallow'; (4) **-ut**: *mar-út-* m. 'storm-god'; (5) with **secondary -t**: the two neuters *yákṛ-t-*[1] (AV.) 'liver', *śákṛ-t-*[2] 'excrement', and perhaps the etymologically obscure m. *nápāt*[3] 'descendant', all three of which are supplemented in the weak cases by the stems *yakán-*, *śakán-* and *náptṛ-* respectively. The inflexion of this group of *-t* stems is the same as that of the radical *-t* stems.

Inflexion.

310. **Sing. N. m.** *taḍít, tánū-nápāt* 'son of himself', *nápāt, prá-ṇapāt* 'great-grandson'. — **f.** *parāvát, pravát, rohít, sarít* (VS. XXXIV. 11). — **n.** *yákṛt* (VS. AV.), *śákṛt.*

A. m. *tánū-nápātam, nápātam.* — **f.** *arvāvátam, parāvátam, pravátam, yoṣítam, rohítam* (AV.), *saṃvátam* (AV.).

I. m. *divítā.* — **f.** *udvátā, devátātā*[4], *nivátā, pravátā, satyátātā*[4], *sarvátātā*[4], *harítā.*

D. f. *devátāte.* There is also the transfer form *avī́rat-e* (from *a-vī́ra-tā-* 'lack of sons').

Ab. f. *arvāvátas, udvátas*[5], *nivátas*[5], *parāvátas, pravátas, saṃvátas.* — **G. f.** *pravátas.*

L. f. *arvāváti, uparátāti, devátāti, parāváti, vṛkátāti.*

V. m. *tanū-napāt, napāt*[6].

Du. N. A. V. m. *nápātā.* — **f.** *harítā.* — **G. f.** *harítos.*

Pl. N. m. *nápātas, marútas, harítas.* — **f.** *āvátas* (AV.), *udvátas, taḍítas, parāvátas* (AV.), *pravátas, yoṣítas* (AV.), *sarítas, harítas.*

A. m. *marútas.* — **f.** *udvátas, nivátas, parāvátas, pravátas, yoṣítas* (AV.), *rohítas, saṃvátas, sarítas, harítas.*

I. m. *marúdbhis.* — **f.** *pravádbhis.* — **D. m.** *marúdbhyas.*

Ab. m. *marúdbhyas.* — **G. m.** *marútām.* — **f.** *pravátām.*

L. m. *marútsu.* — **f.** *udvátsu, nivátsu, pravátsu.*

V. m. *indrā-marutas* 'O Indra and the Maruts', *napātas, marutas.*

Participial Stems in *-at* and *-ant.*

311. **Participles in *-at*** are almost limited to the present active form of stems made with reduplication, viz. those of the third class (457) and of intensives (545). The old reduplicated participle (from *gā-* 'go') *jágat-* 'going', 'living', is used chiefly as a n. substantive meaning 'the animate world'. The analogy of these participles is followed by a few others formed from unreduplicated stems: *dā́ś-at-* 'worshipping', *śā́s-at-* 'instructing'[7]; also *dákṣat-* and *dhákṣat-*, the aor. participle of *dah-* 'burn'. A few others, again, originally participles, having come to be used as substantives, have shifted the accent to the suffix: *vah-át-*[8] 'stream', *veh-át-*[9] (AV. VS.) f. 'barren cow', *vāgh-át-*[10] m. 'sacrificer', *srav-át-*[11] f. 'stream'; like the regular participle *sáśc-at-* (from *sac-* 'accompany'), which as a substantive becomes *saśc-át-* m. 'pursuer'. In

[1] Cp. Lat. *jecur.*

[2] Cp. BRUGMANN, Grundriss 2, p. 559.

[3] The suffix may here have been a primary *-t* added to the root *pā-*: cp. LEUMANN's etymology (1888), Festgruss an Böhtlingk 77 f.; BRUGMANN 2, p. 366.

[4] These forms might be locatives of *devátāti-, satyátāti-, sarvátāti-.*

[5] These forms might be A. pl.

[6] Perhaps *marut* in *evayā́-marut.*

[7] LANMAN 505, would place *dā́sat-* 'injuring' here, but there is no evidence, as only a weak case, *dā́satas* G. sing., occurs.

[8] But *váh-ant-* 'carrying'.

[9] The derivation of this word is obscure.

[10] In one or two passages *vāghát-* still retains its participial sense.

[11] But *sráv-ant-* 'flowing'.

this class masculines are frequent, but only about half a dozen neuter forms occur, and the feminines are limited to three substantives[1] and the adjective *a-saścát* 'unequalled'[2]. The inflexion is like that of the radical *-t* stems, the accent never shifting to the endings.

Inflexion.

312. **Sing. N. m.** 1. **reduplicating class**[3]: *cíkyat, jáhat, júhvat, dádat, dádhat, bápsat* (√*bhas-*), *bíbhyat, bíbhrat.* — 2. **intensives**: *kánikradat* and *kánikrat, kárikrat* (*kṛ-* 'do') and (*ā-*)*cárikrat* (AV.), *ghánighnat* and *jáṅghanat* (√*han-*), *cániścadat* (√*ścand-*), *cárkṛṣat, cákaśat* (√*kāś-*), *cékitat* (√*cit-*), *járbhurat, jágrat, távītvat, dárdrat, dédiśat, dídyat, dávidyutat, dódhuvat, dávidhvat, nánadat, nánnamat, pánīphaṇat, bháribhrat, mármṛjat, mármṛśat, mémyat, rárajat, rérihat, róruvat, várīvṛjat, vávadat, vévidat, véviṣat, śóśucat, sániṣyadat* (√*syand-*), *séṣidhat.* — 3. **non-reduplicating verbs**: *vāghát, śásat*; aor. *dákṣat* and *dhákṣat.* — **N. A. n.** 1. *jágat, dávidyutat, pépiśat, yóyuvat* (AV.). — **N. f.** *vehát* (AV. VS.).

A. m. 1. *á-saścatam* (I. 112⁹), *dádatam, bíbhratam.* — 2. *kárikratam* (AV.), *gánigmatam, dídyatam, nánadatam, pánipnatam, róruvatam* (AV.). — **f.** *a-saścátam* (II. 32³); *vehátam* (AV.).

I. m. *dádatā, śóśucatā.* — **f.** *a-saścátā.* — **n.** *jágatā* (AV.).

D. m. 1. *jújoṣate, júhvate, dádhate, bíbhrate, sáścate.* — 2. *ghánighnate.* — 3. *vāghdte.* — **n.** 1. *jágate* (AV.).

Ab. m. 2. *kánikradatas.*

G. m. 1. *jígatas, dádatas, dádhatas, bápsatas.* — 2. *jáṅghnatas, táritratas, dódhatas, véviṣatas.* — 3. *vāghátas, śásatas, dhákṣatas* (aor.). — **n.** 1. *jágatas.* — 2. *ā-várvṛtatas* (AV.), *vávadatas.* — **L. n.** *jágati.*

Du. N. A. V. m. *a-saścátā, bápsatā, bíbhratā*; *táritratā*; *śásatā*; *dádhatau, bíbhratau.* — **f.** *a-saścátā.* — **G. m.** *píipratos.*

Pl. N. m. 1. *júhvatas, títratas, dádatas, dádhatas, pípratas, bápsatas, bíbhratas, sísratas*[4]. — 2. *kárikratas, jágratas, jóhuvatas, dávidhvatas, dídhyatas, dódhatas, nónuvatas, mármṛjatas, śóśucatas.* — 3. *dáśatas, vāghátas.* — **f.** *a-saścátas, vahátas, sravátas.*

A. m. 1. *jákṣatas* (√*ghas-*). — 2. *jágratas* (AV.), *dódhatas* (AV.), *śáśvasatas, śóśucatas* (AV.). — **f.** *saścátas*; *sravátas.*

I. m. 2. *nánadadbhis, pópruthadbhis, vávadadbhis, śáśvasadbhis.* — 3. *vāghádbhis.* — **G. m.** *jágatām, bíbhyatām* (AV.); *vāghátām.* — **f.** *sravátām.*

V. m. *jagatas, vāghatas.*

313. **Participles in *-ant*** are formed from all present stems (except those of the reduplicating class and of intensives and the few others that follow their analogy), from all future stems, and from aorist stems. Their analogy is followed by *ṛhánt-* 'weak', *pṛ́ṣant-* 'spotted', *bṛhánt-* 'great', *rúśant-* 'brilliant', which have lost their participial function; also by *dánt-*[5] m. 'tooth'. The adjective *mahánt-* 'great', having lost its original participial meaning deviates from the participial declension in lengthening the vowel of the suffix in the strong forms. In the inflexion of this group the distinction between

1 The f. of the regular participles is formed by the suffix *-ī*.

2 But *á-saścant-ī* from *sáścat-*.

3 See below, Verb, 461.

4 There occurs once an anomalous N. pl. with *-ant* from a reduplicated stem: *vavṛdhántas.* See below, Perfect, 492, note on *vāvṛdhvāṃs-*.

5 This word is probably an old pres. participle of *ad-* 'eat', with prehistoric loss of the initial *a* like *s-ánt-* 'being' from *as-* 'be' (25, 1). The RV. has one transfer form, N. *dánta-s* (starting from the A. *dánt-am*); the AV. has others, *dántās* and *dántais.*

strong and weak forms is regularly made, *-ant* appearing in the former only and being reduced to *-at* in the latter, which shift the accent, if resting on the suffix, to the ending. These participles are declined in the m. and n. only, as they form a special f. stem in *-ī*[1]. The m. and n. forms are the same, except of course in the N. A.; the former are very frequent, the latter rare.

Inflexion.

314. The forms occurring, if made from *bhávat-* 'being', would be as follows:

Sing. N. m. *bhávan*[2]. — **n.** *bhávat.* — **A. m.** *bhávantam.* — **I. m. n.** *bhávatā.* — **D.** *bhávate.* — **Ab. m. n.** *bhávatas.* — **G. m. n.** *bhávatas.* — **L.** *bhávati.*

Du. N. A. V. m. *bhávantā* and *bhávantau.* — **n.** *bhávatī.* — **D.** *bhávadbhyām.* — **G. m. n.** *bhávatos.*

Pl. N. m. *bhávantas.* — **n.** *bhávanti.* — **A. m.** *bhávatas.* — **I.** *bhávadbhis.* — **D. m.** *bhávadbhyas.* — **Ab. m.** *bhávadbhyas.* — **G. m. n.** *bhávatām.* — **L. m. n.** *bhávatsu.*

Forms actually occurring are the following. It is unnecessary to enumerate all the m. N. and A. forms, as in the RV. alone 228 forms of the N. sing., 121 of the A. sing., and 166 of the N. pl.[3] occur.

Sing. N. m. Examples are: *árcan, sī́dan; ghnán, yán, sán; páśyan; icchán; kṛṇván, sunván; bhañján; jānán; jānáyan; yúyutsan; kariṣyán.* Also *dán*, 'tooth'[4]; *mahā́n*[5]. — **n.** *anát, ásat*[6], *iṣṇát, éjat, éṣat*[7], *kulāyáyat, cárat, citáyat, tṛpát, dhṛṣát, pátat, patáyat, minát, yát, raghuyát, várdhat, śáṃsat, śíkṣat, śváyat, sát, sunvát;* **adj.** *bṛhát, mahát, rúśat;* **aor.** *sákṣat* (√*sah-*); **fut.** *bhaviṣyát* (AV.). As **adv.** with shift of accent: *dravát* 'swiftly' (*dru-* 'run'), *drahyát* 'firmly' (irregular formation from *dṛh-* 'be firm').

A. m. Examples are: *cárantam; yántam, uśántam, sántam; yúdhyantam; vidhántam; kṛṇvántam; pṛñcántam; gṛṇántam; dítsantam; dántam; bṛhántam, mahā́ntam.*

I. m. *á-ghnatā, ávatā, á-sunvatā, cáratā, jānatā́, tujatā́, púṣyatā, bhindatā́, vanuṣyatā́; datā́, śyāvá-datā* (AV.) 'dark-toothed', *bṛhatā́, mahatā́, rúśatā.* — **n.** *á-dṛpyatā, á-sredhatā, á-heḍatā, ā́satā*[8], *uśatā́, gavyatā́, tvāyatā́, dhṛṣatā́* (adv.), *śucatā́, śravasyatā́, samaryatā́, sumnāyatā́; bṛhatā́, mahatā́, rúśatā.*

D. m. 1. from stems accented on the suffix: *avasyaté, aśvāyaté, iṣayaté, iṣudhyaté, iṣūyaté, uśaté, ṛjūyaté, ṛtāyaté, kṛṇvaté, gavyaté, gṛṇaté, juraté, jānaté, tvāyaté, devayaté, dviṣaté, dhiyāyaté, dhūnvaté, pṛṇaté, pṛcchaté, brahmaṇyaté, mahayaté, mānavasyaté, yajñāyaté, yaté, vanvaté, vidhaté, śṛṇvaté, śravasyaté, sakhīyaté, saté, siñcaté, sunvaté, stuvaté; ṛhaté, bṛhaté, mahaté;* **fut.** *aviṣyaté.* — **n.** *śucaté, sanāyaté.*

2. from stems accented on the radical or the penultimate syllable: *á-ghnate, a-coddte*[9], *á-minate, árcate, árhate, íyakṣate, cárate, cétate, tárate,*

---

[1] On the difference in the form of this f. stem see 201, 377, 455, 461, etc.

[2] On the Sandhi of such nominatives see LANMAN 506.

[3] Lists of the participle stems will be found below under each of the conjugational classes, under the secondary conjugations, and under the future.

[4] Occurring also in several compounds *a-dán* 'toothless', etc.; *ubhayā́-dam* (AV. v. 19[2]) must be emended to *-dann.*

[5] *mahā́m* in II. 24[11], IV. 23[1], IX. 1097 is regarded by BENFEY as N. sing. m. (Göttinger Nachrichten 1878, p. 190).

[6] For *á-sat* (VII. 104[12]); the Pada reads *ásat.*

[7] The Pada reads *ā-íṣat* (x. 89[14]).

[8] Once (IV. 5[14]) with lengthened initial for *á-sat-ā* 'not being', also once *ā́satas* (VII. 104[8]); the Pp. has *ásatā* and *ásataḥ*. See GRASSMANN, Wörterbuch, under *á-sat.*

[9] Wrong accentuation (in v. 44[2]) for *á-codate*; see LANMAN 508 (top).

tṛ́ṣyate, dā́śate, pácate, pipīṣate, púṣyate, yájate, yúdhyate, rā́jate, rīṣate, vádate, śáṃsate, śárdhate, síṣāsate, háryate; a-dáte[1] 'toothless'.

Ab. 1. m. *kṛṇvatás, pṛṇatás, vanuṣyatás; bṛhatás.* — n. *bṛhatás, mahatás.* — 2. m. *á-bhuñjatas, á-vadatas, jíghāṃsatas, rīṣatas.* — n. *á-satas.*

G. m. 1. *arātīyatás, undatás, uśatás, ṛghāyatás, ṛtāyatás, kṛṇvatás, kṣiyatás, gṛṇatás, tujatás, turatás, turaṇyatás, tvāyatás, durhaṇāyatás, dviṣatás, dhṛṣatás, pitūyatás, pṛṇatás, brahmaṇyatás, minatás, miṣatás, yatás, rudhatás, vapuṣyatás, vidhatás, śucatás, satás, saparyatás, sunvatás, stuvatás, huvatás; bṛhatás, mahatás;* fut. *kariṣyatás.*

2. *á-ghnatas, á-jūryatas, á-bhuñjatas, árcatas, á-sunvatas, ínakṣatas, cáratas, cétatas, jáyatas, járatas, jíghāṃsatas, jíjyāsatas, jī́vatas, tū́rvatas, tṛ́ṣyatas, dídāsatas, drávatas, dhámatas, dhrájatas, pī́yatas, bhū́ṣatas, yúdhyatas, rírikṣatas, rébhatas, váyatas, várdhatas, vénatas, śárdhatas, śócatas, síṣāsatas, sīdatas, hárṣatas; rúśatas.*

n. 1. *kṛpayatás, prāṇatás*[2], *miṣatás, yātás, satás; bṛhatás, mahatás.* — 2. *ā́satas*[3], *cáratas, bhávatas, vénatas, síṣāsatas; rúśatas.*

L. m. 1. *yatí, sunvatí; mahatí.* — 2. *īráyati, ubhayā́-dati* (AV.). — n. 1. *mahatí.* — 2. *á-sati.*

Du. N. A. V. a) forms in *-ā*. 1. accented on the suffix: *aśnántā, irajyántā, uśántā, gmántā*[4], *gavyántā, daśasyántā, diśántā, duhántā, pā́ntā, punántā, pṛñcántā, bhujántā, minántā, miṣántā, yántā, yā́ntā, vanvántā, vasnayántā, vājayántā, vy-ántā, vṛdhántā, śṛṇvántā, sántā, saparyántā, sumnayántā; bṛhántā, bṛhantā* (V.), *mahā́ntā.* — 2. accented on the penultimate or antepenultimate: *á-mardhantā, á-yatantā, árhantā, iṣáyantā, kṣáyantā, cárantā, codáyantā, janáyantā, járantā, drávantā, dhámantā, pāráyantā, pípantā, mádantā, rádantā, vádantā, vápantā, váhantā, vājáyantā, vénantā, sádantā, sápantā, sáhantā, sā́dhantā, háyantā.*

b) forms in *-au*. 1. *aśnántau, tirántau, yántau, vṛdhántau, sántau; mahā́ntau.* — 2. *iṣáyantau, krī́ḍantau, kṣáyantau, mádantau* (AV.), *yájantau, rā́jantau.*

N. A. n. *yatī́; bṛhatī́.* — D. m. *mṛḍayádbhyām; mahádbhyām.* — G. m. *járatos.* — n. *saṃ-yatós* (AV.) 'going together'.

Pl. N. m. From the very numerous forms occurring the following may be quoted: *mádantas; ghnántas, yántas, sántas; páśyantas; icchántas; bhindántas; kṛṇvántas; gṛṇántas; devayántas, vājayántas; dípsantas*[5]; aor. *krántas*[6], *bhidántas*[7]; *pṛ́ṣatas* (VS. XXIV. 11), *mahā́ntas*[8]. — V. *uśantas; mahāntas.* — N. A. n. *sánti*[9]; *bṛhánti* (AV. VIII. 9[3]), *mahā́nti.*

A. m. 1. *uśatás, ṛghāyatás, gṛṇatás, taruṣyatás, tvāyatás, pṛṇatás, pṛtanyatás, bhandanāyatás, manāyatás, yatás, rudatás, vanuṣyatás, vājayatás, vidhatás, śṛṇvatás, śravasyatás, śrudhīyatás, sakhīyatás, satás, sasatás, stuvatás; bṛhatás, mahatás; datás.*

2. *á-pṛṇatas, á-prayucchatas, árcatas, kṣáyatas, dhā́vatas, dhrájatas, pátatas, rā́yatas, rīṣatas, rúrukṣatas* (√*ruh-*), *vádatas, vrā́dhatas, śárdhatas, sísṛpsatas; śyāvá-datas* (AV.).

1 On the accent see 90 B c. The dative of *ad-ánt-* 'eating', would be *ad-at-é*.

2 That is, *pra-anatás*.

3 For *ásatas* according to the Pada text.

4 Aor. participle of *gam-* 'go'. In one passage (I. 122[11]) the Pada reads *gmánta*; the sense seems to require the pl. *gmántas*. See Lanman 509.

5 Desiderative of *dabh-* 'injure'; cp. Lanman 508 (gen. masc.).

6 *gmántas* should perhaps be read for *gmánta* in I. 122[11].

7 On the anomalous N. pl. perf. participle, *vavṛdhántas*, see above p. 190, note 4.

8 *ubhayā́-datas* in X. 90[10] is perhaps a metrical shortening for *-dantas*; cp. Lanman 509 (bottom). The AV. has the transfer form *dántās*; cp. p. 190, note 5.

9 The Pada text reads *sánti*; see RPr. IX. 25.

I. m. *á-nimiṣadbhis, á-prayucchadbhis, á-sredhadbhis, uśádbhis, citáyadbhis, tujáyadbhis, devayádbhis, dhávadbhis, patáyadbhis, rébhadbhis, vádadbhis, vājayádbhis, vrájadbhis, śucádbhis, śucáyadbhis, śubháyadbhis, śócadbhis; bṛhádbhis, mahádbhis, rúśadbhis; dadbhis* [1]. — **n.** *śucáyadbhis, standáyadbhis; bṛhádbhis, mahádbhis, rúśadbhis.*

D. m. *uśádbhyas, kṣúdhyadbhyas, gṛṇádbhyas, tvāyádbhyas, páśyadbhyas, prāyádbhyas, vádadbhyas, váhadbhyas, sunvádbhyas; bṛhádbhyas, mahádbhyas; dadbhyás* (AV.). — **Ab. m.** *parā-yádbhyas.*

G. m. 1. *adhvarīyatā́m, uśatā́m, ṛjūyatā́m, gṛṇatā́m, ghnatā́m, juratā́m, devayatā́m, dviṣatā́m, yatā́m, yātā́m, vanuṣyatā́m, vājayatā́m, śatrūyatā́m, śṛṇvatā́m, śravasyatā́m, sakhīyatā́m, satā́m, sasatā́m, sunvatā́m, stuvatā́m, sthātā́m* [2], *bṛhatā́m, mahatā́m; datā́m* (AV.). — **2.** *á-sunvatām, cáratām, jáyatām, nṛ́tyatām, pátatām, vívāsatām, śárdhatām.* — **n.** *rathirāyátām* [3].

L. m. *gṛṇátsu, devayátsu, patáyatsu, mahátsu.* — **n.** *júryatsu.*

Stems in *-mant* and *-vant*.

315. As these two suffixes have the same sense, that of 'possessing', and are inflected exactly alike, the stems formed with them are best treated together in declension. These stems are used in the m. and n. only [4], as they form a separate f. by adding *-ī* to the weak stem. They are inflected like the participles in *-ant* except that they **lengthen the vowel** of the suffix **in the N. sing. m.** and **never shift the accent** from the suffix to **the ending** in the weak cases. Strong and weak forms are as strictly distinguished as in the *-ant* stems [5]. The regular **vocative** of these stems **ends in *-mas* and *-vas*** in the RV., but the AV. has neither [6] in any independent passage, and the VS. has only *bhagavas* and *patnīvas*. The RV. has also three vocatives in *-van*, and the AV. adds five others; but no voc. in *-man* occurs.

Three stems in *-vant* and one in *-mant* have case-forms supplementing the inflexion of stems in *-an* and forming transitions from the latter declension to the former. Thus from *maghávant-* 'bountiful' alone are formed the pl. I.: *maghávadbhis*, D. *maghávadbhyas*, L. *maghávatsu*; also the N. sing. *maghávān* beside the usual *maghávā* from *maghávan-*; from *sáhāvant-* the N. *sáhāvān* beside *sahā́vā*; from *yúvant-* 'young', the A. n. *yúvat* beside the N. m. *yúvā*; from *varimánt-* the I. m. sing. *varimátā* beside forms from *varimán-* 'width' [7].

Inflexion.

316. Sing. N.m. 1. from **stems in *-vant***: *akṣaṇvā́n* [8], *agnivā́n, áṅgirasvān, ánnavān, á-pavīravān, ámavān, árvān, āśīrvān, íḍāvān, iṣávān, ṛ́ghāvān, etā́vān, kakṣī́vān, kṣapā́vān* and *kṣápāvān, ghṛ́ṇīvān, jánivān, tápasvān, tarṣyā́vān, távasvān, táviṣīvān, tā́vān, tuvīrávān* [9], *tvā́vān, daṃsánāvān, dákṣiṇā-*

---

1 The AV. (XI. 3[37]) has the transfer form *dántais*.

2 From the aor. stem *sthā́t-* 'standing'.

3 With irregular accent on the suffix instead of the ending, from *rathirā-yát-*.

4 In two or three instances the m. form seems to be used for the f., as *haviṣmatā* (I. 128[2]) and *ráthavate* (I. 122[11]); see LANMAN 515 (bottom).

5 There seem, however, to be two or three instances of a weak form used instead of a strong: *kṣumáti* (IV. 2[18]), A. pl. n., *krátumatā* (X. 59[1]), N. du. m., *índrāvatas* (IV. 27[4]), N. pl.; see LANMAN 516.

6 In AV. XIX. 34[8] the Mss. read *bhagavas* which is emended to *samábhavas* in the printed text.

7 On the other hand, *árvant-* 'steed', has two forms representing a transition to the *-an* declension: N. *árvā*, A. *árvāṇam*.

8 On the Sandhi of these forms, see LANMAN 517.

9 Probably for **tuvī-ráva-vān*.

vān[1], *dátravān, dā́navān, dā́svān, durhá ṇāvān, devávān, devā́vān, dyumnávān, námasvān, niyútvān, nī́lavān, páyasvān, pavítravān, pávīravān, pastyā̀vān, púraṃdhivān, pūṣaṇvā́n, prajā́vān, práyasvān, pravátvān, prahā́vān, bhágavān, maghávān, matávān, matsarávān, mánasvān, marútvān, máhasvān, māyā́vān, mā́hināvān, mehánāvān, yáśasvān, yātumā́vān, rábhasvān, rásavān, revā́n, vā́javān, vājínīvān, vivakvā́n, vivásvān, vṛ́ṣaṇvān, vṛ́ṣṇyāvān, śácīvān, śarádvān, śáśvān, śíprāvān, śipríṇīvān, śímīvān, sákhivān, sabhā́vān, sárasvān, sáhasvān, sahā́vān* and *sáhāvān, sutā́vān, sūnṛ́tāvān, stavā́n*[2], *svadhā́vān, svádhitīvān, svàrvān, hárivān, hitā́vān, hemyā́vān.*

2. From stems in *-mant*: *abdimā́n, ávimān, aśánimān, íṣumān, udanimā́n, ṛbhumā́n, kakúdmān, krátumān, garútmān, gómān, túviṣmān, tváṣṭṛmān, tvíṣīmān, dyumā́n, dhrájimān, nadanumā́n, paraśumā́n, paśumā́n, pitumā́n, barhíṣmān, mádhumān, vásumān, virúkmān, vṛṣṭimā́n, śárumān, śocíṣmān, suṣumā́n, havíṣmān, hírīmān.*

N. A. n. 1. *apāṣṭhávat, ámavat, arcivát, áśvavat, áśvāvat, ātmanvát, āvṛ́tvat, írāvat, ṛ́ghāvat, etā́vat, kṣáitavat, gopā́vat, grábhaṇavat, ghṛtávat, candrávat, tā́vat, tokávat, tvā́vat, dákṣiṇāvat, dyumnávat, dhānā́vat, dhvasmanvát, námasvat, nī́lavat, nṛvát, padvát, páyasvat, pastyā̀vat, pṛ́ṣadvat, prajā́vat, barhá ṇāvat, yā́vat, yúvat*[3], *ráthavat, rásavat, revát, vayúnavat, vayúnāvat, vā́javat, vipṛ́kvat, vivásvat, viṣávat, vīrávat, śatávat, śaphávat, śáśvat*[4], *sahásravat, sáhasvat, sínavat, svàrvat, híraṇyavat.*

2. *abhiṣṭimát, ṛbhumát, ketumát, krátumat, kṣumát, gómat, jyótiṣmat, tvíṣīmat, dasmát, dā́numat, dyumát, nidhimát, paśumát, pitumát, puṣṭimát, mádhumat, manyumát, yávamat, rayimát, vásumat, svastimát.*

A. m. 1. *apidhā́navantam, apūpávantam, árvantam, áśvāvantam, asthanvántam, ātmanvántam, índrasvantam*[5], *ū́rjasvantam, ū́rṇāvantam, etā́vantam, énasvantam, ójasvantam, ómanvantam, omyā́vantam, kakṣī́vantam, ghṛtávantam, dā́svantam, devávantam, dhānā́vantam, dhī́vantam, nṛvántam, padvántam, párasvantam, prajā́vantam, bhā́svantam, marútvantam, máhiṣvantam, rátnavantam, revántam, vapā́vantam, vayā́vantam, vā́javantam, vā́ravantam, vívasvantam, vīrávantam, vṛ́ṣaṇvantam, śatávantam, śáśvantam, sacanā́vantam, sárasvantam, hárivantam, hástavantam, híraṇyavantam.*

2. *ṛbhumántam, káṇvamantam, ketumántam, kṣumántam, gómantam, jyótiṣmantam, táviṣīmantam, dyumántam, nidhimántam, pitumántam, bándhumantam, bhānumántam, mádhumantam, vásumantam, vā́śīmantam, vṛṣṭimántam, śruṣṭimántam, havíṣmantam, hótṛmantam.*

I. 1. m. *árvatā, áśvāvatā, udanvátā, ṛ́kvatā, kakṣī́vatā, niyútvatā, nṛvátā, marútvatā, yáśasvatā, revátā, viśvádevyāvatā, viṣūvátā, śubhrā́vatā, sáhasvatā.*— **n.** *etā́vatā, candrávatā, prajā́vatā, barhá ṇāvatā, vivásvatā, sūnṛ́tāvatā, háritvatā, śáśvatā.*

2. **m.** *gómatā, jyótiṣmatā, divítmatā, dyumátā, bhṛṣṭimátā, varimátā*[6], *vásumatā, virúkmatā, havíṣmatā.* — **n.** *divítmatā, virúkmatā, havíṣmatā*; as **adv.** *śáśvatā*[7].

D. 1. m. *árvate, áśvāvate, kakṣī́vate, dákṣiṇāvate* 'adroit' and 'bestowing gifts', *datváte, dā́svate, niyutvate*[8], *pūṣaṇváte, marútvate, mā́vate, yuvā́vate, ráthavate*[9],

[1] Representing two words: 1. 'dexterous' (*dákṣiṇa-* 'right hand'); 2. 'possessing sacrifical gifts' (*dákṣiṇā-*).

[2] To be read *stāvā́n* 'thundering', from √*stan-*; see GRASSMANN, s. v.

[3] Transfer form from the *-an* stem *yúvan-*.

[4] Also the Āmreḍita compound *śáśvacchaśvat.*

[5] With the N. *-s* anomalously retained.

[6] Transfer form from the *-an* stem *varimán-*.

[7] See LANMAN 518 (bottom).

[8] Erronously unaccented (I. 135[1]).

[9] The f. *ráthavatyai* should perhaps be read for *ráthavate* in I. 122[11], as the latter form agrees with a f. substantive, and the former is favoured by the metre; cp. LANMAN 519.

vivásvate and *vívasvate*, *śácīvate*, *śáśvate*, *sáhasvate*, *sūnṛtávate*, *svàrvate*, *hárivate*. — n. *padváte*, *reváte*, *śáśvate*.

2. m. *gómate*, *cákṣuṣmate*, *tvíṣīmate*, *divítmate*, *dyumáte*, *barhíṣmate*, *havíṣmate*.

Ab. 1. m. *tvávatas*, *vivásvatas*, *vṛ́ṣṇyāvatas*.

G. 1. m. *árvatas*, *áśvāvatas*, *kakṣívatas*, *jávatas*, *tvávatas*, *dadhanvátas*[1], *dásvatas*, *devávatas*, *dhī́vatas*[2], *niyútvatas*, *nṛvátas*, *prajávatas*, *marútvatas*, *mávatas*, *mehánāvatas*, *yáśasvatas*, *revátas*, *váyasvatas*, *vájavatas*, *vivásvatas* and *vívasvatas*, *vīrávatas*, *śácīvatas*, *śáśvatas*, *sárasvatas*, *sáhasvatas*, *sutávatas*, *sū́rāvatas*, *svadhávatas*, *hṛ́ṣīvatas*. — n. *etávatas*, *yávatas*, *viṣūvátas*, *śáśvatas*.

2. m. *kṣumátas*, *gómatas*, *dyumátas*, *havíṣmatas*. — n. *gómatas*.

L. 1. m. *árvati*, *dákṣiṇāvati* 'bestowing gifts', *nṛváti*, *pastyávati*, *yáśasvati*, *vánanvati*, *vivásvati* and *vívasvati*, *śaryaṇávati*. — n. *áśvāvati*, *śímīvati*, *svàrvati*. — 2. m. *gómati*.

V. m. 1. The normal form in *-vas*[3] occurs in sixteen examples: *ṛṣīvas*, *gnāvas*[4], *taviṣīvas*, *niyutvas*, *patnīvas* (VS.), *bhagavas* (VS. TS.), *marutvas*, *rayivas*, *vajrivas*, *vīravas*, *śaktīvas*, *śacīvas*, *sarasvas*, *sahasvas*, *svadhāvas*, *harivas*. — Of the later V. ending in *-van*, the RV. has three examples: *arvan*, *śatāvan*[5], *śavasāvan*. In the AV. the following five additional forms occur: *marutvan*[6], *vājinīvan*, *vṛṣṇyāvan*, *svadhāvan*, *harivan*[6]. The MS. has *patnīvan*[7]. — 2. There are six examples of the form in *-mas*: *tuviṣmas*, *dyumas*, *bhānumas*, *mantumas*, *śuciṣmas*, *haviṣmas*. — No vocative form in *-man* occurs.

Du. N. A. V. m. 1. with *-ā*: *áṅgirasvantā*, *ánasvantā*, *árvantā*, *índravantā*, *káśāvantā*, *kéśavantā*, *dhármavantā*, *námasvantā*, *niyútvantā*, *pavítravantā*, *marútvantā*, *mitrávárunavantā*, *vájavantā*, *víṣṇuvantā*, *vyácasvantā*, *śáśvantā*[8], *sáptīvantā*; with *-au*: *aṣṭhīvántau*, *yávantau* (AV.), *rómaṇvantau*, *sáhasvantau* (AV.), V. *svádhāvantau* (AV.). — 2. *arcimántā*, *ṛbhumántā*, *krátumantā*[9], *vadhúmantā*.

Ab. 1. m. *aṣṭhīvádbhyām*. — **G.** 1. m. *vājínīvatos*, *śímīvatos*, *sárasvatīvatos*.

Plur. N. V. m. 1. *akṣaṇvántas*, *ánasvantas*, *ámavantas*, *árvantas*, *áśvāvantas*, *āśírvantas*, *íḍāvantas*, *índravantas*, *índrāvantas* (TS. IV. 7. 14[1])[10], *ū́rjasvantas*, *énasvantas*, *kakṣívantas*, *kárṇavantas*, *ghṛtávantas*, *caṣā́lavantas*, *dákṣiṇāvantas* 'bestowing gifts', *dámanvantas*, *dúvasvantas* (VS. XVI. 63), *dráviṇasvantas*, *dhī́vantas*, *námasvantas*, *niyútvantas*, *nṛvántas*, *pátnīvantas*, *padvántas*, *páyasvantas* (VS. XXI. 42), *pavítravantas*, *pájasvantas*, *puṣṭávantas*, *pūṣaṇvántas*, *prajávantas*, *práyasvantas*, *pravátvantas*, *bhágavantas*, *marútvantas*, *máhasvantas* (VS. XXI. 42), *yajñávantas*, *vacanávantas*, *váyasvantas* (VS. III. 18), *vármaṇvantas*, *vīrávantas*, *vṛcī́vantas*, *śáktīvantas*, *śáśvantas*, *śímīvantas*, *sáptīvantas*, *sutávantas*, *sṛkávantas* (TS. IV. 5. 11[2]), *svadhāvantas* (V.), *svàrvantas*, *himávantas*, *hṛ́ṣīvantas*.

2. *añjimántas*, *áyuṣmantas* (TS.), *iṣumantas*, *ṛṣṭimántas*, *kṣumántas*, *jyótiṣmantas*, *tváṣṭṛmantas* (VS. XXVII. 20), *tvíṣīmantas*, *dyumántas*, *mádhumantas*,

[1] 'containing curds'; cp. LANMAN 513.

[2] Also the Āmreḍita compound *dhī́vato-dhīvatas*.

[3] Elsewhere ten vocatives in *-vas* and *-mas* occur: five from perfect participle stems in *-vāṃs*: *khidvas*, *cikitvas*, *titirvas*, *dīdivas*, *mīḍhvas*; four from stems ending in *-van*: *ṛtāvas*, *evayāvas*, *prātaritvas*, *mātariśvas*; and *pumas* from *púmāṃs-*. There are also two in *-yas* from comparative stems in *-yāṃs*: *ojīyas* and *jyāyas*.

[4] In II. 1[5] *gnā́vas* should probably be read *gnāvas* as a vocative.

[5] The Pada text reads *śata-van*; cp. RPr. IX. 10.

[6] These two forms occurring in passages taken from the RV. are substituted for *marutvas* and *harivas* of the RV.

[7] That is, *patnīvāṃn*.

[8] The mysterious form *śā́tapantā* (X. 106[5]) should perhaps be corrected to *śā́tavanta* = *śata-vantā*?

[9] The weak form *krátumatā* seems to be used for *krátumantā* in X. 59[1].

[10] The weak form *indrāvatas* seems to be used for *índrāvantas* in IV. 27[4].

mīḍhúṣmantas, yávamantas, rayimántas, vadhúmantas, vā́śīmantas, śíśumantas, sthivimántas, harṣumántas, havíṣmantas.

N. A. n. 1. *ghṛtávānti.* — 2. *paśumánti.* The Padapāṭha reads *-anti*[1] in these forms, and the lengthening of the vowel seems to be metrical[2]. — The weak form *kṣumáti* (used with *yūthā́*) seems to be used for *kṣumánti* in IV. 2^{18}.

A. m. 1. *árvatas, índrāvatas, ṛtvíyāvatas, kṛśanā́vatas, jánivatas, tápasvatas, tṛṣyā́vatas, tvā́vatas, nṛvátas, pátnīvatas, párasvatas* (VS. XXIV. 28) 'wild asses', *pastyā̀vatas, poṣyā́vatas, prajā́vatas, bhaṅgurā́vatas, yáśasvatas, yātumā́vatas, rábhasvatas, rayivátas, revátas, vánanvatas, vṛcī́vatas, śaryaṇā́vatas, śáśvatas, śímīvatas, sutā́vatas, sūnṛtā́vatas, híraṇyavatas, héṣasvatas.* — 2. *ṛtumátas* (VS. XIX. 61), *gómatas, jyótiṣmatas, dyumátas*[3], *práṣṭimatas, mádhumatas, vadhúmatas, virúkmatas, sūnumátas, svastimátas.*

I. 1. m. *árvadbhis, dákṣiṇāvadbhis, pátnīvadbhis, maghávadbhis*[4], *rábhasvadbhis, revádbhis, vā́javadbhis, śáśvadbhis, śímīvadbhis, sutásomavadbhis.* — n. *ghṛtávadbhis.* — 2. m. *ṛṣṭimádbhis, kṛīḍumádbhis, gómadbhis, barhíṣmadbhis, bhānumádbhis, vidyúnmadbhis, havíṣmadbhis.* — n. *mádhumadbhis.*

D. 1. m. *dúvasvadbhyas* (VS. IX. 35), *bhágavadbhyas* (AV.), *maghávadbhyas*[4], *mā́javadbhyas* (AV.), *sómavadbhyas* (AV.). — 2. m. *asimádbhyas* (VS. XVI. 21), *iṣumádbhyas* (VS. XVI. 22), *mātṛmádbhyas* (AV.), *yātumádbhyas.* — n. *vibhumádbhyas.*

G. m. 1. *árvatām, dákṣiṇāvatām, datvátām* (AV.), *bhaṅgurā́vatām, yātumā́vatām, śáśvatām, śímīvatām, sutā́vatām, himávatām* (AV.). — 2. *gómatām* (AV.).

L. m. 1. *ámavatsu, árvatsu, maghávatsu*[4], *yuṣmā́vatsu.* — 2. *dyumátsu.*

Stems in radical *-th.*

317. There are only three stems in *-th*: *kápṛth-*[5] n. 'penis', *path-*[6] m. path', with its compound *su-páth-* 'fair path', and *abhi-śnáth-* adj. 'piercing'. Among them these three furnish examples of all the cases in the singular, but there are no dual forms, and in the plural only the A. and G. occur.

Sing. N. *kápṛt*; A. *kápṛt*[7]; I. *pathā́*[8], *supáthā*; D. *pathé* (VS.); Ab. *pathás, abhi-śnáthas*; G. *pathás*[9]; L. *pathí.* — Pl. A. *pathás*[10]; G. *pathā́m*[11].

Stems in radical *-d.*

318. About a hundred stems ending in *d* are made in the form of compounds (only seven being simple stems) from the twenty roots *ad-* 'eat', *kṣad-* 'divide', *chad-* 'cover' and 'please', *pad-* 'go', *mad-* 'be exhilarated', *sad-* 'sit', *syad-* 'move on'; *chid-* 'cut off', *nid-* 'revile', *bhid-* 'cleave', *vid-* 'know', *vid-* 'find'; *ud-* 'wet', *nud-* 'push', *mud-* 'rejoice', *rud-* 'weep', *sud-* 'enjoy', *sūd-*

---

1 As also in the only N. pl. n. of the present part. in *-ant, sánti* (314). The SV. also has the short *ă*.

2 Cp. Lanman 521.

3 In VI. 17^{14} the Padapāṭha reads *dyumáta indra* as *dyumátaḥ*; Grassmann explains it as a D. *dyumáte* agreeing with *rāyé*. On the other hand *dyumánta[ḥ]* in AV. XVIII. 1^{57} should probably be emended to *dyumátaḥ*; cp. Whitney's note, and Lanman 521^4.

4 Forms transferred from the *-van* declension.

5 The derivation of this word is uncertain: the *-th* is radical if the word is derived from *prath-* 'extend' (see Grassmann, s. v.); but it is suffixal if the word is connected with Lat. *caper* (cp. Uhlenbeck, Etymologisches Wörterbuch, s. v.). With this possible exception there are no derivative stems in *-th*.

6 This stem supplements *pánthā-* and *pathi-*.

7 *kapṛthá-m* occurs once as a transfer form.

8 Once (I. 129^9) nasalized before a vowel *pathā́ṁ a-*.

9 Once (II. 2^4) with the radical vowel lengthened, *pāthás*.

10 Accented as a weak form.

11 The transfer form *pathīnā́m* also occurs in TS. IV. 2. 55.

'put in order'; *tṛd-* 'pierce', *mṛd-* 'crush'[1]. Of these roots only seven occur as monosyllabic substantives: *nid-* 'contempt', *bhid-* 'destroyer', *vid-* 'knowledge', *úd-* 'wave', *múd-* 'joy', *mṛd-* 'clay', being f., and *pád-* 'foot', m. There is also the monosyllabic n. *hṛ́d-* 'heart'[2].

Strong and weak forms are not distinguished except in *pád-*; and the inflexion is the same in all genders except, of course, the N. A. n. du. and pl.

a. The following peculiarities or irregularities of this declension are to be noted. 1. The weak reduplicated present stem *dád-* of *dā-* 'give', is once treated as a root in the form *āyur-dád-am* (AV.) 'giving long life'. — 2. The vowel of *mád-* is lengthened in *sadha-mā́d-* 'drinking companion', and *soma-mā́d-* 'intoxicated with Soma', of both of which, however, only strong cases occur. The vowel of *pád-* is lengthened not only in the strong cases, but occasionally in others also: *dvipā́t*, N. sing. n., beside *dvipát*, D. *dvipā́de*[3], L. pl. *dvipā́tsu*, while the N. pl. m. is once *dvipádas* (AV.). — 3. The euphonic combination is irregular in the I. pl. of *pád-* which is *paḍbhís*[4] beside the Ab. du. *pad-bhyā́m*. — 4. The stem *hṛ́d-* is found in weak cases only[5]. Its place is taken in the N. A. sing. pl. by *hṛ́d-aya-*, which is also used in other cases (*hṛ́dayāt, hṛ́daye, hṛ́dayeṣu*), though in the RV. almost entirely in late passages. — 5. There are a few transitions to the *a*-declension in the inflexion of these stems. Starting from the strong A. *pā́d-am* are formed the N. sing. *pā́da-s* and the N. pl. *pā́dās*, both in late passages of the RV.[6]. Similarly, starting from the A. *sadha-mā́d-am* are formed the locatives *sadha-mā́de* and *sadha-mā́deṣu*. Beside *nid-ás*, the ordinary Ab. of *níd-*, the form *nidā́yās* occurs once.

Inflexion.

319. The inflexion of these stems is identical with that of the radical *-t* stems. The forms actually occurring, if made from *pád-* 'foot', and *-vid-* m. f. n. 'finding', would be as follows:

Sing. N. *pā́t, -vít.* — **A.** *pā́dam, -vídam.* — n. *-vít.* — **I.** *padā́, -vidā́.* — **D.** *padé, -vide.* — **Ab.** *padás, -vidas.* — **G.** *padás, -vidas.* — **L.** *padí, -vidi.* — **V.** (*sárva*)*-vit.*

Du. N. A. V. *pā́dā*, m. f. *-vídā.* — **I.** *padbhyā́m.* — **Ab.** *padbhyā́m.* — **G.** *padós.* — **L.** *padós.*

Pl. N. *pā́das*, m. f. *-vídas.* — **A.** *padás*, m. f. *-vídas.* — **I.** *padbhís* (AV.), *-vídbhis.* — **D.** *-vídbhyas.* — **G.** *padā́m, -vidā́m.* — **L.** *patsú, -vítsu.*

a. The forms actually occurring are the following:

Sing. N. m. 1. with **lengthened vowel:** *pád-* with its compounds and *sadha-mád-*: *pā́t* (AV.); *a-pā́t, éka-pāt, éka-śiti-pāt* (VS. XXIX. 58) 'having one white foot', *cátuṣ-pāt, tri-pā́t, dvi-pā́t* and *dví-pāt* (AV.), *viśvátas-pāt, śiti-pā́t* (AV.), *sárva-pāt* (AV.), *sahásra-pāt*; *sadha-mā́t* (IV. 21[1]) and the abnormal *sadha-mā́s*[7] (VII. 18[7]).

2. with **unchanged vowel,** being compounds ending in various roots: from *ad-* : *agdhā́t* (TS. III. 3, 8[2]), *karambhā́t, kravyā́t, viśvā́t, havyā́t*; from *chad-* : *prathama-cchát*[8]; from *pad-* : *anu-pát* (VS. XV. 8) 'coming to pass'; from *chid-* : *ukha-cchít*; from *bhid-* : *adri-bhít, ud-bhít, gotra-bhít, pūr-bhít*; from *vid-*: *á-kṣetra-vit, aśva-vít, kratu-vít, kṣetra-vít, gātu-vít, go-vít, draviṇo-vít,*

[1] Compounds formed with *-vid* and *-sad* are the commonest.

[2] The strong form of this word, *hā́rd-*, appears in composition with *dus-* and *su-*. Another word for 'heart', *śrád-* (Lat. *cord-*) n. occurs only in the A. sing. with the verbs *kṛ-* and *dhā-*.

[3] The lengthening here is, however, metrical.

[4] Owing to the confusing influence of the I. pl. *paḍbhís* from *páś-* 'look'.

[5] Its high grade form *-hārd* occurs in the N. sing. m.

[6] Probably also the A. sing. m. *páñca-pādam*; see LANMAN 471[2].

[7] See above 55.

[8] 'appearing first', 'typical' (X. 81[1]); according to Sāyaṇa from *chad-* 'cover' = 'covering first'.

nabho-vít, nātha-vít (AV.), *paśu-vít* (AV.), *purāṇa-vít* (AV.), *prajā-vít* (AV.), *rayi-vít, vaco-vít, vayunā-vít, varivo-vít, vasu-vít, viśva-vít, vīra-vít* (AV.), *śruta-vít, sarva-vít* (AV.), *svar-vít, hiraṇya-vít*; from *sad-* : *adma-sát, antarikṣa-sát, upastha-sát, ṛta-sát, turaṇya-sát, dakṣiṇa-sát* (VS. XXXVIII. 10), *duroṇa-sát, duvaṇya-sát, prāgharma-sát, vara-sát, vyoma-sát, su-saṃ-sát*; *camū-ṣát, dru-ṣát, nṛ-ṣát, vedi-ṣát, śuci-ṣát.* Also *su-hā́rt*[1] (AV. II. 7[5]) 'friendly'.

f. 1. *a-pā́t.* — 2. *ā-cchát* (VS. XV. 5), *pra-cchát* (VS. XV. 5) 'covering'; *sū-yavasā́t* (*-ad*); *saṃ-vít*; *saṃ-sát, su-ā-sát* (AV.)[2].

N. A. n. 1. *-pad-* appears with both unaltered and lengthened vowel: *dvi-pát, cátuṣ-pat* and *tri-pā́t, dvi-pā́t, cátuṣ-pāt.*

2. *hṛ́t* (TS. IV. 4. 7[2]); *prakala-vít* 'knowing very little'; *raghu-ṣyát* 'moving quickly' (√*syad-*).

A. m. 1. *pā́dam*; *a-pā́dam, tri-pā́dam*[3], *dvi-pā́dam* (VS. XIII. 47), *śiti-pā́dam* (AV.), *sahásra-pādam*; *sadha-mā́dam*; *dur-hā́rdam* (AV.). — 2. from *ad-* : *kravyā́dam, viśvā́dam*; from *pad-* : *dvi-pā́dam* (VS. XXVIII. 32) a metre; from *chid* : *pra-cchídam* (VS. XXX. 16) 'cutting to pieces'; from *bhid-* : *ud-bhídam, gotra-bhídam, pūr-bhídam*; from *vid-* : *ahar-vídam, kratu-vídam, kṣetra-vídam, gātu-vídam, go-vídam, varivo-vídam, vasu-vídam, viśva-vídam, saci-vídam, svar-vídam, hotrā-vídam*; from *sad-* : *garta-sádam, su-saṃ-sádam*; *apsu-ṣádam, dru-ṣádam, dhūr-ṣádam, barhi-ṣádam*[4], *vanar-ṣádam*; from *-syad-* : *raghu-ṣyádam, havana-syádam.* — f. 2. *nídam*[5], *mṛ́dam* (VS. XI. 55; TS. IV. 1. 5[2]); *āyur-dádam* (AV.)[6], *upa-sádam, go-vídam* (AV.), *ni-vídam, pari-pádam* 'snare', *pari-ṣádam* (AV.), *pitṛ-ṣádam, barhi-ṣádam*[4], *vaco-vídam, viśva-vídam, saṃ-vídam, saṃ-sádam, sa-mádam* 'battle' ('raging together').

I. m. *padā́*[7]; *ápa-duṣ-padā, cátuṣ-padā, dvi-pádā*; *kṣetra-vídā, varivo-vídā, svar-vídā, su-ṣádā* (AV.). — f. *udā́, mudā́, vidā́*; *upa-vídā, ni-vídā, ni-ṣádā, pra-múdā* (VS. XXXIX. 9), *pra-vídā, saṃ-sádā, svar-vídā.* — n. *hṛdā́*; *cátuṣ-padā* (AV.), *duṣ-pádā, dvi-pádā.* With adverbial shift of accent: *sarva-hṛdā́.*

D. m. *a-páde, kuhacid-víde, kravyā́de, cátuṣ-pade, tad-víde* (AV.), *vedi-ṣáde, sadanā-sáde, sarva-víde* (AV.), *svar-víde.* — f. *nidé, mudé*; *pitṛ-ṣáde, pra-máde* (VS. XXX. 8), *pra-múde* (VS. XXX. 10), *sam-páde* (VS. XV. 8). — n. *hṛdé*; *cátuṣ-pade, dvi-páde*[8].

Ab. m. *padás* (AV.); *dvi-pádas.* — f. *nidás*[9]; *uttāná-padas, saṃ-vídas* (AV.). — n. *hṛdás*; *ṣáṭ-padas* (AV.).

G. m. *éka-padas* (AV.), *dur-hā́rdas* (AV.), *nṛ-ṣádas, yavā́das* (*-adas*), *raghu-ṣyádas* (AV.), *svar-vídas.* — f. *pra-múdas, saṃ-sádas* (AV.). — n. *hṛdás*; *cátuṣ-padas, dvi-pádas.*

L. m. *padí*; *svar-vídi.* — f. *ni-ṣádi, saṃ-sádi.* — n. *hṛdí*[10].

V. m. *viśva-vit, sárva-vit* (AV.).

Du. N. A. V. m. 1. *pā́dā*; *pā́dau.* — 2. V. *ahar-vidā, kavi-cchadā* 'delight-

---

[1] This seems to be the preferable reading (*suhā́rt téna*); the Pada has *su-hā́ḥ*. Otherwise the N. appears as *su-hā́r* in MS. IV. 2[5] (p. 26, l. 19) in *suhā́r ṇaḥ*; see LANMAN's note in WHITNEY's AV. Translation on XIX. 45[2], and Grammar 150 b.

[2] Perhaps also *niṣát* in AV. XX. 132[6. 7], where the edition has *vaniṣád.*

[3] *páñca-pāda-m* (I. 164[12]) is probably a transfer to the *a*-declension; see LANMAN 471[2].

[4] For *barhiṣ-ṣádam*; see above 62.

[5] In the Āmreḍita compound *nídaṃ-nidam.*

[6] From a secondary root *dad-* formed from the present stem of *dā-* 'give'.

[7] BR. take *sádā* in AV. IV. 47 as I. of *sád-* 'position', but owing to the accent it must be taken as an adv. 'always', see WHITNEY's note on the passage.

[8] Beside *dvi-páde* occurring eleven times, *dvi-pā́de* occurs once (I. 121[3]), when the lengthening is metrical.

[9] The transfer form *nidā́yās* occurs once.

[10] On the possibility of *hṛdí* representing an A. sing. n. in two or three passages, see LANMAN 473[4].

ing in sages', *kratu-vidā, vasu-vidā, viśva-vidā, svar-vidā*[1]; *ātma-sádau.* — f. *ud-bhidā, barhi-ṣádā*[2]; *śrānta-sádau* (AV.).

I. m. *padbhyā́m* (AV.). — **Ab. m.** *padbhyā́m.* — **G. m.** *padós* (AV.)[3]. — **L. m.** *padós.* — **f.** *prá-pados* (AV.).

Pl. N. V. m. 1. *a-pā́das, cátuṣ-pādas, dvi-pā́das*[4], *śiti-pā́das*[5]; *sadha-mā́das, soma-mā́das; su-hā́rdas* (AV.). — 2. *ū́rjādas, pūru-ṣā́das, madhv-ádas, yavasā́das, somā́das, havir-ádas; ā-tṛ́das*[6], V. *pra-tṛdas; deva-nídas; ud-bhídas; abhīmoda-múdas* (AV.), *svādú-sam-mudas* (AV.); *anna-vídas* (AV.), *ahar-vídas,* V. *gātu-vidas* (AV.), *ni-vídas* (AV.), *nī-vídas* (AV.), *nīthā-vídas, brahma-vídas* (AV.), *yajur-vídas* (AV.), *vaco-vídas, varivo-vídas, vasu-vídas, viśva-vídas* (AV.), *svar-vídas, hotrā-vídas; adma-sádas, antarikṣa-sádas* (AV.), *apsu-ṣádas* (TS. I. 4. 10[1]), *upa-sádas* (AV.), *paścāt-sádas* (VS. IX. 36), *puraḥ-sádas, śarma-sádas, sabhā-sádas* (AV.), *svādu-saṃ-sádas; camū-ṣádas, divi-ṣádas* (AV.), *dhūr-ṣádas, barhi-ṣádas,* V. *barhi-ṣadas, vanar-ṣádas, vedi-ṣádas* (VS. II. 29); *raghu-ṣyádas.* — **f.** 1. *dur-hā́rdas* (AV.); *nídas, múdas; agha-rúdas* (AV.), *āmā́das* (-*ádas*), *upa-sádas* (AV.), *niṣ-pádas, pra-múdas, viśva-su-vídas, saṃ-sádas, suhutā́das* (-*ádas*), *svar-vídas.*

A. m.[7] *padás; dur-hā́rdas* (AV.), *su-hā́rdas* (AV.); *apsu-ṣádas* (AV.), *kravyā́das, cátuṣ-padas* (AV.), *tvā-nídas, deva-nídas, dvi-pádas* (AV.), *pari-ṣádas, pastya-sádas, bāhu-kṣádas, sattra-sádas* (AV.). — **f.** *nidás, bhídas; ni-vídas, pra-múdas, vasu-vídas, vi-núdas, sa-mádas, sa-syádas, havya-súdas.*

I. m. *padbhís* (AV. TS. VS.), *paḍbhís* in RV. and VS.[8]; *gharma-sádbhis, śatá-padbhis.* — **n.** *hṛdbhís.*

D. m. *antarikṣa-sádbhyas* (AV.), *dakṣiṇā-sádbhyas* (VS. IX. 35), *divi-ṣádbhyas* (AV. TS.), *paścāt-sádbhyas* (VS. IX. 35), *pṛthivi-ṣádbhyas* (AV.).

G. m. *su-hā́rdām* (AV.); *adma-sádām, cátuṣpadām* (VS. TS. AV.), *dvi-pádām, barhi-ṣádām* (VS. XXIV. 18), *śvá-padām* (AV.), *su-ṣádām* (AV.). — **f.** *upa-sádām* (VS. XIX. 14) a kind of ceremony, *pari-pádām, śrānta-sádām* (AV.), *sa-mádām.*

L. m. *patsú.* — **f.** *sa-mátsu.* — **n.** *hṛtsú.*

Stems in derivative *-d.*

320. There are some six stems formed with suffixal *-d,* seemingly all feminines[9], which with one exception (*śarád-*) are of rare occurrence. They are *dṛṣád-* and *dhṛṣád-* (RV[1].) 'nether millstone', *bhasád-* 'hind quarters', with its compound *su-bhasád-* 'having beautiful buttocks', *vanád-*[10] (RV[1].) 'longing', *śarád-* 'autumn'; *kakúd-*[11] 'summit', with its compound *tri-kakúd-* (AV.) 'three-peaked', *kākúd-* 'palate'. The inflexion is like that of radical *-t* stems. The forms occurring are the following:

Sing. N. f. *kakút, kākút, dhṛṣát, bhasát, śarát.* — **m.** *tri-kakút* (VS. AV.).

---

[1] In AV. XVIII. 2[14] occurs the ungrammatical form *pathi-ṣádī* an imitation of *pathi-rákṣī* of RV. X. 14[11].

[2] The form *rapsúdā,* occurring once, is of uncertain meaning and origin.

[3] This form is used with an ablative sense in AV. I. 18[2].

[4] AV. X. 2[6] has *dvi-pádas.*

[5] The transfer form *pā́dās* occurs once in the RV. (I. 163[9]).

[6] Used as ablative infinitive.

[7] There are no N. A. V. forms in the n. pl. Cp. Lanman 474.

[8] Four times in RV. and once in VS. (XXIII. 13) owing to confusion with *paḍbhís,* I. pl. of *pás-* 'look'.

[9] Except the adj. *tri-kakúd-* (AV.), *śiti-kakúd-* (TS.) 'white-humped' and possibly *vanád-.*

[10] This stem occurs only once (II. 4[5]) in the form *vanádas,* N. pl. m. 'Verlangen' (from *van-* 'desire') according to BR.; G. sing. m. of *van-ád-* 'wood-consuming' according to Grassmann.

[11] The origin of this *-d* is obscure. On the relation of this word to *kakúbh-* see Lanman 471[4].

A. f. *kākúdam, dṛṣádam, bhasádam* (AV.), *śarádam*. — **m.** *tri-kakúdam* (AV.). **I.** f. *dṛṣádā, śarádā* (TS. IV. 4. 12[3]). — **D.** f. *śaráde*. — **Ab.** f. *kākúdas*. — **L.** f. *kakúdi* (AV.), *śarádi*. — **Pl. N.** f. *vanádas, śarádas*. — **A.** f. *śarádas*. — **I.** f. *śaradbhis*. — **G.** f. *śarádām* (AV.). — **L.** f. *śarátsu* (AV.).

Stems in radical *-dh*.

321. Stems ending in *-dh* are all radical, simple or compound. There are some fifty derived, with only two or three exceptions, from the following sixteen roots: *bādh-* 'oppress', *sādh-* 'succeed'; *idh-* 'kindle', *vidh-* 'pierce' (= *vyadh-*), *sidh-* 'succeed', *sridh-* 'blunder' (?); *kṣudh-* 'be hungry', *budh-* 'waken', *yudh-* 'fight', *rudh-* 'grow' and 'obstruct'; *ṛdh-* 'thrive', *mṛdh-* 'neglect', *vṛdh-* 'grow', *spṛdh-* 'contend'.

In this declension there occurs no stem distinguishing strong and weak cases. Masculines and feminines are inflected exactly alike. No distinctively neuter forms (N. A. du. pl.) occur, and only four case-forms (G. L. sing.) are found as neuters. There are two monosyllabic m. nouns: *vṛ́dh-* 'strengthening' and (perhaps) *bā́dh-*[1]; besides seven f. substantives: *nádh-*[2] 'bond'; *srídh-* 'foe'; *kṣúdh-* 'hunger', *yúdh-* 'fight'; *mṛ́dh-* 'conflict', *vṛ́dh-* 'prosperity', *spṛ́dh-* 'battle'. Neuter cases occur in the sing. (I. G.) of compounds of *-vidh, -yudh*, and *-vṛdh*.

a. Three or four stems are of doubtful origin: *agnidh-* is probably to be explained as *agni-dh-* 'priest who prepares (*dhā-* 'put') the fire', rather than as a shortened form of *agnídh-* 'fire-kindler' (from *idh-* 'kindle') which does not occur in the RV.[3]; *iṣídh-* 'offering' (RV[1].) is perhaps a shortened form of *niṣ-ṣidh-* 'offering'[4]; *pṛkṣúdh-* (RV[1].) is obscure in meaning and origin; *śurúdh-* f. 'invigorating draught' is perhaps derived from *śṛdh-* 'be defiant' with Svarabhakti[5].

Inflexion.

322. **Sing. N. m.** *agnít, anu-rút* (VS.) and *anū-rút* 'loving'; *uṣar-bhút* 'waking (*budh-*) at morn', *yavīyút*[6] 'eager to fight', *śvā-vít* (AV. VS.) 'porcupine' ('dog-piercer', √*vidh-*), *sam-ít* 'flaming'. — **f.** *kṣút* (AV.); *pra-vṛ́t* 'growth', *vī-rút* 'plant' (AV.), *sam-ít*[7] 'fuel'.

A. m. *vṛ́dham*, and its compounds: *annā-vṛ́dham* 'prospering by food', *āhutī-vṛ́dham* 'delighting in sacrifices', *girā-vṛ́dham* 'delighting in praise', *tugryā-vṛ́dham* 'favouring the Tugryas', *namo-vṛ́dham* 'honoured by adoration', *payo-vṛ́dham* 'full of sap', *parvatā-vṛ́dham* 'delighting in pressing stones', *madhu-vṛ́dham* 'abounding in sweetness', *yajña-vṛ́dham* (AV.) 'abounding in sacrifice', *vayo-vṛ́dham* 'increasing strength', *sadyo-vṛ́dham* 'rejoicing every day', *saho-vṛ́dham* 'increasing strength', *su-vṛ́dham* 'joyous'; *agnídham, anu-rúdham* (VS. XXX. 9), *a-srídham* 'not failing', *uṣar-búdham, goṣu-yúdham*[8] 'fighting for kine', *marmā-vídham* (AV.) 'piercing the vitals', *yajña-sā́dham* 'performing sacrifice', *hṛdayā-vídham* (AV.) 'wounding the heart'. — **f.** *kṣúdham, yúdham, srídham; a-srídham, uṣar-búdham, niṣ-ṣídham, vīrúdham, saṃ-rúdham* (AV.) 'check' (in gambling)[9], *sam-ídham*.

I. m. *su-vṛ́dhā*. — **f.** *kṣudhā́* (AV.), *yudhā́, vṛdhā́; sam-ídhā, su-búdhā* (AV.) 'good awakening', *su-vṛ́dhā* (AV.), *su-ṣam-ídhā* 'good fuel'. — **n.** *payo-vṛ́dhā, yavīyúdhā, sākaṃ-vṛ́dhā* 'growing together'.

1 In *bā́dhas* A. pl. in VI. 11[1] (GRASSMANN); BR. do not acknowledge a m. use of *bā́dh-*, and in VIII. 45[10], IX. 109[6] they would join the word with the preceding *pári*.

2 In *nádbhyas* (X. 60[6]) if derived from *nadh-* = *nah-* 'bind' (BR. s. v. *náh-*); but it is more probably = **nábd-bhyas* from *napt-*, weak stem of *nápāt-*, as also indicated by the accent.

3 See above p. 18, note 6.

4 Cp. *iṣ-kṛti-* for *niṣ-kṛti-*.

5 Cp. above 21.

6 From the intensive stem of *yudh-* 'fight'.

7 In the Āmreḍita *samit-samit*.

8 With the L. pl. *goṣu* instead of the stem *go-*.

9 Cp. WHITNEY's note on AV. VII. 50[5].

D. m. *uṣar-búdhe, ṛtā-vṛ́dhe* 'fostering truth', *puru-niṣṣídhe* 'repelling many (foes)', *mahi-vṛ́dhe* 'greatly rejoicing', *vi-mṛ́dhe* (VS. VIII. 44) 'dispeller of foes', *sam-ṛ́dhe* (AV.) 'welfare', *sa-vṛ́dhe* (VS. XVI. 30) 'growing'. — **f.** *kṣudhé, yudhé* (AV.)[1], *vṛdhé, sam-ídhe.*

Ab. f. *kṣudhás, yudhás, sridhás.*

G. m. *goṣu-yúdhas, vi-mṛdhás*[2] 'foe', *sumatī-vṛ́dhas* (VS. XXII. 12) 'delighting in prayer'. — **f.** *kṣudhás.* — **n.** *hṛdayā-vídhas.*

L. f. *mṛdhí, yudhí, spṛdhí; pra-búdhi* 'awaking'.

Du. N. A. V. m. *a-sridhā, ṛtā-vṛ́dhā,* V. *ṛtā-vṛdhā, namo-vṛ́dhā, puro-yúdhā* 'fighting in front'; *ṛtā-vṛ́dhau.* — **f.** *ṛdū-vṛ́dhā* 'increasing sweetness', *ghṛtā-vṛ́dhā* 'rejoicing in fatness', *payo-vṛ́dhā, vayo-vṛ́dhā, sākaṃ-vṛ́dhā; sam-ídhau* (AV.).

Pl. N.V. m. *ṛtā-vṛ́dhas,* V. *ṛtā-vṛdhas, tugryā-vṛ́dhas, payo-vṛ́dhas, parvatā-vṛ́dhas, vayo-vṛ́dhas, suge-vṛ́dhas* 'rejoicing in good progress', *su-vṛ́dhas; a-sridhas, āyur-yúdhas* (VS. XVI. 60) 'struggling for life', *uṣar-búdhas, goṣu-yúdhas, jñu-bā́dhas* 'bending the knees', *pra-yúdhas* 'assailing', *vṛṣā-yúdhas* 'combating men', *śurúdhas, soma-pari-bā́dhas* 'despising Soma'. — **f.** *kṣúdhas* (AV.), *mṛ́dhas, spṛ́dhas, srídhas* (VS. XXVII. 6) 'foes'; *amitrā-yúdhas* 'fighting with enemies', *a-sridhas, iṣídhas, ṛtā-vṛ́dhas, niṣ-ṣídhas, pari-bā́dhas* 'oppressors', *pari-spṛ́dhas* 'rivals', *vī-rúdhas,* V. *vī-rudhas, śurúdhas, sam-ídhas.*

A. m. *bā́dhas; ṛtā-vṛ́dhas, tamo-vṛ́dhas* 'rejoicing in darkness', *rayi-vṛ́dhas* 'enjoying wealth', *uṣar-búdhas, śurúdhas.* — **f.** *mṛ́dhas, yúdhas, spṛ́dhas, srídhas*[3]; *vī-rúdhas, śurúdhas, sam-ídhas, sam-ṛ́dhas, sa-vṛ́dhas* 'increasing together'[4].

I. f. *sam-ídbhis, vī-rúdbhis* (AV.). — **D. f.** *nád-bhyas*[5]. — **Ab. f.** *vī-rúdbhyas* (AV.).

G. m. *vṛdhā́m; ṛtā-vṛ́dhām, pra-búdhām* 'watchful'. — **f.** *yudhā́m*[6] (AV.), *spṛdhā́m; niṣ-ṣídhām, vī-rúdhām, vī-rudhām*[7] (AV.).

L. f. *yutsú, vī-rútsu.*

Stems in radical *-n.*

323. The radical stems ending in *-n* are formed from half a dozen roots: from *tan-* 'stretch', *ran-* 'rejoice', *van-* 'be pleasant', are formed monosyllabic substantives meaning 'succession', 'joy', 'wood', respectively; from *svan-* 'sound' is formed the adj. *svan-*[8] 'sounding' and the compound *tuvi-ṣván-* 'roaring aloud'; from *san-* 'gain', the compound *go-ṣán-* 'winning cows'. From these six nouns very few case-forms occur. But from *han-* 'strike' no fewer than 35 compounds are made in the RV., and all the singular cases as well as several of the du. and pl. cases are formed. All the stems formed from these six roots[9] are m. except *tán-*, which is f.[10], and only a single n. case-form occurs from a compound of *han-* (*dasyu-ghná*). The distinction between strong and weak forms is made in *-han-* only. Here in the weak cases *a* as

[1] The infinitive *yudháye* is a transition to the *i*-declension, there being no stem *yudhi-*.

[2] With irregular accent; cp. LANMAN 477 (top).

[3] Fifteen times accented *srídhas,* once (IX. 71[8]) *sridhás.*

[4] In VIII. 45[40], IX. 105[6] *pari-bā́dhas* should perhaps be read instead of *pári bā́dhas.*

[5] If from *náh-*, according to BR. (cp. *akṣā-náhas* (A. p. f.); according to WEBER, IS. 13, 109, from *nap-*. It is probably from *napt-* = *nápāt.* See above 321, note on *nádh-*.

[6] In the V. *yudhām pate.*

[7] In the V. *vīrudhām pate.*

[8] The accent of the monosyllabic stems is irregular in remaining on the radical syllable except *tanā́* (beside *tánā*) and *vanā́m*: cp. LANMAN 479[4] and above 94, 1 a.

[9] Other roots in *-n* used as nominal stems have gone over to the *a-* or *ā-*declension; thus *jan-* becomes *-ja-* or *-jā-*.

[10] *-han-* forms a separate fem. stem in *-ī* from its weak form: *-ghn-ī-*.

representing the sonant nasal appears for *an* before consonants, while before vowels the root, by syncopation of its vowel, assumes the form of *-ghn-*. The N. sing. n. of *-han* is *-ha-m*, a transition to the *a*-declension[1] (for *-ha*, which does not occur).

Inflexion.

324. All forms are represented in this declension except Ab. sing., the weak cases of the du., and the D. Ab. pl. The forms made from *-han-* are: **Sing.** N. *-hā́*[2], A. *-hánam*, I. *-ghnā́*, D. *-ghné*, G. *-ghnás*, L. *-ghní*, V. *-han*. — **Du.** N. A. *-hánā*, *-hánau* (VS. TS.), V. *-hanā*. — **Pl.** N. *-hánas*, A. *-ghnás*, I. *-hábhis*. The G. would be *-ghnā́m* and the L. *-hásu* according to the analogy of other stems in this declension. The forms of radical *n*-stems which occur are the following:

Sing. N. m. *aghaśaṃsa-hā́* 'slaying the wicked', *adṛṣṭa-hā́* 'slaying unseen (vermin)', *abhimāti-hā́* 'destroying adversaries', *amitra-hā́* 'killing enemies', *amīva-hā́* 'destroying pains', *aruśa-hā́* 'striking the dark (cloud)', *á-vīra-hā* 'not slaying men', *aśasti-hā́* 'averting curses', *asura-hā́* 'demon-slaying', *ahi-hā́* 'killing the serpent', *kṛṣṭi-hā́* 'subduing nations', *go-hā́* 'killing cattle', *dasyu-hā́* 'destroying the Dasyus', *durṇāma-hā́* (AV.) 'destroying the ill-named', *nṛ-hā́* 'killing men', *puro-hā́* 'destroying strongholds'[3], *pṛśni--hā́* (AV.) 'slaying the speckled (snake)', *mano-hā́* (AV.) 'mind-destroying', *muṣṭi-hā́* 'striking with the fist', *yātu-hā́* (AV.) 'destroying witchcraft', *rakṣo-hā́* 'destroying demons', *vasar-hā́* 'destroying at dawn', *vṛtra-hā́* 'Vṛtra-slaying', *śarya-hā́* 'killing with arrows', *satrā-hā́* 'destroying entirely', *sapatna-hā́* 'slaying rivals', *sapta-hā́* 'slaying seven'. — **n.** Only two transition forms occur: *vṛtra-há-m* and *satrā-há-m*[4].

A. m. *á-pra-haṇam*[5] 'not hurting', *abhimāti-hánam*, *ahi-hánam*, *tamo-hánam* 'dispelling darkness', *dasyu-hánam*, *rakṣo-háṇam*[5], *valaga-hánam* 'destroying secret spells' (VS. v. 23), *mano-hánam* (AV.), *vīra-háṇam*[5] (VS. xxx. 5) 'homicide', *vṛtra-háṇam*[5], *satrā-háṇam*[5], *sapatna-hánam* (AV.).

I. m. *vṛtra-ghnā́*[6]. — **n.** *dasyu-ghnā́*. — **f.** *tanā́* (once) and *tánā*[7] (19 times).

D. m. *ráṇe*[7]; *abhimāti-ghné* (VS. vi. 32), *asura-ghné*[6], *ahi-ghné*, *nṛ-ghné*[6], *makha-ghné* (TS. iii. 2. 4. [1. 2]), 'slayer of Makha', *vṛtra-ghné*[6]. — **f.** *táne*[7].

G. m. *go-ṣaṇas* (in the V. *goṣaṇo napāt*); *asura-ghnás*[6], *vṛtra-ghnás*[6].

L. m. *sváni*[8] (ix. 66[9]), *tuvi-ṣváṇi*; *bhrūṇa-ghní* (AV.) 'killer of an embryo'. Without an ending: *rán*[9].

V. m. *amitra-han*, *ahi-han*, *vṛtra-han*.

Du. N. A. V. *tamo-hánā*, *rakṣo-háṇā*[5], *vṛtra-háṇā*, V. *vṛtra-haṇā*[5]. With *-au*: *rakṣo-háṇau* (VS. v. 25), *valaga-hánau* (VS. v. 25; TS. i. 3. 2[2]).

Pl. N. V. m. V. *tuvi-ṣvaṇas*; *a-bhog-ghánas*[10] 'striking the niggardly one', *punar-háṇas*[5] 'destroying in return', *yajña-hánas* (TS.) 'destroying sacrifice', *śatru-háṇas*[5] 'slaying enemies'.

A. m. *sāta-ghnás* (AV.) 'gain-destroying'. With strong form: *rakṣo-háṇas*[5] and *valaga-hánas* (VS. v. 25; TS. i. 3. 2[2]).

I. m. *vṛtra-hábhis*. — **G. m.** *vanā́m*. — **L. m.** *ráṃsu*[7], *váṃsu*[7].

---

[1] The forms made from *-ghna-*, viz. *-ghnás*, *-ghnám*, *-ghnāya*, *-gnásya*, *-ghne*, are probably to be explained as transition forms starting from the weak stem *-ghn-*.

[2] Formed like the N. of derivative *-an* stems (327).

[3] That is, *puras*, A. pl. of *púr-*, the case termination being retained.

[4] The normal forms would be **vṛtra-há* and **satrā-há*.

[5] See above 47, A b 2 (p. 39).

[6] See above p. 38, note 4.

[7] Against the rule of accentuation in monosyllabic stems (94).

[8] This form may, however, be the 3. sing. passive aor. See below 501, note on *sā́di*.

[9] With loss of the loc. ending as in the *-an* declension (325).

[10] *-ghánas* for *-hánas*, see above 80, 81.

Derivative stems in *-an, -man, -van.*

325. This declension embraces a large number of words, the stems in *-van* being by far the commonest, those in *-an* the least frequent. It is almost limited to masculines and neuters; but some forms of adjective stems serve as feminines, and there is one specifically f. stem, *yóṣ-an-* 'woman'[1].

The distinction **of strong and weak forms** is regularly made. In the strong cases the *a* of the suffix is usually lengthened, e. g. *ádhvān-am;* but in half a dozen *-an* and *-man* stems it remains unchanged; e. g. *arya-máṇ-am.* In the weak cases the *a* is often syncopated before vowel endings, though never when *-man* and *-van* are preceded by a consonant[2], e. g. I. sing. *grā́-vṇ-ā*[3] from *grā́-van-*, 'pressing stone'[4], while before consonant endings the final *n* disappears[5], e. g. *rā́ja-bhis.* In the RV. the syncopation never takes place in the N. A. du. n., nor with one exception (*śata-dā́vn-i*) in the L. sing.

As in all other stems ending in *-n*, the nasal is dropped in the N. sing.; e. g. m. *ádhvā*, n. *kárma.* But there are two peculiarities of inflexion which, being common to these three groups, do not appear elsewhere in the consonant declension. Both the L. sing. and the N. A. pl. n. are formed in two ways. The ending of the L. sing. is in the RV. dropped more often than not, e. g. *mūrdhán-i* and *mūrdhán*, the choice often depending on the metre[6]. The N. A. pl. n. is formed with *-āni* from 18 stems and with *-a* from 19 stems[7] in the RV.; seven of the latter appear with *-ā* in the Saṃhitā text, but with *-a* like the rest in the Pada text. The evidence of the Avesta indicates that there were in the Indo-Iranian period two forms, *nāmān* and *nāmāni*, the former losing its *-n* as usual when final after a long vowel. On this ground the *-ā* form of the Saṃhitā, though the less frequent, would appear to be the older[8].

There are here many supplementary stems and numerous transitions to the *a*-declension.

1. Stems in *-an.*

326. These stems, which are both m. and n., are not numerous. They include some which at first sight have the appearance of belonging to one of the other two groups: *yú-v-an-*[9] 'youth', *śv-án-* 'dog', *ṛji-śv-an*[10] N. of a man, *mātarí-śv-an-*[10] N. of a demi-god, *vi-bhv-an-*[11] 'far-reaching'; *pári-jm-an-*[12] 'going round'. The n. *śīrṣ-án-* is an extended stem from *śíras-* 'head' = *śír(a)s-án-*.

a. Besides the N. pl. *yóṣaṇ-as* 'women', six or seven forms of this declension appear to be **feminine** as agreeing with f. substantives: *vṛ́ṣā* 'raining' (*káśā, vā́k*), *vṛ́ṣaṇam* (*tvácam*), *vṛ́ṣaṇā* (*dyā́vā-pṛthivī́*), *pári-jmānas* 'going round' (*vidyútas*), *rapśád-ūdhabhis* 'having distended udders' (*dhenúbhis*)[13], *vā́ja-karmabhis* (SV. TS.) and *vā́ja-bharmabhis* (VIII. 19[30]) 'bringing rewards' (*ūtíbhis*).

---

[1] The stems in *-van* regularly form their f. in *-varī*, e. g. *pī́-van, pī́-varī;* those in *-an* and *-man* by adding *-ī* to the syncopated stem at the end of compounds; e. g. *sóma-rājñ-ī-*, *páñca-nāmn-ī-* (AV.).

[2] This exception does not apply when *-an* is preceded by two consonants, e. g. *sakth-nā́.*

[3] But also G. sing. *vṛ́ṣaṇ-as* (AV.). The syncopation nearly always takes place in *-an* stems and in nearly half of the *-man* and *-van* stems.

[4] When the accent is on the suffix it is thrown on the ending in these syncopated forms, e. g. *mahnā́* from *mah-án-*.

[5] That is, *a* here represents an original sonant nasal, see p. 17, note [2].

[6] 48 locatives (occurring 127 times) have the *i*, 45 (occurring 203 times) drop it. See LANMAN 535.

[7] But those in *-āni* occur nearly twice as often.

[8] Cp. BRUGMANN, KG. 483 and LANMAN 538.

[9] Cp. the comparative *yav-īyān* and the Avestan *yvan.*

[10] *-śvan* in both these compounds is probably derived from *śū-* 'grow'.

[11] From *bhū-* 'be'.

[12] From *gam-* 'go'.

[13] The f. of *-an* stems at the end of compounds is formed with *-ī* in *ácchidra-ūdhn-ī-* 'having a faultless udder', *sam-rājñ-ī-*

b. In the strong forms the stems *ṛbhu-kṣán-* 'chief of the Ṛbhus', *pūṣán-*, and the f. *yóṣan-*, retain the short *a*, while *ukṣán-* 'ox' and *vṛ́ṣan-* 'bull' fluctuate between *ă* and *ā*. The words *śván-* and *yúvan-* form their weak stems before vowels with Samprasāraṇa, *śún-*, *yū́n-*; the latter is once used in the N. du. m. form *yū́nā* instead of *yúvānā*. In the weak cases syncopation always takes place[1] except in the forms *ukṣáṇas* and *vṛ́ṣaṇas*.

c. A number of *-an* stems have supplementary forms from other stems: *akṣán-* from *ákṣi-*; *asthán-* from *ásthi-*; *áhan-* from *áhas-* and *áhar-*; *āsán-* from *āsyà-*, *ā́s-*, and *āsā́-*; *udán-* from *úd-* and *uda-ká-*; *ū́dhan-* from *ū́dhas-* and *ū́dhar-*; *dadhán-* from *dádhi-*; *doṣán-* from *dós-*; *yakán-* from *yákṛt-*; *yóṣan-* from *yóṣaṇā-* and *yóṣā-*; *śákan-* from *śákṛt-*; *sakthán-* from *sákthi-*. As no stem in *-an* has been found in the N. A. sing. n., such forms appear to have been avoided and to have been purposely replaced by forms from supplementary stems. These forms are the N. A. n. *ákṣi, ásthi* (AV.), *áhar*, *āsyàm*, *udakám*, *ū́dhar*, *yákṛt* (AV.), *śákṛt*, *sákthi*; also *yúvat* instead of **yúva*, as well as *śíras* and *śīrṣá-m* (AV.) instead of **śīrṣá*[2].

d. There are here several transitions to the *a*-declension. The A. sing. *pūṣáṇ-am* is the starting point for the N. *pūṣáṇ-a-s* and the G. *pūṣaṇá-sya-*[3]. The N. A. pl. n. is the starting point in other instances: the two pl. forms *śīrṣā́* and *śīrṣā́ṇi* give rise to the L. sing. *śīrṣé* (AV.) beside *śīrṣáṇi*, as well as to the du. N. A. *śīrṣé* and the N. A. sing. *śīrṣá-m* (AV.); similarly the two plurals *áhā* and *áhāni* led to the G. pl. *áhānām* beside *áhnām*; and *yūṣā́ṇi*, the pl. of *yūṣán-*, which has the appearance of a pl. of a stem *yūṣá-*, led to the formation of an I. sing. *yūṣéṇa* (TS.) beside the regular *yūṣṇā́* (VS.). Again, the weak forms *áśn-as, ahn-ás* etc., gave rise to the transition stems *áśna-* and *áhna-*, from which are formed the I. pl. *áśnais* and the L. sing. *pūrvāhṇé*.

Transition *a*-stems often take the place of *-an* stems at the end of compounds. Thus *-akṣá-* appears in several compounds for *-akṣán-*, and *-vṛṣá-* (AV.) for *-vṛ́ṣan-*; *an-asthán-* once forms the N. sing. m. *an-asthá-s* (VIII. 134); beside the N. sing. m. *bṛhád-ukṣā* appears the D. *bṛhád-ukṣāya* (VS.); beside *rā́jānam* is found the A. m. *adhi-rājá-m* (X. 1289) 'over-lord'; and beside *saptábhis* 'seven', the compound *tri-saptáis*[4].

Inflexion.

327. The normal forms, if made from *rā́jan-* 'king' in the m., and from *áhan-* 'day' in the n., would be as follows:

1. m. **Sing.** N. *rā́jā*. A. *rā́jānam*. I. *rā́jñā*. D. *rā́jñe*. Ab. *rā́jñas*. G. *rā́jñas*. L. *rā́jani* and *rā́jan*. V. *rājan*.

Du. N. A. *rā́jānā* and *rā́jānau*. I. *rā́jabhyām*. D. *rā́jabhyām*. G. *rā́jños*.

Pl. N. V. *rā́jānas*. A. *rā́jñas*. I. *rā́jabhis*. D. *rā́jabhyas*. Ab. *rā́jabhyas* (AV.). G. *rā́jñām*. L. *rā́jasu*.

2. n. **Sing.** N. A. —[5]. I. *áhnā*. D. *áhne*. Ab. G. *áhnas*. L. *áhani* and *áhan*. — **Du.** N. A. *áhanī*. G. *áhnos* (AV.). — **Pl.** N. A. *áhāni*. I. *áhabhis*. D. Ab. *áhabhyas*. G. *áhnām*. L. *áhasu*.

The forms actually occurring are the following:

Sing. N. m. *an-asthā́* 'boneless', *áyaḥ-śīrṣā* 'iron-headed', *a-śīrṣā́* 'headless', *ukṣā́* 'bull', *ṛji-śvā* N. of a man, *tákṣā* 'carpenter', *tápur-mūrdhā* 'burning-headed', *try-udhā́*[6] 'three-uddered', *dvi-bárha-jmā*[7] 'having a double course', *pári-jmā* 'surrounding', *pūṣā́* 'Pūṣan', *plīhā́* (VS.) 'spleen', *bṛhád-ukṣā* 'having great oxen', *majjā́* (VS. AV.) 'marrow', *mātarí-śvā* 'Mātariśvan', *mūrdhā́* 'head', *yúvā* 'youth', *rā́jā* 'king', *ví-bhvā* 'far-reaching', *vi-rā́jā* (TS. v. 7. 4[4]) 'sovereign', *vṛ́ṣā* 'bull', *śvā́* 'dog', *sahásra-śīrṣā* 'thousand-headed'.

'queen', *sóma-rājñ-ī-* 'having Soma as king', *hatá-vṛṣṇ-ī-* 'whose lord has been slain', *rúru-śīrṣṇ-ī-* 'deer-headed', *saptá-śīrṣṇ-ī-* 'seven-headed', *éka-mūrdhn-ī-* (AV.) 'having the head turned in one direction', *síndhu-rājñ-ī-* (AV.) 'having Sindhu as queen'.

[1] The restoration of the *a* seems to be metrically required in a few instances: see LANMAN 525.

[2] The N. sing. n. of the adj. *vṛ́ṣan-* is avoided in several ways: see LANMAN 530 (bottom).

[3] With shifted accent.

[4] On the other hand there are two transitions from the *a*-declension to the *an*-declension in *ni-kāmabhis* beside *ni-kāmais* and *naktá-bhis* for *náktam*, but these forms are due to somewhat artificial conditions; see below, I. pl. p. 206, notes 3 and 4.

[5] Only supplementary forms occur: see LANMAN 530 (bottom).

[6] The metre seems to require *try-ūdhā́* (III, 56[3]).

[7] Here *bárha-* = *bárhas-*.

A. m. *ukṣánam, tákṣāṇam* (VS. xxx. 6), *tri-mūrdhánam* 'three-headed', *tri-śīrṣáṇam* 'three-headed', *pánthānam* (VS. AV.) 'path', *pári-jmānam, pṛthu-gmánam* [1] 'broad-pathed', *plīhánam* (AV.), *majjánam, mātarí-śvānam, mūrdhánam, yúvānam, rájānam* [2], *vṛṣāṇam, śvánam, saptá-śīrṣāṇam* 'seven-headed'. — **With short *a*:** *ukṣáṇam, ṛbhu-kṣáṇam* [3] 'chief of the Ṛbhus', *pūṣáṇam, vṛṣaṇam* [4].

I. m. 1. *ṛjí-śvanā, mātarí-śvanā, vi-bhvánā.* — **2. With syncope:** *áśnā* [5], *pūṣṇá, plīhná* (VS.), *majjñá* (AV.), *mūrdhná* (VS. xxv. 2), *rájñā, vṛṣṇā.* — **3. With Samprasāraṇa:** *śúnā* [6] (AV.). — **n.** *asná* (VS. xxv. 9) 'blood', *áhnā* 'day', *āsná* 'mouth', *udná* 'water', *dadhná* 'curds', *mahná* 'greatness', *yakná* (VS. xxxix. 8) 'liver', *yūṣṇá* (VS. xxv. 9) 'broth', *vi-śīrṣṇá* (Kh. i. 11⁴) 'headless', *śakná* (VS.) 'excrement', *śīrṣṇá* 'head', *sakthná* (VS.) 'thigh'.

D. m. 1. *ṛjí-śvane, pári-jmane, mātarí-śvane, vi-bhváne, vṛṣaṇe* (TS. iii. 2. 5²) [7]. — **2.** *pūṣṇé, prati-dívne* 'adversary at play', *mūrdhné* (VS. xxii. 32), *rájñe, vṛṣṇe* [8]. — **3.** *yúne.* — **n. 1.** *dhúrv-ane* 'hurting'. — **2.** *áhne, āsné, śīrṣṇé.*

Ab. m. 2. *plīhnás* (AV.), *mūrdhnás, vṛṣṇas* [9]. — **n. 2.** *akṣṇás* 'eye', *áhnas, āsnás* [10], *udnás* [11], *údhnas, yaknás* 'liver', *vṛṣṇas* 'shedding rain', *śīrṣṇás.*

G. m. 1. *durgṛ́bhi-śvanas* 'continually swelling', *pári-jmanas, mātarí-śvanas* (VS. i. 2), *vṛṣaṇas* [12] (AV.). — **2.** *áśnas* [13], *ukṣṇás, pūṣṇás, yūṣṇás* (or n.), *rájñas, vṛ́ṣṇas.* — **3.** *yúnas, śúnas.* — **n.** *akṣṇás* (VS. iv. 32; TS.), *asnás* [14] (AV.) 'blood', *asthnás* (AV.) 'bone', *áhnas, udnás, dadhnás, vṛṣṇas, śaknás* (AV.), *śīrṣṇás* [15].

L. m. 1. *ṛjí-śvani, mātarí-śvani, mūrdháni, rájani.* — **2.** *jmán* 'way', *pári-jman, mātarí-śvan* (AV.), *mūrdhán.* — **n. 1.** *áhani, āsáni, udáni, údhani* 'udder', *kṣámaṇi* 'earth', *rājáni, śīrṣáṇi; áhni* (AV.). — **2.** *áhan, āsán, udán, údhan, kṣáman* [16], *gámbhan* (VS. xiii. 30) 'depth', *śīrṣán* [17].

V. m. 1. *uru-jman* (AV.) 'extension', *pari-jman, pṛthu-jman* (AV.), *pūṣan, mūrdhan* (VS. xviii. 55), *yuvan, rājan, vṛṣan, śata-mūrdhan* (VS. xvii. 71; TS.) 'hundred-headed', *satya-rājan* (VS. xx. 4) 'true king'. — **2.** *mātari-śvas* [18].

Du. N. A. V. m. 1. *pári-jmānā*, V. *mitra-rājānā* 'ye kings Mitra (and Varuṇa)', *yúvānā*, V. *yuvānā, rájānā, śvánā.* **With short vowel:** *índrā-pūṣáṇā, pūṣáṇā, vṛṣaṇā*, V. *vṛṣaṇā, somā-pūṣaṇā.* **With weak stem:** *yúnā* (ix. 68⁵) for *yúvānā* (probably through *yúvānā*). — **2. With *au*:** *rájānau, vṛṣāṇau* (AV.), *śvánau*; V. *vṛṣaṇau, somā-pūṣaṇau.*

N. A. n. *áhanī, cákṣaṇī* (AV.) 'eyes', *doṣáṇī* (AV.) 'fore-arms' [19].

I. m. *vṛṣabhyām.* — **D. m.** *soma-pūṣábhyām.* — **G. m.** *pári-jmanos, indrā-pūṣṇós.* — **n.** *áhnos* (AV.). — **L. n.** *akṣṇós* (Kh. i. 11⁸).

---

1 *-gman-* = *-jman-* 'path'.

2 There is also the transfer form *adhi-rājá-m* (x. 128⁹).

3 Perhaps from *kṣā-* = *kṣi-* 'possess'.

4 In the RV. *vṛ́ṣaṇam* occurs 53 times, *vṛ́ṣāṇam* only twice.

5 This form (occurring thrice) may possibly be shortened for *áśmanā* (which occurs twice) from *áśman-* 'stone'.

6 For **śú-an-ā*; hence no shift of accent as in monosyllabic stems.

7 Also *uśán-e* (vi. 20¹¹) according to Benfey, Orient und Occident 2, 242.

8 There is also the transition form *bṛhád-ukṣāya* (VS. viii. 8).

9 Benfey, Gött. Abh. 19, 261, regards *vibhvánā* (x. 76⁵) as = Ab. *vibhvánas.*

10 Also the supplementary forms *āsyát, ās ás.*

11 Also the supplementary form *udakát.*

12 For *vṛ́ṣa-nāma* (ix. 97⁵⁴) Grassmann would read *vṛ́ṣaṇo ná*; cp. Wackernagel 2¹, 68 a, note (p. 160).

13 This form (occurring once) may be shortened for *áśmanas* (occurring four times).

14 With supplementary stem *ásṛ-j-*.

15 The G. *pūṣaṇásya*, occurring once, seems to be a transfer form starting from the A. *pūṣáṇam* (326 d).

16 There are also the transition forms *śīrṣé, pūrvāhṇé*: see Lanman 536.

17 The compound *nemann-íṣ-* 'following guidance' probably contains a loc.

18 Following the analogy of some stems in *-van.*

19 Also the transition form *śīrṣé.*

Pl. N. V. m. *ukṣáṇas* (VS. XXIV. 13), *tigmá-mūrdhānas* 'sharp-edged', *pánthānas* (AV.), *mūrdhánas*, *yúvānas*, *rā́jānas*, *śvā́nas*. — **With short vowel:** *ukṣáṇas*, *ṛbhu-kṣáṇas*, *vṛ́ṣaṇas*.

N. A. n. 1. *akṣáṇi*, *asthā́ni* (TS. IV. 7. 1^{2})[1], *áhāni*, *śīrṣáṇi*, *sakthā́ni*. — 2. *áhā*, *śīrṣā́*[2].

A. m. 1. *mātari-śvānas*, *ukṣáṇas*, *vṛ́ṣaṇas*. — 2. *ukṣṇás*, *jana-rā́jñas* 'king of men', *majjñás* (AV.), *mūrdhnás*, *yamá-rājñas* 'subject to Yama', *rā́jñas*, *vṛ́ṣṇas*. — 3. *yū́nas*, *śúnas*.

I. m. *ukṣábhis*[3], *yúvabhis*, *rā́jabhis*, *vṛ́ṣabhis*, *śvábhis* (Kh. V. 15^{7})[4]. — **n.** *akṣábhis*, *asthábhis*, *áhabhis*, *āsábhis*, *udábhis*, *ū́dhabhis*, *mahábhis*, *vṛ́ṣabhis*, *śákabhis* (TS. V. 7. 23^{1}), *su-kṛ́ta-karmabhis* (Kh. III. 12^{3}) 'doing good deeds'[5].

D. m. *tákṣabhyas* (VS.), *majjábhyas* (TS. VS. XXXIX. 10), *yúvabhyas*, *rā́jabhyas*, *śvábhyas* (AV. VS.). — **n.** *asthábhyas* (VS. XXXIX. 10; TS. V. 2. 12^{2}), *áhabhyas*. — **Ab. m.** *majjábhyas* (AV.). — **n.** *áhabhyas*.

G. m. *vṛ́ṣṇām*, *rā́jñām* (VS. AV.), *śúnām* (AV.). — **n.** *áhnām*[6].

L. m. *majjásu* (AV.), *yamá-rājasu* (AV.), *rā́jasu*. — **n.** *áhasu*, *śīrṣásu*.

2. Stems in *-man*.

328. These stems are about equally divided between the masculine and the neuter gender, the former being agent nouns, the latter verbal abstracts. These stems seem to have been used normally for the f. as well as the m.; for though no simple stem in *-man* occurs as a f., about a dozen of them are used as f. at the end of compounds, while no certain example appears in the RV. of a f. being formed by adding *-ī* to *-man*[7]. A peculiarity of the inflexion of the stems in *-man*, as compared with those in *-an* and *-van*, is that in the syncopated forms of the I. sing. several words drop the *m*, while two drop the *n* of the suffix; e. g. *mahinā́*[8] for *mahimnā́*, and *raśmā́* for *raśmnā́*.

a. The f. forms which occur at the end of compounds are: Sing. N. *purú-śarmā* (VS. X. 9) 'giving wide shelter' (*áditi-*), *sá-lakṣmā* (X. 10^{2}) 'similar'; A. *dyutád-yāmānam* (V. 80^{1}) 'having a shining course' (*uṣásam*); *su-tármāṇam* (VIII. 42^{3}) 'easily conveying across' (*nā́vam*), *su-trā́māṇam* (X. 63^{10}) 'protecting well' (*pṛthivī́m*), *su-śármāṇam* (X. 63^{10}) 'granting secure refuge' (*áditim*); V. *áriṣṭa-bharman* (VIII. 18^{4}) 'yielding security' (*adite*), *pṛthu-yāman* (VI. 64^{4}) 'having a broad path' (*duhitar*); Du. N. *su-jánmanī*[9] (I. 160^{1}) 'producing fair things' (*dhiṣáṇe*); Pl. A. *śúci-janmanas* (VI. 39^{3}) 'of radiant birth' (*uṣásas*); I. *vā́ja-bharmabhis* (VIII. 19^{30}) 'winning rewards' (*ūtíbhis*), *su-kármabhis* (IX. 70^{4}) 'skilful' (fingers); G. *śukrá-sadmanām* (VI. 47^{5}) 'having a bright dwelling-place' (*uṣásām*)[10]. From *nā́man-* 'name' the AV. forms with *-ī* the f. stem *-nāmnī-* at the end of five compounds: *dur-ṇā́mnī-* 'ill-named', *páñca-nāmnī-* 'having five names', *mahā́-nāmnī-* 'great-named', *viśvá-nāmnī-* 'having all names', *sahásra-nāmnī-* 'thousand-named'. The f. *dur-ádman-ī-* (VS. II. 20) 'noxious food' is perhaps similarly formed[11].

[1] In the corresponding passage of VS. (XVIII. 3) *ásthīni*.

[2] Both these might be formed from the transition *a*-stems *áha-*, *śīrṣá-*. This is perhaps the reason why these are the only two plurals of this declension which retain the *ā* in the Pada text; *áha* appears in I. 92^{3}.

[3] The form *ni-kāmabhis* 'eager' for *ni-kāmais* is due to the parallelism of *evayā́vabhis* in X. 92^{9}.

[4] There is also a transition form *áśnais* 'stones', beside the stem *áśan-*.

[5] The unique form *naktábhis* (as if from a stem *naktán-*) is doubtless used for metrical reasons instead of *náktam* in VII. 104^{18}.

[6] There is also the transition form *áhānām*.

[7] The AV. has five stems thus formed at the end of compounds.

[8] Cp. Bloomfield, BB. 23, 105 ff., AJPh. 16, 409—434; Bartholomae IF. 8, Anzeiger 17.

[9] With the ending of the neuter; see Lanman 433 (top).

[10] Possibly also *su-ṣū́mā* (II. 32^{7}) 'bearing well'; but it is derived from *sū́-ma- according to BR. and Grassmann.

[11] The f. *bráhmī-* (IX. 33^{5}) formed from *bráhman-* is quite exceptional, being due to a play on words (see Lanman 528). The form *tmányā* = *tmánā* in sense, occurring twice in the RV., may be an I. sing. f. of *tmán-ī-*: cp. Grassmann and BR.

b. In the strong forms *aryamán-* 'Aryaman', *tmán-* 'self', and *jéman-* 'victorious' retain the short vowel of the suffix. In the weak forms, even when the suffix is preceded by a vowel, about a dozen forms do not syncopate the *a*[1]: I. *ománā, pravád-yāmanā, bhūmánā, bhū́manā, syū́manā, hemánā*; D. *trā́maṇe, dā́mane*; Ab. G. *bhū́manas*; G. *mahimánas, dā́manas, yā́manas, vyómanas*. The forms which, besides syncopating, drop the *m* or the *n* of the suffix are: *prathinā́, preṇā́, bhūnā́, mahinā́, variṇā́*; *drāghmā́, raśmā́*.

c. Beside the *-man* stems there are several transfer stems in *-ma*, which are, however, of rare or late occurrence: *darmá-* 'destroyer' beside *darmán-*; *dhárma-* (AV. etc.) 'law' beside *dhárman-*; *éma-* (VS.) 'course' beside *éman-*; *hóma-* (VS. AV.) 'offering' beside *hóman-* (RV.); *ájma-* 'course' beside *ájman-*; *yā́ma-* 'course' beside *yā́man-*; *priyá-dhāma-* (I. 140[1]) 'fond of home' beside *priyá-dhāman-* (AV.); and occasional forms of *-karma-* at the end of compounds beside the regular *-karman-*: *vīrá-karma-m* (X. 61[5]) 'doing manly deeds'; *viśvá-karmeṇa* (X. 164[4]) 'all-creating' beside *viśvá-karmaṇā*, etc.

Inflexion.

329. The normal forms actually occurring would, if made from *áśman-* 'stone' in the m. and from *kárman-* 'act' in the n., be as follows:

Sing. m. N. *áśmā*. A. *áśmānam*[2]. I. *áśmanā*[3]. D. *áśmane*[4]. Ab. *áśmanas*[5]. G. *áśmanas*[5]. L. *áśmani* and *áśman*. V. *áśman*. — **Du.** N. A. V. *áśmānā*[6]. L. *áśmanos*. — **Pl.** N. V. *áśmānas*. A. *áśmanas*. I. *áśmabhis*. D. *áśmabhyas*. G. *áśmanām*. L. *áśmasu* (AV.).

Sing. n. N. A. *kárma*[7]. I. *kármaṇā*[8]. D. *kármaṇe*[8]. Ab. *kármaṇas*[8]. G. *kármaṇas*[8]. L. *kármaṇi* and *kárman*. — **Du.** N. A. *kármaṇī*. G. *kármaṇos*. — **Pl.** N. A. *kármāṇi*, *kárma*, *kármā*. I. *kármabhis*. D. *kármabhyas*. Ab. *kármabhyas*. G. *kármaṇām*[8]. L. *kármasu*.

Forms which actually occur are the following:

Sing. N. m. *a-karmá* 'wicked', *á-brahmā* 'lacking devotion', *aryamā́* 'Aryaman', *áśmā* 'stone', *a-sremā́* 'faultless', *ātmā́* 'breath', *āśú-hemā* 'speeding swiftly', *iṣṭá-yāmā* 'going according to desire', *usrá-yāmā* 'moving towards brightness', *ṛtá-dhāmā* (VS. IV. 32) 'abiding in truth', *kṛtá-brahmā* 'having performed devotion', *jarimā́* 'old age', *jātú-bharmā* 'ever nourishing', *jemā́* (VS. XVIII. 4) 'superiority', *tṛpála-prabharmā* 'offering what is refreshing', *darmā́* 'demolisher', *dāmā́* 'giver', *dur-ṇā́mā* 'ill-named', *dur-mánmā* 'evil-minded', *dyutád-yāmā* 'having a shining path', *drāghimā́* (VS. XVIII. 4) 'length', *dvi-jánmā* 'having a double birth', *dharmā́* 'arranger', *dhvasmā́* 'darkening', *páka-sthāmā* N. of a man, *pāpmā́* (VS. VI. 35) 'misfortune', *pṛthú-pragāmā* 'wide-striding', *prathimā́* (VS. XVIII. 4) 'width', *brahmā́* 'devout man', *bhujmā́*[9] 'abounding in valleys', *bhūmā́* (TS. VII. 3. 13[1]) 'plenty', *bhū́ri-janmā* 'having many births', *mahimā́* 'greatness', *yajñá-manmā* 'ready for sacrifice', *raghu-yā́mā* 'going quickly', *reṣmā́* (AV.) 'tempest', *vadmā́* 'speaker', *varimā́* 'width', *varṣimā́* (VS. XVIII. 4) 'height', *viśvá-karmā* 'all-creator', *viśvá-sāmā* (VS. XVIII. 39) 'having the form of all Sāmans', *vṛ́ṣa-prabharmā* 'to whom the strong (Soma) is offered', *śatā́tmā* 'possessing a hundred lives', *satyá-dharmā* 'whose laws are true', *satyá-manmā* 'whose thoughts are true', *saptá-nāmā* 'seven-named', *sahásra-yāmā* 'having a thousand courses', *sādhú-karmā* 'acting well', *su-kármā* 'working skilfully', *su-jánimā* 'producing fair things', *su-trā́mā* 'guarding well', *su-dyótmā* 'shining bright', *su-bráhmā* 'accompanied by good prayers', *su-mántu-nāmā* 'bearing a well-known name', *su-mánmā* 'benevolent', *su-váhmā*

---

[1] The vowel has also to be restored in several other forms (see LANMAN 524 f.).

[2] With short vowel *aryamáṇam*, *tmánam*.

[3] Without syncope after vowel *bhū́manā*, etc.; with syncope *mahimnā́*, *mahinā́*, *drāghmā́*, etc.

[4] Also with syncope, *mahimné*, etc.

[5] Also with syncope, *mahimnás*, etc.

[6] Also with short vowel *aryamáṇā*, *jémanā*.

[7] Sometimes *kármā* in the Saṃhitā text.

[8] Also with syncope, *nā́mnā*, etc.

[9] *bhújma* (I. 65[5]) should probably be read *bhujmā́*; see BR., GRASSMANN, LANMAN 530 (top).

'driving well', *su-śármā* (VS. VIII. 8) 'good protector', *su-ṣṭhā́mā* 'having a firm support', *svādu-kṣádmā* 'having sweet food'[1].

N. A. n. *ájma* 'track', *ádma* 'food', *éma* 'course', *kárma* 'deed', *kā́rṣma* 'goal', *kṣádma* 'carving knife', *cárma* 'skin', *jánima* 'birth', *jánma* 'birth', *tókma* 'young blade of corn', *dā́ma* 'cord', *dhárma* 'ordinance', *dhā́ma* 'abode', *nā́ma* 'name', *pátma* 'flight', *bráhma* 'prayer', *bhásma* (TS. VS. XII. 35) 'ashes', *bhū́ma* 'earth', *mánma* 'thought', *márma* 'vital part', *yā́ma* 'course', *lóma* (TS. VS. XIX. 92) 'hair', *vártma* 'path' (Kh. v. 2[1]), *várma* 'mail', *vásma* 'garment', *véma* (VS. XIX. 83) 'loom', *véśma* 'house', *vyòma* 'sky', *śákma* 'power', *śárma* 'refuge', *sádma* 'seat', *sā́ma* 'chant', *sā́ma* 'wealth', *sthā́ma* 'station', *syū́ma* 'strong', *svā́dma* 'sweetness', *hóma* 'oblation'. — With **final vowel lengthened** in the Saṃhitā text: *kármā, jánimī, dhā́mā* (AV.), *bhū́mā, vyòmā, su-ṣṭárīmā*[2] (TS. v. 1. 11[2]) 'forming an excellent couch', *svā́dmā*[3].

A. m. *áśmānam, a-sremā́ṇam, ātmā́nam, ūṣmā́ṇam* (AV.) 'heat', *ojmā́nam* 'power', *omā́nam* 'favour', *klómānam* (VS. XIX. 85) 'right lung', *jarimā́ṇam, tuví-brahmāṇam* 'praying much', *darmā́ṇam, dāmā́nam* 'gift', *dur-mánmānam, dyutád-yāmānam, dvi-jánmānam, dharmā́ṇam, pā́ka-sthāmānam, pāpmā́nam* (VS. XII. 99; TS. I. 4. 41[1]), *puru-tmā́nam* 'existing variously', *purú-ṇāmānam* (AV.) 'having many names', *brahmā́ṇam, bhūmā́nam, mahimā́nam, reṣmā́ṇam* (VS. XXV. 2), *varimā́ṇam, varṣmā́ṇam* 'height', *viśvá-karmāṇam, vi-sarmā́ṇam* 'dispersion', *śatā́tmānam, satyá-dharmāṇam, sadmā́nam* 'sitter', *sahá-sāmānam* 'accompanied by songs', *su-tármāṇam* (TS. I. 2. 2[2]) 'crossing well', *su-dyótmānam, su-bráh-māṇam, su-śármāṇam, somā́nam* 'preparer of Soma', *stāmā́nam* (AV. v. 13[5]) 'track' (?), *svādmā́nam* 'sweetness', *harimā́ṇam* 'jaundice'. — With **short *a***: *aryamáṇam, tmánam* 'breath'.

I. m. *áśmanā, ātmánā* (VS. XXXII. 11), *ūṣmáṇā* (VS. XXV. 9), *tmánā, pāpmánā* (VS. XIX. 11), *bhásmanā* 'chewing', *majmánā* 'greatness', *varṣmáṇā, viśvá-karmaṇā*. — **1.** *ománā, pravád-yāmanā* 'having a precipitous course', *bhūmánā* 'abundance', *śatá-yāmanā* (AV. SV.) 'having a hundred paths'. — **2.** *aryamṇā́* (AV.), *pāmnā́* (AV.) 'scab', *bhūmnā́* (VS. III. 5), *mahimnā́, varimṇā́*[4] (VS. AV.), *śatá-yāmnā*. — **3.** *prathinā́*[5], *preṇā́*[6] 'love', *bhūnā́*[7], *mahinā́*[8], *variṇā́* (TS.)[9]; *drāghmā́, raśmā́*[10]. — **n.** *kármaṇā, jánmanā, dhármaṇā* 'ordinance', *pátmanā, bráhmaṇā, bhásmanā* (VS. VI. 21) 'ashes', *mánmanā, vármaṇā, vidmánā* 'wisdom', *ví-dharmaṇā* 'extension', *śákmanā, śármaṇā, śā́kmanā* 'might', *svá-janmanā* 'self-begotten', *hánmanā* 'stroke'. — **1.** *bhū́manā* 'earth', *syū́manā, hemánā* 'zeal'. — **2.** *dā́mnā* (AV.) 'tie', *dhā́mnā, nā́mnā, lómnā* (AV.) 'hair', *sā́mnā, sutrā́mṇā* (VS. XX. 35) 'protecting well'.

D. m. 1. *ātmáne* (VS. VII. 28), *takmáne* (AV.) a kind of disease, *tmáne, pāpmáne* (AV. VS.), *brahmáṇe, bhū́ri-karmaṇe* 'doing much', *viśvá-karmaṇe* (TS. VS. VIII. 45). — **2.** *aryamṇé, jarimṇé, bhūmné* (VS. XXX. 13) 'plenty', *mahimné*; *án-usra-yāmne* 'not going out during daylight', *usrá-yāmne, su-trā́mṇe* (VS. X. 31), *su-ṣā́mṇe* N. of a man ('having beautiful songs'), *suhávītu-nāmne* 'whose name is to be invoked successfully'. — **n.** *kár-*

---

[1] *su-dhárma* (VS. XXXVIII. 14) 'well supporting' seems to be meant for a V. (wrong accent), but perhaps *su-dhármā* should be read.

[2] *suṣṭárīma* in the Pada text.

[3] See LANMAN 531[1].

[4] Once also the transfer form *varimátā*, according to the declension in *-mant*.

[5] For *prathimnā́* from *prathimán-*.

[6] For *premṇā́* from *premán-*.

[7] For *bhūmnā́* beside *bhūmánā*.

[8] *mahinā́* occurs 35 times, *mahimnā́* only 3 times.

[9] Beside *varimṇā́* (AV.). The TS. twice has *variṇā́*, which in the corresponding passages of the VS. is replaced by *varimṇā́*; cp. LANMAN 533.

[10] In these two forms the *m* being preceded by a consonant remains, the *n* being dropped: = *drāghmnā́* 'breadth', and *raśmnā́* 'rein'. Probably also *dānā́* for *dāmnā́* 'gift', and possibly *áśnā* = *áśmanā*.

mane, jánmane, dhármaṇe, bráhmaṇe, bhármaṇe 'support', *vidmáne, ví-dharmaṇe, śármaṇe.* — 1. *trámaṇe* 'protection', *dā́mane.* — 2. *dhā́mne, sā́mne* 'acquisition'.

Ab. m. *áśmanas, ātmánas, ūṣmáṇas* (VS. VI. 18), *satyá-dharmaṇas* (AV.). — 2. *klomnás* (AV.), *jarimṇás* (AV.), *varimṇás* (AV.). — **n.** *cármaṇas, jánmanas, dhármaṇas, mánmanas, vásmanas* 'nest', *sádmanas.* — 1. *bhū́manas.* — 2. *dā́mnas, dhā́mnas* (VS. VI. 22)[1], *lómnas.*

G. m. *a-mármaṇas* 'having no vital spot', *brahmáṇas, ví-patmanas* 'speeding away', *vípra-manmanas* 'having an inspired mind', *śúci-janmanas* 'of radiant birth', *su-śármaṇas, viśvá-karmaṇas* (VS. XXXI. 17). — 1. *mahimánas.* — 2. *aryamṇás, jarimṇás* (AV.), *mahimnás, sthirá-dhāmnas* (AV.) 'belonging to a strong race'. — **n.** *kármaṇas, jánmanas, dhármaṇas, bráhmaṇas, mánmanas, vármaṇas.* — 1. *dā́manas, bhū́manas, yā́manas, vyòmanas.* — 2. *dhā́mnas, sā́mnas.*

L. m. 1. *áśmani, ātmáni, tmáni, brahmáṇi, mahmáni* (AV.) 'greatness', *su-ṣā́maṇi.* — 2. *áśman, tmán, ātmán* (VS. AV.). — **n.** 1. *ájmani* (AV.), *kármaṇi, cármaṇi* (AV.), *jánmani, dā́mani, dīrghá-prasadmani* 'affording an extensive abode', *dhárīmaṇi* 'established usage', *dhármaṇi, dhā́mani, párīmaṇi* 'abundance', *prá-bharmaṇi* 'presenting', *prá-yāmaṇi* 'setting out', *bráhmaṇi, mánmani, mármaṇi, yā́mani, lákṣmaṇi* (TS. VII. 4. 19[2]) 'mark', *vákmani* 'invocation', *ví-dharmaṇi, véśmani* (AV.), *vyòmani, śármaṇi, sárīmaṇi* 'current of air', *sávīmani* 'impulsion', *su-ṣāmáṇi, stárīmaṇi* 'strewing', *hávīmani* 'invocation', *hómani* 'offering' and 'invocation'. — With **syncope:** *lómni* (AV.), *vi-jā́mni* (AV.) 'knuckle' (?), *sthā́mni* (AV.). — 2. *ájman, á-yāman* 'no expedition', *éman* (VS. TS.), *ódman* (TS. VS.) 'flooding', *kárman, kā́rṣman, cárman, jániman, jánman, dárīman* 'destruction', *dhárman, dhā́man, pátman, bráhman, bhásman* (VS. TS.) 'consuming', *bhā́rman* 'table', *mánman, márman, yā́man, váriman, várīman* 'width, *várṣman, vi-jā́man* 'related to each other', *ví-dharman, vyòman, śárman, śásman* 'song of praise', *sákman* 'attendance', *sádman, sā́man, svā́dman, hávīman.*

V. m. *aryaman, áśman* (TS. IV. 6. 1[1]), *ā́śu-heman* (TS. I. 7. 7[2]), *takman* (AV.), *tri-ṇāman* (TS. AV.) 'three-named', *pāpman* (AV.), *puru-ṇāman, puru-hanman* N. of a seer, *brahman, vi-dharman, viśva-karman, viśva-sāman* N. of a seer, *vṛṣa-karman* 'doing manly deeds', *satya-karman* 'whose actions are true', *sahasra-dhāman* (AV.) 'having thousandfold splendour', *su-dāman* 'giving good gifts', *su-yāman* (AV.), *sva-dharman* 'abiding in one's own customs'.

Du. N. A. V. m. *brahmā́ṇā, satya-dharmāṇā, sa-nāmānā* 'of the same kind', *su-śármāṇā; aryamáṇā, jémanā* 'victorious', *sā́mātmanā* (Kh. III. 22[5]; cp. TB. II. 8. 9[1]) 'endowed with chants', *su-kármaṇā* (VS. XX. 75).

N. A. n. *śármaṇī, jánmanī, sádmanī.* — 1. *dhā́manī, sā́manī* (VS. X. 14). — 2. *nā́mnī* (AV.). — **G. n.** *sádmanos.* — **L. m.** *áśmanos.*

Pl. N. V. *a-dāmā́nas* 'unbound' and 'not giving gifts', *a-dhvasmā́nas* 'undarkened', *ánu-vartmānas* (VS. XVII. 86) 'followers', *á-brahmāṇas, a-raśmā́nas* 'having no reins', *óha-brahmāṇas* 'conveying sacred knowledge', *jarimā́ṇas, brahmā́ṇas* (VS. XXVII. 2), *bhrā́jaj-janmānas* 'having a brilliant birthplace', *mahimā́nas, śúci-janmānas, sátya-dharmāṇas, sá-lakṣmāṇas* (TS. I. 3. 10[1]) 'having the same marks', *su-kármāṇas, su-jánimānas, su-rā́māṇas* (VS. XXI. 42) 'very delightful', *su-śármāṇas, sthā́-raśmānas* 'having firm reins', *svādmā́nas.* — With **short** *a*: *aryamáṇas, mahātmánas* (Kh. III. 12[2]) 'high-minded'.

N. A. n. 1. *ṛk-sāmā́ni* (VS. XVIII. 43), *kármāṇi, cármāṇi, jánimāni, jánmāni, dā́māni* (AV.), *dhármāṇi, dhā́māni, nā́māni, pákṣmāṇi* (VS. XIX. 89) 'eyelashes', *bráhmāṇi, mánmāni, mármāṇi, rómāṇi* 'hair', *lómāni* (AV.), *vártmāni, vármāṇi* (AV.), *śármāṇi, sádmāni, sā́māni.* — 2. *kárma*[2], *jánima, jánma, dhárma,*

[1] BR. and EGGELING suggest that this is a corruption for *dā́mnas* 'bond'.

[2] This and the following forms have short final *a* in the Pada as well as the Saṃhitā text.

dhā́ma, nā́ma, bráhma, bhū́ma, mánma, róma[1], *śárma, sádma.* — 3. *jánimā*[2], *dhármā, nā́mā, bráhmā, bhū́mā, rómā, sádmā*[3].

A. m. *áśmanas, takmánas* (AV.), *brahmáṇas.* — **2.** *dur-ṇā́mnas* (AV.).

I. m. *á-khidra-yāmabhis* 'unwearied in course', *a-dhvasmábhis, áśmabhis, áśma-hanmabhis* 'strokes of the thunderbolt', *āśu-hémabhis, ómabhis, klómabhis* (VS. xxv. 8), *brahmábhis, mayū́ra-romabhis* 'peacock-haired', *vīḷu-pátmabhis* 'flying strongly', *su-kármabhis, su-mánmabhis, su-śármabhis.* — **n.** *ájmabhis, émabhis, kármabhis, tókmabhis* (VS. xix. 81), *trā́mabhis, dhármabhis, dhā́mabhis, nā́mabhis, pátmabhis, bráhmabhis, bhárīmabhis* 'nourishment', *mánmabhis, yā́mabhis, várīmabhis, vā́ja-karmabhis*[4] (SV. TS. iii. 2. 11[1]) 'active in war', *vā́ja-bharmabhis* (viii. 19[30]) 'bringing reward', *ví-gāmabhis* 'strides', *śákmabhis, sā́mabhis, hávīmabhis.*

D. m. *brahmábhyas.* — **n.** *dhā́mabhyas.* — **Ab. n.** *lómabhyas.*

G. m. *brahmáṇām.* — **2.** *dur-ṇā́mnām* (AV.). — **n.** *dhármaṇām, bráhmaṇām, mánmanām, mármaṇām* (Kh. i. 5[5]). — **2.** *áhi-nāmnām*[5] 'animals named snake', *sā́mnām* (AV.).

L. m. *áśmasu* (AV.). — **n.** *kármasu, jánmasu, dhā́masu, vármasu, sádmasu.*

3. Stems in *-van*.

330. The *-van* stems are by far the most numerous of the three groups. They are chiefly verbal adjectives and are almost exclusively declined in the masculine. Hardly a dozen of them make neuter forms, and only five or six forms are used as feminines.

a. The few feminine forms are cases of adjectives agreeing with f. substantives. They are: sing. N. *sa-yúgvā* (x. 130[4]) 'companion' (*gāyatrī́*), *an-arvā́* (ii. 40[6]) 'irresistible' (*áditis*); A. *an-arvā́ṇam* (x. 92[14]) 'irresistible' (*áditim*); du. N. *saṃ-sthā́vānā* (viii. 37[4]) 'standing together' (*ródasī*); pl. I. *índhan-vabhis*[6] (ii. 34[5]) 'flaming' (*dhenúbhis*); G. *sahasra-dā́vnām* (i. 17[5]) 'giving a thousand gifts' (*sumatīnā́m*). The f. of these stems is otherwise formed with *-ī*, which is however never added to *-van*, but regularly to a collateral suffix *-vara*[7]. Twenty-five such stems in *-varī* are found in the RV. and several additional ones in the later Saṃhitās. It is perhaps most convenient to enumerate them here: *agréivarī-*[8] (AV.) 'going in front', *abhi-kṛ́tvarī-* 'bewitching' (AV.), *abhi-bhū́varī-* 'superior', *abhī́tvarī-*[9] (TS. VS.) 'attacking', *uttāna-śī́varī-* (AV.) 'lying extended', *ṛtā́varī-* 'regular', *eva-yā́varī-* 'going quickly', *kṛ́tvarī-* (AV.) 'bewitcher', *talpa-śī́varī-* 'lying on a couch', *niṣ-ṣidhvarī-* 'bestowing', *pī́varī-* 'fat', *pūrva-jā́varī-* 'born before', *pra-sū́varī-* 'furnished with flowers', *bahu-sū́varī-* 'bearing many children', *bhūri-dā́varī-* 'munificent', *mātari-bhvarī-*[10] 'being with her mother', *mātari-śvarī-*[11] (AV.) 'mother-growing', *yújvarī-* 'worshipping', *vákvarī-* 'rolling', *vahya-śī́varī-* (AV.) 'reclining on a couch', *vi-bhā́varī-* 'brilliant', *vi-mṛ́gvarī-* (AV.) 'cleansing', *śákvarī-* ('powerful') a kind of metre, *śárvarī-*[12] '(star-spangled) night', *śruṣṭī́várī-* 'obedient', *śveta-yā́varī-* 'white-flowing', *saṃ-śíśvarī-*[13] 'having a calf in common', *sa-jítvarī-* 'victorious', *sa-yā́varī-* 'accompanying', *sumnā́várī-* 'gracious', *sūnṛtā́varī-*[14] 'glorious', *sṛ́tvarī-* 'streaming', *svadhā́varī-* 'constant'.

---

1 Perhaps singular.

2 The Pada text has always *ă* in this and the following forms.

3 This lengthening is found in neither *-van* stems nor *-an* stems, except *áhā* and *śīrṣā́*, which may be formed from transfer stems and in which the Pada as well as the Saṃhitā text has the long vowel.

4 *vā́ja-karmabhis* is a v. l. of *vā́ja-bharmabhis*, and both adjectives as agreeing with *ūtíbhis* have the value of feminines.

5 The G. *chando-nāmā́nām* (VS. iv. 24) 'named metre' seems to be a transfer to the *a*-declension.

6 Formed from *indhana-* 'fuel', with loss of the final vowel.

7 The f. *atharvī́-*, formed from *átharvan-* 'fire-priest', is quite exceptional.

8 That is, *agra-i-t-varī-*.

9 That is, *abhi-i-t-varī-*.

10 From what only seems to be a *-van* stem which is really = *-bhū-an-*.

11 This seems to be a corruption in AV. v. 2[9] of *mātaribhvarī-* in the corresponding passage of the RV.

12 The f. of *śarvara-* 'variegated' occurring in *api-śarvará-* n. 'early morning'; a stem *śár-van-* does not occur.

13 The f. of what only seems to be a stem in *-van* but is really = *śíśu-an-*.

14 Also *sūnṛtā́vatī-*.

b. In the strong cases there is one instance in which the *a* remains short: *an-arváṇam*[1] (x. 92[14]), and two others in which the weakest stem is used: A. sing. *maghónam* (VS. XXVIII. 9) instead of *maghávānam*, N. pl. *maghónas* (VI. 44[12]) instead of *maghávānas*[2]. In the weak cases when the suffix is preceded by a vowel, the a is always syncopated in the Saṃhitā text except in the forms *dāváne*, *vasuváne* (VS.), and *ṛtāvani*, but it may have to be restored in one or two instances[3].

c. The three words *ṛ́k-van-* 'singing', *maghá-van-* 'bountiful', *sahā́-van-* 'powerful' make a few forms from supplementary stems in *-vant*: I. sing. *ṛ́kvatā*; pl. I. *maghá-vadbhis*, D. *maghávadbhyas*, L. *maghávatsu*; N. sing. *sahā́vān* and *sáhāvān*. Beside *dadhi-krā́van-*, N. of a mythical horse, also occurs the stem *dadhi-krā́-*.

d. Eight or nine words in *-van* show transitions to the *a*-declension by extending the stem with *-a* or, more commonly, by dropping the *n*. Thus *satvaná-m* and *satvanáis* occur beside the numerous regular forms from *sátvan-* 'brave'. The N. sing. m. *anarváṇ-a-s* (v. 51[11], VIII. 31[12]) may have started from the A. *anarváṇ-am* (x. 92[14]), while the n. *anarvá-m* (I. 164[2]) may have been due to the f. (*áditir*) *anarvā́* which appears like the f. of the *a-* declension. Other transitional forms are *ṛkvá-s* beside *ṛ́kvan-*; *ṛ́bhva-m* 'dexterous' beside *ṛ́bhvan-*; *takvá-s* 'swift' beside *tákvan-*; *vákvās*, N. pl., 'rolling' beside *vákvan-*; *vibhā́va-m* 'brilliant' beside *vibhā́van-*; *śikvá-s* (AV.) 'skilful' beside *śíkvan-*.

Inflexion.

331. The normal forms occurring, if made from *grā́van-* 'pressing stone' in the m. and from *dhánvan-* 'bow' in the n., would be:

Sing. m. N. *grā́vā*. A. *grā́vāṇam*. I. *grā́vṇā*. D. *grā́vṇe*. Ab. *grā́vṇas*. G. *grā́vṇas*. L. *grā́vaṇi* and *grā́van*. V. *grā́van*. — **Du.** N. A. V. *grā́vāṇā* and *grā́vāṇau*. I. *grā́vabhyām* (AV.). G. *grā́vṇos*. — **Pl.** N. V. *grā́vāṇas*. A. *grā́vṇas*. I. *grā́vabhis*. D. *grā́vabhyas*. G. *grā́vṇām*. L. *grā́vasu*.

Sing. n. N. A. *dhánva* and *dhánvā*. I. *dhánvanā*. D. *dhánvane*. Ab. G. *dhánvanas*. L. *dhánvani* and *dhánvan*. — **Pl.** N. A. *dhánvāni*, *dhánva*, *dhánvā* (AV.). I. *dhánvabhis*. D. *dhánvabhyas* (VS.). Ab. *dhánvabhyas* (AV.). G. *dhánvanām* (AV.). L. *dhánvasu*.

Forms actually occurring are the following:

Sing. N. m. *agra-yā́vā* 'going in front', *átharvā* 'fire-priest', *adma-sádvā* 'companion at a meal', *ádhvā* 'road', *an-arvā́*[4] 'irresistible', *abhi-yúgvā* (VS. XVII. 86) 'attacking', *abhiśasti-pā́vā* 'protecting from curses', *abhí-satvā* 'surrounded by heroes', *abhyardha-yájvā* 'receiving sacrifices apart', *amatīvā́* 'suffering want', *arātīvā́* 'hostile', *á-rāvā* 'not giving', 'hostile', *árvā* 'steed', *ávatata-dhanvā* (VS. III. 61) 'whose bow is unbent', *āśu-pátvā* 'flying swiftly', *ugrá-dhanvā* 'having a mighty bow', *ṛ́kvā* 'praising', *ṛ́ghāvā* 'impetuous', *ṛṇa-yā́vā* 'pursuing guilt', *ṛṇāvā́* 'guilty', *ṛtā́vā* 'pious', *ṛ́bhvā* 'dexterous', *kṛṣṇā́-dhvā* 'having a black track' (*adhvā*), *kratu-prā́vā* 'granting power', *kṣiprá-dhanvā* 'having an elastic bow', *grāvā́* 'pressing stone', *tákvā* 'bird of prey', *dadhi-krā́vā* N. of a divine horse, *deva-yā́vā* 'going to the gods', *dru-ṣádvā* 'sitting on the wood', *nṛ-ṣádvā* 'sitting among men', *páṭharvā* N. of a man, *pátvā* 'flying', *puru-kṛ́tvā* 'doing much', *pūrva-gátvā* 'leader', *pūrva-yā́vā* 'leader', *pra-tákvā* (VS. v. 32) 'steep', *pra-ríkvā* 'extending beyond', *prāṇa-dā́vā*[5] (AV.) 'breath-giving', *prātar-ítvā* 'coming in the morning', *bāḍha-sṛ́tvā* 'striding mightily', *bṛhád-grāvā* (VS. I. 15) 'like a great stone', *bhū́ri-dā́vā* 'giving much', *maghávā*[6] 'bountiful', *mádvā* 'exhilarating', *mrakṣa-kṛ́tvā* 'rubbing to pieces', *yájvā* 'sacrificer', *yā́vā* 'aggressor', *yuktá-grāvā* 'having yoked the pressing stones', *yúdhvā* 'warlike', *raghu-pátvā* 'flying swiftly', *rárāvā* 'giving abundantly', *rā́vā* (VS. VI. 30) 'giving', *vákvā* 'rolling', *vasu-dā́vā* 'giving goods',

1 This seems to be a metrical shortening; according to GRASSMANN it is an A. of a transfer stem *an-arváṇa-*.

2 The form *kṛ́tvanas* in AV. XIX. 35[5] as N. pl. m. is a conjecture; cp. p. 213, note 2.

3 See LANMAN 524 (bottom).

4 *an-arváṇ-a-s* is a transition to the *a-* declension.

5 Emendation for *prāṇa-dā́vān* in AV. IV. 35[5].

6 Also once *maghá-vān*, transition form from a stem in *-vant*.

vāja-dā́vā 'granting wealth', *vi-jā́vā* 'bodily', 'own', *vi-bhā́vā* 'brilliant', *vi-bhṛ́tvā* 'bearing hither and thither', *vṛ́ṣa-parvā* 'strong-jointed', *vyòmā* (VS. IV. 23) 'heaven'[1], *śubhaṃ-yā́vā* 'flying swiftly', *śúbhvā* 'bright', *śyená-patvā* 'borne by eagles', *śrutárvā* N. of a man, *śruṣṭīvā́* 'obedient', *satīná-satvā* 'truly brave', *satyá-madvā* 'really exhilarated', *sátvā* 'brave', *samádvā* 'eager for battle', *sahā́vā*[2] 'mighty', *sútvā* 'Soma-pressing', *su-dhánvā* 'wielding a good bow', *sṛ́tvā* 'speeding', *soma-pā́vā* 'drinking Soma', *soma-sútvā* 'pressing Soma', *stúbhvā* 'praising', *hítvā* 'speedy'.

N. A. n. *dhánva*[3] 'bow' and 'desert', *párva* (AV.) 'joint', *vi-vásva* 'bright flame', *snā́va* (AV.) 'sinew'.

A. m. *ádhvānam*, *an-arvā́ṇam*, *á-yajvānam* 'not sacrificing', *árvāṇam*, *ṛjíśvānam* N. of a man, *ṛṇāvā́nam*, *ṛtā́vānam*, *grā́vāṇam*, *dadhi-krā́vāṇam*, *dhitā́-vānam* 'bountiful', *pī́vānam* 'fat', *puru-niṣṣídhvānam* 'bestowing many gifts', *puro-yā́vānam* 'going in front', *prātar-yā́vāṇam* 'coming in the morning', *maghávānam*, *muṣīvā́ṇam* 'thief', *śatá-yāvānam* (Kh. I. 3[2]) 'having a hundred ways', *śruṣṭīvā́nam*, *sa-jítvānam* 'victorious', *sátvānam*, *sa-yā́vānam* 'accompanying', *sahā́vānam*, *sṛ́kvāṇam* 'corner of the mouth', *hā́rdvānam* (VS. XXXVIII. 12) 'strengthening hearts'.

I. m. 1. *átharvaṇā*, *abhi-yúgvanā*, *cikitvánā* 'wise', *śatá-parvaṇā* 'having a hundred joints', *śíkvanā* (TS. II. 5. 12[2]) 'skilful'. — **2.** *grā́vṇā*. — **n. 1.** *dhánvanā*, *párvaṇā*. — **2.** *snā́vnā* (AV.).

D. m. 1. *ádhvane*, *á-paścād-daghvane* 'not staying behind', *kṛ́tvane* 'active', *jásvane* 'needy', *drúhvane* 'hostile', *pṛṣṭha-yájvane* 'sacrificing on the ridge', *mádvane*, *yájvane*, *vasuváne* (VS. XXI. 48) 'winning of wealth', *śákvane* (VS. V. 5) 'skilful', *śatá-dhanvane* (VS. XVI. 29) 'having a hundred bows', *śrutárvaṇe*, *sátvane*, *su-kṛ́tvane* 'pious', *su-dhánvane* (VS. XVI. 36), *sthirá-dhanvane* 'having a strong bow'. — **2.** *á-rāvṇe*, *ṛtā́vne*, *oṣiṣṭha-dā́vne* (TS. I. 6. 12[3]) 'giving immediately', *vṛ́ṣa-prayāvṇe* 'going with stallions', *suta-pā́vne* 'Soma-drinker', *su-dā́vne* 'giving abundantly', *soma-pā́vne*, *sva-dhā́vne* 'independent'. — **n. 1.** *turváṇe* 'victory', *dāváne* 'giving', *dhánvane* (VS. XVI. 14).

Ab. m. 1. *ádhvanas* (VS. XXVI. 1; TS.), *pāka-sútvanas* 'offering Soma with sincerity'. — **2.** *á-rāvṇas*, *puru-rā́vṇas* (VS. III. 48) 'loud-roaring'. — **n. 1.** *dhánvanas* (AV.), *párvaṇas*.

G. m. 1. *átharvaṇas*, *ádhvanas*, *á-yajvanas*, *á-stṛta-yajvanas* 'sacrificing indefatigably', *yájvanas*, *vy-àdhvanas* 'striding through'. — **2.** *á-rāvṇas*, *dadhi-krā́vṇas*, *bhūri-dā́vnas*, *yuktá-grāvṇas*, *suta-pā́vnas*, *soma-pā́vnas*; *maghónas*[4]. — **n. 1.** *dhánvanas* 'bow'.

L. m. 1. *átharvaṇi*, *ádhvani*, *ṛtā́vani*, *śrutárvaṇi*, *su-kṛ́tvani*. — **2.** *śata-dā́vni*[5]. — **3. Without ending:** *ádhvan*. — **n. 1.** *túgvani* 'ford', *párvaṇi*. — **3.** *an-arván*, *a-parván*, *dhánvan*, *párvan* (AV.).

V. m. 1. *atharvan* (AV.), *aśva-dāvan* 'giving horses', *dāvan* (AA. V. 2. 2[13]), *maghavan*, *vasu-dāvan*, *víśvato-dāvan* (SV. I. 5. 2. 1[1]) 'giving everywhere', *viśva-dāvan* (AV.) 'giving everything', *satya-satvan* 'truly strong', *satrā-dāvan* 'giving everything', *sahasāvan* 'strong', *suta-pāvan*, *soma-pāvan*, *sva-dāvan* 'having good taste', *sva-dhāvan*, *sva-yāvan* 'going one's own way'. — **2. With -vas:** *ṛtāvas*, *eva-yāvas* 'going quickly', *prātar-itvas*, *vibhāvas*[6].

---

1 As a masculine.

2 Also *sahā́vān* and *sáhāvān* from a stem in *-vant*.

3 Once with final vowel lengthened in the Saṃhitā text, *dhánvā*.

4 Sometimes to be read as *maghá-vanas*; see LANMAN 534.

5 The only example of syncopation in the L. of this declension in the RV. (V. 27[5]), where however the *a* must be metrically restored; there are no examples in the *-an* or *-man* stems, but the AV. has one in the former and three in the latter.

6 *khid-vas* (VI. 22[4]) is perhaps best taken as V. of a stem *khid-vā́ṃs-*; BR. and LANMAN explain it as from *khid-van-*. The V. *mātariśvas* is formed as if from *mātariś-van-* instead of *mātari-śv-an-*; cp. p. 210, notes 10 and 13.

Du. N. A. V. m. *agrādvānā* 'eating (*advan-*) first', *a-druhvāṇā* 'not hostile', *ṛtávānā*, *grávāṇā*, *prātar-yávāṇā*, *maghávānā*, *ratha-yávānā* 'driving in a car', *śubhra-yāvānā* 'driving stately', *śruṣṭīvánā*, *sa-jítvānā*. — **With** ***-au*****:** *ṛtávānau*, *grávāṇau* (AV.). — **I. m.** *grávabhyām* (AV.). — **G. m.** *maghónos*.

Pl. N. V. m. *akṣṇa-yávānas* 'going across', *átharvāṇas*, *an-arváṇas*, *á-yajvānas*, *upa-hásvānas* 'mocking', *ūrdhvá-grāvāṇas* 'lifting the pressing stone', *ŕkvāṇas*, *ṛtávānas*, *grávāṇas*, *ghṛta-pāvānas* (VS. VI. 19) 'drinking ghee', *drúhvāṇas*, *ni-kŕtvānas* 'deceitful', *pari-ṣádvānas* 'besetting', *pívānas* (TS. III. 2. 8[5]), *prá-sthāvānas* 'swift', *prātar-yávāṇas*, *maghávānas*, *raghu-pátvānas*, *vánīvānas*[1] 'demanding', *vasā-pāvānas* (VS. VI. 19) 'drinkers of fat', *śubham-yávānas*, *śruṣṭīvánas*, *sátvānas*, *su-dhánvānas*, *su-śíkvānas* 'shining brightly'. — **Weak form for strong:** *maghónas* (VI. 44[12])[2].

N. A. n. 1. *dhánvāni*, *párvāṇi*, *snávāni* (AV.). — **2.** *dhánva*, *párva*[3]; with long final vowel only *párvā* (AV. XII. 5[42]).

A. m. 1. *ádhvanas*, *á-yajvanas*, *drúhvaṇas* (AV.). — **2.** *á-rāvṇas*, *eva-yávnas*, *grávṇas*, *prātar-yávṇas*; *maghónas*.

I. m. *ádhvabhis*, *á-prayutvabhis* 'attentive', *ŕkvabhis*, *eva-yávabhis*, *grávabhis*, *prātar-yávabhis*[4], *yájvabhis*, *ráṇvabhis* 'agreeable', *śíkvabhis*, *sátvabhis*, *sanítvabhis* 'bestowers', *sa-yávabhis*, *su-pra-yávabhis* 'speeding well', *sva-yúgvabhis* 'allies'. — **n.** *pátvabhis*, *párvabhis*, *vivásvabhis*, *soma-párvabhis* 'times of Soma offerings'.

D. m. *átharvabhyas*, *grávabhyas*, *gharma-pávabhyas* (VS. XXXVIII. 15) 'drinking hot (milk)'[5]. — **n.** *snávabhyas* (VS. XXXIX. 10). — **Ab. n.** *snávabhyas* (AV.).

G. m. 1. *ádhvanām* (VS. V. 33), *an-arváṇām*, *á-yajvanām*, *sátvanām*. — **2.** *grávṇām*, *rárāvṇām*, *vāja-dávnām*[6], *soma-pávnām*; *maghónām*. — **n. 1.** *dhánvanām* (AV.).

L. m. *ádhvasu*, *kŕtvasu*, *grávasu* (Kh. I. 12[3])[7], *yájvasu*[8]. — **n.** *dhánvasu*, *párvasu*.

Stems in *-in*, *-min*, *-vin*.

332. The suffixes *-in*, *-min*, *-vin*, which have the sense of 'possessing', are used to form secondary adjectives. The stems in *-in* are very common, those in *-vin* are fairly frequent, numbering nearly twenty, but there is only one in *-min*: *ṛg-mín-* 'praising'. They are declined in the m. and n. only[9]; but the neuter forms are very rare, amounting to fewer than a dozen altogether. The inflexion presents hardly any irregularities. The vowel of the suffix remains accented throughout[10], and is not liable either to syncope or to lengthening in the G. pl. It is lengthened in the N. sing. m. only[11]. As in all derivative stems ending in *-n*, the nasal disappears in the N. sing. m. n. and before terminations beginning with consonants.

a. There are a few transition forms to the *a*-declension starting from the A. sing. m. in *-in-am* understood as *-ina-m*. Such are *parameṣṭh-ina-m* (AV. XIX. 9[4]) 'most exalted', N. sing. n.; the V. *mahin-a* and the G. *mahina-sya* from *mah-in-* 'mighty', and

[1] From the intensive of √*van-*.

[2] The form *kŕtvano* in AV. XIX. 35[5] is a conjecture for the *kṛṣṇávo* of the Mss.

[3] In Pada as well as Saṃhitā.

[4] Also the supplementary form *maghávadbhis*.

[5] Also the supplementary form *maghávadbhyas*.

[6] The form *sahasra-dávnām* is read as a f. in I. 17[5].

[7] Accented *grāvásu* in the edition.

[8] There is also the transfer form *maghávatsu*.

[9] They form a special f. stem by adding *-ī*; e. g. from *aśv-ín-* 'possessing horses' *aśvin-ī-*.

[10] Except *írin-*, *śákin-*, *sárin-*, and the compounds *kárū-latin-*, *mahā-vaṭūrin-*, *indra-medin-*, from each of which a single form occurs; also the compounds formed with the negative *a-*; e. g. *á-nāmin-*.

[11] It would doubtless be lengthened in the N. A. n. pl. also if that form occurred.

the n. pl. *vanínā-ni* (x. 66⁹)[1] from *van-in-* m. 'forest-tree'. The isolated form *mandi-m* (I. 9²) is a transition to the *i*-declension, starting probably from the I. sing. *mandin-ā* 'exhilarating' understood as *mandi-nā*.

Inflexion.

333. All the case-forms are represented in the m., but in the n. the three singular case-forms, N. A., I., and G. only. As only eight or nine n. forms occur, they may most conveniently be enumerated separately:

Sing. n. N. *á-nāmi* 'unbending', *ubhayā-hastí* 'filling both hands', *tsārí* (AV.) 'hidden', *patatrí* 'winged', *vājí* 'vigorous' (Kh. IV. 6²), *śakalyeṣí* (AV.) 'seeking shavings'[2]. I. *kīriṇā* 'praising', *su-gandhínā*[3] 'fragrant'. G. *pra-hoṣíṇas* 'offering oblations'[4].

The **m.** forms actually occurring, if made from *hast-ín-* 'having hands', would be as follows:

Sing. N. *hastí.* A. *hastínam.* I. *hastínā.* D. *hastíne.* Ab. *hastínas.* G. *hastínas.* L. *hastíni.* V. *hástin.* — **Du.** N. A. *hastínā* and *hastínau.* I. D. *hastíbhyām.* G. L. *hastínos.* — **Pl.** N. *hastínas.* A. *hastínas.* I. *hastíbhis.* D. *hastíbhyas* (VS. AV.). G. *hastínām.* L. *hastíṣu.*

a. The forms actually occurring are:

Sing. N. 1. Stems in *-in*: *aṅkí* 'possessing a hook', *ati-vyādhí* (VS. XXII. 22) 'wounding', *abhyā-vartí* 'coming near', *arthí* 'active', *aśví* 'possessed of horses', *irī*[5] 'powerful', *uj-jeṣí* (VS. XVII. 85) N. of one of the Maruts, *udrí* 'abounding in water', *ṛjīpí* 'moving upwards', *ṛjīṣí* 'receiving the residue of Soma', *ekākí* (VS. TS.) 'solitary', *kapardí* 'wearing braided hair', *kárū-ḷatī*[6] 'having decayed teeth', *kāmí* 'desirous', *kulāyí* (TS. IV. 1. 9⁶) 'forming a nest', *kevalādí* 'eating by oneself alone', *keśí* 'having long hair', *krīḍí* (VS. XVII. 85) 'sporting', *gṛha-medhí* (VS. XVII. 85) 'performing the domestic sacrifices', *candrí* (VS. XX. 37) 'golden', *tsārí* 'hidden', *dyumní* 'majestic', *niṣ-ṣapí* 'lustful', *pakthí* 'cooking the oblation', *patatrí* (TS. I. 7. 7²) 'winged', *parame-ṣṭhí* (VS. VIII. 54) 'most exalted', *pari-panthí* 'waylayer', *pṛṣṭy-āmayí* 'suffering from a pain in the side', *pra-ghāsí* (VS. XVII. 85) 'voracious', *pra-bhaṅgí* 'destroying', *pra-vepaní* 'causing to tremble', *bāhu-śardhí* 'relying on his arms', *brahma-cārí* 'practising devotion', *brahma-varcasí* (VS. XXII. 22) 'eminent in sacred knowledge', *bhadra-vādí* 'uttering auspicious cries', *manīṣí* 'thoughtful', *manthí* (VS. VII. 18) 'stirred Soma juice', *mandí* 'exhilarating', *marāyí* 'destructive' (?), *mahā-hastí* 'having large hands', *māyí* 'crafty', *medí* 'ally', *rathí* 'possessing a car', *rambhí* 'carrying a crutch', *rukmí* 'adorned with gold', *vajrí* 'armed with a bolt', *varmí* 'mailed', *vaśí* 'having power', *vājí* 'vigorous', *vi-rapśí* 'copious', *śata-svī* 'having a hundred possessions', *śākí*[7] 'strong', *śiprí* 'full-cheeked', *śuṣmí* 'roaring', *ślokí* 'sounding', *śvaghní* 'gambler', *ṣoḍaśí* (VS. TS.) 'having sixteen parts', *sárī*[5] 'hastening', *sahasrí* 'thousandfold', *sācí* 'companion', *somí* 'offering Soma', *svabdí* 'bellowing', *hastí* 'having hands'. — **2. stem in *-min*:** *ṛgmí* 'praising'. — **3. stems in *-vin*:** *á-dvayāvī* 'free from duplicity', *á-yudhvī*[8] 'not fighting', *aṣṭrāví* 'obeying the goad', *tarasví* (VS. XIX. 88) 'bold'.

A. 1. *atríṇam* 'devourer', *adhi-kalpínam* (VS. XXX. 18) 'gamble-manager',

[1] Instead of *vanín-as*, probably due to the metre.

[2] The Pada text reads *śakalya-eṣí*; but the Paippalāda recension has the better reading *śākalyeṣu* 'among the shavings': see WHITNEY's note on AV. I. 25².

[3] But this form might be from *su-gandhi-*.

[4] The isolated form *krudhmí* (VII. 56⁸) agreeing with *mánāṃsi* is a N. pl. n. of a stem *krudh-mi-*, rather than of *krudh-mín-* 'angry'.

[5] With abnormal accent.

[6] Accented like a Bahuvrīhi.

[7] Thus accented VS. XVII. 85, but *śā́kī* RV. I. 51⁸: the latter is probably an error as the suffix is accented in the three other forms *śākínam, śākíne, śākínas.*

[8] BÖHTLINGK (pw.) regards this as a gerund: *á-yud-dhvī* 'without fighting'.

abhi-praśnínam (VS. XXX. 10) 'inquisitive', *abhi-mātínam* 'insidious', *arkíṇam* 'praising', *ava-krakṣíṇam* 'rushing down', *á-vājinam* 'a bad horse', *aśvínam*, *ādāríṇam* 'breaking open', *āyínam* (TS. II. 4. 7[1]) 'hurrying up', *iṣmíṇam* 'speeding', *uktha-śaṃsínam* 'uttering verses', *ukthínam* 'praising', *udríṇam*, *ṛjīṣíṇam*[1], *kapardínam*, *karambhíṇam* 'possessing gruel', *kalpínam* (VS. XXX. 18) 'designing', *kalmalīkínam* 'flaming', *kāmínam*, *kāríṇam* 'singing', *kulāyínam*, *kūcid-arthíṇam* 'striving to get anywhere', *catínam* 'lurking', *jana-vādínam* (VS. XXX. 17) 'prattler', *tri-ṣṭhínam* (VS. XXX. 14) 'having a threefold footing', *dyumnínam*, *dhanínam* 'wealthy', *ni-yayínam*[2] 'passing over', *pakṣíṇam* 'winged', *patatríṇam* (VS. XIX. 10), *pari-panthínam*, *pīṭha-sarpíṇam* (VS. XXX. 21) 'cripple', *putríṇam* 'possessing sons', *purīṣíṇam* 'possessing land', *pra-vādínam* (VS. XXX. 13) 'speaking pleasantly', *praśnínam* (VS. XXX. 10) 'questioner', *bahu-vādínam* (VS. XXX. 19) 'talkative', *manīṣíṇam*, *manthínam*, *mandínam*[3], *manyu-ṣāvíṇam* 'pressing Soma with zeal', *māyínam*, *medínam* (TS. IV. 7. 10[4]), *rathínam*, *vaṃśa-nartínam* (VS. XXX. 21) 'pole-dancer', *vajríṇam*, *vanínam* 'bountiful', *vanínam* 'forest tree', *vayākínam* 'ramifying', *varcínam* N. of a demon, *vājínam*, *vi-rapśínam*, *vi-ṣṭīmínam* (VS. XXIII. 29) 'wetting', *śata-gvínam* 'hundredfold', *śatínam* 'hundredfold', *śākínam*, *śuṣmíṇam*, *śṛṅgíṇam* 'horned', *śvanínam* (VS. XXX. 7) 'keeping dogs', *sahasra-poṣíṇam* 'thriving a thousandfold', *sahasríṇam*. — 3. *á-dvayāvinam*, *ubhayāvínam* 'partaking of both', *tarasvínam*, *namasvínam* 'reverential', *māyāvínam* 'employing deceit', *medhāvínam* (VS. XXXII. 14) 'possessed of wisdom', *rakṣasvínam* 'demoniacal'.

I. 1. *arcínā* 'shining', *aśvínā*, *kimīdínā* 'evil spirit', *kīríṇā* 'praising'[4], *balínā* (TS. III. 3. 8[2]) 'strong', *mandínā*, *mahá-vaṭūríṇā*[5] 'very wide', *vaṭūríṇā* 'wide', *vājínā*. — 3. *rakṣasvínā*.

D. 1. *abhyā-vartíne*, *a-mitríṇe* 'hostile', *ava-bhedíne* (VS. XVI. 34) 'splitting', *ā-tatāyíne* (VS. XVI. 18) 'having one's bow drawn', *ā-yudhíne* (VS. XVI. 36) 'warrior', *upa-vītíne* (VS. XVI. 17) 'wearing the sacred cord', *uṣṇīṣíṇe* (VS. XVI. 22) 'wearing a turban', *kapardíne*, *kavacíne* (VS. XVI. 35) 'mailed', *kāríṇe*, *kimīdíne*, *tantrāyíṇe* (VS. XXXVIII. 12) 'drawing out rays', *ni-vyādhíne* (VS. XVI. 20) 'piercing', *ni-ṣaṅgíṇe* (VS. XVI. 20) 'sword-bearer', *pra-sakṣíṇe* 'victorious', *bilmíne* (VS. XVI. 35) 'having a helmet', *bhāmíne* 'angry', *manīṣíṇe*, *mantríṇe* (VS. XVI. 19) 'wise', *mandíne*, *mahíne* 'mighty', *rathíne*, *vajríṇe*, *varūthíne* (VS. XVI. 35) 'wearing armour', *varmíṇe* (VS.), *vi-naṃśíne* (VS. IX. 20) 'vanishing', *vi-rapśíne*, *vy-aśnuv-íne*[6] (VS. XII. 32) a genius of food, *vyādhíne* (VS. XVI. 18) 'piercer', *śākíne*, *śipríṇe*, *śuṣmíṇe*, *ṣoḍaśíne* (VS. VIII. 33), *sv-āyudhíne* (VS. XVI. 36) 'having good weapons'. — 3. *rakṣasvíne*.

Ab. 1. *abhi-prabhaṅgíṇas* 'breaking completely', *patatríṇas*, *manthínas* (TS. VS. XIII. 57), *somínas*.

G. 1. *arthínas*, *ṛjīṣíṇas*, *kapardínas* (TS. VS. XVI. 10), *dhanínas*, *patatríṇas* (TS. IV. 7. 13[1]), *parṇínas* 'winged', *pra-gardhínas* 'pressing onwards', *bhūri-poṣíṇas* 'much-nourishing', *manthínas* (VS. VII. 18), *mandínas*, *māyínas*, *ratnínas* 'possessing gifts', *rasínas* 'juicy', *retínas*[7] 'abounding in seed', *vajríṇas*, *vanínas* 'bountiful', *vanínas* 'forest tree', *varcínas*, *vājínas*, *vi-rapśínas*, *vīḷu-harṣíṇas*

---

1 *ṛjīṣám* in I. 32[6] is possibly a metrically shortened form for *ṛjīṣíṇam*: cp. LANMAN 543[2].

2 As this compound occurs only once beside the simple adj. *yayí-*, which occurs several times, the former is perhaps a transfer from the *i*-declension.

3 *mandí-m* (I. 9[2]) is probably a transition form; but BR. regard it as a contraction in pronunciation of *mandínam*.

4 GRASSMANN in I. 100[9] proposes to read *kīríṇe*.

5 Accented like Bahuvrīhi; but cp. p. 154[5].

6 Formed from the present stem of √*aś-*: *vi-aś-nuv-in-*.

7 From *réta-* for *rétas-* 'seed'.

'refractory', *vrandínas* 'becoming soft', *śatínas, śuṣmíṇas, śṛṅgíṇas, sahasríṇas, somínas.* — 3. *á-dvayāvinas, dvayāvínas* 'double-dealing', *namasvínas.*

L. 1. *dvīpíni* (AV.) 'leopard', *parame-ṣṭhíni* (AV.), *brahma-cāríṇi* (AV.), *māyíni, vājíni, somíni.*

V. 1. *ánā-bhayin* 'fearless', *abhyā-vartin* (VS. XII. 7), *amatrin* 'having a large drinking vessel', *ṛjīpin, ṛjīṣin, tuvi-kūrmin* 'working powerfully', *pra-pathin* 'roaming on distant paths', *yakṣin* 'living', *vajrin, vājin, virapśin, śavasin* 'mighty', *śiprin, śuṣmin, sahasin* 'mighty'. — 3. *ubhayāvin.*

Du. N. A. V. 1. *aśvínā*, V. *áśvinā* and *áśvinā, kumāríṇā* 'having children', *keśínā*, V. *pajra-hoṣiṇā* 'having rich oblations', *parṇínā, putríṇā, purīṣíṇā, pra-sakṣíṇā, manthínā*, V. *māyinā, vajríṇā, vājínā*, V. *vājinā, vi-ghanínā* 'slaying', *śuṣmíṇā, sarathínā* (VS. XXIX. 7; TS.) 'driving in the same car', *sāma-cāríṇā* (Kh. III. 22[5]) 'faring with chants'. — 3. *māyāvínā.* — Forms with *-au*[1]: *aśvínau*, V. *áśvinau* and *aśvinau, patatríṇau* (VS. XVIII. 52), *vājínau.*

I. *aśvíbhyām, índra-medibhyām* (AV.) 'whose ally is Indra'. — **D.** *aśví-bhyām.* — **G.** *aśvínos.* — **L.** *aśvínos.*

Pl. N. V. 1. *aṅkuśínas* 'having a hook', *atríṇas, arkíṇas, arcínas, arthínas, avarokíṇas* (VS. XXIV. 6) 'brilliant', *iṣmíṇas, ukthínas, upa-mantríṇas* 'persuading', *ṛjīṣíṇas, kapardínas, kabandhínas* 'bearing casks', *kāmínas, kāríṇas, kīríṇas, kṛśanínas* 'adorned with pearls', *keśínas, khādínas* 'adorned with rings', *gaṇínas* (TS. I. 4. 11[1]) 'having attendants', *gāthínas* 'singers', *gāyatríṇas* 'singers of hymns', *gharmíṇas* 'preparing the Gharma offering', *daśagvínas* 'tenfold', *drapsínas* 'falling in drops', *dhūmínas* 'smoking', *ni-kāríṇas* (TS. VS. XXVII. 4) 'injurers', *ni-todínas* 'piercing', *ni-rāmíṇas* 'lurking', *ni-ṣaṅgíṇas, pakṣíṇas, patatríṇas, pari-panthínas, pari-paríṇas* (VS. IV. 34) 'adversaries', *parṇínas, pāśínas* 'laying snares', *purīṣíṇas, pra-krīḍínas* 'sporting', *pra-sak-ṣíṇas, balínas, manīṣíṇas, mandínas, mahínas, māyínas, medínas, rathínas, vanínas* 'bountiful', *vanínas* 'forest trees', *varmíṇas, vājínas, vi-rapśínas, vi-rokíṇas* 'brilliant', *viṣāṇínas* 'holding horns' (a people), *vrata-cāríṇas* 'performing vows', *śatagvínas, śatínas, śākínas, śuṣmíṇas, sahasríṇas, somínas, svānínas* 'resounding', *hastínas, hiraṇínas* 'golden'. — 2. *ṛgmíṇas.* — 3. *tarasvínas, dvayāvínas, dhṛṣadvínas* 'bold', *namasvínas, māyāvínas.*

A. 1. *atríṇas, a-rājínas* 'lacking splendour', *arthínas, aśvínas, uktha-śaṃsínas, kāmínas, kāríṇas, grathínas* 'false', *dyumnínas, pakṣíṇas, pra-ghāsínas* (VS. III. 44), *bhāmínas, mandínas, māyínas, mitríṇas* 'befriended', *rathínas, vanínas* 'bountiful', *vanínas* 'forest trees', *vājínas, vrandínas, sahasríṇas, somínas, hastínas* (VS. XXIV. 29), *hiraṇínas.* — 3. *rakṣasvínas.*

I. 1. *aśvíbhis, keśíbhis, ni-ṣaṅgíbhis, patatríbhis, manīṣíbhis, mandíbhis, rukmíbhis, vājíbhis, śuṣmíbhis, hastíbhis.* — 2. *ṛgmíbhis.*

D. 1. *ṛta-vādíbhyas* (VS. V. 7) 'speaking the truth', *krīḍíbhyas* (VS. XXIV. 16), *gṛha-medhíbhyas* (VS. XXIV. 16), *dhanvāyíbhyas* (VS. XVI. 22) 'carrying a bow', *rathíbhyas* (VS. XVI. 26), *śikhíbhyas* (AV.) 'peaked', *śvaníbhyas* (VS. XVI. 27), *sṛkāyíbhyas* (VS. XVI. 21) 'having a spear', *svadhāyíbhyas* (VS. XIX. 36) 'owning the Svadhā'.

G. 1. *kāríṇām, māyínām, vaśínām* (AV.), *vājínām, śṛṅgíṇām.* — 3. *stukā-vínām* 'shaggy'. — **L.** 1. *khādíṣu, dvaríṣu* 'obstructing', *hastíṣu* (AV.).

4. Labial Stems.

a. Stems in (radical) *-p.*

334. These stems are inflected alike in the masculine and feminine, there being no neuters. All the monosyllables are feminine substantives.

[1] According to Lanman 544 the *-ā* forms occur 369 times, the *-au* forms 32 times.

They are: *áp-* 'water', *kṛ́p-* 'beauty', *kṣáp-* 'night', *kṣíp-* 'finger', *ríp-* 'deceit', *rúp-* 'earth', *víp-*[1] 'rod'. Feminine are also the compounds *ā-táp-* 'heating', *pati-ríp-* 'deceiving a husband', *vi-ṣṭáp-* 'summit', *ṛta-sáp-* 'performing worship'. All other compound stems are masculine. They are: *agni-táp-* 'enjoying the warmth of fire', *abhī-lāpa-láp-*[2] (AV.) 'excessively whimpering', *asu-tṛ́p-*[3] 'delighting in lives', *keta-sáp-* 'obeying the will (of another)', *pari-ráp-* 'crying around', *paśu-tṛ́p-*[3] 'delighting in herds', *pra-súp-*[4] 'slumbering', *rīty-àp-* 'having streaming (*rīti-*) water'.

a. The distinction of strong and weak forms appears in *áp-* and its compound *rīty-àp-*, as well as in the two compounds of *sap-* 'serve', *ṛta-sáp-* and *keta-sáp-*. The strong form *ā́pas* is used a few times in the A. pl., but the long vowel in *pari-rā́pas* as A. pl. is due to the metre; on the other hand, the weak form *ap-ás* appears twice in the AV. as N. pl.

b. The A. pl. *apás* is nearly always accented on the ending as a weak case; *kṣapás* similarly appears two or three times, and *vipás* once.

c. No N. sing. m. or f. occurs, but a n. transition form once appears in this case: *viṣṭápa-m* (IX. 113[10]), a form which doubtless started from the A. sing. f. *viṣṭáp-am*. The n. pl. of the same transition stem occurs once as *viṣṭápā* (VIII. 80[5]). Two other transition forms are *kṣapā́bhis* and *kṣipā́bhis*.

Inflexion.

335. The forms actually occurring are the following:

Sing. A. m. *paśu-tṛ́pam.* — **f.** *vi-ṣṭápam.* — **I. m.** *vipā́* 'priest'. — **f.** *apā́, kṛpā́, kṣapā́, vipā́.* — **Ab. f.** *apás; ā-tápas, vi-ṣṭápas.* — **G. m.** *vípas*[5]. — **f.** *apás, kṣapás, ripás, rupás.* — **L. f.** *vi-ṣṭápi.*

Du. N. m. *rīty-ā̀pā; asu-tṛ́pau*[6].

Pl. N. m. *ṛta-sā́pas, keta-sā́pas,* V. *rīti-āpas; vípas; agni-tápas, abhī-lāpa-lápas* (AV.), *asu-tṛ́pas, pra-súpas.* — **f.** *ā́pas,* V. *āpas, ṛta-sā́pas; kṣípas, vípas, rípas; pati-rípas.* The A. form *apás* occurs twice in the AV. for the N.[7].

A. m. *asu-tṛ́pas, pari-rā́pas*[8]. — **f.** *apás* and *ā́pas*[9], *kṣapás* and *kṣápas*[10], *vipás* and *vípas*[11], *rípas.*

I. f. *adbhís*[12]. — **D. f.** *adbhyás*[12] (VS. VI. 9). — **Ab. f.** *adbhyás*[12]. — **G. m.** *vipā́m.* — **f.** *apā́m*[13], *kṣapā́m, vipā́m.* — **L. f.** *apsú*[14].

b. Stems in (radical) *-bh.*

336. Both masculines and feminines occur in this declension, but there are no neuters. The stems comprise five monosyllables formed from roots, together with compounds of three of the latter (*grabh-, śubh-, stubh-*), and *kakúbh-*. The stems are: *kṣúbh-* f. 'push', *gṛ́bh-* f. 'seizing', *nábh-* f. 'destroyer', *śúbh-* f. 'splendour', *stúbh-* adj. 'praising', f. 'praise'; *jīva-gṛ́bh-* m. 'capturing alive', 'bailiff', *sute-gṛ́bh-* 'taking hold of the Soma', *syūma-gṛ́bh-* 'seizing the

---

[1] *víp-* as an adjective is used as a m. also.

[2] An irregular intensive formation.

[3] Cp. KLUGE, KZ. 25, 311 f.

[4] From *svap-* 'sleep'.

[5] With irregular accent.

[6] Cp. LANMAN 482 (middle).

[7] There is also the transition form in the n. *vi-ṣṭápā.*

[8] Metrical for *pari-rápas*, which is the reading of the Pada text in II. 23[3, 14]; see RPr. IX. 26.

[9] *apás* is the regular form occurring 152 times in the RV. and 26 times in the AV. The strong form *ā́pas* is used half a dozen times in books I and X of the RV., and 16 times in the AV.; it also occurs in Kh. III. 9.

[10] *kṣā́pas* 6 or 8 times in RV., *kṣapás* 2 or 3 times.

[11] *vípas* thrice, *vipás* once in RV.

[12] By dissimilation for **ab-bhís*, **ab-bhyás*; cp. JOHANSSON, IF. 4, 134—146. See LANMAN 483. There are also the two transfer forms *kṣapā́bhis* and *kṣipā́bhis*, each occurring once.

[13] On the metrical value of *apā́m* see LANMAN 484 (top).

[14] BR. regard *apásu* in VIII. 4[14] as = *apsú* with inserted *-a-*. See LANMAN 484.

reins'; *rathe-śúbh-* 'flying along in a car'; *anu-ṣṭúbh-* f. 'after-praise', a metre, *ṛta-stúbh-* 'praising duly', *tri-ṣṭúbh-* 'triple praise', a metre, *pari-ṣṭúbh-* 'exulting on every side', *saṃ-stúbh-* (VS.) 'shout of joy', a metre, *gharma-stúbh-* 'shouting in the heat', *chandaḥ-stúbh-* 'praising in hymns', *vṛṣa-stúbh-* 'calling aloud', *su-ṣṭúbh-* 'uttering a shrill cry'; *kakúbh-* f. 'peak', *tri-kakúbh-* 'three-pointed'.

a. The distinction of strong and weak forms does not appear except in the N. and A. pl. of *nábh-*. The inflexion of these stems is incompletely represented, there being no dual forms, and no plural forms the endings of which begin with a consonant.

Inflexion.

337. The forms occurring are:

Sing. N. m. *stúp*; *tri-kakúp*. — **f.** *anu-ṣṭúp* (VS. AV.), *anu-ṣṭúk* (TS. v. 2. 11[1]), *tri-ṣṭúp*; *kakúp* (VS. AV.).

A. m. *rathe-śúbham*, *sute-gṛ́bham*. — **f.** *gṛ́bham*, *śúbham*; *ṛta-stúbham*, *anu-ṣṭúbham*, *tri-ṣṭúbham*; *kakúbham*.

I. m. *stubhā́*; *su-ṣṭúbhā*. — **f.** *kṣubhā́*, *gṛbhā́*, *śubhā́*; *anu-ṣṭúbhā*, *tri-ṣṭúbhā* (VS. XVII. 34; TS. II. 2. 4[8]); *kakúbhā* (VS. XXVIII. 44).

D. m. *gharma-stúbhe*, *syūma-gṛ́bhe*. — **f.** *śúbhe* (AV. VS. XXX. 7); *anu-ṣṭúbhe* (VS. XXIV. 12), *tri-ṣṭúbhe* (VS. XXIV. 12); *kakúbhe* (VS. XXIV. 13).

Ab. m. *jīva-gṛ́bhas*. — **f.** *gṛbhás* (VS. XXI. 43); *anu-ṣṭúbhas* (VS. XIII. 54), *tri-ṣṭúbhas* (AV.).

G. m. *su-ṣṭúbhas*. — **f.** *śubhás*[1] (in *śubhás pátī*, du. N. A. and *śubhas patī*, V.).

L. f. *tri-ṣṭúbhi* (VS. XXXVIII. 18); *kakúbhi* (TS. III. 3. 9[2]; VS. XV. 4).

Pl. N. m. *chandaḥ-stúbhas*, *vṛṣa-stúbhas*, *pari-ṣṭúbhas*, *su-ṣṭúbhas*. — **f.** *nā́bhas*[2], *śúbhas*, *stúbhas*.

A. f. *nábhas*, *stúbhas*; *tri-ṣṭúbhas*, *pari-ṣṭúbhas*; *kakúbhas*.

G. f. *kakúbhām*.

c. Stems in *-m*.

338. There are only about half a dozen stems in *-m* which among them muster a few more than a dozen forms. All are monosyllables except a compound of *nam-* 'bend'. Neuters are *śám-* 'happiness' and perhaps *dám-* 'house'. A possible m. is *hím-* 'cold'; and there are four feminines: *kṣám-*, *gám-*, and *jám-*, all meaning 'earth', and *saṃ-nám-* (AV.) 'favour'. Strong and weak forms are distinguished in *kṣám-*, which lengthens the vowel in the strong cases, and syncopates it in one of the two weak cases occurring; *gám-* and *jám-* are found in weak cases only, where they syncopate the vowel. The forms occurring are the following:

Sing. N. A. n. *śám*. — **I. f.** *kṣamā́*, *jmā́*; **m.** *him-ā́*[3]. — **Ab. f.** *kṣmás*, *gmás*, *jmás*. — **G. f.** *gmás*, *jmás*[4]; **n.** *dán*[5]. — **L. f.** *kṣámi*[6]. — **Du. N. f.** *kṣā́mā*, *dyā́vā-kṣā́mā* 'heaven and earth'. — **Pl. N. f.** *kṣā́mas*; *saṃ-námas* (AV.). — **G. n.** *damā́m*.

---

1 The form *dábhas* in V. 19[4] is regarded by BR. and GRASSMANN as N. sing. m. 'destroyer'. LANMAN 485 thinks it may be a G. sing. f. with wrong accent.

2 Strong form.

3 This is the only form, occurring twice, from a possible stem *him-*, beside *hiména*, from *himá-*. It might, however, be an I. from the latter stem. Cp. 372.

4 Cp. BRUGMANN, Grundriss 2, 580.

5 For **dám-s* (like *á-gan* for **á-gam-s*) occurring only in the expressions *pátir dán* and *pátī dán* and equivalent to *dám-patiḥ* and *dám-patī* at the end of a triṣṭubh line. Cp. BRUGMANN, Grundriss 2, 453.

6 With irregular accent; cp. above 94 a.

5. Stems in Sibilants.

1. a. Stems in radical *s* and *ṣ*.

339. In radical stems ending in *s* and *ṣ*, the sibilants are identical in origin, both being alike etymologically based on the dental *s*, which remains after *ă*, but is cerebralized after other vowels and after *k*. In the RV. there are of radical *s*-stems some 40 derived from about 15 roots; of radical *ṣ*-stems, some 50 derived from about 15 roots; in both groups taken together there are nearly 20 monosyllabic stems, the rest being compounds. Masculine and feminine stems are about equally numerous; but there are altogether only 7 or 8 neuters.

a. The distinction between strong and weak forms appears in three words: *púmāṃs* and *puṃs-* 'male'; *nā́s-* and *nas-* 'nose'; *uktha-śā́s-* and *uktha-śás-* 'uttering verses'. The A. pl. has the accentuation of weak stems in the masculines *jñās-ás*, *puṃs-ás*, *mās-ás* and in the feminines *iṣ-ás*, *uṣ-ás*, *dviṣ-ás*.

b. The stem *ā́s-* 'face' is supplemented in its inflexion by the *an-* stem *ās-án-*; the stem *íṣ-* is supplemented before consonant endings by *iḍā́-*[1]; and *dós-* 'fore-arm' is supplemented by *doṣ-án-* in the dual form *doṣáṇī* (AV. IX. 7[7]).

c. Transitions to the *a-* or *ā*-declension appear in forms made from *ā́s-* 'face', *iṣ-* 'refreshment', *kā́s-* 'cough', *nā́s-* 'nose', *mā́s-* 'month', *ā-śás-* 'hope', *ni-míṣ-* 'winking'. 1. From *ā́s-*, beside and probably through the influence of the I. sing. *ās-ā́*, is formed the adv. *āsayā́* 'before the face of' (as from a stem *āsá-*, and with adverbial shift of accent instead of **āsáyā*). — 2. Forms like G. *iṣ-ás* gave rise to *iṣá-m*; and the supplementary stem *iḍā́-* probably started from the I. sing. *iḍ-ā́*, which itself was probably due to *iḍ-* the form assumed by *íṣ-* before *bh-* endings; the stem *íṣ-* further shows a transition to the *i-* declension in the D. *iṣáye*. — 3. From *kā́s-* 'cough' there is the transition V. *kāse* (AV.). — 4. The strong dual form *nā́s-ā* furnished a transition to an *ā-* stem, from which is formed the dual *nā́se* (AV.). — 5. As *pā́d-am* gave rise to a new N. *pā́da-s*, so from *mā́s-am* arose the new stem *mā́sa-*, from which are formed the N. sing. *mā́sa-s* and the A. pl. *mā́sān*. — 6. In the RV. the stem *ā-śás-* alone is used; but in the AV. appears the A. *āśā́m* (perhaps a contraction for *ā-śásam*) which, understood as *āśā́-m*, was probably the starting point of the *āśā́-*, the only stem in the later language. — 7. From *ni-míṣ-* 'winking' there appear, beside the regular compound forms A. *á-nimiṣ-am*, I. *á-nimiṣ-ā* f. 'non-winking', the transition forms N. *a-nimiṣá-s*, A. *a-nimiṣá-m*, I. *a-nimiṣéṇa*, N. pl. *a-nimiṣā́s*, adj. 'unwinking', with the regular Bahuvrīhi accent (90 B c).

Inflexion.

340. In the N. sing. the sibilant is of course dropped if preceded by a consonant, as *an-ák* 'eyeless', *púmān* 'man'. Otherwise *s* remains, while *ṣ* becomes *ṭ*[2]. Before *bh-* endings, *s* becomes *d* in two forms which occur (*mād-bhís*, *mād-bhyás*)[3] and *r* in the only other one (*dor-bhyā́m*); while *ṣ* becomes *ḍ* in the only example occurring (*vi-prúḍ-bhis*).

The forms actually occurring, if made from *mā́s-*[4] m. 'month' as an *s-* stem, and from *dvíṣ-* f. 'hatred' as a *ṣ*-stem, would be as follows:

Sing. N.[5] *mā́s*; *dvíṭ*. A. *mā́sam*; *dvíṣam*. I. *māsā́*; *dviṣā́*. D. *māsé*; *dviṣé*. Ab. *māsás*; *dviṣás*. G. *māsás*; *dviṣás*. L. *māsí*; *dviṣí*. — **Du.** N. A. *mā́sā*; *dvíṣā*. G. *māsós*. L. *māsós* (AV. TS.). — **Pl.** N. *mā́sas*; *dvíṣas*. A. *māsás*; *dvíṣas* and *dviṣás*. I. *mādbhís*; *dviḍbhís*. D. *mādbhyás* (AV.). Ab. *mādbhyás* (AV.). G. *māsā́m*; *dviṣā́m*. L. *māssú* (AV.).

The forms actually occurring are:

---

1 As *kṣáp-* and *kṣíp-* by *kṣapā́-* and *kṣipā́-* respectively.

2 It becomes *k* only in the n. form *dadhṛ́k* 'boldly', used as an adv. from *dadhṛ́ṣ-*, if the word is derived from *dhṛṣ-* 'be bold'; but the word is perhaps more probably derived from *dṛh-* 'be firm', see BR. s. v. *dadhṛ́k*, and cp. BARTHOLOMAE, IF. 12, Anzeiger p. 28.

3 Cp. J. SCHMIDT, KZ. 26, 340.

4 In this word (derived from *mā-* 'measure') the *s* is really secondary, probably representing the suffix *-as* (*mā́s-* = *mā-as-*); cp. BRUGMANN, Grundriss 2, p. 398.

5 The only V. occurring is *pumas*.

Sing. N. 1. m. *púmān*[1] 'male'; *candrá-mās* 'moon', *dūré-bhās*[2] 'shining to a distance', *su-dā́s*[3] 'worshipping well'. — **f.** *á-jñās* 'having no kindred', *ā-śī́s*[4] 'prayer'. — **n.** *bhā́s* 'light', *mā́s* 'flesh'; *dós* 'arm', *yós* 'welfare', *śaṃ-yós* 'luck and welfare'. — **2. m.** *an-ák*[5] 'blind', *edhamāna-dvíṭ*[6] 'hating the insolent'. — **f.** *vi-prúṭ* (AV.) 'drop'.

A. 1. m. *mā́saṃ* 'month', *púmāṃsam*; *a-yā́sam* 'dexterous', *uktha-śā́sam*[7] 'uttering verses', *su-dā́sam*, *su-bhā́sam* 'shining beautifully', *sv-āśíṣam*[4] 'well-praising', *sv-ā́sam* 'fair-mouthed'. — **f.** *kā́sam*[8] (AV.) 'cough'; *ā-śíṣam*[4], *pra-śíṣam*[4] 'precept'[9]. — **2. m.** *ghṛta-prúṣam* 'sprinkling ghee', *jara-dvíṣam* 'hating decrepitude', *brahma-dvíṣam* 'hating sacred knowledge', *viśvā-púṣam* 'all-nourishing'. — **f.** *íṣam* 'refreshment', *dvíṣam* 'hatred', *pṛ́kṣam* 'satiation'; *á-nimiṣam* 'non-winking', *doṣaṇi-śríṣam* (AV.) 'leaning on the arm', *hṛdaya-śríṣam* (AV.) 'clinging to the heart'. Also the adverbial A. *ā-vy-uṣám* (AV.) 'till the dawn'. — **n.** *dadhṛ́k* 'boldly' as adv.

I. 1. m. *māsā́*. — **f.** *kāsā́* (AV.), *nasā́* (AV.) 'nose', *śāsā́* 'ruler'[10]; *abhi-śā́sā*[11] 'blame', *ava-śā́sā* (AV.) 'wrong desire', *ā-śā́sā* 'hope', *ā-śíṣā*, *niḥ-śā́sā* 'blame', *parā-śā́sā* (AV.) 'calumny', *pra-śíṣā* (AV. VS.). — **n.** *āsā́* 'mouth', *bhāsā́*. — **2. m.** *viśva-púṣā*[12]. — **f.** *iṣā́*, *tviṣā́* 'excitement'; *á-nimiṣā*, *prā-vṛ́ṣā* (AV. TS.) 'rainy season', *preṣā́*[13] 'pressure'. — **n.** *ghṛta-prúṣā*.

D. 1. m. *puṃsé* (AV.); *su-dā́se*. — **n.** *bhāsé* (VS. XIII. 39). — **2. m.** *á-prā-yuṣe*[14] 'not careless'; *á-vi-dviṣe* (AV.) 'for non-enmity', *ṛṣi-dvíṣe* 'hating the seers', *brahma-dvíṣe*; *gav-íṣe* 'wishing for cows', *paśv-íṣe* 'wishing for cattle'; *sākam-úkṣe*[15] 'sprinkling together'. — **f.** *iṣé*[16], *tviṣé*, *pṛkṣé*, *riṣé* 'injury', *préṣe* (VS. V. 7).

Ab. 1. m. *puṃsás*. — **f.** *kāsás* (AV.) — **n.** *āsás*. — **2. f.** *iṣás*, *tviṣás*, *dviṣás*, *riṣás*; *abhi-śríṣas* 'ligature', *ni-míṣas* 'winking'.

G. 1. m. *puṃsás*; *a-śā́sas* 'not blessing', *su-dā́sas*, *sv-ā́sas*. — **f.** *ā-śíṣas* (TS. IV. 6. 6[3]). — **2. m.** *śṛ́ṅga-vṛṣas*[17] a man's name. — **f.** *iṣás*, *uṣás* 'dawn', *dviṣás*, *pṛkṣás*; *abhra-prúṣas* 'sprinkling of the clouds', *ni-míṣas*.

L. 1. m. *puṃsí*, *māsí*. — **f.** *upási* 'in the lap', *nasí* (VS.); *ā-śíṣi* (AV.), *pra-śíṣi* (AV.). — **2. f.** *ni-míṣi*, *prā-vṛ́ṣi*, *vy-úṣi* 'dawn'.

V. m. *pumas*[18].

Du. N. A. 1. m. *uktha-śā́sā*[19], *sū́rya-māsā*[20] 'sun and moon'. — **f.** *nā́sā*[21]. — **I. 1. n.** *dorbhyā́m* (VS. XXV. 3). — **G. 1. f.** *nasós*. — **L. 1. f.** *nasós* (AV. TS.).

Pl. N. 1. m. *a-yā́sas*, V. *ayāsas*, *uktha-śā́sas*[19], *su-saṃśāsas*[22] (AV.) 'well-directing'. — **f.** *ā-śā́sas*; *ā-śíṣas*, *pra-śíṣas*, *vi-śíṣas* (AV.) 'explanations',

---

1 On the Sandhi of this N. see LANMAN 495[1].

2 See LANMAN 495[1].

3 There are also the transition forms *mā́sa-s* and *a-nimiṣá-s*.

4 The root in *ā-śíṣ-* and *pra-śíṣ-*, being a reduced form of *śās-* 'order', is here treated as belonging to the *s*-class.

5 From *an-ákṣ-* 'eyeless'.

6 The N. of *íṣ-* would be **iṭ*: its place is supplied by the extended form *iḍā́*.

7 Strong stem from *śas-* = *śaṃs-* 'proclaim'.

8 Accented *kāsám* (AV. V. 22[11]).

9 Also the transition forms *a-nimiṣám* and *āśā́m* (AV.).

10 Cp. LANMAN 495 (bottom).

11 From *śas-* = *śaṃs-* 'proclaim'.

12 There is also the transition form *a-nimiṣéṇa*.

13 Accented thus as a monosyllabic stem instead of *préṣā* (= *pra-iṣ-ā*).

14 From *pra*+*yu-* 'separate' with *s* as root determinative.

15 Perhaps also *áram-iṣe* (VIII. 46[17]) 'hastening near', Pada *áram iṣe*; cp. LANMAN 496[1].

16 Also the transfer to the *i*-declension *iṣáye*.

17 In a compound vocative with *napāt*.

18 In the f. are found the transfers to the *ā*-declension *iḍe* and *kāse* (AV.).

19 Strong forms; Pp. *uktha-śā́sā*, *-śā́sas*.

20 This might be from the transition stem *-mā́sa-*.

21 There is also the transition form *nā́se* (AV.).

22 There are also the transition forms *mā́sās*, *a-nimiṣā́s*.

saṃ-śíṣas (AV.) 'directions'; *vi-srásas*[1] (AV.) 'falling apart', *su-srásas* (AV.) 'falling off easily', *svayaṃ-srásas* (AV.) 'dropping spontaneously'. — **2. m.** *mákṣas* 'flies', *mū́ṣas* 'mice'; *anṛta-dvíṣas* 'persecuting untruth', V. *a-saca-dviṣas* 'hating non-worshippers', *gav-íṣas, ghṛta-prúṣas, pari-prúṣas* 'sprinkling', *bṛhad-úkṣas* 'shedding copiously', *brahma-dvíṣas, yajña-múṣas* (TS. III. 5. 4[1]) 'sacrifice stealer', *vā́ta-tviṣas* 'having the impetuosity of the wind'. — **f.** *íṣas, tvíṣas, pŕkṣas*; *án-ā-dhṛṣas* (AV.) 'not checking', *ghṛta-prúṣas, ni-míṣas* (AV.), *nemann-íṣas*[2] 'following guidance', *pati-dvíṣas* 'hating her husband', *vy-úṣas* (AV.), *sam-íṣas* 'darts', *sākam-úkṣas, su-pŕkṣas* 'abounding with food'.

A. 1. m. *jñāsás* 'relatives', *puṃsás, māsás*[3]; *an-ā́sas* 'faceless', *án-ūrdhva-bhāsas* 'whose splendour does not rise', *a-yā́sas, a-śā́sas, hṛtsv-ásas* 'throwing into the heart'. — **f.** *ā-śā́sas*; *ā-śíṣas, pra-śíṣas*. — **2. m.** *brahma-dvíṣas*. — **f.** *íṣas* and *iṣás*[4], *uṣás, dvíṣas* and *dviṣás*[5], *pŕkṣas*; *camríṣas*[6], *vi-prúṣas* (AV.).

I. 1. m. *mādbhís*. — **2. f.** *vi-prúḍbhis*[7] (VS.). — **D. 1. m.** *mādbhyás* (AV.). — **Ab. 1. m.** *mādbhyás* (AV.). — **G. 1. m.** *puṃsā́m* (AV.), *māsā́m, vasā́m*[8] 'abodes'; *a-yā́sām*. — **2. f.** *iṣā́m, dviṣā́m*. — **L. 1. m.** *puṃsú*[9] (AV.).

1. b. Stems in derivative *-s*.

a. Stems in *-is* and *-us*.

341. The stems formed with the suffixes *-is* and *-us* may best be treated together, as their inflexion is identical. The *-is* stems, numbering about a dozen, consist primarily of neuters only[10]; these when they are final members of compounds are secondarily inflected as masculines also, but only in a single form (N. sing. *svá-śocis* 'self-radiant') as feminine. The *-us* stems, numbering sixteen (exclusive of compounds) in the RV., include primary masculines (two also as f.) as well as neuters; three of the latter as final members of compounds are also inflected as feminine. Eleven of the *-us* stems are neuter substantives, all but one accented on the radical syllable; four of these are also used as m. adjectives[11] accented in the same way (*árus-, cákṣus-, tápus-, vápus-*). Three of those *-us* stems which are exclusively m. are adjectives accented on the suffix, while two are substantives accented on the root (*náh-us-, mán-us-*)[12].

a. The **N. A. pl. n.** are distinguished as strong forms by lengthening and nasalizing the vowel of the suffix (as in the *-as* stems), e. g. *jyótīṃṣi* and *cákṣūṃṣi*.

b. Among these stems appear a number of transitions to, and a few from, other declensions. 1. The N. sing. n., as in *śoc-is* and *cákṣ-us*, having in some passages the appearance of a N. sing. m. *śoci-s* and *cákṣu-s*, led to formations according to the *i-* and *u-*declension. Such are N. pl. *śocáyas* (AV.) 'flames', V. sing. *pāvaka-śoce* 'shining brightly', *bhadra-śoce* 'shining beautifully', *śukra-śoce* 'shining brilliantly'; N. pl. *arcáyas* 'beams', I. pl. *arci-bhis*. The form of *krav-ís-* 'raw flesh' in the compound *á-kravi-hasta-* 'not having bloody hands' is probably due to the same cause. From *cákṣ-us-* 'eye' is once formed the Ab. *cákṣo-s* and the V. *sahasra-cakṣo* (AV.) 'thousand-eyed'. From *táp-us-* 'hot' is once

---

1 The Mss. read *vi-srasas*; see WHITNEY'S note on AV. XIX. 34³.

2 *neman-* is here probably a locative.

3 There is also the transition form *mā́sān*.

4 *íṣas* occurs 63 times, *iṣás* 7 times in the RV.

5 *dvíṣas* occurs 39 times, *dviṣás* 4 times in the RV.

6 The meaning of this word is perhaps 'libations in ladles'.

7 There is also the transition form *iḍā́bhis* as an I. pl. of *íṣ-*.

8 This word, occurring in this form only, might be a f.

9 *mā́ssu-* occurs Pañc. Br. IV. 4. 1 and *māsú* (like *puṃsú* for *puṃs-sú*) TS. VII. 5. 2². The f. transition form *iḍā́su* occurs as the L. pl. of *íṣ-*.

10 There seems no reason why *ā́m-is-* occurring in L. s. only, should exceptionally be regarded as m. (BR., LANMAN, GRASSMANN).

11 One of these, *tápus-* 'hot', has a single f. form, A. du. *tápuṣā*.

12 See above p. 84, 19.

formed the G. *táṭo-s*; from *van-ús-* 'desiring', as if *vanú-s* in N., the A. sing. *vanú-m* and pl. *vanū́n*; from *ā́y-us-* 'life' occurs not only the L. sing. *ā́yu-n-i*, but several compound forms, V. *dīrghāyo* 'long-lived', *adabdhāyo* (VS.) 'having unimpaired vigour', A. *vṛddhā́yu-m* 'full of vigour', n. *viśvā́yu* 'all-quickening', A. m. *viśvā́yu-m*, D. *viśvā́yave*, G. *viśvā́yo-s*[1]. — 2. There are also some transition forms from three masculines in *-us*, by extension of the stem, to the *a-* declension: from *náh-us-* 'neighbour', starting perhaps from the G. *náhuṣ-as* taken as a N. sing. *náhuṣa-s*, are made the G. *náhuṣa-sya* and the L. *náhuṣe*; from *mán-us-* 'man', starting from the N. pl. *mánuṣ-as* taken as a N. sing. *mánuṣa-s*, come the D. *mánuṣāya* and the G. *mánuṣa-sya*; from *váp-us-* 'beauty', once D. *vápuṣāya* beside the frequent *vápuṣ-e*. — 3. On the other hand, there are a few transitions from the declension of *i-* and *u-* stems to that of stems in *-is* and *-us*. Beside *su-rabhí-* 'fragrant', the superlative form *su-rabhiṣ-ṭamam*[2] occurs once; and beside numerous compounds formed with *tuvi-* appear the stems *túviṣ-mant-* 'powerful' and *tuviṣ-ṭama-* 'strongest'[3]. Beside the G. *dhákṣo-s* and *dákṣo-s*[4] 'burning', there appears once the form *dakṣúṣ-as*[5], which is doubtless due to the false analogy of forms like *tasthúṣas*. Though *mán-us-* 'man' may be an independent formation beside *mán-u-*, the probability is rather in favour of regarding it as secondary (starting from a N. *mánu-s*), because *mánu-* shows eight case-forms, but *mánus-* only three[6]. The stem *á-prāyus-*, occurring only once beside the less rare *á-prāyu-*, probably represents a transition from the latter stem.

Inflexion.

342. The final *s* becomes *ṣ* before vowel endings, and *r* before *-bh*. The inflexion of the n. is the same as that of the m. except in the A. sing., N. A. du. and pl. The only f. forms occurring are in the N. or A. They are the following: N. sing. *svá-śocis* 'self-radiant'; *cákṣus* 'seeing', *á-ghora-cakṣus* 'not having an evil eye', *hradé-cakṣus* 'reflected in a lake'; *citrā́yus* 'possessed of wonderful vitality'; A. du. *tápuṣā* 'hot'; A. pl. *gó-vapuṣas* 'having the form of cows'.

The actual forms occurring, if made from *śocís-* 'glow' in the n., and from *-śocis-* in the m. (when it differs from the n.), and from *cákṣus-* 'eye' as n. and 'seeing' as m., would be as follows:

1. **Sing.** N. *śocís*. A. *śocís*; m. *-śociṣam*. I. *śocíṣā*. D. *śocíṣe*. Ab. *śocíṣas*. G. *śocíṣas*. L. *śocíṣi*. V. *śocis*. — **Pl.** N. A. *śocī́ṃṣi*; m. *-śociṣas*. I. *śocírbhis*. D. m. *-śocírbhyas*. G. *śocíṣām*. L. *śocíṣṣu*.

2. **Sing.** N. *cákṣus*. A. *cákṣus*; m. *cákṣuṣam*. I. *cákṣuṣā*. D. *cákṣuṣe*. Ab. G. *cákṣuṣas*. L. *cákṣuṣi*. — **Du.** N. A. *cákṣuṣī*; m. *cákṣuṣā*. D. *cákṣurbhyām* (VS.). — **Pl.** N. A. *cákṣūṃṣi*; m. *cákṣuṣas*. I. *cákṣurbhis*. D. *cákṣurbhyas* (VS.). G. *cákṣuṣām*.

The forms which actually occur are the following:

Sing. N. m. 1. *á-havis* 'not offering oblations', *kṛṣṇá-vyathis* 'whose path is black'; *citrá-jyotis* (VS. XVII. 80) 'shining brilliantly', *śukrá-jyotis* (VS. XII. 15) 'brightly shining', *satyá-jyotis* (VS. XVII. 80) 'truly brilliant', *su-jyótis* (VS. XXXVII. 21) 'shining well'; *citrá-śocis* 'shining brilliantly', *duróka-śocis* 'glowing unpleasantly', *śukrá-śocis* 'bright-rayed'; *jīvá-barhis* (AV.) 'having a fresh litter', *su-barhís* (VS. XXI. 15) 'having a goodly litter', *stīrṇá-barhis* 'who has strewn the litter'; *svá-rocis* 'self-shining'; *sv-arcís*[7] 'flashing beautifully'. — 2. *cákṣus* 'seeing', *vápus*[8] 'beautyful', *vidús* 'attentive'[9]; *á-dabdha-cakṣus* (AV.) 'having undamaged sight', *kṣitā́yus* 'whose life goes to an end', *dīrghā́yus* 'long-lived', *duḥ-śā́sus* 'malignant', *ví-parus* (AV.) 'jointless', *viśvátaś-cakṣus* 'having eyes on all sides', *sárva-parus* (AV.) 'having all joints', *sahásrāyus* (AV.) 'living a thousand years'.

---

[1] There is probably insufficient reason to assume a primary independently formed stem *-ā́y-u-* beside *ā́y-us-*; cp. LANMAN 569 (bottom).

[2] Retaining the *s* of the N. like *indras-vant-*.

[3] *tuv-is-* as an independent formation would be irregular, since the radical vowel otherwise shows Guṇa before the suffix *-is* (134).

[4] Desiderative adj. from *dah-* 'burn'.

[5] The Pada text has *dhakṣúṣas*.

[6] Cp. LANMAN 570 (bottom).

[7] There are also the transition forms *arcí-s* and *śocí-s*, the neuters becoming masculines of the *i-* declension.

[8] Also the transition forms *cákṣu-s*, *tapú-s*.

[9] This may be an *u*-stem: *vidú-s*.

N. A. n. 1. *arcís* 'flame', *kravís* (AV.) 'raw flesh', *chadís* 'cover', *chardís* 'fence', *jyótis* 'light', *barhís* 'litter', *vartís* 'circuit', *vyáthis* 'course', *śocís* 'lustre', *sarpís* 'clarified butter', *havís* 'oblation'; *vaiśvānará-jyotis* (VS. xx. 23) 'light of Vaiśvānara', *śukrá-jyotis* (TS. iv. 1. 9³), *svàr-jyotis* (VS. v. 32) 'light of heaven'. — **2.** *árus* (AV.) 'wound', *áyus* 'life', *cákṣus* 'eye', *tápus* 'glow', *dhánus* 'bow', *párus* 'joint', *yájus* 'worship', *vápus* 'beauty', *śásus* 'command'; *indra-dhanús* (AV.) 'Indra's bow', *sv-āyús*[1] (VS. iv. 28) 'full vigour'.

A. m. 1. *á-gṛbhīta-śociṣam* 'having unsubdued splendour', *ajirá-śociṣam* 'having a quick light', *ūrdhvá-śociṣam* 'flaming upwards', *citrá-śocisam*, *dīrghāyu-śociṣam* 'shining through a long life', *pāvaká-śociṣam* 'shining brightly', *śīrá-śociṣam* 'sharp-rayed', *śukrá-śociṣam*, *śréṣṭha-śociṣam* 'most brilliant'; *citrá-barhiṣam* 'having a brilliant bed', *vṛktá-barhiṣam* 'having the litter spread', *su-barhíṣam*, *stīrṇá-barhiṣam* (VS. xiv. 49); *dákṣiṇā-jyotiṣam* (AV.) 'brilliant by the sacrificed gift', *hiraṇya-jyotiṣam* (AV.) 'having golden splendour'. — **2.** *janúṣam* 'birth', *dīrghāyuṣam*, *pūrv-āyúṣam* 'bestowing much vitality', *śatáyuṣam*[2] 'attaining the age of a hundred'.

I. 1. n. *arcíṣā*, *kravíṣā*, *chardíṣā* (VS. xiii. 19), *jyótiṣā*, *barhíṣā* (VS. xviii. 63; TS.), *rocíṣā* 'brightness', *śocíṣā*, *sarpíṣā*, *havíṣā*. — **m.** *manthí-śociṣā* (VS. vii. 18) 'shining like mixed Soma', *śukrá-jyotiṣā* (VS.). — **2. n.** *áyuṣā*, *cákṣuṣā*, *janúṣā*, *tápuṣā*, *dhánuṣā* (Kh. iii. 9), *páruṣā*, *yájuṣā*, *śatáyuṣā*, *samiṣṭa-yajúṣā* (VS. xix. 29) 'sacrifice and formula', *sv-āyúṣā* (VS. iv. 28) 'full vigour of life'. — **m.** *tápuṣā*, *náhuṣā* 'neighbour', *mánuṣā* 'man', *vanúṣā* 'eager'.

D. 1. n. *arcíṣe* (TS. VS. xvii. 11), *jyótiṣe* (VS. AV.), *barhíṣe* (VS. ii. 1), *śocíṣe*, *havíṣe*. — **m.** *tigmá-śociṣe* 'sharp-rayed', *pāvaká-śociṣe*, *śukrá-śociṣe*, *vṛktá-barhiṣe*, *stīrṇá-barhiṣe*, *rātá-haviṣe* 'liberal offerer', *su-háviṣe* 'offering fair oblations'. — **2. n.** *áyuṣe* (VS. AV.), *cákṣuṣe*, *janúṣe*, *tápuṣe* (AV.), *yájuṣe* (VS. i. 30), *vápuṣe*. — **m.** *cákṣuṣe*, *mánuṣe*, *vanúṣe*[3].

Ab. 1. n. *jyótiṣas* (AV.), *barhíṣas*, *havíṣas*. — **2. n.** *áyuṣas* (TS. iv. 1. 4³), *cákṣuṣas* (TS. v. 7. 7¹), *janúṣas*, *páruṣas* (TS. iv. 2. 9²), *vápuṣas*. — **m.** *náhuṣas*, *mánuṣas*, *vápuṣas*.

G. 1. n. *kravíṣas*, *chardíṣas*, *jyótiṣas*, *barhíṣas*, *śocíṣas*, *sarpíṣas*, *havíṣas*. — **m.** *pāvaká-śociṣas*, *vṛddhá-śociṣas* 'blazing mightily', *vásu-rociṣas* 'shining brightly', *vṛktá-barhiṣas*[4]. — **2. n.** *áyuṣas*, *cákṣuṣas*, *tápuṣas*, *táruṣas* 'superiority', *páruṣas*, *vápuṣas*. — **m.** *cákṣuṣas*, *náhuṣas*, *mánuṣas*, *vanúṣas*[5]; *iṣṭá-yajuṣas* (VS. viii. 12) 'having offered the sacrificial verses'.

L. 1. n. *arcíṣi*, *āmíṣi*[6] 'raw flesh', *jyótiṣi*, *barhíṣi*, *sádhiṣi* (VS. xiii. 53) 'resting-place', *havíṣi*; *tri-barhíṣi* 'with threefold litter'. — **2. n.** *áyuṣi*[7], *táruṣi*, *páruṣi*, *vápuṣi*.

V. 1. n. *barhis*[8]; *deva-havis* 'oblation to the gods' (VS. vi. 8). — **2. m.** *ékāyus*[9] 'first of living beings'.

Du. N. A. 2. n. *cákṣuṣī* (AV., Kh. iv. 11¹¹), *janúṣī*. — **m.** *cákṣuṣā*, *jayúṣā* 'victorious'. — **D. 2. n.** *cákṣurbhyām* (VS. vii. 27).

---

1 Also the transition form *viśvāyu* 'all-quickening'.

2 Also the transition forms *vanú-m*, *vṛddhāyu-m*, *viśvāyu-m*.

3 Transition forms: *viśvāyave*; *mánuṣāya*, *vápuṣāya*; *á-prāyuṣe* 'not careless'.

4 Also perhaps a transition form *śocé-s*; cp. LANMAN 568.

5 Also the transition forms *tápos*, *viśvāyos*; *náhuṣasya*; *mánuṣasya*; *dhakṣúṣas* (341 b, p. 222).

6 Accounted a m. by BR., GRASSMANN, LANMAN.

7 Also the transition form *áyuni*; and m. *náhuṣe*.

8 Also the transition forms *pāvaka-śoce*, *bhadra-śoce*, *śukra-śoce*.

9 Also the transition forms *adabdhāyo* (VS.), *dīrghāyo*, *sahasra-cakṣo* (AV.).

Pl. N. m. 1. *ágṛbhīta-śociṣas*, *ajirá-śociṣas*, *vā́ta-dhrājiṣas* (Kh. I. 3[3]) 'having the impulse of wind', *vṛktá-barhiṣas*, V. *vṛkta-barhiṣas*, *sádma-barhiṣas* 'preparing the litter', V. *su-barhiṣas*, *su-jyótiṣas* and *su-jyotíṣas*, *svá-rociṣas*[1]. — **2.** *náhuṣas*, *mánuṣas*, V. *manuṣas*, *vanúṣas*, *vápuṣas*.

N. A. n. 1. *arcī́ṃṣi*, *jyótīṃṣi*, *barhī́ṃṣi* (VS. XXVIII. 21), *śocī́ṃṣi*, *havī́ṃṣi*. — **2.** *ā́yūṃṣi*, *cákṣūṃṣi*, *janū́ṃṣi*, *tápūṃṣi*, *párūṃṣi* (TS. VS. AV.), *yájūṃṣi* (VS. AV.), *vápūṃṣi*.

A. m. 1. *su-jyótiṣas*. — **2.** *náhuṣas*, *mánuṣas*, *vanúṣas*[2].

I. 1. n. *havírbhis*[3]. — **2. n.** *dhánurbhis* (AV.), *yájurbhis* (VS. IV. 1), *vápurbhis*. — **D. 1. m.** *ūrdhvá-barhirbhyas* (VS. XXXVIII. 15) 'being above the litter'. — **2. n.** *yájurbhyas* (VS. XXXVIII. 11).

G. 1. n. *jyótiṣām*, *havíṣām* (AV.). — **2. n.** *cákṣuṣām* (AV.), *janúṣām*, *yájuṣām* (AV.), *vápuṣām*. — **m.** *vanúṣām*, *viśvá-manuṣām* 'belonging to all men'.

L. 1. n. *havíṣṣu*.

β. Stems in *-as*.

343. Primarily this declension consists almost entirely of neuters, which are accented on the root, as *mán-as-* 'mind'; but these as final members of adjective compounds may be inflected in all three genders, as N. m. f. *su-mánās*, n. *su-mánas* 'well-disposed'. There are besides a few primary masculines, which are accented on the suffix, being either substantives, as *rakṣ-ás-* 'demon', or adjectives, some of which occur in the f. also (as well as n.), as *ap-ás-* 'active'; and one feminine, *uṣ-ás-* 'dawn'[4].

a. **Strong cases** are regularly distinguished only in the N. A. pl. n., where the vowel of the suffix is lengthened and nasalized[5] (as in the *-is* and *-us* stems), as *aṃhāṃsi* 'troubles'. Otherwise the stem *uṣás-* shows in the A. sing., N. A. du., N. V. pl., strong forms with lengthened vowel in the suffix, which occur beside the unlengthened forms[6], the latter being nearly three times as frequent in the RV. The long vowel is here required by the metre in 20 out of 28 occurrences, and is favoured by the metre in the rest[7]; so that the lengthening may be due to metrical exigencies. The strong form *uṣā́sas*[8] occurs once (X. 39[1]) for the weak *uṣásas* as the G. sing. or A. pl. There is further the single strong form N. du. m. *tośā́sā*[9] 'bestowing abundantly'[10].

b. **Supplementary** stems ending in *-as* beside *-an* are *ṛ́bhvas-* 'skilful' (as well as *ṛ́bhva-*) beside *ṛ́bhvan-*, and *śíkvas-* 'strong' (as well as *śíkva-*) beside *śíkvan-*.

c. There is here a large number of transition forms both to and from the *ā*-declension. Many pairs of stems in *-a* and *-as* are common in both forms and seem therefore to be of independent derivation. But there are also a good many such doublets of which the one is the normal stem, while the other has come into being through mistaken analogy or metrical exigency. 1. In the transitions to the *a*- declension several may be explained as starting from the misleading analogy of contracted forms. To this group belong the following: from *áṅgiras-*, a name of Agni, L. sing. *áṅgire* beside N. pl. *áṅgirās*; from *án-āgas-* 'sinless', A. pl. *án-āgān* beside A. sing. *án-āgām* and N. pl. *án-āgās*; from *ap-sarás-* 'water-nymph', *apsarā́bhyas* (AV.), *apsarā́su* (AV.), *apsarā-patíś* (AV.) beside *apsarā́m* (AV.); from *uṣás-* 'dawn', N. du. *uṣé* (VS.), *uṣā́bhyām* (VS.), beside A. sing. *uṣā́m* and pl. *uṣā́s*; from *jarás-* m. 'old age', f. sing. N. *jarā́* (AV. VS.), D. *jarā́yai* (AV.), beside

---

1 Also the transition forms *arcáyas*, *śocáyas*.

2 Also the transition form *vanún*.

3 Also the transition form *arci-bhis*.

4 The derivation of a few stems ending in *-as* is obscure; as *upás-* 'lap' (only L. sing.), and *riśā́das-* 'destroying enemies'.

5 On the origin of this form as a combination of *-ān-i* and *-ās-i* see Johansson, BB. 18, 3 and cp. GGA. 1890, p. 762.

6 The lengthened vowel never occurs in the Pada text in these forms (excepting of course the N. *uṣā́s*).

7 See Arnold, Vedic Metre, p. 130, 11 (a); cp. Lanman 546.

8 The Pada text has *uṣáṣaḥ*.

9 Here the long vowel appears in the Pada text also. This is the only form made from the stem *tośás-* (from *tuś-* 'drip').

10 The form *sa-psarā́sas* 'enjoying in common(?)', occurring once, must be the pl. of *sa-psará-* (BR., Grassmann), not of *sa-psarás- (Lanman 546, Geldner, VS. 3, 197), because *-as* is never accented in Bahuvrīhi compounds; see Wackernagel 2[1], p. 301 d, note. *su-medhás-* 'very wise' is not a Bahuvrīhi.

A. *jarā́m*[1]; from *sa-jóṣas-* 'united', N. du. *sa-jóṣau* beside pl. *sa-jóṣās*. There is a further group of transitions to the *a*- declension starting not from contracted forms, but from the N. sing. n. understood as m.[2]. From *ávas-* 'favour' is thus formed I. *ávena*; from *krándas-* 'battle-cry', D. *krándāya*[3] (AV.), and the compound *śúci-kranda-m* 'crying aloud'; from *śárdhas-* n. 'troop' the m. forms *śárdha-m*, *śárdhena*, *śárdhāya*, *śárdha-sya*, *śárdhān*[4]; from *héḍas-* n., once (I. 94^{12}) *héḷa-s* N. m., hence A. *héḍa-m* (AV.), L. *héḷe*; also the compound forms N. f. du. *a-dveṣé* 'not ill-disposed', beside *dvéṣas-* 'hate'; *dur-óka-m* (VII. 4^{3}) 'unwonted' beside *ókas-* 'abode'; *vi-dradhé* (IV. 32^{23}) 'unclothed'(?) beside *drádhasī* (TS.) 'garments'; *pṛthu-jráya-m* (IV. 44^{1}) 'far-extending' beside *jráyas* 'expanse'; *puru-péśāsu* 'multiform' beside *péśas* 'form'[5].

2. The second class, comprising transitions to the *-as* declension, consists of the two groups of transfers from the radical *-ā* stems and the derivative *-a* stems. The former group embraces forms of compounds made from *kṣā-* 'abode', *pra-jā́-* 'offspring', *-dā-* 'giving', *-dhā-* 'bestowing', besides *mā́-s* 'moon', starting from the N. in *ā-s* which is identical in form with that of stems in *-às*. The forms of this type are the following: N. pl. *divá-kṣas-as* beside N. sing. *divá-kṣā-s* 'having an abode in heaven'; A. sing. *á-prajas-am* (AV. VS.) 'childless', A. pl. f. *íḍa-prajas-as* (TS. MS.), A. sing. *su-prajás-am* (AV.), N. pl. m. *su-prajás-as* (AV. TS.) 'having a good son' beside N. sing. m. *su-prajā́-s*; V. *draviṇo-das*[6], beside N. sing. *draviṇo-dā́-s*, A. *draviṇo-dā́-m* 'wealth-giving'; *varco-dás-au* (VS.) 'granting vigour'; *reto-dhás-as* (VS.) 'impregnating' beside N. sing. m. *reto-dhā́-s*; A. *vayo-dhás-am* (VS.), I. *vayo-dhás-ā* (VS.), *vayo-dhás-e* (VS.), V. *vayo-dhas*, N. pl. *vayo-dhás-as* (AV.) beside N. sing. *vayo-dhā́-s* 'bestowing vigour'; D. sing. *varco-dhás-e* (AV.) beside N. sing. *varco-dhā́-s* (AV.) and A. sing. f. *varco-dhā́-m* (VS.); of *candrá-mās-*[7] 'moon' all the forms occurring, except the N. sing., which is their starting-point, are transfer forms: A. *candrá-masam* (VS. XXIII. 59^{1}), I. *candrá-masā* (AV.), D. *candrá-mase* (VS.), G. *candrá-masas*, L. *candrá-masi* (AV.), V. *candra-mas* (AV.), N. du. *candrá-masā*, *sū́ryā-candra-másā* and *sū́ryā-candra-másau*.

3. There are further several sporadic transition forms from *-as* stems occurring beside the ordinary corresponding *-a* stem. These may sometimes have started from an ambiguous N. sing., but they seem usually to be due to metrical exigencies. Such forms are the following: *dákṣas-e*, *dákṣas-as*, *pūtá-dakṣas-ā* and *pūtá-dakṣas-as* beside very frequent forms of *dákṣa-* 'skill'; *doṣás-as*[8] (AV.) once beside forms of *doṣā́-* 'evening'; (*viśvā́yu*)-*poṣas-am* beside the common *póṣa-*; N. sing. *sá-bharās*, A. *viśvá-bharas-am* beside the frequent *bhára-* 'supporting'; *veśás-as*[9] (AV.) beside *veśá-* 'neighbour'; *śépas* as A. sing. in AV. (XIV. 2^{38}) for the *śépam* of the RV., from *śépa-* m. 'tail', N. sing. *śépa-s*; N. sing. m. *su-śévās* occurs in the AV. as a variant for *su-śéva-s* 'very dear' of the RV.; *sahásra-śokās* occurs once as N. sing. m. beside the common *śóka-* 'flame'; A. sing. *tuvi-ṣvaṇás-am* and N. pl. *tuvi-ṣvaṇás-as*, beside *svaná-* 'sound'; A. pl. f. *gharmá-svaras-as* beside *svará-* 'roaring'; also the D. *dhruvás-e* (VII. 70^{1}) for *dhruvā́ya* to which it is preferred owing to the metre and the influence of infinitives in *-áse*, and similarly *vṛdhás-e* (V. 64^{5}) parallel to *vṛdhā́ya* (VIII. 83^{6}).

4. There are besides a few quite abnormal transition forms. The occurrence of the very frequent N. pl. m. of *vi-* 'bird' with a singular verb (I. 141^{8}) and once as an A. pl. (I. 104^{1}) may have produced the impression of a n. collective *váyas-* and thus led to the n. pl. *váyāṃsi* (AV.), helped perhaps by the existence of the very frequent n. stem *váyas-* 'food'. The isolated form N. sing. m. *sv-áñcās* is probably lengthened for *sv-áñca-s* (like *su-śévās* for *su-śévas*) which started from the A. sing. m. *sv-áñc-am*. The G. du. *ródas-os* occurs once (IX. 22^{5}), evidently on account of the metre instead of the ordinary *ródasī-os*[10].

---

[1] Lanman 552 thinks that *medhā́-* 'wisdom' in N. *medhā́*, I. *medháyā*, N. pl. *medhā́s*, I. *medhā́bhis* started from *medhā́m* as contracted A. of *medhas-* found in *su-medhás-*. This seems doubtful to me.

[2] In VI. 66^{6} *rókas* might be taken as N. sing. m. (as Grassmann takes it) beside *rokás*, m.

[3] Cp. also the D. *carā́yai* (VII. 77^{1}) beside *caráse* (I. 92^{4}, V. 47^{4}), and *tárāya* (II. 13^{12}) beside *tárase* (III. 18^{3}).

[4] Cp. Lanman 353 and 554, 8.

[5] There is also an *-as* stem extended with *-a* in the D. *ā-jarasā́ya* (X. 85^{43}) 'till old age', based on the adv. compound *ā-jaras-ám* (B.)

[6] Cp. Brugmann, Grundriss 2, p. 398.

[7] From *mā́s-* (A. *mā́s-am*, etc.), where the *s* belongs to the stem. It is formed probably with *-as* from *mā-* 'measure' (*mā-as*), being thus in origin a contracted *-as* stem, in which, however, the N. *mā́s* giving rise to the transition forms was understood as the lengthened form of **mas*.

[8] In *uṣā́so doṣásaś ca* (AV. XVI. 4^{6}) obviously due to parallelism with *uṣásas*.

[9] Clearly owing to the metre instead of *veśā́sas*.

[10] Similarly *akṣ-ós* occurs in AV. V. 11^{10} (but contrary to the metre) for *akṣī-ós*. On the transition forms of the *-as* declension cp. Lanman 546—558.

Inflexion.

344. The **N. sing. m. f. lengthens the vowel** of the suffix; e. g. m. *áṅgirās*[1], f. *uṣā́s*. In about a dozen compounds the long vowel appears (owing to the influence of the m.) in the n. also; e. g. *ū́rṇa-mradās* 'soft as wool'. Before endings with initial *bh* the suffix *-as* becomes *-o*[2]. The forms actually occurring, if made from *ápas-* n. 'work' and *apás-* m. f. 'active', would be as follows:

Sing. N. *ápas*; *apā́s*. A. *ápas*; *apásam*. I. *ápasā*; *apásā*. D. *ápase*; *apáse*. Ab. *ápasas*; *apásas*. G. *ápasas*; *apásas*. L. *ápasi*; *apási*. V. *ápas*; *ápas*. — **Du.** N. A. V. *ápasī*; *apásī* and *apásau*[3]. D. *apóbhyām* (VS.). G. *ápasos* (VS.). — **Pl.** N. *ápāṃsi*; *apásas*. A. *ápāṃsi*; *apásas*. I. *ápobhis*; *apóbhis*. D. *ápobhyas*; *apóbhyas*. Ab. *ápobhyas*. G. *ápasām*; *apásām*. L. *ápassu*; *apássu*[4].

The forms actually occurring are as follows:

Sing. N. m. *áṅgirās*[5] an epithet of Agni, *dámūnās* 'domestic', *nodhā́s* name of a seer, *yaśā́s* 'glorious', *rakṣā́s* 'demon', *vedhā́s* 'ordainer'; **compounds:** *a-cetā́s* 'senseless', *áty-aṃhās* (VS. xvii. 80) 'beyond distress', *ádri-barhās* 'fast as a rock', *á-dvayās* 'free from duplicity', *án-āgās*[6] 'sinless', *an-ūdhā́s* 'udderless', *ánūna-varcās* 'having full splendour', *an-enā́s* 'guiltless', *á-pracetās* 'foolish', *abhibhūty-ójās* 'having superior power', *ámitaujās* 'almighty', *a-rapā́s* 'unhurt', *ávayāta-heḷās* 'whose anger is appeased', *ásamāty-ojās* 'of unequalled strength', *ā-hanā́s* 'exuberant', *uru-cákṣās* 'far-seeing', *uru-vyácās* 'widely extending', *ṛ́ṣi-manās* 'of far-seeing mind', *ṛṣváujās* 'having sublime (*ṛṣvá-*) power', *kārú-dhāyās* 'favouring the singer', *kṛ́tti-vāsās* (VS. iii. 61) 'wearing a skin', *kéta-vedās* 'knowing the intention', *khā́do-arṇās* 'having a devouring flood', *gabhīrá-vepās* 'deeply moved', *gūrtá-manās* 'having a grateful mind', *gūrtá-śravās* 'the praise of whom is welcome', *gó-nyoghās* 'streaming among milk', *ghṛtá-prayās* 'relishing ghee', *jātá-vedās* 'knowing created beings', *tád-apās* 'accustomed to that work', *tád-okās* 'rejoicing in that', *tád-ojās* 'endowed with such strength', *tarád-dveṣās* 'overcoming foes', *tigmá-tejās* (VS. i. 24) 'keen-edged', *trí-vayās* 'having threefold food', *dabhrá-cetās* 'little-minded', *dasmá-varcās* 'of wonderful appearance', *dīrghá-tamās* N. of a seer, *dīrghā́psās* 'having a long fore-part', *dur-óṣās* 'hard to excite', *devá-psarās* 'serving the gods as a feast', *devá-śravās* 'having divine renown', *dvi-bárhās* 'doubly strong', *ná-vedās* 'cognisant', *nṛ-cákṣās* 'watching men', *nṛ-máṇās* 'mindful of men', *ny-ókās* 'domestic', *pāvaká-varcās* 'brightly resplendent', *purū-rávās* (VS. v. 2) N., *pṛthu-jráyās* 'widely extended', *pṛthu-pā́jās* 'far-shining', *prá-cetās* 'attentive', *prá-vayās* 'vigorous', *bāhv-ójās* 'strong in the arm', *bṛhác-chravās* 'loud-sounding', *bṛhád-ravās* (VS. v. 22) 'loud-sounding', *bṛhád-vayās* (TS. i. 5. 10[2]) ,grown strong', *bodhín-manās* 'watchful-minded', *bhū́ri-retās* (VS. xx. 44) 'abounding in seed', *bhū́ry-ojās* 'having great power', *mádhu-vacās* 'sweet-voiced', *máno-javās* 'swift as thought', *mahā-yaśā́s* (Kh. iv. 8[8]) 'very glorious', *mitrá-mahās* 'rich in friends', *raghu-pátma-jaṃhās* 'having a light-falling foot',

---

1 The stems *svá-tavas-* and *sv-ávas-* form the irregular N. *svá-tavān* and *sv-ávān*, VS. *sv-ávā*.

2 Except in f. *uṣádbhis* and m. *svá-tavadbhyas* (VS.); cp. Brugmann, Grundriss 2, p. 713 (bottom).

3 The ending *-au* is here very rare and occurs chiefly in the later Saṃhitās.

4 Represented in f. by *apsarássu* (Kh.) and m. *apásu* if for *apássu*.

5 The *s* of the N. sing. is perhaps lost in *uśánā*; but this form may be a transition, starting from the A. *uśánām* (= *uśánasam*) after the analogy of the f.; another instance is perhaps *an-ehā́* (x. 61[12]).

6 The form *án-āvayās* (AV. vii. 90[3]), meaning perhaps 'not producing conception', may belong to this declension. See Whitney's note. Lanman 443, places it under radical *-ā* stems.

ráthaujās (VS. xv. 15) 'having the strength of a chariot', *riśā́dās* 'destroying enemies', *vásu-śravās* 'famous for wealth', *vā́ta-raṃhās* 'fleet as wind', *ví-cetās* 'clearly seen', *ví-manās* 'very wise', *viśvá-cakṣās* 'all-seeing', *viśvá-dhāyās* 'all-sustaining', *viśvá-bharās*[1] (VS. xi. 32) 'all-supporting', *viśvá-bhojās* 'all-nourishing', *viśvá-manās* 'perceiving everything', *viśvá-vedās* 'omniscient', *viśvá-vyacās* (VS. xiii. 56) 'embracing all things', *viśváujās* 'all-powerful', *ví-hāyās* 'mighty', *vīḷu-dvéṣās* 'hating strongly', *vīḷú-harās* 'holding fast', *vṛddhá-mahās* 'of great might', *vṛddhá-vayās* 'of great power', *vṛddhá-śravās* 'possessed of great swiftness', *śatá-tejās* (VS. i. 24) 'having a hundredfold vital power', *śatá-payās* (TS. VS.) 'having a hundred draughts', *śukrá-varcās* 'having bright lustre', *śraddhā́-manās* 'true-hearted', *śrī́-manās* (VS.) 'well-disposed', *sá-canās* 'being in harmony with', *sá-cetās* 'unanimous', *sa-jóṣās* 'united', *satyá-rādhās* 'truly beneficent', *satyáujās* (AV. VS. TS.) 'truly mighty', *sa-práthās* 'extensive', *sám-okās* 'dwelling together', *sahásra-cakṣās* 'thousand-eyed', *sahásra-cetās* 'having a thousand aspects', *sahásra-pāthās* 'appearing in a thousand places', *sahásra-retās* 'having a thousandfold seed', *sahásra-śokās*[1] 'emitting a thousand flames', *sahásrāpsās* 'thousand-shaped', *su-dáṃsās* 'performing splendid actions', *su-mánās* 'well-disposed', *su-medhā́s*[2] 'having a good understanding', *su-rā́dhās* 'bountiful', *su-réknās* 'having fair possessions', *su-rétās* 'having much seed', *su-várcās* 'splendid', *su-vā́sās* 'having beautiful garments', *sóma-cakṣās* (TS. ii. 2. 12⁴) 'looking like Soma', *stóma-vāhās* 'receiving praise', *spārhá-rādhās* 'bestowing enviable wealth', *sv-áñcās*[1] 'going well', *sv-ápās* 'skilful', *svábhūty-ojās* 'having energy from inherent power', *svá-yaśās* 'glorious through one's own acts', *svàr-cakṣās* 'brilliant as light', *svàr-canās* 'lovely as light', *sv-ójās* 'very strong'.

f. *uṣás* 'dawn'; *áti-cchandās* (TS., VS. xxi. 22) a metre, *á-dvayās*, *ap-sarás* 'water-nymph', *a-repás* 'spotless', *ā-hanás*, *uru-vyácās*, *ū́rṇa-mradās* 'soft as wool', *dvi-bárhās*, *nīcá-vayās* 'whose strength is low', *nṛ-máṇās*, *prá-cetās*, *mádhu-vacās*, *yāvayád-dveṣās* 'driving away enemies', *ví-cchandās* (TS. v. 2. 11¹) 'containing various metres', *ví-hāyās*, *vṛ́ṣa-maṇās* 'manly-spirited', *śukrá-vāsās* 'bright-robed', *sá-cetās*, *sá-cchandās* (TS. v. 2. 11¹) 'consisting of the same metres', *sa-jóṣās*, *sa-práthās*, *sá-bharās*[1] 'furnished with gifts' (?), *sahá-yaśās* (TS. iv. 4. 12²) 'glorious', *su-dáṃsās*, *su-péśās* 'well-adorned', *su-mánās*, *su-medhā́s*[2], *su-vā́sās*.

N. A. n. *áṃhas* 'distress', *áñjas* 'ointment', *a-dveṣás* 'without malevolence', *ánas* 'cart', *an-ehás* 'without a rival', *ándhas* 'darkness' and 'plant', *ápas* 'work', *apás* 'active', *ápnas* 'property', *ápsas* 'hidden part of the body', *ámbhas* 'water', *áyas* 'metal', *a-rakṣás* 'harmless', *a-rapás*, *árṇas* 'flood', *ávas* 'favour', *ā́gas* 'sin', *ā́pas* 'religious ceremony', *úras* 'breast', *ū́dhas* 'udder', *énas* 'sin', *ókas* 'abode', *ójas* 'strength', *kṣódas* 'rushing water', *cánas* 'delight', *cétas* (VS. xxxiv. 3) 'intellect', *chándas* 'metrical hymn', *jáṃhas* 'course', *júvas* 'quickness', *jráyas* 'expanse', *tád-apas*, *tápas* 'heat', *támas* 'darkness', *táras* 'velocity', *téjas* 'sharp edge', *tyájas* 'abandonment', *dáṃsas* 'marvellous power', *dúvas* 'worship', *dráviṇas* 'property', *dvéṣas* 'hostility', *nábhas* 'vapour', *námas* 'obeisance', *pákṣas* 'side', *páyas* 'milk', *pásas* (VS. xx. 9) 'penis', *pā́jas* 'vigour', *pā́thas* 'place', *pī́vas* 'fat', *puru-bhójas* 'greatly nourishing', *péśas* 'ornament', *práthas* 'width', *práyas* 'enjoyment', *psáras* 'feast', *bhárgas* 'radiance', *bhā́sas* 'light', *mánas* 'mind', *máyas* 'joy', *máhas* 'greatness', *mahás* 'great', *mṛ́dhas* 'disdain', *médas* 'fat', *yáśas* 'fame', *rákṣas* 'damage', *rájas* 'region of clouds', *rápas* 'infirmity', *rábhas* 'violence', *rā́dhas* 'bounty', *réknas* 'wealth', *rétas* 'flow', *répas* 'stain', *ródhas* 'bank', *vákṣas* 'breast', *vácas* 'speech', *váyas* 'bird' and

1 Probably a transition form (p. 225, 3, 4).

2 Perhaps a transfer form from *medhā́-*, since the latter stem is common, while the *-as* stem occurs only in *su-medhásam* (once) and *su-medhasas* (four times in a refrain).

'food', *várivas* 'space', *várcas* 'vigour', *várpas* 'figure', *vā́g-ójas* (VS. XXXVI. 1) 'speech-energy', *vā́sas* 'garment', *vā́has* 'offering', *védas* 'wealth', *vépas* 'quivering', *vyácas* 'expanse', *vráyas* 'superior power', *śárdhas* 'troop', *śávas* 'power', *śíras* 'head', *śéṣas* 'offspring', *śrávas* 'renown', *sa-jóṣas*, *sádas* 'seat', *sánas*[1] (Kh. III. 15[15]) 'gain', *sa-práthas*, *sa-bā́dhas* 'harassed', *sáras* 'lake', *sáhas* 'force', *saháujas* (VS. XXXVI. 1) 'endowed with strength', *su-rétas*, *srótas* 'stream', *svá-tavas* 'inherently strong', *háras* 'flame', *hé̱ḷas* 'passion', *hváras* 'crookedness'. — **Ending in -ās**[2] (like m.): *asrī-váyās*[3] (VS. XIV. 18), *uru-práthās* (VS. XX. 39) 'far-spread', *ū́rṇa-mradās*, *gūrtá-vacās* 'speaking agreeably', *devá-vyacās* 'affording space for the gods', *dvi-bárhās*, *viśvá-vyacās* (AV.), *ví-ṣpardhās* (VS. XV. 5) 'emulating', *vīrá-peśās* 'forming the ornament of heroes', *vīḷú-harās*, *sa-práthās* (AV. VS. TS.), *sumánās* (TS. IV. 5. 1[2])[4].

A. m. *jarásam* 'old age', *tavásam* 'strong', 'strength', *tyajásam* 'offshoot', *dámūnasam*, *párīṇasam* (160) 'abundance', *bhiyásam* 'fear', *yaśásam*, *rakṣásam*, *vedhásam*; *a-cetásam*, *ánaṣṭa-vedasam* 'having one's property unimpaired', *án-āgasam*, *ánu-gāyasam* 'followed by shouts', *an-enásam* (TS. I. 8. 5[3]), *an-ehásam*, *apásam*, *á-pratidhṛṣṭa-śavasam* 'of irresistible power', *abhibhūty-ójasam*, *ará-maṇasam* 'obedient', *a-rādhásam* 'not liberal', *a-repásam*, *arcanā́nasam* 'having a rattling carriage' (N. of a man), *ā-hanásam*, *úccaiḥ-śravasam* (Kh. V. 14[5]) 'neighing aloud' (N. of Indra's horse), *upāká-cakṣasam* 'seen close at hand', *uru-cákṣasam*, *uru-jráyasam* 'extending over a wide space', *uru-vyácasam*, *ū́rṇa-mradasam* (VS. II. 2), *ūrdhvá-nabhasam* (VS. VI. 16) 'being above the clouds', *kṣetra-sā́dhasam* 'who divides the fields', *gāthá-śravasam* 'famous through songs', *gāyatrá-cchandasam* (VS. VIII. 47) 'to whom the Gāyatrī metre belongs', *gāyatrá-vepasam* 'inspired by songs', *gír-vaṇasam* 'delighting in invocations', *gír-vāhasam* 'praised in song', *gūrtá-śravasam*, *gó-arṇasam* 'abounding in cattle', *gó-dhāyasam* 'supporting cows', *cikitvín-manasam* 'attentive', *citrá-mahasam* 'possessing excellent bounty', *citrá-rādhasam* 'granting excellent gifts', *jágac-chandasam* (VS. VIII. 47) 'to whom the Jagatī metre belongs', *jātá-vedasam*, *tuvi-rā́dhasam* 'granting many gifts', *tuvi-ṣvaṇásam*[5] 'loud-sounding', *tuvy-ójasam* 'very powerful', *triṣṭúp-chandasam* (VS. VIII. 47), *dā́ndukasam* 'delighting (*ókas-*) in a sacrificial meal', *dyukṣá-vacasam* 'uttering heavenly words', *dvi-bárhasam*, *dví-śavasam* 'having twofold strength', *dhṛṣṇv-ójasam* 'endowed with resistless might', *náryāpasam* 'doing manly (*nárya-*) deeds', *nṛ-cákṣasam*, *paṅkti-rādhasam* 'containing fivefold gifts', *puru-péśasam* 'multiform', *puru-bhójasam*, *puru-várpasam* 'having many forms', *puru-vépasam* 'much-exciting', *prá-cetasam*, *prá-tvakṣasam* 'energetic', *bráhma-vāhasam* 'to whom prayers are offered', *bhū́ri-cakṣasam* 'much-seeing', *bhū́ri-dhāyasam* 'nourishing many', *máno-javasam* (TS. II. 4. 7[1]), *yajñá-vanasam* 'loving sacrifice', *yajñá-vāhasam* 'offering worship', *riśā́dasam*[6], *vā́ja-śravasam* 'famous for wealth', *ví-cetasam*, *vi-joṣasam* 'forsaken', *vi-dveṣásam* 'resisting enmity', *viśvá-dhāyasam*, *viśvá-bharasam*[7], *viśvá-vedasam*, *viśvá-vyacasam*, *viśvā́yu-poṣasam*[7] 'causing prosperity to all men', *viśvā́yu-vepasam* 'exciting all men', *ví-hāyasam*, *vīti-rādhasam* 'granting enjoyment', *sá-cetasam*, *sa-jóṣasam*, *satyá-girvāhasam* 'getting true praise', *satyá-rādhasam* (VS. XXII. 11), *satyá-śavasam* 'truly vigorous',

[1] Though *sánas* does not otherwise occur (*sana-* m. is found as last member of a compound), the context in Khila III. 15[15] seems to require an A.: *ahám gandhárva-rūpeṇa sána ā́ vartayāmi te*.

[2] Cp. LANMAN 560.

[3] Of doubtful meaning; the form may possibly be N. pl. of *asrīvi-*. Cp. BR.

[4] Cp. LANMAN 560; see also the neuters in *ā-s*, LANMAN 445 (mid).

[5] For this form, TS. III. 3. 11[2] has erroneously *tuviṣ-maṇásam*.

[6] Also the transition form *vayo-dhásam* (VS.) 'bestowing strength'.

[7] Probably to be explained as a transition form (p. 225, 3).

sádma-makhasam 'performing sacrifice in a sacred precinct', *sa-práthasam* (VS. XXI. 3), *samudrá-vāsasam* 'concealed in the waters', *samudrá-vyacasam* 'extensive as the sea', *sárva-vedasam* (VS. XV. 55; TS. IV. 7. 13[4]) 'having complete property', *sahásra-cakṣasam*, *sahásra-bharṇasam* 'a thousandfold', *sahásra-varcasam* 'having a thousandfold power', *su-cétasam* 'very wise', *su-dáṃsasam*, *su-péśasam*, *su-prayásam* 'well regaled', *su-bhójasam* 'bountiful', *su-medhásam*[1], *su-rādhasam*, *su-rétasam*, *su-várcasam* (TS. III. 2. 8[5]), *su-śrávasam* 'famous', *sr̥prá-bhojasam* 'having abundant food', *svá-yaśasam*, *sv-ávasam* 'affording good protection', *hári-dhāyasam* 'giving yellow streams', *hári-varpasam* 'having a yellow appearance'. — **Contracted forms:** *uśánām* N. of a seer, *mahām*, *vedhām*.

f. *uṣáṣam* and *uṣāsam*[2], *dhvarásam* 'deceiving'; *án-āgasam*, *an-ehásam*, *a-rakṣásam*, *a-repásam*, *áśva-peśasam* 'decorated with horses', *úd-ojasam* 'exceedingly powerful', *uru-vyácasam*, *cikitvín-manasam*, *puru-bhójasam*, *yāvayád-dveṣasam*, *vāja-peśasam* 'adorned with precious gifts', *viśva-dóhasam* 'yielding all things', *viśvá-dhāyasam*, *viśvá-peśasam* 'containing all adornment', *viśvá-bhojasam*, *śatárcasam* 'having a hundred supports' (*r̥cás-*), *śúci-peśasam* 'brightly adorned', *sahásra-bharṇasam*, *svá-yaśasam*, *hári-varpasam*. — **Contracted forms:** *uṣām*, *jarām*, *medhām* 'wisdom', *vayām* 'vigour'; *án-āgām*, *ap-sarām* (AV.)[3].

I. m. *jarásā*, *tárūṣasā* 'giving victory', *tavásā*, *tveṣásā* 'impulse', *párīṇasā*, *bhiyásā*[4], *yaśásā*, *sáhasā* 'mighty', *havásā* 'invocation'; *an-ehásā*, *a-rakṣásā*, *gó-parīṇasā* 'having abundance of cows', *pr̥thu-pájasā*, *máno-javasā*, *viśvá-peśasā*, *su-péśasā*, *su-śrávasā*, *sv-ápasā* (VS. XXV. 3).

f. *uṣásā*, *yajásā* 'worshipping'; *áti-cchandasā* (VS. I. 27), *a-repásā*, *uru-cákṣasā* (VS. IV. 23).

n. *áñjasā*, *ánasā*, *ándhasā*, *ápasā*, *apásā*, *a-rakṣásā*, *árṇasā*, *ávasā*, *úrasā* (VS.TS.), *énasā*, *ójasā*, *óhasā* 'prospect', *kṣódasā*, *gó-arṇasā*, *cákṣasā* 'brightness', *cétasā*, *chándasā* (VS. TS.), *jávasā* and (once) *javásā*[5] 'with speed', *tánasā* 'offspring', *tápasā*, *támasā*, *tárasā*, *téjasā*, *tyájasā*, *tvákṣasā* 'energy', *dáṃsasā*, *dóhasā* 'milking', *dhāyasā* 'nourishing', *dhrájasā* 'gliding power', *nábhasā*, *námasā*, *páyasā*, *pájasā*, *pívasā*, *péśasā* (VS. XX. 41), *práyasā*, *bāhvòjasā*, *bhrājasā* 'lustre', *mánasā*, *máhasā*, *médasā*, *yaśásā*[6] 'glorious', *rákṣasā*, *rájasā*, *rápasā*, *rādhasā*, *réknasā*, *rétasā*, *vácasā*, *vánasā* 'enjoyment', *váyasā*[7], *várcasā*, *várpasā*, *vāsasā*, *vāhasā*, *védasā*, *vépasā*, *śávasā*, *śírasā* (Kh. I. 9[4]), *śéṣasā*, *śrávasā*, *sáhasā*, *su-dáṃsasā*, *su-rétasā*, *srótasā*, *hárasā*, *héṣasā* 'vigour'[8].

D. m. *taváse*, *duváse* 'worshipper', *yaśáse*, *rakṣáse*, *vedháse*, *śíkvase* 'adroit', *sáhase* 'mighty'; *abhíṣṭi-śavase* 'granting powerful aid', *ukthá-vāhase* 'offering verses', *uru-vyácase*, *r̥tá-peśase* 'having a glorious form', *gāyatrá-vepase*, *gir-vaṇase*, *gir-vāhase*, *ghorá-cakṣase* 'of frightful appearance'[9], *jātá-vedase*, *tád-apase*, *tád-okase*, *dīrghá-yaśase* 'renowned far and wide', *dīrghá-śravase* 'famous far

---

1 Perhaps to be explained as a transition form starting from N. *su-medhā-s*.

2 In Pada text *uṣásam*.

3 Cp. J. SCHMIDT, Heteroklitische nominative singularis auf *-ās* in den arischen sprachen, KZ. 26, 401—409; 27, 284; COLLITZ, BB. 7, 180; PRELLWITZ, BB. 22, 83.

4 Also contracted to *bhīṣā* with adverbial shift of accent occurring 3 times (*bhiyásā* 11 times).

5 In IV. 27[1].

6 Cp. GRASSMANN, s. v. *yaśás-*.

7 Also the transition form *vayo-dhásā* (VS. XV. 7).

8 A few forms in *-as* appear to have the value of instrumentals as agreeing with a word in that case: *vácas* (I. 26[2] etc.), *yajña-vacás* (AV. XI. 3[19]), *śávas* (I. 81[4]); *édhas* (AV. XII. 3[2]); cp. BLOOMFIELD, SBE. 42, 645; see LANMAN 562, and cp. CALAND, KZ. 31, 261.

9 Also the transition form *candrá-mase* (VS. XXX. 21).

and wide', *dyumná-śravase* 'producing a clear sound', *nṛ-cákṣase, ny-òkase, purū-rávase, pṛthu-jráyase, pṛthu-pā́jase, prá-cetase, prá-tavase* 'very strong', *bráhma-vāhase, mṛktá-vāhase* 'carrying off what is injured', N. of a seer, *yajñá-vāhase*[1], *viśvá-cakṣase, ví-hāyase, satyá-rādhase, sahásra-cakṣase, svá-tavase, svá-yaśase.*

f. *uṣáse, vṛdháse* 'furtherance'; *áti-cchandase* (VS. XXIV. 13), *dur-vā́sase* 'ill-clothed', *parjányа-retase* 'sprung from the seed of Parjanya'.

n. *apáse, a-peśáse* 'formless', *ávase, ójase, cákṣase, javáse, tápase, támase, tárase, téjase* (VS. XV. 8), *dákṣase* 'ability', *dhā́yase, dhruváse* 'stopping', *nábhase* (VS. VII. 30), *námase, pā́jase, práyase, psárase, mánase, máhase* (VS. XIX. 8), *yáśase* (VS. XX. 3), *yā́dase* (VS. XXX. 20) 'voluptuousness', *rákṣase, rā́dhase, rétase, vácase, várcase, śárase* (VS. XXXVIII. 15) 'skin of boiled milk', *śávase, śrávase, sáhase, svá-yaśase, hárase.*

Ab. m. *a-rādhásas, jarásas, tavásas, párīṇasas, rakṣásas*[2], *sáhasas.* — **f.** *uṣásas.* — **n.** *áṃhasas*[3], *ánasas, ándhasas, ápasas, árṇasas, ā́gasas* (TS. IV. 7. 15[2]), *énasas, ókasas, ójasas, kṣódasas, jráyasas, tápasas, támasas, dráviṇasas, páyasas, pā́jasas, práthasas, bhā́ṃsasas* 'intestine', *mánasas*[4], *rájasas, rā́dhasas, védasas, sádasas, sárasas, sáhasas.*

G. m. *áṅgirasas, apásas, ápnasas, tavásas, párīṇasas, rakṣásas, vedhásas; án-āgasas, ápāka-cakṣasas* 'shining from afar', *abhí-vayasas* 'refreshing', *a-rakṣásas, upamá-śravasas* 'most highly famed', *kṛṣṇá-jaṃhasas* 'having a black track', *jātá-vedasas, dānā́pnasas* 'having abundance of gifts', *dīrghá-śravasas, dvi-bárhasas, nṛ-cákṣasas, pári-dveṣasas* 'enemy', *puru-bhójasas, pṛthu-śrávasas* 'far-famed', *prá-cetasas, prá-mahasas* 'very glorious', *prayásas* (TS. IV. 1. 8[2]), *bhā́-tvakṣasas* 'having the power of light', *ví-cetasas, vidmanā́pasas* 'working with wisdom', *viśvá-manasas, vṛ́ka-dvarasas*[5], *satyá-rādhasas* (TS. III. 3. 11[1]), *satyá-savasas* (VS. IV. 18) 'having true impulsion', *sa-bā́dhasas, su-prayásas* (VS. XXVII. 15), *svá-yaśasas.* — **f.** *uṣásas*[6].

n. *áṃhasas, ánasas, ándhasas, ápasas, áyasas, árṇasas, árśasas* (VS. XII. 97) 'piles', *ávasas, énasas* (VS. VIII. 13), *ókasas, ójasas, gó-arṇasas, tápasas* (VS. IV. 26; Kh. IV. 11[13]), *támasas, tyájasas, dákṣasas*[7], *dráviṇasas, nábhasas, námasas, páyasas, pā́jasas* (Kh. I. 7[2]), *práyasas, mánasas, médasas, rájasas, rápasas, rā́dhasas, rétasas, vácasas, vápsasas* 'fair form', *váyasas, várpasas, vā́sasas, śávasas*[8], *śrávasas, sádasas, sárapasas*[5], *sáhasas, hárasas*[9]. — **Contracted form:** *nṛ-mánās* (X. 92[14]).

L. m. *áṅgirasi*[10] (VS. IV. 10), *gó-arṇasi, jātá-vedasi, dámūnasi, pṛthu-śrávasi, yajñá-vāhasi* (VS. IX. 37), *satyá-śravasi* 'truly famous', N. of a man. — **f.** *uṣási.* — **n.** *áṃhasi, áñjasi, apási, ávasi, ā́gasi, ókasi, krándasi* 'battle-cry', *cákṣasi, támasi, námasi, páyasi, pā́thasi* (VS. XIII. 53), *mánasi, rájasi, rā́dhasi, rétasi, śrávasi, sádasi, sárasi, héḍasi* (TS. III. 3. 11[4]).

V. m. *áṅgiras, nodhas, vedhas; uktha-vāhas, upama-śravas, kāru-dhāyas,*

---

[1] Also the transition form *vayo-dháse* (VS. XXVIII. 46).

[2] Also the transition form *reto-dhásas* (VS. VIII. 10).

[3] In VI. 3[1] *áṃhas* is probably the stem used instead of the very frequent Ab. *áṃh-as-as*, rather than the Ab. of *áṃh-*, as this would be the only form from such a stem, and the accent would be irregular.

[4] Also the adv., in the sense of the Ab., *medas-tás* (VS. XXI. 60).

[5] Of uncertain meaning.

[6] Once the strong form *uṣā́sas* (X. 39[1]) for the weak.

[7] This, as well as the D. n. *dákṣase*, is a transition form (p. 225, 3).

[8] The stem *śávas* in VIII. 3[6] may be used for the G. Perhaps also *sádas-páti-* stands for *sádasas-páti-*. Cp. LANMAN 563[4].

[9] Transition forms are *śárdhasya, nir-avásya; candrá-masas, reto-dhásas* (VS.); *dákṣasas, doṣásas* (AV.).

[10] Also the transfer forms *áṅgire, héḷe; candrá-masi* (AV.).

gir-vaṇas, *gir-vāhas*[1], *jāta-vedas*, *deva-śravas*, *dhṛṣan-manas* 'bold-minded', *nṛ-cakṣas*, *nṛ-maṇas*, *purū-ravas*, *pra-cetas*[2], *brahma-vāhas*, *mitra-mahas*, *vāja-pramahas* 'superior in strength', *viśva-cakṣas*, *viśva-dhāyas*, *viśva-manas*, *vṛṣa-maṇas*, *satya-rādhas*, *su-draviṇas* 'having fine property', *su-mahas* 'very great', *sva-tavas*, *sv-ojas*[3]. — **f.** *uṣas*; *ā-hanas*, *tigma-tejas* (AV. VS.). — **n.** *draviṇas*, *śárdhas*.

Du. N. A. V. m. *apásā*, *tavásā*, *tośásā*[4] 'showering', *yaśásā*, *vedhasā*; *a-repásā*, *āśu-héṣasā* 'having neighing horses', *īya-cakṣasā* 'of far-reaching sight', *uktha-vāhasā*, *uru-cákṣasā*, *kṛṣṭy-ojasā* 'overpowering men', *gambhīra-cetasā* 'of profound mind', *gó-parīṇasā*, *jātá-vedasā*, *tád-okasā*, *na-vedasā*, *nṛ-cákṣasā*, *nṛ-vā́hasā* 'conveying men', *puru-dáṃsasā* 'abounding in wonderful deeds', *puru-bhojasā*, *pūtá-dakṣasā*[5] 'pure-minded', *pṛthu-pákṣasā* 'broad-flanked', *prá-cetasā*, *prá-mahasā*, *bodhín-manasā*, *mata-vacasā* 'heeding prayers', *mano-javasā*, *yajña-vāhasā*, *riśā́dasā*, *vatsa-pracetasā* 'mindful of Vatsa', *vi-cetasā*, *ví-pakṣasā* 'going on both sides', *vipra-vāhasā* 'receiving the offerings of the wise', *viśvá-bhojasā*, *viśvá-vedasā*, *vy-ènasā* 'guiltless', *śréṣṭha-varcasā* 'having most excellent energy', *sa-jóṣasā*, V. *sátyaujasā* (TS. IV. 7. 15[2]), *sá-manasā* 'unanimous', *samāná-varcasā* 'having equal vigour', *sám-okasā*, *sá-vayasā* 'having equal vigour', *sá-vedasā* 'having equal wealth', *síndhu-vāhasā* 'passing through the sea' (?), *su-dáṃsasā*, *su-prayásā*, *su-rādhasā*, *su-rétasā*, *su-vā́casā* 'very eloquent', *sv-ávasā*, *hitá-prayasā* 'who has offered an oblation of food', *híraṇya-peśasā* 'having golden lustre'[6]. — **With** ***au***: *a-repásau*, V. *jāta-vedasau* (TS. I. 3. 7[2]), *nṛ-cákṣasau*, *prá-cetasau* (VS. XXVIII. 7), *viśvá-śardhasau* 'forming a complete troop', *sá-cetasau* (VS. V. 3; Kh. III. 15[13]), *sa-jóṣasau* (VS. XII. 74), *sá-manasau* (TS. I. 3. 7[2]), *sám-okasau* (TS. I. 3. 7[2])[7]. — **f.** *uṣásā* and *uṣā́sā*[8], *náktoṣā́sā* 'night and morning', *an-ehásā*, *uru-vyácasā*, *nṛ-cákṣasā* (AV.), *bhū́ri-retasā*, *bhū́ri-varpasā* 'multiform', *viśvá-peśasā*, *sá-cetasā*, *sá-manasā*, *su-dáṃsasā*[9], *su-péśasā*. — **With** ***-au***: *ap-sarásau* (AV.), *a-repásau*, *uṣā́sau* (VS. XXI. 50), *yaśásau*; *nṛ-cákṣasau*, *viśvá-śardhasau*, *vy-ènasau* (AV.)[10]. — **n.** *ándhasī*, *krándasī*, *jánasī*, *drádhasī* (TS. III. 2. 2[2]) 'garments', *nábhasī* (AV.), *nā́dhasī* 'refuges', *pákṣasī* (AV.), *pā́jasī*, *rájasī*, *vácasī*, *vā́sasī* (TS. I. 5. 10[1]).

D. m. *sa-jóṣobhyām* (VS. VII. 8).

G. n. *dīkṣā-tapásos*[11] (VS. IV. 2) 'consecration and penance'.

Pl. N. V. m. *áṅgirasas*, *apásas*, *tavásas*, *dámūnasas*, *duvásas* 'restless', *mṛgayásas* 'wild animals', *yaśásas*, *rakṣásas*, *vedhásas*, *śíkvasas*; *á-giraukasas* 'not to be kept back by hymns' (*girā́*), *a-cetásas*, *a-codásas* 'unurged', *ádbhutainasas* 'in whom no fault (*énas*) is visible', *an-avabhrá-rādhasas* 'giving undiminished wealth', *án-āgasas*, *an-ehásas*, *a-repásas*, *á-vicetasas* 'unwise', *a-śéṣasas* 'without descendants', *áśva-rādhasas* 'equipping horses', *á-sāmi-śavasas* 'having complete strength', *ā-hanasas*, *ukthá-vahasas*, *úd-ojasas*, *uru-vyácasas* (VS. XXVII. 16), *kṣetra-sā́dhasas*, *gambhīrá-vepasas*,

---

1 In VI. 24[6] GRASSMANN would read *girvavā́has*, as N.; cp. LANMAN 564[2].

2 TS. I. 5. 11[3] has *praceto rā́jan*; the original passage, RV. I. 24[14], has *pracetā rā́jan* (Pada, *pracetaḥ*); see LANMAN 564[3].

3 Transition forms are *sá-pratha* (TB.), *candra-mas* (AV.), *vayo-dhas*, *draviṇo-das*.

4 With lengthened vowel.

5 Probably to be explained as a transition form (p. 225, 3).

6 Also the transition forms *candrámasā*, *sūryā-candramásā*.

7 Also the transition forms *sūryā-candra-másau*, *varco-dásau* (VS. VII. 27), *sa-jóṣau*.

8 In the Pada text *uṣásā*.

9 In VII. 73[1] *puru-dáṃsā* is perhaps a contracted form.

10 Also the transition forms *uṣé* (VS.), *a-dveṣé*, *vi-dradhé*.

11 There are also in the f. the transition forms *uṣā́bhyām* I. and *ródasos* G.

ghṛṣvi-rādhasas 'granting with joy', *ghorá-varpasas* 'of terrible appearance', *citrá-rādhasas, tád-okasas, tuvi-ṣvaṇásas*[1], *dvi-bárhasas, dhṛṣṇv-òjasas, ná-vedasas, nṛ-cákṣasas, pathi-rákṣasas* (VS. XVI. 60) 'protecting roads', *pūtá-dakṣasas*[1], *pṛthu-pájasas, prá-cetasas, prati-jūti-varpasas* 'assuming any form according to impulse', *prá-tavasas, prá-tvakṣasas, prá-śravasas* 'farfamed', *bāhv-òjasas, bhalānásas* N. of a people, *mádhu-psarasas* 'fond of sweetness', *mádhye-cchandasas* (TS. IV. 3. 11^{3}) 'sun' or 'middle of the year' (Comm.), *yajñá-vāhasas, yutá-dveṣasas* 'delivered from enemies', *riśā́dasas, rukmá-vakṣasas* 'wearing gold ornaments on the breast', *váruṇa-śeṣasas* 'resembling sons of Varuṇa', *vā́ta-raṃhasas, vā́ta-svanasas* 'roaring like the wind', *ví-cetasas, vidmanā́pasas, vidyún-mahasas* 'rejoicing in lightning', *vípra-vacasas* 'whose words are inspired', *vi-mahasas* 'very glorious', *viśvá-dhāyasas, viśvá-mahasas* 'having all splendour', *viśvá-vedasas, ví-ṣpardhasas* 'vying', *ví-hāyasas, vṛddhá-śavasas* 'of great strength', *śréṣṭha-varcasas, sá-cetasas, sa-jóṣasas, satya-śavasas, sa-bharasas*[1], *sá-manasas, sám-okasas, sá-vayasas, sá-srotasas* (VS. XXXIV. 11) 'flowing', *sahá-cchandasas* 'accompanied by metre', *sahásra-pājasas* 'having a thousandfold lustre', *sahaújasas* (VS. X. 4), *su-cákṣasas* 'seeing well', *su-cétasas, su-dáṃsasas, su-pīvásas* 'very fat', *su-péśasas, su-prácetasas* 'very wise', *su-prajásas*[2] (TS. I. 6. 2^{1}; AV.) 'having a good son', *su-mánasas, su-mahasas, su-medhasas*[3], *su-rā́dhasas, sū́ra-cakṣasas* 'radiant as the sun', *sū́rya-tvacasas* (VS. X. 4) 'having a covering bright as the sun', *sū́rya-varcasas* (VS. X. 4) 'resplendent as the sun', *stóma-vāhasas* 'giving praise', *svá-tavasas, sv-ápasas, sv-ápnasas* 'wealthy', *svá-yaśasas, sv-ávasas, hitá-prayasas.* — **Contracted forms:** *áṅgirās, án-āgās*[4], *návedās, sajóṣās.* — **f.** *apásas, uṣásas* and *uṣā́sas*[5], *yaśásas*; *agní-bhrājasas* 'fire-bright', *an-ehásas, ap-sarásas, uru-vyácasas* (TS. IV. 1. 8^{2}), *tṛṣu-cyávasas* 'moving greedily', *dhánv-arṇasas* 'overflowing the dry land', *nṛ-péśasas* 'adorned by men', *prá-cetasas, prá-svādasas* 'pleasant', *mádhv-arṇasas* 'having a sweet flood', *ví-cetasas, su-péśasas, sū́da-dohasas* 'milking sweetness', *sv-ápasas, svá-yaśasas.* — **Contracted forms:** *medhā́s; á-joṣās* 'insatiable', *ná-vedās, su-rā́dhās.*

N. A. n. *áṃhāṃsi, áṅkāṃsi* 'bends', *ándhāṃsi, ápāṃsi, árṇāṃsi, ávāṃsi, ā́gāṃsi, énāṃsi, ókāṃsi, ójāṃsi, kárāṃsi* 'deeds', *chándāṃsi, jávāṃsi, jráyāṃsi, támāṃsi, tvákṣāṃsi, dáṃsāṃsi, dúvāṃsi, dvéṣāṃsi, páyāṃsi, pā́jāṃsi, pā́thāṃsi* (VS. XXI. 46), *péśāṃsi, práyāṃsi, bhā́sāṃsi, mánāṃsi, máhāṃsi, rákṣāṃsi, rájāṃsi, rápāṃsi, rā́dhāṃsi, rétāṃsi, ródhāṃsi, róhāṃsi* 'heights', *vákṣāṃsi, vácāṃsi, váyāṃsi, várāṃsi* 'expanses', *várivāṃsi, várcāṃsi* (VS. IX. 22), *várpāṃsi, vā́sāṃsi, śárdhāṃsi, śávāṃsi, śrávāṃsi, sádāṃsi, sárāṃsi, sáhāṃsi, skándhāṃsi* 'branches', *héḷāṃsi, hvárāṃsi.*

A. m. *áṅgirasas*[6], *dhvarásas, yaśásas, rakṣásas, vedhásas*; *án-āgasas, an-ehásas, á-pracetasas, a-rādhásas, uru-cákṣasas, tuvi-rā́dhasas, pūtá-dakṣasas*[7], *prá-cetasas, bṛhác-chravasas, yajñá-vanasas, riśā́dasas, ví-mahasas, ví-ṣpardhasas, sa-jóṣasas* (VS. III. 44), *sá-manasas* (VS. VII. 25), *su-péśasas, su-rā́dhasas, sv-ápnasas*[8]. — **Contracted forms:** *án-āgās, su-medhā́s*[9]. — **f.** *apásas, uṣásas*[10], *yaśásas*; *a-javásas* 'not swift', *an-apnásas* 'destitute of wealth', *an-ehásas, ap-sarásas, arí-dhāyasas* 'willingly yielding milk', *gharmá-svarasas*[7] 'sounding like (the contents of) a boiler', *tád-apasas, bhū́ri-varpasas, vā́ja-draviṇasas* 'richly

[1] Probably a transition form (p. 225, 3).
[2] Probably a transition form (p. 225, 2).
[3] Probably a transfer form; see p. 227, note [2].
[4] Perhaps also *an-ehā́s* (X. 61^{12}); see LANMAN 551[1].
[5] In the Pada text *uṣásas.*
[6] In I. 112^{18} LANMAN would take *áṅgiras sa* A. pl. m. without ending.
[7] Probably a transition form (p. 225, 3).
[8] Also the transition forms *śárdhān, án-āgān.*
[9] It is somewhat doubtful whether this is a contracted A. pl. (VII. 91^{3}).
[10] Once also *uṣā́sas.* In III. 6^{7} and VIII. 41^{3} LANMAN (566) would take *uṣás* as A. pl. without ending.

rewarded', *vā́ja-śravasas, viśvá-dohasas, viśvá-dhāyasas, su-péśasas*[1]. — **Contracted form:** *uṣā́s* (IX. 41[5]).

I. m. *áṅgirobhis*; *agni-tápobhis* 'having the heat of fire', *svá-yaśobhis.* — **f.** *svá-yaśobhis*; **with -ad- for -o-:** *uṣádbhis* (44 a, 3).

n. *á-yavobhis* (VS. XII. 74) 'dark halves of the month', *árṇobhis, ávobhis, ójobhis, chándobhis* (Kh. v. 3[4]), *tápobhis, támobhis, tárobhis, dáṃsobhis, dvéṣobhis, dhā́yobhis, nábhobhis, námobhis, pákṣobhis* (VS. XXIX. 5; TS. v. 1. 11[2]), *páyobhis, práyobhis, máhobhis, rájobhis, rā́dhobhis, vácobhis, váyobhis, várobhis, śávobhis, śrávobhis, sáhobhis.*

D. m. *áṅgirobhyas;* **with -ad-** for **-o-:** *svá-tavadbhyas* (VS. XXIV. 16). — **n.** *médobhyas* (VS. XXXIX. 10), *rákṣobhyas, váyobhyas* (AV.), *sárobhyas* (VS. XXX. 16). — **Ab. n.** *dvéṣobhyas.*

G. m. *áṅgirasām, apásām, tavásām, yaśásām, vedhásām*; *ádbhutainasām, dasmá-varcasām, mahā́-manasām* 'high-minded', *stóma-vāhasām.* — **f.** *apásām, uṣásām*; *ap-sarásām, nákṣatra-śavasām* 'equalling the stars in number'. — **n.** *chándasām, tárasām* (AV.), *médasām* (VS. XXI. 40), *rákṣasām* (VS. II. 23), *rā́dhasām, védasām*[2].

L. f. *ap-sarássu* (Kh. IV. 8[3]). — **n.** *áṃhassu*[3] (AV.), *ū́dhassu, rájassu, vákṣassu, váyassu* (AV.), *śrávassu, sádassu*[4].

γ. Stems in *-yāṃs*.

345. The primary suffix *-yāṃs* (137)[5] is used to form comparative stems. It is added either directly or with connecting *-ī-* to the root, which is always accented. There are seven duplicate stems formed in both ways: *táv-yāṃs-* and *táv-īyāṃs-* 'stronger'; *náv-yāṃs-* and *náv-īyāṃs-* 'new'; *pán-yāṃs-* and *pán-īyāṃs-* 'more wonderful'; *bhū́yāṃs-* and *bhávīyāṃs-* 'more'; *rábhyāṃs-* and *rábhīyāṃs-* (VS.) 'more violent'; *vásyāṃs-* and *vásīyāṃs-* 'better'; *sáh-yāṃs-* and *sáhī-yāṃs-* 'mightier'. **Strong and weak forms are regularly distinguished.** In the latter the suffix is reduced by loss of the nasal and shortening of the vowel to *-yas*. These stems are declined in the m. and n. only, as they form their f. by adding *-ī* to the weak stem; e. g. *préyas-ī-* 'dearer'. No forms of the dual occur, and in the plural only the N. A. G. are found.

Inflexion.

346. The V. sing. m. ends in *-as*[6]. The forms actually occurring, if made from *kánīyāṃs-* 'younger', would be as follows:

Sing. N. m. *kánīyān*, n. *kánīyas.* A. m. *kánīyāṃsam*, n. *kánīyas.* I. m. n. *kánīyasā.* D. m. n. *kánīyase.* Ab. m. n. *kánīyasas.* G. m. n. *kánīyasas.* L. m. *kánīyasi.* V. m. *kánīyas.* — **Pl.** N. m. *kánīyāṃsas.* A. m. *kánīyasas.* N. A. n. *kánīyāṃsi.* G. m. *kánīyasām.*

The forms which occur are the following:

Sing. N. m. *á-tavyān*[7] 'not stronger', *ójīyān* 'stronger', *kánīyān, jávīyān* 'swifter', *jyā́yān* 'mightier', *tárīyān*[8] 'easily passing through', *távīyān* 'stronger', *távyān* 'stronger', *dhávīyān* 'running fast', *návīyān* 'new', *máṃhīyān* 'more bountiful', *yájīyān* 'worshipping more', *yódhīyān* 'more warlike', *vánīyān* 'imparting more', *várīyān* 'better', *várṣīyān* (VS. XXIII. 48) 'higher', *vásyān*

---

[1] Also the transition forms *íḍa-prajasas* (TS. I. 5. 6[1]; MS. I. 5[3], p. 70).

[2] The form *vayā́m* is perhaps contracted for *vayásām* (I. 165[15] etc.); see LANMAN 552[3].

[3] All the Mss. read *áṃhasu*; see WHITNEY's note on AV. VI. 35[2].

[4] The form *apásu* (VIII. 4[14]) is perhaps for m. *apássu*; cp. WACKERNAGEL I, p. 111, note.

[5] Cp. J. SCHMIDT KZ. 26, 377—400; HIRT, IF. 12, 201 f.

[6] As in the *-mant, -vant* and *-vāṃs* stems.

[7] On the Sandhi of these nominatives see LANMAN 514 (middle).

[8] Cp. REICHELT, BB. 27, 104 f.

'better', *védīyān* 'knowing better', *śréyān* 'better', *sánīyān* (TS. III. 5. 5[3]) 'winning much', *sáhīyān* 'mightier', *skábhīyān* 'supporting more firmly'.

N. A. n. *ŕjīyas* 'straighter', *ójīyas, kánīyas*[1], *jyáyas, távīyas, dávīyas* 'farther', *drághīyas* 'longer', *návīyas, návyas, nédīyas* 'quite near', *préyas* 'dearer', *bhúyas*[2] 'more', *várīyas, várṣīyas, vásīyas* (TS. VS.), *vásyas, śréyas* (TS. VS.), *svádīyas* 'sweeter'.

A. m. *jyáyāṃsam, távyāṃsam, drághīyāṃsam, návyāṃsam, pányāṃsam* 'more wonderful', *várṣīyāṃsam* (AV.), *śáśīyāṃsam*[3] 'more frequent', *śréyāṃsam, sáhīyāṃsam* (AV.).

I. m. *jávīyasā, návyasā, bhúyasā, sáhīyasā* (Kh. I. 1[1]). — **n.** *téjīyasā* 'keener', *tvákṣīyasā* 'very strong', *návīyasā, návyasā, pányasā, bhávīyasā* 'more abundant', *bhúyasā, vásyasā, sáhīyasā*.

D. m. *távyase, návīyase, pánīyase, pányase, bálīyase* (AV.) 'mightier', *várṣīyase* (VS. XVI. 30), *śréyase* (VS. XXXI. 11), *sányase* 'older', *sáhīyase*[4], *sáhyase, hánīyase* (VS. XVI. 40) 'more destructive'. — **n.** *návīyase, návyase, sányase*.

Ab. m. *távīyasas, rábhyasas* 'more violent', *sáhīyasas, sáhyasas*. — **n.** *bhúyasas*.

G. m. *kánīyasas, jyáyasas, távyasas, návīyasas, návyasas, bhúyasas*. — **n.** *návyasas*.

L. m. *várṣīyasi* (VS. VI. 11), *sáhīyasi*. — **V. m.** *ójīyas, jyáyas*.

Pl. N. m. *tíkṣṇīyāṃsas* (AV.) 'sharper', *bhúyāṃsas* (TS. VS. AV.), *śréyāṃsas*. — **n.** *návyāṃsi*.

A. m. *kánīyasas, nédīyasas, bhúyasas, rábhīyasas* (VS. XXI. 46), *várṣīyasas* (AV.), *vásyasas, váhīyasas* 'driving better', *śréyasas* (VS. TS.).

G. m. *á-stheyasām* 'not firm' (137). The f. form *návyasīnām* is twice used owing to metrical exigencies instead of *návyasām* in agreement with *marútām*[5].

δ. Stems in *-vāṃs*.

347. The suffix *-vāṃs*[6] is used to form the stem of the perfect participle active. **Strong and weak stem**[7] are regularly **distinguished**; but the latter assumes two different forms according as it is followed by a vowel or a consonant. The suffix is reduced before vowels, by loss of the nasal and Samprasāraṇa, to *-us* which becomes *-uṣ*; before a consonant (i. e. *bh*), it is reduced, by loss of the nasal and shortening of the vowel, to *-vas*, which becomes *-vat*[8]. The latter form of the stem occurs only three times in the RV. There are thus three stems employed in the inflexion of these participles: *-vāṃs, -vat, -uṣ*. The weakest form of the stem (*-uṣ*) appears instead of the strong twice in the A. sing. m. and once in the N. pl. m. The accent rests on the suffix in all its forms except in compounds formed with the negative *a-* or with *su-* 'well' and *dus-* 'ill', where it shifts to these particles. This declension is restricted to the m. and n., as the f. is formed by adding *-ī* to the weakest stem, as *jagmúṣ-ī-* 'having gone'. There are altogether (including compounds) about 75 stems in *-vāṃs* in the RV.

Inflexion.

348. No specifically n. forms occur except two in the A. sing. No L. has been met with in any number; all the other weak cases are wanting in

1 The form *jávīyas* occurs in VS. XL. 4 (Īśā Up.).

2 Once to be read *bhávīyas*: LANMAN 514[4].

3 Comparative of the root from which *śáś-vat-* 'constant' is derived.

4 To be read *sáhyase* in I. 71[4].

5 See LANMAN 515.

6 On this suffix cp. J. SCHMIDT, KZ. 26, 329—377.

7 On the formation of this perfect stem, see above 181 and below 491.

8 This form was transferred to the N. A. sing. n. in which no consonant (*-bh* or *-s*) followed; cp. 44 a, 3.

the dual as well as the D. Ab. in the plural. The V. sing. m. is regularly formed with *-vas*[1]. The forms actually occurring, if made from *cakṛvāṃs-* 'having done', would be the following:

Sing. N. m. *cakṛvā́n.* A. m. *cakṛvā́ṃsam,* n. *cakṛvát.* I. *cakrúṣā.* D. m. *cakrúṣe.* Ab. *cakrúṣas.* G. *cakrúṣas.* V. m. *cákṛvas.* — **Du.** N. A. m. *cakṛvā́ṃsā.* — **Pl.** N. m. *cakṛvā́ṃsas.* A. m. *cakrúṣas.* I. m. *cakṛvádbhis.* G. m. *cakrúṣām.*

The forms actually occurring are the following:

Sing. N. m. *á-cikitvān*[2] 'not knowing', *á-proṣivān* 'not gone away'[3], *á-rarivān* 'not liberal', *á-vidvān*[4] 'not knowing', *cakṛvā́n* 'having done', *cikitvā́n* 'having noticed', *jaganvā́n* 'having gone', *jaghanvā́n* 'having slain', *jajñivā́n*[5] 'having recognized', *jigīvā́n*[6] 'having conquered', *jujurvā́n* 'having grown old', *jujuṣvā́n* 'having enjoyed', *jūjuvā́n* 'having sped', *tatanvā́n* 'having stretched', *tasthivā́n* 'having stood', *dadaśvā́n*[7] 'having bitten', *dadasvā́n* 'become exhausted', *dadṛśvā́n* 'having seen', *dadvā́n* 'having given', *dadhanvā́n*[8] 'having streamed', *dadhṛṣvā́n* 'having become bold', *dāśvā́n*[4] 'worshipping', *dīdivā́n* 'having shone', *nir-jagmivā́n* (TS. IV. 2. 1[4]) 'having gone out', *papivā́n* 'having drunk'[9], *pupuṣvā́n* 'having made abundant', *babhūvā́n* 'having become', *bibhīvā́n* 'having feared', *mamṛvā́n* 'having died', *mīḍhvā́n*[4] 'bountiful', *yayivā́n* 'having gone', *rarivā́n* 'having given', *rurukvā́n* 'having shone', *vavanvā́n* 'having accepted', *vidvā́n*[4] knowing', *vivikvā́n*[10] 'having divided', *vividvā́n* 'having found', *vividhvā́n*[11] 'having wounded', *śuśukvā́n*[12] 'having shone', *śuśruvā́n,* 'having heard', *sasavā́n* 'having won', *sāsahvā́n* 'having conquered', *sāhvā́n*[4] 'having overcome'.

A. m. *īyivā́ṃsam*[13] 'having gone', *cakṛvā́ṃsam, cakhvā́ṃsam*[14] 'stretching out', *cikitvā́ṃsam, jāgṛvā́ṃsam* 'waking', *jūjuvā́ṃsam, tastabhvā́ṃsam* 'having held fast', *tasthivā́ṃsam, dāśvā́ṃsam*[4], *dīdivā́ṃsam, dúr-vidvāṃsam* 'ill-disposed', *papivā́ṃsam*[15], *paptivā́ṃsam* 'having flown', *pīpivā́ṃsam* 'having swelled', *mamṛvā́ṃsam, ririhvā́ṃsam* 'having licked', *vavṛvā́ṃsam* 'having enclosed', *vāvṛdhvā́ṃsam* 'having grown strong', *vidvā́ṃsam*[4], *(pra-)viviśivā́ṃsam* (TS. IV. 7. 15[1]), *śūśuvā́ṃsam* 'having increased', *sasavā́ṃsam, sasṛvā́ṃsam* 'having sped', *sāsahvā́ṃsam, sú-vidvāṃsam*[4] 'knowing well', *suṣupvā́ṃsam* 'having slept', *suṣuvā́ṃsam* 'having pressed (Soma)'. — **Weak forms for strong:** *cakrúṣam* (X. 137[1]) for *cakṛvā́ṃsam*; *emuṣám* (VIII. 66[10])[16] 'dangerous'.

A. n. *tatanvát* 'extending far', *saṃ-vavṛtvát* 'enveloping'.

I. m. *á-bibhyuṣā* 'fearless', *cikitúṣā* 'wise', *vidúṣā*[4]. — **n.** *á-bibhyuṣā, bibhyúṣā.*

D. m. *á-raruṣe, ūcúṣe*[17] 'pleased', *cakrúṣe, cikitúṣe, jagmúṣe* 'having gone', *jigyúṣe, dadāśúṣe* 'worshipping', *dāśúṣe*[18], *bibhyúṣe, mīḷhúṣe*[18], *vidúṣe*[18], *sedúṣe*[19] 'having sat down'.

Ab. m. *á-raruṣas, jujurúṣas.* — **n.** *tasthúṣas*[20].

---

1 Cp. the *-mant* and *-vant* stems (316) and the *-yāṃs* stems (346).

2 On the Sandhi of these nominatives see LANMAN 512.

3 From *pra* and *vas-* 'dwell'.

4 Without reduplication.

5 From *jñā-* 'know'.

6 From *ji-* 'conquer'.

7 From *daṃś-* 'bite'.

8 From *dhanv-* 'run'.

9 LANMAN adds *paprivā́n*(?).

10 From *vic-* 'separate'.

11 From *vyadh-* 'pierce'.

12 From *śuc-* 'shine'.

13 From *i-* 'go'.

14 From a root *khā-*.

15 LANMAN adds *paprivā́ṃsam*(?).

16 From *am-* 'be injurious', with weak stem, together with anomalous accent, for **em-i-vā́ṃsam*; cp. LANMAN 512[3].

17 From *uc-* 'find pleasure'.

18 Unreduplicated form.

19 From *sad-* 'sit down'.

20 This may be A. pl. m.

G. m. *á-dāśuṣas* 'not worshipping', *á-raruṣas*, *īyúṣas*, *cikitúṣas*, *jagmúṣas*, *jaghnúṣas*, *jānúṣas*[1] 'knowing', *jigyúṣas*, *tatarúṣas* 'having crossed', *tasthúṣas*, *dadúṣas*, *dāśúṣas*[5], *dīdīyúṣas*, *papúṣas*, *bibhyúṣas*, *mamrúṣas* (AV.), *mīḷhúṣas*[5], *vividúṣas* 'having found', *sedúṣas*, *suṣuvúṣas*. — **n.** *vavavrúṣas*[2] 'enveloping'.

V. m. *cikitvas* 'seeing', *titirvas* 'having crossed', *dīdivas* 'shining', *mīḍhvas*[5]. — **With -van:** *cikitvan*[3] (AV.).

Du. N. A. m. *okivāṃsā*[4] 'accustomed to', *jaganvāṃsā*, *jāgṛvāṃsā*, *tasthivāṃsā*, *dīdivāṃsā*, *papivāṃsā*, *vavanvāṃsā*, *vidvāṃsā*[5], *śūśuvāṃsā*, *śuśruvāṃsā*. — **With au:** *vidvāṃsau*[5].

Pl. N. m. *á-vidvāṃsas*, *cakṛvāṃsas*, *cikitvāṃsas*, *jakṣivāṃsas* (TS. I. 4. 44[2]) 'having eaten', *jaganvāṃsas*, *jāgṛvāṃsas*, *jigīvāṃsas*, *tasthivāṃsas*, *titirvāṃsas*, *tuṣṭuvāṃsas* 'having praised', *dadṛvāṃsas* 'having burst', *dāśvāṃsas*[5], *papivāṃsas* (TS. I. 4. 44[2]), *paptivāṃsas*, *mīḍhvāṃsas*[5], *ririkvāṃsas*[6] 'having abandoned', *vidvāṃsas*[5], *śuśukvāṃsas*, *śūśuvāṃsas*, *sasavāṃsas*, *sasṛvāṃsas*, *sāsahvāṃsas*, *sāhvāṃsas*[5], *sú-vidvāṃsas* (TS. IV. 6. 5[2]), *suṣupvāṃsas*. — **Weak form for strong:** *á-bibhyuṣas*[7] (I. 11[5]). The AV. has the **hybrid form** *bhaktivāṃsas*[8]

A. m. *cikitúṣas*, *jagmúṣas*, *jigyúṣas*, *tasthúṣas*, *dāśúṣas*[5], *mīḷhúṣas*[5], *vidúṣas*[5], *sedúṣas*.

I. m. *jāgṛvádbhis*. — **G. m.** *á-dāśuṣām*[5], *jigyúṣām*, *dadúṣām*, *mīḷhúṣām*[5], *vidúṣām*[5].

2. Radical Stems in *-ś*.

349. This declension comprises only radical stems, both monosyllabic and compound, formed from some dozen roots, numbering altogether about sixty. Some forty of these occur in the m., nearly thirty in the f., and half a dozen in the n. Nine monosyllabic stems are f., viz. *dāś-* 'worship', *diś-* 'direction', *dṛś-* 'look', *náś-* 'night', *páś-* 'sight', *píś-* 'ornament', *práś-*[9] 'dispute', *viś-* 'settlement', *vriś-* 'finger'; but only two m., viz. *íś-* 'lord' and *spáś-* 'spy'; all the rest are compounds, about 20 of which are formed from *dṛś-*. The inflexion is the same in all genders: the only n. forms which would differ from the m. and f. (N. A. du. and pl.) do not occur.

a. The only trace of the distinction of strong and weak forms appears in the nasalization of the stem in the N. sing. m. of some half dozen compounds of *-dṛś-* 'look'[10].

b. As the *ś* represents an old palatal (40), it normally becomes the cerebral *ḍ* before terminations beginning with *bh*, as *viḍ-bhis*; but in *diś-* and *-dṛś-* it becomes a guttural, owing doubtless to the influence of the *k* in the N. sing. and L. pl. It regularly becomes *k* before the *-su* of the L. pl., where it is phonetic (43 b 2); it usually also becomes *k* in the N. sing. (which originally ended in *-s*). But in four stems it is represented by the cerebral *ṭ*, e. g. *viṭ*, owing to the influence of forms in which the cerebral is phonetic. In *puro-ḍāś* 'sacrificial cake', the palatal is displaced by the *-s* of the N.[11].

1 Unreduplicated form from *jñā-* 'know'.

2 With anomalous additional reduplicative syllable.

3 AV. VII. 97[1] for *cikitvas* of the corresponding verse of the RV. (III. 29[16]), as if from a *-vant* stem.

4 From *uc-* 'be wont'.

5 Without reduplication.

6 From *ric-* 'leave'.

7 See LANMAN 513[3].

8 In AV. VI. 79[3] for the reading of the edition *bhaktivāṃsaḥ syāma* the Paipp. has *bhakṣīmahi*.

9 From *praś-* 'question'. LANMAN would correct the reading of AV. II. 27[7] to *prāśi*, explaining the word as a compound (*pra-aś-*), where the accent *prāśi* would be regular.

10 That is, *-dṛṅ*, which in its three occurrences in the RV. appears before vowels and doubles the *ṅ*: *-dṛṅṅ*.

11 It cannot, however, have been directly ousted by the N. *-s* (the former existence of which in consonant stems must have been long forgotten), but was doubtless due to the influence of *ā-* stems, such as *draviṇo-dā-s*.

c. There are two transition forms to the *a*-declension from *puro-ḍā́ś-*: *puroḍā́śena* (VS. XIX. 85) and *puroḍāśá-vatsā* (AV. XII. 4[35]) 'having a sacrificial cake as a calf'. The D. infinitive *dṛśáye* is a transition to the *i*-declension, for *dṛś-é*[1].

Inflexion.

350. The normal forms actually occurring, if made from *viś-* f. 'settlement', would be as follows:

Sing. N. V. *viṭ.* **A.** *viśam.* I. *viśā́.* D. *viśé.* Ab. *viśás.* G. *viśás.* L. *viśí.* — **Du.** N. A. *víśā* and *víśau.* — **Pl.** N. *víśas.* A. *víśas.* I. *viḍbhís.* D. Ab. *viḍbhyás.* G. *viśā́m.* L. *vikṣú.*

Forms which actually occur are the following:

Sing. N. m. 1. **with nasalized stem:** *kī-dṛ́ṅ*[2] 'of what kind?', *sa-dṛ́ṅ*[3] 'resembling'; in VS. XVII. 81: *anyā-dṛ́ṅ* 'of another kind', *ī-dṛ́ṅ* 'such', *práti-sadṛṅ* 'similar'[4]. — 2. ending **in -*k*:** *ī-dṛ́k* (AV.), *etā-dṛ́k* 'such', *tā-dṛ́k* 'such', *divi-spṛ́k* 'touching heaven', *ni-spṛ́k*[5] 'caressing', *yā-dṛ́k* 'of what kind', *raṇvá-saṃdṛk* 'appearing beautiful', *svar-dṛ́k* 'seeing light', *hiraṇya-saṃdṛk* 'resembling gold', *hṛdi-spṛ́k* 'touching the heart'. — 3. ending **in -*ṭ*:** *spáṭ*; *vi-ṣpáṭ* 'spy'. — 4. ending **in -*s*:** *puro-ḍā́s* 'sacrificial cake' (occurs twice).

f. 2. ending **in -*k*:** *dík* (VS. AV.), *nák*; *án-apa-spṛk* (AV.) 'not refusing', *upa-dṛ́k* 'aspect', *raṇvá-saṃdṛk*, *saṃ-dṛ́k* 'appearance', *su-dṛ́śīka-saṃdṛk* 'having a beautiful appearance'. — 3. ending **in -*ṭ*:** *víṭ*; *ví-pāṭ* ('fetterless') N. of a river.

N. A. n. *etā-dṛ́k*[6], *su-saṃdṛ́k* 'handsome'; *tā-dṛ́k* may be a neuter in v. 44[6].

A. m. *spáśam*; *puro-ḍā́śam*; *upari-spṛ́śam* 'reaching above', *divi-spṛ́śam*, *hṛdi-spṛ́śam*; *tveṣá-saṃdṛśam* 'of brilliant appearance', *piśáṅga-saṃdṛśam* 'of reddish appearance', *raṇvá-saṃdṛśam*, *su-saṃdṛ́śam*; *dūre-dṛ́śam* 'visible far and wide', *su-dṛ́śam* 'well-looking', *svar-dṛ́śam*; *dūrá-ādiśam*[7] 'announcing far and wide'. — **f.** *díśam*, *prā́śam* (AV.), *víśam*; *ā-díśam* 'intention', *ṛta-spṛ́śam* 'connected with pious works', *piśáṅga-saṃdṛśam* (AV.), *pra-díśam* 'direction', *ví-pāśam*, *śukra-píśam* 'radiantly adorned', *saṃ-dṛ́śam*.

I. m. *viśva-píśā* 'all-adorned', *su-saṃdṛ́śā*[8]. — **f.** *dāśā́*[9], *diśā́*, *piśā́*, *viśā́*; *pra-díśā*. — **n.** *divi-spṛ́śā*, *dūre-dṛ́śā*.

D. m. *ánar-viśe* 'seated on the car', *ī-dṛ́śe*, *divi-spṛ́śe*, *dū-ḍā́śe* (AV.) 'irreligious', *dūre-dṛ́śe*. — **f.** *diśé* (AV. VS.), *viśé*; *saṃ-dṛ́śe*[10].

Ab. m. *svar-dṛ́śas*. — **f.** *diśás* (AV.), *viśás*; *saṃ-dṛ́śas*, *saṃ-spṛ́śas* (VS. XXXVIII. 11).

G. m. *upa-spṛ́śas* (AV.) 'touching', *divi-spṛ́śas*, *práti-prāśas*[11] (AV.) 'counter-disputant', *su-dṛ́śas*, *svar-dṛ́śas*, *hiraṇya-saṃdṛśas*, *hṛdi-spṛ́śas*. — **f.** *diśás* (AV.), *viśás*. — **n.** *sā́dana-spṛ́śas* 'coming into one's house'.

L. m. *divi-spṛ́śi*. — **f.** *diśí* (AV.), *dṛśí*, *prāśí* (AV.), *viśí*; *pra-díśi*, *ví-pāśi*, *saṃ-dṛ́śi*. — **V. m.** *tveṣa-saṃdṛk*.

Du. N. A. V. m. *ṛta-spṛ́śā*, *divi-spṛ́śā* and *divi-spṛśā*, *mithū-dṛ́śā* 'appearing alternately', *svar-dṛ́śā*. — **f.** *mithū-dṛ́śā*. — **With -*au*:** *víśau*.

Pl. N. m. *spáśas*; *upari-spṛ́śas* (AV.), *ṛta-spṛ́śas*, *divi-spṛ́śas*, *mandi-ni-spṛ́śas* 'fond of Soma', *ratha-spṛ́śas* 'touching the chariot', *hṛdi-spṛ́śas*; *dūre-*

[1] Cp. LANMAN 490[1].

[2] *kīdṛ́ṅṅ i-* (x. 108[3]).

[3] *sadṛ́ṅṅ* always before *a-* in RV. In TS. II. 2. 8[6] (B) the final *k* is preserved before *s*: *sadṛ́ṅk samānáis*.

[4] Also *sadṛ́ṅ*: all four before *ca*. Cp. LANMAN 456[1] and 463[1].

[5] From *ni-spṛ́ś-*, BR., GRASSMANN, LANMAN; from *ni-spṛ́h-* 'desirous of' (loc.), BÖHTLINGK (pw.).

[6] The form *manānák* (x. 61[6]), perhaps the same as *manā́k* 'a little', is explained by GRASSMANN as *manā-náś* 'dispelling wrath'.

[7] For *dūré-ā-diśam*.

[8] In the Īśā Upaniṣad (VS. XL. 1) also occurs *īśā́*.

[9] Cp. LANMAN 490 (bottom).

[10] There is also the transition form *dṛśáye*.

[11] Cp. WHITNEY's note on AV. II. 27[1]. The accent should be *prati-prā́śas*.

dṛ́śas, *yakṣa-dṛ́śas* 'having the appearance of a Yakṣa', *su-dṛ́śas*, *svar-dṛ́śas*; *tveṣá-saṃdṛ́śas*, *su-saṃdṛ́śas*; *viśva-piśas*, *su-piśas* 'well adorned'; *sú-sadṛśas* 'handsome'. — f. *díśas*, *víśas*; *ā-díśas*, *ud-díśas* (VS. VI. 19) 'upper quarters', *upa-spṛ́śas*, *pra-díśas*, *vi-díśas* (VS. VI. 19) 'intermediate quarters', *saṃ-dṛ́śas*.

A. m. *spáśas*; *ahar-dṛ́śas* 'beholding the day', *bhīmá-saṃdṛśas* 'of terrible appearance', *svar-dṛ́śas*, *hiraṇya-saṃdṛśas*. — f. *díśas*, *víśas*, *vríśas*; *ā-díśas*, *pra-díśas*, *saṃ-dṛ́śas*.

I. m. *su-saṃdṛ́gbhis*. — f. *paḍbhís*[1] (IV. 2[12]) 'with looks', *viḍbhís*. — **D.** f. *digbhyás* (VS. VI. 19). — **Ab.** f. *digbhyás*, *viḍbhyás*. — **G.** f. *diśā́m*, *viśā́m*; *ā-diśā́m*. — **L.** f. *dikṣú* (AV. VS.), *vikṣú*.

6. Radical stems in *-h*.

351. This declension comprises some 80 stems formed from about a dozen roots. All three genders appear in its inflexion; but the neuter is rare, being found in only two stems and never in the plural. Of monosyllabic stems six or seven are f., one m., and one n. All the remaining stems are compounds, about three-fourths of which are formed from the three roots *druh-*, *vah-* and *sah-* (over 30 from the last). The origin of the two stems *uṣṇíh-* (AV.) a metre, and *sarádh-*[2] 'bee' is obscure.

a. The distinction of strong and weak appears in compounds of *vah-* and *sah-*[3], the vowel being lengthened in the N. A. sing. and N. pl. m.; also in the N. A. du. m. forms *indra-vā́hā*, *indra-vā́hau*, *anaḍ-vā́hau*; and in the f. sing. N. *dakṣiṇā-vā́ṭ* and A. *havya-vā́ham*. The strong stem *-vāh-* twice appears in weak cases, while it is metrically shortened 18 times in strong cases[4]. The word *anaḍ-váh-* 'ox' (lit. 'cart-drawer') distinguishes three stems, the strong one being *anaḍ-vā́h-*, and the weak *anaḍ-úh-* before vowels and *anaḍ-út-*[5] before consonants.

b. As *h* represents both the old guttural aspirate *gh* and the old palatal *jh*, it should phonetically become *g* and *ḍ* respectively before *bh*. But the cerebral appears for both in the only two case-forms that occur with a *-bh* ending: *saráḍbhyas* from *saráh-*, and *anaḍ-úḍbhyas* (AV.) from *anaḍ-váh-*, where the dental *d* takes the place of the cerebral by dissimilation. Before the *-su* of the L. pl., *k* would be phonetic; but here again, in the only form occurring, the cerebral appears: *anaḍútsu*[6]. On the other hand the phonetic *k* appears in the N. sing. in the six forms *-dhak*, *-dhúk*, *-dhrúk*[7], *-rúk*, *-spṛ́k*, *uṣṇík* (AV.)[8]; while the unphonetic *ṭ* appears in the two forms *-vā́ṭ* and *-ṣā́ṭ*[9]. The word *anaḍ-váh-* forms, instead of **anaḍ-vā́ṭ*, the anomalous *anaḍvā́n* as if from a stem in *-vant*.

c. The stem *mahá-* is perhaps a transfer to the *a*-declension from the far more frequent but defective *máh-* 'great'. Several cases are formed from it: sing. N. *mahá-s*, G. *mahásya*, L. *mahé*; pl. N. *mahā́* and *mahā́ni*, n., G. *mahā́nām*. The D. sing. *maháye*, used as an infinitive, is a transfer to the *i*-declension from *máh-*.

Inflexion.

352. The forms actually occurring, if made from *sáh-* 'victorious', would be as follows:

1 BLOOMFIELD is of opinion that here, as well as in the 5 other passages in which this form occurs in the RV., it means 'with feet': Johns Hopkins University Circular, 1906, p. 15—19.

2 That the *h* here represents an original guttural is shown by the N. pl. *sarághas* (ŚB.) and the derivatives *sarághā-* and *sā́ragha-* (TB.).

3 The Pada text has always *vāh-* on the one hand, but *sāh-* on the other.

4 Cp. LANMAN 498 (middle).

5 For *anaḍ-úḍ-* by dissimilation.

6 The dental again by dissimilation for the cerebral *ṭ*.

7 Occurring respectively in *uśá-dhak* 'burning with eagerness', in three compounds of *duh-* 'milk', and in five compounds of *druh-* 'injure'. These three forms, together with *uṣar-bhút*, are the only examples of the restoration of initial aspiration in the declension of the RV.

8 The derivation of this word (AV. VS.), is uncertain; it occurs in the RV. only in the extended form of *uṣṇihā-*.

9 When the final *h* becomes *ṭ*, the initial *s* is cerebralized.

Sing. N. *ṣáṭ*. V. m. f. *ṣāṭ*. A. m. f. *sā́ham*. I. *sahā́*. D. *sahé*. Ab. *sahás*. G. *sahás*. L. *sahí*. — **Du.** N. A. V. m. f. *sā́hā* and *sā́hau*. N. A. n. *sahí*. — **Pl.** N. V. m. f. *sā́has*. A. m. *sáhas* and *sahás*, f. *sáhas*. D. m. f. *ṣaḍ-bhyás*[1]. G. m. *sahā́m*. L. m. *ṣaṭsú*[1].

The forms actually occurring are the following:

Sing. N. m. 1. with -*k*: *uśá-dhak* 'burning with eagerness'; *go-dhúk* 'milkman', *prati-dhúk*[2] (AV. TS.) 'fresh milk'; *akṣnayā-dhrúk* 'injuring wrongly', *a-dhrúk* 'free from malice', *antaka-dhrúk* 'demon of death', *abhi-dhrúk* 'inimical', *asma-dhrúk* 'inimical to us'.

2. with -*ṭ*: *ṣā́ṭ*; *abhī-ṣā́ṭ* 'overpowering', *ṛṣi-ṣā́ṭ* 'overcoming the seer', *janā-ṣā́ṭ* 'overcoming men', *turā-ṣā́ṭ* 'overpowering quickly', *niṣ-ṣā́ṭ* 'overpowering', *nī-ṣā́ṭ*[3] (AV.) 'overcoming', *purā-ṣā́ṭ* 'victorious from of old', *pṛtanā-ṣā́ṭ* 'conquering hostile armies', *prāśu-ṣā́ṭ* 'finishing swiftly', *bhuri-ṣā́ṭ*[4] 'bearing much', *rayi-ṣā́ṭ* 'ruling over wealth', *vane-ṣā́ṭ* 'prevailing in woods', *vīra-ṣā́ṭ*[5] 'ruling men', *viśvā-ṣā́ṭ*[6] (AV.) 'all-conquering', *vṛthā-ṣā́ṭ* 'conquering easily', *śatrū-ṣā́ṭ*[7] (AV.) 'overcoming foes', *satrā-ṣā́ṭ* 'always conquering'; *turya-vā́ṭ* (TS. IV. 3. 3²) 'four-year-old ox', *ditya-vā́ṭ*[8] (VS. XIV. 10; TS. IV. 7. 10¹) 'two-year-old ox', *paṣṭha-vā́ṭ* (VS. XIV. 9) 'four-year-old ox'[9], *madhyama-vā́ṭ* 'driving at middling speed', *havir-vā́ṭ* 'conveying the oblation', *havya-vā́ṭ* 'conveying the offering'. — **Irregular form:** *anaḍ-vā́n* (AV. TS. VS.) 'ox'[10].

f. 1. *uṣṇík* (VS. AV.) a metre, *gartā-rúk*[11] 'ascending the car-seat', *sabar-dhúk* 'yielding nectar'. — **2.** *dakṣiṇā-vā́ṭ* 'borne to the right'[12]. — **n. 1.** *puru-spṛ́k* 'much desired'.

A. m. 1. Strong forms with *-vā́ham* and *-sā́ham* (after *ă*) or *-ṣā́ham* (after *ĭ* or *ṛ*): *anaḍ-vā́ham*, *turya-vā́ham* (VS. XXVIII. 28), *ditya-vā́ham* (VS. XXVIII. 25), *paṣṭha-vā́ham* (VS. XXVIII. 29), *vīra-vā́ham* 'conveying men', *svasti-vā́ham* 'bringing welfare', *havya-vā́ham* (also f.); *pra-sā́ham* 'victorious', *yajña-sā́ham*[13] 'mighty in sacrifice', *viśvā-sā́ham*, *satrā-sā́ham*; *abhimāti-ṣā́ham* 'conquering adversaries', *ṛtī-ṣā́ham* 'subduingassailants', *nṛ-ṣā́ham* 'overcoming men', *pṛtanā-ṣā́ham*[14]. — **With metrical shortening** of *-sā́h-* or *-ṣā́h-* : *ṛtī-ṣáham*, *pṛtanā-ṣáham*[14]; *carṣaṇī-sáham*[15] 'ruling over men', *prā-sáham*, *vibhvā-sáham* 'overcoming the rich', *sadā-sáham* 'always holding out'. — **2.** *a-drúham*, *puru-spṛ́ham*. — **f.** *gúham* 'hiding-place', *drúham* 'fiend', *míham* 'mist'; *uṣṇíham* (VS. XXVIII. 25); *parī-ṇáham* 'enclosure'.

I. m. *dhanvā-sáhā* 'skilled in archery', *puru-spṛ́hā*, *viṣu-drúhā* 'injuring in various parts'. — **f.** *guhā́*[16], *druhā́*, *mahā́* 'great'; *uṣṇíhā* (VS. XXI. 13); *prā-sáhā*[17] 'might', *vi-srúhā* 'plant'. — **n.** *mahā́*.

D. m. *druhé*[18], *mahé*; *a-drúhe*, *abhi-drúhe*, *abhimāti-ṣā́he*[19] (TS. V. 2. 7³), *carṣaṇī-sáhe*[15], *satrā-sā́he*[20]. — **f.** *mahé*; *uṣṇíhe* (VS. XXIV. 12); *go-dúhe*[21]. — **n.** *mahé*.

[1] To be inferred from *anaḍúdbhyas* and *anaḍútsu*.

[2] There is no evidence to show the gender of this word.

[3] For *ni-ṣā́ṭ*.

[4] For *bhūri-ṣā́ṭ*.

[5] For *vīra-ṣā́ṭ*.

[6] For *viśva-ṣā́ṭ*.

[7] For *śatru-ṣā́ṭ*.

[8] Here *ditya-* seems to be = *dvitī́ya-*.

[9] Probably from *paṣṭha-* = *pṛṣṭha-* 'back'. The TS. (IV. 3. 3² etc.) has *paṣṭha-vā́t* with dental *t* for cerebral *ṭ*.

[10] There is also the transfer form *mahá-s*, supplying the place of a N. of *máh-*.

[11] For *garta-rúk*.

[12] The N. of *saráh-* 'bee', occurs as *saráṭ* in TS. V. 3. 12² (B) and in ŚB. XIII. 3. 1⁴.

[13] For *yajña-sā́ham*.

[14] With unphonetic cerebral after *ā* owing to the influence of the N. *pṛtanā-ṣā́ṭ*.

[15] The *s* is here not cerebralized after *ī*.

[16] *gúhā* which occurs 53 times (beside *guhā́*, once) is used adverbially, 'in secret', with retracted accent.

[17] From *prā-sáh*, beside *pra-sā́h-*.

[18] This form is perhaps f.

[19] Strong form for weak.

[20] Strong form for weak (II. 21²), but the Pada text has *satrā-sáhe*.

[21] There is also a transfer to the *i*-declension: *mahā́ye* (as an infinitive).

Ab. m. *druhás, mahás; ṛtī-ṣáhas.* — **f.** *druhás*[1]. — **n.** *mahás.*

G. m. *druhás, mahás*[2]; *a-drúhas, anaḍúhas* (AV.), *pṛtanā-ṣáhas;* with strong form: *abhimāti-ṣā́has*[3]. — **f.** *druhás, mihás; prā-sáhas.* — **n.** *mahás; puru-spṛ́has.*

L. m. *anaḍúhi* (AV.)[4]. — **f.** *upā-náhi* (AV.) 'shoe', *parī-ṇáhi* (AV.).

V. 1. m. *turā-ṣāṭ* (VS. x. 22), *pṛtanā-ṣāṭ* (AV.), *havya-vāṭ.* — **2. m.** *go-dhuk* (AV.). — **f.** *á-dhruk*[5].

Du. N. A. V. 1. m. *anaḍ-vā́hau, indra-vā́hā* and *indra-vā́hau* 'conveying Indra', *dhūr-ṣā́hau* (VS. iv. 33) 'bearing the yoke'; **shortened:** *carṣaṇī-sahā, rathā-sā́hā* 'drawing the chariot'. — **2. m.** *a-drúhā, án-abhidruhā* 'not inimical', *puru-spṛ́hā.* — **f.** *a-drúhā, a-druhā.* — **n.** *mahī́.*

Pl. N. V. 1. m. *anaḍ-vā́has* (AV.), *indra-vā́has, turya-vā́has* (VS. xxiv. 12), *ditya-vā́has* (VS.), *paṣṭha-vā́has* (VS.), *pṛṣṭi-vā́has* (AV.) 'carrying on the sides', *vajra-vā́has* 'wielding a thunderbolt', *vīra-vā́has, saha-vā́has* 'drawing together', *suṣṭhu-vā́has* 'carrying well', *havya-vā́has; abhimāti-ṣā́has, śatrū-ṣā́has;* **shortened:** V. *carṣaṇī-sahas.* — **2. m.** *drúhas, mahás*[6]; *a-drúhas,* V. *a-druhas, go-dúhas, puru-spṛ́has,* V. *puru-spṛhas.*

f.[7] *míhas, rúhas* 'sprouts'; *a-drúhas, ā-rúhas* (AV.) 'shoots', *ghṛta-dúhas* 'giving ghee', *puru-drúhas* 'injuring greatly', *puru-spṛ́has, pra-rúhas* (AV.) 'shoots', *mano-múhas* (AV.) 'bewildering the mind', *vi-srúhas.*

A. m. *druhás*[8], *mahás*[8], *a-drúhas, anaḍúhas* (AV.), *puru-spṛ́has.* — **f.** *drúhas, níhas*[9] (AV. VS.) 'destroyers', *míhas, rúhas* (AV.); *akṣā-náhas* 'tied to the axle', *a-drúhas, upā-rúhas* 'shoots', *pra-rúhas* (AV.), *saṃ-díhas* 'mounds'.

D. m. *anaḍúdbhyas* (AV.) — **f.** *saráḍbhyas* 'bees'. — **G. m.** *mahā́m*[10], *carṣaṇī-sáhām* (VS. xxviii. 1). — **L. m.** *anaḍútsu.*

7. Stems in semivowels: *r, y, v.*

353. This group forms a transition from the consonant to the vowel declension inasmuch as the stem often assumes a vocalic form before endings with initial consonant, and in some cases takes endings which otherwise appear in the vowel declension only. The *-r* stems are nearest the consonant declension as their radical division conforms almost without exception to that type; their derivative division, however, has several points in common with the inflexion of vowel stems.

1. Stems ending in *-r.*

354. **A. Radical stems.** Here the stems ending in radical *r* must be distinguished from those in which the *r* belongs to a suffix. The radical stems numbering over 50 are formed from some sixteen roots, the vowel of which is nearly always *i* or *u.* Only three of these stems contain *a* and only two *ā.* Nearly a dozen are monosyllabic, but the rest (numbering over 40) are compounds, almost a dozen of which are formed with *-tur.*

1 *áṃhas* (vi. 3[1]) is probably not an Ab. of *áṃh-* 'distress' (which does not occur elsewhere), but by haplology for *áṃhas-as,* which is very frequent.

2 There is also the transition form *mahásya.*

3 The Pada text has *-sáhas.*

4 There is also the transition form *mahé* (m. n.).

5 See Whitney's note on AV. vii. 73[6].

6 With irregular accent.

7 There are no neuters except the transition forms *mahā́* and *mahā́ni.*

8 With irregular accent as if weak forms. Cp. above 94, note 6 and Lanman 501 (middle).

9 The derivation of this word is uncertain: it is explained by Mahīdhara as = *nihantṛ-.* Whitney (AV. ii. 6[5]) would emend to *nidas.*

10 There is also the transition form *mahā́nām.*

The inflexion is the same in all genders except the N. A. neuter. A peculiarity is the lengthening of the radical *i* and *u* when a consonant ending follows or originally followed[1].

a. The distinction of strong and weak appears in *dvā́r-* f. 'door', which is reduced to *dúr-* in weak cases; in *tár-* and *stár-* 'star', from which are made *tā́ras* and *stṛ́bhis*; and in the n. *svàr* 'light' two weak cases, the D. and G. sing., are formed from the contracted stem *sūr-*.

b. There are here a few transitions to the *a*-declension: *śatá-durasya* and *śatá-dureṣu* 'having a hundred doors', which started from weak cases like *dúras*; *su-dhúra-s*, N. sing. m. 'well-yoked', due to the A. *su-dhúr-am*; perhaps also the A. sing. f. *án-apa-sphurā-m* 'not pushing away', which occurs beside the N. pl. *án-apa-sphur-as*[2]. On the other hand the N. pl. m. *vandhúr-as* 'car-seats' seems to be a transition from the *a*-declension, as *vandhúra-* is probably the older stem.

c. The form *yan-túr-am* 'guide', which occurs twice for *yan-tā́r-am* has been formed as if from *-túr* owing to the parallelism with *ap túram* which once appears beside it[3].

Inflexion.

355. The forms actually occurring, if made from *púr-* f. 'stronghold', would be as follows:

Sing. N. *pū́r*. A. *púram*. I. *purā́*. D. *puré*. Ab. *purás*. G. *purás*. L. *purí*. — **Du.** N. A. *púrā* and *púrau*. — **Pl.** N. V. *púras*. A. *púras*. I. *pūrbhís*. D. *pūrbhyás* (VS.). G. *purā́m*. L. *pūrṣú*.

The forms actually occurring are as follows:

Sing. N. m. *gī́r* 'praising', *vā́r*[4] 'protector'; *muhur-gī́r* 'swallowing suddenly'; *dúr-āśī́r* 'badly mixed'; *rajas-tū́r* 'traversing the air', *ratha-tū́r* 'drawing a chariot', *viśva-tū́r* 'all-surpassing', *su-pra-tū́r* 'very victorious'[5]. — f. *gī́r* 'praise', *dvā́r* (AV.) 'door', *dhū́r* 'burden', *pū́r*; *amā-jū́r* 'aging at home', *ā-śī́r*[6] (AV. TS.) 'mixture'.

N. A. n. *vā́r* 'water', *súar*[7] 'light'[8], *súvar* (TS. II. 2. 12[1]).

A. m. *túram* 'promoter'; *ap-túram*[9] 'active', *āji-túram* 'victorious in battles', *rajas-túram*, *ratha-túram*, *vṛtra-túram* 'conquering enemies'; *a-júram* 'unaging', *apa-sphúram* 'bounding forth', *ṛta-júram* 'grown old in (observing) the law', *gávāśiram* 'mixed with milk', *yávāśiram* 'mixed with corn', *sahásra-dvāram* 'having a thousand doors', *su-dhúram* 'well yoked'[10]. — f. *gíram*, *dvā́ram* (AV.), *dhúram*, *púram*; *ā-śíram*, *upa-stíram* 'cover', *saṃ-gíram* 'assent'.

I. m. *bándhurā*[11] (AV.) 'binder'(?). — f. *girā́*, *dhurā́*, *purā́*; *abhi-pra-múrā* 'crushing', *abhi-svárā* 'invocation', *ā-śírā*. — n. *viśva-túrā*.

D. m. *giré*; *niṣ-ṭúre* 'overthrowing'. — f. *upa-stíre*. — n. *sūré*.

Ab. f. *dhurás*; *ni-júras* 'consuming by fire'.

G. m. *gávāśiras*, *yávāśiras*, *radhra-túras* 'encouraging the obedient'. — f. *amā-júras*. — n. *sū́ras*[12]; *rásāśiras* 'mixed with juice'.

---

1 That is, the *-s* of the N. sing. m. and f. This rule also applies in *vā́r* (I. 132[3]) if Grassmann is right in explaining this form as a N. sing. m. meaning 'protector', from *vár-* (*vṛ-* 'cover'); but BR., s. v. *vā́r-*, regard this form as a corruption.

2 In the later language *dvā́r-* f. and *púr-* f. went over to the *a*-declension as *dvāra-* n. and *pura-* n., while *vā́r-* n. went over to the *i*-declension as *vāri-*.

3 See Lanman 486 (bottom).

4 If this form is not a corruption.

5 There is also the transition form *su-dhúra-s*.

6 From *śṛ-* 'mix'.

7 This is the only declensional form of this word occurring in the AV.

8 Neuter compounds ending in *-r* are avoided; thus the AV. has the transition form *náva-dvāra-m*, N. n.

9 For *ap-(a)-s-túram* 'getting over work'.

10 There is also the anomalous form *yantúram* for *yantā́ram*.

11 Probably a transfer from the *a*-declension.

12 With the accentuation of a dissyllabic stem (*súar*). In VIII. 61[17] for *sū́ra ā́* the Pada text has *sū́re ā́*, but it is probably the G. *sū́ras*. In I. 66[10], 69[10] the uninflected form *súar* seems to be used in a G. sense.

L. f. *dhurí*, *purí*. — n. *súar*[1].

Du. N. A. m. *vṛtra-túrā*, *sanā-júrā* 'long grown old', *su-dhúrā*. — f. *dvā́rā*; *mithas-túrā* 'alternating'; with *au*: *dvā́rau*, *dhúrau*.

Pl. N. V. m. *gíras*, *gíras*, *múras* 'destroyers'; *ap-túras*, *ā-múras* 'destroyers'; *gávāśiras*, *try-ā́śiras* 'mixed with three (products of milk)', *dádhy-āśiras* 'mixed with curds'; *dur-dhúras* 'badly yoked', *dhiyā-júras* 'grown old in devotion', *niṣ-ṭúras*, *bandhúras* (AV.), *vandhúras* 'seat of the chariot', *vṛtra-túras* (VS. VI. 34). — f. *gíras*, *gíras* (AV.), *tā́ras* 'stars'[2], *dvā́ras*[3], *dvāras*, *púras*; *án-apasphuras* 'not struggling', *amā-júras*, *mithas-túras*.

A. m. *gíras*; *ā-múras*, *gávāśiras*, *mithas-túras*, *yávāśiras*, *saṃ-gíras*, *su-dhúras*. — f. *gíras*, *dúras*[4], *dhúras*, *púras*, *psúras*[5] 'victuals'; *ni-púras*[6] (VS. AV.), *parā-púras*[6] (VS. AV.), *vi-ṣṭíras* 'expansion', *saṃ-stíras* 'contraction'.

I. m. *ratha-tū́rbhis*. — f. *gīrbhís*, *pūrbhís*[7], *stṛ́bhis*[8] 'stars'. — D. n. *vārbhyás* (VS.). — G. m. *sám-āśirām* 'mixed'. — f. *girā́m*, *purā́m*. — L. m. *tūrṣú*. — f. *gīrṣú*, *dhūrṣú*, *pūrṣú*. — n. *pṛtsu-túrṣu*[9] 'victorious in battle'.

356. B. **Derivative stems.** — Derivative stems ending in *r* consist of two groups, the one formed with the suffix *-ar*, the other with *-tar*. The former is a small group containing only eight stems, the latter is a very large one with more than 150 stems. Both groups agree in regularly distinguishing **strong and weak cases.** The strong stem ends in *-ar* or *-ār*, which in the weak forms is reduced to *r* before vowels and *ṛ* before consonants. Both groups further agree in dropping the final of the stem in the N. sing. m. f., which case always ends in *-ā*[10]. They resemble the vowel declension in adding the ending *-n* in the A. pl. m., and *-s* in the A. pl. f. and in inserting *n* before the *-ām* of the G. pl. They have the peculiar, ending *-ur* in the G. sing.[11].

a. Stems in *-ar*.

357. There are only five simple m. and f. stems in *-ar*, viz. *uṣ-ár-* f. 'dawn', *dev-ár-* m. 'husband's brother', *nánānd-ar-* f. 'husband's sister', *nár-*[12] m. 'man', *svásar-*[13] f. 'sister'; and the two compounds *svàr-ṇar-* m. 'lord of heaven' and *saptá-svasar-* 'having seven sisters'. Of these, *uṣár-* shows only case-forms according to the consonant declension, while *nár-* and *svásar-* have some according to the vowel declension also. Of *nánāndar-* only the G. and L. sing. and of *devár-* only the A. sing. and the N. and L. pl. occur. Nearly all case-forms are represented by these five stems taken together. There are also the three neuters *áh-ar-* 'day', *ū́dh-ar-* 'udder', and *vádh-ar-* 'weapon', which occur in the N. A. sing. only. The first two supplement the *-an* stems *áh-an-* and *ū́dh-an-* in those cases.

---

[1] This form is used 5 times as a L. sing. dropping the *-i* like the *-an* stems, as *áhan* beside *áhani*.

[2] Strong form of *tár-* = *stár-* 'star'. The gender is uncertain.

[3] Once the weak form *dúras*.

[4] The strong form *dvā́ras* is once used. The accentuation of a weak case, *durás*, occurs once.

[5] Occurring only in X. 26³; it is a n. sing. according to BR.

[6] The meaning and derivation of these two words is uncertain; see WHITNEY's note on AV. XVIII. 2²⁸.

[7] From *púr-* 'stronghold' and *púr-* 'abundance'.

[8] Weak form, accented like a dissyllabic stem. In Kh. I. 11⁶ normally accented, but spelt with *ri* as *stribhís*.

[9] With L. pl. ending kept in the first member.

[10] In this they resemble the N. m. of nouns of the *-an* declension.

[11] Except *nár-as* and *usr-ás*.

[12] This word is probably derived with the suffix *-ar*; cp. BRUGMANN, Grundriss 2, p. 359.

[13] Here *-sar* is probably a root; cp. BRUGMANN, op. cit., 2, p. 8, footnote.

Inflexion.

358. **Sing. N.** m. *hatá-svasā* (AV.) 'whose sisters have been slain'. — f. *svásā*; *saptá-svasā* 'having seven sisters'. — n. *áhar*, *ū́dhar*, *vádhar*.

A. m. *deváram*, *náram*. — f. *svásāram*. — **I.** f. *svásrā*. — **D.** m. *náre*; *svàr-ṇare*. — f. *svásre*. — **Ab.** f. *svásur*[1]. — **G.** m. *náras*. — f. *usrás*, *nánāndur* (AV.), *svásur*. — **L.** m. *nári*. — f. *usrí*[2] and *usrā́m*[3], *nánāndari*[4]. — **V.** f. *uṣar*.

Du. N. A. m. *nárā*, **V.** *narā* and *narau*. — f. *svásārā* and *svásārau*. — **L.** f. *svásros*.

Pl. N. m. *devāras*, *náras*, **V.** *naras*, *suar-ṇaras*. — f. *svásāras*. — **A.** m. *nṝn*[5]. — f. *usrás*, *svásṝs*. — **I.** m. *nṛ́bhis*. — f. *svásṛbhis*. — **D.** m. *nṛ́bhyas*. — **Ab.** m. *nṛ́bhyas*. — **G.** m. *narā́m*[6] and *nṛṇā́m*[7]. — f. *svásrām*[6] and *svásṝṇām*. — **L.** *devṛ́ṣu*, *nṛ́ṣu*.

b. Stems in *-tar*.

359. This group includes two subdivisions, the one forming its strong stem in *-tar*, the other in *-tār*. The former consists of a small class of five names of relationship: three masculines, *pi-tár-* 'father', *bhrā́-tar-* 'brother', *náp-tar-*[8] 'grandson', and two feminines, *duhi-tár-* 'daughter', and *mā-tár-* 'mother'; and the m. and f. compounds formed from them. The second class consists of more than 150 stems (including compounds), which are either agent nouns accented chiefly on the suffix, or participles accented chiefly on the root. These are never used in the f., which is formed with *-ī* from the weak stem of the m., e. g. *jánitr-ī-* 'mother' (377).

a. This declension is almost restricted to the m. and f. gender. The only n. stems are *dhar-tár-* 'prop', *dhmā-tár-* 'smithy', *sthā-tár-* 'stationary', *vi-dhar-tár-* 'meting out'; and from these only about half a dozen forms occur. The only oblique cases met with are the G. *sthātúr* and the L. *dhmātárī* (Pada *-tári*). The N. A. sing. which might be expected to appear as *-tár*, seems to have attained to no fixity of form, as it was of extremely rare occurrence. It seems to be represented by the following variations: *sthātar* (VI. 49⁶), *sthātṝn* (I. 72⁶), *sthātúr* (I. 58⁵, 68¹, 70⁷), *dhartári* (IX. 86⁴²; II. 23¹⁷), *vi-dhartári* (VIII. 59²; IX. 47⁴)[9].

Inflexion.

360. The inflexion is exactly the same in the m. and f. except that the A. pl. m. ends in *-tṝn*, but the f. in *-tṝs*.

The forms actually occurring, if made from *mātár-* f. 'mother', as representing a name of relationship, and from *janitár-* m. 'begetter', as representing an agent noun, would be as follows:

Sing. N. *mātā́*; *janitā́*. A. *mātáram*; *janitā́ram*. I. *mātrā́*; *janitrā́*. D. *mātré*; *janitré*. Ab. *mātúr*; *janitúr*. G. *mātúr*; *janitúr*. L. *mātári*; *janitári*. V. *mâtar*; *jánitar*.

Du. N. A. *mātárā* and *mātárau*; *janitā́rā* and *janitā́rau*. I. *janitṛ́bhyām* (VS.). D. *janitṛ́bhyām*. G. *mātrós*; *janitrós*. L. *mātrós*; *janitrós*.

[1] The ending *-ur* in this declension appears to represent original *-ṛz* through *-ṛr*; cp. LANMAN 426, BRUGMANN, KG. p. 381 (middle).

[2] The metre requires *uṣári*. As to the *sr* cp. 57, 1 *a*.

[3] The ending *-ām* is a transfer from the *ī-* declension. The metre requires *uṣárām* in which *-ām* is added direct to the stem.

[4] The metre requires *nánāndri* (x. 85⁴⁶).

[5] On *nṝn* as a metrically shortened form for other cases see PISCHEL, VS. I, p. 42 f.

[6] The only two forms in the derivative *-(t)ar* declension in which *-ām* is added direct to the stem.

[7] Often to be read as *nṝṇā́m*; see LANMAN 43.

[8] In the RV. this stem occurs in weak forms only, being supplemented in the strong by *nápāt*. The TS. (I 3. 4¹) however has the strong form *náptāram* with long vowel, like *svásāram*.

[9] See LANMAN 422 f.

Pl. N. *mātáras*; *janitāras*. A. *mātṝs*; *janitṝn*. I. *mātṛ́bhis*; *janitṛ́bhis*. D. *mātṛ́bhyas*; *janitṛ́bhyas*. Ab. *mātṛ́bhyas*; *janitṛ́bhyas*. G. *mātṝṇā́m*; *janitṝṇā́m*. L. *mātṛ́ṣu*; *janitṛ́ṣu*. V. *mā́taras*; *jánitāras*.

Forms actually occurring are the following:

Sing. N. 1. m. *pitā́*, *bhrā́tā*; *dákṣa-pitā* (TS. IV. 3. 4[1]; VS. XIV. 3) 'having Dakṣa as father', *tri-mātā́* 'having three mothers', *dvi-mātā́* 'having two mothers', *hatá-bhrātā* (AV.) 'whose brothers have been slain', *hatá-mātā* (AV.) 'whose mother has been slain'. — **f.** *duhitā́*, *mātā́*; *a-bhrātā́* 'brotherless', *síndhu-mātā*[1] 'having a stream as mother'.

2[2]. **m.** *anv-ā-gantā́* (VS. XVIII. 59)[3], *avitā́* 'protector', *upa-sattā́* (TS. VS. AV.) 'attendant', *kroṣṭā́* 'jackal' ('yeller'), *janitā́*, *jaritā́* 'praiser', *trātā́* 'protector', *tváṣṭā* 'fashioner', *dātā́* 'giver', *dhartā́* 'supporter', *netā́* 'leader', *prati-grahītā́* (VS. VII. 48) 'receiver', *prati-dhartā́* (VS. XV. 10) 'one who keeps back', *pra-vaktā́* (Kh. IV. 8[8]) 'speaker', *voḍhā́* and *vóḍhā* 'driving'; etc.

A. 1. m. *pitáram*, *bhrā́taram*; *ádri-mātaram* 'having a rock for a mother', *jā́-mātaram* 'son-in-law', *síndhu-mātaram*. — **f.** *duhitáram*, *mātáram*, *saptá-mātaram* 'having seven mothers'.

2. m. *adhi-vaktā́ram* 'advocate', *anu-kṣattā́ram* (VS. XXX. 11) 'doorkeeper's mate', *abhi-ṣektā́ram* (VS. XXX. 12) 'consecrator', *abhi-sartā́ram* (VS.) 'assistant', *ava-sātā́ram* 'liberator', *avitā́ram*, *ástāram* 'shooter', *ā-yantā́ram* 'restrainer', *iṣ-kartā́ram* 'arranging', *upa-manthitā́ram* (VS. XXX. 12) 'churner', *upa-ṣektā́ram* (VS. XXX. 12) 'pourer-out', *kártāram* 'agent', *kṣattā́ram* (VS. XXX. 13) 'door-keeper', *gántāram* 'going', *goptā́ram* (Kh. V. 3[3]) 'protector', *céttāram* 'attentive', *janitā́ram* (VS. XIII. 51), *jaritā́ram*, *jétāram* 'victorious', *joṣṭā́ram* (VS. XXVIII. 10) 'cherishing', *tarutā́ram* 'victor', *trātā́ram*, *tváṣṭāram*, *dātā́ram* 'giver', *dā́tāram* 'giving', *dhartā́ram*, *ni-dātā́ram* 'one who ties up', *niṣ-kartā́ram* (TS. IV. 2. 7[3])[4], *netā́ram* 'leader', *panitā́ram* 'praising', *pari-veṣṭā́ram* (VS. XXX. 12) 'waiter', *pavitā́ram* 'purifier', *pura-etā́ram* (VS. XXXIII. 60) 'leader', *peśitā́ram* (VS. XXX. 12) 'carver', *pra-karitā́ram* (VS. XXX. 12) 'sprinkler', *pra-ṇetā́ram* 'leader', *pra-dātā́ram* (VS. VII. 46; TS.) 'giver', *pra-hetā́ram* 'impeller', *bodhayitā́ram* 'awakener', *bhettā́ram* (TS. I. 5. 6[4]) 'breaker', *mandhātā́ram* 'pious man', *marḍitā́ram* 'comforter', *yantā́ram* 'ruler', *yántāram* 'restraining', *yātā́ram* 'pursuer', *yoktā́ram* (VS. XXX. 14) 'exciter', *rakṣitā́ram* 'protector', *vanditā́ram* 'praiser', *vi-bhaktā́ram* 'distributor', *vi-moktā́ram* (VS. XXX. 14) 'unyoker', *śamitā́ram* (VS. XXVIII. 10) 'slaughterer', *śṛtaṃ-kartā́ram* (TS. III. 1. 4[4]) 'cooking thoroughly', *śrotā́ram* 'hearer', *sanitā́ram* 'bestower', *sam-eddhā́ram*[5] 'kindler', *savitā́ram* 'stimulator', *stotā́ram* 'praiser', *hantā́ram* 'slayer', *has-kartā́ram* 'inciter', *hétāram* 'driver', *hótāram* 'invoker'.

I. 1. m. *náptrā*, *pitrā́*, *bhrā́trā* (AV.). — **f.** *duhitrā́*, *mātrā́* (VS. AV.). — **2. m.** *ástrā*, *tváṣṭrā* (AV.), *dhātrā́* 'establisher', *pra-savitrā́* (VS. X. 30) 'impeller', *savitrā́*.

D. 1. m. *náptre*, *pitré*. — **f.** *duhitré*, *mātré*. — **2. m.** *ástre* (AV.), *kartré* (AV.), *kroṣṭré* (AV.), *jaritré*, *jóṣṭre* (VS. XVII. 56), *tváṣṭre* (VS. XXII. 20), *dātré*, *dhartré* (VS. XVII. 56; TS. IV. 6. 3[2]), *dhātré* (AV.), *prati-grahītré* (VS. VII. 47), *rakṣitré* (AV.), *vi-dhātré* (AV.) 'disposer', *śamitré* (TS. IV. 6. 3[3]), *savitré*, *stotré*, *hantré* (VS. XVI. 40), *hótre*.

Ab. 1. m. *pitúr*, *bhrā́tur*, *vi-jāmātur* 'son-in-law'. — **f.** *duhitúr*, *mātúr*. — **2. m.** *ástur*, *tváṣṭur* (AV.), *dhātúr*, *savitúr*, *hótur*.

---

1 On the Sandhi of these nominatives in *-ā* see LANMAN 423—5.

2 The nominatives of the m. agent nouns are so numerous (140 in the RV. alone) that examples only can be given here.

3 Used with the A., an example of incipient use as a periphrastic future: = 'will follow'.

4 RV. X. 140[5] and VS. XII. 110 have *iṣ-kartā́ram* in the same passage.

5 For **edh-tā́ram*, from *idh-* 'kindle'.

G. 1. m. *náptur*, *pitúr*, *bhrā́tur*. — **f.** *duhitúr*, *nánāndur* (AV.), *mātúr*. — **2. m.** *abhi-kṣattúr* 'carver', *avitúr*, *ástur*, *utthātúr* (AV.) 'resolving', *kartúr* (Kh. IV. $5^{6.16}$), *cettúr* (AV.), *janitúr*, *jaritúr*, *trātúr*, *tváṣṭur*, *dātúr*, *dhātúr* (VS. TS. AV.), *ni-dhātúr* 'one who lays down', *netúr*, *néṣṭur* 'leader', *mandhātúr*, *yantúr* (VS. IX. 30), *vanditúr*, *vāvā́tur* 'adherent', *vóḍhur*[1] 'draught-horse', *śamitúr*, *sanitúr*, *savitúr*, *sotúr* 'presser of Soma', *stotúr*, *hótur*.

L. 1. m. *pitári*. — **f.** *duhitári*, *mātári*. — **2. m.** *netári*, *vaktári* (AV.) 'speaker', *sotári*. — **With** metrically **protracted** *-ī*: *etárī*[2], *kartárī*, *vaktárī*[3].

V. 1. m. *jā́mātar*, *pitar*, *bhrā́tar*. — **f.** *duhitar*, *mātar*. — **2. m.** *ava-spartar* 'preserver', *avitar*, *janitar*, *jaritar*, *trātar*, *tvaṣṭar*, *dartar* 'breaker', *doṣā-vastar* 'illuminer of the dark', *dhartar*, *dhātar*, *netar*, *neṣṭar*, *pra-ṇetar*, *pra-yantar* 'bringer', *yajña-hotar* 'offerer at a sacrifice', *vi-dhartar* 'ruler', *vi-dhātar*, *vi-śastar* (AV.) 'slaughterer', *sanitar*, *savitar*, *su-sanitar* 'liberal giver', *sotar*, *stotar* (VS. XXIII. 7; TS. VII. 4. 20), *sthātar* 'guider', *hotar*.

Du. N. A. V.[4] **1. m.** *pitárā*, *bhrā́tarā*; *ihéha-mātarā* 'whose mother is here and there', *dákṣa-pitarā*, *mātárā-pitárā*[5] 'father and mother', *síndhu-mātarā*. — **f.** *duhitárā*, *mātárā*, *sam-mātárā* 'twins'. — **With** *-au*: **m.** *pitárau*, *sam-mātárau* (AV.). — **f.** *duhitárau* (AV. Kh. III. 15^{13}), *mātárau*. — **2. m.** *avitā́rā*, *a-snātā́rā* 'not (fond of) bathing', *uṣṭā́rā* 'ploughing bulls', *gántārā*, *coditā́rā* 'instigators', *janitā́rā*, *dhartā́rā*, *ni-cetā́rā* 'observers', *pretā́rā* 'lovers', *yantā́rā* 'guides', *rakṣitā́rā*, *śamitā́rā*, *sthā́tārā*, *hótārā*. — **With shortened vowel:** *manotárā* 'disposers'. — **With** *-au*: *anu-ṣṭhātárau* (AV.) 'undertakers', *kṣattā́rau* (AV.) 'carvers', *goptā́rau* (AV.), *dātā́rau*, *rakṣitā́rau*, *hótārau* (VS. XX. 42), *hotā́rau* (TS. IV. 1. 8^{2}). — **With shortened vowel:** *dhánutarau*[6] 'running swiftly', *savātárau* (VS. XXVIII. 6) 'having the same calf'[7].

I. 2. m. *hótṛbhyām* (VS. XXI. 53). — **D. 1. m.** *pitṛ́bhyām*[8]. — **G. 1. m.** *pitróś*. — **f.** *mātróś*. — **2. m.** *pra-śāstróś* (VS.) 'directors'. — **L. 1. m.** *pitróś*. — **f.** *mātróś*[9].

Pl. N. 1. m. *pitáras*, V. *pítaras*, *bhrā́taras*; *dákṣa-pitaras*, *dákṣa-pitāras*[10] (TS. I. 2. 3^{1}), *gó-mātaras* 'having a cow for mother', *pṛ́śni-mātaras* 'having Pṛśni for a mother', *síndhu-mātaras*, *su-mātáras* 'having a beautiful mother'. — **f.** *duhitáras*, *mātáras*, V. *mā́taras*; *a-bhrātáras* and *a-bhrā́taras* (AV.). — **2. m.** *agní-hotāras* 'having Agni for a priest', *abhi-kṣattā́ras*, *abhi-svartā́ras* 'invokers', *ástāras*, *upa-kṣetā́ras* 'dwelling near', *gántāras*, *cetā́ras* 'avengers', *jaritā́ras*, *joṣṭā́ras*, *trātā́ras*, *daditā́ras* (VS. VII. 14) 'keepers', *dātā́ras*, *dhartā́ras*, *dhā́tāras*, *ni-cetā́ras* 'observing' and 'observers', *ninditā́ras* 'scorners', *nṛ-pātā́ras* 'protectors of men', *nétāras* and *netā́ras*, *panitā́ras*, *pari-veṣṭā́ras* (VS. VI. 13), *pavītā́ras* 'purifiers', *pura-etā́ras* (VS. XVII. 14; TS. IV. 6. 1^{4}), *pra-jñātā́ras* 'conductors', *pra-ṇetā́ras*, *prāvitā́ras* 'promoters', *pretā́ras*, *yantā́ras*, *rakṣitā́ras*, *vantā́ras* 'enjoyers', *vi-dhātā́ras*, *vi-yotā́ras* 'separators', *śamitā́ras*, *śrótāras*, *sanitā́ras*, *sotā́ras*, *stotā́ras*, *sthātā́ras*, *svā́ritāras* 'roaring', *hétāras*, *hótāras*[11].

---

[1] For **váh-tur*, from *vah-* 'draw'.

[2] GRASSMANN takes this form (V. 41^{10}; VI. 12^{4}) as a N. f. of *etár-* 'one who approaches or asks'.

[3] The Pada text has *i* in all these forms. Cp. NEISSER BB. 20, 44.

[4] In the RV. the ending *-ā* occurs 176 times, *-au* only 10 times: LANMAN 427 (mid.).

[5] A Dvandva compound in which both members are inflected.

[6] The shortening is probably metrical.

[7] This is the interpretation of the commentator; but the derivation of the word is obscure.

[8] No form in *-bhyām* with the Ab. sense occurs.

[9] These G. L. forms as well as *svásros* must be pronounced trisyllabically in the RV. except *mātrós* in VII. 3^{9}. See LANMAN 428.

[10] With long grade vowel.

[11] The form *vasu-dhā́taras* (AV. V. 27^{6}) may be N. pl. with shortened vowel, but WHITNEY regards it as a comparative N. sing. 'greater bestower of wealth'. See his note on AV. V. 27^{6}.

A. 1. m. *pitṝn*[1]; *dákṣa-pitṝn*, *pṛ́śni-mātṝn*. — **f.** *mātṝ́s*[2]. — **2. m.** *ástṝn*, *a-snātṝ́n*, *kartṝ́n* (AV.; Kh. IV. 5[30]), *goptṝ́n* (AV.), *jaritṝ́n*, *trātṝ́n*, *dātṝ́n*, *pātṝ́n* (AV.) 'drinkers', *pra-voḍhṝ́n* 'carrying off', *stotṝ́n*, *sthātṝ́n*, *hótṝn*.

I. 1. m. *nápṭṛbhis*, *pitṛ́bhis*, *bhrā́tṛbhis*; *saptá-mātṛbhis*. — **f.** *mātṛ́bhis*. — **2. m.** *ástṛbhis*, *kartṛ́bhis*, *dhātṛ́bhis*, *partṛ́bhis* 'with aids', *setṛ́bhis* 'bindings', *sotṛ́bhis* and *sótṛbhis*, *hetṛ́bhis*, *hótṛbhis*.

D. 1. m. *pitṛ́bhyas*. — **f.** *mātṛ́bhyas*. — **2. m.** *kṣattṛ́bhyas* (VS. XVI. 26) 'charioteers', *rakṣitṛ́bhyas* (AV.), *stotṛ́bhyas*, *saṃ-grahītṛ́bhyas* (VS. XVI. 26) 'drivers'.

Ab. 1. m. *pitṛ́bhyas*. — **f.** *mātṛ́bhyas*.

G. m. 1. *pitṝṇā́m*[3]. — **2.** *unnetṝṇā́m* (VS. VI. 2) kind of Soma priests, *jaritṝṇā́m*, *dātṝṇā́m*[4] (AV.), *dhātṝṇā́m*, *stotṝṇā́m*, *hótṝṇām*. — **With ṛ: 1.** *pitṛṇā́m* (TS. I. 3. 6[1] etc.); **2.** *dhātṛṇā́m* (TS. IV. 7. 14[3]), *netṛṇā́m* (TS. I. 3. 6[1])[5].

L. 1. m. *pitṛ́ṣu* (AV.). — **f.** *mātṛ́ṣu*. — **2. m.** *hótṛṣu*.

2. Stems in *y* and *v*.

361. These stems, of which there are only five, form a transition to the vowel declension because, while taking the normal endings like the ordinary consonant declension, they add *-s* in the N. sing. m. f. and show a vowel before the endings with initial consonant. There are no neuter forms[6].

a. Stem in *-āy* (*-ai*).

362. This type is represented by only one word, usually stated in the form of *rái-*, which never appears in any case. This word, which is both m. and (rarely) f., means 'wealth', being in origin doubtless connected with the root *rā-* 'give'. The stem appears as *rāy-* before vowels and *rā-* before consonants. The forms occurring are: **Sing.** A. *rā́m*. I. *rāyā́*. D. *rāyé*. Ab. *rāyás*. G. *rāyás*[7]. — **Pl.** N. *rā́yas*. A. *rāyás*[8]. G. *rāyā́m*.

a. The inflexion of *rā́y-* is supplemented by *rayí-*, m. f., from which occur the additional cases sing. N. *rayís*, A. *rayím*, I. *rayyā́* and *rayiṇā́*; pl. I. *rayíbhis*, G. *rayīṇā́m*.

b. There are three forms which seem to be irregular compounds of *rāy-*: sing. G. *ṛdhád-rayas* ('increasing wealth') N. of a man, D. *bṛhád-raye* 'having much wealth', and du. N. *śatá-rā* 'having a hundred goods'. In the first two forms the vowel of the stem has probably been shortened metrically[9]; in the third form, the stem as it appears before consonants has been used.

b. Stems in *-av* (*-o*) and *-āv* (*-au*).

363. There are two stems in *-av*, viz. *gáv-* m. 'bull', f. 'cow', and *dyáv-* m. f. 'heaven', 'day'. Both distinguish **strong forms**, in which the vowel is lengthened; both take *-s* in the N. sing. before which the end of the stem assumes the form of *-au*. Both show various irregularities in their inflexion.

---

1 On the Sandhi of these accusatives see LANMAN 429.

2 Once with m. ending *mātṝ́n* (X. 35[2]).

3 With *n* before the ending *-ām* as in the vowel declension, and accent shifted to the ending as in the *i-* and *u-* declension when those vowels are accented.

4 See WHITNEY's note on AV. V. 24[3].

5 Also *udgātṛṇā́m* (TS. III. 2. 9[5]) and *bhrā́tṛṇām* (TS. II. 6. 6[2]). See BENFEY, Vedica, p. 1—38; IS. 13, 101; LANMAN 430.

6 Except the isolated *dyavī* occurring once as V. du. of *dyáv-* 'heaven'.

7 The G. a few times has the irregular accent *rā́yas*.

8 Accented thus 22 times as a weak case in the RV., and four times *rā́yas* as a strong case (also VS. II. 24). The SV. I. 4. 1. 4[1] has the A. pl. *rā́s* in the variant *adhad rā́ḥ* for *adhatta* of RV. VIII. 96[13].

9 According to BR. and GRASSMANN, they are formed from the stems *bṛhád-ri-* and *ṛdhád-rī-*. Cp. LANMAN 431.

The **inflexion of** ***gáv-***, which is almost complete (the only forms not represented being the weak cases of the dual) is as follows:

Sing. N. *gáus.* A. *gā́m.* I. *gávā.* D. *gáve.* Ab. *gós.* G. *gós.* L. *gávi.* — **Du.** N. A. *gā́vā* and *gā́vau.* — **Pl.** N. *gā́vas.* A. *gā́s.* I. *góbhis.* D. *góbhyas.* G. *gávām* and *gónām.* L. *góṣu.* V. *gāvas.*

a. Three of these forms, *gā́m, gā́s, gós* must, in the RV., be read as dissyllables in a few instances, though this is doubtful in the case of *gā́s*[1].

b. The normal G. pl. *gávām*, which is by far the commoner, occurring 55 times in the RV., is found only 3 times at the end of a Pāda (which in two of these instances ends iambically); the irregular G. *gónām*[2], occurring 20 times in the RV., is found at the end of a Pāda only. The use of the latter form thus seems to have arisen from metrical exigencies.

c. It is to be noted that from the point of view of accentuation the stem is not treated as a monosyllable, since the Udātta never shifts to the ending in weak cases.

d. There are three compounds formed from this stem: *á-gos*[3] G. sing. m. 'having no cows'; *pṛ́śni-gāvas*[4] N. pl. m. 'having dappled cows'; *rúśad-gavi* L. sing. f. 'having bright cows'.

364. The **strong form** of *dyáv-* (in which the *y* has often to be read as *i*) is ***dyáv-***, which appears as *dyáu-* before the *-s* of the N., and with loss of the final *u*, in the A. sing. *dyā́m*[5]. The normal stem *dyáv-* appears in weak cases only, in the contracted Ab. G. *dyós*[6] and the L. *dyávi*; it is otherwise entirely displaced by the Samprasāraṇa form *div-* (from which the accent shifts to the ending in weak cases) before vowels and *dyú-* before consonants.

The **weak grade stem** ***div-*** has not only entirely ousted *dyáv-* from the I. D. sing., and largely from the Ab. G. L. sing., but has even encroached on the strong forms: *dívam* occurring (21 times) beside *dyā́m* (79 times), and *dívas* (once) beside *dyā́vas* (22 times) in the N. pl. Similarly *dyú-*[7] has displaced *dyáv-* in the weak plural forms: A. *dyū́n* (for **dyávas*) and I. *dyúbhis* (for **dyó-bhis*).

The **inflexion of** ***dyáv-*** is less complete than that of *gáv-*, the D. Ab. G. L. pl. being wanting as well as all the weak cases of the dual. The forms occurring are the following:

Sing. N. *dyáus.* A. *dyā́m; dívam.* I. *divā́.* D. *divé.* Ab. *dyós; divás*[8]. G. *dyós; divás*[9]. L. *dyávi; diví*[10]. V. *dyàus* and *dyàus*[11]. — **Du.** N. A. V. *dyā́vā*[12]; *dyavī*[13]. — **Pl.** N. V. *dyā́vas; dívas*[14] (once). A. m. *dyū́n;* f. *dívas*[15] (twice). I. m. *dyúbhis*[16].

a. The A. *dyā́m* seems to require dissyllabic pronunciation in a few instances. The form *dyáus* occurs once (I. 71⁸) as an Ab. instead of *dyós.* The form *dívam* doubtless made its way into the A. sing. owing to the influence of the very frequent weak cases *divás* etc., which taken together occur more than 350 times in the RV.

---

1 See LANMAN 431 (bottom). The form *gā́vas* is actually used for the A. in Kh. II. 6[15].

2 Formed on the analogy of the vowel declension.

3 This might be formed from the reduced stem *á-gu-*.

4 There is also from the reduced stem *-gu-* the A. sing. m. *pṛ́śni-gum*, as the N. of a man.

5 For **dyā́[u]m* like *gā́m* for **gā́[u]m*.

6 Like *gós* for **gávas*.

7 Based on *diu-*.

8 In the RV. *dyós* occurs only twice as Ab., *divás* 50 times.

9 In the RV. *dyós* occurs 4 times as G., *divás* 180 times.

10 *dyávi* occurs 12 times, *diví* 118 times in the RV.

11 *dyàus*, that is, *díaus* occurs only once and is to be read as a dissyllable.

12 In the G. du. of the Dvandva *divás-pṛthivyós*, the G. sing. takes the place of the G. du., which would be *divós*.

13 The neuter form used once for the m.

14 Also twice in AV.

15 Also 3 or 4 times in AV.

16 *dyū́n* and *dyúbhis* occur only in the RV. or in verses borrowed from the RV.

b. Starting from *div-ás* etc. a transition stem **divá-** according to the *a-* declension came into being. From this occur the forms *divá-m* 'heaven' and *divé-dive* 'every day', and in compounds *tri-divá-m* (AV.) 'third heaven', *tri-divé*, *su-divá-m* (AV.) 'bright day'.

c. It is to be noted that the accentuation of forms from *div-* follows the rule of monosyllables, while that of forms from *dyáv-* and *dyú-*, as may be inferred from *dyávi* and *dyúbhis*, does not, being the same as that of *gáv-*.

d. The following case-forms of compounds of **dyáv-** occur: sing. N. *pra-dyáus* (AV.) 'highest heaven', I. *pra-divā*, Ab. *pra-divas*, L. *pra-divi*; *áhar-divi* 'day by day'; du. N. A. *pṛthivī-dyā́vā* 'earth and heaven', *dyā́vā-kṣā́mā*, *dyā́vā-pṛthivī́*, *dyā́vā-bhū́mī* 'heaven and earth', *vṛṣṭi-dyāvā* 'having a raining sky'; pl. N. *vṛṣṭi-dyāvas*, *su-divas*.

365. There are two stems in *-āv*, viz. **nā́v-** (*náu-*) f. 'ship', and **glā́v-** (*gláu-*) m. or f. 'lump'. The inflexion is very incomplete, as no dual and only two plural forms are found; but as far as can be judged from the forms occurring it is quite regular, the accentuation being that of monosyllabic stems. The forms of *nā́v-* are:

Sing. N. *náus*. A. *nā́vam*, *su-nā́vam* 'good ship' (VS. XXI. 7). I. *nāvā́*[1]. G. *nāvás*. L. *nāví*. — **Pl.** N. *nā́vas*. I. *naubhís*.

From *glā́v-* occur only the two forms N. sing. *gláus* (AV.) and I. pl. *glaubhís* (VS. XXV. 8)[2].

B. Vowel stems.

366. The vowel declension comprises stems ending in *a*, *i*, *u*, both long and short. These differ considerably in their inflexion according as they are radical or derivative. The radical stems, which virtually all end in the long vowels *ā*, *ī*, *ū*[3], are allied to the consonant declension in taking the normal endings; but they add *-s* in the N. sing. m. f. The derivative stems, which end in both long and short vowels, modify the normal endings considerably; though they for the most part add *-s* in the N. sing. m. f., those in *-ā* and *-ī* regularly drop it.

1. a. Stems in radical *-ā*.

367. Radical *ā-* stems are frequent in the RV., but become less common in the later Saṃhitās where they often shorten the final vowel to *ă* and are then inflected like derivative *a*-stems. The great majority of the forms occurring are nominatives or accusatives, other cases being rare and some not occurring at all. In the RV. the N. sing. forms with *ā* occur ten times oftener than those with the shortened vowel *ă*, and five times oftener than the forms with *ā* in the AV. On the other hand, the AV. has only slightly more forms with *ā* than with *ă*, and no m. forms at all from *ā-* stems in the oblique cases[4]. This tendency to give up the *ā* forms in the later Saṃhitās may be illustrated by the fact that the forms of the RV. N. sing. *carṣaṇi-prā́-s* 'blessing men', *nāma-dhā́-s* 'name-giver', *prathama-jā́-s* 'first-born', V. *soma-pā-s* 'soma-drinker', are replaced in the AV. by *carṣaṇi-prá-s*, *nāma-dhá-s*, *prathama-já-s*[5], V. *soma-pa* respectively.

This declension includes stems formed from about thirty roots. Of these, four appear as monosyllables in the m.: *jā́-* 'child', *trā́-* 'protector', *dā́-* 'giver', *sthā́-* 'standing'; and seven in the f.: *kṣā́-*[6] 'abode', *-khā́-* 'well', *gnā́-*[7] 'divine

1 There is also the transition form according to the *ā-* declension I. sing. *nāvā́yā*, the accentuation of which indicates that it started from *nāvā́*.

2 The N. pl. *glā́vas* also occurs in the AB.

3 These, however, by being shortened often appear secondarily as *ă*, *ĭ*, *ŭ*, when they are inflected like derivative stems. Radical *ĭ* *ŭ* and *ṛ* stems have joined the consonant declension by almost always adding the root determinative *-t*.

4 See LANMAN 435[1].

5 The form *prathama-jā́-s*, however, also occurs in the AV.

6 From *kṣā-* = *kṣi-* 'dwell', 'rule'.

7 Perhaps formed with suffixal *ā* from a root **gan-* and sometimes to be pronounced as a dissyllable (*ganā́-*), but inflected as if a radical stem.

woman', *jā́-* 'child', *jyā́-* 'bowstring', *mā́-* 'measure', *vrā́-*[1] 'troop'; the rest appear only at the end of compounds: *-krā́-*[2] 'doing', *-krā́-*[3] 'scattering', *-kṣā́-* 'ruling', *-khā́-* 'digging', *-khyā́-* 'seeing', *-gā́-* 'going', *-gā́-* 'singing', *-jā́-* 'born', *-jñā́-* 'knowing', *-jyā́-* 'power', *-tā-* 'stretching', *-dā́-* 'giving', *-drā́-* 'sleeping', *-dhā́-* 'putting', *-dhā́-* 'sucking', *-pā́-* 'guarding', *-pā́-* 'drinking', *-prā́-* 'filling'[4], *-bhā́-* 'appearing', *-mā́-* 'measuring', *-yā́-* 'going', *-vā́-* 'blowing', *-sā́-* 'winning'[5], *-sthā́-* 'standing', *-snā́-* 'bathing', *-hā́-* 'starting'.

These stems are inflected in the m. and f. only. There are no distinctively n. forms[6], as the stem shortens the radical vowel to *ă* in that gender and is consequently inflected according to the derivative *a*-declension.

a. Three anomalously formed m. derivative stems in *-ā* follow the analogy of the radical *ā*-stems. 1. From the adverb *tá-thā* 'thus' is formed the N. sing. *á-tathā-s* 'not saying "yes"'. 2. *uśánā-*, N. of a seer, forms its A. *uśánām* and D. *uśáne*[7]; the N. sing. being irregularly formed without *-s*, has the appearance of a N. sing. f. from a derivative *ā*-stem[8]. 3. The strong stem of *pathi-* 'path' is in the RV. *pánthā-* only: N. sing. *pánthā-s* (+ AV.), A. *pánthā-m* (+ AV.), N. pl. *pánthās*. The AV. also uses the stem *pánthān-*, from which it forms N. sing. *pánthā* (once), A. *pánthānam* (once), and N. pl. *pánthānas*. Though the stem *pánthān-* never occurs in the RV., the evidence of the Avesta points to its having been in use beside *pánthā-* in the Indo-Iranian period[9]. The A. *pánthām*[10], as a contraction of *pánthānam*, may have been the starting point of the N. sing. *pánthā-s*.

Inflexion.

368. The forms occurring in the oblique cases are so rare that some endings, such as those of the L. sing., G. L. du. and G. pl. are not represented at all. The m. always takes *-s* in the N. sing., but the f. often drops it, doubtless owing to the influence of the f. of derivative *ā*-stems. Excepting the few forms occurring in the D. and G. sing.[11], the N. sing. with *-s* is the only case in which the inflexion of the radical stems can be distinguished in the f.[12] from that of the derivative *ā*-stems in form[13]. The forms actually occurring would, if made from *jā́-* 'offspring', be the following:

Sing. N. m. f. *jā́-s*, f. also *jā́*. A. m. f. *jā́-m*. I. f. *j-ā́*. D. m. f. *j-é*. G. m. *j-ás*. V. m. *jā́-s*.

Du. N. A. V. m. *jā́*, *jáu*. I. *jā́-bhyām*[14].

Pl. N. m. f. *jā́s*. A. f. *jā́s*. I. m. f. *jā́-bhis*. D. f. *jā́-bhyas*. Ab. m. *jā́-bhyas*. L. f. *jā́-su*.

The forms actually occurring are the following:

Sing. N. m. *jā́-s*[15] 'child', *dā́-s*[16] 'giver', *sthā́-s* 'standing'. — *dadhi-krā́-s*[17],

---

[1] From an extended form of the root *vṛ-* 'surround'.

[2] An extension with *-ā* of *kṛ-* 'do'.

[3] An extension with *-ā* of *kṝ-* 'scatter'.

[4] The root *mlā-* 'soften' occurs in the modified form of *-mnā-* in *carma-mnā́-* 'tanner'.

[5] Four of these roots, *khā-*, *gā-*, *jā-*, *sā-*, are collateral forms of others ending in a nasal, *khan-*, *gam-*, *jan-*, *san-*; cp. DELBRÜCK, Verbum, p. 92 f., LANMAN 442.

[6] Five N. sing. m. forms with *-s* are found in agreement with n. substantives.

[7] There is also a L. sing. *uśáne*, which is formed as if from an *a*-stem.

[8] The starting-point of this may have been *uśánām* as a contracted A. for *uśánasam*.

[9] See LANMAN 441.

[10] The analogy of *pathi-* is followed by *mathi-* 'churning-stick', which once has the A. form *mánthā-m*.

[11] There are otherwise only the f. transition forms L. sing. *āpayā́yām*, N. of a river, and *puro-dhā́yām* (AV.).

[12] The N. sing. with *-s* is about as common as that without it in the RV., the latter occurring in late hymns; in the AV. the former are less common.

[13] But on etymological grounds other cases may commonly be distinguished as belonging to either one group or the other; thus A. f. *á-gopām* 'having no herdsman' must be regarded as a radical *ā*-form, because the m. is almost without exception *go-pā́-m*, and not as a derivative f. from *go-pā́-*.

[14] Contrary to the rule generally applicable to monosyllable stems, the accent remains on the radical syllable throughout.

[15] LANMAN 443 thinks *gā́-s* in x. 127⁸ is a N. sing. 'singer' (*gā-* 'sing'), but it is probably the A. pl. of *gó-* 'cow'.

[16] Also *dhā́-s* in TS. II. 6. 4[4].

[17] These compounds are arranged according to the alphabetical order of the roots.

N. of a divine horse. — *ṛbhu-kṣā́-s* 'lord of the Ṛbhus'. — *bisa-khā́-s* 'digging up lotus fibres'. — *agre-gā́-s* (VS. XXVII. 31; Kh. v. 6[1]) 'going before', *an-ā-gā́-s* 'not coming', *puro-gā́-s* 'leader', *samana-gā́-s* 'going to the assembly'. — *sāma-gā́-s* 'singing chants'. — *adri-jā́-s* 'produced from stones', *apsu-jā́-s* 'born in the waters', *ab-jā́-s* 'born in water', *abhra-jā́-s* (AV.) 'born from clouds', *ṛta-jā́-s* 'truly born', *ṛte-jā́-s* 'produced at the rite', *go-jā́-s* 'born from the cow', *tapo-jā́-s* (VS. XXXVII. 16) 'born from heat', *divi-jā́-s* 'born in the sky', *deva-jā́-s* 'god-born', *dvi-jā́-s* 'twice-born', *nakṣatra-jā́-s* (AV.) 'star-born', *nabho-jā́-s* 'produced from vapour', *nava-jā́-s* 'newly born', *purā-jā́-s* 'primeval', *pūrva-jā́-s* 'born before', *prathama-jā́-s* 'first-born', *bahu-pra-jā́-s* 'having numerous progeny', *manuṣya-jā́-s* 'born of men', *vane-jā́-s* 'born in woods', *vāta-jā́-s* (AV.) 'arisen from wind', *sana-jā́-s* 'born long ago', *saha-jā́-s* 'born together', *saho-jā́-s* 'produced by strength', *su-pra-jā́-s* 'having good offspring', *hiraṇya-jā́-s* (AV.) 'sprung from gold'. — *ṛta-jñā́-s* 'knowing the sacred law'. — *parama-jyā́-s* 'holding supreme power'. — *apāna-dā́-s* (TS. VS.) 'giving the downward air', *ātma-dā́-s* 'granting breath', *āyur-dā́-s* (TS. VS) 'granting long life', *āśīr-dā́-s* (VS. XVIII. 56) 'fulfilling a wish', *ojo-dā́-s* 'granting power', *go-dā́-s* 'giving kine', *cakṣur-dā́-s* (TS. IV. 6. 1[5]) 'giving sight', *draviṇo-dā́-s* 'giving wealth', *dhana-dā́-s* 'giving booty', *prāṇa-dā́-s* (VS. TS.) 'life-giving', *bala-dā́-s* 'giving power', *bhūri-dā́-s* 'giving much', *rāṣṭra-dā́-s* (VS. X. 2) 'giving dominion', *varivo-dā́-s* (VS. TS.) 'giving space', *varco-dā́-s* (VS. TS.) 'giving vigour', *vasu-dā́-s* (AV.) 'giving wealth', *vyāna-dā́-s* (VS. TS.) 'giving breath', *sahasra-dā́-s* 'giving a thousand', *saho-dā́-s* 'giving strength', *svasti-dā́-s* 'giving happiness', *havir-dā́-s* (AV.) 'giving oblations', *hiraṇya-dā́-s* 'yielding gold'. — *abhi-dhā́-s* (VS. XXII. 3) 'surrounding', *kiye-dhā́-s* 'containing much', *cano-dhā́-s* (VS. VIII. 7) 'gracious', *dhāma-dhā́-s* 'founder of dwellings', *dhiyaṃ-dhā́-s* 'devout', *nāma-dhā́-s* 'name-giving', *bhāga-dhā́-s* (TS. IV. 6. 3[1]) 'paying what is due', *ratna-dhā́-s* 'procuring wealth', *reto-dhā́-s* 'impregnating', *vayo-dhā́-s* 'bestowing strength', *varco-dhā́-s* (AV.) 'granting vigour', *viśvá-dhā-s* (VS. I. 2) 'all-preserving', *sarva-dhā́-s* 'all-refreshing'. — *adhi-pā́-s* 'ruler', *apāna-pā́-s* (VS. XX. 34) 'protecting the downward breath', *abhiśasti-pā́-s* 'defending from imprecations', *abhiṣṭi-pā́-s*[1] 'protecting with assistance', *āprīta-pā́-s* (VS. VIII. 57) 'guarding when gladdened', *āyuṣ-pā́-s* (VS. XXII. 1) 'life-protector', *ṛta-pā́-s* 'guarding divine order'; *go-pā́-s* 'herdsman', *á-gopā-s* 'lacking a cowherd', *devá-gopā-s* 'having the gods for guardians', *su-gopā́-s* 'good protector', *sóma-gopā-s* 'keeper of Soma'; *cakṣuṣ-pā́-s*[2] (VS. II. 6) 'protecting the eyesight', *tanū-pā́-s* 'protecting the person', *nidhi-pā́-s* (AV. VS.) 'guardian of treasure', *paras-pā́-s*[2] 'protecting afar', *paśu-pā́-s* 'keeper of herds', *prāṇa-pā́-s* (VS. XX. 34) 'guardian of breath', *vrata-pā́-s* 'observing ordinances', *śevadhi-pā́-s* 'guarding treasure', *sti-pā́-s* 'protecting dependents', *sva-pā́-s*[3] (AV.) 'protector of his own'. — *án-ṛtu-pā-s* 'not drinking in time', *ṛtu-pā́-s* 'drinking at the right season', *pūrva-pā́-s* 'drinking first', *suta-pā́-s* 'drinking the Soma-juice', *soma-pā́-s* 'drinking Soma', *hari-pā́-s* 'drinking the yellow (Soma)'. — *antarikṣa-prā́-s* 'traversing the air', *kratu-prā́-s* 'granting power', *carṣaṇi-prā́-s* 'satisfying men', *rodasi-prā́-s*[4] 'filling heaven and earth'. — *ṛṇa-yā́-s* 'exacting obligations', *eva-yā́-s* 'going quickly', *tura-yā́-s* 'going swiftly', *deva-yā́-s* 'going to the gods'. — *ap-sā́-s* 'giving water', *aśva-sā́-s* 'giving horses', *dhana-sā́-s* "winning wealth', *vāja-sā́-s* 'winning booty', *śata-sā́-s* 'gaining a hundred', *sahasra-sā́-s* 'gaining a thousand'; *go-ṣā́-s* 'acquiring cattle', *nṛ-ṣā́-s* 'procuring men', *su-ṣā́-s* 'gaining

1 In *abhiṣṭipā́si* (II. 20[2]), where the Pada text reads *abhiṣṭi-pā́ asi*. See LANMAN 443 (bottom).

2 On the Sandhi in this compound cp. 78 c.

3 The Pada text of AV. III. 3[1] divides *sva-pā́ḥ*; but the correct division may be *su-apā́ḥ*; see WHITNEY's note.

4 For *rodasī-prā́-s*.

easily', *svar-ṣā́-s* 'winning light'. — *ádhara-sthā-s*[1] (Kh. II. 8[2]) 'subordinate', *ṛta-sthā́-s* (AV.) 'standing right', *rocana-sthā́-s* 'abiding in light', *sūpa-sthā́-s*[2] (VS. XXI. 60; TS. I. 2. 2[3]) 'forming a good lap'; *aṅge-ṣṭhā́-s* (AV.) 'situated in a member of the body', *adhvare-ṣṭhā́-s* 'standing at the sacrifice', *giri-ṣṭhā́-s* 'mountain-dwelling', *ni-ṣṭhā́-s* 'excelling', *puru-ni-ṣṭhā́-s* 'excelling among many', *bhuvane-ṣṭhā́-s*[3] (AV.) 'being in the world', *maṃhane-ṣṭhā́-s* 'liberal', *madhyame-ṣṭhā́-s* (AV. VS. TS.) 'standing in the middle', *rathe-ṣṭhā́-s* 'standing on a car', *vandane-ṣṭhā́-s* 'mindful of praises', *vandhure-ṣṭhā́-s* 'standing on the car-seat', *savya-ṣṭhā́-s*[4] (AV.), *hari-ṣṭhā́-s* 'borne by bay horses'. — *ghṛta-snā́-s* 'sprinkling ghee'. — Also the **abnormal forms** *á-tathā-s* 'not saying "yes"', *pánthā-s* 'path'.

f. *kṣā́-s* 'abode', *gnā́-s* 'divine woman', *vrā́-s*[5] (I. 124[8]) 'troop'. — *ṛta-pā́-s, ṛte-jā́-s, kula-pā́-s* (AV.) 'chief of a family', *go-dhā́-s*[6] 'sinew', *go-pā́-s* (AV.) 'female guardian', *go-ṣā́-s, divi-jā́-s, divo-jā́-s* 'born from heaven', *vane-jā́-s, vayo-dhā́-s* (AV.), *vasu-dā́-s* (AV.), *śata-sā́-s, samana-gā́-s, sahasra-sā́-s*[7]. — **Without -s in the Pada** but with hiatus in the Saṃhitā[8]: *jyā́* 'bowstring'; *ni-drā́* 'sleep', *pra-pā́* 'place for watering', *śrad-dhā́* 'faith', *sva-dhā́*[9] 'self-power'; *un-mā́* (TS.) 'measure of height', *prati-mā́* (TS.) 'counter-measure', *pra-mā́* (TS.) 'fore-measure', *vi-mā́* (TS.) 'through-measure'[10]. — **Without -s** as in the derivative *ā-* declension: *jā́* (AV.), *mā́* (TS. IV. 3. 7[1]) 'measure'. — *ápa-gā*[11] (AV.) 'going away', *abhi-bhā́* 'apparition', *á-saṃjñā* (AV.) 'discord', *upa-jā́* (AV.) 'distant posterity', *go-dhā́*[12], *dur-gā́* (AV.) 'hard to go upon', *devá-gopā, dyu-kṣā́* 'heavenly', *pra-jā́* 'offspring', *prati-mā́* 'image', *pra-pā́* (AV. III. 30[6]), *pra-mā́* 'measure', *madhu-dhā́*[13] 'dispensing sweetness', *śrad-dhā́* (AV.), *sana-jā́, svá-gopā* 'guarding oneself', *sva-dhā́*.

n. With -s and agreeing with n. substantives: *sthā́-s* 'stationary'; *indra-jā́-s* (AV.) 'descended from Indra', *śata-sā́-s, su-pra-yā́-s* 'pleasant to tread on', *soma-jā́-s*[14] (AV.) 'Soma-born'.

A. m. *jā́m, trā́m* 'protector', *sthā́m*. — *dadhi-krā́m, rudhi-krā́m* N. of a demon. — *tamo-gā́m* 'roaming in the darkness', *tavā-gā́m* 'moving mightily', *svasti-gā́m* 'leading to prosperity'. — *sāma-gā́m*. — *agra-jā́m* 'first-born', *ab-jā́m, nabho-jā́m, purā-jā́m, prathama-jā́m, bhareṣu-jā́m* 'existing in battles'. — *án-aśva-dām* 'not giving horses', *án-āśīr-dām* 'not giving a blessing', *a-bhikṣa-dā́m*[15] 'giving without being asked', *upa-dā́m* (VS. XXX. 9) 'giving a present', *jani-dā́m* 'giving a wife', *draviṇo-dā́m, dhana-dā́m, rabho-dā́m* 'bestowing strength', *vasu-dā́m, saho-dā́m, havir-dā́m* (AV.). — *ratna-dhā́m* (AV., VS. IV. 25), *reto-dhā́m* (VS. VIII. 10), *vayo-dhā́m, varivo-dhā́m* 'granting space', *varco-dhā́m* (VS. IV. 11), *vipo-dhā́m* 'inspiring'. — *abhiśasti-pā́m, go-pā́m, tanū-pā́m, ni-ṣikta-pā́m* 'protecting the infused (semen)', *vrata-pā́m*. — *añjas-pā́m* 'drinking instantly', *śṛta-pā́m* 'drinking boiled milk', *soma-pā́m*. — *antarikṣa-prā́m, kakṣya-prā́m* 'filling out the girth',

---

1 The Ms. reads *ádhira-sthā nīnaśat*.

2 That is, *su-upa-sthā́-s*.

3 While Kh. III. 22[2] has in the same verse *bhūmane-ṣṭhāḥ* (sic).

4 The Pada reads *savya-sthāḥ*; see APr. II. 95, and cp. WHITNEY's note on AV. VIII. 8[23].

5 N. sing. GRASSMANN and LANMAN, N. pl. ROTH and SĀYAṆA.

6 The derivation is uncertain.

7 The above are the only N. sing. f. forms written with *-s* in the Pada text.

8 It may therefore be assumed that the N. was formed with *-s*.

9 Cp. RPr. II. 29. With regard to *sva-dhā́*, the Saṃhitā text is inconsistent, writing it contracted with a following vowel in *svadhā́sīt* (I. 165[6]) and *svadhā́mitā* (V. 34[1]), where it must be pronounced with hiatus.

10 All these four compounds of *mā-* 'measure' occur in TS. IV. 4. 11[3]; see TPr. X. 13, IS. 13, 104, note [2].

11 BR. would accentuate *apa-gā́*; cp. WHITNEY's note on AV. I. 34[5].

12 Probably *go-dhā́s* in X. 28[11]; cp. LANMAN 445.

13 Also *maryā́dā* 'limit' if *maryā́-dā*, but the derivation is doubtful.

14 These forms must be regarded as m. used as n. Cp. the *-ās* forms of *-as* stems used as n. (344).

15 According to the Pada text *abhi-kṣa-dā́m* ('destroying').

carṣaṇi-prā́m, *ratha-prā́m* 'filling a car', *rodasi-prā́m*[1]. — *ap-sā́m*, *urvarā-sā́m* 'granting fertile land', *kṣetra-sā́m* 'procuring land', *dhana-sā́m*, *sadā-sā́m* 'always gaining', *sahasra-sā́m*; *go-ṣā́m*, *svar-ṣā́m*. — *rocana-sthā́m*, *sv-āsa-sthā́m* (VS. II. 2) 'offering a good seat'; *giri-ṣṭhā́m*, *nare-ṣṭhā́m* 'serving for a man[2] to stand on', *ni-ṣṭhā́m*, *karma-niṣṭhā́m* 'diligent in religious acts', *pathi-ṣṭhā́m* (AV.) 'being on the way', *pathe-ṣṭhā́m*[3] 'standing in the way', *pari-ṣṭhā́m* 'surrounding', *parvate-ṣṭhā́m* 'dwelling on the heights', *barhi-ṣṭhā́m*[4] 'standing on the sacrificial grass', *rathe-ṣṭhā́m*, *rayi-ṣṭhā́m* (AV.) 'possessed of wealth', *hari-ṣṭhā́m*. — Also the **abnormal** derivative **forms** *pánthām*, *mánthām* 'churning-stick'.

f. *kṣā́m*, *khā́m* 'well', *gnā́m*, *jā́m*, *jyā́m*, *vrā́m*. — *á-gopām*, *antarikṣa-prā́m*, *ava-sā́m* 'liberation', *áśva-sām*, *upa-vā́m* (AV.) 'act of blowing upon', *uru-ṣā́m* 'granting much', *ṛta-jñā́m*, *tiro-dhā́m* (AV.) 'concealment', *dur-dhā́m* 'disarrangement', *dhana-sā́m*, *pra-jā́m*, *prati-dhā́m* (AV.) 'draught', *prati-ṣṭhā́m* 'standpoint', *pra-vā́m* (AV.) 'blowing forth', *pra-hā́m* 'advantage', *yakṣmo-dhā́m*[5] (AV.) 'maker of disease', *vāja-sā́m*, *śrad-dhā́m*, *sabhā́m*[6] 'assembly', *su-prajā́m*, *sva-jā́m* 'self-born', *sva-dhā́m*, *svar-ṣā́m*.

I. f. *apa-dhā́* 'concealment', *abhi-khyā́* 'splendour', *a-sthā́* 'without standing'[7], *āśīr-dā́* (VS.) 'fulfilment of a wish', *prati-dhā́*, *prati-ṣṭhā́*[8], *sva-dhā́*.

D. m. *dé*; *kīlāla-pé* 'drinking (the beverage called) *kīlāla*', *dhiyaṃ-dhé* 'devout', *paśu-ṣé* 'bestowing cattle', *rāyas-poṣa-dé* (VS. V. 1) 'granting increase of wealth', *śuci-pé* 'drinking the clear (Soma)', *śubhaṃ-yé* 'flying swiftly along', *havir-dé*.

f. *kṣé*; *śrad-dhé*[9]. — Also the **infinitives** *pra-khyái* 'to see', *vi-khyái* 'to look about'; *parā-dái* 'to give up'; *vayo-dhái* 'to strengthen'; *prati-mái*[10] 'to imitate'; *ava-yái* 'to go away', *ā-yái* 'to approach', *upa-yái* 'to come near', *pra-yái* 'to go forward; *ava-sái*[11] 'to rest'[12].

G. m. *kṛṣṭi-prás* 'pervading the human race', *paśu-ṣás*[13].

V. m. *ṛta-pā-s* (TS. III. 2. 8[1]), *ṛtu-pā-s*, *puro-gā-s* (TS. V. 1. 11[4]), *bhū́ri-dā-s*, *śukra-pūta-pā-s* 'drinking bright and purified (Soma)', *śuci-pā-s*, *śrotra-pā-s* (VS. XX. 34) 'protecting the ear', *suta-pā-s*, *soma-pā-s*[14].

Du. N. A. V. m. *kakṣya-prā́*, *go-pā́*, *gharmye-ṣṭhā́* 'being in a house', *chardiṣ-pā́* 'protecting a house', *jagat-pā́* 'protecting the living', *tanū-pā́*, *tapuṣ-pā́* 'drinking warm beverage', *draviṇo-dā́*[15], *paras-pā́*, *purā-jā́*, *púru-trā* 'protecting much', *vāja-dā* 'bestowing vigour', *śuci-pā*, *su-gopā́*, *soma-pā́*, *sti-pā́*. — **With** **-au**: *á-krau*[16] 'inactive', *a-doma-dháu* (AV.) 'not causing inconvenience', *adhva-gáu* 'travelling', *go-páu*, *go-pau*, *madhu-pau* 'drinking Soma', *rayi-dáu* 'bestowing wealth', *suta-pau*[17].

---

[1] For *rodasī-prā́m*.

[2] The D. case-form of *nṛ́-* 'man' being retained in the compound.

[3] The L. of the stem *patha-* = *pathi-* being retained in the compound.

[4] *barhi-* for *barhiṣ-*: see 62.

[5] With the N. case-form retained in the compound; see WHITNEY's note on AV. IX. 8[9].

[6] The derivation of this word is uncertain.

[7] Used adverbially = 'at once'.

[8] Cp. LANMAN 447[1]. There are also the transition forms *jyáyā*, *prajáyā*.

[9] Also the transition form *prajáyai*.

[10] The infinitive *prati-mé* is probably a locative.

[11] These dative infinitives are formed by combining the full root with the ending *-e*, while in the ordinary datives the radical *ā* is dropped before the ending.

[12] See below, the Dative Infinitive, 584.

[13] The form *jás-* in *jás-pati-* (I. 185[8]) 'lord of the family' is probably a f. G. of *jā́-*; and *gnā́s* probably G. of *gnā́-* in *gnā́s-páti-* 'husband of a divine woman'. There are also the transition forms *jyáyās* and *pra-jáyās*.

[14] There are also in the f. the transition forms *gaṅge*, *śrad-dhe*, *tiro-dhe* (AV.) 'concealment'.

[15] The Pada text reads *draviṇo॰dáu*.

[16] Some of these duals in *-au* may be formed from radical stems with shortened *-ă*; cp. LANMAN 450[1].

[17] There are also the f. transition forms *ṛdū-pé* 'drinking what is sweet', *pūrva-jé* 'born before', *sv-āsa-sthé* 'sitting on a good seat'.

I. Only four compounds of *-pā* in TS. III. 2. 10[1]: *kratu-pā́bhyām* 'watching one's intentions', *cakṣuṣ-pā́bhyām*, *vāk-pā́bhyām* 'protecting speech', *śrotra-pā́bhyām*[1].

Pl. N. V. m. *ṛbhu-kṣā́s.* — *agni-jā́s* (AV.) 'fire-born', *á-pra-jās* 'childless', *apsu-jā́s* (AV.), *oṣadhi-jā́s* (AV.) 'born among herbs', *khala-jā́s* (AV.) 'produced on a threshing-floor', *deva-jā́s*, *purā-jā́s*, *prathama-jā́s*, *pravāte-jā́s* 'grown in an airy place', *raghu-jā́s* 'produced from a racer', *śaka-dhūma-jā́s* (AV.) 'produced from cow-dung', *su-pra-jā́s*, *sva-jā́s.* — *ṛta-jñā́s*, *ṛta-jñā́s*, *pada-jñā́s* 'knowing the track'. — *aśva-dā́s* 'giving horses', *āśīr-dā́s* (VS. VIII. 5), *go-dā́s*, *draviṇo-dā́s*, *dhana-dā́s*, *vara-dā́s* (AV.) 'granting boons', *vastra-dā́s* and *vāso-dā́s* 'giving garments', *hiraṇya-dā́s.* — *jani-dhā́s*[2] (x. 29[5]), *dhiyaṃ-dhā́s*, *ratna-dhā́s*, *reto-dhā́s*, *vayo-dhā́s.* — *payo-dhā́s* 'sucking milk'. — *kula-pā́s* 'heads of the family'; *go-pā́s*, *índra-gopās* 'protected by Indra', *devá-gopās*, *vāyú-gopās* 'protected by Wind', *su-gopā́s*; *tanū-pā́s*, *paśu-pā́s*, *vrata-pā́s.* — *agre-pā́s* 'drinking first', *añjas-pā́s*, *payas-pā́s* 'drinking milk', *manthi-pā́s*[3] (VS. VII. 17) 'drinking the stirred Soma', *soma-pā́s*, *sóma-pās* (AV.), *haviṣ-pā́s* 'drinking offerings'. — *carma-mnā́s*[4] 'tanners'. — *jma-yā́s* 'going on the earth'. — *dhana-sā́s*, *sadā-sā́s*, *sahasra-sā́s.* — *pṛthivi-ṣṭhā́s*[5] 'standing on the earth', *rathe-ṣṭhā́s*[6], *harmye-ṣṭhā́s*[6] 'dwelling in the house'. — *ghṛta-snā́s* 'sprinkling ghee'. — Also the abnormal derivative *pánthās*[7].

f. *gnā́s*, *vrā́s.* — *á-gopās*, *ava-sthā́s* 'female organs', *áhi-gopās* 'guarded by the dragon', *ā́-tās* 'frames', *ṛta-jñā́s* (AV.), *giri-jā́s* 'mountain-born', *jaraṇi-prā́s*[2], *devá-gopās*, *deva-yā́s*, *pada-jñā́s* (AV.), *pra-jā́s*, *prathama-jā́s*, *pra-yā́s* 'advance', *manuṣya-jā́s* (AV.), *vakṣaṇe-ṣṭhā́s* 'being in Agni' (?), *vāja-dā́s*, *śuṣma-dā́s* 'bestowing strength', *su-gopā́s*, *soma-pā́s*, *svayaṃ-jā́s*[8] 'self-born'.

A. m. There is no certain example: *vane-jā́s* (x. 79[7]) is possibly one[9].

f. *kṣā́s*, *gnā́s*, *jā́s.* — *án-agni-trās* 'not maintaining the sacred fire', *anu-ṣṭhā́s* 'following in succession', *aśva-dā́s*, *deva-yā́s*, *pari-jā́s* (AV.) 'places of origin', *pari-ṣṭhās* 'impediments', *pra-jā́s*, *manuṣya-jā́s*, *vi-ṣṭhā́s* 'positions', *sahá-gopās* 'accompanied by herdsmen', *su-gā́s* 'easy to traverse', *sva-dhā́s.*

I. m. *agre-pā́bhis.* — **f.** *gnā́bhis*; *ṛtu-pā́bhis*, *ratna-dhā́bhis*, *prajā́bhis*, *śrad-dhā́bhis*, *sva-dhā́bhis.*

D. f. *pra-jā́bhyas.* — **Ab. m.** *bhūri-dā́bhyas*[10].

L. f. *kṣā́su*, *gnā́su*, *jā́su*; *ā́-tāsu*[11], *pra-jā́su*, *sabhā́su.*

1 b. Stems in Radical *-a*.

369. These consist almost entirely of stems in radical *ā* which has been shortened to *ă*. With the exception of *khá-*[12] 'aperture' they occur at the end of compounds only. They are: *-kṣá-* 'dwelling', *khá-*, *-gá-* 'going', *-gá-* 'singing', *-já-* 'born', *-jya-* 'bowstring', *-ta-* 'stretching', *-tra-*[13] 'protecting', *-dá-* 'giving'[14], *-dá-* 'binding', *-dhá-* 'putting', *-pá-* 'guarding', *-pá-* 'drinking', *-prá-* 'filling', *-mná-*

---

1 In the L. du. there also occur the f. transition forms *jaṅgháyos* (AV.) and *sva-dháyos.*

2 Of doubtful meaning.

3 The stem is *manthi-pá-* according to BR.

4 From √*mlā-*: 'softening hides'.

5 *Pṛthivi-* = *pṛthivī-*.

6 With the L. ending retained in the first member of the compound.

7 The form *pánthāsas* also occurs once. It is doubtful whether the plurals *dyu-kṣā́sas* and *priya-sā́sas* are to be regarded as formed from *ā-* stems. Such plurals are probably made from *a-* stems.

8 There is also the f. transition form *náva-gvās.*

9 Cp. LANMAN 451[4].

10 In the G. occur the f. transition forms *pra-jñānām* (AV.) 'fore-knowing', *vi-bhā́nām* 'radiant'.

11 Probably from *tā-* = *tan-* 'stretch'.

12 The nominatives *drá-s* and *vrá-s* in AV. XI. 73 (also *nyá-s*, 74) are of unknown meaning (see WHITNEY's note).

13 Cp. GARBE in KZ. 23, 476, 480.

14 Perhaps also *-dra-* 'running' in *kṛṣṇa-drá-m* (AV.).

'thinking', *-mla-*[1] 'softening', *-sá-* 'winning', *-sthá-* 'standing'; also *-grá-*[2] 'swallowing', *-gva-*[3] 'going', *-há-*[4] 'slaying'.

These stems are inflected in the m. and n. only. This is the form assumed in the n. by all radical *ā*-stems (367).

Inflexion.

370. The inflexion of the radical *a*-stems is identical with that of the derivative *a*-stems (371). The forms which occur are the following:

Sing. N. m. *dyu-kṣá-s* 'dwelling in heaven'. — *su-khá-s* 'having a good (axle) hole'. — *agre-gá-s* 'going in front', *āśuṃ-gá-s* (AV.) 'swift-going', *ṛju-gá-s* (AV.) 'going straight on', *pataṃ-gá-s*[5] 'going by flight', *vala-gá-s* (AV.) 'hidden in a cave'[6], *śitiṃ-gá-s* (AV. XI. 5^{12}) 'white-goer', *su-gá-s* 'easy to traverse'. — *dáśa-gva-s*[7] 'going in tens', *náva-gva-s*[7] 'going in nines'[8]. — *a-já-s* 'unborn', *adhṛ́-ja-s* 'irresistible', *eka-já-s* (AV.) 'produced alone', *jarāyu-já-s* (AV.) 'viviparous', *ni-já-s* (AV.) 'familiar'[9], *prathama-já-s* (AV.) 'first-born', *samudra-já-s* (AV.) 'sea-born', *stamba-já-s* (AV.) 'shaggy' (?). — *an-ānu-dá-s* 'not giving way', *dānu-dá-s* 'dripping', *dāyā-dá-s* (AV.) 'receiving (*ā-da-*) inheritance (*dāya-*)', *prāṇa-dá-s* 'life-giving'. — *nāma-dhá-s* (AV.) 'name-giver'. — *ākūti-prá-s* (AV.) 'fulfilling wishes', *kāma-prá-s* (AV.) 'fulfilling desire', *carṣaṇi-prá-s* (AV.) 'satisfying men', *pṛthivī-prá-s* (AV.) 'earth-filling'[10]. — *apnaḥ-sthá-s* 'possessor', *go-ṣṭhá-s* (AV.) 'cow-pen', *puru-niṣṭhá-s* 'excelling among many'. — *śatru-há-s* (AV.) 'slaying enemies', *sahasra-há-s* (AV.) 'slaying a thousand'.

N. A. n. *khám* 'aperture'. — *a-doma-dám* (AV.) 'not causing inconvenience', *antári-kṣam* 'air', *kṛṣṇa-drám* (AV.) 'black runner' (?)[11], *tuvi-kṣám* 'destroying many', *dur-gám* 'impassable', *dyu-kṣám*, *prathama-jám* (AV. VS.), *váta-gopam* (AV.) 'guarded by the wind', *vṛtra-hám* 'slaying foes', *satrā-hám* 'always destroying', *sadhá-stham* 'abode', *su-gám* , *su-mnám* 'benevolent'.

A. m. *atithi-gvám* ('to whom guests go') N. of a man, *an-ānu-dám*, *arāti-hám* (AV.) 'destroying adversity', *aśva-pám* (VS. XXX. 11) 'groom', *á-sva-gam* (AV.) 'homeless', *eka-jám*, *garbha-dhám* (VS. TS.) 'impregnator', *gṛha-pám* (VS. XXX. 11) 'guardian of a house', *go-pám* 'herdsman', *carma-mnám* (VS.) 'tanner', *tri-ṣṭhám* 'having three seats', *dáśa-gvam*, *dāva-pám* (VS. XXX. 19) 'forest-fire guard', *dyu-kṣám*, *pataṃ-gám*, *prathama-jám* (VS. XXXIV. 51), *madhu-pám* 'honey-drinker', *vana-pám* (VS. XXX. 19) 'wood-ranger', *vala-gám* (AV.), *vitta-dhám* (VS. XXX. 11) 'possessing wealth', *su-khám*, *su-gám* (AV.), *hasti-pám* (VS. XXX. 11) 'elephant-keeper'.

I. m. *rathe-ṣṭhéna* 'standing on a car'. — **n.** *antári-kṣeṇa*, *ṛtá-jyena* 'whose bowstring is truth', *kāma-préṇa*, *su-géna* (AV.), *su-mnéna*.

D. m. *atithi-gvā́ya*, *dyu-kṣā́ya*, *pataṃ-gā́ya*, *rathe-ṣṭhā́ya*[12]. — **n.** *parás-pāya* (VS.) 'protecting from afar', *su-mnā́ya*. — **Ab. m.** *ṛśya-dā́t* (X. 39^8) 'pit for antelopes'. — **n.** *antári-kṣāt*[13], *dur-gā́t*, *sadhá-sthāt*.

---

1 In the form of *-mna-* in *carma-mná-* 'tanner'.

2 An extension of *gṛ-* 'swallow'; cp. *-krā-* and *vrā-* among the radical *ā-* stems.

3 In its original form perhaps *-gvā-*; a reduced form *-gu-* appears in *vanar-gú-* 'forest-roaming'.

4 A reduced form of *han-* 'slay'.

5 See Bartholomae, BB. 15, 34 and cp. BB. 18, 12.

6 The etymology and meaning are somewhat doubtful; cp. IS. 4, 304.

7 These two compounds as well as *atithi-gvá-* and *éta-gva-*, are with more probability derived from a reduced form of *go-* 'cow' by Bloomfield, AJPh. 17, 422—27; cp. above p. 153 (mid.).

8 The compound *puro-gavá-s* 'leader' possibly = **puro-gvá-s*; but it is probably a governing compound; cp. above, p. 176^1.

9 See Whitney's note on AV. III. 5^2.

10 Also *paśu-ṣá-s* (V. 41^1) if it is N. sing. and not a G. of *paśu-ṣā́-*.

11 Cp. Whitney's note on AV. IX. 7^4.

12 *svajā́ya* (AV.) is analyzed by the Commentator as *sva-jā́ya* 'self-born', but is explained by Whitney (AV. VI. 56^2) as 'constrictor' (from *svaj-* 'embrace').

13 See Lanman 337.

G. m. *a-jásya, atithi-gvásya*[1]. — **n.** *antári-kṣasya, asthi-jásya* (AV.) 'produced in the bones', *tanū-jásya* (AV.) 'produced from the body', *su-mnásya*.
L. m. *dáśa-gve, náva-gve, ratha-saṃgé* 'encounter of war-cars', *saṃ-sthé* 'presence', *saṃ-gé* 'conflict', *su-khé, svar-gé* 'going to heaven'. — **n.** *antári-kṣe, khé*. — *karañja-hé* 'pernicious to the Karañja tree', *dur-gé, bhayá-sthe* 'perilous situation', *sadhá-sthe, su-mné*. — V. m. *eka-ja, dyu-kṣa, pataṃ-ga* (AV.), *soma-pa* (AV.) 'drinking Soma'.
Du. N. A. m.[2] *éta-gvā* 'going swiftly'. — A. n. *sadhá-sthe*.
Pl. N. V. m. *ājya-pā́s* (VS. xxi. 40) 'drinking clarified butter', *éta-gvās, tanū-jā́s* (AV.), *tapo-jā́s* (AV.) 'produced by austerity', *dáśa-gvās, náva-gvās, pataṃ-gā́s, vala-gā́s* (AV.), *su-gā́s*. — Also four forms with **āsas**: *dáśa-gvāsas, dyu-kṣásas, náva-gvāsas, priya-sā́sas*[3] 'granting desired objects'.
N. A. n. 1. *áṃsa-trā* 'armour protecting the shoulder', *antárikṣā, dur-gā́, prathama-jā́*[4] (AV.), *sadhá-sthā, su-gā́, su-mnā́*. — 2. *khā́ni*. — *antári-kṣāṇi, ararín-dāni*[5], *dur-gā́ṇi, sadhá-sthāni, su-gā́ni, su-mnā́ni*.
A. m. *go-pā́n, tapo-jā́n, dur-gā́n* (AV.), *pataṃ-gā́n, pū́rva-jā́n* (TS.) 'born before', *śŕta-pā́n* 'drinking boiled milk', *saha-jā́n* (TS.) 'born at the same time', *su-gā́n, soma-pā́n* (AV.).
I. m. 1. *tuvi-grébhis* 'swallowing much', *mithó-avadya-pebhis* 'mutually averting calamities', *ratna-dhébhis* 'preserving wealth', *sāma-gébhis* (AV.) 'reciting chants', *su-gébhis*. — 2. *ă-tais*[6] 'frames', *dáśa-gvais, náva-gvais, dhana-sáis* 'winning wealth', *náva-gvais, pataṃ-gáis, su-kháis*. — n. 1. *madhu-pébhis, su-gébhis, su-mnébhis*. — 2. *su-mnáis*.
D. m. *pū́rva-jébhyas*. — G. m. *dvi-jánām* (AV.) 'twice-born', *sākaṃ-jánām* 'being born together'. — L. m. *draviṇo-déṣu* 'giving wealth', *su-khéṣu*. — n. *dur-géṣu, sadhá-stheṣu, su-géṣu, su-mnéṣu*.

2 a. Derivative stems in -a.

BENFEY, Vollständige Grammatik p. 293—317. — WHITNEY, Grammar 326—334 (p. 112—116). — LANMAN, Noun-Inflection 329—354.

371. This is the most important of the declensions as it embraces more than one-half of all nominal stems. It is also the most irregular inasmuch as its ending diverge from the normal ones more than is elsewhere the case. This is the only declension in which the N. A. n. has an ending in the singular. Here the I. D. Ab. G. sing. are peculiar; and in the plural, the A., the G., one of the forms of the I. and of the N. A. n. do not take the normal endings. The final vowel of the stem is also modified before the endings with initial consonant in the du. and pl. Three of the peculiar case-endings of the sing. (I. Ab. G.) are borrowed from the pronominal declension, while in the pl. two of the case-endings (G. and N. A. n.) are due to the influence of the stems in -*n*. This is the only declension in which the Ab. sing., as a result of taking the pronominal ending, is distinguished from the G. As elsewhere in the vowel declension, the N. sing. m. here adds the ending -*s* throughout; but the V. sing. shows the bare stem unmodified. This declension includes

---

[1] *svajásya* in AV. x. 4.10.15 is according to WHITNEY 'constrictor', not *sva-jásya* 'self-born'; cp. p. 254, note 12.
[2] Some of the m. duals given under the radical ā-declension ought possibly to be placed here.
[3] There is no reason to suppose that any of these are plurals of ā- stems, since the first three appear as *ă-* stems only and *priya-sá-* does not otherwise occur. The pl.

pánthāsas, occurring once beside the ordinary *panthās* formed from the anomalous derivative ā- stem *pánthā-*, proves nothing regarding radical ā- stems.
[4] This is the reading of the Pada text, the Saṃhitā having -*já ṛ-* (70 a).
[5] A word of uncertain meaning.
[6] Two other forms, *átās* and *átāsu* are formed from the f. stem of this word, *á-tā-*, which is probably a radical ā- stem.

m. and n. stems only, as the corresponding f. follows the derivative *ā*-declension. There is here no irregularity in the accent, which remains on the same syllable in every case except the V., where it of course shifts to the first.

Inflexion.

372. The inflexion of the n. differs from that of the m. in the N. sing. and the N. A. du. and pl. only. In the G. L. du. *y* is inserted between the final *-a* of the stem and the ending *-os*. The forms actually occurring, if made from *priyá-* 'dear', would be the following:

Sing. N. m. *priyá-s*, n. *priyá-m*. A. *priyá-m*. I. *priyéṇa* and *priyā́*. D. *priyā́ya*. Ab. *priyā́t*. G. *priyásya*. L. *priyé*. V. *príya*.

Du. N. A. m. *priyā́* and *priyáu*, n. *priyé*. V. m. *príyā* and *príyau*. I. D. Ab. *priyā́bhyām*. G. L. *priyáyos*.

Pl. N. m. *priyā́s* and *priyā́sas*, n. *priyā́* and *priyā́ṇi*. A. m. *priyā́n*, n. *priyā́* and *priyā́ṇi*. I. *priyáis* and *priyébhis*. D. Ab. *priyébhyas*. G. *priyā́ṇām*. L. *priyéṣu*. V. *príyās* and *príyāsas*.

Owing to the enormous number of words belonging to this declension, only forms of commonest occurrence will be given below as examples under each case.

Sing. N. m. This case is formed in the RV. by 1845 *a*-stems and occurs more than 10000 times. The most frequent substantive is *índras* N. of a god, found more than 500 times; next in order come *sómas* (220) N. of a plant, *devás* (203) 'god', *mitrás* (132) N. of a god, *váruṇas* (94) N. of a god.

A. m. After the N. sing. m., the A. sing. m. is the commonest declensional form in the RV., being made from 1357 stems[1] and occurring nearly 7000 times. The nouns most frequently found in this case are *índram* (335), *sómam*, (212), *yajñám* (183) 'sacrifice', *vā́jam* (123) 'vigour', *sū́ryam* (90) 'sun', *hávam* (88) 'invocation', *vṛtrám* (82) N. of a demon, *stómam* (77) 'praise'[2].

N. A. n. This is the only declension in which these cases take an ending. They here add *-m*, being thus identical in form with the A. sing. m.[3]. They are very frequently used, being formed from about 950 stems and occurring, taken together, more than 4000 times. Examples are: *ṛtám* (70) 'sacred order', *ghṛtám* (47) 'clarified butter', *padám* (46) 'step', *rátnam* (44) 'wealth', *sakhyám* (43) 'friendship', *dráviṇam* (41) 'wealth', *satyám* (40) 'truth'[4].

I. m. n. 1. The usual form of this case ending in *-ena* is very frequent, being formed from more than 300 stems nearly equally divided between m. and n. The commonest forms are: **m.** *sū́ryeṇa* (37), *índreṇa* (34), *vájreṇa* (33) 'thunderbolt', *yajñéna* (13). — **n.** *ghṛténa* (31)[5].

a. The **final vowel** appears **lengthened** in about twenty-five forms: *amṛ́tenā* (AV.) 'ambrosia', *á-śivenā* 'malevolent', *ā́jyenā* 'melted butter', *ṛténā*, *kā́vyenā* 'wisdom', *kúliśenā* 'axe', *pétvenā* 'ram', *taviṣéṇā* 'strong', *dákṣiṇenā* 'right', *dáivyenā* 'divine', *bákureṇā* 'bagpipe', *bhadréṇā* (AV.) 'excellent', *mártyenā* 'mortal', *mā́rutenā* 'consisting of storm-gods', *ravā́thenā* 'roar', *váruṇenā*, *vithuréṇā* 'staggering', *vi-ravéṇā* 'roar', *vīryèṇā* 'heroic power', *vṛjánenā* 'might', *vṛṣabhéṇā* 'bull', *sahasyènā* 'mighty', *sā́yakenā* 'missile', *sū́ryeṇā*, *skámbhanenā*

1 The pronominal forms *tám* and *yám* occur 509 and 259 times respectively in the RV.

2 On the occasional elision of the *-m* before *iva* and subsequent contraction, see LANMAN 331.

3 For this reason there is in some instances not sufficient evidence for determining whether a word is m. or n.; cp. LANMAN 331 (middle).

4 On occasional elision of the final *-m* and subsequent contraction, see LANMAN 331.

5 The final vowel is twice nasalized: *ghanénam̐ ékas* (I. 33⁴) and *téjanenam̐ ékam* (I. 110⁵).

'support'[1]. These forms regularly occur where the metre at the end of a Pāda favours a long vowel; e. g. *skámbhanenā jánitrī* (III. 31[12]), but *kámbhanena skábhīyān* (X. 111[5]); on the other hand, the long vowel appears to be used arbitrarily at the beginning of a Pāda, though the short vowel here is much more frequent. Hence the *ā* seems to be a survival and not to be due to metrical exigencies.

2. There are also more than a dozen forms made with the **nominal ending -ā.** In the m. there are no quite certain examples beyond *yajñā́*; possibly also *krāṇā́* 'acting', *ghanā́* 'club', *dānā́* 'gift'[2], *camasā́*[3] 'cup'. The n. forms are *kavitvā́* and *kavitvanā́* 'by wisdom', *taraṇitvā́* 'by energy', *mahitvā́* and *mahitvanā́* 'by greatness', *ratna-dhéyā* 'by distribution of wealth', *ráthyā* 'belonging to a car', *vīryā̀* 'with heroism', *sakhyā́* 'with friendship', *sarva-rathā́* 'with the whole line of chariots', *su-hávā* 'with good invocation'[4]. — This ending is also preserved in a few **instrumental adverbs**: *anā́* 'hereby', *uccā́* 'above', *paścā́* 'behind', *sánā* 'from of old'[5].

D. m. n. This case, which has the abnormal ending *-āya*, is of very frequent occurrence, being formed in the RV. from over 300 stems in the m. and from nearly 150 in the n. The commonest forms are: **m.** *índrāya* (188), *mádāya* (76) 'exhilaration', *devā́ya* (26), *mártyāya* (25), *mitrā́ya* (23), *váruṇāya* (23), *yájamānāya* 'sacrificing', *sū́ryāya* (11); **n.** *suvitā́ya* (34) 'welfare', *sakhyā́ya* (29), *tokā́ya* (21) 'offspring', *tánayāya* (18) 'line of descendants'[6].

a. The normal form would have been for example **yajñā́i* = *yajñá-e*[7]. This would in Sandhi have become **yajñā́y*, which was ultimately extended with *-a*, owing to the frequent combination with a following *a* in Sandhi (e. g. *yajñā́y-a pi* for *yajñā́y api*), or with the shortened form of the preposition *ā́*[8].

Ab. m. n. These are the only nominal stems in which the Ab. is formally distinguished from the G. Instead of the normal ending *-as*, they take the *-d* which appears in the pronominal declension (e. g. *má-d* 'from me'), lengthening the *-a* of the stem before it[9]. This Ab. in *-ād* is formed in the RV. from over 200 stems, nearly equally divided between m. and n. Some of the n. forms are used as adverbs. Forms of common occurrence are: **m.** *samudrā́t* (15) 'sea', *upásthāt* (9) 'lap', *índrāt* (8); **n.** *antári-kṣāt*[10] (15) 'air'; *dūrā́t* (19) 'from a distance', *paścā́t* (26).

G. m. n. These are the only nominal stems in which the G. sing. does not end in *-s*[11]. Instead of the normal ending *-as*, they add *-sya*[12] which is

---

1 In all these forms the Pada text has the short final vowel *ă*; see RPr. VIII. 21 and cp. APr. III. 16. The pronominal forms *ténā*, *yénā*, *svénā* also appear, and always with the short vowel in the Pada text; on the other hand, *enā́* is always *enā́* in the Pada, while the unaccented *enā*, beside *ena*, has the short vowel in the Pada. See LANMAN 332 (bottom).

2 See LANMAN 334 (middle).

3 Nasalized in *camasā́ṁ iva* (X. 25[4]), Pada *camasā́n*. On these forms see LANMAN 335.

4 This form of the instrumental also appears a few times in the pronoun *tvā́* beside the usual *tváyā*; it also occurs in a few compounds, as *tvā́-datta-* and *tvā́-dāta-* 'given by thee'; cp. LANMAN 334 (middle).

5 Perhaps also *nīcā́* 'below', cp. *nīcā́is*; but it may be the I. of *nyàñc-*.

6 Such D. forms are twice nasalized before vowels: *tad-vaśā́yaṁ eṣá* (II. 14[2]) and *savā́yaṁ evá* (I. 113[1]).

7 The normal ending *-e* is actually used in the pronominal declension, e. g. *tásmai* = *tásma-e*.

8 See JOHANSSON, BB. 20, 96 ff. and BARTHOLOMAE, Arische Forschungen 2, 69; 3, 63.

9 Cp. JOHANSSON, BB. 16, 136 and BRUGMANN, Grundriss 2, 588.

10 This is really a radical *a*- stem; see above, 370.

11 In the G. sing. of stems in *-ar* and *-tar*, the final *r* seems to represent original *-s*; see above 358, note on *svásur*.

12 The *y* is never to be read as *i*; possibly however about five times in the pronominal *asyá*. The final *-a* in two or three instances undergoes protraction of a purely metrical character: see LANMAN 338[3].

otherwise found in the pronominal declension only. This case is very common, being formed in the RV. from over 500 stems in the m. and 175 in the n., occurring altogether over 3300 times[1]. Among the frequent forms[2] are: **m.** *índrasya* (123), *sū́ryasya* (93), *sómasya* (88), *devásya* (60), *yajñásya* (55), *sutásya* (53) 'pressed'; **n.** *ṛtásya* (187), *bhúvanasya* (39) 'world', *amṛ́tasya* (35)[3].

L. m. n. This case is formed with the normal ending *-i*, which combines with the final *-a* of the stem to *-e*. It is formed in the RV. from 373 stems in the m., and over 300 in the n., occurring altogether about 2500 times. Among the frequent forms are: **m.** *adhvaré* (68) 'sacrifice', *suté* (53), *upá-sthe* (49), *máde* (48), *dáme* (40) 'house', *índre* (33), *yajñé* (28), *jáne* (26) 'man', *gṛhé* (23) 'house'; **n.** *vidáthe* (49) 'assembly', *ágre* (43) 'front', *sádane* (35) 'seat', *padé* (33), *duroṇé* (31) 'abode', *mádhye* 'middle' (29).

V. m. n. In this case the bare stem (always accented on the first syllable) is employed. It is formed in the RV. from about 260 stems, occurring about 2500 times in the m.; but in the n. there is no undoubted example[4]. The AV. however has four or five n. vocatives. Among the commonest forms are: **m.** *sóma* and *soma* (240), *deva* (132), *śū́ra* (94) 'hero', *pavamāna* (63) 'bright Soma', *puru-hūta* (49) 'much invoked', *varuṇa* (45), *mitra* (35), *yaviṣṭha* (29) 'youngest', *vṛṣabha* (27) 'bull', *ugra* (23) 'mighty', *amṛta* (12)[5]; **n.** *antarikṣa*[6] (AV. VI. 130^{4}), *tráikakuda* 'coming from the three-peaked (mountain)' and *dévāñjana* (AV. XIX. 44^{6}) 'divine ointment', *talpa* (AV. XII. 2^{49}) 'couch', *viṣa* (AV. IV. 6^{3}) 'poison'[7].

Du. N. A. V. m. The ending of these cases in the RV. is ordinarily *-ā*, much less frequently *-au*[8]. The former is taken by over 360 stems occurring about 1150 times, the latter by fewer than 90 stems occurring about 170 times. The ending *-ā* is therefore more than seven times as common as *-au*. The rule is that *-ā* appears before consonants[9], in pausa at the end of a Pāda[10], or within a Pāda in coalescence with a following vowel; while *-au*[11] occurs in the older parts of the RV. only before vowels in the Sandhi form of *-āv*, within a Pāda. Examples of this rule are *tā́ vām* (I. 184^{1}); *ṛtāvṛdhā* | (I. 47^{3b}); *dasrā́t*[12] (I. 116^{10c}) for *dasrā ā́t*; *mitrā́gním* (I. 14^{3}) for *mitrā́ agním*; but *tā́v*[13] *aparám* (I. 184^{1}). Hiatus, when the metre requires two

---

1 The pronominal genitives *asya* and *asyá*, *tásya*, *yásya*, *víśvasya* occur over 900 times in the RV.; cp. LANMAN 338.

2 The commonest G. in *-sya* is the pronominal *asyá* which (accented or unaccented) occurs nearly 600 times in the RV.

3 The final vowel is once nasalized at the end of a Pāda in *ṛtásyaṁ ékam* (VIII. 89^{5}); cp. RPr. II. 31.

4 Cp. LANMAN 339.

5 There are two instances of the final *-a* being nasalized: *ugraṁ ókas* (VII. 25^{4}) and *puru-ṣṭutaṁ éko* (VIII. $15^{3.11}$); cp. RPr. XIV. 20. There is a purely metrical lengthening of the final vowel in *vṛṣabhā* (VIII. $45^{22.38}$), *sīmā* (VIII. 4^{1}), and *hāriyojanā* (I. 61^{16}); perhaps also *maryā* (I. 6^{3}); cp. LANMAN 339.

6 Properly a radical *a-* stem.

7 By a syntactical peculiarity the N. *índraś ca* is some ten times coupled with a vocative *vā́yo*, *ágne* etc. See LANMAN 340 (top).

8 In the AV. *-au* is more than twice as common as in the RV.; it is there sometimes a various reading for *-ā* of the RV. In the independent Mantra portions of the TS. there are at least seven forms in *-ā* and fourteen in *-au*. In the Khilas *-ā* is nearly three times (32) as common as *-au* (12).

9 *-au* occurs 23 times before a consonant within a Pāda; mostly in passages showing signs of lateness. Cp. LANMAN 576.

10 *-au* occurs 5 times at the end of an odd Pāda before a consonant; and 4 times as *-āv* at the end of an odd Pāda before a vowel. At the end of an even Pāda *-au* occurs 4 times.

11 LANMAN 343 enumerates the forms in *-au* which occur in the RV.

12 At the end of an odd Pāda *-ā* is always written in the Saṃhitā contracted with a following vowel, but must always be read with hiatus.

13 This is the normal use of *-au*, which in 70 per cent of its occurrences is found as *-āv* before a vowel within a Pāda; in the AV. the percentage is only 26.

syllables, is thus removed[1] by the use of *-āv*, except when *u* or *ū* follows[2]. In the latter case the Saṃhitā text writes *-ā u-*[3], e. g. *ubhā́ upāṃśú* (x. 83[7]), though the Pada always has *-au u-*.

There are seven or eight passages of the RV. in which *-ā* is written with hiatus before other vowels (*a- i- o-*)[4], but those passages are all obscure or corrupt[5].

a. About a dozen forms, occurring altogether some 20 times, shorten the dual *-ā* to *a*, mostly owing to the metre, but in a few instances against the metre. In the forms *asura, āditya, deva, dhṛta-vrata, mitra, varuṇa, indrā-varuṇa, mitrā-varuṇa*[6] the Pada text has *-ā*; but in *pā́ura* (v. 74[4]) and *vīra* (vi. 63[10]) the short vowel appears in the Pada also[7]. A similar shortening occurs in the first member of the dual compounds *indră-vāyū* (i. 2[4]) and *mitră-rājānā* (v. 62[3]).

N. A. n. This form takes the normal ending *-ī*, which combines with the final *-a* of the stem to *-e*. It is made in the RV. from about 30 nominal stems. The vocative does not occur. Only seven of these n. forms are found more than once, *śṛ́ṅge* 'two horns' being the commonest (5)[8].

a. The n. *nákta-* 'night' is irregular in forming its du. N. as a m. in the compound *uṣā́sā-náktā* 'dawn and night', in agreement with which a f. adjective is used, owing doubtless to the predominance of 'Dawn', in the combination. In ii. 39[4], *yugéva nábhyeva* 'like two yokes, like two naves', though analyzed by the Pada as *yugā́ iva* and *nábhyā iva*, must be explained as regular n. forms *yugé* and *nábhye+va*.

I. D. Ab. Before the normal ending *-bhyām*[9] which forms these cases, the final *-a* of the stems is lengthened, e. g. *nā́satyābhyām*. In the RV. this form is made from only about a dozen nominal stems in the m. and three in the n. The cases can of course only be distinguished exegetically.

I. m. *kárṇābhyām* (AV.) 'ears', *dáṃṣṭrābhyām* (TS. AV.) 'teeth', *dakṣiṇa-savyā́bhyām* (AV.) 'right and left', *dáśa-śākhābhyām* 'having ten fingers', *mitrā́-váruṇābhyām*[10], *yuktā́bhyām* 'yoked', *vrīhi-yavā́bhyām* (AV.) 'rice and barley', *śubhrā́bhyām* 'shining', *sūryā-candramásābhyām* (AV.)[10] 'sun and moon', *hástābhyām* 'hands', *haryatā́bhyām* 'desirable'. — **n.** *ṛk-sāmā́bhyām* 'hymn and chant', *śṛ́ṅgābhyām* (AV.).

D. m. *tveṣā́bhyām* 'violent', *nā́satyābhyām* 'truthful', *nicirā́bhyām* 'attentive'.

Ab. m. *áṃsābhyām* 'shoulders', *kárṇābhyām*. — **n.** *pārśvā́bhyām* (AV.) 'sides', *prá-padābhyām* 'tips of the feet', *máta-snābhyām* certain internal organs.

G. L. These cases take the normal ending *-os*, between which and the stem *y* is inserted. In the RV. only eight nominal[11] forms occur with the genitive sense, and twelve with the locative sense. One form, *dhvasrā́yos* (ix. 58[3]), seems to be used as an Ab. There are one or two others which anomalously drop the final *-a* of the stem, instead of inserting *y*, before the ending *-os*[12].

---

1 In two instances hiatus is removed by nasalization: *upásthām̐ ékā* (i. 35[6]) and *jánānām̐ ásamā* (vi. 67[1]).

2 There are 40 instances of this in the RV.; see LANMAN 575.

3 This is also the practice of the Brāhmaṇas; see AUFRECHT, AB. 427; cp. Sarvānukramaṇī, ed. MACDONELL, p. x. In the AV. (as in the later language) *-āv u-* is regularly written (except *muṣkā́ upā́vadhīt*, xx. 136[2]).

4 See LANMAN 341[4].

5 Except vii. 70[4] where *devā́ óṣadhīṣu* (Pada *devau*) is written, *o-* being treated like *u-*, perhaps owing to its labial character.

6 See RPr. iv. 39, 40.

7 The shortening of the du. *-ā* at the end of odd Pādas before *r*, occurring in four passages (ii. 37; vi. 68[2]; viii. 66[11]; x. 66[13]) is due to Sandhi; see 70.

8 These neuter duals are enumerated by LANMAN 343.

9 To be read *-bhiām* in two or three forms.

10 In this compound only the second dual takes the proper case-ending.

11 There are also the pronominal forms G. L. m. *ayós, ubháyos, táyos, yáyos*; *táyos* also as G. n.

12 Also the pronominal forms *av-ós, en-ós, y-ós*. Cp. LANMAN 344.

The forms occurring are:

G. m. *índrā-váruṇayos*, *īśānáyos* 'ruling', *deváyos*, *mitráyos*, *mitrá-váruṇayos*, *yamáyos* 'twins', *váruṇayos*, *vaikarṇáyos* 'descendants of Vikarṇa'. — n. *páṣy-òs* (for **páṣyà-y-os*) 'pressing stones', *purāṇ-y-ós*[1] (for **purāṇá-y-os*) 'ancient'.

L. m. *áṃsayos*, *áśvayos*, *upākáyos* 'closely connected', *kárṇayos* (AV.), *jámbhayos* (TS. IV. I. 10³) 'jaws', *tuvi-jātáyos* 'of powerful nature', *dáṃṣṭrayos* (AV.), *nadáyos* 'roarers', *mitráyos*, *muṣkáyos* 'testicles', *váruṇayos*, *váhiṣṭhayos* 'drawing best', *ví-vratayos* 'refractory', *sthūráyos* 'strong', *hástayos*.

Pl. N. V. m. Here there are two forms. In the more common form the normal ending -*as* coalesces with the final of the stem to -*ās*, e. g. *devā́s*. The less common form appears to be made by adding the normal ending -*as* over again[2], e. g. *devā́s-as*. The form in -*ās* is about twice as frequent in the RV. as that in -*āsas*[3], the former being made from 808 stems, the latter from 403. In the original parts of the AV. -*ās* is 24 times as frequent as -*āsas*, the former occurring 1366 times, the latter only 57 times[4]. Both forms frequently occur side by side, the choice of the one or the other being often no doubt determined simply by the metre; e. g. *bṛhád vadema vidáthe suvī́rāḥ* (II. 1¹⁶) 'abounding in heroes we would speak aloud in the assembly', but *suvī́rāso vidátham ā́ vadema* (II. 12¹⁵) 'abounding in heroes we would speak to the assembly'.

Examples of the most frequent forms made with the two endings are:
1. *devā́sas* (86), *jánāsas* (41), *sómāsas* (41), *sutā́sas* (29), *ādityā́sas* (24) 'Ādityas', *yajñíyāsas* (21) 'holy', *amŕ̥tāsas* (11). — 2. *devā́s* and *devā́s* (311), *sómās* (42), *ādityā́s* (39), *sutā́s* (27), *jánās* (24), *amŕ̥tās* (22), *yajñíyās* (10).

N. A. n.[5] Here, as in the N. m. there are two forms, a shorter and a longer, the former being the older and original, as well as the more frequent one. The older form is made not by adding the normal ending -*i*, but by lengthening the final -*a* of the stem, e. g. *havyā́* 'oblations'[6]. The later form ends in -*āni* and is doubtless due to transitions from the stems in -*an*[7] which form the n. pl. N. A. with both -*ā* and -*āni*, e. g. *nā́mā* and *nā́māni*. The form in -*ā* is in the RV. made from 394 stems, that in -*āni* from 280, the proportion of the occurrences of the former being roughly three to every two of the latter. The proportion in the AV. is almost exactly reversed, the form in -*ā* being there made from 102 stems, that in -*āni* from 158[8]. The two forms are so common side by side that when two n. plurals occur in the same Pāda, the one generally ends in -*āni* and the other in -*ā*[9]; e. g. *yā́ te bhīmā́ni ā́yudhā* (IX. 61³⁰) 'thy terrible weapons'. This phenomenon

---

[1] With *y* inserted though -*a* is dropped.
[2] See BRUGMANN, Grundriss 2, p. 661, where several examples are given of endings being repeated in other languages.
[3] The form in -*āsas* seems to be an Indo-Iranian innovation, as there are no certain traces of it in other Indo-European languages; cp. BRUGMANN l. c.
[4] In the original Mantra portions of the TS. the pl. in -*ās* is very numerous, but I have noted only 11 forms in -*āsas*. In the Khilas, forms in -*ās* are three times (30) as numerous as in -*āsas* (10).
[5] There is no example of a V. in the RV., and only one, *cittā́ni* (III. 2⁴), in the AV. where the Mss. have *cittā́ni*.
[6] This form in -*ā* is commonly supposed to have started from a N. sing. f. in -*ā* as a collective; this would account for the agreement of the singular verb with this pl. in Greek; cp. also *sárvā tā́ ... astu* (RV. I. 162⁸); see BRUGMANN, Grundriss 2, p. 682.
[7] The G. *áhanām* is an example of the transference of another case from an -*an* stem.
[8] In the independent Mantra portions of the TS. the forms in -*ā* seem to outnumber those in -*āni* in about the same proportion as in the RV.: there are at least 20 forms of the former and 14 of the latter. In the Khilas the two forms are almost equally divided, as 10 examples of -*ā* and 12 of -*āni* occur.
[9] Similarly, the form in -*ā* appears beside n. pl. forms in -*īni*, -*ūni* or even -*āṃsi*, -*īṃṣi*, -*ūṃṣi*; e. g. *bhū́rīṇi bhadrā́* (I. 166¹⁰);

is clearly due to the influence of metre. The *-ā* here seems never to be shortened to *-ă*, as is so frequently the case in the N. A. n. pl. of *-an* stems[1]. Nor does it avoid hiatus (like the *-ā* of the N. A. du. m.), though coalescence with a following vowel sometimes takes place[2].

Examples of the commonest forms are: 1. *havyā́* (44), *bhúvanā* (36), *duritā́* (31) 'distresses', *sávanā* (30), *ukthā́* (25) 'praises'. — 2. *bhúvanāni* (57), *vṛtrā́ṇi* (36) 'foes', *vratā́ni* (34) 'laws', *havyā́ni* (25), *kṛtā́ni* (20) 'done'.

A. m. The ending of this case is not the normal *-as*, but *-n*, before which the final vowel of the stem is lengthened[3], e. g. *áśvā-n*. The form is frequent, being made from more than 250 stems in the RV. That the ending was originally *-ns* is shown by the treatment of *-ān* in Sandhi, where it becomes *-ām̐* before vowels and the sibilant itself occasionally survives before *c-* and *t-*[4].

I. m. n. In this case there are two forms, the one adding the normal ending *-bhis* (before which the final vowel of the stem becomes *-e*), while the other ends in *-ais* (which does not appear in any other declension). The form in *-ais* is only slightly commoner in the RV., being made from 221 stems, while that in *-bhis* is made from 211. In the AV., however, the former is 5 times as frequent as the latter[5]. The two forms[6] often appear in the same Pāda; e. g. *upamébhir arkáis* (I. 33[2]) 'with highest songs'. The choice is often due to the metre; e. g. *yātám áśvebhir aśvinā* (VIII. 5[7]) 'come with your steeds, O Aśvins', and *ādityáir yātam aśvinā* (VIII. 35[13]) 'with the Ādityas come, O Aśvins'.

In the RV. the m. forms are roughly twice as numerous as the n. Examples of the most frequent forms are: 1. *arkáis* (43); *ukthái̇s* (35), *yajñáis* (34), *deváis* (31), *áśvais* (30), *stómais* (25). — 2. *devébhis* (52), *stómebhis* (26), *vā́jebhis* (21).

D. m. n. This case is formed with the normal ending *-bhyas*, before which the final *-a* of the stem appears as *-e*. In the RV. it is made from over 40 stems in the m., but from only one in the n. In about half the forms occurring the ending has to be read as a dissyllable *-bhias*. The forms occurring are: *ajárebhyas* 'unaging', *ámavattarebhyas* 'mightier', *áraṇebhyas* (Kh. V. 1[2]) 'foreign', *arbhakébhyas* 'small', *ādityébhyas*, *āśinébhyas* 'aged', *āśv-àpastarebhyas* 'working more quickly', *ū́mebhyas* 'helpers', *gárbhebhyas* 'infants', *gṛhébhyas*, *jánebhyas*, *jīvébhyas* 'living', *jñātébhyas* (Kh. III. 16[1]) 'known', *tāvakébhyas* 'thy', *dáśa-kakṣyebhyas* 'having ten girths', *dáśa-yoktrebhyas* 'having ten traces', *dáśa-yojanebhyas* 'having ten teams', *devébhyas*, *pajrébhyas* 'strong', *párvatebhyas* 'mountains', *pasprdhānébhyas* 'striving', *pitu-kṛ́ttarebhyas* 'procuring more nourishment', *píśunebhyas* 'treacherous', *putrébhyas* 'sons', *púruṣebhyas* 'men', *pū́rvebhyas* 'former', *bādhitébhyas* 'oppressed', *bharatébhyas* 'descendants of Bharata', *mártye-*

sávanā purū́ṇi (III. 36[8]); *ūrdhvā́ śocíṃṣi prásthitā rájāṃsi* (III. 4[4]); *rabhasā́ vápūṃṣi* (III. 1[8]).

[1] There seems no sufficient reason to assume that in *viśvéd áha* (I. 92[3]) as compared with *áhā víśvā* (I 130[2]), *áha* is formed from the transition stem *áha-* rather than from *áhan-*; cp. LANMAN p. 348.

[2] On some probable mistakes made by the Pada in contracted forms see LANMAN 348.

[3] This lengthening is at least Indo-Iranian: BRUGMANN, Grundriss 2, p. 672[2].

[4] See above 77; and cp. LANMAN 346 on the Sandhi of *-ān* in general.

[5] In the independent Mantra portions of the TS. the proportion is about the same as in the AV. The following four forms with *-bhis* occur: *étaśebhis* (I. 2. 4[1]), *devébhis* (III. I. 4[3]), *rudrébhis* (II. I. 11[2]), *su-yámebhis* (IV. 7. 15[3]). In the Khilas 5 forms in *-ais* to 7 in *-ebhis* occur. The latter are: *amīva-cā́tanebhis* (I. 11[7]), *ārtavébhis* (III. 16[6]), *ukthébhis* (V. 6[3]), *ṛṣvébhis* (III. 1[7]), *kárvarebhis* (I. 5[1]), *ráthebhis* (I. 11[7]), *sāraghébhis* (I. 11[7]). In the later language the form in *-bhis* survives in the pronominal *ebhis* alone.

[6] On the origin of the two forms cp. BRUGMANN, Grundriss 2, p. 717.

bhyas, *mānavébhyas* 'men', *mánuṣebhyas* 'men', *mánebhyas* 'descendants of Māna', *yajatébhyas* 'adorable', *yajñíyebhyas*, *ráthebhyas* 'chariots', *vidúṣṭarebhyas* 'very wise', *víprebhyas* 'seers', *vy-àśvebhyas* 'horseless', *śaśamānébhyas* 'toiling', *suvidatríyebhyas* 'bountiful', *sóma-rabhastarebhyas* 'intoxicated with Soma', *somyébhyas* 'preparers of Soma', *stenébhyas* 'thieves'. — **n.** *bhúvanebhyas* 'beings'.

Ab. m. n. This case is formed like the D. with the normal ending *-bhyas* from nearly two dozen stems in the RV. about equally divided between the m. and n. In more than half of these forms the ending must be pronounced as a dissyllable. The forms occurring are: **m.** *ántebhyas* 'ends', *ásurebhyas* 'divine spirits', *ugrébhyas*, *gṛhébhyas*, *jánebhyas*, *jīvébhyas* 'living beings', *devébhyas*, *párvatebhyas*, *makhébhyas* 'vigorous', *víprebhyas*, *śūrebhyas*, *śyenébhyas* 'eagles'. — **n.** *anyá-kṛtebhyas* 'done by others', *āntrébhyas* entrails', *duritébhyas*, *nakhébhyas* 'nails', *padébhyas*, *párthivebhyas* 'terrestrial spaces', *bhúvanebhyas*, *mṛdhrébhyas* 'contempt', *vánebhyas* 'forest trees', *harmyébhyas* 'houses'.

G. m. n. Instead of the normal ending *-ām* these stems almost invariably add the ending *-nām*, before which the final vowel is lengthened as in the *-i*, *-u* and *-ṛ* stems. This ending (like *-āni* in the n. pl.) must have been due to the influence of the *-n* stems[1]. The case is thus formed in the RV. from over 100 stems in the m. and over 20 in the n. In nearly half these forms the final syllable may be metrically read as *aam*[2]. Two-thirds of these resolutions are, however, not necessary as they occur at the end of octosyllabic Pādas which may be catalectic; but many undoubted resolutions are required within the Pāda[3]. Among the forms of most frequent occurrence are **m.** *devánām* (148), *jánānām* (34), *yajñíyānām* (12), *ādityánām* (11), *adhvaráṇām* (10). — **n.** *dhánānām* (13).

a. The organic form e. g. from *devá-* would have been *devám* (= *devá-ām*). Not more than three or four examples of this survive in the RV., and only two of these seem undoubted: *yūthyàm áśvānām* (VIII. 56[4]) 'of horses belonging to the herd' and *caráthām* in *gárbhaś ca sthātáṃ gárbhaś caráthām* (I. 70[3]) 'offspring of things that are stationary, offspring of things that move'[4]. There are further some half dozen forms written with final *-ān* or *-āñ* which seem to stand for the G. pl. in *-ām*: *devāñ jánma* (I. 71[3]; VI. 11[3]) 'the race of the gods' (Pada *devān*); *devāñ jánmanā* (X. 64[14]) 'with the race of the gods' (Pada *devān*); *viśa á ca mártān* (IV. 2[3]) 'and hither to the dwellings of mortals' (= *mártām*); *coṣkūyáte viśa índro manuṣyān* (VI. 47[16]) 'Indra protects the tribes of men'.

L. m. n. This case adds the normal ending *-su* before which (as before *-bhis* and *-bhyas*) *-e* takes the place of the final vowel of the stem and cerebralizes the following sibilant. It is formed from some 123 stems in the m. and some 92 in the n.[5] It is almost invariably[6] to be read with hiatus, even before *u-*[7].

Among the most frequently occurring forms are: **m.** *devéṣu* (99), *vájeṣu* (41), *yajñéṣu* (35), *adhvaréṣu* (27), *mártyeṣu* (25), *sutéṣu* (16). — **n.** *vidátheṣu* (33), *váneṣu* (20), *sávaneṣu* (14), *bhúvaneṣu* (12), *ukthéṣu* (10).

---

1 See LANMAN 352 c; BRUGMANN, Grundriss 2, p. 691.

2 LANMAN (352, bottom) enumerates the forms in which resolution takes place.

3 LANMAN 352[4], gives a list of the forms in which resolution is required; cp. ARNOLD, Vedic Metre 143 (p. 92).

4 Perhaps also *hiṃsānām* (X. 142[1]) if G. pl. of a participle *hiṃsāna-*, and *śāsám* if G. of *śāsá-* 'ruler' (II. 23[12]). *vanám* (X. 46[5]) is G. pl. of *ván-* rather than *vána-*. Cp. LANMAN 353.

5 The gender is doubtful in some instances.

6 The only undoubted exception to this rule in the RV. occurs in a late hymn (X. 121[8]), where *devéṣv ádhi* must be read. Cp. LANMAN 354.

7 On the probable origin of the ending *-su* cp. BRUGMANN, Grundriss 2, p 700.

2 b. Derivative Stems in -*ā*.

LANMAN, Noun-Inflection 335—365. — WHITNEY, Sanskrit Grammar p. 131—137. — Cp. COLLITZ, die herkunft der *ā*-deklination, BB. 29, p. 81—114.

373. The derivative *ā*-declension corresponds to the derivative *a*-declension, for the m. adjectives of which it furnishes the f. stems. It includes more feminines than any other declension. Like the *a*-declension it has many irregularities of inflexion, every case in the singular, except the A., and two cases in the plural showing some abnormal feature. The N. sing. shares with the derivative *ī*-declension the peculiarity of not adding the ending *-s*; the I. sing. has an alternative form borrowed from the pronominal declension; the D. Ab. G. L. sing. are formed under the influence of the derivative *ī*-stems; and the V. sing. ends in *-e* instead of appearing in the form of the bare stem. In the plural the N. has to a limited extent the same alternative form in *-āsas* as the m. of the *a*-declension, and the G. is similarly formed with *-nām*.

As in the *a*-declension, the accent remains in the same position throughout except the V., where it of course shifts to the first syllable.

Inflexion.

374. The forms actually occurring, if made from *priyá-* 'dear', would be as follows:

Sing. N. *priyā́*. A. *priyā́m*. I. *priyā́* and *priyáyā*. D. *priyā́yai*. Ab. G. *priyā́yās*. L. *priyā́yām*. V. *príye*.

Du. N. A. *priyé*. I. Ab. *priyā́bhyām*. G. L. *priyáyos*.

Pl. N. *priyā́s* and *priyā́sas*. V. *príyās*. A. *priyā́s*. I. *priyā́bhis*. D. Ab. *priyā́bhyas*. G. *priyā́ṇām*. L. *priyā́su*.

Sing. N. This case never adds the normal ending *-s*[1]. It is formed in the RV. from 424 stems and occurs more than 1000 times. Examples of the most frequent forms are: *yóṣā* (24) 'maiden', *dákṣiṇā* (24) 'good milch cow', *íḷā* (17) 'refreshment', *jāyā́* (17) 'wife', *su-bhágā* (13) 'beautiful', *sūnṛ́tā* (10) 'joyful', *citrā́* (9) 'brilliant'.

a. At the end of odd Pādas the final *-ā* of this N. is regularly written with Sandhi, but must always be read with hiatus; coalescence with *e-* and *ṛ-* is, however, twice avoided by nasalization[2], while twice[3] the *-ā* is shortened before *ṛ-*.

b. Within a Pāda the *-ā* is written with Sandhi in 160 instances in the RV., but is pronounced (unlike the *-ā* of the N. A. du. m.) with hiatus in 23 of these instances; while the nominatives *īṣā́* 'car-pole' and *manīṣā́* 'devotion' are written as well as pronounced with hiatus[4], the former once, the latter four times.

A. This case, which is formed with the normal ending *-m*, is in the RV. made from over 200 nominal stems occurring more than 400 times. Examples of the most frequent forms are: *manīṣā́m* (21), *jāyā́m* (11), *ámīvām* (9) 'distress', *yóṣām* (7), *yóṣaṇām* (6) 'maiden'.

a. This case is often identical in form with the L. sing. f. of stems in *-ī*; thus *pūrvyā́m* may be the A. of *pūrvyā́-* 'previous' or L. of *pūrvī́-* 'much'. In one instance at least elision of the *-m*, followed by contraction, takes place[5]: *śatatamā́viveṣīḥ* (VII. 19[5]) for

[1] The stem *gnā́-* 'woman', though originally dissyllabic, came to be regarded as a radical *ā*-stem and accordingly forms its N. sing. *gnā́-s* (IV. 9[4]).

[2] *śā́śadānā́m̐ véṣi* (I. 123[10]) and *yā́m̐ ṛṇaṃcayé* (V. 30[14]).

[3] *priyá ṛ-* (I. 151[4]), *ṛju-hásta ṛ-* (V. 41[15]). Cp. 70.

[4] *īṣā́ dákṣo* (VIII. 5[29]); *manīṣā́ abhí* (I. 101[7]); *manīṣā́ iyám* (V. 11[5]; VII. 70[7]); *manīṣā́ asmát* (VII. 34[1]); cp. RPr. II. 29. LANMAN 356 suggests that the comparative frequency of this hiatus justifies the restoration of the augment in Pādas short of a syllable; e. g. *prá sā́ [a]vāci* (VII. 58[6]).

[5] On some contractions in which *-m* has probably been elided but explained wrongly by the Pada as containing nominatives in *-ā*, see LANMAN 356.

śatatamám aviveṣīḥ. In two or three instances the metre seems to require *-ām* to be read as *-aam*[1].

I. There are **two forms** of this case. In the one, the normal ending *-ā* is added directly to the stem and, by contracting with its final *-ā*, produces a form identical in appearance with the N., e. g. *jihvā́* (= *jihvā́-ā*) 'tongue'. In the other, *y* is interposed between the ending *-ā* and the final *-ā* of the stem, which is shortened, e. g. *jihvá-y-ā*. The latter form is due to the influence of the regular pronominal I. sing. f., e. g. *táyā*[2]. This form is already slightly the more common in the RV.[3], being made from 113 stems[4] as compared with 95 which take the older form with *-ā*. In the later Saṃhitās the I. in *-ā* is very rare in original passages, the AV. using only five such forms independently[5]. Both forms are (unlike the N. pl. m. in *-āsas* and *-ās*) comparatively seldom made from the same stem, as *jihvā́* and *jihváyā*. Two thirds of the total number of 95 stems which have the older form, end in the suffixes *-tā* and *-yā*, as *puruṣá-tā* 'after the manner of men', *hiraṇyáyā́* 'golden'. The choice of the alternative forms is, as elsewhere, often determined by the metre[6].

Examples of the commonest forms are: 1. *doṣā́* (13) 'evening', *barhánā* (13) 'might', *manīṣā́* (13), *maṃhánā* (11) 'willingness', *śravasyā́* (7) 'desire to praise'[7]. — Also *āśīr-dā́yā* (TS. III. 2. 8[4]) 'fulfilment of blessing', *viśvá-psnyā* (TS. I. 5. 3[3]; VS. XII. 10) 'omniform'. — 2. *dhā́rayā* (53) 'stream', *jihváyā* (24), *māyáyā* (20) 'craft'.

a. There are some instrumentals sing. f. formed from derivative *a-* stems, which are used as adverbs with shift of accent to the ending. Such are: *a-datrayā́* 'without a gift' (*a-datra-*), *ubhayā́* 'in both ways' (*ubháya-*), *ṛtayā́* 'in the right way' (*ṛtá-*), *dakṣiṇā́* 'on the right' (*dákṣiṇa-*), *naktayā́* 'by night' (*nákta-*), *madhyā́* 'in the middle' (*mádhya-*), *samanā́* 'together' (*sámana-*), *svapnayā́* (AV.) 'in dream' (*svápna-*)[8].

D. This case is anomalously formed by adding *-yai* to the stem, e. g. *jarā́-yai*[9]. It is not of common occurrence, being made from only 14 nominal[10] stems in the RV. The forms occurring are: *a-gótāyai* 'lack of cows', *a-vīratāyai* 'lack of sons', *ukhā́yai* (TS. IV. 1. 9[3]) 'pot', *uttānā́yai* (TS. IV. 1. 4[1]; Kh. V. 16[4]) 'supine', *ghóṣāyai* N. of a woman, *carā́yai* 'for going', *jarā́yai* (AV.) 'old age', *tvá-yatāyai* 'presented by thee', *ducchúnāyai* 'mischievous demon', *putrá-kāmāyai* (Kh. IV. 13[1]) 'desiring sons', *pūtá-kratāyai* N. of a woman, *manā́yai* 'eagerness', *viśpálāyai* N. of a woman, *śivā́yai* 'auspicious', *śvetanā́yai* 'dawn', *sūnṛ́tāyai* 'joy', *sūryā́yai* 'sun-goddess'.

a. Two forms have been preserved in which the D. is made by adding the normal ending *-e* directly to the stem with the *-ā* of which it coalesces to *-ai*: *mahīyái* (I. 113[6]) 'greatness', *sv-apatyái*[11] (I. 54[11]) 'accompanied with fair offspring'. These are formed like the D. infinitives from radical *ā*-stems such as *vi-khyái* (584).

b. In one passage (VII. 1[19]) the form *a-vīrate*, for *a-vīratāyai* 'lack of sons',

---

1 See LANMAN 357 (top).

2 Cp. BRUGMANN, Grundriss 2, p. 629, 783.

3 The corresponding later form in the Avesta is much commoner than the older: BRUGMANN 2, p. 629.

4 This number given by LANMAN 357 includes some pronominal stems. BRUGMANN'S statement (2, p. 629) that the form in *-ayā* is less common than the form in *-ā* in Vedic, is not applicable even to the RV.

5 The forms are *dakṣiṇā́*, *devátā*, *doṣā́*, *sumnayā́*, *vitta-kāmyā́*; only the last is peculiar to the AV.

6 Euphony also has some influence; thus *hiraṇyayayā́* does not occur.

7 LANMAN 358 enumerates the homophonous instrumentals.

8 These forms may have been due to the influence of the pronominal adverb *a-y-ā́* 'in this way' (with adverbial shift of accent, cp. *táyā* etc.); see J. SCHMIDT, Pluralbildung 212 ff., and BRUGMANN, Grundriss 2, p. 629; otherwise BARTHOLOMAE, BB. 15, 20 f.

9 Formed in the Indo-Iranian period, probably under the influence of the derivative stems in *-ī* originally *-yā*, i. e. *-yái* for *-yā-e*.

10 Also *svā́yai* from the possessive pronoun *svá-*.

11 BRUGMANN, Grundriss 2, p. 600, thinks this form may be shortened for *sv-apatyā́yai*.

takes the ending *-e* direct, but with elision of the stem vowel, as in the radical *ā*-declension[1].

Ab. This case is formed anomalously by adding the ending *-yās* to the stem[2]. It is rare, being made in the RV. from only seven stems, the AV. having three additional examples. The forms occurring are: *ūrdhvā́yās* (AV.) 'upright', *kanā́yās* 'maiden', *jihvā́yās*, *dákṣiṇāyās*, *dur-évāyās* 'ill-disposed', *dur-háṇāyās* 'mischief'. *dáivyāyās* 'divine', *dhruvā́yās* (AV.) 'firm', *nílāyās* 'disgrace', *vy-adhvā́yās* (AV.)[3] 'lying half-way'.

G. This case is formed in the same way as the Ab., but is much more frequent, being made from 26 stems in the RV. The forms occurring are: *ághnyāyās* and *aghnyā́yās* 'cow (not to be killed)', *íḷāyās*, *ukhā́yās*, *usríyāyās* 'ruddy cow', *ū́rmyāyās* 'night', *kanā́yās*, *kā́ṣṭhāyās* 'course', *jihvā́yās*, *dákṣiṇāyās*, *darśatā́yās* 'conspicuous', *dū́rvāyās* 'Dūrvā grass', *dhiṣáṇāyās* 'offering', *dhíṣamāṇāyās*[4] 'longing', *pájrāyās* 'vigorous', *pári-takmyāyās* 'wandering', *máhināyās* 'mighty', *rasā́yās* a mythical river, *vayā́yās* 'branch', *viśpálāyās*, *śaśvattamā́yās* 'most recent', *śíphāyās* N. of a river, *śucā́yās* 'pure', *sabar-dúghāyās* 'yielding nectar', *sehānā́yās*[5] 'victorious', *súrāyās* 'intoxicating liquor', *sūryā́yās*.

L. This case is formed by adding the anomalous ending *-yām* to the stem, e. g. *bhadrā́-yām*. It is not common, being formed from only 16 or 17 stems in the RV. The forms occurring are: *āpayā́yām*[6] N. of a river, *āmā́yām* 'raw', *uttānā́yām* 'outstretched', *usríyāyām*, *(á)-gatāyām* 'come', *grīvā́yām* 'neck', *jūrṇā́yām* 'ancient', *návāyām* 'new', *pári-takmyāyām*, *bhadrā́yām* 'beneficent', *yamúnāyām* N. of a river, *varatrā́yām* 'thong', *váśāyām* (Kh. II. 10[5]) 'cow', *śiṃśápāyām* N. of a tree, *śíriṇāyām* 'night', *sabhā́yām* (TS. I. 8. 3[1]) 'assembly', *súrāyām*, *su-ṣómāyām*[7] N. of a river, *hariyūpī́yāyām* N. of a locality.

V. This case has the abnormal ending *-e*[8] and is in the RV. formed from over 50 stems; e. g. *áśve*. The original form must have been the bare stem with the final vowel shortened; e. g. **áśva*, but of this there is no certain survival. The form *amba* which occurs in the RV. three times (unaccented) may originally have been an exclamation, and it can have this sense alone in one of the three passages of the RV. (x. 97[2]), where it is used with a plural. In the two other passages it may very well mean 'O mother' (II. 41[16]; x. 86[7]). The VS. (XXIII. 18) and the TS. (VII. 4. 19[1]) have the V. *ámbe* as from a stem *ámbā* 'mother'[9].

The forms occurring are: *ághnyāsye*[10] (Kh. IV. 5[26. 32]) 'cow-faced', *aghnye*, *apve* N. of a disease, *amartye* 'immortal', *ámbike* (TS. VS.) 'mother', *ambitame* 'most motherly', *áśve* 'mare', *áśva-sūnṛte* 'rich in horses', *áditya-varṇe*[11] (Kh. II. 6[6]) 'sun-coloured', *ārjīkīye* N. of a river, *íḷe* goddess of devotion, *íṣṭake* (TS. IV. 2. 9[2]) 'brick', *ugra-putre* 'having mighty sons', *uttare* 'mightier', *uttāna-parṇe* 'having extended leaves', *uru-vraje* 'extending afar', *ūrmye*, *ṛṣve* 'exalted', *kadha-priye* 'ever pleased', *kā́ṇe* 'one-eyed', *kāma-dughé* (TS. IV. 2. 9[6]) 'cow of plenty', *kṛtye* (Kh. IV. 5[25]) 'magic', *ghóra-rūpe* (Kh. IV. 5[26]) 'of awful form', *gaṅge* 'Ganges', *ghore* 'awful', *citre*, *citrā-maghe* 'having brilliant gifts', *jāye*, *dūrve* (TS. IV. 2. 9[2]), *deva-jūte* 'impelled by the gods'

1 This forms a transition to the consonant declension like *devátāte* beside *devátātaye*; cp. LANMAN 359[2].

2 Like the D. it is due to the influence of the stems in derivative *-ī*, to the fuller form of which, *-yā-*, the normal ending *-as* was added.

3 Also the pronominal *svā́yās* 'own'.

4 Participle, perhaps desiderative, of *dhī-* 'think'.

5 Perfect participle middle of *sah-* 'conquer'.

6 A transition form from the radical *ā*-declension, see p. 249, note 11.

7 Also the pronominal form *svā́yām*.

8 The origin of this ending is uncertain; cp. BRUGMANN 2, 541.

9 This is a common stem in post-Vedic Sanskrit.

10 The ed. has *aghnyā́sye*.

11 The ed. has *ādityá-varṇe*.

devi-tame[1] 'most divine', *dhiṣaṇe* 'goddess of devotion', *nadī-tame* 'best of rivers', *pathye* 'path' (as goddess), *pastye* 'goddess of the house', *putra-kāme*, *puru-priye* 'much beloved', *pṛthu-jāghane* 'broad-hipped', *pṛthu-ṣṭuke* 'having broad braids of hair', *priye* (TS. VII. 1. 6[8]), *brahma-saṃśite* 'sharpened by prayer', *marud-vṛdhe* N. of a river, *yamune*, *rāke* N. of a goddess, *vapuṣṭame* (Kh. IV. 7[7]) 'most beautiful', *vára-rūpe* (Kh. IV. 5[26]) 'of excellent form', *vi-kaṭe* 'monstrous', *vivasvad-vāte* (TS. IV. 4. 12[4]) 'desired by Vivasvat', *viśva-rūpe* (TS. IV. 2. 5[2]) 'omniform', *viśva-vāre* 'possessed of all goods', *śaravye* 'arrow', *śītike* 'cool', *śúṅge* (Kh. V. 15[8]) N. of a goddess, *śubhre* 'shining', *sa-dānve* 'associated with demons', *sarame* N. of a goddess, *sīte* 'furrow', *su-jāte* 'well-born', *su-putre* 'having good sons', *su-bhage*, *su-lābhike* 'easy to win', *su-snuṣe* 'having fair daughters-in-law', *sū-nṛte*, *sūrya-varṇe* (Kh. IV. 7[7]) 'sun-coloured', *sūrye*, *stóma-trayastriṃśe* (TS. IV. 4. 12[4]), *háriklike* (Kh. V. 15[1]) 'yellowish', *hiraṇya-parṇe* (Kh. IV. 7[7]) 'gold-winged', *hlādike* 'refreshing'.

Du. N. A. V. These cases are identical in form, having final *-e* which doubtless contains the same dual ending *-ī* as N. A. V. du. of the *a-* declension[2]. They are of frequent occurrence, being made from over 130 stems in the RV. The ending *-e* is Pragṛhya, being distinguished by the Pada text with an appended *iti* from the *e* of the V. sing. f.; e. g. V. du. f. *śubhre iti*, but V. sing. f. *śubhre*.

Examples of the most frequent forms are: *ubhé* (66) 'both', *su-méke*[3] (8) 'well-established', *devá-putre* (7) 'having gods as sons', *vi-rūpe* (7) 'of different forms', *śípre* (5) 'cheeks'. The compound *sítāsite* 'black and white' occurs in a Khila (p. 171[5]).

I. Ab. These cases, made with the ending *-bhyām*, are identical in form with the I. D. Ab. m. n. of the *a-* declension. They are represented by only two forms in the RV.: *śíprābhyām* (X. 105[5]) which seems to be I.[4], and *nā́sikābhyām* (X. 163[1]) 'nostrils', Ab. No form with a D. sense occurs.

G. L. Both these cases add, with interposing *-y-*, the normal ending *-os* to the final *-ā* of the stem, which is shortened. They are thus identical in form with the G. L. du. m. n. of the *a-* declension. There are only four nominal forms in the RV. and AV.: in the G. sense *jáṅghayos* (AV.) 'legs', *yamáyos* 'twins'; and in the L. sense *uttānáyos*, *svadháyos* 'homestead'[5].

Pl. N. V. The regular form ends in *-ās* and is very common, being formed from nearly 260 stems in the RV. Examples of the commonest forms are: *bhadrā́s* (19), *dhā́rās* (16), *manīṣā́s* (10)[6].

There is, however, a **second form in *-āsas*** which occurs nearly 20 times in the RV. Considering the rarity of this form here, while it is the commoner as N. pl. m. in the *a-* declension, the probability is that its introduction was due to those very numerous masculines. The forms occurring are: *á-tandrāsas* 'indefatigable', *a-mṛ́tāsas* (AV.) 'immortal', *dur-mitrā́sas* 'unfriendly', *paspṛdhānā́sas* 'vying'[7], *pā́rthivāsas*[8] 'terrestrial', *pāvakā́sas* 'pure', *bhejānā́sas*[9] 'having obtained', *vanvānā́sas*[10] (SV.) 'having obtained', *vaśā́sas*,

1 Superlative of *devī-*, the final being shortened as in the simple vocative *devi*.

2 Cp. BRUGMANN, Grundriss 2, 286 (p. 643).

3 Cp. WINDISCH in Festgruss an O. v. BÖHTLINGK 114 f.

4 The pronominal form *tā́bhyām* (X. 88[15]) has a locative meaning.

5 There are also the pronominal forms *ayós* and *yáyos*. In III. 54[2] the Pada text reads *āyós* probably for *ayós*.

6 In two or three passages the Pada text seems to confuse forms in *-ās* with others in *-ā*; see LANMAN 362.

7 Perfect participle middle of √*spṛdh-*.

8 Cp. LANMAN 362.

9 Perfect participle middle of *bhaj-* 'share'.

10 The variant of the SV. for *bhejānā́sas* of the RV.

vāśrā́sas 'roaring', *vidānā́sas*[1] 'being found', *vṛdhā́sas* 'helping', *ā-śuṣāṇā́sas*[2] 'stimulating', *śū́ghanā́sas*[3] 'swift', *sámmitāsas* (AV.) 'corresponding', *smáyamānāsas* 'smiling', *hávamānāsas* 'calling'[4].

A. This case is formed with the normal ending *-as* which coalesces with the final of the stem to *-ās*, e. g. *sūnṛ́tās*. It is very frequent, being made from more than 160 stems in the RV. Examples of the commonest forms are: *māyā́s* (22), *pṛ́tanās* (13) 'battles', *usrā́s* (12) 'dawns', *dhā́rās* (11), *usríyās* (10)[5]. Two instances occur of forms in *-āsas* being wrongly used as A. pl. f.: *saṃvidānā́sas* (x. 30[14]) 'united' and *araṃ-gamā́sas* (AV. xiii. 2[33]) 'ready to help'.

I. This case is always formed by adding the ending *-bhis* directly to the stem, e. g. *sūnṛ́tā-bhis*. It is made from over 80 stems in the RV. Examples of the most frequent forms are: *māyā́bhis* (13), *citrā́bhis* (8), *dhā́rābhis* (7), *hótrābhis* (7) 'libations', *íḷābhis* (6). The form *drā́ghiṣṭhābhis* (iii. 62[17]) 'for longest times'[6] is used adverbially.

D. Ab. These cases are formed with the same ending *-bhyas* (sometimes to be read as two syllables) added directly to the stem. In the RV. only 4 datives and 11 ablatives occur from nominal stems[7]. The forms occurring are: **D.** *aghnyā́bhyas, usríyābhyas, ducchúnābhyas, devátābhyas* (TS. iv. 2. 9[6]) 'deities', *vṛtā́bhyas* 'movements'. — **Ab.** *ádharābhyas* 'lower', *ā́śābhyas* 'regions', *úttarābhyas, uṣṇíhābhyas* 'nape of the neck', *kī́kasābhyas* 'cartilages of the breast-bone', *gúdābhyas* 'intestines', *grīvā́bhyas, daṃsánābhyas* 'wondrous powers', *dhiṣáṇābhyas* 'Soma bowls', *vakṣáṇābhyas* 'bellies', *śyāvyā̀bhyas* 'darkness'.

G. This case being made with the abnormal ending *-nām* is identical in form with the G. pl. m. of the *a*-declension. It is formed in the RV. from 22 stems. There is no certain example here of forms with the normal ending *-ām* which is found in a few genitives of the *a*- declension (372). There are only a couple of instances in which the resolution of the final syllable as *-aam* seems required by the metre[8]. The G. of *kanyā̀-* 'girl' always appears in the contracted form of *kanī́nām*[9] (occurring five times) in the RV.[10]

The forms actually occurring are: *ákṣarāṇām* 'speech', *ághnyānām, a-niveśanā́nām* 'affording no place of rest', *á-bhayānām* 'free from danger', *áśma-vrajānām* 'whose pen is a rock', *ā́śānām* (TS. iv. 4. 12[3]), *urvárāṇām* 'arable fields', *usrā́ṇām, usríyāṇām, kā́ṣṭhānām, kṛtyā́nām* (Kh. iv. 5[30]), *jihmā́nām* 'transverse', *divyā́nām* 'heavenly', *dúghānām* 'milch kine', *devátānām* (Kh. ii. 4[1]), *deva-senā́nām* 'hosts of the gods', *dhiṣáṇānām, nā́vānām, navyā̀nām* 'navigable rivers', *pastyā̀nām* 'abodes', *manīṣā́ṇām, rā́myāṇām* 'nights', *sámānām* 'years', *sūnṛ́tānām* 'songs of joy', *stíyānām* 'still waters'.

L. This case is formed by adding the ending *-su* directly to the stem. The final *-u* though always combined with a following vowel both at the end of an internal Pāda or within a Pāda, is invariably to be read with hiatus

---

1 Participle middle, with passive sense, of *vid-* 'find'.

2 Participle middle of √*śvas-*.

3 This word (AV.) is of uncertain derivation.

4 There are besides two or three doubtful instances which may be m.; see Lanman 362.

5 In several instances *-ās* is most probably to be read where the Pada text has *-ā*, see Lanman 363. In a few forms the resolution of *-ās* as *-aas* or *-aās* seems necessary; Lanman l. c.

6 Cp. *aparī́bhyas* 'for future times'.

7 There are also the pronominal forms *ābhyás* and *ābhyas, tā́bhyas, yā́bhyas*.

8 *dhānā́nām* in viii. 59[12] and *pṛ́tanānām* in viii. 59[1]. In *sūnṛ́tānām* (i. 3[11]) the metre seems to require the shortening of the final of the stem: *sūnṛ́tānām*; Lanman 364.

9 This is a form of some importance as showing how the suffix *-ī* arose from *-yā-*.

10 It also occurs once in Kh. i. 5[7].

in the RV.; e. g. *svásu urvárāsu* (x. 50³) for *svásūrvárāsu*¹. This case is formed from over 50 nominal stems in the RV. The forms occurring are: *aghásu* 'evil', *amṛ́tāsu*, *ávarāsu* 'later', *āmásu*, *ártanāsu* 'uncultivated', *íḷāsu*, *úparāsu* 'neighbouring', *urvárāsu*, *usríyāsu*, *ū́rmyāsu*, *kanyàsu*, *kāṣṭhāsu*, *kṛṣṇā́su* 'black', *grīvā́su* (TS. IV. 2. 5³), *cittá-garbhāsu* 'visibly pregnant', *citrā́su*, *jagmānā́su*² 'having gone', *jātā́su* 'born', *tū́gryāsu* 'descended from Tugra', *dúryāsu* 'abodes', *devátāsu* (TS. I. 6. 4³), *dhíṣṇyāsu* 'fireplaces', *dhruvā́su* 'unchangeable', *návāsu*, *pathyā̀su*, *pádyāsu* 'footsteps', *pastyā̀su*, *páñca-janyāsu* 'relating to the five tribes', *puru-péśasu* 'multiform', *pū́rvāsu* 'earlier', *pṛ́tanāsu*, *pradhanyā̀su* 'forming the spoil', *priyā́su*, *mádyāsu* 'fond of exhilaration', *madhyamā́su* 'middlemost', *manuṣyā̀su* 'human', *mandrā́su* (TS. IV. 1. 8²), *mártyāsu* 'mortal', *mahinā́su* 'mighty', *yajñíyāsu* 'devout', (*prá-*)*yatāsu* 'presented', *yóṣaṇāsu*, *rámyāsu*, *ropaṇákāsu* a kind of bird, *vakṣáṇāsu* 'bellies', *vṛddhā́su* 'great', *vṛdhasānā́su*³ 'growing', *śayā́su* 'resting-places', *śúṣkāsu* 'dry', *śyāvā́su* 'nights', *śrutā́su* 'famous', *sánayāsu* 'old', *saptá-śivāsu* 'blessing the seven (worlds)', *sirā́su* 'streams', *su-vṛjánāsu* 'dwelling in fair regions', *hávyāsu* 'to be invoked'.

3. a. Stems in radical -*ī*.

LANMAN, Noun-Inflection 365—400. — WHITNEY, Sanskrit Grammar 348—359.

375. This declension consists primarily of fewer than 50 m. and f. nouns derived from 9 roots. Only four of these words appear as monosyllables, the rest being compounds. The analogy of this primary group (A) is closely followed both in inflexion and accentuation by a second group of about 80 polysyllabic stems which, though formed with derivative -*ī*, are for the sake of clearness best treated as a division (B) of this declension. The normal endings as they appear in the inflexion of consonant stems are taken throughout this declension. The G. pl., however, with the exception of a single form occurring only once (*dhiyā́m*), takes the ending -*nām*; and the N. sing. always adds -*s*. Accentuation on the final syllable of the stem is characteristic of this declension; and except in monosyllabic stems the acute remains on that syllable throughout⁴. Before vowel endings the -*ī* is split to -*iy* in the monosyllabic nouns; e. g. *dhíy-am*; this is also the case in compounds formed with these nouns, except -*dhī́* when it is accented, e. g. *jana-śríyam*, *nā́nā-dhiyas*, but *ā-dhíam*; in compounds formed with roots it is split only when two consonants precede; e. g. *yajña-príyam*, but *yajña-níam*; in the secondary group it is split in *samudrī́-* and partly in *cakrī́-*, e. g. *samudríyas* and *cakríyau*, but *cakrías*. Otherwise the *ī* is always written as *y*, but is in the RV. invariably⁵ to be pronounced as a vowel; e. g. *nadyàm* pronounced *nadíam*⁶.

A. The stems belonging to the primary group are: 1. the monosyllabic feminines *dhī́-* 'thought', *bhī́-* 'fear', *śrī́-* 'glory'; and the m. *vī́-* 'receiver' (which occurs only once in the N. sing.). — 2. Compounds (mostly Bahuvrīhis) formed with the first three: *ā-dhī́-* f. 'care', *itthā́-dhī́-* 'right devout', *dīrghādhī́-*

---

¹ Cp. the L. pl. of the *a*-declension.
² Perfect participle middle of *gam-* 'go'.
³ Participle middle from *vṛdh-* 'grow'.
⁴ There are one or two exceptions to this rule in compound words in the A group, and a few others, in the AV., in the B group.
⁵ There are only two exceptions in the RV.: A. sing. *staryàm* (VII. 68⁸) in a late verse (cp. LANMAN 379¹) and N. pl. *nadyàs* (VII. 50⁴). The AV. has six such forms: *aśvataryàs, nadyàs, naptyàs, nādyàs, pippalyàs, vṛkṣa-sarpyàs*.
⁶ The resolved forms are therefore always given below, spelt with *i* in this declension. This will not lead to any confusion with the written forms of the Saṃhitā text in which the *ī* of the stem always appears as *iy* or *y*.

'having a far-reaching mind' (*ā-dhī́-*), *dur-ā-dhī́-* 'malevolent', *dūrá-ādhī-*[1] 'longing for the distance', *sv-ādhí-* 'attentive', *dū-ḍhī́-*[2] 'malevolent', *nānā-dhī́-* 'of various intent', *viśváto-dhī-* 'all-attending', *su-dhī́-* 'devout'; *avadya-bhī́-* f. 'fear of blame'; *agni-śrī́-* 'fire-bright', *adhvara-śrī́-* 'adorning the sacrifice', *kṣatra-śrī́-* 'blessing dominion', *ghṛta-śrī́-* 'glittering with ghee', *jana-śrī́-* 'blessing men', *darśata-śrī́-* 'of beauteous splendour', *márya-śrī́-* 'adorned like a wooer', *yajña-śrī́-* 'beautifying the sacrifice', *su-śrī́-* 'glorious', *hari-śrī́-* 'of golden glory'. — 3. Compounds[3] formed with the roots *krī-* 'buy', *nī-* 'lead', *prī-* 'love', *mī-* 'diminish', *vī-* 'move' and 'cover', *śī-* 'lie', *śrī-* 'mix': *pra-krī́-* (AV.) 'purchasable', *sadyaḥ-krī́-* (AV.) 'bought on the same day'; *agre-ṇī́-* (VS.) 'leading', *ṛta-nī́-* 'leading the rite', *grāma-ṇī́-* 'leading the community', *pada-nī́-* (AV.) 'following the steps of another', *pra-ṇī́-* f. 'furtherance', *pra-ṇenī́-*[4] 'powerfully furthering', *mana-nī́-* 'spirit-leading', *yajña-nī́-* 'leading the sacrifice', *vaśa-nī́-* m. 'commander', *vrata-nī́-* 'carrying out the ordinance', *sadha-nī́-* 'accompanying', *sen ī-nī́-* m. 'leader of an army', *skambha-nī́-* (VS.) 'furnishing a prop'; *abhi-prī́-* 'gladdening', *kadha-prī́-* 'gladdening whom?', *pari-prī́-* 'dear', *brahma-prī́-* 'prayer-loving', *yajña-prī́-* 'sacrifice-loving'; *manyu-mī́-* 'rage-obstructing', *vāta-pra-mī́-* 'surpassing the wind'; *takva-vī́-* m. '(swiftly darting) bird', *deva-vī́-* and *devá-vī́-* 'god-refreshing', *pada-vī́-* m. 'leader', *parṇa-vī́-* 'moving with wings', *pratī-vī́-*[5] 'gladly accepting', *hiraṇya-vī́-* 'gold-bringing'; *pra-vī́-* (VS.) 'wound round'; *jihma-śī́-* 'lying prostrate', *patsu-taś-śī́-*[6] 'lying at the feet', *madhyama-śī́-* 'lying in the midst', *syona-śī́-* 'lying on a soft couch'; *abhi-śrī́-*[7] 'admixture', *gaṇa-śrī́-*[7] 'mixing in troops'.

B. This secondary group comprises upwards of 80 polysyllabic stems, accented on the final vowel, which are all substantives except about half a dozen. It includes fewer than a dozen masculines. Of the remainder, which are feminine, more than half are names of female beings; about 30 are the f. form of m. stems that are not accented on the final vowel, as *puruṣī́-* 'woman' beside *púruṣa-* 'man'. There are also some f. adjectives corresponding to m. in *-ya*, as *svarī́-* beside *svaryà-* 'resounding'. This derivative group closely follows the analogy of the third division of the radical group (compounds ending in roots with final accented *-ī*); it joined the radical declension doubtless owing to the accentuation of the final vowel.

The m. stems are: *ahī́-* 'serpent', *upāvī́-* (VS.)[8] 'encouraging', *dakṣī́-*[9] 'flaming'; *prāvī́-*[8] 'attentive', *dus-prāvī́-* 'unfriendly', *su-prāvī́-* 'very attentive'; *yayī́-*[10] 'going'; *rathī́-* 'charioteer', *á-rathī-* 'not a charioteer'; *sahásra-starī-* 'having a thousand barren cows', *híraṇya-vāśī́-* 'wielding a golden axe'.

The f. stems are: *atharī́-* 'flame', *atharvī́-* 'priestess' (m. *átharvan-*), *á-durmaṅgalī-* 'not unlucky', *aparī́-* pl. 'future days' (m. *ápara-*), *apasī́-* (VS.) 'industrious' (m. *apásya-*), *ambī́-* 'mother', *arāyī́-* 'demoness' (m. *árāya-*), *aruṇī́-* 'dawn', *aśvatarī́-* (AV.) 'she-mule', *aṣṭa-karṇī́-* 'cow with notched ear', *ā-pathī́-* 'impediment', *enī́-* 'doe' (m. *éta-*), *oṇī́-* 'breast', *kalyāṇī́-* 'fair woman' (m. *kalyā́ṇa-*), *kavaṣī́-* 'creaking' (m. *kaváṣa-*), *kilāsī́-* 'spotted deer' (m. *kilā́sa-*), *kumārī́-* (AV.) 'girl', *kūdī́-* (AV.) 'fetter', *kṛṣṇī́-* 'night', *kṣoṇī́-* 'flood', *khārī́-* 'measure', *gandharvī́-* 'female Gandharva', *gaurī́-* 'buffalo cow', *cakrī́-* 'wheel', *tandrī́-*

---

[1] For *dūrá-ādhī-*.
[2] From *dus-dhī́-*.
[3] Mostly Tatpuruṣas, generally with accusative sense; some Karmadhārayas.
[4] An intensive formation from *nī-* 'lead'.
[5] 'Coming towards', *práti*, with lengthened final vowel.
[6] From *patsu-tás*, an adverb anomalously formed by adding the suffix *-tas* to the L. pl. of *pád-* 'foot'.
[7] Formed directly from the root *śrī-* = 'mix', and not from the substantive *śrī́-*.
[8] From *upa* and *pra+av-* 'favour'.
[9] To be assumed as the stem of the V. *dakṣi*, Pada text *dhakṣi*.
[10] The final vowel is here perhaps radical in origin.

(AV.) 'weariness' (m. *tándra-*), *tapanī́-* 'heat' (m. *tápana-*), *tila-piñjī́-*[1] (AV.) N. of a plant (m. *tila-piñja-*), *tīkṣṇa-śṛṅgī́-* (AV.) 'sharp-horned' (m. *tīkṣṇá-śṛṅga-*), *dūtī́-* 'messenger', *dehī́-* 'dam', *nadī́-* 'stream', *naptī́-* 'daughter' (m. *nápt̥r-*), *nāḍī́-* 'pipe', *nāndī́-* 'joy', *niṣṭigrī́-* N. of Indra's mother, *palālī́-*[1] (AV.) 'stalk', *pippalī́-* (AV.), 'berry' (m. *píppala-*), *puruṣī́-* 'woman' (m. *púruṣa-*), *prapharvī́-* 'voluptuous girl', *maṇḍūkī́-* 'female frog' (m. *maṇḍū́ka-*), *mayūrī́-* 'peahen' (m. *mayū́ra-*), *mahi-nadī́-* 'great stream', *mahiṣī́-* (TS.) 'buffalo cow', *meṣī́-* 'ewe', *yamī́-* 'Yamī', *yayī́-*[2] 'quick', *yātudhānī́-* 'sorceress' (m. *yātudhā́na-*), *rathī́-* 'female charioteer' (m. *rátha-* 'car'), *lakṣmī́-* 'mark', *lalāmī́-* 'speckled mare' (m. *lalā́ma-*), *vakṣī́-* 'flame', *vi-keśī́-* (AV.) 'shaggy hog', *vibālī́-* N. of a river, *vi-liptī́-* (AV.) 'cow', *vi-līḍhī́-* (AV.) 'female monster', *viśva-rūpī́-* 'brindled cow' (m. *viśvá-rūpa-*), *vṛkī́-* 'she-wolf' (m. *vṛ́ka-*), *vṛkṣa-sarpī́-* (AV.) 'tree-serpent', *veśī́-* 'needle', *vyasta-keśī́-* (AV.) 'shaggy hog', *śakaṭī́-* 'cart' (*śákaṭa-*), *śabalī́-* (TS.) 'cow of plenty' (m. *śabála-*), *sakthī́-* 'thigh' (n. *sákthi-*), *sasarparī́-* 'trumpet', *sahasra-parṇī́-* (AV.) N. of a plant (m. *sahásra-parṇa-*), *siṃhī́-* 'lioness', *su-maṅgalī́-*[3] 'lucky woman' (m. *su-maṅgála-*), *sūrmī́-* 'pipe', *sṛṇī́-* 'sickle', *starī́-* 'barren cow', *sphigī́-* 'hip', *hastinī́-*[4] (AV.) 'female elephant', *hiraṇya-keśī́-* 'gold-haired' (AV.) (m. *hiraṇya-keśa-*).

a. There are further a few f. adjectives in *-ī* from m. stems in *-ya*: *ā́pī-* 'watery' (m. *ā́pya-*), *samudrī́-*[5] 'belonging to the sea' (m. *samudríya-*), *svarī́-* 'resounding' (m. *svaryà-*).

α. There are a few transition forms from the *i*-stems: *karkaryàs*[6] (AV.) from *karkarī́-* 'lute' (*karkarí-*); N. sing. *arīs*[7] (VS. VI. 36) from *arī́-* 'faithful' beside the usual *arí-*; and the stems *yayī́-*, *sakthī́-*, *sṛṇī́-* also occur beside *yayi-*, *sakthi-*, *sṛ́ṇi-* respectively. The only certain transition from the derivative *ī-* declension to the radical *ī-* declension is represented by *strī́-* 'woman', originally a dissyllable[8], from which occur the forms A. sing. *striyam*, N. A. pl. *striyas*, I. *strībhis*. Other transition forms are probably *pṛśanias* G. sing. N. pl., *yahvias* A. pl., *suparṇias*[9] N. A. pl.

Inflexion.

376. The forms actually occurring if made from *dhī́-* 'thought', *yajña-śrī́-* m. f. 'adorning the sacrifice', *senā-nī́-* m. 'leader of an army', *rathī́-* m. f. 'charioteer' respectively, would be the following:

A. 1. sing. N. *dhī́s*. A. *dhíyam*. I. *dhiyā́*. D. *dhiyé*. G. *dhiyás*. — **Pl.** N. *dhíyas*. A. *dhíyas*. I. *dhībhís*. G. *dhīnā́m*[10]. L. *dhīṣú*.

2. sing. N. *yajña-śrī́s*. A. *yajña-śríyam*. I. *yajña-śríyā*. D. *yajña-śríye*. G. *yajña-śríyas*. — **Du.** N. A. *yajña-śríyā* and *yajña-śríyau* (AV.). — **Pl.** N. *yajña-śríyas*. A. *yajña-śríyas*. I. *yajña-śrī́bhis*.

3. sing. N. *senā-nī́s*. A. *senā-níam*. D. *senā-níe*. G. *senā-nías*. — **Du.** N. A. *senā-níā*. G. *senā-níos*. — **Pl.** N. *senā-nías*. A. *senā-nías*. D. *senā-nī́bhyas*. G. *senā-nī́nām*.

B. Sing. N. *rathī́s*. A. *rathíam*. I. *rathíā*. D. *rathíe*. G. *rathías*. V. *ráthi*. — **Du.** N. A. *rathíā*. I. f. *rathī́bhyām*. G. f. *rathíos*. L. *rathíos*. — **Pl.** N. *rathías*. A. *rathías*. I. *rathī́bhis*. D. f. *rathī́bhyas*. G. *rathī́nām*. L. f. *rathī́ṣu*.

---

1 In these words the accent is shifted to a vowel ending in weak cases.

2 The final vowel in this word is perhaps radical in origin (from *yā-* 'go').

3 The V. pl. *su-hastias* (IX. 46[4]), presupposes a stem *su-hastī́-*, but as the form is a m., the reading ought perhaps to be emended to *suhastiās* with BR.

4 *hastinī-* (IX. 3[17]) means 'having a hand'.

5 GRASSMANN regards this as a f. of an adjective *samudrá-*.

6 See WHITNEY on AV. IV. 37[5].

7 See LANMAN 371[3].

8 In I. 122[7] *starīs* seems to be the equivalent of *strī́*. See pw. s. v.

9 Cp. LANMAN 372[2].

10 The form *dhīnā́m* occurs 7 times in the RV., *dhiyā́m* only once.

The forms actually occurring are the following:

Sing. N. A. 1. m. *vís.* — **f.** *dhís, bhís, śrís.* — **2. m.** *itthā́dhīs, kṣatra-śrís, ghṛta-śrís, darśata-śrís, dūrá-ādhīs, márya-śrīs, viśváto-dhīs, sv-ādhís.* — **f.** *abhi-śrís.* — **3. m.** *agre-ṇís* (VS. VI. 2), *grāma-ṇís, takva-vís, deva-vís* and *devā-vís, patsu-taś-śís, pada-nís* (AV.), *pada-vís, pari-vís* (VS. VI. 6), *parṇa-vís, pra-krís* (AV.), *pra-ṇenís, madhyama-śís, manyu-mís, yajña-nís, yajña-prís* (VS. XXVII. 31), *vaśa-nís, sadyaḥ-krís, senā-nís, skambha-nís* (VS. I. 19), *syona-śís.* — **f.** *pra-krís* (AV.), *vrata-nís.* — **B. m.** *á-rathīs*[1], *prāvís, su-prāvís, rathís*[2] *sahásra-starīs, hiraṇya-vāśīs.* — **f.** *á-dur-maṅgalīs, aruṇís, kalyāṇís, kṛṣṇís, kṣoṇís*[3], *gandharvís, gaurís, jā́trís*[4] (AV.), *tandrís* (AV.), *dūtís, naptís, nāḍís, mahiṣís*[5] (TS. I. 2. 12^2), *yamís, yātudhānís* (AV.), *rathís, lakṣmís, lalāmís, viśva-rūpís* (TS. I. 5. 6^2), *vṛkís, śakaṭís, śabalís* (TS. IV. 3. 11^5), *sasarparís, siṃhís* (TS. I. 2. 12^2), *su-maṅgalís*[6], *starís*[7].

Acc. A. 1. f. *dhíyam, bhíyam, śríyam.* — **2. m.** *dur-ādhíam, sv-ādhíam, adhvara-śríyam, kṣatra-śríyam, ghṛta-śríyam, jana-śríyam, yajña-śríyam, su-śríyam, hari-śríyam*[8]. — **f.** *abhi-śríyam.* — **3. m.** *gāthā-níam, grāma-ṇíam* (VS. XXX. 20), *yajña-níam; devā-víam, pratī-víam; abhi-príyam, ghṛta-príyam* (AV.), *brahma-príyam.* — **f.** *devā-víam*[9]. — **B. m.** *rathíam, su-prāvíam.* — **f.** *atharvíam, arāyíam, kumāríam* (AV.), *kūdíam* (AV.), *gauríam, nadíam, naptíam, nāndíam, prapharvíam, yamíam, lakṣmíam* (AV.), *lalāmíam* (AV.), *vibālíam, viliptíam* (AV.), *vilīḍhíam* (AV.), *viśva-rūpíam, vṛkíam, siṃhíam, sūrmíam, staríam*[10], *sphigíam, svaríam.*

I. A. 1. f. *dhiyā́, bhiyā́, śriyā́.* — **2. m.** *dū-ḍhíā.* — **f.** *avadya-bhiyā́*[11], *ā-dhiā́*[12] (AV.). — **B. m.** *rathíā.* — **f.** *tila-piñjiā́*[12] (AV.), *palāliā́*[12] (AV.), *maṇḍūkíā, veśíā, sahasra-parṇiā́*[12] (AV.), *sūrmíā, sphigíā.* — The form *tapanī́* may be a contraction for *tapaníā*[13].

D. A. 1. f. *dhiyé, śriyé.* — **2. m.** *itthā́-dhiye, dur-ādhíe, dū-ḍhíe.* — **f.** *ā-dhíe.* — **3. m.** *gaṇa-śríye* (VS. XXII. 30), *yajña-príye; jihma-śíe, senā-níe* (VS. XVI. 17). — **B. m.** *rathíe, su-prāvíe*[14]. — **f.** *nāndíe, meṣíe, vṛkíe.*

G.[15] **A. 1. f.** *dhiyás.* — **2. m.** *dū-ḍhías, su-dhías.* — **n.** *sv-ādhías*[16]. — **3. m.** *gaṇa-śríyas; gāthā-nías, manyu-mías*[17]. — **B. m.** *ahías, su-prāvías.* — **f.** *atharías, ápias*[18], *nadías, niṣṭi-grías, pṛśanías, meṣías, sṛṇías.*

L. f. *gaurī́* (IX. 12^3) and *sarasī́* (VII. 103^2) may be locatives containing the normal ending *-i.*

---

1 There is also the transition form *arís* (VS. VI. 36).

2 On *rathíva* occurring once or twice for *rathír iva*, cp. LANMAN 375 (bottom).

3 The N. sing. once (I. 180^5) appears without the *-s* as *kṣoṇī́.* This word has other forms also according to the derivative *ī-* declension; cp. LANMAN 372 (bottom).

4 The reading of the Mss. in AV. XX. 48^2 is *jā́trīs;* the edition has *jánis.*

5 This is a transition from the derivative *ī-* declension for the *máhiṣī* of the RV.

6 The AV. has *su-maṅgalī́* three times; cp. LANMAN 377 (top).

7 There are also the transition forms *árātīs* (VI. 45), *śakvarís* (TS. IV. 4. 4^1), *devís* (AV. VI. 59^2); *variantís* (I. 140^9) is a purely metrical lengthening; cp. LANMAN 377^2.

8 This form is also once (Vāl. II. 10) used in agreement with a neuter substantive (*gotrám*).

9 In agreement with *tvácam* (IX. 74^5).

10 This form is once (VII. 68^8) pronounced *staryàm*, being one of the two only examples in the RV. of the *ī* in this declension being pronounced as *y* before a vowel.

11 Accented as if *-bhiyā́* were used independently; the form occurs in a late hymn (X. 107^3).

12 Irregular accentuation of the ending.

13 Otherwise it may be an I. of the derivative *ī*-declension.

14 Cp. LANMAN 382^3.

15 There is no example of an ablative.

16 This seems to be the only actual n. form of this declension in the RV.

17 The form *ahi-ghnyás* (AV.) is a transition form with shift of accent from the derivative *ī*-declension.

18 The form *aruṇís* (I. 121^3) may be contracted for *aruṇías.*

V. B. m. *dakṣi*[1]. — f. *arāyi, mahe-nadi*[2], *yami, lakṣmi* (AV.).

Du. N. A. A. 2. f. *abhi-śrlyā, ghṛta-śrlyā.* — 3. m. *mana-nīā, sadha-nīā; senānī-grāmaṇyàu* (VS. XV. 15). — f. *abhi-śrlyau* (AV.). — **B.** m. *rathīā.* — f. *cakrlyā, nadīā, naptīā, yamīā, sakthīā, sṛṇīā; cakrlyau* (SV.), *nādyàu* (AV.), *sakthīau* (AV.)[3].

I. B. f. *kṣoṇībhyām.* — **G. A.** 3. m. *yajña-nīos.* — **B.** f. *oṇīos*[4], *cakrīos.* — **L. B.** f. *oṇīos, naptīos.*

Pl. N. V. A. 1. f. *dhlyas, śrlyas*[5]. — 2. m. *dīrghādhiyas, durādhias, dūḍhias, nānā-dhiyas, su-dhiyas, sv-ādhias; agni-śrlyas, adhvara-śrlyas, su-śrlyas.* — f. *ādhias, vyādhias*[6] (AV.). — 3. m. *grāma-ṇīas* (AV.), *devā-vīas, pada-vīas, sadha-nīas; abhi-prlyas, kadha-prlyas, gaṇa-śrlyas, pari-prlyas.* — f. *abhi-śrlyas, ā-prlyas* (AV.), *pra-ṇīas, vāta-pramiyas.* — **B.** m. *ahīas, āpathīas, rāthīas, su-hastīas*[7]. — f. *apasīas* (VS. x. 7), *arāyīas* (AV.), *aruṇīas, enīas, kalyāṇīas, kavaṣīas* (VS. XX. 40, 60), *gaurīas, tīkṣṇa-śṛṅgīas, nadīas, nāḍīas* (AV.), *mayūrīas, yātu-dhānīas* (AV.), *rathīas, lakṣmīas* (AV.), *vakṣīas, vi-keśīas* (AV.), *vyasta-keśīas* (AV.), *samudrlyas, sahasra-parṇīas* (AV.), *starīas.* — With *ī* **pronounced as *y*:** once *nadyàs* (VII. 50[4]) and 6 forms in the AV., *aśvataryàs, nadyàs, naptyàs, nāḍyàs, pippalyàs, vṛkṣa-sarpyàs.*

Acc. A. 1. f. *dhlyas, bhlyas* (AV.), *bhiyás* (TS. IV. 1. 7[3] = VS. XXVII. 7), *śrlyas.* — 2. m. *durādhīas, dūḍhias, su-śrlyas*[8]. — f. *ādhias* (AV.). — 3. m. *sadha-nīas.* — **B.** m. *ahīas, duṣprāvīas, rathīas.* — f. *arāyīas* (AV.), *aṣṭa-karṇīas, kilāsīas, khārīas, dehīas, nadīas, naptīas, meṣīas, yamīas, yātu-dhānīas, samudrlyas, sambādha-tandrīas* (AV.) 'affliction and exhaustion', *starīas*[9].

I. A. 1. f. *dhībhis, śrībhis*[10]. — 2. m. *sv-ādhībhis.* — 3. m. *gaṇa-śrībhis*[11]. — **B.** m. *hiraṇya-vāśībhis.* — f. *kalyāṇībhis, kṣoṇībhis, nadībhis, naptībhis.*

D.[12] **A.** 3. m. *ṛta-nībhyas*[11], *śva-nībhyas*[11] (VS. XVI. 27), *senā-nībhyas*[11] (VS. XVI. 26). — **B.** f. *aparībhyas, nadībhyas* (VS. XXX. 8).

G. A. 1. f. *dhīnām* and *dhiyām, śrīṇām.* — 3. f. *hiraṇya-vīnām.* — **B.** m. *ahīnām, nadīnām* 'invokers', *rathīnām*[13]. — f. *aruṇīnām, krimīṇām* (AV.), *nadīnām, puruṣīṇām, svarīṇām.*

L. A. 1. f. *dhīṣú.* — **B.** f. *aparīṣu, aruṇīṣu, nadīṣu*[14].

3. b. Stems in derivative -ī.

LANMAN, Noun-Inflection 365—400. — WHITNEY, Sanskrit Grammar 362—366.

377. 1. This declension embraces a very considerable number of stems which are formed by means of the suffix *-ī* (originally *-yā*) and, except seven masculines, are restricted to the f. gender. It largely supplies the f. form of words requiring inflexion in more than one gender. Feminine stems are thus made from nouns in *-a*, e. g. *devī-* (m. *devá-*); from adjectives in *-u*; e. g. *pṛthv-ī-* (m. *pṛthú-*); from present participles in *-ant*; e. g. *mád ant-ī-*

---

[1] Pada *dhakṣi*; cp. RPr. IV. 41.

[2] Treated as a compound in the Pada (VIII. 74[15]) though *mahe* is V.

[3] The AV. shows no example of *-īā.* It has three transition forms *āṇḍiau, phálgunyau, akṣyàu.*

[4] Cp. APr. III. 61.

[5] Also the transition form *striyas.*

[6] This would be *vyā-dhiyas* in the RV. where in compounds ending in *-dhī-* the *ī* if unaccented is split.

[7] See above, 375 B a α, note 3.

[8] Also the transition form to the derivative *ī*-declension *deva-śrīs* (TS. IV. 6. 3[2] = VS. XVII. 56) 'worshipping the gods'.

[9] Also the transition form *striyas*; on *yahvīas* and *suparṇīas* see 375 a α.

[10] Also the transition form *strībhis* (accented as a monosyllabic stem).

[11] Metrical shortening; see LANMAN 372[3].

[12] There is no example of an Ab. m. or f.

[13] The accent of the G. *atasīnām* 'beggars' would seem to require a stem *atasí-* and not *atasi-*.

[14] There is also the transition form *strīṣú* accented as a monosyllable.

(m. *mádant-*), *-ánt*, e. g. *adat-ī́-* (m. *adánt-*), or *-at*, e. g. *píprat-ī-* (m. *píprat-*); from perfect participles in *-vāṃs*, e. g. *jagmúṣ-ī-* (m. *jaganvā́ṃs-*); from comparatives in *-yāṃs*, e. g. *návīyas-ī-* (m. *návīyāṃs-*); from words in *-tar* (*-tṛ*), e. g. *avitr-ī́-* (m. *avitár-*); from adjectives in *-mant*, e. g. *dhenu-mát-ī-* (m. *dhenu-mánt-*), and *-vant*, e. g. *áma-vat-ī-* (m. *áma-vant-*); from nouns in *-an*, e. g. *sam-rā́jñ-ī-* (m. *rā́jan-*), *-van*, e. g. *ṛtá-var-ī-* (m. *ṛtá-van-*); from adjectives [1] in *-in*, e. g. *arkíṇ-ī-* (m. *arkín-*); from compounds ending in *-añc*, e. g. *arvā́c-ī-* (m. *arvā́ñc-*), in *-dṛś*, e. g. *su-dṛ́ś-ī-*, in *-pad*, e. g. *a-pád-ī-*, and in *-han*, e. g. *á-pati-ghn-ī-*.

2. There is besides a large group of **miscellaneous f. stems** of an independent character, having no corresponding m.[2], e. g. *śác-ī-* 'might'.

3. The **seven m. stems**[3], of which five are proper names, are: *Tiraśćī́-*, *Námī-*, *Pṛ́thī-*, *Mā́talī-*, *Sóbharī-*; *rā́ṣṭrī-* 'ruler', *sirī́-* 'weaver'.

a. The stems of this declension (in contrast with those of the B group of the radical *ī-* declension) do not normally accent the suffix. The exceptions to this rule are of a definite character.

1. When in the first f. group there is a corresponding m. accented on a final syllable which is liable to be reduced in such a way as to be incapable of bearing the accent, the acute is thrown forward on the *-ī*; e. g. m. *urú-*, f. *urv-ī́-*; m. *netár-*, f. *netr-ī́-*; m. *ad-ánt-*, f. *ad-at-ī́-*; m. *praty-áñc-*, f. *pratīc-ī́-*; m. *-han-*, f. *-ghn-ī́-*. When the m. ends in *-á*, the accent also in several stems remains on the corresponding *-ī*; thus m. *devá-*, f. *devī́-*; *pāpá-* 'evil', f. *pāpī́-*[4]; m. *puro-gavá-* 'leader', f. *puro-gavī́-*; m. *rāmá-* 'night', f. *rāmī́-*; m. *vamrá-* 'ant', f. *vamrī́-*. More usually, however, the accent of such feminines is thrown back on the first syllable[5]; thus m. *āyasá-* 'made of iron', f. *ā́yasī-*; m. *aruṣá-* 'red', f. *áruṣī-*; m. *gāndharvá-* 'belonging to the Gandharvas', f. *gā́ndharvī-*; m. *taviṣá-* 'strong', f. *táviṣī-* 'strength'; m. *paruṣá-* 'reed', f. *páruṣṇī-* 'reedy', N. of a river; m. *palitá-* 'grey', f. *páliknī-*; m. *mahiṣá-*[6] 'buffalo', f. *máhiṣī-*; m. *rohitá-* 'ruddy', f. *róhiṇī-* 'ruddy cow', m. *śaṃ-gayá-* 'procuring prosperity for the household', f. *śaṃ-gáyī-*; m. *śyāvá-* 'brown', f. *śyā́vī-*; m. *śyetá-* 'white', f. *śyénī-* 'white cow'.

2. Again, the miscellaneous group of feminines hardly ever accents the final *-ī* of the stem except when it is a proper name, a shift of accent having here probably taken place to indicate a change of meaning; thus *araṇyānī́-* 'Forest-goddess', *arundhatī́-*[7] (AV.) N. of a plant and a star, *indrāṇī́-* 'Indra's wife', *rodasī́-* N. of the Aśvins' wife, *vadhri-matī́-* N. of a mythical female, *varuṇānī́-* 'Varuṇa's wife', *śavasī́-* N. of Indra's mother, *sinīvālī́-* N. of a goddess; and the river names *añjasī́-*, *asiknī́-*[8] (but *ásiknī-* 'black' and 'night'), *go-mat-ī́-* (but *gó-mat-ī-* 'rich in cows'), *śutudrī́-*.

Inflexion.

378. The inflexion of the derivative *ī-* stems stands in marked contrast with that of the radical *ī-* stems in three respects: (1) **no *-s* is added in the N. sing.** masculine or feminine; (2) the **endings diverge considerably from the normal** ones, the Sing. A. taking *-m*, the D. *-ai*, the Ab. G. *-ās*, the L. *-ām*, the du. N. A. *-ī*, the pl. N. A. *-s*; (3) stems accented on the final vowel **shift the acute** to the ending in the weak cases of the sing., in the G. L. du., and the G. pl.

1 Adjectives ending in *-a* do not form their f. in *-ī* unless they are accented on the final syllable, when the accent almost always shifts to the first syllable; e. g. *áruṣī-* from *aruṣá-*; but *pāpá-* has *pāpī́-* beside *pāpā́-*.

2 A list of these is given by GRASSMANN, Wörterbuch 1722—23.

3 Cp. ZUBATÝ, zu den altindischen männlichen *ī*-stämmen, Sitzungsberichte d. Böhm. Ges. d. Wiss. 1897, XIX (treats also of the radical *ī*-stems used in the masc.).

4 Beside *pāpā́-*. The great majority of adjectives and all participles ending in *-a* form their f. with *-ā*.

5 This is the converse of the accentuation in the B group of the radical *-ī* declension, where the m. in unaccented *-a* throws the acute on the final *-ī* of the f.

6 Similarly *varūtṛ́-* 'protector', f. *várūtr-ī-*.

7 Originally a present participle **á-rundhat-ī-* 'not hindering'.

8 *ásiknī-* also occurs once as the N. of the river.

The forms actually occurring, if made from *deví-* 'goddess', would be as follows:

Sing. N. *deví.* A. *devím.* I. *devyā́.* D. *devyái.* Ab. *devyā́s.* G. *devyā́s.* L. *devyā́m.* V. *dévi.*

Du. N. A. *deví,* V. *dévī.* D. Ab. *devíbhyām.* G. L. *devyós.*

Pl. N. *devís.* A. *devís.* I. *devíbhis.* D. *devíbhyas.* Ab. *devíbhyas.* G. *devīnā́m.* L. *devíṣu.* V. *dévīs.*

Forms actually occurring are the following:

Sing. N. The **m.** forms are: *nā́mī, pṛ́thī, mā́talī, rā́ṣṭrī, sóbharī.* The **f.** forms are very common, being made from nearly 300 stems in the RV. Among the most frequent are: *pṛthiví* 'earth' (57), *deví* (48), *sárasvatī* (43) N. of a goddess, *mahí* 'great' (35), *ucchántī* 'shining' (16), *yatí* 'going' (14), *jánitrī* 'mother' (10), *bṛhatí* 'great' (10), *ghṛtā́cī* 'filled with ghee' (9), *maghónī* 'bountiful' (9), *strí*[1] 'woman' (3)[2].

A. m. *nā́mīm.* — The **f.** is formed from over 100 stems in the RV. Among the commonest forms are: *pṛthivī́m* (62), *mahī́m*[3] (35), *devī́m* (18), *táviṣīm* (13), *urvī́m* (9) 'wide', *pipyúṣīm*[4] (9) 'swelling'[5].

I. This case is formed with the normal ending *-ā.* The only **m.** form is *nā́myā.* But there are about 40 f. forms in the RV. In more than two-thirds of these the suffix is pronounced as a vowel[6] *-iā* (in oxytones *-iā́*), in the rest as a semivowel *-yā* (in oxytones *-yā́*). The stem *śámī-* 'labour' has, beside *śámyā,* the contracted form *śámī,* which also appears in the compound *su-śámī* 'with great care'. At the end of a Pāda and before vowels[7] this I. *śámī* is shortened to *śámi*[8]. The forms occurring are: 1. *áṇvyā* 'subtile', *aśvābhidhā́nyā* (AV.) 'halter', *áśvāvatyā* 'furnished with horses', *ásiknyā*[9] (AV.), *kuṇḍṛṇā́cyā* 'house lizard', *kumbhyā́* (TS. III. 2. 8[4]) 'jar', *gātú-mátyā* 'spacious', *gāyatryā́* (TS. II. 2. 4[8]) a metre, *ghṛtā́cyā, citántyā* 'observing', *citáyantyā* 'appearing', *jágatyā* (TS. II. 21. 4[8]), a metre, *tmányā* 'by oneself', *dávidyutatyā* 'glittering', *devā́cyā* 'directed towards the gods', *dáivyā* (AV.) 'divine', *návyasyā* 'new', *pátnyā* 'wife', *mádhu-matyā* 'accompanied by sweetness', *róhiṇyā, vásvyā* 'good', *vā́javatyā* 'rich in treasure', *vā́syā* (AV.) 'knife', *viśvá-bheṣajyā* (AV.) 'all-healing', *viśvā́cyā* 'universal', *víśvyā* 'everywhere' (adv.), *śácyā* 'might', *śámyā, śarmayántyā* 'protecting', *śímyā* 'work', *satrā́cyā* 'attentive', *samī́cyā* (Kh. III. 10[5]) a goddess, *sárasvatyā* (AV.), *sóma-vatyā* 'accompanied with Soma', *stóbhantyā* 'praising', *háriṇyā* 'yellow', *hiraṇyáyā*[10] 'golden'. — **Oxytones with shift of accent:** *annādyā́* (AV.) 'proper food', *asiknyā́, devyā́, purāṇyā́* 'ancient', *pṛthivyā́, mahyā́, samānyā́* 'similar', *sādhāraṇyā́*[11] 'common', *sūcyā́* 'needle', *sautrāmaṇyā́* (AV.) a kind of Indra sacrifice. The TS. and VS. also have *urvyā́* as an **adverb** 'afar', which in the RV. appears only in the modified form *urviyā́.*

D. The ending looks like *-ai,* e. g. *devy-ái;* but it is doubtless in origin the normal ending *-e* fused with the suffix *-yā,* i. e. *-yai* = *-yā-e*[12]. Only 13 forms (all f.) occur in the RV. These are, besides a few others from the later

[1] Cp. WIEDEMANN, BB. 27, 211, footnote.

[2] In the AV. there are also the transition forms *á-durmaṅgalī, su-maṅgalī́, nadī́.* In RV. I. 180[5] *kṣoṇī́* has perhaps dropped its *-s* owing to the following *s-*.

[3] Perhaps to be read uncontracted as *mahíam* in X. 50[5]; *vā́ṇīm* (II. 11[8]) is also to be read as *vā́ṇiam.*

[4] Perfect participle of *pī-* 'swell'.

[5] There is also the transition form *nadī́m* (AV.).

[6] The vocalic pronunciation seems to be the commoner in the AV. also; cp. LANMAN 381.

[7] This also occurs in the compound *urvi-ūtíḥ* (VI. 24[2]), if *urvi-* = the adv. instr. *urvyā́.*

[8] The compound *su-śámi* also occurs once in the TS. VS. as well as the RV.

[9] Probably an error for *ásiknyās;* see WHITNEY on AV. V. 13[8].

[10] For *hiraṇyáyyā.*

[11] Cp. LANMAN 368 (top).

[12] An indication of this origin is perhaps to be found in the fact that of the 13 stems in the RV. taking this dative only one, *-patnyai,* has the vocalic pronunciation *-iai*

Saṃhitās: 1. *arvā́cyai* (VS. XXII. 24) 'hitherward', *ávācyai* (VS. XXII. 24) 'downward', *á-vyatyai* 'not desiring', *íyatyai* 'so great', *údīcyai* (VS. XXII. 24) 'northern', *jágatyai* (VS. XXIV. 12), *jāryái* (TS. III. 2. 2^{2}) 'mistress', *jū́ryantyai* 'aging', *jyā́yasyai* 'elder', *dhenumátyai* 'yielding milk', *parjánya-patnyai*[1] 'having Parjanya for a husband', *paśumátyai* 'consisting of cattle', *pratī́cyai* (VS. XXII. 24) 'western', *prā́cyai* (VS. XXII. 24) 'eastern', *yaśo-bhagínyai* (VS. II. 20) 'rich in glory', *rā́tryai* (VS. XXIV. 25) 'night', *vā́javatyai*, *viś-pátnyai*, *sahá-patnyai*[1] (AV.) 'united with the husband'. — 2. **Oxytones**: *indrāṇyái* (VS. XXXVIII. 3), *urvyái* (VS. XXII. 27), *kalyāṇyái*[2] (AV.) 'good', *gāyatryái* (VS. XIII. 54), *devyái*, *pṛthivyái*, *bṛhatyái*, *mahyái*, *rājāsandyái* (VS. XIX. 16) 'Soma stand', *sinīvālyái*, *striyái*[3] (AV.), *hiraṇya-keśyái*[4] (AV.) 'gold-haired'.

Ab. The ending looks like *-ās*, e. g. *pṛthivy-ā́s*; but it is doubtless the normal ending *-as* fused with the suffix *-yā*, i. e. *-yās* = *-yā-as*[5]. Only five forms occur in the RV., besides a few others in the later Saṃhitās: *avadyávatyās* (AV.) 'disgraceful', *urváśyās* N. of a nymph, *jágatyās* (VS. XIII. 56), *jī́vantyās*[5] 'living', *dur-admanyā́s* (VS. II. 20) 'bad food', *pátantyās* 'flying', *pṛthivyā́s*, *bṛhatyā́s* (AV.), *mahyā́s*[6].

G. The ending is the same as in the Ab. and of similar origin. m. *tiraścyā́s*[7], *pṛ́thyās*, *sóbharyās*. — f. The forms occurring in the RV.[8] are: 1. *aṃśu-mátyās*[9] N. of a river, *aṃhu-bhédyās* (VS. XXIII. 28) 'having a narrow slit', *uśīnárāṇyās* N. of a people, *ūrjáyantyās* 'vigorous', *óṣadhyās* (VS. I. 25) 'plant', *táviṣyās*, *dā́numatyās* 'rich in drops', *mā́ṃs-pácanyās* 'flesh-cooking', *rā́tryās*, *vivásvatyās* 'shining', *śámyās*, *śóśucatyās* 'shining', *sū́ṣyantyās* 'about to bear'. — 2. *urvyā́s* 'earth', *devyā́s*, *pṛthivyā́s*, *mahatyā́s* 'great', *yatyā́s*, *yātyā́s* 'going', *vadhrimatyā́s* N. of a woman, *striyā́s*[10].

L. This case seems to be formed with the ending *-ām*, e. g. *devy-ā́m*; but it may be due to the fusion of a particle *-*am*[11] with the suffix *-yā*. It is formed from 15 stems in the RV., where the pronunciation *-iām* is considerably less than half as common[12] as *-yām*. Forms occurring are: 1. *ásiknyām*, *ucchántyām*, *údīcyām* (TS. II. 4. 14^{1}), *jágatyām* (VS. XXXVIII. 18), *jahnā́vyām* 'race of Jahnu', *dṛṣádvatyām* N. of a river, *nā́ryām* (Kh. IV. 13^{3}) 'woman', *páruṣṇyām* N. of a river, *prā́cyām* (TS. II. 4. 14^{1}), *yavyā́vatyām* 'rich in streams', *rā́tryām*, *varaṇā́vatyām* (AV.) N. of a river, *vasā́vyām* 'treasury', *śácyām*, *sárasvatyām* N. of a river, *soma-kráyaṇyām* (VS. VIII. 54) 'serving as the price of Soma'. — 2. *araṇyānyā́m*, *āṣṭryā́m* 'fire-place', *āsandyā́m* (AV.) 'stool', *gavīnyā́m* (Kh. IV. 13^{3}) 'groin', *gāyatryā́m* (VS. AV.), *catvāriṃśyā́m* 'fortieth', *jyeṣṭhaghnyā́m* (AV.) N. of an asterism, *devyā́m*, *narācyā́m* (AV.) N. of a river, *pṛthivyā́m*, *striyā́m* (AV.)[13].

(and here the *i* is preceded by two consonants).

1 To be pronounced *-iai*.

2 This is an emendation for the reading *kalyāṇyài* of the edition; cp. LANMAN 383^{2}.

3 With split *ī* as in the radical *ī*- stems.

4 There are also the transition forms *bhiyái*, *śriyái* (VS. XIX. 94), *hriyái* (VS. XIV. 35) from the radical *ī*- declension, and from the *i*- declension *devá-hūtyai*, *turyái*, *nírṛtyai*, *puṣṭyái*, *bhujyái*, *bhṛtyái*, *śrútyai*.

5 *-yās* is read *-iās* 4 times out of 25 in the RV.: *pṛthiviā́s* 3 times and *jī́vantiās* once, always for metrical reasons, cp. LANMAN 384 (top).

6 There are also the transition forms from the *i*-declension, *nā́bhyās*, *bhū́myās*, *hetyā́s*; and from the AV. *á-bhūtyās*, *á-rātyās*, *á-śastyās*, *ā́hūtyās*, *kṛṣyā́s*, *deva-hetyā́s*, *rā́tryās*, *śīrṣaktyā́s*; probably also *yónyās* (VI. 121^{4}), Pada *yónyā*.

7 Pronounced *tiraściā́s*. But cp. ROTH, ZDMG. 48, 115 (bottom).

8 This case is formed from more stems in the AV. than in the RV.; cp. LANMAN 355.

9 In about 15 per cent of the following genitives the ending is pronounced *-iās*.

10 There are also half a dozen transition forms from the *i*- declension in the RV.: *anumátyās*, *árātyās*, *nírṛtyās*, *pṛ́śnyās*, *bhū́myās* (once with crasis in *bhū́myopári* X. 75^{3}), *yuvatyā́s*; there are many others in the AV.; as *jāmyā́s* (also Kh. V. 5^{19}); see LANMAN 385^{2}.

11 Cp. BRUGMANN, Grundriss 2, 265 (p. 619).

12 It is much less common than this is in the AV.

13 There are also two transition forms

V. This case is formed, by shortening the final, from 38 stems (all f.) in the RV. Examples are: *devi* (23), *sarasvati* (16), *pṛthivi* (11), *maghoni* (9), *vibhāvari* 'radiant' (8), *mahi* (6). From the TS.: *ámbāli* (VII. 4. 19^1) 'mother', *kāmpīla-vāsini* (VII. 4. 19^1; VS.) 'living in Kāmpīla', *darvi* (I. 8. 4^1) 'ladle', *patni* (IV. 4. 12^4), *máṇḍūki* (IV. 6. 1^2; VS.) 'frog', *deva-yajani* (VS.) 'whereon gods are adored'.

Du. N. A. V. This form in the RV. ends in *-ī* exclusively, being made probably with the ending *-i* (like the f. du. of the derivative *-ā* stems), which coalesces with the *-ī* of the stem[1]. There is only one **m.** form, the V. *mādhvī* 'fond of sweetness', an epithet of the Aśvins. The f. is very frequent, being made from 76 stems in the RV. and from over 20 in the VS. The commonest forms in the RV. are: *ródasī* (87) 'the two worlds', *dyā́vā-pṛthivī́* (65) 'heaven and earth', *mahī́* (27), *urvī́* (20), *pṛthivī́* (20), *devī́* (13), *samī́cī́* (11) 'united', *bṛhatī́* (10), *yahvī́* (6) 'active', *akṣī́* (6) 'eyes', *pṛthvī́* (5). From the TS.: N. *chándasvatī* 'desiring' and *sū́rya-patnī* (IV. 3. 11^1) 'having the sun as husband', V. *úrvī*, *rodasī*, *patnī* (IV. 7. 15^6).

a. The *-ī* is twice metrically shortened in *pṛthivi* (II. 31^5; III. 54^4) and in *máhi* (IV. 56^9; X. 93^1).

b. In the AV. three stems of this declension form transition duals[2] according to the radical *ī-* declension: *akṣyàu*, *āṇḍyàu*, *phálgunyau*[3]; in other texts: *gavīnyàu* (TS. III. 3. 10^1) 'the groins', *pátnyau* (VS. XXXI. 22), *rébhatyau* and *su-párṇyau* (Kh. I. 37).

I. *akṣī́bhyām* (AV.), *kumbhī́bhyām* (VS. XIX. 27), *jóṣṭrībhyām* (VS. XXI. 51) 'cherishing', *mádhūcībhyām* (VS.) 'sweetness-loving', *mádhvībhyām* (VS.).

D. *ródasībhyām*. — **Ab.** *akṣī́bhyām*, *dyā́vāpṛthivī́bhyām* (VS. XXXVII. 18).

G. *akṣyós*[4] (AV.; TS. III. 2. 5^5), *ā́rtniyos* (TS. IV. 5. 2^3) 'ends of the bow', *ā́rtnyos* (VS. XVI. 9), *divas-pṛthivyós*[5], *niṇyós*[6] 'secret', *pari-nṛ́tantyos* (AV.) 'dancing round', *ródasyos*[7]. — **L.** *akṣyós* (AV.), *aráṇyos*, *árjunyos*, *dyā́vāpṛthivyós* (VS. XX. 10), *pátantyos*, *ródasyos*, *samīcyós*.

Pl. N. V. The ending seems to be simply *-s*, but it is doubtless the normal ending *-as*, which originally coalesced with the suffix *-yā* to *-yās*, the latter then contracting to *-īs*. In the **m.** the only example is *sirī́s*. But the **f.** is very frequent, being formed from 166 stems in the RV., and occurring in the independent parts of the TS. at least 25 and of the VS. at least 40 times. The commonest forms are: *devī́s* (43), *pūrvī́s* (36) 'many', *óṣadhīs* (27), *vā́ṇīs* (12) 'songs', *pátnīs* (11), *mahī́s* (11), *bhātī́s* (8) 'shining', *yahvī́s* (7), *devayántīs* (6) 'serving the gods', *vásvīs*[8] (6). In the Khilas occur the 7 forms *a-lakṣmī́s* (II. 6^6), *āṇī́s* (IV. 8^5), *devī́s* (III. 10^2), *pāvamānī́s* (III. 10^1) N. of certain hymns, *bahvī́s* (II. 8^4 etc.) 'many', *svastyáyanīs* (III. 10^1), *hiraṇyáyīs* (V. 15^{11}).

a. Transitions from this to the radical *ī-* declension are almost unknown to the RV.: *stríyas* is the only certain example, and *pṛśanyàs* and *suparṇyàs* are probably such; the tendency to use such transition forms is only incipient even in the AV.[9], where *urvyàs*[10] (once) and *rudatyàs* (once) occur[11]. In the Khilas also, occur the three forms *ghṛtā́cyas* from the radical *ī-* declension: *śriyā́m* (AV.) and *dūtyā́m*; five from the *i-* declension: *púraṃdhyām*, *bhū́myām*, *bhṛtyā́m*, *yuvatyā́m*, *sáṃgatyām*; besides at least 10 additional ones from the AV.: *ávyām*, *ā́kūtyām*, *cíttyām*, *devá-hūtyām*, *nā́bhyām* (+ VS. XXIV. 1), *pṛṣṭyā́m*, *bhū́tyām*, *yónyām* (+ VS.), *védyām*, *sámityām*.

1 Cp. BRUGMANN, Grundriss 2, 287 (p. 644).

2 There are also the transition forms from the radical *ī-* declension *kṣoṇī́* and once *nadī́*.

3 This form in *-yau* becomes universal in the post-Vedic language.

4 The Mss. in AV. V. 4^{10} read *akṣós*; see WHITNEY's note.

5 With the first member of the Dvandva inflected in the sing. G.

6 Either the G. of *niṇī́-* (m. *niṇyá-*) or shortened for *niṇyáyos*.

7 Once (VI. 24^3) used in the sense of an Ab.

8 *éka-patnīs* (AV. X. 8^{39}) 'having one husband' is N. pl. f., not N. sing. m.

9 There seem to be no such transitions in the TS.; but there are at least 3 to the *i-* declension: *óṣadhayas* (IV. 1. 4^4), *revátayas* (IV. 2. 11^1), *pátnayas* (V. 2. 11^2).

10 Beside *urvī́s* which occurs 9 times.

11 And yet this form is the only one in the post-Vedic language.

(II. 8[4]), *bahvyàs* (III. 11[2]), *pāvamānyás* (III. 10[3]). The VS. has about 10 such forms: *devyàs* (XXXVII. 4) beside *devī́s*, *pátnyas* (XXIII. 36) beside *pátnīs* (VI. 34), *phálavatyas* (XXII. 22), *bahvyàs* (XIX. 44) beside *bahvī́s*, *mahā́nāmnyas* (XXIII. 35), *maitrāvaruṇyàs* (XXIV. 2), *maitryàs* (XXIV. 8), *vatsataryàs* (XXIV. 5), V. *vamryas* (XXXVII. 4), *vaiśvadevyàs* (XXIV. 5), *sārasvatyàs* (XXIV. 4).

b. There are no transitions from the radical *ī-* declension to this one in the RV., and in the AV. only *nadī́s* (beside *nadyàs*) and *lakṣmī́s* (beside *lakṣmyàs*). But the transitions from the *i-* declension are numerous: *aṅgúlīs* (AV.), *avánīs*, *ājánīs*, *ūtī́s*, *ṛṣṭī́s* (AV.), *dhamánīs* (AV.), *nā́ktīs*, *nā́bhīs* (AV.), *nírṛtīs*, *niṣkṛtīs*, *pā́rṣṇīs* (AV.), *púraṃdhīs*, *pṛṣṭī́s* (AV.), *bhū́mīs*, *viśvá-kṛṣṭīs*, *śréṇīs*[1], *sáyonīs*.

A. This case is identical in form with the N., and its origin is doubtless similar. It is very frequent, being made from more than 100 stems in the RV. The commonest forms are: *pūrvī́s* (40), *óṣadhīs* (24), *mahī́s* (18), *bṛhatī́s* (12), *dā́sīs* (9) 'demonesses', *pátnīs* (7), *pṛ́ṣatīs* (7)[2] 'dappled mares'.

I. This case is fairly frequent, being made from 32 stems in the RV. The commonest forms are: *śácībhis* (36), *táviṣībhis* (13), *śámībhis* (8), *óṣadhībhis* (6), *pṛ́ṣatībhis*[3] (5). The TS. has also *sīmībhis* (V. 2. 12[1]), *sūcī́bhis* (V. 2. 11[1, 2]); the VS. *aruṇī́bhis* (XII. 74), *jágatībhis* (I. 21), *sthālī́bhis* (XIX. 27) 'cooking-pots'.

D. This case is rare, being formed from only three stems in the RV. and a few others in the later Saṃhitās: *āvyādhínībhyas* (VS. XVI. 24) 'assailing bands', *óṣadhībhyas*, *keśínībhyas* (AV.) 'hairy', *gandharvá-patnībhyas* (VS. AV.) 'having Gandharvas for spouses', *ghoṣíṇībhyas* (AV.) 'noisy', *táviṣībhyas*[4], *tíṣṭhantībhyas* (VS. XXII. 25) 'standing', *tṛṃhatī́bhyas* (VS. XVI. 24) 'piercing', *mā́nuṣībhyas* (TS. IV. 1. 4[3]; VS. XI. 45) 'human', *vṛṣaṇyántībhyas* 'desiring a male', *śáśvatībhyas*[5] (AV.) 'everlasting', *srávantībhyas* (VS. XXII. 25) 'flowing', *hrādúnībhyas* (VS. XXII. 26) 'hail'.

Ab. Only three forms of this case occur in the RV.: *óṣadhībhyas*, *padvátībhyas* 'possessed of feet', *bṛhatī́bhyas*.

G. This case, which as is usual in the vowel declension takes the ending *-nām*, is found in only one m. form, *sóbharīṇām*; but it is fairly common in the f., being formed from 34 stems in the RV. The oxytones which number only six[6], throw the accent (as in the *i*-declension) on the ending: *bahvīnā́m*, *bhañjatīnā́m* 'breaking', *bhātīnā́m*, *bhuñjatīnā́m* 'gladdening', *mahīnā́m*[7], *yatīnā́m*. This rule does not, however, hold in the SV. and VS., which have *mahī́nām* (VS. I. 70; IV. 3); nor in the AV. where the forms *nārāśaṃsī́nām* 'eulogies' and *rāthajiteyī́nām* 'chariot-conquering' occur. Of the remaining 28 genitives in the RV.[8] the commonest are: *śáśvatīnām* (10), *óṣadhīnām*[9] (9), *mā́nuṣīṇām* (8), *śácīnām* (4), *īyúṣīṇām*[10] (3) 'having departed'. From the VS.: *āvyādhínīnām* (XVI. 21).

L. This case is fairly common, being formed from 30 stems (all f.) in the RV. The most frequent forms are: *óṣadhīṣu* (20), *mā́nuṣīṣu* (8), *nā́huṣīṣu* 'neighbouring', *jágatīṣu* (2) 'females', *táviṣīṣu* (2), *yahvī́ṣu* (2), *róhiṇīṣu*[11] (2). The rest occur only once each[12]. From Khila III. 15[17]: *śúddha-dantīṣu* 'white-toothed'.

---

1 This form should perhaps be read as *śréṇayas* in V. 597.

2 Also the transitions from the radical *ī-* declension *aruṇī́s* and *yātudhā́nīs* (AV.).

3 The stems forming this case in the RV. are enumerated by LANMAN 396.

4 *nā́rī-* 'woman', by shortening its final vowel, forms its D. according to the *i-* declension: *nā́ribhyas*.

5 Irregularly accented on the final of the stem, otherwise, *śáśvatī-*.

6 Or 7 including *strī́- : strīṇā́m*.

7 On the exceptions *mahī́nām* (X. 134[1]), *yatī́nām* (I. 158[6]), *devayatī́nām* (I. 36[1]), see LANMAN 398 (bottom).

8 The G. *návyasīnām* is once used in agreement with the m. *marútām*.

9 *kanī́nām*, with contracted *-yā-*, is the only G. pl. of *kanyā-* in the RV., *kanyā́nām* occurs once in the AV.; see LANMAN 399 (top).

10 Perfect participle of *i-* 'go'.

11 There is also the transfer form from the *i-* declension *svā́hākṛtīṣu*, in which the long vowel is perhaps metrical. On the other hand *strīṣú* (accent) is a transfer to the radical *ī*-declension.

12 LANMAN enumerates the stems, 399 (bottom).

4. a. Radical stems in -*i*.

379. No nominal *i*-stems are derived from roots originally ending in -*i*, as these (some six or seven) have all joined the consonant declension by adding a determinative -*t*[1]. There are, however, about a dozen stems in which *i* is probably radical in a secondary sense, as representing a reduced form of roots ending in -*ā*[2]. These are with one or two exceptions m. compounds formed with -*dhi* = *dhā-* 'put': *api-dhí-* 'covering', *ā-dhí-* 'pledge', *utsa-dhí-* 'receptacle of a spring', *uda-dhí-* 'receptacle of water', *upa-dhí-* 'part of the wheel between nave and felly', *garbha-dhí-* 'nest', *ni-dhí-* 'treasury', *pari-dhí-* 'fence', *prati-dhí-* 'cross-piece of car-pole', *pra-dhí-* 'felly', *śeva-dhí-* 'treasure', *sá-dhi-* 'abode'; perhaps also *óṣa-dhi-* f. as a shortened form of *óṣa-dhī-* 'plant'. Besides these there is *prati-ṣṭhí-* f. 'resistance', from *sthā-* 'stand', and probably the reduplicated stem *yayí-* 'speeding', in which the -*i* is secondarily reduced through the older form *yayī́-* from the -*ā* of the root *yā-* 'go'. These few stems have nothing distinctive in their inflexion, which follows that of the derivative *i*-stems in every particular.

The forms which occur from these words are the following:

Sing. N. *ā-dhí-s*, *óṣa-dhi-s*, *nidhí-s*, *pari-dhí-s*, *prati-ṣṭhí-s*, *yayí-s*, *sá-dhi-s*. — **A.** *utsa-dhí-m*, *uda-dhí-m*, *óṣa-dhi-m*, *garbha-dhí-m*, *ni-dhí-m*, *pari-dhí-m*, *pra-dhí-m*, *yayí-m*, *śeva-dhí-m*. — **I.** *yayínā*. — **Ab.** *uda-dhés*. — **Du. N.** *upa-dhī́*, *pra-dhī́*. — **Pl. N.** *óṣa-dhayas*, *ni-dháyas*, *pari-dháyas*, *prati-dháyas*, *pra-dháyas*. — **A.** *api dhín*, *uda-dhī́n*, *ni-dhī́n*, *pari-dhī́n*, *pra-dhī́n*. — **I.** *ni-dhíbhis*. — **G.** *ni-dhīnā́m*. — **L.** *ni-dhíṣu*.

4. b. Derivative stems in -*i*.

LANMAN, Noun Inflection 365—400. — WHITNEY, Grammar 335—340, 343. — Cp. REICHELT, Die abgeleiteten *i-* und *u*-stämme, BB. 25, 238—252.

380. This declension embraces a large number of m. and f. stems. There are comparatively few neuter stems; and, except the N. A. sing. and pl., neuter forms are rare, not occurring at all in several cases. The regular inflexion is practically the same in all genders, except that the N. A. sing. and pl. n. differ from the m. and f., and the A. pl. m. and f. differ from each other. There are several peculiarities here as regards the formation of the stem, the endings, and accentuation. The final vowel of the stems shows Guṇa in three of the weak cases of the singular (D. Ab. G.) as well as in the V. sing. and the N. pl. m. f., while it is abnormally strengthened in the L. sing. The normal ending -*as* of the Ab. G. sing. is reduced to -*s*, while that of the L. sing. is lost. Oxytone stems, when the vowel is changed to *y*, throw the accent on a following vowel not as Svarita but as Udātta; and even on the -*nām* of the G. pl., though the stem vowel in that case does not lose its syllabic value.

a. The only word which distinguishes strong forms is **sákhi-** 'friend', which takes Vṛddhi in its strong stem *sákhāy-*. These strong forms are frequent: **Sing. N.** *sákhā*[3], **A.** *sákhāyam*. **Du. N. A.** *sákhāyā*[4] and *sákhāyau*. **Pl. N.** *sákhāyas*. This word has two further irregularities, the simple stem *sákhi-* adding -*e* in the D. *sákhy-e*, and the abnormal ending -*ur* in the Ab. G. *sákhy-ur*. The other forms occurring are regular: **Sing. I.** *sákhyā*, **V.** *sákhe*. **Pl. A.** *sákhīn*, **I.** *sákhibhis*, **D. Ab.** *sákhibhyas*, **G.** *sákhīnām*. Eight compounds in the RV.[5] are inflected in the same way (also *sóma-sakhā*, VS. IV. 20); but of four others, which have joined the *a-* declension, there occur the forms **A.** *drāvayát-sakha-m* (X. 39[10]), **N.** *yāvayat-sakhá-s* (X. 26[5]), **A.** *patayát-sakha-m*) and *mandayát-sakha-m* (I. 4[7]).

[1] See above, stems in derivative -*t* (307).
[2] Cp. LINDNER 56 and LANMAN 453.
[3] See J. Schmidt, KZ. 29, 526, note 1.
[4] *sákhāyā* occurs 6 times (also VS. XXVIII. 7), *sákhāyau* only once.
[5] See LANMAN 400[3].

b. 1. The stem *páti-*, when it means 'husband' and is uncompounded, shows irregular inflexion in the Sing. D. and G. (like *sákhi-*) and the L.: D. *pátye*, G. *pátyur*[1], L. *pátyau*. When it means 'lord'[2] or is compounded, it is regular: D. *pátaye, bṛ́haspátaye*, G. *pátes, prajā́-pates* (TS.), L. *gó-patau*. — 2. The stem *jáni-* 'wife' also takes the abnormal ending *-ur* in the G. sing.: *jányur*[1]. This stem has the further irregularity of forming its N. sing. *jánī* according to the derivative *ī-* declension. — 3. The stem *arí-* 'devout' is irregular in forming several cases like the radical *ī-* stems (except in accentuation): Sing. A. *aryám* (beside *arím*), G. *aryás*[3]. Pl. N. A. m. f. *aryás*. The VS. has also the N. sing. *arī́s* beside the *arís* of the RV.

c. Twenty-seven stems in the RV. show forms according to the derivative *ī-* declension in the D. Ab. G. L. sing. f.[4], perhaps from a desire to add a distinctively f. ending in a declension which does not distinguish genders in these cases. There is a steady increase of such forms in the later Saṃhitās; thus while the RV. has only 7 datives in *-ai* from *i-* stems, the VS. has about 40.

d. In the RV. 4 or 5 stems show the influence of the *n-* declension in the incipient use of the ending *-nī* in the N. A. n. du., and *(ī)-ni* in N. A. n. pl.; and in the I. sing., stems taking the ending *-nā* are already 5 times as numerous as those adding the normal *-ā*.

Inflexion.

381. The N. sing. m. f. always takes *-s*[5], the A. simply *-m*. The D. Ab. G. V. gunate the suffix, to which the Ab. G. add only *-s* instead of *-as*. The L. sing. has an altogether abnormal form ending in *-ā* or *-au*. The N. pl. m. f. gunates the *-i*, to which the normal ending *-as* is added. The A. pl. in the m. adds *-n*, in the f. *-s*, before which the vowel is lengthened. The G. pl. always takes *-nām*, lengthening the preceding vowel. The frequent adjective *śúci-* 'bright' may be used to illustrate the forms actually occurring in the three genders:

Sing. N. m. f. *śúcis*, n. *śúci*. A. m. f. *śúcim*, n. *śúci*. I. m. *śúcyā, śúcinā*, f. *śúcyā, śúcī, śúci*. D. m. f. n. *śúcaye*. Ab. m. f. *śúces*. G. m. f. n. *śúces*. L. m. f. n. *śúcā, śúcau*. V. m. f. *śúce*.

Du. N. A. V. m. f. n. *śúcī*. I. m. f. n. *śúcibhyām*. D. m. *śúcibhyām*. Ab. m. f. *śúcibhyām*. G. m. f. *śúcyos*. L. m. f. n. *śúcyos*.

Pl. N. m. f. *śúcayas*. N. A. n. *śúcī, śúci, śúcīni*. A. m. *śúcīn*, f. *śúcīs*. I. m. f. *śúcibhis*. D. m. f. *śúcibhyas*. Ab. m. f. n. *śúcibhyas*. G. m. f. *śúcīnām*. L. m. f. n. *śúciṣu*.

Forms actually occurring are the following:

Sing. N. m. This form is very frequent, being made from nearly 250 stems in the RV. The commonest examples are: *agnís* (389) 'fire', *kavís* (90) 'sage', *háris* (58) 'tawny', *bṛ́has-pátis* (52) 'Lord of Prayer', *śúcis* (38) 'bright', *ṛ́ṣis* (32) 'seer', *bráhmaṇas-pátis* (23) 'Lord of Prayer', *átithis* (20) 'guest'[6].

a. The stem *ví-* 'bird', besides the regular N. *ví-s*, which occurs 6 times, has the anomalously gunated form *vé-s*[7], which occurs 5 times in the RV.

b. The pronominal forms *ná-ki-s* (50) and *mā́-ki-s* (13) 'no one' are old nominatives which have become indeclinable.

N. f. This form is frequent, being made from 136 stems in the RV. The commonest examples are: *áditis* (78) 'freedom', *su-matís* (22) 'benevolence', *rātís* (22) 'gift', *nā́bhis* (19) 'navel', *matís* (18) 'thought', *yuvatís* (18) 'maiden', *bhū́mis* (12) 'earth', *prá-matis* (11) 'providence'[8].

---

1 This ending is probably due to the analogy of the words of relationship, *pitúr* etc.; cp. KZ. 25, 289 and 242 f.

2 The VS., however, has *pátye víśvasya bhū́manas* 'lord of the whole world'.

3 Cp. BB. 25, 242; OLDENBERG, ZDMG. 54, 49—78.

4 Cp. REICHELT, BB. 25, 234—238, and J. SCHMIDT, KZ. 27, 382.

5 Except the irregular m. *sákhā* and the f. *jánī* (*jánis* in AV. XX. 48[2] is an emendation).

6 There is also the transition form from the radical *ī-* declension *véṣa-śrī-s* 'beautifully adorned' (TS.).

7 Cp. REICHELT, BB. 25, 250.

8 Also the transition forms from the *ī-* declension *araṇyā́nis, óṣadhis, naptís* (AV.), *rā́tris* (AV., VS. XXXVII. 21).

N. A. n. This form has no ending[1]. It is made from 37 stems in the RV. The commonest examples are: *máhi* (84) 'great', *bhū́ri* (47) 'much', *sv-astí* (35) 'welfare', *hā́rdi* (9) 'heart'[2]. From other Saṃhitās: *án-abhiśastī* (VS. v. 5) 'blameless', *a-mení* (VS. xxxviii. 14) 'not casting', *ásthi* (AV., VS.) 'bone', *a-sthūrí* (VS. ii. 27) 'not single-horsed', *ātma-sáni* (VS. xix. 48) 'life-winning', *éka-nemi* (AV.) 'having one felly', *krívi* (VS. x. 20) 'active' (?), *kṣatra-váni* (VS. i. 17) 'devoted to warriors', *gāyatrá-vartani* (TS. iii. 1. 10[1]; VS. xi. 8) 'moving in Gāyatrī measures', *dádhi* (AV., VS., Kh. iii. 16[2]) 'sour milk', *paśu-sáni* (VS. xix. 48) 'cattle-winning', *pṛ́śni* (AV.) 'dappled', *brahma-váni* (VS. i. 17) 'devoted to Brahmans', *loka-sáni* (VS. xix. 48) 'causing space', *vádhri* (AV.) 'emasculated', *vā́ri*[3] (VS. xxi. 61) 'choiceworthy', *sajāta-váni* (VS. i. 17) 'conciliating relations'.

A. m. This form is very frequent, being made from 205 stems in the RV. and occurring more then 1200 times. The commonest examples are: *agním* (269), *rayím* (180) 'wealth', *yónim* (61) 'receptacle', *pátim* (49) 'lord' or 'husband', *áhim* (40) 'serpent', *ádrim* (30) 'rock', *kavím* (28), *átithim* (25), *bṛ́haspátim* (25), *hárim* (24), *ūrmím* (23) 'wave', *púraṃdhim* (8) 'bountiful', *yayím* (2) '(speeding) cloud', *arím*[4] (2) 'devout'[5].

f. This is a frequent form, being made from 156 stems in the RV. and occurring more than 600 times. It is thus about half as common as the m. The examples occurring oftenest are: *su-matím* (41), *su-ṣṭutím* (35) 'excellent praise', *vṛṣṭím* (26) 'rain', *matím* (22), *rātím* (20), *bhū́mim* (19), *púraṃdhim* (5), *rayím* (4)[6].

I. m. This case is formed in two ways. 1. Five stems in the RV. add the normal ending *ā*, before which the *-i* is generally pronounced as *y*, but half a dozen times as a vowel: *pátyā* 'husband', *sákhyā*, *ūrmyā́*[7], *pavyā́* 'felly', *rayyā́*[8]. — 2. Owing to the influence of the *n*-declension 25 stems in the RV. add *-nā* instead of the normal *-ā*: *agnínā*, *áṅghriṇā* (VS. ii. 8) 'foot', *ádriṇā*, *asínā* 'sword', *áhinā*, *ūrmíṇā*, *kavínā*, *kāśínā* 'fist', *kiki-dīvínā* 'blue jay', *jamádagninā* N. of a seer, *devā́pinā* N. of a man, *dhāsínā* 'draught', *paṇínā* 'niggard', *pátinā* 'lord', *pápriṇā* 'delivering', *paridhínā* (VS. xviii. 63; TS. v. 7. 7[2]) 'fence', *pāṇínā* (VS. i. 16) 'hand', *pṛ́śninā* (Kh. iii. 15[7]), *bṛ́has-pátinā*, *maṇínā* 'gem', *yayínā*, *rayíṇā*, *raśmínā* 'rein', *vádhriṇā*, *vavríṇā* 'vesture', *vastínā* (VS. xxv. 7) 'bladder', *vṛ́ṣa-nābhinā* 'having strong naves', *vṛṣṇínā* 'strong', *śúcinā*, *sásninā* 'bountiful'.

f. This case is formed in two ways. 1. About 30 stems in the RV. add the normal ending *-ā*, before which the *-i* is pronounced as a vowel in about three-fourths of the occurrences of this form, and as *y* in the rest[9]. The forms occurring are (a) oxytones: *aśītyā́* 'eighty', *ūtyā́* 'aid', *kīrtyā́*[10] (AV.) 'fame', *paṅktyā́* (VS. xxiii. 33) a metre, *pītyā́* 'draught', *puṣṭyā́* (AV. TS.) 'prosperity', *matyā́*, *mithatyā́* 'emulation', *vasatyā́* 'abode', *vṛṣṭyā́*, *sanyā́* (VS. v. 7; TS. iv. 2. 1[2]) 'gain', *su-kīrtyā́* 'praise', *su-matyā́*, *su-ṣṭutyā́*, *svastyā́* (VS.

[1] The only *i*- stem taking *-m* is the pronominal *kí-m*, probably owing to the false analogy of *ká-m*.

[2] Lanman 377 enumerates the forms.

[3] The Pada text reads *vā́ri*. According to BR. *vā́ry ā́* here stands for *vā́ryam ā́*.

[4] Also *aryám* formed like a radical *ī*-stem (though differently accented).

[5] There are also the transitions from the *ī*-declension *pṛ́thim* and *sóbharim*.

[6] Also the transfers from the *ī*- declension *araṇyānim*, *oṇím*, *óṣadhim*, *rā́trim* (AV.), *snīhitim* (SV.).

[7] Pronounced *ūrmiā́*, sometimes also *pátiā*, *sákhiā*.

[8] *ghṛ́ṇīva* (ii. 33[6]) possibly stands for *ghṛ́ṇī-iva* (Pada *-i-iva*), *ghṛ́ṇī* then possibly being a contracted I. for *ghṛ́ṇyā*; cp. Lanman 379 (middle).

[9] On the other hand *-yā* is pronounced 5 times as often as *-iā* in the AV.; see Lanman 380.

[10] All the Mss. but one read *kírtyā* or *kīrtyā*; see Whitney's note on x. 6[27].

viii. 15; TS. i. 4. 44[1]); **(b) otherwise accented:** *abhi-śastyā* (AV.) 'curse', *árātyā* (AV.) 'malignity', *ávartyā* 'distress', *aśányā* 'thunderbolt', *ákūtyā* 'purpose', *ábhūtyā* 'ability', *íṣṭyā* 'sacrifice', *jálpyā* 'whispering', *tŕptyā* (AV.) 'satisfaction', *tvíṣyā* 'brilliance', *devá-hūtyā* 'invocation of the gods', *dhrā́jyā* 'impulse'; *nā́bhyā* (VS. xxv. 9), *pā́rṣṇyā* 'heel', *púraṃdhyā*, *púṣṭyā* (TS. iii. 1. 5[1]), *prá-matyā*, *bhū́tyā* (AV.) 'growth', *bhū́myā*, *rámhyā* 'speed', *rījyā* 'direction', *rúcyā* (AV.) 'lustre', *vícyā* 'seduction', *śáktyā* (VS. xi. 2; TS. iv. 1. 5[3]) 'power', *sú-bhūtyā* (AV.) 'welfare', *sŕṇyā* 'sickle', *svádhityā* (AV.) 'knife', *hárṣyā* 'excitement'.

2. **A contracted form in** *-ī*[1] is made by 35 stems in the RV. and occurs more than twice as often as the uncontracted *-yā*. The forms occurring are: *á-cittī* 'thoughtlessness', *á-prabhūtī* 'little effort', *a-vyathī́* 'sure-footedness', *ā́hutī* 'oblation', *ūtī́*, *ṛju-nītī́* 'right guidance', *cíttī* 'understanding', *júṣṭī* 'favour', *dī́dhitī* 'devotion', *du-ṣṭutī́* and *dú-ṣṭutī* 'faulty hymn', *dhītī́*[2] 'thought', *ní-śitī* 'kindling', *pári-viṣṭī* 'attendance', *puró-jitī* 'previous acquisition', *prá-ṇītī* 'guidance', *prá-bhūtī* 'violence', *prá-yatī* 'offering', *prá-yutī* 'absence', *matī́*, *vartanī́* 'felly', *viṣṭī́* 'effort', *vī́tī* 'enjoyment', *vṛṣṭī́*, *śaktī́* and *śáktī*, *śruṣṭī́*[3] 'willingness', *sá-hūtī* 'joint invocation', *su-dītī́* 'bright radiance', *sú-nītī* 'good guidance', *su-matī́*, *sú-mitī* 'being well fixed', *su-śastī́* (Kh. ii. 10[2]) 'good recitation', *su-ṣṭutī́*, *hásta-cyutī* 'quick motion of the hand'. Also *su-paptanī́* (i. 182[5])[4] 'with swift flight' (in Pada with *-ī*); perhaps also the two forms *hetī́* (vi. 18[10]) 'missile' and *-iṣṭī* (i. 180[4]) 'desire', which occurring before *r-* are given by the Pada as *hetíḥ*[5] and *-iṣṭiḥ*.

a. This form is further **shortened to** *-i* in about a dozen words[6] in the RV., occurring altogether some 25 times: *iṣáṇi* 'setting in motion', *úpa-śruti* 'giving ear to', *upā́bhṛti* 'bringing near', *tri-viṣṭí* 'thrice' (= adv.), *ni-tikti* 'haste', *prá-yukti* 'impulse', *váṣaṭ-kṛti* 'exclamation vaṣaṭ', *sadhá-stuti* 'joint praise', *su-vṛktí* 'excellent praise', *su-śastí* 'good praise', *sv-astí*, *havíṣ-kṛti* 'preparation of the oblation'. Perhaps also *á-smṛti* (AV. vii. 106[1]) 'through forgetfulness'.

b. A few forms follow the analogy of the m. in **adding** *-nā*: *dhāsínā* 'abode', *nā́bhinā*, *prétinā* (VS. xv. 6) 'advance'.

n. There is no certain instance of a neuter I.: *śúcinā* (ii. 38[8]) is perhaps an example, but it may be taken as a masculine.

D. m. The stem regularly takes Guṇa before adding the normal ending *-e*; e. g. *ŕṣay-e*. This is a form of frequent occurrence, being made from 44 stems in the RV. The commonest examples are: *agnáye* (48), *átraye* (12) N. of a seer, *sanáye* (12), *gŕ́ṣvaye* (6) 'gladdening', *dabhī́taye* (5) N. of a man[7]. From the VS.: *brā́hmaye* 'holy', *bhuvantáye* (xvi. 19) 'earth-extender' (?), *vṛṣṭi-vánaye* (xxxviii. 6) 'rain-winning', *sandháye* (xxx. 9) 'agreement'.

a. The only two stems not taking Guṇa are *páti-* 'husband' and *sákhi-*, which make *pátye* and *sákhye*[8]. When compounded *páti-* 'lord' forms its D. regularly as *-pataye*; e. g. *bŕ́has-pátaye*[9], *prajā́-pataye* (VS. xi. 66) 'Lord of Creatures', *aṃhasas-pátaye*

1 This form is, except in two instances, written with *y* before *ā*, but is to be read with hiatus; it coalesces in the written text with *i* or *ī*, but is not always to be so pronounced.

2 This is the only contracted form occurring in the independent parts of the AV.

3 The form *sadhrī́* (ii. 13[2]) is probably an adverb 'to the same goal' from *sádhri-* (Lindner p. 112), or it might be an inst. f. of *sadhri-* (Lanman 380[3]).

4 See RPr. vii. 15.

5 Cp. Lanman 380[4].

6 These occur eight times at the end of a line or stanza, four times at the end of an internal Pāda before vowels, two or three times within a Pāda before vowels.

7 The stems which form this dative are enumerated by Lanman 382.

8 These words are never pronounced as *pátie* and *sákhie*.

9 This is the only compound in the RV. formed with the D. of *páti-*.

(VS. VII. 30) 'Lord of distress', *bhúvana-pataye* (VS. II. 2) 'Lord of the world', *bhúva-pataye* (VS. II. 6) 'Lord of the atmosphere', *vācás-pátaye* (VS. VII. 1) 'Lord of speech', *saṃveśá-pataye* VS. II. 20) 'Lord of rest'; also in the expressions *kṣétrasya pátaye* (AV.) 'Lord of the Field' and (*bhūtásya pátaye* (AV.) 'Lord of the world', which are virtually compounds[1]; similarly *diśā́m pátaye* (VS. XVI. 17)[2]; but *pátye*[3] *viśvasya bhū́manas* (VS. XVII. 78) 'Lord of all the earth'.

f. This form is made like the m.; e. g. *iṣṭáy-e*. It is very frequent, being formed from 50 stems and occurring over 500 times in the RV. The commonest examples are: *ūtáye* (88), *pītáye* (67), *sóma-pītaye* (49) 'draught of Soma', *vā́ja-sātaye* (34) 'winning of booty', *sātáye* (34) 'acquisition', *vītáye* (31), *devá-vītaye* (22) 'feast for the gods', *iṣṭáye* (20) 'impulse'[4].

a. The form *ūtī́* is frequently used as a dative, similarly *án-ūtī* 'no help' once and *vītī́* twice. *svastí* occasionally has this value at the end of a Pāda and when it alternates with *svastáye* in V. 51[12. 13], but it may be intended for an adverb[5].

b. In the RV. seven stems in *-i* (all but 2 of which occur in Maṇḍala X), follow the analogy of derivative *ī-* stems and take the ending *-ai*: *turyái* 'victory', *devá-hūtyai* 'invocation of the gods', *nírṛtyai* 'dissolution', *puṣṭyái*, *bhujyái* 'favour', *bhṛtyái* 'support', *śrútyai* 'blessing'. The AV. forms such datives from at least 11 stems; the TS. has *á-samartyai* (III. 3. 8²) 'non-injury', *dúr-iṣṭyai* (III. 2. 8³) 'failure in sacrifice', *śáktyai* (IV. 1. 1¹); the VS. has nearly 40: *á-kṣityai* (VI. 28) 'imperishableness', *áditya*i (I. 30) 'Aditi', *ánu-matyai* (XXIV. 32) 'assent', *á-bhittyai* (XI. 64) 'not bursting', *abhi-śastyai* (II. 5), *á-bhūtyai* (XXX. 17) 'wretchedness', *á-rāddhyai* (XXX. 9) 'mischance', *á-riṣṭyai* (II. 3) 'safety', *áva-ṛtyai* (XXX. 12) 'distress', *á-hantyai* (XVI. 18) 'non-killing', *ā́kūtyai* (IV. 7), *ā́rtyai* (XXX. 9. 17) 'trouble', *útkrāntyai* (XV. 9) 'upstriding', *étyai* (XXVII. 45) 'arrival', *kṛṣyái* (IX. 22) 'tillage', *dúr-iṣṭyai* (II. 20), *dhrā́jyai* (VI. 18), *nā́bhyai* (XXXIX. 2), *níṣkṛtyai* (XXX. 9) 'atonement', *paṅktyái* (XIII. 58), *práti-ṣṭhityai* (XV. 10) 'firm footing', *prá-sityai*[6] (II. 20 'attack', *prā́yaś-cittyai* (XXXIX. 12) 'expiation', *prétyai* (XXVII. 45), *bhū́tyai* (XII. 65), *bhū́mya* (XXIV. 26), *matyái* (XXIV. 39), *mahyái* (XXII. 20), *rayyái* (IX. 22), *víviktyai* (XXX. 13) 'separation', *vṛ́ṣṭyai* (XVIII. 28), *védyai* (XIX. 16) 'altar', *vyùṣṭyai* (XXII. 34) 'dawn', *vyṛ̀ddhyai* (XXX. 17) 'failure', *śā́ntyai* (III. 43) 'quiet', *su-kṣityái* (XXXVII. 10) 'secure dwelling', *hetyái* (XVI. 18) 'missile'.

n. The only form which seems to occur is *śúcaye*.

Ab. m. The stem takes Guṇa, to which *-s* only, instead of *-as*, is added; e. g. *ádres*. It is not common, being formed from only 8 or 9 stems in the RV.: *agnés* (TS. IV. 2. 10⁴; Kh. IV. 6⁵), *áhes*, *udadhés* 'water-receptacle', *girés* 'mountain', *ghṛ́ṇes* 'heat', *tiráści-rājes* (AV.) 'striped across', *parṇa-dhés* (AV.) 'feather-holder', *prajā́pates* (TS. IV. 1. 11⁴), *plāśés* (AV.) 'intestine', *yónes*, *vṛṣā́-kapes* 'man-ape', *śatá-m-ūtes*[7] 'granting a hundred aids', *sám-ṛtes* 'conflict'.

f. This form is made in the same way as in the m. from 11 stems in the RV.: *ádites*, *ápītes* 'entering (*iti-*) into (*api*)', *abhí-śastes*, *abhí-hrutes* 'injury', *ámates* 'indigence', *árātes*, *ā́hutes* (AV.), *dhāsés* 'abode', *dhūrtés* 'injury', *nṛ́tes*[8] (AV.), *pári-ṣūtes* 'oppression', *bhū́mes* (AV.), *vasatés*, *srutés* 'course'.

a. The RV. has three forms according to the derivative *ī-* declension: *nā́bhyās* (X. 90¹⁴), *bhū́myās* (I. 80⁴), *hetyā́s* (X. 87¹⁹). Besides these the AV. has: *á-bhūtyās*, *á-rātyās*, *á-śastyās* 'imprecation', *ā́hutyās*, *kṛṣyā́s*, *deva-hetyā́s* 'divine weapon', *śīrṣaktyā́s* 'headache'; probably also *yónyās* in *yónyeva* (VI. 121⁴) for *yónyā iva*.

G. m. The regular form of this case is identical with that of the Ab., but is much more frequent, being made from 42 stems in the RV. The commonest examples are: *agnés* (55), *vés* (14), *ádres* (10), *paṇés* (8), *bṛ́has-pátes* (6), *sūrés* (5) 'patron', *átres* (4), *kavés* (4), *dhāsés* (4) 'draught', *bhū́res* (4); *pátes* 'lord'

[1] Equivalent to *kṣetra-pati-* (K.) and *bhūta-páti-* (AV.).

[2] And a number of other epithets in VS. XVI. 17—23.

[3] *pátye* otherwise means 'husband'.

[4] LANMAN 382 enumerates the stems which take this dative.

[5] Cp. LANMAN 383 (top).

[6] Used in the sense of the ablative with *pāhi* 'protect from'.

[7] Cp. RICHTER, IF. 9, 5.

[8] This form *nṛ́tes* is probably an error for *dṛ́tes* 'skin'; see WHITNEY's note on AV. VI. 18³.

occurs once. Elsewhere are found: *jamád-agnes* (VS. III. 62; Kh. V. 3[6]), *prajā́pates* (TS. III. I. 4[1]; Kh. III. 15[13]), *yayés*[1] (Kh. I. 10[2]).

a. The two stems *ari-* and *ávi-* 'sheep' do not take Guṇa, and add the normal ending *-as*: *aryás*[2] which occurs nearly 40 times, and *ávyas* which occurs nearly 20 times. The stem *páti-*, when meaning 'husband', and *sákhi-* do not take Guṇa either, but add the anomalous ending *-ur*: *pátyur, sákhyur*[3].

f. This case, identical in form with the m., is made from 11 stems in the RV.: *ádites, abhí-śastes, ámates, iṣṭés, kṛṣṭés* 'tillage', *devá-vītes, nírṛtes, puṣṭés, pṛ́śnes, vṛṣṭés, vratátes* 'creeper'. This form is also made by at least 8 stems in the AV.

a. Six stems in the RV. form genitives according to the derivative *ī-* declension, occurring 17 times altogether: *ánu-matyās, árātyās, nírṛtyās, pṛ́śnyās, bhū́myās, yuvatyā́s*. In the AV. such forms are made from at least 16 stems and occur over 50 times: *jāmyā́s* 'akin' etc. One of these, *ádityās,* occurs also in the TS. (I. 6. 5[1]) and VS. (I. 11).

n. The only example is *bhū́res*, which occurs 16 times.

L. This case in all genders ends very anomalously in *-ā* or *-au*. The latter. ending occurs more than twice as often as the former in the RV. (272 times to 126), while in the N. A. dual *-ā* is nearly 7 times as frequent as *-au* (1145 times to 171)[4]. The general conditions under which the parallel L. forms *-ā* and *-au* occur[5] are the same as apply to the dual *-ā* and *-au*: *-ā* appears before consonants, *-au* (as *-āv*) before vowels, e. g. *vír yónā vasatā́v iva* (IX. 62[15]) 'a bird in the receptacle as in a nest'. But while the dual *-ā* is the regular form at the end of a Pāda, the L. *-au* is almost exclusively found in that position[6]. As in the dual N. A. and the perfect sing. 1 and 3, the *ā*-form is doubtless the earlier. It is most probably derived from a locative form with Guṇa (like the D. Ab. G. V. sing.), e. g. **agnáy-i*, which dropped the ending (like some other locatives), **agnáy* then losing its *y*[7] before consonants and lengthening its *-a*: *agnā́*. The later form *agnáu* must have been due to the influence of the *u-* stems, the inflexion of which is closely parallel to that of the *i-* stems, through the Sandhi form *-ā* which is common to both[8].

m. 1. The *-ā* form is made from 7 stems and occurs 40 times in the RV.: *agnā́, ājā́* 'contest', *ūrmā́, kukṣā́* 'belly', *ghṛ́ṇā, yónā, su-rabhā́*[9] 'fragrant'. The AV. TS. VS. have no *-ā* form in independent passages, but Kh. III. 15[19] has *agnā́*.

2. The form in *-au* is taken by 27 stems in the RV.: *agnáu, ádrau, aratáu*[10] 'manager', *aratnáu* 'elbow', *ājáu, āṇáu* 'pin of the axle', *ūrmáu, gábhastau* 'hand', *giráu, gó-patau* 'lord', *jīráu*[11] 'stream', *tṛkṣáu* N. of a prince, *dhvasánau* 'sprinkler', *námucau* N. of a demon, *nī́pātithau* N. of a man, *paṇáu, pṛt-sutáu* 'hostile attack', *médhyātithau* N. of a seer, *yajñá-patau* 'lord of sacrifice', *yónau, ráthavītau* N. of a man, *vánas-pátau*[12] 'lord of

---

1 Emendation for *yaydis*.

2 Once or twice to be pronounced *ariás*.

3 Cp. WACKERNAGEL, KZ. 25, 289 f.

4 Cp. LANMAN 514.

5 See LANMAN 385 ff.; and cp. for the dual 340 ff. and 574—576.

6 The L. *-ā* appears only 5 times at the end of a Pāda, and then only in the two forms *devátātā* and *sárvatātā*.

7 Cp. the N. *sákhā* for **sákhāy*. The old L. may be preserved in feminines like *agnā́y-ī-* 'she who is beside Agni'; cp. IF. 12, 3.

8 Cp. MERINGER, BB. 16, 224.

9 LANMAN 388[2], suggests the possibility of restoring *ājáyi* in I. 112[10] and *yónayi* in X. 46[6]. The n. L. *a-pratā́* is used adverbially = 'without recompense' (VIII. 32[16]); cp. BARTHOLOMAE, IF. 9, 255 f.

10 BR. would read *aratnáu*.

11 *jīrí-* may be f. as there is nothing to show the gender of the word.

12 The form *vánaspátau* occurs in Kh. II. 10[5] also.

the forest', *śalmaláu* 'silk-cotton tree', *sánitau* 'attainment', *sáṃvaraṇau* 'descendant of Saṃvaraṇa', *syūma-raśmau* N. of a man, *svádhitau*. The AV. also forms the L. in *-au* from at least 16 stems; among them appears the uncompounded *pátau* (AV. III. 18³) 'husband'[1] as a variant for *jáne* in the corresponding passage of the RV. (x. 145⁴). The TS. has *áhau* (v. 6. 1² = AV. III. 13¹).

f. 1. The form in *-ā* is made from 21 stems in the RV.: *avánā* 'river-bed', *ājá*, *úditā* 'sunrise', *kṣétra-sātā* 'acquisition of land', *gó-ṣātā* 'winning of cows', *toká-sātā* 'attainment of offspring', *devá-tātā* 'worship of the gods', *dyumná-sātā* 'obtainment of strength', *nā́bhā*, *nṛ́-ṣātā* 'capture of men', *nemá-dhitā* 'conflict', *pītā́*, *prá-bhṛtā* 'offering', *medhá-sātā* 'receiving the oblation', *yā́ma-hūtā* 'invocation by prayer', *śū́ra-sātā* 'battle', *sám-ṛtā*, *sarvá-tātā* 'perfect prosperity', *sātā́*[2], *srutā́*, *svàr-ṣātā* 'attainment of heaven'. The AV. has *nā́bhā* (VII. 62¹); and the SV. reads *śáṃtātā* 'beneficent', as a variant for *śáṃtāti* of RV. VIII. 18⁷. The TS. and VS. have no independent L. f. in *-ā*.

2. The form in *-au* is more than twice as frequent, being made from 49 stems in the RV. The commonest examples are *sātáu* (17), *vā́ja-sātau* (16), *vyùṣṭau* (16) 'flush of dawn', *abhíṣṭau* (10) 'help', *su-matáu* (14), *gáviṣṭau* (7) 'fight', *iṣṭáu* (6), *rātáu* (5), *pūrvá-hūtau*[3] (5) 'first invocation'. The AV. makes this form from 7 stems in independent passages. The TS. has *úditau* (I. 8. 12³), *pūrvá-cittau* (IV. 2. 10²) 'first thought'; the VS. *ratha-nābháu* (XXXIV. 5) 'chariot nave', *rā́trau* (XXIII. 4) 'night'; and Kh. I. 11⁴ *śū́ra-sātau*.

a. There are 5 locatives f. formed according to the derivative *ī-* declension with the ending *-ām*: *púraṃdhyām*, *bhū́myām*, *bhṛtyā́m*, *yuvatyā́m*, *sám-gatyām* 'assembly'. The AV. has 9 more: *ávyām*, *ā́kūtyām*, *cíttyām*, *devá-hūtyām*, *pṛṣṭyā́m* 'rib', *bhū́tyām*, *yónyām*, *védyām* (+ VS. XXVIII. 12), *sámityām* 'assembly'. The VS. has *sanyā́m* (VIII. 54).

b. The locative *védī*[4] occurring twice (VI. 1¹⁰; II. 3⁴) is the only one formed from an *i-* stem with the normal ending *-i* (= *védi-i*). The form *práṇītī* may also possibly be a L. in III. 51⁷.

L. n. The only form in *-ā* is *a-pratā́* (VIII. 32¹⁶) 'without recompense' (used adverbially), and the only one in *-au* is *saptá-raśmau* (AV. IX. 5¹⁵) 'seven-rayed'.

V. This case regularly gunates the final vowel in the m. and f. It is very frequent in the m., being formed from 72 stems and occurring over 1100 times in the RV. In the f. it is not common, being formed from only 11 stems and occurring only 27 times in the RV.

m. The commonest examples are: *ágne*[5] (799), *pate* (35), *bṛ́has-pate*[6] (32), *kave* (26), *brahmaṇas-pate* (17), *vanas-pate* (14), *āghṛṇe* (13) 'glowing', *sat-pate* (13) 'lord of the seat', *sakhe* (11)[7]. In Kh. I. 5⁷ the anomalously formed compound *bhuvanas-pate*[8] 'lord of the world' occurs; in the VS. *aṅghāre* (IV. 27) a guardian of Soma, *dṛ́te* (XXXVI. 18) 'bag', *drā́pe* (XVI. 47) 'causing to run', *bámbhāre* (IV. 27) a guardian deity of Soma, *bhuvas-pate* (IV. 34) 'lord of the earth', *śáteṣudhe* (XVI. 13) 'hundred-quivered', *sapte* (XXIX. 2) 'steed'.

a. The V. *sobhare* is a transfer from the *ī-* declension; and the compounds *pāvaka-śoce, bhadra-śoce, śukra-śoce* are transfers from the *-is* declension, doubtless meant to avoid the unusual form *-śocis* in the V.

---

1 The RV. has only the form *pátyau* 'husband'.

2 For this form in VI. 46¹ the SV. and VS. have the variant *sātáu*.

3 This form occurs also in AV. V. 1¹.

4 Cp. RPr. I. 28; II. 35.

5 Written with Pluti VS. VIII. 10: *ágnā̃i*.

6 Once (IX. 80¹) with double accent *bṛ́has-páte*.

7 In *mahe-mate* 'O great-souled' (Indra), the first member is anomalously gunated as well as the second; cp. *mahe-nadi* 'O great stream'.

8 Formed like *vanas-pate*.

f. The forms occurring in the RV. are: *adite, anumate, asu-nīte* 'spirit-world', *iṣṭe, upa-māte*[1] 'granting (of wealth)', *ṛjīte* 'radiant', *bhūme, mate, yuvate, satyatāte*[1] 'truth', *sv-aṅgure* 'fair-fingered'. The AV. has *darve*[2] 'spoon'; the VS. *svadhite.*

a. There is also the transfer *oṣadhe* from the *ī-* declension.

Du. N. A. V. This form ends in *-ī*[3] and can be used in all genders alike. The **m.** is very frequent, being made from 72 stems in the RV. The commonest examples are: *indrāgnī́* (78) 'Indra and Agni', *hárī* (78), *pátī* (33), *śubhás-pátī* (21) 'lords of light'. Elsewhere also occur: *sa-tátī* (TS. III. 2. 2[2]) 'continuous'; *bhū́ri-raśmī* (Kh. IV. 22[8]) 'many-rayed'; *viśva-vyáparī* (Kh. II. 22[8]) 'extending (?) everywhere'. The final vowel is shortened in *sakṣáṇi* (x. 32[1]) 'united'.

f. The forms occurring in the RV. are: *itá-ūtī* 'extending from hence', *ūtī́, ṛ́jītī, jāmī́, dárvī, dyā́vā-bhū́mī* 'heaven and earth', *dhārayát-kavī* 'protecting the wise', *púraṃdhī, bhujī́* 'patrons', *yuvatī́, vásu-dhitī* 'treasuries', *śúcī, sá-yonī* 'of the same origin', *su-prátūrtī* 'very victorious', *srutī́.*

n. The only two regular forms are *śúcī*[4] and *tigmá-hetī* (AV.) 'having a keen thrust'; also *máhi* (with shortened final)[5]. There are besides one or two secondary forms with *-nī* made under the influence of the *n-* declension: *ákṣiṇī* (AV.) 'eyes' and perhaps *háriṇī* (IX. 70[7]) from *hári*[6].

I. m. *indrāgníbhyām, dámpatibhyām* (AV.) 'husband and wife', *háribhyām.*— **f.** *vartaníbhyām, śróṇibhyām* (VS. XXV. 6) 'hips'. — **n.** *sákthibhyām* 'thighs'.

D. m. *indrāgníbhyām, índra-bṛhaspátibhyām* (VS. VII. 23) 'Indra and Bṛhaspati', *háribhyām*[7].

Ab. m. *kukṣíbhyām* (AV. VS.) *pāṇíbhyām* (AV.). — **f.** *pā́rṣṇibhyām, śróṇibhyām.* — **G. m.** *indrāgnyós, háryos.* — **f.** *yuvatyós.*

L. m. *kukṣyós, gábhastyos*[8], *háryos.* — **f.** *jāmyós; gavīnyós* (AV.) 'groins', *pā́rṣṇyos* (AV.). — **n.** *sákthyos* (VS. XXIV. 1).

Pl. N. V. This form gunates the final vowel of the stem, adding the normal ending *-as* in the m. and f.; e. g. *agnáy-as, ūtáy-as.* It is of very frequent occurrence, but is nearly twice as common in the m. as the f.

m. This form is made from 109 stems in the RV. and occurs 523 times. The commonest examples are: *kaváyas* (45), *váyas* (38), *sūráyas* (36), *hárayas* (31), *agnáyas* (27), *ádrayas* (26), *ṛ́ṣayas* (26), *śúcayas* (18), *pátayas* (16), *raśmáyas* (16), *váhnayas* (15) 'conveyers'. In the VS. also occur: *ajāváyas* 'goats and sheep' (III. 43), *vṛ́ṣa-pāṇayas* (XXIX. 44) 'strong-hoofed', *vrīháyas* (XVIII. 12) 'rice-plants'.

a. The stem *arí-*, being the only *i-* stem that does not take Guṇa, forms its N. pl. like the B group of the radical *ī-* stems (except the accent): *ary-ás,* which occurs 16 times in the RV.

b. The form *á-hrayas* 'shameless' is a transfer from the radical *ī-* declension, and *sóbharayas* 'descendants of Sobharī' from the derivative *ī-* declension.

f. This form is made from 66 stems and occurs 290 times in the RV. The commonest examples are: *ūtáyas* (42), *dhītáyas* (21), *matáyas* (20), *árātayas* (18), *rātáyas* (18), *kṛṣṭáyas* (17), *kṣitáyas* (13) 'races', *jánayas* (12), *vṛṣṭáyas* (12).

a. The stem *arí-* has the same anomalous form as in the m.: *ary-ás,* which occurs 4 times in the RV.

---

1 Agreeing with *agne.*

2 The VS. (II. 49) has *darvi* from *dárvī-* = *dárvi-*. The VS. (VIII. 43) also has *vi-śruti* which seems to be an irregular V. for *vi-śrute*; cp. pw. s. v.

3 The derivative *-i, -u* and *-ī* stems are the only ones which do not take *-ā* or *-au* in the dual.

4 Occurring in x. 85[12] and possibly IV. 56[5].

5 Occurring x. 97[54] and perhaps also IV. 56[5].

6 BR. and GRASSMANN place this form under *hárita-*.

7 No n. forms occur in the D. Ab. dual.

8 This word may be f. also.

b. About 10 *i*- stems in the RV. have also N. pl. forms according to the derivative *ī*- declension: *avánīs*[1] 'streams', *ājánīs* 'births', *ūtī́s*[1], *náktīs* 'nights', *nírṛtīs*, *níṣkṛtīs*, *púraṃdhīs*, *bhū́mīs*[1], *viśvá-kṛṣṭīs*[1] 'dwelling among all men', *sá-yonīs*. The AV. also has: *aṅgúlīs*, *ṛṣṭī́s* 'spears', *dhamánīs* 'tubes', *nā́bhīs*, *pā́rṣṇīs*, *pṛṣṭī́s*.

c. The stems *yayí*- 'speeding', *śubhrí*- 'shining', *karkarí*- 'lute' form their N. pl. according to the radical *ī*-declension: *yayíyas*, *śubhríyas* (AV.), *karkaryàs* (AV.).

d. Some *ī*-stems have transfer forms according to the *i*-declension: *ambáyas*, *aruṇáyas*, *kṣoṇáyas*; *óṣadhayas*, *śákvarayas* (TS. V. 4. 12[2]; VS. XVIII. 22). The TS. has also: *garbhíṇayas* (II. 1. 2[6]), *pátnayas* (V. 2. 11[2] etc.), *revátayas* (V. 2. 11[1]), *várūtrayas* (IV. 1. 6[2]).

N. A. n. 1. The **normal form**, in which the ending *-i* coalesces with the final of the stem to *-ī*, is made from 4 stems in the RV.: *a-pratī́*[2] 'irresistible', *krúdhmī* 'irascible', *trī́* 'three', *śúcī*. The final **vowel** of this form is further **shortened** in six stems: *apratí*, *a-sthūrí* 'not single-horsed', *jā́mi*, *bhū́ri*, *śámi*[3] 'work', *surabhí*. The AV. has also *máhi* (besides *apratí* and *bhū́ri*). The forms in *-ī* and *-i* (which are of about equal frequency) taken together occur about 50 times in the RV.

2. There is a **secondary form** (following the analogy of the *n*-stems) in *-īni*, which is taken by 4 stems having the primary form also: *apratī́ni*, *bhū́rīṇi*, *śúcīni*, *surabhī́ṇi*. These forms occur about 14 times. The AV. has also *ákṣīṇi* and *ásthīni*; the latter form occurs in the TS. as well (V. 7. 2[1]); the VS. has *śíṅgīni* (XXXIX. 8) 'entrails'.

A. m. The ending *-n* here (as in the *-a* and *-u* declension) represents original *-ns*, which in one half (42) of the total occurrences (84) of these forms in *-īn* in the RV. is preserved as *-ṃs* or (before vowels) *-ṃr*. This A. is made from 31 stems in the RV[4]. The commonest examples are *sūrī́n* (14), *vánas-pátīn* (11), *paṇī́n* (9), *raśmī́n* (6), *sákhīn* (5), *girī́n* (4)[5]. The TS. also has *ádhi-patīn* (I. 6. 6[4]) 'lords', *áhīn* (IV. 5. 1[2]; VS. XVI. 5); the VS. has *tittirī́n* (XXIV. 20) 'partridges', *lājī́n*[6] (XXIII. 8) 'parched grain', *śācī́n*[6] (XXIII. 8) 'groats'.

a. The stem *arí*- is the only one which does not take *-n*, but adds the normal ending *-as* instead, the A. *aryás* (which occurs 7 times in the RV.) being thus identical with the N. pl. The stem *ví*- in its only occurrence (I. 104[1]) in the A. pl. uses the N. pl. form *váyas*.

f. This form, which is made by adding simple *-s* (instead of *-as*), e. g. *bhū́mīs*, occurs from 42 stems in the RV. The commonest examples are ***árātīs*** (16), ***kṛṣṭī́s*** (16), ***kṣitī́s*** (8), ***carṣaṇī́s*** (7) 'people', ***púraṃdhīs*** (7), ***avánīs*** (6), ***áśastīs*** (5)[7]. The TS. has ***abhiṣṭī́s*** (V. 4. 14[2]), *ámatīs* (III. 1. 4[4]), ***yónīs*** (I. 5. 3[3]), ***vyùṣṭīs*** (IV. 3. 11[4]); and ***śácīs*** occurs in a Khila (p. 171, 6)[8].

a. As in the m., the stem *arí*- has *aryás* (occurring 4 times). Two N. forms, *citrótayas* (X. 140[3]) 'granting wonderful gifts' and *śúcayas* (AV. V. 1[3]), appear to be used for the A.

I. m.[9] This form is made with the regular ending *-bhis* from 40 stems in the RV. The commonest examples are ***ádribhis*** (43), ***raśmíbhis*** (36), ***pathíbhis*** (28) 'paths', ***háribhis*** (23), ***sákhibhis*** (15), ***sūríbhis*** (14), ***agníbhis*** (10), ***añjíbhis*** (10) 'ornaments', ***ṛ́ṣibhis*** (10), ***víbhis***[10] (9). — From the VS.: ***plāśíbhis*** (XXV. 8).

---

[1] Beside *avánayas*, *ūtáyas*, *bhū́mayas*, *viśvá-kṛṣṭayas*.

[2] The Pada text has *aprati*.

[3] BR. set up a n. stem *śámi*- beside f. *śámī*-. GRASSMANN recognizes *śámī*- only, making *śámi* always the I. sing. with shortened final vowel. Cp. the I. sing. of *śámī*- above (p. 274).

[4] LANMAN 395 enumerates the stems which take this accusative.

[5] On the Sandhi of the final *-n* in this form see LANMAN 394 f.

[6] Written with pluti in the text as *lājī́3n*, *śācī́3n*.

[7] The stems which take this form in the RV. are enumerated by LANMAN 395[3].

[8] See SCHEFTELOWITZ' note, p. 171 (bottom).

[9] No n. form occurs.

[10] Not accented as a monosyllabic stem.

f. This form is made in the same way as the m. from 48 stems in the RV. The commonest examples are: *ūtíbhis* (100), *svastíbhis* (82), *matíbhis* (37), *dhītíbhis* (27), *su-vṛktíbhis* (18).

a. The form *ūtí* is used 9 times as an I. pl. in the RV., as is shown both by the sense and by the forms agreeing with it; e. g. *tvābhir ūtī* (II. 20[2]) 'with thine aids'.
b. A transfer from the *ī*-declension is *araṇíbhis* 'tinder-sticks'.

D. m. This form is made with *-bhyas* from 9 stems in the RV.: *áśva-patibhyas* (VS. XVI. 24) 'masters of horses', *ṛ́ṣibhyas*[1], *gaṇá-patibhyas* (VS. XVI. 25) 'lords of troops', *dáśāvanibhyas* 'having ten courses', *pátibhyas*, *yátibhyas* N. of a race, *raśmíbhyas* (VS. XXII. 28), *ví-bhyas*[2], *vrā́ta-patibhyas* (VS. XVI. 25) 'lords of companies', *śúcibhyas*, *śvá-patibhyas* (VS. XIV. 28) 'masters of dogs', *sákhibhyas*, *sanibhyas*, *sandhibhyas* (VS. XXIV. 25), *sūríbhyas*.

f. *kṣitíbhyas*, *carṣaṇíbhyas*, *deva-jāmíbhyas* (VS. XXIV. 24) 'sisters of the gods'. There is also the transfer from the *ī*-declension *nā́ribhyas* 'women'.

Ab. m. This case, identical in form with the D., is made from 12 stems in the RV.: *agníbhyas*, *átribhyas*, *kavā́ríbhyas* 'niggardly', *giríbhyas*, *paṇíbhyas*, *pavíbhyas*, *plāśíbhyas*, *yónibhyas* (VS. XIII. 34), *vánas-pátibhyas*, *víbhyas*[2], *sákhibhyas*, *saníbhyas*, *sthivíbhyas* 'bushels'. — **f.** *aṃhatíbhyas* 'distresses', *aṅgúlibhyas* (AV.), *kṣitíbhyas*, *carṣaṇíbhyas*, *jánibhyas*, *dhamánibhyas* (AV.) 'blasts'. — **n.** *asthíbhyas*[3] (AV. II. 33[6]).

G. m. This form is made from 28 stems in the RV.: **(a) oxytones** are *agnīnā́m*, *kavīnā́m*, *girīṇā́m*, *carṣaṇīnā́m*, *deva-jāmīnā́m* (AV.), *nidhīnā́m* 'treasures', *paṇīnā́m*, *pathīnā́m*, *maṇīnā́m* (AV.), *mathīnā́m*[4], *rayīṇā́m*, *vāpīnā́m*[5] (AV.), *vīnā́m*, *sanīnā́m*[6]; **(b) otherwise accented:** *átrīṇām*, *dvīnām*, *áhīnām*, *ṛ́ṣīṇām*, *gandhā́rīṇām* N. of a people, *carā́ṇīnām* 'active', *tuviṣváṇīnām* 'loud-roaring', *dhúnīnām* 'roaring', *mahi-ṣvā́ṇīnām* 'very noisy', *múnīnām* 'seers', *vánas-pátīnām*, *vi-mahīnām* 'very great', *vyátīnām* 'steeds', *śúcīnām*, *sákhīnām*, *hárīṇām*, *havir-máthīnām*[7] 'disturbing sacrifices'. Also *gṛhá-patīnām* (VS. IX. 39) 'householders', *dhárma-patīnām* (VS. IX. 39) 'guardians of law'.

f. This form is made from 18 stems in the RV.[8]: **(a) oxytones:** *kavīnā́m*, *kṛṣṭīnā́m*, *kṣitīnā́m*, *carṣaṇīnā́m*, *jāmīnā́m*, *dur-matīnā́m* 'hatred', *dhautīnā́m* 'wells', *puṣṭīnā́m*, *matīnā́m*, *rayīṇā́m*, *su-kṣitīnā́m*, *su-matīnā́m*, *su-ṣṭutīnā́m*; **(b) otherwise accented:** *arā́tīnām*[9] (Kh. I. 5[5]), *úpa-stutīnām* 'invocations', *jánīnām*, *nírṛtīnām*, *márīcīnām* 'particles of light', *śúcīnām*.

L. m. This form is made with the ending *-su*, which becomes *-ṣu*, from 16 stems in the RV.: *á-kaviṣu* 'not wise', *agníṣu*, *añjíṣu*, *á-samātiṣu* 'incomparable', *ājíṣu*, *āpíṣu* 'kinsmen', *ṛ́ṣiṣu*, *khādíṣu* 'rings', *giríṣu*, *nidhíṣu*, *pathíṣu*, *pavíṣu*, *yóniṣu*, *raśmíṣu*, *śubhríṣu*, *sūríṣu*.

f. This form is made from 21 stems, all but three of which (*a-vyathí-*, *jāmí-*, *śubhrí-*) end in *-ti-*: *abhí-mātiṣu* 'plots', *a-vyathíṣu*, *iṣṭíṣu*, *ūtíṣu*, *ṛṣṭíṣu*, *kṛṣṭíṣu*, *kṣitíṣu*, *gáv-iṣṭiṣu*, *jāmíṣu*, *dív-iṣṭiṣu* 'devotions', *devá-hūtiṣu*, *páriṣṭiṣu* 'distresses', *puṣṭíṣu*, *prá-ṇītiṣu*, *prá-tūrtiṣu* 'speedy motions', *prá-yuktiṣu*, *prá-śastiṣu* (TS. I. 7. 7[1]; VS. IX. 6) 'praises', *yā́ma-hūtiṣu*, *rātíṣu*, *vyúṣṭiṣu*, *śubhríṣu*, *sātíṣu*. The form *nā́riṣu*[10] is a transfer from the *ī*- declension.

n. The only example that occurs is *bhū́riṣu*.

---

1 Once accented *ṛṣíbhyas* in Vālakhilya XI. 6, doubtless an error.

2 Not accented as a monosyllabic stem.

3 With wrong accent for *ásthibhyas*; cp. *asthábhyas* (VS. XXIII. 44).

4 Vāl. 5[8]; BR. and GRASSMANN would read *matīnā́m*, which is actually the reading of the Kashmir Ms.: SCHEFTELOWITZ, Die Apokryphen des Ṛgveda 40.

5 See WHITNEY'S note on AV. XIX. 24[6].

6 Also the numeral *trīṇā́m*.

7 In about a dozen out of 128 occurrences resolution of *-ām* to *-aam* seems necessary.

8 Resolution of *-ām* to *-aam* seems to be necessary in 4 out of 98 occurrences.

9 Wrong accent for *árātīnām*.

10 On the other hand *svā́hā-kṛtīṣu* is a transfer from this to the *ī*-declension.

5. a. Radical ū-stems.

LANMAN, Noun-Inflection 400—419. — WHITNEY, Grammar 348—352.

382. This declension comprises strictly speaking only m. and f. stems; for the few distinctively n. forms which occur are made only from stems in which the *ū* is shortened and which therefore in form belong to the *ŭ-* declension. The normal endings, as they appear in the inflexion of consonant stems, are taken throughout. The G. pl., however, adds the ending *-nām* to compound stems[1]; and the N. sing. always has *-s*.

This declension contains seven monosyllabic stems, one of which is m., five f., and one m. and f.; two reduplicated f. substantives and one adjective; and about 60 compounds, almost exclusively adjectives, made with the roots *jū-* 'speed', *dyū-* (*di̯u̯-*) 'play', *pū-* 'purify', *bhū-* 'be', *śū-* 'swell', *sū-* 'bring forth', *hū-* 'call', and with the modified forms *krū-*, *gū-* 'go', *drū-* 'run', *snū-* 'drip', which may be treated as roots. The stems occurring are: 1. **monosyllables**: m. *jú-* 'speeding', 'steed', *sū-* 'begetter'; f. *dū-* 'gift', *bhū́-* 'earth', *bhrū́-* 'brow', *sū́-* 'mother', *syū́-* 'thread' (VS.), *srū́-* 'stream'. 2. **reduplicated stems**: *juhū́-* 'tongue', *juhū́-* 'sacrificial spoon', *jógū-* 'singing aloud'. 3. **compounds** (in the alphabetical order of the roots): *apī-jū́-* 'impelling', *kaśo-jū́-* 'hastening to the water (?)', N. of a man, *dhī-jū́-* 'inspiring the mind', *nabho-jū́-* 'cloud-impelling', *mano-jū́-* 'swift as thought', *yātu-jū́-* 'incited by 'demons', *vayo-jū́-* 'stimulating strength', *vasū-jū́-* 'procuring goods', *viśva-jū́-* 'all-impelling', *sadyo-jū́-* 'quickly speeding', *senā-jū́-* 'swift as an arrow'. — *eka-dyū́-* m. N. of a seer, *kama-dyū́-* f. N. of a woman. — *agre-pū́-*[2] 'drinking first', *uda-pū́-* 'purified by water', *keta-pū́-* (VS. TS.) 'purifying the will', *ghṛta-pū́-* 'clarifying ghee', *madhu-pū́-* 'purifying itself by sweetness', *vāta-pū́-* 'purified by the wind', *viṣṇā-pū́-* m. N. of a man, *su-pū́-* 'clarifying well', *sva-pū́-* 'broom'. — *án-ābhū-* 'disobedient', *abhi-bhū́-* 'superior', *ā-bhū́-* 'present', *pari-bhū́-* 'surrounding', *punar-bhū́-* 'being renewed', *puro-bhū́-* 'being in front', *pra-bhū́-* 'excelling', *mayo-bhū́-* 'causing pleasure', *vi-bhū́-* 'far-extending', *viśvā-bhū́-* 'being everywhere', *viśvá-śambhū-* 'beneficial to all', *śam-bhū́-* 'beneficent', *sacā-bhū́-* 'associate', *su-bhū́-* 'good', *svayam-bhū́-* 'self-existing', *sv-ābhū́-* 'helping well'. — *surā-śū́-* 'exultant with liquor'. — *a-sū́-* 'not bringing forth', *a-sūsū́-* (AV.) 'barren', *nava-sū́-* 'having recently calved', *pūrva-sū́-* 'bringing forth first', *prā-sū́-* 'bringing forth', *yama-sū́-* 'bringing forth twins', *raha-sū́-* 'bringing forth secretly', *rāja-sū́-* 'king-creating', *viśva-sū́-* 'all-generating', *vīra-sū́-* 'hero-bearing', *sakṛt-sū́-* 'bringing forth once', *su-ṣū́-* 'bringing forth easily'. — *ā-hū́-* 'invoking', *u-hū́-*[3] 'crying aloud', *varṣā-hū́-* (VS.) f., *sumna-hū́-* (TS.) 'invoking favour', *su-hū́-* (VS.) 'invoking well'. — *mitra-krū́-* f. a kind of demon. — *agre-gū́-*[4] 'moving forwards'. — *raghu-drū́-* 'running swiftly'[5]. — *ghṛta-snū́-* 'dripping ghee'[6].

a. **Vocalic pronunciation.** Before vowels the *ū* has regularly a vocalic value in pronunciation. In monosyllabic stems it is always written as *-uv*; generally also in compounds even when preceded by a single consonant. In the minority of compounds (some 9 stems in the RV.) it is written as *v*, but pronounced as a vowel. In the latter instances it is always given as *u* below; e. g. *vibhvā* as *vibhúā*.

b. **Accentuation.** Except in the monosyllabic stems, which follow the general rule, the accent remains throughout on the same syllable, which is almost always the radical one.

---

1 The monosyllabic and the reduplicated stems, on the other hand, added *-ām*, as far as can be inferred from *bhuvām* and *jóguvām*, the only examples which occur.

2 *-pū-* here = *-pā-* 'drink'.

3 Perhaps an onomatopoetic word.

4 *-gū-* here = *gā-* 'go'.

5 Cp. LANMAN 402.

6 About a dozen of the above compounds (all but 3 or 4 of them being formed with *bhū-*) also shorten the final of the stem, which is then inflected like an *ŭ-* stem.

Inflexion.

383. The inflexion is identical in the m. and f. Several of the cases do not occur at all in the m., viz. Ab. L. V. sing., I. D. Ab. G. L. du., D. Ab. pl. In the monosyllabic stems several cases are wanting in both genders, viz. A. D. V. sing., and all the cases of the pl. except the N. A. G. The forms actually occurring, if made from *bhū́-* f. 'earth' and the adjectives *ā-bhū́-* 'present' and *vi-bhū́-* 'far-reaching', would be as follows:

1. **Sing.** N. *bhū́s*. I. *bhuvā́*. Ab. *bhuvás*. G. *bhuvás*. L. *bhuvi* (VS.). **Du.** N. *bhúvā*. I. *bhūbhyā́m* (VS.). L. *bhuvós*. **Pl.** N. *bhúvas*. A. *bhúvas*. G. *bhuvām* (VS.).

2. **Sing.** N. *ābhū́s*; *vibhū́s*. A. *ābhúvam*; *vibhúam*. I. *ābhúvā*; *vibhúā*. D. *ābhúve*; *vibhúe*. Ab. f. *vibhúas* (AV.). G. m. *ābhúvas*.

Du. N. A. *ābhúvā*. **Pl.** N. *ābhúvas*; *vibhúas*. A. m. f. *ābhúvas*; f. *vibhúas*. I. m. f. *ābhū́bhis*. G. m. f. *ābhū́nām*. L. m. f. *ābhū́ṣu*.

The forms actually occurring are:

Sing. N. m. *jū́s* (VS. IV. 17), *sū́s*; *eka-dyū́s*. — *uda-pū́s* (AV.), *keta-pū́s* (VS. IX. 1; TS. IV. 1. 1[3]), *madhu-pū́s* (AV.), *vāta-pū́s* (AV.). — *abhi-bhū́s*, *pari-bhū́s*, *puro-bhū́s*, *pra-bhū́s* (AV.), *mayo-bhū́s*, *vi-bhū́s* (AV.), *viśvá-śambhūs*, *śam-bhū́s* (VS. AV.), *sacā-bhū́s*, *su-bhū́s* (VS. AV.), *svayam-bhū́s*. — *sumna-hū́s* (TS. IV. 6. 3[4]), *su-hū́s* (VS. I. 30) 'invoking well'. — **f.** *bhū́s*, *sū́s*, *syū́s* (VS. V. 21); *juhū́s* (AV. VS.). — *kama-dyū́s*. — *abhi-bhū́s* (AV.), *punar-bhū́s*, *pra-bhū́s* (VS. AV.), *mayo-bhū́s*, *śam-bhū́s* (AV.). — *pra-sū́s* (AV.), *yama-sū́s*, *raha-sū́s*, *vīra-sū́s*, *su-ṣū́s*. — *varṣā-hū́s* (VS. XXIV. 38) 'frog'.

A. m. 1. *kaśo-júvam*, *mano-júvam*, *vasū-júvam*; *abhi-bhúvam* (AV.), *ā-bhúvam*, *mayo-bhúvam*, *viśvá-śambhuvam*, *śambhúvam*, *sacā-bhúvam*, *sv-ābhúvam*; **2.** *viṣṇī-púam*; *vi-bhúam*, *su-bhúam*. — **f.** *juhúam* 'sacrificial spoon'; **1.** *kama-dyúvam*, *viśva-júvam*, *sacā-bhúvam*; **2.** *a-súam*[1], *viśva-súam* (AV.), *sakṛt-súam*.

I. m. 1. *mano-júvā*, *senā-júvā*, *sv-ābhúvā*; **2.** *vi-bhúā*. — **f.** *bhuvā́*; *juhúā* 'tongue' and 'spoon'; **1.** *punar-bhúvā* (AV.), *mayo-bhúvā* (TS. I. 8. 3[1]; VS. III. 47). — **n. 1.** *mayo-bhúvā*; **2.** *su-púā* (VS. I. 3).

D. m. 1. *abhi-bhúve*, *vi-bhúve* (VS. XXII. 30), *viśvā-bhúve*, *sacā-bhúve*; **2.** *viṣṇā-púe*, *vi-bhúe*, *su-bhúe*.

Ab. f. *bhuvás*; *a-sūsúas* (AV.). — **G. m.** *śam-bhúvas*, *sacā-bhúvas*[2]. — **f.** *bhuvás*. — **L. f.** *bhuvi* (VS.). — **V. f.** *júhu* (AV.).

Du. N. A. m. *mano-júvā*; *mayo-bhúvā*, *śam-bhúvā*, *sacā-bhúvā*; *ghṛta-snúvā*[3]. — **f.** *srúvā*; *apī-júvā*; *punar-bhúvā*, *viśvá-śambhuvā*, *viśvá-śambhuvau* (VS. X. 9), *śambhúvā*, *sacā-bhúvā*. — **I. f.** *bhrūbhyā́m* (VS.). — **L. f.** *bhruvós*.

Pl. N. m. *júvas*; **1.** *á-duvas*, *ā-bhúvas*, *u-húvas*, *nabho-júvas*, *pari-bhúvas*, *mano-júvas*, *mayo-bhúvas*, *raghu-drúvas*, *vayo-júvas*, *śam-bhúvas*, V. *sacā-bhuvas* (VS. III. 47), *sadyo-júvas*, *su-bhúvas*, *sv-ābhúvas*[4]; **2.** *vi-bhúas*, *su-bhúas*; *surā-śúas*. — **f.** *dúvas*, *bhúvas*; *juhúas* 'tongues' and 'spoons'; **1.** V. *agre-guvas* (VS.), V. *agre-puvas* (VS.), *dhī-júvas*, *punar-bhúvas*, *mayo-bhúvas*, *mitra-krúvas*; V. *viśva-śambhuvas* (VS. IV. 7); **2.** *ghṛta-púas*, *nava-súas*, *pra-súas*, *vi-bhúas*, *su-bhúas*.

A. m. *án-ābhuvas*, *mayo-bhúvas*[5]. — **f.** *dúvas*, *bhúvas*; *ā-bhúvas*, *ā-húvas*,

---

[1] The transition form *a-sū́m* (VS.) under the influence of the derivative *ī-* stems also occurs. The form *ayogū́m* (VS. XXX. 5) is perhaps of the same kind.

[2] The AV. has also the transition form *punar-bhúv-ās*.

[3] Cp. LANMAN 413 (middle).

[4] There are also the transfers from the *u-* declension *á-prāyuvas*, *madhyāyúvas*, *mitrā-yúvas*, *śramayúvas*.

[5] In II. 14[3] *jū́s* is perhaps contracted for *júas*.

ghṛta-snúvas, *mayo-bhúvas*, *sanā-júvas*; *pra-súas*, *rāja-súas* (VS. x. 1) 'king-creating', *vi-bhúas*[1].

I. m. *ā-bhū́bhis*. — **f.** *juhū́bhis* 'tongues' and 'spoons'; *sva-pū́bhis*.

G. m. *jóguvām*; *yātu-jū́nām*. — **f.** *bhuvām*[2] (VS. xxxvii. 18); *pūrva-sū́nām*.

L. m. *ā-bhū́ṣu*, *puru-bhū́ṣu* 'appearing to many'. — **f.** *pra-sū́ṣu*.

5. b. Derivative *ū*- stems.

LANMAN, Noun-Inflection 400—419. — WHITNEY, Sanskrit Grammar 355—359, 362—364.

384. This declension is almost entirely restricted to f.[3] stems, which (like the derivative or B group of the radical *ī*- declension) accent the final vowel and in inflexion are practically identical with the radical stems. The f. stems which it comprises may be divided into **two groups.** The **first** contains about 18 oxytone f. substantives corresponding in several instances to m. or n. stems in *-u* accented on the first syllable: *a-grū́*- (m. *á-gru*-) 'maid', *kadrū́*- (m. *kádru*- 'brown') 'Soma vessel', *kuhū́*- (AV.) 'new moon', *guggulū́*- (n. *gúggulu*-) (AV.) N. of an Apsaras, *guṅgū́*- N. of a goddess, *camū́*- 'bowl', *jatū́*- (n. *jatu*-) (AV. VS.) 'bat', *tanū́*- 'body', *dhanū́*- (*dhánu*-) 'sandbank' (AV.), *nabhanū́*- 'well', *nṛtū́*- 'dancer', *pṛdākū́*- (m. *pṛ́dāku*-) 'serpent' (AV.), *prajanū́*- (AV.) 'organ of generation', *vadhū́*- 'bride', *śvaśrū́*- (m. *śváśura*-) 'mother-in-law', *saraṇyū́*- N. of a goddess; also *kyā́mbū*-[4] (n. *kiyā́mbu*-) an aquatic plant (AV.). The **second group** comprises oxytone f. adjectives corresponding to m. oxytones: *aṃhoyū́*- 'troublesome', *aghāyū́*- 'malicious', *apasyū́*- 'active', *abhi-dipsū́*- 'wishing to deceive', *avasyū́*- 'desiring favour', *asita-jñū́*- (AV.) 'black-kneed', *āyū́*- 'active', *udanyū́*- 'seeking water', *caraṇyū́*- 'movable', *cariṣṇū́*- 'moving', *jighatsū́*- 'hungry', *tanū́*- 'thin', *didhiṣū́*- 'wishing to gain', *dur-haṇāyū́*- 'meditating harm', *duvasyū́*- 'worshipping', *devayū́*- (VS.) 'devoted to the gods', *dravitnū́*- 'speeding', *patayālū́*- 'flying', *panasyū́*- 'glorious', *pārayiṣṇū́*- 'victorious', *pṛtanāyū́*- 'hostile', *pṛśanāyū́*- 'tender', *phalgū́*- 'reddish', *babhrū́*- 'reddish brown', *bībhatsū́*- 'loathing', *makhasyū́*- 'cheerful', *madhū́*-[5] 'sweet', *mandrayū́*- 'gladdening', *mahīyū́*- 'joyous', *mumukṣū́*- 'wishing to free', *vacasyū́*- 'eloquent', *vi-panyū́*- 'admiring', *śundhyū́*- 'radiant', *sanāyū́*- 'wishing for gain', *sūdayitnū́*- 'yielding sweetness'; also *su-drū́*- 'having good wood' (*dru*-)[6].

a. **Vocalic pronunciation.** Before vowels the *-ū* has almost invariably a vocalic value in pronunciation. It is written as *uv* in the substantives *agrū́*- and *kadrū́*-, and in adjectives when the *-ū* is preceded by *y*, also in *bībhatsū́*-[7]. Otherwise though always written as *v* it is (except four or five times at the most in the RV.)[8], here also to be pronounced as a vowel. Hence the forms written in the Saṃhitā with simple *v* are given below with *ú*.

b. **Accentuation.** The derivative *ū*-stems not only accent the final syllable[9] but

---

[1] VS. xxiv. 25 has the form *sīcā-pū́s* a kind of bird.

[2] In the V. *viśvāsām bhuvām pate*.

[3] There are only five m. forms: N. *prāśū́s* 'guest', *átapta-tanūs* 'whose body is not cooked', *sárva-tanūs* (AV.) 'whose body is entire'; A. *kṛka-dāśúam* a kind of demon; I. pl. *makṣū́bhis* 'swift'.

[4] This is the only f. stem in this declension not accented on the final vowel; but TA. vi. 4[1] has the normally accented *kyāmbū́*-.

[5] The corresponding m. in this instance is not oxytone, *mádhu*-.

[6] Also as a substantive f. 'good beam'. BR. and pw. however regard *su-drúam* as A. of a m. substantive *su-drú*- 'starkes Holz'.

[7] This is the regular practice in the TS. even when a single consonant precedes the *-ū*, e. g. *tanúv-am*; cp. IS. 13, 105 f.

[8] *tanvàs* 3 times, *camvòs* once, *tanvàm* perhaps once; cp. LANMAN 408 (top).

[9] Except the f. *kyā́mbū*- (AV.) and the two m. Bahuvrīhis *átapta-tanū*- and *sárva-tanū*-.

retain the accent on that syllable throughout their inflexion. In this respect they agree with the B group of the radical *ī*- declension and differ from the ordinary derivative *ī*- declension.

c. **Transition forms.** There is an incipient tendency here to be affected by the analogy of the derivative *ī*-stems. The only certain example in the RV. is the L. *śvaśruā́m* (X. 85[46]) for **śvaśrúi*; the I. *dravitnuā́* is perhaps another instance [1]. But the AV. has at least 10 such forms: A. *kuhū́m, tanū́m, vadhū́m*; D. *agrúvai, vadhvái, śvaśruái*; Ab. *punar-bhúvās*; G. *urvāruā́s* [2] 'gourd', *pṛdākuā́s, śvaśruā́s*; L. *tanúām*. The VS. has A. *puṃścalū́m*, D. *tanvài*, G. *tanvā̀s*.

Inflexion.

385. In the L. sing. the *-i* may be dropped in the RV. In the later Saṃhitās *-m* sometimes appears in the A. for *-am*, and *-ai*, *-ās*, *-ām* are occasionally taken as the endings of the D. G. L. respectively. The ending *-ām* appears once in the RV. also. The forms actually occurring, if made from *tanū́*- f. 'body', would be as follows:

Sing. N. *tanū́s*. A. *tanúam*. I. *tanúā*. D. *tanúe*. Ab. *tanúas*. G. *tanúas*. L. *tanúi* and *tanū́*. V. *tánu*.

Du. N. A. *tanúā*. D. *tanū́bhyām*. L. *tanúos*.

Pl. N. *tanúas*. A. *tanúas*. I. *tanū́bhis*. D. *tanū́bhyas*. G. *tanū́nām*. L. *tanū́ṣu*.

The forms actually occurring are:

Sing. N. m. *prāśū́s, á-tapta-tanūs, sárva-tanūs* (AV.). — **f.** *asita-jñū́s* (AV.), *kuhū́s* (TS. AV.), *kṛ́ambūs* [3] (AV.), *guggulū́s* (AV.), *guṅgū́s, jatū́s* (VS.), *tanū́s, dhanū́s* (AV.), *nṛtū́s, patayālū́s* (AV.), *pṛdākū́s* (AV.), *phalgū́s* (VS. XXIV. 4), *madhū́s* (AV.), *vadhū́s, śundhyū́s, śvaśrū́s, saraṇyū́s*.

A. m. *kṛkadāśúam* [4]. — **f.** *cariṣṇúam, jighatsúam* (AV.), *tanúam* [5], *pṛdākúam* [6] (AV.), *vadhúam, su-drúam* [7]; *avasyúvam, dur-haṇāyúvam, deva-yúvam* (VS. I. 12), *makhasyúvam, vacasyúvam, śundhyúvam, su-drúvam* (SV.). — **With ending *-m*** for *-am*: *kuhū́m* (TS. AV.), *tanū́m* (TS. AV.), *puṃś-calū́m* (VS. XXX. 5), *vadhū́m* (AV.; Kh. IV. 5[1]).

I. f. *tanúā* [8], *vadhúā; duvasyúvā*. — **D. f.** *tanúe* [9]. — **With ending *-ai***: *agrúvai* (AV.), *tanvài* (VS. XXIII. 44), *babhrvái* (VS. XX. 28), *vadhvái* [10] (AV.), *śvaśruái* (AV.). — **Ab. f.** *kadrúvas; tanúas*.

G. f. *agrúvas, śundhyúvas; tanúas* [11], *vadhúas*. — **With ending *-ās***: *tanvā̀s* (VS. III. 17), *pṛdākuā́s* (AV.), *śvaśruā́s* (AV.).

L. f. *camúi, tanúi* [12]. — **Without ending:** *camū́* [13], *tanū́* [14]. — **With ending *-ām***: *śvaśruā́m; tanvā̀m* [15] (AV.), *tanúvām* [16] (TS. I. 7. 12[2]).

V. f. *bábhru, vádhu*.

---

[1] Because the accent is shifted to the ending as in the derivative *ī*- declension; cp. Lanman 404.

[2] See Lanman 411[1].

[3] The TA. has the normal accentuation *kyāmbū́-*; the corresponding stem in the RV. is *kiyā́mbu-* n.

[4] That the word is m. is probable because *sárvam* seems to agree with it (I. 297). The A. m. *ábhīruam* 'fearless' is a transfer from the *u*- declension.

[5] The AV. has *tanvàm* once, *tanúam* 16 times. The TS. regularly has *tanúvam* (I. 8. 10[2], etc.).

[6] The Mss. all read *pṛdākvàm*; see Whitney's note on AV. X. 4[17].

[7] As an adj. in VII. 32[20], 'made of good wood'; as a subst. in X. 28[8] 'good beam'.

[8] The AV. has *tanúā* 4 times, *tanvā̀* 5 times. The TS. has *tanúvā* (I. 1. 10[1] etc.) In RV. X. 24[1] *camū́* is once perhaps a contracted I.; see Lanman 409 (top).

[9] The AV. has *tanúe* 6 times, *tanvè* 7 times. The TS. has *tanúve*.

[10] The AV. has *vadhvái* and *vadhuái* once each.

[11] The AV. has *tanúas* 10 times, *tanvàs* 4 times. The TS. has *tanúvas*.

[12] Three or four times *tanúī*, metrically lengthened (the Pada has *i*); cp. Lanman 411 (bottom). The TS. (IV. 3. 13[1]) has *tanúvi*.

[13] *camū́* occurs 6 times, *camúi* once.

[14] *tanū́* occurs once, *tanúi* 3 times.

[15] This should doubtless be read *tanvā̀m*; see Lanman 412.

[16] This form in TS. IV. 2. 6[3] is a variant for the G. sing. *tanvàs* of RV. X. 97[10].

Du. N. A. f[1]. *camúā, tanúā.* — D. f. *hanúbhyām*[2] (TS. VII. 3. 16[1]). — L. *camúos*[3].

Pl. N. f. 1. *agrúvas; camúas, jatúas* (AV.), *tanúas*[4], *pṛdākúas* (AV.), *prajanúas* (AV.). — 2. *aṃho-yúvas, apasyúvas, avasyúvas, āyúvas, udanyúvas, caraṇyúvas* (AV.), *didhiṣúas, panasyúvas, pārayiṣṇúas, pṛtanāyúvas, pṛśanāyúvas, bībhatsúvas, makhasyúvas, mandrayúvas, mahīyúvas, mumukṣúas, sanāyúvas, sūdayitnúas.* — *yuva-yús* (IV. 41[8]), agreeing with N. f. *dhíyas*, appears to be a contracted form for *-yú-as*[5].

A. f. 1. *agrúvas; tanúas*[6], *nabhanúas, vadhúas*[7]. — 2. *abhi-dipsúas, dravitnúas; vi-panyúvas, śundhyúvas*[8]. — I. m. *makṣúbhis*[9]. — f. *tanúbhis.* — D. f. *tanúbhyas.* — G. f. 1. *tanúnām, vadhúnām* — 2. *aghāyúnām*[10] (AV.), *babhrúṇām, bībhatsúnām.*

L. f. 1. *camúṣu, tanúṣu.* — 2. *babhrúṣu.*

6. a. Radical *u-* stems.

386. There are not many *u-* stems derived from roots originally ending in *-u*, as several of these (about nine) have joined the consonant declension by adding the determinative *-t*[11]. Some eight stems are, however, formed from roots in *-u*, all of them but one (*dyú-*) being compounds. These are: *dyú-* 'day', *abhí-dyu-* 'heavenly'; *mitá-dru-*[12] 'firm-legged', *raghu-drú-* 'running swiftly'; *á-prā-yu-*[13] 'assiduous'; *ádhri-gu-*[14] 'irresistible', *vanar-gú-* 'forest-roaming'; *su-ṣṭú-* 'highly praised'[15]. There are besides some 12 stems in which *u* is radical in a secondary sense as representing the shortened form of the vowel of three roots ending in *-ū*[16]. These are: *dhī-jú-* 'inspiring the mind', from *jū-* 'impel'; *su-pú-* 'clarifying well', from *pū-* 'purify'; and compounds of *bhū-* 'be': *á-pra-bhu-* 'powerless', *abhi-bhú-* 'superior', *ā-bhú-* 'empty', *ud-bhú-* 'persevering', *pari-bhú-* 'surrounding', *puru-bhú-* 'appearing in many places', *pra-bhú-* 'powerful', *mayo-bhú-* 'delighting', *vi-bhú-* 'far-extending', *śam-bhú-* 'beneficent', *su-bhú-* 'good'.

387. The inflexion of these words is identical with that of derivative *u-* stems. Forms which occur are the following:

Sing. N. m. *ádhri-gus, á-pra-bhus, pra-bhús, mayo-bhús, mitá-drus, vanar-gús, vi-bhús, śam-bhús*[17]. — n. *á-pra-bhu, á-prāyu, ā-bhú, ud-bhú* (AV.), *pra-bhú, mayo-bhú, raghu-drú, vi-bhú, śam-bhú, su-bhú.*

A. m. *ádhri-gum, abhí-dyum, abhi-bhúm* (AV.), *ā-bhúm, pra-bhúm, vi-bhúm*[18].

I. m. *mayo-bhúnā.* — n. *su-púnā* (AV.).

---

1 There are also two m. transfers from the *u-* declension, *madhūyuvā* and *paśvā*; cp. LANMAN 403 and 413 (mid).

2 This is really a transition form from the derivative *u-* declension.

3 *camúos* occurs 14 times, *camvòs* possibly once (IX. 96[21]).

4 Once *tanvàs*; see LANMAN 408 (top). The TS. has *tanúvas.*

5 On *ratha-yús* (X. 70[5]) standing possibly for *-yús* = *yú-as*, see LANMAN 415[2].

6 RV. 20 times, AV. 3 times *tanúas*; RV. twice, AV. once *tanvàs*. The TS. has *tanúvas*. On WEBER's conjecture (IS. 13, 58) *viśvàs* as A. pl. of **viśú-* see LANMAN 416[3].

7 The Mss. of the AV. once read *badhvàs* (= *vadhúas*).

8 On *ratha-yús* (VII. 2[5]) for *-yús* = *yúas*, see LANMAN 416[3]. The VS. (XXI. 25) has *jatús.*

9 This is only a metrical lengthening of the stem vowel (Pada *ŭ*).

10 Cp. LANMAN 418[3].

11 See above, stems in derivative *-t* (307).

12 From *dru-* 'run'. On *sádru-* see WHITNEY's note on AV. XV. 7[1].

13 From *yu-* 'separate', 'keep away'.

14 'going unrestrained', from *gu-* 'go' = *gā-*.

15 The words *sabar-dhú-* 'yielding nectar', and *á-smṛta-dhru-* 'not caring for enemies', seem to be compounded with *-duh* (*-dhuk*) and *-druh* (*-dhruk*: see pw.).

16 They are therefore transfers from the radical *ū-* declension, all the N. A. neuters of which are thus formed.

17 *sabar-dhús* (VS. V. 26; Kh. IV. 5[20]) = *sabar-dhúk.*

18 *sabar-dhúm* A. f. = *sabar-dúham.*

D. m. *ádhri-gave, abhí-dyave.*

G. m. *pra-bhós, su-ṣṭós.* — L. n. *ud-bháu* (VS. xv. 1), *mitá-drau.*

V. m. *adhri-go, pra-bho* (AA. iv. 1 = Kh. v. 4)[1].

Du. N. A. V. m. *ádhri-gū*[2], *abhí-dyū* (Kh. i. 3[4]), *pari-bhú* (AV.), *puru-bhú, puru-bhū, vanar-gú, śam-bhú, śam-bhū.*

Pl. N. m. *ádhri-gāvas*[3], *abhí-dyavas, dhī-jávas, mitá-dravas*[4], *vi-bhávas,* V. *ví-bhv-as*[5]. — n. *mayo-bhú.*

A. m. *mayo-bhún, dyún, vi-bhún* (VS. xx. 23).

I. m. *dyúbhis; á-prā-yubhis, abhí-dyubhis, vanar-gúbhis* (AV.), *vi-bhúbhis.*

6. b. Derivative *u-* stems.

LANMAN, Noun-Inflection 400—419. — WHITNEY, Sanskrit Grammar 335—346.

388. This declension embraces a large number of nouns of all genders. The masculine stems greatly preponderate, being about four times as numerous as the feminine and neuter stems taken together; while the neuters considerably outnumber the feminines. Thus the N. and A. sing. are formed by about 430 stems in the m., by 68 in the n., and by 46 in the f. in the RV. The normal inflexion which is practically the same in all genders, except the N. A. sing. du. pl. n., is closely parallel to that of the *i-* stems (380). The stem takes Guṇa in the same cases; but while in the *i-* declension only one word (*arí-*) ever uses the unmodified stem, 8 or 9 words may do so here. The endings, too, are closely analogous; but while in the *i-* declension the ending of the L. sing. is always dropped, it is here retained in several words; and while the *n-* declension has affected only the I. sing. of the *i-*declension, it has here affected all the other cases of the singular which take vowel endings. Finally, the accentuation is exactly parallel to that of of the *i-* stems.

a. Adjectives in *-u* often use this stem for the feminine also; e. g. *cáru-* 'dear'; otherwise they form the f. in *-ū*, as *tanú-* m., *tanū́-* f. 'thin'; or in *-ī*, as *urú-* m., *urv-ī́-* f. 'broad', *pṛthú-* m., *pṛthv-ī́-* f. 'broad', *bahú-* m., *bahv-ī́-* f. 'much', *mṛdú-* (AV.) m., *mṛdv-ī́-* (VS.) f. 'soft'.

b. The 8 stems which are analogous to *arí-* in having forms that attach the normal endings to the unaltered stem are: *paśú-, pitú-; kṛ́tu-, krátu-, mádhu-, vásu-, śíśu-, sahásra-bāhu-.*

c. Oxytone stems when the final vowel is changed to *v*, throw the accent on a following vowel not as Svarita but as Udātta; they also shift it to the *-nām* of the G. pl. even though the stem vowel does not in that case lose its syllabic value; e. g. *paśū-nā́m.*

d. Transition forms. 1. There are in the RV. only three forms which follow the analogy of the derivative *ī-* declension: D. *iṣv-ai*, G. *iṣv-ās, su-vā́stv-ās*, all in late passages; the AV. also has *rájjv-ām*[6]. — 2. Transitions to the *ū-* declension appear in the A. *á-bhīrvam*, from *á-bhīru-*, and in several words formed with the suffix *-yu* which make their N. pl. or du. as *-yuvas, -yuvā.* — 3. Besides some 46 I. forms m. and n. sing., there are several transitions to the *n-* declension in the remaining cases of the sing., all neuter forms (except the m. G. *cáruṇas*): D. *mádhune*; Ab. *mádhunas, sā́nunas*; G. *cáruṇas, dā́nunas, drúṇas, mádhunas, vásunas*; L. *ā́yuni, sā́nuni*; also a few other forms from the later Saṃhitās.

Inflexion.

389. The N. sing. m. f. always takes *-s*, the A. simply *-m*. The D. Ab. G. sing. sometimes attach the normal endings to the unmodified stem; but

1 In the f. V. *pṛthu-ṣṭo* 'broad-tufted', the *u* of the stem *stu-* = *stukā-* 'tuft' may be radical.

2 *á-smṛta-dhrū* = *ásmṛta-druhā.*

3 For *ádhri-gavas* owing to the false analogy of *gā́vas* 'cows'.

4 There are also the forms according to the radical *ū-* declension *á-prāyuvas, raghu-drúvas.*

5 See LANMAN 414[2].

6 The Mss. in AV. vi. 121[2] read *rájvām*. the only form of this word which occurs in the RV. is the N. sing. *rájjus.*

they generally gunate the stem, which then adds only *-s* instead of *-as* in the Ab. G. The L. sing. sometimes gunates the stem and adds *-i*, but generally takes Vṛddhi without an ending. The V. always gunates the stem. The N. pl. m. f. nearly always gunates the *-u*, to which the normal ending *-as* is added. The A. pl. in the m. adds *-n*, in the f. *-s*, before which the vowel is lengthened. The G. pl. always takes *-nām*, lengthening the preceding vowel. The N. A. V. du. m. f. have no ending, simply lengthening the final vowel. The adjective *mádhu-* 'sweet' may be used to illustrate the forms actually occurring:

Sing. N. m. f. *mádhus*, n. *mádhu*. A. m. f. *mádhum*, n. *mádhu*. I. m. f. n. *mádhvā*, m. n. *mádhunā*. D. m. f. n. *mádhave*, m. *mádhve*. Ab. m. f. n. *mádhos*, m. n. *mádhvas*, n. *mádhunas*. G. m. f. n. *mádhos*, m. n. *mádhvas*; n. *mádhunas*. L. m. f. n. *mádhau*, m. n. *mádhavi*, n. *mádhuni*. V. m. f. *mádho*, n. *mádhu*.

Du. N. A. V. m. f. *mádhū*, n. *mádhvī*. I. m. *mádhubhyām*. D. m. *mádhubhyām*. Ab. m. n. *mádhubhyām*. G. m. *mádhvos*, n. *mádhunos* (AV.). L. m. f. *mádhvos*.

Pl. N. V. m. f. *mádhavas*; *mádhvas*. N. A. n. *mádhū*, *mádhu*; *mádhūni*. A. m. *mádhūn*; *mádhvas*, f. *mádhūs*; *mádhvas*. I. m. f. n. *mádhubhis*. D. m. f. n. *mádhubhyas*. Ab. m. f. *mádhubhyas*. G. m. f. n. *mádhūnām*. L. m. f. n. *mádhuṣu*.

The forms actually occurring are the following:

Sing. N. m. This form is very frequent, being made from 250 stems in the RV. and occurring nearly 900 times. The commonest examples are: *índus* (64) 'drop', *víṣṇus* (34) 'Viṣṇu', *su-krátus* (32) 'skilful', *vásus* (25) 'good', *ketús* (23) 'brightness', *ṛbhús* (21) 'deft', *vāyús* (20) 'wind', *viśvā́yus* (18) 'kind to all men', *sūnús* (18) 'son', *síndhus* (17) 'river', *cā́rus* (16) 'dear', *asmayús* (16) 'desiring us', *devayús* (15) 'devoted to the gods', *mánus* (15) 'man'. — *íṣus* 'arrow', otherwise f., is once (VIII. 66^{7}) m.

a. The form *yús* 'moving' is perhaps a corruption in VIII. 18^{13}, where BLOOMFIELD (JAOS. 1906, p. 72) would read, for *ririṣīṣṭa yúr*, *ririṣīṣṭāyúr* = *ririṣīṣṭa āyúr*.

b. In VII. 86^{3} *didṛ́kṣū́po* perhaps stands for *didṛ́kṣus*+*úpo*; but the Pada reads *didṛ́kṣu*, and desiderative adjectives otherwise accent the final syllable; cp. LANMAN 405 (bottom).

f. This form is made from 31 stems and occurs 73 times in the RV. The commonest examples are *dhenús* (22) 'cow', *síndhus* (11), *śárus* (4) 'arrow', *vasūyús* (3) 'desiring goods', *íṣus* (2), *gātús* (2) 'course', *cā́rus* (2), *jīvā́tus* (2) 'life'[1].

N. A. n. This form, which has no ending, is made from 68 stems and occurs over 400 times in the RV. The commonest examples are *mádhu* (77) ('sweetness'), *vásu* (77) 'wealth', *urú* (51) 'wide', *cā́ru* (27), *sā́nu* (18) 'summit', *pṛthú* (15) 'broad', *tri-dhā́tu* (13) 'threefold', *purú* (13) 'much'. The RV. once has *páśu* and the VS. (XXIII. 30) *paśú* 'animal'. In other Saṃhitās occur *tā́lu* (VS.) 'palate', *trápu* (AV. VS.) 'tin'.

a. The final *-u* is metrically lengthened in *purū́* (12 times), *mithū́* (twice) 'wrongly', and *urū́* (once)[2].

b. The metre seems to require the forms *ā́yu* (III. 49^{2}), *jarā́mṛtyu* (AV. XIX. 30^{1}), *jiṣṇú* (AV. III. 19^{1}), *pārayiṣṇú* (AV. VIII. 2^{28}), *bahú* (AV. XX. 135^{12}), instead of the corresponding forms with *-s*, *ā́yus* etc., of the Saṃhitā text.

A. m. This form is made from 179 stems and occurs over 700 times in the RV. The commonest examples are: *krátum* (55) 'ability', *ketúm* (34), *gātúm* (33) 'course' and 'song', *índum* (27), *śíśum* (26) 'child', *síndhum* (22),

---

[1] LANMAN 406 enumerates the stems which form this N.

[2] The Pada text here always has *purú*, *mithú*, *urú*. Cp. RPr. VII. 9, 19, 31; IX. 3.

āśúm (20) 'swift', *urúm* (18), *manyúm* (18) 'wrath', *vāyúm* (18), *aṃśúm* (17) 'shoot', *sūnúm* (17), *dásyum* (15) 'fiend', *paśúm* (15), *bhānúm* (15) 'lustre', *bhujyúm* (15) N. of a man, *śátrum* (15) 'enemy'.

f. This form is made from 15 stems and occurs 50 times in the RV.: *á-dhenum* 'yielding no milk', *aruṇá-psum* 'of ruddy appearance', *íṣum*, *krúmum* N. of a river, *cā́rum*, *jásum* 'resting-place', *jigatnúm* 'speeding', *jīrádānum* 'sprinkling abundantly', *jīvā́tum*, *dhánum* 'sandbank', *dhenúm*, *bhujyúm* 'viper', *vasūyúm*, *śárum*, *síndhum*.

I. m. This case is formed in two ways. 1. Four stems in the RV. add the **normal ending** *-ā*, before which the *-u* is almost invariably pronounced as *v*: *paraśv-ā́* 'axe', *paśv-ā́*; *krátv-ā*[1], *śíśv-ā*. — 2. Owing to the influence of the *n-* declension 30 stems in the RV. add *-nā* instead of the normal *-ā*: *aṃśúnā*, *aktúnā* 'light', *an-āśúnā* 'not swift', *a-bandhúnā* 'kinless', *índunā*, *iṣuṇā́* (Kh. IV. 7[3])[2], *urúṇā*, *ṛjúnā* 'straight', *ṛtúnā* 'fixed time', *ketúnā*, *krátunā*[3], *cetúnā* 'heed', *jiṣṇúnā* 'victorious', *tri-dhā́tunā*, *dhūmá-ketunā* 'smoke-bannered', *dhṛṣṇúnā* 'bold', *paśúnā*, *bhānúnā*, *mánunā*, *manyúnā*, *ripúṇā* 'deceiver', *vagnúnā* 'roar', *vahatúnā* 'bridal procession', *vāyúnā*, *vi-bhindúnā* 'splitting', *víṣṇunā*, *vṛ́ṣa-psunā* 'of strong appearance', *sādhúnā* 'straight', *su-cetúnā* 'benevolence', *sétunā* (TS. III. 2. 2[1]) 'bridge', *stanayitnúnā* 'thunder', *snúnā*[5] 'summit'.

f. This form is made from 7 stems in the RV. by adding the normal ending *-ā*, before which the *u* is pronounced as a vowel in five stems: *cikitvā́* (AV.), *panvā́* 'praise'; *á-dhenvā*, *íṣvā* (AV.; Kh. IV. 5 3[1]), *mádhvā*, *mehatnvā́* N. of a river, *rájjvā* (AV.) 'rope', *śárvā*, *su-sártvā* N. of a river, *hánvā* 'jaw'.

a. Six oxytone stems and also *mithu-* form instrumentals with interposed *-y-*; they are used adverbially with shift of accent to the ending: *anu-ṣṭhuyā́* 'immediately', *amuyā́* 'thus', *āśuyā́* 'quickly', *dhṛṣṇuyā́* 'boldly', *raghuyā́* 'swiftly', *sādhuyā́* 'rightly'; *mithuyā́* 'falsely'.

n. This case is made in two ways. 1. The **normal ending** *-ā* is added directly to the stem. Of this formation there is only one example: *mádhvā*[4] 'honey'. — 2. Owing to the influence of the *n-* declension 15 stems in the RV. add *-nā*: *urúṇā*, *kṛdhúnā* 'defective', *ghṛtá-snunā* 'dripping with ghee', *jarā́yuṇā* 'after-birth', *títaünā* 'sieve', *tṛṣúṇā* 'greedy', *tri-dhā́tunā*, *dā́nunā* 'fluid', *drúṇā*[5] 'wood', *dhṛṣṇúnā*, *purūrúṇā* 'far and wide', *pṛthúnā*, *mádhunā*, *vásunā*, *sā́nunā*, *svādúnā* 'sweet'.

D. m. This case is formed in two ways. 1. The ending *-e* is added to the **unmodified stem** in three words in the RV.: *krátve*[6], *śíśve*, *sahásra-bāhve*[7] 'having a thousand arms'. — 2. The ending *e* is added to the **gunated final** vowel in over 60 stems in the RV. The commonest examples are: *mánave* (36), *vāyáve* (23), *víṣṇave* (13), *manyáve* (12), *āyáve* (10) 'living', *sūnáve* (10), *dásyave* (9), *ripáve* (7), *mṛtyáve* (6) 'death', *pūráve* (5)[8] 'man'.

f. This case is made in the same way as the second form of the m. from only three stems in the RV.: *jīvā́tave*, *dhenáve*, *śárave*.

n. This case is formed in three ways. 1. The ending *-e* is added to the

---

1 Twice out of 59 occurrences pronounced *krátuā*. The form *krátvā* occurs VS. XXXIII. 72 and twice in the Khilas (III. 16[2]; V. 6[3]); and in Kh. IV. 53[6] *kartvā́* is perhaps meant for *krátvā*.

2 For the *íṣvā* of AV. V. 54.

3 The form *krátunā* occurs 12 times, *krátvā* 59 times, in the RV.

4 This form also occurs in VS. XX. 56 etc., TS. IV. 1. 8[1] (twice) and Kh. V. 6[4].

5 The words *snú-* and *drú-* are not accentuated as monosyllabic stems because they are the reduced form of the dissyllables *sā́nu-* and *dā́ru-*.

6 *krátve* also occurs VS. XIV. 8; XXXVIII. 28.

7 Pronounced *-bāhue*.

8 LANMAN 409 enumerates the stems which take this dative.

unmodified stem in one word: *páśv-e*[1]. — 2. The ending *-e* is added to the gunated stem in two words: *uráve, viśvā́yave.*

3. Owing to the influence of the *n-* declension *-ne* is added to the stem in one word in the RV.: *mádhune.* The AV. also has *kaśípune* 'mat'.

Ab. m. This case is formed in two ways. 1. The normal ending *-as* is added to the unmodified stem in one word only: *pitv-ás* 'draught'. — 2. The ending *-s* is added to the gunated stem in 20 words in the RV.: *aṃhós* 'distress', *adhvaryós* 'officiating priest', *ṛtós*, *kṛśā́nos* N. of a divine archer, *kṣipaṇós* 'archer', *gántos* 'course', *tanayitnós* 'thundering', *tanyatós* 'thunder', *devayós, ninitsós* 'wishing to blame', *pūrós, babhrós* (Kh. v. 15[11]) 'brown', *manyós, mṛtyós, ririkṣós* 'wishing to injure', *vaniṣṭhós* 'intestine', *vāyós, víṣṇos, śátros, síndhos, snós.*

f. This case is made in the same way as the second form of the m. The only two examples are: *dhános* and *vástos* 'dawn'. There is also one transition form due to the influence of the *ī-* declension: *íṣv-ās.*

n. This case is made in three ways. 1. The ending *-as* is added to the unmodified stem in one word only: *mádhvas.* — 2. The ending *-s* is added to the gunated stem: *urós, drós*[2], *mádhos* (Kh. IV. 12[1]; TS. IV. 4. 12[1]), *sā́nos, svādós.* — 3. Under the influence of the *n-* declension *-nas* is added to the stem: *mádhunas, sā́nunas.*

G. m. This case is made in two ways. 1. The ending *-as* is added to the unmodified stem in six words: *paśvás, pitvás; krátvas, mádhvas, vásvas, śíśvas*[3]. — 2. The prevailing form is made by adding *-s* to the gunated stem, and appears in 70 words. The commonest examples are[4]: *āyós* (22), *víṣṇos* (14), *síndhos* (13), *aktós* (11), *vāyós* (10), *dásyos* (8), *mános* (8), *śátros* (5), *kārós* (4) 'singer'.

a. There is a single transition form according to the *n-* declension *cā́ruṇas*, which occurs only once (VIII. 5[14]).

f. This case is formed in one way only, like the second form of the m., from 5 stems: *aktós, dhenós, vástos, saráyos* N. of a river, *síndhos.*

n. This case is made like the Ab. n. 1. *mádhvas*[5], *vásvas.* — 2. The commonest form, made from 8 stems in the RV.: *urós, kṣós* 'food', *gúggulos* (AV.) 'bdellium', *cā́ros, mádhos* (+ AV.), *vásos* (+ AV.), *vā́stos* (+ AV.) 'dwelling', *sādhós, svādós.* — 3. *cā́ruṇas, dā́nunas, drúṇas*[6], *mádhunas*[7], *vásunas*[8].

L. m. This case is formed in two ways. 1. The normal ending *-i* is added to the gunated final vowel in 7 stems: *ánavi* 'non-Aryan man', *trasádasyavi* N. of a king, *dásyavi, druhyávi* N. of a man, *pávīravi* N. of a man, *víṣṇavi, sūnávi.* — 2. More usually the ending is dropped, leaving the final stem vowel with Vṛddhi instead of Guṇa. This form of the L. is taken by 19 stems in the RV.: *aktáu* 'at night', *āyáu, uráu, krátau, caráu* 'pot', *druhyáu, párśau* N. of a man, *paśáu,*

[1] The stem *páśu-* occurs once in the N. as a neuter, and *páśve* must owing to the accent be taken as the D. of that stem; the m. stem is *paśú-*, D. *paśáve.*

[2] The form *drós* also occurs in Kh. IV. 5[11].

[3] Possibly 4 other words written with *-os*, should be pronounced with *-uas*: *dhṛṣṇúas* (X. 22[3]), *ripúas* (IV. 3[13]), *píprúas* (VI. 22[7]), *viṣṇúas* (VIII. 31[10]).

[4] LANMAN 410 gives a list of the stems taking this form of the genitive.

[5] Pronounced *mádhuas* twice out of 67 occurrences.

[6] There is no certain evidence as to the gender of *drú-* 'wood', but, as it is a reduced form of *dā́ru-* which is n., it may be assumed to be n. There is also the form *drós.*

[7] *mádhvas* occurs 67 times, *mádhos* 13 times, *mádhunas* 9 times in the RV. The VS. has all three forms in independent passages.

[8] *vásvas* occurs 38 times, *vásos* 8 times, *vásunas* 11 times in the RV.

púṣṭi-gau N. of a man, *pūtá-kratau* N. of a man, *pūráu*, *mánau* and *manáu*[1], *yádau* N. of a man, *śrúṣṭi-gau* N. of a man, *síndhau*, *sétau* 'bond', *svárau*[2] 'sacrificial post'.

f. This case is made in one way only, like the second form of the m. The only example in the RV. is *síndhau*; the AV. has *śárau*[3] and *sū́tau* 'birth'.

n. This case is formed in three ways. **1.** With the **ending** *-i* added to the gunated stem only in *sā́navi*, which occurs 9 times. When the adjective *ávya-* or *avyáya-* 'made of sheep's wool' immediately follows, the L. of this word appears as *sā́no*. The Pada here always has *sā́nau*, but as the metre requires a short syllable it seems likely that the ending has been dropped to avoid a disagreeable sequence of syllables in *sā́navy ávye*, but without leaving the lengthened form of the stem (*sā́nāv*) because of the metre. A parallel form appears to be *vásto* in the formula *vásta usrā́s* 'at break of dawn', which occurs 5 times in the RV.[4]. — **2.** As in the m., the usual form is that in *-au* formed from 8 stems: *a-rajjáu* 'not consisting of ropes', *uráu*, *ghṛ́ṣau* 'lively', *pṛtháu*, *mádhau*, *vásau*, *vīḷáu* 'stronghold', *sā́nau*. — **3.** According to the *n-* declension: *ā́yuni*, *dā́ruṇi* (AV.), *drúṇi* (Kh. I. 5[10]), *sā́nuni*[5].

V. m. This case, which gunates the final vowel, is formed from 58 stems. The commonest examples are: *indo* (144), *vaso* (62), *śata-krato* (47) 'having a hundred powers', *vāyo* (43), *sūno* (36), *su-krato* (22)[6].

f. This case which has the same form as the m., is made from 6 stems: *adri-sāno* 'dwelling on mountain tops', *dur-haṇo* 'ugly-jawed', *pṛthu-ṣṭo* 'having a broad tuft of hair', *sindho*, *su-bāho* 'having strong arms', *sva-bhāno* 'self-luminous'.

n. The V. n. seems to have been identical in form with the N. judging by the only example which occurs: *gúggulu*[7] (AV. XIX. 38[2]).

Du. N. A. V. m. This form, which is made by lengthening the final vowel, occurs from 69 stems. The commonest examples are: *indra-vāyū́* (22) 'Indra and Vāyu', *vājinī-vasū* (21) 'rich in swift mares', *bāhū́* (20) 'arms', *vṛ́ṣaṇ-vasū* (18) 'possessing great wealth', *indrā-viṣṇū* (13) 'Indra and Viṣṇu'. The TS. has also *ágnā-viṣṇū* (I. 8. 22[1]) 'O Agni and Viṣṇu'. There are besides two forms in which the final vowel is shortened[8]: *jigatnú* (VII. 65[1]) 'speeding' and *su-hántu* (VII. 19[4])[9] 'easy to slay'.

f. This form is made in the same way as the m. but is much rarer, occurring from 5 stems only: *jigatnū́*, *dhenū́*, *sá-bandhū* 'akin', *samānábandhū* 'having the same kin', *hánū*.

n. This form adds the regular ending *-ī*. The only example in the RV. is *urv-ī́*. The VS. has according to the *n-* declension *jā́nu-n-ī* (XX. 8) 'knees'.

I. m. *aṃśúbhyām* (VS. VII. 1), *an-āmayitnúbhyām* 'curative', *nṛ-bāhúbhyām* 'man's arms', *bāhúbhyām*. — **f.** *hánubhyām* (VS. XI. 78)[10].

D. m. *indra-vāyúbhyām* (VS. VII. 8), *indrā-víṣṇubhyām* (VS. VII. 23), *bāhúbhyām*.

---

1 Accented *manáu* only when followed by *ádhi*.

2 A possible m. L. with *n* would be *rájjuni*, an emendation for *rajani* of the Mss. (AV. XX. 133[3]). For the reading of AV. XX. 131[12] *vaniṣṭháu* the Mss. have *vaniṣṭhā* which, if correct, would be a unique example of *-ā* in the L. of the *u-* declension.

3 Emendation for *sárau* of the Mss.; see WHITNEY's note on AV. V. 25[1].

4 See KAEGI, Festgruss an Böhtlingk 48 f.

5 *sā́navi* occurs 9 times, *sā́no* (*ávye*) 8 times, *sā́nau* 10 times, *sā́nuni* once.

6 The V. *vibhāvaso* in Kh. II. 8[2] is wrongly accented.

7 The Mss. read *guggulú* or *gugguló*. See WHITNEY's note on the passage.

8 In both Saṃhitā and Pada text.

9 The RV. three times has the curious A. m. du. *bāhávā* = *bāhū́* apparently from a stem *bāháva-*.

10 *hánūbhyām*, a transition to the *ū-* stems, in TS. IV. 1. 10[2]; VII. 3. 16[1].

Ab. m. *ūrúbhyām* 'thighs', *bāhúbhyām.* — **n.** *jā́nubhyām* (AV.).

G. m. *ūrvós*[1], *bāhvós*[1]. — **n.** according to the *n*- declension: *jā́nunos* (AV.).

L. m. *ūrvós* (AV.), *bāhvós*[1]. — **f.** *hánvos*[1].

Pl. N. V. m. This case is formed in two ways. **1.** The ending *-as* is added to the **unmodified stem.** Of this formation the only example is *mádhv-as* (occurring 4 times). — **2.** The ending *-as* is added to the **gunated stem,** e. g. *aktáv-as.* This form is very frequent, being made from 161 stems and occurring over 700 times in the RV. The commonest examples are: *índavas* (67), *ṛbhávas* (57), *vásavas* (46), *sudā́navas* (42) 'bounteous', *síndhavas* (34), *āśávas* (30), *adhvaryávas* (27), *āyávas* (27), *kārávas* (18), *mitá-jñavas* (2) 'firm-kneed'.

f. This case is formed in the same two ways as the m. **1.** Of this formation there are only two examples: *mádhv-as, śata-kratv-as.* — **2.** The regular form is made from 15 stems in the RV.: *an-aśrávas* 'tearless', *á-bhīravas* 'fearless', *a-reṇávas* 'dustless', *íṣavas, tri-dhā́tavas, dhenávas, párśavas, vasūyávas, śáravas, saniṣyávas* 'desirous', *sá-manyavas* and *sa-manyávas* 'unanimous', *síndhavas, su-ketávas, svá-setavas* 'forming one's own bridge', *hánavas.*

N. A. n. This form is made in two ways. **1.** Twelve stems take **no ending,** four of them also lengthening the final vowel sometimes. These forms occur 76 times altogether in the RV., 48 times with short, 28 times with long vowel. The words occurring are: *urú, ṛjú, cā́ru, tri-dhā́tu, purú*[2], *bahú, mádhu, vásu, vīḷú, sā́nu, su-dhā́tu* 'manifold', *su-hántu*; *urū́, purū́*[3], *vásū*[4], *vīḷū́.* The Pada text always has the short vowel. — **2.** The more usual form follows the *n*- declension, adding *-ni,* before which the final vowel is lengthened. It is made by 14 stems[5] and occurs 127 times altogether in the RV.: *aghāyū́ni* (Kh. IV. 5[3]) 'malicious', *aṇū́ni* (AV.) 'minute', *alā́būni* (AV.)[6] 'gourds', *áśrūṇi* (AV.) 'tears', *karkándhūni* (VS. XIX. 23) 'jujube berries', *cā́rūṇi, tri-dhā́tūni, dā́nūni* 'fluid', *dā́rūṇi, devayū́ni, purū́ṇi, pṛthū́ni, bahū́ni, mádhūni, yuvayū́ni* 'longing for you both', *vásūni, vā́stūni, śmáśrūṇi, sā́nūni.*

A. m. This case is made in two ways. **1.** The normal ending *-as* is added to the unmodified stem. The only two examples of this formation are *paśv-ás* and *kṛ́tv-as*[7] 'times'. — **2.** The usual form is made from 43 stems with the ending *-n,* before which the vowel is lengthened. The original ending *-ns* still survives as *-ṃr* 45 times before vowels and once as *-ṃś* before *ca*[8]. The commonest examples are *śátrūn* (43), *dásyūn* (27), *síndhūn* (23), *aktū́n* (9), *ṛtū́n* (8), *paśū́n* (5)[9]. From the VS.: *ākhū́n* (XXIV. 26) 'moles', *nyáṅkūn* (XXIV. 27) 'antelopes', *madgū́n* (XXIV. 22) 'diver-birds', *malímlūn* (XI. 78; TS.) 'robbers', *rúrūn* (XXIV. 27) 'antelopes'. From the Khilas: *íṣūn* (III. 16[8]).

f. This like the m. is formed in two ways. **1.** The only example is *mádhv-as,* which occurs twice. — **2.** The ending *-s* is added, before which the vowel is lengthened. The only two examples in the RV. (occurring 5

---

[1] To be pronounced *ūruós, bāhuós, hánuos* in the RV.

[2] *purú* seems to be the only form of this kind in the AV., where it occurs once (XIX. 49[4]).

[3] *purū́* occurs 24 times, *purú* 12 times (all but once at the end of a Pada).

[4] *vásū* occurs twice, *vásu* 19 times (12 times at the end of a Pāda).

[5] Half of these also take the form without *n* in the RV.

[6] The Mss. in AV. XX. 134[1] read *álābūni.*

[7] The A. of a noun *kṛ́tu-* 'making', used adverbially: *bhū́ri kṛ́tvas* (III. 18[4]) 'many times', *śáśvat kṛ́tvas* (III. 54[1]) 'innumerable times', *dáśa kṛ́tvas* (AV. XI. 2[9]) 'ten times'.

[8] On the Sandhi of these accusatives in *-ūn* see LANMAN 415 (bottom) and 416 (top).

[9] LANMAN 416 enumerates the stems which form this A.

times) are: *íṣūs* and *dhenū́s*. The Khila after RV. x. 9 has the form *várenya-kratūs* 'intelligent', but the text of Kh. III. 13[1] reads *várenya-kratus*[1].

I. m. This form is frequent, being made from 50 stems and occurring over 200 times. The commonest examples[2] are: *vásubhis* (24), *aktúbhis* (17), *ṛtúbhis* (15), *āśúbhis* (12), *pāyúbhis* (12) 'protectors', *índubhis* (11), *bhānúbhis* (7), *ṛbhúbhis* (6), *síndhubhis* (5), *snúbhis*[3] (5).

f. This case, formed in the same way as the m., is rare, only 3 examples occurring in the RV.: *éka-dhenubhis* 'excellent cows', *tri-dhā́tubhis, dhenúbhis*.

n. *a-reṇúbhis* 'dustless', *áśrubhis* (VS. xxv. 9), *karkándhubhis* (VS. xxi. 32), *jarā́yubhis* (AV.), *bahúbhis, mádhubhis* (Kh. I. 11[7]), *vásubhis, śmáśrubhis* (VS. xxv. 1; SV.) 'beards', *su-mántubhis* 'benevolent'.

D. m. *a-śatrúbhyas* 'foeless', *ṛtúbhyas* (VS. xxii. 28), *ṛbhúbhyas, guṅgúbhyas* 'descendants of Guṅgu', *tṛ́tsubhyas* 'the Tṛtsus' (a tribe), *dáśābhīśubhyas*, 'having ten reins', *dásyubhyas, paśúbhyas, pūrúbhyas, bahúbhyas, mṛgayúbhyas* (VS. xvi. 27) 'hunters', *vásubhyas, síndhubhyas*.

f. There is no example in the RV. The AV. has two: *íṣubhyas, dhenúbhyas*. — **n.** *sā́nubhyas* (VS. xxx. 6).

Ab. m. *aktúbhyas, jatrúbhyas* 'cartilages of the breast bone', *jighatsúbhyas* (AV.) 'seeking to devour', *dásyubhyas, bahúbhyas, bhṛ́gubhyas* 'Bhṛgus', *mṛtyúbhyas* (AV.), *sá-bandhubhyas* (AV.). — **f.** *dhánubhyas, síndhubhyas*.

G. m. This case is formed from 23 stems in the RV., 12 being oxytones and 11 otherwise accented: **1.** *ṛtūnā́m, ṛbhūṇā́m, ṛṣūṇā́m* 'flames', *carūṇā́m, devayūnā́m, paśūnā́m* (AV. VS. TS.), *pitūnā́m, purūṇā́m, prāśūnā́m* 'very swift', *babhrūṇā́m, bahūnā́m, yātūnā́m* 'spectres', *ripūṇā́m, stāyūnā́m* (VS.) 'thieves'. — **2.** *abhí-kratūnām* 'insolent', *abhī́śūnām* 'reins', *ahy-árṣūṇām* 'gliding like a snake', *krátūnām, tṛ́tsūnām, dásyūnām* (AV.), *píyārūṇām* (AV.) 'mischievous', *bhṛ́gūṇām, mánūnām, vásūnām, śátrūṇām, sá-bandhūnām* (AV.), *síndhūnām, svárūṇām* 'sacrificial posts'. — **f.** *dhenūnā́m; síndhūnām*. — **n.** *mádhūnām, yā́śūnām* 'embraces', *vásūnām*.

L. m. *aṃśúṣu* (VS. VIII. 57), *aktúṣu, ánuṣu, āśúṣu, druhyúṣu, paśúṣu* (AV.), *pūrúṣu, bāhúṣu, yáduṣu, ví-bandhuṣu* (AV.) 'kinless', *viśvá-bhānuṣu* 'all-illumining', *śátruṣu, síndhuṣu*. — **f.** *vástuṣu, síndhuṣu*[4]. — **n.** *urúṣu, vā́stuṣu, śmáśruṣu, sā́nuṣu, snúṣu*[5] (VS. TS.).

II. Pronouns.

BENFEY, Vollständige Grammatik 773—780 (p. 333—340). — WHITNEY, Sanskrit Grammar 490—526 (p. 185—199). — PISCHEL, ZDMG. 35, 714—716. — DELBRÜCK, Syntaktische Forschungen 5, 204—221; cp. BRUGMANN, KG. 494—525, and Die Demonstrativa der indogermanischen Sprachen, Leipzig 1904.

390. The pronouns occupy a special position in declension, as being derived from a limited class of roots with a demonstrative sense, and as exhibiting several marked peculiarities of inflexion. These peculiarities are in some degree extended to a certain number of adjectives.

1. Personal Pronouns.

391. These are the most peculiar of all, as being for each person derived from several roots or combinations of roots, as being specially anomalous in inflexion, as not distinguishing gender and, to some extent,

---

1 The m. A. *sindhūn* occurs once (x. 35[2]) in the sense of a f.

2 LANMAN 416 (bottom) enumerates the stems taking this case.

3 Accentuated like a dissyllable as elsewhere.

4 *āyúṣu* (I. 58[3]) is perhaps a transfer form for *āyū́ṣu*; cp. LANMAN 419[1].

5 With dissyllabic accent as usual.

not even number. Some resemble neuters in form; a few have no apparent case-ending; in two of them the acc. pl. masc. does duty as fem. also.

The forms of the first and second person[1] which occur are:

1. **Sing.** N. *ahám*[2]. A. *mā́m*, *mā*. I. *máyā*. D. *máhyam*, *máhya*, *me*[3]. Ab. *mád*[4]. G. *máma*, *me*. L. *máyi*[5].

Du. N. *vā́m* (RV[1]).[6]. A. *nau*. D.[7] *nau*. Ab. *āvád* (TS.). G.[8] *nau*.

Pl. N. *vayám*. A. *asmā́n*[9], *nas*[3]. I. *asmā́bhis*. D. *asmábhyam*, *asmé* (RV.), *nas*. Ab. *asmád*. G. *asmā́kam*[10], *asmā́ka*[11] (RV[1].), *nas*. L. *asmé*, *asmā́su*[12].

2. **Sing.** N. *tvám*[13]. A. *tvā́m*, *tvā*. I. *tváyā*, *tvā́* (RV.). D. *túbhyam*, *túbhya*, *te*[14]. Ab. *tvád*. G. *táva*, *te*. L. *tvé*[15] (RV. VS.), *tváyi* (AV. VS. TS.).

Du. N. *yuvám*. A. *yuvā́m*, *vām*. I. *yuvábhyām*, *yuvā́bhyām*. D. *vām*. Ab. *yuvád* (RV[1].). G. *yuvós* (RV. and Kh. I. 12[1]), *yuváyos* (TS. III. 5. 4[1]), *vām*.

Pl. *yūyám*[16]. A. *yuṣmā́n*[17], f. *yuṣmā́s* (VS[2].), *vas*[18]. D. *yuṣmábhyam*, *vas*. Ab. *yuṣmád*. G. *yuṣmā́kam*[10], *yuṣmā́ka* (RV[2].), *vas*. L. *yuṣmé*.

a. The usual stems representing these personal pronouns in derivation or as first member of a compound are *ma-*, *asma-*; *tva-*, *yuva-*, *yuṣma-*; e. g. *mā́-vant-* 'like me', *asma-drúh-* 'hating us', *tvā́-vant-* 'like thee', *tvá-yata-* 'presented by thee'; *yuva-yú-* 'desiring you two', *yuvá-dhita-* 'established by you two', *yuvā́-datta-* 'given by you two'; *yuṣma-yánt-* 'desiring you', *yuṣmá-ūta-* 'supported by you'; *yuṣmā́-datta-* 'given by you'[19].

b. The forms *mad-*, *asmad-*, *tvad-* occur a few times as first member of compounds; thus *mát-kṛta-* 'done by me', *mát-sakhi-* 'my companion', *mat-tás* (AV.) 'from me'; *asmát-sakhi-* 'having us as companions', *asmád-rāta-* (VS.) 'given by us'; *tvát-pitṛ-* (TS.) 'having thee as father'; *tvád-yoni-* (AV.) 'derived from thee', *tvád-vivācana-* (TS.) 'having thee as umpire'.

c. *aham-*, *mām-*, *mama-*; *asme-*; *tvām-* are also sometimes found as first member of compounds; thus *aham-uttará-* (AV.) 'struggle for precedence', *aham-pūrvá-* 'eager to be first', *ahaṃ-yú-* 'proud'; *mām-paśyá-* (AV.) 'looking at me'; *mama-satyá-* 'dispute as to ownership'; *asmé-hiti-* 'errand for us'; *tvā́ṃ-kāma-* 'desiring thee', *tvā́m-āhuti-* (TS.) 'offering to thee'.

2. Demonstrative Pronouns.

392. *Tá-* 'that', which also serves as the personal pronoun of the third person, 'he', 'she', 'it', is typical, in its inflexion, of the adjectival pronoun. It has the special peculiarity of using the stem *sa-* for the nom. masc. and fem. sing. and, in the RV., for the loc. sing. masc. and neut. The general **peculiarities of the adjectival pronominal declension**, as distinct from

[1] Cp. Gaedicke, Akkusativ 12—14.

[2] On the formation of *ahám* cp. J. Schmidt, KZ. 36, 405 ff. — All the nominatives of the personal pronouns are formed with *-am* as also the N. sing. of the demonstrative *ay-ám* and the reflexive *svayám*.

[3] The unaccented forms of the personal pronoun (85) may be accompanied by accented words in agreement with them; e. g. *te jáyataḥ* 'of thee when conquering'; *vo vṛtā́bhyaḥ* 'for you that were confined'; *nas tribhyáḥ* 'to us three'.

[4] *mád* is two or three times unaccented in the AV.

[5] Cp. Bartholomae, ZDMG. 50, 725.

[6] This seems to be the only nom. form (VI. 55[1]) occurring in the Saṃhitās. The nom. in the ŚB. is *āvám*, in the AB. *āvām*; the acc. in the ŚB. is *āvā́m*. The form *vā́m* must be an abbreviation of *āvā́m*.

[7] The AB. has *āvābhyām*.

[8] The ŚB. has *āváyos*.

[9] *asmā́n* and *yuṣmā́n* are new formatives according to the nominal declension; cp. Brugmann, KG. 519, 2, note.

[10] *asmā́kam* and *yuṣmā́kam* are properly acc. n. of the possessives *asmā́ka-*, *yuṣmā́ka-*; cp. Brugmann, KG. 524, 4.

[11] Occurs only in I. 173[10].

[12] *asmā́su* is a new formation according to the inst. *asmā́-bhis*.

[13] *tvám* must often be read as *túam*.

[14] *te*, originally only loc., is used as dat. and gen.; similarly *me*; the loc. *asmé* is also used as dat.

[15] Cp. Bartholomae, loc. cit.

[16] Originally **yūṣ-ám* where *y* was substituted for the sibilant owing to the influence of *vayám*; cp. Bartholomae, op. cit. 726, note; Brugmann, KG. 513 and note 3, 518.

[17] *yuṣmā́n* is a new formation according to the nominal declension (like *asmā́n*).

[18] The inst. was originally in all probability *yuṣmā́* (like *tvā́*), which later became *yuṣmā́bhis* (like *asmā́bhis*).

[19] This compound may preserve the old inst.

the nominal *a-* declension, are that 1. in the singular they take *-d* instead of *-m* in the nom. and acc. neut.; the element *-sma-* in the dat., abl., loc. masc. and neut.; the element *-sya-* in the dat., abl, gen., loc. fem.; the suffix *-in* in the loc. masc. and neut.[1]; 2. in the plural they take *-e* for *-ās* in the nom. masc.; *s* for *n* in the gen. before *-ām*.

1. The inflexion of *tá-* accordingly is as follows:

Sing. N. m. *sá-s*[2], f. *sā́*, n. *tá-d*. A. m. *tá-m*, f. *tā́-m*, n. *tá-d*. I. m. *ténā*[3], f. *táyā*. D. m. n. *tá-smai*, f. *tá-syai*. Ab. m. n. *tá-smāt*, f. *tá-syās*. G. m. n. *tá-sya*, f. *tá-syās*. L. *tá-smin*[4], *sá-smin* (RV.), f. *tá-syām*.

Du. N. A. m. *tā́*, *táu*, f. *té*, n. *té*. I. m. f. *tā́-bhyām*[5]. Ab. m. *tā́-bhyām*. G. m. n. *táyos*. L. m. *táyos*.

Pl. N. m. *té*, f. *tā́s*, n. *tā́*, *tā́ni*. A. m. *tā́n*, f. *tā́s*, n. *tā́*, *tā́ni*. I. m. n. *té-bhis*, *táis* (AV.; Kh. II. 10[4]), f. *tā́-bhis*. D. m. n. *té-bhyas*, f. *tā́-bhyas*. G. m. *té-ṣām*, f. *tā́-sām*. L. m. *té-ṣu*, f. *tā́-su*.

a. The stem *tá-* is frequently used in derivation, especially that of adverbs; e. g. *tá-thā* 'thus', *tā́-vant-* 'so great', *tá-ti* (AV.) 'so many', and in the compound *tā-dṛ́ś-* 'such'.

b. The neuter form *tád* is often used as the first member of a compound; thus *tád-anna-* 'having that food'; *tád-apas* 'accustomed to that work'; *tad-id-artha-* 'having just that as an object'; *tád-okas-* 'delighting in that'; *tád-ojas-* 'possessing such power'; *tad-vaśá-* 'having a desire for that'; *tad-vid-* (AV.) 'knowing that'.

2. Two other demonstrative pronouns are formed from *tá-*. a. One of them, *etá-*, formed by prefixing the pronominal element *e-*[6], means 'this here'. It is inflected exactly like *tá-* and is of common occurrence. The forms which occur are:

m. Sing. m. N. *eṣás* or *eṣá*[2] A. *etám*. I. *eténa*. D. *etásmai* (TS.). Ab. *etásmāt* (AV.). G. *etásya* (AV.). — **Du.** N. *etā́*, *etáu*. — **Pl.** N. *eté*. A. *etā́n*. I. *etébhis*, *etáis* (AV.). D. *etébhyas*.

f. Sing. N. *eṣā́*. A. *etā́m*. I. *etáyā*. L. *etásyām*. — **Du.** N. *eté*. — **Pl.** N. *etā́s*. A. *etā́s*. I. *etā́bhis* (AV.). L. *etā́su* (AV.).

n. Sing. N. *etád*. — **Pl.** N. *etā́* (+VS.), *etā́ni*.

a. The stem used in derivation and composition is *eta-*; thus *etā́-vant-* 'so great'; *etā-dṛ́ś-* 'such'.

b. The other secondary demonstrative, *tyá-*, is derived from *tá-* with the suffix *-ya*[7] and means 'that'. It is common in the RV., but rare in the later Saṃhitās[8]. It is used adjectivally, being nearly always accompanied by its substantive. It is never found at the beginning of a sentence except when followed by *u*, *cid*, *nú*, or *sú*[9].

The forms occurring are:

m. Sing. N. *syá*[10] (+VS.). A. *tyám*. G. *tyásya*. — **Du.** N. *tyā́*. — **Pl.** N. *tyé*. A. *tyā́n*. I. *tyébhis*.

f. Sing. N. *syā́*. A. *tyā́m*. I. *tyā́* (for *tyáyā*). G. *tyásyās*. — **Du.** N. *tyé*. — **Pl.** N. *tyā́s*. A. *tyā́s*.

n. Sing. N. *tyád* (+TS.). — **Pl.** *tyā́*, *tyā́ni*.

393. The demonstrative which appears as ***ayám*** in in the nom. sing. masc. and means 'this here', employs the pronominal roots *a-* and (in various modifications) *i-* in its inflexion, the latter being used in nearly all the

[1] This suffix is once found in the RV., in the form of *-min*, attached to *yādṛ́ś-* 'having what appearance', though the stem ends in a consonant.

[2] On the Sandhi of *sá-* and *eṣá-* see 78.

[3] The Pada text always reads *téna*.

[4] *sásmin* occurs nearly half as often as *tásmin* in the RV.

[5] In IX. 66[2] this form (f.) seems to have a loc. sense; see LANMAN 343[4].

[6] According to BRUGMANN, KG. 495, 6, note 3, originally loc. sing. of *a-*.

[7] Cp. BRUGMANN, KG. 401 and 495, 2.

[8] It occurs two or three times also in B.

[9] Cp. GRASSMANN, s. v. *tyá-*.

[10] *syá-* and *tyá-* are often to be read with Vyūha.

nom. and acc. forms, the former in the other cases. The acc. sing. masc. and fem. starts from *i-m*[1], the acc. of *i-*, and is followed by the nom. acc. du. and pl., all these forms having the appearance of being made from a stem *ima-*. The nom. sing. fem. is formed from *i-*[2], and the nom. acc. sing. neut. from *i-d* (the N. A. n. of *i-*), both with the suffix *-am* added. The nom. sing. masc. is formed from *a-* with the suffix *-am* and interposing *-y-*. The remaining cases formed from *a-*[3] are inflected throughout like *tá-*.

The **inflexion** of this pronoun is accordingly as follows:

Sing. N. m. *a-y-ám*, f. *i-y-ám*, n. *i-d-ám*. A. m. *im-ám*, f. *im-ā́m*, n. *i-d-ám*. I. m. *e-nā́*[3], f. *ayā́*[4]. D. m. *a-smái*[5], f. *a-syái*. Ab. m. *a-smā́t*[6], f. *a-syā́s*. G. m. *a-syá*[7], f. *a-syā́s*. L. m. *a-smín*, f. *a-syā́m*.

Du. N. A. m. *imā́*, *imáu*, f. *imé*, n. *imé*. D. m. *ā-bhyā́m* (RV[1].). Ab. m. *ā-bhyā́m*. G. m. *a-y-ós* (RV.)[8]. L. m. *a-y-ós*[9] (RV.).

Pl. N. m. *imé*, f. *imā́s*, n. *imā́*, *imā́ni*. A. m. *imā́n*, f. *imā́s*, n. *imā́*, *imā́ni*. I. m. *e-bhís*, f. *ā-bhís*[10]. D. m. *e-bhyás*, f. *ā-bhyás*. G. m. *e-ṣā́m*, f. *ā-sā́m*. L. m. *e-ṣú*, f. *ā-sú*.

394. The corresponding demonstrative employed to express remoteness, 'that there', 'yon', appears in the nom. sing. masc. fem. as ***asáu***. The pronominal root employed throughout its inflexion is *a-*, but always in an extended form only. The fundamental stem used in every case, excepting the nom. sing., is *a-m*, acc. masc. of *a-*; this is extended by the addition of the particle *u* to *amu-*, which has become the stem in the oblique cases of the sing. (with long *u* in the acc. fem.); in the plur. *amū́-* is the fem. and *amī́-* the masc. stem (except the acc.). The nom. sing. forms are quite peculiar. In the masc. and fem. the pronominal root *a-* seems to be compounded with *sa-* extended by the particle *u*: *a-sá-u* and *a-sā́-u*[11]; while the neut. has the pronominal *-d* extended with the suffix *-as*: *a-d-ás*. Only one dual form has been noted, and several plural case forms are wanting. The forms found in the Saṃhitās are the following:

m. Sing. N. *asáu*. A. *amúm*. I. *amúnā* (VS.). D. *amú-ṣmai*. Ab. *amú-ṣmāt* (AV. TS.). G. *amú-ṣya*[12]. L. *amú-ṣmin* (AV.). — **Pl.** N. *amī́*[13]. A. *amū́n* (AV.). D. *amī́bhyas* (AV.). G. *amī́-ṣām*.

f. Sing. N. *asáu*. A. *amū́m*. I. *amuyā́*[14]. D. *amú-ṣyai* (VS.). G. *amú-ṣyās* (AV.). — **Du.** N. *amū́* (AV.). — **Pl.** N. *amū́s*. A. *amū́s*.

n. Sing. N. *adás*. — **Pl.** N. *amū́* (AV.).

395. A defective unaccented pronoun of the third person meaning 'he', 'she', and in the AV. 'it', is ***e-na-***[15]. It occurs almost exclusively in the

---

1 Cp. BRUGMANN, KG. 495, 10.

2 From *i-* is also formed the acc. *ī-m* and the neut. *i-d*, both used as particles.

3 The Pada text always reads *enā́* (the unaccented *ena* occurs twice). This and all other oblique cases formed from *a-*, when used as nouns may lose their accent; see 85 β 3; cp. GRASSMANN, s. v. *idám*. On *ayám* see BRUGMANN, KG. 498, 3.

4 This inst. is fairly frequent in the RV.; instead of it *anáyā* occurs twice (IX. 65[12. 27]), being probably a later correction to obviate the hiatus. Otherwise no forms of *ana-* (*anéna*, *anáyā*, *anáyos*) occur in the Saṃhitās. But *anéna* (n.) occurs in Kh. III. 16[7].

5 *asmai* and *asya* are accented on the first syllable, the former four or five times, the latter about ten times, when specially emphatic at the beginning of a Pāda in the RV.

6 The abl. according to the nominal declension, *ā́t*, is used as a conjunction.

7 The form *imásya* also occurs once.

8 To be read as *āyós*.

9 Seems to be wrongly read as *āyós* in the Pada text; cp. LANMAN 344[3].

10 *ābhís* occurs ten times in the RV.; it is thrice accented *ā́bhis* and thrice unaccented: cp. note 5.

11 Cp. BRUGMANN, KG. 495, 6; 498, 4.

12 This is the only instance of *-sya* being added to any but an *a-* stem.

13 This form is Pragṛhya (70). On its origin cp. IF. 18, 64, note.

14 Used adverbially, with shifted accent.

15 The same *e-* (loc. of *a-*) as in *é-ka-* 'one', *e-vá* 'thus'; cp. BRUGMANN, KG. 495, 6.

acc. (the great majority of occurrences being masc. sing.). Otherwise it is found only twice in the inst. sing. and three or four times in the gen. dual. The forms occurring are: **m. Sing.** A. *enam.* I. *enena* (AV.). — **Du.** A. *enau* (AV.). G. *enos* (RV.), *enayos* (AV.). — **Pl.** A. *enān.*

f. Sing. A. *enām*[1]. **Du.** A. *ene.* **Pl.** A. *enās.* — **n.** N. *enad* (AV.; Kh. IV. 6[5]).

396. Another demonstrative found nearly twenty times in the RV., but otherwise occurring only once in the AV., is the unaccented pronoun ***tva-***[2] meaning 'one', 'many a one', generally repeated, in the sense of 'one — another'. The forms occurring are: **m. Sing.** N. *tvas.* A. *tvam.* I. *tvena.* D. *tvasmai.* **Pl.** N. *tve*[3]. — **f. Sing.** N. *tvā.* D. *tvasyai.* — **n. Sing.** N. *tvad.*

a. The pronoun ***avá-***[4] 'this' is found two or three times in the RV., and only in the gen. du. form *avós* in combination with *vām,* meaning 'of you two being such' (used like *sa,* e. g. *sá tvám* 'thou as such').

b. The pronoun ***áma-***[5] 'this' occurs only once in the AV.: *ámo 'hám asmi* (XIV. 2[71]), 'this am I'.

3. Interrogative Pronoun.

397. The interrogative *ka-,* 'who?', 'which?', 'what?' used both as substantive and adjective, is quite regular in its declension, excepting the alternative neuter form *kí-m*[6], which instead of the pronominal *-d* has the nominal *-m* (never elsewhere attached to a stem in *-i*). The forms occurring are:

m. Sing. N. *kás.* A. *kám.* I. *kéna.* D. *kásmai.* Ab. *kásmāt* (AV.). G. *kásya.* L. *kásmin.* — **Du.** *káu.* — **Pl.** N. *ké.* I. *kébhis.* L. *késu* (VS.).

f. Sing. N. *kā́.* A. *kā́m.* I. *káyā.* G. *kásyās* (AV. VS.). — **Pl.** N. *kā́s.* A. *kā́s.* L. *kā́su.*

n. Sing. N. A. *ká-d*[7] (RV.) and *kí-m.* — **Pl.** N. A. *kā́* and *kā́ni.*

a. In forming **derivatives**, which are numerous, the stem of the interrogative employed is not only *ka-,* but also *ki-* and *ku-;* e. g. *ká-ti* 'how many?'; *kí-yant-* 'how great?'; *kú-ha* 'where?'. The neuter form *kim* is twice used in this way: *kiṃ-yú-* 'desiring what?'; *kim-máya-* 'consisting of what?'.

b. In the formation of **compounds** *kad* occurs twice as first member: in *kat-payá-* 'greatly swelling', and *kád-artha-* 'having what purpose?'. *kim* is similarly used a few times in the later Saṃhitās; thus *kiṃ-śilá-* (VS. TS.) 'being in stony ground', *kiṃ-kará-* (AV.) 'servant'.

4. Relative Pronoun.

398. The relative pronoun *ya-* 'who', 'which', 'what' is perfectly regular in its declension. The forms occurring are:

m. Sing. N. *yás*[8]. — A. *yám.* I. *yénā*[9] and *yéna.* D. *yásmai.* Ab. *yásmāt*[10]. G. *yásya.* L. *yásmin.* — **Du.** N. A. *yā́, yáu.* D. *yā́bhyām.* G. *yáyos.* L. *yáyos* and *yós*[11] (RV.). — **Pl.** N. *yé.* A. *yā́n.* I. *yébhis, yáis* (AV.; Kh. I. 9[2]). D. *yébhyas.* G. *yéṣām.* L. *yéṣu.*

---

1 This form occurs once (VIII. 6[19]) at the beginning of a sentence and is then accented as *enā́m.*

2 The unaccented adverb *tvadānīm* (MS. IV. 2[2]) 'sometimes', is derived from this pronoun.

3 See WHITNEY's note on AV. VIII. 9[9] in his translation.

4 This pronoun also occurs in the Avesta; cp. BRUGMANN 495, 10.

5 From this pronoun are derived the inst. and abl. adverbs (with shifted accent) *amā́* 'at home' and *avā́t* 'from near at hand'.

6 The nom. masc. is preserved as a petrified form in *ná-kis* and *mā́-kis* 'no one', 'nothing', 'never'.

7 The relative frequency of *kád* to *kím* in the RV. is as 2 to 3.

8 *yás* is the commonest declensional form in the RV., occurring more than 1000 times.

9 *yénā* is twice as common in the RV. as *yéna;* the Pada text, however, always reads *yéna* (cp. LANMAN 332).

10 The ablative according to the nominal declension, *yā́t,* is used as a conjunction.

11 *yós* for *yáyos,* like *yuvós* for *yuváyos;* cp. BB. 23, 183; ZDMG. 50, 589.

f. Sing. N. *yā́.* A. *yā́m.* I. *yáyā.* G. *yásyās.* L. *yásyām.* — **Du.** N. *yé* (TS. AV.). G. *yáyos.* L. *yáyos.* — **Pl.** N. *yā́s.* A. *yā́s.* I. *yā́bhis.* D. *yā́bhyas.* G. *yā́sām.* L. *yā́su.*

n. Sing. N. A. *yád.* — **Du.** *yé.* — **Pl.** *yā́, yā́ni.*

a. The stem of *yá-* is used in the formation of many derivatives; e. g. *yá-thā* 'as'; it also appears as first member of a compound in *yā-dṛ́ś-* 'which like'. The neuter form *yad* is once used similarly in the RV.: *yát-kāma-* 'desiring what'.

b. The relative receives the indefinite meaning of 'whoever'[1] by the addition of *káś ca, káś cid,* or *cid* alone; e. g. *yád vo vayáṃ cakṛmā́ kác cid ā́gaḥ* (II. 27[14]) 'whatever sin we have committed against you'; *yát kíṃ ca duritám máyi* (I. 23[12]) 'whatever sin (there is) in me'; *yé cid dhí tvā́m ṛ́ṣayaḥ pū́rva ūtáye juhūré* (I. 48[14]) 'whatever early seers have called on thee for aid'.

5. Indefinite Pronouns.

399. a. In the RV. there are found the two **simple indefinite pronouns** *sama* (unaccented) 'any', 'every' and *simá-* 'every', 'all'. The six forms of the former which occur are: **m. Sing.** A. *samam.* D. *samasmai.* Ab. *samasmāt.* G. *samasya.* L. *samasmin.* — **Pl.** N. *same.* From *simá-* are met with the five forms: **Sing.** V. *síma.* N. *simás.* D. *simásmai* (neut.). Ab. *simásmāt.* — **Pl.** *simé.*

b. **Compound indefinite pronouns** are formed by combining the particles *ca, caná,* or *cid* with the interrogative; thus *káś ca* 'any', 'any one'; *káś caná* 'any one soever', 'every'; *káś cid* 'any', 'some'; 'any one', 'some one'.

6. Reflexive Pronouns.

400. 1. The reflexive adjective is ***svá-*** 'own', which refers to the first and second as well as the third person of all numbers; e. g. *yád, indrāgnī, mádathaḥ své duroṇé* (I. 108[7]) 'when, O Indra and Agni, ye rejoice in your own abode'.

2. The substantive reflexive is ***sva-y-ám*** 'self', which is derived from *svá-* with the suffix *-am* and interposing *y* (as *a-y-ám* from *a-*). It is properly used as a nom. referring to all three persons; e. g. *svayáṃ yajasva diví, deva, devā́n* (x. 7[6]) 'do thou thyself, O god, worship the gods in heaven'. Sometimes, however, the nominative nature of the pronoun is forgotten and *svayám* is used agreeing in sense with another case; e. g. *vatsám .. svayáṃ gātúṃ .. icchámānam* (IV. 18[10]) 'the calf himself seeking a way'.

3. Other cases than the nom. are regularly expressed in the RV. by ***tanū́-*** 'body'; e. g. *svayáṃ gātúṃ tanvà icchámānam* (IV. 18[10]) 'himself seeking a way for himself (*tanvè*)'; *yajasva tanvàm* (x. 7[6]) 'worship thyself'; *mā́ hāsmahi prajáyā, mā́ tanū́bhiḥ* (x. 128[5]) 'may we suffer no harm with (regard to our) offspring or ourselves'. The reflexive adjective and a possessive gen. may be added; e. g. *ágne, yájasva tanvàṃ táva svā́m* (VI. 11[2]) 'Agni, worship thine own self'[2].

4. There are one or two instances in the RV. of the incipient use of ***ātman-*** 'soul' in a reflexive sense; thus *bálaṃ dádhāna ātmáni* (IX. 113[1]) 'putting strength into himself'; *yákṣmaṃ sárvasmād ātmánas .. ví vṛhāmi* (x. 163[6]) 'I expel the disease from (thy) whole self'. The acc. *ātmā́nam,* though not met with in the RV. as a reflexive, is frequently found so used in the later Saṃhitās[3]; also in Kh. III. 10[3].

a. In the formation of compounds *sva-* several times appears in the substantive as well as the adjective sense as first member; e. g. *svá-yukta-* 'self-yoked'; *sva-yúgvan-* 'own companion'. *svayám* is also thus used in a few compounds; thus *svayaṃ-jā́-* 'self-born'; *svayam-bhū́-* 'self-existent'.

1 Cp. DELBRÜCK, Syntaktische Forschungen 5, 569—570.

2 Cp. DELBRÜCK op. cit. 135, and GRASSMANN, s. v. *svá-* and *tanū́-*.

3 See DELBRÜCK op. cit. 155.

7. Possessive Pronouns.

401. Possessive pronouns are of rare occurrence because the genitive of the personal pronoun is generally used to express the sense which they convey.

a. The possessives of the **first person** are *mámaka-* (RV.) 'my', *māmaká-* 'my', (both formed from the genitive of the personal pronoun *máma*)[1], and *asmā́ka-* 'our'. The commonest form of the latter is the N. A. neut. *asmā́kam*, which is used as the gen. plur. of the personal pronoun[2]. The other forms occurring are *asmā́kena, asmā́kāsas*, and *asmā́kebhis*. The VS. also has the form *āsmākás* (IV. 24) 'our' from a secondary derivative[3].

b. The possessives of the **second person** are *tāvaká-* (RV.) 'thy', (from *táva*), met with only in the form *tāvakébhyas*; *tvá-*[4] (RV.) 'thy', found only in the inst. pl. *tvā́bhis* (II. 20[2]); and *yuṣmā́ka-* 'your', the N. A. neut. of which is used as the gen. pl. of the personal pronoun of the second person; it otherwise occurs only in the RV. in the two forms *yuṣmā́kena* and *yuṣmā́kābhis*.

c. Besides being used reflexively, ***svá-*** is fairly often employed as a simple possessive, generally as that of the **third person**, 'his', 'her', 'their', but also of the second, 'thy', 'your', and of the first, 'my', 'our'. It is, however, inflected like an ordinary adjective, having only two isolated forms according to the pronominal declension[5]. The forms which occur are:

m. sing. N. *svás*. A. *svám*. I. *svéna* and *svénā*[6] D. *svā́ya*. Ab. *svā́t*. G. *svásya*. L. *své* and *svásmin* (RV.). — **Pl.** N. *svā́s* (AV.). A. *svā́n* (AV.). I. *svébhis* and *sváis*. D. *svébhyas* (Kh. V. 1[2]). G. *svā́nām* (AV.; Kh. II. 10[4]). L. *svéṣu*.

f. sing. N. *svā́*. A. *svā́m*. I. *sváyā*. D. *svā́yai*. Ab. *svā́yās*. G. *svásyās* (RV.). L. *svā́yām*. — **Pl.** N. *svā́s*. A. *svā́s*. I. *svā́bhis*. L. *svā́su*.

n. sing. N. A. *svám*. — **Pl.** A. *svā́*.

8. Pronominal derivatives and compounds.

402. A certain number of derivatives are formed from the roots or stems of simple pronouns by means of suffixes which modify the pronominal sense. There are also a few pronominal compounds.

a. With the **suffix *-ka***, conveying a diminutive or contemptuous meaning, derivatives are formed from the pronouns *tá-*, *yá-*, *sá-*, and *asáu*; thus *ta-ká-* (RV.) 'that little', of which the forms A. sing. m. *taká-m* and n. *taká-d* occur; *yá-ka-* 'who', 'which', the only forms met with being N. m. *yakás*, f. *yakā́* (VS. XXIII. 22, 23), and N. pl. m. *yaké* (RV.); *sa-ká-* (RV. AV.) 'that little', of which only N. sing. f. *sakā́* occurs; N. sing. f. *asakáu* 'that little' (VS. XXIII. 22, 23).

b. With the comparative **suffix *-tara*** derivatives are formed from *i-*, *ká-*, and *yá-*; and with the superlative **suffix *-tama***, from the latter two; thus *í-tara-* 'other'; *ka-tará-* 'which of two?'; *ya-tará-* 'who or which of two'; *ka-tamá-* 'who or which of many?', *ya-tamá-* 'who or which of many'.

c. With ***-ti*** derivatives with a numerical sense are formed from *ká-*, *tá-*, and *yá-*; thus *ká-ti* 'how many?', *tá-ti* (AV.) 'so many'; *yá-ti* 'as many'. No inflected forms of these words occur.

---

1 Cp. BRUGMANN, KG. 524, 2.
2 Op. cit. 524, 4.
3 Formed like *māmaká-* beside *mámaka-*.
4 Used as a possessive probably under the influence of *svá-*; cp. BRUGMANN, op. cit. 524, 2.
5 That is, *svásyās* and *svásmin*.
6 The Pada text always reads *svéna*.

d. With ***-yant,*** expressing the quantitative meaning of 'much', derivatives are formed from *i-* and *ki-*: *í-yant-* 'so much' (n. N. sing. *íyat,* pl. *íyānti;* f. D. sing. *íyatyai*); *kí-yant-* 'how much?' (sing. N. n. adv. *kíyat,* D. m. *kíyate,* L. *kíyāti* for *kíyati*; N. f. *kíyatī*).

e. With ***-vant*** are formed derivatives from personal pronouns with the sense of 'like', 'attached to', and from others in the quantitative sense of 'great'; thus *tvā́-vant-* 'like thee', *mā́-vant-* 'like me'; *yuvā́-vant-* (RV.) 'devoted to you two' (only D. *yuvā́vate*); *yuṣmā́-vant-* (RV.) 'belonging to you' (only L. pl. *yuṣmā́vatsu*); *etā́-vant-* and *tā́-vant-* 'so great'; *yā́-vant-* 'as great'; *ī́-vant-* 'so great' (sing. N. n. *ī́vat,* D. m. n. *ī́vate,* G. *ī́vatas;* pl. A. m. *ī́vatas*); *kī́-vant-* 'how far?' (G. *kī́vatas*).

f. With *-dṛś, -dṛśa, -dṛkṣa* are formed the following pronominal compounds: *ī-dṛ́kṣa-* (VS.) and *ī-dṛ́ś-* (VS. TS.) 'such'; *etā-dṛ́kṣa-* (VS.) and *etā-dṛ́ś-* 'such' (N. sing. n. *etādṛ́k*); *kī-dṛ́ś-* 'what like?' (N. sing. m. *kīdṛ́ṅ*); *tā-dṛ́ś-* 'such' (N. sing. m. *tā-dṛ́k*); *yā-dṛ́ś-* 'what like' (sing. m. N. *yādṛ́k,* L. *yādṛ́śmin*).

9. Pronominal Adjectives.

403. Certain adjectives derived from pronominal roots or allied to pronouns in sense conform in varying degrees to the pronominal declension.

1. The adjectives which **strictly** adhere to the **pronominal** type of inflexion are *anyá-* 'other', and (as far as can be judged by the few forms occurring and by the usage of the later language) the derivatives formed with *-tara* and *-tama* from *ká-* and *yá-*. The specifically pronominal cases of the latter which have been met with are: **sing.** N. n. *katarád* (AV.), *yatarád; katamád, yatamád* (AV.); D. m. *katamásmai* (VS.); G. f. *katamásyās* (AV.); L. f. *yatamásyām* (AV.); **Pl.** N. m. *katamé* (AV.), *yatamé* (AV.). No such form of *ítara-* has been found. The forms of *anyá-* which occur are:

m. sing. N. *anyás.* A. *anyám.* I. *anyéna.* D. *anyásmai* (AV.). G. *anyásya.* L. *anyásmin.* — **Pl.** N. *anyé.* A. *anyā́n.* I. *anyébhis* and *anyáis.* D. *anyébhyas* (AV.). G. *anyéṣām.* L. *anyéṣu.*

f. sing. N. *anyā́.* A. *anyā́m.* I. *anyáyā.* D. *anyásyai.* G. *anyásyās.* L. *anyásyām.* — **Du.** N. *anyé.* — **Pl.** N. *anyā́s.* A. *anyā́s.* I. *anyā́bhis.* G. *anyā́sām.* L. *anyā́su.*

n. sing. N. *anyád.* — **Du.** I. *anyā́bhyām* (AV.). — **Pl.** N. *anyā́.*

2. The three adjectives *éka-* 'one', *víśva-* 'all', *sárva-* 'whole' are **partially pronominal,** following this declension except in the nom. acc. sing. neut., which takes the nominal *-m.* Thus sing. G. f. *ékasyās,* L. m. *ékasmin*[1], pl. N. m. *éke,* but sing. N. n. *ékam;* sing. D. *víśvasmai*[2], Ab. *víśvasmāt*[2], L. *víśvasmin*[2], pl. N. m. *víśve,* G. m. *víśveṣām,* f. *víśvāsām,* but sing. N. n. *víśvam;* sing. D. m. *sárvasmai* (AV.), f. *sárvasyai* (AV.; AA. III. 2 5), Ab. m. *sárvasmāt,* pl. N. m. *sárve,* G. *sárveṣām* (AV.), f. *sárvāsām* (AV.), but sing. N. n. *sárvam.*

3. More than a dozen other adjectives which have pronominal affinities in form or sense **occasionally** show **pronominal** case-forms (but never *-d* in the N. A. sing. n.).

a. A few adjectives formed with the comparative and superlative **suffixes** ***-ra*** **and** ***-ma*** have such endings; thus *ápara-* 'lower' has *ápare* in the N. pl m. beside *áparāsas*; *úttara-* 'higher', 'later', forms the L. sing. f. *úttarasyām*

[1] The AV. once has *éke* as a loc. sing.; see WHITNEY's note on AV. XIX. 56[2] in his translation.

[2] The RV. has the nominal forms D. *víśvāya,* Ab. *víśvāt,* L. *víśve,* once each; *víśvāt* (n.) also occurs Kh. II. 6[18].

(AV.), N. pl. m. *úttare*; Ab. L. sing. *úttarasmāt* and *úttarasmin* beside *úttarāt* and *úttare*; *úpara-* 'lower' has *úpare* beside *úparās* and *úparāsas* in the N. pl. m.; *avamá-* 'lowest' has L. sing. f. *avamásyām*; *upamá-* 'highest' has sing. L. f. *upamásyām*; *paramá-* 'farthest' has sing. f. G. *paramásyās* and L. *paramásyām* (+VS.); *madhyamá-* 'middlemost' has sing. L.f. *madhyamásyām*.

b. A few other adjectives with a **comparative or pronominal sense** have occasional pronominal endings. Thus *pára-* 'ulterior' has sing. D. m. *párasmai* (AV.), Ab. m. *párasmāt* (+AV. VS.), G. f. *párasyās*, G. pl. m. *páreṣām*; L. sing. m. *párasmin* beside *páre*; and N. pl. m. *páre* beside *párāsas*. *pū́rva-* 'prior' has sing. m. D. *pū́rvasmai*, Ab. *pū́rvasmāt*, G. pl. m. *pū́rveṣām*, f. *pū́rvāsām*; and the N. pl. m. *pū́rve* is very common beside the very rare *pū́rvāsas*. *néma-* 'other'[1] has m. L. sing. *némasmin*, N. pl. *néme*, but N. sing. n. *némam* and G. pl. m. *nemānām* (unaccented). *svá-* 'own', otherwise following the nominal declension, has once sing. G. f. *svásyās* and once L. n. *svásmin*. *samāná-* 'similar', 'common', has once Ab. sing. n. *samānásmāt* beside *samānā́t*.

c. A few adjectives which are **numerical in form or meaning** have occasional pronominal forms; thus *prathamá-* 'first', has G. sing. f. *prathamásyās* (AV.); *tṛtī́ya-* 'third' has L. sing. f. *tṛtī́yasyām*[2] (AV.); *úbhaya-* 'of both kinds' has m. pl. G. *úbhayeṣām*, and N. *úbhaye* beside *úbhayāsas* and *úbhayās*[3]; *kévala-* 'exclusive' has once N. pl. m. *kévale*.

III. Numerals.

BENFEY, Vollständige Grammatik 764—771. — WHITNEY, Sanskrit Grammar 475—488. — Cp. BRUGMANN, KG. 441—451.

404. The series of the numerals is based on the decimal system of reckoning. The names of the first ten cardinals, which are of an adjectival character, form the foundation of the rest either by compounding or derivation; the ordinals and numerical adverbs being further derived from the corresponding cardinals.

A. Cardinals.

405. The names of the **first ten cardinals** are: *éka-* 'one'; *dvá-* 'two'; *trí-* 'three'; *catúr-* 'four'; *páñca* 'five'; *ṣáṣ-* 'six'; *saptá* 'seven'; *aṣṭā́* 'eight'; *náva* 'nine'; *dáśa* 'ten'.

a. The numbers intermediate **between 'ten' and 'twenty'** are Dvandva compounds formed by prefixing the accented unit to *dáśa* 'ten': *ékā-daśa*[4] ('one and ten') 'eleven'; *dvā́-daśa*[5] 'twelve'; *tráyo-daśa*[6] (AV. VS. TS.) 'thirteen'; *cátur-daśa*[7] 'fourteen'; *páñca-daśa* 'fifteen'; *ṣó-ḍaśa*[8] (VS. TS.) 'sixteen'; *saptá-daśa* (TS.) 'seventeen'; *aṣṭá-daśa* (TS.) 'eighteen'; *náva-daśa* (VS.) 'nineteen'.

b. The remaining cardinals are substantives. The names of the **decades from 'twenty' to 'ninety'** are either old Dvandva compounds or derivatives formed with the suffix *-ti*. They are *viṃ-śatí-* 'twenty'; *triṃ-śát* 'thirty';

---

1 Cp. NEISSER, BB. 30, 303.

2 The pronominal endings are recognized as alternative in the later language as regards *dvitī́ya-* and *tṛtī́ya-*; the Bṛhaddevatā (VIII. 95) has *prathamasyām* as well as *dvitīyasyām*.

3 *ubhá-* 'both' is declined in the dual only: N. A. m. *ubhā́* and *ubhāú*, f. *ubhé*, I. *ubhā́bhyām* (once in RV.), G. *ubháyos* (twice in RV.).

4 With *ékā-* for *éka-* under the influence of *dvā́-daśa*.

5 Here the N. m. du. form *dvā* is retained instead of the stem form *dva-*.

6 In this and other numeral compounds the N. m. plural form remains in every case; e. g. *tā́n ... tráyas-triṃśatam ā́ vaha* (I. 45[2]) 'bring those thirty-three'.

7 As first member of a compound *catúr-* is regularly accented *cátur-*.

8 For *ṣaṣ-daśa*, see above 43, b, 3; 56, b.

catvāriṃ-śát 'forty'; *pañcā-śát* 'fifty'; *ṣaṣ-ṭí-* 'sixty'; *sapta-tí-* 'seventy'; *aśī-tí-* 'eighty'; *nava-tí-* 'ninety'. The last four are abstract fem. nouns derived from the simple cardinal (except *aśī-tí-*) [1] and meaning originally 'hexad etc. (of tens)'. The others are fem. compounds, the first member of which is 'two', 'three', 'four', or 'five', and the second a remnant of the IE. word for 'ten'; thus *triṃ-śát* meant 'three tens'. *viṃśatí-* was probably in origin an old dual of this formation which ended in *-ī* but was transformed by the influence of *ṣaṣṭí-* etc. to a singular fem. in *-ti* [2].

c. The **numbers** intermediate **between these decades** are Dvandva compounds formed by prefixing the accented unit to the decade; thus *aṣṭá-viṃśati-* (VS.) 'twenty-eight'; *éka-triṃśat* (VS.) 'thirty-one'; *tráyas-triṃśat* 'thirty-three'; *náva-catvāriṃśat* (TS.) 'forty-nine'; *náva-ṣaṣṭi-* (TS.) 'sixty-nine'; *návāśīti-* (TS.) 'eighty-nine'; *páñca-navati-* (TS.) 'ninety-five'; *ṣáṇ-ṇavati-* (TS.) 'ninety-six'; *aṣṭā́-navati-* (TS.) 'ninety-eight'.

α. In the TS., the number preceding a decade is also expressed by *ékān ná* 'by one not' = 'minus one'; thus *ékān ná viṃśati-* 'twenty less one' = 'nineteen'; *ékān ná catvāriṃśát* 'thirty-nine'; *ékān ná ṣaṣṭí-* 'fifty-nine'; *ékān nā́śītí-* 'seventy-nine'; *ékān ná śatám* 'a hundred less one', 'ninety-nine' [3].

β. Intermediate numbers may also be expressed by adding together unit and decade with or without *ca*; e. g. *náva ca navatíṃ ca* 'ninety and nine'; *navatíṃ náva* 'ninety-nine'.

d. The numbers expressing **'a hundred'** and its multiples are *śatá-* '100'; *sahásra-* '1000'; *a-yúta-* (AV. TS.) '10 000'; *ni-yúta-* (TS.; Kh. IV. 12 [8]) '100 000'; *pra-yúta-* (VS. TS.) '1 000 000'; *árbuda-* (TS.; Kh. IV. 12 [8]) '10 000 000'; *nyàrbuda-* (AV. VS. TS.) '100 000 000' [4].

α. Intermediate numbers are compounded in the same way with *śatá-* as with the preceding decades; e. g. *éka-śatam* 'a hundred and one'; *cátuḥ-śatam* 'a hundred and four'; *triṃśác-chatam* 'a hundred and thirty'.

β. Multiples may be expressed in two ways. Either the larger number is put in the dual or plural multiplied by the smaller one used adjectivally; e. g. *dvé śaté* (VII. 18²²) 'two hundred'; *ṣaṣṭíṃ sahásrā* (VI. 26⁶) 'sixty thousand'; *tríṇi śatā́ trī́ sahásrāṇi triṃśác ca náva ca* (III. 9⁹) 'three thousand three hundred and thirty-nine'. Or the multiplier may be prefixed to the larger number, forming with it a possessive compound accented on the final syllable; e. g. *tráyastriṃśat triśatā́ḥ ṣaṭsahasrā́ḥ* (AV.) 'six thousand three hundred and thirty-three'. Numbers below a hundred are sometimes used multiplicatively in these two ways; e. g. *navatī́r náva* (I. 84¹³) 'nine nineties' = 'eight hundred and ten'; *tri-saptá-* [5] 'thrice seven'; *tri-ṇavá-* (VS.) 'having thrice nine'.

Inflexion.

406. With regard to their inflexion, which in many respects is peculiar, the cardinals may be divided into **three groups**.

a. The first group comprises the **first four numerals**. These are the only cardinals which, like other adjectives, distinguish the genders. They also distinguish the numbers as far as the sense admits: *éka-* 'one', while inflected chiefly in the singular, forms a plural also in the sense of 'some'; *dvá-* 'two' is of course inflected in the dual only; and *trí-* 'three' and *catúr-* 'four' in the plural only.

1. ***éka-*** is declined like the second group of pronominal adjectives [6]. The only form of the abl. sing. [3] met with follows the nominal declension,

---

[1] *aśī-* is radically related to *aṣṭáu*, cp. 56, a.

[2] Cp. Brugmann, KG. 443, 1.

[3] In the TS. (B.) are also met with *ékasmān ná pañcāśát* and *ékasyai ná pañcāśát* (VII. 4. 7³) 'forty-nine': Whitney 477, b.

[4] In TS. VII. 2²⁰ these numerals, followed by *samudrá-*, *mádhya-*, *ánta-*, *parārdhá-*, occur in succession: we may infer from the first few that each successive number is equal to ten times the preceding one; cp. Whitney 475, c. The contents of TS. VII. 2. 11—20 are almost entirely numerals.

[5] Inflected according to the *a-* declension: inst. *trisaptáis*.

[6] See above 403, 2.

viz. *ékāt*, used in the compound numerals *ékān ná triṃśát* 'twenty-nine' etc. occurring in the TS. A single dual case, from *éka-* in the sense of 'a certain', appears in *éke yuvatī* (AV. x. 7[42]) 'a certain pair of maidens'. The forms to be found in the Saṃhitās are: **m.** sing. N. *ékas.* A. *ékam.* I. *ékena.* G. *ékasya.* L. *ékasmin*; pl. N. *éke.* D. *ékebhyas.* — **f.** N. *ékā.* A. *ékām.* I. *ékayā.* G. *ékasyās*; du. N. *éke* (AV.); pl. N. *ékās* (AV.). — **n.** N. sing. *ékam*; pl. *ékā.*

2. ***dvá-*** 'two', declined in the dual only, is quite regular. The forms occurring are: **m.** N. *dvā́, dváu.* I. *dvā́bhyām.* G. *dváyos.* L. *dváyos.* — **f.** N. *dvé.* I. *dvā́bhyām.* — **n.** N. *dvé.* L. *dváyos.*

a. The dual form *dvā́* is retained in the first member of the numeral compound *dvā́-daśa* 'twelve'. Otherwise *dvi-* is used as the stem of *dva-* in derivation, e. g. *dvi-dhā* 'twofold'; and as the first member of compounds, e. g. *dvi-pád-* 'biped'.

3. The cardinal ***trí-*** 'three' is, in the masc. and neut., inflected like a regular *i-* stem. The fem. stem is *tisṛ́-*: the gen. pl. is once (v. 69[2]) written *tisṛṇā́m* (though the *ṛ* is actually long metrically)[1]. The forms occurring are: **m.** N. *tráyas.* A. *trī́n.* I. *tribhís.* D. *tribhyás.* G. *trīṇā́m.* L. *triṣú.* — **f.** N. *tisrás.* A. *tisrás.* I. *tisṛ́bhis.* D. *tisṛ́bhyas.* G. *tisṝṇā́m*[2]. L. *tisṛ́ṣu.* — **n.** N. A. *trí, trī́ṇi.*

a. The stem used in derivation and compounding is regularly *tri-*, e. g. *tri-dhā* 'in three ways'; *tri-pád-* 'three-footed'. But *tṛ-* appears in *tṛ-tá-* (AV.) 'third', as a N., and in the secondary ordinal *tṛ-t-ī́ya-* 'third'; and in numeral compounds *trim* appears in *triṃ-śát* 'thirty', and *tráyas* in *tráyo-daśa* 'thirteen', and *tráyas-triṃśat* 'thirty-three'.

4. ***catúr-*** 'four' has the stem *catvā́r-* in the strong forms of the masc. and neut. In the gen. it has the peculiarity of taking *n* before the ending *ām*, though the stem ends in a consonant[3]. The fem. stem is *cátasṛ-*, which is inflected like *tisṛ́-* and shifts its accent like *páñca*. The forms occurring are: **m.** N. *catvā́ras.* A. *catúras.* I. *catúrbhis.* D. *catúrbhyas* (AV.). G. *caturṇā́m*[4]. — **f.** N. *cátasras.* A. *cátasras.* I. *catasṛ́bhis*[5]. — **n.** N. A. *catvā́ri.*

a. The stem used in derivation and compounding is regularly *catur-*; e. g. *catur-dhā́* 'in four ways'; *cátur-daśa* 'fourteen'; *cátuṣ-pad-*[6] 'four-footed'. But it is once *catvārim-* (from the n. pl.) in the numeral compound *catvāriṃśát* 'forty'.

b. The second group, comprising the cardinals from 'five' to 'nineteen', though used adjectivally, does not distinguish gender, and takes no ending in the nom. and acc. These numerals also share the same peculiarities of accentuation[7].

5. N. A. *páñca* 'five'. I. *pañcábhis.* D. *pañcábhyas.* L. *pañcásu.*

6. *ṣáṣ-* 'six': N. A. *ṣáṭ.* I. *ṣaḍbhís.* D. *ṣaḍbhyás*[8].

7. N. A. *saptá* 'seven'. I. *saptábhis.* D. Ab. *saptábhyas.* G. *saptānā́m.*

8. That the cardinal for 'eight' was an old dual[9] is indicated by its forms in the N. A. *aṣṭā́, aṣṭáu* and in the only other cases occurring, I. *aṣṭā-bhís*, D. *aṣṭā-bhyás* (TS.). According to the analysis of the Pada text in a late passage of the RV. (x. 27[15]), *aṣṭóttarā́ttāt* contains the N. *aṣṭá*, doubtless because it is preceded by *saptá* and followed by *náva* and *dáśa*.

a. The stem used in compounding has mostly the dual form *aṣṭā*; thus *aṣṭā́-pad-* 'eight-footed', *aṣṭā́-vandhura-* 'eight-seated'[10]; *aṣṭā́-daśa-* (TS.) 'eighteen', *aṣṭā-viṃśá-* (AV.)

---

1 See above 12, 13; cp. BENFEY, Vedica und Verwandtes 4.

2 On the accentuation, see 94, 2 a.

3 It shares this peculiarity with *ṣaṇ-ṇā́m*, the gen. plur. of *ṣáṣ-*, which however does not seem to occur in any of the Saṃhitās.

4 With accent on the final syllable like the genitives of *páñca* etc.

5 G. *catasṛṇā́m* and L. *catasṛ́ṣu* occur in B.

6 On the Sandhi, see above 78.

7 That is, of accenting *-á* before the terminations *-bhis, -bhyas, -su*, and the final syllable in the gen. See above, 93.

8 Cp. note 3.

9 Cp. BRUGMANN, KG. 441, 8.

10 These are the only two occurrences in the RV., for in *aṣṭa-karṇá-* (x. 62[7]) the first member is doubtless a past participle.

'twenty-eightfold', *aṣṭā-cakra-* (AV.) 'eight-wheeled', *aṣṭā-pakṣa-* (AV.) 'eight-sided', *aṣṭā-yogá-* (AV.) 'yoke of eight'. The form *aṣṭa-* begins to appear in the AV. in the derivative *aṣṭa-dhā́* 'in eight ways'; and in the compounds *aṣṭa-kŕ̥tvas* 'eight times', *aṣṭá-yoni-* 'having eight wombs', *aṣṭa-vr̥ṣá-* 'eight times chief'.

9. N. A. *náva* 'nine'. I. *navábhis*. D. *navábhyas* (TS.). G. *navānā́m*.

10. N. A. *dáśa* 'ten'. I. *daśábhis*. D. *daśábhyas* (TS.). G. *daśānā́m*. L. *daśásu*.

11. N. A. *ékādaśa* 'eleven'. D. *ekādaśábhyas* (TS.).

12. N. A. *dvā́daśa* 'twelve. D. *dvādaśábhyas* (TS.).

13. N. A. *tráyodaśa* 'thirteen'. I. *trayodaśábhis* (TS.). D. *trayodaśábhyas* (TS.).

14. N. A. *cáturdaśa* 'fourteen'. D. *caturdaśábhyas* (TS.).

15. N. A. *páñcadaśa* 'fifteen'. D. *pañcadaśábhyas* (TS.).

16. N. A. *ṣóḍaśa* (VS.) 'sixteen'. D. *ṣoḍaśábhyas* (TS.).

17. 18. The N. of the cardinals for 'seventeen' and 'eighteen' does not seem to occur in Mantras. D. *saptadaśábhyas* (TS.); *aṣṭādaśábhyas* (TS.).

19. N. A. *návadaśa* (VS.) 'nineteen'. I. *navadaśábhis* (VS.). D. *ékān ná viṃśatyái* (TS.).

c. The **third group** of cardinals, comprising the numbers from 'twenty' onwards, are substantives inflected regularly according to the declension of the stem final; e. g. N. *viṃśatí-s* 'twenty', A. *viṃśatí-m*, I. *viṃśaty-ā́*; N. *triṃśát* 'thirty', A. *triṃśát-am*, I. *triṃśát-ā*, L. *triṃśát-i*. The decades 'twenty' to 'ninety' and their compounds are fem. and nearly always inflected in the sing.; but if the sense requires it they may be used in the plural; e. g. *náva navatī́ḥ* 'nine nineties'; *navānā́m navatīnā́m* (I. 191[13]) 'of nine nineties'.

a. *śatá-* 'a hundred' and *sahásra-* 'a thousand' are neuters, which may be declined in all numbers; e. g. *dvé śaté* 'two hundred'; *saptá śatā́ni* 'seven hundred'.

Syntactical employment of the Cardinals.

407. a. The numerals from **'one' to 'nineteen'** are used **adjectivally**; e. g. *tráyo vīrā́ḥ* (III. 56[8]) 'three heroes'; *saptábhiḥ putráiḥ* (X. 72[9]) 'with seven sons'; *jáneṣu pañcásu* (III. 37[9]) 'among the five races'. The bare stem (in the numerals of the second group) is, however, sometimes used in the oblique cases; e. g. *saptá hótr̥bhiḥ* (III. 10[4]) 'with seven priests'; *ádhi páñca kr̥ṣṭíṣu* (II. 2[10]) 'over the five tribes'.

a. Exceptionally these numerals are, however, to be met with governing a genitive; e. g. *dáśa kaláśānām* (IV. 32[19]) 'ten jars'.

b. The **third group** of numerals (from 'twenty' upwards), as singular **substantives**, is treated in two ways.

1. They may govern a genitive; e. g. *pañcāśátam áśvānām* (V. 18[5]) 'fifty horses'; *ṣaṣṭím áśvānām* (VIII. 46[29]) 'sixty horses'; *śatáṃ gónām* (I. 126[2]) 'a hundred kine'. So also when *śatá-* and *sahásra-* are in the du. or pl.; e. g. *gávāṃ śatā́ni* (VII. 103[10]) 'hundreds of kine'; *sahásrāṇi gávām* (VIII. 51[2]) 'thousands of kine'.

2. They may, remaining singular, agree in case with the following plural, being then used adjectivally (not appositionally, because they always precede the substantive in this use); e. g. *triṃśád devā́ḥ* (III. 9[9]) 'thirty gods'; *triṃśátaṃ yójanāni* (I. 123[8]) 'thirty leagues'; *triṃśátā háribhiḥ* (II. 18[5]) 'with thirty bays'; *śaténa háribhiḥ* (II. 18[6]) 'with a hundred bays'; *śatám púraḥ* (IV. 27[1]) 'a hundred forts'; *sahásraṃ hárayaḥ* (IV. 46[3]) 'a thousand bays'. The following word, agreeing with *sahásra-*, may be in the singular as a collective; thus *śúnaś cic chépaṃ níditaṃ sahásrād yū́pād amuñcaḥ* (V. 2[7]) 'Śunaḥśepa, who was bound, thou didst release from a thousand posts'.

a. *śatá-* and *sahásra-* have, in their adjectival use, the peculiarity of sometimes either being put in the plural themselves or retaining the N. A. neuter sing. form (like *páñca*) when in agreement with an inst. pl.; e. g. *śatā́ púraḥ* (I. 53[8]) 'a hundred forts'; *sahásrāṇy ádhirathāni* (x. 98[9]) 'a thousand wagonloads'; *śatám pūrbhiḥ* (vi. 48[8]) 'with a hundred forts'; *sahásram ṛ́ṣibhiḥ* (i. 189[8]) 'with a thousand seers'.

β. The numeral pronouns *káti* 'how many?', *táti* 'so many', *yáti* 'as many', remain uninflected in agreement with nominatives and accusatives plural, which are the only cases found occurring with them in the Saṃhitās[1].

B. Ordinals.

408. The ordinals, being all adjectives ending in *-a*, are declined throughout in the masc. and neut. according to the nominal *a*-declension. The feminine is formed with *-ī*[2], except in the first four, which take *-ā*, viz. *prathamā́-*[3], *dvitī́yā-*, *tṛtī́yā-*[3], *turī́yā-* (TS.). The ordinals may best be divided into **four groups** according to the formation of their stems.

1. The ordinals from **'first' to 'tenth'** are formed with various suffixes, viz. *(-t)-īya*, *-tha*, *-thamá*, *-má*, the first four in a somewhat irregular manner.

a. *pra-thamá-* 'first' was doubtless formed from *pra-* with the superlative suffix *-tama*[4], meaning 'foremost', the initial of the suffix being probably changed under the influence of other ordinals formed with *-tha* (*ṣaṣṭhá-*, etc.).

b. The next three ordinals are formed with the suffix *-īya*: *dvit-ī́ya-* 'second', *tṛt-ī́ya-* 'third', secondarily through *dvi-tá-* 'second', and *tṛ-tá-* 'third', both used as names; *tur-ī́ya-* 'fourth' for **ktur-ī́ya-* (beside *catur-thá-*). The latter when used in the fractional sense is accented *túrīya-* (AV.) 'quarter'[5].

c. The ordinal for 'sixth', besides the alternative forms for 'fourth' and 'seventh', is formed with *-tha*: *ṣaṣ-ṭhá-* (AV. VS.), *catur-thá-* (AV. VS.), *saptá-tha-* (RV.).

d. The ordinals for 'fifth' and 'seventh' to 'tenth' are formed with *-ma*: *pañca-má-* (AV. VS.), *sapta-má-* (VS.) beside *saptá-tha-*, *aṣṭa-má-*, *nava-má-*, *daśa-má-*.

2. The stems of the ordinals for **'seventh' to 'nineteenth'** are the same as those of the cardinals, except that they are accented on the final syllable. In inflexion they differ from the cardinals in following the ordinary nominal *a-* declension; thus from *ekādaśá-* 'eleventh' are formed: sing. m. A. *ekādaśám*; pl. N. *ekādaśā́sah*, A. *ekādaśā́n*, I. *ekādaśáis*.

3. The ordinals for **'twentieth' to 'ninetieth'** (including their compounds) seem, judged by some three examples met with in the Saṃhitās (and some four others in B.), to have been abbreviated forms of the cardinals, ending in *-á*: *eka-viṃśá-* 'twenty-first' (B.) 'consisting of twenty-one' (VS.), *catvāriṃśá-* (RV.) 'fortieth', *aṣṭā-catvāriṃśá-* (VS.) 'forty-eighth'; *catus-triṃśá-* (B.) 'thirty-fourth', *dvā-pañcāśá-* (B.) 'fifty-second', *eka-ṣaṣṭá-* (B.) 'sixty-first'.

4. The ordinals for **'hundredth' and 'thousandth'** are formed with the superlative suffix *-tama*: *śata-tamá-*; but *sahasra-tamá-* has been noted in B. passages only (TS. ŚB.).

C. Numeral Derivatives.

409. A number of derivatives, chiefly adverbs, are formed from the cardinals.

a. There are a few **multiplicative adjectives** derived with the suffixes *-a*, *-ya*, *-taya*, *-vaya*; thus *tray-á-* 'threefold' (from *tri-*); *dva-yá-* 'twofold'; *dáśa-taya-* 'tenfold'; *cátur-vaya-* 'fourfold'.

b. Multiplicative adverbs are formed in three different ways. 'Once'

1 Cp. Delbrück 50.

2 Inflected like stems in derivative *-ī*: 377.

3 Both *prathamā́-* and *tṛtī́yā-* have one form each according to the pronominal declension in the AV. (403, 3, c).

4 Cp. the adverbial acc. *pra-tamā́m* (B.) 'specially'. See Brugmann, KG. 447, 1.

5 Similarly in B. passages *cáturtha-* quarter', *tṛ́tīya-* 'third'.

is expressed by *sa-kṛ́t*, which originally seems to have meant 'one making'. The next three are formed with the suffix *-s*: *dvi-s* 'twice'; *trí-s* 'thrice', *catúṣ* (AV.) 'four times' (for **catúr-s*, cp. Av. *čathru-š*)[1]. Others are expressed by the cardinal and the form *kṛ́tvas* 'times' (probably = 'makings', acc. pl. of **kṛ́tu-*), which, except in *aṣṭa-kṛ́tvas* (AV.) 'eight times', is a separate word; thus *dáśa kṛ́tvas* (AV.) 'ten times', *bhū́ri kṛ́tvas* (RV.) 'many times'[2].

c. **Numeral adverbs of manner** are formed with the suffix *-dhā*; thus *dvi-dhā́* 'in two ways or parts'; similarly *tri-dhā́* and *tre-dhā́*, *catur-dhā́*, *pañca-dhā́* (AV.), *ṣoḍhā́*[3], *sapta-dhā́* (AV. VS. TS.), *aṣṭa-dhā́* (AV.), *nava-dhā́* (AV.), *sahasra-dhā́*.

VII. THE VERB.

BENFEY, Vollständige Grammatik 788—920. — WHITNEY, Sanskrit Grammar 527—1073. — DELBRÜCK, Das altindische Verbum, Halle 1874. — AVERY, Contributions to the history of verb-inflection in Sanskrit, JAOS. x. (1876), 219—276; 311—324. — JUL. V. NEGELEIN, Zur Sprachgeschichte des Veda. Das Verbalsystem des Atharva-Veda, Berlin 1898.

410. **General characteristics.** — The verbal system comprises the two groups of forms which include, on the one hand, the finite verb and, on the other, the nominal formations connected with the verb. The former group represents the forms made with personal endings, viz. indicative, subjunctive, injunctive, optative, and imperative. The latter group consists of infinitives (nouns of action) and participles (agent nouns). These differ from ordinary nouns inasmuch as they participate in the characteristics of the verb, governing cases, being connected with particular tenses, being used in different voices, and being liable to tmesis when compounded with prepositions.

A. The finite verb distinguishes the **primary conjugation** of the root and the **secondary conjugation** of derivative formations, viz. desiderative, intensive, causative, and denominative. The latter class does not, however, differ in origin from the former; but doubtless because (in contrast with the present stems of the primary conjugation) it preserves the distinctive meaning of the stem, it extends the form of the present stem beyond the present system to the whole conjugation.

The finite verb further distinguishes voice, tense, mood, number, and person.

a. There are two **voices**, active and middle, which are distinguished throughout the inflexion of the verb (largely also in the participle, though not in the infinitive). The middle forms may be employed in a passive sense, except in the present system where there is a special passive stem inflected with middle terminations. Some verbs are conjugated in both active and middle; e. g. *kṛṇó-ti* and *kṛṇu-té* 'makes'; others in one voice only, e. g. *ás-ti* 'is'; others partly in one and partly in the other; e. g. pres. *várta-te* 'turns', but perf. *vavárt-a* 'has turned'.

b. There are five **tenses** in ordinary use, viz. the present, the imperfect, the perfect, the aorist, and the future. The terms imperfect, perfect, and aorist are here used in a purely formal sense, that is, as corresponding in formation to the Greek tenses bearing those names. No Vedic tense has an imperfect meaning, while the perfect sense is generally expressed by the aorist.

c. Beside the indicative there are four **moods**, the subjunctive, the injunctive, the optative, and the imperative, all formed from the stem of the

[1] Cp. BRUGMANN, KG. 450, 1.
[2] Cp. WHITNEY 1105, a.
[3] For *ṣaṣ-dhā́*; cp. above 43, b, 3; 56, b; and p. 307, note 8.

present, the perfect, and the aorist. The imperfect has no moods; and the only modal form occurring in the future is the unique subjunctive *kariṣyás*, from *kṛ-* 'make'.

d. The finite verb is, as in other languages, used in **three persons** in all tenses and moods excepting the imperative, where the first persons are supplied from the subjunctive. As in declension, the three numbers, singular, dual, and plural, are in regular use throughout.

B. The **nominal verb-forms** comprise:

a. Participles. The tense-stem of the present, future, aorist, and perfect each forms an active and a middle participle; e. g. *gácchant-*, *gáccha-māna-* 'going'; *kariṣyánt-* 'going to do', *yakṣyá-māṇa-* 'going to sacrifice'; *kránt-*, *krāṇá-* 'making'; *cakṛvā́ṃs-*, *cakrāṇá-* 'having done'. Besides these, there are passive participles, present, perfect, and future. The present form is made from the passive stem in *-ya*; e. g. *stūyá-māna-* 'being praised'. The perfect passive participle, on the other hand, is formed from the root; e. g. *kṛ-tá-* 'made'; as is also (with few exceptions) the future passive participle or gerundive; e. g. *vánd-ya-* 'praiseworthy'.

b. Gerunds. These are stereotyped cases (chiefly instrumentals) of verbal nouns, and have the value of indeclinable active participles with a prevailingly past sense; e. g. *gatvī́* and *gatvā́ya* 'having gone'.

c. Infinitives. There are about a dozen differently formed types of infinitives, which are cases of verbal nouns made directly or with a suffix from the root, and hardly ever connected with a tense stem; e. g. *ídh-am* 'to kindle'; *gán-tavái* 'to go'.

A. The Finite Verb.

411. All forms of the finite verb[1] may be classed under **four groups**: (1) the **present system**, comprising the present tense together with its moods and participles, and its augmented past tense, the imperfect; (2) the **perfect system**, comprising the perfect tense together with its moods and participles, and its augmented past tense, the pluperfect[2] (494); (3) the **aorist system**, comprising the aorist tense together with its moods and participles; (4) the **future system**, comprising the future tense[3] together with its participles, and its augmented past form, the conditional[4].

Personal Endings.

412. The characteristic feature of the finite verb is the addition of personal endings[5]. These are divided into active and middle; in each of which groups, again, **primary and secondary forms** are to be distinguished. The primary forms appear throughout the present and future indicative, but in the middle only of the perfect indicative[6]. The secondary forms appear in augmented indicatives, in injunctives (which are identical in form with unaugmented past indicatives), in the imperative (several forms of which are identical with the injunctive)[7], and in the optative. The subjunctive fluctuates between the primary and the secondary endings, but the latter are about

[1] Over 18000 occurrences of verb-forms have been noted by AVERY (221) in the RV.

[2] This term is used in a purely formal sense, as this rare tense has not a pluperfect meaning.

[3] There is no periphrastic future in the Saṃhitās.

[4] There is only a single occurrence of this formation in the Saṃhitās.

[5] Cp. AVERY 225 f.; BRUGMANN, KG. 771—798.

[6] The 3. pl. has here the peculiar ending *-re*.

[7] Cp. BRUGMANN, KG. 729.

twice as frequent as the former[1]. The perfect indicative active has some of the regular secondary endings (*-va, ma, -ur*), but the rest are of a peculiar type.

Active endings.

Primary. Sing. 1. *-mi*[2]. 2. *-si*. 3. *-ti*[3]. Du. 1. *-vas*[4]. 2. *-thas*[5]. 3. *-tas*[5]. Pl. 1. *-masi, -mas*[6]. 2. *-tha, -thana*[7]. 3. *-anti*[8].

Secondary. Sing. 1. *-m*. 2. *-s*[9]. 3. *-t*[10]. Du. 1. *-va*. 2. *-tam*. 3. *-tām*. Pl. 1. *-ma*. 2. *-ta, -tana*[11]. 3. *-an, -ur*[12].

Middle endings.

Primary. Sing. 1. *-e*. 2. *-se*[13]. 3. *-te*[14]. Du. 1. *-vahe*[15]. 2. *-āthe*[16]. 3. *-āte*[16]. Pl. 1. *-mahe*[17]. 2. *-dhve*[18]. 3. *-ante*[19].

Secondary. Sing. 1. *-i*[20]. 2. *-thās*[21]. 3. *-ta*[22]. Du. 1. *-vahi*. 2. *-āthām*[23]. 3. *-ātām*[23]. Pl. 1. *-mahi*. 2. *-dhvam*[24]. 3. *-anta*[25].

a. Beside the perfect endings containing *r*, act. du. 2. *-athur*, 3. *-atur*, pl. 3. *-ur*, middle *-re*, some verbs have endings with initial *r* in the 3. pl. mid. ind. and opt. of most tenses. These endings are *-re* and *-rate* in the pres. ind.; *-rire* in the perf. ind.; *-ran* in the opt. pres. and the ind. imperfect, pluperfect, and aorist; *-ram* in the ind. aor.; *-ranta* in the pluperfect; *-rata* in the opt. In the AV. *-rām* and *-ratām* appear in the 3. pl. impv. mid.[26].

b. More than twenty roots have forms in which certain endings are added to the root with the connecting vowel *i* or less commonly *ī*. These roots are *an-* 'breathe', *am-* 'injure', *as-* 'be', *īḍ-* 'praise', *īś-* 'rule', *cud-* 'impel', *jan-* 'beget', *tu-* 'be strong', *dhvan-* 'sound', *brū-* 'speak', *vam-* 'vomit', *vas-* 'clothe', *vṛṣ-* 'rain', *śnath-* 'pierce', *śru-* 'hear',

---

1 Avery 227 (middle).

2 The subjunctive has *-āni* and instead of it (13 times) *-ā*; cp. Avery 225 (mid.) and Brugmann, KG. 772.

3 The perf. ind. has the peculiar endings 1. *-a* or *-au*, 2. *-tha*, 3. *-a* or *-au* in the sing.

4 This ending does not occur in the RV.; cp. Delbrück, Verbum p. 24.

5 The perf. act. du. has the peculiar endings 2. *-athur*, 3. *-atur*.

6 *-masi* occurs 109 times in the RV., being more than 5 times as frequent as *-mas* (cp. Whitney 548; Avery 226), but in the AV. *-mas* has become commoner than *-masi* in the proportion of 4 to 3. On these endings cp. Neisser, BB. 30, 311—315.

7 In the RV. *-tha* occurs more than 6 times as often as *-thana* (Avery 226). The perf. ind. has the peculiar ending *-a*.

8 The *an* is replaced by *a* (for the sonant nasal) in reduplicated verbs and a few others treated as such; cp. Delbrück, Verbum p. 51 (mid).

9 The impv. act. adds *-dhi, -hi, -āna, -tāt* or no ending.

10 The 3. impv. has *-tu* instead of *-t*; in the RV. and TS. also *-tāt*; see 418 b.

11 In the RV. *-ta* occurs more than 4 times as often as *-tana* (560 occurrences to 125: Avery 226).

12 In the ind. perf., the ind. *s*-aorist, and the optative, *-ur* always appears, sometimes also in the imperfect; cp. Delbrück, Verbum p. 52. The impv. has *-antu*, which loses its *n* under the same conditions as *-anti*.

13 In the AV. *-sai* is the only form of the subjunctive (Whitney 561, a).

14 *-tai* occurs once in the RV. for *-te* in the subjunctive; it is the usual form in the AV. In the RV. *-e* sometimes occurs for *-te* in the ind. pres.; it is the only ending in the perf. ind.

15 The subjunctive has *-vahai*.

16 In the *a-* conjugation *-ethe* and *-ete*; *aithe* and *-aite* appear in the RV. as subjunctives in several forms; *-aite* occurs once as an indicative; cp. Whitney 547, c and 561, a; Delbrück, Verbum 106 and p. 45 (mid.).

17 *-mahai* is the usual form in the subjunctive in the RV. and AV.

18 In the RV. once *-dhvai* in the subjunctive.

19 In the impv. *-antām* and *-atām*.

20 In the optative (*īy*)-*a*.

21 In the impv. *-sva*.

22 In the impv. *-tām*.

23 In the *a*-conjugation *-ethām* and *-etām*.

24 Once *-dhva* in the RV.

25 In the impv. *-antām*; both this ending and *-anta* lose their *n* under the same conditions as *-anti*. The perf. ind. has *-re*.

26 See Delbrück, Verbum 76—78; Avery 226; Brugmann, KG. 797; cp. also Bollensen, ZDMG. 22, 599; Kuhn, KZ. 18, 400; Benfey, Ueber die Entstehung und Verwendung der im Sanskrit mit *r* anlautenden Personalendungen. Abh. d. Ges. d. Wiss. zu Göttingen 15, Göttingen 1870; Windisch, Berichte der sächsischen Gesellschaft d. Wiss. 1889, p. 1 ff.; Zimmer, KZ. 30, 224 ff.

śvas- 'breathe', *sidh-* 'repel', *stan-* 'thunder', *stambh-*[1] 'prop'. There are also a few 3. plurals in *-i-re*, viz. *ṛṇvire, pinvire, śṛṇviré, sunviré* and *hinviré*, in which the connecting vowel *i* appears[2].

The Augment.

413. The augment[3] (originally doubtless an independent temporal particle) consists of the syllable *a-*, which is prefixed to the imperfect, pluperfect, aorist, and conditional, giving to those forms the signification of past time. It invariably bears the acute when the verb is accented, like the preposition immediately preceding a verb in a principal sentence (111). The augment sometimes appears lengthened before *n, y, r* or *v*, the only examples being *ā́-naṭ*, from *naś-* 'attain'; *ā́-yunak* (beside *a-yunak*), *ā́-yukta* (beside *á-yukta*), and *ā́-yukṣātām*, from *yuj-* 'join'; *ā́-riṇak* and *ā́-raik*, from *ric-* 'leave'; *ā́-var*, from *vṛ-* 'cover'; *ā-vṛṇi*, from *vṛ-* 'choose'; *ā́-vṛṇak*, from *vṛj-* 'turn'; *ā-vidhyat* (beside *á-vidhyat*), from *vyadh-* 'wound'. The only one of these forms written with *ā* in the Pada text is *ā́-var* (but once also *a-var*). There is also one passage (II. 17. 9) in which the metre seems to require that *yás té 'vidhat* should be read *yás ta ā́vidhat*[4].

a. With the initial vowels *i, u, ṛ* the augment irregularly **contracts to the Vṛddhi vowels** *ai, au, ār*; e. g. *áicchas*, 2. sing. imperf. of *iṣ-* 'wish'; *áunat*, 3. sing. imperf. of *ud-* 'wet'; *ā́rta*, 3. sing. aor. of *ṛ-* 'go'. This appears to be a survival of a prehistoric contraction of *ā* with *i, u, ṛ* to *āi, āu, ār*, which is otherwise almost invariably represented by *e, o, ar*[5].

b. The augment is **very often dropped.** This optional loss is to be explained as a survival from the Indo-European period when, being an independent particle, the augment could be dispensed with if the past sense was clear from the context. In the RV. the number of examples in which the augment is wanting (about 2000) is considerably more than half that of forms in which it is prefixed (about 3300), more than one half of these unaugmented forms being aorists. In the AV. the number of forms which lose the augment is less than half that of those which retain it, more than four fifths of these unaugmented forms being aorists. In sense, the forms which drop the augment are either indicative or injunctive. The indicatives have for the most part a past, but often also (generally when compounded with prefixes) a present meaning. In the RV., the indicative and injunctive unaugmented forms are about equal in number[6]; the injunctives being used in nearly one-third of their occurrences with the prohibitive particle *mā́*. In the AV. about nine-tenths of the unaugmented forms are injunctive, some four-fifths of these being construed with *mā́*.

Formation of the Moods.

414. 1. Subjunctive[7]. The subjunctive is a very common mood in the RV. and the AV., occurring three or four times as often as the optative. It is formed from the present, the perfect, and the aorist[8]. The stem is formed by adding *a* to the indicative stem. When a strong and weak stem are distinguished, the *a* is attached to the former; while it coalesces to *ā* with the final of the stem in the *a-* conjugation. Thus the subjunctive stem of

1 Avery 226.

2 Avery 227 (top).

3 Cp. Avery 225; Brugmann KG. 626.

4 Whitney 585, a.

5 Cp. above 19 a, 4. 5.

6 Whitney 587, a. According to Avery 225, the unaugmented forms of the RV. have a historical sense in 488 instances only.

7 See especially W. Neisser, Zur vedischen Verballehre (Inaugural-Dissertat.), Göttingen 1882 = BB. 7 (1883), 211—241.

8 Only a single form of the future subjunctive occurs.

the root *duh-* 'milk' is *dóh-a-*; of *yuj-* 'join' *yunáj-a-*; but of *bhū-* 'be' *bháv-ā-*. Owing to the analogy of the *a-* conjugation, other verbs sometimes add *ā* instead of *a*, e. g. *brav-ā-thá* from *brū-* 'speak'[1]. The subjunctive is on the whole inflected like an indicative, but with fluctuations between the primary and the secondary endings, besides some variations in the endings themselves. Thus in the active, (1) the ending of the 1. sing. is *-āni*, of which the *ni* is dropped thirteen times in the RV., e. g. *dóh-āni, yunáj-āni, bháv-āni; bháv-ā*; (2) the 1. du. and 1. 3. pl. have the secondary endings *-va*, *-ma*, *-an* only; e. g. *dóh-āva, dóh-āma, dóh-an; bháv-āva, bháv-āma, bháv-ān*; (3) the 2. 3. sing. may take the secondary endings as well as the primary; e. g. *dóh-a-si* or *dóh-a-s; bháv-ā-ti* or *bháv-ā-t*[2].

In the **middle**, (1) the only secondary ending is found in the 3. pl., *-anta*, which occurs beside and more frequently than *-ante*; (2) the ending *-ai*, which is normal in the 1. sing. (being = *a* + *e*), has spread from that person to forms in which *e* would be normal. Thus the 1. du. has *-āvahai* only; in the 1. pl., *-āmahai* is the usual form in the RV. and AV. beside the rarer *-āmahe*; in the 2. sing., *-sai* always appears for *-se* in the AV., though it does not occur in the RV.; in the 2. pl., *-dhvai* occurs once for *-dhve*[3] in the RV.; in the 2. 3. du., *-aithe* and *-aite* occur several times in the RV., being doubtless intended for subjunctive modifications[4] of the indicative *-ethe* and *-ete* of the *a-* conjugation; in the 3. sing., *-tai* occurs once in the RV. for *-te*, and is the usual form in the AV.

a. The **subjunctive endings** in combination with the *-a* of the stem are accordingly the following:

	Active				Middle		
	sing.	du.	pl.		sing.	du.	pl.
1.	*āni*, *-ā*	*-ā-va*	*-ā-ma*	1.	*-ai*	*-ā-vahai*	*-ā-mahai*, *-ā-mahe*
2.	*-a-si*[5], *-a-s*[6]	*-a-thas*	*-a-tha*	2.	*-a-se*, *-a-sai*	*-aithe*	*-a-dhve*, *-a-dhvai*
3.	*-a-ti*[7], *-a-t*	*-a-tas*	*-a-n*	3.	*-a-te*, *-a-tai*	*-aite*	*-a-nte*, *-a-nta*.

415. **Injunctive.** The unaugmented forms of past tenses used modally, are sometimes called improper subjunctives[8], but they are more suitably termed injunctives, as they appear to have originally expressed an injunction. This is borne out by the fact that since the IE. period the second and third persons imperfect (except the 2. sing. act.) had come to be used as regular imperatives expressing a command[9]. But the unaugmented forms of the imperfect that could be distinguished from the regular imperative (as *bháras*, *bhárat*, *bharan*) and especially unaugmented aorists[10], are often used in a sense fluctuating between that of the subjunctive (requisition) and of the optative (wish)[11]. Thus *bháratu* 'let him bear', but *bhárat* 'may he bear', *bhū́t* 'may he be'.

416. **Optative.** This mood, which is comparatively rare in the Saṃhitās, is formed from the present, the perfect, and the aorist. The stem is formed with *-yā́* or *-ī*, which, when strong and weak stem are distinguished,

---

[1] Cp. Whitney 560e; Brugmann, KG. 719.

[2] The subjunctive in *ā* is in origin an old injunctive: Brugmann, KG. 716 (end).

[3] In the form *mādayādhvai* 'may ye rejoice'.

[4] *kṛṇvaite*, however, appears once as an indicative; see Delbrück, Verbum p. 45.

[5] In the aor. subj., *-si* occurs only once in the RV.

[6] In the *a-* conjugation *ā* appears throughout: *-āsi*, *-ās*, etc.

[7] In the aor. subj., *-ti* occurs only six times in the RV.

[8] Whitney 563.

[9] The 3. sing. and pl., e. g. *bhárat-u* and *bhárant-u*, are explained as injunctives and the particle *u*: Brugmann, KG. 729, 1.

[10] The aorist injunctives were probably used originally with the prohibitive particle *mā́* only: Brugmann, KG. 716, 2 (end).

[11] Cp. Whitney 575.

are attached to the latter. In the *a-* conjugation *-ī* is added (coalescing with *a* to *e*) throughout; in other verbs *-ī* is added in the middle only, and *-yā́* (often to be read as *-iā́*) in the active only[1].

a. Roots ending in *ā* usually change that vowel to *e* before *-yā*: e. g. *de-yā́m* (perhaps to be explained as *dāi̯ā́m*)[2] 'I would give'. But *ā* is sometimes retained, as in *yā-yā́m* 'I would go'.

b. The endings are the secondary ones. There are, however, some irregularities in the 1. sing. and the 3. pl. 1. The 3. pl. mid. always takes *-ran* instead of *-an*. 2. The 3. pl. act. always takes *-ur*, before which the *ā* of *-yā* is dropped, while in the *a-* conjugation *y* is interposed between *e*[3] and *-ur*. 3. The 1. sing. mid. has the peculiar ending *a* with *y* interposed between it and the modal *-ī*. 4. The 1. sing. act. of the *a-* conjugation attaches *-am* instead of *-m* (the termination *-em* being unknown), interposing *y* between it and the *e*[3] of the stem.

a. The **endings of the optative** in combination with the modal suffix are accordingly the following:

1. Graded conjugation.

Active			Middle		
sing.	du.	pl.	sing.	du.	pl.
1. *-yā́-m*	*-yā́-va*	*-yā́-ma*	1. *-ī-y-á*	*-ī-váhi*	*-ī-máhi*
2. *-yā́-s*	*-yā́-tam*	*-yā́-ta*	2. *-ī-thā́s*	*-ī-y-ā́thām*	*-ī-dhvám*
3. *-yā-t*	*-yā́-tām*	*-y-úr*	3. *-ī-tá*	*-ī-y-ā́tām*	*-ī-r-án*

2. a- conjugation.

1. *-e-y-am*	*-e-va*	*-e-ma*	1. *-e-y-a*	*-e-vahi*	*-e-mahi*
2. *-e-s*	*-e-tam*	*-e-ta*	2. *-e-thās*	*-e-y-āthām*	*-e-dhvam*
3. *-e-t*	*-e-tām*	*-e-y-ur*	3. *-e-ta*	*-e-y-ātām*	*-e-r-an.*

417. Precative. This is a form of the optative which adds an *-s* after the modal suffix in several persons, and is made almost exclusively from aorist stems. In the RV. there occur a few forms of the precative in three persons (1. 3. sing., 1. pl.) active, and in two persons (2. 3. sing.) middle; thus **active**: 1. sing. *bhū-yā-s-am* (aor.) 'may I be'; 3. sing. *aś-yās* (for **aś-yā-s-t*) 'may he attain' (aor.); *babhū-yās* 'may he be' (perf.); 1. pl. *kri-yā-s-ma* 'may we do' (aor.); **middle**: 2. sing. *maṃ-s-ī-ṣ-ṭhā́s* (aor.) and 3. sing. *maṃ-s-ī-ṣ-ṭa* (aor.), from *man-* 'think'.

418. Imperative. This mood has no mood-sign of its own, as all the first persons are subjunctives and the second and third persons are mostly old injunctives. The purely injunctive forms are the 2. 3. du. and 2. pl. active and middle, ending in *-tam*, *-tām*, *-ta*; *-āthām*, *-ātām*, *-dhvam*. The 3. sing. pl. act. in *-tu*[4] and *-antu*[5], and the 3. pl. mid. in *-antām*[5] may be modifications of injunctives. The imperative has, however, distinctive forms of its own in the 2. sing. act.: *-dhi*, *-hi*, *-āna*, *-tāt*; and in the middle: 2. sing. *-sva* and 3. sing. *-tām* or *-ām*.

a. The **2. sing. act.** in the *a*-conjugation has no ending, employing the bare stem (like the vocative singular of the *a-* declension); e. g. *bhára* 'support'; *neṣa* 'lead' (aor. of √*nī-*). In the graded conjugation, when a strong and weak stem are distinguished, the ending is attached to the latter: *-dhi* is added after both consonants and vowels, *-hi* (the later form of *-dhi*) after vowels only; thus *ad-dhí* 'eat'; *śru-dhí* and *śṛṇu-dhí* 'hear'; *i-hí* 'go', *jāgṛ-hí* 'awake', *pipṛ-hi* 'save', *śṛṇu-hí* 'hear'. In the *nā-* class, *-hi* is added

1 On the accentuation cp. above 9 and 24 a.

2 Cp. Brugmann, KG. 555 (bottom).

3 The *e* (for *a*) is here probably due to the influence of the other forms *-es*, *-et*, etc.: Brugmann, KG. 728.

4 Cp. Brugmann, KG. 729, 1; IF. 18, 71; Delbrück, Vergl. Syntax 2, p. 357.

5 The ending *-antu* and *-antām* lose their *n* under the same conditions as *-anti* (p. 314, note [8]).

only when the root ends in a vowel, but *-āna*[1] when it ends in a consonant; thus *pu-nīhí* 'purify', but *aś-āna* 'eat'.

b. The ending **-tāt** occurs some twenty times in the RV. When strong and weak stem are distinguished, it is added to the latter; e. g. *vit-tā́t* 'thou shalt regard', *dhat-tāt* 'thou shalt place', *kṛṇu-tāt* 'thou shalt make', *punī-tāt* 'thou shalt purify', etc.[2] Its use is almost restricted to the 2. sing. It is, however, once[3] found in the RV. and once in the TS. in the sense of the 3. sing., once as 2. du. in the RV., once as 2. pl. in the TS., and once as 1. sing. in AV.[4]. It appears to have the value of a future imperative, expressing an injunction to be carried out at a time subsequent to the present. It may originally have been identical with the abl. *tā́d* 'after that', 'then'; *kṛṇu-tāt* would thus have meant 'do (it) then'[5].

I. The Present System.

419. This group consists of a present indicative together with a subjunctive, an injunctive, an optative, an imperative, and participles, besides a past augmented tense called the imperfect because formed analogously to the Greek tense. This is the most important system, as its forms are about three times as common as those of the three other systems taken together[6]. Hence roots are generally classified according to the manner in which their stems are formed in the present system. Here **two** distinct **conjugations** may be conveniently distinguished.

The **first or *a*- conjugation**, all the stems in which end in *-a*, retains the stem unaltered (like the *a*- declension) in every tense, mood, and participle, accenting the same syllable throughout the present indicative, its moods and participles, as well as the unaugmented imperfect[7]. The secondary conjugations in *-a* (desideratives, intensives, causatives, denominatives) as well as the future[8], follow this conjugation in their inflexion.

The **second or graded conjugation** is characterized by shift of accent between stem and ending, accompanied by vowel gradation. Minor differences consist in the loss of *n* in the 3. pl. middle, in the addition of another suffix (*-āna* instead of *-māna*) in the middle participle, in the employment of an ending in the 2. sing. impv. act., and in vowel gradation, with shift of accent, in the modal suffix of the optative.

a. The first or *a*- conjugation.

420. The **special characteristics** of this conjugation are:

1. The *-a* of the stem is lengthened before the endings of the 1. du. and pl. which begin with *v* and *m*; e. g. *jayāmasi* 'we conquer'; while the initial *a* of the endings of the 3. pl. *-anti*, *-ante*, *-an*, *-anta*, is dropped; e. g. *bhára-nti* 'they bear'.

2. The optative sign is throughout *-ī*, which combines with the *-a* of the present stem to *e*; e. g. *bháves*.

3. The 2. sing. impv. act. has no ending except the comparatively few instances (about sixteen) in which *-tāt* is added.

---

1 On the origin of this peculiar imperative form cp. BRUGMANN, KG. 839, 5.

2 See DELBRÜCK, Verbum 38.

3 Op. cit. 77; WHITNEY 571, b. AVERY, however (225, bottom), states that it occurs 5 times in the RV. as a 3. sing.

4 WHITNEY, loc. cit.

5 BRUGMANN, KG. 732.

6 WHITNEY 600, a.

7 But when the augment was added, it received the accent just like the verbal preposition in a principal sentence (the verb itself remaining unaccented).

8 Also aorist stems ending in *-a*.

4. The 2. 3. du. mid. substitute *e* for the *ā* of the endings *-āthe*, *-āte*; e. g. 2. *vahethe* 'ye two travel', 3. *vardhete* 'they two thrive'.

5. The middle participle regularly ends in *-māna*.

a. **Five classes** or types may be distinguished in the present stems of the *a-* conjugation. These are: 1. Stems in which the radical syllable has a strong grade accented vowel[1]; e. g. *bhára-ti*, from *bhṛ-* 'bear'. 2. Stems in which the radical syllable has a weak grade vowel, the thematic *a* being accented[2]; e. g. *rujá-ti*, from *ruj-* 'break'. 3. Stems formed with the suffix *-ya*, being either (a) ordinary transitive or intransitive verbs[3], e. g. *ás-ya-ti* 'throws'; or (b) passives, e. g. *nī-yá-te* 'is led'. 4. Stems ending in *-aya*, being either (a) causatives (*-áya*) or (b) denominatives (*-ayá*)[4]. 5. Stems formed with the suffix *-sa*, added to the reduplicated root, being desideratives; e. g. *pí-pā-sa-* 'desire to drink'. The last two classes, which retain the present stem throughout their inflexion, constitute three of the secondary conjugations which will be treated separately below (541—570).

1. The radically accented *a-* class (*bháva-*).

421. This is by far the **commonest type** of the *a-* conjugation, about 300 such present stems occurring in the Saṃhitās[5]. The radical vowel takes Guṇa, unless it is medial and long by nature or position; thus from *ji-* 'conquer' : *jáy-a-*; *nī-* 'lead' : *náy-a-*; *bhū-* 'be' : *bháv-a-*; *budh-* 'awake' : *bódh-a-*; *sṛp-* 'creep' : *sárpa-*; but *jinv-* 'quicken' : *jínv-a-*; *krīḍ-* 'play' : *krī́ḍ-a-*. Roots with medial *a* remain unchanged, e. g. *vad-* 'speak' : *vád-a-*.

a. There are, however, several irregularities in the formation of the present stem: 1. *ūh-* 'consider' takes Guṇa: *óha-* (but *ūh-* 'remove' remains unchanged: *ūha-*); *guh-* 'hide' lengthens its vowel: *gū́ha-*; *kram-* 'stride' lengthens its vowel in the active: *krā́ma-* (but *krama-* in the middle); *kṛp-* 'lament' retains its vowel unchanged: *kṛ́pa-*. — 2. The roots *daṃś-* 'bite' and *sañj-* 'hang' lose their nasal: *dáśa-*, *sája-*. — 3. *gam-* 'go', *yam-* 'reach', *yu-* 'separate' form their stem with the suffix *-cha-*: *gáccha-*, *yáccha-*, *yúccha-*. — 4. Four stems are transfers from the reduplicating class[6]: *piba-* from *pā-* 'drink', *tíṣṭha-* from *sthā-* 'stand', *sī́da-*[7] (for **si-sad-a-*) from *sad-* 'sit', *śáśca-*[8] (for **sá-sac-a-*) from *sac-* 'accompany'; four others[9] are transfers from the *nu-* class, being either used beside or having entirely superseded the simpler original stems: *i-nv-a-* from *i-* 'send', beside *i-nó-ti*; *ji-nv-a-* from *ji-* 'quicken', beside *ji-nó-ṣi*; *hi-nv-a-* from *hi-* 'impel', beside *hi-nó-ti*; *pinv-a-* 'fatten' was doubtless originally **pi-nu-* from the root *pī-*[10].

422. Present indicative. The forms of this tense which actually occur, if made from *bháva-*, would be as follows:

Active. Sing. 1. *bhávā-mi*, 2. *bháva-si*, 3. *bháva-ti*. Du. 1. *bhávā-vas* (TS.), 2. *bháva-thas*, 3. *bháva-tas*. Pl. 1. *bhávā-masi* and *bhávā-mas*, 2. *bháva-tha*[11], 3. *bháva-nti*.

Middle. Sing. 1. *bháv-e*, 2. *bháva-se*, 3. *bháva-te*[12]. Du. 1. *bhávā-vahe*, 3. *bháv-ete*. Pl. 1. *bhávā-mahe*[13], 2. *bháva-dhve*, 3. *bháva-nte*.

The forms which actually occur are the following:

---

[1] The first class of the Indian grammarians.

[2] The sixth class of the Indian grammarians.

[3] The fourth class of the Indian grammarians.

[4] The nominal *a* preceding the *-ya* is here sometimes dropped or changed to *ā* or *ī*. See below 562. Some of these verbs in *-aya*, having lost their special stem meaning, are treated as a class (the tenth) of primary verbs.

[5] See WHITNEY 214—216, cp. 744.

[6] *dádā-* occasionally appears for the regular *dádā-*, from *dā-* 'give'.

[7] See ROZWADOWSKI, BB. 21, 147.

[8] A reminiscence of its reduplicative origin is the loss of the nasal (the sonant becoming *a*) in the ending of the 3. pl.: *śáścati*, *śáścata*.

[9] *ṛṇv-á-*, beside *ṛ-ṇó-ti* from *ṛ-* 'send', is a similar transfer to the sixth class.

[10] See WHITNEY, Roots, under *pinv*.

[11] *vádā-thana* is the only example of the ending *-thana* in the indicative of the *a-* conjugation.

[12] The RV. once has *śóbhe* as 3. sing. for *śóbhate*.

[13] DELBRÜCK, Verbum p. 30 (top), AVERY p. 235, WHITNEY 735, b, and GRASSMANN, under *man* 'think', give *manāmahé* (IX. 41²),

Present Indicative.

Active. Sing. 1. *acāmi, árcāmi, avāmi, ūhāmi* (AV. VS.), *khánāmi, gácchāmi* (AV.), *carāmi, codāmi, jánāmi, jayāmi, tapāmi* (AV.). *tiṣṭhāmi* (AV.), *dahāmi, dhā́vāmi* (AV.), *náyāmi* (AV. TS.), *pacāmi* (AV.), *patāmi, píbāmi*[1], *bhajāmi, bhárāmi, bhavāmi* (AV.), *mándāmi* (TS. IV. 2. 6[1]), *yacchāmi* (AV.), *yajāmi* (AV.), *yācāmi, rapāmi, rā́jāmi, rohāmi* (AV.), *vádāmi, vapāmi* (AV.), *váhāmi, śáṃsāmi, śikṣāmi, śumbhāmi, sajāmi, sapāmi, sīdāmi*[1] (AV.), *svadāmi, harāmi.*

2. *atasi, arṣasi, arhasi, ávasi, ínvasi*[2], *ū́hasi, kṣayasi, cárasi, jayasi, jínvasi*[2], *jū́rvasi, tapasi* (AV.), *tarasi, tiṣṭhasi*[1], *tū́rvasi, dāśasi, dhanvasi, dhā́vasi, náyasi, pátasi, pinvasi*[2], *píbasi*[1], *bhávasi, bhū́ṣasi, madasi* (AV.), *yácchasi, yájasi, rákṣasi, rā́jasi, rohasi, vañcasi* (AV.), *vádasi, vapasi, varṣasi* (AV.), *váhasi, śaṃsasi, śikṣasi, sárpasi* (AV.); *saścasi*[1], *sīdasi*[1], *harasi* (AV.).

3. *acati* (AV.), *ájati, ánati* (AV.), *ayati, árcati, ardati* (AV.), *arṣati, arhati, ávati, ínvati*[2], *īṣati, īhati* (Kh. II. 10[5]), *ūhati, éjati, oṣati, krándati, krāmati* (AV.), *krīḷati, kṣáyati, kṣarati, khanati* (AV.), *khā́dati, gácchati, gūhati* (AV.), *cárati, cétati, jáyati, jínvati*[2], *jī́vati, jūrvati, jrayati, tapati, tárati, tiṣṭhati*[1], *tsárati* (AV.), *dadati*[1], *dahati* (AV.), *dā́śati, dā́sati, dhámati, dhāvati* 'runs' and 'washes', *nákṣati, nándati* (AV.), *náyati, navati* (AV.) 'praises', *pácati, pátati, pinvati*[2], *píbati*[1], *píyati, bódhati, bhájati, bhánati, bhárati, bhárvati, bhávati, bhāsati* (AV.), *bhū́ṣati, bhédati, mádati, márdhati, mehati* (AV.), *yácchati, yájati, yátati, yabhati* (TS. VII. 4. 19[2]), *yámati, yācati* (AV.), *yúcchati, rákṣati, rádati, rapati, rā́jati, rādhati, réjati, rebhati, ródhati, roṣati, róhati, váñcati* (AV.), *vádati, vápati, varjati, vardhati, varṣati* (AV.), *vasati* 'dwells', *vahati, vā́śati, vénati, śaṃsati, śā́sati*[3], *śíkṣati, śundhati, śúmbhati, śócati* (AV. TS.), *sarjati, sárpati, sādhati, sī́dati*[1], *sédhati, skandati, stobhati, sphūrjati* (AV.), *sredhati, hárati, hiṃsati*[4] (Kh. IV. 5[11]).

Du. 1. *cárāvas* (TS. I. 5. 10[1]). — 2. *acathas, árcathas, arhathas, ávathas, invathas*[2], *karṣathas, kṣáyathas, gácchathas, ghoṣathas, cetathas, janathas, jínvathas*[2], *jī́vathas, jū́rvathas, tiṣṭhatas*[1], *dhámathas, nakṣathas, nayathas, pátathas, pínvathas*[2], *bhárathas, bhávathas, bhūṣathas, mádathas, yajathas, yátathas, rakṣathas* (AV. TS.), *rā́jathas, rohathas, vanathas, varathas, vahathas, śíkṣathas, sadathas, sā́dhathas, sīdathas*[1], *svádathas.*

3. *invatas*[2], *ejatas* (AV.), *kṣayatas, khādatas* (AV.), *gácchatas* (AV.), *ghoṣatas, cáratas, tíṣṭhatas*[1] (AV.), *dravatas* (AV.), *dhā́vatas* 'wash', *nakṣatas, pácatas* (AV.), *pinvatas*[2], *píbatas*[1], *bhávatas, bhū́ṣatas, manthatas, mardhatas, yacchatas* (AV.), *yúcchatas, rakṣatas, rā́jatas, vardhatas* (AV.), *vasatas, váhatas.*

Pl. 1. *árcāmasi, árhāmasi, khanāmasi* (AV.), *cárāmasi* and *cárāmas* (AV.), *janāmasi, jayāmasi, tarāmasi, dáyāmasi* (AV.), *dahāmasi* (AV.), *namāmasi* (AV.), *náyāmasi* and *nayāmas* (AV.), *pibāmas*[1] (AV.), *bódhāmasi, bhajāmas* (AV.), *bharāmasi, mádāmasi* and *madāmas, methāmasi, yájāmasi* and *yájāmas, vádāmasi* and *vadāmas, vasāmasi* (AV.), *śaṃsāmas* (AV.), *sajāmasi* (AV.), *harāmasi* (AV.) and *hárāmas* (AV.).

2. *ájatha*[5], *ávatha, éjatha, krī́ḷatha, kṣáyatha, khādatha, gácchatha, caratha* (AV.), *cetatha, jínvatha*[2], *tákṣatha, tū́rvatha, dhāvatha* (AV.), *náyatha, naśatha, patatha, pinvatha*[2] (TS. III. 1. 11[8]), *bháratha, bhávatha, bhū́ṣatha, mádatha, moṣatha, rákṣatha, rā́jatha, rejatha, vahatha, sárpatha.* — **With -*thana*** only *vádathana.*

3. *acanti* (AV.), *ajanti, árcanti, árṣanti, árhanti, ávanti, krandanti,*

but this is due to Sandhi (108), *manāmahé* *'ti* standing for *manāmahe áti* (Pp.).

[1] A transfer from the reduplicating class.

[2] A transfer from the *nu-* class.

[3] A transfer from the root class for *śā́sti.*

[4] A transfer from the infixing class.

[5] The Saṃhitā lengthens the final vowel in at least ten of the following forms.

krāmanti (AV.), *krīḷanti*, *krόśanti*, *kṣáranti*, *kṣodanti*, *khananti* (AV.), *khā́danti* (AV.), *gacchanti*, *gámanti*, *gūhanti*, *cáranti*, *jáyanti*, *járanti*, *jinvanti*[1], *jī́vanti*, *tákṣanti*, *tápanti*, *taranti*, *tiṣṭhanti*[2], *trásanti*, *tsáranti*, *dabhanti*, *dahanti*, *dāsanti* (AV.), *drávanti*, *dhanvanti*, *dhámanti*, *dhāvanti*, *dhū́rvanti*, *nakṣanti*, *nandanti*, *namanti*, *náyanti*, *naśanti* 'they attain', *níkṣanti* (AV.), *nindanti*, *pácanti*, *pátanti*, *pinvanti*[1], *píbanti*[2], *pī́yanti*, *bhajanti*, *bhananti*, *bháranti*, *bhávanti*, *bhūṣanti*, *majjanti*, *mádanti*, *mánthanti*, *maranti*, *mardhanti*, *mimanti*[2] (*mā-* 'bellow'), *mehanti*, *yácchanti*, *yájanti*, *yācanti* (AV.), *yodhanti* (AV.), *rákṣanti*, *ráṇanti*, *rádanti*, *rājanti*, *rebhanti*, *róhanti*, *vádanti*, *vananti*, *vápanti*, *várdhanti*, *várṣanti*, *valganti* (AV.), *váśanti*, *vasanti* (AV.), *váhanti*, *vénanti*, *śáṃsanti*, *śíkṣanti*, *śócanti*, *ścótanti*, *sapanti*, *sarpanti* (AV.), *sī́danti*[2], *sedhanti*, *skandanti*, *stobhanti*, *srávanti*, *svádanti*, *sváranti*, *háranti* (AV.), *hiṃsanti*[3].

Indicative Middle.

Sing. 1. *aje*, *áme*, *arce*, *ī́kṣe*, *gacche* (TS. I. 1. 10[2]), *daye* (AV. TS.), *name*, *níkṣe* (AV.), *bādhe* (AV.), *bháre*, *bhikṣe*, *mande*, *yáje*, *rabhe*, *lábhe* (AV.), *vade*, *vánde*, *varte*, *śraye* (AV.), *sáhe* (AV.), *stáve*, *svaje* (AV.), *háve*.

2. *arṣase* (AV.), *ohase*, *garhase*, *gāhase*, *cákṣase*, *cayase*, *jarase*, *joṣase* (AV.), *tiṣṭhase*[2], *tośase*, *dohase*, *nakṣase*, *nayase*, *pavase*, *pinvase*[1], *bā́dhase*, *bhrājase*, *maṃhase*, *mandase*, *modase*, *yacchase*, *yajase*, *yamase*, *rakṣase*, *ramase* (AV.), *rócase*, *rohase*, *várdhase*, *vahase*, *śúmbhase*, *śobhase*, *sácase*, *stávase*, *harṣase*.

3. *ajate*, *ayate*, *ī́kṣate* (AV.), *ī́śate*, *ī́ṣate*, *ejate*[4], *edhate*, *óhate*, *kṛpate*, *kalpate* (AV.), *kramate*, *krīḍate* (AV.), *gacchate*, *gāhate*, *gūhate*, *ghoṣate*, *cáyate*, *cétate*, *codate*, *cyávate* (AV.), *járate*, *jṛ́mbhate*, *tandate*, *tíṣṭhate*[2], *tejate*, *tośate*, *dákṣate*, *dadate*[2] (AV.), *dadhate*[2] (TS. II. 2. 12[4]), *dóhate*[5], *dyotate* (AV.), *dhāvate*, *nákṣate*, *námate*, *náyate* (AV.), *náśate*, *násate*, *pácate* (AV.), *páyate*, *pávate*, *pínvate*[1], *píbate*[2], *práthate*, *plávate*, *bā́dhate*, *bhájate*, *bhandate*, *bhayate*, *bhárate*, *bhikṣate*, *bhójate*, *bhrā́jate*, *bhreṣate*, *máṃhate*, *madate* (AV.), *márate*, *modate*, *yájate*, *yatate*, *yamate*, *yojate*, *raṃhate*, *rakṣate*, *rapśate*[6], *rámate*, *rambate*, *réjate*, *rócate*, *rohate*, *láyate* (AV.), *vañcate* (AV.), *vadate*, *vanate*, *vándate*, *vapate*, *várate* 'covers', *vártate*, *várdhate*, *varṣate* (AV.), *vāsate* (x. 37[3]), *váhate*, *vépate*, *vyathate*, *śapate* (AV.), *śikṣate*, *śúmbhate*, *śrayate* (AV.), *sácate*, *sahate*, *sādhate*, *sécate*, *sévate*, *stárate*, *śayate*, *stávate*, *smayate*, *syándate*, *svādate*, *hárṣate*, *hávate*, *hāsate*[7], *hvárate*. — **With -e for -te:** *joṣe*, *tośé*[8], *mahe*, *śáye*, *séve*, *stáve*.

Du. 1. *sácāvahe*.

2. *jayethe*, *jarethe*, *rakṣethe*, *varethe*, *vahethe*, *śrayethe*, *sacethe*.

3. *carete*, *javete*, *tarete*, *namete*, *bādhete* (AV.), *bháyete*, *bharete*, *methete*, *yatete*, *rejete*, *vádete*, *vartete*, *vardhete*, *vepete*, *vyathete*, *sacete*, *smayete*, *havete*.

Pl. 1. *kṣadāmahe* (AV.), *cáyāmahe*[9] (AV.), *jarāmahe*, *nákṣāmahe*, *návāmahe*, *náśāmahe*, *bādhāmahe*, *bhájāmahe*, *bháyāmahe*, *bharāmahe*, *mánāmahe*[10], *mándāmahe*, *marāmahe*, *yájāmahe*, *yācāmahe*, *rabhāmahe*, *vánāmahe*, *vándāmahe*, *sahāmahe* (AV.), *starāmahe*, *stávāmahe*, *svajāmahe*, *hávāmahe*.

2. *cayadhve*, *dhavadhve*, *bādhadhve*, *bháradhve*, *mandadhve*, *váhadhve*, *śayadhve*, *sácadhve* (AV.).

1 Transfer from the *-nu* class.

2 A transfer form from the reduplicating class.

3 A transfer from the infixing nasal class.

4 In *ápejate* in IV. 48[2], V. 64[3]: Pp. *ápa ījate*.

5 *dohā́te* (X. 133[7]), DELBRÜCK, Verbum 97, and AVERY 233, is a mistake for *dóhate* (a transfer from the root class).

6 Cp. BARTHOLOMAE, IF. 10, 18.

7 From *hās-* 'go emulously', a secondary form of *hā-* 'leave' (IX. 27[5]; X. 127[3]); cp. p. 322, note 3. This form is given by AVERY 258 as subjunctive of the *s-* aorist of *hā-*.

8 (IV. 38[1]). With irregular accent, like that of similar forms in the graded conjugation.

9 Conjecture for *cayásmahe*, AV. XIX. 48[1]: see WHITNEY'S note on the passage in his Translation.

10 See note on *bhávāmahe*, above, p. 319, note 13.

3. *áyante, īkṣante* (AV. TS.), *īṣante, édhante, kṣódante, gácchante* (TS. IV. 2. 6[2]), *cétante, cyávante, jáyante, jarante* 'sing', *tíṣṭhante*[1], *dádante*[1] (AV.), *dhavante, nakṣante, namante, navante, pávante, píbante*[1], *plavante* (AV.), *bādhante, bhajante, bháyante, bhárante, bhrā́jante, módante* (AV.), *yájante, yatante, yā́cante, rakṣante, rante*[2], *rapśante* (AV.), *rabhante, ramante, réjante, rócante, vadante, várante, vártante, várdhante, vahante, vyathante, śayante, śúmbhante, śrayante, sácante, sápante, sáhante, stávante, spárdhante, svajante, svadante, hárante, hávante, hā́sante*[3] (AV.).

Present Subjunctive[4].

423. **Active.** Sing. 1. *ajāni* (TS. VII. 4. 19[1]; VS. XXIII. 19), *carāṇi, jīvāni* (AV.), *tarāṇi* (AV.), *náyāni, pacāni, bhajāni, rā́jāni, vádāni* (AV.), *váhāni, hárāṇi* (AV.). — **Without** *-ni*: *arcā*.

2. a. **With** *-si*: *ájāsi, gácchāsi* (AV.), *jayāsi, tiṣṭhāsi*[1] (AV.), *nayāsi* (AV.), *píbāsi*[1], *bhájāsi, bhávāsi, bhāsāsi* (AV.), *yájāsi, vadāsi, vahāsi*.

b. **With** *-s*: *ávās, gacchās, jáyās, jī́vās* (AV.), *jū́rvās*[5], *tiṣṭhās*[1], *bhárās, vadās* (AV.), *vánās* (AV.), *várdhās, śíkṣās*.

3. a. **With** *-ti*: *ájāti, ejāti* (AV.), *gácchāti, jayāti, jī́vāti, tápāti, tíṣṭhāti*[1], *dabhāti, dahāti, dhanvāti, náyāti, pácāti, pátāti, padāti, píbāti*[1], *bódhāti, bhájāti, bhárāti, bhávāti, marāti, yájāti, rakṣāti* (AV.), *vadāti, vahāti* (AV.), *śáṃsāti, śápāti* (AV.), *śumbhāti* (AV.), *śráyāti* (AV.), *sīdāti*[1], *svádāti, svarāti*.

b. **With** *-t*: *árcāt, árṣāt, árhāt, ávāt, invāt*[6], *ejāt, gácchāt, ghóṣāt, janāt* (AV. VI. 81[3]), *jīvāt, tíṣṭhāt*[1], *dáśāt* (AV.), *dā́sāt, dhāvāt* (AV.), *náyāt* (AV.), *níndāt, pácāt, pátāt, píbāt*[1], *bhajāt* (AV.), *bhárāt, bhū́ṣāt, yácchāt, yajāt, réṣāt* (AV.), *róhāt* (AV.), *várdhāt, vahāt* (AV. TS.), *śáṃsāt, śápāt* (AV.), *śíkṣāt, sarpāt* (AV.), *skándāt* (TS. I. 6. 2[2]), *smárāt* (AV.), *hárāt* (AV.).

Du. 1. *cárāva, jáyāva, píbāva*[1], *vánāva, śáṃsāva*.

2. *ávāthas, tarāthas* (AV.), *tiṣṭhāthas*[1], *náyāthas* (AV.), *píbāthas*[1], *bhávāthas* (AV.), *vadāthas, smarāthas*.

3. *cárātas*[7], *píbātas*[1], *váhātas, śápātas*.

Pl. 1. *árcāma, krámāma, khánāma* (TS. IV. 1. 2[3]), *takṣāma, namāma* (TS. V. 7. 4[4]), *patāma* (Kh. p. 171. 6), *bhajāma, bhárāma, bhávāma, madāma, manthāma, marāma, yajāma, rādhāma, vadāma, vardhāma, váśāma, śreṣāma*[8], *hárāma*.

2. *ávātha, gacchātha, jayātha, jīvātha* (TS. V. 7. 4[4])[9], *yacchātha* (AV.), *váhātha*.

3. *árcān, krī́ḷān, gácchān, ghóṣān, cárān, jī́vān* (AV.), *dāsān* (AV.), *patān, yacchān* (AV.), *vádān, várdhān*[10], *vahān, śíkṣān* (AV.), *sídān*[1] (AV.), *harān* (AV.).

Middle. Sing. 1. *gácchai* (AV.), *mánai, marai, stávai*. — 2. *vardhāse; nayāsai* (AV.). — 3. *jarāte, tíṣṭhāte*[1], *pavāte, bhayāte, yájāte, váhāte, śráyāte, svajāte; carātai* (AV.), *jayātai* (TS. AV.), *yajātai, śrayātai* (AV.), *svajātai* (AV.).

---

1 A transfer form from the reduplicating class.

2 According to ROTH, ZDMG. 20, 71, for **raṇ-ante*; WHITNEY, Roots = *r-ante*, under *r* 'go'; also GRASSMANN, under root *ar*.

3 From *hās-* 'go emulously': see WHITNEY's note on AV. IV. 36[5].

4 No forms of the 2. 3. pl. subj. middle occur in this class.

5 DELBRÜCK p. 37 (top) gives *tákṣās*, which I cannot trace.

6 A transfer from the *-nu* class.

7 DELBRÜCK, Verbum 82, gives *tiṣṭhātas*, but I cannot trace it.

8 Perhaps from *śriṣ-* = *śliṣ-* 'clasp': cp. WHITNEY, Roots.

9 DELBRÜCK 48 gives *pibātha* also.

10 *várdhān* (I. 70[4]; VI. 17[11]) as well as *árcān* (IV. 55[2]; V. 31[5]) are given as indicatives by DELBRÜCK, Verbum 91; cp. p. 327, note 3.

Du. 1. *rabhāvahai* (TS. IV. 4. 7[2]), *sácāvahai, sahāvahai.* — 3. *yátaite.*
Pl. 1. *nááāmahai, bhajāmahai* (AV.), *yájāmahai, vánāmahai.*

Present Injunctive.

424. Active. Sing. 1. *cyávam, takṣam, tíṣṭham*[1], *bhojam, yojam.*
2. *ávas, eṣas* (AV.), *oṣas, gūhas, caras, tíṣṭhas*[1] (AV.), *dáhas, namas* (AV.), *madas* (AV.), *yamas, vadas* (VS. XXIII. 25), *vanas, vapas, váras, vasas, venas, śocas.*

3. *arcat, arṣat* (AV.)[3], *karṣat, krandat, krāmat*[4] (AV.), *kṣarat, cárat, cetat, códat, janat, jáyat, jóṣat, takṣat, tandrat*[5], *tapat, tamat, tárat, tíṣṭhat*[1], *dadat*[1], *dábhat, dásat, dáśat, dásat, drávat, nákṣat, nayat, naśat, pácat, pátat, pinvat*[2], *píbat*[1], *próthat, bódhat, bhárat, bhavat* (AV.), *bhásat, bhraṃśat* (AV.), *madat* (AV.)[6], *minat, yámat*[7], *raṇat, rádat, rápat, rādhat, rejat, reṣat, rodhat, vádat, várat, vártat, várdhat, váśat, śakat, śardhat, śíkṣat, śnáthat, śramat, sadat, sárpat, saścat*[1], *svájat.*

Pl. 3. *arcan, cáran, dabhan, dhāvan, nákṣan, náśan* ('lose' and 'reach'), *bharan* (AV.), *bhavan* (AV.), *yaman, ráṇan, vaman, vardhan, śásan, sādhan*[8], *sīdan*[1].

Middle. Sing. 2. *gūhathās* (AV.), *bādhathās, rabhathās* (AV.).
3. *īśata, bharata, rocata, várdhata, sacata, sádhata.*

Pl. 3. *ámanta, áyanta, caranta, cyavanta, jananta, tíṣṭhanta*[1], *nakṣanta, namanta, náyanta, navanta, naśanta, nasanta, pinvanta*[2], *pravanta, bhájanta, bhananta, bháranta, bhikṣanta, yakṣanta, yavanta, raṇanta, ranta* (I. 61[11]; VII. 39[3])[9], *ramanta, réjanta, vanta*[10], *váranta* ('cover'), *vardhanta, vrādhanta, śócanta, sácanta, sapanta, sádhanta, stávanta, smayanta, hávanta.*

Present Optative.

425. Active. Sing. 1. *careyam* (AV.), *bhaveyam* (TS. IV. 7. 12[2]), *vadheyam* (AV.), *śíkṣeyam.* — 2. *áves, bhaves, mades, vanes.* — 3. *ávet, gácchet* (AV.), *caret, taret, pátet, bhávet* (AV.), *yacchet* (AV.), *lábhet* (AV.), *vadet* (AV.), *vaśet*[11] (AV.), *sravet, haret* (AV.). — **Du. 3.** *grásetām.*

Pl. 1. *krāmema, kṣayema* (AV.), *khanema* (TS. IV. 1. 2[4]), *gacchema* (AV. TS.), *cayema, carema, jáyema, jívema, tárema, tiṣṭhema*[1], *dáśema, patema* (TS. IV. 7. 13[1]), *bharema* (AV. TS.), *bhávema, bhūṣema, mádema, mahema, yatema, rapema, róhema* (AV.), *vatema, vadema, śíkṣema, sapema, sīdema*[1] (AV.), *hárema* (AV.). — 3. *táreyur, yáceyur* (AV.), *vaheyur, saheyur* (ŚA. XII. 32).

Middle. Sing. 1. *saceya.* — 3. *ajeta, kalpeta* (ŚA. XII. 20), *kṣameta, jareta, bhikṣeta, yajeta, vadeta, śáṃseta* (AV.), *saceta, saheta* (ŚA. XII. 20), *staveta.*

Du. 1. *sacevahi* (AV.).

Pl. 1. *gāhemahi, bhajemahi, bharemahi, yátemahi, rabhemahi, sácemahi.* — 3. **With ending** ***-rata***: *bharerata.*

Present Imperative.

426. Active. Sing. 2. *aca, ája, árca, árṣa, áva, inva*[2], *ūha* (AV.), *óṣa, karṣa, kranda, krāma, kṣára, khāda* (AV. TS.), *gáccha, gada* (AV.), *cára,*

1 Transfer form from the reduplicating class.
2 A transfer from the *-nu* class.
3 AV. X. 4[1], some Mss. *riṣat*: see WHITNEY's note in his Translation.
4 Emendation for *kṣāmat*, AV. VII. 63[1]: see WHITNEY's Translation.
5 II. 30[7], perhaps to be emended to *tandat.*
6 AV. XX. 49[2] emendation for *mada.*
7 DELBRÜCK 56 (top) adds *rákṣat.*
8 DELBRÜCK, Verbum 89 (p. 63), takes *háran* as an unaugmented imperfect, but it seems to occur only as a N. sing. m. participle.
9 According to DELBRÜCK 113 for **raṇ-anta*; WHITNEY, Roots, *r-anta.* Cp. p. 322, note 2.
10 DELBRÜCK l. c., for **van-anta.*
11 AV. XII. 4[27]: should probably be *vaset.* Cp. p. 324, note 3.

códa, jáya, jinva[1], *jīva, jūrva, jóṣa, tápa, tara, tíṣṭha*[2], *daśa* (AV.), *dáha, dŕṃha* (AV.), *drava, dhanva, dhama, dhāva, nama, náya, níkṣa* (AV.), *pata, pava, pinva*[1], *píba*[2], *protha, bódha, bhája, bhára, bháva, bhūṣa, mada, mántha* (AV.), *manda, myakṣa, mrada, yáccha, yája, yábha* (AV.), *yoja, rákṣa, ráṇa, ráda, rāja* (AV.), *róha, vada, vadha* (AV.), *vapa, várdha, vaśa*[3] (AV.), *vasa* (AV.), *váha, vāñcha*[4] (AV.), *śáṃsa, śárdha, śíkṣa, śumbha, śóca, śraya* (AV. TS.), *sára, sarpa, saha* (ŚA. XII. 31), *sádha, sída*[2], *sédha, skanda* (AV.), *stana* (AV.), *srava, svada, svapa, svara, hara, hinva*[1]. — **With ending** ***-tāt***: *avatāt, oṣatāt, gacchatāt* (AV.), *jinvatāt*[1] (AV.), *dahatāt, dhāvatāt* (AV.) 'run', *bhavatāt, yacchatāt, yācatāt, rákṣatāt, vahatāt, śrayatāt* (TS. VII. 4. 19[2]).

3. *ajatu, añcatu* (AV.), *arcatu, arṣatu* (AV.), *ávatu, invatu*[1], *īṣatu* (AV.), *ejatu, éṣatu* (AV.), *oṣatu* (AV.), *krandatu, krāmatu* (TS. VII. 3. 11[1]), *krośatu* (AV.), *gacchatu, caratu* (AV.), *jayatu, jinvatu*[1], *jívatu* (AV.), *tapatu, tiṣṭhatu*[2], *dahatu* (AV.), *dṛṃhatu* (AV.), *dravatu* (AV.), *dhāvatu, nakṣatu* (AV.), *nayatu, patatu* (AV.), *píbatu*[2], *bódhatu, bhavatu, bhūṣatu, manthatu* (AV.), *mándatu, yacchatu, yajatu, rákṣatu, rājatu* (AV.), *rohatu, vadatu* (AV.), *vapatu* (TS. AV.), *várdhatu, varṣatu* (Kh. II. 13[6]), *vasatu* (AV.), *vahatu, śíkṣatu, śocatu, sarpatu, sídatu*[2], *sedhatu, hinvatu*[1]. — **With ending** ***-tāt***: *gacchatāt, smaratāt* (AV.).

Du. 2. *ajatam, ávatam, invatam*[1], *oṣatam, gácchatam, jáyatam, jaratam, jínvatam*[2], *takṣatam, tápatam, tíṣṭhatam*[2], *túrvatam, dahatam* (AV.), *dhāvatam, nayatam, patatam, pínvatam, píbatam*[2], *bódhatam, bhajatam, bháratam, bhávatam, bhūṣatam, maṃhatam* (Kh. I. 10[2]), *yacchatam, yátatam, rákṣatam, rohatam* (TS. I. 8. 12[3]), *vánatam, vardhatam, váhatam, venatam, śíkṣatam, sīdatam*[2], *sédhatam*.

3. *ayatām* (AV.), *ávatām, invatām*[1], *krośatām* (AV.), *gacchatām, cetatām, jáyatām* (AV.), *jívatām* (AV.), *drávatām, pibatām*[2] (AV.), *bharatām* (AV.), *bhavatām, madatām, mehatām* (AV.), *yacchatām, rakṣatām, váhatām, veṣṭatām* (AV.), *sídatām*[2].

Pl. 2. *árcata, arṣata*[5], *avata, gacchata, gūhata, carata, codata, janata, jayata, jinvata*[1], *jívata, takṣata, tapata, tarata, tíṣṭhata*[1], *trasata, dakṣata, dŕṃhata, dhāvata, náyata, nindata, pácata, patata* (AV.), *pinvata*[1], *píbata*[2], *bhájata* (AV.), *bhárata, bhávata, bhūṣata, madata, mánthata, yácchata, yajata, yācata, rákṣata, rohata, vadata, vanata, vapata, vardhata, vahata, vrajata* (AV.), *śaṃsata, śundhata* (Kh. III. 16[6]), *śumbhata, śócata* (AV.), *sacata, sarpata, saścata*[2], *sídata*[2], *sédhata, stobhata, sredhata, harata* (AV.). — **With ending** ***-tana***: *bhajatana*.

3. *árcantu, árṣantu, ávantu, kasantu* (AV.), *krośantu* (AV.), *kṣarantu, gacchantu, carantu, jáyantu, jīvantu, takṣantu, tapantu* (AV. TS.), *tiṣṭhantu*[2], *trasantu* (AV.), *dahantu, drávantu, dhanvantu* (AV.), *dhāvantu* (AV.), *dhūrvantu, namantu* (AV. TS.), *nayantu, pacantu, patantu, píbantu*[2], *bódhantu, bhajantu* (AV.), *bharantu* (AV.), *bhávantu, mathantu* (AV.), *madantu, manthantu* (AV.), *mándantu, yácchantu, yajantu, yácchantu, rákṣantu, radantu, rohantu, lapantu* (AV.), *vádantu, vapantu, vardhantu, várṣantu* (AV.; Kh. II. 5), *vasantu* (AV.), *váhantu, vāñchantu, śundhantu, śumbhantu* (AV.), *śroṣantu, sajantu* (AV.), *sarpantu* (AV.), *sídantu*[2], *sedhantu, stobhantu, sravantu, svádantu, svarantu, harantu* (AV.).

Middle. Sing. 2. *ácasva* (AV.), *edhasva* (AV.), *kalpasva, kramasva, gacchasva* (AV.), *codasva, cyavasva* (AV. TS.), *járasva, tapasva, dayasva* (AV.),

---

1 Transfer from the *-nu* class.
2 Transfer from the reduplicating class.
3 AV. III. 4[7], perhaps to be read *vasa*.
4 AVERY 243 adds *vena*(?).
5 The form *arṣata* in AV. VI. 28[2] is a corruption: see WHITNEY's note in his Translation.

nakṣasva, nabhasva (AV.), *namasva, nayasva, pávasva, pinvasva*[1], *pibasva*[2], *prathasva, plavasva*[3] (Kh. II. 16), *bā́dhasva, bhajasva, bhárasva, mádasva* (AV.), *mandasva*[4], *yajasva, yatasva, rakṣasva, rabhasva, ramasva, vadasva, vándasva, vártasva, várdhasva, váhasva, śocasva, śrayasva, śvañcasva, sácasva, sáhasva, sīdasva*[2], *sevasva* (AV.), *syandasva, svajasva* (AV.), *svádasva, hárṣasva.*

3. *edhatām* (TS. VII. 4. 19[2]), *kalpatām* (AV.), *gacchatām, jaratām, tiṣṭhatām*[2] (AV.), *dadatām*[2], *dayatām* (AV.), *dyotatām* (AV.), *nabhatām* (AV.), *pávatām, pinvatām*[1], *prathatām, bā́dhatām, bhayatām* (AV.), *yajatām, rabhatām* (AV.), *ramatām* (AV.), *rocatām, vanatām, vartatām, várdhatām, śrayatām* (AV.), *sacatām, sahatām* (AV.).

Du. 2. *kalpethām* (TS. IV. 2. 5[1]), *gāhethām* (AV.), *codethām, cyavethām* (AV.), *jarethām, bā́dhethām, yajethām, rabhethām* (AV.), *vartethām* (AV.), *várdhethām, vahethām, śrayethām, sacethām* (AV.), *smarethām.*

3. *kalpetām* (TS. IV. 4. 11[1]), *śrayetām, sacetām.*

Pl. 2. *ajadhvam, kṣámadhvam, gacchadhvam, cyavadhvam* (TS. IV. 7. 13[4]), *tiṣṭhadhvam*[2], *nayadhvam, namadhvam, pavadhvam, pinvadhvam*[1], *pibadhvam*[2], *bādhadhvam, bhajadhvam* (AV.), *bharadhvam, modadhvam, yacchadhvam, yajadhvam, rabhadhvam, rámadhvam, vadadhvam, vartadhvam, śrayadhvam, sacadhvam* (AV.), *sáhadhvam, syandadhvam* (AV.), *svajadhvam, harṣadhvam* (AV.). — With ending **-dhva**: *yájadhva.*

3. *ayantām* (AV.), *kálpantām* (TS. IV. 4. 11[1]), *jayantām, tiṣṭhantām*[2], *namantām, pávantām*[5], *bādhantām* (TS. IV. 2. 6[4]), *bharantām* (AV.), *yajantām, yatantām, radantām* (AV.), *rabhantām* (AV.), *ramantām* (AV.), *layantām, vartantām, vardhantām, śrayantām, sacantām, sādhantām, syandantām, hárṣantām* (AV.).

Present Participle.

427. a. The active form made with the suffix *-ant*[6] is very common. Stems of forms which occur are: *ájant-, átant-, árcant-, árṣant-, árhant-, ávant-, ínvant-*[1], *úkṣant-, éjant-, éṣant-, ódant-, óṣant-* (AV.), *kálpant-*[7] (AV.), *kū́jant-* (AV.), *krándant-, krā́mant-, krīḷant-, krósant-, kṣáyant-, kṣárant-, khánant-* (AV.), *khā́dant-* (AV.), *gácchant-, gū́hant-, ghóṣant-, cátant-, cárant-, cétant-, céṣṭant-* (AV.), *jájhjhant-, jáñjant-, jáyant-, járant-, jínvant-*[1], *jī́vant-, jū́rvant-, tákṣant-, tápant-, tárant-, tiṣṭhant-*[2], *tū́rvant-*[8], *dáśant-, dáhant-, dā́sant-, drávant-, dhámant-, dhā́vant-, dhū́rvant-, dhrájant-, nákṣant-, nádant-* (AV.), *náyant-, návant-, pácant-, pátant-, pínvant-*[1], *píbant-*[2], *pṛ́ṣant-, próthant-, bhájant-, bhárant-, bhárvant-, bhávant-, bhā́sant-, bhū́ṣant-, bhrā́jant-, mádant-, mī́vant-* (AV.), *méhant-* (AV.), *mrócant-, yákṣant-, yácchant-, yájant-, yátant-, yā́cant-, yúcchant-, yéṣant-, rákṣant-, rádant-, rápant-* (TS. VII. 1. 11[1]), *rā́jant-, rébhant-*[9], *róhant-, lápant-* (AV.), *vátant-, vádant-, vápant-, várdhant-, várṣant-* (AV.), *vásant-, váhant-, vénant-, véṣant-, vrájant-, vrā́dhant-, śáṃsant-, śápant-, śárdhant-, śā́sant-, śíkṣant-, śócant-, śváyant-*[10], *sánant-, sápant-, sárjant-* (AV.), *sárpant-, sā́dhant-, sā́hant-* or *sáhant-, sī́dant-*[2], *sédhant-, skándant-* (AV.), *stóbhant-, srávant-, srédhant-, háyant-, hárant-, hárṣant-, héṣant-.*

b. The middle participles almost invariably formed with the suffix **-māna** are also numerous: *átamāna-, ámamāna-* (AV.), *áyamāna-, ī́kṣamāṇa-* (AV.), *ī́ṣamāṇa-, kálpamāna-* (TS. IV. 2. 10[2]), *kṛ́pamāṇa-, krákṣamāṇa-, krósamāna-, kṣámamāṇa-,*

1 Transfer from the *-nu* class.

2 Transfer form from the reduplicating class.

3 Accented *plavásva.*

4 AVERY 243 adds *yacchasva* (?).

5 AVERY 246 adds *pinvantām* (?).

6 On the declension of these stems see 314.

7 If *kálpat*, AV. XI. 5[26], is with WHITNEY in his Translation emended to *kálpan.*

8 From *tūrv-* a secondary form of *tur-*.

9 Fem. *rébhatyau* (Kh. I. 37).

10 The form *śváyat*, VII. 50[1], seems to be regarded by DELBRÜCK (p. 56, middle) as an injunctive of *śvi-*.

khánamāna-, *gáhamāna-*, *gūhamāna-*, *cáyamāna*, *jánamāna-*, *járamāṇa-*, 'singing' and 'approaching', *jásamāna-*, *jéhamāna-*, *túñjamāna-*, *téjamāna-*, *tóśamāna-* (AV.), *dákṣamāṇa-* (AV.), *dásamāna-*, *dyótamāna-*, *dhāvamāna-*, *nákṣamāṇa-*, *námamāna-*, *náyamāna-*, *návamāna-*, *nādhamāna-*, *pávamāna-*, *pínvamāna-*[1], *píbdamāna-*, *práthamāna-* (AV. TS.), *próthamāna-*, *bādhamāna-*, *bhándamāna-*, *bháyamāna-*, *bháramāṇa-*, *bhíkṣamāṇa-*, *bhrājamāna-*, *máṃhamāna-*, *mándamāna-*, *méghamāna-*, *módamāna-*, *yácchamāna-*, *yájamāna-*, *yátamāna-*, *yācamāna-* (AV.), *yādamāna-*, *ráṃhamāṇa-*, *rákṣamāṇa-*, *rábhamāṇa-*, *rámbamāṇa-*, *rāsamāna-* (AV.), *réjamāna-*, *rócamāna-*, *vándamāna-*, *vártamāna-*, *várdhamāna-*, *váhamāna-*, *vépamāna-* (AV.), *vyáthamāna-*, *śíkṣamāṇa-*, *śúmbhamāna-*, *śóbhamāna-*, *śráyamāṇa-*, *śróṣamāṇa-*, *śváñcamāna-*, *sácamāna-*, *sáhamāna-*, *stávamāna-*, *spárdhamāna-*, *smáyamāna-*, *syándamāna-*, *hárṣamāṇa-*, *hávamāna-*, *hāsamāna-*.

a. A few middle participles in *-āna* instead of *-māna*, seem to be formed from present stems of this class: thus *cyávāna-*, *prathāná-*, *yátāna-* and *yatāná-*, *śúmbhāna-*[3]; but it is probably better to class them as somewhat irregular or isolated root aorist participles[4].

Imperfect Indicative.

428. It is to be noted that the longer ending of the 2. pl. active never occurs in the imperfect of this or any other class of the *a-* conjugation. Unaugmented forms are fairly common; used injunctively they are in the 3. sing. very nearly as frequent (424) as the regular subjunctive[5] (423).

Active sing. 1. *ágaccham* (AV.), *acaram*, *atakṣam*, *ataram*, *anamam*, *anayam*, *apinvam*[1], *abharam*, *abhavam*, *abhedam*, *arodham*, *aroham*, *asīdam*; *āvam*; *yamam*.

2. *ákrandas*, *akṣaras*, *agacchas*, *ácaras*, *ájanas*, *ájayas*, *átaras*, *átiṣṭhas*[2], *ádahas*, *adhamas*, *ánayas*, *ápinvas*[1], *apibas*[2], *ábhajas*, *ábharas*, *ábhavas*, *ámadas*, *áyajas*, *áraṃhas*, *áradas*, *avadas*, *ávapas*, *ávahas*, *áśikṣas*, *ásadas*, *ásarpas* (AV.), *asīdas*[2], *asedhas*, *asravas*; *ājas*, *āvas*; *tapas* (AV.), *bháras*.

3. *ákrandat*, *ákrāmat*, *ákṣarat*, *akhanat* (AV.), *ágacchat*, *ágūhat*, *ácarat*, *ácalat* (AV.), *acetat*, *ájanat*, *ájayat*, *ajinvat*[1], *átakṣat*, *atapat*, *atarat*, *átiṣṭhat*[2], *ádadat*[2] (AV.), *ádahat*, *adāśat*, *ádṛṃhat* (AV.), *ádravat*, *adhamat*, *anamat*, *ánayat*, *ápacat*, *ápatat* (AV.), *ápinvat*[1], *ápibat*[2], *abhajat*, *abharat*, *ábhavat*, *ábhūṣat*, *ámadat*, *amanthat*, *ámandat*, *ámūrchat* (AV.), *áyacchat*, *árakṣat*, *arapat*, *arohat*, *ávapat*, *ávaśat*, *ávasat*, *ávahat*, *ávenat*, *áśayat*, *áśāsat*[6] (Kh. I. 9[4]), *áśocat*, *asajat*, *asadat*, *ásīdat*[2], *asedhat*, *askandat* (AV.), *áharat* (AV.); *ājat*, *ārcat*, *āvat*; *áirat* ($\sqrt{}$*īr-*)[7], *auhat* (*ūh-* 'push'); *krándat*, *carat* (AV.), *takṣat*, *tsárat*, *dṛṃhat*, *nakṣat*, *nayat*, *pibat*[2], *bhárat*, *rébhat*, *váhat*.

Du. 2. *ájinvatam*[1], *átakṣatam* (AV.), *ápinvatam*[1], *áprathatam*, *ábhavatam*, *ámanthatam*, *aradatam*, *áśikṣatam*, *ásaścatam*[2], *ásīdatam*[2]; *ājatam*, *āvatam*; *airatam*[7] (*īr-* 'set in motion').

3. *atiṣṭhatām*[2] (AV.), *ábhavatām* (TS. IV. 7. 15[6]), *avardhatām*; *āvatām*; *auhatām* (AV. VS. TS.).

Pl. 1. *átakṣāma*, *ábharāma* (AV.). — **2.** *átakṣata*, *átiṣṭhata*[2], *ánadata* (TS. V. 6. 1[2]), *ánayata*, *ápinvata*[1], *ábhavata*, *avartata* (AV.), *ávalgata* (TS. V. 6. 1[2]), *ásarpata*; *āvata*; *auhata* (AV.).

3. *ákaṣan* (AV.), *akrāman*[8] (AV.), *ákṣaran*, *akhanan* (AV.), *agūhan*,

---

[1] Transfer from the *-nu* class.

[2] Transfer form from the reduplicating class.

[3] Cp. WHITNEY 741 a, and LINDNER, Nominalbildung 54 (top).

[4] Cp. Root Aorist 506.

[5] See WHITNEY 743.

[6] Transfer from the root class.

[7] Transfer from the root class, in which the verb *īr-* is also middle.

[8] *akramus* is given by AVERY 249 as an impf. of this class with *-us*, but it is doubt-

ácaran (AV.), *acalan* (AV.), *ajanan*, *ájayan* (AV.), *átakṣan*, *átaran*, *átiṣṭhan*[1], *atrasan*, *ádāśan*, *adravan*, *adhrajan*, *anakṣan*, *ánaman* (AV.), *ánayan*, *ápinvan*[2], *apiban*[1] (AV.), *ábharan*, *ábhavan*, *ábhūṣan*, *ámadan*, *ámandan*, *áyacchan* (AV.), *áyācan* (AV.), *árakṣan*, *árājan* (AV.), *ávadan*, *ávapan* (AV.), *ávardhan*[3], *ávahan*, *aveṣan* ($\sqrt{}$*viṣ-*), *áśaṃsan*, *aśikṣan* (AV.), *aśrayan* (AV.), *áṣṭhīvan*[4] (AV.), *ásredhan*, *ásvaran*; *ājan*, *āyan* (AV.), *ārcan*[3], *āvan*[5], *áijan* (*ej-* 'stir'), *auhan*[6] (AV.); *jinvan*, *tákṣan*, *tsáran* (AV.), *dádan*[1] (AV.), *bharan*, *bhūṣan*, *śróṣan*, *sīdan*[7].

Middle. Sing. 1. *atiṣṭhe*[1] (AV.). — 2. *ágāhathās* (AV.), *ápavathās*, *ámandathās*, *árocathās*; *gáhathās* (AV.).

3. *akalpata*[8] (AV.), *atakṣata*, *apinvata*[2], *abādhata*, *ámaṃhata*[9], *ámanthata*, *ámandata*, *áraṃhata*, *arakṣata*, *árocata*, *ávartata*, *avardhata*, *ávalgata* (AV.), *áśapata*; *ājata*, *āyata*; *áikṣata*[10] (AV.), *auhata* (*ūh-* 'remove'); *cakṣata*, *janata*, *nakṣata*, *niṃsata*, *bādhata*, *rejata*.

Du. 2. *ábādhethām*, *árabhethām* (AV.). — 3. *akṛpetām*, *aprathetām*, *ábhyasetām*[11], *árejetām*; *áikṣetām*[10].

Pl. 3. *ákalpanta* (AV.), *akṛpanta*, *ákhananta*, *ágacchanta*, *ajananta*, *atiṣṭhanta*[1], *ádadanta*[1], *adhavanta*[12], *anamanta* (TS. IV. 6. 2[6]), *ánayanta*, *ánavanta*, *apacanta*, *aprathanta*, *ábhajanta*, *abhayanta*, *ábharanta*, *áyajanta*, *aramanta*, *árejanta*, *avadanta*, *ávartanta*, *ávardhanta*, *avepanta* (AV.), *ávradanta*, *áśamanta* (TS. IV. 6. 3[2]), *ásacanta*, *ásapanta*, *ásahanta*; *áikṣanta*[10] (AV. TS.); *īṣanta*, *kṛpanta*, *jananta*, *navanta*, *prathanta*, *bhájanta* (AV.), *bhananta*, *mananta*, *vapanta*.

2. The suffixally accented *á-* class (*tudá-*)[13].

429. Nearly one hundred roots belong to this class. The radical vowel is almost always medial, being regularly *i*, *u* or *ṛ*. If the vowel is final, which is very rare, it is almost invariably short. As the *-a* is accented, the radical vowel appears in its weak form; e. g. *huv-á-* (but according to the radically accented class, *háv-a-*) from *hū-* 'call'.

a. There are, however, some irregularities in the formation of the present stem. 1. Several roots instead of appearing in their weak form, are nasalized: *kṛt-* 'cut': *kṛntá-*; *tṛp-* 'be pleased': *tṛmpá-*; *piś-* 'adorn': *piṃśá-*; *muc-* 'release': *muñcá-*; *lip-* 'smear': *limpá-*; *lup-* 'break': *lumpá-*; *vid-* 'find': *vindá-*; *sic-* 'sprinkle': *siñcá-*. A few other roots occasionally have nasalized forms according to this class: thus *tundate*, beside the regular *tudáti* etc., from *tud-* 'thrust'; *dṛṃhéthe*, beside *dṛ́ṃhata*, etc., from *dṛh-* 'make firm'; *śumbhánt-*,

less an aorist: see WHITNEY, Roots, under $\sqrt{}$*kram*.

1 Transfer form from the reduplicating class.

2 Transfer from the *-nu* class.

3 *ārcān* (IV. 55[2]; V. 31[5]) and *várdhān* are given as indicatives by DELBRÜCK 91, followed by AVERY 249. Cp. p. 322, note 10.

4 From *ṣṭhīv-* 'spue', originally **sthīv-*: cp. v. NEGELEIN 24, note 6: the root is there wrongly given as *ṣṭīv*.

5 *āsthan* (AV. XIII. 1[5]) is given by v. NEGELEIN 18, note 1 as imperfect of *as*; but see WHITNEY's note on AV. XIII. 1[5].

6 *akṛpran* being formed with the ending *-ran* (DELBRÜCK 124) is doubtless an aorist; cp. WHITNEY, Roots under $\sqrt{}$*kṛp-*. See below, 500.

7 *sran* (IV. 2[19]) according to DELBRÜCK, Verbum 89 (p. 63, middle), followed by AVERY 249, for **asara-n*; but *avasran* is 3. pl. aor. of *vas-* 'shine' with ending *-ran* (not *ava-sran*: accent!). Cp. WHITNEY, Roots, under *vas* 'shine'.

8 DELBRÜCK 176 and AVERY 247 give *akṛnvata* as (once) a 3. sing. If this is correct, the form would be a transfer for *akṛṇuta*.

9 *ámata* is given by DELBRÜCK 101 and AVERY 247 as belonging to this class (presumably from the root *am-*), but it is doubtless 3. sing. mid. aor. of *man-* 'think'; see WHITNEY, Roots, under $\sqrt{}$*man*.

10 From *īkṣ-* 'see'.

11 From *bhyas-* 'fear'.

12 VII. 18[15]: from *dhav-* 'run' = *dhanv-*.

13 Cp. E. LEUMANN, Die Herkunft der 6. Praesensklasse im Indischen (Actes du X. Cong. Intern. Orient. II. 1, 39—44; IF. 5, Anz. 109; KZ. 34, 587 ff.).

beside *śúmbhate* and *śóbhate*, from *śubh-* 'shine'; *śṛnthati* (TS[1].), beside the regular *śrathnās* etc., from *śrath-* 'loosen'. — 2. Four roots form their stem with the suffix *-chá*: *iṣ-* 'wish': *i-cchá-*; *ṛ-* 'go': *ṛ-cchá-*; *práś-*[1] 'ask': *pṛcchá-*; *vas-* 'shine': *u-cchá-*. — 3. Two stems are transfers from the nasal class of the second conjugation: *pṛṇá-*, beside *pṛ-ṇā-*, from *pṛ-* 'fill'; *mṛṇá-*, beside *mṛ-ṇā-*, from *mṛ-* 'crush'; *ṛñjá-* 'stretch' has become the regular stem beside 3. pl. *ṛñjate*; and 2. pl. *umbha-ta* (AV.), appears beside *ubh-ná-*, from *ubh-* 'confine'. — 4. Beside the normal *-nu* stem *ṛ-ṇu*, the root *ṛ-* also has the transfer stem *ṛṇv-á-*. — 5. While roots ending in *i* or *ū* change these vowels into *iy* or *uv* before *-á* (e. g. *kṣiy-á-*, from *kṣi-* 'dwell', *yuv-á-* from *yu-* 'join'), the TS. has *kṣy-ánt-* beside RV. *kṣiyánt-* 'dwelling'.

b. The present stems *chyá-* (AV.) 'cut up', *dyá-* (AV.) 'divide', *śyá-* 'sharpen', *syá-* 'bind', though regarded by the Indian grammarians as belonging to the *-ya* class, should most probably be classified here, because the *a* is accented, *i* appears beside *ā* in various forms from these roots, and *-yá* is here often to be read as *-ia*, while this is never the case in the *-ya* class.

430. The inflexion is exactly the same as that of *bhāva-*. The forms which actually occur are the following:

Present Indicative.

Active. Sing. 1. *icchā́mi, ukṣā́mi* (AV.), *kirā́mi* (AV.), *khidā́mi* (AV.), *girāmi*[2] (AV.), *cṛtā́mi* (AV.), *tirā́mi, dyā́mi* (AV.), *diśā́mi* (TS. AV.), *dhuvā́mi* (AV.), *pṛcchā́mi, muñcā́mi, rujā́mi, limpā́mi* (AV.), *vindā́mi, viśā́mi* (AV.), *vṛścā́mi* (AV.), *vṛhā́mi, siñcā́mi, sulā́mi* (TS. VII. 4. 19[4]), *suvā́mi, sṛjā́mi, spṛśā́mi, syā́mi* (AV. TS.).

2. *icchasi* (AV.), *ucchasi* (TS. IV. 3. 11[5]), *tirasi, kṣipasi* (AV.), *tṛmpási, pṛcchasi, mṛṇasi, vindasi, vṛścasi, suvási.*

3. *anáti* (AV.), *icchati, ucchati, ṛcchati* (AV.), *ṛṇvati, kṛntáti* (AV.), *kṛṣati* (TS. IV. 2. 5[6]), *kṣiyati* (AV.), *khidáti, girati* (AV.), *chyati* (TS. V. 2. 12[1]), *dyati* (AV.), *piṃśati, pṛcchati, pṛṇáti, miṣati, muñcati* (AV.), *yuváti, rujáti, ruváti, vindáti, viśati* (AV.), *vṛścati, vṛhati, siñcati* (AV.), *suváti, sṛjáti, sphuráti* (AV.), *syati.*

Du. 2. *ṛṇvathas, bhasáthas, muñcathas, viśathas* (AV.), *vṛhathas, sṛjáthas.*

3. *icchatas* (AV.), *muñcatas* (AV.), *siñcatas.*

Pl. 1. *girā́mas* (AV.), *cṛtā́masi* (AV.), *tirā́masi, dyā́masi* (AV.), *nudā́masi* (AV.) and *nudā́mas* (AV.), *pṛcchā́mas* (AV.), *mṛśā́masi, vṛhā́masi* (AV.) and *vṛhā́mas* (AV.), *suvā́masi* (AV.), *sṛjā́masi* (AV.) and *sṛjā́mas* (AV.), *spṛśā́masi.*

2. *muñcátha, siñcátha* (TS. AV.).

3. *anánti* (AV.), *icchánti, ukṣánti, ucchánti, ṛcchánti, ṛñjánti, ṛṣánti, kṣiyánti* (AV.), *khidánti* (AV.), *cṛtánti, tiranti, tuñjánti, pṛcchánti, miṣanti, mucánti, muñcanti, mṛśánti, rujánti, vindanti, viśánti, vṛścánti, śumbhánti, siñcánti, suvánti, sṛjánti, spṛśánti, sphuránti, syanti.*

Middle. Sing. 1. *iṣe* 'send', *nude* (AV.), *pṛcché, muñce* (AV.), *mṛje, vindhe, viśé* (AV.), *śuṣe, siñce, huvé.*

2. *icchase, ṛñjáse, juṣáse* (AV.), *pṛcchase, mṛśáse, yuvase, vindáse, siñcáse.*

3. *icchate* (AV.), *ukṣáte, ṛñjáte, kirate, kṛṣáte* (AV.), *tiráte, tundate, turáte* (TS. II. 2. 12[4]), *nudate* (AV.), *piṃśáte, pṛcchate, pṛñcáte, muñcate, mṛśate, yuváte, vindáte, vindháte, viśáte, vṛścate* (AV.), *sṛjate.* — **With ending -e:** *huvé.*

Du. 2. *dṛṃhéthe, nudethe* (AV. TS.), *yuvethe, vindethe* (Kh. I. 12[8]).

3. *tujete.*

Pl. 1. *nudā́mahe* (AV.), *yuvā́mahe, riśā́mahe, sicā́mahe, huvā́mahe.*

3. *icchante* (AV.), *ukṣánte, tiránte, vijánte* (AV.), *vindante* (AV.), *viśánte, vṛścante* (AV.), *sṛjante* (AV.).

---

[1] The suffix *-cha* has in this instance attached itself throughout the conjugation to the root, which thus becomes for practical purposes *pracch-* (but *praś-ná-* 'question'); cp. *prec-or* and *posco* for **porc-sco* in Latin.

[2] From *gṛ-* 'swallow'.

Present Subjunctive.

431. **Active.** Sing. 1. *sṛjā́ni*; *mṛkṣā́*. — 2. *kirā́si*, *muñcāsi* (AV.), *rujā́si*; *siñcā́s*. — 3. *tirāti*, *bhṛjjā́ti*, *mṛḷāti*, *mṛdhāti*, *vanā́ti*, *vidhāti*, *viśā́ti* (AV.), *suvā́ti*, *sṛjāti* (AV.); *icchāt*, *ucchā́t*, *ṛcchāt*, *nudāt* (ŚA. XII. 29), *pṛcchā́t*, *pṛṇā́t*, *muñcāt* (AV.), *mṛḷā́t*, *mṛśā́t* (AV.), *vṛścā́t*, *siñcāt*, *sṛjā́t*, *spṛśāt* (AV.).

Du. 1. *viśā́va* (AV.). — 3. *mṛḷātas*.

Pl. 2. *viśā́tha* (AV.). — 3. *ucchān*, *pṛcchā́n*, *sphurā́n*.

Middle. Sing. 1. *pṛcchai*, *viśā́i* (TS. III. 5. 6[1]). — 2. *yuvāse*. — 3. *juṣā́te*, *tirāte*. — Du. 2. *pṛṇā́ithe*. — 3. *yuvā́ite*. — Pl. 1. *siñcāmahai*.

Present Injunctive.

432. **Active.** Sing. 2. *icchas* (AV.), *guhas*, *rujás*, *vṛhas*, *vṛścas*, *sicas*, *sṛjás*.

3. *ucchat*, *kṛntát*, *kṣipát*, *khidat*, *juṣát*, *mṛṇat* (AV.), *ruját*, *rudhat*, *ruvát*, *vidhat*, *viśat*, *vṛhat*, *siñcat*, *sṛját*[1], *spṛśat* (AA. V. 2[2]), *sphurat*, *huvat*.

Pl. 3. *tṛpán*, *vidhán*, *vindan*.

Middle. Sing. 3. *juṣata*, *tirata*. — Pl. 3. *icchánta*, *iṣanta*, *juṣánta*, *tiránta*, *nudánta*, *bhuránta*, *yuvanta*, *vidhanta*, *sṛjanta*.

Present Optative.

433. **Active.** Sing. 1. *udeyam*[2] (AV.), *tireyam* (Kh. I. 9[5]), *vindeyam* (Kh. II. 6[2]). — 3. *icchet*, *ucchet* (AV.), *khidét* (AV.), *pṛcchet*, *lumpét* (AV.), *siñcét* (AV.), *sṛjét* (AV.). — Du. 1. *vṛheva*. — 2. *tiretam*. — Pl. 1. *iṣema*, *kṣiyema* (AV.), *rujema*, *ruhema* (Kh. II. 4[1]), *vanéma*, *vidhéma*, *viśema*, *huvéma*. — 2. *tireta*; *tiretana*.

Middle. Sing. 1. *huvéya*. — 3. *iccheta* (AV.), *juṣéta*.

Pl. 1. *vanemahi*, *vidhemahi*. — 3. *juṣerata*.

Present Imperative.

434. **Active.** Sing. 2. *icchá*, *ucchá*, *ubja* (AV.), *kira*, *kṛntá* (AV.), *kṣipa*, *kṣiya* (AV.), *khida* (AV.), *cṛta*, *chya* (AV.), *tira*, *tuda*, *tṛmpá*, *nuda* (AV.), *piṃśá* (AV.), *pṛccha*, *pṛñca*[3] (AV.), *pṛṇa*, *pruṣa*, *muñcá*, *mṛṇá*, *mṛḷá*, *mṛśa*, *yuva*, *rikha*, *rujá*, *ruva*, *viśa*, *vinda*, *vṛścá*, *vṛhá*, *śṛṇa* (AV.), *siñca*, *suva*[4], *sṛjá*, *spṛśa*, *sphura*, *sya*. — **With ending -tāt:** *mṛḍatāt* (AV.), *vṛhatāt*, *viśatāt* (TS. VII. 1. 6[6]), *suvatāt*.

3. *icchatu*, *ukṣatu* (AV.), *ucchatu*, *ubjatu* (AV.), *ṛcchatu*, *kirátu* (TS. III. 3. 11[5]), *kṛṣatu* (AV.), *cṛtatu* (AV.), *tiratu* (Kh. II. 11[2]), *tṛmpatu*, *diśatu* (AV.), *dyatu* (AV.), *nudatu* (AV.), *piṃśatu*, *muñcatu* (AV. TS.), *mṛḷatu*, *viśátu* (AV. TS.), *vindatu* (AV.), *vṛścatu* (AV.), *siñcatu*, *suvatu*, *syatu*. — **With -tāt:** *viśatāt* (Kh. IV. 6[1]; 8[3]).

Du. 2. *ukṣatam*, *ubjátam*, *tiratam*, *tṛmpatam*, *nudatam* (AV.), *bṛhatam* (AV.), *muñcátam*, *mṛḷátam*, *viśatam* (AV.), *vṛhatam*, *siñcatam*, *sṛjátam*, *sphuratam* (AV.), *syatam*.

3. *juṣatām* (Kh. I. 3[1]), *tṛmpatām*, *dyatām* (AV.), *muñcatām*, *viśatām* (TS. VII. 3. 13[1]), *suvatām* (AV.), *syatām*.

---

1 AVERY adds *sṛdhat*(?): perhaps the aor. injunctive *sridhat* is meant.

2 With Samprasāraṇa. This verb otherwise follows the radically accented *a*-class.

3 Transfer from the infixing nasal class (√*pṛc*-): that it would have been accented *pṛñcá* is to be inferred from the fem. part. *pṛñcat-ī-* (RV. AV.), though the AV. has also *pṛ́ñcat-ī-*.

4 In AV. VII. 14[3] *suvā* appears in the Pp. as *sva*.

Pl. 2. *icchata, ukṣata, ucchata, umbhata* (AV.), *ṛñjáta, khudáta, gṛṇáta* (AV.), *tirata, tudata* (AV.), *nudata, piṃśata, pṛcchata, pṛṇata, muñcáta, mṛḷáta, mṛṇáta* (AV.), *viśata* (AV.), *vṛhata, śundhata, siñcata, sṛjáta, spṛśáta.*

3. *ukṣantu* (AV.), *ucchántu, ubjantu, ṛcchantu, ṛdantu, kṛṣantu, chyantu* (TS. v. 2. 12[1]), *tirantu, tudantu* (AV. TS.), *diśantu* (Kh. III. 10[2]), *nudantu* (AV.), *bhurantu, muñcántu, mṛḷantu, viśantu, siñcantu, suvantu, sṛjantu.*

Middle. Sing. 2. *icchasva, kṛṣasva, gurasva, juṣásva, nudásva, pṛcchasva* (Kh. II. 13[1]), *pṛṇásva, mṛśásva, yuvásva, vindásva* (AV.), *viśásva, vṛṣasva, siñcasva, sṛjasva, spṛśasva* (AV.); *syasva.*

3. *icchatām* (AV.), *juṣátām, nudatām* (AV.; ŚA. XII. 9), *pṛṇatām, muñcatām* (AV.), *viśatām, sṛjatām* (AV.).

Du. 2. *ukṣéthām, juṣéthām, nudéthām, pṛṇethām, vṛṣethām, sṛjethām* (AV. TS.). — 3. *juṣétām.*

Pl. 2. *kramádhvam* (TS. IV. 6. 5[1]), *juṣádhvam, tiradhvam, pṛṇádhvam, viśadhvam* (AV.), *siñcádhvam, sṛjádhvam, syadhvam.*

3. *juṣántām, muñcantām* (AV.), *riśantām, vijantām* (AV.), *vṛścantām* (AV.), *spṛśantām* (AV.).

Present Participle.

435. Active. *icchánt-, ukṣánt-* (AV.), *ucchánt-, ubjánt-, ṛṣánt-, kṛntánt-, kṛṣánt-, kṣipánt-, kṣiyánt-, khidánt-* (AV.), *guhánt-, citánt-, juránt-, tiránt-, tujánt-, tudánt-, tṛpánt-, diśánt-, dṛṃhánt-* (AV.), *nudánt-, nuvánt-, pṛcchánt-, pruṣánt-* (AV.), *bhujánt-, mithánt-, miṣánt-, muñcánt- mṛjánt-, mṛśánt-, riśánt-, rujánt-, rudhánt-, ruvánt-, vidhánt-, viśánt-, vṛścánt-, śucánt-, śumbhánt-, śuṣánt-* and *śvasánt-, siñcánt-, suvánt-, sṛjánt-, sphuránt-, huvánt-*[1] (*hū-* 'call').

Middle. *icchámāna-, ukṣámāṇa-, uśámāna-* ($\sqrt{}$*vaś-*), *uṣámāṇa-* (*vas-* 'wear'), *guhámāna-, juṣámāṇa-, dhṛṣámāṇa-, nṛtámāna-, pṛcchámāna-, bhurámāṇa-, muñcámāna-* (AV. TS.), *yuvámāna-, vijámāna-* (AV.), *śucámāna-.*

Imperfect Indicative.

436. Active. Sing. 1. *atiram* (TS. IV. 1. 10[3]), *ápṛccham, árujam.*

2. *átiras, anudas, apṛṇas, ámuñcas, amṛṇas, arujas, avindas, avṛhas, ásṛjas, ásphuras, ásyas* (AV.); *áicchas, áucchas; vindas, vṛścas, sṛjas.*

3. *ákṛntat, akhidat, ájuṣat, átirat, aduhat* (TS. IV. 6. 5[4]), *ápiṃśat, apṛṇat, ámuñcat, amṛṇat, amṛśat* (AV.), *arujat, ávidhat, ávindat, áviśat, ávṛścat, ásiñcat, asuvat, ásṛjat, aspṛśat, asphurat, asyat; áicchat* (AV.), *áukṣat, áucchat, aubjat; tudat, tṛṃhát, ruját, likhat* (AV.), *vindat, vṛścát, śyat, siñcat, sṛját.*

Du. 2. *atiratam, amuñcatam, ámṛṇatam, avindatam* (Kh. I. 3[1]), *asiñcatam.*

3. *ámuñcatām, ásiñcatām* (AV.).

Pl. 1. *áicchāma.* — 2. *ápiṃśata* ($\sqrt{}$*piś-*), *apṛcchata, ámuñcata, asṛjata.* — 3. *ápiṃśan, ápīṣan*[2] (AV. IV. 6[7]), *ávindan, áviśan* (AV.), *ávṛścan* (AV.), *ásiñcan, ásṛjan, aspṛśan* (AV.); *ārdan* ($\sqrt{}$*ṛd-*); *áukṣan; ukṣan, rujan.*

Middle. Sing. 1. *ájuṣe* (AV.), *avije, áhuve.* — 2. *amuñcathās, aviśathās* (AV.). — 3. *ajuṣata, amuñcata, ásiñcata* (AV.), *asṛjata; dṛṃhata.*

Du. 2. *anudethām, ávindethām.*

Pl. 2. *ajuṣadhvam.* — 3. *ájuṣanta, atiranta, atviṣanta, ánudanta* (AV.), *amuñcanta* (AV.), *ájuvanta* (AV.), *avindanta, aviśanta, ásṛjanta, aspṛśanta* (AV.), *áhuvanta; áiṣanta* (*iṣ-* 'send'); *gṛṇanta, juṣanta.*

---

[1] The fem. is regularly formed from the strong stem in *-ant*; but the weak stem in *-at* appears in *siñcat-ī́-*, beside *siñcánt-ī-*.

[2] Anomalous form for **ápiṃṣan*, from *piṣ-* 'crush'.

3. The *ya-* class [1].

437. The present stems formed with this suffix fall into **two groups.** In the first, consisting of about 70 transitive or intransitive verbs, the suffix is unaccented; in the second, consisting of rather more than 80 verbs with a passive meaning, the suffix is accented. In all probability both groups were identical in origin, with the accent on the suffix. This is indicated by the fact that the root though accented in the first group appears in its weak form; and that this group consists largely of intransitive verbs and to some extent of verbs with a passive sense. The latter are manifestly transfers from the *-yá* or passive group with change of accent. Thus *jáyate* 'is born' is an altered passive beside the active *jánati* 'begets'. The accent moreover occasionally fluctuates. Thus the passive *mucyáte* 'is released' once or twice occurs (in the RV. and AV.) accented on the root; and there is no appreciable difference of meaning between *kṣíyate* and *kṣīyáte* 'is destroyed'; *jíyate* and *jīyáte* 'is overcome'; *pácyate* and *pacyáte* 'is cooked'; *míyate* and *mīyáte* (AV.) 'is infringed' [2].

A. The radically accented *ya-* class.

438. The root nearly always appears in a weak form. Thus roots that otherwise contain a nasal, lose it: *dṛṃh-* 'make firm' : *dṛ́h-ya-*. The root *vyadh-* 'pierce' takes Samprasāraṇa: *vídh-ya-*. The root *spaś-* 'see' loses its initial: *páś-ya-*. Several roots ending in *ā* shorten the vowel before the suffix: *dhā-* 'suck' : *dhaya-*; *mā-* 'exchange' : *maya-*; *vā-* 'weave' : *váya-*; *vyā-* 'envelope' : *vyáya-*; *hvā-* 'call' : *hváya-* [3].

a. Several other roots usually stated as ending in *ā* remain unchanged: *gā-* 'sing' : *gáya-*; *glā-* 'be weary' : *gláya-* (AV.); *trā-* 'save' : *tráya-*; *pyā-* 'fill up' : *pyáya-*; *rā-* 'bark' : *ráya-*; *vā-* 'blow' : *váya-*; *śrā-* 'boil' : *śráya-* [4].

b. The root *śram-* 'be weary' lengthens its vowel: *śrā́mya-* [5].

c. The final of roots in *-ṝ* sometimes becomes both *īr* [6] and *ūr*; thus *jṝ-* 'waste away' becomes *jū́rya-* and *jīrya-* (AV.); *tṝ-* 'cross' : *tū́rya-* and *tírya-* [7] (AV.). The root *pṝ-* 'fill' because of its initial labial becomes *pū́rya-* only.

439. The forms actually occurring in this class are the following:

Present Indicative.

Active. Sing. 1. *asyāmi* (AV.), *íṣyāmi*, *nahyāmi*, *páśyāmi* (AV.), *vídhyāmi* (AV.), *hváyāmi*.

2. *ásyasi*, *iṣyasi*, *ucyasi* (√*uc-*), *gāyasi*, *náśyasi*, *páśyasi*, *púṣyasi*, *ráṇyasi*, *rāyasi*, *riṣyasi*, *haryasi*.

3. *ásyati*, *íyati* (RV[1].), *íṣyati*, *krudhyati* (AV.), *gāyati*, *jī́ryati* (AV.), *jūryati*, *tanyati*, *dásyati*, *dáhyati* (AV.), *dīyati*, *dī́vyati* (AV.), *duṣyati* (SA. XII. 23), *dhayati*, *naśyati*, *nṛ́tyati* (AV.), *páśyati*, *púṣyati*, *raṇyati*, *riṣyati*, *vayati* (AV.), *vāyati*, *vidhyati*, *vyayati*, *śimyati* (TS. V. 2. 12[1]), *śuṣyati* (Kh. IV. 5[38]), *sidhyati*, *haryati*, *hṛṣyati*, *hváyati*.

Du. 2. *dīyathas*, *raṇyathas*. — **3.** *asyatas* (AV.), *naśyatas*, *páśyatas*, *púṣyatas*, *riṣyatas* (AV.), *vayatas* (AV.), *vāyatas*, *śrā́myatas* (AV.).

---

[1] Cp. LORENTZ, IF. 8, 68—122.

[2] Also in Brāhmaṇa passages of the TS. *ricyate* 'is left' beside *ricyáte* (V.), *lúpyate* 'is lost' beside *lupyáte* (AV.), *hīyate* 'is left' beside *hīyáte* (V.).

[3] These are reckoned by the native grammarians as ending in *e* and belonging to the *a-* class. This seems preferable from the point of view of vowel gradation: see 27, a, 3.

[4] Such roots are reckoned by the native grammarians as ending in *-ai* and belonging to the *a-* class. The latter form is preferable from the point of view of gradation. Cp. 27, a, 1; BB. 19, 166.

[5] In B. this analogy is followed by several roots in *-am*.

[6] In the *á-* class *-ṝ* becomes *-ir*, e. g. *tṝ-* : *tirá-*.

[7] Only in an emendation *ava-tíryatī* (AV. XIX. 9[8]) for *ávatīryatīs*, Pada *ávatīḥ yatīḥ*.

Pl. 1. *asyāmasi*, *páśyāmasi* and *paśyāmas* (AV.), *vidhyāmas* (AV.), *vyayāmasi* (AV. TS.), *haryāmasi*, *hváyāmasi*.

2. *ásyatha*, *páśyatha*, *púṣyatha*, *riṣyatha*, *háryatha*.

3. *ásyanti* (AV.), *áryanti*, *gáyanti*, *jūryanti*, *dasyanti*, *dīyanti*, *dháyanti* (AV.), *naśyanti* (AV.), *náhyanti*, *nṛ́tyanti* (AV.), *páśyanti*, *puṣyanti*, *ráṇyanti*, *riṣyanti*, *váyanti*, *vāyanti*, *vidhyanti* (AV. TS.), *śrāmyanti*, *háryanti*, *hváyanti*.

Middle. Sing. 1. *iṣye*, *padye* (AV.), *gáye*, *nahye* (TS. I. 1. 10[1]), *mánye*, *mṛṣye*, *vyaye* (AV.), *hvaye*.

2. *íyase* (*i*- 'go'), *jáyase*, *tráyase*, *dáyase*, *pátyase*, *pyāyase*, *mányase*, *míyase*, *múcyase*.

3. *iṣyate*, *íyate*, *ṛjyate*, *kṣīyate*, *jáyate*, *jíyate*, *tṛṣyate* (AV.), *dáyate*, *dīpyate* (AV.), *pácyate*, *pátyate*, *pádyate*, *páśyate*, *púṣyate* (AV.), *budhyate* (AV.), *manyate*, *mīyate*, *mṛṣyate*, *ríyate*, *haryate*.

Du. 3. *jāyete* (AV.), *hváyete*.

Pl. 1. *hváyāmahe*. — 2. *trāyadhve*. — 3. *íyante*, *kṣíyante*, *jāyante*, *trāyante*, *pádyante*, *manyante* (AV.), *mayante*, *mṛṣyante*, *yúdhyante*, *rīyante*, *hváyante*.

Present Subjunctive.

440. Active. Sing. 1. *páśyāni* (AV.). — 2. *páśyāsi*, *haryāsi* (AV.); *paśyās* (AV.); *riṣyās*, *háryās*. — 3. *riṣyāti*; *páśyāt*, *púṣyāt*, *riṣyāt* (TS. I. 6. 2[1]).

Pl. 1. *páśyāma* (AV.). — 3. *páśyān*.

Middle. Sing. 1. *yúdhyai*. — 2. *paśyāsai* (AV.). — 3. *manyāte*, *múcyātai* (AV.). — Pl. 1. *hvayāmahai* (AV.).

Present Injunctive.

Active. Sing. 2. *dívyas*. — 3. *gáyat*, *dīyat*, *páśyat*, *vidhyat*. — Pl. 3. *páśyan*.

Middle. Sing. 2. *manyathās*. — 3. *jāyata*, *manyata*. — Pl. 3. *dáyanta*.

Present Optative.

Active. Sing. 1. *vyayeyam*. — 2. *paśyes*. — 3. *dasyet*, *dhayet* (AV.), *riṣyet*. — Du. 3. *hvayetām* (TS. III. 2. 4[1]). — Pl. 1. *páśyema*, *púṣyema*, *búdhyema* (AV.), *riṣyema*.

Middle. Sing. 3. *paśyeta*, *manyeta* (AV.), *mīyeta* (ŚA. XII. 20). — Pl. 1. *jáyemahi*.

Present Imperative.

441. Active. Sing. 2. *asya*, *gáya*, *dīya*, *dṛ́hya*, *naśya*, *nahya* (AV.), *nṛtya* (AV.), *páśya*, *yudhya*, *vaya*, *vídhya*, *śuṣya* (AV.), *sívya* (AV.), *harya*, *hvaya*. — With ending *-tāt*: *asyatāt* (AV.).

3. *asyatu*, *ucyatu* (AV.), *tṛpyatu* (AV.), *naśyatu*, *nṛtyatu* (AV.), *rádhyatu* (AV.), *vidhyatu* (AV.), *śuṣyatu*, *sīvyatu*, *hváyatu* (AV.).

Du. 2. *asyatam*, *iṣyatam* (AV.), *dīyatam*, *nahyatam* (AV.), *puṣyatam* (AV.), *vidhyatam*, *háryatam*. — 3. *asyatām* (AV. TS.), *nahyatām* (ŚA. XII. 32), *vidhyatām*.

Pl. 2. *iṣyata*, *gāyata*, *jasyata*, *náśyata* (AV.), *nahyata* (AV.), *páśyata*, *puṣyata*, *muhyata* (AV.), *vayata*, *vídhyata*, *haryata*. — With ending *-tana*: *nahyatana*.

3. *gāyantu* (AV.), *tṛpyantu* (AV.), *naśyantu* (AV.), *puṣyantu*, *múhyantu*, *médyantu*, *vyayantu* (AV.), *śimyantu* (TS. V. 2. 11[1]), *haryantu* (AV.), *hváyantu* (AV.).

Middle. Sing. 2. *jáyasva*, *tráyasva*, *dayasva*, *dṛhyasva*, *nahyasva* (AV.), *padyasva*, *paśyasva*, *pyāyasva*, *budhyasva* (TS. AV.), *manyasva* (TS. AV.), *vyayasva*, *hvayasva* (AV.).

3. *ṛdhyatām*, *jáyatām*, *tráyatām*, *dīpyatām* (TS. IV. 7. 13[4]), *padyatām* (AV.), *pyāyatām* (TS. AV.), *manyatām* (TS. AV.), *medyatām* (AV.), *rádhyatām* (AV.), *śíyatām* (AV.) 'lie', *hvayatām* (AV.).

Du. 2. *trāyethām, manyethām, hvayethām* (AV.). — 3. *trāyetām.*

Pl. 2. *asyadhvam, jāyadhvam* (AV.), *tráyadhvam, dayadhvam, nahyadhvam* (AV.), *budhyadhvam, sīvyadhvam.* — 3. *jāyantām, tráyantām, padyantām* (AV.), *pyāyantām, manyantām* (AV. TS.), *vyayantām* (TS. III. 3. 11³), *hvayantām* (TS. III. 2. 4¹).

Present Participle.

442. **Active.** *ásyant-, íṣyant-, ṛ́jyant-, (á-)kupyant-* (AV.), *kṣúdyant-, gāyant-, gṛ́dhyant-*[1], *tṛ́ṣyant-, dīyant-, nṛ́tyant-, páśyant-, píyant-, púṣyant-, yásyant-, yúdhyant-, rāyant-, (á-)lubhyant-* (AV.), *váyant-, vídhyant-* (AV.), *vyáyant-, śímyant-* (TS. V. 2. 12¹), *sívyant-, háryant-*; and the compound *án-ava-glāyant-* (AV.) 'not relaxing'.

Middle. *íyamāna-, kāyamāna-, cāyamāna-, jāyamāna-, trāyamāṇa-, dáyamāna-, náhyamāna-, pátyamāna-, pádyamāna-, páśyamāna-, pūryamāṇa-, pyāyamāna-, búdhyamāna-, mányamāna-, yúdhyamāna-, rādhyamāna-* (AV.), *vā́śyamāna-* (AV.), *háryamāṇa-, hváyamāna-.*

Imperfect Indicative.

443. **Active. Sing.** 1. *adīyam, ápaśyam, avyayam.* — 2. *apaśyas, áyudhyas.* — 3. *agāyat, adhayat, anṛtyat* (AV.), *ápaśyat, ayudhyat, avayat* (AV.), *ávidhyat, avyayat, áharyat, áhvayat; ásyat.*

Du. 3. *ápaśyatām.*

Pl. 1. *ápaśyāma.* — 3. *ajūryan*[2], *ápaśyan, ávayan* (AV.), *ahvayan* (AV.); *ásyan* (AV.).

Middle. Sing. 2. *ájāyathās, aharyathās; jāyathās.* — 3. *ájāyata, apatyata, amanyata, arajyata* (AV.); *jāyata.*

Du. 2. *áhvayethām* (AV.). — 3. *áhvayetām.*

Pl. 3. *ájāyanta, ánahyanta* (AV.), *apadyanta* (AV.), *ápaśyanta, ámanyanta, ahvayanta; jāyanta, dáyanta.*

B. The suffixally accented *yá-* class (passive).

DELBRÜCK, Verbum 184 (p. 166—169). — AVERY, Verb-Inflection 274—275. — WHITNEY, Sanskrit Grammar 768—774; Roots 230—231. — v. NEGELEIN 38—40.

444. Any root that requires a passive forms its present stem by adding accented *-yá* (which never needs to be pronounced *-ia*). The root appears in its weak form, losing a nasal and taking Samprasāraṇa; thus *añj-* 'anoint': *aj-yá-* be anointed'; *vac-* 'speak' : *uc-yá-* 'be spoken'. Final vowels undergo the changes usual before *-ya* in verbal forms: final *i* and *u* being lengthened, *ā* mostly becoming *ī*, *ṛ* being generally changed to *ri*, and *ṝ* becoming *īr*[3]. Thus *mi-* 'fix' : *mīya-*; *su-* 'press' : *sūyá-*; *dā-* 'give' : *dī-yá-* (but *jñā-* 'know' : *jñā-yá-*); *kṛ-* 'make' : *kri-yá-*; *śṝ-* 'crush' : *śīrya-*.

a. The root *tan-* 'stretch' forms its passive from *tā-* : *tā-yá-*. Similarly *jan-* 'beget' makes its present stem from *jā-* : *jā́ya-te*, which has, however, been transferred to the radically accented *ya-* class. *mri-yá-te* 'dies' (√*mṛ-*)[4] and *dhriyáte* (√*dhṛ-*) 'is steadfast', though passives in form, are not so in sense[5].

445. The inflexion is identical with that of the radically accented *ya-* class in the middle, differing from it in accent only. No forms of the optative are found in the RV. or AV. The forms actually occurring are the following:

---

1 *ávatīryatīs* (AV. XIX. 9⁸) is a corrupt reading: see WHITNEY'S Translation; cp. p. 331, note 7.

2 AVERY 249 adds *adhayan*(?).

3 No example of *ūr* seems to occur in in the Saṃhitās, but *pūr-ya-* from *pṝ-* 'fill' is found in the *-ya* class.

4 This root has a transitive sense ('crush') only in its secondary form *mṛṇ-*, and in the AV. in the imperative forms *mṛṇīhi* and *mṛṇīta*.

5 Cp. above 437.

Present Indicative.

Sing. 1. *hīye* (*hā-* 'leave'). — **2.** *acyase* (*añc-* 'bend', AV.), *ajyáse* (√*aj-* and √*añj-*), *idhyáse*, *ucyáse* (√*vac-*), *nīyase*, *pūyase*, *badhyáse* (AV.), *mucyáse* (AV.), *mṛjyáse*, *yujyáse*, *ricyase*, *rudhyase* (*rudh-* 'hinder'), *śasyáse* (√*śaṃs-*), *sicyáse*, *stūyase*, *hūyáse* (*hū-* 'call'). — **3.** *ajyáte* (√*aj-* and √*añj-*), *asyate* (AV.), *idhyáte*, *ucyáte* (√*vac-*), *udyate* (*ud-* 'wet' and *vad-* 'speak'), *upyáte* (√*vap-*), *uhyate* (√*vah-*), *ṛcyáte* (*arc-* 'praise'), *kriyáte*, *kṣīyáte* 'is destroyed', *gamyáte* (AV.), *gṛhyate* (AV.), *chidyate* (AV.), *jīyáte* (AV.)[1], *tapyate*, *tāyáte*, *tujyáte*, *dabhyate*, *dīyáte* 'is given' (AV.), *dīyate* 'is divided' (AV.), *duhyate*, *dṛśyate*, *dhamyate*, *dhīyate* (*dhā-* 'put'), *dhriyate*, *nīyáte*, *pacyáte*, *pīyate* 'is drunk' (AV.), *pūyate*, *pṛcyáte*, *badhyáte* (√*bandh-*)[2], *mathyáte* (AV.), *mucyáte*, *mṛjyáte*, *mriyáte*, *yujyáte*, *ricyate*, *ribhyate*[3], *lupyáte* (AV.), *vacyáte* (√*vañc-*), *vidyáte* 'is found', *vṛjyáte*[4], *śasyáte* (√*śaṃs-*), *śiṣyate*, *śīryate*, *śrūyate*, *sicyáte*, *sūyáte* 'is pressed', (√*su-*), *sṛjyáte*, *hanyáte*, *hūyáte* 'is called'.

Du. 3. *ucyete* (√*vac-*).

Pl. 1. *tapyāmahe* (AV.), *panyámahe*. — **3.** *upyánte* (√*vap-*), *ṛcyánte*, *ṛdhyante* (AV.), *kriyánte*, *jñāyante*, *tṛhyánte* (AV.), *dahyante* (AV.), *duhyánte* (AV.), *bhriyante*, *mīyánte* 'are fixed' (√*mi-*, AV.), *mriyante* (AV.), *yujyante*, *vacyánte* (√*vañc-*, AV.), *vīyante* (√*vī-*, AV.), *śasyánte* (√*śaṃs-*), *śīryante* (AV.), *sṛjyante* (AV.), *hanyánte*, *hūyante*.

Present Subjunctive.

446. Sing. 3. *uhyáte*, *bhriyāte*, *śiṣyātai*[5] (AV.).
Du. 2. *ūhyáthe*[6].

Present Injunctive.

Sing. 3. *sūyata* (√*su-*).

Present Imperative.

Sing. 2. *idhyásva* (AV. TS.), *dhīyasva* (AV.), *dhriyasva* (AV.), *mucyasva* (Kh. II. 11[4]), *mriyásva* (AV.), *vacyasva* (√*vañc-*).

3. *ṛdhyatām* (AV.), *tāyatām* (AV.), *dhīyatām* (AV.), *dhūyatām* (AV.), *dhriyatām* (AV.), *pṛcyatām*, *badhyatām* (AV.), *mucyatām* (AV.), *hanyátām* (AV.), *hīyatām*.

Pl. 2. *pṛcyadhvam* (AV. TS.), *yujyadhvam*, *vicyadhvam* (AV.).

3. *tapyantām* (AV.), *tṛhyantām* (AV.), *pṛcyantām* (AV.), *badhyantām*, *bhajyantām* (√*bhañj-*, AV.), *vacyantām*, *vṛścyantām*, *hanyantām* (AV.).

Present Participle.

447. *acyámāna-* (AV), *ajyámāna-*, *idhyámāna-*, *udyámāna-* (√*vad-*, AV.), *upyámāna-* (√*vap-*, AV.), *uhyámāna-*, *ṛcyámāna-*, *kṛtyámāna-* (AV.), *kriyámāṇa-*, (*á-*)*kṣīyamāṇa-*, *gīyámāna-*, *guhyámāna-*, *tapyámāna-*, *tāyámāna-*, *tujyámāna-*, *tṛhyámāṇa-*, *dadyámāna-*[7], *dīyámāna-* (AV.), *duhyámāna-* (AV.), *dhīyámāna-*, *nahyámāna-* (AV.), *nidyámāna-*, *nīyámāna-*, *pacyámāna-*, *piśyámāna-* (AV.), *pūyámāna-*, *pṛcyámāna-*, *badhyámāna-*, *bhajyámāna-*, *mathyámāna-*, *madyámāna-*, *mīyámāna-* (*mi-* 'fix'), *mṛjyámāna-*, *yamyámāna-*, *vacyámāna-* (√*vañc-*),

---

1 From √*jyā-* or √*jī-* 'scathe'.

2 *bhidyate*, AV. XX. 131[1], is an emendation.

3 *līyate*, AV. XX. 134[3.4], is an emendation.

4 The forms *vṛścate*, *vṛścante*, *vṛścantām* appear occasionally to stand for *vṛścyate*, *vṛścyante*, *vṛścyantām* in the AV. See v. NEGELEIN 40; BLOOMFIELD, SBE. 42, 418.

5 Emendation in AV. II. 31[3], for *uchiṣātai*, the reading of the text.

6 A 3. pl. mid. in *-antai* once occurs in the TS. in the form *jāyantai*: WHITNEY 760 a.

7 From the weak present stem *dad-* of *dā-* 'give'.

vīyámāna- (AV.), *śasyámāna-*, *sicyámāna-*, *sṛjyámāna-*, *stūyámāna-*, *hanyámāna-* (AV.), *hiṃsyámāna-*, *hūyámāna-* (*hū-* 'call'); from the causative of √*bhaj-*: *bhājyámāna-* (AV. XII. 4[28]).

Imperfect Indicative.

448. Sing. 3. *anīyata*, *ámucyata*, *aricyata*. — **Pl. 3.** *átapyanta* (AV. TS.), *apacyanta*, *apṛcyanta*, *ásicyanta* (AV.); *acyanta*.

b. The second or graded conjugation.

449. The **chief characteristic** of this conjugation is **vowel gradation** in the base[1] consequent on shift of accent. The base has a strong grade vowel in the singular indicative (present and imperfect) active, throughout the subjunctive, and in the 3. sing. imperative active. **Minor peculiarities** are: 1. loss of *n* in the endings of the 3. pl. mid. (*-ate*, *-ata*, *-atām*); 2. formation of the 2. sing. imperative active with a suffix, generally *-dhi*; 3. vowel gradation in the modal suffix of the optative (act. *-yā*; mid. *-ī*); 4. formation of the middle participle with *-āna*.

a. The second conjugation comprises five distinct **classes** falling into two main groups in which *α*) the vowel of the root (simple or reduplicated) is graded; *β*) the vowel of the suffix (nearly always containing a nasal) is graded.

α. 1. The root class.

450. The base is formed by the root itself, to which the personal endings are directly attached (in the subjunctive and optative with the intervening modal suffix). The radical vowel is accented and takes Guṇa in the strong forms. More than a hundred roots are comprised in this class[2].

a. A good many irregularities are met with in this class, with regard to both the base and the endings. 1. Vṛddhi is taken in the strong forms by *mṛj-* 'wipe' (e. g. *mā́rj-mi*), and before consonants by roots ending in *-u*, i. e. by *kṣṇu-* 'whet', *nu-* 'praise', *yu-* 'unite' (AV.), *stu-* 'praise'; e. g. *stáu-mi*[3], *á-stau-t*[4], but *á-stav-am*. — 2. The Guṇa vowel, along with the accent, is retained in the root of *śī-* 'lie' (middle) throughout the weak forms; e. g. sing. 1. *śáy-e*, 2. *śé-ṣe*. In the 3. pl. this verb at the same time inserts *r* before the endings: *śé-rate*, *śé-re* (AV.), *śé-ratām*, *á-śe-rata*, *á-śe-ran*[5]. — 3. Several roots form a base with the connecting vowel *i* or *ī*[6] before consonant endings. The roots *an-*[7] 'breathe', *rud-*[8] 'weep', *vam* 'vomit', *śvas-* 'blow', *svap-*[9] 'sleep' insert *i* before all terminations beginning with a consonant, except in 2. 3. impf., where they insert *ī*: e. g. *áni-ti*, *ā́nī-t*; *avamī-t*; *śvasi-ti*. The roots *īḍ-* 'praise' and *īś-* 'rule' add *i* in some forms of the 2. pers. middle: *ī́ḍi-ṣva*; *ī́śi-ṣe* (beside *ī́k-ṣe*), *īśi-dhve*. The 3. pl. *ī́śi-re* is, owing to its accent[10], probably to be accounted a present rather than a perfect[11]. Occasional (imperative sing.) forms with connecting *i* from other roots also occur: *jáni-ṣva* 'be born', *vasi-ṣva* 'clothe', *śnathi-hi* 'pierce', *stani-hi* 'thunder'. The root *brū-* 'speak' regularly inserts *ī* in the strong forms before terminations beginning with consonants; e. g. *brávī-mi*. The same *ī* also appears in the form *tavī-ti* from *tu-* 'be strong'; in *amī-ṣi* and in the TS.[12] *amī-ti*, *amī-ṣva*, *āmī-t* from *am-* 'injure'; and in *śamī-ṣva* (VS.), from *śam-*

1 Cp. BRUGMANN, KG. 211.

2 Several roots of this class show transfers to the *a-* conjugation: cp. WHITNEY 625 a.

3 The RV. has once 2. sing. *sto-ṣi* (X. 22[4]), a form which AVERY 275 takes to be a 3. sing. aor. pass. injunctive.

4 Vṛddhi on the other hand once appears even in the weak form 3. pl. impf. *anāvan*. On the Vṛddhi in these verbs, cp. v. NEGELEIN 10 a.

5 There are some transfer forms according to the *a-* conjugation from the stem *śáy-a-*, including the isolated active form *áśayat*, which is common. Nearly a dozen roots besides *śī-* retain the accent on the radical syllable throughout. See 97, 2 a.

6 This *ī* is, however, in reality originally part of a dissyllabic base: cp. BRUGMANN, KG. 212, 2.

7 The AV. has also forms according to the *a-* conjugation: *ána-ti*, etc.

8 The RV. has no such forms from *rud-* and *svap-*.

9 The AV., however, has the form *svap-tu*.

10 See 97, 2 a and 484.

11 The 3. sing. impf. of this verb is in the MS. *aiśa* (like *aduha*), cp. WHITNEY 630.

12 WHITNEY 634.

'labour'. — 4. A few roots undergo peculiar shortenings in the weak forms: *as-* 'be' loses its vowel[1] (except where protected by the augment)[2], e. g. *s-más* 'we are'; *han-*[3] 'slay' in the weak forms loses its *n* before terminations beginning with consonants (except *m, y* or *v*), but syncopates its *a* before terminations beginning with vowels, when *h* reverts to the original guttural *gh-*; e. g. *ha-thá*, but *han-yāma*; *ghn-ánti*, part. *ghn-ánt-*; the root *vaś-* 'be eager', takes Samprasāraṇa; e. g. 1. pl. *uś-mási*, part. *uś-āná-*[4], but 1. sing. *váś-mi*. The root *vas-* 'clothe' similarly takes Samprasāraṇa once in the participle *uṣ-āṇá-* (beside the usual *vásāna-*). — 5. With regard to endings, the root *śās-* 'order' loses the *n* in the 3. pl. active (as well as middle) and in the participle, being treated like roots of the reduplicating class (457)[5]: 3. pl. impv. *śās-atu* (TS.), part. *śās-at-*[6]. The root *duh-* 'milk' is very anomalous in its endings: middle impv. 3. sing. *duh-ām*, 3. pl. *duh-rām* and *duh-ratām*; ind. 3. pl. mid. *duh-ré* and *duh-ráte* beside the regular *duh-até* (with irregular accent)[7]; active imperf. 3. sing. *á-duh-a-t*[8] beside *á-dhok*, 3. pl. *a-duh-ran* beside *á-duh-an* and *duh-úr*[9]; and in the 3. opt. the entirely anomalous sing. *duh-ī-yát* (RV.) and pl. *duh-īyán* (RV.) (for *duh-yát* and *duh-yúr*).

Present Indicative.

451. A final or prosodically short medial radical vowel takes Guṇa in the singular; elsewhere it remains unchanged, excepting the changes of final vowels required by internal Sandhi, and the irregular shortenings mentioned above (450, a 4). The ordinary endings are added directly[10] to the root. But the 3. sing. mid. ends in *-e* nearly as often as in *-te*; and anomalous endings appear in the 3. persons of the roots *īś-*, *duh-*, *śās-*, *śī-*[11].

The forms actually occurring would, if made from *i-* 'go' and *brū-* 'speak', be as follows:

Active. Sing. 1. *é-mi*. 2. *é-ṣi*. 3. *é-ti*. — Du. 2. *i-thás*. 3. *i-tás*. — Pl. 1. *i-mási* and *i-más*. 2. *i-thá* and *i-thána*. 3. *y-ánti*.

Middle. Sing. 1. *bruv-é*. 2. *brū-ṣé*. 3. *brū-té* and *bruv-é*. — Du. 2. *bruv-āthe*. 3. *bruv-áte*. — Pl. 1. *brū-máhe*. 2. *brū-dhve*. 3. *bruv-áte*.

The forms which actually occur are the following:

Active. Sing. 1. *ádmi*, *ásmi*, *émi*, *kṣṇaumi*, *dvéṣmi* (AV.), *pāmi* 'protect', *mārjmi*, *yāmi*, *yaumi* (AV.) 'join', *vaśmi*, *vāmi*, *śāsmi* (AV.), *staumi* (AV. TS.), *hanmi*, *harmi*. — **With connecting *ī*-:** *brávīmi*.

2. *átsi*, *ási*, *éṣi*, *kárṣi* (AV.), *cakṣi* (= **cakṣ-ṣi*), *chantsi* (√*chand-*), *dárṣi* (*dṛ-* 'pierce'), *párṣi* (*pṛ-* 'pass'), *pāsi* ('protect'), *bhāsi*, *yāsi*, *vakṣi* (*vaś-* 'desire'), *véṣi* (√*vī-*), *śāssi*, *sátsi*, *stoṣi*[12], *hámsi*. — **With imperative sense**[13]: *kṣéṣi* (*kṣi-* 'dwell'), *jéṣi*, *jóṣi* (= **joṣ-ṣi* : *juṣ-* 'enjoy'), *dárṣi*, *dhákṣi* (*dah-* 'burn'), *nakṣi* (*naś-* 'attain'), *néṣi*, *párṣi*, *prāsi*, *bhakṣi* (*bhaj-* 'divide'), *matsi*, *māsi*, *yákṣi* (*yaj-* 'sacrifice'), *yámsi* (*yam-* 'reach'), *yāsi*, *yótsi* (*yudh-* 'fight'), *rátsi* (*rad-* 'dig'), *rāsi*, *vákṣi* (*vah-* 'carry'), *véṣi* (√*vī-*), *śróṣi*, *sakṣi* (*sah-* 'prevail'), *sátsi*, *hoṣi* (*hu-* 'sacrifice'). — **With connecting *ī*-:** *amīṣi*, *brávīṣi*.

---

1 It is, however, preserved in an altered form in the 2. sing. impv. act.: *e-dhi* for **az-dhi* (62, 4, 6, p. 57). This verb has the further anomalies of losing its *s* in the 2. sing. pres. *a-si*, and in inserting *ī* in the 2. 3. sing. impf. *āsī-s*, *āsī-t*. It has no middle.

2 Cp. v. NEGELEIN 83; VAN WIJK, IF. 18, 59.

3 Limited to the active in this conjugation in the RV.

4 The only middle form.

5 There are also some transfer forms according to the *a-* conjugation: 3. sing. *śāsati*.

6 Similarly from *dāś-* 'worship' the part. *dāś-at-*.

7 In the middle participle the *h* of the root reverts to the guttural *gh*: *dúgh-āna-*.

8 Transfer to the *a-* conjugation.

9 The MS. has further anomalous endings in the imperf. mid.: 3. sing. *a-duh-a* and 3. pl. *a-duh-ra*, probably as parallel to the present *duhe* and *duhre*: WHITNEY 635.

10 Excepting the few forms of roots which may take connecting *i* or *ī* (450, a 3).

11 See above 450, a 2, 3, 5; cp. JOHANSSON, KZ. 32, 512; NEISSER, BB. 20, 74.

12 See 450, a 1, note 3.

13 Some of these have no corresponding root present or root aorist; cp. WHITNEY, Sanskrit Grammar 624; BARTHOLOMAE, IF. 2, 271; NEISSER, BB. 7, 230 ff., 20, 70 ff.; BRUGMANN, IF. 18, 72; DELBRÜCK, Verbum 30; Syntaktische Forschungen 5, 209.

3. *átti, ásti, éti, kṣeti, takti* (*tak-* 'rush'), *dāti* (*dā-* 'share'), *dāṣṭi* (*dāś-* 'worship'), *dvéṣṭi, pāti, bhárti, bhāti, mārṣṭi* (ŚA. XII. 9), *yāti, rāṣṭi* (*rāj-* 'rule'), *réḷhi* (*rih-* 'lick'), *vaṣṭi* (*vaś-* 'desire'), *vāti, véti, stauti* (AV.; Kh. v. 3[2]), *hánti*. — **With connecting *-i-* or *-ī-***: *ániti, śvásiti; amīti* (TS. VS.), *tavīti* (*tu-* 'be strong'), *brávīti*.

Du. 2. *itháḥ, kṛtháḥ, pāthás, bhūthás, yāthás, vīthás, sthás* (*as-* 'be'), *hathás* (√*han-*).

3. *attas, etas*[1] (AV.), *kṣitás, dviṣṭas* (AV.), *pātas, psātás* (AV.), *bhūtas, yātas, vātas, stas, snātas, hatás, hnutas*.

Pl. 1. *admasi* (AV.), *imási, uśmási*[2] (√*vaś-*), *stumási, smási, hanmasi* (AV.); *dviṣmás, brūmás* (AV.), *mṛjmas* (AV.), *yāmas, rudhmas* (AV.), *vidmas* (Kh. IV. 5[33]), *stumas* (AV.), *smas, hanmas*.

2. *itha, kṛtha, gathá* (RV[1].)[3], *nethá*[4], *pāthá* 'protect'[5], *yāthá, stha, hathá; pāthána, yāthána, sthána*.

3. *adanti, amánti, uśánti, kṣiyánti, ghnánti* (√*han-*), *dānti* (*dā-* 'cut'), *duhanti, dviṣánti* (AV.), *pānti*[6], *bruvánti, bhānti, mṛjánti, yánti, yānti, rihánti, rudánti, vānti, vyánti* (√*vī-*), *sánti*.

Middle. Sing. 1. *iye* (*i-* 'go'), *íḷe, íśe, uvé*[7], *duhe, bruve, mṛje* (AV.), *yujé, yuve* (*yu-* 'join'), *suve* (*sū-* 'beget')[8], *hnuve*.

2. *íkṣe, kṛṣé, cakṣe* (= **cakṣ-ṣe*), *dhukṣe* (AV.), *brūṣe, vitsé* (*vid-* 'find'), *śéṣe*. — **With connecting *-i-***: *íśiṣe*.

3. *áste, íṭṭe* (√*īḍ-*), *īrte, íṣṭe* (√*īś-*), *cáṣṭe* (√*cakṣ-*), *brūté, váste, śāste, śiṅkte*[9] (√*śiñj-*), *sūte, hate* (ŚA. XII. 27). — **With ending *-e***: *íśe*[10], *cité* (*cit-* 'perceive'), *duhé, bruve, vidé* ('finds'), *śáye*[11].

Du. 2. *ásāthe, íśāthe, cakṣāthe, vasāthe*. — 3. *āsāte, iyāte, duhāte, bruvāte, śayāte, sávāte*.

Pl. 1. *ásmahe* (AV.), *ímahe, īśmahe* (AV.), *mṛjmáhe* (AV.), *yujmahe, śāsmahe, śémahe* (AV.), *hūmáhe*. — 2. **With connecting *-i-***: *īśidhve* (AV.). — 3. *ásate, írate, íḷate, íśate, óhate* (√*ūh-*), *gṛhate*[12], *cákṣate, duhaté*[13], *dviṣáte* (AV.), *níṃsate, bruváte, rihaté*[13], *vásate, śāsate, suvate*. — **With ending *-re***: *duhré, śére* (AV.); **with *-rate***: *duhrate, śérate* (AV. TS.).

Present Subjunctive.

452. In the AV. several forms are irregularly made with *ā*, as if following the *a-* conjugation. No examples of the 2. du. and pl. mid. are found. The forms which actually occur, if made from *brū-* 'speak', would be:

Active. Sing. 1. *brávāṇi, brávā*. 2. *brávasi, brávas*. 3. *brávati, brávat*. — Du. 1. *brávāva*. 2. *brávathas*. 3. *brávatas*. — Pl. 1. *brávāma*. 2. *bravatha*. 3. *brávan*.

Middle. Sing. 1. *bravé*. 2. *bravase*. 3. *brávate*. — Du. 1. *bravāvahai*. 3. *brávaite*. — Pl. 1. *brávāmahai, bravāmahe*. 3. *brávanta*.

The forms which actually occur are the following:

Active. Sing. 1. *ásāni* (AV.), *brávāṇi; ayā, bravā, stávā*.

1 With irregular strong radical vowel.
2 Once anomalously *śmási*.
3 With loss of nasal as in √*han-*.
4 With irregular strong radical vowel: cp. v. NEGELEIN 33.
5 Once from *pā-* 'drink', in I. 86[1]?
6 Thirteen times from *pā-* 'protect', once (II. 11[14]) from *pā-* 'drink' (probably subj. aor.).
7 This form occurring only once in the RV. seems to be formed from a doubtful root *u* 'proclaim'; cp. WHITNEY, Roots, under *u*.
8 *huvé*, sing. 1. and 3., should perhaps be placed here rather than in the *á-* class; on this form cp. OLDENBERG, ZDMG. 59, 355 ff.; NEISSER, BB. 25, 315 ff.
9 *śiṅte* (AV.).
10 AVERY 234 gives *íṣe* only, apparently instead of *íśe*. The form *īṣé* would be 3. sing. mid. perfect.
11 On these forms cp. v. NEGELEIN 10[2]; NEISSER, BB. 20, 74.
12 Placed by WHITNEY, Roots, doubtfully under the aorist of √*grah-*.
13 With irregular accent.

2. *ayasi* (AV.), *ásasi*, *bravasi*; *áyas* (AV.), *ásas*, *kṣáyas* (*kṣi-* 'dwell'), *ghásas*, *dánas*, *parcas*, *bravas*, *védas*, *śákas*, *hánas*; with *-ā-*: *áyās* (AV.).
3. *áyati*, *ásati*, *vayati* (√*vī-*), *védati*, *hanati*; *adat* (AV.), *áyat*, *ásat*, *írat*[1], *kṣayat*, *ghasat*, *cayat*, *déhat*, *dohat* (I. 164[26]), *dvéṣat* (AV.), *pāt* ('protect'), *brávat*, *védat* (*vid-* 'know'), *stávat*, *hánat* (AV. TS.); with *-ā-*: *ayāt* (Kh. III. 1[8]), *asāt* (AV.), *rodāt* (Kh. 2. 11[1]).

Du. 1. *hánāva*. — 2. *ásathas*, *vedathas*. — 3. *pátas* 'protect' (IV. 55[7]).

Pl. 1. *ayāma*, *ásāma*, *kṣáyāma*, *dveṣāma* (AV.), *brávāma*, *stávāma*, *hánāma*. — 2. *ásatha*[2], *stavatha*; with *-ā-*: *bravātha* (AV.), *hanātha* (AV.). — 3. *ayan*, *ásan*, *brávan*, *yavan* ('join', AV. III. 17[2]), *hánan* (AV.); with *-ā-*: *ádān* (AV.), *ayān* (AV.).

Middle. Sing. 1. *stuṣé*[3]. — 2. *āsase*. — 3. *āsate*, *idhaté*[4], *dóhate*, *dvéṣate* (TS. IV. 1. 10[3]), *várjate*; **with** *-tai*: *áyātai* (AV.), *ásātai* (AV.); with secondary ending *-ta*: *īśata*. — **Du.** 1. *bravāvahai*. — 3. *brávaite*. — **Pl.** 1. *íḷāmahai*, *brávāmahai*; *īḷāmahe*. — 3. *hánanta*.

Present Injunctive.

Active. Sing. 2. *vés*. — 3. *vet* (X. 53[9]), *staut*; without ending: *dán*, *rāṭ*, *han*. — **Pl.** 3. *yan*, *san*.

Middle. Sing. 3. *vasta*, *sūta*. — **Pl.** 3. *īḷata*, *vasata*.

Present Optative.

453. **Active. Sing.** 1. *iyām*, *yāyām*, *vidyām*, *syám*. — 2. *syás*. — 3. *adyāt* (AV.), *iyāt*, *brūyāt*, *vidyát*, *syát*, *hanyát* (AV.).

Du. 2. *brūyātam* (TS. IV. 7. 15[6]), *vidyātam*, *syātam*. — 3. *syātām*.

Pl. 1. *iyāma*, *turyáma*, *vidyáma*, *syáma*, *hanyáma*. — 2. *syáta*; *syátana*. — 3. *adyúr*, *vidyúr*, *syúr*.

Middle. Sing. 1. *íśīya*, *śáyīya* (AV.). — 3. *āsīta*, *īḷīta*, *īśīta*, *duhīta*, *bruvīta*, *śáyīta*, *stuvītá*. — **Pl.** 1. *bruvīmahi*, *vasīmahi*, *stuvīmahi*.

Present Imperative.

454. The endings are added directly to the root, which appears in its weak form except in the 3. sing. act., where it is strong and accented[5]. In the 2. sing. act., *-dhi* is added to a final consonant, *-hi* to a vowel; *-tāt*, which occurs only three times, may be added to either a consonant or a vowel. In the mid., *-ām* 3. sing., *-rām* and *-ratām* 3. pl., occasionally appear for *-tām* and *-atām*[6].

Active. Sing. 2. *addhí*, *edhi* (*as-* 'be'), *taḍhí* (√*takṣ-*), *psāhi* (AV.), *mṛḍḍhi* (AV.), *viddhí* ('find' and 'know'), *śādhi* (√*śās-*); *ihi*, *jahí*[7], *pāhí* 'protect', *brūhí*, *bhāhi*, *yāhí*, *vāhí*, *vihí*[8], *vīhí*, *stuhí*, *snāhi* (AV.); **with connecting** *-i-*: *anihi* (VS. IV. 25), *śnathihi*, *śvasihí* (AV.), *stanihi*; **with** *-tāt*: *brūtāt* (TS. I. 6. 4[3]), *vittát*, *vītāt*. — 3. *attu*, *ástu*, *etu*, *dveṣṭu* (AV.), *pātu* 'protect', *psātu* (AV.), *mārṣṭu* (AV. TS.), *yātu*, *vaṣṭu* (√*vaś-*), *vātu*, *vétu*, *vettu* (AV.), *sastu*, *stautu* (AV.), *snautu* (TS. III. 5. 5[2]), *sváptu* (AV.), *hántu*; **with connecting** *-ī-*: *brávītu*.

---

[1] AVERY 230 here adds *ṛdhat*, which I regard as a root aor. subjunctive.

[2] *vidátha*, AV. I. 32[1], seems to be a corruption for *védatha*; cp. WHITNEY's note.

[3] For *stuṣ-a-i*: cp. AVERY 238; DELBRÜCK, Verbum p. 181[3]; NEISSER, BB. 27, 262—280; OLDENBERG, ZDMG. 55, 39.

[4] With irregular accent and weak root (VII. 1[8]) for **indhate*, beside *inádhate* formed from √*idh-* according to the infixing nasal class.

[5] This is also irregularly the case in six or seven forms of the 2. pl., before both *-ta* and *-tana*: *éta*, *neta*, *stota*; *étana*, *bravītana*, *sotana*, *hantana*.

[6] In *duhām*, *vidām* (AV.), *śayām* (AV.); *duhrām* (AV.), *duhratām* (AV.).

[7] For **jha-hi*, from *han-* 'slay': see 32, 2 c, and cp. V. NEGELEIN, Zur Sprachgeschichte 8[2].

[8] Metrically shortened for *vīhi*, from √*vī-*.

Du. 2. *attam* (AV.), *itam* (AV. TS.), *pātám* 'protect', *brūtam* (AV.), *yātám*, *vittám*, *vītám*, *stam* (*as-* 'be'), *stutam*, *hatám*. — 3. *itām*, *dugdhām* (√*duh-*), *pātām* 'protect', *sastām*, *stām* (AV.), *hatām* (AV.).

Pl. 2. *attá*, *itá* and *éta*, *pātá* 'protect', *brūta*, *yātá*, *śasta* (*śas-* 'cut'), *sta* (VS. AV.), *stota*, *hatá*; with **-tana**: *attana*, *itana* and *étana*, *yātána*, *śāstána*, *sotana* (*su-* 'press'), *hantana*; with connecting **-ī-**: *bravītana*.

3. *adantu*, *ghnantu*, *drāntu*, *pāntu* 'protect', *bruvantu*, *yantu*, *yāntu*, *vāntu* (AV.), *vyántu* (√*vī-*) and *viyantu* (TS.), *śāsatu* (TS. v. 2. 12[1]), *śvásantu* (AV.), *santu*, *svápantu* (AV.).

Middle. Sing. 2. *īrṣva*, *cakṣva* (= _*cakṣ-ṣva_), *trásva*, *dhukṣva*[1], *mṛkṣva* (√*mṛj-*, AV.), *stuṣvá* (AV.); with connecting **-i-**: *īḷiṣva*, *jániṣva*, *vásiṣva*.

3. *āstām*, *yutām* (AV.), *vastām*, *śetām* (AV.); with **-ām**: *duhām*, *vidām* (*vid-* 'find', AV.), *śayām* (AV.).

Du. 2. *īrāthām*, *cakṣāthām* (TS.), *duhāthām* (AV.), *vasāthām* (TS.). — 3. *duhātām* (AV.). — Pl. 2. *ādhvam*[2] (√*ās-*), *īrdhvam*, *trádhvam*, *mṛḍḍhvam* (AV.). — 3. *īratām*, *stuvatām* (AV.); with **-rām**: *duhrām* (AV.); with **-ratām**: *duhratām* (AV.).

Present Participle.

455. The active participle is formed by adding *-ánt*[3] to the weak root; thus *y-ánt-* from *i-* 'go'; *duh-ánt-* from *duh-* 'milk'; *s-ánt-* from *as-* 'be'. The strong stems of the participles of *dāś-* 'worship' and *śās-* 'order' lose the *n*: *dáś-at-*[4] and *śáś-at-*[5]. The middle participle is formed by adding the suffix *-āná* to the weak form of the root; thus *iy-āná-* from √*i-*; *uś-āná-* from √*vaś-*; *ghn-āná-* (AV.) from √*han-*. In a few examples, however, the radical vowel takes Guṇa; thus *oh-āná-* from *ūh-* 'consider'; *yodh-āná-* from *yudh-* 'fight'; *śáy-āna-* from *śī-* 'lie'; *stav-āná-* from *stu-* 'praise'. The final of √*duh-* reverts to the original guttural in *dúgh-āna-* beside the regular *dúhāna-*. The root *ās-* 'sit' has the anomalous suffix *-īna* in *ás-īna-* beside the regular *ās-āná-*. Several of these participles in *-āna* alternatively accent the radical vowel instead of the final vowel of the suffix; thus *víd-āna-* beside *vid-āná-* 'finding'.

Active. *adánt-*, *anánt-*, *uśánt-*, *kṣiyánt-*[6] 'dwelling', *ghnánt-* (√*han-*), *duhánt-*, *dviṣánt-*, *dhṛṣánt-*, *pánt-* 'protecting', *bruv-ánt-*, *bhánt-*, *yánt-*, *yánt-*, *rihánt-*, *rudánt-*, *vánt-*[7] (AV.), *vyánt-* (√*vī-*), *sánt-*, *sasánt-*, *stuvánt-*, *snánt-*, *svapánt-*; with loss of ***n***: *dáśat-*, *śásat-*.

Middle. *adāná-*, *āsāná-* and *ásīna-*, *índhāna-*, *iyāná-* (VS. x. 19; TS. I. 8. 14[2]), *íḷāna-*, *írāṇa-*, *íśāna-* and (once) *īśāná-*, *uśāná-*[8], *uṣāṇá-*[9] (*vas-* 'wear'), *óhāna-* and *ohāná-* (√*ūh-*), *kṣṇuvāná-*[10], *ghnāná-* (AV.), *dihāná-*, *dúghāna-* and *duhāná-* and *dúhāna-*, *dhṛṣāṇá-* (AV.), *nijāná-*, *bruvāṇá-*, *mṛjāná-*, *yuvāná-* (*yu-*

[1] DELBRÜCK 61 and AVERY 242 wrongly give this form as *dukṣva*.

[2] In AV. (IV. 14[2]) and TS. (IV. 6. 5[1]) some Mss. read *āddhvam*. VS. XVII. 65 has *ādhvam*.

[3] The feminine is formed with *-ī* from the weak stem; thus *ghnat-ī-*, *duhat-ī-*, *yat-ī-*, *yāt-ī-*, *bhāt-ī-*, *rudat-ī-*, *sat-ī-* (AV.), *snāt-ī-*. But the AV. has *yántī-* (beside *yatī-*) and *svapántī-*; see WHITNEY, Index Verborum 374[4].

[4] The verb *dāś-* may have lost its nasal in the 3. pl. act., but there is no evidence of this, as the only form preserved according to the root class is 3. sing. *dāṣṭi*.

[5] As in 3. pl.

[6] *kṣyántam* TS. IV. 1. 2[5].

[7] *apa-vān* AV. XIX. 50[4] is probably N. sing. of this part.; see WHITNEY's note and cp. LANMAN 484[2].

[8] The RV. has once the transfer form *uśámāna-*.

[9] Once, beside the regular *vásāna-*. The RV. has also once the transfer form *uṣámāṇa-*.

[10] The form *gṛhāṇá* (x. 103[12]), doubtless 2. sing. impv. of the *nā-* class, is regarded by GRASSMANN as a participle.

'join'), *yodhāná-*, *rihāṇá-*, *vásāna-* 'wearing', *vidāna-* and *vidāná-*, *vyāná-* (√*vī-*), *śáyāna-*, *śā́sāna-* (AV. TS.), *súvāna-* (*sū-* 'bring forth', AV.), *stuvāná-* and *stavāná-*, *svāná-* (*su-* 'press', SV.)[1].

Imperfect Indicative.

456. **Active. Sing. 1.** *adoham* (Kh. v. 15^{14}), *apām* ('protect'), *ábravam*, *avedam*, *ahanam*; *ādam* (VS. xii. 105), *ā́yam*, *āsam*, *airam* (√*īr-*).

2. *ápās*, *áyās*; *áis* (AV.); *ves* (√*vī-*); **with connecting -ī-:** *abravīs* (AV.); *āsīs*; **without ending:** *áhan*; *han*.

3. *ápāt*, *áyāt*, *avāt* (AV.), *astaut*; *áit*[2]; **with connecting -ī-:** *ábravīt*, *avamīt*; *ā́nīt*, *ā́sīt*[3]; **without ending:** *adhok*, *ávet* (AV.), *áhan*; *ās* (= **ās-t*, from *as-* 'be'); *han*[4].

Du. 2. *áyātam*, *ahatam*; *ā́stam*, *áitam*; *yātam* (AV.). — **3.** *abrūtām* (AV.); *āttām* (VS. xxi. 43), *ā́stām*, *aitām* (AV. VS.).

Pl. 1. *atakṣma*, *ápāma*. — **2.** *ataṣṭa*; *áita*; *abravīta*; *áyātana*, *ásastana*; *áitana*; *ábravītana*. — **3.** *ádihan* (AV.), *anāvan*, *abruvan*, *avyan* (√*vī-*); *ā́yan* (*i-* 'go'), *ā́san*; *asan*[5] (*as-* 'throw'), *-ghnan* (Kh. i. 2^2); **with ending -ur:** *atviṣur*, *apur* (*pā-* 'protect'); *asur* (*as-* 'throw', i. 179^2); *cákṣur*, *duhur*.

Middle. Sing. 3. *acaṣṭa*, *atakta*, *ávasta* (AV.), *ásūta*; *áiṭṭa* (√*īḍ-*); *mṛṣṭa* (i. 174^4), *sūta*.

Pl. 2. *árādhvam*. — **3.** *aghnata* (AV.), *acakṣata*, *ajanata*, *ámṛjata* (AV.), *aśāsata*; *āsata*, *áirata*. **With ending -ran:** *aduhran* (AV.), *áśeran*.

α. 2. The Reduplicating Class.

457. This class is less than half as frequent as the root class, comprising fewer than 50 verbs. The endings are here added to the reduplicated root, which is treated as in the root class, taking Guṇa in the strong forms. The stem shows the same peculiarity as the desiderative in reduplicating *r̥̄* (= *ar*) and *ā̆* with *i*. Here, however, this rule is not invariable. All the roots with *r̥* except one reduplicate with *i*. They are *r̥-* 'go': *i-y-ar-*[6]; *ghr̥-* 'drip': *jighar-*; *tr̥̄-* 'cross': *titr̥-*; *pr̥̄-* 'fill' and *pr̥-* 'pass': *pipar-*; *bhr̥-* 'bear': *bibhar-*; *sr̥-* 'run': *sisar-*; *pr̥c-* 'mix': *pipr̥c-*; but *vr̥t-* 'turn': *vavart-*. While nine roots reduplicate *ā̆* with *a*, thirteen do so with *i*. The latter are: *gā-* 'go': *jigā-*; *ghrā-* 'smell': *jighrā-*; *pā-* 'drink': *piba-*; *mā-* 'measure': *mimā-*; *mā-* 'bellow': *mimā-*; *śā-* 'sharpen': *śiśā-*; *sthā-* 'stand': *tiṣṭha-*; *hā-* 'go forth': *jihī-*[7]; *vac-* 'speak': *vivac-*; *vaś-* 'desire': *vivaś-*[8]; *vyac-* 'extend': *vivyac-*; *sac-* 'accompany': *siṣac-*[9]; *han-* 'strike': *jighna-*. Three of these, however, *pā-*, *sthā-*, *han-*, have permanently gone over to the *a-* conjugation, while a fourth, *ghrā-*, is beginning to do so. Contrary to analogy the accent is not, in the majority of verbs belonging to this class, on the root in the strong forms, but on the reduplicative syllable. The latter is further accented in the 3. pl. act. and mid., as well as in the 1. du. and pl. mid. Doubtless as a result of this accentuation, the verbs of this class lose the *n* of the endings in the 3. pl. act. and mid.; e. g. *bibhr-ati*[10] and *jihate*.

---

[1] To be pronounced thus in the RV., though always written *suvāná-*.

[2] The form *aitat* (AV. xviii. 3^{40}) seems to be a corruption of *áit*; see Whitney's note in his Translation.

[3] Cp. v. Negelein 8^1; Reichelt BB. 27, 89. VS. viii. 46 has the transfer form *āsat*.

[4] *árudat* (AV.) is a transfer to the *a-* conjugation. In i. 77^2 *vés*, 3. sing., seems to be an aor. form = **vé-s-t*.

[5] Unaugmented form iv. 3^1.

[6] With *-y-* interposed between reduplication and root.

[7] With *ī* for *ā*; inflected in the middle only.

[8] Also *vavaś-*.

[9] Also *saśc-*.

[10] That is, *a* replaces the sonant nasal.

a. There are a number of irregularities chiefly in the direction of shortening the root in weak forms. 1. Roots ending in *ā* drop their vowel before terminations beginning with vowels[1]: e. g. √*mā*: *mim-e*, 3. pl. *mim-ate*. √*dā*- and √*dhā*-, the two commonest verbs in this class, drop the *ā* in all weak forms. — 2. The root *vyac*- takes Samprasāraṇa; e. g. 3. du. *viviktás*; analogously *hvar*- 'be crooked', makes some forms with Samprasāraṇa, when it reduplicates with *u*; e. g. *juhūrthās*, 2. sing. mid. injunctive. — 3. The verbs *bhas*- 'chew', *sac*- 'accompany', *has*- 'laugh', syncopate the radical vowel; thus *babhas-at*, 3. sing. subj., but *báps-ati*, 3. pl. ind.; *sáśc-ati*, 3. pl. ind. pres., *saśc-ata*, 3. pl. inj.; *jákṣ-at*-, pres. part. — 4. The *ā* of *śā*- 'sharpen', *mā*- 'measure', *mā*- 'bellow', *rā*- 'give', *hā*- 'go away' (mid.), and (in AV.) *hā*- 'leave' (act.)[2], is usually changed to *ī* before consonants; e. g. *śiśīmási*, *mimīte*, *rarīthās*[3], *jihīte*, *jahīta* (AV.); while the roots *dā*- 'give' and *dhā*- 'put' drop their vowel even here[4]; e. g. *dád-mahe*, *dadh-mási*. — 5. The initial of *ci*- 'observe' reverts to the original guttural throughout; e. g. *cikéṣi* (AV.). — 6. When the aspiration of *dadh*-, the weak base of *dhā*-, is lost before *t*, *th*, *s*, or *dhv*, it is thrown back on the initial; e. g. *dhat-sva*. — 7. The roots *dī*- 'shine', *dhī*- 'think', *pī*- 'swell', reduplicate with *ī*; e. g. *ádīdet*; *ádīdhet*; *ápīpet*. — 8. There are a number of transfers from this to other classes. Thus *cakṣ*- 'see', originally a syncopated reduplicative base (= **cakās*-), has become a root inflected according to the root class; *jakṣ*- 'eat', also originally a reduplicated base (*jaghas*-), has become a root from which is formed the past passive participle *jag-dhá*-, and which in the later language is inflected both in the root-class and the *a*- class. The weak bases *dad*- and *dadh*- show an incipient tendency to become roots[5], from which a number of transfer forms according to the *a*- conjugation are made, such as 3. sing. mid. *dada-te*, 3. pl. ind. act. *dádhanti*, 3. pl. impv. act. *dadha-ntu*, 3. sing. mid. *dadha-te*, 2. du. *dadhethe* (AV.). The roots *pā*- 'drink', *sthā*-, *han*-, form only transfer stems according to the *a*- class: *piba*-, *tiṣṭha*-, *jighna*-; while *ghrā*-, *mā*- 'bellow', *rā*-, *bhas*-, *sac*- make occasional forms from transfer stems according to the *a*- class: *jighra*-, *mima*-, *rára*-, *bápsa*-, *sáśca*-.

Inflexion.

458. The forms actually occurring would, if made from *bhṛ*- 'bear', be the following:

Active. Sing. 1. *bíbharmi*. 2. *bíbharṣi*. 3. *bíbharti*. — Du. 2. *bibhṛthás*. 3. *bibhṛtás*. — Pl. 1. *bibhṛmási* and *bibhṛmás*. 2. *bibhṛthá*. 3. *bíbhrati*.

Middle. Sing. 1. *bibhré*. 2. *bibhṛṣé*. 3. *bibhṛté*. — Du. 1. *bíbhṛvahe*. 2. *bibhrā́the*. 3. *bibhrā́te*. — Pl. 1. *bíbhṛmahe*. 2. *bibhṛdhve*. 3. *bíbhrate*.

The forms which actually occur are the following:

Present Indicative.

Active. Sing. 1. *íyarmi*, *jáhāmi*, *jígharmi*, *juhómi*, *dádāmi*, *dádhāmi*, *píparmi* ('fill', AV.), *bíbharmi*, *vivakmi* (√*vac*-), *śiśāmi*.

2. *iyárṣi*[6], *cikéṣi* (AV.), *jáhāsi* (AV.), *jígāsi*, *dádāsi*, *dádhāsi*, *píparṣi*, *bíbharṣi*, *mamatsi*, *vavákṣi* (√*vaś*-), *vivekṣi*[7] (*viṣ*- 'be active'), *siṣakṣi* (√*sac*-), *sisarṣi*[8].

3. *íyarti*, *jáhāti*, *jígāti*, *jígharti*, *juhóti*, *dádāti*[9], *dádhāti*, *píparti* 'fills' and 'passes', *bábhasti* (AV.), *bíbharti* and (once) *bibhárti*, *mímāti* 'bellows', *mimeti* (*mā*- 'bellow', SV.), *yuyoti* 'separates', *vavarti* (= *vavart-ti*, II. 38[6]), *vívakti*, *vivaṣṭi* (√*vaś*-), *viveṣṭi* (*viṣ*- 'be active'), *sásasti* (VS.) and *sasásti* (TS. VII. 4. 19[1]), *siṣakti* (√*sac*-), *sisarti*.

Du. 2. *dhatthás*, *ninīthás*, *pipṛthas*, *bibhṛthás*. — **3.** *dattás* (AV.), *dádhātas*[10] (AV.), *bibhītás* (AV.), *bibhṛtás*, *mimītas*, *viviktás* (√*vyac*-), *viviṣṭas*.

Pl. 1. *juhūmási*, *dadmasi*, *dadhmási*, *bibhṛmási*, *śiśīmási*; *jahimas*[11] (AV.), *juhumás*, *dadmas* (AV.), *dadhmas*, *bibhṛmas* (AV.), *viviṣmas*. — **2.** *dhatthá*,

1 This of course does not take place in the transfer verbs according to the *a*- conjugation.

2 In the RV. *hā*- 'leave', has only forms with *ā* (never *ī*).

3 But *rarāsva* (AV.).

4 The vowel of *hā*- 'leave' is also dropped in the 3. pl. opt. act. *jahyur* (AV.).

5 From the former is made the past passive participle *dat-tá*- 'given'.

6 This is the accentuation in MAX MÜLLER's and AUFRECHT's editions, both in Saṃhitā and Padapāṭha.

7 Cp. NEISSER, BB. 30, 303.

8 With imperative sense.

9 Also the transfer form *dádati*.

10 With strong base, for *dhattás*.

11 With base weakened to *jahi*- for *jahī*-.

piprthá, bibhrthá. — 3. *jahati, jighrati* (AV.), *júhvati, dádati, dádhati*[1], *dīdyati*[2] (AV.), *piprati, bapsati* (√*bhas-*), *bibhrati*[3], *sáścati.*

Middle. Sing. 1. *juhvé, dadé* (AV. TS.), *dadhé, mime.* — 2. *datse* (AV.), *dhatsé.* — 3. *jíhīte, juhuté, datté*[4], *dhatté*[5], *mímīte, śíśīte*[6]; **with -e:** *dadhé* (+ AV.).

Du. 1. *dádvahe.* — 2. *dadhā́the.* — 3. *jihāte, dadhā́te*[7], *mimāte*[8] (v. 82[6]).

Pl. 1. *dádmahe, mimīmahe* (AV.). — 2. *jihīdhve* (AV.). — 3. *jíhate, dadhate*[9], *mimate* ('measure'), *sisrate.*

Present Subjunctive.

459. **Active. Sing.** 1. *dadhāni, bibharāṇi* (TS. I. 5. 10[1]). — 2. *juhuras, dádas, dadhas, dīdhyas* (AV.), *viveṣas.* — 3. *piprati; dadat, dádhat, dídayat, dīdāyat*[10] (AV.), *babhasat, bibharat* (AV.), *yuyávat* 'separate'.

Du. 2. *dádhathas, bapsathas* (Kh. I. 11[1]).

Pl. 1. *jahāma, juhavāma, dadhāma.* — 3. *dádan* (AV.), *dádhan, yuyavan.*

Middle. Sing.[11] 2. *dádhase.* — 3. *dádhate*; with *-tai·* *dadātai* (AV.). — **Du.** 1. *dadhāvahai* (TS. I. 5. 10[1]). — **Pl.** 1. *dadāmahe.* — 3. *juhuranta*[12].

Present Injunctive.

Active. Sing. 2. *dadās* (AV.), *bibhes* (AV.). — 3. *jigāt, dadāt* (AV.), *vivyak.*

Pl. 1. *yuyoma*[13] (AV.).

Middle. Sing. 2. *juhūrthās* (√*hvṛ-*). 3. *jihīta.*

Pl. 3. *saścata.*

Present Optative[14].

Active. Sing. 2. *mimīyās* (x. 56[2]). — 3. *jahyāt*[15] (ŚA. XII. 11); *juhuyā́t* (AV.), *dadyāt* (AV.), *bibhīyāt, bibhṛyāt, mamanyāt, mimīyāt* (*mā-* 'measure'). — **Du.** 3. *yuyuyā́tām.* — **Pl.** 1. *juhuyā́ma.* — 3. *jahyur*[15] (AV.).

Middle. Sing. 3. *dádhīta* and *dadhītá.* — **Pl.** 1. *dadīmahi, dadhīmáhi.* — 3. *dadīran.*

Present Imperative.

460. **Active. Sing.** 1. *jáhāni* (AV.). — 2. *daddhí, piprgdhi* (√*pṛc-*), *mamaddhí, mamandhi, yuyodhi, viviḍḍhi* (√*viṣ-*), *śiśādhi.* — **With -hi:** *cikīhi* (*ci-* 'note', AV.), *didīhí* and *dīdihí* (√*dī-*), *dehí* (√*dā-*), *dhehí, piprhí, bibhṛhi* (AV. TS.), *mimīhí* (*mā-* 'measure'), *rirīhí*[16] (√*rā-*), *śiśīhí.* — **With -tāt:** *jahītāt* (AV.), *dattāt, dhattāt, piprtāt* (TS. IV. 4. 12[1]). — 3. *ciketu* (TS. III. 3. 11[5]), *jáhātu, jigātu, juhotu* (TS. III. 3. 10[1]), *dádātu, dádhātu, pipartu* ('fill' and 'pass'), *bibhartu* (AV. TS.), *mimātu, yayastu, yuyotu, śiśātu, siṣaktu.*

---

1 Also the transfer form *dádhanti.*

2 Regarded by DELBRÜCK, Verbum p. 133[3], as an intensive.

3 There is also a transfer form *mimanti* 'bellow'.

4 Also the transfer form *dadate.*

5 Also the transfer form *dadhate.*

6 There is also the transfer form *rarate* from √*rā-*.

7 Also the transfer form *dadhete* (AV.).

8 By AVERY 237[4] given as 3. sing. subjunctive middle.

9 TS. I. 5. 10[4], III. 1. 8[2] has the transfer form *dádante.*

10 Pp. *dīdayat*; see WHITNEY's note on AV. III. 8[3].

11 *śaśvacái* (RV. III. 33[10]) is probably sing. 1 perfect subj. (p. 361); but occurring beside the aorist form *naṃsai*, it may be an aorist, to which tense WHITNEY, Roots, doubtfully assigns it.

12 *dīdayante* (AV. XVIII. 37[3]) is perhaps a subjunctive.

13 With the strong base *yuyo-* for *yuyu-*.

14 AVERY 241 gives here several forms which it is better to class as optatives perfect.

15 With weak base *jah-*, for *jahī-*, which here loses its final vowel like *dadā-* and *dadhā-*.

16 The only form in which √*rā-* reduplicates with *i.*

Du. 2. *jahītam* (AV.), *jigātam*, *dattám*, *dhattám*, *piprtám*, *mimītám*, *yuyutám* and *yuyotam*[1], *śiśītám*, *sisrtam*. — 3. *cikitām* (*ci-* 'note', AV.), *dattām*, *dhattām*, *piprtām*, *bibhrtām*, *mimītām*, *śiśītām*.

Pl. 2. *íyarta*[2], *jahīta* (AV.), *jigāta*, *juhuta* and *juhóta*[3], *dattá* and *dádāta*[4], *dhattá* and *dádhāta*[5], *ninikta* (√*nij-*), *piprkta*, *piprtá*, *bibhīta* (AV.), *bibhrtá* (TS. IV. 2. 3[2]), *yuyóta*[1], *śiśīta*, *sisakta*; *jigātana*, *juhótana*[3], *dadātana*[4], *dhattana* and *dádhātana*[5], *pípartana*[6], *bibhītana*, *mamattána*, *yuyótana*[1], *vivaktana*. — 3. *dadatu* (AV.), *dadhatu*[7].

Middle. Sing. 2. *jihīṣva*, *datsva* (AV.), *dhatsva*, *mimīṣva* (AV.), *rarāsva* (AV.). — 3. *jihītām*[8].

Du. 2. *jihāthām* (TS. I. 1. 12[1]), *dīdhīthām* (AV.), *mimāthām*, *rarāthām*.

Pl. 2. *juhudhvam* (TS. IV. 6. 1[5]), *rarīdhvam*. — 3. *jihatām*, *dadhatām*, *sisratām* (Kh. I. 3[6]).

Present Participle.

461. Active. As the suffix *-ant* drops its *n* (like the endings of the 3. pl. act.) strong and weak stem are not distinguished. The feminine stem of course lacks *n* also; e. g. *bíbhrat-ī-*. Stems occurring are: *cíkyat-* (*ci-* 'note')[9], *jáhat-*, *jígat-*, *júhvat-*, *títrat-* (*tr-* 'cross'), *dádat-*, *dádhat-*, *dídyat-*, *dídhyat-*, *bápsat-*, *bíbhyat-*, *bíbhrat-*, *saścát-* ('pursuer') and *sáścat-*[10] ('helping'), *sísrat-*[11].

Middle. *jíhāna-*, *júhvāna-*, *dádāna-*, *dádhāna-*, *dídyāna-*, *dídhyāna-*, *pípāna-* (*pā-* 'drink', AV.) and *pipānā-*[12], *pípyāna-*[13] (√*pī-*), *mímāna-*, *rárāṇa-*[14], *śíśāna-*.

Imperfect Indicative.

462. All the verbs of this class occurring in the 3. pl. act. take the ending *-ur* except *bhr-*, which has the normal *-an*. The verbs *dā-*, *dhā-*, *hā-* show the irregularity (appearing elsewhere also) of using the strong instead of the weak base in the 2. pl. act.

Active. Sing. 1. *ádadām*, *ádadhām*. — 2. *ádadās*, *ádadhās*[15], *ádīdes*, *ávives* (√*viṣ-*); *bíbhes* (AV.), *vivés* (√*viṣ-*), *śíśās*. — 3. *aciket* (√*ci-*), *ájahāt*, *ajīgāt*, *ádadāt*[16], *ádadhāt*, *ádīdet*, *ábibhar*, *abibhet*, *ávivyak*[17], *aśíśāt*; *vivés* (√*viṣ-*).

Du. 2. *adattam*, *adhattam*. — 3. *áviviktām*, *ámimātām* (AV.)[18].

Pl. 2. *ádadāta*[19], *ádadhāta*[19] and *ádhatta*; *ájahātana*[19], *ádattana*. — 3. *abíbhran*; *ajahur*, *ájuhavur*, *adadur*, *adadhur*, *ámamadur*, *avivyacur*; *jahur*, *dadur*, *dīdhyur* (AV.), *vivyacur*.

Middle. Sing. 2. *ádhatthās*, *ámimīthās*; *dīdīthās* (AV.). — 3. *ájihīta*, *adatta*, *adhatta*, *ápiprata*[20], *ámimīta*; *śíśīta*. — Pl. 3. *ajihata*, *ájuhvata*[21].

---

[1] With strong base *yuyo-* for *yuyu-*.
[2] With strong base *iyar-* for **iyr-*; cp. v. NEGELEIN 65[4] f.
[3] With strong base for weak.
[4] Strong base *dádā-* for *dad-*.
[5] Strong base *dádhā-* for *dadh-*.
[6] Strong base *pípar-* for *pipr-*.
[7] Also the transfer form *dadhantu*.
[8] There is also the 3. sing. transfer form *dadatām*.
[9] *cíkyat* (IV. 38[4]), nom. sing. m., is given by v. NEGELEIN 77[2] as *cíkyat* and explained as a pluperfect form.
[10] When compounded with the negative particle, *saścat-* remains unchanged in the fem. if accented *a-saścát-*, but has *n* if accented on the prefix: *á-saścant-ī-*.
[11] For inflected forms of these stems see 312.

[12] With irregular accent.
[13] The anomalous transfer form *bibhrámāṇa-* takes the place of **bíbhrāṇa-*.
[14] But perfect *raráṇá-*.
[15] There is no sufficient reason for regarding *ádadhās* in X. 739, as a 3. sing. (AVERY 248; DELBRÜCK, Verbum 50, 59).
[16] There is also the transfer form *dádat*. v. NEGELEIN 67[2] gives *dádhāt* (RV. AV.) which seems a misprint for *dádhat*.
[17] There is also the unaugmented transfer form *vivyácat*.
[18] WHITNEY, Sanskrit Grammar 665, quotes *ajahitām* from the TS. (mantra?).
[19] With strong base instead of weak.
[20] Anomalous form instead of **ápiprta*.
[21] Also the transfer form *adadanta*. WHITNEY 658 also mentions the unaugmented 3. pl. *jihata*.

β. 1. The infixing nasal class.

463. This class, which includes fewer than 30 verbs, is characterized by the accented syllable *ná* preceding the final consonant of the root in the strong forms. That syllable in the weak forms becomes a simple nasal varying according to the class to which the following consonant belongs.

1. The infix, appearing in forms outside the limits of the present stem, has become part of the root in *añj-* 'anoint', *bhañj-* 'break', and *hiṃs-* 'injure'. — 2. There are a few transfers to the *á-* class, in which some of these verbs come to be inflected in the later language[1], and in which several verbs are regularly nasalized in the present stem (429, a, 1). — 3. Instead of the regular *-ná-*, the root *tṛh-* 'crush' infixes *-né-* in the strong forms; thus 3. sing. *tṛṇe-ḍhi*. — 4. In the 3. pl. ind. mid. irregular accentuation of the final syllable occurs exceptionally in each of the forms *añjaté*, *indhaté*, *bhuñjaté*[2].

Present Indicative.

464. The forms actually occurring, if made from *yuj-* 'join', would be the following:

Active. Sing. 1. *yunájmi*. 2. *yunákṣi*. 3. *yunákti*. — Pl. 1. *yuñjmas*. 3. *yuñjánti*.

Middle. Sing. 1. *yuñjé*. 2. *yuṅkṣe*. 3. *yuṅkté*. — Du. 2. *yuñjā́the*. 3. *yuñjā́te*. — Pl. 2. *yuṅgdhvé*. 3. *yuñjáte*.

The forms which actually occur are the following:

Active. Sing. 1. *anajmi* (AV.), *chinadmi* (AV.), *tṛṇadmi* (√*tṛd-*), *bhinádmi*, *yunájmi*, *ruṇadhmi* (*rudh-* 'obstruct'). — 2. *pṛṇákṣi* (√*pṛc-*), *bhinátsi*, *yunakṣi*, *vṛṇákṣi* (*vṛj-* 'twist'). — 3. *anakti*, *unátti* (√*ud-*), *kṛṇatti* (*kṛt-* 'spin'), *gṛṇatti*[3] (AV.x. 7[43]), *chinátti* (AV.), *tṛṇatti*, *pináṣṭi* (√*piṣ-*), *bhanákti* (√*bhañj-*), *bhiṇátti*, *yunákti* (AV.), *riṇákti* (√*ric-*), *ruṇáddhi*, *vṛṇákti*, *hinásti* (√*hiṃs-*, AV. ŚA.).

Pl. 1. *añjmas*. — 3. *añjánti*, *undánti*, *piṃṣánti*, *pṛñcánti*, *bhindánti*, *yuñjánti*, *viñcanti* (*vic-* 'sift'), *vṛñjanti*.

Middle. Sing. 1. *añje*, *ṛñje* (*ṛj-* 'direct'), *pṛñce* (AV.), *yuñjé*, *vṛñjé*. — 2. *yuṅkṣe* (AV.). — 3. *aṅkté*[4], *indhé* (= *ind-dhé*, √*idh-*), *pṛṅkté*, *yuṅkté*[5], *rundhé* (= *rund-dhé*, AV.), *vṛṅkte*, *hiṃste*[6] (AV.). — **With ending -e:** *vṛñjé*.

Du. 2. *añjā́the* (Kh. v. 6[4]; VS. xxxiii. 33), *yuñjā́the*. — 3. *añjā́te* (VS. xx. 61), *tuñjā́te*, *vṛñjā́te* (AV.).

Pl. 2. *aṅgdhvé*. — 3. *añjáte* and *añjaté*, *indháte* and *indhaté*, *ṛñjate*, *tuñjáte*, *pṛñcáte*, *bhuñjáte* and *bhuñjaté*, *yuñjáte*, *rundhate* (AV.), *vṛñjate*.

Present Subjunctive.

465. The weak base is once used instead of the strong in the form *añj-a-tas* for **anaj-a-tas*; and the AV. has once the double modal sign *ā* in the form *tṛṇáh-ān*.

Active. Sing. 2. *bhinádas*. — 3. *ṛṇádhat*, *bhinádat*, *yunájat*. — **Du.** 1. *riṇácāva*. — 3. *añjatas*. — **Pl.** 3. *anájan*, *yunájan*, *vṛṇajan*; *tṛṇáhān* (AV.).

Middle. Sing. 3. *inádhate*, *yunájate*. — **Pl.** 1. *bhunájāmahai*, *ruṇadhāmahai*.

Present Injunctive.

Active. Sing. 2. *piṇák* (√*piṣ-*), *bhinát*. — 3. *piṇak*, *pṛṇák*, *bhinát*, *riṇak* (√*ric-*).

Middle. Pl. 3. *yuñjata*.

---

[1] Thus *ud-* 'wet' : *unátti* is inflected as *unda-ti* in B. and S.; and *yuj-* 'join' : *yunákti* as *yuñja-ti* in U. and E., beside the old forms.

[2] In the RV. *añjaté* occurs once, *añjáte* 12 times, *indhaté* 4 times, *indháte* 15 times, while *bhuñjaté* and *bhuñjáte* occur once each.

[3] *úd gṛṇatti* 'ties up', is here only a corruption of the corresponding *út kṛṇatti* of RV. x. 130[2], seemingly a form of *grath-* 'tie'.

[4] AV. *aṅté*.

[5] AV. *yuṅte*.

[6] With irregular accent.

Present Optative.

Active. Sing. 3. *bhindyāt* (AV.). — **Middle. Sing. 3.** *pṛñcītá.*

Present Imperative.

466. The only ending of the 2. sing. act. is *-dhi*, no form with *-tāt* having been met with. As usual, the strong base sometimes appears in the 2. pl. act.: *unátta, yunákta; anaktana, pinaṣṭana.*

Active. Sing. 2. *aṅdhi*[1] (√*añj-*), *undhi* (= *unddhi*), *chindhi* (= *chind-dhi*), *tṛndhí* (= *tṛnddhí*), *pṛṅdhi* (= *pṛṅgdhi*), *bhaṅdhi* (= *bhaṅgdhi*), *bhindhí* (= *bhinddhí*), *yuṅdhi* (= *yuṅgdhi*, AV.), *rundhi* (= *runddhi*, AV.), *vṛṅdhi* (= *vṛṅgdhi*). — 3. *anáktu, chinάttu* (AV.), *tṛṇéḍhu*[2] (AV.), *pṛṇáktu, bhanaktu* (AV.), *bhinattu* (AV.), *yunáktu* (AV.), *vinaktu* (√*vic-*, AV.), *vṛṇaktu, hinástu* (Kh. IV. 5[15]).

Du. 2. *aṅtam* (= *aṅktam*, AV.), *chintám* (= *chinttám*, AV.), *pṛṅktám.* — 3. *aṅktām* (VS. II. 22).

Pl. 2. *unátta*[3], *bhintta* (TS. IV. 7. 13[2]), *yunákta, vṛṅkta; anaktana, pinaṣ-ṭana.* — 3. *añjantu, undantu* (AV.), *yuñjántu* (AV.), *vṛñjantu* (AV.).

Middle. Sing. 2. *aṅkṣva*[4] (AV.), *yuṅkṣvá, vṛṅkṣva* (AV.). — 3. *indhām*[5] (= *inddhām*, AV.), *yuṅtām* (= *yuṅktām*, AV.), *rundhām* (= *runddhām*, AV.). — **Du. 2.** *yuñjāthām.* — **Pl. 2.** *indhvam* (= *inddhvam*), *yuṅgdhvám.* — 3. *indhatām.*

Present Participle.

467. **Active.** *añjánt-, undánt-* and *udat-í-* (AV.), *ṛñjánt-, ṛndhánt-, kṛntatí-* (AV.), *piṃṣatí-, pṛñcánt-* and *pṛñcatí-*[6], *bhañjánt-* and *bhañjatí-, bhindánt-* and *bhindatí-* (AV.), *bhuñjatí-, yuñjatí-, viñcánt-, (á-)hiṃsant-.*

Middle. *añjāná-, índhāna-, tuñjāná-, tundāná-*[7] (AV.), *pṛñcāná-, bhindāná-, yuñjāná-* (TS. IV. 1. 1[1]), *rundhāná-, śumbhāná-*[8], *híṃsāna-.*

Imperfect Indicative.

468. **Active. Sing. 2.** *átṛṇat*[9] (AV.), *abhanas*[10] (AV.), *ábhinat, ariṇak* (√*ric-*), *avṛṇak; unap* (√*ubh-*), *ṛṇak* (Kh. IV. 6[9]), *piṇak, bhinát.* — 3. *átṛṇat, apṛṇak* (√*pṛc-*), *ábhinat, ayunak* and *āyunak, avinak* (√*vic-*, AV.), *ávṛṇak* (√*vṛj-*); *áunat* (√*ud-*); *bhinát, riṇák, vṛṇák.* — **Du. 2.** *atṛntam* (= *atṛnttam*). — **Pl. 3.** *átṛndan, ábhindan, avṛñjan; āñjan, āyuñjan* (TS. I. 7. 7[2]).

Middle. Sing. 3. *ainddha* (√*idh-*, AV.). — **Pl. 3.** *ayuñjata, arundhata* (AV.); unaugmented: *añjata.*

β. 2. The *nu-* class.

DELBRÜCK, Verbum p. 154—157. — AVERY, Verb-Inflection 232 ff. — WHITNEY, Sanskrit Grammar p. 254—260; Roots 213. — v. NEGELEIN, Zur Sprachgeschichte 57—60; 63—64; 94.

469. More than thirty verbs follow this class in the Saṃhitās. The stem is formed by adding to the root, in the strong forms, the accented syllable *-nó*, which in the weak forms is reduced to *-nu.*

---

[1] For *aṅg-dhi.* The final consonant of the root is regularly dropped before the ending *-dhi.*

[2] Cp. v. NEGELEIN, Zur Sprachgeschichte 61[3].

[3] The AV. has the transfer form *umbhata* (√*ubh-*) according to the *á-* class.

[4] AV. XIX. 45[5]: *ākṣva* emended to *ā-aṅkṣva*; see WHITNEY's note on the passage.

[5] v. NEGELEIN 63, note [1], thinks this form may be the starting point of the ending *-ām* in the imperatives 3. sing. *vid-ām* and *dúh-ām.*

[6] AV. also *pṛ́ñcatī-.*

[7] √*tud-* otherwise follows the *á-* class.

[8] √*śubh-* otherwise follows the *a-* or *á-* class.

[9] From √*tṛd-*. The MSS. have *átriṇat*: see WHITNEY's note on AV. XIX. 32[4].

[10] For **abhanak-s* (√*bhañj-*): see WHITNEY, Grammar 555, and his note on AV. III. 6[3]. Cp. above 66, c, β 2 (p. 61).

a. Several irregularities occur with regard to root, suffix, and ending. 1. The root *śru-* 'hear' is dissimilated to *śṛ-*[1] before the suffix: *śṛ-ṇu-*, *śṛ-ṇó-*. — 2. The root *vṛ-* 'cover' assumes the anomalous form of *ūr-* (with interchange of vowel and semivowel): *ūr-ṇu-*, beside the regular *vṛ-ṇu-*[2]. — 3. Four roots ending in *-n*, *tan-* 'stretch', *man-* 'think', *van-* 'win', *san-* 'gain', seem to form their stem with the suffix *-u*, being assigned by the Indian grammarians to a separate class, the eighth; but this appearance has probably been brought about by the *-an* of the root having originally been reduced to the nasal sonant: *ta-nu-* for **tṇ-nu-*[3]. — 4. In place of the regular and very frequent *kṛ-ṇu-*, there appears in the tenth book of the RV. the anomalous stem *kuru-*, once in the form *kur-mas* (x. 51^{7}), 1. pl. pres. ind., and twice in the form *kuru* (x. 19^{2}, 145^{2}), 2. sing. impv. act. The strong form of this stem, *karó-*[4], which has the additional anomaly of Guṇa in the root, appears in the AV., where however the forms made from *kṛṇó-*, *kṛṇu-* are still upwards of six times as common as those from *karó-*, *kuru-*[5]. The isolated form *taru-te* 'attains', which occurs once in the RV. (x. 76^{2}), seems to be analogous in formation to *karó-ti*, but it may be connected with the somewhat frequent nominal stem *taru-*[6]. — 5. The *u* of the suffix is dropped, in all the few forms which occur in the 1. pl. ind. act. and mid., before terminations beginning with *m*: *kur-más*, *kṛṇ-mási* (AV.), *tan-masi* (TS.), *hin-mas* (AV.), *hin-masi* (AV.); *kṛṇ-mahe*, *man-mahe*[7]. When the *-nu* is preceded by a consonant, the *u* becomes *uv* before vowel endings; e. g. *aśnuv-anti* (but *sunv-ánti*). — 6. In the 3. pl. mid., six verbs of this class take the ending *-re*[8] with connecting vowel *-i-*: *inv-ire*, *ṛṇv-ire*, *pinv-ire*[9], *śṛṇv-iré*, *sunv-iré*, *hinv-iré*. The connecting vowel *-i-* is also taken by *śru-* in the 2. sing. mid. *śṛṇv-i-ṣé* (for **śṛṇu-ṣe*) used in a passive sense. — 7. Five stems of this class, *i-nu-*, *ṛ-ṇu-*, *ji-nu-*, *pi-nu-*, *hi-nu-*, have come to be used frequently even in the RV. as secondary roots following the *a-* conjugation. Of these *pinv-a-* occurs almost exclusively in the RV. as well as the AV.; *inv-a-* alone is met with in the AV.; and *jinv-a-* and *hinv-a-* are commoner in the RV. than *ji-nu-* and *hi-nu-*.

Present Indicative.

470. The forms actually occurring, if made from *kṛ-* 'make', would be as follows:

Active. Sing. 1. *kṛṇómi.* 2. *kṛṇóṣi.* 3. *kṛṇóti.* — Du. 2. *kṛṇuthás.* 3. *kṛṇutás.* — Pl. 1. *kṛṇmási* and *kṛṇmás.* 2. *kṛṇuthá.* 3. *kṛṇvánti.*

Middle. Sing. 1. *kṛṇvé.* 2. *kṛṇuṣé.* 3. *kṛṇuté* and *kṛṇvé.* — Du. 2. *kṛṇvāthe.* — Pl. 1. *kṛṇmahe.* 3. *kṛṇváte*[10].

The forms which actually occur are the following:

Active. Sing. 1. *ūrṇomi* (AV.), *ṛṇomi*, *kṛṇómi*, *kṣiṇómi* (AV. TS.), *minomi* (*mi-* 'fix', AV.), *vṛṇomi* ('choose', Kh. II. 6^{5}), *śaknomi* (AV.), *śṛṇómi*, *hinómi.* — **With -u-:** *karomi* (AV. TS.), *tanomi.*

2. *āpnóṣi* (AV.), *inoṣi*, *kṛṇóṣi*, *jinóṣi*, *stṛṇóṣi*, *hinóṣi*; *tanóṣi*, *vanóṣi.*

3. *aśnoti* (*aś-* 'attain'), *āpnóti* (VS. AV.), *inóti*, *unoti* (RV[1].), *ūrṇoti*, *ṛṇoti*, *ṛdhnoti*, *kṛṇóti*, *cinóti* 'gathers', *dāśnóti*, *dunoti* (AV.), *dhūnoti*, *minoti* (AV.), *vṛṇóti*, *śaknoti* (AV.), *śṛṇóti*, *sunóti*, *skunóti* (AV.), *hinóti*; *karoti* (AV. TS. VS.), *tanóti*, *vanoti*, *sanóti.*

Du. 2. *aśnuthas* (Kh. I. 9^{2}), *ūrṇuthas*, *kṛṇuthás*, *vanuthás.* — **3.** *aśnutás*, *ūrṇutás*, *kṛṇutas*, *sunutás*; *tanutas* (Kh. III. 22^{6}).

Pl. 1. *kṛṇmási* (AV.), *hinmas* (AV.), *hinmasi* (AV.); *kurmás*, *tanmasi* (TS. IV. 5. 11^{1}). — **2.** *aśnutha*, *kṛṇuthá*, *dhūnuthá*, *sunuthá.* — **3.** *aśnuvanti*,

---

1 Cp. DELBRÜCK, Verbum p. 154[1].

2 Cp. BRUGMANN, KG. 674.

3 Cp. BRUGMANN, KZ. 24, 259; DELBRÜCK p. 156.

4 Perhaps starting from the aorist *á-kar* and following the analogy of *kṛṇó-*; cp. BRUGMANN, KG. 656, 3.

5 WHITNEY 715.

6 Occurring in *táru-* 'swift'(?), *taru-tṛ́-* 'conqueror', *táru-tra-* 'victorious', *táru-ṣa-* 'victor', and the verbal stem *táruṣya-* 'cross', 'overcome'.

7 Thus *kṛṇ-mahe* is not the only example (DELBRÜCK 174, BRUGMANN, KG. 673) of this phenomenon. There is no example in the Saṃhitās of the 1. du. in *-vas* and *-vahe*; but **kṛṇ-vás*, **kṛṇ-váhe* must be presupposed to account for the loss of the *-u* before *-mas* and *-mahe*: BRUGMANN, KG. 673.

8 Like *duh-re* in the root class.

9 This is the only form (besides the participle *pinv-āná-* and *pinv-ánt-*, *pinv-at-ím* in AV.) in which the stem *pinu-* appears. All others are made from the transfer stem *pinva-*.

10 Sometimes accented *kṛṇvaté.*

ṛṇvánti, kṛṇvánti[1], *cinvánti* (TS. I. 1. 7[2]), *dabhnuvanti, dunvanti* (AV.), *prusṇuvanti, śaknuvánti* (AV.), *śṛṇvánti, sunvánti, hinvánti*; *kurvanti* (AV.), *tanvánti*.

Middle. Sing. 1. *aśnuve, kṛṇvé, hinvé*; *kurve* (AV.), *manvé* (AV.), *vanve*. **2.** *aśnuṣe, ūrṇuṣe, kṛṇuṣé, cinuṣé, dhūnuṣé*; *tanuṣe* (AV.). — **With connecting vowel -*i*-:** *śṛṇv-i-ṣé*.

3. *aśnuté, ūrṇuté, kṛṇuté, dhūnute, prusṇute, śṛṇute*; *kurute* (AV.), *tanute, tarute, vanuté*. — **With ending -e:** *śṛṇvé, sunvé, hinvé*.

Du. 2. *tanvāthe*. — **Pl. 1.** *kṛṇmahe, manmahe*. — **3.** *aśnuvate, kṛṇváte, vṛṇváte* and *vṛṇvaté, spṛṇvaté, hinváte*; *kurváte* (AV.), *tanvaté* and *tanváte* (AV.). — **With ending -re:** *inv-i-re, ṛṇv-i-re, pinv-i-re, śṛṇv-i-ré, sunv-i-ré, hinv-i-ré*.

Present Subjunctive.

471. Active. Sing. 1. *kṛṇavā, hinavā*; *sanávāni* (AV.). — **2.** *ṛṇávas, kṛṇávas, tṛpṇávas, śṛṇávas*; *karavas* (AV.). — **3.** *aśnavat*[2], *kṛṇávat, cinavat, dhūnavat, prusṇávat, śṛṇávat, sunávat*; *vanávat*. — **With double modal sign *ā*:** *karavāt* (AV.), *kṛṇavāt* (AV. XX. 132[5]). — **With ending -*tai*:** *aśnavātai*[3] (AV.). — **Du. 1.** *aśnavāva, kṛṇavāva*.

Pl. 1. *aśnávāma, kṛṇávāma, minavāma, śaknávāma, sunavāma, spṛṇavāma*. — **2.** *sanávatha*; **with double modal sign:** *kṛṇavātha* (VS.). — **3.** *aśnavan, kṛṇávan, śṛṇávan*.

Middle. Sing. 1. *aśnavai* (VS. XIX. 37), *kṛṇávai, sunávai*; *manávai*. — **2.** *kṛṇavase*; *vanavase*. — **3.** *kṛṇávate*; *manávate*.

Du. 1. *kṛṇavāvahai*; *tanavāvahai*. — **2.** *aśnávaithe*. — **3.** *kṛṇvaite*[4].

Pl. 1. *aśnávāmahai* (X. 97[17])[5], *kṛṇávāmahai, stṛṇavāmahai* (AV.). — **3.** *aśnavanta, kṛṇávanta*.

Present Injunctive.

Active. Sing.[6] **2.** *ṛṇos*. — **3.** *ūrṇot*. — **Pl. 3.** *ṛṇvan, minván, hinván*; *vanvan*.

Middle. Sing. 2. *tanuthās*. — **3.** *ṛṇutá*. — **Pl. 3.** *kṛṇvata*; *manvata*.

Present Optative.

Active. Sing. 1. *sanuyām*. — **3.** *śṛṇuyát* (AV.). — **Pl. 1.** *cinuyāma, śṛṇuyāma*; *vanuyáma, sanuyáma*.

Middle. Sing. 3. *kṛṇvīta*[7]; *manvīta* (AV.).

Present Imperative.

472. Active. Sing. 2. *śṛṇudhí*. — **With ending -*hi*[8]:** *akṣṇuhi* (*akṣ*- 'mutilate', AV.), *aśnuhi, āpnuhí* (AV.), *inuhi, ūrṇuhi, kṛṇuhí, cinuhí, tṛpṇuhi, dabhnuhi* (AV.), *dhūnuhi, dhṛṣṇuhí, śṛṇuhí, spṛṇuhi, hinuhi*; *tanuhi, sanuhi*. — **With ending -*tāt*:** *kṛṇutāt, hinutāt*. — **Without ending:** *inú, ūrṇu, kṛṇu, dhūnu* (AV.), *śṛṇú, sunú, hinu*; *kuru, tanu*. — **3.** *aśnotu, āpnotu* (AV.), *ūrṇotu* (AV.), *kṛṇótu, cinotu, minotu, śṛṇótu, sunotu*; *karotu* (TS. VS.), *tanotu* (AV.), *sanotu*.

Du. 2. *aśnutam, kṛṇutám, tṛpṇutám, śṛṇutám, hinótam*[9]. — **3.** *aśnutām* (AV. TS.), *kṛṇutām* (AV.).

---

[1] *skṛṇvanti* after *pari*: *pariṣkṛṇvánti* (IX. 14[2]), *pári ṣkṛṇvanti* (IX. 64[23]).

[2] The form *arṇavat*, AV. V. 2[8] (√*ṛ*-), is a corruption of *avṛṇot* in RV.

[3] The TS. has once *aśnavatai* (WHITNEY 701).

[4] Irregular for *kṛṇávaite*.

[5] Omitted by AVERY 238.

[6] The injunctive form *aśnavam*, AV. XIX. 55[6], is a conjecture; see WHITNEY's note on the passage.

[7] *ūrṇvītá* occurs in TS. VI. 1. 3[3] and *ūrṇuvīta* in K. (WHITNEY 713).

[8] Cp. WHITNEY 704.

[9] With strong stem.

Pl. 2. *ūrṇuta*, *kṛṇutá* and *kṛṇóta*[1], *tṛpṇuta*, *dhūnuta*, *śṛṇutá* and *śṛṇota*[1], *sunutá* and *sunóta*[1], *hinuta* (AV.) and *hinóta*[1]; *tanota*[1] (AV. TS.). — With ending **-tana**: *kṛṇótana*[2], *śṛṇotana*[2], *sunótana*[2], *hinotana*[2] (x. 30[7]). — 3. *aśnuvantu*, *ūrṇuvantu*, *kṛṇvántu*, *cinvantu* (TS. v. 2. 11[2]), *śṛṇvántu*, *hinvantu*; *vanvántu*, *sanvantu*.

Middle. Sing. 2. *ūrṇuṣva*, *kṛṇuṣvá*, *cinuṣva* (AV.), *dhūnuṣva* (AV.), *śṛṇuṣvá*; *tanuṣva*, *vanuṣva*. — 3. *aśnutām* (AV.), *kṛṇutám*; *tanutām* (TS. I. 6. 3[3]), *manutām*, *vanutām* (AV.).

Du. 2. *kṛṇvāthām* (AV.). — Pl. 2. *kṛṇudhvám*, *sunudhvam*; *tanudhvam*, *vanudhvam* (AV.). — 3. *ṛṇvatām* (AV.); *kurvatām* (AV.), *tanvátām* (AV.), *vanvatām* (AV.).

Present Participle.

473. **Active.** *ūrṇuvánt-* and *ūrṇvánt-*, f. *-vatī́-*, *ṛṇvánt-*, *kṛṇvánt-*[3], f. *-vatī́-*, *cinvánt-*, f. *-vatī́-*, *dunvánt-* (AV.), *dhūnvánt-*, *pinvánt-* (AV.), *minvánt-*, *vṛṇvánt-*, *śṛṇvánt-*, f. *-vatī́-*, *sunvánt-*, *hinvánt-*, f. *-vatī́-*; *kurvánt-* (AV.), f. *-vatī́-* (AV.), *tanvánt-*, f. *-vatī́-* (AV.), *vanvánt-*.

Middle. *ūrṇvāná-*, *kṛṇvāná-*, *cinvāná-* (TS. IV. 2. 10[1]), *dhūnvāná-*, *pinvāná-*, *sunvāná-*, *hinvāná-*; *kurvāṇá-* (AV.), *tanvāná-*, *manvāná-*, *vanvāná-*.

Imperfect Indicative.

474. **Active. Sing.** 1. *aśṛṇavam*; *kṛṇavam*. — 2. *ákṛṇos*, *ávṛṇos*, *áśṛṇos*, *ásaghnos*, *ainos*, *áurṇos*; *akaros* (AV.), *ávanos*, *ásanos*. — 3. *ákṛṇot*, *ádhūnot*, *avṛṇot*, *āpnot* (AV. TS.), *ārdhnot* (AV.), *ainot*, *áurṇot*; *akarot* (VS. AV.), *atanot*, *asanot*. — Du. 2. *akṛṇutam*, *adhūnutam*.

Pl. 2. *akṛṇuta* and *akṛṇota*; *akṛṇotana*. — 3. *ákṛṇvan*, *acinvan* (AV.), *aśaknuvan*, *aśṛṇvan* (AV.); *ṛṇvan*, *minvan*; *akurvan* (AV.), *avanvan*, *ásanvan*.

Middle. Sing. 2. *adhūnuthās*; *kuruthās* (AV.). — 3. *akṛṇuta*, *ádhūnuta*; *kṛṇuta*; *akuruta* (AV.), *atanuta* (AV.), *ámanuta*.

Pl. 2. *ákṛṇudhvam*. — 3. *ákṛṇvata*[4], *avṛṇvata*; *akurvata* (AV.; Kh. II 13[5]), *átanvata*, *amanvata*, *avanvata* (AV.).

β. 3. The *nā-* class.

DELBRÜCK, Verbum p. 151—153. — AVERY, Verb-Inflection 232 ff. — WHITNEY, Sanskrit Grammar p. 260—263; Roots 214. — v. NEGELEIN, Zur Sprachgeschichte 49—57. — Cp. J. SCHMIDT, Festgruss an Roth 179 ff.; BARTHOLOMAE, IF. 7, 50—81; BRUGMANN, IF. 16, 509 ff.

475. Nearly forty verbs belong to this class in the Saṃhitās. The stem is formed by adding to the root, in the strong forms, the accented syllable *-nā́*[5], which in the weak forms is reduced to *-nī* before consonants and *-n* before vowels.

a. There are some **irregularities** with regard to the root, the suffix, and the endings. 1. The root shows a tendency to be **reduced** in various ways. The roots *jī-* 'overpower', *jū-* 'hasten', *pū-* 'purify', are shortened; e. g. *jināmi*, *junāsi*, *punā́ti*. The root *grabh-* 'seize' and its later form *grah-* take

---

[1] With strong stem instead of weak. Thus in four out of seven verbs there is an alternative strong form; and in one other (*tanota*) the strong is the only form occurring.

[2] Thus all the forms occurring with *-tana* have a strong stem. WHITNEY 704 also mentions *karóta* besides the 2. du. *kṛṇotam*, but I do not know whether these forms occur in mantra passages.

[3] *skṛṇvánt-* in *pari-ṣkṛṇván* (IX. 39[2]).

[4] In X. 134 *akṛṇvata* has the appearance of being used for the 3. sing. (= *akṛṇuta*).

[5] The suffix may originally have been *-nai* of which *-nī* would be the weak grade (27); but BRUGMANN, Grundriss 2, 597, note, disagrees with this view. He thinks *-nī* has displaced earlier *-ni*, KG. p. 512.

Samprasāraṇa; e. g. *gṛbhṇā́mi* and *gṛhṇā́mi* (AV.). Four roots which, in forms outside the present system appear with a nasal[1], drop the nasal here; thus *bandh-* 'bind' : *badhnā́mi* (AV.); *manth-* 'shake' : *mathnāmi* (AV.); *skambh-* 'make firm' : *skabhnā́ti*; *stambh-* 'prop' : *stabhnā́ti* (AV.). The root *jñā-* 'know', also loses its nasal; e. g. *jā-nā-mi*[2]. — 2. The **strong form** of the suffix, *-nā*, appears **in certain 2. persons** impv. act., which should have the weak form *-nī*; e. g. 2. pl. *punā́-ta* for *punī-tá*. On the other hand *-nī* appears once instead of *-nā* in 3. sing. injv. *minīt*[3] (AV.). — 3. A few roots ending in consonants take the **peculiar ending** *-ānā́* in the 2. sing. impv. act.; e. g. *gṛh-āṇā́*[4]. — 4. **Transfers** to the *a-* conjugation are made from five roots. These are rare in the case of *gṛ-* 'sing' : *gṛṇā́-ta* 2. pl. ind., *gṛṇa-nta* 3. pl. impf.; *mi-* 'damage' : *mina-t* 3. sing. injv., *amina-nta* 3. pl. impf.; *śṛ-* 'crush' only *śṛṇa* (AV.) 2. sing. impv. But *pṛ-* 'fill' and *mṛ-* 'crush' form the regular *á-* stems *pṛṇá-* and *mṛṇá-* (beside *pṛṇā́-* and *mṛṇā-*), ten forms being made from the former, and five from the latter in the RV.[5]

Present Indicative.

476. The forms actually occurring, if made from *grabh-* 'seize', would be the following:

Active. Sing. 1. *gṛbhṇā́mi*. 2. *gṛbhṇā́si*. 3. *gṛbhṇā́ti*. — Du. 2. *gṛbhṇīthas*. 3. *gṛbhṇītás*. — Pl. 1. *gṛbhṇīmási* and *gṛbhṇīmás*. 2. *gṛbhṇītha* and *gṛbhṇīthána*. 3. *gṛbhṇánti*.

Middle. Sing. 1. *gṛbhṇé*. 2. *gṛbhṇīṣé*. 3. *gṛbhṇīté*. — Pl. 1. *gṛbhṇīmáhe*. 3. *gṛbhṇáte*.

The forms which actually occur are the following:

Active. Sing. 1. *aśnā́mi* ('eat', AV. VS.), *iṣṇāmi* (AV.), *kṣiṇā́mi* (AV.), *gṛṇāmi* (*gṛ-* 'sing'), *gṛṇā́mi* (AV. VI. 71[3], *gṛ-* 'swallow'), *gṛbhṇā́mi*, *gṛhṇā́mi* (AV. TS.), *jānā́mi*, *jinā́mi*, *punāmi*, *pṛṇā́mi* (AV.), *badhnāmi*[6] (*bandh-* 'bind', AV. TS.), *mathnāmi* (AV.), *mināmi*, *riṇāmi* (AV.), *śṛṇā́mi* (AV.), *sināmi* (AV.), *stabhnāmi*, *stṛṇāmi* (AV.). — **2.** *aśnā́si* (AV.), *iṣṇāsi*, *junāsi*, *pṛṇā́si*, *riṇā́si*, *śṛṇāsi*. — **3.** *aśnā́ti*, *krīṇā́ti*, *kṣiṇāti* (*kṣi-* 'destroy'), *gṛṇā́ti*, *gṛbhṇā́ti*, *gṛhṇā́ti* (AV.), *jānā́ti*, *jinā́ti*, *junā́ti*, *punā́ti*, *pṛṇā́ti*, *minā́ti*, *muṣṇāti* (AV.), *riṇā́ti*, *śṛṇā́ti*, *sinā́ti*, *skabhnā́ti*, *stabhnā́ti* (AV.), *hruṇāti*.

Du. 2. *riṇīthas*. — **3.** *gṛṇītás*, *pṛṇītas*.

Pl. 1. *gṛṇīmási*, *junīmási*, *minīmási*, *śṛṇīmasi* (AV.); *jānīmás*. — **2.** *jānītha*; *stṛṇīthána* (AV.). — **3.** *aśnánti* (AV.), *kṣiṇánti*, *gṛṇánti*, *gṛbhṇánti*, *gṛhṇánti* (AV. TS.), *jānánti*, *jinanti*, *junánti*, *punánti*, *pṛṇánti*, *prīṇanti*, *badhnánti* (AV.), *bhrīṇánti*[7], *minánti*, *riṇánti*, *śrīṇánti*, *stṛṇánti*.

Middle. Sing. 1. *gṛṇé*, *gṛbhṇe*, *gṛhṇé* (AV.), *vṛṇé*. — **2.** *gṛṇīṣé*[8], *vṛṇīṣé* (AV.), *śrīṇīṣe*, *hṛṇīṣe*. — **3.** *krīṇīte* (AV.), *kṣiṇīte* (AV.), *gṛṇīté*, *punīte*, *prīṇīté*, *riṇīte*, *vṛṇīté*, *śrathnīté*, *stṛṇīte*, *hṛṇīte*. — **With -e** for *-te*: *gṛṇe*.

Pl. 1. *gṛhṇīmahe* (TS. V. 7. 9[1]), *punīmahe* (Kh. III. 10[4]), *vṛṇīmáhe*[9]. —

[1] Cp. Brugmann, Grundriss 2, 627.

[2] Originally **janā-* with nasal sonant, **jṇ-nā-*; see Brugmann, KG. 666 (p. 511).

[3] On this form see v. Negelein 56, note [1].

[4] On the origin of this ending see Brugmann, Grundriss 2, p. 975.

[5] Beside seven present stems of this class there appear denominative stems in *-āya* from the same roots. Cp. v. Negelein 50—52.

[6] Given, along with a number of cognate forms, as from the root *bādh-*, by v. Negelein 57.

[7] The only form occurring of the root *bhrī-* 'consume'.

[8] The form *gṛṇīṣé* also occurs in the RV. as a 1. sing. ind., 'I praise', being formed from an anomalous aorist stem *gṛṇī-ṣ-*.

[9] According to Whitney 719, once *vṛṇīmahé*, with reference doubtless to RV. V. 20[3], where, however, *vṛṇīmahé 'gne* is only the Sandhi accentuation for *vṛṇīmahe ágne* (see above 108 and p. 319, note [13]).

3. *aśnate*[1], *gṛbhṇate*, *gṛhṇate* (AV.), *jānate*, *punáte* (AV.) and *punaté*, *badhnáte*, *riṇaté*, *vṛṇáte*.

Present Subjunctive.

477. In the 2. 3. sing., subjunctive forms are indistinguishable from the indicative present, if formed with primary endings, and from the injunctive, if formed with secondary endings, as the modal sign *a* is merged in the strong stem; thus *gṛbhṇáti* may be 3. sing. indicative or subjunctive; *gṛbhṇás* may be 2. sing. injunctive or subjunctive. In such forms therefore the sense or construction of the sentence can alone decide their value. These as well as unmistakable subjunctives are rare in this class.

Active. **Sing. 2.** *gṛbhṇás*, *junás*. — **3.** *pṛṇāti* (x. 2[4], cp. 2[5]), *pṛṇāt* (AV.). — **Pl. 1.** *junāma*, *mināma*.

Middle Du. 1. *krīṇāvahai* (TS. I. 8. 4[1]). — **Pl. 1.** *jānāmahai* (AV.).

Present Injunctive.

Active. **Sing. 1.** *kṣiṇām*. — **2.** *riṇās* (AV. XX. 135[11]). — **3.** *jānāt*[2], *minīt*[3] (AV. VI. 110[3]). — **Pl. 3.** *minan*, *riṇán* (VIII. 7[28]), *ścamnan*.

Middle. **Sing. 2.** *hṛṇīthās*. — **3.** *gṛṇīta*, *gṛbhṇīta*, *vṛṇīta*. — **Pl. 1.** *stṛṇīmáhi*[4].

Present Optative.

In the middle some forms of the optative cannot be distinguished from unaugmented forms of the imperfect, as the modal sign *-ī* is merged in the suffix *-nī*. The forms actually occurring are very few, being found in the 2. 3. sing. only.

Active. **3.** *aśnīyāt* (AV.), *gṛhṇīyát* (AV.), *jinīyát* (AV.), *pṛṇīyát*.

Middle. **2.** *jānīthās* (Kh. IV. 5[30]). — **3.** *vṛṇīta* (TS. I. 1. 2[1] = *vurīta*, VS. IV. 8).

Present Imperative.

478. The regular ending of the 2. sing. act. is *-hi*, while *-dhi* never occurs. Three verbs take *-tāt* as well. One of these, *grah-*, and three others ending in a consonant, *aś-*, *bandh-*, *stambh-*, take the peculiar ending *-āná*.

Active. **Sing. 2.** *gṛṇāhi*[5] (TS. IV. 4. 12[5]), *gṛṇīhí*, *gṛbhṇīhi* (AV.), *gṛhṇāhi*[5] (AV.), *jānīhí*, *punāhí*[6] (SV.), *punīhí*, *pṛṇīhi* (AV.), *mṛṇīhí*, *śṛṇāhí*[6] (SV.), *śṛṇīhí*[7], *stṛṇīhi*[8] (AV.). — **With -tāt:** *gṛhṇītāt* (AV.), *jānītāt*[9] (TS. AV.), *punītāt*. — **With -āna:** *aśāna*[10], *gṛhāṇa*[10] (x. 103[12]), *badhāna* (AV.), *stabhāná* (AV.) — **3.** *gṛṇātu*, *gṛhṇātu*, *jānātu* (AV.), *punātu*, *pṛṇātu* (AV.), *badhnātu* (AV.), *śṛṇátu* (AV.), *sinātu* (AV.).

Du. 2. *aśnītám*, *gṛṇītam* (TS. IV. 1. 8[2]), *gṛhṇītam* (AV.), *pṛṇītám*, *śṛṇītám*, *stṛṇītám*. — **3.** *gṛṇītām*, *punītām* (AV.).

---

[1] *gṛṇaté* (AV. IV. 21[2]), given by v. NEGELEIN as a finite form *gṛṇate* (unaccented), is the dat. sing. of the participle.

[2] This form is accented *jánāt* in the Khila (III. 21) after RV. X. 103 (AUFRECHT's Ṛigveda[2], 682), but it is correct in the corresponding passage of the AV. (III. 2[6]).

[3] For *mināt*.

[4] There seems to be no certain example of a 3. pl. AVERY 240 gives *gṛbhṇata*, but this form (IX. 14[7]) appears to have an imperf. sense; he adds *vṛṇata* with a query, but I cannot trace the form.

[5] With strong base instead of *gṛṇīhi*, *gṛhṇīhi*.

[6] With strong base and irregular accent.

[7] Also the transfer form *śṛṇa* (AV. XIX. 45[1]).

[8] WHITNEY 723 quotes *stṛṇāhi* from the TS. [VI. 3. 1[2]].

[9] v. NEGELEIN 57, line 6, seems to regard *jñātát* (AV. XIX. 15[6]), given as *jñātāt* (unaccented), as an anomalous imperative; but it is the ablative of the past participle.

[10] Both forms are omitted by AVERY 243; the latter is regarded by GRASSMANN as a participle.

Pl. 2. *gṛṇīta*[1], *gṛbhṇīta*, *jānītá*, *punītá* and *punīta*[2], *pṛṇītá*, *mathnīta* (AV.), *mṛṇīta* (AV.), *stṛṇīta* (AV.). — With **-tana**: *punītána*, *pṛṇītana*, *śrīṇītana*. — 3. *aśnantu* (AV.), *gṛṇantu* (AV. TS.), *gṛhṇantu* (AV.). *jānantu* (AV.), *punántu*, *mathnantu* (AV.), *badhnantu* (AV.), *śṛṇantu*, *śrīṇantu* (AV.), *sinantu* (AV.).

Middle. **Sing.** 2. *gṛbhṇīṣva* (Kh. IV. 5[26]), *pṛṇīṣva* (Kh. II. 8[1]), *vṛṇīṣvá*. — 3. *stṛṇītām*, *hṛṇītām*.

Pl. 2. *jānīdhvam* (AV.), *vṛṇīdhvám*. — 3. *jānatām*[3], *vṛṇatām* (AV.).

Present Participle.

479. **Active.** *aśnánt-*, f. *-atī-* (AV.), *iṣṇánt-*, *uṣṇánt-*, *gṛṇánt-*, *gṛhṇánt-* *jānánt-*, f. *-atī-*, *jinánt-* (AV.), *punánt-*, f. *-atī-*, *pṛṇánt-*[4], *prīṇánt-*, *mathnánt-*, *minánt-*, f. *-atī-*, *muṣṇant-*, *mṛṇánt-*, *riṇánt-*, *śrīṇánt-*, *skabhnánt-*, *stṛṇánt-*, f. *-atī-* (AV.).

Middle. *ápnāna-*, *iṣṇāná-*, *gṛṇāná-*, *gṛhṇāná-* (AV.), *jānāná-*, *drūṇāná-*, *punāná-*, *prīṇāná-*, *mināná-*, *riṇāná-*, *vṛṇāná-*, *śṛṇāná-*, *śrathnāná-* (AV.), *śrīṇāná-*, *stṛṇāná-*, *hṛṇāná-*.

Imperfect Indicative.

480. **Active.** **Sing.** 1. *ajānām*, *āśnām*. — 2. *ákṣiṇās*, *agṛbhṇās*, *apṛṇās*, *áminās*, *amuṣṇās*, *aramṇās*, *ariṇās*, *astabhnās*; *ubhnás*, *riṇás*, *śrathnās*. — 3. *agṛbhṇāt*, *agṛhṇāt* (AV.), *ajānāt* (AV.), *ápṛṇāt*, *aprīṇāt*, *ábadhnāt*, *ámathnāt*, *amināt*, *amuṣṇāt*, *áramṇāt*, *áriṇāt*, *aśṛṇāt*, *ástabhnāt*, *ástṛṇāt*; *āśnāt* (AV.), *aubhnāt*; *jānāt*, *badhnāt* (AV.).

Du. 2. *ámuṣṇītam*, *ariṇītam*, *avṛṇītam*. — **Pl.** 2. *áriṇīta*. — 3. *akrīṇan* (AV.), *agṛbhṇan*, *agṛhṇan* (AV. TS.), *ajānan*[5], *apunan*, *ábadhnan*, *aśrathnan*, *ástṛṇan*; *āśnan*[6] (AV.); *áśnan* (x. 176[1]), *riṇán* (x. 138[1]).

Middle. **Sing.** 1. *ávṛṇi*. — 3. *ábadhnīta* (TS. I. 1. 10[2]), *ávṛṇīta*, *áśrīṇīta*. — **Pl.** 1. *avṛṇīmahi*. — 3. *agṛbhṇata*[7], *ájānata* (TS. II. 1. 11[3]); *gṛbhṇata*.

II. The Perfect System.

BENFEY, Vollständige Grammatik p. 372—381. — DELBRÜCK, Verbum 112—134. — AVERY, Verb-Inflection 249—253. — WHITNEY, Sanskrit Grammar p. 279—296; Roots 219—221. — v. NEGELEIN, Zur Sprachgeschichte 70—78.

481. Like the present system, the perfect has, besides an indicative, the subjunctive, optative and imperative moods, as well as participles and an augmented tense, the pluperfect. It is of very frequent occurrence, being taken by nearly 300 verbs in the Saṃhitās. It is formed in essentially the same way from all roots, its **characteristic** feature being **reduplication**.

1. The Reduplicative Syllable[8].

482. The reduplicative vowel is as a rule short. It is, however, long in more than thirty verbs. These are *kan-* 'be pleased' : *cā-kan*; *kḷp-* 'be adapted' : *cā-kḷp-*; *gṛ-* 'wake' : *jā-gṛ-*; *gṛdh-* 'be greedy' : *jā-gṛdh-*; *tṛp-* 'be pleased' : *tā-tṛp-*; *tṛṣ-* 'be thirsty' : *tā-tṛṣ-*; *dhṛ-* 'hold' : *dā-dhṛ-*; *nam-* 'bend' : *nā-nam-*;

---

1 Also the transfer form according to the *á-* class, *gṛṇáta* (AV. v. 27[9]).

2 With strong instead of weak base.

3 In Khila II. 10[6] wrongly *jānītām*.

4 With fem. *pṛṇántī-*, a transfer to the *á-* class.

5 v. NEGELEIN 57 also gives the unaugmented form *jānan* (RV. AV.), which I cannot trace (the participle nom. sing. m. *jānán* is common).

6 In *prāśnan* (AV. XI. 33[2]) the Pada text reads *pra-āśnan*.

7 Also the transfer forms *aminanta* and *gṛṇanta* (VIII. 37).

8 On the reduplicative syllable see v. NEGELEIN 70; cp. BRUGMANN, Grundriss 2, 846.

mah- 'be liberal' : *mā-mah-*; *mṛj-* 'wipe' : *mā-mṛj-*; *mṛś-* 'touch' : *mā-mṛś-*; *radh-* 'be subject' : *rā-radh-*; *ran-* 'rejoice' : *rā-ran-*; *rabh-* 'grasp' : *rā-rabh-*; *vañc-* 'be crooked' : *vā-vak-*; *van-* 'win' : *vā-van-*; *vaś-* 'desire' : *vā-vaś-*; *vas-* 'clothe' : *vā-vas-*; *vāś-* 'roar' : *vā-vaś-*; *vṛj-* 'twist' : *vā-vṛj-*; *vṛt-* 'turn' : *vā-vṛt-*; *vṛdh-* 'grow' : *vā-vṛdh-*; *vṛṣ-* 'rain' : *vā-vṛṣ-*; *śad-* 'prevail' : *śā-śad-*; *sah-* 'prevail' : *sā-sah-*; *skambh-* 'prop' : *cā-skambh-*; *dī-* 'shine' : *dī-dī-*; *dhī-* 'think' : *dī-dhī-*; *pī-* 'swell' : *pī-pī-*; *hīḍ-* 'be hostile' : *jī-hīḍ-* (AV[1].); *jū-* 'be swift' : *jū-ju-*; *tu-* 'be strong' : *tū-tu-*; *śū-* 'swell' : *śū-śu-*[1].

a. The reduplication of *ṛ* (= *ar*) and *ḷ* (= *al*) is always *ă*[2]; e. g. *kṛ-* 'make' : *cakṛ-*; *gṛdh-* 'be greedy' : *jā-gṛdh-*; *kḷp-* 'be adapted' : *cā-kḷp-*.

b. The reduplication of *ā*, *ī*, *ū* is made with *ă*, *ĭ*, *ŭ* respectively; e. g. *khād-* 'chew' : *ca-khād-*; *bhī-* 'fear' : *bibhī-*; *budh-* 'know' : *bu-budh-*.

There are, however, certain exceptions to this rule.

1. Roots containing *ya* or *va* and liable to Samprasāraṇa in other forms (such as the past passive participle), reduplicate with *i* and *u* respectively[3]. Those with *ya* are: *tyaj-* 'forsake' : *ti-tyaj-*; *yaj-* 'sacrifice' : *i-yaj-*; *vyac-* 'extend' : *vi-vyac-*; *syand-* 'move on' : *si-ṣyand-* (AV.). Similarly *cyu-* 'stir' : *ci-cyu-*[4] (beside *cu-cyu-*), and *dyut-* 'shine' : *didyut-*[4]. Those with *va-* are: *vac-* 'speak' : *u-vac-*; *vad-* 'speak' : *u-vad-*; *vap-* 'strew' : *u-vap-*; *vah-* 'carry' : *u-vah-*; *svap-* 'sleep' : *su-ṣvap-*. The three roots *yam-* 'reach', *van-* 'win', *vas-* 'wear', however, have the full reduplication: *ya-yam-*, *va-van-*, *vā-vas-*; and *vac-* 'speak' has it optionally: *va-vac-* beside *u-vac-*[5]. — a. The roots *bhū-* 'be', *sū-* 'generate', and *śī-* 'lie', reduplicate with *a*: *ba-bhū-*; *sa-sū-* (beside *su-ṣū-*, AV.); *śa-śī-* (in the participle *śa-śay-āná-*)[6].

c. In roots beginning with vowels, the reduplication coalesces with the initial of the root to a long vowel; e. g. *an-* 'breathe' : *ān-*; *av-* 'favour' : *āv-*; *aś-* 'eat' : *āś-*; *as-* 'be' : *ās-*; *ah-* 'say' : *āh-*; *ṛ-* 'go' : *ār-* (= *a-ar-*); *āp-* 'obtain' : *āp-*; *īḍ-* 'praise' : *īḍ-*; *īr-* 'set in motion' : *īr-*; *ūh-* 'consider' : *ūh-*. But if the root begins with *i* or *u*, the reduplicative syllable is separated, in the sing. act., from the strong radical syllable by its own semivowel: *i-* 'go' : 3. pl. *īy-úr*, but 2. sing. *i-y-é-tha*; *uc-* 'be pleased': 2. sing. mid. *ūc-i-ṣé*, but 3. sing. act. *u-v-óc-a*[7].

α. Five roots beginning with prosodically long *a*, reduplicate not with *a*, but with the syllable *ān-*. Only two of these, both containing a nasal, viz. *aṃś-* 'attain' and *añj-* 'anoint', make several forms; the former, 3. sing. *ān-áṃś-a* and *ān-áś-a*, pl. 1. *ān-aś-ma*, 2. *ān-aś-á*, 3. *ān-aś-úr*; mid. sing. 1. 3. *ān-aś-é*; subj. pl. 1. *ān-áś-ā-mahai*; opt. sing. 1. *ān-aś-yām*[8]; the latter, *ān-añja* (VS. VIII. 29; TS. III. 3. 10[2]); mid. sing. 1. *ān-aj-é*, pl. 3. *ān-aj-re*; subj. sing. 1. *ān-aj-ā*; opt. 3. sing. *ān-aj-yāt*. The root *ṛdh-* (reduced from *ardh-*) 'thrive', which has a nasalized present stem[9], makes the forms *ān-ṛdh-úr* (AV.) and *ān-ṛdh-e*. Through the influence of these nasalized verbs, their method of reduplication spread to two others which show no trace of a nasal anywhere. Thus from *arc-* 'praise' occur the forms *ān-ṛc-úr* and *ān-ṛc-é*; and from *arh-* 'deserve', *ān-ṛh-úr* (TS[1].) beside *arh-ire* (RV[1].). There are besides two isolated forms of doubtful meaning, probably formed from

1 The quantitative form of the stem is governed by the law that it may not contain (except in the 1. sing. act.) two prosodically short vowels; the only exceptions in the weak stem being the two irregular forms *tatane*, 1. sing. mid., and *jajanúr*, 3. pl. act. Thus *sah-* reduplicates *sāsah-* and once *sasāh-* (weak). Cp. BENFEY's articles 'Die Quantitätsverschiebungen in den Samhita- und Pada-Texten', GGA. 19 ff.

2 In most of the forms from *a-* and *ṛ-* roots, the Pada text has *a*.

3 These verbs originally had the full reduplication *ya-* and *va-* as is shown by the evidence of the Avesta, which has this only; cp. BARTHOLOMAE, IF. 3, 38 (§ 59).

4 Due to the vocalic pronunciation of the *y*: *cịu-* and *dịut-*.

5 This root thus shows the transition from the full to the Samprasāraṇa reduplication.

6 Cp. BRUGMANN, Grundriss 2, 846.

7 These are the only two examples to be met with in the Saṃhitās of this form of reduplication.

8 Beside *āśatur*, *āśāthe*, etc., from *aś-*, the unnasalized form of the same root. Cp. BRUGMANN, Grundriss 2, p. 1211[4].

9 Thus *ṛṇádhat*, *ṛndhyām*, *ṛndhánt-*, according to the infixing nasal class.

nasalized roots: *ān-ṛj-úr* (AV[1].), from *ṛj-* 'attain' (with present stem *ṛñj-*)[1], and *an-āh-a*[2], 2. pl. act., perhaps from *aṃh-* 'compress'[3].

This form of reduplication evidently arose from a radical nasal having originally been repeated along with the initial vowel, which is lengthened as in many other stems (*cā-kan*, etc), while the root itself is shortened by dropping the nasal[4]. In the modal forms *ánaj-ā, ănaj-yāt, ăn-áś-āmahai* the reduplicative vowel seems to have been shortened because *ān-* came to be regarded as containing an augment (like *ānaṭ*, aorist of *naś-* 'attain')[5].

d. A few **irregularities in** regard to **consonants** also appear in the formation of the reduplicative stem. 1. The root *bhṛ-* 'bear' reduplicates with *j* (as if from √*hṛ-*), making the stem *ja-bhṛ-*, forms from which occur nearly thirty times in the RV., beside only two forms from the regular stem *ba-bhṛ-*. — 2. In forming their stem, the five roots *ci-* 'gather', *ci-* 'observe', *cit-* 'perceive', *ji-* 'conquer', *han-* 'smite', revert to the original guttural (as in other reduplicated forms) in the radical syllable: *ci-ki-*, *ci-kit-*, *ji-gi-*, *ja-ghan-*.

e. The root *vid-* 'know' **loses** its **reduplication** along with the perfect sense[6]. Thus *véd-a* 'I know'; *vid-vā́ṃs-* 'knowing'. Some half dozen other roots show isolated finite forms without reduplication; and four or five more have unreduplicated participial forms. Thus *takṣ-* 'fashion' makes *takṣ-athur* and *takṣ-ur*; *yam-* 'guide': *yam-átur*; *skambh-* 'prop': *skambh-áthur, skambh-ur*[7]; *nind-* 'blame': *nind-ima*[7]; *arh-* 'be worthy': *arh-ire*; *cit-* 'perceive': *cet-atur* (AV. VS. SV.)[8]. Three unreduplicated participles are common: *dāś-vā́ṃs-* and *dāś-i-vā́ṃs-* (SV.) 'worshipping', beside the rare *dadāś-vā́ṃs-*; *mīḍh-vā́ṃs-* 'bountiful'; *sāh-vā́ṃs-* 'conquering', beside *sāsah-vā́ṃs-*. There also occurs once the unreduplicated *jāni-vā́ṃs-* (in the form *vi-jānúṣ-aḥ*) beside *jajñivā́ṃs-* 'knowing' (from √*jñā-*); and the isolated vocative *khid-vas* may be the equivalent of **cikhid-vas*, from *khid-* 'oppress'[9].

2. The Root.

483. Like the present and imperfect, the **perfect is strong in the sing. act.** Here the root, as a rule, is strengthened, while it remains unchanged in the weak forms. But if it contains a medial *a* or a final *ā*, it remains unchanged in the strong forms (except that *a* is lengthened in the 3. sing.), while it is reduced in the weak.

In the strong stem, the radical vowel takes Guṇa, but in the 3. sing. a final vowel takes Vṛddhi instead of Guṇa[10]. Thus *viś-* 'enter' makes *vivéś-*; *druh-* 'be hostile', *dudróh-*; *kṛt-* 'cut', *cakárt-*; but *bhī-* 'fear', 1. 2. *bibhé-*, 3. *bibhái-*; *śru-* 'hear', 1. 2. *śuśró-*, 3. *śuśráu-*; *kṛ-* 'make', 1. 2. *cakár-*, 3. *cakā́r-*[11]. In the weak stem, on the other hand, the root remains unchanged; thus *viviś-*, *dudruh-*, *cakṛt-*, *bibhī-*, *śuśru-*, *cakṛ-*.

a. Some irregularities occur in the treatment of the radical vowel. 1. The verb

---

1 According to both the infixing nasal class, 3. pl. *ṛñjate*, and the *á-* class, 3. sing. *ṛñjáti*.

2 Probably for **ānaha*; cp. the weak stem *sasāh-* beside *sāsah-*.

3 Cp. DELBRÜCK, Verbum 145, and WHITNEY, Roots, under *aṅh* 'be narrow or distressing'.

4 Except in the form *ān-áṃśa* (cp. ἤνεγκ-ται) beside *ān-āśa* (= -ήνοκ-ε).

5 Cp. the Greek aor. inf. ἐν-εγκ-εῖν and the perfect ἐν-ήνεγκ-ται.

6 Cp. BEZZENBERGER, GGA. 1879, p. 818; J. SCHMIDT, KZ. 25, 3; BRUGMANN, Grundriss 2, 848.

7 With the strong (nasalized) form of the root beside *caskabh-āná-* (AV.), and *ninid-úr*.

8 With strong radical syllable.

9 DELBRÜCK, Verbum 148, adds *dabhúr*, but this is rather aorist (beside perf. *debhur*).

10 On the origin of this distinction between the 1. sing. and the 3. sing. cp. J. SCHMIDT, KZ. 25, 8 ff. and STREITBERG, IF. 3, 383—386.

11 This distinction is invariable in the RV., and the rule seems to be the same in the AV. WHITNEY 793 d mentions *cakāra* as an exception, but this form is 3. sing. in all the passages given in his AV. Index; and *jagrāha* (AV. III. 18[3]) is evidently a corruption; see WHITNEY's note and cp. p. 356, note 9.

mṛj- 'wipe' takes Vṛddhi instead of Guṇa throughout the strong stem: *mamārj-*[1]. — 2. Two instances of the strong stem being used in weak forms occur in the RV.: pl. 1. *yuyopimá* and 3. *vivesur*[2] beside the regular *viviśur*. — 3. The radical vowel of *bhū-* remains unchanged in the strong as well as the weak forms, interposing *v* before vowels; thus sing. 2. *babhū-tha*, pl. 3. *babhū-v-úr*. — 4. The weak stem of *tṝ-* 'cross' appears in the RV. as *titir-* and *tutur-*; thus sing. 3. *tatār-a*, but pl. 3. *titir-ur*, part. *titir-vāṃs-*, opt. sing. 3. *tutur-yā́t*[3].

a. **Roots containing medial *a*** leave the radical syllable unchanged in sing. 1. 2., lengthening the vowel in sing. 3.; they reduce it in the weak stem by contraction, syncopation, or loss of nasal.

1. The roots with initial ***ya-*** and ***va-***, which reduplicate with the vowels *i* and *u*[4] respectively, **take Samprasāraṇa**, the result being contraction to *ī* and *ū*. Thus from *yaj-* 'sacrifice': strong stem *i-yáj-*, weak *īj-* (= *i-ij-*)[5]; *vac-* 'speak' : *u-vác-* and *ūc-* (= *u-uc-*); *vad-* 'speak' : *u-vád-* and *ūd-*; *vap-* 'strew' : *u-vap-* and *ūp-*; *vas-* 'dwell' : *u-vás-* and *ūṣ-*; *vah-* 'carry' : *u-váh-* and *ūh-*. The root *vā-* 'weave' is similarly treated in the form pl. 3. *ū-v-ur* (= *u-u-v-ur*). Samprasāraṇa of the root also appears in the weak stem of *svap-* 'sleep' and of *grabh-* and *grah-* 'seize' : *su-ṣváp-* and *su-ṣup-*; *ja-grábh-*, *ja-gráh-* and *ja-gṛbh-*, *ja-gṛh-*. The roots *yam-*[6], *van-*, *vas-* 'wear' have the full reduplication throughout; *yam-* taking Samprasāraṇa and contracting in the weak stem, *van-* syncopating its *a*, and *vas-* retaining it throughout: *ya-yam-* and *yem-* (= *ya-im*); *va-ván-* and *va-vn-*; *vā-vas-* (both strong and weak).

2. More than a dozen roots containing *a* between single consonants and reduplicating their initial without change, **contract** the reduplication and root to a single syllable with **medial *e***. The type followed by these verbs was doubtless furnished by *sad-* 'sit', which forms the weak stem *sed-* (= **sazd-*), beside the strong *sa-sád-*, and supported by *yam-*, with its weak stem *yem-* (= *ya-im*) beside the strong *yayam-*[7]. The other stems showing this contraction are formed from *tap-* 'heat', *dabh-* 'harm', *nam-* 'bend', *pac-* 'cook', *pat-* 'fall', *yat-* 'stretch', *yam-* 'guide', *rabh-* 'seize', *labh-* 'take', *śak-* 'be able', *śap-* 'curse', *sap-* 'serve'. The roots *tan-* 'stretch' and *sac-* 'follow' also belong to this class in the AV., but not in the RV. The root *bhaj-* 'divide' though not reduplicating with an identical consonant in its strong stem *ba-bhaj-*, follows the analogy of this group in forming the weak stem *bhej-*.

3. Four roots of this form, however, simply **syncopate** the radical *a* without contracting. These are *jan-* 'beget' : *jajñ-*, strong *jaján-*; *pan-* 'admire' : *papn-*, strong *papan-*; *man-* 'think' : *mamn-*[8]; *van-* 'win' : *vavn-*, strong *vāvan-*. Three others have this syncopated as well as the contracted form: *tan-* 'stretch' : *tatn-* and *ten-* (AV.); *pat-* 'fall' : *papt-* and *pet-*; *sac-* 'follow' : *saśc-* and *sec-* (AV.). Syncopation of medial *a* also takes place in four roots with initial guttural: *khan-* 'dig' : *cakhn-* (AV.), strong *cakhán-*; *gam-* 'go' : *jagm-*, strong *jagám-*; *ghas-* 'eat' : *jakṣ-*, strong *jaghás-*; *han-* 'smite' : *jaghn-*, strong *jaghán-*.

4. In a few roots with medial *a* and a penultimate **nasal**, the latter **is lost** in the weak stem[9]. Thus *krand-* 'cry out' : *cakrad-*; *taṃs-* 'shake' : *tatas-*; *skambh-* 'prop' : *caskabh-* (AV.), strong *caskámbh-*; *stambh-* 'prop' :

[1] The same irregularity appears in the present stem.

[2] Cp. BRUGMANN, Grundriss 2, p. 1223[1].

[3] Cp. v. NEGELEIN 74[1].

[4] But they had the full reduplication in the IIr. period; cp. BRUGMANN, Grundriss 2, p. 1220[3].

[5] In the one form *yejé* (beside *ījé*), *yaj-* follows the analogy of *yam-*, preserving a trace of the old reduplication *ya-*.

[6] The analogy of *yam-* is followed by *yaj-* in the one form *yejé* (beside *ījé*); cp. note [5].

[7] See BARTHOLOMAE, Die ai. *ē*-Formen im schwachen Perfect, KZ. 27, 337—366; BRUGMANN, Grundriss 2, p. 1222; cp. v. NEGELEIN 71[3].

[8] The strong stem does not occur.

[9] Cp. BRUGMANN, Grundriss 2, p. 1217[4].

tastabh-, strong *tastámbh-*. Similarly, from *dambh-*, the nasalized form of *dabh-*[1] 'harm', is formed *dadabh-*, strong *dadámbh-* (AV.); and from *rambh-*, the nasalized form of *rabh-*[2] 'seize', *rărabh-*. From *daṃś-* 'bite', only the participle *dadaśvā́ṃs-* occurs. The root *bandh-* 'bind', both loses its nasal and contracts, forming the weak stem *bedh-* (AV.) beside the strong *babándh-* (AV.).

b. Roots with final *ā* retain that vowel in the strong stem, but in the weak reduce it to *i*[3] before consonants and drop it before vowels. Thus *dhā-* 'put' employs *dadhā́-* in the strong forms, *dadhi-* and *dadh-* in the weak.

3. Endings.

484. The endings in the indicative active are all peculiar (excepting the secondary *-va*[4] and *-ma*), while in the middle they are identical (excepting the 3. sing. *-e* and 3. pl. *-re*)[5] with the primary middle endings of the present. They are the following:

	Active				Middle	
	sing.	du.	pl.	sing.	du.	pl.
1.	*-a*	[*-vá*]	*-má*	*-é*	[*-váhe*]	*-máhe*
2.	*-tha*	*-áthur*[6]	*-á*	*-sé*	*-ā́the*	*-dhvé*
3.	*-a*	*-átur*[6]	*-úr*[7]	*-é*	*-ā́te*	*-ré*

Roots ending in *-ā* take the anomalous ending *-au*[8] in the 1. and 3. sing. act.; e. g. *dhā-* 'put' : *da-dháu*. The only exception is the root *prā-* 'fill', which once forms the 3. sing. *pa-prā́* (I. 69^1) beside the usual *pa-práu*.

a. Consonant endings. These are, as a rule, added directly to the stem. No forms with *-vá* or *-váhe* occur in the Saṃhitās; *-máhe* is always added direct, as is also *-dhvé* in the only form in which it occurs, *dadhi-dhvé*. The remaining consonant endings, *-tha*, *-ma*, *-se*, *-re*, are nearly always added direct to stems ending in vowels, but frequently with the connecting vowel *-i-* to stems ending in consonants.

1. Roots with final *ā* always add the endings directly to the stem, which reduces the radical vowel to *i*[9] in the weak forms; e. g. *dadā́-tha*; *dadhi-má*, *dadhi-ṣé*, *dadhi-ré*[10].

2. Roots with final *ī* and *ū* also always add these endings direct to the stem; e. g. *ji-* 'conquer' : *jige-tha*; *nī-* 'lead' : *niné-tha*; *su-* 'press' : *suṣu-má*; *cyu-* 'move' : *cicyu-ṣé*; *hu-* 'sacrifice' : *juhu-ré*; *hū-* 'call' : *juhū-ré*. The only exception is *bhū-*, which (doubtless owing to the fondness of this verb for *-ūv-*) forms *babhū́v-i-tha* twice in the RV. beside the usual *babhū́-tha*, and *babhūv-i-má* once in the AV.

1 From which is formed the weak stem *debh-*.

2 From which is formed the weak stem *rebh-*.

3 See Delbrück, Verbum 147 (p. 120); Brugmann, Grundriss 2, 844 (p. 1206—8); cp. v. Bradke, IF. 8, 123—137; 156—160; Reichelt, BB. 27, 94.

4 No perfect form with *-va* is, however, found in the Saṃhitās.

5 Both of these, however, occasionally appear in the present ind. mid.

6 The a is here probably not connecting vowel but identical with the *a* of the 2. pl.; *a-tur* getting its *r* from the 3. pl. *-ur*, and *-a-thur* being then formed like *-thas* beside *-tas*: cp. Brugmann, KG. p. 597.

7 That *r* (and not *s*) is here original is shown by the evidence of the Avesta; cp. Brugmann, KG. 797 (p. 597).

8 This has not been satisfactorily explained; cp. Brugmann, Grundriss 2, p. 1223^3.

9 This *i* as the reduced form of *ā* (cp. *hi-tá-* etc., from *dhā-*), occurring in such very common verbs as *dā-* 'give' and *dhā-* 'put', was probably the starting point for the use of *i* as a connecting vowel in other verbs; but cp. Brugmann, Grundriss 2, p. 1208^1; cp. also IF. 8, 123—160.

10 The vowel is dropped before *-re* in *dadh-re*, which occurs once beside the very common *dadhi-ré*. Similarly the stem of *dā-* 'give', is shortened before the ending *-rire* in *dad-rire*, which occurs once (with passive sense).

3. **Roots with final** *-ṛ* add the endings *-tha*, *-ma*, and *-ṣe* direct (excepting two or three forms), but *-re* always with connecting *-i-*; thus *kṛ-* 'do' : *cakár-tha*, *cakṛ-ma*, *cakṛ-ṣé*, but *cakr-i-ré*. Connecting *-i-* before the other endings appears in *ār-i-tha*, *ār-i-má* (*ṛ-* 'go'); and in *jabhr-i-ṣe* (*bhṛ-* 'bear').

4. **Roots with final consonant** add *-tha*, *-ma*; *se*, *-re* direct if the last syllable of the stem is prosodically short, but with the connecting vowel *-i-* if that syllable is long[1]. Thus *tatán-tha*; *jagan-ma*, *jagṛbh-má*, *yuyuj-ma*; *dadṛk-ṣé*, *vivit-se*; *cākḷp-ré*, *tatas-ré*, *duduh-ré*, *paspṛdh-ré*, *yuyuj-re*, *vivid-ré* and others; but *ās-i-tha*, *uvóc-i-tha*, *vivéd-i-tha*; *ūc-i-má*, *papt-i-má*, *sed-i-ma*; *tatn-i-ṣe*; *īj-i-ré*, *jagm-i-re*, *tatakṣ-i-ré*[2], *yet-i-ré*. The only exception is *vét-tha*, which as an old form inherited from the IE. period (Greek οἶσ-θα) without reduplication, remained unaffected by the influence of reduplicated forms.

a. Six roots ending in consonants add *-rire*[3] instead of *-re*: *cikit-rire* (beside the more usual *cikit-ré*), *jagṛbh-rire* (once beside the usual *jagṛbh-ré*), *bubhuj-riré* (once), *vivid-rire* (once beside *vivid-ré*), *sasṛj-rire* (once), and *duduh-rire* (once in the SV. for the common *duduh-ré* of the RV.)[4].

b. **Vowel endings.** Before terminations beginning with vowels final radical vowels are variously treated. 1. *ī*, if preceded by one consonant, becomes *y*, if preceded by more than one, *iy*: e. g. from *bhī-* 'fear', *bibhy-atur*, *bibhy-ur*; but from *śri-* 'resort', *śiśriy-e*. — 2. Final *ū* ordinarily becomes *uv*; e. g. *yu-* 'join' : *yuyuv-é*; *śru-* 'hear' : *śuśruv-e*; *śū-* 'swell' : *śūśuve*. But *ū* becomes *v* in *hū-* 'call', e. g. *ju-hv-é*; and *ūv* in *bhū-* 'be' and *sū-* 'bring forth', even in strong forms[5]; e. g. 3. sing. *ba-bhūv-a*, *sasūv-a*[6]. — 3. Final *-ṛ* becomes *r*; e. g. from *kṛ-* 'make', *cakr-á*, *cakr-é*. But *-ṝ* becomes *ir* in *titir-ur* from *tṝ-* 'cross', and in 3. sing. *tistir-e*, part. *tistir-āṇá-*, from *stṝ-* 'strew' (the only root with a *ṛ* vowel preceded by two consonants that occurs in the perfect).

Perfect Indicative.

485. The forms actually occurring, if made from *kṛ-* 'make', would be the following:

Active. Sing. 1. *cakára*[7]. 2. *cakártha*. 3. *cakā́ra*. — Du. 2. *cakráthur*. 3. *cakrátur*. — Pl. 1. *cakṛmá*. 2. *cakrá*. 3. *cakrúr*.

Middle. Sing. 1. *cakré*. 2. *cakṛṣé*. 3. *cakré*. — Du. 2. *cakrā́the*. 3. *cakrā́te*. — Pl. 1. *cakṛmáhe*. 2. *cakṛdhvé*. 3. *cakriré*[8].

The forms which actually occur are the following:

Active. Sing. 1. *āsa*, *uvápa* (TS. I. 5. 3[2]), *cakara*, *ciketa* (*cit-* 'observe'), *jagama*, *jagrábha*, *jagráha* (AV.)[9], *jaghása* (AV. VI. 117[2])[10], *jihīḷa*[11], *tatápa*, *dudróha*, *papana*, *babhūva*, *bibháya*, *mimaya* (*mī-* 'diminish'), *raraṇa*, *riré̄bha*, *viveśa*, *véda*[12], *śiśraya*, *śuśráva*. The TS. (III. 5. 5[1]) has the Vṛddhi form *vavāra* (*vṛ-* 'cover').

---

[1] This is in accordance with the rhythmic rule that the stem may not have two prosodically short vowels in successive syllables.

[2] The strength of this rhythmic rule is well illustrated by the same root *vac-* having the two collateral forms *vavak-ṣé* and *ūc-i-ṣé*; cp. also the unique lengthening, in a weak form, of the radical *a* in *sa-sāh-i-ṣe* (beside the usual *sāsah-*) and the Guṇa in *yuyop-i-má*.

[3] The additional *r* may have come into use under the influence of forms from roots in *ṛ*, like *dadhr-ire* from √*dhṛ-*.

[4] The ending *-rire* is once also added to a root ending in a vowel: *dad-rire*, from √*dā-*.

[5] Instead of the normal *āv*.

[6] This is the only perfect form of √*sū-* occurring.

[7] The 1. and 3. of *dhā-* 'put' would both be *dadháu*; of *vid-* 'find', both *vivéda*.

[8] The 3. pl. of *vid-* 'find' would be *vividré*.

[9] AV. III. 18[3] reads *jagrā́ha*, but this must be emended to *jagráha*; see WHITNEY's note.

[10] *jaghā́sa* here is a misprint for *jaghása*: see WHITNEY's note on the passage.

[11] Also in AV. IV. 32[5], but written *jīhīḍa* in the Saṃhitā text, but *ji-* in Pada. See WHITNEY's note.

[12] Unreduplicated form.

2. *iyatha*[1] and *iyetha*, *cakártha*, *jagántha* (*gam-* 'go'), *jaghántha*, *jabhartha*, *jigetha* (*ji-* 'conquer'), *tatántha*, *dadātha*, *dadhártha* (*dhṛ-* 'hold'), *dadhā́tha*, *ninétha*, *papātha* (*pā-* 'drink'), *paprā́tha*[2], *babhū́tha*, *yayantha* (*yam-* 'guide'), *yayā́tha*, *vāvántha*, *vavártha* (*vṛ-* 'cover'), *vivyáktha* (*vyac-* 'extend'), *véttha*[10], *sasáttha* (*sad-* 'sit'). — **With connecting -*i*-:** *ā́pitha* (AV.), *ā́ritha* (*ṛ-* 'go'), *ā́vitha* (*av-* 'favour'), *ā́sitha* (*as-* 'be'), *uvócitha* (*uc-* 'be pleased'), *cakartitha* (*kṛt-* 'cut'), *tatárditha* (*tṛd-* 'split'), *dudohitha*, *dudróhitha* (AV.), *babhū́vitha*, *rurójitha*, *rurodhitha*, *ruróhitha* (AV.), *vavákṣitha*, *vivéditha* (*vid-* 'find'), *vivéśitha*.

3. *āna*, *ānáṃśa* and *ānā́śa* (*aṃś-* 'attain'); *ā́pa*, *āra* (*ṛ-* 'go'), *āva*, *ā́śa* (*aś-* 'eat'), *ā́sa* (*as-* 'be' and *as-* 'throw'), *ā́ha* (*ah-* 'say'), *iyā́ya* (*i-* 'go'), *uvā́ca* (*vac-* 'speak'), *uvā́sa* (*vas-* 'shine'), *uvāha*, *uvóca* (*uc-* 'be pleased'), *cakarta* (*kṛt-* 'cut'), *cakárśa* (*kṛś-* 'be lean', AV.), *cakā́ra*, *cakrāma*, *cakhā́da*, *cakhā́na* (VS. V. 23), *cacákṣa*, *cácarta* (*cṛt-* 'bind', AV.), *cacā́ra* (AV.), *cacchanda*, *caskánda*, *cāskámbha*, *cikā́ya* (*ci-* 'gather'), *cikāya* (*ci-* 'observe'), *cikéta*[3] (*cit-* 'perceive'), *jagā́ma*, *jagrā́ha*, *jaghā́na*, *jaghā́sa*, *jajā́na*, *jajā́ra* (AV.), *jabhā́ra*[4], *jigā́ya* (*ji-* 'conquer'), *jujóṣa*, *juhā́va* (*hū-* 'call'), *tatákṣa*, *tatarda*, *tatarha* (AV.), *tatā́na*, *tatā́pa*, *tatāra*, *tatsāra* (*tsar-* 'approach stealthily'), *tastámbha*, *tātāna* (RV[1].), *tityā́ja*, *tutā́va* (*tu-* 'be strong'), *tutóda*, *dadámbha* (*dambh-* 'harm', AV.), *dadárśa*, *dadā́bha* (*dabh-* 'harm'), *dadā́ra* (*dṛ-* 'split'), *dadā́śa* (*dāś-* 'worship'), *dadharṣa*, *dādhā́ra*, *didéva* (*dīv-* 'play', AV.), *didéśa* (AV.), *didyóta* (AV.), *dīdā́ya* (VS. XII. 34), *nanāśa* (*naś-* 'be lost'), *nanā́ha*[5] (AV.), *nānāma*, *ninā́ya*, *papā́ca* (AV.), *papāta* (AV.), *papāda*, *paprā́*[6], *pipéśa*, *pipeṣa*, *pīpāya*, *pupóṣa*, *babándha* (VS. AV.), *babarha* (*bṛh-* 'make strong', AV.), *babhañja*[7] (*bhañj-* 'break'), *babhā́ja*, *babhū́va*, *bibhāya*, *bibhéda*, *mamanda* (*mand-* 'exhilarate'), *mamárṣa*, *mamā́tha* (*math-* 'shake', AV.), *mamā́da* (*mad-* 'exhilarate'), *mamā́ra* (*mṛ-* 'die'), *mamā́rja* (*mṛj-* 'wipe', AV.), 1. *mimā́ya* (*mā-* 'bellow'), 2. *mimā́ya* (*mi-* 'fix'), 3. *mimāya* (*mī-* 'damage'), *mīmā́ya* (*mī-* 'damage', AV.), *mimetha* (*mith-* 'alternate'), *mimyákṣa*, *mumóda*, *yayāma*, *yuyója* (AV.), *yuyódha*, *yuyópa*, *rarákṣa*, *rarā́da*, *rarā́dha*, *riréca*, *ruroca*, *rurója*, *ruroha* (AV.), *vavakṣa*, *vavanda*, *vavárta*, *vavárdha*, *vavarha*, *vavāca*[8] (*vac-* 'speak'), *vavāra* (*vṛ-* 'cover'), *vavrā́ja*, *vāvárta*, *vāvā́na*, *vivā́ya* (*vī-* 'be eager'), *vivéda*, *vivéśa*, *vivéṣa*, *vivyāca*, *véda*[10], *śaśāka* (AV.), *śaśā́pa* (AV.), *śiśrāya* (*śri-* 'resort'), *śuśoca*, *śuśrāva*, *sasarja*, *sasā́da*, *sasā́na*, *sasā́ra*, *sasūva*, *sāsā́ha*, *siṣedha*, *siṣāya*, *suṣā́va* (*su-* 'press'). — **With the ending -*au*:** *tastháu*, *dadáu*, *dadháu*, *papáu* (*pā-* 'drink'), *papráu*, *yayáu*.

Du. 2. *ārathur*, *āváthur*, *āsathur*, *īyathur*, *īṣáthur*, *ūpáthur* (√*vap-*), *ūháthur* (√*vah-*), *cakráthur*, *cakhyathur* (*khyā-* 'see'), *jagṛbháthur*, *jagmáthur*, *jigyathur* (*ji-* 'conquer'), *jijinváthur*[9], *takṣathur*[10], *tastháthur*, *dadáthur*, *dadhathur*, *ninyathur*, *papáthur* (*pā-* 'drink'), *paprathur*, *pipinváthur*[11], *pipyathur* (*pī-* 'swell'), *petathur* (√*pat-*), *babhūváthur*, *mimikṣáthur*, *yayathur*, *yemáthur* (√*yam-*), *riricáthur*, *vidáthur*[10], *vividáthur*, *vivyáthur* (*vyā-* or *vī-* 'envelope'), *sedáthur* (√*sad-*), *skambháthur*[10].

[1] The irregularity of this form which occurs once in the RV. and once in the AV. beside the regular *iyétha* is hard to explain.

[2] In VI. 17[7] this form stands for the 2. sing. of *prath-* 'extend'; see NEISSER, BB. 30, 302.

[3] Occurs twice in the RV. also with the irregular accent *cíketa*.

[4] It is very doubtful whether *jahā́* VIII. 45[37] is 3. sing. perfect of *hā-* 'leave' (cp. DELBRÜCK, Verbum p. 124), like *paprā́*. PISCHEL, Vedische Studien I, 163 f., thinks this word with the following *kó* should be read *jáhāko* 'abandoning'. ROTH thinks (pw.) *jahā́* is an interjection.

[5] Overlooked by WHITNEY, Roots, under √*nah-*: AV. VI. 133[1].

[6] The only occurrence of *ā* for *au* unless *jahā́* is a verbal form.

[7] Omitted by AVERY 250.

[8] RV[1]. beside the ordinary *uvā́ca*.

[9] From *jinv-* 'quicken', a secondary root starting from the present stem *ji-nu-* of *ji-* 'quicken'; see 469, a, 7.

[10] Unreduplicated form.

[11] From *pinv-* 'fatten', which started from a present stem of the *-nu* class; see 469, a, 7.

Du. 3. *āpatur, āvatur, āśatur* (*aś-* 'attain'), *āsatur, īyátur, ūhátur* (√*vah-*), *cakratur, cikyatur* (*ci-* 'observe'), *cetatur*[1], *jagmatur, jajñátur* (*jan-* 'beget'), *jahatur* (*hā-* 'leave'), *tatakṣátur, tasthátur, dadatur, paprátur* (*prā-* 'fill'), *petátur, babhūvátur, mamátur* (*mā-* 'measure'), *mimikṣátur* (*mikṣ-* 'mix'), *yamátur*[2], *yematur* (√*yam-*), *vavakṣátur, vāvṛdhatur, sasratur*[3] (√*sṛ-*, AV.), *siṣicatur, sedátur* (√*sad-*).

Pl. 1. *ānaśma* (*aṃś-* 'attain'); *cakṛmá, jaganma, jagṛbhmá, tasthi-má* (√*sthā-*), *dadhi-má, yuyujma, rarabhmá, rari-má* (*rā-* 'give'), *vavanmá, vidmá*[4], *śuśruma* (AV.), *suṣuma*. — **With connecting -*i*-:** *ārimá, āsimá* (*as-* 'be', AV.), *ūcimá* (√*vac-*), *ūdimá* (√*vad-*), *ūṣimá* (*vas-* 'dwell', AV.), *cerimá* (√*car-*, AV.), *jaghnimá* (√*han-*, AV.), *jihiṃsimá* (AV. TS.), *dadāśimá, nindima*[5], *nīnima*[6] (TS. III. 2. 8[3]), *paptima, babhūvima* (AV.), *yuyopimá*[7], *yemimá, vavandima, vidmá*[8], *śekimá* (√*śak-*, AV.), *saścima, suṣūdima* (√*sūd-*), *sedima*[5] (√*sad-*).

2. *anāha*[9] (RV[1].), *ānaśá* (*aṃś-* 'attain'); *ūṣá* (*vas-* 'shine'), *cakrá, jagmá*[10] (AV. TS. VS.), *dadá, babhūvá, yayá, vidá*[8], *śaśāsá, seka* (√*śak-*), *sedá* (√*sad-*).

3. *ānaśúr* (*aṃś-* 'attain'), *ānṛcúr* (√*arc-*), *ānṛdhúr* (AV.), *ānṛhúr* (TS. III. 2. 8[3]); *āpúr, ārúr, āśur* (*aś-* 'attain'), *āsúr* (*as-* 'be'), *āhúr, īyúr, īṣur* (*iṣ-* 'send'), *ūcúr, ūdur* (*und-* 'wet', AV.), *ūvur* (*vā-* 'weave'), *ūṣúr* (*vas-* 'shine'), *ūhúr* (√*vah-*), *cakramúr, cakrúr, cakhnúr* (*khan-*, AV.), *cāklpur* (AV.), *cikitur, cikyúr* (*ci-* 'perceive'), *cerúr* (√*car-*, AV.), *jagṛbhúr, jagṛhúr* (AV.), *jagmúr, jaghnúr* (√*han-*, AV.), *jajanúr*[11] and *jajñúr* (*jan-* 'beget'), *jabhrur* (√*bhṛ-*), *jahúr* (*hā-* 'leave'), *jaharur*[12] (√*hṛ-*, AV.), *jāgṛdhúr, jigyur* (*ji-* 'conquer'), *jugupur*[13], *jujuṣúr, jūjuvur* (√*jū-*), *takṣur*[14], *tatakṣúr, tastabhúr, tasthúr, tātṛpur* (AV.), *tātṛṣúr, titirur* (√*tṝ-*), *tuṣṭuvúr, dadāśúr, dadúr, dadhúr, dādhṛṣur* (AV.), *didyutur* (TS. II. 2. 12[6]), *duduhur, dudruvur* (AV.), *debhur* (*dabh-* 'harm'), *nanakṣúr, ninidúr, papur* (*pā-* 'drink'), *paptúr* (*pat-* 'fall'), *paprur* (*prā-* 'fill'), *pipiśur, pipyur* (√*pī-*), *babhūvúr, bibhidúr, bibhyur* (*bhī-* 'fear'), *bedhúr* (*bandh-*, AV.), *mamur* (*mā-* 'measure'), *mamrur* (*mṛ-* 'die'), *māmṛjur, māmṛśúr, mimikṣúr* (√*myakṣ-*), *mimyúr* (*mi-* 'fix'), *yamur*[14], *yayur, yuyudhur, yemúr, rāradhur* (√*rādh-*), *riripur, rurucúr, ruruhúr, vavakṣúr, vavṛjur, vavrur* (*vṛ-* 'cover'), *vāvaśúr* (*vaś-* 'desire'), *vāvṛtúr, vāvṛdhúr, vidúr*[8], *vividur, viviśúr* and (once) *viveśur*[15], *viviṣur, śaśāsur, śaśramur, śāśadúr, śūśuvur, śekúr* (√*śak-*), *saścur, sasrúr, siṣyadúr* (√*syand-*, AV.), *sisicur, suṣupur* (√*svap-*), *suṣuvur* (VS. XX. 63), *susruvur* (AV.), *sedúr* (√*sad-*), *sepur, skambhur*[14].

Middle. Sing. 1. *īje, īdhe* (*idh-* 'kindle'), *īṣé* (*īṣ-* 'move'), *ūhé* (*ūh-* 'consider'), *caké* (*kā-* = *kan-* 'be pleased'), *cakre, jigye* (*ji-* 'conquer'), *tatane*[16], *tasthe, titviṣe, dade, mame* (*mā-* 'measure'), *māmahe, raré* (√*rā-*), *śepé* (√*śap-*), *saśce.*

---

1 AV. III. 21[2]; SV. I. 2. 2. 1[10], explained by BENFEY, SV. Glossary, as 3. du. perf. without reduplication. WHITNEY, note on AV. III. 21[2], thinks it is a corruption for *cetatu*, but quotes WEBER as taking it for 3. du. perf. from *cat-* 'frighten into submission'.

2 Unreduplicated form with present meaning (VI. 67[1]).

3 *sisratur* (RV[1].) is an anomalous 3. du. pres. ind. of *sṛ-*, according to the reduplicating class with perfect ending instead of **sisṛtás*.

4 The form *viviṣma* which AVERY gives with a query is probably an error for *viviṣmas* 1. pl. pres. (VI. 23[5. 6]).

5 Cp. IF. 3, 9f.; ZDMG. 48, 519.

6 The metre requires *ninīma* (see BR. under *nī-* 'lead').

7 With strong radical syllable.

8 Unreduplicated form.

9 This form (VI. 48[5]) may be 2. pl. from a root *aṃh-* for **ānaha*.

10 Cp. WHITNEY's note on AV. VI. 97[4].

11 This form without syncope occurs once in the RV., *jajñúr* twice.

12 WHITNEY on AV. III. 9[6] would emend this irregular form, the reading of all the Mss., to *jahrur*.

13 This is the only finite form of this secondary root, and it occurs in a late hymn (VII. 103[9]); the past participle *gupitá-* also occurs twice in the tenth book. This √*gup-* was doubtless evolved from the denominative *gopā-yá-* 'act as a cowherd'.

14 Unreduplicated form occuring once.

15 With irregular strong vowel.

16 With unsyncopated vowel occurring once; 3. sing. *tatne*.

2. *cakṛṣé, cicyuṣé, tasthi-ṣe* (AV.), *dadṛkṣé* (*dṛś-* 'see'), *dadhi-ṣé, papṛṣe, yuyukṣé* (√*yuj-*, AV.), *rari-ṣe, ririkṣé* (√*ric-*), *vavakṣé* (√*vac-*), *vavṛṣé* (*vṛ-* 'choose'), *vivitse* (*vid-* 'find'). — **With connecting -*i*-:** *ūciṣé* (√*uc-* and √*vac-*), *ūpiṣe* (√*vap-*), *ūhiṣe* (√*vah-*), *jajñiṣé* (√*jan-*), *jabhriṣe, tatniṣe, bedhiṣe* (AV.), *śepiṣé* (√*śap-*, AV.), *sasāhiṣe*[1].

3. *ānajé* (√*añj-*), *ānaśé* (√*aṃś-*), *ānṛce, ānṛdhe*; *āse* (*as-* 'throw'), *ījé* (√*yaj-*), *īḷé* (√*īḍ-*), *īdhé* (√*idh-*), *īṣé* (*īṣ-* 'move'), *ūce* (*uc-* 'be pleased'), *ūpe* (√*vap-*), *ūhé*[2] (*ūh-* 'consider'), *caké* (√*kā-*), *cakradé* (√*krand-*), *cakramé, cakré, cakṣadé* (*kṣad-* 'divide'), *cāklpé* (AV.), *cikité* (√*cit-*), *cukṣubhé* (*kṣubh-* 'quake', AV.), *cucyuve, jagṛhe*[3], *jagmé* (√*gam-*), *jajñé* (√*jan-*), *jabhre* (√*bhṛ-*), *jigye* (√*ji-*), *jihīḷe* (√*hīḍ-*), *jujuṣé, juhvé* (*hū-* 'call'), *tatakṣé, tate* (√*tā-* 'stretch' = √*tan-*), *tatne* (√*tan-*), *tatre* (*trā-* 'protect'), *tasthe* (√*sthā-*), *titviṣé, tistiré*[2] (*stṝ-* 'strew'), *dádṛśe, dadé, dadhanvé*[4], *dadhé, dadhré* (*dhṛ-* 'hold'), *dadhvase* (*dhvaṃs-* 'scatter'), *duduhe, dudhuve* (√*dhū-*, AV.), *nanakṣé*[5], *nunudé, neme* (√*nam-*), *papṛkṣé*[6], *pape*[2] (*pā-* 'drink'), *pápṛathe* (RV^{1}.) and *papṛathé* (RV^{2}. AV^{1}.), *papre*[7] (√*prā-*, AV.), *paspaśé* (*spaś-* 'see'), *pipiśé, pipiṣe, pipīḷe, pipye* (*pī-*'swell'), *pece* (√*pac-*), *babādhé, babhre* (√*bhṛ-*), *bedhé* (√*bandh-*, AV.), *bhejé* (*bhaj-* 'divide'), *mamé* (*mā-* 'measure'), *māmahe, māmṛjé, mimikṣé*[8], *yuyujé, yuyuvé* (*yu-* 'join'), *yejé*[9] (√*yaj-*), *yeme* (√*yam-*), *rarapśé, rārabhe* (√*rambh-*), *riricé, rurucé, rebhé* (√*rabh-*, AV.), *vavakṣé* (√*vakṣ-*), *vavande, vavné* (√*van-*), *vavré* (*vṛ-* 'cover'), *vāvaśe* (*vaś-* 'desire'), *vāvase* (VIII. 4^{8}, *vas-* 'clothe')[10], *vāvṛje, vāvṛté, vāvṛdhé, vidé* (*vid-* 'know'), *vividé* (*vid-* 'find'), *vivyé* (*vyā-* 'envelope'), *vivye* (*vī-* 'be eager'), *śaśamé* (VS. XXXIII. 87), *śaśrathe, śaśré* (*śṛ-* 'crush'), *śiśriyé* (*śri-* 'resort'), *śuśruve, śūśuve* (*śū-* 'swell'), *śepé* (√*śap-*, AV.), *sasāhé*[11] and *sasāhe*[12], *sasṛjé, sasré* (*sṛ-* 'flow'), *sasvajé, sisice, siṣyade* (√*syand-*, AV.), *suṣuvé* (*sū-* 'bring forth').

Du. 2. *āśāthe* (√*aś-* 'attain'), *ījāthe* (AV.), *ūhyáthe*[13] (IV. 56^{6}), *cakramāthe, cakráthe, cikéthe*[14] (*ci-* 'note'), *dadáthe, dadháthe, mamnáthe* (√*man-*), *rarāthe* (*rā-* 'give'), *riricáthe, sasráthe* (√*sṛ-*).

3. *áśāte*[15], *cakrāte, dadháte, paspṛdhāte, bhejáte* (*bhaj-* 'divide'), *mamáte* (*mā-* 'measure'), *mamnáte* (*man-* 'think'), *yuyudháte, yemáte* (√*yam-*), *rebháte* (√*rabh-*, AV.), *vāvṛdháte*[16], *sasvajāte.*

Pl. 1. *bubhujmáhe, mumucmáhe, vavṛmáhe* (*vṛ-* 'choose'), *śāśadmahe* (*śad-* 'prevail'), *sasṛjmáhe.* — **2.** *dadhidhvé.*

3. *ānajre* (√*añj-*); *cāklpré, cikitré* (√*cit-*), *jagṛbhré*[17], *jahi-re* (√*hā-*, AV.), *juhuré, juhūré, tatasré* (√*taṃs-*), *tasthi-re, dádṛśre, dadhi-ré, dadhre, duduhré, nunudré, paspṛdhré, pipiśre, mami-ré* (*mā-* 'measure'), *mumucré, yuyujré, riricré,*

---

1 With strong radical vowel: cp. p. 356, note 2.

2 With passive sense.

3 Omitted by AVERY 250.

4 From *dhanv-* a transfer root from *dhan-* 'run'. Cp. WHITNEY, Roots 81.

5 From *nakṣ-* 'attain', a secondary form of *naś-* 'attain'; cp. WHITNEY, Roots 87.

6 IV. 43^{7}. This form (which is perhaps rather to be taken as 1. sing.) may be formed from *prakṣ-*, a secondary form of *prach-* 'ask'; cp. BENFEY, O. u. O. 3, 256; DELBRÜCK p. 126^{4}; WHITNEY, Roots, and BR. s. v. *prach-*.

7 *papré*, given by AVERY 250 with a query, does not seem to occur in the RV.

8 From *mikṣ-*, a desiderative formation from *miś-*; cp. WHITNEY, Roots.

9 *yeje* occurs three times in the RV. (only with *ā-* and *pra-*), *ījé* occurs twice as 3. sing., once as 1. sing.

10 WHITNEY, Roots, under *vas-* 'clothe'. This form is placed by BR. and GRASSMANN under a root *vas-* 'aim'.

11 X. 104^{10} (AVERY *sāsahe*), Pada text *sasahé*.

12 VIII. 96^{15}, (AVERY *sāsāhe*), Pada text *sasahe* cp. RPr. 580, 582, 587, 589.

13 This seems to be an anomalous form for *ūhāthe* (*ūh-* 'consider'; cp. GRASSMANN).

14 Irregular form (RV^{1}.) for **ciky-āthe*.

15 Thus irregularly accented V. 66^{2}. This form, *āśāte*, also occurs five times unaccented.

16 The AV. has also the transfer form *vāvṛdhéte*.

17 See notes on AV. XVIII. 34^{6} in WHITNEY's Translation.

rurudhre, vāvakre (*vañc-* 'move crookedly')[1], *vāvaśre*[2] (*vāś-* 'bellow'), *vivijre, vidre*[3], *vividré, vivipre, viviśre, śāśadré.* — **With connecting -i-:** *arhire*[3], *áśire* (Kh. I. 11[1]), *ījiré* (√*yaj-*), *īdhiré* (√*idh-*), *īriré*[4], *īṣiré*[5] (*iṣ-* 'send', AV.), *ūciré* (√*vac-*, AV.), *ūhiré* (√*vah-*), *cakriré, cacakṣiré* (VS. XL. 10 : Up.), *jagmire, jajñiré* (√*jan-*), *jabhriré* (√*bhṛ-*), *jihīḍiré* (√*hīḍ-*), *tatakṣiré, tatniré* (√*tan-*), *tastriré*[6] (√*stṛ-*, AV.), *teniré* (√*tan-*, VS. TS. AV.), *dadhanviré*[7], *dadhire* (Kh. I. 4[3]), *dadhrire* (√*dhṛ-*), *papire* (*pā-* 'drink'), *bedhire* (√*bandh-*, AV.), *bhejiré* (√*bhaj-*), *mimikṣire* (√*mikṣ-* 'mix', and √*myakṣ-*), *yetiré* (√*yat-*), *yemire* (√*yam-*), *rurucire* (Kh. I. 12[1]), *rebhiré* (√*rabh-*), *lebhiré* (√*labh-*), *vavakṣire, vavandiré, vavāśire, saściré* (√*sac-*), *secire* (√*sac-*, AV.), *sedire* (√*sad-*). — **With ending -rire:** *cikitrire* (√*cit-*), *jagṛbhriré, dadrire* (√*dā-*), *bubhujriré, vividrire, sasṛjrire.*

Moods of the Perfect.

486. Modal forms of the perfect are of rare occurrence in the Saṃhitās except the RV. They are made from the perfect stem in the same way as from the present stem. It is, however, not always possible to distinguish modal forms of the perfect from those of other reduplicated stems (present reduplicating class, reduplicated aorist, and intensive) either in form (because the reduplication is in many instances the same) or in meaning (because the perfect is often used in a present sense).

Perfect Subjunctive.

487. The normal method of forming the stem is to add *-a-*[8] to the strong perfect stem, accented on the radical syllable. In the active the secondary endings are more usual; e. g. *tuṣṭáv-a-t.* If the primary endings are added in the active, the reduplicative syllable is in several forms[9] accented, as *jújoṣ-a-si*[10]. In about a dozen forms, nearly all with secondary endings, the weak stem[11] is employed, but whether the reduplicative syllable was then accented is uncertain, because the examples that occur are unaccented. Middle forms, numbering not many more than a dozen, occur only in the 3. sing., with the ending *-te,* and in the 3. pl. with the ending *-anta.*

Active. Sing. 1. *anajā*[12]. — 2. *jújoṣasi, dīdáyasi, papṛcāsi*[13]; *cakradas, cākánas, cikitas* (√*cit-*), *jújoṣas, tatanas, dadāśas, dīdáyas, papráthas, piprayas, bubodhas, mamádas, māmáhas, mumucas*[14], *rāránas, sāsáhas, súṣūdas.*

3. *ciketati* (√*cit-*), *jújoṣati, dádāśati, dadhárṣati, dīdeśati*[15], *dīdáyati, búbodhati, mumocati, vavártati; cākánat, cākḷpat* (AV.), *ciketat* (√*cit-*), *jaghánat, jabhárat, jugurat* (*gur-* = *gṛ-* 'greet'), *jújoṣat, jūjuvat*[14], *tatánat, tuṣṭávat, dádāśat, dadhánat, dadhárṣat, papráthat, paspárśat, pipráyat, mamádat* (AV.), *mamandat, dīdáyat, mumucat*[14], *mumurat* (*mur-* = *mṛ-* 'crush'), *mumócat, rāránat, vavártat* and *vavṛtat*[14], *vāvanat* (TS. II. 4. 5[1]), *vividat*[14], *śuśravat, śūśuvat*[14], *sāsáhat, suṣūdat.*

---

1 With reversion to the original guttural.

2 With shortening of the radical vowel.

3 Without reduplication.

4 In RV. regularly *erire,* Pp. *ā-īrire* (but in I. 6[4] for *eriré* the accentuation should be *érire* = *á īrire*). The AV. has once *sam-īhiré* (XIV. 1[46]).

5 *īśire* with irregular accent is probably to be regarded as a present (450, 2).

6 IF. 8, Anzeiger 13.

7 From the secondary root *dhanv-* = *dhan-* 'run'.

8 Two subjunctive forms with double modal sign *-ā-* occur: *papṛcāsi* and *vāvṛdhāti.*

9 Cp. the accentuation of the reduplicating class.

10 Except the forms *dīdáyasi, dīdáyati, dadhárṣati* and *vavártati.*

11 The two roots *muc-* and *dhṛṣ-* make subjunctive forms from both the strong and weak stem.

12 RV. V. 54[1]: this form (Pp. *anaja*) is regarded by DELBRÜCK 126[b] and AVERY 251 as a 2. pl. ind.

13 With double modal sign *-ā-*.

14 With weak radical syllable.

15 Always *ā-dīdeśati* in relative clauses.

Du. 2. *ciketathas, jújoṣathas; ninīthas*[1] (I. 181[1]).

Pl. 1. *cākánāma, tatánāma, śūśávāma.* — 2. *jújoṣatha, bubodhatha.* — 3. *jujuṣan*[2], *jújoṣan, tatánan, papráthan, mamádan.*

Middle. Sing. 1. *śaśvacái*[3] (√*śvañc-*). — 3. *jújoṣate*[4], *tatápate, dadhṛṣate*[2], *yuyójate, vāvṛdhate*[2], *śaśámate* (*śam-* 'labour'). — **Pl.** 1. *anáśāmahai.*

Perfect Injunctive.

488. There are a few singular active and 3. pl. middle forms which must be classed as injunctives, being identical in form with the corresponding unaugmented persons of the pluperfect. These are: **Sing.** 2. *śaśās* (= **śaśās-s*). — 3. *dūdhot* (*dhū-* 'shake'), *siṣet*[5] (*si-* 'bind'); *sasvár* (= **sasvar-t*, from *svar-* 'sound'); with connecting *-ī-*: *dadharṣīt.*

Pl. 3. *cákramanta, cākánanta, tatánanta, dadabhanta, paprathanta, māmahanta, rurucanta*[2], *vāvṛdhánta*[2], *vivyacanta.*

Perfect Optative.

489. This mood is formed by adding the accented optative modal suffix combined with the endings (416a) to the weak perfect stem. The active forms are the commonest, occurring more than twice as often as those of the middle.

a. There are a few irregularities in the formation of this mood. 1. The radical vowels of *pā-* 'drink', *śru-* 'hear', and *kṛ-* 'make', being treated as before the *-ya* of the passive (444), the stems of these roots appear before the optative suffix as *papī-, śuśrū-*, and *cakri-*. — 2. The vowel of the reduplicative syllable *ān-* is shortened (as if it contained the augment) in *ănajyāt* (√*añj-*). — 3. A connecting *-ī-* is interposed in *jakṣ-ī-yát*, while the radical *i* is combined with the ending in *śiśrītá*. — 4. A transfer according to the analogy of the *a-* conjugation is *ririṣes*; possibly also *siṣet*[6].

Active. Sing. 1. *ānaśyām; jagamyām, papṛcyām, riricyām, vavṛtyám.*

2. *cakriyās*[7], *juguryās* (*gur-* = *gṛ-* 'greet'), *pupusyās, pupūryās* (*pur-* = *pṛ-*, 'fill'), *babhūyās, rurucyās, vavṛtyās, viviśyās, śuśrūyás*[8].

3. *anajyāt; cacchadyāt, jakṣīyát*[9] (*ghas-* 'eat'), *jagamyāt, jagāyāt* (*gā-* 'go'), *jagṛbhyāt, juguryát, tutujyát, tuturyát* (√*tur-* = *tṝ-*), *ninīyāt*[10], *papatyāt* (AV.), *papīyāt*[11] (*pā-* 'drink'), *papṛcyāt, babhūyát, mamadyat, riricyāt, vavṛtyāt, sasadyāt* (AV.), *sasṛjyāt, sāsahyāt.*

Du. 2. *jagamyātam, śuśrūyátam.*

Pl. 1. *tuturyāma, vavṛtyāma, śūśuyáma, sāsahyáma.*

3. *jagamyur, tatanyur, dadhanyur, mamṛdyur, vavṛjyúr, vavṛtyur.*

Middle. Sing. 1. *vavṛtīya.* — 2. *cakṣamīthās, vāvṛdhīthás.* — 3. *jagrasīta, dudhuvīta, māmṛjīta, vavṛtīta, śiśrītá* (*śri-* 'resort'), *śuśucīta.*

Pl. 1. *vavṛtīmahi.*

There also occurs in the middle one **precative** form: **Sing.** 2. *sāsah-ī-ṣ-ṭhás.*

Perfect Imperative.

490. The regular perfect imperative is formed like the present imperative of the reduplicating class, the 3. sing. active being strong. Hardly more

---

1 Abnormal form without modal sign or strong radical vowel; cp. HIRT, IF. 12, 220.

2 With weak radical syllable.

3 This form occurs only once (III. 33[10]) beside the *s*-aor. *naṃsai*, and may therefore be an irregular redupl. aorist, to which it is doubtfully assigned by WHITNEY 863 a.

4 SV. *jujóṣate.*

5 This form, however, might be a transfer present optative from *sā-* (the collateral form of the root *si-*) according to the reduplicating class; or a reduplicated aorist injunctive (GRASSMANN and WHITNEY 868 a).

6 See note 5 on this form.

7 Cp. v. NEGELEIN 66.

8 With lengthened radical vowel.

9 With interposed *-ī-*.

10 Cp. HIRT, IF. 12, 220.

11 With change of the final radical vowel *ā* to *ī*.

than twenty regular forms occur, nearly all of them being active. There are also some irregular imperatives, being transfer forms which follow the analogy of the *a-* conjugation, made from either the strong or the weak perfect stem..

Active. Sing. 2. *cākandhi, cikiddhi* (√*cit-*), *dididḍhi*[1] (√*diś-*), *piprīhí, mumugdhí* (√*muc-*), *śaśādhi* (√*śās-* 'order'), *śuśugdhí* (√*śuc-*).

3. *cākantu, dídeṣṭu*[1], *babhūtu*[2], *mamáttu, mumoktu, rārantu.*

Du. 2. *jajastám*[3] (*jas-* 'be exhausted'), *mumuktam, vavṛktam.*

Pl. 2. *jujuṣṭana, didiṣṭana* (√*diś-*), *vavṛttana*[4].

Middle. Sing. 2. *dadhiṣvá, mimikṣvá*[5], *vavṛtsva*[6].

Pl. 2. *dadhidhvam, vavṛddhvam*[7] (VIII. 20[18]). — 3. With the unique ending *-rām*: *dadṛśrām* (AV[1].)[8] 'let be seen'.

a. The transfer forms are:

Active. Du. 2. *jujoṣatam, mumócatam.* — **Pl. 2.** *mumócata*[9], *rarāṇátā*[10] (I. 171[1]).

Middle. Sing. 2. *pipráyasva, māmahasva, vāvṛdhasva, vāvṛṣasva.* — **Pl. 3.** *māmahantām.*

Perfect Participle.

WHITNEY, Sanskrit Grammar 802—807. — DELBRÜCK, Verbum 229. — LINDNER 84 and 216.

491. There is an active and a middle participle, and both occur frequently. Both are formed from the weak stem of the perfect, being accented on the suffix. The strong form is made by adding the suffix *-vā́ṃs* to the unstrengthened perfect stem; e. g. *cakṛ-vā́ṃs-, jaghan-vā́ṃs-.* If the stem is reduced to a monosyllable, the suffix is nearly always added with the connecting vowel *-i-*[11], as *papt-i-vā́ṃs-* from *pat-* 'fall'. Unreduplicated stems, however, do not take the connecting vowel[12], as *vidvā́ṃs-.* The weak stem of the active participle is identical in form with the 3. pl. ind. act. if written with *-uṣ* instead of *-ur*; e. g. *cakruṣ-.* The middle participle is formed by adding the suffix *-āná* to the weak perfect stem; thus from *cakṛ-* is made *cakr-āṇá-.*

Active.

492. *cakṛvā́ṃs-*[13], *cakhvā́ṃs-*[14], *cikitvā́ṃs-* (f. *cikitúṣī-*), *jaganvā́ṃs-* (f. *jagmúṣī-*), *jagṛbhvā́ṃs-, jagmivā́ṃs-* (TS. IV. 2. 1[4] for RV. X. 1[1] *jaganvā́ṃs-*), *jaghanvā́ṃs-* (f. *á-jaghnuṣī-*), *jānivā́ṃs-*[15], *jigīvā́ṃs-* (*ji-* 'conquer'), *jujurvā́ṃs-*

---

1 WHITNEY, Roots 73, doubtfully assigns this and the cognate forms *dideśati, didiṣṭa* to the reduplicating present class.

2 With *ū* unchanged, as elsewhere in strong forms.

3 Beside ind. *jajāsa* (AV.). WHITNEY, Roots 53, assigns this form to the reduplicated aor. beside 3. sing. *ajījasata* (ŚB.).

4 Given by AVERY 268 as a reduplicated aorist in the form of *vavṛtana* (sic).

5 For **mimikṣ-ṣva*. WHITNEY, Roots 120, assigns this form to the reduplicating present class.

6 WHITNEY, Roots 164, assigns this form to the reduplicating present class.

7 Written *vavṛdhvam.*

8 Cp. WHITNEY's note on AV. XII. 3[33].

9 Perhaps also *suṣūdáta* (AV. I. 26[4]) placed by WHITNEY, Roots 188, under the perfect, but, Sanskrit Grammar 871, doubtfully under the reduplicated aorist.

10 Owing to the strong radical vowel this should perhaps be regarded rather as a 2. pl. subjunctive. (The final vowel is long in the Pada text also.) The accent of these transfer forms was perhaps, except when the radical syllable was strong, normally on the thematic *-a-*. Cp. WHITNEY, Sanskrit Grammar 815.

11 Not, however, in *dadvā́ṃs-*, nor in the problematic form *cakhvā́ṃsam* (II. 14[4]), which seems to be formed from a root *khā-*.

12 Except *viśivā́ṃs-* (AV.).

13 With the weak stem in the acc. sing. *cakrúṣam* (X. 137[1]).

14 Without connecting vowel.

15 Only the weak stem of this participle occurs in the form *vi-jānúṣ-aḥ*; cp. above 482 e.

(*jur-* = *jṛ-* 'waste away'), *jujuṣvā́ṃs-*, *jūjuvā́ṃs-*, *tatanvā́ṃs-*, *tastabhvā́ṃs-*, *tasthi-vā́ṃs-* (f. *tasthúṣī-*), *titirvā́ṃs-*[1], *tuṣṭuvā́ṃs-* (√*stu-*), *dadaśvā́ṃs-* (*daṃś-* 'bite'), *dadasvā́ṃs-*, *dadāvā́ṃs-*[2] (AV.), *dadīśúṣ-*, *dadivā́ṃs-* (AV.), *dadṛvā́ṃs-* (f. *dadrúṣī-*[3], AV., *dṛ-* 'pierce'), *dadṛśvā́ṃs-* (f. *dadṛśúṣī-*), *dadvā́ṃs-* (*dā-* 'give'), *dadhanvā́ṃs-*, *dadhṛṣvā́ṃs-*, *dīdivā́ṃs-*, *papivā́ṃs-* (*pā-* 'drink'), *paprvā́ṃs-* (f. *paprúṣī-*; *pṛ-* 'fill'), *pīpivā́ṃs-* (f. *pipyúṣī-*; *pī-* 'swell'), *pupuṣvā́ṃs-*, *babhūvā́ṃs-* (f. *babhūvúṣī-*), *bibhīvā́ṃs-* (f. *bibhyúṣī-*), *mamandúṣī-*, *mamṛvā́ṃs-* (f. *mamrúṣī-*; *mṛ-* 'die'); *yayi-vā́ṃs-* (√*yā-*), *rari-vā́ṃs-* (f. *rarúṣī-*, AV.), *ririkvā́ṃs-*[4] (√*ric-*), *ririhvā́ṃs-*, *rurukvā́ṃs-*[4] (√*ruc-*), *vavanvā́ṃs-*, *vavarjúṣī-*[5], *vavṛvā́ṃs-*[6] (*vṛ-* 'cover'), *vavṛtvā́ṃs-*, *vāvṛdhvā́ṃs-*[7], *vivikvā́ṃs-*[4] (*vic-* 'sift'), *vividvā́ṃs-*, *vividhvā́ṃs-* (√*vyadh-*), *śuśukvā́ṃs-*[4] (√*śuc-*), *śuśruvā́ṃs-*, *śūśuvā́ṃs-*, *sasavā́ṃs-*[8], *sasṛvā́ṃs-* (f. *sasrúṣī-*), *sāsahvā́ṃs-*, *suṣupvā́ṃs-* (√*svap-*), *suṣuvā́ṃs-*, *sedúṣ-* (*sad-* 'sit').

a. **With connecting -*i*-**: *ārivā́ṃs-* presupposed by f. *ārúṣī-* (*ṛ-* 'go'), *īyivā́ṃs-* (f. *īyúṣī-*), *ūṣivā́ṃs-* (*vas-* 'dwell'), *ūṣúṣī-* (TS. IV. 3. 11[5]: *vas-* 'shine'), *okivā́ṃs-*[9] (weak stem *ūc-úṣ-*, √*uc-*), *jakṣivā́ṃs-* (*ghas-* 'eat', VS. AV. TS.), *jajñivā́ṃs-*[10] (√*jñā-*), *paptivā́ṃs-*, *viviśivā́ṃs-* (TS. IV. 7. 15[1]). Also the negative compound *á-saścivāṃs-* presupposed by the feminine *á-saścuṣī-*.

b. **Without reduplication**: *dāśvā́ṃs-*, *vidvā́ṃs-* (f. *vidúṣī-*), *sāhvā́ṃs-*; perhaps also *khidvā́ṃs-* in the voc. *khidvas*. Similarly formed is *mīḍhvā́ṃs-* (f. *mīḷhúṣī-*) 'bountiful', though the root is not found in independent use. With irregular connecting -*i*-: *dāśivā́ṃs-* (SV.), *viśivā́ṃs-* (AV.), and the negative compound *á-varjivāṃs-* presupposed by the f. *á-varjuṣī-* (AV.).

Middle.

493. *ākṣāṇá-* (√*ákṣ-*), *ānajāná-* (√*añj-*), *ānaśāná-* (√*aṃś-*, AV.), *ārāṇá-*, *āpāná-*, *ījāná-* (√*yaj-*), *ūcāná-* (√*vac-*), *cakamāná-*[11] (AV.), *cakāná-* (√*kā-*), *cakramāṇá-*, *cakrāṇá-*, *cakṣadāná-*, *caskabhāná-* (AV.), *cikitāná-* (√*cit-*), *jagrasāná-*, *jagmāná-*, *jajñāná-* (√*jan-*), *jāhṛṣāṇá-*, *jihīḷāná-*, *jujuṣāṇá-*, *juhurāṇá-*[12] (√*hvṛ-*), *jūjuvāná-*, *tatṛdāná-*, *tastabhāná-*, *tasthāná-*, *tātṛpāṇá-*, *tātṛṣāṇá-*, *titviṣāṇá-*, *tistirāṇá-* (√*stṛ-*), *tuṣṭuvāná-*, *tūtujāná-*[13], *tepāná-* (√*tap-*), *dadāná-*, *dadṛśāná-*, *dadrāṇá-* (*drā-* 'run'), *dādṛhāṇá-*, *didyutāná-*, *duduhāná-*, *papāná-* (*pā-* 'drink'), *paprathāná-*, *paspaśāná-*, *paspṛdhāná-*, *pipriyāṇá-*, *pīpyāná-*, *babṛhāṇá-*, *babhrāṇá-*, *bubudhāná-*, *bhejāná-*, *māmahāná-*, *mumucāná-* (AV.), *yuyujāná-*, *yemāná-* (√*yam-*), *rarāṇá-*, *rārakṣāṇá-*, *rārahāṇá-* (*raṃh-* 'hasten'), *riricāná-*, *rurucāná-*, *rebhāṇá-* (AV.), *lebhāná-* (√*labh-*), 1. *vāvaśāná-* (*vaś-* 'desire'), 2. *vāvaśāná-* (*vāś-* 'bellow'), 1. *vāvasāná-* (*vas-* 'wear'), 2. *vāvasāná-* (*vas-* 'dwell'), 3. *vāvasāná-* (*vas-* 'aim'), *vāvṛdhāná-*, *vāvṛṣāṇá-*, *vivyāná-* (√*vyā-*), *śaśamāná-*[11], *śaśayāná-*[14] (*śī-* 'lie'), *śaśāná-* (*śā-* 'sharpen', AV.), *śaśramāṇá-*,

[1] There also occurs the weak stem *tatarúṣ-*, from √*tṝ-*.

[2] With strong stem instead of weak.

[3] Given under *drā-* 'run' in the AV. Index Verborum, but translated by WHITNEY, AV. V. 13[8], as from *dṛ-* 'pierce'.

[4] With reversion to the original guttural.

[5] With strong radical vowel.

[6] The anomalous gen. sing. with an additional reduplicative syllable, *va-vavrúṣ-as* appears once (I. 173[5]); cp. ZDMG. 22, 605.

[7] There occurs once (IV. 2[17]) the anomalous participle with pres. suffix *vavṛdhántas* (GRASSMANN, Aorist).

[8] From *san-* 'gain'. The metre seems almost invariably to require this participle to be read *sasanvā́ṃs-* (cp. the f. *sasanúṣī-* in B.); see ARNOLD, Vedic metre p. 144[2].

[9] With strong radical vowel and reversion to the original guttural.

[10] The *i* may here perhaps more correctly be regarded as a reduced form of the basic vowel, as in *dadi-*, *tasthi-* etc.

[11] The *a* is not syncopated in *kam-* or *śam-*.

[12] Doubtfully assigned by WHITNEY, Roots, to the reduplicating class.

[13] More frequently with the intensive accent *tū́tujāna-*.

[14] With the double irregularity of strong radical syllable and reduplication with *a*.

śāśadāna-[1] (*śad-* 'prevail'), *śiśriyāṇá-* (*śri-* 'resort'), *śuśucāná-*, *śúśujāna-*[2], *śúśuvāna-*[3], *sasṛjāná-*, *sasrāṇá-*[4], *sasvajāná-*, *sāsahāná-*[5], *siṣmiyāṇá-*, *siṣvidāná-*, *suṣupāṇá-* (√*svap-*), *suṣvāṇá-* (*su-* 'press'), *sehāná-* (√*sah-*)[5].

Pluperfect.

BENFEY, Vollständige Grammatik p. 353. — Abhandlungen der königl. Gesellschaft der Wissenschaften zu Göttingen 15, p. 151—154. — DELBRÜCK, Verbum 419. — AVERY, Verb-Inflection 253. — WHITNEY, Sanskrit Grammar 817—820.

494. This tense, which is a pluperfect in form but not in meaning, is an augmented preterite made from the perfect stem. As in the perfect, the strong stem is used in the singular active, the weak elsewhere. The endings are the secondary ones; in the 3. pl. *-ur* always appears in the active and *-iran* in the middle. There is some difficulty in distinguishing this tense from the imperfect of the reduplicating class and from the reduplicating aorist[6]. Though its sense is the same as that of the imperfect, its forms may usually be distinguished (when the reduplication would be identical in both tenses) by the fact that the verb in question is not otherwise conjugated according to the reduplicating present class. On the other hand, the sense helps to distinguish the pluperfect from the aorist, when the reduplication would be identical in both tenses. With the aid of these criteria some sixty forms may be classed as belonging to the pluperfect. The augment is, as in other past tenses, dropped in several instances. The *-s* and *-t* of the 2. 3. sing. are in some forms preserved by an interposed *-ī-* (as in the aorist). Several transfer forms according to the *a-* conjugation are met with in this tense.

495. **Active. Sing.** 1. *acacakṣam*, *ajagrabham*, *atuṣṭavam*; *ápiprayam*[7] (TS. V. 1. 11[3]; VS. XXIX. 7); *cakaram*, *ciketam* (√*cit-*), *jagrabham* (AV.).

2. *ájagan*[8]; *áiyes*[9] (V. 2[8]); *cākán*, *nanámas*. — **With** *-ī-*: *ábubhojīs*, *dvivesīs*, *ávivesīs*; *jíhiṃsīs*[10] (AV.).

3. *ájagan*[11], *aciket* (√*cit-*); *rārán*[12]. — **With** *-ī-*: *acucyavīt*[13], *ájagrabhīt*, *arirecīt*, *ávāvacīt*, *avāvarīt*[14]. — **With thematic** *-a-*: *acakrat*, *acikitat* and *aciketat* (√*cit-*), *adadhāvat*[15] 'ran', *aśuśravat*[16] (MS.), *ásasvajat*; *cakradat*, *jagrabhat* (VS. XXXII. 2), *tastámbhat* (I. 121[3]).

Du. 2. *átataṃsatam*[17], *amumuktam*; *mumuktam*. — 3. *avāvaśītām* (*vaś-* 'desire').

Pl. 2. *ájaganta*; *ájagantana*, *ajabhartana*[18]. — **With** *-ī-*: *acucyavītana*[13].
3. *ácucyavur*, *áśiśrayur*, *aśuśravur*[19], *ábībhayur* (Kh. I. 7[5]).
Middle. Sing. 1. *áśuśravi*. — 3. *didiṣṭa* (√*diś-*).
Du. 2. *ápaspṛdhethām*[17].

1 With the intensive accent.

2 With the intensive accent and regarded by WHITNEY, Roots 174, and by LINDNER, Nominalbildung p. 54, as an intensive.

3 With the intensive accent and assigned by LINDNER, l. c., to the intensive, but by WHITNEY, Roots 175, to the perfect.

4 Once also anomalously with *-māna*: *sasṛmāṇá-*.

5 *sāsahāná-* once in RV., *sehāná-* thrice, from √*sah-*.

6 On such doubtful forms see specially DELBRÜCK, Verbum 158 (p. 135 f.).

7 WHITNEY 866 also quotes *apiprayan* from the TS.

8 For **á-jagam-s*.

9 BENFEY (p. 152) and DELBRÜCK, Verbum p. 123 and 128, regard this form as a pluperfect of *i-* 'go' (= *á-iy-e-s*), WHITNEY, Roots, as pluperfect of *iṣ-* or *eṣ-* 'move' (= *á-iy-eṣ*), ROTH and GRASSMANN as aorist of √*īṣ-*.

10 With irregular accent.

11 For **á-jagam-t*.

12 From *ran-* 'rejoice' (I. 122[12]).

13 Cp. WHITNEY 868 a.

14 From *vṛ-* 'cover'; cp. DELBRÜCK, Verbum p. 122[4].

15 WHITNEY regards this form as an aorist, but the reduplicative vowel is that of the pluperfect, while the sense (IX. 877) does not seem decisive.

16 WHITNEY 866.

17 Transfer form.

18 With strong radical vowel.

19 These three are, however, classed by WHITNEY 861, and Roots, as aorists.

Pl. 3. *ácakriran, ajagmiran, ápeciran* (√*pac-*, AV.); *avavṛtran*; *ásasṛgram*[1]. — **Transfer forms** according to the *a-* conjugation: *átitviṣanta, ádadṛhanta, ádadṛṃhanta* (TS. IV. 6. 2[4]), *ávāvaśanta* (*vāś-* 'bellow'); *cakṛpánta, dádhṛṣanta* (AV.), *vāvaśanta* (*vāś-* 'bellow'). — **With ending *-ranta*:** *avavṛtranta.*

Periphrastic Perfect.

496. This formation made with the reduplicated perfect of *kṛ-* 'make' which governs the acc. of a fem. substantive in *-ā* derived from a secondary (causative) verbal stem, is found only once in the Mantra portion of the Vedas: *gamayā́ṃ cakāra* (AV. XVIII. 2[27]) 'he caused to go' (lit. 'he made a causing to go'). In the Brāhmaṇa portions of the Saṃhitās (TS. MS. K.), such periphrastic forms (made even with an aorist) are occasionally met with.[2]

III. The Aorist System.

497. The aorist is of frequent occurrence in the Vedas, being made from about 450 roots. An augmented tense taking the secondary endings and forming moods and participles, it is distinguished from the imperfect by lack of a corresponding present[3] (e. g. 3. sing. aor. *á-kar*, 3. sing. imp. *á-kṛṇot*, 3. sing. pres. *kṛṇóti*) and by difference of meaning (*ákar* 'he has done', *ákṛṇot*, 'he did').

There are three distinct types of aorist.

1. The **simple aorist** adds the endings to the root either directly or with the connecting vowel *-a-*. It thus resembles the imperfect of the root-class or of the accented *á-* class. This type of aorist is formed by nearly 170 roots. Some nine or ten roots have, beside the regular forms of the simple aorist, a certain number of other forms which have the appearance of indicatives present. They seem to represent a transition to the formation of a new present stem. The most striking example is the aorist stem *voca-* from which the 3. sing. *vocati* occurs several times.

2. The **reduplicated aorist** resembles the imperfect of the reduplicating present class. It is, however, distinguishable from the latter not only in meaning, but by a certain peculiarity of reduplication and by being nearly always formed with a connecting *-a-*. This type of aorist is taken by about 85 roots.

3. The **sigmatic aorist** inserts *-s-*, with or without an added *-a*, between the root and the endings. It is taken by rather more than 200 roots.

Thus each of the three types has one form following the analogy of the graded conjugation, and another following that of the *a-* conjugation. The sigmatic aorist has, however, further subdivisions.

Upwards of 50 roots take more than one form of the aorist. One verb, *budh-* 'wake', has even forms from five varieties of the aorist; from two of the first type, e. g. *á-bodh-i* and *budhá-nta*; from one of the second, e. g. *a-būbudh-a-t*; and from two of the third, e. g. *á-bhut-s-i* and *bódh-i-ṣ-a-t.*

1 With reversion to the original guttural.

2 See WHITNEY, Sanskrit Grammar 1073 a, b; JACOBI, KZ. 35, 578—587; BÖHTLINGK, ZDMG. 52, article 11; DELBRÜCK, Altindische Syntax 426[4] f.; LUDWIG, Sitzungsber. d. kgl. Böhm. Ges. d. W., phil.-hist. Kl. Nr. XIII.

3 There are, however, sometimes sporadic forms from the same stem as the aorist beside the normal ones; thus the 2. du. pres. *kṛ-thás* occurs besides the numerous regular forms of the *nu-* class.

1. Simple Aorist.

A. Root Aorist.

BENFEY, Vollständige Grammatik 840. — AVERY, Verb-Inflection 253—256. — WHITNEY, Sanskrit Grammar, 299—304; Roots 222 f.; AV. Index Verborum 380.

498. This form of the simple aorist is taken by about 100 roots (and by more than 80 of these in the RV.), the commonest being those with medial *a* (nearly 30 in number). It is inflected in both the active and the middle voice. The root is strong in the indicative active singular, but weak elsewhere. Roots ending in vowels, however, show a tendency to retain the strong vowel throughout the indicative active except the 3. plural.

a. Roots ending in *ā*, of which there are some eight, retain the *ā* throughout the indicative active except the 3. pl., where they drop it before the ending which in these verbs is invariably *-ur*. In the middle indicative, the radical vowel is weakened to *i*[1].

The forms which occur from these roots, if made from *sthā-* 'stand', would be the following:

Active. Sing. 1. *ásthām.* 2. *ásthās.* 3. *ásthāt.* — Du. 2. *ásthātam.* 3. *ásthātām.* — Pl. 1. *ásthāma.* 2. *ásthāta.* 3. *ásthur.*

Middle. Sing. 2. *ásthithās.* 3. *ásthita.* — Pl. 1. *ásthimahi.* 3. *ásthiran.*

b. Roots ending in *ṛ*, of which there are some ten, take Guṇa throughout the indicative active except the 3. pl. Roots ending in *ĭ* and *ŭ* (of which, however, few dual and plural forms occur) show the same tendency. The root *bhū-* 'be' retains its *ū* throughout (as in the perfect), interposing *v* between it and a following *a*. The forms met with from *kṛ-* 'make' are the following:

Active. Sing. 1. *ákaram.* 2. *ákar.* 3. *ákar.* — Du. 2. *kartam* (AV.). 3. *ákartām.* — Pl. 1. *ákarma.* 2. *ákarta.* 3. *ákran.*

Middle. Sing. 1. *akri.* 2. *ákṛthās.* 3. *ákṛta.* — Pl. 3. *ákrata.*

The forms which actually occur are the following:

Indicative Active.

499. **Sing. 1.** *ákaram, ágamam*[2], *agām* (*gā-* 'go'), *ágrabham, adhām, ápām*[3] (*pā-* 'drink'), *abhuvam*[4], *abhedam, arodham* (*rudh-* 'hinder'), *áśravam, asthām* (AV.); *karam, gamam, gām* (AV.), *dām*[5], *dhām* (AV.), *vam*[6] (*vṛ-* 'cover').

2. *agās, adās*[7], *ápās, aprās, ábhūs, áśres, ásthās*; *gās, dās, dhās, bhūs, sthās.* — **With loss of ending:** *akar, ákrān* (√*krand-*), *ágan*[8], *ághas, avar* (*vṛ-* 'cover'), *aspar*; *ānaṭ*[9], *āvar* (*vṛ-* 'cover'); *kar, kran*[10] (√*kram-*), *bhet* (√*bhid-*), *vár, várk*[11].

3. *ágāt, acet*[12] (*ci-* 'collect'), *ádāt*[12], *ádhāt* (*dhā-* 'put'), *adhāt* (*dhā-* 'suck', AV.), *ápāt, aprāt* (AV.), *ábhūt, áśret* (√*śri-*), *áśrot, ásthāt,*

[1] As in the perfect before consonant endings and in the past passive participle, e. g. *ta-sthi-ṣe* (AV.), and *sthi-tá-* from *sthā-* 'stand'.

[2] This might also be the sing. 1. of the thematic aorist *ágama-t* etc.

[3] No forms of *pā-* 'protect' are made according to this aorist, while *pā-* 'drink' (present stem *piba-*) has no forms from the root in the present system except *pānti* (RV[1].) and *pāthás* (AV[1].), but perhaps even these are rather to be taken as meant for aorist forms; cp. p. 369, note [1] and p. 368, note [10].

[4] With the usual absence of Guṇa in this root; later *abhūvam.*

[5] There is also the transfer form *ádam* (I. 126[2]), which though not analyzed in the Pada text, appears to stand for *á-adam* as indicated by both sense and accent.

[6] For *varam* formed by false analogy as a first person to 2. sing. *vaḥ* (for **var-s*) appearing as if formed with the *-s* of 2. sing.

[7] There is also the transfer form *ádas* (I. 121[8]), which though not analyzed in the Pada text, is shown by both sense and accent to stand for *á-adas.*

[8] For **á-gam-s.*

[9] For **ā-naś-s* from *naś-* 'attain', where **ānak* would have been phonetic (54, 6).

[10] For **kram-s.*

[11] For **varj-s* from √*vṛj-*.

[12] There is also the transfer form *ádat*

asrat[1] (VS. VIII. 28); *gāt*, *dā́t*, *dhā́t*[2], *bhūt*, *sthāt*. — **With loss of ending:** *ákar*, *akran*[3] (√*kram*-), *ákrān* (√*krand*-), *agan*, *aghas*, *ácet* (*cit*- 'observe'), *atan*, *adar* (*dṛ*- 'pierce'), *abhet*, *ábhrāṭ* (√*bhrāj*-), *amok* (√*muc*-, AV.), *ámyak* (√*myakṣ*-), *ávart*[4], *avṛk*[5] (AV.), *ástar*; *ā́naṭ*, *ā́var*; *kar*, *gan*, *naṭ* (√*naś*- 'attain', AV.), *bhét*, *vár*, *vark*, *skan* (√*skand*-).

Du. 2. *agātam* (AV.), *ábhūtam*, *amuktam* (Kh. I. 12[6]); *kartam* (AV.), *gātam* (AV.), *dātam*, *dhātam*, *spartam*.

3. *ákartām*, *agātām* (AV.), *ádhātām* (VS. XX. 57), *ánaṣṭām* ('reach'), *ápātām* (VS. XXXVIII. 13), *abhūtām*; *gātām* (AV.), *dātām*.

Pl. 1. *ákarma*, *áganma*, *ágāma*, *ádarśma* (TS. III. 2. 5[4]), *adāma*[6], *ápāma*, *ábhūma*[7], *asthāma* (AV.), *áhema* (√*hi*-); *dhāma*, *bhūma* (AV.).

2. *ákarta*, *agāta* (AV.), *ábhūta*; *abhūtana*, *áhetana*; *karta* (AV.) and *kṛta*[8] (AV.), *gāta* (AV.), *sthāta* (AV.).

3. *ákran* (√*kṛ*-), *ákṣan*[9] (√*ghas*-), *ágman*, *ábhūvan*, *avṛjan*, *avṛtan*[10] (AV.), *avran*, *áśriyan* (√*śri*-), *áśravan* (AV.), *aśvitan*, *ahyan* (√*hi*-), *āsthan*[11] (AV.); *kran* (AV.), *kṣan* (√*ghas*-), *gman*, *vran*. — **With ending -ur:** *ákramur*, *águr*, *ádur*, *ádhur*, *apur* (I. 164[7]), *áyamur*, *ásthur*; *gur*, *dabhúr*, *dúr*, *dhur*, *nṛtur*[12], *mandur*, *sthur*.

Indicative Middle.

500. **Sing. 1.** *akri*, *ajani*, *ayuji*, *avri* (*vṛ*- 'choose'), *ahvi* (√*hū*-, AV.).

2. *ákṛthās*, *agathās* (VS. III. 19), *adhithās*, *áyukthās*, *ásthithās*.

3. *akṛta*, *ágata* (AV.), *ádiṣṭa*, *adhita*, *apṛkta* (√*pṛś*-), *ámata* (√*man*-), *amṛta* (AV.), *áyukta*, *ávṛkta* (√*vṛj*-), *avṛta* ('choose' and 'cover'), *ásṛṣṭa*, *askṛta* (X. 127[3]), *ásthita*, *áspaṣṭa* (√*spaś*-), *áśīta* (*śī*- 'sharpen'); *ā́yukta*; *ārta* (*ṛ*- 'go'), *āṣṭa* (*aś*- 'attain'); *arta* (*ṛ*- 'go'), *kṛta*, *gūrta* (*gur*- 'greet'), *gdha*[13], *mṛta* (AV.).

Du. 1. *gánvahi*. — **3.** *adhītām*[14] (√*dhā*-).

Pl. 1. *áganmahi*, *adimahi* (TS. I. 8. 6[2]) and *adīmahi*[14] (VS. III. 58)[15], *adhīmahi*[14] (√*dhā*-), *apadmahi* (VS. IV. 29), *ámanmahi*, *ayujmahi*, *áhūmahi*; *dhīmahi*[14] (√*dhā*-).

2. *ácidhvam* (*ci*- 'note'), *ámugdhvam* (√*muc*-), *ayugdhvam*.

3. *akrata*[16], *ágmata*, *atnata*; *ārata*, *ā́śata* (*aś*- 'attain'); *yujata*. — **With the ending -ran:** *akṛpran*[17], *agṛbhran*, *ajuṣran*, *ádṛśran*, *apadran*, *abudhran*, *áyujran*, *avasran*[18] (*vas*- 'shine'), *áviśran*, *avṛtran*, *ásṛgran*[19], *ásthiran*, *aspṛdhran*. — **With ending -ram:** *ádṛśram*, *ábudhram*, *ásṛgram*[19].

(I. 127[6], II. 124, V. 32[8]) which, though not analyzed in the Pada text, appears to stand for *ā́-adat*.

1 For **asras-t*: see Sandhi p. 61[3].

2 Also the transfer form (*práti*) *dhat* (IV. 27[5]).

3 For **akram-t*.

4 For **ávart-t* from *vṛt*- 'turn'.

5 Seemingly with anomalously weak root for **avṛk-t*. But the form really stands by haplology for the 3. sing. mid. *avṛkta*: *ápāvṛk támaḥ* (AV. XIII. 29) 'he has wasted away the darkness': see WACKERNAGEL, KZ. 40, 544—547.

6 That is, in *ā́dāma* (V. 30[15]), which though not analyzed in the Pada text, must stand for *ā́-adāma*.

7 *arudhma* is quoted in WHITNEY's Roots as occurring in the MS. [I. 6[5]: 94, 6].

8 Emendation for *kṛtám* (AV. XIX. 44[1]).

9 For *ágh(a)san*.

10 Misprinted as *acṛtan* in the text of AV. III. 31[1]: see WHITNEY's note.

11 Transfer form probably for *asthur* from *sthā*- 'stand'; see AJP. 12, 439; IF. 5, 388; KZ. 22, 435; WHITNEY, Sanskrit Grammar 847, and his note on AV. XIII. 1[5].

12 This form might be regarded as an unaugmented perfect.

13 For *gh(a)s-ta*, from √*ghas*-; cp. p. 56, 3.

14 With *ī* for *i*; cp. BRUGMANN, Grundriss 2, p. 896; v. NEGELEIN 6[1]; OLDENBERG, ZDMG. 63, 297.

15 From *dā*- 'share'.

16 There is also the transfer form *kránta* (I. 141[3]).

17 Cp. BLOOMFIELD, Johns Hopkins University Circular, Dec. 1906, p. 10.

18 Cp. p. 327, note 7.

19 With reversion to the original guttural.

Passive Indicative of the Root Aorist.

DELBRÜCK, Verbum 181[4]. — AVERY, Verb-Inflection 275. — WHITNEY, Sanskrit Grammar 842—845; Roots 240. — v. NEGELEIN, Zur Sprachgeschichte 4. — Cp. OSTHOFF, IF. 3, 390; HIRT, IF. 17, 64 f.

501. There is a peculiar middle form, made from about 45 roots in the Saṃhitās (40 of them occurring in the RV.), which is used with a predominantly passive meaning[1]. When it is formed from verbs with a neuter signification, like *gam-* 'go', the sense remains unaltered (as in the past passive participle). It is a 3. sing. indicative, in which the augmented root takes the ending *-i*. This *-i*, otherwise the ending of the 1. sing. middle, appears to be used in the regular 3. sing. perfect middle (e. g. *dadhe*, 1. and 3. sing.), and sometimes in the 3. sing. present middle (e. g. *śáye*, 1. and 3. sing.). The **characteristic** feature of this passive form is the **strengthening of the root** as compared with other middle forms, e. g. *ákāri* beside *akri* (1. sing. mid.)[2].

a. A prosodically short **medial** *i*, *u* or *ṛ* takes **Guṇa**, while *a* is normally lengthened; a **final** *i*, *u* or *ṛ* takes **Vṛddhi**, while final *ā* interposes a *y* before the ending. The accent in unaugmented forms is always on the root. The forms actually occurring are: **Sing. 3.** *ákāri*, *agāmi*, *áceti*, *ácchedi*, *ájani*[3], *ájñāyi*, *átāpi*, *ádarśi*, *ádhāyi*, *ápādi* (AV.), *ápāyi* ('drink'), *aprāyi* (AV. VS.), *ábodhi*, *ábhrāji*, *amāyi* ('measure'), *ámodi*, *ámyakṣi*, *áyāmi*, *áyāvi*[4] (VS. XXVIII. 15), *áyoji*, *árādhi*, *aroci*, *avahi* (Kh. v. 15[3]), *avāci*, *ávāri* ('cover'), *avedi* ('find'), *áśoci*, *áśrāyi* (√*śri-*), *ásarji*, *ásādi*, *ásāvi* (√*su-*), *ástāri*, *ástāvi*, *áhāvi*; *ceti*, *jáni*, *jāni*, *tāri*, *darśi*, *dāyi* ('give'), *dáyi* ('bind'), *dhấyi*, *pấdi*, *védi* ('find'), *sấdi*[5]. — **Used injunctively**: *ghóṣi*, *ceti*, *chedi*, *tāri*, *dhấyi*, *bhāri*, *bhedi* (VS. XI. 64), *móci* (AV.), *yoji*, *reci*, *roci*, *vandi*, *varhi*, *vāci*, *śaṃsi*, *śāri*, *śeṣi* (*śiṣ-* 'leave', AV.), *śrấvi*, *sarji*, *sādi*, *hāyi* (*hā-* 'leave', AV.); also the **unique form** *jārayấyi* 'let him be embraced', from the secondary stem *jāra-ya-* 'play the lover'.

Root Aorist Subjunctive.

502. **Active. Sing.** 1. *kárāṇi*, *gamāni*, *gāni*, *bhuvāni*. — 2. *kárasi*; *káras*, *gamas*, *gás*[6], *tárdas*, *dás*, *dhás*, *párcas*, *pás* (IV. 20[4] 'drink'), *prás*, *bhúvas*[7], *yamas*, *váras* ('choose'), *śásas*, *sthás*.

3. *karati*, *jóṣati*, *darśati* (AV.), *dáti*, *dháti*, *padāti*[8], *bhédati*, *rādhati*, *varjati*, *stháti*; *kárat*, *gámat*, *garat* (*gṛ-* 'swallow', AV.), *gāt*, *jóṣat*, *dát*, *dhāt*, *padāt*[8] (AV.), *máthat*[9] (AV. VII. 50[5]), *yamat*, *yodhat*, *rādhat*, *várat* ('choose'), *vártat*, *śrávat*, *sághat*, *sāt*, *sthāt*, *spárat*. — **Without Guṇa**: *ṛ́dhat*, *bhúvat*, *śrúvat* (RV[1].).

Du. 2. *karathas*, *gamathas*, *darśathas*, *pāthás*[10] (AV. VII. 29[1]), *bhūthás*[11], *śravathas*. — 3. *karatas*, *gamatas*, *bhūtas*[11], *śrávatas*, *sthấtas*.

---

1 In one or two passages this form seems to have a transitive meaning; cp. WHITNEY, Sanskrit Grammar 845 (end).

2 Cp. BRUGMANN, Grundriss 2, 1054, 3.

3 This augmented form always occurs in the RV. with short radical vowel, beside the unaugmented *jāni* as well as *jani*.

4 From *yu-* 'separate'.

5 The form *sváni* (VI. 46[14]) may be the 3. sing. passive aorist (BR. and doubtfully WHITNEY, Roots 201), but GRASSMANN, s. v. *sváni*, regards it as a neut. substantive in *-i*. Cp. NEISSER, BB. 30, 305 ff.

6 The 2. 3. sing. with secondary endings from roots ending in *ā* cannot be distinguished from injunctives.

7 Formed without Guṇa as in the ind. aor. and perfect.

8 With double modal sign *-ā-*.

9 This form has a subjunctive sense ('might shake'); it might otherwise be an injunctive of the *a-* aorist.

10 Assigned by WHITNEY, Roots, to the present of the root class.

11 Both *bhūthás* (VI. 67[5]) and *bhūtas* (X. 27[7]) seem to be meant for subjunctives formed anomalously without mood sign, instead of **bhúvathas* and **bhúvatas*.

Pl. 1. *kárāma, gamā́ma, gāma, dhāma, rādhāma.* — 3. *karanti, gámanti, pānti*[1] (II. 11[14]); *káran, gáman, garan, dárśan, bhúvan, yaman.*

Middle. Sing. 2. *kárase, joṣase* (AV.). — 3. *idhaté*[2] (RV[1].), *kárate, bhójate, yojate, várjate, stárate.* — Du. 2. *dhéthe*[3], *dhaithe.* — Pl. 1. *kárāmahe, gámāmahai, dhāmahe, manāmahe* (VS. IV. 11), *starāmahe.* — 3. *yavanta* (*yu-* 'separate').

Root Aorist Injunctive.

503. Active. Sing. 1. *karam* (AV.), *gām, dhām* (VS. I. 20), *bhuvam, bhojam, yojam, sthām.*

2. *jes, bhūs, bhés* (√*bhī-*, VS. I. 23 etc.; TS. IV. 5. 10[1]). — With loss of ending: *kar* (TS. I. 3. 7[2]), *dhak* (*dagh-* 'reach'), *bhet* (√*bhid-*), *rok* (√*ruj-*, VS.), *var* ('cover'), *vark* (√*vṛj-*), *star, spar.*

3. *bhū́t, śret, ut-thā́t* (√*sthā-*, Kh. II. 11[3]). — With loss of ending: *gan* (VS. XXVII. 31; TS. V. 6. 1[4]), *dhak* (√*dagh-*), *nak* and *naṭ* (*naś-* 'attain'), *vár, vark, skán* (√*skand-*), *stan*[4].

Pl. 1. *gāma, chedma*[5], *daghma, bhūma, bhema*[5], *hóma*[5] (*hū-* 'call'). — 3. *bhūvan, vrán.* — With ending *-ur*: *kramur, gur, dabhúr, dur, dhúr, sthur.*

Middle. Sing. 1. *náṃśi* (*naṃś-* = *naś-* 'attain'). — 2. *dhṛthās* (AV.), *nutthā́s, bhitthās* (VS. XI. 68), *mṛthā́s* (*mṛ-* 'die'), *mṛṣṭhās* (√*mṛṣ-*), *rikthās* (√*ric-*), *vikthās* (√*vij-*, VS. I. 23). — 3. *arta* (√*ṛ-*), *aṣṭa* (*aś-* 'attain'), *vukta* (TS. IV. 3. 11[4]), *vikta* (√*vij-*), *vṛta* (*vṛ-* 'choose'). — Pl. 1. *dhīmahi*[6] (√*dhā-*). — 3. *aśata* (ŚA. XII. 19).

Root Aorist Optative.

504. Active. Sing. 1. *aśyā́m* (*aś-* 'attain'), *ṛdhyām* (AV.), *deyām*[7], *dheyām*[7], *vṛjyām, śakyām.* — 2. *avyās, aśyās, ṛdhyās, gamyās, jñeyās, bhūyā́s, mṛdhyās, sahyās.* — 3. *bhūyāt*[8] (AV.).

Du. 1. *yujyāva.* — 3. *yujyā́tām.*

Pl. 1. *aśyā́ma, ṛdhyā́ma, kriyāma, bhūyā́ma, vṛjyā́ma, sāhyāma*[9], *stheyāma*[7]. — 3. *aśyur* (*aś-* 'attain'), *dheyur, sahyur.*

Middle. Sing. 1. *aśīya, murīya* (*mṛ-* 'die', AV.). — 3. *arīta* (√*ṛ-*) *uhīta-*[10] (√*vah-*), *vurīta* (*vṛ-* 'choose'). — Du. 2. *ṛdhāthe.*

Pl. 1. *aśīmáhi, idhīmahi, ṛdhīmáhi, naśīmahi* ('reach'), *nasīmahi, pṛcīmahi, mudīmahi, yamīmahi, sīmahi*[11] (*sā-* 'bind').

a. Precative forms of the root aorist are common in the active, being made from about twenty roots in the Saṃhitās.

Active. Sing. 1. *āpyāsam*[12] (AA. V. 3. 2[3]) *ṛdhyāsam* (VS. VIII. 9), *jīvyā́sam* (AV. VS.), *priyāsam*[13] (AV.), *bhūyā́sam, bhrājyāsam* (AV.), *bhriyāsam* (VS. II. 8), *rādhyāsam* (VS. XXXVII. 3), *vadhyāsam* (VS. AV.), *śrūyāsam* (AV.). — 3. *avyā́s, aśyās* ('reach'), *ṛdhyās, gamyā́s, daghyās, peyās* ('drink'), *bhūyā́s, yamyās, yūyās*[14] *yu-* 'separate'), *vṛjyās, śrūyās, sahyās.*

[1] Assigned by WHITNEY, Roots, to the present of the root class.

[2] With weak and unaccented root.

[3] A transfer form for **dhā́the.*

[4] This form may, however, perhaps preferably be classed as an imperfect injunctive along with *stanihi* as pres. impv., as in WHITNEY's Roots. These are the only forms of the simple verb beside the aor. *astānīt* (AV.).

[5] With strong radical vowel.

[6] Probably to be explained as the injunctive corresponding to the augmented indicative *adhīmahi* (see 500, note 14); it might, however, be the 1. pl. opt. mid. with loss of *ā* before the modal *-ī-*.

[7] For *dā-iyām, dhā-iyām, sthā-iyāma.*

[8] The RV. has no forms of the 3. sing. in *-yāt*, but only the somewhat numerous precatives in *-yās* = **-yās-t.*

[9] With irregular strong radical vowel, Padapāṭha *sahyāma*; cp. RPr. IX. 30.

[10] Aor. opt. in WHITNEY, Sanskrit Grammar 837 b, but pres. opt. in 'Roots' 157.

[11] With loss of *ā* before the modal *-ī-*.

[12] Accented *ā́pyāsam* in the ed. (B. I.).

[13] WHITNEY, in AV. III. 54, would emend this form to *bhriyāsam*: see his note on that passage.

[14] According to AVERY 241, 3. sing. pres. opt.

Du. 2. *bhūyāstam* (VS. II. 7). — Pl. 1. *ṛdhyā́sma* (AV.), *kriyāsma*, *bhūyāsma* (AV. VS.), *rādhyāsma* (AV.). — 2. *bhūyāsta*[1] (TS. III. 2. 5^6).

Middle. Sing. 3. *padīṣṭá*, *mucīṣṭa*[2].

Root Aorist Imperative.

505. The active forms of this mood are fairly numerous, occurring in all the 2. and 3. persons; but middle forms occur in the 2. pers. only, ten in the sing. and two in the pl. In the 2. persons active of all numbers, several forms irregularly strengthen the root, which is then nearly always accented.

Active. Sing. 2. *kṛdhí*, *gadhi*, *bodhí*[3], *yandhí* (√*yam-*), *yódhi*[4], *randhi* (= *rand-dhi*; √*randh-*), *viḍḍhi* (√*viś-*, AV.), *vṛdhí* 'cover', *śagdhí* (√*śak-*), *śrudhí*, *spṛdhí*. — **With ending -*hi*:** *gahi*, *pāhi* (AV.), *māhi* 'measure', *sāhi* 'bind'.

3. *gantu*, *dātu*, *dhātu*, *pā́tu* (AV.), *bhū́tu*, *śrótu*, *sótu* (*su-* 'press').

Du. 2. *kartam*[5] (AV.) and *kṛtám*, *gatám* and *gantám*[5], *jitam*, *dātam*, *dhaktam* (√*dagh-*), *dhātam*, *pātam* (AV.), *bhūtám*, *bhṛtam* (VS. XI. 30), *yantám*[5], *riktam* (√*ric-*), *varktam*[5] (√*vṛj-*), *vartam*[5] (*vṛ-* 'cover'), *voḷhám*[6], *śaktam*, *śrutám*, *sitam* (*si-* 'bind'), *sutám*, *sthātam*, *spṛtam*.

3. *gantām*[5] (VS. IX. 19), *ghástām* (VS. XXI. 43), *dātām*, *pātā́m*, *voḷhā́m*[6].

Pl. 2. *kárta*[5] and *kṛta*, *gata* and *gánta*[7], *gātá*, *dāta*, *dhā́ta*[8], *pāta* (AV.), *bhūtá*, *yánta*[5], *varta*[9] (√*vṛt-*), *śasta* (√*śaṃs-*), *śruta* and *śróta*[10], *sóta*[5] (√*su-*), *sthāta*, *heta*[5] (√*hi-*). — **With ending -*tana*:** *kártana*[5], *gántana*[5], *gātana*, *dhātana*, *dhetana*[11], *pātana* (AV.), *bhūtana*, *yantana*[5], *sotana* (√*su-*).

3. *gámantu*, *dāntu* (*dā-* 'cut', AV. XII. 3^3), *dhāntu*, *pāntu* (AV.), *śruvantu*.

Middle. Sing. 2. *kṛṣvá*, *dhiṣvá* (√*dhā-*), *yukṣvá*; **accented on the root:** *mátsva*, *yákṣva*, *rā́sva*, *váṃsva* (*van-* 'win'), *sákṣva*[12] (I. 42^1, √*sac-*); unaccented *dīṣva* (*dā-* 'give', VS. XXXVIII. 3), *māsva* 'measure'.

Pl. 2. *kṛdhvam*, *voḍhvam*[13] (VS.).

Root Aorist Participle.

506. Of the active form of the participle of the root aorist few examples occur. But the middle form is common, nearly forty examples being met with in the RV. The accent here generally rests on the final syllable of the suffix *-āna*, but in several examples it is on the radical syllable.

Active. *ṛdhánt-*, *kránt-*, *gmánt-*, *citánt-*, *pā́nt-*, *bhidánt-*, *sthā́nt-*; also *dyutánt-*[14] as first member of a compound.

Middle. *arāṇá-*, *idhāná-*, *urāṇá-* 'choosing', *ū́hāna-* (√*vah-*), *krāṇá-*[15], *citāna-*, *cyávāna-*, *juṣāṇá-*, *tṛṣāṇá-*, *dṛśāná-* and *dṛ́śāna-*, *dyutāná-* and *dyútāna-*, *dhuvāná-* (TS. IV. 4. 12^5), *nidāná-*, *piśāná-*, *pṛcāná-*, *prathāná-*, *budhāná-*, *bhiyāná-*, *manāná-*, *mandāná-*, (*vi-*)*mā́na-* (TS. IV. 6. 3^3), *yatāná-* and *yátāna-*, *yujāná-*,

1 AV. XVIII. 4^{86} has the corrupt reading *bhūyāstha*; see WHITNEY's note on that passage.

2 The form *grabhīṣṭa* is a 2. pl. injv. beside the 1. pl. ind. *agrabhīṣma* according to the *iṣ-* aorist.

3 From both *bhū-* 'be' for **bhū-dhi* and *budh-* 'awake' for **bód-dhi* instead of **bud-dhi*.

4 For **yód-dhi* instead of **yuddhi*.

5 With strong root.

6 For *vah-tam*, *vah-tām* through **vaẓh-tam*, **vaẓh-tām*.

7 Once (VI. 49^{11}) accented *gantá*.

8 With the accent of strong forms.

9 For *vart-ta* (like *varti* for *vart-ti*).

10 Always *śrutā* or *śrótā*; also *sótā* (cp. RPr. VII. 14 f.).

11 With *e* for *ā*.

12 *sákṣva* (III. 37^7) is from √*sah-*, being an *s-* aor. form, for **sah-s-sva* beside 1. sing. mid. *asākṣi* and *sā́kṣi*.

13 For *vah-dhvam* through **vaẓh-dhvam*.

14 In *dyutád-yāman-* 'having a shining track'.

15 Cp. BB. 20, 89.

rucānā-, *rúhāṇa-*, *vásāna-* 'dwelling', *vipānā-*, *vrāṇā-* 'covering', *śubhānā-* and *śúmbhāna-*, *śvitānā-*, *sacānā-*, *suvānā-*[1] and *svānā-* (SV.) (*su-* 'press'), *sṛjānā-*, *spṛdhānā-*, *hiyānā-*[2]. As members of compounds only, *-cetāna-* and *-hrayāṇa-*[3] occur.

B. *a-* Aorist.

AVERY, Verb-Inflection 256 f. — WHITNEY, Sanskrit Grammar p. 305—308; Roots 224; AV. Index Verborum 380. — v. NEGELEIN, Zur Sprachgeschichte 32—34.

507. This form of the simple aorist is taken by nearly 60 roots, chiefly by such as contain a medial vowel. In the RV. less than half as many verbs form the *a-* aorist as form the root-aorist; and it is more frequent in the AV. than in the RV. The root generally appears in the weak form, the stem being made with an added *-a*, which in unaugmented forms is normally accented. This form of the aorist therefore resembles an imperfect of the *á-* class. Middle forms are of rare occurrence in this aorist.

a. A certain number of irregularities occur in the formation of the stem. 1. The radical vowel of *śās-* 'order' is reduced to *i*[4], e. g. *śiṣat*[5] (IV. 2[7]). — 2. Some half dozen roots containing a medial *a* followed by a nasal, drop the nasal; these are *krand-* 'cry out', *taṃs-* 'shake', *dhvaṃs-* 'scatter', *bhraṃś-* 'fall', *randh-* 'make subject', *sraṃs-* 'fall'. — 3. On the other hand *ṛ-* 'go' and *sṛ-* 'flow' take Guṇa and accent the radical syllable, as *áranta* (unaugmented 3. pl.) and *sárat*. — 4. Several roots form transfer stems from the root aorist. Some half dozen do this by reducing a final radical *ā* to *a*. This is regularly the case in *khyā-* 'see', *vyā-* 'envelope', *hvā-* 'call'; e. g. *ákhyat*, *ávyat*, *áhvat*; but from *dā-* 'give', *dhā-* 'put', and *sthā-* 'stand', only occasional transfer forms occur; thus *ádat*; *adhat* (SV.) and *dhat*; *āsthat* (AV[1].). On the other hand, occasional transfer forms are made from *kṛ-* 'make', and *gam-* 'go', in which the radical syllable remains strong; e. g. *ákarat* (AV.) and *ágamat*.

Indicative.

508. The forms of the indicative actually occurring, if made from *vid-* 'find', would be as follows:

Active. Sing. 1. *ávidam*. 2. *ávidas*. 3. *ávidat*. — Pl. 1. *ávidāma*. 2. *ávidata*. 3. *ávidan*.

Middle. Sing. 1. *ávide*. 3. *ávidata*. — Pl. 1. *vidāmahi*. 3. *ávidanta*.

The forms which actually occur are the following:

Active. **Sing. 1.** *ákhyam*, *agṛbham* (Kh. III. 15[5]), *átṛpam* (AV. TS.), *atṛham* (AV.), *anijam* (AV.), *ámucam* (AV.), *áruham* (TS. VS. AV.), *ávidam*, *ávṛdham* (Kh. IV. 8[5]), *aśakam* (VS. II. 28), *ásanam*, *ásaram*, *ahyam*[6] (√*hi-*, AV.), *ahvam* (AV.); *ápam* (AV.); *aram*, *vidam*.

2. *ákaras* (AV.), *ákṛtas* (*kṛt-* 'cut'), *ákhyas* (TS. AV.), *áruhas*, *ávidas*, *asadas* (TS. VS. AV.), *ásaras*; *ápas*; *káras*, *guhas*, *druhas*, *bhúvas*[7], *mucas* (AV.), *vidás*.

3. *ákarat*[8] (AV.), *akramat* (AV.), *ákhyat*, *ágamat*[8] (AV.), *ágṛdhat*, *acchidat* (AV.), *atanat*, *átasat* (VS. AV.), *adṛpat*[9] (AV.), *adhat*[10] (√*dhā-*, SV.), *ámucat*,

[1] Always written thus in the RV., but to be pronounced *svanā-*.

[2] Hardly any of these participles occur in any of the other Saṃhitās: *rucānā-* (VS. XII. 1), *rúhāṇa-* (TS. IV. 1. 2[4]), *svānā-* (SV.).

[3] In *á-cetāna-* 'thoughtless', and *á-hrayāṇa-* 'bold'.

[4] As in the weak forms of the present stem.

[5] At the same time accenting the radical syllable.

[6] Though the other forms from √*hi-* follow the root-aorist (*áhema*, *ahyan*, etc.), this is probably to be regarded as a transfer form, since the regular form according to the root aorist ought to be **áhayam*.

[7] A transfer form, *bhúva-s*, following *bhuv-am* as if from a stem *bhúva-*.

[8] Transfers from the root aorist, following the 1. sing. *ákar-am*, *ágam-am*.

[9] Emendation in AV. XX. 136[5].

[10] Transfer from the root aorist for *a-dhāt*.

árudat (AV.), *arudhat*, *áruhat*, *ávidat*, *avṛtat* (AV.), *avṛdhat*, *avyat*[1] (√*vyā*-), *áśakat* (AV.), *aśucat*, *áśramat* (AV.), *ásadat*, *ásanat*, *ásarat*, *ásicat* (TS. III. 2. 8[4]), *ásṛpat* (AV.), *áhvat*[1]; *ádat*[2] (√*dā*-), *ápat*, *ārat*, *āsthat*[3] (AV[1].); *tṛṣat* (AV.), *dhat*[4] (√*dhā*-), *bhúvat*[1], *vidát*, *sadat* (AV.), *sánat*, *sárat*.

Pl. 1. *aruhāma* (VS. VIII. 52), *ávidāma*, *ásanāma*, *áhvāma*; *vṛdhāma*[5] (AV. V. 1[9]). — 2. *ávyata*[1]; *ārata*.

3. *akhyan*, *akraman* (AV.), *agaman* (AV.), *acchidan* (AV.), *ádṛśan* (TS. IV. 5. 1[3]), *arudhan* (AV.), *áruhan*, *ávidan*, *avṛjan*, *avṛdhan* (VS. XXXIII. 60), *aśakan* (AV.), *ásadan*, *asanan*, *asaran*, *asican*; *ápan*, *āran*, *āsthan*[6] (AV. XIII. 1[5]); *khyán*, *dhvasán*[7], *vidán*, *sadan*.

Middle. Sing. 1. *áhve*; *hve* (AV.). — 3. *akhyata*, *ávyata*[1]; *ārata*; *vyata*[1]. — Pl. 1. *śiṣāmahi* (√*śās*-). — 3. *avidanta* (AV.), *ahvanta*; *áranta*, *kránta*[1].

a- Aorist Subjunctive.

509. The forms of this mood are rare and almost restricted to the active.

Active. Sing. 2. *vidási*; *vidás*. — 3. *mucāti*; *vidát*.

Du. 1. *ruháva*. — 2. *vidāthas*. — 3. *gamātas* (AV. X. 7[42]).

Pl. 1. *arāma*; *radhāma*, *riṣāma*, *sadāma*. — 2. *gamātha* (AV.), *riṣātha*, *vidātha*; *riṣāthana*.

Middle. Sing. 3. *mucāte*, *śiṣātai*[8] (*śiṣ*- 'leave', AV. II. 31[3]).

Pl. 1. *śiṣāmahe*[9] (AV. SV.).

a- Aorist Injunctive.

510. Active. Sing. 1. *aram*, *khyam*, *dárśam*, *radham*, *riṣam*, *ruhám*, *vidam*, *sanam*.

2. *kradas*, *krudhas* (AV.), *khyás*, *guhas*, *gṛdhas* (AV. VS.), *druhas* (AV.), *mucás*, *vidas*, *riṣas* (VS. XI. 68; TS. IV. 1. 9[1]), *śiṣas* ('leave'), *sadas*, *sṛpas* (AV.).

3. *kṣudhat* (AV.), *khyat*, *gṛdhat* (AV.), *tanat*, *tamat*, *tṛṣat* (AV.), *dasat*, *dhṛṣát* (Kh. IV. 1), *bhraśat*, *mucat*, *riṣat*, *rudhat*, *rúhat*[10], *vidát*, *śiṣat*[11], *śramat*, *śriṣat*, *śrúvat*[12], *sadat*, *sánat*[10], *sṛpat* (AV.), *sridhat*.

Pl. 3. *aran*, *khyan*, *gáman* (VS. XVII. 78), *tṛpán*, *tṛṣan* (VS. VI. 31), *dṛśan*, *druhan*, *riṣan*, *vidan*, *śakan* (AV.).

Middle. Sing. 3. *vidata* (AV. XIII. 2[31]).

Pl. 1. *arāmahi* (AV.); *gṛhāmahi*. — 3. *aranta*, *budhánta*, *mṛṣanta*, *vidánta*.

a- Aorist Optative.

511. This mood is rare and confined to the active in the RV., though three or four middle forms occur in the later Saṃhitās.

Active. Sing. 1. *āpeyam*[13] (AV.), *gameyam*, *dṛśeyam*, *bhideyam* (AV.),

---

1 Transfer form.

2 A transfer form: see p. 366, note 12.

3 See p. 327, note 5.

4 *práti dhat* (IV. 27[5]).

5 WHITNEY, note on AV. V. 1[9], would instead of *ávim vṛdhāma* read (with Paipp.) *ávīvṛdhāma*.

6 A transfer form from √*sthā*-; cp. WHITNEY's note on AV. XIII. 1[5].

7 With loss of medial nasal, from √*dhvaṃs*-.

8 This form is probably a corrupt reading for the passive *śiṣyātai*: see WHITNEY's note on AV. II. 31[3].

9 For *śiṣāmahi* of RV. VIII. 24[1].

10 With accent on the radical syllable.

11 From *śāṣ*- 'order', with accent on the root.

12 It is hard to decide whether this form, which occurs only once (I. 127[3]) beside the regular *śrávat*, should be classed here as an injunctive of the *a*- aorist, or as an irregular subjunctive of the root-class following the analogy of *bhúvat* (cp. 502).

13 In *prāpeyam* (AV. III. 20[9]), analyzed in the Pada text as *prá āpeyam*; cp. WHITNEY's note on the passage.

vidéyam[1] (AV.), *śákeyam* (Kh.IV. 8[4]), *sanéyam*. — 2. *games* (VS.). — 3. *ṛdhet* (AV.), *gamét*, *yamet*[2] (AV.), *videt*, *sanet*, *set*[3] (VS. IX. 5, 6).

Pl. 1. *aśema* ('attain'), *ṛdhema* (AV.), *gaméma*, *dṛśema* (AV.), *puṣema*, *bhujema*, *ruhema*, *videma* (AV.), *śakéma*, *sadema*, *sanéma* and *sánema*, *srasema*[4].

Middle. Sing. 1. *videya* (VS. IV. 23). — Pl. 1. *gamemahi*. There is also one precative form: 3. sing. *videṣṭa* (AV.) 'may she find'.

a- Aorist Imperative.

512. This mood is also of rare occurrence and is restricted to the active, excepting two middle plural forms.

Active. Sing. 2. *kara*[5] (RV[1].), *bhuja* (TS. IV. 5. 1[4]), *muca*, *ruha* (AV.), *sada*, *sána*[6], *sára*. — 3. *sadatu*.

Du. 2. *aratam*, *karatam*[7] (RV[1].), *khyatam*, *ruhátam*, *vidatam*, *sádatam*. 3. *aratām*, *karatām*[8], *sadatām*.

Pl. 2. *khyáta*, *sadata*; *sadatana*. — 3. *sadantu*.

Middle. Pl. 2. *mucadhvam*. — 3. *sadantām* (AV.).

a- Aorist Participle.

a. There are hardly more than a dozen certain examples of the participle of this aorist.

Active. *tṛpánt*-, *dhṛṣánt*-, *riṣant*- or *rīṣant*-[9], *vṛdhánt*-, *śiṣánt*- (*śās*- 'order'), *śucánt*-, *sádant*-[10], *sánant*-[10]; and as first member of compounds: *kṛtánt*-, *guhánt*-, *vidánt*-[11].

Middle. *guhámāna*-, *dhṛṣámāṇa*-, *nṛtámāna*-, *śucámāna*-; possibly also *dásamāna*-[12]. Probably three participles in *-āna* are to be regarded as belonging to this aorist: *dhṛṣāṇá*- (AV.), *vṛdhāná*-, *sridhāná*-.

2. Reduplicated Aorist.

Delbrück, Verbum 143 f. — Avery, Verb-Inflection 266—268. — Whitney, Sanskrit Grammar 856—873; Roots 224; Atharvaveda, Index Verborum 380. — v. Negelein, Zur Sprachgeschichte 68 f.

513. This type of aorist is formed from nearly 90 verbs in the Saṃhitās. Though it has come to be associated with the secondary conjugation in *-áya* (causative), it is not in form (with a few slight exceptions) connected with that stem, being made directly from the root. It is, however, in sense **connected with the causative**, inasmuch as it has a causative meaning when the corresponding verb in *-aya* has that meaning. As an augmented reduplicated form, it has affinities with the imperfect of the reduplicating present class and with the pluperfect. It may, however, be distinguished from the imperfect by the long reduplicative vowel, by the thematic *-a-* which nearly always appears in the stem, and often by the meaning; and from the

1 Emendation in AV. XIX. 4[2] for *vide yám*; see Whitney's note.

2 A probable conjecture for *yame* in AV. XVIII. 2[3].

3 From *sā*- 'gain', as if *sa*- (*sa-īt*). Cp. v. Negelein 34.

4 With loss of the radical nasal, from √*sraṃs*-.

5 A transfer from the root aorist (otherwise *kṛdhi*). Avery 243 adds *gama*(?).

6 With accent on the root instead of the second syllable; always *sánā*: cp. RPr. VII. 14, 19, 33.

7 A transfer form from the root aorist (otherwise *kṛtám*).

8 A transfer form from the root aorist.

9 Once with the short, six times with the long vowel in the Saṃhitā text (Pp. always *i*): see APr. 583, 584, 588.

10 With accent on the root as also *rīṣant*- and *rīṣant*-.

11 In *kṛtád-vasu*- 'disclosing wealth', *guhád-avadya*- 'concealing faults', *vidád-vasu*- 'winning wealth'.

12 As occurring beside the *a*- aorist injunctive form *dasat* (510).

pluperfect by difference of reduplication when the root contains *a* or *ṛ*, and often by meaning.

a. The **characteristic feature** of this aorist is the almost invariable **quantitative sequence** of a **long** reduplicative and a **short** radical vowel (– ⏑). The vowels *ă*, *ṛ̆*, *ḷ*[1], as well as *ĭ*, are reduplicated with *i*[2], which (unless it becomes long by position) is lengthened if the radical vowel is (or is made) prosodically short; e. g. *á-jījan-a-t* from *jan-* 'beget'; *á-vīvṛdh-a-t* from *vṛdh-* 'grow', but *cikṣip-a-s* from *kṣip-* 'throw'.

In order to bring about this trochaic rhythm, the radical vowel has to be shortened or the nasal dropped in the roots *vāś-* 'bellow', *sādh-* 'succeed', *hīḍ-* 'be hostile', *krand-* 'cry out', *jambh-* 'crush', *randh-* 'subject', *syand-* 'flow', *sraṃs-* 'fall'; e. g. *avīvaśat*, *acikradat*. In *jīhvaratam* (TS.) the reduplicative vowel, being already long by position, is unnecessarily lengthened.

1. In a few forms the reduplicative vowel is, contrary to the prevailing rhythmic rule, left short: *jigṛtám* and *jigṛtá* (beside *ájīgar*); *didhṛtam* and *ririṣas* (beside *rīriṣas*). On the other hand, in the isolated injunctive form *didīpas*[3], the radical vowel remains long, and in *ámīmet* both the reduplicative and the radical syllable are long (beside *mīmayat* with the regular rhythm).

2. The *p* of the causative stems *jñā-paya-*, *sthā-paya-*, *hā-paya*, *ar-paya-* (*ṛ-* 'go'), is retained in the aorist, the radical vowel being at the same time reduced to *i* in the first three: *ajijñipat* (TS.), *átiṣṭhipat*, *jīhipas*; the *ṣ* of the causative stem *bhīṣaya-* is also retained: *bībhiṣ-as* (TS.).

3. The root *dyut-* 'shine', reduplicates with *i*: *adidyutat*[4]. In the aorist formed from the causative stem *arpaya-*, the reduplicative *i* appears after, instead of before, the radical vowel, doubtless owing to the difficulty caused by the initial *a* and the augment: *arp-i-p-am* (AV.). The initial *a* also led to the anomaly of reduplicating the whole of the root *am* 'injure', and then prefixing the augment: *ām-am-at*.

4. There are three anomalous aorists formed from *naś-* 'be lost', *pat-* 'fall', and *vac-* 'speak', in which besides an irregular reduplicative vowel, the radical *a* is syncopated (*a-pap-t-at*, *á-ne-ś-an*) or contracted (*á-voc-at*). As beside the former two the regular reduplicated aorists *apīpatat* and *anīnaśat* occur, and as all three have the regular reduplicative vowel *a* of the perfect[5], they appear to have been originally pluperfects which before being shortened had the form of **á-papat-at*[6], **á-nanaś-at*, **á-vavac-at*[7]. But they all came to be regarded as aorists. This is undoubted in the case of *ávocat* owing to its numerous mood forms; *ápaptat*, moreover, has an imperative form beside it; and *áneśan* (TS VS.) has a distinctly aoristic meaning.

b. The reduplicated aorist in the **great majority** of forms makes its stems **with a thematic -*a*-**. Before this, a final *ṛ* regularly, and *ī* and *u* in two or three forms, take Guṇa; e. g. *adīdhar-a-t* (√*dhṛ-*), *bībhay-a-t* (√*bhī-*), *cucyav-a-t* (√*cyu-*), *dudráv-a-t* (√*dru-*). The inflexion of this aorist stem is like that of an imperfect of the *a-* conjugation.

c. About a **dozen roots**, however, have occasional forms from stems made **without thematic -*a*-**, the inflexion then being like that of an imperfect of the reduplicating class. These roots are *mā-* 'bellow'; *śri-* 'resort'; *tu-* 'be strong', *dru-* 'run', *dhū-* 'shake', *nu-* 'praise', *pū-* 'cleanse', *yu-* 'separate',

---

1 In √*kḷp-*, the only root in which it occurs.

2 In the reduplicating present class *ṛ̆* is almost invariably, and *ă* predominantly, reduplicated with *i* (457).

3 In form this might be a pluperfect. A similar reversal of the ordinary rhythm appears in the three forms *átatamsatam* (I. 120[7]), *adadhāvat* (IX. 877), *vavákṣat* (SV. I. 1, 2, 2, 3 var. lect. for *vavákṣa* of RV. X. 115[1]) each occurring once, but owing to the reduplicative vowel they should rather be accounted pluperfects. Cp. p. 364, note [15].

4 See 514, note [1].

5 That is, *neś-* for *nanaś-*, on the analogy of *sed-* for **sazd-* in the perfect: this form of contraction would be unique in an original aorist.

6 Like *a-sasvaj-at*; becoming *a-papt-at* like *a-cakr-at* beside *cakar-am*.

7 The cause of the anomalous contraction may be due to the awkwardness of combining the augment with the reduced reduplicative syllable *u-* of the perfect (**a-uvac-at*). The accentuation of the augment would also favour the second syllable taking Samprasāraṇa: *á-va-uc-at*.

sū- 'generate', *sru-* 'flow'; *gṛ-* 'waken', *dhṛ-* 'hold'; *svap-* 'sleep'; e. g. *aśiśre-t* (TS.), *ádudro-t*, *ájīgar*, *siṣvap*. Beside forms made thus, occur others made from several of these roots with the thematic *-a-*; and those made from the roots ending in *ŭ* (the majority), cannot be distinguished in form from pluperfects. The number of forms of this type which can with certainty be classed as aorists is therefore very small.

d. Besides the indicative all the moods are represented in this aorist, but **no participial form** has been found.

Reduplicated Aorist Indicative.

514. The forms actually occurring would, if made from *jan-* 'beget' with thematic *-a-*, be the following:

Active. Sing. 1. *ájījanam.* 2. *ájījanas.* 3. *ájījanat.* — Du. 2. *ajījanatam.* — Pl. 1. *ájījanāma.* 2. *ájījanata.* 3. *ájījanan.*

Middle. Sing. 3. *ájījanata.* — Pl. 2. *ájījanadhvam.* 3. *ájījananta.*

The forms actually occurring (including those made without thematic *-a-*) are:

Active. Sing. 1. *acīkṛṣam*, *ajīgamam* (TS. VS. AV.), *ajījabham* (AV.), *atiṣṭhipam* (AV.), *adūduṣam* (AV.), *anīnaśam*, *apīparam* (*pṛ-* 'pass', AV.), *ámīmadam* (AV.), *avocam*, *áśīśamam* (*śam-* 'be quiet', AV.); *arpipam* (AV.),

2. *acikradas*, *ájījanas*, *átiṣṭhipas*, *átītaras* (AV.), *atītṛpas* (AV.), *anīnaśas* ('be lost', AV.), *apīparas* (AV.), *abūbhuvas* (AV.), *ámīmadas* (AV.), *arūrupas* (AV.), *ávīvṛdhas* (AV.), *áśīśamas* (AV.); *jihvaras* (AV.), *didyutas*[1], *rūrupas* (AV.), *śūśucas* (TS. IV. 1. 4^3), *siṣvapas.* — **Without thematic *-a-*:** *tūtos*[2], *susros*; *ajīgar*[3] (*gṛ-* 'swallow'), *ájīgar* (*gṛ-* 'waken'); *dīdhar*, *siṣvap.*

3. *acikradat*, *acīkḷpat* (AV.), *acīcarat* (AV.), *ácukrudhat*, *acucyavat*[4] (K.), *ajijñipat* (TS. II. 1. 11^3), *ájījanat*, *ájīhiḍat* (AV.), *átiṣṭhipat*, *ádidyutat*[1], *adīdharat*, *adūduṣat*, *ánīnaśat*, *ápaptat* and *ápīpatat*, *abūbudhat*, *amūmuhat* (AV.), *árīramat*, *árūrucat*, *avīvaśat* ('has bellowed', √*vāś-*), *avīvipat*, *avīvṛtat*, *ávīvṛdhat*, *ávocat*, *aśiśriyat*[5] (AV.), *áśiśvitat*, *áśīśamat* (AV.), *asiṣyadat* (√*syand-*); *āmamat* (√*am-*); *jījanat*, *didyutat* (VS. XXXVIII. 22), *dīdharat*, *dudrávat*, *néśat*[6], *bībhayat*, *vavṛtat*, *vócat*, *śiśnáthat.* — **Without thematic *-a-*:** *ádudrot*, *ánūnot*, *ápupot*, *ámīmet*[7] (*mā-* 'bellow'), *áśiśret*[8], *asuṣot* (√*sū-*, MS.), *ásusrot* (VS. XVIII. 58; TS. V. 7. 7^1); *tūtot*, *dūdhot* (*dhū-* 'shake'); *ájīgar* (*gṛ-* 'waken'), *aśiśnat* (√*śnath-*); *dīdhar.* — **Du. 2.** *árūrujatam* (Kh. I. 5^{10}).

Pl. 1. *átītṛpāma* (VS. VII. 29), *atītṛṣāma*, *apaptāma* (Kh. III. 19), *apīpadāma* (AV.), *ávīvṛtāma* (AV.), *ávocāma.*

2. *ájījapata*[9] (VS. IX. 12), *arūrucata* (VS. XXXVII. 15).

3. *ácikradan*, *ájījanan*, *atitrasan* (AV.), *adīdharan* (AV.), *anīnaśan* (AV.), *ánešan* (VS. XVI. 10; TS. IV. 5. 1^4),), *apaptan*, *apīparan* (*pṛ-* 'cross'), *ámīmṛṇan* (AV.), *ávīvatan*, *avīvaran* (AV.), *avīvaśan* (*vāś-* 'bellow'), *avīvipan*, *ávīvṛdhan*, *ávocan*, *áśīśaman* (AV.), *áśūśubhan*, *asisrasan* (√*sraṃs-*, AV.), *asīṣadan* (√*sad-*, VS. XII. 54; TS. IV. 2. 4^4); *jījanan*, *paptan.*

---

[1] Reduplicated with *i* owing to the vocalic pronunciation of the *y* (*diut-*) as in the perfect: see 482 a 1.

[2] Classed by Whitney, Sanskrit Grammar 868 a, as an aorist, but Roots 63, as pluperfect; similarly *tūtot* below.

[3] Occurring only in RV. I. 163^7 = VS. XXIX. 18 = TS. IV. 6. 7^3.

[4] Whitney 866 (Mantra?).

[5] This form occurs only once (AV. VI. 31^3), as a variant for *dhīyate* in RV. X. 189^3 (= SV.) and for *śiśriye* in TS. I. 5. 3^1. See Whitney's note on AV. VI. 31^3.

[6] This form occurs once in the RV. (VI. 1^{17}) as a past tense (along with three other unaugmented forms: *rócata, arta, tiṣṭhat*) and twice as an injunctive. Bartholomae, KZ. 27, 360, note [1], regards it as a pluperfect.

[7] Whitney 868 a; v. Negelein 69^1.

[8] Occurs TS. I. 8. 10^2 with other aorists.

[9] From the causative stem *jāpaya-* of *ji-* 'conquer'.

Middle. Sing. 3. *ávīvarata* (*vṛ-* 'cover', AV.; TS. v. 6. 1[3]). — **With ending** *-i* for *-ta*: *atītape*.

Pl. 2. *ávīvṛdhadhvam*. — 3. *átītṛpanta* (VS. xix. 36), *ábībhayanta*, *ámīmadanta*, *ávīvaśanta* (√*vāś-*), *ávīvṛdhanta*, *ávocanta*, *ásiṣyadanta* (√*syand-*), *ásūṣudanta* (TS. i. 8. 10[2]); *jījananta*.

Reduplicated Aorist Subjunctive.

515. This mood is of rare occurrence, only about a dozen forms having been noted. The active is represented in all the persons of the sing. and the 1. pl. only; the middle by a single dual form.

Active. Sing. 1. *rāradhā*, *vocā*. — 2. *tītapāsi* (AV.), *vocāsi* (VS. xxiii. 51). — 3. *cīklpāti*, *pispṛśati*[1], *vócati*[2], *vocāti*, *sīṣadhāti*[3] (√*sādh-*).

Pl. 1. *cukrudhāma*, *rīramāma*, *vocāma*, *sīṣadhāma* (√*sādh-*).

Middle. Du. 1. *vocāvahai*.

Reduplicated Aorist Injunctive.

516. Forms of this mood are of common occurrence in the active, in which voice more than fifty have been found; but in the middle only five have been noted.

Active. Sing. 1. *cukrudham*, *jījanam*, *dīdharam*, *vocam*.

2. *cikradas*, *cikṣipas*, *jihvaras*, *jīhipas* (caus. *hā-paya-*), *tītṛṣas* (TS. iii. 2. 5[3]), *didīpas*, *didyutas*, *dīdharas*, *nīnamas*, *nīnaśas*, *paptas*, *pispṛśas*, *pīparas* (*pṛ-* 'cross'), *bībhiṣas* (TS. iii. 2. 5[2]), *mīmṛṣas*, *rīradhas*, *rīriṣas*, *vīvijas*, *vocas*, *śiśnathas*, *śiśráthas*, *śūśucas* (AV.), *sīṣadhas* (√*sādh-*).

3. *cucyavat*, *tiṣṭhipat*, *dīdharat*, *dudravat*, *dūduṣat*, *neśat*, *paptat* (AV.), *pīparat* (*pṛ-* 'cross', RV[1].) and *pīpárat* (*pṛ-* 'cross', RV[1]. = TS. i. 6. 12[3]), *pīparat* (*pṛ-* 'fill'), *mīmayat*[4], *rīradhat* (√*randh-*), *rīriṣat*, *vocat*, *śiśrathat*, *siṣvadat* (√*svād-*). — **Without thematic** *-a-*: *nūnot* (*nu-* 'praise'), *yūyot* (*yu-* 'separate'), *susrot*.

Du. 2. *jihvaratam*[5] (VS. v. 17) and *jīhvaratam*[5] (TS. i. 2. 13[2]), *rīradhatam*[5].

Pl. 2. *rīradhata*[5], *rīriṣata*[5] (i. 89[9] = VS. xxv. 22).

3. *cikṣipan* (AV.), *paptan*, *rīraman*, *vocan*, *śūśucan* (VS. xxxv. 8).

Middle. Sing. 1. *vóce*. — 2. *bībhiṣathās*[6].

Pl. 3. *jījananta*, *vócanta*, *sīṣapanta* (*sap-* 'serve').

Reduplicated Aorist Optative.

517. The forms of this mood are rare, numbering altogether (including a precative) not more than a dozen. The majority of these come from *vac-* 'speak', and the rest from two other roots, *cyu-* 'stir' and *riṣ-* 'hurt'.

Active. Sing. 1. *vocéyam*. — 2. *ririṣes*, *vocés*. — 3. *vocet* (AV.).

Du. 2. *vocetam*. — **Pl.** 1. *vocéma*[7]. — 3. *vocéyur*.

Middle. Sing. 1. *voceya*. — **Pl.** 1. *cucyuvīmáhi*[8], *vocemahi*. — 3. *cucyavīrata*[8], There is also the **precative sing.** 3. *rīriṣ-ī-ṣ-ṭa*[9] (vi. 51[7]) or *ririṣ-ī-ṣ-ṭa* (viii. 18[13]).

---

1 As if from an indicative 3. sing. **apispṛk*.

2 Like an indicative present in form.

3 These forms refute the statement of HIRT, IF. 12, 214 f., that the reduplicated, as well as the root and *a-* aorist, has no subjunctive, but only injunctive forms. Cp. 502, 509.

4 This form seems to have an injunctive sense in RV. x. 27[22], its only occurrence.

5 Reckoned here an injunctive form (not imperative) because accompanied by *mā́*: cp. DELBRÜCK, Altindische Syntax p. 361[1].

6 Formed from the causative stem *bhīṣáya-* of *bhī-* 'fear'.

7 This form occurs six times in the RV., three times unaccented and three times accented *vocéma*. AVERY 268 wrongly states *vocéma* to occur five times and *vócema* (sic) once.

8 Without thematic *-a-*.

9 In the Pada text *ririṣīṣṭa*.

Reduplicated Aorist Imperative.

518. Forms of this mood are rare, numbering hardly more than a dozen. They occur in the active only.

Active. Sing. 2. *vocatāt.* — **3.** *vocatu.* — **Du. 2.** *jigṛtám* (*gṛ-* 'waken'), *didhṛtam*, *vocatam.* — **Pl. 2.** *jigṛtá*, *didhṛtá*, *paptata*[1] (I. 88[1]), *vocata*, *suṣūdáta* (AV. I. 26[4])[2]. — **3.** *pūpurantu* (*pṛ-* 'fill'), *śiśrathantu.*

3. Sigmatic Aorist.

519. The general tense sign of this aorist is an *s* added to the root. This *s* in the vast majority of verbs (more than 200) comes immediately before the endings. When such is the case, the stem may be formed in three different ways: the *s* being added **1.** direct to the root, e. g. *a-jai-ṣ-am* (*ji-* 'conquer'); **2.** with a connecting *-i-*, e. g. *a-kram-i-ṣ-am* (*kram-* 'stride'); **3.** with an additional *s-* prefixed to the connecting *-i-*, e. g. *a-yā-s-i-ṣ-am* (*yā-* 'go'). The inflexion of these three varieties (A) follows that of the graded conjugation. In a small number of verbs the stem is formed by adding *-s* extended with a thematic *a*; e. g. *á-ruk-ṣa-t* (*ruh-* 'mount'). The inflexion of this fourth form (B) of the sigmatic aorist is like that of an imperfect of the *a-* conjugation.

Of the four varieties of the sigmatic aorist, the first two, the *s-* aorist and the *iṣ-* aorist, are very common, each being formed by nearly 100 roots. The other two are rare, the *siṣ-* aorist being made from only six, and the *sa-* aorist from only nine roots.

A. 1. The *s-* aorist.

DELBRÜCK, Verbum 177—179. — AVERY. Verb-Inflection 257—259. — WHITNEY, Sanskrit Grammar 878—897; Roots 225—226; Atharvaveda, Index Verborum 380. — v. NEGELEIN, Zur Sprachgeschichte 83—84.

520. In this form of the sigmatic aorist, the radical vowel as a rule takes **Vṛddhi** (*a* being lengthened) **in the active.** In the middle, on the other hand, excepting final *ī̆* and *u* (which take Guṇa), the radical vowel remains unchanged. Thus in the active there occur the forms 1. sing. *a-jai-ṣam* (√*ji-*), *a-bhār-ṣam* (√*bhṛ-*), 3. sing. *á-raik* (√*ric-*), 3. pl. *á-cchānt-sur* (√*chand-*); while in the middle we find 1. sing. *a-vit-si* (√*vid-*), *á-bhut-si* (√*budh-*), *a-sṛk-ṣi* (√*sṛj-*), *a-nū-ṣi* (*nū-* 'praise'), beside forms with Guṇa from roots ending in *ī̆* or *u* such as 3. pl. *a-he-ṣ-ata* (√*hi-*), *a-ne-ṣ-ata* (√*nī-*), 1. sing. *a-sto-ṣi* (√*stu-*).

a. There are, however, some irregularities. **1.** In a few active injunctive forms Guṇa appears instead of Vṛddhi, e. g. sing. 2. *je-s* (√*ji-*), pl. 1. *jé-ṣma.* — **2.** In two or three middle forms of *sah-* 'overcome', the *a* is lengthened, e. g. sing. 1. *sāk-ṣi*[3]. — **3.** The root is shortened in a few middle forms; thus the *ā* of *dā-* 'cut', is reduced to *i* in sing. 1. opt. *di-ṣ-īya*, and the nasal of *gam-* 'go' and *man-* 'think' is dropped in the forms *a-ga-smahi* and *ma-sīya.* — **4.** After a consonant other than *n m r*, the tense sign *s* is dropped before *t*, *th*, and *dh*; thus *á-bhak-ta* beside *á-bhak-ṣ-i* (√*bhaj-*); *pat-thās* (AV.) beside *pat-s-i* (√*pad-*, AV.); *á-sto-ḍhvam*[4] (√*stu-*), where the *s* on becoming *ẓ* cerebralized the following dental before disappearing (**á-sto-ẓ-dhvam*).

In addition to the indicative, all the moods of this form of the aorist occur. There is also a participle, but it is rare.

[1] An imperative form like this justifies the classification of *ápaptat* etc. as an actual aorist, apart from its possible origin as a pluperfect.

[2] Pada text *susūdáta*. It is perhaps better to class this form here (cp. WHITNEY, Sanskrit Grammar 871) than as a transfer form of the perfect imperative from √*sūd-* (Roots 188), though the reduplicative vowel is short. Cp. p. 362, note 9.

[3] Also in the active subjunctive form *sākṣāma*, where the *a* would normally remain short, as the radical vowel in this mood takes Guṇa only.

[4] The only example in this aorist of the ending *-dhvam.*

Indicative.

521. The only point in which the inflexion differs from that of the imperfect of the graded conjugation is that the 3. pl. active invariably ends in *-ur*.

a. The following peculiarities and irregularities are moreover to be noted. 1. In the active: in the RV.[1] the endings *-s* and *-t* of the 2. 3. sing. disappear, and the tense sign also, unless the root ends in a vowel; e. g. *a-hār* (AV.), 3. sing. from √*hṛ-*, = **a-hār-s-t*, but *a-hā-s*, 3. sing. from *hā-* 'leave' = **a-hā-s-t*. The AV. and TS., however, less often than not, insert a connecting *-ī-* before these endings, thus preserving both the latter and the *s* of the tense stem; e. g. *a-naik-ṣ-ī-t* (√*nij-*, AV.), *a-tāṃ-s-ī-t* (√*tan-*, TS.). In four forms in which the *-ī-* is not inserted, the *-s* and *-t*, as distinctive of the 2. and 3. persons, abnormally take the place of the *-s* of the stem or the final consonant of the root: *a-śrai-t* (AV.) for **a-śrai-s-t* (√*śri-*); *á-hai-t* (AV.) for **á-hai-s-t* (√*hi-*); *a-vā-t* (AV. VIII. 1[21]) for **a-vās-t*[2] (*vas-* 'shine'); 2. sing. *srā-s* (AV.) for **srāj-s-s*[3] (√*sṛj-*). The RV. also has *a-yā-s* for **a-yāj-s-s* (*yaj-* 'sacrifice') beside the phonetically regular form in the 3. sing. *a-yāṭ* for **a-yāj-s-t*. — 2. In the middle nine first and one or two third persons singular appear in which the stem is made with the addition of *-s*, but which have both the ending and the meaning of the present; and the *-s* is added to a present stem and not to the aorist form of the root. Thus formed are from a present stem of 1. the *a-* class: *arca-s-e* 'I praise', *yaja-s-e* 'I worship' (VIII. 25[1]); 2. the *á-* class, nasalized: *ṛñja-s-e*[4] 'I strive after'; 3. the *ya-* class: *gāy-i-ṣe*[5] 'I sing'; 4. the *nā-* class: *gṛṇī-ṣ-é*[6] 'I praise'; *punī-ṣ-é* 'I purify'; 5. the root class: *kṛ-ṣ-e* 'I make', *hi-ṣ-e* 'I impel', *stu-ṣ-é*[7] 'I praise'[8]; 6. the intensive: *cárkṛ-ṣ-e* which (like *stuṣé*[9] in I. 122[7]) is a 3. sing. with a passive sense: 'is praised'.

522. The forms of the indicative actually occurring would, if made from *bhṛ-* 'bear' in the active and *stu-* 'praise' in the middle, be as follows:

Active. Sing. 1. *ábhārṣam*. 2. *ábhār*, *abhārṣīs* (AV.). 3. *ábhār*; *abhārṣīt* (AV. TS.). — Du. 2. *ábhārṣṭam*. 3. *abhārṣṭām*. — Pl. 1. *ábhārṣma*. 2. *ábhārṣṭa*. 3. *ábhārṣur*.

Middle. Sing. 1. *ástoṣi*. 2. *ástoṣṭhās*. 3. *ástoṣṭa*. — Du. 3. *ástoṣātām*. — Pl. 1. *ástoṣmahi*. 2. *ástoḍhvam*. 3. *ástoṣata*.

The forms which actually occur are the following:

Active. Sing. 1. *akārṣam* (AV.), *ajaiṣam* (√*ji-*), *áprākṣam* (√*prach-*, AV.), *abhārṣam*, *áyāṃsam* (√*yam-*), *ayāsam*, *áspārṣam* (*spṛ-* 'win'), *áhārṣam* (√*hṛ-*).

2. *akrān* (√*krand-*), *aghās*[10] (√*ghas-*, AV. XX. 129[16]), *áhās* (*hā-* 'leave', AV. II. 10[7]). — **With irregular *-s*:** *ayās* (√*yaj-*), *srās* (√*sṛj-*, AV.). — **With connecting *-ī-*:** *arātsīs* (*rādh-* 'succeed', AV.), *avātsīs*[11] (*vas-* 'dwell', AV.); *bhaiṣīs* (AV.).

3. With loss of the ending *-t*: *ajais*[12] (√*ji-*), *aprās* (√*prā-*), *ahās* (*hā-* 'leave'). — With loss of both tense sign and ending: *ákrān*[13] (√*krand-*), *ákṣār* (√*kṣar-*), *acait* (√*cit-*), *acchān* (√*chand-*), *atān* (√*tan-*), *atsār* (√*tsar-*), *ádyaut* (√*dyut-*), *adhāk* (√*dah-*), *aprāk* (*pṛc-* 'mix', AV.), *aprāṭ* (√*prach-*), *abhār*, *ayāṭ* (√*yaj-*), *áyān* (√*yam-*), *araut*[14] (√*rudh-*, AV.), *ávāṭ* (√*vah-*), *avāt*[15] (*vas-* 'shine', AV.), *aśvait* (√*śvit-*), *asyān* (√*syand-*), *ásrāk* (√*sṛj-*), *ásvār* (√*svar-*), *ahār* (√*hṛ-*, AV.); *áraik* (√*ric-*); *dyaut*, *vāṭ* (√*vah-*). —

[1] and the Kāṭhaka, WHITNEY 888.

[2] In *avāt* the *t* may, however, represent the final *s* of the root, the form possibly standing for **a-vāt-s-t*; see above 44 a 2, and WHITNEY, Sanskrit Grammar 167.

[3] The phonetically regular form would be **srāk*. Cp. p. 61 (middle).

[4] Also the participle *ṛñjas-āná-*.

[5] From *gāya-*, with *-i-* for *-a-*.

[6] From the weak stem.

[7] These three forms seem to represent the transition of aorist stems to employment as present stems.

[8] The form *stuṣé* is frequent as a 1. sing.; in one passage (I. 122[7]), however, it appears to be a 3. sing. with a passive sense: 'is praised'.

[9] On *stuṣé* in general, see OLDENBERG, ZDMG. 59, 355 ff., NEISSER, BB. 30, 315—325.

[10] Cp. above 499, *ághas* sing. 2. 3.

[11] Cp. v. NEGELEIN 83, note 5; above 44, a 1.

[12] For **ajais-t*.

[13] For **ákrānd-s-t*.

[14] For **araudh-s-t*.

[15] Cp. *avāt-s-ī-s* (AV.) from *vas-* 'dwell'. Cp. note 2 and p. 36 (top).

With irregular *-ī*: *aśrait* (√*śri-*, AV.), *áhait* (√*hi-*, AV.). — With connecting *-ī-*: *atāṃsīt* (√*tan-*, TS. IV. 7. 13[5]; VS. XV. 53), *anaikṣīt* (√*nij-*, AV.); *rautsīt* (√*rudh-*, Kh. IV. 7[5]).

Du. 2. *ásrāṣṭam*[1] (√*sṛj-*, AV.). — **3.** *abhārṣṭām* (VS. XXVIII. 17), *asvārṣṭām* (√*svar-*).

Pl. 1. *ájaiṣma*, *ábhaiṣma*. — **2.** *ácchānta*[2] (√*chand-*), *anaiṣṭa* (TS. V. 7. 2[4]). — **3.** *ácchāntsur*, *ábhaiṣur*, *amatsur* (√*mad-*), *ayāsur*, *ávākṣur* (√*vah-*, AV.)[3].

Middle. Sing. 1. *ádikṣi* (√*diś-*), *ádiṣi*[4] (*dā-* 'give', AV.), *anūṣi* (√*nū-*), *ábhakṣi* (√*bhaj-*), *ábhutsi* (√*budh-*), *ámāsi* (*mā-* 'measure', AV.), *ámukṣi* (√*muc-*, AV.), *avitsi* (*vid-* 'find'), *asākṣi*[5] (√*sah-*), *asṛkṣi*, *astoṣi*; *maṃsi* (√*man-*), *vṛkṣi*[6] (√*vṛj-*, AV.), *sākṣi*[5].

2. *ájñāsthās* (AV.), *átapthās*[7] (AV. IX. 5[6]), *apṛkthās* (√*pṛc-*, AV.), *ámukthās* (√*muc-*, AV.).

3. *apṛkta* (√*pṛc-*), *ábhakta* (√*bhaj-*), *ámaṃsta* (VS. V. 40), *amatta* (√*mad-*), *ayaṃsta* (√*yam-*), *ayaṣṭa* (√*yaj-*), *áraṃsta* (√*ram-*), *árabdha* (√*rabh-*), *asakta* (√*saj-*), *ásṛṣṭa* (√*sṛj-*), *astoṣṭa*.

Du. 3. *anūṣātām*, *amaṃsātām* (VS. XXXVIII. 13), *áyukṣātām* (√*yuj-*).

Pl. 1. *agasmahi*[8] (√*gam-*), *apṛkṣmahi* (√*pṛc-*, AV.), *abhutsmahi* (√*budh-*), *ávikṣmahi* (√*viś-*), *asṛkṣmahi* (√*sṛj-*, TS. I. 4. 45[3]; VS. XX. 22).

2. *ástoḍhvam* (for **á-stoṣ-dhvam* from *stu-* 'praise').

3. *akraṃsata* (AV.), *ádṛkṣata* (√*dṛś-*), *ádhukṣata* (√*duh-*), *ádhūrṣata*[9] (*dhvṛ-* 'injure'), *adhūṣata*, *ánūṣata*, *aneṣata* (√*nī-*), *ábhutsata* (√*budh-*), *amaṃsata* (√*man-*), *amatsata* (√*mad-*), *ayaṃsata* (√*yam-*), *ayukṣata* (√*yuj-*), *araṃsata* (AV.), *árāsata*, *alipsata*, *ávikṣata* (√*viś-*), *avṛtsata* (√*vṛt-*), *avṛṣata* (*vṛ-* 'choose', AV. III. 3[5]), *asakṣata* (*sac-* 'accompany'), *ásṛkṣata* (√*sṛj-*), *ástoṣata*, *ahāsata*, *ahūṣata* (*hū-* 'call'), *ahṛṣata* (√*hṛ-*), *aheṣata* (√*hi-*).

s- Aorist Subjunctive.

523. This mood is quite common in the RV., but decidedly less so in the other Saṃhitās. Its forms are, however, frequent only in the active, in which all persons are represented except the 1. du. The middle is much less common, about 20 forms occurring altogether; only one of these is found in the dual, and two in the plural. The root regularly takes Guṇa throughout before the tense sign[10], in the middle as well as the active. The primary endings are frequent, being used almost exclusively[11] in the du. and the 2. pl.

In the middle 3. sing. and pl. the exceptional ending *-tai* occurs in two forms in later Saṃhitās (AV. TS.).

Active. Sing. 1. *stoṣāṇi*. — **2.** *darṣasi* (*dṛ-* 'split'); *jéṣas* (√*ji-*), *vákṣas* (√*vah-*). — **3.** *neṣati* (√*nī-*(, *parṣati* (*pṛ-* 'take across'), *pāsati* ('protect'), *matsati* (√*mad-*), *yoṣati* (*yu-* 'separate'), *vakṣati* (√*vah-*), *sakṣati* (√*sah-*, AV.); *ákṣat* (*aś-* 'attain', X. 11[7]), *kṣeṣat* (*kṣi-* 'dwell'), *chantsat* (√*chand-*), *jéṣat* (√*ji-*), *dárṣat* (*dṛ-* 'split'), *dāsat* (*dā-* 'give'), *drāsat*

1 Emendation for *ásrāṣṭram* of the Mss., AV. IV. 28[4]; see Whitney's note.

2 For **acchānt-s-ta*.

3 Avery 257 adds the form *aveṣan*, which occurs twice in the RV., regarding it doubtless as an *s-* aorist of √*vī-*. It would as such have the double anomaly of absence of Vṛddhi and the ending *-an*. It is probably 3. pl. impf. of √*viṣ-* in both passages (I. 170[2]; X. 114[1]). Grassmann in X. 114[1] regards it as aorist of √*vī-*.

4 Cp. v. Negelein 834.

5 With anomalous long vowel.

6 See Whitney's note on AV. VI. 30[2].

7 For **á-tap-s-thās*.

8 With loss of the radical nasal (*a* taking the place of the sonant nasal).

9 With interchange of the radical vowel and semivowel: see 50, b.

10 The *a* of *sah* is lengthened in the forms *sákṣāma* and *sākṣate*.

11 Excepting only the 3. du. act. *yakṣatām*.

(*drā-* 'run'), *nakṣat* (*naś-* 'reach'), *néṣat* (√*nī-*), *pákṣat* (√*pac-*), *párṣat* ('take across'), *préṣat* (√*prī-*), *bhakṣat* (√*bhaj-*), *bharṣat* (√*bhṛ-*), *mátsat* (√*mad-*), *yáṃsat* (√*yam-*), *yákṣat* (√*yaj-*), *yāsat*, *yóṣat* (*yu-* 'separate'), *rā́sat*, *váṃsat* (√*van-*), *vákṣat* (√*vah-*), *valṣat* (Kh. v. 15[16]), *véṣat*[1] (√*vī-*)[2], *sakṣat* (*sac-* 'accompany'[3] and *sah-* 'overcome'[4]), *satsat* (√*sad-*), *sarṣat* (√*sṛ-*, AV.), *stoṣat*, *srakṣat* (√*sṛj-*, VS. XXI. 46).

Du. 2. *dā́sathas*, *dhāsathas*, *párṣathas* (*pṛ-* 'take across'), *vákṣathas* (√*vah-*, AV.), *varṣathas* (*vṛ-* 'cover').

3. *pāsatas* ('protect'), *yaṃsatas* (√*yam-*), *yakṣatas* (√*yaj-*), *yoṣatas* (*yu-* 'separate', AV.), *vakṣatas* (√*vah-*). — **With -tām:** *yakṣatām* (√*yaj-*).

Pl. 1. *jéṣāma* (√*ji-*), *váṃsāma* (√*van-*), *sā́kṣāma*[5] (√*sah-*), *stoṣāma*. — 2. *dhāsatha*, *neṣatha*, *párṣatha* ('take across'), *mátsatha*. — 3. *parṣan* ('take across'), *yaṃsan* (√*yam-*), *rā́san*, *vákṣan*, *śéṣan* (*śī-* 'lie').

Middle. Sing. 1. *naṃsai*, *máṃsai* (√*man-*). — 2. *dṛ́kṣase*[6], *pṛkṣase*[6] (√*pṛc-*), *maṃsase* (√*man-*). — 3. *kraṃsate*, *trāsate*, *darṣate* (*dṛ-* 'split'), *máṃsate* (√*man-*), *yaṃsate* (√*yam-*), *yakṣate* (√*yaj-*), *rāsate*, *vaṃsate* (√*van-*), *sākṣate*[5] (√*sah-*)[7]. — **With ending -tai:** *mā́sātai* (AV.).

Du. 2. *trā́sāthe* (for **trā́saithe*). — **Pl. 3.** *náṃsante* (√*nam-*), *máṃsante* (√*man-*). — **With ending -tai:** *maṃsatai*[8] (TS. VII. 4. 15[1]).

s- Aorist Injunctive.

524. Injunctive forms are of fairly common occurrence, especially after *mā́*. Judged by the extremely few accented forms occurring, the accent was on the radical syllable. All the forms occurring in the 1. sing. act. are irregular in one way or another: nearly all of them take Guṇa instead of Vṛddhi, while *yūṣam* (AV.) only lengthens the radical vowel (*yu-* 'separate'). Three first persons from roots in *-ā* substitute *e*[9] for that vowel, as *yeṣam* from *yā-* 'go'; the same substitution takes place in the 1. pl. *geṣma* (AV.), *deṣma* (VS.), and 3. pl. *stheṣur* (AV.).

Active. Sing. 1. *jeṣam*[10] (√*ji-*, VS. IX. 13 etc.), *yūṣam* (*yu-* 'separate', AV.), *stoṣam*[10]; from roots ending in *-ā*: *geṣam* (*gā-* 'go', VS. V. 5), *yeṣam* (*yā-* 'go'), *stheṣam*[9] (*sthā-* 'stand', VS. II. 8).

2. *jes*[10]; *bhāk* (√*bhaj-*), *yāṭ* (√*yaj-*), *yaus* (*yu-* 'separate'), *hvār* (√*hvar-*, VS. I. 2). — **With connecting -ī-:** *hāsīs* (Kh. IV. 8[5]; AA. II. 7).

3. *dhāk* (√*dah-*), *bhāk* (√*bhaj-*), *bhār* (√*bhṛ-*), *mauk* (√*muc-*, VS. I. 25), *hās*[11] (*hā-* 'leave'). — **With connecting -ī-:** *tāpsīt* (VS. XIII. 30), *vākṣīt* (√*vah-*, AV.), *hāsīt* (TS. VII. 3. 13[1]; AV.), *hvārṣīt* (√*hvar-*, VS. I. 2).

Du. 2. *tāptam* (√*tap-*, VS. V. 33), *yauṣṭam* (*yu-* 'separate'), *srāṣṭam* (√*sṛj-*, AV.).

---

1 As appearing in immediate juxtaposition with *préṣat* (I. 180[6]), this form appears to be an aorist subjunctive of *vī-*, not a present injunctive of √*viṣ-* (*véṣati*).

2 AVERY 258 gives *śiṣat*, among these forms, as occurring once. He doubtless means *ni-śiṣat* (IV. 2[7]) which occurs beside the subjunctives *bhárāt* and *udīrat*. But it cannot be an *s-* aorist (which would be *śikṣat*). WHITNEY, Roots, takes it as an *a-* aorist of *śiṣ-* 'leave', GRASSMANN, Wörterbuch 1392, as an aorist of *śās-*. Cp. above 510.

3 In I. 129[10] ('accompany').

4 In V. 30[6] ('conquer').

5 With lengthened radical vowel.

6 Weak radical vowel instead of Guṇa.

7 AVERY 258 adds *hāsate*, also WHITNEY, Grammar 893 a; but this form is doubtless a 3. sing. mid. pres. of *hās-* 'hasten', a secondary form of *hā-* 'leave' according to the *a-* class; also *hāsante* (AV. IV. 36[5]). Cp. p. 321, note 7.

8 See WEBER's ed. of the TS., p. 310, 15, note 12.

9 Made perhaps from an *i-* form of roots ending in *-ā*. Cp. WHITNEY, Grammar 894 c.

10 Formed perhaps under the influence of the subjunctives *jéṣat* and *stoṣat*.

11 Unnecessarily regarded by DELBRÜCK, Verbum p. 60 (80) as from *hṛ-* 'take'.

Pl. 1. *yauṣma* (*yu-* 'separate', VS. IV. 22). — **With Guṇa only:** *geṣma*[1] (*gā-* 'go', AV.), *jéṣma* (√*ji-*), *deṣma*[1] (*dā-* 'give', VS. II. 32). — 2. *naiṣṭa* (√*nī-*), *yauṣṭa* (√*yu-* 'separate', AV.), *śāpta*[2] (TS. III. 3. 9^{1}). — 3. *jaiṣur* (√*ji-*, AV.), *dhāsur*, *yauṣur* (*yu-* 'separate'), *stheṣur*[1] (AV. XVI. 4^{7}), *hāsur*.

Middle. Sing. 1. *gāsi* (*gā-* 'sing'), *nikṣi* (√*nij-*, AV.), *patsi* (√*pad-*, AV.), *bhakṣi* (√*bhaj-*, VII. 41^{2}), *meṣi* (*mī-* 'diminish', AV.), *yaṃsi* (√*yam-*), *yakṣi* (√*yaj-*), *váṃsi* (√*van-*), *vṛkṣi* (√*vṛj-*).

2. *cyoṣṭhās* (√*cyu-*), *chitthās* (√*chid-*, AV.), *patthās* (√*pad-*, AV.), *bhitthās* (TS. IV. 1. 9^{2}), *maṃsthās* (√*man-*, AV.; VS. XIII. 41), *meṣṭhās* (√*mī-*, AV.), *raṃsthās* (√*ram-*, AV.), *hāsthās* (*hā-* 'go forth', AV.).

3. *kṣeṣṭa* (*kṣi-* 'destroy', AV.), *neṣṭa* (√*nī-*, AV.), *pāsta* (*pā-* 'drink', AV.), *maṃsta* (√*man-*, AV.), *māṃsta*[6] (√*man-*, AV. XI. 2^{8}), *meṣṭa* (*mī-* 'fail', AV.), *hāsta* (*hā-* 'be left', AV.).

Du. 2. *sṛkṣāthām* (√*sṛj-*, VS. XIX. 7).

Pl. 1. *yutsmahi*[3] (√*yudh-*, AV.), *hāsmahi* (*hā-* 'be deprived of').

3. *dhukṣata* (√*duh-*), *nūṣata*, *matsata* (√*mad-*), *mukṣata* (√*muc-*), *sakṣata* (√*sac-* 'accompany').

s- Aorist Optative.

525. This mood occurs in the middle only in this form of the sigmatic aorist. The **2. 3. sing. always** appears **with** the **precative** *s* excepting the one form *bhakṣīta* in the SV. (I. 1. 2. 4^{2}).

Sing. 1. *diṣīya*[4] (*dā-* 'cut'), *bhakṣīyá* (√*bhaj-*), *masīya*[5] (√*man-*), *mukṣīya*, *rāsīya*, *sākṣīya*[6] (√*sah-*, AV.), *stṛṣīya* (√*stṛ-*, AV.)

2. *maṃsīṣṭhās* (√*man-*). — 3. *darṣīṣṭa* (*dṛ-* 'tear'), *bhakṣīta* (SV.), *maṃsīṣṭa* (√*man-*), *mṛkṣīṣṭa* (*mṛc-* 'injure').

Du. 2. *trāsīthām* (for **trās-īyāthām*).

Pl. 1. *dhukṣīmáhi* (√*duh-*, TS. I. 6. 4^{3}), *bhakṣīmáhi* (√*bhaj-*), *maṃsīmáhi* (√*man-*), *vaṃsīmáhi* and *vasīmahi*[5] (√*van-*, IX. 72^{8}), *sakṣīmáhi* (√*sac-*). — 3. *maṃsīrata*.

s- Aorist Imperative.

526. No certain regular forms of the imperative occur in the active. Two or three, such as *yauṣṭam*, *naiṣṭa*, might have been classed here, but as they occur with *mā́* only, they have been placed among the injunctives. There are, however, the two transfer forms in the 2. sing. *neṣa* (√*nī-*, AV.) and *parṣā* (*pṛ-* 'take across')[7]. The only forms of the imperative occurring in the middle are three made from *rā-* 'give' and one from *śah-* 'conquer'.

Middle. Sing. 2. *sákṣva*. — 3. *rāsatām*. — **Du.** 2. *rāsāthām*. — **Pl.** 3. *rāsantām*.

s- Aorist Participle.

527. Only two or three forms of the active participle are found. These are *dákṣant-* and *dhákṣant-* from *dah-* 'burn', and *sákṣant-* from *sah-* 'prevail'. In the middle there are no regular forms. There is one doubtful example in which the stem is extended with *-a-* and accordingly adds the suffix *-māna*, as in the *a-* conjugation: *dhí-ṣ-a-māṇa-* (*dhī-* 'think').

There are, besides, a dozen stems irregularly formed by adding *s* to the root with an intermediate *-a-*, and taking the regular ending *-āna*. These forms

---

1 See p. 380, note 9.

2 For *śāp-s-ta*.

3 A somewhat doubtful reading: see Whitney's note on AV. VII. 52^{2}.

4 With the radical *ā* weakened to *i*.

5 Root weakened by loss of nasal (*a* taking the place of the sonant nasal).

6 With irregular lengthening of the radical vowel.

7 See Whitney, AV. Index Verborum 382.

may be accounted as belonging to the *s*- aorist. All but two of them occur in the RV. They are: *arśasānā*- 'injuring', *óhasāna*- (√*ūh*-) 'lying in wait', *jrayasānā*- (√*jri*-) 'far-extending', *dhiyasānā*- (√*dhī*-) 'attending', *namasānā*- (√*nam*-) 'rendering homage' (AV.), *bhiyásāna*- (√*bhī*-) 'fearing' (AV.), *mandasānā*- (√*mand*-) 'rejoicing', *yamasānā*- (√*yam*-) 'being driven' (with passive sense), *rabhasānā*- (√*rabh*-) 'agile', *vṛdhasānā*- (√*vṛdh*-) 'growing', *śavasānā*- (√*śū*-) 'strong', *sahasānā*- (√*sah*-) 'mighty'.

A. 2. The *iṣ*- Aorist.

DELBRÜCK, Verbum p. 179—180. — AVERY, Verb-Inflection 259—261. — WHITNEY, Sanskrit Grammar 898—910; Roots 226—227; AV. Index Verborum 380. — v. NEGELEIN, Zur Sprachgeschichte 85—86.

528. About 80 roots take this form of the sigmatic aorist in the RV. and about a dozen others in the AV.

The *-s* is here added to the root with the connecting vowel *-i-*. The radical vowel as a general rule takes **Guṇa throughout**; but in the active a final vowel takes Vṛddhi and a medial *-a* is sometimes lengthened. No roots with final *-ā* and few with final *-ī̆* take this aorist. The terminations are the same as those of the *s*- aorist, excepting that the 2. and 3. sing. act. end in *-īs* (= *iṣ-s*) and *-īt* (= *iṣ-t*). Active and middle forms, though frequent, are rarely both made from the same root, occurring thus in about fifteen verbs only. This is the only aorist from which a few forms are made in the secondary conjugation[1].

Besides the indicative, all the moods are represented in this aorist, but **no participial forms** have been met with.

Indicative.

529. In the active all persons are represented except du. 1. 2. and pl. 2.; but in the middle only sing. 2. and 3. occur besides a single form of sing. 1 (Kh.), du. 3. and pl. 3. (VS.).

a. A few **irregularities** occur in the formation of this tense[2]. 1. The forms *atārima* (beside the normal *átāriṣma*) and *avādiran*[3] (AV.), are probably to be regarded as irregular forms with abnormal **loss** of the aoristic ***-s***. — 2. The root *grabh*- 'seize' takes the **connecting vowel** *ī*[3] (as it does in other verbal forms) instead of *-i-*, as *agrabhīṣma*. — 3. In the sing. 1. act., the **ending *-īm*** appears instead of *-iṣam* in the three forms *ákramīm*, *vádhīm*, and *agrabhīm* (TS.), doubtless owing to the analogy of the 2. and 3. sing. *-īs* and *-īt*[4]. — 4. The abnormal **ending *-ait*** appears in the 3. sing. in *ásarait*[5] (AV.) beside *asārīt* (AV.)[6].

The normal forms occurring, if made from *kram*- 'stride', would be as follows:

Active. Sing. 1. *ákramiṣam*. 2. *ákramīs*. 3. *ákramīt*. — Du. 3. *ákramiṣṭām*. — Pl. 1. *ákramiṣma*. 3. *ákramiṣur*.

Middle. Sing. 1. *ákramiṣi* (Kh.). 2. *ákramiṣṭhās*. 3. *ákramiṣṭa*. — Du. 3. *ákramiṣātām*. — Pl. 3. *ákramiṣata* (VS.).

The forms which actually occur are the following:

[1] From causatives *dhvanayīt*, *ailayīt* (√*il*-, AV.), from a desiderative *īrtsīs* (√*ṛdh*-, AV.).

[2] The weak form of the root appears in the injunctive *nudiṣṭhās* (AV.) and the optative *truciṣīya* (AV.) and *gmiṣīya* (VS.), which syncopates the radical vowel as in the root aor. and the perfect of this verb.

[3] Cp. WHITNEY 904 d.

[4] Cp. DELBRÜCK, Verbum p. 188.

[5] This abnormal ending also occurs in the secondary conjugation in the denominative aor. *ásaparyait* (AV.): see below 570.

[6] Both these forms also show the irregularity of taking Guṇa instead of Vṛddhi.

Active. Sing. 1. *akāniṣam, akāriṣam, akramiṣam, acāyiṣam* (AV.), *acāriṣam, abhāriṣam* (√*bhṛ-*, AV.), *avadhiṣam* (AV.), *avādiṣam* (AV.), *áśaṃsiṣam, asāniṣam; ā́śiṣam* (*aś-* 'eat', AV.); *rāviṣam.* — **With ending -īm:** *akramīm, agrabhīm* (TS.); *vádhīm.*

2. *akramīs, adṛṃhīs* (VS. VI. 2), *ávadhīs, avarṣīs*[1], *astarīs* (√*stṛ-*, AV.); *āśīs*[2] (*aś-* 'eat', AV.), *áukṣīs* (*ukṣ-* 'grow'); *kramīs, vádhīs.*

3. *ákārīt, ákramīt, ágrabhīt, ágrahīt* (AV.), *átārīt, adṛṃhīt* (MS. IV. 13^{8}), *anayīt*[2] (√*nī-*, AV.), *ámandīt, ayāsīt, áyodhīt, arāvīt, ávadhīt, ávarṣīt* (√*vṛṣ-*, AV.), *áśaṃsīt, aśarīt*[3] (AV.), *asāvīt, astānīt* (AV.), *ásvanīt; āvīt, āśīt* (*aś-* 'eat', AV.); *járvīt* (*jūrv-* 'consume'), *tārīt, vádhīt.* — **With ending -ait:** *aśarait*[4] (AV.).

Du. 3. *ámanthiṣṭām; jániṣṭām.*

Pl. 1. *agrabhīṣma, átāriṣma* and *atārima*[5], *ávadhiṣma* (VS. IX. 38).

3. *atakṣiṣur, átāriṣur, adhanviṣur, ánartiṣur, ánindiṣur, apāviṣur, ámandiṣur, amādiṣur, arājiṣur, arāṇiṣur* (*ran-* 'rejoice'), *árāviṣur, avādiṣur, asāviṣur; ā́kṣiṣur*[6] (I. 163^{10}), *āniṣur* (√*an-*, AV., TS.), *áviṣur* (√*av-*). — **With -ran:** *avādiran* (AV.).

Middle. Sing. 1. *aikṣiṣi* (Kh. I. 1^{1}: √*īkṣ-*). — **2.** *ájaniṣṭhās* (AV.), *aśamiṣṭhās* (*śam-* 'labour'), *aśayiṣṭhās, áśramiṣṭhās; jániṣṭhās.*

3. *akrapiṣṭa* (√*kṛp-*), *ájaniṣṭa, adhāviṣṭa, anaviṣṭa, aprathiṣṭa, arociṣṭa* (VS. XXXVII. 15), *avasiṣṭa* (*vas-* 'wear'), *áśamiṣṭa, ásahiṣṭa; áuhiṣṭa* (*ūh-* 'consider'); *krámiṣṭa, jániṣṭa, práthiṣṭa, mándiṣṭa, yamiṣṭa.*

Du. 3. *ámandiṣātām.* — **Pl. 3.** *ágṛbhīṣata* (VS. XXI. 60).

iṣ- Aorist Subjunctive.

530. Active forms of this mood are fairly common, but are almost exclusively limited to the 2. and 3. sing. Middle forms are very rare, occurring only in the pl., where not more than four examples have been noted.

Active. Sing. 1. *daviṣāṇi*[7]. — **2.** *aviṣas, kániṣas, tāriṣas, rakṣiṣas, vádhiṣas, vádiṣas* (AV.), *véṣiṣas, śaṃsiṣas.*

3. *káriṣat, jambhiṣat, jóṣiṣat, tāriṣat, níndiṣat* (AV.), *páriṣat* ('take across'), *bódhiṣat, márdhiṣat, yāciṣat, yodhiṣat, rakṣiṣat, vaniṣat* (AV.), *vyathiṣat* (VS. VI. 18), *śaṃsiṣat* (TS. V. 6. 8^{6}), *saniṣat, sáviṣat*[8] (*sū-* 'vivify').

Pl. 3. *saniṣan*[9] (AV. V. 3^{5}).

Middle. Pl. 1. *yāciṣāmahe, saniṣāmahe.* — **3.** *vaniṣanta*[10] (TS. IV. 7. 14^{1}), *sániṣanta.*

iṣ- Aorist Injunctive.

531. Forms of the injunctive are commoner than those of the subjunctive. In the active they are found almost exclusively in the 2. 3. sing., 2. du. and 2. 3. pl.; in the middle nearly a dozen forms occur, all but one in the sing.

The forms of this mood have the accent on the root (as in the unaugmented indicative).

Active. Sing. 1. *śáṃsiṣam, hiṃsiṣam* (VS. I. 25).

---

1 AVERY 259 adds *ávarhīs* as occurring once.

2 See WHITNEY's note on AV. XI. 3^{26}.

3 With Guṇa instead of Vṛddhi of final vowel; cp. BARTHOLOMAE, Studien 2, 165.

4 See WHITNEY's note on AV. VI. 66^{2}, where the reading *aśarīt* is better supported; cp. his note on AV. VI. 65^{1}.

5 With loss of the aoristic *-s.*

6 From *akṣ-* 'attain' (WHITNEY, Roots 1) a secondary form of √*aś-*; otherwise a *siṣ*-aorist from *aś-* 'attain'.

7 Cp. v. SCHROEDER, WZKM. 13, 119—122.

8 This form occurs also in two passages of the AV.; in a third (AV. I. 18^{2}) *sāviṣak* appears instead of it. Cp. WHITNEY's note on this passage, and his Grammar 151 a.

9 The corresponding passage of the RV. (X. 128^{3}) has *vanuṣanta*, and of the TS. (IV. 7. 14^{1}) *vaniṣanta.*

10 See preceding note.

2. *avīs*, *kramīs* (AV.), *jīvīs* (AV.), *tarīs*, *barhīs*, *máthīs*, *mardhīs*, *moṣīs*, *yā́vīs*, *yodhīs*, *rakṣīs* (AV.), *randhīs*, *lekhīs* (VS. v. 43), *vádhīs*, *śocīs* (VS. XI. 45), *sā́vīs*, *spharīs*, *hiṃsīs* (VS. AV.). — **With** *-ais*: *śarais* (√*śṛ*-, AV.).

3. *aśīt* (*aś*- 'eat'), *gārīt* (*gṛ*- 'swallow'), *cārīt*, *jīvīt* (AV.), *tārīt*, *dāsīt* (*das*- 'waste'), *barhīt*, *máthīt*, *vadhīt* (TS. IV. 2. 9[1]; VS. XIII. 16), *veśīt*, *svānīt*, *hiṃsīt*.

Du. 2. *tā́riṣṭam*, *mardhiṣṭam*, *hiṃsiṣṭam* (AV. VS.).

Pl. 1. *śramiṣma*. — **2.** *grabhīṣṭa*, *vadhiṣṭa*, *hiṃsiṣṭa* (AV. TS.); *mathiṣṭana* (AV.), *rā́ṇiṣṭana* (√*ran*-), *vadhiṣṭana*. — **3.** *jāriṣur* (*jṛ*- 'waste away'), *jīviṣur* (AV.), *tāriṣúr*[1] (AV.), *vadhiṣur* (AV.), *vādiṣur* (AV.), *hiṃsiṣur* (AV.).

Middle. Sing. 1. *rādhiṣi* (AV.). — **2.** *kṣaṇiṣṭhās*[2] (AV.), *nudiṣṭhās*[3] (AV.), *marṣiṣṭhās* (√*mṛṣ*-), *vadhiṣṭhās* (Kh. II. 11[3]), *vyathiṣṭhās* (AV.). — **3.** *paniṣṭa*, *paviṣṭa*, *bādhiṣṭa*. — **Pl. 1.** *vyathiṣmahi* (AV.).

iṣ- Aorist Optative.

532. This mood is rare, occurring in the middle only and being formed from hardly a dozen roots. Though the ending is accented, the root appears in a weak form in *gmiṣīya*[4] (VS.) and *ruciṣīya* (AV.). The **2.** and **3. sing.** take the **precative** *-s-*.

Middle. Sing. 1. *edhiṣīyá* (AV.), *gmiṣīya*[3] (VS. III. 19), *janiṣīya* (AV.)[5], *ruciṣīya*[3] (AV.). — **2.** *modiṣīṣṭhās* (AV.). — **3.** *janiṣīṣṭa*, *vaniṣīṣṭa*.

Du. 1. *sahiṣīvahi* (AV.). — **Pl. 1.** *edhiṣīmáhi* (AV.), *tāriṣīmahi*, *mandiṣīmahi* (VS. IV. 14; TS. I. 2. 3[1] etc.), *vandiṣīmáhi*, *vardhiṣīmáhi* (VS. II. 14, XXXVIII. 21), *sahiṣīmahi* (AV.), *sāhiṣīmáhi* (Pada text *sahiṣīmáhi*).

iṣ- Aorist Imperative.

533. Forms of this mood are rare, occurring in the active only and being made from six or seven roots at the most. Among these forms, two only are distinctively imperative, *aviḍḍhí* and *aviṣṭu*; a few others can be distinguished by having the accent on the ending; the rest, being unaccented and used without *mā́*, cannot be distinguished from injunctives.

Sing. 2. *aviḍḍhí*. — **3.** *aviṣṭu*. — **Du. 1.** *aviṣṭám*, *kramiṣṭam*, *gamiṣṭam*, *caniṣṭám*, *cayiṣṭam* (*ci*- 'gather'), *yodhiṣṭam* (√*yudh*-), *vadhiṣṭam*, *śnathiṣṭam*. — **3.** *aviṣṭām*. — **Pl. 2.** *avitá*[6]; *aviṣṭána*, *śnathiṣṭana*.

A. 3. The *siṣ*- Aorist.

DELBRÜCK, Verbum p. 179. — AVERY, Verb-Inflection 261. — WHITNEY, Sanskrit Grammar 911—916; Roots 227. — v. NEGELEIN, Zur Sprachgeschichte 86.

534. This aorist, which is inflected exactly like the *iṣ*- aorist, is formed by only six or seven roots in the Saṃhitās. Middle forms occur in the optative only.

Indicative.

Sing. 1. *ayāsiṣam*. — **Du. 3.** *ayāsiṣṭām* (VS. XXVIII. 14). — **Pl. 2.** *áyāsiṣṭa*. — **3.** *agāsiṣur* (*gā*- 'sing'), *ayāsiṣur*[7].

Subjunctive.

Sing. 3. *gāsiṣat* (*gā*- 'sing'), *yāsiṣat*.

---

1 With accent on the ending instead of the root.

2 Cp. BRUGMANN, KZ. 24, 363 f.

3 With weak form of root.

4 Cp. ZIMMER, KZ. 30, 222.

5 The Kāṭhaka has the forms *janiṣeyam* and *janiṣeya* made from a secondary *-a-* stem (WHITNEY 907).

6 This may be regarded as a form irregularly lacking *ṣ* = *aviṣṭá*.

7 *ā́kṣiṣur* is formed from *aś*- 'attain', according to DELBRÜCK, Verbum p. 179; according to WHITNEY, Sanskrit Grammar 913, and Roots 1, from the secondary root *akṣ*-; see above p. 383, note 6.

Optative.

Middle. Sing. 1. *vaṃsiṣīya*[1] (*van-* 'win', AV.). — **2.** *yāsiṣīṣṭhās*[2]. — **Pl. 1.** *pyāsiṣīmahi*[3] (AV.; VS. II. 14; MS. IV. 9[10] [p. 181, 9]).

Injunctive.

Sing. 1. *raṃsiṣam*[4] (SV. I. 4. 1. 2[5]). — **Du. 2.** *hāsiṣṭam* (AV.). — **3.** *hāsiṣṭām* (AV.). — **Pl. 2.** *hāsiṣṭa* (AV.). — **3.** *hāsiṣur* (AV.).

Imperative.

Du. 2. *yāsiṣṭám.* — **Pl. 2.** *yāsīṣṭa*[5] (I. 165[15]).

B. The *sa-* Aorist.

DELBRÜCK, Verbum p. 179. — AVERY, Verb-Inflection 262. — WHITNEY, Sanskrit Grammar 916—920; Roots 227. — v. NEGELEIN, Zur Sprachgeschichte 86.

535. In the Saṃhitās this form of the sigmatic aorist is taken by only nine roots, which end in *j ś ṣ* or *h* and contain the medial vowels *i u* or *ṛ*. The thematic *a* doubtless came to be employed in these few verbs to avoid a difficult agglomeration of consonants when the endings were added. The inflexion is like that of an imperfect of the *á-* class of the first conjugation, the *-sá-* being accented[6] in unaugmented forms. Besides the indicative, only forms of the injunctive and imperative occur, altogether fewer than a dozen. **No subjunctive, optative, or participial forms** have been noted.

Indicative.

536. Neither forms of any person of the dual nor of the 2. pl. occur in the indicative of this type of the *s-* aorist. The active forms greatly predominate, the middle being represented in the 3. sing. and pl. by only three or four forms altogether.

Active. Sing. 1. *avṛkṣam* (√*vṛh-*). — **2.** *adhukṣas* (√*duh-*, VS. I. 3), *arukṣas* (√*ruh-*, AV.); *rukṣas* (√*ruh-*, AV.). — **3.** *ákrukṣat* (√*kruś-*), *aghukṣat* (√*guh-*), *adukṣat*[7] and *ádhukṣat* (√*duh-*), *ámṛkṣat* (√*mṛś-*, AV.) *árukṣat* (√*ruh-*), *áspṛkṣat* (√*spṛś-*, AV.; VS. XXVIII. 18). — **Pl. 1.** *amṛkṣāma* (√*mṛj-* 'wipe'), *arukṣāma* (√*ruh-*, AV.). — **3.** *ádhukṣan* (√*duh-*); *dukṣan*[8] and *dhukṣán* (√*duh-*).

Middle. Sing. 3. *ádhukṣata*[9]; *dukṣata*[8] and *dhukṣata.* — **Pl. 3.** *amṛkṣanta* (√*mṛj-*).

Injunctive.

Active. Sing. 2. *dukṣas, mṛkṣas* (√*mṛś-*). — **3.** *dvikṣat* (√*dviṣ-*, AV.). — **Pl. 2.** *mṛkṣata* (√*mṛś-*).

Middle. Sing. 3. *dukṣata*[8] and *dhúkṣata* (√*duh-*), *dvikṣata* (√*dviṣ-*, AV.). — **Pl. 3.** *dhukṣánta* (√*duh-*).

Imperative.

Active. Du. 2. *mṛkṣatam* (√*mṛj-*). — **3.** *yakṣatām* (√*yaj-*).
Middle. Sing. 2. *dhukṣásva* (√*duh-*).

1 In the Mss. *vaṃśiṣīya*; see WHITNEY's note on AV. IX. 1[14].
2 With precative *s*.
3 In the Mss. *pyāśiṣīmahi*; see WHITNEY's note on AV. VII. 81[5].
4 Variant for *rāsīya* of the RV.
5 With *ī* for *i*. AVERY 261 gives the form as *yāsiṣṭá*.
6 Three forms occur accented thus; the root is, however, accented in *dhúkṣata*.
7 See above 32 b.
8 See above 32 b.
9 In IX. 110[8] the form *ádhukṣata* seems to be a 3. pl.

IV. The Future System.

Delbrück, Verbum p. 183—184. — Avery, Verb-Inflection 262. — Whitney, Sanskrit Grammar 931—941; Roots 228 f.; AV. Index Verborum 380. — v. Negelein, Zur Sprachgeschichte 86—87.

537. The stem is formed by adding *-syá*[1] or (rather less frequently with connecting *-i-*) *-iṣyá*[1] to the root, which gunates a final or a prosodically short medial vowel. As the subjunctive frequently has a future sense, and even the present indicative may have it, the occasion for the use of actual future forms seldom arises in the RV., which forms a future stem from only fifteen roots, while the AV. does so from more than thirty (about eight of these occurring in the RV. also)[2]. There is only one subjunctive and one conditional form, but some twenty participles occur.

a. In the following stems the suffix **-sya** is **added direct**: *kṣi-* 'abide' : *kṣe-ṣyá-*[3]; *ji-* 'conquer' : *je-ṣyá-*; *dah-* 'burn' : *dhak-ṣyá-*; *yaj-* 'sacrifice' : *yak-ṣyá-*; *vac-* 'speak' : *vak-ṣyá-*; *sū-* 'bring forth : *sū́-ṣya-*[4]. In the AV. also occur: *i-* 'go' : *e-ṣyá-*; *kṛt-* 'cut' : *kart-sya-*; *kram-* 'stride' : *kraṃ-syá-*; *gup-* 'protect' : *gop-sya-*; *dā-* 'give' : *dā-syá-*; *nī-* 'lead' : *ne-ṣya-*; *mih-* 'mingere' : *mek-ṣyá-*[5]; *yā-* 'go' : *yā-syá-*; *yuj-* 'join' : *yok-ṣya-*[6]; *rādh-* 'succeed' : *rāt-sya-*; *vah-* 'carry' : *vak-ṣyá-*; *vṛt-* 'turn' : *-vart-syá-*[7]; *śad-* 'fall' : *śat-sya-*; *sah-* 'prevail' : *sāk-ṣya-*[8]; *hā-* 'leave' : *hā-sya-*; *hu-* 'sacrifice' : *ho-ṣyá-*. In the VS. *bandh-* 'bind' : *bhant-syá-*.

b. In the following stems the suffix is added **with connecting -i-**: *av-* 'favour' : *av-iṣyá-*[9]; *as-* 'shoot' : *as-iṣyá-*; *kṛ-* 'do' : *kar-iṣyá-*; *jan-* 'beget' : *jan-iṣya-*; *bhū-* 'be' : *bhav-iṣyá-*; *man-* 'think' : *man-iṣyá-*; *vā-* 'weave' : *vay-iṣyá-*[10]; *san-* 'acquire' : *san-iṣyá-*; *sṛ-* 'hasten' : *sar-iṣyá-*; *stu-* 'praise' : *stav-iṣyá-*. From **causative** stems: *dhṛ-* 'support' : *dhāray-iṣyá-*; *vas-* 'clothe oneself' : *vāsay-iṣyá-*.

The AV. has the following additional stems: *gam-* 'go' : *gam-iṣya-*; *dhṛ-* 'maintain' : *dhar-iṣyá-*; *naś-* 'disappear' : *naś-iṣya-*; *pat-* 'fly' : *pat-iṣyá-*; *mṛ-* 'die' : *mar-iṣya-*; *vad-* 'speak' : *vad-iṣya-*; *vṛt-* 'turn' : *vart-iṣya-*[11]; *svap-* 'sleep' : *svap-iṣyá-*[12]; *han-* 'slay' : *han-iṣyá-*. From **causative** stems: *duṣ-* 'spoil' : *dūṣay-iṣya-*; *vṛ-* 'cover' : *vāray-iṣya-* 'shield'.

538. a. **Subjunctive.** The only subjunctive form occurring is *kar-iṣyā́(-s)* in IV. 30[23].[13]

b. **Conditional.** The only example occurring is formed from *bhṛ-* 'bear' : *á-bhar-iṣya-t* 'he was going to bear off' (II. 30[2]).

c. **Participles.** A good many participial forms occur. The following stems are met with:

Active. *av-iṣyánt-*[14], *as-iṣyánt-*, *e-ṣyánt-* (AV.)[15], *kar-iṣyánt-*, *kṣe-ṣyánt-*, *khan-iṣyánt-* (TS.), *je-ṣyánt-*[16] (AV.), *dā-syánt-* (AV.), *dhak-ṣyánt-*, *pat-iṣyánt-* (AV.),

1 On the origin of this suffix see Brugmann, Grundriss 2, 747 (p. 1092), who connects the *-iṣya* form with the *iṣ-* aorist; and v. Negelein, Zur Sprachgeschichte 86.

2 According to Whitney 937 the future is formed from over 60 roots in the TS. but I am uncertain how many of these occur in independent Mantra passages.

3 This is the only stem in which *-syá* is to be read *-sia* : *kṣeṣiántas*.

4 This stem has the double irregularity of accenting the root and not taking Guṇa: cp. the perfect *sasūva*.

5 The Mss. read *mekṣāmi* in AV. VII. 102[1]: cp. Whitney's note.

6 Doubtful reading see note 3 p. 387 on *yokṣye*.

7 See Whitney's note on AV. XV. 6[7].

8 An emendation: see note on *sākṣye*.

9 Cp. Delbrück, Verbum p. 184.

10 Op. cit. p. 183.

11 In the form *ánvartiṣye* for *ánu-vartiṣye*; see p. 11, 18.

12 See Whitney's note on AV. XIX. 479.

13 The form *kariṣyā́* (I. 1659) is probably to be explained as the same subjunctive (= *kariṣyā́s*): cp. BR. sv. *kariṣyā́*.

14 Cp. Delbrück, Verbum p. 183.

15 In *praiṣyán* (AV. V. 22[14]), Pp. *pra-eṣyán*, but Whitney = *pra-iṣyan*.

16 In AV. XV. 20[1] nearly all the Mss. read *jyeṣyán* (as if from √*jyā-*) for *jeṣyán*.

bhar-iṣyánt- (TS.), *bhav-iṣyánt-* (AV. VS.), *yā-syánt-* (AV.), *vac-* 'speak': *vak-ṣyánt-*, *vay-iṣyánt-*, *san-iṣyánt-*, *sar-iṣyánt-*, *sú-ṣyant-*, *han-iṣyánt-*.

Middle. *kraṃsyá-māṇa-* (AV.), *janiṣyá-māṇa-* (VS. xviii. 5), *yakṣyá-māṇa-*, *staviṣyá-māṇa-* (AV.).

Future Indicative.

539. The future is inflected, in both active and middle, like the present of the *a-* conjugation. The forms actually met with in the Saṃhitās would, if made from *kṛ-* 'do', be the following:

Active. Sing. 1. *kariṣyámi.* 2. *kariṣyási.* 3. *kariṣyáti.* — Du. 2. *kariṣyathas* (TS.). 3. *kariṣyatas* (AV.). — Pl. 1. *kariṣyámas* and *kariṣyámasi* (AV.). 2. *kariṣyátha.* 3. *kariṣyanti* (AV.).

Middle. Sing. 1. *kariṣyé.* 2. *kariṣyase.* 3. *kariṣyate.*

The forms actually occurring are the following:

Active. Sing. 1. *eṣyāmi* (AV.), *kariṣyāmi* (AV.), *kartsyāmi* (AV.), *cariṣyāmi* (VS. i. 5), *jeṣyámi*, *bhantsyámi* (√*bandh-*, VS. xxii. 4)[1], *mekṣyámi*[2] (AV.), *vakṣyámi* (√*vac-*), *staviṣyámi.*

2. *kariṣyási*, *jeṣyasi* (VS. xxiii. 17), *bhaviṣyasi* (AV.), *mariṣyasi* (AV.), *rātsyasi* (√*rādh-*, AV.), *vakṣyasi* (√*vac-*, TS. ii. 6. 12[5]), *saniṣyasi*, *haniṣyasi* (AV.).

3. *kariṣyati*, *gamiṣyati* (AV.), *naśiṣyati* (AV.), *neṣyati* (AV.), *patiṣyati* (AV.), *bhaviṣyáti*, *mariṣyati* (AV.), *vadiṣyati* (AV.), *saniṣyati*, *sthāsyati* (VS. vi. 2), *haniṣyati* (AV.).

Du. 2. *kariṣyathas* (TS. iv. 1. 9[2]). — **3.** *mariṣyatas* (AV.), *vakṣyatas* (√*vah-*, AV.).

Pl. 1. *bhariṣyāmas* (VS. xi. 16), *vakṣyámas* (√*vac-*), *svapiṣyámasi* (AV.).

2. *kariṣyátha*, *bhaviṣyatha*, *sariṣyatha* (AV.).

3. *gopsyanti* (√*gup-*, AV.), *śatsyanti* (√*śad-*, AV.), *hāsyanti* (√*hā-*, AV.).

Middle. Sing. 1. *dhariṣyé* (AV.), *maniṣye*, *yokṣye*[3] (AV.), *vartiṣye*[4] (AV.), *sākṣye*[5] (√*sah-*, AV.). — **2.** *staviṣyase.* — **3.** *janiṣyate*, *staviṣyate* (AV.).

Periphrastic Future.

540. Of this formation, common in the later language, there seems to be an incipient example in VS. xviii. 59 = TS. v. 7. 7[1]: *anvāgantā́ yajñápatir vo átra* 'the sacrificer is following after you here', a modification of AV. vi. 123[1, 2]: *anvāgantā́ yájamānaḥ svastí*, which Whitney translates 'the sacrificer follows after well-being'[6].

V. Secondary Conjugation.

541. As opposed to the primary conjugation, there are four derivative formations in which the present stem is used throughout the inflexion of the verb and is everywhere accompanied by the specific sense connected with that stem. The forms which occur outside the present system are, however, rare. The four derivative formations are the desiderative, the intensive, the causative, and the denominative.

1. The Desiderative.

Delbrück, Verbum p. 184—186. — Avery, Verb-Inflection 230, 268—270. — Whitney, Sanskrit Grammar 1026—1040; Roots 233f. — v. Negelein, Zur Sprachgeschichte 88—90.

542. Though the least frequent of the secondary conjugations, the desiderative is perhaps best dealt with first, as being akin in derivation and

1 In AV. iii. 9[5] Roth and Whitney's edition reads *bhartsyámi*; but Whitney, note on that passage, would emend this to *bhantsyámi* (√*bandh-*), and Shankar Pandit reads *bhatsyámi.*

2 Whitney's emendation for *mekṣāmi* of the Mss.; see his note on AV. vii. 102[1].

3 All the Mss. in AV. xix. 13[1] read *yokṣe* (but Paipp. *yokṣye*).

4 In *ánvartiṣye* (AV. xiv. 15[6]) given under the root *art-* by Whitney, AV. Index Verborum; see p. 386, note 11.

5 The Mss. in AV. ii. 27[5] read *sākṣe.*

6 Cp. Whitney, Sanskrit Grammar 946.

meaning **to the future**[1], the last of the primary verbal formations treated above (537—540). The desiderative is formed from the root with an accented reduplicative syllable and the suffix *-sa*, which expresses the desire for the action or condition denoted by the root; e. g. ***pā-*** 'drink' : ***pí-pā-sa-*** 'desire to drink'. Desiderative stems from fewer than sixty roots are met with in the Saṃhitās.

The **characteristic reduplicative vowel is *i***, which appears in all stems except those formed from roots containing *ŭ* (which reduplicate with *u*); and the root generally remains unchanged. Thus *jñā-* 'know' : *ji-jñā-sa-* (AV.); *jyā-* 'overpower' : *jí-jyā-sa-*; *dā-* 'give' : *dí-dā-sa-*; *pā-* 'drink' : *pi-pā-sa-*; *tij-* 'be sharp' : *tí-tik-ṣa-*; *nid-* 'blame' : *ní-nit-sa-*; *bhid-* 'split' : *bí-bhit-sa-*; *miś-* 'mix' : *mí-mik-ṣa-*; *riṣ-* 'hurt' : *rí-rik-ṣa-*; *nī-* 'lead' : *ni-nī-ṣa-*; *prī-* 'love' : *pí-prī-ṣa-*; *guh-* 'hide' : *ju-guk-ṣa-*[2]; *duh-* 'milk' : *dú-duk-ṣa-*[2]; *muc-* 'release' : *mú-muk-ṣa-*; *yudh-* 'fight' : *yú-yut-sa-*; *ruh-* 'ascend' : *rú-ruk-ṣa-*; *bhū-* 'be' : *bú-bhū-ṣa-*; *tṛd-* 'pierce' : *tí-tṛt-sa-*; *tṛp-* 'delight' : *tí-tṛp-sa-*; *dṛś-* 'see' : *dí-dṛk-ṣa-*; *vṛt-* 'turn' : *ví-vṛt-sa-*; *sṛp-* 'creep' : *sí-sṛp-sa-*.

a. A few desideratives **reduplicate with a long vowel**: *tur-* (= *tṝ-*) 'cross' : *tú-tūr-ṣa-*; *bādh-* 'oppress' : *bī-bhat-sa-*; *man-* 'think' : *mī-māṃ-sa-* (AV.) 'investigate'. On the other hand, two desideratives abbreviate the reduplicative syllable by dropping its consonant; thus *yaj-* 'sacrifice' : *í-yak-ṣa-* for **yí-yak-ṣa-*[3]; *naś-* 'attain' : *í-nak-ṣa-*, for **ní-nak-ṣa-*, perhaps through the influence of *íyak-ṣa-*; and the RV. has one desiderative form from *āp-* 'obtain' in which the reduplication is dropped altogether: *ap-santa*.

b. The **radical vowel is lengthened** when *i*, *u*, or *ṛ* is final (the latter becoming *īr*); thus *ci-* 'see' : *ci-kī-ṣa-*; *ji-* 'conquer' : *jí-gī-ṣa-*; *yu-* 'unite' : *yú-yū-ṣa-*; *śru-* 'hear' : *śú-śrū-ṣa-*; *kṛ-* 'make' : *ci-kīr-ṣa-* (AV.); *hṛ-* 'take' : *jí-hīr-ṣa-* (AV.); *dhvṛ-* 'injure' : *dú-dhūr-ṣa-* with *ū* because vowel and semivowel have interchanged[4].

α. A **few roots with medial *a*** followed by *n* or *m* **lengthen** the vowel; thus *man-* 'think' : *mī-māṃ-sa-* (AV.); *han-* 'smite' : *jí-ghāṃ-sa-*; *gam-* 'go' : *ji-gāṃ-sa-* (AV.); two others do so after dropping the nasal, viz. *van-* 'win' : *ví-vā-sa-*; and *san-* 'gain' : *sí-ṣā-sa-*[5].

c. In nearly a dozen roots, on the other hand, the **radical vowel is weakened.**

1. In a few roots final *ā* is **reduced to *ī*** and, in one instance, even *i*[6]; thus *gā-* 'go' : *ji-gī-ṣa-* (SV[1].); *pā-* 'drink' : *pí-pī-ṣa-* (RV.) beside *pi-pā-sa-*; *hā-* 'go forth' : *ji-hī-ṣa-*[7] (AV.); *dhā-* 'put' : *dí-dhi-ṣa-* (RV.) beside *dhít-sa-*.

2. Half a dozen roots containing *ā* or *a* shorten the root **by syncopation** resulting in contraction with the reduplicative syllable; *dā-* 'give' : *dít-sa-*, for *dí-d[ā]-sa-*, beside *dí-dā-sa-*; *dhā-* 'put' : *dhí-t-sa-*, for *dí-dh-[ā]-sa-*, beside *di-dhi-ṣa-*; *dabh-* 'harm' : *dí-p-sa-*, for *dí-d[a]bh-sa-*; *labh-* 'take' : *lí-p-sa-* (AV.), for *lí-l[a]bh-sa-*; *śak-* 'be able' : *śí-k-ṣa-*, for *śí-ś[a]k-ṣa-*; *sah-* 'prevail' : *sí-k-ṣa-*, for *si-s[a]k-ṣa-*; similarly initial *ā* in *āp-* 'obtain' : *íp-sa-*[8] (AV.); and in *ṛdh-* 'thrive' : *írt-sa-* (AV.) the initial *ṛ* is treated as if it were *ar-*[9].

α. In a few roots the consonants undergo exceptional changes; thus palatals revert to the original guttural in *ci-* 'note' : *ci-kī-ṣa-*; *cit-* 'perceive' : *ci-kit-sa-*; *ji-* 'conquer' : *ji-gī-ṣa-*;

1 Cp. v. NEGELEIN 86.
2 See above 32 b.
3 Cp. v. NEGELEIN 68, note 2. The *i* being the reduplicative vowel, cannot be explained in the same way as that of the perfect *i-yáj-* for **ya-yáj-*, where *i-* has the nature of Samprasāraṇa.
4 Cp. √*dīv-* : *dyū-tá-* etc., below 573 α.
5 As in the past participle 574, 2 a.
6 As in the past participle 574, 3.
7 In AV. xx. 127[2] the Mss. read *jihīṣate* probably for *jihīḍate*.
8 Cp. BRUGMANN 2, 854, 1027.
9 v. NEGELEIN (89, note 2) thinks *īrtsá-* can only be explained from *ī-īrdh-sa-*.

han- 'slay': *jí-ghāṃ-sa-*. In *ghas-* 'eat' the final *s* becomes *t* before the *s* of the suffix: *ji-ghat-sa-*[1] (AV.).

β. The desiderative suffix *-sa* is never added in the RV. with the connecting vowel *-i-*; but there is one example of this formation in the AV., viz. *pat-* 'fly': *pi-pat-i-ṣa-*[2].

Inflexion.

543. The desiderative is inflected regularly like verbs of the *a-* conjugation in both voices, having the moods and participles of the present tense, as well as an imperfect. No forms outside the present system occur in the RV. with the exception of the perfect from *miś-*, *mi-mikṣ-ur*[3] etc. (in which, however, the desiderative stem is treated as a root) besides two aorist forms and one passive participle in the AV.[4].

The forms of the **present indicative**, active and middle, which actually occur, would if made from *vi-vā-sa-* 'desire to win', be as follows:

Active. Sing. 1. *vivāsāmi*. 2. *vivāsasi*. 3. *vivāsati*. — Du. 2. *vivāsathas*. 3. *vivāsatas*. — Pl. 1. *vivāsāmas*. 3. *vivāsanti*.

Middle. Sing. 1. *vivāse*. 2. *vivāsase*. 3. *vivāsate*. — Pl. 1. *vivāsāmahe*. *vivāsante*.

544. Forms occurring elsewhere in the present system are the following:

a. **Subjunctive**. Active. Sing. 3. *jíghāṃsāt* (TS.), *títṛpsāt*, *dípsāt* (TS. AV.), *nínitsāt*, *vivāsāt*. — Pl. 3. *íyakṣān*, *títṛtsān*, *vivāsān*.

b. **Injunctive**. Active. Sing. 3. *ínakṣat*, *cíkitsat*, *vivāsat*. — Middle. Pl. 3. *apsanta*, *dídhiṣanta*, *síkṣanta*.

c. **Optative**. Active. Sing. 1. *dítseyam*, *vivāseyam*. — 3. *vivāset*. — Pl. 1. *dídhiṣema*, *vivāsema*. — Middle. Sing. 1. *dídhiṣeya*.

d. **Imperative**. Active. Sing. 2. *cikitsa*, *dīpsa* (AV.), *mimikṣa*, *vivāsa*. — 3. *cíkitsatu* (AV.). — Du. 2. *mímikṣatam*, *síṣāsatam*. — 3. *mimikṣatām*. — Pl. 2. *cikitsata* (TS.), *vivāsata*. — 3. *dídhiṣantu*.

e. **Participles**. Active. *ínakṣant-*, *íyakṣant-*, *ípsant-* (AV.), *ī́rtsant-* (AV.), *cíkitsant-*, *jíghāṃsant-*, *dítsant-*, *dípsant-*, *dúdukṣant-*, *pipīṣant-*, *búbhūṣant-*, *yúyutsant-*, *yúyūṣant-*, *riríkṣant-* (√*riṣ-*), *rúrukṣant-* (√*ruh-*), *vivāsant-*, *síṣāsant-*, *sísṛpsant-*, *síkṣant-*. — Middle. *íyakṣamāṇa-*, *ī́rtsamāna-* (AV.), *jígiṣamāṇa-*, *múmukṣamāṇa-*, *lípsamāna-* (AV.), *síkṣamāṇa-* (TS.), *śúśrūṣamāṇa-*; and with *-āna-*: *dídhiṣāṇa-*.

f. **Imperfect**. Active. Sing. 2. *ásiṣāsas*. — 3. *ajíghāṃsat*, *asiṣāsat*. — Pl. 3. *áyuyutsan*, *ásiṣāsan*; *dudukṣan*, *bíbhitsan*.

g. **Aorist**. Sing. 2. *acikitsīs* (AV.), *ī́rtsīs* (AV.).

h. **Passive**. No finite form of the passive seems to occur in the Saṃhitās; of participles, no certain form of the present occurs, *mīmāṃsyámāna-* (AV. IX. 6[24])[5] being a conjecture; and of the past only one form has been noted: *mīmāṃsitá-* (AV. IX. 6[24])[6].

i. **Gerundive**. Two regular forms occur: *didṛkṣ-éṇya-* 'worthy to be seen' and *śuśrūṣ-éṇya-* (TS.) 'worthy to be heard'. There are also one or two irregular formations: *didṛkṣ-éya-* 'worthy to be seen' and *papṛkṣ-éṇya-* 'to be asked' (unless from aorist stem)[7].

k. **Verbal adjective**. A considerable number (more than a dozen in the RV.) of verbal adjectives are formed from the desiderative stem with the

---

[1] See above 44 a, 1.
[2] The desiderative of *jīv-* 'live', *jijīv-i-ṣa-*, occurs in VS. XL. (Īśā Up.).
[3] According to Grassmann, perf. des. of *mih-* 'mingere'; cp. Whitney, Roots, s. v. *mikṣ*.
[4] In all these forms the stems have lost their distinct desiderative meaning: cp. Whitney 1033.

[5] Cp. Whitney's note in his translation; in his grammar 1039 he quotes *rurutsyamāna* (√*rudh-*) from K. 37, 12 (*apa-*).
[6] Whitney 1037 quotes the gerund *mīmāṃ-sitvā* from K.
[7] See below, Gerundive 580.

suffix *-u*. They have the value of a present participle governing a case; thus *iyakṣ-ú-* 'wishing to sacrifice'; *jigīṣ-ú-* 'wishing to conquer'; *didhiṣ-ú-* 'desiring to win'; *dips-ú-* 'wishing to injure'; *vivakṣ-ú-* (AV.) from *vac-* 'speak'; *siṣās-ú-* 'eager to win'[1].

2. Intensives.

Delbrück, Verbum p. 130—134. — Avery, Verb-Inflection 230, 270—272. — Whitney, Sanskrit Grammar 1000—1025; Roots 232 f. — v. Negelein, Zur Sprachgeschichte 78—80. — Lindner, Altindische Nominalbildung 10 (p. 48) and 21 c (participles). — Burchardi, Die Intensiva des Sanskrit und Avesta. Teil I. Halle 1892; Teil II. BB. 19, 169—225.

545. The intensive or, as it is also often called, the frequentative implies intensification or repetition of the sense expressed by the root[2]. It is a common formation, being made from over 90 roots in the Saṃhitās. The stem is derived from the root by means of a **reduplicative syllable,** the characteristic feature of which is that it always **has a strong form.** The reduplicative syllable may be formed in three different ways: 1. radical *ĭ ŭ* are always reduplicated with a Guṇa vowel, and *ă* and *ṛ* (*ar*) often with *ā*; 2. roots containing *ṛ* or *a* followed by *r l n m* more usually reduplicate with *a* and liquid or nasal; 3. a considerable number of intensives interpose the vowel *ī* between the reduplicative syllable and the root.

1. a. Roots containing *ĭ* or *ŭ* **reduplicate with *e* or *o*;** thus *cit-* 'perceive' : *cékit-*; *tij-* 'be sharp' : *té-tij-*; *diś-* 'point' : *dé-diś-*; *nij-* 'wash' : *né-nij-*; *nī-* 'lead' : *ne-nī-*; *piś-* 'adorn' : *pé-piś-*; *mī-* 'damage' : *mé-mī-*; *rih-* 'lick' : *re-rih-*; *vij-* 'tremble' : *ve-vij-*; *vid-* 'find' : *vé-vid-*; *viṣ-* 'be active' : *ve-viṣ-*; *vī-* 'enjoy' : *ve-vī-*; *sidh-* 'repel' : *se-ṣidh-*; *gu-* 'sound' : *jo-gu-*; *dhū-* 'shake' : *do-dhu-*; *nu-* 'praise' : *no-nu-*; *pruth-* 'snort' : *po-pruth-*; *bhū-* 'be' : *bo-bhū-*; *yu-* 'join' : *yó-yu-*; *yu-* 'separate' : *yó-yu-*; *ru-* 'cry' : *ro-ru-*; *ru-* 'break' : *ro-ru-*; *śuc-* 'gleam' : *śó-śuc-*; *sū-* 'generate' : *so-ṣū-*; *sku-* 'tear' : *co-ṣkū-*; *hū-* 'call' : *jo-hū-*.

b. More than a dozen roots with medial *ă* (ending in mutes or sibilants, and one in *m*), as well as three with final *-ṛ*, **reduplicate with *ā*:** *kāś-* 'appear' : *cā-kaś-*; *gam-* 'go' : *jā-gam-*; *nad-* 'sound' : *nā́-nad-*; *pat-* 'fall' : *pā-pat-*; *bādh-* 'oppress' : *bā-badh-*; *raj-* 'colour' : *rā́-raj-*; *randh-* 'make subject' : *rārandh-*; *rap-* 'chatter' : *rā-rap-*; *lap-* 'prate' : *lā́-lap-*; *vac-* 'speak' : *vā-vac-*; *vad-* 'speak' : *vā-vad-*; *vaś-* 'be eager' : *vā-vaś-*; *vāś-* 'bellow' : *vā́-vaś-*; *śvas-* 'blow' : *śā-śvas-*; *gṛ-* 'wake' : *jā-gṛ-*; *dṛ-* 'split' : *dā-dṛ-*; *dhṛ-* 'hold' : *dā-dhṛ-*; also *cal-* 'stir' : *cā-cal-* (AV.).

2. All other roots containing *ṛ* (and *dṛ-* and *dhṛ-* alternatively) and several with medial *a* followed by *r l*, or a nasal, **reduplicate with *-ar*, *-al*** or ***-an*, *-aṃ*.** Thus:

a. *kṛ-* 'commemorate' : *car-kṛ-* and *car-kir-*; *kṛṣ-* 'drag' : *car-kṛṣ-*; *gṝ-* 'swallow' : *jár-gur-* and *jal-gul-*; *tṛ-* 'cross' : *tar-tṛ-* (RV.); *dṛ-* 'split' : *dár-dṛ-* and *dar-dir-*; *dhṛ-* 'hold' : *dár-dhṛ-*; *bṛh-* 'make strong' : *bár-bṛh-*; *bhṛ-* 'bear' : *jar-bhṛ-*[3]; *mṛj-* 'wipe' : *mar-mṛj-*; *mṛś-* 'touch' : *már- mṛś-*; *vṛt-* 'turn' : *var-vṛt-*; *sṛ-* 'flow' : *sar-sṛ-*; *hṛṣ-* 'be excited' : *jar-hṛṣ-*.

b. *car-* 'move' : *car-car-* (AV.); *cal-* 'stir' : *-cal-cal-* (MS.) beside *-cā-cal-* (AV.); *phar-* 'scatter' (?) : *par-phar-*; *kram-* 'stride' : *caṅ-kram-*; *gam-* 'go' : *jaṅ-gam-*; *jambh-* 'chew up' : *jañ-jabh-*; *taṃs-* 'shake' : *tan-tas-*; *daṃś-* 'bite' : *dan-daś-*; *nam-* 'bend' : *nan-nam-*; *yam-* 'reach' : *yaṃ-yam-*; *stan-* 'thunder' : *taṃ-stan-* (AV.).

---

[1] Grassmann, p. 1727, gives a list of the desiderative adjectives in *-su* occurring in the RV. (about 15); four occur in the AV.: *cikitsú-*, *jighatsú-*, *dipsú-*, *bībhatsú-*; cp. Whitney 1038.

[2] The specific meaning of the formation is wanting in the intensives of *gṛ-* 'wake', *cit-* 'perceive', *nij-* 'wash', *viṣ-* 'work'.

[3] The palatal *j* in the reduplication is like that of *bhṛ-* in the perfect form *ja-bhāra* (482 d).

α. A few intensives show irregularities in the reduplicative syllable; thus *ṛ-* 'go': *al-ar-* (dissimilation); *gāh-* 'plunge': *jaṅ-gah-* (from a root which otherwise has no nasal in inflected forms)[1]; *bādh-* 'oppress': *bad-badh-* (only example of a final mute being reduplicated); *gur-* 'greet' and *bhur-* 'quiver' reduplicate with *a*: *jar-gur-* and *jar-bhur-*[2].

β. In a few roots containing *ṛ* or *r* the radical syllable varies; thus *gṝ-* 'swallow': *jar-gur-* and *jal-gul-*; *car-* 'move': *car-cur-* beside *car-car-*; *tṛ-* 'cross': *tar-tur-* beside *tar-tar-*.

3. Over **twenty roots** with final or penultimate nasal, *ṛ*, or *ŭ*, interpose an *ī* (or *ĭ* if the vowel would be long by position) between the reduplicative syllable and the root:

a. *krand-* 'cry out': *kan-i-krand-* and *kan-i-krad-*; *gam-* 'go': *gan-ī-gam-* (but *gan-i-gm-at*); *pan-* 'admire': *pán-ī-pan-*; *phaṇ-* 'spring': *pán-ī-phaṇ-*; *ścand-* 'shine': *can-i-ścad-*; *san-* 'gain': *san-ī-ṣan-*; *skand-* 'leap': *kan-i-ṣkand-* and *can-i-ṣkad-*; *syand-* 'flow': *sán-i-ṣyad-*; *svan-* 'sound': *san-i-ṣvan-*; *han-* 'slay': *ghan-ī-ghan-*.

b. *kṛ-* 'make': *kar-i-kṛ-* and *car-i-kṛ-* (AV.)[3]; *tṛ-* 'cross': *tar-ī-tṛ-*; *bhṛ-* 'bear': *bhar-ī-bhṛ-*; *vṛ-* 'cover': *var-ī-vṛ-*; *vṛj-* 'twist': *vár-ī-vṛj-*; *vṛt-* 'turn': *var-ī-vṛt-*.

c. *tu-* 'be strong': *táv-ī-tu-*; *dhū-* 'shake': *dáv-i-dhu-*; *nu-* 'praise': *náv-ī-nu-*; *dyut-* 'shine': *dáv-i-dyut-*.

a. Primary Form. Present Indicative.

546. With the exception of eight or nine verbs, which take a secondary form (inflected in the middle only and identical in appearance with a passive), the intensive is inflected like the third conjugational class. The only difference is that *ī* may be inserted between the root and terminations beginning with consonants; it is common in the 1. and 3. sing. ind. act., and is also sometimes found to occur in the 2. 3. du. ind. and the 2. 3. sing. imperative and imperfect active[4]. The forms actually found, if made from the intensive of *nij-* 'wash', would be the following in the indicative:

Active. Sing. 1. *nénej-mi* and *nénej-ī-mi*. 2. *nének-ṣi*. 3. *nének-ti* and *nénej-ī-ti*. — Du. 2. *nenej-ī-thas*[5]. 3. *neṇik-tás*. — Pl. 1. *nenij-mas* and *nenij-masi* (AV.). 3. *nénij-ati*.

Middle. Sing. 1. *nenij-é*. 3. *nenik-té*. — Du. 3. *nenij-āte*. — Pl. 3. *nénij-ate*.

The forms actually met with are:

Active. Sing. 1. *carkarmi*, *veveṣmi* (AV.); *cākaśīmi*, *jóhavīmi*, *dardar-īmi*. — **2.** *alarṣi*, *jāgarṣi* (Kh. II. 3), *dárdarṣi*, *dárdharṣi*. — **3.** *álarti*, *kánikranti*, *ganīganti*, *jaṅghanti*, *varīvarti* and *várvarti*[6]; *-calcalīti* (MS. III. 1 3[1]); *carcarīti* (AV.), *cákaśīti*, *jarbhurīti*, *jalgulīti* (TS.), *jóhavīti*, *tartarīti*, *dardarīti*, *dodhavīti*, *nánnamīti*[7], *nónavīti*, *pāpatīti*, *bobhavīti*, *yaṃyamīti*, *rārajīti* (AV.), *rārapīti*, *róravīti*, *lālapīti* (AV.), *vāvadīti*, *soṣavīti*.

Du. 2. *tartarīthas*[8]. — **3.** *jarbhṛtás*.

Pl. 1. *nonumas* and *nonumasi* (AV.). — **3.** *jágrati* (AV.), *dávidyutati*, *nānadati*, *bharibhrati*, *várvṛtati*.

Middle. Sing. 1. *joguve*. — **3.** *tétikte*, *dédiṣṭe*, *nánnate*[9], *nenikté*,

---

[1] Though it has in nominal derivatives; see WHITNEY, Roots, s. v. *gāh*; cp. BURCHARDI, BB. 19, 179; v. NEGELEIN 79.

[2] Cp. p. 390, note 3.

[3] In the participle *kárikr-at* and *-çárikr-at* (AV.).

[4] This *ī* never occurs if the reduplication contains *ī*: thus *no-nav-ī-ti* and *nav-ī-no-t*, but never **navī-nav-ī-ti*. Cp. DELBRÜCK, Verbum p. 131; v. NEGELEIN 79.

[5] For **nenik-thás*; the only 2. du. which occurs is *tartar-ī-thas* for **tartṛ-thás*.

[6] For *várvart-ti*, *varīvart-ti*; cp. GRASSMANN, s. v. *vṛt*.

[7] See note 9.

[8] Cp. note 5.

[9] With loss of nasal (*a* = sonant nasal) for **nánnan-te* (I. 140[6]). AUFRECHT, RV[2]., and MAX MÜLLER, RV[2]., write *námna-te* (also Padapāṭha); but the participle *nánnamat* (VIII. 43[8]), AUFRECHT *nánn-*, MAX MÜLLER *náṃn-*; the 3. sing. *nánnamīti* (V. 83[5]) AUFRECHT[2], *náṃnamīti* MAX MÜLLER[2]; similarly *nánnamāne* (X. 82[1]) AUFRECHT, *námnamāne* MAX MÜLLER (also Pp.).

sarsṛte; with -*e* for -*te*: *cékite*, *jáṅgahe*, *joguve*, *badbadhé*[1] and *bābadhe*, *yoyuve*, *sarsré*. — Du. 3. *sarsrāte*. — Pl. 3. *dédiśate*.

547. a. **Subjunctive. Active. Sing.** 1. *jaṅghánāni*. — 2. *jāgarāsi*[2] (AV.); *jaṅghanas*, *jalgulas*. — 3. *caniṣkadat*, *cárkṛṣat*, *cékitat*, *jáṅghanat*, *jāgarat* (AV.), *dardirat*, *davidyutat*, *parpharat*, *bárbṛhat*, *mármṛjat*, *marmṛśat*, *saniṣvaṇat*. — Du. 1. *jaṅghánāva*. — Pl. 1. *carkirāma*, *vevidāma*. — 3. *carkiran*, ('commemorate'), *cākaśān*[2] (AV.), *pāpatan*, *śóśucan*.

Middle. Du. 3. *tantasaite*. — Pl. 3. *jáṅghananta*, *jarhṛṣanta*, *nonuvanta*, *marmṛjanta*, *śośucanta*.

b. **Optative.** No certain form occurs in the RV.[3], and only two or three in other Saṃhitās: Sing. 3. *veviṣyāt* (AV.). — Pl. 1. *jāgṛyāma* (VS. TS. MS.), *jāgriyāma* (TS. I. 7. 10[1]).

c. **Imperative.** Examples of forms of all the 2. and 3. persons are found excepting the 3. pl., but no middle form has been met with.

Active. Sing. 2. *carkṛdhi* (AV.) 'remember', *jāgṛhí*, *dardṛhí*, *dādṛhí*, *nenigdhi* (AV.), *barbṛhi*[4]; *jaṅghanīhi* (AV.), *cākaśīhi* (VS. TS.), *taṃstanīhi* (AV.). — With -*tāt*: *carkṛtāt*, *jāgṛtāt*[5]. — 3. *dardartu*, *marmartu*, *veveṣṭu* (AV.); *vāvadītu* (AV.), *johavītu* (AV.). — Du. 2. *jāgṛtam*. — 3. *jāgṛtām* (AV.). — Pl. 2. *jāgṛta* (AV.), *caṅkramata*[6].

548. **Participle. Active.** *kánikradat-*, *kárikrat-*, *ghánighnat-*, -*cárikrat-* (AV.), *cákaśat-*, *cékitat-*, *jáṅghanat-*, *járbhurat-*, *jágrat-*, *dáridrat-* (TS. IV. 5. 10[1]), *dárdrat-*, *dávidyutat-*, *nánnamat-*, *nánadat-*, *pánipnat-*, *pánīphaṇat-*, *pépiśat-*, *bóbhuvat-* (AV.), *mármṛjat-*, *yóyuvat-* (*yu-* 'ward off'), *rérihat-*, *róruvat-*, *vávaśat-* (*vāś-* 'roar'), *véviṣat-*, *śóśucat-*, *séṣidhat-*.

Middle[7]. *cékitāna-*, *jáñjabhāna-* (AV.), *járbhurāṇa-*, *járhṛṣāṇa-*, *dándaś-āna-*, *nánnamāna-*, *pépiśāna-* (AV. TS.), *bábadhāna-*, *mémyāna-*, *yóyuvāna-* (*yu-* 'join'), *rórucāna-*, *śóśucāna-*, *sársrāṇa-*.

a. The participles *badbadhāná-* and *marmṛjāná-* (beside *mármṛjāna-*), though irregularly accented, unmistakably belong to the intensive. *kánikrat* once (IX. 63[20]) appears as an abbreviated form of *kánikrad-at*. The participle *jáṅghan-at-* syncopates the radical vowel in the gen. sing.: *jáṅghn-at-as*; another form of the intensive participle from the same root syncopates the radical vowel throughout: *ghánighn-at-*; also *pánipn-at-*. The obscure form *cākán* (X. 29[1]) may be the nom. of an intensive participle with anomalous accent for *cákan-at*[8].

549. **Imperfect.** Altogether (including unaugmented forms, some of which are used injunctively) about thirty forms of the imperfect occur, among them only four examples of the middle. In the active all persons are represented except the 1. du. and the 2. pl.; but in the middle only the 3. sing. and pl. are met with.

Active. Sing. 1. *acākaśam*; *dediśam*. — 2. *ajāgar*, *adardar*; *dardar*. — 3. *adardar*, *adardhar*, *avarīvar*; *kániṣkan*, *dardar*, *dávidyot*, *návīnot*; *ájohavīt*, *áyoyavīt*, *ároravīt*, *ávāvacīt*.

Du. 2. *adardṛtam*. — 3. *avāvaśītām*. — Pl. 1. *marmṛjmá*. — 3. *acarkṛṣur* (AV.), *ájohavur*, *adardirur*, *anonavur*.

---

1 With irregular accent.

2 With double modal sign.

3 Cp. WHITNEY 1009 a.

4 For *barbṛh-hi*, the final *h* being dropped after being cerebralized before -*dhi* : **barbṛẓ-ḍhi* (58, 1 b, α; 62, 4 e).

5 This form occurs once in the AV. as a 1. person: cp. WHITNEY 1011 a.

6 With anomalous connecting -*a-* for **caṅkran-ta*.

7 The participles *rārah-āṇá-*, *vārakṣ-āṇá-*, and *jāhṛṣ-āṇá-* (beside *járhṛṣ-āṇa-*) are probably perfect participles, although no other perfect forms with *ā* in the reduplicative syllable occur from these roots (*rah-*, *rakṣ-*, *hṛṣ-*); cp. WHITNEY 1013.

8 I regard it as 3. sing. perf. inj. = **cākán-t* (488). Cp. BARTHOLOMAE, IF. 7, 111, GRASSMANN, under the root *kā-*; WHITNEY, Sanskrit Grammar 1013 b; Roots 17.

Middle. Sing. 3. *ádediṣṭa, ánannata*[1]. — Pl. 3. *marmṛjata*[2].

550. a. **Perfect.** A few perfect forms with intensive reduplication and present sense are met with:

Active. Sing. 1. *jāgara.* — 3. *jāgára, davidhāva* (*dhū-* 'shake'), *nónāva*[3] (*nu-* 'praise').

The only perfect **participle** occurring is *jāgṛvā́ṃs-*.

b. **Aorist.** The only trace of an aorist being formed from the intensive is *cárkṛ-ṣ-e* 'thinks of', 3. sing. mid., formed like *hi-ṣ-e* and *stu-ṣ-e.* It occurs three times in the RV., always with a present sense.

c. **Causative.** A causative formed from the intensive is once found in the **participle** *varīvarj-áyant-ī-* (AV.) 'twisting about' (√*vṛj-*).

b. Secondary Form.

551. The rare secondary form of the intensive is identical in meaning with the primary. In form it is indistinguishable from a passive, the suffix *-yá* being added to the primary stem and the inflexion being the same as that of the passive. Altogether about a dozen forms have been met with from nine roots. The only persons represented are the 2. and 3. sing. and 3. pl. indicative; and there is also a present participle. The forms actually occurring are the following:

Present indicative. Sing. 2. *coṣkūyáse.* — 3. *dediśyáte* (AV. VS.), *nenīyáte* (VS.), *marmṛjyáte, rerihyáte, vevijyáte, vevīyate.* — Pl. 3. *tartūryante* (√*tṝ-*), *marmṛjyánte.*

Participle. *carcūryámāṇa-* (√*car-*), *nenīyámāna-*, *marmṛjyámāna-*.

3. The Causative.

DELBRÜCK, Verbum p. 209—216. — AVERY, Verb-Inflection 262—268. — WHITNEY, Sanskrit Grammar p. 379—386; Roots 235 f. — v. NEGELEIN 44—48.

552. The causative verb expresses that its object is caused to perform the action or to undergo the state denoted by the root; e. g. *páram evá parāvátaṃ sapátnīṃ gamayāmasi* (x. 145[4]) 'we cause our rival to go to the far distance'. It is by far the commonest of the secondary conjugations, being formed from over 200 roots in the Saṃhitās; but of about 150 causative stems appearing in the RV. at least one-third lack the causative meaning. The stem is formed by adding the suffix *-áya* to the root, which as a rule is strengthened. Those verbs in which the root, though capable of being strengthened, remains unchanged, have not a causative[4], but an iterative sense, being akin in formation to denominatives[5] (which sometimes even have the causative accent). The whole group may originally have had this meaning, from which the causative sense was developed till it became the prevalent one[6]. This may perhaps account for an iterative formation, the reduplicated aorist, having specially attached itself to the causative. Both the iterative and the causative form are occasionally made from the same root; e. g. *patáya-ti* 'flies about' and *pātáya-ti* 'causes to fly' beside the simple verb *páta-ti* 'flies'.

---

1 See p. 391, note 9.

2 *ávāvaśanta* (√*vāś-*) is probably a pluperfect (p. 365, top).

3 WHITNEY 1018 quotes also *dodrāva* (*dru-* 'run') from the TS., and *yoyāva* (*yu-* 'separate'), and *leláya* (*lī-* 'be unsteady') from the MS. (I. 86); the latter form is irregular in accent. Cp. BÖHTLINGK's Lexicon, s. v. 3. *lī*.

4 Cp. WHITNEY 1042 b.

5 Cp. v. NEGELEIN 44.

6 Cp. BRUGMANN, KG. 698.

553. The **root is strengthened** in different ways according to the nature and position of its vowel.

Initial or **medial** *i u ṛ ḷ* (if not long by position) **take Guṇa**; thus

a. *cit-* 'perceive' : *cet-áya-* 'teach'; *mih-* 'mingere' : *meh-áya-* 'cause to rain'; *riṣ-* 'be hurt' : *reṣ-áya-* 'injure'; *vid-* 'know' : *ved-áya-* 'cause to know'; *vip-* 'tremble' : *vep-áya-* 'shake'; *viś-* 'enter' : *veś-áya-* 'cause to enter'; *viṣṭ-* 'wrap' : *veṣṭ-áya-* (AV.) 'involve'; *snih-* 'be moist' : *sneh-áya-* 'destroy';

b. *kup-* 'be agitated' : *kop-áya-* 'shake'; *krudh-* 'be angry' : *krodh-áya-* 'enrage'; *kṣud-* 'be agitated' : *kṣod-aya-* 'shake'; *ghuṣ-* 'sound' : *ghoṣ-áya-* 'proclaim'; *cud-* 'impel' : *cod-áya-*, id.; *juṣ-* 'enjoy' : *joṣ-áya-* 'caress'; *jyut-* 'shine' : *jyot-áya-* (AV.) 'enlighten'; *tuś-* 'drip' : *toś-aya-* 'bestow abundantly'; *dyut-* 'shine' : *dyot-aya-* 'illumine'; *puṣ-* 'thrive' : *poṣ-aya-* 'nourish'; *budh-* 'be awake' : *bodh-áya-* 'waken'; *muh-* 'be dazed' : *moh-áya-* 'bewilder'; *yudh-* 'fight' : *yodh-áya-* 'cause to fight'; *yup-* 'efface' : *yop-áya-*, id.; *ruc-* 'shine' : *roc-áya-* 'illumine'; *rud-* 'weep' : *rod-áya-* 'cause to wail'; *ruh-* 'rise' : *roh-áya-* 'raise'; *lubh-* 'desire eagerly' : *lobh-áya-* 'allure'; *śuc-* 'flame' : *śoc-áya-* 'set on fire'; *śubh-* 'shine' : *śobh-aya-* (AV.) 'adorn'; *śuṣ-* 'grow dry' : *śoṣ-áya-* (AV.) 'make dry';

c. *ṛd-* 'dissolve' (intr.) : *ard-áya-* 'destroy'; *kṛś-* 'be lean' : *karś-áya-* 'emaciate'; *tṛp-* 'be pleased' : *tarp-áya-* 'delight'; *dṛś-* 'see' : *darś-áya-* (AV.) 'show'; *nṛt-* 'dance' : *nart-áya-* 'cause to dance'; *bṛh-* or *vṛh-* 'tear' : *barh-áya-* 'thrust'; *mṛc-* 'injure' : *marc-áya-*, id.; *mṛj-* 'wipe' : *marj-áya-*, id.; *vṛj-* 'turn' : *varj-aya-* (AV.) 'cause to turn'; *vṛt-* 'roll' : *vart-áya-* 'cause to revolve'; *vṛdh-* 'grow' : *vardh-áya-* 'augment'; *vṛṣ-* 'rain' : *varṣ-áya-* 'cause to rain'; *śṛdh-* 'be bold' : *śardh-áya-* 'cause to be bold'; *hṛṣ-* 'be excited' : *harṣ-áya-* 'excite';

d. *kḷp-* 'be adapted' : *kalp-áya-* 'arrange'.

554. The following verbs, mostly lacking the causative meaning, leave the **root unchanged**: *il-* 'be quiet' : *il-áya-* (AV.) 'cease'; *cit-* 'observe' : *cit-áya-* 'stimulate' (also *cet-áya-*); *riṣ-* 'be injured' : *riṣ-aya-* id. (beside *reṣ-áya-*); *vip-* 'quiver' : *vip-áya-* 'agitate' (also *vep-aya-*);

tuj- 'be eager' : *tuj-áya-* id.; *tur-* 'overwhelm' : *tur-áya-* id.; *tuṣ-* 'be content' : *tuṣ-áya-* id.; *dyut-* 'shine' : *dyut-aya-* id. (beside *dyot-aya-* 'illumine'); *ruc-* 'shine' : *ruc-aya-* id. (beside *roc-áya-* 'illumine'); *śuc-* 'shine' : *śuc-áya-* id. (beside *śoc-áya-* 'illumine'); *śubh-* 'shine' : *śubh-áya-* id. (also *śobh-aya-* 'adorn' AV.). The vowel is **lengthened** in *duṣ-* 'spoil' : *dūṣ-áya-* id.

kṛp- 'lament' : *kṛp-áya-* id.; *mṛḍ-* 'be gracious' : *mṛḷ-áya-*[1] id.; *spṛh-* 'be eager' : *spṛh-aya-* id. In the case of *grabh-* 'grasp', the root is even **weakened**: *gṛbh-áya-* id.

a. **Vowels long** by nature or position remain **unchanged**, but the stem, in this case, usually has the causative sense: *iṅg-* 'move' : *iṅg-áya-* 'set in motion'; *īkṣ-* 'see' : *īkṣ-áya-* 'cause to see'; *īṅkh-* 'swing' : *īṅkh-áya-* 'shake'; *īr-* 'set in motion' : *īr-áya-* id.; *jīv-* 'live' : *jīv-áya-* 'animate'; *dīp-* 'shine' : *dīp-áya-* 'kindle'; *pīḍ-* 'press' : *pīḍ-aya-* (AV.) 'distress'; *vīḍ-* 'be strong' (in *vīḷ-ú-* 'strong') : *vīḷ-áya-* 'make strong'[2];

ukṣ- 'grow up' : *ukṣ-aya-* 'strengthen'; *kūḍ-* (does not occur in the simple form) : *kūḷ-aya-* 'scorch'; *śundh-* 'purify' : *śundh-aya-* id.; *sūd-* 'make pleasant' : *sūd-áya-* id.; *sphūrj-* 'rumble' : *sphūrj-áya-* id.;

dṛṃh- 'make firm' : *dṛṃh-aya-* (AV.) 'hold fast';

a. Two roots with medial *ī* take Guṇa: *srīv-* 'fail' : *srev-áya-* beside *srīv-aya-*[3] (AV.) 'lead astray'; *hīḍ-* 'be hostile' : *heḷaya-* in the participle *á-heḷayant-* 'not angry'; while

[1] Cp. v. NEGELEIN 46, note [1].

[2] DELBRÜCK 189, 4 regards *vīḷáya-* as a denominative.

[3] In AV. VI. 73[2] all the Mss. but one have *śrīv-*.

two others already have it in the root: *rej-* 'tremble' : *rej-áya-* 'shake'; *med-* 'be fat' : *med-áya-* 'fatten'.

555. An initial or a **medial *a*** (if not long by position) is **lengthened** in some thirty roots: *am-* 'be injurious' : *ām-áya-* 'be injured'; *kam-* 'desire' : *kām-áya-* 'love'; *cat-* 'hide oneself' : *cāt-áya-* 'drive away'; *chad-* 'cover'[1] : *chād-áya-* id.; *tan-* 'stretch' : *tān-aya-* (AV.) 'make taut'; *tap-* 'burn' : *tāp-áya-* (AV.) 'cause to burn'; *tras-* 'be terrified' : *trās-aya-* (AV.) 'terrify'; *naś-* 'be lost' : *nāś-áya-* 'destroy'; *pad-* 'go', 'fall' : *pād-áya-* 'cause to fall'; *phaṇ-* 'bound' : *phāṇ-aya-* 'cause to bound'; *bhaj-* 'divide' : *bhāj-aya-* 'cause to share'; *bhraś-* 'fall' : *bhrāś-áya-* 'cause to fall'; *man-* 'think' : *mān-aya-*[2] (AV.) 'esteem'; *yat-* 'stretch' : *yāt-áya-* 'unite'; *yam-* 'guide' : *yām-aya-* (Pp. *yăm-*) 'present'; *lap-* 'prate' : *lāp-aya-* (AV.) 'cause to cry'; *vat-* 'apprehend' : *vāt-áya-* 'inspire'; *van-* 'win' : *vān-aya-* (AV.) 'conciliate' (Pp. *văn-*); *vas-* 'dwell' : *vās-áya-* 'cause to stay'; *vas-* 'wear' : *vās-áya-* 'clothe'; *vas-* 'shine' : *vās-aya-* 'illumine'; *śat-*[3] 'cut in pieces' : *śāt-áya-* (AV.) id.[4]; *śvas-* 'snort' : *śvās-aya-* (AV.) 'cause to resound'; *spaś-* 'see' : *spāś-áya-* 'show'; *svap-* 'sleep' : *svāp-aya-* 'send to sleep'.

a. Five or six other causatives **optionally retain the *a***: *gam-* 'go' : *gam-áya-* and *gām-aya-* (RV[1].) 'bring'; *das-* 'waste away' : *das-aya-* and *dās-aya-* (AV.) 'exhaust'; *dhvan-* 'disappear' : *dhvan-aya-* (RV.) and *dhvān-aya-* (RV.) 'cause to disappear'; *pat-* 'fall' : *pat-áya-* 'fly about' (in RV. only once, I. 169[7], 'cause to fall') and *pāt-áya-* 'cause to fall'; *mad-* 'be exhilarated' : *mad-áya-* (AV.) and *mād-áya-* 'rejoice'; *ram-* 'rest' : *ram-áya-* and *rām-áya-* 'cause to rest'.

556. Some twenty-five roots with initial or medial ***a*** (**short** by position) remain **unchanged**, as the causative meaning is mostly absent: *an-* 'breathe' : *-an-áya-* (AV.) 'cause to breathe'; *chad-* 'seem' : *chad-áya-* id.; *jan-* 'beget' : *jan-áya-* id.; *tvar-* 'make haste' : *tvar-áya-* (AV.) 'quicken'; *dam-* 'control' : *dam-áya-* id.; *dhan-* 'set in motion' : *dhan-áya-* id.; *dhvas-* 'disperse' (intr.) : *dhvas-áya-* 'scatter' (tr.); *nad-* 'roar' : *nad-áya-* 'cause to resound'; *nam-* 'bend' (tr. and intr.) : *nam-aya-* 'cause to bend', 'strike down'; *pan-* 'admire' : *pan-áya-* id.; *prath-* 'spread out' : *prath-áya-* id.; *mah-* 'be great' : *mah-áya-* 'magnify'; *raj-* 'colour' : *raj-aya-* (AV.) id.; *raṇ-* 'rejoice' : *raṇ-áya-* id. and 'gladden'; *vyath-* 'waver' : *vyath-áya-* 'cause to fall'; *śam-* 'be quiet' : *śam-áya-* (AV.) 'appease'; *śnath-* 'pierce' : *śnath-aya-* id.; *śrath-* 'loosen' : *śrath-áya-* id.; *stan-* 'thunder' : *stan-áya-* id.; *svad-* 'enjoy', 'sweeten' : *svad-áya-* id.; *svan-* 'sound' : *svan-aya-* id.; *svar-* 'sound' : *svar-áya-* (AV.) id.[5]

a. If **long** by nature or position medial ***ă*** **remains unchanged,** the causative sense being more often lacking than present: thus *arc-* 'shine' : *arc-aya-* 'cause to shine'; *kāś-* 'appear' : *kāś-áya-* (AV.) 'cause to be viewed'; *krand-* 'roar' : *krand-áya-* 'cause to roar'; *cakṣ-* 'see' : *cakṣ-aya-* 'cause to appear'; *chand-* 'seem' : *chand-aya-* id.; *jambh-* 'chew up', 'crush' : *jambh-áya-* id.; *taṃs-* 'set in motion' : *taṃs-áya-* id.; *dambh-* 'destroy' : *dambh-áya-* id.; *bādh-* 'oppress' : *bādh-aya-* (AV.) 'force'; *bhakṣ-* 'partake of' : *bhakṣ-áya-* id.; *maṃh-* 'bestow' : *maṃh-áya* id.; *mand-* 'gladden' : *mand-áya-* 'satisfy'; *yāc-* 'ask' : *yāc-áya-* (AV.) 'cause to be asked for'; *raṃh-* 'hasten' : *raṃh-áya-* (AV.) id.; *randh-* 'make subject' : *randh-áya-* id.; *rāj-* 'rule' : *rāj-aya-* (AV. TS.) 'be king'; *rādh-* 'succeed' : *rādh-aya-* (AV.) 'make successful'; *vakṣ-* 'grow' : *vakṣ-aya-* 'cause to grow';

---

1 Finite forms of the simple root *chad-* do not occur; the part. *channa-* is found in B.

2 In AV. XV. 10[2] the reading should be *mānayet*; see WHITNEY's note.

3 In AV. IV. 18[4] *śāpaya*, which would be the causative of *śap-*, is probably a wrong reading; cp. WHITNEY's note.

4 No form or derivative of the simple root *śat-* occurs in V.; see WHITNEY, Roots, s. v. *śat*.

5 Occurring only in the participle *svaráyantam* (AV. XIII. 2[2]), which WHITNEY translates 'shining'.

śaṃs- 'proclaim' : *śaṃs-áya-* 'cause to proclaim'; *śvañc-* 'spread' : *śvañc-áya-* 'cause to spread out'; *syand-* 'flow' : *syand-aya-* id.; *sraṃs-* 'fall' : *sraṃs-aya-* (AV.) 'cause to fall'.

557. **Final *i*, *ŭ*, *ṛ* take Guṇa or Vṛddhi,** the latter being commoner.

a. The only example of a causative stem from a root ending in an *i*-vowel is that of *kṣi-* 'possess', which takes Guṇa: *kṣay-áya-* 'cause to dwell securely'.

b. Final *ŭ* takes Guṇa or Vṛddhi: *cyu-* 'waver' : *cyāv-áya-* 'shake'; *dru-* 'run' : *drav-aya-* 'flow' and *drāv-áya-* 'cause to flow'; *bhū-* 'become' : *bhāv-áya-* (AV.) 'cause to become'; *yu-* 'separate' : *yav-aya-* and *yāv-áya-* id.; *śru-* 'hear' : *śrav-áya-* and *śrāv-áya-* 'cause to hear'; *śru-*[1] 'dissolve' : *śrav-áya-* and *śrāv-aya-* (Pp. *śrav-*) 'cause to move'; *sru-* 'flow' : *srāvaya-* (AV.) 'cause to flow'.

c. Final *ṛ* usually takes Vṛddhi; thus *ghṛ-* 'drip' : *ghār-aya-* (AV.) 'cause to drip'; *dhṛ-* 'hold' : *dhār-áya-* id.; *pṛ-* 'pass' : *pār-áya-* id.; *pṛ-* 'fill' : *pūr-áya-* (AV.) 'fulfil'; *mṛ-* 'die' : *mār-áya-* (AV.) 'kill'; *vṛ-* 'confine' : *vār-áya-* id. Two causatives have the Guṇa as well as the Vṛddhi form: *jṛ-* 'waste away' : *jar-áya-* and *jār-áya-* (Pp. *jar-*) 'wear out', 'cause to grow old'; *sṛ-* 'flow' : *sar-áya-* id. and *sār-aya-* 'cause to flow'. One root in *-ṛ* takes Guṇa only: *dṛ-* 'pierce' : *dar-áya-* 'shatter'.

558. **Roots ending in *-ā*** form their causative stem **by adding *-páya***; thus *kṣā-* 'burn' : *kṣā-paya-* (AV.) id.; *glā-* 'be weary' : *glā-paya-* (Pp. *glăp-*) 'exhaust'; *dā-* 'give' : *dā-paya-* (AV.) 'cause to give'; *dhā-* 'put' : *dhā-páya-* 'cause to put'; *dhā-* 'suck' : *dhā-páya-* 'suckle'; *mlā-* 'relax' (intr.) : *mlā-páya-* (AV.) 'relax' (tr.); *vā-* 'blow' : *vā-páya-* 'fan'; *sthā-* 'stand' : *sthā-paya-* 'set up'; *snā-* 'wash' (intr.) : *snā-páya-* 'bathe' (tr.)[2]. In three roots the *ā* is shortened: *jñā-* 'know' : *jña-paya-* (AV.) 'cause to know'; *śrā-* 'boil' : *śra-páya-* (AV. TS.) 'cook'; *snā-* 'wash' : *sna-páya-* (AV.) beside *snā-páya-* 'bathe' (tr.).

a. A few roots ending in other vowels take *-paya*. Two stems are formed by adding the suffix to the guṇated root: *kṣi-* 'possess' : *kṣe-paya-* 'cause to dwell' beside *kṣay-áya-*; *ṛ-* 'go' : *arpaya-* 'cause to go'. In the VS. two roots in *i* substitute *ā* for that vowel before *-paya*: *ji-* 'conquer' : *jā-paya-* 'cause to win'; *śri-* 'resort' : (*ud-*)*śrā-paya-* (VS[1].) 'raise'.

α. Two roots with initial *p* and ending in *-ā* do not form their causative stem with *-paya*, but add the ordinary suffix *-aya* with interposed *y*: *pā* 'drink' : *pāy-áya-*, 'cause to drink'; *pyā-* 'overflow' : (*ā-*)*pyāy-áya-* (AV.) 'fill up'. This seeming irregularity is doubtless due to the original form of the root[3].

Inflexion.

559. The causative is inflected regularly like the verbs of the *a-* conjugation in both voices. It is to be noted, however, that in the 1. pl. pres. the termination *-masi* occurs in the RV. and AV. ten times as often as *-mas*; that in the 2. pl. no forms in *-thana* are met with; and that in the 3. sing. mid. *e* never appears for *-ate*.

a. The forms of the **present indicative** active and middle, which actually occur, would if made from *kalpáya-* be the following:

Active. Sing. 1. *kalpayāmi.* 2. *kalpáyasi.* 3. *kalpáyati.* — Du. 2. *kalpáyathas.* 3. *kalpayatas.* — Pl. 1. *kalpayāmasi* and *kalpáyāmas.* 2. *kalpáyathă.* 3. *kalpáyanti.*

Middle. Sing. 1. *kalpáye.* 2. *kalpáyase.* 3. *kalpáyate.* — Du. 2. *kalpáyethe.* 3. *kalpáyete.* — Pl. 1. *kalpayāmahe.* 3. *kalpáyante.*

Forms that occur elsewhere in the present system are the following:

[1] This root, of which only three forms occur in the RV., seems to be only a varied spelling for *sru-* 'flow'.

[2] The causative stem *hā-paya-*, from *hā-* 'forsake' is presupposed by the aorist *jīhipas.*

[3] See above 27 a 1 and 4.

b. Subjunctive. Active. Sing. 1. *cetáyāni* (TS. III. 2. 10[2]; MS. IV. 5[8]), *randhayāni*. — **2.** *codáyāsi, mṛḷáyāsi, randháyāsi* (AV.), *vartayāsi* (TS. VII. 4. 20[1]); *janáyās* (AV.), *yāvayās* (AV.), *yodháyās*. — **3.** *ardayāti* (AV.), *kalpáyāti, tarpayāti* (AV.), *pādayāti* (AV.), *pārayāti, pūrayāti* (AV.), *māráyāti* (AV.), *mṛḷáyāti, rājayāti* (TS. II. 4. 14[2]), *sūdayāti*; *kalpayāt* (AV.), *codáyāt, pāráyāt, marcáyāt, sādayāt, sāydyāt* (TS. I. 8. 6[2]). — **Du. 1.** *īráyāva*. — **2.** *dhāpayāthas* (AV.), *pādayāthas* (AV.), *vāsayāthas* (AV.), *sādayāthas* (AV.). — **3.** *kūḷayātas*. — **Pl. 1.** *īrayāma, dhārayāma*. — **2.** *chaddáyātha, vardhayātha* (AV.). — **3.** *śrapáyān* (TS. IV. 1. 5[4]). — **Middle. Sing. 2.** *kāmáyāse, codáyāse, joṣáyāse, mādáyāse, yātayāse, mādayāthās* (AV. IV. 25[6]). — **3.** *codayāte, chandayāte, dhārayāte, mādáyāte, vartayāte*; *īṅkháyātai* (AV.), *cetáyātai* (TS. I. 1. 13[2]), *dhārayātai* (AV.), *rājayātai* (AV.), *vārayātai* (AV.). — **Du. 1.** *īṅkhayāvahai, kalpayāvahai, janayāvahai* (AV.). — **3.** *mādáyaite*. — **Pl. 2.** *kāmáyādhve, mādayādhve*; *mādayādhvai*.

c. Optative. This mood is very rare, only four forms occurring in the RV. and two in the AV. **Sing. 2.** *janayes* (Kh. II. 10[4]), *dhārayes*. — **3.** *mānayet* (AV.), *vādayet* (AA. III. 2. 5), *veśayet* (AV.), *spṛhayet*. — **Pl. 1.** *citáyema, marjayema*.

d. Imperative. Forms of this mood are common, nearly 120 occurring in the RV.; of these, however, quite one half are in the 2. sing. act. No forms of the 3. sing. and du. mid. are met with in the RV. No impv. in *-tāt* is found in the RV. and only one in the AV.: 2. sing. *dhārayatāt*[1]. The forms actually occurring, if made from *kalpáya-*, would be the following:

Active. Sing. 2. *kalpáyā* and *kalpayatāt* (AV.). 3. *kalpayatu*. — Du. 2. *kalpáyatam*. 3. *kalpayatām*. — Pl. 2. *kalpáyatā*. 3. *kalpáyantu*.

Middle. Sing. 2. *kalpáyasva*. — Du. 2. *kalpáyethām*. — Pl. 2. *kalpáyadhvam*. 3. *kalpayantām*.

e. Participles. The **active** participle in *-ant*, with fem. in *-ī*, is common; e. g. *jan-áyant-*, f. *jan-áyant-ī-* 'producing'. The **middle** participle, which is always formed with *-māna*, is rare. In the RV. are found only *maháya-māna-* 'glorifying', *yātáya-māna-* 'reaching', *vardháya-māna-* 'increasing', and in the AV. only *kāmáya-māna-* 'desiring'; in the TS. (IV. 2. 6[2]) *cātáya-māna-*.

f. Imperfect. Forms of this tense, both augmented and unaugmented, are frequent. In the RV. some 130 occur in the active, about two-thirds of which are in the 2. and 3. sing. Middle forms are rare except in the 3. pl. In the active the 1. and 3. du., and 1. and 2. pl. are wanting; in the middle all the 1. persons and the 3. du. are unrepresented. Some 50 unaugmented forms are used as injunctives in the RV.[2] The forms actually occurring, if made from *janáya-*, would be the following:

Active. Sing. 1. *ajanayam*; *janayam*. 2. *ájanayas*; *janáyas*. 3. *ájanayat*; *janáyat*. — Du. 2. *ájanayatam*. — Pl. 3. *ájanayan*; *janayan*.

Middle. Sing. 2. *ajanayathās*; *janáyathās*. 3. *ájanayata*; *janayata*. — Du. 2. *ájanayethām*. — Pl. 2. *ajanayadhvam*. 3. *ájanayanta*; *janáyanta*.

560. Outside the present system very few causative forms occur. These are found in the following formations.

a. Future. Only four forms occur in the RV. and AV. **Active.** Sing. 1. *dūṣayiṣyāmi* (AV.). 3. *dhārayiṣyáti*. — **Middle.** Sing. 2. *vāsayiṣyáse* 'wilt adorn thyself'. 3. *vārayiṣyate* (AV.) 'will shield'.

b. Perfect. The only example of a periphrastic perfect occurring in the Saṃhitās is made from a causative stem: *gamayáṃ cakāra* (AV.).

c. Aorist. The **reduplicated** aorist has attached itself to the causative, probably because the intensive character of the reduplicated form became

---

1 In K. the forms *yamayatāt* and *cyāvayatāt* occur; and in pl. 2. the unexampled ending *-dhvāt* in *vārayadhvāt*: Whitney 1043 d.

2 See Avery 264.

associated with the originally iterative meaning of the causative. But in form it is unconnected with the causative stem, being derived directly from the root; and more than one-third of the verbs which form it in the RV., and about one-fifth in the AV., have no causative stem in *-aya*. There are, however, eight forms which are actually made from the causative stem: Sing. 1. *arp-ip-am* (AV.) from *ar-paya-*; 2. *jīhip-as* from *hā-paya-*[1] 'cause to depart'; *atiṣṭhip-as* and 3. *átiṣṭhip-at* from *sthā-paya-* 'fasten'; *ajijñip-at* (TS.) from *jñā-paya-* 'cause to know'; Pl. 2. *ájījap-ata* (VS.) from *jāpaya-* 'cause to conquer' (√*ji-*); Sing. 2. act. *bībhiṣ-as* (TS.) and mid. *bībhiṣ-athās* from *bhī-ṣaya-* 'frighten', anomalous causative of *bhī-* 'fear'.

a. There are besides three *iṣ*-aorists formed from the causative stem: *vyathay-īs* (AV.) from *vyathaya-* 'disturb'; *ailay-īt* (AV.) from *ilaya-* 'has quieted down'; *dhvanay-īt*[2] from *dhvanaya-* 'envelope'.

561. **Nominal derivatives.** a. The only present **passive participle** appears in the form *bhāj-yá-māna-* (AV. XII. 5^{28}). There are also a few past participles: *ghār-i-ta-* (AV.) 'smeared'; *cod-i-tá-* 'impelled'; *-veś-i-ta-* (AV.) 'caused to enter'.

b. A few **gerundives** in *-āyya* are formed from causative stems: *trayay-ā́yya-* 'to be guarded'; *panay-ā́yya-* 'admirable'; *spṛhay-ā́yya-* 'desirable'[3].

c. Ten **infinitives** formed with *-dhyai* from the causative stem are met with in the RV.: *iṣáyadhyai*, *īráyadhyai*, *taṃsayádhyai*, *nāśayádhyai*, *mandayádhyai*, *mādayádhyai*, *riṣayádhyai*, *vartayádhyai*, *vājayádhyai*, *syandayádhyai*[4].

d. Four **gerunds** formed with *-tvā* from causative stems are met with in the AV.: *arpay-i-tvā́*, *kalpay-i-tvā́*, *sāday-i-tvā́*, *sraṃsay-i-tvā́*.

e. Finally several **ordinary nouns** are derived from the causative stem with various suffixes; a few verbal nouns in **-ana**: *árp-aṇa-* (AV.) 'thrusting'; *-bhī́-ṣ-aṇa-* 'frightening'; one or two agent nouns in **-tṛ́**, f. *-tr-ī*: *coday-i-tr-ī-* 'stimulator'; *bodhay-i-tṛ́-* 'awakener'; a few adjectives in **-á** as second members of compounds: *ati-pārayá-* 'putting across'; *ni-dhārayá-* 'putting down'; *vācam-īṅkhayá-* 'voice-impelling'; *viśvam-ejaya-* 'all-stimulating'; an adjective in **-ālu**: *patay-ālú-* (AV.) 'flying'; five adjectives in **-iṣṇu**: *tāpay-iṣṇú-* 'tormenting'; *namay-iṣṇu-* 'bending'; *patay-iṣṇú-* 'flying'; *pāray-iṣṇú-* 'rescuing'; *māday-iṣṇú-* 'intoxicating'; seven adjectives in **-itnú**: *-āmay-itnú-* 'making ill'; *tanay-itnú-* 'thundering'; *drāvay-itnú-* 'speeding'; *poṣay-itnú-* 'nourishing'; *māday-itnú-* 'intoxicating'; *sūday-itnú-* 'streaming sweetness'; *stanay-itnú-* m. 'thunder'; and three adjectives in **-u**: *dhāray-ú-* 'streaming'[5]; *bhāvay-ú-* 'animating'; *manday-ú-* 'rejoicing'.

4. The Denominative.

DELBRÜCK, Verbum p. 201—209, 216—218. — AVERY, Verb-Inflection 272—274. — WHITNEY, Sanskrit Grammar 1053—1068. — v. NEGELEIN, Zur Sprachgeschichte 40—44. — Cp. BRUGMANN, KG. 693—696.

562. The denominative is nearly always formed from a nominal stem with the suffix *-ya*. The latter is normally accented; but a certain number of unmistakable denominatives, such as *mantrá-ya-te* 'takes counsel', have the causative accent and thus form a connecting link between the regular denominatives and the causatives[6] The formation is a frequent one, more than a hundred denominative stems occurring in the RV., and in the AV. about

[1] The stem *hā-paya-* does not itself otherwise occur in V.; cp. p. 396 note [2].

[2] The TS. IV. 6. 9^2 has instead *dhvanayit*.

[3] See below 579.

[4] Cp. DELBRÜCK, Verbum 211; and below 585, 7.

[5] WHITNEY, Roots, s. v. *dhṛ*; according to BR. and GRASSMANN to be analyzed as *dhāra-yú-*.

[6] There can be little doubt that the denominative suffix *-ya* is identical with that of the causative as well as that of the verbs of the fourth class; cp. WHITNEY 1055 a; v. NEGELEIN 44; BRUGMANN, KG. 690, 694.

thirty (or about fifty if those which form present participles or derivative nouns only are included). The general meaning of the denominative is that the subject expressed by the inflexion stands in some relation to the noun from which the stem is formed. It may usually be rendered by 'be or act like'; 'regard or treat as'; 'turn into or use as'; 'wish for'.

Denominatives formed with *-ya* are best classified according to the final of the nominal stem to which the suffix is added.

563. **Stems in -a,** which usually remains unchanged; thus *amitra-yá-* 'act like an enemy', 'be hostile'; *indra-ya-* 'behave like Indra'; *kṣema-yá-* 'take a rest'; *jāra-ya-* 'treat like a lover', 'caress'; *deva-yá-* 'serve the gods'; *yuṣma-yá-* 'seek you'; *vasna-yá-* 'deal with the price', 'bargain'.

With the causative accent: *(pary-)aṅkhá-ya-*[1] 'clasp (round)'; *arthá-ya-* 'have as a desire'; *ṛtá-ya-* 'act according to sacred order'; *kulāyá-ya-* 'build a nest'; *nīḷá-ya-* 'bring together'; *pālá-ya-* (AV.) 'act as guardian', 'protect'; *mantrá-ya-* 'take counsel'; *mṛgá-ya-* 'treat as a wild animal', 'hunt'; *vavrá-ya*; 'put in hiding', 'shrink from'; *vājá-ya-* 'act like a steed', 'race' (beside *vāja-yá-*)- *vīrá-ya-* 'play the man'; *sa-bhāgá-ya-* (AV.) 'apportion'[2].

a. One or two denominatives are from nominal stems extended with *-a*: *iṣ-á-ya-* 'have strength' (*iṣ-*)[3]; *ūrj-á-ya-* 'have strength' (*ū́rj-*)[4].

a. The **-a** is, however, **often lengthened:** *aghā-yá-* 'plan mischief'; *ajirā-ya-* 'be swift'; *amitrā-yá-* (AV.) 'be hostile' (Pp. *-āyá-*); *aśvā-yá-* 'desire horses'; *ṛtā-yá-* 'observe sacred order' (beside *ṛtá-ya-*); *tilvilā-yá-* 'be fertile'; *tudā-yá-* (AV.) 'thrust'; *dhūpā-yá-*[5] (MS. AV.) 'be like smoke', 'fume'; *priyā-yá-* 'become friends'; *mathī-yá-* (AV.) 'shake'; *muṣā-ya-*[6] (AV.) 'steal'; *yajñā-yá-* 'sacrifice'; *rathirā-yá-* 'be conveyed in a car'; *randhanā-ya-*[7] 'make subject'; *vṛṣā-yá-* 'act like a bull'[8]; *śamā-yá-* 'be active' (*śáma-*); *śubhā-yá-* 'be beautiful'[9]; *śrathā-ya-* 'make loose' (Pp. *-āya-*)[10]; *satvanā-yá-* (AV.) 'act like a warrior'; *sumnā-yá-* 'show benevolence'; *skabhā-yá-* 'make firm'. In most of these examples the Pada text has a short *a*.

a. The denominative *ojā-yá-* 'employ force' is formed from *oja-*, shortened for *ójas-* 'strength'.

b. The **-a** of the nominal stem **is sometimes changed to -ī**: *adhvarī-yá-* 'perform the sacrifice' (*adhvará-*); *caranī-yá-* 'follow a course' (*cárana-*), 'pursue'; *taviṣī-yá-* 'be strong' (*taviṣá-*); *putrī-yá-* 'desire a son' (*putrá-*); *rathī-yá-* 'drive in a car' (*rátha-*); *śapathī-yá-* (AV.) 'utter a curse' (*śapátha-*). In nearly every instance here the Pada text has *i*. Even in the Saṃhitā text the AV. has *putri-yá-* 'desire a son', and the RV. the denominative participle (with shifted accent) *ánni-yant-* 'desiring food' (*ánna-*).

a. For the *-a* of the nominal stem *e* is substituted in *vare-yá-* 'play the wooer' (*vára-*), 'woo'.

c. The final **-a** of the nominal stem **is sometimes dropped**[11]: *adhvar-yá-* 'perform sacrifice' (beside *adhvarī-yá-*); *kṛpaṇ-yá-* 'be eager'; *taviṣ-yá-* 'be

---

1 Regarded as a causative by GRASSMANN, s. v. *aṅkh.*

2 DELBRÜCK 189, 1 regards the form *hástayatas* as a denominative; but the accent would be unique: its explanation by BR. and GRASSMANN as a compound, *hásta-yatas* 'wielded by the hand', is doubtless the correct one.

3 Cp. DELBRÜCK 189, 2.

4 GRASSMANN regards this verb as a causative: see Wörterbuch, s. v. *ūrjáy.*

5 See WHITNEY's note on AV. IV. 19[6].

6 See WHITNEY on AV. IV. 21[2].

7 Based on *randhana*, an assumed derivative of the root *randh-*.

8 Beside *vṛṣaṇ-yá-*, from *vṛṣa-*, the form which *vṛ́ṣan-* assumes before terminations or before second members of compounds beginning with consonants.

9 From *śubha-*, an assumed derivative of *śubh-* 'shine'.

10 There is also a causative form *śratháya-*, from *śrath-* 'loosen'.

11 Cp. v. NEGELEIN 40.

mighty' (beside *taviṣī-yá-*); *turaṇ-yá-* 'be speedy'; *daman-ya-*[1] 'overpower'; *bhuraṇ-yá-* 'be active'; *vithur-yá-* 'stagger'; *saraṇ-yá-* 'hasten'. There are several other denominatives which presuppose nouns in *-ana*: thus *dhiṣaṇ-yá-* 'pay attention'; *riṣaṇ-yá-* 'commit faults'; *ruvaṇ-ya-* 'roar'; *huvan-ya-* 'call'. The derivation of *iṣaṇ-yá-* beside *iṣaṇa-ya-* 'impel' is perhaps similar; but the nominal stem on which this denominative is based may be *iṣáṇi-* 'impulse'[2].

564. **Stems in -ā**, which usually remains unchanged: *gopā-yá-* 'act as herdsman', 'protect'; *jmā-yá-* 'speed to earth'; *ducchunā-yá-* 'desire mischief'[3]; *pṛtanā-yá-* 'fight'; *bhandanā-yá-* 'strive for glory'; *manā-yá-* 'feel attachment'; *raśanā-yá-* (AV.)[4] 'put on a girdle'. Similar stems are to be assumed in *ṛghā-yá-* 'tremble', and *hṛṇā-yá-* 'be wrathful'; and *dhiyā-yá-* 'pay attention' is based on *dhiyā-*[5] = *dhī-* 'thought'.

α. The -ā of the nominal stem is once shortened, if *kṛpa-yá-* (RV[1].) 'mourn'[6] is a denominative and different from the causative *kṛpáya-* (554). The *ā* is dropped in *pṛtan-yá-* 'fight' beside *pṛtanā-yá-*.

a. There are more than a dozen denominatives with *ā* preceding *-ya-*, **without any corresponding noun in ă**; thus *aśā-yá-* 'attain'[7]; *tudā-yá-* (AV.) 'thrust'; *damā-yá-* 'tame'[7]; *naśā-ya-*[8] (x. 40[6]) 'reach'; *panā-ya-* 'boast of'; *vasā-yá-* 'invest oneself with'; *vṛṣā-ya-* 'cause to rain'[9]. Seven such denominatives, however, appear beside present bases according to the ninth class in *-nā*: *gṛbhā-yá-* 'seize' (*gṛbh-ṇā-*); *mathā-yá-* 'shake' (*math-nā-*); *pruṣā-yá-* 'drip' (*pruṣ-ṇánt-*, VS.); *muṣā-yá-* 'steal' (*muṣ-ṇā-*); *śrathā-ya-* 'loosen' (*śrath-nā-*); *skabhā-yá-* 'fasten' (*skabh-nā-*); *stabhā-yá-* 'support' (*stabh-nā-*).

565. **Stems in -i**, which is nearly always lengthened (though usually short in the Pada text): *arātī-yá-* (RV. VS.) 'be malevolent', but *arāti-yá-* (AV. and RV. Pp.); *kavī-yá-* 'be wise'; *janī-yá-* 'seek a wife', but *jani-yá-* (AV.); *dur-gṛbhī-ya-* 'be hard to grasp'; *mahī-yá-* 'be delighted'; *rayī-yá-* 'desire wealth'; *sakhī-yá-*[10] 'seek friendship'.

α. In a few instances the *i* is either treated as *a* or takes Guṇa of which the final element is dropped (*-a-ya* = *-ay-ya*): thus *iṣaṇa-ya-* 'set in motion' (*iṣáṇi-* 'impulse'); *kīrtá-ya-* (AV.) 'make mention of' (*kīrti-*); *ahuna-yá-* 'resound' (*dhúni-* 'sounding'); *suṣva-yá-* and *suṣvá-ya-* 'flow' (*súṣv-i-*[11] 'pressing'). Perhaps formed in the same way are *śrudhī-yá-* 'obey' and *hṛṇī-yá-* 'be angry'[12].

β. *pátya-* 'be a lord', 'rule', probably in origin a denominative of *páti-* 'lord', is treated like a verb of the fourth class as if from a root *pat-*.

566. **Stems in -u**, which (except *gātu-yá-* twice) is **always long** (though always short in Pp.): *asū-yá-* 'grumble'; *ṛjū-yá-* 'be straight'; *kratū-yá-* 'exert the intellect'; *gātū-yá-* and *gātu-yá-* 'set in motion'; *pitū-yá-* 'desire nourishment'; *valgū-yá-* 'treat kindly'; *vasū-yá-* 'desire wealth'; *śatrū-yá-* 'play the enemy', 'be hostile'; *sukratū-ya-* 'show oneself wise'. Moreover, *iṣū-ya-* 'strive', may be derived from *íṣu-* 'arrow'; and nouns in *-u* are presupposed by *aṅkū-yá-* 'move tortuously', and *stabhū-yá-* 'stand firm'.

a. In *go-*, the only **stem in -o**, the diphthong becomes *-av* before the denominative suffix: *gav-yá-* 'desire cows'.

1 From an assumed adjective derivative *damana-*.

2 Cp. DELBRÜCK 189, 4.

3 The Pada text wrongly *ducchunayá-*.

4 Cp. WHITNEY's note on AV. XIV. 2[74].

5 Which perhaps became an independent noun through the influence of the instrumental form in such compounds as *dhiyā-jūr-* 'growing old in devotion'.

6 Cp. GRASSMANN, s. v. *kṛpay*.

7 Cp. DELBRÜCK 199 (p. 217, middle).

8 DELBRÜCK, l. c., regards *naśāya-* (X. 40[6]) as a denominative, BR. as causative of *naś-*.

9 To be distinguished from *vṛṣāyá-* 'act like a bull'.

10 Cp. v. NEGELEIN 41 (middle).

11 From the reduplicated root *su-* 'press'.

12 According to DELBRÜCK 205, p. 57, also *duhīya-* in the forms *duhīyát* and *duhīyán* (optatives GRASSMANN, Wörterbuch, and WHITNEY, Roots, s. v. *duh*). Cp. 450, a 5.

567. **Consonant stems** usually remain unchanged before the suffix.

a. The only stem ending in *-j* is *bhiṣáj-* 'physician': *bhiṣaj-yá-* 'play the physician', 'heal'.

b. There is one denominative, *iṣudh-yá-* 'implore', which seems to presuppose a stem in ***-dh***, viz. *iṣudh-*[1], but is probably a denominative from *iṣu-dhi-* (like *pátya-* 'from *páti-*) 'put in the arrow', 'aim'[2].

c. Denominatives formed from stems in ***-n*** are *ukṣaṇ-yá-* 'act like a bull'; *udan-yá-* 'irrigate'; *brahmaṇ-yá-* 'be devout' ('act like a *brahmán*'); *vṛṣaṇ-yá-*[3] 'act like a bull', 'be lustful'.

d. A denominative formed from a stem in ***-ar*** is *vadhar-yá-* 'hurl a bolt' (*vádhar-*). Stems in *-ar* are further presupposed in *rathar-yá-* 'ride in a car'; *śrathar-yá-* 'become loose'; *sapar-yá-* 'worship'.

e. The consonant stems most frequently used to form denominatives are those in ***-as***: *apas-yá-* 'be active'; *avas-yá-* 'seek help'; *canas-yá-* 'be satisfied'; *duvas-yá-* 'adore'; *namas-yá-* 'pay homage'; *nṛ-maṇas-yá-* 'be kindly disposed to men'; *manas-yá-* 'bear in mind'; *vacas-yá-* 'be audible'; *varivas-yá-* 'grant space'; *śravas-yá-*[4] 'hasten'; *sa-canas-yá-* 'cherish'; *su-manas-yá-* 'be gracious'; *sv-apas-yá-* 'act well'. Stems in *-as* are further presupposed by *iras-yá-* 'be angry'; *daśas-yá-* 'render service to'; *panas-yá-* 'excite admiration'; *sacas-yá-* 'receive care'. A few denominatives have further been formed from stems in *-a* following the analogy of those in *-as*; thus *makhas-yá-* 'be cheerful' (*makhá-*) and *su-makhas-yá-* (TS.) 'be merry'; *mānavas-yá-* 'act like men' (*mānavá-*). The stem *aviṣ-yá-*, appearing in the participle *aviṣyánt-* 'helping willingly', apparently a denominative (beside *aviṣyā́-* 'desire', *aviṣyú-* 'desirous'), seems to be formed from **av-is-* = *áv-as-* 'favour'[5].

f. A few denominatives are formed from stems in ***-us***: *taruṣ-yá-* 'engage in fight' (*tár-us-*); *vanuṣ-yá-* 'plot against' (*van-ús-* 'eager'); *vapuṣ-ya-* 'wonder' (*váp-us-* 'marvellous'). This analogy is followed by *uru-ṣ-yá-* 'seek wide space' from a stem in *-u* (*urú-* 'wide').

568. There are a few **denominative forms** made **without a suffix** direct from nominal stems, but they nearly always have beside them denominative stems in *-ya*; thus *bhiṣák-ti* (VIII. 79[2]) 'heals' 3. sing. from *bhiṣáj-* 'act as physician' (also m. 'physician'); *a-bhiṣṇak* (X. 131[5]), 3. sing. impf. of *bhiṣṇaj-* 'heal'. Similarly there appear the forms sing. 2. *iṣaṇa-s*, 3. *iṣaṇa-t*, pl. 3. *iṣaṇa-nta* beside *iṣaṇ-yá-*; pl. 3. *kṛpáṇa-nta* beside *kṛpaṇ-yá-*; pl. 1. *taruṣe-ma*, 3. *táruṣa-nte*, *taruṣa-nta* beside *taruṣ-yá-*; pl. 3 *vanuṣa-nta* beside *vanuṣ-yá-*. Possibly the form *vánanvati* is a denominative meaning 'is at hand', from a noun **van-anu-*, beside the simple verb *van-* 'win'[6].

Inflexion.

569. The denominative is regularly inflected throughout the present system according to the *a-* conjugation in both voices. The commonest form is the 3. sing. active and middle.

The forms of the **present indicative** active and middle that actually occur would, if made from *manas-yá-* 'bear in mind', be the following:

Active. Sing. 1. *manasyāmi* (AV.). 2. *manasyási*. 3. *manasyáti*. — Du. 2. *manasyáthas*. 3. *manasyátas*. — Pl. 1. *manasyā́masi* and *manasyā́mas*. 2. *manasyatha*. 3. *manasyánti*.

Middle. Sing. 1. *manasyé*. 2. *manasyáse*. 3. *manasyáte*. — Du. 2. *manasyethe*. 3. *manasyéte* (AV.). — Pl. 1. *manasyā́mahe*. 3. *manasyánte*.

1 Cp. DELBRÜCK 194.
2 Cp. GRASSMANN, s. v. *iṣudhy*.
3 Beside *vṛṣāyá-*; cp. p. 399, note 8.
4 According to BR. derived from *śravas-* from *śru-* = *sru-* 'flow', but GRASSMANN from *śru-* 'hear'.
5 Cp. GRASSMANN, s. v. *aviṣy*.
6 Cp. DELBRÜCK p. 218.

Forms that actually occur elsewhere in the present system are the following:

a. Subjunctive. Active. Sing. 1. *namasyā*. — 2. *uruṣyā́s, kīrtáyās* (AV.), *śravasyā́s*. — 3. *apasyā́t, arātīyā́t* (TS. IV. 1. 10³; VS. XI. 80), *arātīyā́t* (AV.), *uruṣyā́t, caraṇyā́t* (AV.), *durasyā́t* (AV.), *duvasyā́t, pṛtanyā́t, vanuṣyā́t, vareyā́t, vasūyā́t, śravasyā́t, saparyā́t*. — Du. 3. *varivasyā́tas*. — Pl. 3. *pṛtanyā́n* (AV.), *saparyā́n, saraṇyā́n*. — Middle. Sing. 2. *arthā́yāse, nīḷā́yāse*. — 3. *aṅkhā́yāte*.

b. Injunctive. Active. Sing. 2. *iraśyas, riṣaṇyas, ruvaṇyas*. — Pl. 3. *turaṇyan, duvasyan, namasyan, saparyan*. — Middle. Sing. 3. *panāyata*. — Pl. 3. *ṛghāyánta, ṛtayanta, kṛpáṇanta, taruṣanta, dhunayanta*[1], *rucayanta, vanuṣanta, suṣváyanta*.

c. Optative. Active. Sing. 2. *daśasyes*. — 3. *uruṣyet, caraṇyet* (TS. I. 8. 22¹), *daśasyet, duvasyét*. — Pl. 1. *iṣayema, taruṣema, saparyéma*. — Middle. Sing. 3. *manasyéta* (AV.).

d. Imperative. Active. Sing. 2. *iṣaṇya, uruṣyá, gātuyá, gūrdhaya, gopāyá* (AV. TS.), *gṛbhāya, daśasyá, duvasya, namasyá, varivasyá, vājaya* (TS. I. 7. 8¹), *śrathāya, saparya*. — 3. *uruṣyatu, gopāyatu*ᵃ (AV.), *bhiṣajyatu* (TS. V. 2. 12²). — Du. 2. *uruṣyátam, gopāyátam, canasyátam, daśasyátam*. — 3. *uruṣyátām*. — Pl. 2. *iṣaṇyata, uruṣyata, gṛbhāyáta* (AV.), *gopāyata* (AV.), *daśasyata, duvasyáta, namasyáta, riṣaṇyata, saparyata*. — 3. *uruṣyantu, gopāyantu* (AV.), *varivasyantu*. — Middle. Sing. 2. *arthayasva, vīráyasva* (AV. TS.), *vṛṣāyasva* (AV.). — Pl. 2. *tilvilāyádhvam, vīráyadhvam*. — 3. *dhunayantām*.

e. Participle. The present participle active in *-ant* (with fem. *-ant-ī*) is very common, while the middle form in *-māna*, occurs fairly often.

α. Examples of the active are *aghāyánt-, aṅkūyánt-, adhvarīyánt-, amitrayánt-, arātīyánt-, aśvāyánt-, iṣaṇyánt-, iṣáyant-, iṣūyánt-, udanyánt-, ūrjáyant-, ṛghāyánt-, ṛtáyant-, ṛtāyánt-, gavyánt-, gopāyánt-* (AV.), *taviṣīyánt-, daśasyánt-, duvasyánt-, devayánt-, namasyánt-, pāláyant-* (AV.), *putrīyánt-, pṛtanāyánt-, pṛtanyánt-, bhandanāyánt-, bhuraṇyánt-, mathāyánt-, muṣāyánt-, yajñāyánt-, yuṣmayánt-, rathirāyánt-, rathīyánt-, vasūyánt-, vasnayánt-, vājáyant-* and *vājayánt-, vṛṣaṇyánt-, śatrūyánt-, śīkāyánt-* (VS.) 'dripping', *sakhīyánt-, satvanāyánt-* (AV.), *saparyánt-, sumnāyánt-, suṣváyant-, hṛṇāyánt-* 'angry'.

β. Examples of the middle are *ṛghāyámāṇa-, ṛjūyámāna-, ojāyámāna-, kaṇḍūyámāna-* (TS.), *kavīyámāna-, caraṇīyámāna-, taviṣyámāṇa-, priyāyámāṇa-* (AV.), (*á-prati-)manyūyamāna-* (AV.), *raśanāyámāna-, vṛṣāyámāṇa-, samanayámāna-, sumakhasyámāna-* (TS.), *sumanasyámāna-, stabhūyámāna-, svapasyámāna-, hṛṇīyámāna-* 'angry'.

f. Imperfect. Active. Sing. 2. *arandhanāyas*. — 3. *apṛtanyat, áskabhāyat* (AV.); *uruṣyat, damanyat, dhūpáyat* (AV.); *abhiṣṇak*. — Du. 3. *uruṣyátām*. — Pl. 3. *anamasyan, asaparyan; turaṇyan, vapuṣyan, saparyan* (TS. II. 2. 12⁴). — Middle. Sing. 3. *ápriyāyata*. — Du. 2. *avīrayethām*. — Pl. 3. *iṣaṇayanta*.

570. Outside the present system no denominative form occurs in the RV. except *ūnayīs* (+AV.), 2. sing. *iṣ-* aorist (used injunctively with *mā́*)

---

[1] The form *bhurájanta* (IV. 43⁵) is according to pw. = *bhrajanta* for *bhrajjanta* (*bhrajj-* 'be roasted'). Cp. note in OLDENBERG's Ṛgveda.
[2] This denominative is derived from the very frequent *go-pā́-* 'cowherd', of which two transition forms according to the *a-* declension (*go-pá-*) occur in the RV. To the denominative must be due the secondary root *gup-* 'protect' (*jugupur* once, *gupitá-* twice in the RV.). Cp. p. 358, note ¹³. How *gup-* should be a denominative of *go-* 'cow' (v. NEGELEIN 43, note ⁵) is not clear.

from *ūnaya-* 'leave unfulfilled' (*ūná-*). A few other forms occur in the later Saṃhitās. Thus the AV. has the peculiar form *ásaparyait* (AV. XIV. 2^{20})[1], probably 3. sing. aorist, with *-ait* for *-īt*[2]. The VS. (II. 31) has the 3. pl. aorist *á‿a-vṛṣāy-iṣ-ata* 'they have accepted'. The TS. has the 2. pl. aor. *pāpay-iṣ-ṭa* 'lead into evil' (used injunctively with *mā́*). The TS. (III. 2. 8^3) has also the future participles *kaṇḍūyiṣyánt-* 'about to scratch', *meghāyiṣyánt-* 'about to be cloudy', *śīkāyiṣyánt-* 'about to drip', with the corresponding perfect participles passive *kaṇḍūyitá-*, *meghitá-*, *śīkitá-*.

B. Nominal Verb Forms.

571. A large number of nominal formations partake of the verbal character inasmuch as they express time (present, past, or future); or the relations between subject and object, implying transitive or intransitive action, and active, middle, or passive sense. Such formations are participles (including verbal adjectives), infinitives, and gerunds. The participles formed from tense-stems having already been treated[3], only those that are formed directly from the root remain to be dealt with. These are the verbal adjectives which have the value either of past passive participles or of future passive participles (otherwise called gerundives).

a. Past Passive Participles.

572. The past passive participle is formed by adding, in the great majority of instances, the **suffix** ***-tá***[4] (with or without connecting *-i-*), or far less commonly the **suffix** ***-ná*** (directly) to the root. When formed from a transitive verb, it has a passive as well as a past sense; e. g. *as-* 'throw' : *as-tá-* 'thrown'; *dā-* 'give' : *dat-tá-* 'given'. But when formed from an intransitive verb, it has a neuter past sense; e. g. *gam-* 'go' : *ga-tá-* 'gone'; *pat-* 'fall' : *pat-i-tá-* (AV.) 'fallen'.

573. When ***-tá*** **is added direct**, the root tends to appear in its weak form. Very frequently, however, the form in which the root is generally stated, if ending in vowels, remains unchanged, while those ending in consonants are usually modified only in so far as is required by the rules of internal Sandhi; thus √*mlā-* : *mlā-tá-* 'softened'; √*yā* : *yā-tá-* 'gone'; √*rā-* : *rā-tá-* 'given'; √*ji-* : *ji-tá-* 'conquered'; √*śri-* : *śri-tá-* 'leaning on'; √*prī-* : *prī-tá-* 'rejoiced'; √*bhī-* : *bhī-tá-* 'frightened'; √*yu-* 1. 'yoke' and 2. 'ward off' : *-yu-ta-*; √*śru-* : *śru-tá-* 'heard'; √*stu-* : *stu-tá-* 'praised'; √*bhū-* : *bhū-tá-* 'become'; √*hū-* : *hū-tá-* 'called'; √*kṛ-* : *kṛ-tá-* 'made'; √*bhṛ-* : *-bhṛ-ta-* 'borne'; √*vṛ-* : *vṛ-tá-* 'covered' and 'chosen'; √*mṛc-* : *mṛk-tá-*[5] (RV.) 'injured'; √*sic-* : *sik-tá-* 'poured out'; √*tij-* : *tik-tá-* 'sharp'; √*yuj-* : *yuk-tá-* 'yoked'; √*mṛj-* : *mṛṣ-ṭá-* 'rubbed'; √*sṛj-* : *sṛṣ-ṭá-* 'discharged'; √*cit-* : *cit-tá-* 'perceived'; √*vṛt-* : *vṛt-tá-* 'turned'; √*mad-* 'be exhilarated' : *mat-tá-* (AV.); √*idh-* : *id-dhá-* 'kindled'; √*krudh-* : *krud-dhá-* 'angry'; √*tap-* : *tap-tá-* 'hot'; √*rip-* : *rip-tá-* (RV.) 'besmeared'; √*diś-* : *diṣ-ṭá-* 'shown'; √*naś-* : *naṣ-ṭá-* 'lost'; √*juṣ-* : *juṣ-ṭá-* (RV^1.) 'gladdened' and *júṣ-ṭa-* 'welcome'; √*piṣ-* : *piṣ-ṭá-* 'crushed'; √*kas-* : *vi-kas-ta-* 'split'; √*guh-* : *gū-ḍhá-*[6] 'hidden'; √*tṛh-* : *tṛ-ḍhá-* 'crushed'; √*dah-* : *dag-dhá-*[7] 'burnt'; √*dih-* : *dig-dhá-* (AV.) 'besmeared'; √*duh-* : *dug-dhá-* 'milked'; √*dṛh-*

[1] Cp. v. NEGELEIN 41; BÖHTLINGK, ZDMG. 52, 510 ff.

[2] As in the AB. form *agrabhaiṣam* beside *agrabhīt*; cp. v. NEGELEIN 41, note 2.

[3] See under declension 311—313, and in the account of the various tenses (present, perfect, aorist, future).

[4] Cp. REICHELT, BB. 27, 95—97.

[5] Only in the compounds *á-mṛkta-* and *mṛktá-vāhas-*.

[6] In roots in *-h* which cerebralize the suffix, the vowel is lengthened as compensation for the loss of the cerebral *ẓ*: cp. p. 51, note 2.

[7] In the RV. only in *agni-dagdhá-* 'burnt with fire'.

: *dṛ-ḍhá-* 'firm'; √*druh-* : *drug-dhá-* 'hurtful'; √*nah-* : *nad-dhá-* 'bound'; √*muh-* : *mug-dhá-* and *mū-ḍhá-* (AV.) 'bewildered'; √*rih-* : *rī-ḍhá-* (RV.) 'licked'; √*ruh-* : *rū-ḍhá-* (AV.) 'ascended'; √*sah-* : *sā-ḍhá-* 'overcome'.

a. Occasional irregularities in the form of the root are not due to the ordinary rules of internal Sandhi. Thus some roots show an interchange of vowel and semi-vowel: *dīv-* 'play' : *dyū-tá-* (AV.); *sīv-* 'sew' : *syū-tá-*; *mīv-* 'push' : *-mūta-* (VS. AV.) instead of **myū-ta-*[1]; *hvṛ-* 'make crooked' has *hru-tá-* 'crooked', beside the regular *-hvṛ-ta-* (RV.); sometimes a long vowel appears in the root: *svad-* 'sweeten' : *svāt-tá-*; *gur-* 'greet' : *gūr-tá-*; *śṛ-* 'mix' : *-śīr-ta-*, beside *śrī-tá-* from *śrī-* 'mix', the usual form of the root; *dā-* 'give', beside the regular form *-dā-ta-* in *tvā́-dāta-* (RV.) 'given by thee', otherwise always has *dat-tá-*, formed from *dad-*, the weak form of the present base.

574. **Roots** which contain the syllables *ya, ra, va* (initial or medial) are generally **weakened** by Samprasāraṇa; those which contain a nasal (medial or final), by dropping it; those which end in *ā* or *yā*, by shortening the former to *ī* or *i*, the latter to *ī*. Thus:

1. *yaj-* 'sacrifice' : *iṣ-ṭá-*; *vyadh-* 'pierce' : *vid-dhá-*; *prach-* 'ask' : *pṛṣ-ṭá-*; *bhraś-* 'fall' : *bhṛṣ-ṭá-* beside *bhraṣ-ṭá-* (AV.); *vac-* 'speak' : *uk-tá-*; *vap-* 'strew' : *up-tá-*; *vas-* 'shine' : *uṣ-ṭá-*; *vah-* 'carry' : *ū-ḍhá-*; *svap-* 'sleep' : *sup-tá-* (AV. VS.).

a. A shortening akin to Samprasāraṇa appears in *av-* 'favour' : *-ū-ta-*; *vā-* 'weave' : *u-tá-*; *śrā-* 'boil' : *śṛ-tá-* beside *śrā-tá-*.

2. A medial nasal is **dropped** in *añj-* 'anoint' : *ak-tá-*; *umbh-* 'confine' : *ub-dhá-*; *daṃś-* 'bite' : *daṣ-ṭá-* (AV.); *baṃh-* 'make firm' : *-bā-ḍha-*; *śundh-* 'purify' : *śud-dhá-*. Final *n* and *m* are dropped (the radical *a* representing the sonant nasal) in *kṣan-* 'wound' : *-kṣa-ta-*; *tan-* 'stretch' : *ta-tá-*; *man-* 'think' : *ma-tá-*; *han-* 'smite' : *ha-tá-*; *gam-* 'go' : *ga-tá-*; *nam-* 'bend' : *na-tá-*; *yam-* 'reach' : *ya-tá-*.

a. A few roots in *-an* have *ā* instead of *-an*[2]: *khan-* 'dig' : *khā-tá-*; *jan-* 'be born' : *jā-tá-*; *van-* 'win' : *-vā-ta-*; *san-* 'gain' : *sā-tá-*; while some roots in *-am* and one in *-an*, retaining the nasal, have *ān*: *dhvan-* 'sound' : *dhvāntá-* (VS. XXXIX. 7); *kram-* 'stride' : *krān-tá-* (AV.); *śam-* 'be quiet'; *śān-tá-* (AV.); *śram-* 'be weary' : *śrān-tá-*; *dham-* 'blow' has the irregular *dhmā-tá-* and *dham-i-tá-*.

3. **Final** *ā* **is shortened** to *ī* in *gā-* 'sing' : *gī-tá-*; *dhā-* 'suck' : *dhī-tá-*; *pā-* 'drink' : *pī-tá-*[3]; to *i* in *dā-* 'bind' : *-di-ta-*; *dhā-* 'put' : *-dhi-ta-* and *hi-tá-*; *mā-* 'measure' : *mi-tá-*; *śā-* 'sharpen' : *śi-tá-*; *sā-* 'bind' : *si-tá-*; *sthā-* 'stand' : *sthi-tá-*.

Final *yā* **is shortened** to *ī* in *jyā-* 'overpower' : *jī-tá-* (AV.); *vyā-* 'envelope' : *vī-tá-*; *śyā-* 'coagulate' : *śī-tá-*.

a. Internal shortening of *ā* to *i* appears in *śās-* 'order' : *śiṣ-ṭá-*; and medial *a* entirely disappears in *ghas-* 'eat' : *-gdha-* (TS.) and in the compounded form of *dattá-* 'given', which becomes *-t-ta-* . *deva-ttá-* 'given by the gods'; *vy-ā-tta-* (AV. VS.), n. 'the opened mouth'; *pári-tta-* (VS. IX. 9) 'deposited'; *-pratī-tta-* (AV.) 'given back'. The same syncopated form appears in the compound participle of *dā-* 'divide' : *áva-tta-* (VS.) 'cut off'.

575. When *-tá* is added, as it is in many verbs, **with connecting** *-i-*, the root is not weakened (excepting four instances of Samprasāraṇa)[4]. It is thus added to a number of roots ending in consonants and to all secondary verbs.

a. The **roots** to which it is thus regularly added are those that end:

1. **in two consonants**: thus *ukṣ-* 'sprinkle' : *ukṣ-i-tá-*; *ubj-* 'force' : *ubj-i-tá-* (AV.); *nind-* 'revile' : *nind-i-tá-*; *rakṣ-* 'protect' : *rakṣ-i-tá-*; *śumbh-* 'beautify' : *-śumbh-i-ta-* (AV.); *hiṃs-* 'injure' : *hiṃs-i-tá-* (AV.); but *takṣ-* 'fashion' has *taṣ-ṭá-*;

---

1 See above 50 b.

2 Representing the long sonant nasal.

3 The more correct way of stating these roots would be *gai-, dhai-, pai-*; cp. 27 a.

4 In *gṛbh-ī-tá-* from *grabh-* 'seize' and *gṛh-ī-ta-* (AV.) from *grah-* id.; *ukṣ-i-tá-* from *vakṣ-* 'increase'; *ud-i-tá-* from *vad-* 'speak'; *śṛth-i-tá-* from *śrath-* 'slacken'.

2. **in voiceless aspirates:** *likh-* 'scratch' : *likh-i-tá-* (AV.); *grath-* 'tie' : *grath-i-tá-*; *nāth-* 'seek aid' : *nāth-i-tá-*; *math-* 'stir' : *math-i-tá-*;

3. **in cerebral** *ḍ*: *īḍ-* 'praise' : *īḷ-i-tá-*; *hīḍ-* 'be hostile' : *hīḷ-i-tá-*;

4. **in semivowels:** *car-* 'move' : *car-i-tá-*[1]; *jīv-* 'live' : *jīv-i-tá-*.

b. The suffix is also added with *-i-* to a number of **roots** ending **in simple consonants,** especially sibilants, about which no rule can be stated. Such are the following participles arranged according to the final of the root: *yāc-* 'ask' : *yāc-i-tá-* (AV.); *pat-* 'fall' : *pat-i-tá-* (AV.); *rad-* 'dig' : *rad-i-tá-* (AV.); *vad-* 'speak' : *ud-i-tá-*; *vid-* 'know' : *vid-i-tá-* (AV.)[2]; *dudh-* 'stir up' : *dúdh-i-ta-* (RV.); *nādh-* 'seek aid' : *nādh-i-tá-*; *bādh-* 'oppress' : *bādh-i-tá-*; *pan-* 'admire' : *pan-i-tá-*; *kup-* 'be agitated' : *-kup-i-ta-*; *gup-*[3] protect' : *gup-i-tá-* beside *gup-tá-* (AV.); *yup-* 'obstruct' : *yup-i-tá-* (AV.); *rup-* 'break' : *-rup-i-ta-*; *dṛp-* 'rave' : *-dṛp-i-ta-* and *-dṛp-ta-*; *lap-* 'prate' : *lap-i-tá-* (AV.); *grabh-* 'seize' : *gṛbh-ī-tá-* and *grah-* 'seize' : *gṛh-ī-tá-* (AV.); *skabh-* 'prop' : *skabh-i-tá-*; *stabh-* 'prop' : *stabh-i-tá-*; *dham-* 'blow' : *dham-i-tá-* (beside *dhmā-tá-*);

aś- 'eat' : *aś-i-tá-*; *piś-* 'adorn' : *piś-i-tá-* (AV.) beside *piṣ-ṭá-*; *iṣ-* 'send' : *iṣ-i-tá-*; *īṣ-* 'move' : *-īṣ-i-ta-*; *tviṣ-* 'be stirred' : *tviṣ-i-tá-*; *dhṛṣ-* 'dare' : *dhṛṣ-i-tá-* beside *dhṛṣ-ṭá-*; *pruṣ-* 'sprinkle' : *pruṣ-i-tá-*; *muṣ-* 'steal' : *muṣ-i-tá-*; *hṛṣ-* 'be excited' : *hṛṣ-i-tá-*; *gras-* 'devour' : *gras-i-tá-*.

α. The verb *hā-* 'leave' forms its past participle anomalously (like *dā-* 'give') from the reduplicated present base: *jah-i-tá-* (cp. the pres. part. *jáh-at-*).

β. In the AV. is once (IX. 6[38]) found a past passive participle extended with the possessive suffix *-vant*, which gives it the sense of a perfect participle active: *aś-i-tā-vant-* (Pp. *aśitá-vant-*) 'having eaten'.

c. **Secondary verbs,** almost exclusively causatives[4], add ***-ita*** after dropping *-aya-*; thus *arp-aya-* 'cause to go' : *arp-itá-* and *árp-ita-*; *īṅkh-áya-* 'cause to quake' : *īṅkh-itá-*; *cod-áya-* 'set in motion' : *cod-itá-*; *vīḷ-áya-* 'make strong' : *vīḷ-itá-*; *śnath-aya-* 'pierce' : *śnath-itá-*; *svan-aya-* 'resound' : *-svan-ita-*.

The only past passive participle formed from a denominative is *bhām-itá-* 'enraged', from *bhā́ma-* 'wrath'.

576. The **suffix *-ná*** is **always attached directly** to the root, which as a rule remains unweakened. Among roots ending in consonants, it is taken by those in *d*, besides two or three in the palatals *c* and *j*; among roots in vowels, it is taken by those ending in the long vowels *ā*, *ī*, *ṝ*, besides one in *ū*.

a. The final of **roots in *-d*** is assimilated to the *n* of the suffix; thus *chid-* 'cut off' : *chin-ná-*; *tud-* 'push' : *tun-ná-*; *tṛd-* 'pierce' : *-tṛṇ-ṇa-* (VS. XXXVI. 2); *nud-* 'push' : *-nun-na-* (SV.) beside *nut-tá-*; *pad-* 'go' : *pan-ná-* (AV.); *bhid-* 'split' : *bhin-ná-*; *vid-* 'find' : *vin-ná-* (AV.) beside *vit-tá-*; *sad-* 'sit' : *san-ná-* (VS. AV.) beside *sat-tá-*; *skand-* 'leap' : *skan-ná-*; *syand-* 'move on' : *syan-ná-*; *svid-* 'sweat' : *svin-ná-*. The original participle of *ad-* 'eat' survives only (with change of accent) in the neuter noun *án-na-* 'food'.

b. The **roots in palatals** which take *-na* are: *pṛc-* 'mix' : *-pṛg-ṇa-* (RV[1].) beside *pṛk-tá-*; *vraśc-* 'cut up' : *vṛk-ṇá-*; *ruj-* 'break' : *rug-ṇá-*.

c. **Roots in *-ā*** remain unchanged or weaken the final to *ĭ*: *drā-* 'sleep' : *-drā-ṇa-* (AV.); *dā-* 'divide' : *di-ná-*; *hā-* 'leave' : *hī-ná-*; final *-yā* is shortened to *-ī*: *śyā-* 'coagulate' : *śī-ná-* (VS.) beside *śī-tá-*.

d. **Roots in *-ī* and *-ū*** remain unchanged: *kṣī-* 'destroy' : *-kṣī-ṇa-* (AV.);

[1] Also *ār-i-tá-* if derived from a somewhat doubtful root *ār-* 'praise'; cp. WHITNEY, Roots, s. v. *ār*.

[2] *mad-i-tá-* is probably from the causative of *mad-* 'be exhilarated'.

[3] See p. 402, note [2].

[4] No examples of past participles from desideratives (except *mīmāṃsitá-*, AV.) and intensives seem to occur in the Saṃhitās.

pī- 'swell' : *pī-ná-* (AV.); *blī-* 'crush' : *-blī-na-* (AV.); *lī-* 'cling' : *-lī-na-* (AV.); *dū-* 'burn' : *dū-ná-* (AV.).

e. **Roots in -ṝ** change that vowel to *-īr* or (generally when a labial precedes) *-ūr* before *-na*: *gṝ-* 'swallow' : *gīr-ṇá-*; *jṝ-* 'waste away' : *jīr-ṇá-* (AV.) and *jūr-ṇá-*; *tṝ-* 'pass' : *tīr-ṇá-*; *pṝ-* 'fill' : *pūr-ṇá-* beside *pūr-tá-*; *mṝ-* 'crush' : *mūr-ṇá-* (AV.); *śṝ-* 'crush' : *śīr-ṇá-* (AV.) beside *śūr-tá-* (RV. I. 174⁶)[1]; *stṝ-* 'strew' : *stīr-ṇá-* beside *-stṛ-ta-*.

b. Future Passive Participles (Gerundives).

577. Verbal adjectives formed with certain suffixes have acquired the value of future participles passive, expressing that the action of the verb is or ought to be suffered. There are **four forms** of such gerundives in use in the RV.: that derived with the primary suffix *-ya*, which is common, and those derived with the secondary suffixes *-áy-ya*, *-én-ya*, and *-tv-a*, about a dozen examples of each of which are met with. In the AV. are also found two instances each of gerundives in *-tavyà* and *-anīya*.

578. By far the most frequent form of **gerundive** is that **in *-ya***, about 40 examples occurring in the RV. and about 60 in the AV. This suffix is nearly always to be read as *-ia*, which accounts for the treatment of final radical vowels before it. The root, being accented, appears in a strong form, excepting a few instances in which there is the short radical vowel *i u* or *ṛ*.

1. In the following examples a **final short vowel** remains unchanged, a *-t-*[2] being interposed: *-í-t-ya-* 'to be gone'; *apa-mi-t-ya-* (AV. VI. 117¹) 'to be thrown away' (? *mi-* 'fix')[3]; *śrú-t-ya-* 'to be heard'; *-kṛ-t-ya-* 'to be made'; *car-kṛ́-t-ya-* 'to be praised' (*kṛ-* 'commemorate').

2. Otherwise **final** *ī*, *ū*, *ṛ* regularly take Guṇa or Vṛddhi, the final element of which always appears as *y*, *v*, *r* as before a vowel; thus from *lī-* 'cling' : *a-lā́y-ya-*[4], an epithet of Indra; *nu-* 'praise' : *náv-ya-* 'to be praised'; *bhū-* 'be' : *bháv-ya-* and *bhāv-yá-* 'future'; *hū-* 'call' : *háv-ya-* 'to be invoked'; *vṛ-* 'choose' : *vā́r-ya-* 'to be chosen'.

3. **Final -ā** coalesces with the initial of *-ia* to *e*, between which and *-a* a phonetic *y* is interposed; thus *dā-* 'give' : *dé-ya-* (= *dā́-i-y-a-*) 'to be given'; *khyā-* 'see' : *-khye-ya-* (AV.); *mā-* 'measure' : *mé-ya-* (AV.). In the RV., however, the form *jñā-ya-* once occurs in the compound *bala-vi-jñā-yá-* (x. 103⁵) 'to be recognized by his might'.

4. A **medial vowel** either remains unchanged or, if short, may take Guṇa, and *a* is sometimes lengthened; thus *íḍ-ya-* 'to be praised'; *gúh-ya-* 'to be hidden'; *-dhṛṣ-ya-* 'to be assailed'; *dvéṣ-ya-* (AV.) 'to be hated' (√*dviṣ-*); *yódh-ya-* 'to be fought' (√*yudh-*); *árdh-ya-* 'to be completed' (√*ṛdh-*); *márj-ya-* to be purified' (√*mṛj-*); *cákṣ-ya-* 'to be seen'; *dábh-ya-* 'to be deceived'; *ráṃh-ya-* 'to be hastened'; *rā́dh-ya-* 'to be won'; *vánd-ya-* 'praiseworthy'; *śáṃs-ya-* 'to be lauded'; *-sā́d-ya-* from *sad-* 'sit'; *-mā́d-ya-* from *mad-* 'be exhilarated'; *vā́c-ya-* 'to be said' (√*vac-*).

579. Hardly a dozen **gerundives**, almost restricted to the RV., are formed **with *-áy-ya***[5] (which with one exception is always to be read *-áyia*): *dakṣ-áyya-* 'to be conciliated'; *pan-áyya-* 'to be admired'; *vid-áyya-* 'to be

---

1 The form *-śīr-ta-* is also found in the MS.: Whitney, Roots, s. v. √*śṛ-* 'crush'.

2 Cp. the *-t* added to roots ending in *-i*, *-u*, *-ṛ* to form nominal stems (308).

3 The meaning is uncertain: Whitney translates the word by 'borrowed'. See his notes in his Translation.

4 Cp. Grassmann, s. v.

5 Cp. Lindner, Nominalbildung 22; Delbrück, Verbum 233; Whitney 966 c; Bartholomae, BB. 15, 179 n. 1; BB. 20, 85.

found'; *śrav-áyya-* 'glorious'; *-hnav-áyya-* 'to be denied'. A few are formed **from secondary verbs**; from causatives: *trayay-áyya-* 'to be guarded' (√*trā-*)[1]; *panay-áyya-* 'admirable' (√*pan-*); *spṛhay-áyya-* 'desirable' (√*spṛh-*); from a desiderative: *di-dhi-ṣ-áyya-* 'to be conciliated (√*dhā-*); from an intensive: *vi-tan-tas-áyya-* 'to be hastened' (√*taṃs-*). Akin to these gerundives is the anomalous form *stuṣé-yya-* 'to be praised', derived direct from the infinitive *stuṣé* 'to praise'[2].

580. More than a dozen **gerundives** are formed **with *-en-ya*** (generally to be read *-enia*): *īkṣ-éṇya-* 'worthy to be seen', *īḷ-énya-* 'praiseworthy', *-car-éṇya-* 'to be acted', *dṛś-énya-* 'worthy to be seen', *-dviṣ-enya-* 'malignant', *ā-bhūṣ-éṇya-* 'to be glorified', *yudh-énya-* 'to be combatted', *vár-eṇya-* 'desirable'. **From the aorist stem** is formed *-yaṃs-énya-* 'to be guided' (√*yam-*); and perhaps *papṛkṣ-éṇya-*[3] 'desirable' (√*prach-*). A few are also derived from secondary verbs; **from desideratives**: *didṛkṣ-éṇya-* 'worthy to be seen' (√*dṛś-*), *śuśrūṣ-éṇya-* (TS.) 'deserving to be heard'; **from intensives**: *mar-mṛj-énya-* 'to be adorned', *vāvṛdh-énya-* 'to be glorified'; **from a denominative**: *sapary-éṇya-* 'to be adored'.

581. About a dozen gerundives, almost restricted to the RV.[4], end in ***-tv-a*** (generally to be read as *-tu-a*), which seems to be the infinitive stem in *-tu* turned into an adjective by means of the suffix *-a*: *kár-tva-* 'to be made', *ján-i-tva-* and *ján-tva-* 'to be born', *jé-tva-* 'to be won', *nán-tva-* 'to be bent', *bhám-ī-tva-* 'future', *vák-tva-* 'to be said', *sán-i-tva-* 'to be won', *só-tva-* 'to be pressed', *snā́-tva-* 'suitable for bathing', *hán-tva-* 'to be slain', *hé-tva-* 'to be driven on' (√*hi-*).

a. In the AV. there begins to appear a gerundive in ***-tav-yà***. It probably started from the stem of the predicative infinitive in *-tav-e*, which was turned into an adjective by means of the suffix *-ia*[5]. The only examples of this formation are *jan-i-tav-yà-* 'to be born' (AV. IV. 23^7) and *hiṃs-i-tav-yà-* 'to be injured' (AV. V. 18^6).

b. There are also two examples in the AV. of a new gerundive in ***-an-ī́ya***, which is derived from a verbal noun in *-ana* with the adjective suffix *-īya*. These are *upa-jīv-anī́ya-* 'serving for subsistence' = 'to be subsisted on' (AV. VIII. 10^{22}); *ā-mantr-aṇī́ya-* 'fit for address' (*ā-mántraṇa-*) = 'worthy to be addressed' (AV. VIII. 10^7)[6].

c. Infinitive.

A. LUDWIG, Der Infinitiv im Veda, Prag 1871. — J. JOLLY, Geschichte des Infinitivs im Indogermanischen (München 1873), especially p. 111—137. — DELBRÜCK, Das altindische Verbum (1874), p. 221—228; Altindische Syntax p. 410—425. — AVERY, Verb-Inflection in Sanskrit, JAOS. 10, 275—276 (1876). — BRUNNHOFER, Über die durch einfache flectirung der wurzel gebildeten infinitive des Veda, KZ. 30 (1890), 504—513. — BARTHOLOMAE, Zur bildung des dat. sing. der *a*-stämme, BB. 15. 221—247. — v. NEGELEIN, Zur Sprachgeschichte des Veda (1898), 91. — FRITZ WOLFF, Die infinitive des Indischen und Iranischen. Erster teil: Die ablativisch-genetivischen und die accusativischen infinitive, Gütersloh 1905.

582. The infinitive, all the forms of which are old cases of nouns of action, is very frequently used, occurring in the RV. alone about 700 times. The case-forms which it exhibits are those of the **accusative, dative, ablative-genitive, and locative.** Only the first two are common, but the dative is by far the commonest, outnumbering the accusative in the proportion of 12 to 1 in the RV. (609 to 49)[7], and of 3 to 1 in the AV.[8] Infinitives are

[1] Cp. GRASSMANN, s. v., and WHITNEY 1051 f.

[2] See BRUGMANN, KG. 809.

[3] See BENFEY, Vollständige Grammatik 904 and 860.

[4] A few of these are also found in B., also an additional one, *hó-tva-* 'to be sacrificed', in the MS. (I. 9^3).

[5] Cp. BRUGMANN, KG. 809.

[6] The gerundive meaning in these two verbal adjectives is probably only incipient. The second is expressly connected with the verbal noun *ā-mántraṇa-*.

[7] AVERY 231.

[8] WHITNEY 986.

formed chiefly from radical stems or stems in *-tu*, only a few dative and locative forms being made from other stems. It is somewhat remarkable that the acc. form in *-tum* which is the only infinitive in the later language, hardly occurs in the RV., being found there only five times[1], while the dative infinitive, which is more than seven times as frequent as all the rest in the RV., has almost disappeared even in the Brāhmaṇas. The formations which are restricted to the infinitive meaning are the datives in *-tavai*, *-dhyai*, and (the very few) in *-ṣe*, besides a small number of locatives in *-sáni*. In other forms it is often difficult to draw a strict line of demarcation between the infinitive[2] and ordinary case uses[3].

1. Dative Infinitive.

583. This infinitive ends in *-e*, which when added to the *ā* of a root or stem combines with it to *-ai*. It has the final meaning of '(in order) to', 'for (the purpose of)'[3]. This dative is commonly used without an object; hence a dative often appears beside it by **attraction** instead of an accusative; e. g. *asmábhyaṃ dṛśáye sū́ryāya púnar dātām ásum* (x. 14[12]) 'may they two grant us life again, for the sun, that we may see (it)', i. e. 'that we may see the sun' (= *dṛśáye sū́ryam*). When used with *kṛ-* 'make' or verbs of wishing, and when predicative, this infinitive acquires a passive meaning; e. g. *agníṃ sam-ídhe cakártha* (i. 113[9]) 'thou hast made (= caused) the fire to be kindled'; *yád īm uśmási kártave* (x. 74[6]) 'what we wish to be done'; *brahmadvíṣaḥ . . . hántavā́ u* (x. 182[3]) 'Brahma-haters (are) to be slain'[4].

584. From roots are formed some 60 dative infinitives.

a. About a dozen are made from **roots ending in long vowels, chiefly *-ā*,** and one in *-ī*. All of these are found only compounded with prefixes, excepting *bhū-*, which appears once in the simple form. Two of them drop *ā* before the *-e*[5]. These infinitives are: *vi-khyái* 'to look abroad'; *parā-dái* 'to give up'; *prati-mái* 'to imitate' (iii. 60[4]); *-yái* 'to go'; *ava-sái* (iii. 53[20]) 'to rest'; *śrad-dhé* (i. 102[2]) 'to trust' (with the dat. particle *kám*); *pra-mé* (ix. 70[4]) 'to form'; *pra-hyè* (x. 109[3]) 'to send' (√*hi-*); *-míy-e* 'to diminish' (√*mī-*); *bhuv-é* and *-bhv-é* 'to be' (√*bhū-*); *-tír-e* 'to cross' (√*tṝ-*); *-stír-e* (√*stṝ-* 'spread').

b. The rest are formed from **roots** ending in **consonants.** The uncompounded forms are: *tviṣ-é* 'to arouse', *dṛś-é* 'to see', *bhuj-é* 'to enjoy', *mah-é* 'to be glad', *mih-é* 'to make water', *mud-é* 'to rejoice', *muṣ-é* 'to rob', *muh-é* 'to be bewildered', *yuj-é* 'to yoke', *yudh-é* 'to fight', *ruc-é* 'to shine', *vṛdh-é* 'to thrive', *śubh-é* 'to shine'.

The compounded forms are much more frequent. They are: *-áj-e* 'to drive', *-ídh-e* 'to kindle', *-krám-e* 'to stride', *-grábh-e* 'to seize', *-cákṣ-e* 'to see', *-tír-e* 'to cross', *-túj-e*[6] 'to procure', *-dábh-e* 'to injure', *-díś-e* 'to point', *-dṛ́ś-e* 'to see', *-dhṛ́ṣ-e* 'to be bold' (+ AV. TS.), *-nám-e* 'to bend', *-náś-e* (+ VS.) 'to attain', *-níkṣ-e* 'to pierce', *-núd-e* 'to thrust', *-pṛ́c-e* 'to fill', *-pṛ́cch-e* 'to ask'; *-bádh-e* 'to bind' (AV.), *-búdhe* (TS. i. 2. 3[1]) 'to awake', *-mṛ́ṣe* 'to forget', *-yákṣ-e* 'to speed', *-yúj-e* 'to yoke', *-rábh-e* 'to seize', *-rúj-e* 'to break', *-vác-e* 'to speak' (√*vac-*), *-víd-e* 'to find', *-vídh-e* 'to pierce' (√*vyadh-*), *-víṣ-e* 'to seize', *-vṛ́j-e* 'to put round', *-vṛ́t-e* 'to turn', *-śás-e* 'to proclaim', *-sád-e* 'to sit', *-súd-e* 'to enjoy', *-skád-e* 'to leap', *-skábh-e* 'to prop', *-spṛ́ś-e* 'to touch', *-syád-e* 'to flow', *-sváj-e* 'to embrace'[7].

---

1 Avery 230.
2 Whitney 970 l; Wolff p. 1.
3 Cp. Whitney 982. On the uses of the infinitive, cp. Brugmann, KG. 805—811.
4 Cp. Whitney 982, a—d.
5 That is, *śrad-dhé* and *pra-mé*, which might, however, be explained as locatives.
6 In viii. 4[15] the dative, accented *túj-e*, occurring independently, appears to be a substantive.
7 Cp. the list in Ludwig p. 56—58.

a. One infinitive is also formed from a reduplicated root: *śiśnáth-e* (III. 31[13]) 'to attack'; but according to GRASSMANN[1] it is the locative of a substantive meaning 'attack'.

585. The remaining dative infinitives are formed **from verbal nouns** derived with nine different suffixes.

1. Some 25 of these are datives of **stems in *-as***[2]. They are the following: *áyas-e* (I. 57[3]) 'to go', *arhás-e* 'to be worthy of', *ṛcás-e* 'to praise', *ṛñjás-e* 'to strive after', *kṣádas-e*[3] 'to partake of', *cákṣas-e* 'to see', *carás-e* 'to fare', *javás-e*[4] (III. 50[2]) 'to speed', *jīvás-e* 'to live', *tujás-e* 'to hurl', *dohás-e* 'to milk', *dhā́yas-e* 'to cherish', *dhruvás-e* 'to sit firmly', *puṣyás-e* 'to thrive', *bháras-e*[3] 'to bear', *bhiyás-e* 'to fear', *bhojás-e* 'to enjoy', *rājás-e* 'to shine', *vṛñjás-e* 'to turn aside', *vṛdhás-e* 'to further', *śobhás-e* 'to shine', *śriyás-e* 'to be resplendent', *sáhyas-e*[5] 'to conquer', *spáras-e* 'to help to', *spūrdhás-e* 'to strive after', *harás-e* 'to seize'.

a. Three roots form an infinitive stem with *-s* only instead of *-as*: *ji-ṣ-é* 'to conquer', *upa-prak-ṣ-é*[6] (V. 47[6]) 'to unite', *stu-ṣ-é* 'to praise'[7].

2. Some half dozen are formed from **stems in *-i***: *iṣ-áy-e*[8] (VI. 52[15]) 'to refresh', *tuj-áy-e* (V. 46[7]) 'to breed', *dṛś-áy-e* 'to see', *mah-áy-e* 'to rejoice', *yudh-áy-e* 'to fight', *san-áy-e* 'to win'; *cit-áy-e*[9] (VS.) 'to understand'.

3. Four or five are formed from **stems in *-ti***: *iṣ-ṭáy-e* 'to refresh', *pī-táy-e* 'to drink', *vī-táy-e* 'to enjoy', *sā-táy-e* 'to win'; perhaps also *ū-táy-e* (*nṝn*) 'to help (his men)'.

4. Over 30 dative infinitives are formed from **stems in *-tu*** (added to the guṇated root, in some instances with connecting vowel), from which acc. and abl. gen. infinitives are also formed:

a. *át-tav-e* 'to eat', *áṣ-ṭav-e* 'to attain', *ás-tav-e* (VS.; TS. IV. 5. 1[2]) 'to shoot', *é-tav-e* 'to go', *ó-tav-e* 'to weave' (√*vā-*), *kár-tav-e* 'to make', *gán-tav-e* and *gā́-tav-e* 'to go', *dā-tav-e* 'to give', *práti-dhā-tav-e* 'to place upon', *dhā́-tav-e* 'to suck', *pák-tave* (AV.) 'to cook', *pát-tav-e* 'to fall', *pā́-tav-e* 'to drink', *bhár-tav-e* 'to bear away', *mán-tav-e* 'to think', *yán-tav-e* 'to present', *yáṣ-ṭav-e* 'to sacrifice', *yā́-tav-e* 'to go', *yó-tav-e* 'to ward off', *vák-tav-e* 'to speak', *prá-van-tav-e* 'to win' (√*van-*), *vár-tav-e* 'to restrain', *vás-tav-e* 'to shine', *vā́-tav-e* (AV.) 'to weave', *vét-tav-e* (AV.) 'to find', *vó-ḷhav-e* 'to convey', *pári-śak-tav-e* 'to overcome', *sár-tav-e* 'to flow', *sū́-tav-e* 'to bring forth', *sé-tav-e* (AV.) 'to bind', *só-tav-e* 'to press', *stó-tav-e* 'to praise', *hán-tav-e* 'to slay'.

β. *áv-i-tav-e* 'to refresh', *cár-i-tav-e* 'to fare', *jīv-ā́-tav-e* (TS. IV. 2. 6[5]; VS. XVIII. 67) 'to live', *sávi-tav-e* 'to bring forth', *stár-ī-tav-e* (AV.) 'to lay low', *sráv-i-tav-e* 'to flow', *háv-i-tav-e* 'to call'.

5. Over a dozen infinitives are formed from **stems in *-tavā́*** (added like *-tu* to the gunated root), which are doubly accented.

a. *é-tavái* 'to go' (also *áty-*, *ánv-*, *etavái*), *ó-tavái* 'to weave', *gán-tavái* 'to go' (also *úpa-gantavái*), *dā́-tavái* 'to give', *pári-dhā-tavái* (AV.) 'to envelope', *pā́-tavái* 'to drink', *ápa-bhar-tavái* 'to be taken away', *mán-tavái* 'to think', *mā́-tavái* 'to low', *sár-tavái* 'to flow', *sū́-tavái* (AV.) 'to bring forth'), *hán-tavái* 'to slay'[10].

---

1 s. v. *śiśnátha*.

2 As a rule the suffix, but in half a dozen instances the root, is accented.

3 According to GRASSMANN, 2. sing. middle.

4 According to GRASSMANN, dat. of the substantive *jávas* meaning 'swiftness'.

5 According to GRASSMANN, dat. of the comparative *sáhyas*.

6 DELBRÜCK, Verbum, and AVERY accent *-prákṣe*. Cp. OLDENBERG. Ṛgveda, note on V. 47[6].

7 See DELBRÜCK p. 181 (I, 5); cp. above, p. 378, note 1.

8 Cp. however, DELBRÜCK 207.

9 Perhaps more probably a substantive, according to BR.: 'for understanding'.

10 The MS. has *kártavái*, cp. WHITNEY 982 d and WOLFF 7 (p. 9).

β. *jív-i-tavái* (AV.) 'to live' (Pp. *-ta vái*), *yám-i-tavái* 'to guide', *sráv-i-tavái* 'to flow'.

6. There seems to be only one certain example of a dative infinitive formed from a **stem in -tyā**: *i-tyái* 'to go'[1].

7. Some 35 dative infinitives almost limited to the RV.[2] are formed from **stems in -dhyā** added to verbal bases ending in *a* (generally accented), and seem to have the termination *-dhyai*: *iyá-dhyai* 'to go' (√*i-*), *irá-dhyai*[3] 'to seek to win', *iṣá-dhyai* and *iṣáya-dhyai* 'to refresh', *īrayá-dhyai* 'to set in motion', *kṣára-dhyai* 'to pour out', *gáma-dhyai* 'to go', *gṛṇá-dhyai* (AA. v. 2. 1^{10}) 'to praise', *cará-dhyai* 'to fare', *jará-dhyai* 'to sing', *taṃsayá-dhyai* 'to attract', *tará-dhyai* to overcome', *duhá-dhyai* 'to milk', *dhiyá-dhyai* 'to deposit' (√*dhā-*), *nāśayá-dhyai* 'to cause to disappear', *píba-dhyai* 'to drink', *pṛṇá-dhyai* 'to fill', *bhára-dhyai* 'to bear', *mandá-dhyai* 'to delight in', *mandayá-dhyai* 'to rejoice', *mādayá-dhyai* 'to delight in', *yája-dhyai*[4] 'to worship', *riṣayá-dhyai* 'to injure oneself', *vandá-dhyai* 'to praise', *vartayá-dhyai* 'to cause to turn', *váha-dhyai* 'to guide', *vājayá-dhyai* 'to hasten', *vāvṛdhá-dhyai* (from the perfect) 'to strengthen', *vṛjá-dhyai* 'to turn to', *śayá-dhyai* 'to lie', *śucá-dhyai* 'to shine', *sacá-dhyai* 'to partake', *sáha-dhyai* 'to overcome', *stavá-dhyai* 'to praise', *syandayá-dhyai* 'to flow', *huvá-dhyai* 'to call'. The TS. has also one of these infinitives ending in *-e*: *gamá-dhye* (I. 3. 6^{2}).

8. Five dative infinitives are formed from **stems in -man**: *trá-maṇ-e* 'to protect', *dá-man-e* 'to give', *dhár-maṇ-e* (x. 88^{1}) 'to support', *bhár-maṇ-e* 'to preserve', *vid-mán-e*[5] 'to know'.

9. Three dative infinitives are formed from **stems in -van**: *tur-váṇ-e* 'to overcome' (√*tṝ-*), *dā-ván-e* 'to give', *dhúr-vaṇ-e* 'to injure' (√*dhvṛ-*).

2. Accusative Infinitive.

586. This infinitive is an accusative in sense as well as in form, being used only as the object of a verb. It is primarily employed as a supine with verbs of motion[6] to express purpose. It is **formed in two ways.**

a. More than a dozen radical stems in the RV. and several others in the AV. form an accusative infinitive with the **ending -am**[7].

The root nearly always ends in a consonant and appears in its weak form. It is not always easy to distinguish these infinitives from substantives, but the following include all the more certain forms: *sam-ídham* 'to kindle', *vi-cṛ́t-am* 'to unfasten', *pra-tír-am* (√*tṝ-*) 'to prolong', *prati-dhā́m* 'to place upon' (AV.), (*vi-*, *sam-*)-*pṛ́cch-am* 'to ask', *pra-míy-am* 'to neglect' (√*mī-*), *yám-am*[8] 'to guide', *yúdh-am* (AV.) 'to fight', *ā-rábh-am* 'to reach', *ā-rúh-am* 'to mount', *ā-víś-am* 'to enter', *śúbh-am* 'to shine', *ā-sád-am* 'to sit down'[9].

b. Five accusative infinitives from **stems in -tu** (of which the dative

---

[1] In x. 106^{4} *bhujyái*, occurring beside *puṣṭyái*, is doubtless a substantive; other cases of the word are also met with: see GRASSMANN, s. v. *bhuji*. The MS. I. 6^{3} has also *sā́ḍhyai* (from *sah*+*ti*); *róhiṣyai*, which occurs in the TS. I. 3. 10^{2} is doubtless a substantive; see DELBRÜCK 201 and WHITNEY 977.

[2] This infinitive form occurs once only in the AV. in a Rigvedic passage.

[3] An intensive formation from √*rādh-* (64, 1).

[4] *yajádhyai* TS. IV. 6. 3^{3}; VS. XVII. 57.

[5] WHITNEY 974 also quotes *dár-maṇe*.

[6] Cp. WOLFF 32, 40.

[7] The only roots in vowels taking it are *dhā-*, *mī-*, *tṝ-*.

[8] Occurs three times in the RV., always dependent on *śakéma*.

[9] Perhaps also *sam-óh-am* (strong radical vowel) and *upa-spíj-am*. Cp. the list in WOLFF, p. 87—90. There are several quite doubtful examples from the AV., as *niḥ-khid-am* (conjecture), *pra-táṅk-am*, *saṃ-rúdh-am*. See WHITNEY's notes in his Translation on AV. IV. 16^{2}; V. 18^{7}; VII. 50^{5}.

form is much commoner)[1] occur in the RV. and about the same number of others in the AV.: *át-tum* (AV.) 'to eat', *ó-tum* 'to weave', *kár-tum* (AV.) 'to make', *ni-kartum* (Kh. IV. 5[25]) 'to overcome', *khán-i-tum* (VS. XI. 10) 'to dig', *dā́-tum* 'to give', *drás-ṭum* (AV.) 'to see', *prás-ṭum* 'to ask', *prá-bhar-tum* 'to present', *yā́c-i-tum* (AV.) 'to ask for', *ánu prá-voḷhum* 'to advance, *spárdh-i-tum* (AV.) 'to contend with'[2].

3. Ablative-Genitive Infinitive.

587. This infinitive is **formed in two ways,** like the accusative infinitive, either from a radical stem or from a verbal noun in *-tu* (from which a dative and an acc. infinitive are also formed)[3]. The former, therefore, ends **in *-as*,** the latter **in *-tos*.** As these endings are both ablative and genitive in form, the cases can only be distinguished syntactically. The ablative use is by this criterion shown to preponderate considerably.

a. The *-as* form **has the ablative sense** almost exclusively, as is indicated by its being employed with words governing the ablative, viz. the adnominal prepositions *ṛté* 'without', *purā́* 'before', and the verbs *pā-* 'protect' *trā-* 'rescue', *bhī-* 'fear'. It occurs with the same kind of **attraction** as appears with the dative infinitive: thus *trā́dhvaṃ kartā́d ava-pád-as* (II. 29[6])[4] 'save us from the pit, from falling down (into it)'. There are six such ablatives in the RV.: *ā-tṛ́d-as* 'being pierced', *ava-pád-as* 'falling down', *sam-pṛ́c-as* 'coming in contact', *abhi-śríṣ-as* 'binding', *abhi-śvás-as* 'blowing', *ati-ṣkád-as* 'leaping across'.

α. There seems also to be at least one example (II. 28[6]) of the genitive use, viz. *ni-míṣ-as* .. *íśe* 'I am able to wink', the construction of $\sqrt{}$*īś-* being the same as with the genitive infinitive in *-tos* (b *α*). Another instance is perhaps *ā-pṛ́c-as* 'to fill' (VIII. 40[9]).

b. Of the infinitives in *-tos* occurring in the RV. some **six** are shown by the construction to be **ablatives.** They are: *é-tos* 'going', *gán-tos* 'going', *jáni-tos* 'being born', *ní-dhā-tos* 'putting down', *śár-ī-tos* 'being shattered', *só-tos* 'pressing', *hán-tos* 'being struck'; perhaps also *vás-tos* (I. 174[3])[5].

α. **Three** infinitives in *-tos* **have the genitive sense,** viz. *kár-tos* 'doing' (with *madhyā́*)[6], *dā́-tos* 'giving', and *yó-tos* 'warding off' (both with *īś-* 'have power'). In two passages in which *íśe* governs the infinitive **attraction** of the object appears as with the dative infinitive: *íśe rāyáḥ suvī́ryasya dā́tos* (VII. 4[6]) 'he has power over wealth (and) brave sons, over giving (them)', i. e. 'he has power to give wealth and brave sons'; also *yásya* .. *íśe* .. *yótos* (VI. 18[11]) 'whom he can ward off'[7].

4. Locative Infinitive.

588. This form of the infinitive is rare, since thirteen or fourteen examples at the most occur. Several of these are, however, indistinguishable in meaning from ordinary locatives of verbal nouns[8].

a. Five or six of these locatives are formed from **radical stems:** *vy-úṣ-i* 'at the dawning', *saṃ-cákṣ-i* 'on beholding', *dṛś-í* and *saṃ-dṛ́ś-i* 'on seeing', *budh-í* 'at the waking'. As these nearly always govern a genitive, they are preferably to be explained as simple locatives of verbal nouns.

1 See above 585, 4.
2 See the list in Wolff p. 68—71.
3 Above 585, 4 and 586.
4 Cp. also VIII. 1[12]: *purā́ jatrúbhya ā-tṛ́das* 'before the cartilages being pierced'.
5 See Wolff 11.
6 On this word see Wolff 14, who thinks it governs the ablative rather than the genitive.
7 See Delbrück, Altindische Syntax p. 418, and cp. Wolff 58.
8 Cp. Delbrück 212 (p. 227) and Whitney 985.

b. One locative infinitive is formed from a stem in *-tar*: *dhar-tár-i* 'to support' and *vi-dhar-tár-i* 'to bestow'.

c. Eight locatives with a genuine infinitive meaning are formed from stems in *-san* in the RV. They are: *gr̥-ṇī-ṣáṇ-i*[1] 'to sing', *tar-ī-ṣáṇ-i* 'to cross', *ne-ṣáṇ-i* 'to lead', *par-ṣáṇ-i* 'to pass', *abhi-bhū-ṣáṇ-i* 'to aid', *śū-ṣáṇ-i* 'to swell', *sak-ṣáṇ-i* 'to abide' (√*sac-*)[2], *upa-str̥-ṇī-ṣáṇ-i*[1] 'to spread'.

α. The form *iṣáṇ-i* (II. 2⁹), seems to be derived from *iṣ-* 'emit' for *iṣ-ṣáṇ-i*[3].

d. Gerund.

589. A considerable number (upwards of 120) of forms ending in *-tvī́*, *-tvā́*, *-tvā́ya*, *-tyā́*, *-yā̆* occur in the RV. and AV. in the sense of gerunds expressing an action which accompanies or more often precedes that of the finite verb. They are doubtless old cases[4] (the first most probably a locative, the rest instrumentals) of verbal nouns formed with *-tu*, *-ti*, *-i*, all of which are also employed in the formation of infinitives[5]. The first three are formed from the simple root, the last two from the compounded root.

590. A. a. Of the gerunds formed from the simple root, those in *-tvī́* are the commonest in the RV., there being fifteen altogether in the RV. They hardly ever occur in any of the other Saṃhitās. They appear to be old locatives[6] of stems in *-tu*, which as a rule is added directly to the root, but in two instances with connecting *-i-*. They are *kr̥-tvī́* 'having made', *khā-tvī́* (TS. IV. 1. 1⁴) 'having dug', *ga-tvī́* 'having gone', *gū-ḍhvī́* 'having concealed', *jani-tvī́* 'having produced', *juṣ-ṭvī́* 'liking', *pī-tvī́* 'having drunk', *pū-tvī́* 'having cleansed', *bhū-tvī́* 'having become', *vr̥-tvī́* 'enclosing', *vr̥k-tvī́* 'having overthrown' (√*vr̥j-*), *viṣ-ṭvī́* 'working' (√*viṣ-*), *vr̥ṣ-ṭvī́* 'showering', *skabhi-tvī́* 'having propped', *ha-tvī́* 'having smitten', *hi-tvī́* 'having abandoned' (√*hā-*).

b. The gerund in *-tvā́*, an old instrumental of a verbal noun in *-tu*, is formed by nine roots in the RV. and about thirty more in the AV. Those found in the RV. are: *pī-tvā́* 'having drunk', *bhit-tvā́* 'having shattered', *bhū-tvā́* 'having become', *mi-tvā́* 'having formed' (√*mā-*), *yuk-tvā́* 'having yoked', *vr̥-tvā́* 'having covered', *śru-tvā́* 'having heard', *ha-tvā́* 'having slain', *hi-tvā́* 'having abandoned' (√*hā-*). The forms occurring in the AV. include two formed from secondary verbal stems and three others formed with the connecting vowel *-ĭ-*. They are: *iṣ-ṭvā́* 'having sacrificed' (√*yaj-*), *kalpay-i-tvā́* 'having shaped', *kr̥-tvā́* 'having made', *krī-tvā́* 'trading', *ga-tvā́* 'having gone', *gr̥h-ī-tvā́* 'having seized', *jag-dhvā́* 'having devoured' (√*jakṣ-*), *ci-tvā́* 'having gathered', *cāy-i-tvā́* 'noting', *tīr-tvā́* 'having crossed' (√*tr̥̄-*), *tr̥-ḍhvā́* 'having shattered'[7] (√*tr̥h-*), *dat-tvā́* 'having given', *dr̥ṣ-ṭvā́* 'having seen', *pak-tvā́* 'having cooked', *pū-tvā́* 'having purified', *bad-dhvā́* 'having bound', *bhak-tvā́* 'sharing', *mr̥ṣ-ṭvā́* 'having wiped off', *rū-ḍhvā́* 'having ascended', *lab-dhvā́* 'taking', *vit-tvā́* 'having found', *vr̥ś-tvā́* 'cutting off' (√*vraśc-*)[8], *sup-tvā́* 'having slept', *stab-dhvā́* 'having established', *stu-tvā́* 'having praised', *snā-tvā́* 'having bathed', *sraṃsay-i-tvā́* 'letting fall', *hiṃs-i-tvā́* 'having injured'. One gerund in *-tvā* also occurs though compounded with a prefix: *praty-arpay-i-tvā́* (AV.) 'having sent

---

[1] Formed from the present base.
[2] From √*sac-*, BR., DELBRÜCK, Verbum 213; from √*sah-*, WHITNEY 978.
[3] See BÖHTLINGK, pw. s. v. *iṣáṇi*, and cp. WHITNEY 978, OLDENBERG, note on II. 2⁹.
[4] Cp. v. NEGELEIN, Zur Sprachgeschichte 91.
[5] Cp. BARTHOLOMAE. BB. 15, 227, 239; BRUGMANN, Grundriss 2, 1090.
[6] BARTHOLOMAE, loc. cit.
[7] *tr̥ṣ-ṭvā́* in AV. XIX. 34⁶ is probably to be read *triṣ ṭvā* 'thrice thee'; see WHITNEY's Translation.
[8] See note on AV. VIII. 3² in WHITNEY's Translation (RV. has *vr̥k-tvā́*).

in opposition'. From the Khilas: *janay-i-tvā́* (I. 4[8]); from the VS. *i-tvā́* (XXXII. 12), *vid-i-tvā́* (XXXI. 18) 'having known', *spṛ-tvā́* (XXXI. 1) 'pervading'.

c. The rarest gerund in the RV. is that in **-tvā́ya**, being formed from only seven roots. It appears to be a late formation, occurring only in the tenth Maṇḍala, excepting one example in the eighth (VIII. 100[8]) in a hymn which is marked by ARNOLD[2] as belonging to the latest period of the RV. Two of these gerunds (*gatvā́ya* and *hatvā́ya*) recur in the AV., which, however, has no additional examples of this type. These forms have the appearance of being datives of stems in *-tva*, but the use of the dative in this sense is in itself unlikely, as that case is otherwise employed to express the final meaning of the infinitive. Hence BARTHOLOMAE[3] explains the forms as a metrical substitute for a fem. inst. in *-tvā́yā* (from the stem *-tvā*), or for a loc. of *-tva* with enclitic *ā* added. There seems to be another possible explanation. Three of the seven forms occurring appear instead of the corresponding forms in *-tvā* of the older Maṇḍalas. Owing to this close connexion and the lateness as well as the rarity of these forms, we may here have a tentative double formation, under the influence of compound gerunds formed with *-ya* which end in *-āya*, such as *ā-dā́ya* 'taking'.

The forms occurring are *kṛ-tvā́ya* (VS. XI. 59; TS. IV. 1. 5[4]) 'having made', *ga-tvā́ya* 'having gone', *jag-dhvā́ya* 'having devoured', *ta-tvā́ya* (VS. XI. 1) 'having stretched', *dat-tvā́ya* 'having given', *dṛṣ-ṭvā́ya* 'having seen', *bhak-tvā́ya* 'having attained', *yuk-tvā́ya* 'having yoked', *vṛ-tvā́ya* (TS. IV. 1. 2[3]; VS. XI. 19) 'having covered', *ha-tvā́ya* 'having slain', *hi-tvā́ya* 'having abandoned'.

591. B. **When the verb is compounded**, the suffix is regularly either *-yā̆* or **-tyā̆**. In at least two-thirds of these forms the vowel is long in the RV.[4]

a. Nearly 40 roots in the RV. and about 30 more in the AV., when compounded with verbal prefixes, take the suffix **-ya**[5]. Four roots take it also when compounded with nouns or adverbs. The forms occurring in the RV. are in the alphabetical order of the radical initial: *ā-ác-yā* 'bending', *pra-árp-ya* 'setting in motion', *prati-íṣ-yā* 'having sought for', *abhi-úp-ya* 'having enveloped' (√*vap-*), *vi-kṛ́t-ya* 'having cut in pieces', *abhi-krám-ya* 'approaching', *abhi-khyā́-ya* 'having descried', *abhi-gū́r-yā* 'graciously accepting', *saṃ-gṛ́bh-yā* 'gathering', *prati-gṛ́h-yā* 'accepting', *anu-ghúṣ-yā* 'proclaiming aloud', *abhi-cákṣ-yā* 'regarding', *prati-cákṣ-ya* 'observing' and *vi-cákṣ-ya* 'seeing clearly', *ni-cā́y-yā* 'fearing', *pari-táp-yā* 'stirring up' (heat), *vi-tū́r-yā* 'driving forth', *ā-dā́-ya* 'taking' and *pari-dā́-ya* 'handing over', *ati-dī́v-ya* 'playing higher', *anu-dṛ́ś-ya* 'looking along', *abhi-pád-ya* 'acquiring', *pra-prúth-yā* 'puffing out', *vi-bhíd-yā* 'shattering', *abhi-bhū́-ya* 'overcoming', *vi-mā́-ya* 'disposing' and *sam-mā́-ya* 'measuring out', *sam-mī́l-ya* 'closing the eyes', *vi-múc-yā* 'unyoking', *ā-múṣ-yā* 'appropriating', *anu-mṛ́ś-yā* 'grasping', *ā-yú-ya*[6] 'taking to oneself', *ā-rábh-ya* 'grasping' and *saṃ-rábh-yā* 'surrounding oneself with', *ni-rúdh-yā* 'having restrained', *abhi-vṛ́t-ya* 'having overcome' and *ā-vṛ́t-yā* 'causing to roll towards', *abhi-vlág-yā* 'pursuing', *ni-ṣád-yā̆* 'having sat down', *vi-ṣáh-ya* 'having conquered', *ava-sā́-ya* 'having unyoked', *saṃ-hā́-ya* 'preparing oneself' (*hā-* 'go'). Compounds formed with adverbs are: *punar-dā́-ya* 'giving back', *mitha-spṛ́dh-ya* 'vying together'; and with nouns, *karṇa-gṛ́h-ya* 'seizing by the ear', *pāda-gṛ́h-ya* 'grasping by the foot', *hasta-gṛ́h-ya* 'grasping by the hand'.

1 The MS. has also the form *sam-īray-i-tvā́*: WHITNEY 990 a.

2 Vedic Metre p. 283.

3 BB. 15, p. 239, 12.

4 Cp. WHITNEY 993 a.

5 On the gerund in *-ya* cp. NEISSER, BB. 30, 308—311.

6 *-yú-ya* is also compounded with *ni-* and *vi-*.

The additional roots thus compounded in the AV. are: *ud-úh-ya* 'having carried up', *ā-krám-ya* 'stepping into' and *pari-krám-ya* 'striding about', *saṃ-gír-ya* 'swallowing up', *saṃ-gṛ́h-ya*[1] 'having grasped'[2], *vi-cchíd-ya* 'having cut asunder', *upa-dád-ya* 'putting in' (*dā-* 'give')[3], *abhi-dhā́-ya* 'encircling', *vi-dhū́-ya* 'shaking off', *parā-ṇī-ya* 'leading away', *ā-pád-ya* 'arriving at' and *pra-pád-ya* 'going forward', *sam-pā́-ya* 'drinking up', *vi-bhā́j-ya* 'having apportioned', (caus. of √*bhaj-*), *sam-bhū́-ya* 'combining', *ni-májj-ya* 'having immerged' (√*majj-*), *apa-mā́-ya* 'having measured off'[4], *apa-mṛ́j-ya* 'having wiped off', *saṃ-rábh-ya* 'taking hold together', *ā-rúh-ya* 'ascending', *saṃ-lúp-ya* 'having torn up'[5], *upa-víś-ya* 'sitting down', *pari-viṣ-ya* 'attending upon', *saṃ-śā́-ya* 'sharpening', *ā-sád-ya* 'sitting upon' and *ni-ṣád-ya* 'sitting down', *saṃ-síc-ya* 'having poured together', *apa-sídh-ya* 'driving away', *saṃ-sív-ya* 'having sewed', *niḥ-sṛ́p-ya* 'having crept out', *ati-ṣṭhā́-ya* 'excelling', *prati-ṣṭhā́-ya* 'standing firm', *ut-thā́-ya* 'arising'. From the VS.: *ni-śír-ya* (XVI. 13) 'having broken off', *saṃ-sṛ́j-ya* (XI. 53) 'having mingled', *ati-hā́-ya* (XXV. 43) 'having missed'.

b. Roots which end in a short vowel, either originally or after losing a nasal, add **-tyā** (nearly always in RV.) or **-tya** instead of *-yā̆*, when compounded. The following gerunds are thus formed in the RV.: *-i-tyā* 'having gone' with *api-*, *abhi-* and *ā-*, *-i-tya* with *abhi-* and *prati-*; *ā-gá-tyā* 'having come' (√*gam-*), *ā-dṛ́-tyā* 'regarding', *ā-bhṛ́-tyā* 'bringing', *vi-há-tyā* 'having driven away' (√*han-*); and with adverbial prefixes *araṃ-kṛ́-tyā* 'having made ready', *akhkhalī-kṛ́-tya* 'shouting'. From the Khilas: *aty-ā́-hṛ-tya* (IV. 5[29]).

The AV. has the following gerunds from nine additional roots *nir-ṛ́-tya* 'separating' (?)[6], *abhi-jí-tya* 'having conquered', and *saṃ-ji-tya* 'having wholly conquered', *ā-tá-tya*[7] 'having expanded', *apa-mí-tya* 'having borrowed' (√*mā-*), *ud-yá-tya* 'lifting up', *pra-ā́-vṛ-tya* 'having enveloped', *upa-śrú-tya* 'having overheard', *ud-dhṛ́-tya* 'having taken up' (√*hṛ-*); also in composition with a substantive: *namas-kṛ́-tya*. The VS. has *upa-stú-tya* (XXI. 46) 'having invoked' and *pra-stú-tya* (XXI. 46) 'having lauded'.

VIII. INDECLINABLES.

1. Prepositions.

Gaedicke, Der Akkusativ im Veda (Breslau 1880), p. 193—210. — Whitney, Sanskrit Grammar 1077—1089, 1123—1130. — Delbrück, Altindische Syntax p. 440—471. — Cp. Benfey, Vollständige Grammatik 241 and 784. — Brugmann, KG. p. 457—480. — J. S. Speijer, Vedische und Sanskrit-Syntax, Grundriss I. 6, 87.

592. **Two classes** of prepositions are to be distinguished. The first class embraces the genuine or **adverbial** prepositions. These are words with a local sense which, being primarily used to modify the meaning of verbs, came to be connected independently with the cases governed by the verbs thus modified. They show no signs of derivation from inflexional forms or (except *tirás* and *purás*) forms made with adverbial suffixes. The second class embraces what may be called **adnominal** prepositions. These are words which are not compounded with verbs, but govern cases only. As regards form, they almost invariably end in case terminations or adverbial suffixes.

[1] *-gṛ́hya* also appears compounded with *ni-*, *vi-* and *prati-*.

[2] The gerund *ā-ghrā́-ya* (AV. XIX. 8[5]), the reading of the text, is not found in the Mss. and is doubtless wrong; cp. Whitney's Index Verborum.

[3] From the present base of √*dā-*, cp. Whitney 992 a.

[4] *apa-mā́-ya* is a conjectural reading.

[5] v. Negelein 92 gives *-vidh-ya* (√*vyadh-*) and *-śuṣ-ya* as occurring in the AV., but they are not to be found in Whitney's Index verborum.

[6] See note on AV. X. 2[2] in Whitney's Translation.

[7] Conjectural reading in AV. XX. 136[3]; see Whitney's Index Verborum.

A. Adverbial Prepositions.

593. Of the twenty-two included in this class[1], eight are never used adnominally, viz. *ápa*[2] 'away'; *úd* 'up', 'out'; *ní* 'down', 'into'; *nís* 'out'; *párā* 'away'; *prá* 'forth'; *ví* 'asunder' (often = 'dis-', 'away'); *sám*[3] 'together'[4]. Three others, for the most part employed adnominally, are restricted in their adverbial use to combination with particular verbs, viz. *áccha* 'towards', *tirás* 'across', *purás* 'before'. The remaining eleven, being employed both adverbially and adnominally, are: *áti* 'beyond'; *ádhi* 'upon'; *ánu* 'after'; *antár* 'within'; *ápi* 'on'; *abhí* 'against'; *áva* 'down'; *ā́* 'near'; *úpa* 'up to'; *pári* 'around'; *práti* 'towards'.

a. When combined with verbs[5] these **prepositions are not compounded in the principal sentence**[6]. Generally speaking, they immediately precede the verb; but they are also often separated from it, e. g. *ā́ tvā viśantu* (I. 5[7]) 'may they enter thee'. Occasionally the preposition follows the verb, e. g. *indro gā́ avṛṇod ápa* (VIII. 63[3]) 'Indra disclosed the cows'. Two prepositions are not infrequently combined with the verb[7]; no certain instances of three being thus used can be quoted from the RV., though a few such instances occur in the AV.[8] On the other hand, a preposition sometimes appears quite alone[9]; the verb 'to be', or some other verb commonly connected with it, can then be supplied without difficulty; e. g. *ā́ tū́ na indra* (I. 10[11]) 'hither, pray, (come) to us, Indra'. Or the preposition appears without the verb in one part of the sentence, but with it in another; e. g. *pári mā́m, pári me prajā́m, pári naḥ pāhi yád dhánam* (AV. II. 7[4]) 'protect me, protect my projeny, protect what wealth (is) ours'. As the verb normally stands at the end of the sentence, the preposition would naturally come after the object. Hence as a rule it follows the noun governed by the verb (though it is also often found preceding the noun). Primarily used to define the local direction expressed by the verb which governs a case, prepositions gradually became connected with particular cases. In the RV. it is still often uncertain whether the adverbial or the adnominal sense is intended. Thus *dāśvā́ṃsam úpa gacchatam* (I. 47[3]) may mean either 'do ye two go-to the pious man' or 'do ye two go to-the pious man'. When used adnominally the preposition only

1 On the relative frequency of these prepositions in the RV. and AV. see WHITNEY, Sanskrit Grammar 1077 a.

2 On the relation of *ápa, ápi, úpa, ní, pári* to corresponding Greek prepositions see J. SCHMIDT, KZ. 26, 21 ff.

3 *sám* seems in a few passages to have attained an independent prepositional use with the instrumental: *sám uṣádbhiḥ* (I. 6[3]), *sám pátnībhiḥ* (II. 16[8]), *sám ṛ́kvabhiḥ* (VIII. 97[12]), *sáṃ jyótiṣā jyótiḥ* (VS. II. 9), *sám ā́yuṣā* (TS. I. I. 10[2]); but in all these examples the case perhaps depends on the compound sense of the verb. BR. do not recognize the prepositional use, cp. DELBRÜCK p. 459; on the other hand, see GRASSMANN s. v. *sám* and WHITNEY 1127. *sám* is used with the inst. in Kh. I. 47.

4 The adverbs *āvís* and *prādúr* 'in view' are used with √*as*-, √*bhū*- and √*kṛ*- only.

5 Though a certain number of verbs are never actually met with in the RV. and AV. in combination with prepositions (cp. DELBRÜCK p. 433), there can be litte doubt that practically all verbs except denominatives were capable of combining with prepositions. On the other hand, some verbs occur only in combination with prepositions (DELBRÜCK, loc. cit.).

6 *áccha, tirás, purás* seem never to be compounded with the verb even in dependent clauses; see DELBRÜCK p. 469 (mid.).

7 When there are two, *párā* always immediately precedes the verb; *ā́* and *áva* nearly always; *úd, ní, prá* usually. On the other hand, *abhí* is all but invariably the first of the two; *ádhi* and *ánu* are nearly always so, *úpa* and *práti* usually; cp. DELBRÜCK 234.

8 Cp. DELBRÜCK 235. Three prepositions combined with a verb are common in B.; the last is then almost invariably *ā́* or *áva*.

9 On the elliptical imperative use of prepositions cp. PISCHEL, VS. I. 13, 19 f.; BRUGMANN, IF. 18, 128; DELBRÜCK, Vergleichende Syntax 3, 122 f.

defines the local meaning of the case. It cannot be said to 'govern' the case, except perhaps when *á* 'up to' or *purás* 'before' are connected with the ablative.

594. The fourteen **genuine prepositions** which are used adnominally are **almost** entirely **restricted to** employment with the **accusative, locative, and ablative.** Six are used with the accusative only, viz. *áccha, áti, ánu, abhí, práti* and *tirás*; one (*ápi*) with the locative only; one (*áva*) with the ablative only (and that very rarely).

The remaining six take the accusative and one or both of the other two cases: *pári* takes the ablative also; *úpa* the locative also; *ádhi, antár, á, purás* take both the locative and the ablative also. The first two[1] of these six belong primarily to the sphere of the accusative, the last four to that of the locative. Thus it appears that the genuine prepositions were at the outset practically associated with these two cases only. The ablative came to be used secondarily with *pári* in the sense of 'from (around)'; and similarly with locative prepositions, *ádhi* = 'from (upon)', *antár* = 'from (within)', *á* = 'from (on)'. In all these, the sense of the ablative case combined with the original meaning of the preposition to form a new double notion. But in *purás* 'before' and in *á*, when it means 'up to', which are both used before the case, the ablative sense has completely disappeared.

The following is a detailed account of the genuine prepositions in their alphabetical order.

áccha 'towards'.

595. In combination with verbs of motion and of speaking[2], *áccha*[3] expresses direction in the sense of '(all the way) to'[4]. Used **adnominally with** the same meaning, it takes the **accusative,** which either precedes or follows. It is rare except in the RV.[5] Examples of its use are: *prá yātana sákhīm̐r ácchā* (I. 165^{13}) 'proceed hither to your friends'; *úpa prāgāt .. ácchā pitáram mātáraṃ ca* (I. 163^{13}) 'he has come forward hither to his father and mother'; *kám ácchā yuñjāthe rátham* (V. 74^{3}) 'to (go to) whom do ye two yoke your car?'; *ácchā ca tvā‿enā́ námasā vádāmasi* (VIII. 21^{6}) 'and to thee we speak with this devotion'; *préyám agād dhiṣáṇā barhír áccha* (TS. I. 1. 2^{1} = MS. I. 1^{2} = K. I. 2) 'this bowl has come forward hither to the litter'.

áti 'beyond'.

596. Adverbially *áti* is frequently used in the sense of 'beyond', 'over', 'through', with verbs of motion. Whether it is used adnominally with these and cognate verbs is somewhat uncertain. There are, however, a few distinct instances of such use[6] of *áti* in other connexions **with the accusative;** e. g. *śatáṃ dāsā́m̐ áti srájaḥ* (VIII. 56^{3}) 'a hundred slaves (beyond =) in addition to garlands'; *purvī́r áti kṣápaḥ* (X. 77^{2}) 'through many nights'; *kád asya‿áti vratáṃ cakṛmā* (X. 12^{5}) 'what have we done (beyond =) contrary

[1] In regard to *úpa* the sense of 'motion to' seems to be the primary one; for it is used twice as often with the acc., and its position before the loc. is less primitive.

[2] It is once (VIII. 33^{13}) also used with *śru-* 'hear' in the sense of 'listen to'.

[3] The final *a* is short only at the end of a Pāda and in I. 31^{17} and IX. 106^{1}; otherwise always *ácchā*.

[4] In the SV. it is once used with the locative in the v. r. *sádaneṣu áccha* for *sádanāni áccha* (RV. IX. 91^{1}).

[5] It is used with over twenty roots in the RV. and with only two in the AV. (Whitnev 1078). In the TS. it occurs with *i-* 'go' (IV. 1. 8^{1}; II. 2. 12^{3}) and with *vad-* 'speak' (IV. 5. 1^{2} = VS. XVI. 4).

[6] The adnominal use survives through the Brāhmaṇas into the Mahābhārata.

to his ordinance?'; *yó devó mártyām̐ áti* (AV. XX. 127[7]) 'the god who (is) beyond mortals'.

ádhi 'upon'.

597. The general meaning of *ádhi* in its adverbial use is 'upon', e. g. *ádhi gam* 'come upon', then 'find out', 'learn'.

In **adnominal use** the proper sphere of *ádhi* is the **locative,** with which it is almost always connected. Here, however, there is sometimes an uncertainty whether the preposition belongs to the verb or the noun; e. g. *nákasya pṛṣṭhé ádhi tiṣṭhati* (I. 125[5]) 'he stands upon the ridge of the firmament'. When referring to a person *ádhi* means 'beside', 'with' (from the notion of wielding sway over); e. g. *yán, nāsatyā, parāváti yád vā sthó ádhi turváśe* (I. 47[7]) 'when, O Nāsatyas, ye are at a distance or with Turvaśa'.

a. From the locative the use of *ádhi* extended to the **ablative,** with which it is less frequently connected. It then primarily has the compound sense 'from upon'; e. g. *átaḥ . . . á gahi divó vā rocanád ádhi* (I. 6[9]) 'thence come, or from the bright realm of heaven'. Often, however, the simple ablative meaning alone remains; e. g. *hṛ́dayād ádhi* (X. 163[3]) 'from the heart'; *púruṣād ádhi* (VS. XXXII. 2) 'from Puruṣa'. A somewhat extended sense is occasionally found; e. g. *yám . . . káṇva īdhá ṛtád ádhi* (I. 36[11]) 'whom Kaṇva kindled (proceeding from =) in accordance with sacred order'; *má paṇír bhūr asmád ádhi* (I. 33[3]) 'be not niggardly with regard to us'.

b. From the locative the use of *ádhi* further spread to the **accusative,** though in a very limited way, to express the sphere on or over which an action extends; e. g. *pṛthú prátīkam ádhy édhe agníḥ* (VII. 36[1]) 'Agni has been kindled over the broad surface'. Otherwise, when taking the accusative in the sense of 'upon' with verbs of motion, *ádhi* nearly always belongs to the verb.

a. In the RV. only, *ádhi* is used seven times with the (following) instrumental singular or plural of *snú-* 'height', to express motion along and over = 'across'; e. g. *cakrám . . . ádhi ṣṇúnā bṛhatá vártamānam* (IV. 28[2]) 'the wheel rolling across the mighty height'. This is probably to be explained as the instrumental of the space (by =) through which motion takes place (e. g. *váto antárikṣeṇa yāti* 'the wind goes through the air', I. 161[14]), the preposition that regularly means 'upon' being added to define the action as taking place 'over' as well as 'along'. The VS. has the regular locative of *snú-* with *ádhi*: *pṛthivyá ádhi snúṣu* (XVII. 14) 'on the heights of the earth'.

ánu 'after'.

598. In its adverbial use *ánu* primarily means 'after', e. g. *ánu i-* 'go after', 'follow'; from this fundamental sense are developed various modifications such as 'along', 'through'.

In its **adnominal use** *ánu* takes the **accusative only.** When the influence of the verb is still felt, it means 'after', 'along', 'throughout'; e. g. *párā me yanti dhītáyo gávo ná gávyūtīr ánu* (I. 25[16]) 'my prayers go abroad like kine (seeking) after pastures'; *úpa prá yanti dhītáyaḥ ṛtásya pathyà ánu* (III. 12[7]) 'forth go my prayers along the paths of sacred order'; *yát páñca mánuṣām̐ ánu nṛmṇám* (VIII. 9[2]) 'the might which (exists) throughout the five peoples'; similarly *pṛthivím ánu* (VS. XIII. 6) 'throughout the earth', *vánaspátīm̐r ánu* (VS. XIII. 7) 'in all trees', *pradíśó 'nu* (VS. XXXII. 4) 'throughout the regions'.

When used in closer connexion with nouns *ánu* expresses:

a. sequence in time: 'after' or (with plurals) 'throughout'; e. g. *pū́rvām ánu práyatim* (I. 126[5]) 'after the first presentment'; *ánu dyū́n* 'throughout the days' = 'day after day'.

b. conformity: 'after' = 'in accordance with'; e. g. *svám ánu vratám* (I. 128[1]) 'according to his own ordinance'; *amṛ́tām̐ ánu* (VS. IV. 28) 'after the manner of immortals'; *ánu jóṣam* (TS. I. 1. 13[2] = VS. II. 17) 'for (= to suit) thy enjoyment'. This is the commoner independent use.

antár 'between'.

599. In its adverbial use, which is not frequent, *antár* means 'between', 'within', 'into'; e. g. *antáś car-* 'move between or within'; *antáḥ páś-* 'look into'; *antár gā-* 'go between', 'separate'; *antar-vidvā́n* 'knowing (the difference) between', 'distinguishing'.

The **fundamental** and by for the most frequent **adnominal use** of *antár* is connected **with the locative** in the sense of 'within', 'among'; e. g. *antáḥ samudré* 'within the ocean'; *apsú‿antár* 'within the waters'; *antár devéṣu* 'among the gods'; *gárbhe antáḥ* (VS. XXXII. 4) 'within the womb'; *mātṛ́tamāsu‿antáḥ* (TS. I. 8. 12[2] = VS. X. 7) 'in the best of mothers'.

a. From the locative its use extends in a few instances to the **ablative** in the sense of 'from within'; e. g. *antár áśmanaḥ* 'from within the rock'; *eṣá yayau paramā́d antáḥ ádreḥ* (IX. 87[8]) 'it has come from the highest stone'.

b. From the locative its use further extends, in several instances, to the **accusative**, in the sense of 'between' (expressing both motion and rest), generally in connexion with duals or two classes of objects; e. g. *mahā́n sadhásthe dhruvá ā́ níṣatto 'ntár dyā́vā* (III. 6[4]) 'the great one who has sat down in the firm seat between the two worlds'; *índra ít somapā́ éka̋ḥ .. antár devā́n mártyāṃś ca* (VIII. 2[4]) 'Indra is the one Soma-drinker (between =) among gods and mortals'[1].

ápi 'upon'.

600. In its adverbial use with verbs of motion *ápi* generally means 'into', e. g. *ápi gam-* 'go into', 'enter'; but this sense assumes various modifications which may be expressed by 'on', 'over', 'up'; e. g. *ápi dhā-* 'put upon', 'close up'; *ápi nah-* 'tie up'; *ápi-ripta-* 'smeared over' = 'blind'.

In its adnominal use, which is rare, *ápi* is connected with the **locative only.** It then has the sense of 'on'; e. g. *ayám, agne, tvé ápi yáṃ yajñáṃ cakṛmā́ vayám* (II. 5[8]) 'this (is), O Agni, the sacrifice which we have offered on thee'[2].

abhí 'towards'.

601. In its adverbial use *abhí* means 'towards' with verbs of motion, e. g. *abhí dru-* 'run towards'; it further commonly makes verbs of action transitive, e. g. *krand-* 'roar' : *abhí krand-* 'roar at'; it also sometimes, especially with *bhū-* 'be', comes to have the sense of superiority: *abhí bhū-* 'overcome'.

The **adnominal** use of *abhí* is fairly frequent, though in many individual instances difficult to distinguish from its adverbial use. It is connected **with the accusative only,** in the sense of 'to'; e. g. *úd īrṣva nāri‿abhí jīvalokám* (X. 18[8]) 'Arise, O woman, to the world of the living'. The sense of 'over' (implying dominion), abstracted from one of its secondary adverbial uses, is occasionally found; e. g. *víśvā yáś carṣaṇī́r abhí* (I. 86[5]) 'who (is) over all men'.

---

1 In the later language *antár* is not infrequently used with the genitive (as well as the locative). An example of this occurs as early as VS. XL. 5 (= Īśā Upaniṣad 5): *tád antár asya sárvasya, tád u sárvasya‿asya bāhyatáḥ* 'it is within this all and it is without this all'.

2 The adverb *ápi* begins to be employed secondarily in the RV. (though rarely) as a conjunctional particle meaning 'also'; cp. Brugmann, KG. 588, 5.

áva 'down'.

602. In its adverbial use, *áva* generally means 'down'. e. g. *áva gam-* 'come down'; but is has also the extended sense of 'away', 'off', e. g. *áva sṛj-* 'discharge'.

In its adnominal use, which is very rare and doubtful, it is connected with the ablative in the sense of 'down from'. In the following two examples, especially the second, the case seems to be directly dependent on the preposition: *vṛṣṭím áva divá invatam* (VII. 64²) 'send rain down from heaven'; *yé te pánthāno áva diváḥ* (AV. VII. 55¹) 'which (are) thy paths down from the sky'[1].

ā́ 'near'.

603. The adverbial use of *ā́* with verbs expressing either physical or mental motion is very common in the sense of 'near', 'hither', 'towards', 'to', 'upon'; e. g. *ā́ aj-* 'drive hither'; *ā́ krand-* 'cry to'; *ā́ dhī-* 'think upon', 'attend to'. Less commonly, when used with verbs expressing rest or occurrence, it means 'in' or 'at'; e. g. *ā́ kṣi-* 'dwell in', *ā́ jan-* 'be born at' a place.

When used **adnominally**, *ā́* regularly follows the case, excepting only one sense of the ablative. It is **primarily and most commonly connected with the locative**, when it has the sense of 'on', 'in', 'at', 'to'; e. g. *upásthā ā́* 'on the lap'; *dadhúṣ ṭvā bhṛ́gavo mā́nuṣeṣu ā́* (I. 58⁶) 'the Bhṛgus brought thee to men'.

a. From the locative its use extended to the **ablative**, with which it is used fairly often. It is generally used after this case, when it primarily has the compound sense of 'from on' (cp. *ádhi*); e. g. *parvatā́d ā́* 'from (on) the mountain'. It also means, secondarily, 'away from'; e. g. *yáś cid dhí tvā bahúbhya ā́ sutā́vām̐ āvívāsati* (I. 84⁹) 'who entices thee away from many (others) with his Soma draught'. This secondary meaning is sometimes further extended to express preference; e. g. *yás te sákhibhya ā́ váram* (I. 4⁴) 'who is a boon to thee (in distinction) from friends', i. e. 'who is better to thee than friends'.

α. In about a dozen instances in the RV., *ā́* is used before the ablative to express 'up to'[2]; e. g. *yatī́ giríbhya ā́ samudrā́t* (VII. 95²) 'going from the mountains up to the sea'; *ā́ nimrúcaḥ* (I. 161¹⁰) 'till sunset'[3]. This reversal of meaning is probably due to the reversal of the natural order of the words: *samudrā́d ā́* 'from the sea' thus becoming *ā́ samudrā́t* 'to the sea'.

b. The use of *ā́* is further extended to the **accusative**, with which it is least frequently connected, generally meaning 'to', 'upon', to express the goal with verbs of motion; e. g. *antár īyase .. yuṣmā́m̐ś ca devā́n víśa ā́ ca mártān* (IV. 2³) 'thou goest mediating to you, the gods, and to the people, the mortals'; *mātárā sídatām barhír ā́* (I. 142⁷) 'may the two mothers seat themselves upon the litter'; *éhy ā́ naḥ* (AV. II. 5⁴) 'come hither to us'; *devā́nāṃ vakṣi priyám ā́ sadhástham* (TS. V. 1. 11¹ = VS. XXIX. 1) 'bring (it) to the dear abode of the gods'. In closer connexion with nouns, *ā́* is used to express purpose in the phrases *jóṣam ā́* 'for enjoyment', and *váram ā́* 'for pleasure'.

úpa 'up to'.

604. In its adverbial use *úpa* is in sense akin to *abhí* and *ā́*, expressing 'near to'; e. g. *úpa gam-* 'go near to'. The fundamental meaning of close

---

[1] Cp. DELBRÜCK p. 451.
[2] With very few exceptions this is the only use of *ā́* to be found in B.; in C. also *ā́* is found only before the ablative, but with the old sense of 'from' as well as 'up to'.
[3] It is occasionally found after the ablative in this sense; see GRASSMANN s. v. *ā́*.

contiguity is often coupled with the idea of subordination or inferiority; e. g. *úpa sad-* 'sit down close to', 'approach reverentially'; *upa ās-* 'sit under',' adore'.

In its adnominal use *úpa* is most frequently connected with the accusative (which it more often precedes than follows) in the sense of 'to'; e. g. *á yāhi .. úpa bráhmāṇi vāghátaḥ* (I. 3[5]) 'come to the prayers of the worshipper'.

a. It is also used (about half as frequently in the RV.) before the locative in the sense of 'beside', 'upon', 'at': *yá úpa sū́rye* (I. 23[17]) 'who (are) beside the sun'; *úpa dyávi* '(upon =) up to the sky' (from below); *úpa jmánn úpa vetasé áva tara* (VS. XVII. 6 = MS. II. 10[1]) 'descend upon the earth, upon the reed'.

α. Quite exceptionally (only three times) *úpa* occurs in the RV. with the (following) instrumental. In two passages it expresses sequence of time in the phrase *úpa dyúbhis* (V. 53[3]; VIII. 40[8]) 'day by day'. Once it expresses conformity: *yásmai víṣṇus tríṇi padā́ vicakramá úpa mitrásya dhármabhiḥ* (Vāl. IV[3]) 'for whom Viṣṇu strode forth his three steps in accordance with the ordinances of Mitra'. These abnormal senses of *úpa* are parallel to those of *ánu* (598 a, b), and the construction to that of *ádhi* (597 α).

tirás 'across'.

605. Adverbially *tirás* is used in the sense of 'aside', but only with the two verbs *dhā-* 'put' and *bhū-* 'be', in the Saṃhitās[1]; thus *tiró dhā-* 'put aside', 'conceal'; *tiró bhū-* 'disappear'; e. g. *ajakāvám tiró dadhe* (VII. 50[1]) 'I put away the scorpion'; *má tiró 'bhūt* (AV. VIII. 1[7]) 'may it not disappear'.

Adnominally *tirás* is used fairly often in the RV., and a few times in the AV., in the sense of 'across', 'over', 'through', 'past', with (nearly always before) the accusative[2]; e. g. *á yé tanvánti raśmíbhis tiráḥ samudrám* (I. 19[8]) 'who spread with their rays across the ocean'; *náyanti duritá tiráḥ* (I. 41[3]) 'they lead him through (so as to escape) dangers'; *tiró víśvām̐ árcato yāhy arvā́ṅ* (X. 89[16]) 'come hither past (leaving behind) all singers'.

a. Figuratively *tirás* occasionally means 'contrary to'; e. g. *devā́nām cit tiró váśam* (X. 171[4]) 'even against the will of the gods'; *yó no .. tiráś cittā́ni jíghāṃsati* (VII. 59[8]) 'who desires to slay us contrary to expectations' (= 'unawares'), *yó no .. tiráḥ satyā́ni .. jíghāṃsāt* (TS. IV. 3. 13[3]) 'who may desire to slay us contrary to oaths'.

pári 'around'.

606. In its adverbial use *pári* generally means 'around', e. g. *pári i-* 'go around'; figuratively it also means 'completely', e. g. *pári vid-* 'know fully' (cp. πέρι οἶδε).

Its adnominal use starts from the accusative, with which case it is, however, not very commonly connected. Here, too, it is not always certain that the preposition does not belong to the verb. It nearly always immediately precedes the accusative in the sense of 'around', 'about'; e. g. *pári dyā́m anyád īyate* (I. 30[19]) 'the other (wheel) goes around the sky'. The following is one of the two instances in which *pári* comes after the accusative[3]: *havāmahe śraddhā́m madhyáṃdinam pári* (X. 151[5]) 'we invoke Śraddhā (about =) at noon'[4].

a. Its use then extends to the ablative, with which it is much more frequently connected. Here it has primarily the compound sense of 'from around'; e. g. *divás pári* (I. 47[6]) 'from the sky (which is) around'; *támasas pári* (I. 50[10]) 'from the surrounding darkness'. The original meaning (as in

[1] In the ŚB. and later *tirás* is used with *kṛ-* 'do' also.

[2] It is found at least once in the AV. (XII. 3[39]) and occasionally in the ŚB. in the sense of 'away from' = 'without the knowledge of'.

[3] Cp. GRASSMANN, s. v. *pári*, 784 (bottom).

[4] Like the German preposition 'um'.

ádhi) then disappears, leaving only the ablative sense 'from'; e. g. *tvám adbhyás tvám áśmanas pári .. jāyase* (II. 1[1]) 'thou art born from the waters, from the rock'.

purás 'before'.

607. Adverbially *purás* is combined with *kṛ-* 'do', and *dhā-* 'put' only, in the sense of 'in front'; e. g. *índraḥ kṛṇotu prasavé rathám puráḥ* (I. 102[9]) 'may Indra place (our) car in front in the enterprise'; *índraṃ víśve devā́so dadhire puráḥ* (I. 131[1]) 'the all-gods placed Indra in the forefront'.

Adnominally *purás* occurs about nine times in the RV., in the sense of 'before' and connected **with the accusative, the ablative, and the locative;** e. g. *ásadan mātáram puráḥ* (X. 189[1]) 'he has sat down before his mother'; *ná gardabhám puró áśvān nayanti* (III. 53[23]) 'they do not place the ass before the horse' (*áśvāt*); *yáḥ sṛ́ñjaye puró .. samidhyáte* (IV. 15[4]) 'who is kindled before Sṛñjaya'.

práti 'against'.

608. Used adverbially *práti* means 'towards', 'against', e. g. *práti i-* 'go towards or against'; *práti mā-* 'counterfeit', 'imitate'. From this sense the notion of equality was developed, as in *práti as-* 'be a match for'; e. g. *índra, nákiṣ ṭvā práty asty eṣām, víśvā jātány abhy àsi tā́ni*[1] (VI. 25[5]) 'O Indra, none of them is equal to thee; thou art superior to all these beings'. The verb *as-* often being omitted, *práti* appears to be used like an adjective; e. g. *índraṃ ná mahnā́ pṛthivī́ caná práti* (I. 55[1]) 'not even the earth (is) equal to Indra in greatness'. The preposition further comes to express adverbially the sense of 'back'; e. g. *práti ūh-* 'thrust back'; *práti brū-* 'reply'.

Adnominally *práti* is used **with the accusative only,** altogether about a dozen times in the RV. With verbs of motion[2] or of calling it means 'towards', 'to' (though here there is sometimes a doubt whether it does not rather belong to the verb); e. g. *práti tyáṃ cā́rum adhvaráṃ gopīthā́ya prá hūyase* (I. 19[1]) 'thou art summoned to the beloved sacrifice to drink the milk'. With verbs of protecting it means 'against' = 'from'; e. g. *ágne rákṣā ṇo áṃhasaḥ, práti ṣma, deva, rī́ṣataḥ* (VII. 15[13]) 'O Agni, protect us from distress, against injurers, O god'. Sometimes it means 'over against', 'opposite'; e. g. *ábodhy agníḥ .. práti .. āyatī́m uṣásam* (V. 1[1]) 'Agni has awakened in face of the coming Dawn'. It expresses conformity in the phrase *práti váram* 'according to desire' (cp. *ánu* b, *úpa* a, α).

a. In the phrase *práti vástoḥ* 'at dawn', occurring three times in the RV., the preposition seems to take the ablative, but *vástoḥ* may here be meant for an adverbial form[3].

B. Adnominal Prepositions.

609. This class of words which is never compounded with verbs, but only governs oblique cases (with the exception of the dative), cannot be clearly distinguished from adverbs such as *ūrdhvám* (which from B. onwards is also used as a preposition with the ablative in the sense of 'above' and 'after'). It is to be noted that several of them govern the genitive and the instrumental, cases practically never connected with the genuine prepositions in the Saṃhitās. The following is an account of these words arranged in their alphabetical order[4].

---

1 Both *abhi* and *práti* primarily express direction 'towards', but the former tends to imply superiority or attack ('at'), the latter comparison and equality or repulsion ('back').

2 In B. *práti* is regularly used after the accusative, though apparently never connected with verbs of motion: here it expresses approximate position = 'about', 'at', 'on'; it also means 'in regard to', 'in equality with'.

3 Cp. BR., and DELBRÜCK p. 463.

4 Though several of these (*avás, āré, parás, sácā, sanitúr, sanutár, samáyā, sumád,*

adhás 'below'.

610. With the **accusative** *adhás* occurs only once in the RV., in the sense of 'below': *tisráḥ pṛthivī́r adhó astu* (VII. 104[11]) 'may he be below the three earths'. It is also found once with the **ablative** (or genitive) in the same sense: *adháḥ . . padóḥ* (X. 166[2]) 'below (my) feet'. The latter use also occurs once in the SV. and once in the AV.: *yé te pánthā adhó diváḥ* (SV. I. 2. 2. 3[8]) 'thy paths which are below the sky'; *adhás te áśmano manyúm úpāsyāmasi yó gurúḥ* (AV. VI. 42[2]) 'we cast thy fury under a stone that (is) heavy'.

antarā́ 'between'.

611. This word occurs five times in the RV. **with a following accusative** in the sense of 'between', e. g. *antarā́ dámpatī* 'between husband and wife'. It also occurs a few times in the AV. and VS. before duals; e. g. *antarā́ dyā́vāpṛthiví* 'between heaven and earth'.

abhítas 'around'.

612. This adverb is employed in a few passages of the RV. and AV. in the sense of 'around' with the **accusative**; e. g. *sáro ná pūrṇám abhíto vádantaḥ* (VII. 103[7]) 'talking as round a brimful lake'; *yé devā́ rāṣṭrabhṛ́to 'bhíto yánti sū́ryam* (AV. XIII. 1[35]) 'the kingdom-bearing gods who go around the sun'.

avás 'down from'.

613. In the RV. *avás* occurs four times with the **ablative** (cp. *áva*) in the sense of 'down from'; e. g. *aváḥ sū́ryasya bṛhatáḥ púrīṣāt* (X. 27[21]) 'down from the vast misty region of the sun'. It is further employed four or five times with the **instrumental**; e. g. *avó divā́ patáyantam pataṃgám* (I. 163[5]) 'a bird flying down from heaven'. The latter use seems to be analogous to that of *ádhi* with the instrumental (597 α).

upári 'above'.

614. This adverb occurs three times in the RV. **after the accusative** in the sense of 'above', 'beyond'; e. g. *tisráḥ pṛthivī́r upári* (I. 34[8]) 'above the three earths'. It is also found once with the instrumental in the combination *bhū́myopári*, i. e. *bhū́myā upári* (X. 75[3]) 'beyond the earth'. It is, however, more likely that here we have an irregular euphonic combination for *bhū́myā[ḥ] upári*[1] and that the case governed by the preposition is the **genitive**. This would account for the frequent use of *upári* with the genitive in the later language, while the instrumental would be unique.

ṛté 'without'.

615. This word[2] is used fairly often in the RV., and occasionally in the later Saṃhitās, before or after the **ablative** (sometimes separated from it) in the sense of 'without'; e. g. *ná ṛté tvát kriyate kíṃ caná* (X. 112[9]) 'without thee nothing is done'; *yébhyo ná 'rté pávate dhā́ma kíṃ caná* (TS. IV. 6. 1[4] = VS. XVII. 14) 'without whom no dwelling is purified'.

---

smád) disappear in C., there is nevertheless in the later language a large increase in their numbers, greatly supplemented by the periphrastic use of nouns and by the prepositional gerunds. Cp. SPEIJER, Vedische und Sanskrit-Syntax 89—93.

1 See GRASSMANN, s. v. *upári*; cp. above p. 65 (top).

2 In origin an old locative. On some other words representing old case-forms, used prepositionally (*arvā́k* etc.), cp. WHITNEY 1128.

parás 'beyond'.

616. In the RV. *parás* is used with the accusative, instrumental, ablative, and locative; but in the later Saṃhitās it seems to be found with the ablative only.

a. It takes the **accusative** six or seven times in the sense of 'beyond', not only locally, but also to express superiority or excess; e. g. *áti sū́ryam paráḥ śakunā́ iva paptima* (IX. 107[20]) 'we have flown away like birds beyond the sun'; *nahí devó ná mártyo mahás táva krátum paráḥ* (I. 19[2]) 'for neither god nor mortal (goes) beyond the might of thee, the great'.

b. It is employed nearly three times as frequently with the **instrumental**, for the most part in the sense of 'beyond'; e. g. *paró mā́trayā* (VII. 99[1]) 'beyond measure'. In some passages this sense is somewhat modified. Thus the word twice means 'over' (as opposed to *avás*); e. g. *yás te aṃśúr avás ca yáḥ paráḥ srucā́* (X. 17[13]) 'thy juice which (fell) down from and over the ladle'. Twice, moreover, it expresses 'without'; e. g. *paró māyā́bhis* (V. 44[2]) 'without wiles'.

c. With the **locative** it occurs only once in the sense of 'beyond': *yé triṃśáti tráyas paró devā́so barhír ā́sadan* (VIII. 28[1]) 'the gods who, three in excess of thirty, have seated themselves upon the litter'.

d. It is found in three passages of the RV., as well as a few times in the AV. and the VS., with the **ablative** in the senses of 'beyond', far 'from', and 'away from'; e. g. *paró diváḥ* (AV. IX. 4[21]) 'beyond the sky'; *asmā́t . . paráḥ* (VIII. 27[18]) 'far from him'; *tvát paráḥ* (AV. XII. 3[39]) 'apart from thee'; *paró mū́javató 'tīhi* (VS. III. 61) 'go away beyond (Mount) Mūjavat'. The last example may probably be an instance of the accusative with *parás* = 'beyond (the tribe of) the Mūjavants'[1].

purástād 'in front of'.

617. This adverb is used two or three times in the Saṃhitās with the **genitive** in the sense of 'before', 'in front of'; e. g. *sámiddhasya purástāt* (III. 8[2]) 'in front of the kindled one'; *vā́jaḥ purástād utá madhyató naḥ* (TS. IV. 7. 12[2] = VS. XVIII. 34) 'strength be before us and in the midst of us'.

purā́ 'before' (time).

In the RV. *purā́* is used some twenty times, and in the later Saṃhitās occasionally, before or after the **ablative.** It has primarily the sense of 'before' (of time); e. g. *purā́ nú jarásaḥ* (VIII. 67[20]) 'before old age'; *purā́ krūrásya visṛ́paḥ* (TS. I. 1. 9[3] = VS. I. 28) 'before the departure of the cruel (foe)'. This sense is, however, often modified to express exclusion, sometimes equivalent to 'without', 'except', 'in preference to', e. g. *purā́ saṃbādhā́d abhy ā́ vavṛtsva* (II. 16[8]) 'turn to us before (= so as to save us from) distress'; *purā́ mát* (AV. XII. 3[46]) 'except me'.

bahirdhā́ 'outside'.

618. This adverb[2] is once used in the VS. with the **ablative** in the sense of 'outside', 'from': *idám ahám taptáṃ vā́r bahirdhā́ yajñā́n nissṛjāmi* (VS. V. 11) 'this heated water I eject from the sacrifice'.

sácā 'with'.

619. The use of *sácā* is almost restricted to the RV., where it is common before and after the **locative,** meaning 'in association with', 'beside', 'at',

1 The word *mū́javant-* occurs in the plural as the name of a tribe in AV. V. 22[5] etc.

2 It is used fairly often in B. and S. The simple form *bahis* 'outside' (used also with abl.) is frequent in B. and later.

'in'; e. g. *índra íd dháryoḥ sácā* (I. 7[2]) 'Indra with his two bays'; *mādáyasva suté sácā* (I. 81[8]) 'rejoice at the pressed libation'; *námucāv āsuré sácā* (VS. XX. 68) 'along with the demoniac Namuci'[1].

sanitúr 'apart from'.

620. This adverb is used two or three times[2] in the RV. after the **accusative** in the sense of 'beside', 'apart from'; e. g. *pátiṃ sanitúr* (V. 12[3]) 'without a lord'.

sanutár 'far from'.

621. Allied to the preceding word, *sanutár* appears once in the RV. with the **ablative** in the sense of 'far away from': *kṣétrād apaśyaṃ sanutáś cárantam* (V. 2[4]) 'far from the field I saw him wandering'.

sahá 'with'.

622. This adverb is common in the RV. as well as the later Saṃhitās, before and after the **instrumental** in the sense of 'with'; e. g. *sahá ṛṣibhiḥ* (I. 23[24]) 'together with the seers'; *jarā́yuṇā sahá* (VS. VIII. 28) 'with the after-birth'; *sahá pátyā* (TS. I. 1. 10[2]) 'with (my) husband'; *mánasā sahá* (AV. I. 1[2]) 'together with divine mind'.

sākám 'with'.

623. In the same sense as, but less frequently than, *sahá*, the adverb *sākám*[3] is used before and after the **instrumental**; e. g. *sākáṃ sū́ryasya raśmíbhiḥ* (I. 47[7]) 'together with the rays of the sun'; *sākáṃ gan mánasā yajñám* (VS. XXVII. 31) 'may he come with thought to the sacrifice'; *sākáṃ jarā́yuṇā pata* (AV. I. 11[6]) 'fly with the afterbirth'.

sumád 'with'.

624. This word occurs four times as an adverb[4] in the RV. with the sense of 'together'. It is found once governing the **instrumental** in the sense of 'with': *jāyā́ pátiṃ vahati vagnúnā sumát* (X. 32[3]) 'the wife weds the husband with a shout of joy'.

smád 'with'.

625. Besides being used adverbially some half dozen times in the RV. with the sense of 'together', 'at the same time', *smád*[5] also occurs about as often with the **instrumental**, meaning 'with'; e. g. *smát sūríbhiḥ* (I. 51[15]) 'together with the princes'.

2. Adverbs.

GRASSMANN, Wörterbuch 1737—1740. — WHITNEY, Sanskrit Grammar 1097—1117.

626. Adverbs are most conveniently grouped as those which are formed with adverbial suffixes and those which are formed with case-endings. The former class may be best described according to the suffixes alphabetically arranged, the latter according to the ordinary sequence of the cases.

---

1 Though not found in the AV., *sácā* survives in the TB. (I. 2. 1[8]).

2 Cp. BR. and GRASSMANN, s. v.

3 On other adverbs of similar meaning, with case-endings (*samáyā*, *sarátham*) used prepositionally, see WHITNEY 1127.

4 *sumád* also appears as the first member of a compound in *sumád-aṃśu-*, *sumád-gaṇa-*, *sumád-ratha-*.

5 *smád* also appears as the first member of six or seven compounds.

A. Adverbial suffixes.

627. ***-as*** forms adverbs chiefly of a **local or temporal meaning**; thus *tir-ás* 'across', *par-ás* 'beyond', *pur-ás* 'before', *sa-dív-as* and *sa-dy-ás* 'to-day', 'at once'; *śv-ás* 'to-morrow', *hy-ás* 'yesterday'; also *mith-ás* 'wrongly'.

628. ***-tas*** expresses the **ablative sense** of 'from'. It forms adverbs:

a. **from pronouns**; e. g. *á-tas* 'hence', *amú-tas* 'from there', *kú-tas* 'whence?', *tá-tas* 'thence', *yá-tas* 'whence', and, with accent on the suffix, *i-tás* 'from hence', *mat-tás* (AV.) 'from me'.

b. **from adjectives and substantives**; e. g. *anyá-tas* 'from another place', *dakṣiṇa-tás* 'from the right', *sarvá-tas* 'from all sides'; *agra-tás* 'in front', *hṛt-tás* 'from the heart', etc.; the suffix is added to a locative case-form in *patsu-tás* 'at the feet', beside *pat-tás* 'from the feet'.

c. **from prepositions**: *ánti-tas* 'from near', *abhí-tas* 'around', *parí-tas* (AV.) 'round about'.

a. These adverbs in *-tas* are sometimes used *as* equivalents of ablatives; e. g. *áto bhū́yas* 'more than that'; *tátaḥ ṣaṣṭhā́t* (AV.) 'from that sixth'. On the other hand, the ablative sense is sometimes effaced, the locative meaning taking its place; e. g. *agra-tás* 'in front'.

629. ***-tāt*** (an old ablative of *ta-* 'this')[1] has an **ablative or a locative meaning**. It is attached to adverbial case-forms and adverbial or adnominal prepositions; thus *údak-tāt* 'from above', *prā́k-tāt* 'from the front'; *ārā́t-tāt* 'from afar', *uttarā́t-tāt* 'from the north', *parākā́t-tāt* 'from a distance'; *paścā́-tāt* 'from behind'; *adhás-tāt* 'below', *avás-tāt* 'below', *parás-tāt* 'beyond', *purás-tāt* 'in or from the front', and with inserted *s* (probably due to the influence of the preceding forms) *upári-ṣ-ṭāt* '(from) above'.

630. ***-ti*** in *án-ti* 'near', *í-ti* 'thus'; probably also in *á-ti* 'beyond', *prá-ti* 'towards'.

631. ***-tra*** or ***-trā́*** has a **local sense**, and is mostly attached to pronominal stems or stems allied to pronouns in sense; thus *á-tra* 'here', *amú-tra* (AV.) 'there', *kú-tra* 'where?', *tá-tra* 'there', *yá-tra* 'where'; *anyá-tra* 'elsewhere', *ubhayá-tra* 'in both places', *viśvá-tra* 'everywhere'; *asma-trā́* 'among us', *sa-trā́* 'in one place', 'together'; *dakṣiṇa-trā́* 'on the right side', *puru-trā́* 'in many places', *bahu-trā́* 'amongst many'; *deva-trā́* 'among the gods', *pāka-trā́* in simplicity', *puruṣa-trā́* 'among men', *martya-trā́* 'among mortals', *śayu-trā́* 'on a couch'.

a. These adverbs in *-trā́* are sometimes used *as* equivalents of locatives; e. g. *yátrā́dhi* 'in which', *hásta ā́ dakṣiṇa-trā́* 'in the right hand'. This locative sense also sometimes expresses the goal; e. g. *pathó devatrā́ .. yā́nān* (x. 73⁷) 'roads that go to the gods'.

632. ***-thā*** forms adverbs of **manner**, especially from pronominal stems; thus *á-thā* (more usually with shortened vowel, *átha*) 'then', *i-t-thā́* 'thus', *imá-thā* 'in this manner', *ka-thā́* 'how'; *tá-thā* 'thus', *yá-thā* 'in which manner'; *anyá-thā* 'otherwise', *viśvá-thā* 'in every way'; *ūrdhvá-thā* 'upwards', *pūrvá-thā* 'formerly', *pratná-thā* 'as of old'; *ṛtu-thā́* 'regularly', *nāmá-thā* (AV.) 'by name'; *evá-thā* 'just so'.

a. ***-thám*** occurs beside *-thā* in *i-t-thám* 'thus', and *ka-thám* 'how?'.

633. ***-dā*** forms adverbs of **time** almost exclusively from pronominal roots; thus *i-dā́* 'now', *ka-dā́*[2] 'when?', *ta-dā́* 'then', *ya-dā́* 'at what time'; *sá-dā* 'always'; *sarva-dā́* (AV.) 'always'.

a. ***-dam*** occurs beside *-dā* in *sá-dam* 'always'; and ***-dā́-nīm***, an extended form of *-dā*, appears in *i-dā́-nīm* 'now', *ta-dā́-nīm* 'then', *viśva-dā́-nīm* 'always'.

[1] In the RV. *tā́t* itself is once used independently in the sense of 'in this way'.

[2] In the RV. nearly always accented *kádā* when followed by *caná* = 'never'.

b. *di-*, which occurs only in *yá-di* 'if'[1], is perhaps related to *-dā*.

634. *-dhā* forms adverbs **from numerals** or words of cognate meaning, with the sense of '**(so many) times**', 'in (so many) ways', '-fold'; thus *eka-dhā́* (AV.) 'singly', *dvi-dhā* 'in two ways', *tri-dhā* and *tre-dhā́* 'triply', *catur-dhā́* 'fourfold', *ṣo-ḍhā́* 'in six ways', *dvādaśa-dhā́* (AV.) 'twelvefold'; *kati-dhā́* 'how many times?', *tati-dhā́* (AV.) 'in so many parts', *puru-dhā́*[2] 'variously', *bahu-dhā́* 'in many ways', *viśvá-dhā*[2] 'in every way', *śaśva-dhā́* 'again and again'; *priya-dhā́* (TS.) 'kindly', *pre-dhā́* (MS.) 'kindly', *bahir-dhā́* (VS.) 'outward', *mitra-dhā́* (AV.) 'in a friendly manner'; *á-dhā* and (with shortened final) *á-dha* 'then', *a-d-dhā́* ('thus' =) 'truly'; *sáma-dhā*[3] (Kh. I. 11[4]) 'in the same way'.

a. *sa-dha-*, occurring as the first member of several compounds, in the sense of ('in one way' =) 'together', is probably formed with the same suffix, the final vowel being shortened[4]; in independent use it appears as *sahá* 'with'[5]. With the same original suffix appear to be formed other adverbs in *-ha*; thus *i-há* 'here' (Prākrit *idha*), *kú-ha* 'where?', *viśvá-ha*[6] and *viśvá-hā*[7] 'always', *sama-ha* 'in some way or other'.

635. *-va*, expressing **similarity of manner**, forms two adverbs: *i-va* 'like', 'as'[8]; *e-vá*, often with lengthened final, *e-vā́* 'thus'. *-vám* appears beside *-va* in *e-vám* 'thus', which occurs once in the RV. (x. 151[3]) instead of *evá*, and a few times in the AV. with *vid-* 'know'; it is also found in the SV. (I. 3. 1. 1[10]): *ná ki evám̐ yáthā tvám* 'there is nothing such as thou'.

636. *-vát* forms adverbs meaning '**like**' from substantives and adjectives; e. g. *aṅgiras-vát* 'like Aṅgiras', *manu-vát* 'as Manu (did)'; *purāṇa-vát*, *pūrva-vát*, *pratna-vát* 'as of old'. In origin it is the accusative neuter (with adverbial shift of accent) of the suffix *-vant*, which is used to form adjectives of a similar meaning (e. g. *tvā́-vant-* 'like thee').

637. *-śás* is used to form adverbs of measure or manner with a **distributive sense**, often from numerals or words implying number; thus *śata-śás* (AV.) 'by hundreds', *sahasra-śás* 'by thousands'; *śreṇi-śás* 'in rows'; similarly *ṛtu-śás* 'season by season', *deva-śás* 'to each of the gods', *parva-śás* 'joint by joint', *manma-śás* 'each as he is minded'.

638. *-s* forms two or three **multiplicative adverbs**: *dvi-s* 'twice', *tri-s* 'thrice', and probably *catúr* for **catúr-s* (cp. Zend *cathruš*) 'four times'. The same suffix forms a few other adverbs: *adhá-s* 'below' (cp. *ádha-ra* 'inferior'), *avá-s* 'downwards' (from *áva* 'down'), *-dyú-s*[9] (from *dyú-* 'day') in *anye-dyú-s* (AV.) 'next day' and *ubhaya-dyú-s* (AV.) 'on both days'; perhaps also in *āvi-s* 'openly' and *bahi-s* 'outside'[10].

639. *-hi* forms a few adverbs of **time** from pronominal roots; thus *kár-hi* 'when?', *tár-hi* 'then?'[11]. The first part of these words seems already to contain an adverbial suffix *-r*[12] (thus *ká-r* = Lat. *cūr*)[13].

640. There are also some **miscellaneous adverbs** consisting of isolated

---

1 Cp. BRUGMANN, KG. 585.

2 The final vowel of *purudhā́* and *viśvádhā* appears shortened before a double consonant in the RV.

3 Cp. *sama-ha*.

4 As in *ádha, purudhá, viśvádha*.

5 See above 58, 2 a (p. 52).

6 Just as *viśvádha* beside *viśvádhā*; but cp. BRUGMANN, KG. 582.

7 On the other hand *viśvā́hā* 'always' is = *viśvā áhā* 'all days' ('*alle Tage*') with a single accent, like a compound; see GRASSMANN, s. v.

8 In the late parts of the RV. and in the AV. *iva* has often to be read as *va*; cp. ARNOLD, Vedic Metre 129, but see OLDENBERG, ZDMG. 61, 830.

9 See MERINGER, IF. 18, 257; cp. RICHTER, IF. 9, 238; SCHULZE, KZ. 28, 546.

10 Cp. BRUGMANN, KG. 584.

11 *amúr-hi, etár-hi, yár-hi* also occur in B.

12 Cp. *avá-r*, which occurs once beside the usual *avá-s*.

13 Cp. BRUGMANN, KG. 583.

words or small groups, mostly of obscure origin, formed with other suffixes. The latter in alphabetical order are:

-a : *kv-à* (always *kú-a*) 'where?' and *a-dy-á*[1] 'to-day'.

-ar : *pún-ar* 'again' and *sasv-ár* 'secretly'.

-ā : *antar-á* 'between', *pur-á* 'before'; perhaps also in *nắnā* 'variously', which may be = *nắ-nā* 'so and so' from the pronominal root *na-*[2].

-it : *dakṣiṇ-ít* 'with the right hand'; and *-vít* in *cikit-vít* 'with deliberation'.

-u : *jắt-u* 'ever', *míth-u* 'wrongly', *múh-u* 'suddenly'; *anu-ṣṭh-ú* 'at once' ('standing after', from √*sthā-*, cp. *su-ṣṭh-ú* 'in good state').

-ur : *múh-ur* 'suddenly'.

-k : *jyó-k* 'long'. In several other adverbs *-k* with more or less probability represents the final of a root; thus *niṇík* 'secretly' (probably from **niṇi-ac-* adj. 'secret'), *madrík* 'towards me' (contracted from *madríak*, neut. adv. of *madríac-* adj. 'turned to me'); *ānu-ṣák* 'in succession' ('following after' : √*sac-*); *āyu-ṣák* 'with the cooperation of men' (*sac-* 'follow'); *uśá-dhak* 'with eager consumption' ('eagerly burning' : √*dah-*).

-tár : *prā-tár* 'early' and *sanu-tár* 'away' (621).

-túr : *sani-túr* 'away' (620).

-nám : *nū-nám* 'now' and *nānā-nám* 'variously' (642 d).

B. Adverbial Case-forms.

641. A large number of case-forms of nominal and pronominal stems, often not otherwise in use, are employed as adverbs. They become such when no longer felt to be case-forms[3]. Forms of all the cases appear with adverbial function.

Nominative. Examples of this case are *prathamám* 'firstly', *dvitíyam* 'secondly'; e. g. *divás pári prathamáṃ jajñe agnír, asmád dvitíyam pári jātávedāḥ* (x. 45[1]) 'Agni was first born from heaven, secondly he, Jātavedas, (was born) from us'. Such adverbs are to be explained as originally used in **apposition** to the verbal action: 'as the first thing, Agni was born'. A masculine form has become stereotyped in *kí-s* as an interrogative adverb; its negative forms *ná-kis* and *má-kis* are often used in the sense of 'never' or simply 'not'.

642. Accusative. Adverbs of this form are to be explained from various meanings of the accusative. The following are examples of nominal forms representing:

a. the **cognate accusative**: *ṛcá kapótaṃ nudata praṇódam* (x. 165[5]) 'by song expel the pigeon as expulsion'; *citráṃ bhānty uṣásaḥ* (vi. 65[2]) 'the Dawns shine brightly' (= 'a bright scil. shining'); *marmṛjmá te tanvàm bhúri kṛ́tvaḥ* (iii. 18[4]) 'we adorned thy form many times' (originally 'makings'); similarly *dhṛṣṇú* 'boldly', *purú* 'much', 'very', *bhúyas* 'more'; and the comparative in *-taram* added to verbal prefixes; e. g. *vi-taráṃ ví kramasva* (iv. 18[11]) 'stride out more widely'; *saṃ-taráṃ sáṃ śiśādhi* (AV. vii. 16[1]) 'quicken still further'; *prá táṃ naya pra-tarám* (x. 45[9]) 'lead him forward still further'; *úd enam ut-taráṃ naya* (AV. vi. 5[1]) 'lead him up still higher'; so also *ava-tarám, paras-tarám, parā-tarám* 'further away', and the fem. accusatives *saṃ-tarắm* and *paras-tarắm* (AV.).

[1] Cp. REICHELT, BB. 25, 244.

[2] Cp. op. cit. 839; PERSSON, IF. 2, 200 ff., 'auf diese (oder) jene Weise'; BARTHOLOMAE, IF. 10, 10—12, originally 'separatim'.

[3] On the distinction between case function and adverbial use see BRUGMANN, KG. 571.

b. the **appositional accusative**; thus *oṣá-m* 'quickly' (lit. 'burningly'), *kā́ma-m* 'according to desire'; *nā́ma* 'by name[1]', *rūpá-m* 'in form', *satyá-m* 'truly'.

c. the **accusative of direction**; e. g. *ágra-m* (*i-*) '(go) to the front of', 'before'; *ásta-m* (*gam-*) '(go) home'.

d. the **accusative of distance and time**; e. g. *dūrá-m* 'a long way off', 'far'; *nákta-m* 'by night', *sāyá-m* 'in the evening', *cirá-m* '(for a) long (time)', *nítya-m* 'constantly', *pū́rva-m* 'formerly'.

α. There are also some adverbs derived from obsolete nominal stems, which would seem for the most part to have belonged originally to the sphere of the cognate accusative; thus *ára-m* 'sufficiently' (from **ára-* 'fitting'), *ála-m* (AV.) id.; *tūṣṇī́-m* 'in silence', *nānānā́-m* (from *nā́nā*) 'variously', *nūná-m* (from *nū́*) 'now'; *sākā́-m* 'together' (from **sākā́-* 'accompaniment': *sac-* 'follow'[2].

β. Finally a number of accusative adverbs are formed from pronominal stems; thus *adás* 'there', 'thither'; *id* 'just', 'even'; *idā́m* 'here', 'now'; *īm* 'ever' (e. g. *yá īm* 'whoever'); *ká-d*, an interrogative particle; *ká-m*, a particle emphasizing a preceding dative or (unaccented) the particles *nú*, *sú*, *hí*; *kí-m* 'why?'; *-kī-m* 'ever' (in *mā́-kīm* 'never'); *kuv-id* 'whether?'; *ci-d* 'even'; *tá-d* 'then'; *yá-d* 'if', 'when', 'that'; *sī-m* 'ever' (*yát sīm* 'whenever'); *smá-d* and *smá-d* 'together'.

643. **Instrumental.** With the ending of this case (sometimes plural) are formed adverbs from substantives, adjectives, and pronouns, the latter two groups being at first probably used with the ellipse of a substantive. Various senses of the instrumental case are expressed by these adverbs. Usually they imply **manner or accompanying circumstances**; e. g. *táras-ā* 'with speed'; *sáhas-ā* 'forcibly'; *táviṣī-bhis* 'with might'; *návyas-ā* 'anew'; *enā́* 'in this (way)', 'thus'. Not infrequently they express extension of space or time; e. g. *ágreṇa* 'in front'; *aktú-bhis* 'by night'; *dív-ā* 'by day' (but *div-ā́* 'through the sky'); *doṣā́* 'in the evening'.

a. The **substantive instrumentals** are chiefly formed from feminine **stems in *-ā*** not otherwise in use, but corresponding mostly to masculines or neuters in *-a*; thus *a-datrayā́* 'without (receiving) a gift' (*dátra-* 'gift'); *āsayā́* 'before the face of', 'openly' (**ā́sā- = ās-* 'face'); *ṛtayā́* 'in the right way' (**ṛtā́- = ṛtá-*); *naktayā́* 'by night' (**náktā- = nákta-*); *sumnayā́* 'piously' (**sumnā́- = sumná-*); *svapnayā́* (AV.) 'in a dream' (**svápnā- = svápna-*).

α. Several of these feminines are instrumentals from stems in *-tā* and identical in form with the stem; thus *tiraścá-tā* 'through'; *devá-tā* 'among the gods'; *bāhú-tā* 'with the arms'; *sasvár-tā* 'in secret'; *dvi-tā́* 'in two ways' may have a similar origin (*dvi-tā́-* 'two')[3]. We have perhaps also old instrumentals of feminine stems in *-ā* in *tādī́tnā* 'then' = 'at that time'; and in *vṛ́thā* 'according to choice', 'at will' (**vṛ́-thā-* 'choice', from *vṛ-* 'choose').

β. In a few examples the instrumental seems more probably to be that of a radical stem with adverbial shift of accent rather than from a stem in *-ā*; thus *gúh-ā* 'in secret', rather inst. of *gúh-* 'hiding'[4], than of a stem **gúh-ā-*[5]; similarly *mṛ́ṣ-ā* 'in vain' (**mṛ́ṣ-* 'neglect' : inst. *mṛṣ-ā́*); *sác-ā* 'together' (**sác-* 'accompaniment' : inst. *sac-ā́*). In *a-sthā́* (RV¹.), perhaps meaning 'at once', we seem to have an instrumental adverb from a radical *ā*-stem *a-sthā́-* ('no standing') = 'without delay'.

b. The **adjective instrumentals** end either in *-ā* (plural *-ais*) or *-yā*. The former are derived from *a-* stems and a few consonant stems in *-c*; the latter are anomalous feminines from *u-* stems and one or two *ī-* stems:

α. *apākā́* 'afar' (*ápāka-* 'far'); *īrmā́* 'quickly' (*īrmá-*); *uccā́* and *uccáis* 'on high' (*uccá-*); *dakṣiṇā́* 'to the right' (*dákṣiṇa-*); *parācáis* 'for away' (**parācá-*); *paścā́* 'behind' (**paścá-*); *madhyā́* 'in the midst' (*mádhya-*); *śánais* 'slowly'

---

[1] Cp. Gray, IF. 11, 307 ff.; Foy, IF. 12, 172.

[2] For some other adverbs of obscure origin, which were originally accusatives, see Whitney 1111 f.

[3] Cp. Benfey, SV. Glossary, and Grassmann, Wörterbuch, s. v.

[4] The normal inst. of which would be *guh-ā́*.

[5] Cp. RV. 1. 67[6] *guhā́ gúhaṃ gās* and in the next stanza *gúhā bhávantam*.

(*śána-) and śánakais id.; sánā[1] 'from of old' (sána-); samanā́ 'in the same way' (sámana-); tiraśc-ā́ 'across'; nīc-ā́ 'downwards'; prāc-ā́ 'forwards'.

β. anu-ṣṭhu-y-ā́[2] 'at once' (anu-ṣṭhú 'following', adv. from sthā- 'stand'); āśu-y-ā́ 'swiftly' (āśú-); dhṛṣṇu-y-ā́ 'boldly' (dhṛṣṇú-); mithu-y-ā́ 'falsely' (míthu, adv. from mith- 'be hostile'); raghu-y-ā́ 'rapidly' (raghú-); sādhu-y-ā́ 'straight' (sādhú-); also urviy-ā́ (for urvy-ā́) 'far', from urvī́ f. of urú- 'wide'; and viśvy-ā 'everywhere', from *viśvī-, irregular f. of viśva- 'all', beside the regular inst. f. viśvayā, which itself seems once (VIII. 68[2]) to be used adverbially.

c. **Pronominal instrumentals** are formed from several stems in *-a* and one in *-u*. Some appear in the masculine (or neuter) form of *-ā* or the feminine of *-yā*; so *anā́* 'thus' (*aná-* 'that'); *amā́* 'at home' (*áma-* 'this'); *a-yā́* 'thus' (*a-* 'this'); *enā́* 'thus' (*ena-* 'this'); *ka-yā́* 'how?' (*ká-* 'who?'); *ubhayā́* 'in both ways' (*ubháya-* 'both'). From *amú-* 'that' is formed the adverb *amu-y-ā́* 'in that way', with the anomalous interposition of *y*[3]. To the influence of the latter word is probably due the form *kuhayā́* 'where?' (RV[1].) beside the usual *kúha* 'where?'.

644. a. Dative. The adverbial use of this case is rare. Examples are: *aparā́ya* 'for the future' (from *ápara-* 'later'); *várāya* 'according to wish' (*vára-* 'choice').

b. Ablative. This case is on the whole used adverbially fairly often. It is, however, seldom formed from substantives, as *ārā́t* 'from a distance', *āsā́t* 'from near'; or from pronouns, as *ā́t* 'then', *tā́t* 'thus', *yā́t* 'as far as'. It is most commonly formed from adjectives; thus *dūrā́t* 'from afar'; *nīcā́t* 'from below'; *paścā́t* 'from behind'; *sākṣā́t* 'visibly'; and with shifted accent: *adharā́t* 'below' (*ádhara-*); *apākā́t* 'from afar' (*ápāka-*); *amā́t* 'from near' (*áma-*); *uttarā́t* 'from the north' (*úttara-*); *sanā́t*[4] and *sanakā́t* 'from of old' (*sána-*).

c. Genitive. The adverbial use of this case is very rare. Examples are *aktós* 'by night' and *vástos* 'in the morning'.

d. Locative. Several forms of this case have an adverbial meaning; thus *ágre* 'in front'; *abhi-svaré* 'behind' (lit. 'within call'); *astam-īké* 'at home'; *āké* 'near'; *āré*[5] 'afar'; *ṛté* 'without'; *dūré* 'afar'; and in the plural *aparī́ṣu* 'in future'.

3. Particles.

WHITNEY, Sanskrit Grammar 122, 132—133. — DELBRÜCK, Altindische Syntax p. 240—267. — Cp. BRUGMANN, KG. 817—855.

645. Other adverbial words, the derivation of which is obscure and the meaning of which is abstract or general, may be classed as particles. They form **three groups**, the emphatic, the conjunctional, and the negative, the first being the most numerous. The emphatic particles, as throwing stress on a preceding word, are either enclitic or incapable of beginning a sentence; the conjunctional particles, except *utá*, are of a similar nature; but the negatives, having a strongly antithetical meaning, generally occupy an emphatic position in the sentence.

646. The **emphatic particles** may usually be translated by such words as 'just', 'indeed', or rendered merely by stress on the word they follow.

1 In the last three adverbs the accent does not shift to the final syllable.

2 These anomalous forms are due perhaps to the influence of the pronominal *amu-y-ā́*.

3 The anomalous interposition of *y* is perhaps due to the influence of the numerous adverbs in *-yā* from stems in *-a*, *amú-* being an isolated pronominal *u-* stem.

4 *sanā́t* occurs also AA. V. 2. 2[15].

5 On *āré*, *ārā́t*, *ṛté* cp. NEISSER, BB. 19, 140.

They are *aṅgá*; *áha*[1], *gha*, *ha* (the last two less emphatic than *áha*); *smā̆*; *svid* (generally following an interrogative) = 'pray'; *vái*, nearly always following the first word of a sentence. Three particles which emphasize the preceding word more strongly in the sense of 'certainly', 'in truth', are *kíla* (+ AV.), *khálu* (RV[1]., not in AV.), *bhála* (RV[1]. AV[1].). In the RV. *tú* usually emphasises exhortations = 'pray', but sometimes also statements = 'surely'; once (VI. 29[5]) it seems to mean 'but', which is its sense in its single occurrence in the AV. The particle *ná*, when it means 'as it were', 'like', was in origin probably an emphatic particle = 'truly'[2].

647. There are several **conjunctional particles,** some of which are compounded. *ū̆*[3] 'now', 'again', is commonly used deictically and anaphorically after pronouns and verbs. Both *u-tá* and *ca* mean 'and'. *ca* when compounded with the negative particle as *caná* originally meant 'not even', but the negative sense generally disappears and *caná* turns the interrogative pronoun into an indefinite, as *káś caná* 'some one'[4]. *ca* when compounded with *íd*, that is *céd*, means 'if'. *nū̆* 'now' generally follows the first word of the sentence. The disjunctive particle is *vā* 'or'. *hí* (generally following the first word of a sentence) expresses the reason for an assertion = 'for', 'because'; it is also used with imperatives, when it means 'then'. It occurs once in the RV. (VI. 48[2]) compounded with the negative *ná*, but without change of meaning: *hiná* 'for'.

648. The **negative particle** which denies assertions is *ná* 'not'. Its compound *néd* (= *ná íd*) expresses an emphatic 'not'; it is, however, usually employed in the final sense of 'in order that not', 'lest'. Its compound *ná-kis* often means 'never', and *ná-kīm*, in the only two stanzas in which it occurs (VIII. 78[4. 5]), has the same sense. The negative also occurs twice (X. 54[2]; 84[3]) compounded with *nú* as *nanú*, which expresses a strong negative = 'not at all', 'never'. When it is compounded with *hí* as *nahí*, the latter word retains the meaning of both particles: 'for not'.

mā́ 'not' is the **prohibitive particle** regularly used with the injunctive[5]. It is compounded with the petrified nom. *-kis* and acc. *-kīm* to *mā́-kis* and *mā́-kīm*. The former frequently and the latter in its only two occurrences mean 'never'.

a. Adverbial words occurring in compounds only.

649. A limited number of words of an adverbial character have either entirely lost or, in a few instances, nearly lost their independent character, being found in combination **with** half a dozen particular **verbs** or as the first member of nominal compounds. In two or three examples the original independence of such words can still be traced.

650. A few mostly **onomatopoetic** reduplicative words appear only compounded with the roots *kṛ-* 'do' and *bhū-* 'be', the prefixed form generally ending in *-ā*, once in *-ī*: thus *akhkhalī-kṛ́tya*[6] (VII. 103[3]) 'croaking', *alalā-*

---

[1] Another frequent particle of the same meaning, *id*, has already been mentioned among the pronominal accusative adverbs.

[2] Greek *ναί*, Lat. *nae*, cp. Lith. *nei* 'as it were' (cp. BRUGMANN, KG. 839); this sense of *ná* is generally explained as derived from the negative = 'not (precisely)': see WHITNEY 1122 h; cp. BB. 22, 194 ff.

[3] On the Sandhi of *u*, see above 71, 1 b.

[4] Cp. DELBRÜCK, op. cit. p. 544.

[5] It is not used with the ordinary subjunctive, nor the imperative, nor the optative except in the form *bhujema*; see DELBRÜCK p. 361 (top). In the Khilas it occurs two or three times with the 2. impv.; *paśya* (III. 15[17]), *tiṣṭha* (IV. 5[25]), and once at least with the subj.: *vadāti* (I. 9[5]): MS. *vádeti*.

[6] This is the only instance of the prefix ending in *-ī* instead of *-ā* in the RV. In the AV. *-ī* appears before forms of *kṛ-* in the nominal compounds *vātī-kṛta-* and *vātī-kārá-*, designations of a disease.

bhávant- (IV. 18[6]) 'sounding merrily'; *jañjaṇā-bhávant-* (VIII. 43[8]) 'sparkling'; *kikirā́ kṛṇu* (VI. 53[7]) 'tear to tatters'; *maṣmaṣā́-karam* (AV. v. 23[8]) 'I have crushed', *masmasā́ kuru* (VS. XI. 80) and *mṛsmṛsā́ kuru* (MS. II. 7[7]) 'crush', *malmalā-bhávant-* (MS. II. 13[19]; TS. I. 4. 34[1]) 'glittering', *bharbharā́-bhavat* (MS. II. 2[1]: B.) 'became confounded'; *bibibā-bhávant-* (MS. I. 6[5]: B.) 'crackling'.

651. The adverb *āvís* 'openly', 'in view', is found in combination with the verbs *as-*, *bhū-* and *kṛ-* only. With the latter it means 'make visible', e. g. *āvíṣ karta* (I. 86[9]) 'make manifest'. With the two former, which are sometimes omitted, it means 'become visible', 'appear'; e. g. *āvís sánti* (VIII. 8[23]) 'being manifest'; *āvír agnír abhavat* (I. 143[2]) 'Agni became manifest'.

prā-dúr, lit. 'out of doors', begins to appear in the AV. in combination with √*bhū-*, meaning 'become manifest', 'appear'.

652. The word *śrád*, which originally probably meant 'heart'[1], is often found in combination with *dhā-* 'place', in the sense of 'put faith in', 'credit', nearly always, however, separated from the verb by other words, e. g. *śrád asmai dhatta* (II. 12[5]) 'believe in him'; *śrád asmai, naro, vácase dadhātana* (VS. VIII. 5) 'give credence, O men, to this utterance'. It also appears in the substantive *srad-dhā́-* 'faith'. The word is once also found with √*kṛ-* in the sense of 'entrust': *śrád víśvā vā́ryā kṛdhi* (VIII. 75[2]) 'entrust all boons (to us)'.

653. The **interjection** *híṅ* is compounded with *kṛ-* 'make' in the sense of 'utter the sound *híṅ*', 'murmur'; thus *gáur . . híṅṅ akṛṇot* (I. 164[28]) 'the cow lowed'; *hiṅ-kṛṇvatī́* (I. 164[27]) 'lowing'; *hiṅ-kṛtāya svā́hā* (VS. XXII. 7) 'hail to the sound *híṅ*'; *tásmā uṣā́ hiṅ-kṛṇoti* (AV. IX. 6[45]) 'for him the dawn utters *híṅ*'.

654. A few **substantives**, after assuming an **adverbial** character, are found compounded with participial forms. *ásta-m* 'home', which still appears as a noun in the RV., though commonly used adverbially in the accusative with verbs of motion, is combined like a verbal prefix with participles of *i-* 'go' in the AV.: *astaṃ-yánt-* 'setting', *astam-eṣyánt-* 'about to set', *ástam-ita-* (AV. XVII. 1[23])[2] 'set'. The noun *námas-* 'obeisance' is similarly compounded in the gerund with *kṛ* -'make' in the AV.: *namas-kṛ́tya*[3]. In the RV. itself names of parts of the body, with no tendency otherwise to adverbial use, are thus compounded with the gerund of *grah-* 'seize': *karṇa-gṛ́hya* 'seizing by the ear', *pāda-gṛ́hya* 'seizing by the foot', *hasta-gṛ́hya* 'grasping the hand'[4]. The transition to this use was probably supplied by nouns compounded with past participles, as *sáhas-kṛta-* 'produced by force'.

655. There are besides a few **monosyllabic adverbial particles** which occur as prefixes **compounded with nominal forms only.** By far the most frequent of these is the negative prefix, which appears in the form of *an-* before vowels and *a-* before consonants. It is compounded with innumerable substantives and adjectives, but rarely with adverbs, as *a-kútrā* 'to the wrong place', *a-punár* ('not again' =) 'once for all'; *án-eva* (AV[1].) 'not so'.

656. *sá-*, as a prefix expressive of accompaniment, is employed as a reduced form of the verbal prefix *sam*[5], and interchanges with *saha-*; e. g. *sá-cetas-* 'accompanied by wisdom', 'wise', beside *sahá-cchandas-* 'accompanied with songs'.

1 See UHLENBECK, Kurzgefasstes Etymologisches Wörterbuch der altindischen Sprache, Amsterdam 1888—89, s. v. *śraddhā́*.

2 For some other later nominal compounds of this kind see WHITNEY 1092 c.

3 This is the regular form in the later language, but the independent form *namas kṛtvā* is occasionally found; cp. Bṛhaddevatā, I. 1, critical note in my edition.

4 Cp. WHITNEY 990 b and above 591 a (p. 413, bottom) and 591 b.

5 Cp. above 250.

657. ***dus-*** (appearing also, according to the euphonic combination, as *dur-*, *duś-*, *duṣ-*)[1], means 'ill', 'hard to'; e. g. *dur-gá-* '(place) difficult of access', *dur-yúj-* 'ill-yoked', *dur-matí-* 'ill-will'; *duś-cyavaná-* 'hard to shake'; *duṣ-kṛtá-* 'ill-done'; *duṣ-ṣáha-* 'irresistible'.

658. ***su-*** 'well', 'easy to' is compounded with a much larger number of words than *dus-*[2]; e. g. *su-kára-* 'easy to accomplish'; *su-kṛ́t-* 'acting well', *su-gá-* 'easy of access', *su-matí-* 'good-will', *su-yúj-* 'well-yoked'. It is, however, still found in a state of transition in the RV., where it occurs independently more than 200 times[3], being then connected in sense with the verb only[4]; e. g. *asmā́n sú jigyúṣaḥ kṛtam* (I. 17[7]) 'make us well victorious'[5].

4. Interjections.

659. A certain number of words having the nature of interjections occur in the Saṃhitās. They are of two kinds, being either exclamations or imitative sounds.

a. The **exclamations** are *báṭ* (RV.) 'truly', *bata* (RV.) 'alas!', *hánta* 'come' used exhortatively with the subjunctive, and *hayé* 'come', before vocatives, *hiruk* 'away!', *hurúk* (RV.) 'away!', *hái* (AV.) 'ho!'. Perhaps *uvé* (x. 86[7])[6].

b. Interjections of the **onomatopoetic** type are: *kikirā́* (RV.) used with *kṛ-* 'make the sound *kikirā́*' = 'tear to tatters'; *kikkiṭā́* (TS.) used in invocations (TS. III. 4. 2[1]); *ciścā́* (RV.) 'whiz!' (of an arrow) used with *kṛ-* 'make a whizzing sound'; *phā́ṭ* (AV. VS.) 'crash!', *phál* (AV. xx. 135[3]) 'splash!'; *bā́* (TS. = AV.) 'dash!'; *bhúk* (AV. xx. 135[1]) 'bang!', *śál* (AV. xx. 135[2]) 'clap!

1 See GRASSMANN, Wörterbuch, columns 614—619.

2 Op. cit., columns 1526—1560.

3 In the AV. it is still used independently, but only 14 times.

4 See GRASSMANN, op. cit., s. v. *sú*.

5 The Pada text of AV. XIX. 49[10] treats *sv ápāyati* 'may he go well away' as a compound: *su-ápāyati*; but this is doubtless an error for *sú | ápa | ayati*. See WHITNEY's note on this passage in his Translation of the AV.

6 See NEISSER, BB. 30, 303; cp. above p. 337, note 7.

ADDENDA AND CORRIGENDA.

It should be noted, in addition to what is said at the end of § 1 (p. 2), that when the abbreviations 'VS.' etc. indicate the occurrence of a form in a later Veda, they only mean that the form in question is not found in the RV., while it may occur in parallel passages of one or more of the other Saṃhitās also. The symbols '+ VS.' etc. are intended to draw attention to the fact that the form indicated occurs in a later Saṃhitā as well as in the RV. — In the enumeration of words, stems, inflected forms, and suffixes, initial alphabetical order is the principle followed. But it is occasionally varied for clearness of grouping. Thus the arrangement, in the case of compounds, is sometimes according to the final member (e. g. 308, 375 A, 591 a) or, in the case of roots, according to the medial or final vowel (e. g. 421, 483). The principle is also departed from when examples only of very frequent forms are given. Thus the nom. forms of present participles are arranged in the order of the conjugational classes (314); the nom. and other cases of the *a*-declension are given according to frequency of occurrence (372). Adverbs are classed according to the alphabetical order of the suffixes (626—640) or the sequence of the cases (641—644). — The principle of giving the meanings of words has been followed throughout the work. But this has been modified in two ways in the enumeration of inflected forms. In declension the meaning is given only with the first occurrence of a case-form of any word found in the same paragraph (e. g. 372). It seemed impossible to follow the same method in lists of inflected verbal forms. For, owing to the modifications of sense due to context and compounding with prepositions, the meaning could not be satisfactorily stated by giving it with the first occurrence of forms from the same root. The meaning has therefore been stated with the root only or when forms from different roots might be confused (e. g. 444, 445). But as the index gives the meaning of every root and enumerates all paragraphs containing forms from that root, the general sense of all such forms may easily be ascertained. — As regards references, figures without an added 'p.' always indicate paragraphs when books are divided into paragraphs; e. g. 'Delbrück, Verbum 184 (p. 166—169)'; otherwise they refer to the page. When pages have to be referred to they are for the convenience of the reader often divided into quarters; thus Lanman 372[3] means the third quarter of p. 372 in Lanman's Noun-Inflection.

P. 23, line 19 *for* orignal *read* original. — P. 51, note [2], for **guẓḍhá* read **guẓḍha-*. — P. 56, l. 27, *for* AV. *read* Av. and *for* 'weak *read* weak. — P. 58, l. 4 from below, for *cak[an]anta* read *cāk[an]antu*. — P. 60, l. 2, *for* appears *read* appears as. — P. 61, l. 7, *for* become *read* becomes; l. 34, for (*a-yās* read *a-yās*; l. 36, *for* fall') *read* 'fall'. — P. 66, § 72, 2 b: cp. Oldenberg, ZDMG. 63, 298. — P. 67, l. 30, *for* There seems to be no certain instance of this in the RV. *read* This is of regular and, as far as *d* is concerned, of very frequent occurrence in the RV., e. g. *tán* (for *tád*) *mitrásya* (I. 115^5); l. 31, after *cakrán ná*

(x. 95[12. 13]) *for* however *read* too. — P. 70, l. 17, *insert* often also *after* But *s.* — P. 83, l. 27, *for* Reduplicated stems *read* Reduplicated present stems; l. 28, *after* 'invoking' *add* but perfect *śiśriyāṇá-* 'having resorted to'. — P. 99, l. 2 from below, *insert* (AV.) *after ma-mád-a-t*; note [3], for *ri-hatẹ́* read *rih-até.* — P. 100, last line: on *dása-māna-* cp. p. 373 note [12]. — P. 109, l. 3 from below, for *vevij-á* read *vevij-á-* and for *carā-car-á* read *carā-car-á-.* — P. 119, l. 21, for *jigīṣ-ú* read *jigīṣ-ú-.* — P. 141, l. 2 from below, for *medh-i-rá-* read *medh-i-rá-.* — P. 146, l. 6, *for* 204 *read* 244. — P. 156, l. 20, for *váruṇas* read *váruṇaś* and l. 22, for *pitárā-* read *pitárā.* — P. 157, l. 26, *for* occurs *read* occur. — P. 169, l. 21, after *puruṣa-vyāghrá-* add (VS.). — P. 192, l. 9 from below, for *mahā̃ntas* read *mahā́ntas.* — P. 197, note [7], *for* 55 *read* 66 c *β*. — P. 199, note [8], *add* Cp. OLDENBERG, ZDMG. 63, 300—302. — P. 202, I. sing.: OLDENBERG, ZDMG. 63, 289, would place the form *rā́ṇā* (IX. 7[7]) here. — P. 209, l. 25, *for* 'width *read* width. — P. 215, note [5], *for* Bahuvrīhi *read* a Bahuvrīhi. — P. 238, note [1], *add* Cp. OLDENBERG, ZDMG. 63, 300—302. — P. 255, l. 11, for *āsas* read *-āsas;* § 371, l. 3, *for* ending *read* endings. — P. 257, lines 9 and 12: on *krāṇā́, dānā́,* and *sakhyā́* (as acc. pl.) cp. OLDENBERG, ZDMG. 63, 287—290. — P. 264, l. 3 from below: according to OLDENBERG, ZDMG. 63, 293, also *śatruhátyai.* — P. 279, l. 10, *for i*-declension *read ī*-declension. — P. 304, l. 9 from below, for *ātman-* read *ātmán-.* — P. 315 *delete* 1 *after* 414. — P. 317, l. 20, for *-yāt* read *-yā́t.* — P. 320, sing. 3.: *yámati* should perhaps be classed as a root aor. subj., though this form seems to have a distinctly indicative sense in the two passages in which it occurs; du. 2. for *sadathas* read *sádathas,* which form should perhaps rather be classed as a root aor. subj.; pl. 1., delete *dáyāmasi* (AV.). — P. 321, l. 2, delete *gámanti*: see p. 369 top; l. 12: the shift of accent is insufficient (cp. *híṃs-te*) for the treatment of *hiṃsanti* as a transfer form (cp. p. 100, l. 13): it should preferably be placed in 464 after *vṛñjanti.* — P. 321, Indicative Middle: Sing. 1., delete *daye* (AV. TS.). — Sing. 3., delete *bhójate, yojate, stárate* (p. 369, top); read *váhate* before *vāsate,* and *śayate* before *śikṣate.* — Du. 3., add *śobhete.* — Pl. 1, delete *starāmahe* (p. 369, top). — P. 323, § 424, Sing. 1., delete *bhojam, yojam* (503). — Sing. 2., delete *yamas, váras* (502). — Sing. 3. delete *yamat, rādhat, śakat* (502), *tamat, dásat, śramat, sadat* (510), *minat* (477), *śnáthat* (452); for *várat* read *varat* ('cover'): — Pl. 3., delete *yaman* (502), *vaman, śásan* (452), add *śróṣan.* — Middle. Pl. 3., delete *yavanta* (502). — P. 324, l. 4, for *yoja* read *yója;* last line, delete *dayasva* (AV.). — P. 325, § 427 a, delete *śā́sant-* (455) and *sánant-* (512). — P. 326, l. 1, for *cáyamāna* read *cā́yamāna-;* § 428, Sing. 3., delete *asadat* (508). — P. 328, l. 3, : *śṛṇa- read* Four; l. 4 add *gṛ-* 'sing' : *gṛṇá-* (AV.) beside *gṛṇā́-,* and *śṛ-* 'crush' *for* Two (AV.) beside *śṛṇā́-.* — § 430, Sing. 2., read *kṣipasi* (AV.) before *tirasi;* Middle. Sing. 1., delete *mṛje* and *śuṣe* (451). — P. 329, § 431, Sing. 3., delete *pṛṇā́t;* § 432, delete *guhas, rudhat, tṛpán* (510) and add *bhuját* (*bhuj-* 'bend'). — P. 330, l. 11, add *medátām;* l. 14, *after* TS. IV. 6. 5[1] *add* = AV. VS. MS. — § 435, delete *kṣiyánt-, mṛjánt-* (455), *citánt-* (506), *guhánt-, śucánt-* (512), *śuṣánt-, śvasánt-* (455); *insert* 'bending' after *bhujánt-;* Middle, delete *guhámāna-, dhṛṣámāṇa-, nṛtámāna-, śucámāna-* (512). — § 436, Sing. 2., add *adyas.* — P. 332, l. 1, add *dayāmasi* (AV.); l. 7, add *daye* (AV. TS.); § 441, add *rāya.* — P. 333, l. 12, delete *cā́yamāna-.* — P. 337, lines 6 and 8, delete *bhūthás* and *bhūtás* (502), and (AV.) after *psātás;* Middle. Sing. 1., for *mṛje* (AV.) read *mṛje;* add *śuṣe* (√*śvas-* 'blow'). — P. 338, l. 2., delete *parcas, śákas* (502); l. 5, add *śnathat;* l. 10, add *váman, śā́san;* l. 12, delete *várjate* (502). — § 454, Act. Sing., add *drāhi* (AV.) and *drātu* (AV.) and after *psāhi* delete (AV.); note [4], *add* Perhaps root aor. subj.; cp. 502 (p. 369). —

P. 339, l. 6, delete *sotana* (*su-* 'press'): cp. 505. — § 455, Act., delete *dhṛṣánt-* (512), add *mṛjánt-*, *śuṣánt-*, *śvasánt-*; Middle., delete *dhṛṣāṇá-* (AV.), add *tvakṣāṇá-*. — P. 340, l. 3, delete *svāná-* (*su-* 'press', SV.): cp. 506. — P. 342, l. 11, delete *píprati*. — P. 343, l. 12, *for* TS. IV. 6. 1[5] *read* TS. IV. 6. 1[4]. — P. 345, § 467, delete *kṛntatí-* and *śumbhāná-*. — P. 350, l. 11, for *pṛṇāt* (AV.) read *pṛṇát*; l. 16, add *minat* (for *mināt*). — P. 359, l. 23, *delete* VS. XXXIII. 87; l. 24, after *śṛ-* 'crush' *add* AV.; l. 26, after 'bring forth' *add* AV.; note [11], for *sāsahe* read *sāsahé*. — P. 361, l. 10, add *cākán* before *sasvár*. — P. 362, l. 6: *cākantu* though sing. in form is pl. in meaning and stands by haplology for *cākanantu*: cp. p. 58, l. 4 from below. — P. 364, l. 12, read *-ran* or *-iran* for *-iran*; l. 9 from below, delete *ávāvacīt* (549). — P. 366, l. 5 from below, delete *ákrān* (√*krand-*): see 522 (*s*-aor.). — P. 367, l. 2, delete *ákrān* (√*krand-*): see 522 (*s*-aor.); l. 22, delete *apṛkta* (√*pṛc-*): see 522 (*s*-aor.). — P. 368, § 502, l. 3, add *śákas*; l. 6, for *yamat* read *yámat*; l. 7, add *śákat*; l. 9, after *pāthás* add 'drink'. — P. 369, l. 5 from below: on *āpyāsam* (AA. v. 3. 2) see KEITH, Aitareya Āraṇyaka, p. 157, note [10], and Index IV, √*āp-*. — P. 374, l. 22, add *bībhiṣ-athās*. — P. 383, l. 8, delete *ayāsīt*. — P. 384, l. 4 from below, *add* 3. *ayāsīt*. — P. 397, l. 2 and l. 24, *add vīḷáyāsi* and *vīḷáyasva*.

LIST OF ABBREVIATIONS.

AA. = Aitareya-Āraṇyaka.
AB. = Aitareya-Brāhmaṇa.
AJPh. = American Journal of Philology.
APr. = Atharva-Prātiśākhya.
ASL. = Ancient Sanskrit Literature.
AV. = Atharva-Veda.
Av. = Avesta.
B. = Brāhmaṇa.
BB. = BEZZENBERGER's Beiträge.
BI. = Bibliotheca Indica.
BR. = BÖHTLINGK and ROTH (St. Petersburg Dictionary).
C. = Classical Sanskrit.
GGA. = Göttingische Gelehrte Anzeigen.
IE. = Indo-European.
IF. = Indogermanische Forschungen.
IIr. = Indo-Iranian.
IS. = Indische Studien.
JAOS. = Journal of the American Oriental Society.
K. = Kāṭhaka.
KG. = BRUGMANN's Kurze Vergleichende Grammatik.
Kh. = Khila.
KZ. = KUHN's Zeitschrift.
MS. = Maitrāyaṇī Saṃhitā.
N. = (Proper) Name.
O. u. O. = Orient und Occident.
Pp. = Pada-pāṭha.
pw. = Petersburger Wörterbuch (BÖHTLINGK's Smaller Lexicon).
Paipp. = Paippalāda.
RPr. = Rigveda-Prātiśākhya.
RV. = Rigveda.
S. = Sūtra.
ŚA. = Śāṅkhāyana-Āraṇyaka.
ŚB. = Śatapatha-Brāhmaṇa.
SBE. = Sacred Books of the East.
SV. = Sāma-Veda.
TB. = Taittirīya-Brāhmaṇa.
TPr. = Taittirīya-Prātiśākhya.
TS. = Taittirīya-Saṃhitā.
Up. = Upanishad.
V. = Vedic.
VPr. = Vājasaneyi-Prātiśākhya.
VS. = (1) Vājasaneyi-Saṃhitā; (2) Vedische Studien.
Wb. = Wörterbuch.
WZKM. = Wiener Zeitschrift für die Kunde des Morgenlandes.
YV. = Yajur-Veda.
ZDMG. = Zeitschrift der Deutschen Morgenländischen Gesellschaft.

I. SANSKRIT INDEX.

The references in both Indexes are to paragraphs.

a-, *an-*, negative particle compounded with nouns 251, 655.

√*aṃś-* 'attain', pr. 470, sj. 471, impv. 472; pf. 482 c α, 485, sj. 487, opt. 489, pt. 493; root aor. 500, inj. 503; opt. 504, prec. 504; *a*-aor. opt. 511; *s*-aor. sj. 523; inf. 585, 4.

√*aṃh-* 'compress', pf. 482 c α; p. 358, n. 9.

akramīm, 1. s. aor. √*kram-* 66 c β 2.

√*akṣ-* 'mutilate', pr. impv. 472; pr. pt. 473; *iṣ*-aor. 529.

ákṣan, root aor. of *ghas-* 499.

aṅkhaya- den., sj. 569 a.

√*ac-* 'bend', pr. 422, impv. 426; ps. pr. 445, pt. 447, impf. 448; gd. 591 a.

acchā́ 'towards', prep. with acc. 595.

√*aj-* 'drive', pr. 422, sj. 423, opt. 425, impv. 426, pt. 427, impf. 428; ps. 445, pt. 447; inf. 584 b.

√*añj-* 'anoint', pr. 464, sj. 465, impv. 466, pt. 467, impf. 468; pf. 482 c α, 485, sj. 487, opt. 489, pt. 493; ps. 445, pt. 447; pp. 574, 2.

√*at-* 'wander', pr. 422, pt. 427.

áti 'beyond', prep. with acc. 596.

√*ad-* 'eat', pr. 451, sj. 452, opt. 453, impv. 454, pt. 455, impf. 456; pp. 576 a; inf. 585, 4, 586 b.

adánt- 'eating', inflected 295 c.

adhás 'below', prep. with acc. abl. 610.

ádhi 'upon', prep. with loc. abl. acc. inst. 597.

√*an-* 'breathe', pr. 422, 430, 451, impv. 454, pt. 455, impf. 456; pf. 482 c, 485; *iṣ*-aor. 529; cs. 556.

anákṣ- 'eyeless' 340.

anaḍváh- 'ox' 351 a.

anáśāmahai, pf. sj. √*aṃś-* 482 c α.

ánu 'after', prep. with acc. 598.

antár 'between', prep. with loc. abl. acc. 599.

antarā́ 'between', prep. with acc. 611.

anyá- 'other' 403, 1.

áp- 'water' 334.

apád- 'footless' 319 a.

ápas- n. 'work' and *apás-* 'active', inflected 344.

ápi 'upon', prep. with loc. 600.

abhanas, 2. s. impf. √*bhañj-* 66 c 2; p. 345, note 10.

abhí 'towards', prep. with acc. 601.

abhítas 'around', prep. with acc. 612.

√*am-* 'injure', pr. 422, 451, inj. 424, pt. 427; red. aor. 514; cs. 555.

amba, f. voc. 374 (p. 265).

ayám 'this', inflected 393.

ayās 2. s. aor. √*yaj-* 66 c 2, 522.

arātīya- den., sj. 569 a.

arí- devout', inflected 380 b 3.

√*arc-* 'shine', 'praise', pr. 422, sj. 423, inj. 424, impv. 426, pt. 427, impf. 428; ps. 445, pt. 447; pf. 482 c α, 485; cs. 556; inf. 585, 1.

artháya- den., sj. 569 a, impv. 569 d.

√*arh-* 'deserve', pr. 422, sj. 423, pt. 427; pf. 485; inf. 581, 1.

arhire, 3. pl. pf. 482 c α.

√*av-* 'favour', pr. 422, sj. 423, inj. 424, opt. 425, impv. 426, pt. 427, impf. 428; pf. 482 c, 485; root aor. opt., prec. 504; *iṣ*-aor. 529, sj. 530, inj. 531, impv. 533; ft. 537, pt. 538; pp. 574, 1 α; inf. 585, 4.

avá- 'this', pron., inflected 396.

áva 'down', prep. with abl. 602.

avayā́s, nom. of *avayā́j-* 66 c β 1; 302.

avás 'down from', prep. with abl. 613.

ávi- 'sheep' p. 283 (top).

√*aś-* 'eat', pr. 476, opt. 477, impv. 478, pt. 479, impf. 480; pf. 482 c, 485; *iṣ*-aor. 529, inj. 531; pp. 575 b.

áśman- 'stone', inflected 329.

√1. *as-* 'be', pr. 451, sj. 452, inj. 452, opt. 453, impv. 454, pt. 455, impf. 456; pf. 482 c, 485.

√2. *as-* 'throw', pr. 439, impv. 441, pt. 442, impf. 443, 456; pf. 485; ft. 537; ps. 445; pp. 572; inf. 585, 4.

asáu 'that', inflected 394.

askṛta, root aor. of *kṛ-* 'make' 500.

asmā́ka 'of us' 390, 1.

asrat 3. s. aor. √*sras-* 66 c β 2; 499.

√*ah-* 'say', pf. 482 c, 485.

ahám 'I', inflected 391, 1.

ā́ 'near', prep. with loc. abl. acc. 603.

ā́d 'then', Sandhi of 67.

ān- pf. red. syllable 482 c α.

-āná pf. pt. suffix 491.

√*āp-* 'obtain', pr. 470, impv. 472, impf. 474, pt. 479; pf. 482 c, 485, pt. 493; prec. 504; *a*-aor. 508, opt. 511; des. 542, sj. 544.

ābhū́- 'present', inflected 383.

√*ār-* 'praise' (?), pr. 439.

ā́vayās, nom. of *ā́vayāj-* 302.

āvis 'openly', adv. with √*as-*, √*bhū-*, √*kṛ-* 651.

√*ās-* 'sit', pr. 451, sj. 452, opt. 453, impv. 454, pt. 455, impf. 456.

√*i-* 'go', pr. 422, 439, 451, sj. 452, inj. 424, 452, opt. 453, impv. 426, 454, pt. 427, 442, 455; impf. 428, 456; pf. 482 c, 485, pt. 492; plup. 495; ft. 537, 539, pt. 538; gdv. 578, 1; inf. 585, 1, 4, 5, 6, 7, 587 b; gd. 590 b, 591 b.

√*iṅg-* 'move' cs. 554 a.

iḍ- 'refreshment' 304.

√*idh-* 'kindle', pr. 464, sj. 465, impv. 466; pf. 485; root

aor. sj. 502, opt. 504, pt. 506; ps. 445, impv. 446, pt. 447, 455, 467, impf. 468; pp. 573; inf. 584 b, 586 a.
√*inv-* 'send', pr. 422, 470, sj. 423, impv. 426, 472, pt. 427, impf. 474.
iyatha, 2. s. pf. √*i-* 485.
√*il-* 'be quiet', cs. 554, aor. 560 a.
√1. *iṣ-* 'desire', pr. 430, sj. 431, inj. 432, opt. 433, impv. 434, pt. 435, impf. 436; gd. 591 a.
√2. *iṣ-* 'send', pr. 430, 439, 476, inj. 432, impf. 436, impv. 441, pt. 442, 479; 485; pp. 575 b.
iṣaṇaya- den., impf. 569 f.; inf. 585, 1 α 3; 588 c α.
iṣaṇya- den., impv. 569 d.
iṣaya- den., opt. 569 c.

√*ī-* = √*i-*, pr. 451.
√*īkṣ-* 'see', pr. 422, pt. 427, impf. 428; *iṣ*-aor. 529; cs. 554; gdv. 580 a.
īṅkh- 'swing', cs. 554 a, sj. 559 b, pp. 575 c.
√*īḍ-* 'praise', pr. 451, sj. 452, inj. 452, opt. 453, impv. 454, pt. 455; pf. 482 c, 485; pp. 575 a 3; gdv. 578, 4, 580.
√*īr-* 'set in motion', pr. 451, sj. 452, impv. 454, impf. 428, 456, pt. 455; pf. 482 c, 485; cs. 554 a, sj. 559 b.
√*īś-* 'be master', pr. 422, 451, inj. 424, opt. 453, pt. 455, impf. 428; 'be able to' with inf. 587 a α, b α.
√*īṣ-* 'move', pr. 422, inj. 424, impv. 426, pt. 427; pp. 575 b.
√*īh-* 'desire', pr. 422; pf. 485.

u particle 647; Sandhi of 71 b.
√*u-* 'proclaim' 451, 470.
√*ukṣ-* 'sprinkle', pr. pt. 427; *iṣ*-aor. 529; cs. 554 a; pp. 575 a 1.
√*uc-* 'be pleased', pr. 437, impv. 441; pf. 482 c, 485, pt. 492.
√*ud-* 'wet', pr. 464, impv. 466, pt. 427, 467, impf. 468; pf. 485; ps. 445.
úpa 'up to', prep. with acc. loc. inst. 604.
upári 'above', prep. with acc. 614.
√*ubj-* 'force', pr. impv. 434, pt. 435, impf. 436; pp. 575 a 1.
√*ubh-* 'confine', pr. impv. 434, impf. 468, 480.
uruṣyá- den., sj. 569 a, opt. 569 c, impv. 569 d, impf. 569 f; pp. 574, 2.

ulokā- p. 59, note 1.
√*uṣ-* 'burn', p. 422, inj. 424, impv. 426, pt. 427, 479.
uṣás- f. 'dawn' 44 a 3; 344 (p. 233).

ūti- 'aid', d. s. = inf. 585, 3 contracted dat. s. p. 282; inst. s. = inst. pl. p. 287.
ūnaya- den., aor. 570.
√1. *ūh-* 'remove'. pr. 422, impv. 426, impf. 428.
√2. *ūh-* 'consider', pr. 422, 451 (3. pl.), pt. 455; pf. 482 c, 485; *s*-aor. pt. 527; *iṣ*-aor. 529.

√*ṛ-* 'go', pr. 430, 458, 470, sj. 431, 471, inj. 471, impv. 434, 460, 472, pt. 473, impf. 474; pf. 482 c, 485, pt. 492, 493; root aor. 500, inj. 503, opt. 504, pt. 506; *a*-aor. 508, sj. 509, inj. 510, impv. 512; red. aor. 514; intv. 545, 2, 546; cs. 558 a, aor. 560, pp. 575 c, gd. 590 b, 591 a, b.
ṛghāyá- den., inj. 569 b.
√*ṛj-* 'direct', pr. 430, 439, 464, impv. 434, pt. 442, 467, impf. 468.
√*ṛṇv-* 'go', pr. 430.
ṛtaya- den., inj. 569 b.
ṛté 'without', prep. with abl. 615.
√*ṛd-* 'stir', pr. 422, impv. 434, impf. 436; cs. 553 c, sj. 559 b.
√*ṛdh-* 'thrive', pr. 470, sj. 464, impv. 441, pt. 467, impf. 474; pf. 485; root aor. sj. 502, opt. 504, prec. 504, pt. 506; *a*-aor. opt. 511; des. 542, pt. 544; ps. 445, impv. 446; gdv. 578, 4.
√*ṛś-* 'injure'(?), *s*-aor. pt. 527.
√*ṛṣ-* 'rush', pr. 422, 430, sj. 423, inj. 424, impv. 426, pt. 427, 435.

éka- 'one' 403, 2, 406 a 1.
éka-pad- 'one-footed' 319 a.
√*ej-* 'stir', pr. 422, sj. 423, impv. 426, pt. 427, impf. 428.
√*edh-* 'thrive', pr. 422, impv. 426; *iṣ*-aor. opt. 532.
ena- 'he, she, it', inflected 395.

okivā́ṃs- pf. pt. 492 a.

ká- 'who?', pron. 397.
kaṇḍūya- den., ft. and pp. 570.
√*kan-* 'enjoy, pr. pt. 442; pf. 482, sj. 487, inj. 488, impv. 490; plup. = pf. inj. 495; *iṣ*-aor. 529, sj. 530.
kánīyāṃs- 'younger', inflected 346.
√*kam-* 'love', pf. pt. 493; cs. 555, sj. 559 b, pt. 559 e.
kárman- 'act', inflected 329.
√*kaṣ-* 'scratch', impf. 428.
√*kas-* 'open', pr. impv. 426; pp. 573.
√*kā-* = √*kan-* 'enjoy', pf. 485, pt. 493.
√*kāś-* 'appear', intv. 545, 1, 546, 547, pt. 548, impf. 549; cs. 556 a.
kīrtáya- den., sj. 569 a.
√*kup-* 'be angry', pr. pt. 442; cs. 553 b; pp. 575 b.
√*kūj-* 'hum', pr. pt. 427.
√*kūḍ-* 'burn', cs. 554 a, sj. 559 b.
√1. *kṛ-* 'make', pr. 451, 470 (inflected), sj. 471, inj. 471, opt. 471, impv. 472, pt. 473, impf. 474; pf. 482 a, 485 (inflected), opt. 489, pt. 492, 493; plup. 495; root aor. (inflected) 498, 499, 500, sj. 502, inj. 503, opt. 504, prec. 504, impv. 505, pt. 506; *a*-aor. 508, impv. 512; *s*-aor. 522; ft. 537, 539 (inflected), sj. 538, pt. 538; des. 542 b; intv. 545, 3, pt. 548; ps. 445, pt. 447, aor. 501; pp. 573; gdv. 578, 1, 581; inf. 585, 4, 586 b, 587 b; gd. 590 a, b, c, 591 b.
√2. *kṛ-* 'commemorate', *iṣ*-aor. 529; intv. 545, 2, 546, 547, aor. 550 b, gdv. 578, 1.
√1. *kṛt-* 'cut', pr. 430, inj. 432, impv. 434, pt. 435, impf. 436; pf. 485; *a*-aor. 508, pt. 512; ft. 537, 539; gd. 591 a.
√2. *kṛt-* 'spin', pr. 464; ps. pr. pt. 447.
√*kṛp-* 'lament', pr. 422, pt. 427, impf. 428; plup. 495; root aor. 500; *iṣ*-aor. 529; cs. 554.
kṛpáṇa- den., sj. 569 a.
√*kṛś-* 'be lean', pr. impv. 434; pf. 485; cs. 553 c.
√*kṛṣ-* 'plough', pr. 422, 430, inj. 424, impv. 426, pt. 435; pf. 485; red. aor. 514; intv. 545, 2, 547, impf. 549.
√*kṝ-* 'scatter', pr. 430, sj. 431, impv. 434; *iṣ*-aor. sj. 530.
√*kḷp-* 'be adapted', pr. 422, opt. 425, impv. 426, pt. 427, impf. 428; pf. 482, 485; sj. 487; red. aor. 514, sj. 515; cs. 553 d, 559 (inflected), sj.

559 b, impv. 559 d (inflected); gd. 590 b.
√*krakṣ-* 'crash', pr. pt. 427.
kránta, root aor. √*kṛ-*, p. 367, n. [16].
√*krand-* 'cry out', pr. 422, inj. 424, impv. 426, pt. 427, impf. 428; pf. 485, sj. 487; plup. 495; *a*-aor. inj. 510; red. aor. 514, inj. 516; *s*-aor. 522; intv. 545, 3, 546, pt. 548; cs. 556 a.
√*kram-* 'stride', pr. 422, sj. 423, inj. 424, opt. 425, impv. 426, 434, pt. 427, impf. 428; pf. 485, inj. 488, pt. 493; root aor. 66, 4 *α*, 499, inj. 503; *a*-aor. 508; *s*-aor. 522, sj. 523; *iṣ*-aor. 529 (inflected), inj. 531, impv. 533, ft. 537; intv. 547 c; pp. 574, 2; inf. 584 b; gd. 591 a.
√*krī-* 'buy', pr. 476, sj. 477, impf. 480; gd. 590 b.
√*krīḍ-* 'play', pr. 422, sj. 423, pt. 427.
√*krudh-* 'be angry', pr. 439; *a*-aor. inj. 510; red. aor. 512, sj. 515, inj. 516; cs. 553 b; pp. 573.
√*kruś-* 'cry out', pr. 422, impv. 426, pt. 427; *sa*-aor. 536.
√*kṣad-* 'divide', pr. 422; pf. 485, pt. 493; inf. 585, 1.
√*kṣan-* 'wound', *iṣ*-aor. inj. 531; pp. 574, 2.
√*kṣam-* 'endure', pr. opt. 425, impv. 426, pt. 427; pf. opt. 489.
√*kṣar-* 'flow', pr. 422, inj. 424, impv. 426, pt. 427, impf. 428; *s*-aor. 522; inf. 585, 7.
√*kṣā-* 'burn', cs. 558.
√1. *kṣi-* 'possess', pr. 422, 430, 451, sj. 452, opt. 425, 433, pt. 427, 435, 455, impv. 434, *s*-aor. sj. 523; ft. 537, pt. 538; cs. 557 a, 558 a.
√2. *kṣi-* 'destroy', pr. 439, 470, 476, inj. 477, impf. 480; *s*-aor. inj. 524; ps. 445, pt. 447.
√*kṣip-* 'throw', pr. 430, inj. 432, impv. 434, pt. 435; red. aor. inj. 516.
√*kṣī-* = *kṣi-* 'destroy', pp. 576 d.
√*kṣud-* 'be agitated', 'crush', pr. 422, pt. 442; cs. 553 b.
√*kṣudh-* 'be hungry', cs. aor. inj. 510.
√*kṣubh-* 'quake', pf. 485.
√*kṣṇu-* 'whet', pr. 451, pt. 455.

√*khan-* 'dig', pr. 422, sj. 423, opt. 425, pt. 427, impf. 428, pf. 485; ft. pt. 538; pp. 574, 2; inf. 586 b; gd. 590 a.
√*khā-* = *khan-*, pf. pt. 492.
√*khād-* 'chew', pr. 422, impv. 426, pt. 427; pf. 482 b, 485.
√*khid-* 'tear', pr. 420, inj. 432, opt. 433, impv. 434, pt. 435, impf. 436; pf. pt. 482 d, 492 b.
√*khud-* 'futuere', pr. impv. 434.
√*khyā-* 'see', pf. 485; *a*-aor. 508, inj. 510, impv. 512; gdv. 578, 3; inf. 584 a; gd. 591 a.

√*gad-* 'say', pr. impv. 426.
√*gam-* 'go', pr. 422, 451, sj. 423, opt. 425, impv. 426, pt. 427, impf. 428; pf. 485, opt. 489, pt. 492, 493; plup. 495; periphr. pf. 496, 560 b; root aor. 499, 500, sj. 502, inj. 503, opt. 504, prec. 504, impv. 505, pt. 506; *a*-aor. 508, sj. 509, inj. 510, opt. 511; red. aor. 514; *s*-aor. 522, *iṣ*-aor. opt. 532, impv. 533; ft. 537, 539, periph. ft. 540; des. 542; intv. 545, 1, 3, 546; cs. 555 a; ps. 445, aor. 501; pp. 572, 574, 2; inf. 585, 4, 5, 7, 587 b; gd. 590 b, c.
√*garh-* 'chide', pr. 422.
√1. *gā-* 'go', pr. 458, inj. 459, impv. 460, pt. 461, impf. 462; pf. 489; root aor. 499, sj. 502, inj. 503, impv. 505; *s*-aor. inj. 524; des. 542 c; inf. 585, 4.
√2. *gā-* 'sing', pr. 439, inj. 440, impv. 441, pt. 442; *s*-aor. inj. 524; *siṣ*-aor. 534; pr. pt. 447; pp. 574, 3.
gātuyá- den., impv. 569 d.
√*gāh-* 'plunge', pr. 422, opt. 425, impv. 426, pt. 427, impf. 428; intv. 545, 2 *α*, 546.
√*gu-* 'sound', intv. 545, 1, 546.
√*gup-* 'protect', pf. 485 (cp. p. 358, note [13]); ft. 537, 539; pp. 575 b.
√*gur-* 'greet', pr. impv. 434; pf. sj. 487, opt. 489; root aor. 500; intv. 545, 2 *α*; pp. 573 a; gd. 591 a.
√*guh-* 'hide', pr. 422, inj. 424, impv. 426, pt. 427, impf. 428; *a*-aor. 508, inj. 510, pt. 512 a; *sa*-aor. 536; des. 542; ps. pt. 447; pp. 573; gdv. 578, 4; gd. 590 a.
gūrdhaya- den., impv. 569 d.
√1. *gṛ-* 'sing', pr. 476, inj. 477, impv. 434, 478, pt. 479, impf. 436; inf. 585, 7, 588 c.
√2. *gṛ-* 'awake', pf. 482; red. aor. 512, impv. 518; intv. 545, 1 b, 546, 547, pt. 548, impf. 549, pf. 550.
√*gṛdh-* 'be greedy', pr. pt. 442; pf. 482, 485; *a*-aor. 508, inj. 510.
gṛbhāya- den., impv. 569 d.
√*gṝ-* 'swallow', pr. 430, 479; root aor. sj. 502; red. aor. 514; *iṣ*-aor. inj. 531; intv. 545, 1 b, 2 a, 547; pp. 576; gd. 591 a.
gó- 'cow', inflected 365.
gopāyá- den., impv. 569 d; p. 402, n. [2].
gdha, 3. s. root aor. √*ghas-*, p. 367, note [13].
gnā́- 'woman', 367 (bottom); p. 263, note [1].
√*grath-* 'tie', pr. 464; pp. 575 a 2.
√*grabh-* 'seize', pr. 476 (inflected), sj. 477, inj. 477, impv. 478, impf. 480; pf. 485, opt. 489, pt. 492; plup. 495; root aor. 499, 500; *a*-aor. 508; *iṣ*-aor. 529; cs. 554; pp. 575 b; inf. 584 b; gd. 591 a
√*gras-* 'devour', pr. opt. 425; pf. opt. 489, pt. 493; pp. 575 b.
√*grah-* 'seize', pr. 476, opt. 477, impv. 478, pt. 479, impf 480; pf. 485; *a*-aor. inj. 510; *iṣ*-aor. 529; pp. 575 b; gd. 590 b, 591 a.
grā́van- 'pressing-stone', inflected 331.
√*glā-* 'be weary', pr. pt. 412; cs. 558.

√*ghas-* 'eat', pr. sj. 452; pf. 485, opt. 489, pt. 492; root aor. 499, impv. 505; *s*-aor. 522; des. 542 (p. 389, top); pp. 574, 3 *α*.
√*ghuṣ-* 'sound', pr. sj. 423, pt. 427; cs. 553 b; ps. aor. 501; gd. 591 a.
√*ghṛ-* 'drip', pr. 458; cs. 557 c, ps. pt. 561 a.
√*ghrā-* 'smell', pr. 458.

√*cakṣ-* 'see', pr. 422, 451, impv. 454, impf. 428, 456; pf. 485; plup. 495; cs. 556 a; gdv. 578, 4; inf. 584 b, 585, 1, 588 a; gd. 591 a, b.
cákṣus- 'eye', inflected 342.
√*cat-* 'hide', pr. pt. 427; cs. 555, pt. 559 e.

cátuṣpad- 'four-footed' 319 a.
√*can-* 'be pleased', *iṣ*-aor. impv. 533.
canasyá- den., impv. 569 d.
car- 'move', pr. 422, sj. 423, inj. 424, opt. 425, impv. 426, pt. 427, impf. 428; pf. 485; red. aor. 514; *iṣ*-aor. 529, inj. 531; ft. 539; intv. 545, 2 b, 546, 551; pp. 575 a 3; gdv. 580; inf. 585, 1, 4, 7.
caraṇya- den., sj. 569 a, opt. c.
carmamná- 'tanner' p. 38 n. 1; p. 249 note 4.
√*cal-* 'stir', impf. 428; intv. 545, 2, 546.
cākán inj. pf. 488 (cp. p. 392 note 8).
√*cāy-* 'note', pr. pt. 427; *iṣ*-aor. 529; gd. 590 b, 591 a.
√1. *ci-* 'gather', pr. 422, 470, sj. 452, 471, opt. 425, 471, impv. 472, pt. 473, impf. 474; pf. 485; root aor. 499; *iṣ*-aor. impv. 533; gd. 590 b.
√2. *ci-* 'note', pr. 458, impv. 460, pt. 461, 462; pf. 485; root aor. 500; des. 542.
√*cit-* 'perceive', pr. 422, 451, inj. 424, impv. 426, pt. 427, impf. 428; pf. 485, sj. 487, impv. 490, pt. 492, 493; plup. 495; root aor. 499, pt. 506; *s*-aor. 522; des. 542, sj. 544; intv. 545, 1, 546, 547, pt. 548; cs. 553, 554, sj. 559 b, opt. 559 c; ps. aor. 501; pp. 573; inf. 585, 2.
√*cud-* 'impel', pr. 422, inj. 424, impv. 426; cs. 553 b, sj. 559 b, ps. pt. 561 a, pp. 575 c.
√*cṛt-* 'bind', pr. 430, impv. 434; pf. 485; inf. 586 a.
cetatur pf. √*cit-*, p. 358 n. 1.
√*ceṣṭ-* 'stir', pr. pt. 427.
√*cyu-* 'move', pr. 422, inj. 424, impv. 426; pf. 482 b 1, 485; plup. 495; red. aor. 514, inj. 516, opt. 517; *s*-aor. inj. 524; cs. 557 b.

√*chad-* or *chand-* 'seem', pr. 451; pf. 485, opt. 489; *s*-aor. 522, sj. 523; cs. 556, 556 a, sj. 559 b.
√*chad-* 'cover', cs. 555.
√*chā-* 'cut up', pr. 430, impv. 434.
√*chid-* 'cut off', pr. 464, impv. 466; root aor. inj. 503; *a*-aor. 508; *s*-aor. inj. 524; ps. 445, aor. 501; pp. 576 a; gd. 591 a.
√*jakṣ-* 'eat', gd. 590 b, c.
√*jajh-*, pr. pt. 427.
√*jañj-* pr. pt. 427.
√*jan-* 'generate', pr. 422, sj. 423, inj. 424, impv. 426, 454, pt. 427, impf. 428, 456; pf. 485, pt. 493; root aor. 500; red. aor. 514 (inflected), inj. 516; *iṣ*-aor. 529, opt. 532; ft. 537, 539; cs. 556, sj. 559 b, opt. 559 c, pt. 559 e, impf. 559 f (inflected); pp. 574, 2; gdv. 580, 581; inf. 587 b; gd. 590 a.
jáni- 'wife' 380 b 2.
janitár- 'begetter' 390.
√*jambh-* 'chew', red. aor. 514; *iṣ*-aor. 530; intv. 545, 2, pt. 548; cs. 556 a.
√*jas-* 'be exhausted', pr. impv. 441, pt. 427; pf. impv. 490.
jahā́, 3. s. pf.? p. 357 note 4.
jahi, 2. s. impv. √*han-* 32 c; p. 50 note 9.
jā́- 'offspring', inflected 368.
√*jā-* 'be born', pr. 439, inj. 440, opt. 440, impv. 441, pt. 442, impf. 443.
jānivā́ṃs- pf. pt. 482 d.
jāraya- den., ps. aor. 501.
√*ji-* 'conquer', pr. 422, 451, sj. 423, inj. 424, opt. 425, impv. 426, pt. 427, impf. 428; pf. 485, pt. 492; root aor. inj. 503, impv. 505, red. aor. 514; *s*-aor. 522, sj. 523, inj. 524; ft. 537, 539, pt. 538; des. 542, pt. 544; cs. 558 a; pp. 573; gdv. 581; inf. 585, 1 α; gd. 591 b.
√*ji-* or *jinv-* 'quicken', pr. 422, 470, impv. 426, pt. 427, impf. 428; pf. 485.
√*jīv-* 'live', pr. 422, sj. 423, opt. 425, impv. 426, pt. 427; prec. 504; *iṣ*-aor. inj. 531; cs. 554 a; pp. 575 a 3; gdv. 581 b; inf. 585, 1, 4, 5.
√*juṣ-* 'enjoy', pr. 422, 430, 451, inj. 424, 432, sj. 431, opt. 433, impv. 426, 434, pt. 435, impf. 436; pf. 485, sj. 487, impv. 490, pt. 492, 493; root aor. 500, sj. 502, pt. 506; *iṣ*-aor. sj. 530; cs. 553 b, sj. 559 b; pp. 573; gd. 590 a.
√*jū-* 'be swift', pr. 422, 476, sj. 477; pf. 482, 485, sj. 487, pt. 492, 493; inf. 585, 1.
√*jūrv-* 'consume', pr. 422, sj. 423, impv. 426, pt. 427; *iṣ*-aor. 529.
√*jṛ-* 'sing', pr. 422 (p. 322), sj. 423, opt. 425, impv. 426 (top), pt. 427; inf. 585, 7.
√*jṛmbh-* 'gape', pr. 422.
√*jṝ-* 'waste away', pr. 422, 439, impv. 426, pt. 427, 435, impf. 443; pf. 485, pt. 492; *iṣ*-aor. inj. 531; cs. 557 c; pp. 576 e.
√*jeh-* 'pant', pr. pt. 427.
√*jñā-* 'know', pr. 476, sj. 477, opt. 477, impv. 478, pt. 479, impf. 480; pf. pt. 492, 492 a; root aor. opt. 504; red. aor. 514; *s*-aor. 522; des. 542; cs. 558, aor. 560; gdv. 578, 3; ps. 445, aor. 501.
√*jyā-* 'overpower', pr. 439, 476, opt. 477, pt. 479; des. 542; ps. 445; pp. 574, 2.
√*jyut-* 'shine', cs. 553 b.
√*jri-* 'go', pr. 422; *s*-aor. pt. 527.

tá- 'that', inflected 392, 1.
√*taṃs-* 'shake', pf. 485; plup. 495; *a*-aor. 508; intv. 545, 2 b; sj. 547, gdv. 579; cs. 556 a; inf. 585, 7.
√*tak-* 'rush', pr. 451, impf. 456.
√*takṣ-* 'fashion', pr. 422, sj. 423, inj. 424, impv. 426, 454, pt. 427, impf. 428, 456; pf. 485; *iṣ*-aor. 529; pp. 575 a 1.
√1. *tan-* 'stretch', pr. 470, sj. 471, inj. 471, impv. 472, pt. 473, impf. 474; pf. 485, sj. 487, inj. 488, opt. 489, pt. 492; root aor. 499, 500; *a*-aor. 508, inj. 510; *s*-aor. 522; cs. 555; pp. 574, 2; gd. 591 b.
√2. *tan-* 'roar', pr. 439.
tanū́- 'body', inflected 385; = 'self' 400, 3.
√*tand-* 'be weary', pr. 422, inj. (?) 424.
√*tap-* 'be hot', pr. 422, sj. 423, inj. 424, impv. 426, pt. 427, impf. 428; pf. 485, sj. 487, pt. 493; red. aor. 514, sj. 515; *s*-aor. 522, inj. 524; cs. 555; ps. 445, impv. 446, pt. 447, impf. 448; aor. 501; pp. 573; gd. 591 a.
√*tam-* 'faint', *a*-aor. inj. 510.
taruṣa- den., inj. 569 b, opt. 569 c.
tā́t, abl. adv. 'in this way' 629.
tij- 'be sharp', pr. 422, pt. 427; des. 542; intv. 545, 1, 546; pp. 573.

tirás 'across', prep. with acc. 605.
tilvilāyá- den., impv. 569 d.
√*tu-* 'be strong', pr. 451; pf. 482, 485; red. aor. 514; intv. 545, 3.
√*tuj-* 'urge', pr. 430, 464, pt. 427, 435, 467; pf. opt. 489, pt. 493; cs. 554; ps. 445, pt. 447; inf. 584 b, 585, 1, 2.
√*tud-* 'thrust', pr. 430, impv. 434, pt. 435, 467, impf. 436; pf. 485; pp. 576 a.
√*tur-* = *tṝ-* 'pass', pr. 430, opt. 453; des. 542; cs. 554; gd. 591 a.
turaṇya- den., inj. 569 b, impf. 569 f.
√*tuś-* 'drip', pr. 422, pt. 427; cs. 553 b.
√*tuṣ-* 'be content', cs. 554.
√*tūrv-* 'overcome', pr. 422, impv. 426, pt. 427.
√*tṛd-* 'split', pr. 464, impf. 468; pf. 485, pt. 493; root aor. sj. 502; des. 542, sj. 544; pp. 576 a; inf. 587 a.
√*tṛp-* 'be pleased', pr. 430, sj. 471, impv. 434, 441, 472, pt. 435; pf. 482, 485, pt. 493; *a*-aor. 508, inj. 510, pt. 512; red. aor. 514; des. 542, sj. 544; cs. 553 c, sj. 559 b.
√*tṛṣ-* 'be thirsty', pr. 439, pt. 442; pf. 482, 485, pt. 493; root aor. pt. 506; *a*-aor. 508, inj. 510; red. aor. 514, inj. 516.
√*tṛh-* 'crush', pr. sj. 465, impf. 436; pf. 485; *a*-aor. 508; ps. 445, impv. 446, pt. 447; pp. 573; gd. 590 b, c.
√*tṝ-* 'pass', pr. 422, 430, 470, sj. 423, 431, inj. 424, 432, opt. 425, 433, impv. 426, 434, pt. 427, 435, 461, impf. 428, 436; pf. 485, opt. 489, pt. 492; red. aor. 514; *iṣ*-aor. 529, sj. 530, inj. 531, opt. 532; intv. 545, 2, 3, 546, 551; ps. aor. 501; pp. 576 e; inf. 584 a, 585, 7, 9, 586 a, 588 c; gd. 590 a.
√*tyaj-* 'forsake', pf. 482 b 1, 485.
√*tras-* 'be terrified', pr. 422, impv. 426, impf. 428; red. aor. 514; cs. 555.
√*trā-* 'rescue', pr. 439, impv. 441, 454, pt. 442; pf. 485; *s*-aor. sj. 523, opt. 525, cs. gdv. 561 b, 579; inf. 585, 8.
tripád- 'three-footed' 319 a.
trivṛ́t- 'threefold', inflected 306.
tva- 'many a one', inflected 396.
√*tvakṣ-* 'fashion', pr. pt. 455.
tvám 'thou', inflected 391, 2.
√*tvar-* 'make haste', cs. 556.
√*tviṣ-* 'be stirred', impf. 436, 456; pf. 485, pt. 493; plup. 495; pp. 575 b; inf. 584 b.
√*tsar-* 'approach stealthily', pr. 422, impf. 428; pf. 485; *s*-aor. 522.

√*daṃś-* 'bite', pr. impv. 426, pt. 427; pf. pt. 492; intv. 545 2 b, pt. 548; pp. 574, 2.
√*dakṣ-* 'be able', pr. 422, impv. 426, pt. 427; gdv. 579.
√*dagh-* 'reach to', root aor. inj. 503; prec. 504, impv. 505.
dán, g. of *dám-* 'house', p. 37 (bottom); 66, 4 α; 338.
√*dan-* 'straighten'?, pr. sj. 452, inj. 452.
dánt- 'tooth' 313.
√*dabh-* or *dambh-* 'harm', pr. 422, 470, sj. 423, inj. 424, impv. 472; pf. 485, inj. 488; root aor. 499, inj. 503; des. 542, sj. 544; cs. 556 a; ps. 445; gdv. 578, 4; inf. 584 b.
√*dam-* 'control', cs. 556.
damanya- den., impf. 569 f.
daśasyá- den., opt. 569 c, impv. 569 d.
√*das-* or *dās-* 'waste', pr. 422, 439, sj. 423, inj. 424, pt. 427, opt. 440; pf. pt. 492; *a*-aor. inj. 510, pt. 512; *iṣ*-aor. inj. 531; cs. 555.
√*dah-* 'burn', pr. 422, 439, 451, sj. 423, inj. 424, impv. 426, pt. 427, impf. 428; *s*-aor. 522, inj. 524, pt. 527; ft. 537, pt. 538; pp. 573.
√1. *dā-* 'give', pr. 422, 458, sj. 459, inj. 424, 459, opt. 459, impv. 426, 460, pt. 461, impf. 428, 462; pf. 485, pt. 492; root aor. 499, 500, sj. 502, inj. 503, opt. 504; impv. 505; *a*-aor. 508; *s*-aor. 522, sj. 523, inj. 524; ft. 537, pt. 538; des. 542; cs. 558; ps. 445, aor. 501; pp. 572, 573 α, 574, 3 α; gdv. 578, 3; inf. 584 a, 585, 4, 5. 8, 9, 586 b, 587 b; gd. 590 b, c, 591 a.
√2. *dā-* 'divide', pr. 422, 430, 451, impv. 426, 434, inj. 440, impv. 441, pt. 442, impf. 436; pf. pt. 493; root aor. impv. 505; *s*-aor. inj. 525; ps. 445, pt. 447; pp. 574, 3 α, 576 c.
√3. *dā-* 'bind', impf. 443; ps. aor. 501; pp. 574, 3.
√*dāś-* 'make offering', pr. 422, 451, 470, sj. 423, opt. 425, pt. 455, impf. 428; pf. 485, sj. 487, pt. 492, 492 b.
√*diś-* 'point', pr. 430, opt. 434, pt. 435; pf. 485, sj. 487, impv. 490; plup. 495; root aor. 500; *s*-aor. 522; intv. 545, 1, 546, impf. 549, 551; pp. 573; inf. 584 b.
√*dih-* 'smear', pr. sj. 452, pt. 455, impf. 456; pp. 573.
√1. *dī-* 'fly', pr. 439, inj. 440, impv. 441, pt. 442, impf. 443.
√2. *dī-* 'shine', pr. 458, sj. 459, impv. 460, pt. 461, impf. 462; pf. 482, 485, sj. 487, pt. 492.
√*dīp-* 'shine', pr. 439, impv. 441; red. aor. inj. 516; cs. 554 a.
√*dīv-* 'play', pr. 439, inj. 440; pf. 485; pp. 573 α; gd. 591 a.
√*du-* or *dū-* 'burn', pr. 470, pt. 473; *iṣ*-aor. sj. 530; pp. 576 d.
√*dudh-* 'stir up', pp. 575 b.
durasyá- den., sj. 569 a.
duvasyá- den., sj. 569 a, opt. 569 c, impv. 569 d.
√*duṣ-* 'spoil', pr. 439; red. aor. 514, inj. 516; ft. cs. 537, 560; cs. 554.
dus- 'ill', adverbial particle as first member of compounds 251, 657.
√*duh-* 'milk', pr. 422, 451, sj. 452, opt. 453, impv. 454, pt. 455, impf. 436, 456; pf. 485, pt. 493; *s*-aor. 522, inj. 524, opt. 525; *sa*-aor. 536; des. 542, pt. 544; ps. 445, pt. 447; pp. 573; inf. 585, 1, 7.
dūḍábha-, Sandhi of, p. 70 note 3; 81, 1 b.
√1. *dṛ-* 'pierce', pr. 451; pf. 485, pt. 492; root aor. 499; *s*-aor. sj. 523, opt. 525; intv. 545, 1, 2, 546, 547, pt. 547, impf. 549; cs. 557 c.
√2. *dṛ-* 'heed', gd. 591 b.
√*dṛp-* 'rave', *a*-aor. 508; pp. 575 b.
√*dṛś-* 'see', pf. 485, pt. 492, 493; root aor. 499, 500, sj. 502, pt. 506; *a*-aor. 508, inj. 510, opt. 511; *s*-aor. 522, sj. 523; des. 542, gdv.

544 i, 580; cs. 553 c; ps. 445, aor. 501; gdv. 580; inf. 584 b, 585, 2, 586 b, 588 a; gd. 590 b, c, 591 a.
√*dṛh-* 'be firm', pr. 430, impv. 426, 441, pt. 435, impf. 428, 436; pf. pt. 493; plup. 495; *iṣ*-aor. 529; cs. 554 a; pp. 573.
devī-, inflected 378.
dehi, pr. impv. √*dā-* 'give' 62, 4 b.
dyáv- 'heaven', inflected 364.
√*dyut-* 'shine', pr. 422, impv. 426, pt. 427; pf. 482 b 1, 485, pt. 493; root aor. pt. 506; red. aor. 514, inj. 516; intv. 545, 3, 546, pt. 547, impf. 549; cs. 553 b, 554.
dyaus, accentuation of voc. 85, 93, 364 note [11] (p. 247).
√1. *drā-* 'run', pr. impv. 454; pf. pt. 493; *s*-aor. sj. 523; intv. pt. 547.
√2. *drā-* 'sleep', pp. 576 c.
√*dru-* 'run', pr. 422, impv. 426, pt. 427, impf. 428; pf. 485; red. aor. 514, inj. 516; cs. 557 b.
√*druh-* 'be hostile', pf. 485; *a*-aor. 508, inj. 510; pp. 573.
√*drū-* 'hurl'(?), pr. pt. 479.
dvipád- 'two-footed' 319 a.
dviṣ- 'hatred', inflected 340.
√*dviṣ-* 'hate', pr. 451, sj. 452, impv. 454, pt. 455; *sa*-aor. inj. 536; gdv. 578, 4, 580.
dvīpá- 'island' 255, 4.

√*dhan-* 'run', pf. sj. 487, opt. 489; cs. 556.
√*dhanv-* 'run', pr. 422, sj. 423, impv. 426; pf. 485, pt. 492; *iṣ*-aor. 529.
dhánvan- 'bow', inflected 331.
√*dham-* or *dhmā-* 'blow', pr. 422, impv. 426, pt. 427, impf. 428; ps. 445; pp. 574, 2, 575 b.
√*dhav-* 'flow', impf. 428.
√1. *dhā-* 'put', pr. 422, 458, sj. 459, opt. 459, impv. 460, pt. 461, impf. 462; pf. 485, impv. 490; root aor. 499, 500; *a*-aor. 508; *s*-aor. sj. 523, inj. 524; des. 542, sj. 544, gdv. 579; cs. 558, sj. 559 b; ps. 445, impv. 446, pt. 447, aor. 501, sj. 502, inj. 503, opt. 504, impv. 505; pp. 574, 3; inf. 584 a, 585, 4, 5, 7, 586 a, 587 b; gd. 591 a.
√2. *dhā-* 'suck', pr. 439, opt. 440; root aor. 499; cs. 558; pp. 574; inf. 585, 1, 4.
√1. *dhāv-* 'run', pr. 422, sj. 423, inj. 424, impv. 426, pt. 427; plup. 495.
√2. *dhāv-* 'wash', pr. 422, impv. 426; *iṣ*-aor. 529.
dhī- 'thought', inflected 376.
√*dhī-* 'think', pr. sj. 459, pt. 461, impf. 462; pf. 482; *s*-aor. pt. 527.
dhunaya- den., inj. 569 b, impv. 569 d.
√*dhū-* 'shake', pr. 430, 470, sj. 441, impv. 446, 472, pt. 473, impf. 474; pf. 485, inj. 488, opt. 489; root aor. pt. 506; red. aor. 514; *s*-aor. 522; intv. 545, 1, 3, 546, pf. 550; gd. 591 a.
dhūpáya- den., impf. 569 f.
√*dhūrv-* 'injure', pr. 422, impv. 426, pt. 427.
√*dhṛ-* 'hold', red. aor. 514, inj. 516, impv. 518; pf. 482, 485; root aor. inj. 503; ft. 537, 539; intv. 545, 1, 2, 546, impf. 549; cs. 557 c, sj. 559 b, opt. 559 c, ft. 537, 560; ps. 445, impv. 446; inf. 585, 1, 8, 588 b.
√*dhṛṣ-* 'dare', pr. impv. 472; pf. 485, sj. 487, inj. 488, pt. 492; plup. 495; *a*-aor. inj. 510, pt. 512; pp. 575 b; gdv. 578, 4; inf. 584 b.
√*dhraj-* 'sweep', pr. pt. 427, impf. 428.
√*dhvaṃs-* 'scatter', pf. 485; *a*-aor. 508; cs. 556.
√*dhvan-* 'sound', cs. 555, aor. 560 α; pp. 574, 2 α.
√*dhvṛ-* 'injure', *s*-aor. 522; des. 542; inf. 585, 1.

ná 'like', Sandhi of 67, p. 63 note 9.
nákis, indecl. pron., old nom. sing. 381 b (p. 279, bottom).
nákta- n. 'night', irreg. nom. du. 372.
√*nakṣ-* 'attain', pr. 422, inj. 424, impv. 426, pt. 427, impf. 428; pf. 485.
√*nad-* 'sound', pr. pt. 427, impf. 428; intv. 545, 1 b, 546, pt. 548; cs. 556.
nádbhyas, dat. of *nápāt-* 62, 3 b; 321 note 7.
√*nand-* 'rejoice', pr. 422.
√*nabh-* 'burst', pr. impv. 426.
√*nam-* 'bend', pr. 422, sj. 423, inj. 424, impv. 426, pt. 427, impf. 428; pf. 482, 485; plup. 495; red. aor. inj. 516; *s* aor. sj. 523; pt. 527; intv. 545, 2, 546, pt. 548, impf. 549; cs. 556; pp. 574, 2; gdv. 581; inf. 584 b.
√1. *naś-* 'be lost', pr. 439, inj. 424, impv. 441; pf. 485; red. aor. 514, inj. 516; ft. 537, 539; cs. 555, inf. 585, 7; pp. 573.
√2. *naś-* 'obtain', pr. 451, sj. 423, inj. 424; root aor. 499, inj. 503, opt. 504, *s*-aor. sj. 523; des. 542 a, sj. 544; inf. 584 b.
√*nas-* 'unite', pr. 422, inj. 424; root aor. opt. 504.
√*nah-* 'bind', pr. 439, impv. 441, pt. 442, impf. 443; pf. 485; ps. pt. 447; pp. 573.
√*nāth-* 'seek aid', pp. 575 a 2.
√*nādh-* 'seek aid', pr. part. 427; pp. 575 b.
nā́v- 'ship', inflected 365.
√*niṃs-* 'kiss', pr. 451, impf. 428.
√*nikṣ-* 'pierce', pr. 422, impv. 426; inf. 584 b.
√*nij-* 'wash', pr. impv. 460, pt. 455; *a*-aor. 508; *s*-aor. 522, inj. 524; intv. 545, 1, 546 (inflected), 547.
√*nind-* 'revile', pr. 422, sj. 423, impv. 426; pf. 485; root aor. pt. 506; *iṣ*-aor. 529, sj. 530; des. 542, sj. 544; ps. pt. 447; pp. 575 a 1.
√*nī-* 'lead', pr. 422, 451, 458, sj. 423, inj. 424, impv. 426, pt. 427, impf. 428; pf. 485; sj. 487 (cp. p. 361 note [1]), opt. 489; *s*-aor. 522, sj. 523, inj. 524, impv. 526; *iṣ*-aor. 529; ft. 537, 539; des. 542; intv. 545, 1, 551; ps. 445, pt. 447, impf. 448; inf. 588 c; gd. 591 a.
nīḷáya- den., sj. 569 a.
√1. *nu-* 'praise', pr. 422, inj. 424, pt. 427, impf. 428, 456, pt. 435; red. aor. 514, inj. 516; *s*-aor. 522, inj. 524; *iṣ*-aor. 529; intv. 545, 1, 546, 547, impf. 549, pf. 550; gdv. 578, 2.
√2. *nu-* 'move', pr. 422, impf. 428.
√*nud-* 'push', pr. 430, sj. 431, inj. 432, impv. 434, pt. 435, impf. 436; pf. 485; root aor. inj. 503; *iṣ*-aor. inj. 531; pp. 576 a; inf. 584 b.
√*nṛt-* 'dance', pr. 439, impv. 441, pt. 442; root aor. 499; *a*-aor. pt. 512; *iṣ*-aor. 529; cs. 553 c.

√*pac-* 'cook', pr. 422, 439, sj. 423, inj. 424, impv. 426, pt. 427, impf. 428; pf. 485; plup. 495; *s*-aor. sj. 523; ps. 445, pt. 447, impf. 448; inf. 585,4; gd. 590 b.
paḍbhís, inst. pl. 42 c, 43 b 1, 62, 4 b (p. 57) note 3, 350 (p. 238 note 1).
√1. *pat-* 'fly', pr. 422, sj. 423, inj. 424, opt. 425, impv. 426, pt. 427, impf. 428; pf. 485, opt. 489, pt. 492; red. aor. 514, inj. 516, impv. 518; ft. 537, 539, pt. 538; des. 542; intv. 545, 1, 546, 547; cs. 555 a; pp. 572, 575 b; inf. 585, 4.
√2. *pat-* 'rule', pr. 439, pt. 442, 565 β, impf. 443.
páti- 'husband', inflected 380 b; in compounds 280; accentuation p. 95 α, p. 96, 3.
√*pad-* 'go', pr. 439, sj. 423, impv. 441, pt. 442, impf. 443; pf. 485; root aor. 500, sj. 502, prec. 504; red. aor. 514; *s*-aor. inj. 524; cs. 555, sj. 559 b; ps. aor. 501; pp. 576 a; inf. 587 a; gd. 591 a.
pád- 'foot', inflected 319.
√*pan-* 'admire', pf. 485; *iṣ*-aor. inj. 531; intv. 545, 3, pt. 548; cs. 556, gdv. 561 b; ps. 445; pp. 575 b; gdv. 579.
panāya- den., inj. 569 b.
paprā́, 3. s. pf. √*prā-* 484.
parás 'beyond', prep. with acc. inst. loc. abl. 616.
pári 'around', prep. with acc. abl. 606.
√*paś-* 'see', pr. 439, sj. 440, inj. 440, opt. 440, impv. 441, pt. 442, impf. 443.
√1. *pā-* 'drink', pres. 422, sj. 423, inj. 424, impv. 426, pt. 427, 461, impf. 428; pf. 485, opt. 489, pt. 492, 493; root aor. 499, sj. 502, prec. 504, impv. 505, pt. 506; *s*-aor. inj. 524; des. 542, pt. 544; cs. 558 α; ps. 445, aor. 501; pp. 574, 3; inf. 585, 3, 4, 5, 7; gd. 590 a, b; 591 a.
√2. *pā-* 'protect', pr. 451, sj. 452, impv. 454, pt. 455, impf. 456; *s*-aor. sj. 523.
pāpaya- den., aor. inj. 570.
√*pi-* or *pī-* 'swell', pr. 422, 470, pt. 442, 461, 473; pf. 482, 485, pt. 492, 493; pp. 576 d.
√*pinv-* 'fatten', pr. 422, inj. 424, impv. 426, pt. 427, impf. 428; pf. 485.
√*pibd-* 'stand firm', pr. pt. 427.
√*piś-* 'adorn', pr. 430, impv. 434, impf. 436; pf. 485; root aor. pt. 506; intv. 545, 1 a, pt. 548; ps. pt. 447; pp. 575 b.
√*piṣ-* 'crush', pr. 464, inj. 465, impv. 466, impf. 436, pt. 467, impf. 468; pf. 485; pp. 573.
√*pīḍ-* 'press', pf. 485; cs. 554 a.
púr- 'stronghold', inflected 355.
purás 'before', prep. with acc. abl. loc. 607.
purástād 'in front of', prep. with gen. 617.
purā́ 'before', prep. with abl. 617.
puroḍā́ś- 42 c, 66 c β 1 (p. 61, mid.), 349 b, 350.
√*puṣ-* 'thrive', pr. 439, sj. 440, opt. 440, impv. 441, pt. 442; pf. 485, opt. 489, pt. 492; *a*-aor. opt. 511; cs. 553 b, inf. 585, 1.
√*pū-* 'cleanse', pr. 422, 476, sj. 423, impv. 426, 478, pt. 427, 479, impf. 428, 480; red. aor. 514; *iṣ*-aor. 529, inj. 531; ps. 445, pt. 447; gd. 590 a, b.
√*pṛ-* 'pass', pr. 451, 458, impv. 460; red. aor. 514, inj. 516; *s*-aor. sj. 523, impv. 526; *iṣ*-aor. sj. 530; cs. 557 c, sj. 559 b; inf. 588 b.
√*pṛṇ-* 'fill', pr. 430, sj. 431, impv. 434, impf. 436; inf. 585, 7.
√*pṛc-* 'mix', pr. 430, 464, inj. 465, opt. 465, impv. 434, 460, 466, pt. 467, impf. 468; pf. sj. 487, opt. 489; root aor. sj. 502, opt. 504, pt. 506; *s*-aor. 522, sj. 523; ps. 445, impv. 446, pt. 447, impf. 448; pp. 576 b; inf. 584 b, 587 a.
pṛtanya- den., sj. 569 a, impf. 569 f.
√*pṛṣ-* 'sprinkle', pr. pt. 427, = adj. 'spotted' 313.
√*pṝ-* 'fill', pr. 458, 476, sj. 477, opt. 477, impv. 460, 478, pt. 442, 479, impf. 462, 480; pf. opt. 489, pt. 492; red. aor. inj. 516, impv. 518; cs. 557 c, sj. 559 b; pp. 576 e.
√*pyā-* 'fill up', pr. 439, impv. 441, pt. 442; *siṣ*-aor. opt. 534; cs. 558 α.
√*prakṣ-* = *prach-* 'ask', pf. 485 (cp. p. 359 note 6); inf. 585, 1 α.
√*prach-* 'ask', pr. 430, sj. 431, opt. 433, impv. 434, part. 435, impf. 436; *s*-aor. 522; gdv. 544 i, 580; pp. 574, 1; inf. 584 b, 586 a, b.
práti 'against', prep. with acc. 608.
pratyáñc-, inflected 299.
√*prath-* 'spread', pr. 422, impv. 426, pt. 427, impf. 428; pf. 485 (cp. p. 357 note 2), sj. 487, inj. 488, pt. 493; root aor. pt. 506; *iṣ* aor. 529; cs. 556.
√*prā-* 'fill', pr. 451; pf. 485; root aor. 499, sj. 502; *s*-aor. 522; ps. aor. 501.
prādúr- 'out of doors', adv. compounded with √*bhū-* 651.
priyá- m., inflected 372.
priyā́- f., inflected 374.
priyāya- den., impf. 569 f.
√*prī-* 'please', pr. 476, pt. 479, impf. 480; pf. sj. 487, impv. 490, pt. 493; plup. 495; root aor. prec. 504; *s*-aor. sj. 523; des. 542; pp. 573.
√*pru-* 'flow', pr. inf. 424.
√*pruth-* 'snort', pr. inj. 424, impv. 426, pt. 427; pf. 485; intv. 545, 1; gd. 591 a.
√*pruṣ-* 'sprinkle', pr. 470, sj. 471, impv. 434, pt. 435; pp. 575 b.
√*plu-* 'float', pr. 422, impv. 426.
√*psā-* 'devour', pr. 451, impv. 454.

√*phaṇ-* 'spring', intv. 545, 3, pt. 548; cs. 555.
√*phar-* 'scatter', intv. 545, 2, 547 a.

√*baṃh-* 'make firm', pp. 574, 2.
√*bandh-* 'bind', pr. 476, impv. 478, impf. 480; pf. 485; ft. 537, 539; ps. 445, impv. 446, pt. 447; inf. 584 b, 590 b.
bahirdhā́ 'outside', prep. with abl. 618.
√*bādh-* 'oppress', pr. 422, inj. 424, impv. 426, pt. 427, impf. 428; pf. 485; *iṣ*-aor. inj. 531; des. 542; intv. 545, 1 b, 2 α, 546, pt. 548; cs. 556 a; pp. 575 b.
√*budh-* 'wake', pr. 422, 439, sj. 423, inj. 424, opt. 440, impv. 426, 441, pt. 442; pf. 482 b, sj. 487, pt. 493; root aor. 500, pt. 506;

a-aor. inj. 510; red. aor. 514; *s*-aor. 522; *iṣ*-aor. sj. 530; ps. aor. 501; inf. 584 b, 588 a.
√*bṛh*- 'make big', pr. impv. 434; pf. 485, pt. 493; *iṣ*-aor. inj. 531; intv. 545, 2, 547 a.
bodhi, impv. of √*bhū*- and √*budh*- 32 c, 505 note 3.
√*brū*- 'say', pr. (inflected) 451, sj. (inflected) 452, opt. 453, impv. 454, pt. 455, impf. 456.
√*blī*- 'crush', pp. 576 d.

√*bhakṣ*- 'partake of', cs. 556 a.
√*bhaj*- 'divide', pr. 422, 451, sj. 423, inj. 424, opt. 425, impv. 426, pt. 427, impf. 428; pf. 485, pt. 493; *s*-aor. 522, sj. 523, inj. 524, opt. 525; cs. 555, ps. pt. 447, 561, gd. 591 a; ps. pr. pt. 447; gd. 590 b, c.
√*bhañj*- 'break', pr. 464, impv. 466, pt. 467, impf. 468; pf. 485; ps. impv. 446.
√*bhan*- 'speak', pr. 422, inj. 424, impf. 428.
√*bhand*- 'be bright', pr. 422, pt. 427.
√*bharv*- 'devour', pr. 422.
bhávant- 'being', inflected 314.
√*bhas*- 'devour, pr. 430, 458, sj. 459, inj. 424, pt. 461.
√*bhā*- 'shine', pr. 451, impv. 454, pt. 455.
bhāmaya- 'be angry', den., pp. 575 c.
√*bhās*- 'shine', pr. 422, sj. 423, pt. 427.
√*bhikṣ*- 'beg', pr. 422, inj. 424, opt. 425, pt. 427.
√*bhid*- 'split', pr. 422, 464, sj. 465, inj. 465, opt. 465, impv. 466, pt. 467, impf. 428, 468; pf. 485; root aor. 499, sj. 502, inj. 503, pt. 506; *a*-aor. opt. 511; *s*-aor. inj. 524; des. 542, impf. 544; ps. aor. 501; pp. 576 a; gd. 590 b, 591 a.
bhiṣaj- 'heal', den., pr. 568.
bhiṣajya- den., impv. 569 d.
bhiṣṇaj- 'heal', den., impf. 568, 569 f.
√*bhī*- 'fear', pr. 422, 458, sj. 423, inj. opt. 459, impv. 426, 460, pt. 427, 461, impf. 428, 462; pf. 482 b, 485, pt. 492; plup. 495; root aor. inj. 503, pt. 506; red. aor. 514, inj. 516; *s*-aor. 522, pt. 527; cs. aor. 560; inf. 585, 1.
√*bhuj*- 'enjoy', pr. 464, sj. 465, pt. 467; pf. 485; root aor. sj. 502, inj. 503; *a*-aor. opt. 511, impv. 512; inf. 584 b, 585, 1.
√*bhur*- 'quiver', pr. inj. 432, impv. 434, pt. 435; intv. 545, 2 α, 546, pt. 548.
√*bhū*- 'be', pr. 422, sj. 423, inj. 424, opt. 425, impv. 426, pt. 427, impf. 428; pf. 482 b 1, 485, opt. 489, pt. 492; root aor. 499, sj. 502, inj. 503, opt. 504, prec. 504; *a*-aor. 508; red. aor. 514; ft. 537, 539, pt. 538; des. 542, pt. 544; intv. 545, 1, 546, pt. 548; cs. 557 b; pp. 573; gdv. 578, 2, 581; inf. 584 a, 588 c; gd. 590 a, b, 591 a.
bhū- 'earth', inflected 383.
√*bhūṣ*- 'adorn', pr. 422, sj. 423, opt. 425, impv. 426, pt. 427, impf. 428; gdv. 580.
√*bhṛ*- 'bear', pr. 422, 451, 458 (inflected), sj. 423, 459, inj. 424, opt. 425, 459, impv. 426, 460, pt. 427, 461, impf. 428, 462; pf. 482 d, 485, sj. 487, pt. 493; plup. 495; root aor. prec. 504, impv. 505; *s*-aor. (inflected) 522, sj. 523, inj. 524; *iṣ*-aor. 529; cond. 538, ft. pt. 538; intv. 545, 2, 546; ps. 445, sj. 446, aor. 501; pp. 573; inf. 585, 585, 4, 5, 7, 8, 586 b; gd. 591 b.
√*bhṛjj*- 'roast', pr. sj. 431.
√*bhyas*- 'fear', impf. 428.
√*bhraṃś*- 'fall', pr. inj. 424; *a*-aor. inj. 510; cs. 555; pp. 574.
√*bhrāj*- 'shine', pr. 422, pt. 427; root aor. 499, prec. 504; ps. aor. 501.
√*bhrī*- 'consume', pr. 476.
√*bhreṣ*- 'totter', pr. 422.

√*maṃh*- or *mah*- 'be great', pr. 422, opt. 425, impv. 426, pt. 427, impf. 428; pf. 482, 485, sj. 487, inj. 488, impv. 490, pt. 493; cs. 556, 556 a, pt. 559 e; inf. 584 b, 585, 2.
√*majj*- 'sink', pr. 422; gd. 591 a.
madgú- 38 c, 44 a 3 α (p. 36), 62, 4 b note 3 (p. 57).
√*math*- or *manth*- 'stir', pr. 422, 476, sj. 423, impv. 426, 478, pt. 479, impf. 428, 480; pf. 485; root aor. sj. 502; *iṣ*-aor. 529, inj. 531; ps. 445, pt. 447; pp. 575 a 2.
√*mad*- or *mand*- 'exhilarate', pr. 422, 451, 458, sj. 423, inj. 424, opt. 425, impv. 426, 460, pt. 427, impf. 428, 462; pf. 485, sj. 487, opt. 489, impv. 490, pt. 492; root aor. 499, impv. 505, pt. 506; red. aor. 514; *s*-aor. 522, sj. 523, inj. 524, pt. 527; *iṣ*-aor. 529, opt. 532; cs. 555 a, 556 a, sj. 559 b; ps. pt. 447; pp. 573; gdv. 578, 4; inf. 585, 7.
mádhu- 'sweet', inflected 389.
madhyá- 'in the midst of' 587 b α.
√*man*- 'think', pr. 422, 439, 470, sj. 423, 440, 471, inj. 440, 471, opt. 440, 459, 471, impv. 441, 472, pt. 442, 473, impf. 443, 474; pf. 485; root aor. 500, sj. 502, pt. 506; *s*-aor. 522, sj. 523, inj. 524; ft. 537, 539; des. 542, ps. 544 h, pp. 544 h; cs. 555, opt. 559 c; pp. 574, 2; inf. 585, 4, 5.
manasyá- den., pr. (inflected) 569, opt. 569 c.
mantraṇ̄ya- gdv. 581 b.
√1. *mā*- 'measure', pr. 451, opt. 459, impv. 460, pt. 461, impf. 462; root aor. impv. 505, pt. 506; *s*-aor. 522; ps. aor. 501; pp. 574, 3; gdv. 578, 3; inf. 584 a; gd. 590 b, 591 a.
√2. *mā*- 'exchange', pr. 439; gd. 591 b.
√3. *mā*- 'bellow', pr. 422, 458; pf. 585; red. aor. 514, inj. 516; inf. 585, 5.
mā́, prohibitive particle used with injunctive 648.
mātár- 'mother', inflected 360.
mā́s- 'month' 44, 3, 340 (inflected).
√*mi*- 'fix', pr. 470, sj. 471, inj. 471, impv. 472, part. 473, impf. 474; pf. 485; ps. 445, pt. 447; gdv. 578, 1.
√*mikṣ*- 'mix', pf. 485 (cp. p. 359 note 8), impv. 490.
√*migh*- 'mingere', pr. pt. 427.
√*mith*- 'alternate', pr. 422, pt. 435; pf. 485.
√*miś*- 'mix', des. 542, impv. 544.
√*miṣ*- 'wink', pr. 430, pt. 435; inf. 587 a α.
√*mih*- 'mingere', pr. 422, impv. 426, pt. 427; ft. 537, 539; cs. 553 a; inf. 584 b.
√*mī*- 'damage', pr. 439, 476, subj. 477, inj. 477, opt. 440, pt. 479, impf. 480; pf. 485; *s*-aor. inj. 524;

intv. 545, 1, pt. 548; inf. 584 a, 586 a.
mīḍhvāṃs-, pf. pt. 492 b.
√*mīl-* 'wink', gd. 591 a.
√*mīv-* 'push', pr. pt. 427; pp. 573 α.
√*muc-* 'release', pr. 430, 439, sj. 431, 440, impv. 434, pt. 435, impf. 436; pf. 485, sj. 487, pt. 493; plup. 495; root aor. 499, 500, prec. 504; *a*-aor. 508, sj. 509, inj. 510, impv. 512; *s*-aor. 522, inj. 524, opt. 525, des. 542, pt. 544; ps. aor. 501; gd. 591 a.
√*mud-* 'be merry', pr. 422, impv. 426, pt. 427; pf. 485; root aor. opt. 504; *iṣ*-aor. opt. 532; ps. aor. 501; inf. 584 b.
√*mur-* = *mṛ-* 'crush', pf. sj. 487.
√*muṣ-* 'steal', pr. 422, 476, pt. 479, impf. 480; *iṣ*-aor. inj. 531; pp. 575 b; inf. 584 b; gd. 591 a.
√*muh-* 'be dazed', pr. impv. 441; red. aor. 514; cs. 553 b; pp. 573; inf. 584 b.
√*mūrch-* 'thicken', impf. 428.
√1. *mṛ-* 'die', pr. 422, sj. 423; pf. 485, pt. 492; root aor. 500, inj. 503, opt. 504; ft. 537, 539; cs. 557 c; ps. 445, impv. 446; pp. 576 e.
√2. *mṛ-* 'crush', pr. impv. 478, pt. 479; intv. 547 c.
√*mṛkṣ-* 'stroke', pr. sj. 431.
√*mṛc-* 'injure', *s*-aor. opt. 525; cs. 553 c; sj. 559 b; pp. 573.
√*mṛj-* 'wipe', pr. 451, impv. 454, pt. 455, impf. 456; pf. 482, 485, opt. 489; *sa*-aor. 536; intv. 545, 2, 547, pt. 548, impf. 549, 551, gdv. 580; cs. 553 c, opt. 559 c; ps. 445, pt. 447; pp. 573; gdv. 578, 4; gd. 590 b.
√*mṛḍ-* 'be gracious', pr. sj. 431, impv. 434; cs. 554, sj. 559 b.
mṛṇ- 'crush', pr. 430, inj. 432, impv. 434, impf. 436; red. aor. 514.
√*mṛd-* 'crush', pf. opt. 489.
√*mṛdh-* 'neglect', pr. 422, sj. 431; root aor. opt. 504; *iṣ*-aor. sj. 530, inj. 531.
√*mṛś-* 'touch', pr. 430, sj. 431, impv. 434, pt. 435; impf. 436; pf. 482, 485; *sa*-aor. 536; intv. 545, 2, 547 a; gd. 591 a.
√*mṛṣ-* 'not heed', pr. 439; pf. 485; root aor. inj. 503; *a*-aor. inj. 510; red. aor. inj. 516; *iṣ*-aor. inj. 531; inf. 584 b.
meghāya- den., ft. and pp. 570.
√*med-* 'be fat', pr. impv. 441; cs. 554 α.
√*myakṣ-* 'be situated', pr. impv. 426; pf. 485; root aor. 499; ps. aor. 501.
√*mruc-* 'set', pr. pt. 427.
√*mlā-* 'relax', cs. 558; pp. 573.

yá- 'who', rel. pron. 398.
√*yakṣ-* 'press on'(?), pr. inj. 424, pt. 427; inf. 584 b.
√*yaj-* 'sacrifice', pr. 451, opt. 425, impv. 426, pt. 427, impf. 428; pf. 482 b 1, 485, pt. 493; root aor. impv. 505; *s*-aor. 522, sj. 523, inj. 524; *sa*-aor. impv. 536; ft. 537; des. 542, sj. 544; pp. 574; inf. 585, 4, 7; gd. 590 b.
yajñaśrī-, inflected 376.
√*yat-* 'stretch', pr. 422, sj. 423, opt. 425, impv. 426, pt. 427; pf. 485; root aor. pt. 506; cs. 555, sj. 559 b, pt. 559 e.
√*yabh-* 'futuere', pr. 422, impv. 426.
√*yam-* 'reach', pr. 422, 451, sj. 423, inj. 424, opt. 425, impv. 426, pt. 427, impf. 428; pf. 482 b 1, 485, pt. 493; root aor. 499, sj. 502, opt. 504, prec. 504, impv. 505; *a*-aor. opt. 511; *s*-aor. 522, sj. 523, inj. 524, pt. 527; *iṣ*-aor. 529; intv. 545, 2, 546; cs. 555; ps. pt. 447, aor. 501; pp. 574, 2; aor. gdv. 580; inf. 585, 4, 5β, 586 a; gd. 591 b.
√*yas-* 'be heated', pr. impv. 460, pt. 442.
√*yā-* 'go', pr. 451, opt. 453, impv. 454, pt. 455, impf. 456; pf. 485, pt. 492; *s*-aor. 522, sj. 523, inj. 524; *siṣ*-aor. 534, sj., opt., impv. 534; ft. 537, pt. 538; pp. 573; inf. 584 a, 585, 4.
√*yāc-* 'ask', pr. 422, opt. 425, impv. 426, pt. 427, impf. 428; *iṣ*-aor. sj. 530; cs. 556 a; pp. 575 b; inf. 586 b.
√*yād-* 'unite'(?), pr. pt. 427.
√1. *yu-* 'unite', pr. 430, 451, sj. 431, 452, inj. 432, impv. 434, 454, pt. 435, 455, impf. 436; pf. 485; des. 542, pt. 544; intv. 545, 1, 546, pt. 548; pp. 573; gd. 591 a.
√2. *yu-* 'separate', pr. 422, 458; sj. 459, inj. 459, opt. 459, impv. 426, 460, pt. 427; root aor. sj. 502, prec. 504; red. aor. inj. 516; *s*-aor. sj. 523, inj. 524; *iṣ*-aor. inj. 531; intv. 545, 1, pt. 548, impf. 549; cs. 557 b, sj. 559 b; ps. aor. 501; pp. 573; inf. 585, 4, 587 b.
√*yuj-* 'join', pr. 451, 464 (inflected), sj. 465, inj. 465, impv. 426, 466, pt. 467, impf. 468; pf. 485, sj. 487, pt. 493; root aor. 500, sj. 502, inj. 503, opt. 504, impv. 505, pt. 506; *s*-aor. 522; ft. 537, 539; ps. 445, impv. 446, aor. 501; pp. 573; inf. 584 b; gd. 589 b, c.
√*yudh-* 'fight', pr. 422, 439, 451, sj. 440, impv. 441, pt. 442, 455, impf. 443; pf. 485; root aor. sj. 502, impv. 505; *s*-aor. inj. 524; *iṣ*-aor. 529, sj. 530, inj. 531, impv. 533; des. 542, pt. 544; cs. 553 b, sj. 559 b; gdv. 578, 4, 580; inf. 584 b, 585, 2, 586 a.
√*yup-* 'obstruct', pf. 485; cs. 553 b; pp. 575 b.
yuṣmāka 'of you' 391, 2.
yūyám 'you', pron. 49 a, 391, 2.
√*yeṣ-* 'be heated', pr. pt. 427.

√*raṃh-* 'hasten', pr. 422, pt. 427, impf. 428; pf. pt. 493; cs. 556 a; gdv. 578, 4.
√*rakṣ-* 'protect', pr. 422, sj. 423, impv. 426, pt. 427, impf. 428; pf. 485, pt. 493; *iṣ*-aor. 530; pp. 575 a 1.
√*raj-* or *ranj-* 'colour', impf. 443; intv. 545, 1 b, 546; cs. 556.
rathī- m. f. 'charioteer', inflected 376.
√*rad-* 'dig', pr. 422, 451, inj. 424, impv. 426, pt. 427, impf. 428; pf. 485; pp. 575 b.
√*radh-* or *randh-* 'make subject', pr. impv. 441; pf. 482; root aor. impv. 505, *a*-aor. sj. 509, inj. 510; red. aor. sj. 515, inj. 516; *iṣ*-aor. inj. 531; intv. 545, 1 b; cs. 556 a, sj. 559 b.
√*ran-* 'rejoice', pr. 422, 439, inj. 424, impv. 426; pf. 482, 485, sj. 487, impv. 490; plup. 495; *iṣ*-aor. 529, inj. 531; cs. 556.
randhanāya- den., impf. 569 f.
√*rap-* 'chatter', pr. 422, inj.

424, opt. 425, pt. 427, impf. 428; intv. 545, 1 b, 546.
√*rapś-* 'be full', pr. 422; pf. 485.
√*rabh-* or *rambh-* 'grasp', pr. 422, sj. 423, inj. 424, opt. 425, impv. 426, pt. 427, impf. 428; pf. 482, 485, pt. 493; *s*-aor. 522, pt. 527; inf. 584 b, 586 a; gd. 591 a.
√*ram-* 'rejoice', pr. 422, inj. 424, impv. 426, impf. 428, 480; red. aor. 514, sj. 515, inj. 516; *s*-aor. 522, inj. 524; *siṣ*-aor. inj. 534; cs. 555 a.
√*ramb-* 'hang down', pr. 422, pt. 427.
√1. *rā-* 'give', pr. 451, impv. 460, pt. 461, impf. 456; pf. 485, impv. 490, pt. 492, 493; root aor. impv. 505; *s*-aor. 522, sj. 523, opt. 525, impv. 526; pp. 573.
√2. *rā-* 'bark', pr. 439, pt. 442.
√*rās-* 'give', pr. pt. 427.
√*rāj-* 'be kingly', pr. 422, 451, sj. 423, inj. 424, 452, impv. 426, pt. 427, impf. 428; *iṣ*-aor. 529; cs. 556 a, sj. 559 b; inf. 585, 1.
√*rādh-* 'succeed' pr. 422, sj. 423, impv. 441, pt. 442; pf. 485; root aor. sj. 502, prec. 504; *s*-aor. 522; *iṣ*-aor. inj. 531; ft. 537, 539; cs. 556 a; ps. aor. 501; gdv. 578, 4; inf. 585, 7.
√*ri-* or *rī-* 'flow', pr. 439, 476, inj. 477, pt. 479; impf. 480.
√*rikh-* 'scratch', pr. impv. 434.
√*ric-* 'leave', pr. 464, sj. 465, inj. 465, impf. 468; pf. 485, opt. 489, pt. 492, 493; plup. 495; root aor. inj. 503, impv. 505; *s*-aor. 522; ps. 445, impf. 448, aor. 501.
√*rip-* 'smear', pf. 485; pp. 573.
√*ribh-* 'sing', pr. 422, pt. 427, impf. 428; ps. 445; pf. 485.
√*riś-* 'tear', pr. 430, impv. 434, pt. 435.
√*riṣ-* 'be hurt', pr. 439, sj. 423, 440, inj. 424, opt. 440; *a*-aor. sj. 509, inj. 510, pt. 512; red. aor. inj. 516, opt. 517, prec. 517; des. 542, pt. 544; cs. 553, 554; inf. 585, 7.
riṣaṇya- den., inj., impv. 569 b, d.
√*rih-* 'lick', pr. 451, pt. 455; pf. pt. 492; intv. 545, 1 a, pt. 548, 551; pp. 573.
√1. *ru-* 'cry', pr. 430, inj. 432, impv. 434, pt. 435; *iṣ*-aor. 529; intv. 545, 1 a, pt. 548, impf. 549.
√2. *ru-* 'break', *iṣ*-aor. 529; intv. 545, 1, 546, pt. 548.
√*ruc-* 'shine', pr. 422, inj. 424, impv. 426, pt. 427, impf. 428; pf. 485, inj. 488, opt. 489, pt. 492, 493; root aor. pt. 506; red. aor. 514; *iṣ*-aor. 529, opt. 532; intv. pt. 548; cs. 553 b, 554; inf. 584 b.
rucaya- den., inj. 569 b.
√*ruj-* 'break', pr. 430, sj. 431, inj. 432, opt. 433, impv. 434, pt. 435, impf. 436; pf. 485; root. aor. inj. 503; red. aor. 514; pp. 576 b; inf. 584 b.
√*rud-* 'weep', pr. 451, sj. 452, pt. 455; *a*-aor. 508; cs. 553 b.
√1. *rudh-* 'grow', pr. 422, inj. 424, pt. 435, impf. 428.
√2. *rudh-* 'obstruct', pr. 451, 464, sj. 465, impv. 466, pt. 467, impf. 468; pf. 485; root. aor. 499; *a*-aor. 508, inj. 510; *s*-aor. 522; ps. 445; gd. 591 a.
√*rup-* 'break', red-aor. 514; pp. 575 b.
ruvaṇya- den., inj. 569 b.
√*ruṣ-* 'be vexed', pr. 422.
√*ruh-* 'ascend', pr. 422, sj. 423, opt. 425, impv. 426, pt. 427, impf. 428; pf. 485; root aor. pt. 506; *a*-aor. 508, sj. 509, inj. 510, opt. 511; *sa*-aor. 536; des. 542, pt. 544; cs. 553 b; pp. 573; inf. 586 a; gd. 590 b, 591 a.
√*rej-* 'tremble', pr. 422, inj. 424, pt. 427, impf. 428; cs. 554 α.

√*lap-* 'prate', pr. impv. 426, pt. 427; intv. 545, 1 b, 546; cs. 555; pp. 575 b.
√*labh-* 'take', pr. 422, opt. 425; pf. 485, pt. 493; des. 542, pt. 544; gd. 590 b.
√*likh-* 'scratch', impf. 436; *iṣ*-aor. inj. 531; pp. 575 a 2.
√*lip-* 'smear', pr. 430; *s*-aor. 522.
√*lī-* 'cling', pr. 422, impv. 426; pp. 576 d; gdv. 578, 2.
√*lup-* 'break', pr. opt. 433; ps. 445; gd. 591 a.
√*lubh-* 'desire', pr. pt. 442; cs. 533 b.

√*vakṣ-* 'increase', pr. 430, impv. 434, pt. 435, impf. 436; pf. 485; cs. 556 a.
√*vac-* 'speak', pr. 458, impv. 460; pf. 482 b 1, 485, pt. 493; red. aor. 514, sj. 515, inj. 516, opt. 517, impv. 518; ft. 537, 539, pt. 538; intv. 545, 1 b, impf. 549; ps. 445, aor. 501; pp. 574, 1; gdv. 578, 4, 581; inf. 584 b, 585, 4.
√*vañc-* 'move crookedly', pr. 422; pf. 482, 485; ps. 445, impv. 446, pt. 447.
√*vat-* 'apprehend', pr. opt. 425, pt. 427; red. aor. 514; cs. 555.
√*vad-* 'speak', pr. 422, sj. 423, inj. 424, opt. 425, 433, impv. 426, pt. 427, impf. 428; pf. 485; *iṣ*-aor. 529, sj. 530, inj. 531; ft. 537, 539; intv. 545, 1 b, 546, 547 c, opt. 559 c; ps. pt. 447, pp. 575 b.
√*vadh-* 'slay', pr. opt. 425, impv. 426; root aor. prec. 504; *iṣ*-aor. 529, sj. 530, inj. 531, impv. 533.
√*van-* 'win', pr. 422, 470: sj. 423, 431, 471, inj. 424, 471, opt. 425, 433, 471, impv. 426, 472, pt. 473, impf. 474; pf. 482, 485, sj. 487, pt. 492; root aor. impv. 505; *s*-aor. sj. 523, inj. 524, opt. 525; *iṣ*-aor. sj. 530, opt. 532; *siṣ*-aor. opt. 534; des. 542, 543 (inflected), sj. 544; cs. 555; pp. 574, 2 α; inf. 585, 4.
vanuṣa- den, inj. 569 b.
vanuṣyá- den., sj. 569 a.
√*vand-* 'greet', pr. 422, impv. 426, pt. 427; pf. 485; *iṣ*-aor. opt. 532; ps. aor. 501; gdv. 578, 4; inf. 585, 7.
√1. *vap-* 'strew', pr. 422, inj. 424, impv. 426, pt. 427, impf. 428; pf. 482 b 1, 485; ps. 445, pt. 447; pp. 574, 1; gd. 591 a.
√2. *vap-* 'shear', pr. (2. s., 3 pl. act.) 422.
vapuṣya- den., impf. 569 f.
vam, 1. s. aor. of √*vṛ-* 'cover' 66 c β 2, 499.
√*vam-* 'vomit', pr. sj. 452, impf. 456.
varivasyá- den., sj. 569 a, impv. 569 d.
vareyá-, den., sj. 569 a.
√*val-*, *s*-aor. sj. 523.
√*valg-* 'bound', pr. 422, impf. 428.
vavṛdhánt-, anom. pf. pt., p. 363 note 7.

√*vaś-* 'desire', pr. 422, 451, 458, sj. 423, inj. 424, opt. 425, impv. 426, 454, pt. 455, impf. 428, pt. 435; pf. 482, 485; intv. 545, 1.
√1. *vas-* 'shine', pr. 430, sj. 431, inj. 432, opt. 433, impv. 434, pt. 435, impf. 436; pf. 485, pt. 492, 493; plup. 495; root aor. 500; *s*-aor. 522; cs. 555; pp. 574; inf. 585, 4, 588 a.
√2. *vas-* 'wear', pr. 451, inj. 452, opt. 453, pt. 435, impv. 454, pt. 455, impf. 456; pf. 482, 485, pt. 493; *iṣ*-aor. 529; cs. 555, ft. 537, 560.
√3. *vas-* 'dwell', pr. 422, inj. 424, impv. 426, pt. 427, impf. 428; pf. 485, pt. 492, 493; root aor. pt. 506; *s*-aor. 522; cs. 555, sj. 559 b.
√*vah-* 'carry', pr. 422, 451, sj. 423, opt. 425, impv. 426, pt. 427, impf. 428; pf. 482 b 1, 485; root aor. opt. 504, impv. 505, pt. 506; *s*-aor. 522, sj. 523, inj. 524; ft. 537, 539; ps. 445, sj. 446, pt. 447; pp. 574; inf. 585, 4, 7, 586 b; gd. 591 a.
√1. *vā-* 'blow', pr. 439, 451, impv. 454, pt. 455, impf. 456; cs. 558.
√2. *vā-* 'weave', pr. 439, impv. 441, pt. 442, impf. 443; pf. 485; ft. 537, pt. 538; pp. 574, 1 α; inf. 585, 4, 5, 586 b.
-vāṃs, pf. pt. suffix, 181, 347, 491.
vā́c-, inflected, p. 180.
vājaya- den., impv. 569 d; inf. 585, 7.
√*vāñch-* 'desire', pr. impv., 426.
vā́m 'we two' 391, 1.
√*vāś-* 'bellow', pt. 442; pf. 482, 485, pt. 493; plup. 495; red. aor. 514; intv. 545, 1 b, pt. 548, impf. 549.
√*vās* = 3. *vas-* (?) pr. 422.
vi- 'bird' 381 a.
√*vic-* 'sift', pr. 464, impv. 466, pt. 467, impf. 468; pf. pt. 492; ps. impv. 446.
√*vij-* 'tremble', pr. 430, impv. 434, pt. 435, impf. 436; pf. 485; root aor. inj. 503; red. aor. inj. 516; intv. 545, 1 a, 551.
√1. *vid-* 'know', pr. 451, sj. 452, opt. 453, impv. 454, impf. 456; pf. 485, pt. 492 b; cs. 553; pp. 575 b; inf. 585, 8; gd. 590 b.
√2. *vid-* 'find', pr. 430, 451, inj. 432, opt. 433, impv. 434, 454, pt. 455, impf. 436; pf. 485, sj. 487, pt. 492; *a*-aor. (inflected) 508, sj. 509, inj. 510, opt. 511, prec. 511, impv. 512, pt. 512; *s*-aor. 522; intv. 547 a; ps. 445, aor. 501; pp. 576 a; gdv. 579; inf. 584 b, 585, 4; gd. 590 b.
víd- 'finding', inflected, 319.
√*vidh-* 'worship', pr. sj. 431, inj. 432, opt. 433, pt. 435, impf. 436.
√*vindh-* 'lack', pr. 430.
vasūya- den., sj. 569 a.
√*vip-* 'tremble', pr. 422, pt. 427, impf. 428; pf. 485; root aor. pt. 506; red. aor. 514; cs. 553 a, 554.
vibhū́-, inflected, 383.
viś-, inflected, 350.
√*viś-* 'enter', pr. 430, sj. 431, inj. 432, opt. 433, impv. 434, pt. 435, impf. 436; pf. 483, 485, opt. 489, pt. 492, 492 b; plup. 495; root aor. 500, impv. 505; *s*-aor. 522; *iṣ*-aor. 531; cs. 553 a, opt. 559 c, pp. 561 a; inf. 586 a; gd. 591 a.
viśvátaspad- 'having feet on every side', 319 a.
√*viṣ-* 'be active', pr. 458, sj. 459, impv. 460, pt. 427, impf. 428, 462; pf. 485; *iṣ*-aor. sj. 530; intv. 545, 1 a, 546, 547 b, pt. 548; inf. 584 b.
√*viṣṭ-* or *veṣṭ-* 'wrap', pr. impv. 426; cs. 553.
√*vī* 'enjoy', pr. 451, sj. 452, inj. 452, impv. 454, pt. 455; impf. 456; pf. 485; *s*-aor. sj. 523; intv. 545, 1 a, 551; ps. 445, pt. 447, inf. 585, 3.
√*vīḍ-* 'make strong', cs. 554 a.
vīráya- den., impv. 569 d, impf. 569 f.
vīḷáya-., sj. 559 b, impv. 559 d, pp. 575 c.
√1. *vṛ-* 'cover', pr. 422, 470, inj. 424, 471, impv. 472, pt. 473, impf. 474; pf. 485, pt. 492; plup. 495; root aor. 499, 500, inj. 503, impv. 505, pt. 506; red. aor. 514; *s*-aor. sj. 523; intv. 545, 3; cs. 557 c, sj. 559 b; ft. 537, 560; ps. aor. 501, pp. 573; inf. 585, 4; gd. 590 a, b, c, 591 b.
√2. *vṛ-* 'choose', pr. 470, 476, inj. 477, opt. 477, impv. 478, pt. 479, impf. 480; pf. 485; root aor. 500, sj. 502, inj. 503, opt. 504, pt. 506; *s*-aor. 522; pp. 573; gdv. 578, 2, 580.
√*vṛj-* 'twist', pr. 422, 464, sj. 465, impv. 466, impf. 468; pf. 482, 485, opt. 489, impv. 490, pt. 492, 492 b; root aor. 499, 500, sj. 502, inj. 503, opt. 504, prec. 504, impv. 505; *a*-aor. 508; *s*-aor. 522, inj. 524; intv. 545, 3, cs. 550 c; cs. 553 c; inf. 584 b, 585, 1, 7; gd. 590 a.
√*vṛt-* 'turn', pr. 422, 458, inj. 424, impv. 426, pt. 427, impf. 428; pf. 482, 485, sj. 487, opt. 489, impv. 490, pt. 492; plup. 495; root aor. 499, 500, sj. 502, impv. 505; *a*-aor. 508; red. aor. 514; *s*-aor. 522; ft. 537, 539; des. 542; intv. 545, 2, 3, 546; cs. 553 c, sj. 559 b; pp. 573; inf. 584 b, cs. 585, 7; gd. 591 a.
√*vṛdh-* 'grow', pr. 422, sj. 423, inj. 424, impv. 426, pt. 427, impf. 428; pf. 482, 485, sj. 487, inj. 488, opt. 489, impv. 490, pt. 492, 493; *a*-aor. 508, pt. 512 a; red. aor. 514; *s*-aor. pt. 527; *iṣ*-aor. opt. 532; cs. 553 c, sj. 559 b, pt. 559 e; intv. gdv. 580; inf. 584 b, 585, 1, 7.
√*vṛṣ-* 'rain', pr. 422, impv. 426, 434, pt. 427; pf. 482, impv. 490, pt. 493; *iṣ*-aor. 529; cs. 553 c; gd. 590 a.
vṛṣāya- den., impv. 569 d, aor. 570.
√*vṛh-* 'tear', pr. 430, inj 432, opt. 433, impv. 434, impf. 436; pf. 485; *sa*-aor. 536; cs. 553 c; ps. aor. 501.
védi-, loc. sing. p. 284 (mid.).
√*ven-* 'long', pr. 422, inj. 424, impv. 426, pt. 427, impf. 428.
√*vyac-* 'extend', pr. 458, inj. 459, impf. 462; pf. 482 b 1, 485, inj. 488.
√*vyath-* 'waver', pr. 422, pt. 427; *iṣ*-aor. sj. 530, inj. 531; cs. 556, aor. 560 α.
√*vyadh-* 'pierce', pr. 439, inj. 440, impv. 441, pt. 442, impf. 443; pf. pt. 492; pp. 574, 1; inf. 584 b.
√*vyā-* 'envelope', pr. 439, opt. 440, impv. 441, pt.

442, impf. 443; pf. 485, pt. 493; *a*-aor. 508; pp. 574, 3.
√*vraj*- 'proceed', pr. impv. 426, pt. 427; pf. 485.
√*vrad*- 'weaken', impf. 428.
√*vraśc*- 'cut up', pr. 430, sj. 431, inj. 432, impv. 434, pt. 435, impf. 436; ps. impv. 446; pp. 576 b; gd. 590 b.
√*vrādh*- 'stir up', pr. inj. 424, pt. 427.
√*vlag*- pursue(?) gd. 591 a.
√*vlī*- 'crush' = √*blī*-.

√*śaṃs*- 'praise', 422, sj. 423, opt. 425, impv. 426, pt. 427, impf. 428; root aor. impv. 505; *iṣ*-aor. 529, sj. 530, inj. 531; cs. 556 a; ps. 445, pt. 447, aor. 501; gdv. 578, 4; inf. 584 b.
√*śak*- 'be able', pr. 470, sj. 471, impf. 474; pf. 485; root aor. sj. 502, opt. 504, impv. 505; *a*-aor. 508, inj. 510, opt. 511; des. 542, 2, pt. 544; inf. 585, 4.
√*śat*- 'cut in pieces', cs. 555.
√1. *śad*- 'prevail', pf. 482, 485, pt. 493.
√2. *śad*- 'fall', ft. 537, 539.
√*śap*- 'curse', pr. 422, sj. 423, pt. 427, impf. 428; pf. 485; *s*-aor. inj. 524.
√1. *śam*- 'labour', pr. 439, impv. 441, pt. 442; pf. 485, sj. 487, pt. 493; *iṣ*-aor. 529.
√2. *śam*- 'be quiet', impf. 428; red. aor. 514; cs. 556; pp. 574, 2 *α*.
√*śas*- 'cut', pr. impv. 454.
√*śā*- 'sharpen', pr. 458, impv. 460, pt. 461, impf. 436, 462; pf. pt. 493; pp. 574, 3; gd. 591 a.
√*śās*- 'order', pr. 422, 451, sj. 452, impv. 454, pt. 455, impf. 428, 456; pt. 485, inj. 488, impv. 490; root aor. sj. 502; *a*-aor. 508, sj. 509, inj. 510, pt. 512 a; pp. 574, 3 *α*.
√*śikṣ*- = des. of *śak*- 'be able', pr. 422, sj. 423, inj. 424, opt. 425, impv. 426, pt. 427, impf. 428: these forms strictly speaking belong to 543, 544.
√*śiñj*- 'twang', pr. 451.
śitipád- 'white-footed' 319 a.
√*śim*- 'labour' = √1. *śam*-.
√*śiṣ*- 'leave', *a*-aor. sj. 509, inj. 510; ps. 445, sj. 446, aor. 501.
√1. *śī*- 'lie', pr. 422, 451, opt. 453, impf. 428, 456, impv. 441, 454, pt. 455; pf. 482 b 1 a, pt. 493; *s*-aor. sj. 523; *iṣ*-aor. 529; inf. 585, 7.
√2. *śī*- 'sharpen' = √*śā*-, root aor. 500.
śīkāya- den., ft. and pp. 570.
√*śuc*- 'gleam', pr. 422, inj. 424, impv. 426, pt. 427, impf. 428; pf. 485, pt. 492, 493, opt. 489, impv. 490; *a*-aor. 508, pt. 512 a; red. aor. 514, inj. 516; *iṣ*-aor. inj. 531; intv. 545, 1 a, 547 a, pt. 548; cs. 553 b, 554; ps. aor. 501; inf. 585, 7.
śúci-, inflected, 381.
√*śuj*- pf. pt. 493 (p. 364 note 2).
√*śundh*- 'purify', pr. 422, impv. 426, 434; cs. 554 a; pp. 574, 2.
√*śubh*- or *śumbh*- 'beautify', 422, 430, sj. 423, impv. 426, pt. 427, 435; root aor. pt. 506; red. aor. 514; cs. 553 b, 554; pp. 575 a 1; inf. 584 b, 585, 1, 586 a.
√*śuṣ*- 'dry', pr. 439, impv. 441; cs. 553 b.
√*śū*- or *śvi*- 'swell', pr. pt. 427; pf. 482, 485, sj. 487, opt. 489, pt. 492, 493 (p. 364 note 3); *s*-aor. pt. 527; inf. 588 c.
√*śṛṇ*- = √*śṝ*- 'crush', pr. impv. 434.
√*śṛdh*- 'be defiant', inj. 424, impv. 426, pt. 427; cs. 553 c.
√*śṝ*- 'crush', 476, impv. 478; pt. 479, impf. 480; pf. 485; *iṣ*-aor. 529, inj. 531; ps. 445, aor. 501; pp. 573 *α*, 576 e; inf. 587 b; gd. 591 a.
śocis-, inflected, 342.
√*ścand*- or *cand*- intv. 545, 3.
√*ścam*- 'labour'(?), pr. inj. 477.
√*ścut*- 'drip', pr. 422.
√*śnath*- 'pierce', pr. sj. 452, impv. 454; red. aor. 514, inj. 516; *iṣ*-aor. impv. 533; cs. 556; cs. pp. 575 c; inf. 584 b.
√*śyā*- 'coagulate', pp. 574, 3, 576 c.
√*śrath*- 'slacken', pr. 476, pt. 479, impf. 480; pf. 485; red. aor. inj. 516, impv. 518; cs. 556.
śrathar-yá- den. 567 d.
śrathāya- den. 564 a, 569 d.
śrád- 'heart', used adverbially with √*kṛ*- and √*dhā*-, 652.
√*śram*- 'be weary', pr. 439; pf. 485, pt. 493; *a*-aor. 508, inj. 510; *iṣ*-aor. 529, inj. 531; pp. 574, 2 *α*.
śravasyá- den., sj. 569 a.
√*śrā*- (*śrī*-, *śṛ*-) 'boil', pr. 476, pt. 479, impf. 480; cs. 558, sj. 559 b; pp. 574, 1 *α*.
√*śri*- 'resort', pr. 422, sj. 423, impv. 426, pt. 427, impf. 428; pf. 485, opt. 489, pt. 493; plup. 495; root aor. 499; red. aor. 514; *s*-aor. 522; ps. aor. 501; cs. 558 a; pp. 573.
√*śriṣ*- 'clasp', pr. sj. 423; *a*-aor. inj 510; inf. 587 a.
√*śrī*- 'mix', pr. 476; pp. 573 *α*; inf. 585, 1.
√*śru*- 'hear', pr. 451, 470, sj. 471, opt. 471, impv. 472, pt. 473, impf. 474; pf. 485, sj. 487, opt. 489, pt. 492; plup. 495; root. aor. 499, sj. 502, prec. 504, impv. 505; *a*-aor. inj. 510, des. 542 b, pt. 544, gdv. 544 i, 580; cs. 557 b; ps. 445, aor. 501; pp. 573; gdv. 578, 1, 579; gd. 590 b, 591 b.
√*śruṣ*- 'hear', pr. inj. 424, impv. 426, pt. 427, impf. 428.
√*śvañc*- 'spread', pr. impv. 426, pt. 427; pf. sj. 487 (cp. p. 361 note 3); cs. 556 a.
śván-, accentuation, p. 80 (bottom).
√*śvas*- 'blow', 451, impv. 454, pt. 455; intv. 545, 1 b; cs. 555; inf. 587 a.
√*śvit*- 'be bright', root aor. 499, pt. 506; red. aor. 514; *s*-aor. 522.

ṣáṭ 'six' 43 a 2.
ṣāṭ 53 a 2.
√*ṣṭhīv*- 'spue', impf. 428.

sa-, adv. particle in compounds, 250, 656.
sákhi-, inflected, 380 a.
√*sagh*- 'be equal to', impf. 474; root aor. sj. 502.
√*sac*- 'accompany', pr. 422, 458, sj. 423, inj. 424, 459, opt. 425, impv. 426, 460, pt. 427 b, 461, impf. 428; pf. 485, pt. 492; root aor. impv. 505, pt. 506; *s*-aor. 522, sj. 523, inj. 524, opt. 525; inf. 585, 7, 588 c.
sacā́ 'with', prep. with loc., 619.

√*saj-* and *sañj-* 'hang', pr. 422, impv. 426, impf. 428; *s*-aor. 522.
√*sad-* 'sit', pr. 422, 451, sj. 423, inj. 424, opt. 425, impv. 426, pt. 427, impf. 428; pf. 485; opt. 487, pt. 492; *a*-aor. 508, inj. 510, opt. 511, impv. 512, pt. 512; red. aor. 514; *s*-aor. sj. 523; cs. sj. 559 b; ps. aor. 501; pp. 576 a; gdv. 578, 4; inf. 584 b, 586 a; gd. 591 a.
sadha- 'together', adv. 634 a.
sadhamā́s, nom. of *sadhamā́d-* 66 c β, 319 a.
√*san-* 'gain', 470, sj. 471, opt. 471, impv. 472, impf. 474; pf. 485, pt. 492; *a*-aor. 508, inj. 510, opt. 511, pt. 512; *iṣ*-aor. 529, sj. 530; ft. 537, 539, pt. 538; des. 542, sj. 544; intv. 545, 3; pp. 574, 2; gdv. 581; inf. 585, 2, 3.
sanitúr 'apart from', prep. with acc. 620.
sanutár 'far from', prep. with abl. 621.
√*sap-* 'serve', pr. 422, inj. 424, opt. 425, pt. 427, impf. 428; pf. 485; red. aor. inj. 516.
saparyá- den., sj. 569 a, opt. 569 c, impv. 569 d, impf. 569 f; aor. 570; gdv. 580.
sám 'with', prep. with. inst. 593 note 3; adv. 'together' as first member of compounds 250.
sama- 'any', pron. 399.
saraṇyá- den., sj. 569 a.
sarvapā́d- 'all-footed' 319 a.
√*sas-* 'sleep', pr. 458, impv. 454, pt. 455, impf. 456.
sáh-, inflected, 352.
√*sah-* 'prevail', pr. 422, 451, 2, sj. 423, opt. 425, impv. 426, pt. 427, impf. 428; pf. 482, 485, sj. 487, opt. 489, pt. 492, 492 b, 493; root aor. opt. 504, prec. 504; *s*-aor. 522, sj. 523, opt. 525, pt. 527; *iṣ*-aor. 529, opt. 532; ft. 537, 539; des. 542, pt. 544; pp. 573; inf. 585, 1, 7; gd. 591 a.
sahá 'with' prep. with inst. 622; in compounds 656.
sahásrapad- 'thousand-footed', 319 a.
√*sā-* 'bind', pr. 430, impv. 434, impf. 436; root aor. sj. 502, opt. 504, impv. 505; *a*-aor. opt. 511; cs. sj. 559 b; pp. 574, 3; inf. 584 a; gd. 591 a.
sākám 'with', prep. with. inst. 623.
√*sādh-* 'succeed', pr. 422, inj. 424, impv. 426, pt. 427, red. aor. sj. 515, inj. 516.
√*si-* 'bind', 476, impv. 478; pf. 485, sj. 487; root aor. impv. 505; inf. 585, 4.
√*sic-* 'pour', pr. 422, 430, sj. 431, inj. 432, opt. 433, impv. 434, pt. 435, impf. 436; pf. 485; *a*-aor. 508; ps. 445, pt. 447, impf. 448; pp. 573; gd. 591 a.
√1. *sidh-* 'repel', pr. 422, impv. 426, pt. 427, impf. 428; pf. 485; intv. 545, 1, pt. 548; gd. 591 a.
√2. *sidh-* 'succeed', pr. 439.
sīda-, present base of *sad-* 'sit', p 57 note 8.
√*sīv-* 'sew', pr. impv. 441, pt. 442; pp. 573 α; gd. 591 a.
sú 'well', adv. particle, as first member of compounds, 251, 658.
√*su-* 'press', pr. 430, 470, sj. 471, impv. 472, pt. 473; pf. 485, pt. 492, 493; root aor. impv. 505, pt. 506; ps. 445, inj. 446, aor. 501; gdv. 581; inf. 585, 4, 587 b.
sumád 'with', prep. with. inst., 624.
suṣvā́ya- den., inj. 569 b.
√*sū-* 'generate', pr. 430, 451, sj. 431, inj. 452, impv. 434, pt. 435, 455, impf. 436, 456; pf. 482 b 1, 485; red. aor. 514; *iṣ*-aor. 529, sj. 530, inj. 531; ft. 537, pt. 538; intv. 545, 1, 546; inf. 585, 4, 5.
√*sūd-* 'put in order', pf. 485, sj. 487; red. aor. 514, impv. 518; cs. 554 a, sj. 559 b.
√*sṛ-* 'flow', pr. 458, impv. 426, 460, pt. 461; pf. 485, pt. 492, 493; *a*-aor. 508; *s*-aor. sj. 523; ft. 537, 539, pt. 538; intv. 545, 2, 546, pt. 548; cs. 557 c; inf. 585, 4, 5.
√*sṛj-* 'emit', pr. 422, 430, sj. 431, inj. 432, opt. 433, impv. 434, pt. 427, 435, impf. 436; pf. 485, opt. 489, pt. 493; plup. 495; root aor. 500; *s*-aor, 522, sj. 523, inj. 524; ps. 445, pt. 447, aor. 501; pp. 573; gd. 591 a.
√*sṛp-* 'creep', pr. 422, sj. 423, inj. 424, impv. 426, pt. 427, impf. 428; *a*-aor. 508, inj. 510; des. 542, pt. 544; gd. 591 a.
senānī́-, inflected, 376.
√*sev-* 'attend upon', pr. 422, impv. 426.
√*skand-* 'leap', pr. 422, sj. 423, impv. 426, pt. 427, impf. 428; pf. 485; root aor. 499, inj. 503; intv. 545, 3, 547, impf. 549; pp. 576 a; inf. 584 b, 587 a.
√*skabh-* or *skambh-* 'prop', pr. 476, pt. 479; pf. 482, 485, pt. 493; pp. 575 b; inf. 584 b; gd. 590 a.
skabhāya- den., impf. 569 f.
√*sku-* 'tear', pr. 470; intv. 545, 1, 551.
√*skṛ-* = *kṛ-* 'make', p. 55 note 10.
√*stan-* 'thunder', pr. impv. 426, 454; root aor. inj. 503 (or. pr. inj. 452); *iṣ*-aor. 529; intv. 545, 2, 547; cs. 556.
√*stabh-* or *stambh-* 'prop', pr. 476, impv. 478, impf. 480; pf. 485, pt. 492, 493; plup. 495; pp. 575 b; gd. 590 b.
√*stu-* 'praise', pr. 422, 451, sj. 423, 452, inj. 424, 452, opt. 425, 453, impv. 454, pt. 427, 455; impf. 456; pf. 485, sj. 487, pt. 492, 493; plup. 495; *s*-aor. 522 (inflected), sj. 523, inj. 524; ft. 537, 339; ps. 445, pt. 447, pp. 573; gdv. 579; inf. 585, 1 α, 4, 7; gd. 590 b, 591 b.
√*stubh-* 'praise', pr. 422, impv. 426, pt. 427.
√*stṛ-* 'strew', pr. 470, 476, sj. 471, inj. 477, impv. 478, pt. 479, impf. 480; pf. 485, pt. 493; root aor. 499, sj. 502, inj. 503; *s*-aor. opt. 525; *iṣ*-aor. 529; ps. aor. 501; pp. 576 e; inf. 584 a, 585, 4, 588 c.
√*sthā-* 'stand', pr. 422, sj. 423, inj. 424, opt. 425, impv. 426, pt. 427, impf. 428; pf. 485, pt. 492, 493; root aor. 498 (inflected), 499, 500, sj. 502, inj. 503, opt. 504, impv. 505, pt. 506; *a*-aor. 508; red. aor. 514, inj. 516; *s*-aor. inj. 524; ft. 539; cs. 558, aor. 560; pp. 574, 3; gd. 591 a.

√*snā-* 'bathe', pr. 451, impv. 454, pt. 455; cs. 558; gdv. 581; gd. 590 b.
√*snih-* 'be moist', cs. 553.
√*snu-* 'distil', pr. impv. 454.
√*spaś-* 'see', pf. 485, pt. 493; root aor. 500; cs. 555.
√*spṛ-* 'win', pr. 470, sj. 471, impv. 472; root aor. 499, sj. 502, inj. 503, impv. 505; *s*-aor. 522; inf. 585, 1; gd. 590 b.
√*spṛdh-* 'contend', pr. 422, pt. 427; pf. 485, pt. 493; plup. 495; root aor. 500, pt. 506; inf. 585, 1, 586 b; gd. 591 a.
√*spṛś-* 'touch', pr. 430, sj. 431, inj. 432, impv. 434, impf. 436; pf. sj. 487; red. aor. sj. 515, inj. 516; *sa*-aor. 536; inf. 584 b.
√*spṛh-* 'be eager', cs. 554, opt. 559 c, gdv. 561 b, 579.
√*sphur-* 'jerk', pr. 430, sj. 431, inj. 432, impv. 434, pt. 435, impf. 436.
√*sphūrj-* 'rumble', pr. 422; cs. 554 a.
√*sphṛ-* 'jerk', *iṣ*-aor. inj. 531.
smád 'with', prep. with inst., 625.
√*smi-* 'smile', pr. 422, inj. 424, pt. 427; pf. pt. 493.
√*smṛ-* 'remember', pr. sj. 423, impv. 426.
√*syand-* 'move on', pr. 422, impv. 426, pt. 427; pf. 482 b 1, 485; red. aor. 514; *s*-aor. 522; intv. 545, 3; cs. 556 a; pp. 576 a; inf. 584 b, 585, 7.
√*sras-* 'fall', root aor. 66 c 2, 499; *a*-aor. opt. 511; red. aor. 514; cs. 556 a; gd. 590 b.
srās, 2. s. *s*-aor. √*sṛj-*, 522.
√*sridh-* 'blunder', pr. 422, impv. 426, pt. 427, impf. 428; *a*-aor. inj. 510, pt. 512.
√*srīv-* 'fail', cs. 554 a α.
√*sru-* 'flow', pr. 422, opt. 425, impv. 426, pt. 427, impf. 428; pf. 485; red. aor. 514, inj. 516; cs. 557 b; inf. 585, 4, 5.
svá- 'own' 400, 1; 'his' etc. 401 c.
√*svaj-* 'embrace', pr. 422, sj. 423, inj. 424, impv. 426; pf. 485, pt. 493; plup. 495; inf. 584 b.
svátavas-, 44, 3, dat. pl. p. 226 note [2], and p. 233.
√*svad-* and *svād-* 'sweeten', pr. 422, sj. 423, impv. 426; red. aor. inj. 516; cs. 556; pp. 573 α.
√*svan-* 'sound', *iṣ*-aor. 529, inj. 531; intv. 545, 3, sj. 547; cs. 556; cs. pp. 575 c.
√*svap-* 'sleep', pr. impv. 426, 454, pt. 455; pf. 482 b 1, 485, pt. 492, 493; red. aor. 514; ft. 537, 539; cs. 555; pp. 574; gd. 590 b.
svayám 'self' 400, 2.
√*svar-* 'sound', pr. 422, sj. 423, impv. 426, impf. 428; pf. inj. 488; *s*-aor. 522; cs. 556.
√*svid-* 'sweat', pf. pt. 493; pp. 576 a.

√*han-* 'strike', pr. 451, sj. 452, inj. 452, opt. 453, impv. 454, pt. 455; pf. 485, sj. 487, pt. 492; ft. 537, 539, pt. 538; des. 542, sj. 544; intv. 545, 3, 546, 547, pt. 548, 548 a; ps. 445, impv. 446, pt. 447, impf. 456; pp. 574, 2; gdv. 581; inf. 585, 4, 5; gd. 590 b, c, 591 b.
√*har-* 'be gratified', pr. 439, sj. 440, impv. 441, pt. 442, impf. 443.
hastín-, inflected 333.
√1. *hā-* 'leave', pr. 458, sj. 459, opt. 459, impv. 460, pt. 461, impf. 462; pf. 485; *s*-aor. 522, inj. 524; *siṣ*-aor. inj. 534; ft. 537, 539; cs. p. 396 note [2]; ps. 445, impv. 446, aor. 501; pp. 575 b α, 576 c; gd. 590 a, b, c.
√2. *hā-* 'go forth', pr. 458, inj. 459, impv. 460, pt. 461, impf. 462; red. aor. inj. 516; *s*-aor. 522, inj. 524; des. 542 c 1; cs. aor. 560; gd. 591 a.
√*hās-* 'go emulously', pr. pt. 427.
√*hi-* 'impel', pr. 470, inj. 471, impv. 472, pt. 427, 473; root aor. 499, impv. 505; pt. 506; *a*-aor. 508; *s*-aor. 522; gdv. 581; inf. 584 a.
√*hiṃs-* 'injure', pr. 422, 464, impv. 466, pt. 467; pf. 485; plup. 495; *iṣ*-aor. inj. 531; ps. pt. 447; pp. 575 a 1; gdv. 581 a; gd. 590 b.
√*hinv-* = *hi-* 'impel', pr. impv. 426.
√*hīḍ-* 'be hostile', pf. 482, 485, pt. 493; red. aor. 514; cs. 554 α; pp. 575 a 3.
√*hu-* 'sacrifice', pr. 451, 458, sj. 459, opt. 459, impv. 460, pt. 461, impf. 462; ft. 537; ps. aor. 501.
√*hū-* 'call', pr. 422, 430, 451, 458, inj. 424, 432, opt. 433, pt. 427, 435, impf. 436; pf. 485; root aor. 500, inj. 503; *a*-aor. 508; *s*-aor. 522; intv. 545, 1, 546, 547, impf. 549; ps. 445, pt. 447; pp. 573; gdv. 578, 2; inf. 585, 4, 7.
√1. *hṛ-* 'take', 422, 451, sj. 423, opt. 425, impv. 426, pt. 427, impf. 428; pf. 485; *s*-aor. 522; des. 542; inf. 585, 1; gd. 591 b.
√2. *hṛ-* 'be angry', pr. 476, inj. 477, impv. 478, pt. 479.
√*hṛṣ-* 'be excited', pr. 422, 439, impv. 426, pt. 427; pf. pt. 493; intv. 545, 2, 547, pt. 548; cs. 553 c; pp. 575 b.
√*heṣ-* 'whinney', pr. pt. 427.
√*hnu-* 'hide', pr. 451; gdv. 579.
√*hrī-* 'be ashamed', root aor. pt. 506.
√*hvā-* 'call', pr. 439, sj. 440, opt. 440, impv. 441, pt. 442, impf. 443.
√*hvṛ-* 'be or make crooked', pr. 422, 476, sj. 459, inj. 459; pf. 485, pt. 493; red. aor. 514, inj. 516; *s*-aor. inj. 524; pp. 573 α.

II. GENERAL INDEX

Ablative: sing. masc. formed in two, neuter in three ways from der. *u*-stems 389.

Accusative: pl. masc. and fem. formed in two ways from der. *u*-stems 389; appositional 642b; cognate 642 a; of direction 642 c; of distance and time 642 d.

Accentuation 83—111; aorist 505 (root aor.), 507 (*a*-aor.), 535 (*sa*-aor.); augment 96; causative 552; denominative 562; double 85 a, 91 (p. 96), 105 a; lack of 85 b; irregular monosyllabic 94, 1 a, 368 n. 14 (rad. *ā*-stems), 362 n. 7 (*rā́y*-), 364 c (*dyā́v*-, *dyú*-), 376, p. 272 n. 10. 14 (*strī́*-); normal nominal 384 b (der. *ū*-stems), 382 b (radical *ū*-stems); shift of 22, 29 38 d, 58 d, 107 (case-forms as adverbs), 299, 319, and 389 (inst. as adv.), 311 (participles as substantives), 314 (nom. neut. of participles as adv.), 374 (inst. adverbs p. 264 mid.), p. 273 n. 1 (fem. of *a*-stems), 94, 2—4 (oxytones), 377, 3 a and 378 (der. *ī*-stems), 380 (der. *i*-stems), 388 c (der. *u*-stems), 94, 1 (monosyllabic stems), 334 b (*áp*-), 364 c (*div*-), 93 a α (cardinals); systems of 84.

Adjectives: fem. of 299 (*añc*-stems), 326 a n. 13 (*an*-stems), 330 a (*van*-stems), 332 note 9 (*in*-stems), 345 (*yāṃs*-stems), 347 (*vāṃs*-stems), 375 a, p. 270 (*ya*-stems), 377, 1 (various stems), 388 a (*u*-stems).

Adverbs: two classes 626; formed from nouns 442 α, 643 a, 643 b, from pronouns 642 d β, 643 c, from numerals 634; multiplicative 638; miscellaneous 640; of manner 632; of time 639; with the case-ending of the abl. 644 b, of the acc. 642, 642 a, 642 d β, of the dat. 644 a, of the gen. 644 c, of the instr. 372 (p. 257), 374 (p. 264), 374 (f. pl. p. 267), of the loc. 643, 644 d, of the nom. 641.

Alternative nominal stems 253, 318 a 4, 328 c, 332 a.

Āmreḍita compounds 257, 6, 258, 319 (p. 198 note 5); accentuation of 88; Sandhi in 57 b γ, 78, 1 c.

Anudātta accent 83, 84.

Anunāsika for final *n* 77 1 b, 77, 2 d.

Anusvāra for *m* 75, 2, 3, for *n* 77, 2 a b c; in the intensive reduplicative syllable 60b.

Aoristic *s*: added to present stem 521 a 2; lost 520 a 4, 529 a.

Archaic Sandhi in compounds 81.

Aspirates: two in the same syllable avoided 32, 40 a.

Assimilation: of *s* 53, 57, 78; of final consonants 74; of final *t* to *l* and palatals 76, 1, 2; of final media to following nasal 74 a; final *m* to following mutes 75, 2, to *y l v* 75, 4.

Attraction with the dative and ablative infinitive 583, 587.

Augment 413; lengthened 413; dropped 413 b; irregular Sandhi of 413 a.

Breathing *h*: represents sonant aspirates, guttural, palatal, cerebral, dental, labial 58; when final becomes *k* or *ṭ* 66 b 6 δ, 351 b.

Case-endings, normal 295 c.

Case-forms: as adverbs (treated in the order of the cases) 641—644; strong and weak 295 d, 297, 298, 301, 313, 315, 323, 325, 326b, 328b, 330 b, 334 a, 336 a, 338, 339 a, 341 a, 343 a, 344 (p. 230 note 6), 345, 347, 349 a, 351 a, 354 a, 356, 363, 380 a.

Causative stem: nominal derivatives in -*ana*, -*tṛ*, -*a*, -*ālu*, -*iṣṇu*, -*itnu*, -*u* 561 e; formed with suffix -*paya* 558, the *p* of which sometimes retained in the reduplicated aorist 513 a 2.

Cerebralization: of *n*, in verbal forms after the *r* of prepositions 47 A a; after *ṛ*, *r*, *ṣ*, in the second member of nominal compounds 47 A b, 81, 2 e; in a following word 47 A c; of initial *t* 78, 2 b.

Cerebrals: their origin 42, unexplained 43 c, 47 B c; Prakritic 42 b, 47 B; representing old palatals 43; *ṭ* for final *ṣ* 66 b 6 β, *ṭ* and *ḍ* for *ṣ* 42 d; *ṣ* for palatal *ś* 56.

Compounds: characteristic features 241, consisting of phrases 293, 3, gender 241 a, Sandhi 81, suffixes 256, tmesis p. 143 (bottom), 260; first member consisting of adverbs 247, 274 b, 278 c, 289 b, nouns with case-endings 242, 248, 275, 277, 278 a, 280, 287, 355 (p. 242 note 9), 368 (p. 252 notes 2, 3, 13, p. 253 note 6), particles 251, 278 c, 284, 289 c, prepositions 249, 274a, 278d, 283, 298a, 292,1, alternative stems 244, 245, present stems 292, 2 a, b; last member consisting of alternative stems 253, or present stems 272.

Conjugation: irregularities of the *a*-class 421 a, of the *á*-class 429 a, of the *ya*-class 438, of the *yá*-class (passive) 444 a, of the root class 450 a, of the redu-

plicated class 457 a, of the infixing nasal class 463, 1, of the *nu*-class 469 a, of the *nā*-class 475 a.
Consonants lost: 81, 2 a, in final group 66 c, 521 a; mute between nasal and mute 62, 3 c; *t* between two consonants 62, 3 b, *s* between two mutes 355 note 9, 520 a 4, *m* or *n* in the inst. of *-man* stems 328 b.
Contraction: in secondary Sandhi 70, 3; in the perfect 483 a 2; in declension 344 (p. 229, 230, 232, 233), 374 (gen. pl. of *kanyā*).

Dative: sing. masc. formed in two, neut. in three ways, in der. *u*- stems 389.
Denominative: with causative accent 563; formed from stems in *-a* 563, in *-ā* 564, in *-i* 565, in *-u* 566, in *-o* 566 a, in consonants 567; formed without a suffix 568; inflexion 569; participles 569 e.
Dentals: cerebralized 42 a, c, 47 A; replace cerebral and labial 44 a 3 β; *s* cerebralized 57, palatalized 53 a 1, 3, 54, changed to *t* 44 a, 522, unchanged before *r* or *ṛ* 57, 1 α, 2 a α, unchanged in Āmreḍita compounds 57, 2 b γ; *n* replaces *m* 46 d β, 66, 4 α; *n* before *p* 77, 2 a, before *l* 77, 2 e.
Dissimilation 43 b 1, b 2 p. 55 note 8, 351 notes 5 and 6, 469 a 1, 545, 2 α (p. 391 top).
Dissyllabic pronunciation 363 a (*gā̆m* etc.), 364 a (*dyā̆m*), 372 (gen. pl. of *a*-stems).
Doubling of final *n* 77.
Dravidian influence 42.
Dvandvas: accentuation 262, 267 note 7; gender 264, 266; plural 265; singular 266.

Elision: of final *a* before *e* and *o* 70, 2 a, after *e* and *o* 72, of *a* before ending of gen. loc. du. 372 (p. 260 top); of final *m* 70, 3 b, 75, followed by contraction 372 notes 2 and 4 (p. 256): of *y* and *v* 72, 1 b, 73; of *r* 79, 1 b; of *s* 78, 1 b.
Enclitics 85 b 1.
Endings: in declension 295 c, abnormal fem. loc. *-ām*, gen. *-ās*, dat. *-ai* 374, 385; in conjugation, *-āna* 2. sing. impv. 475, 3, *-ām* 3. sing. impv. mid. 454, *-i* for *-ta* 3. sing. red. aor. p. 376 (top), *-iran* 494, 495, 529, *-ur* 3. pl. 456, 494, 499, 503, *-au* 1. 3. sing. pf. 484, 485, *-e* 3. sing. mid. for *-te* 422, 430, 451, 458, 464, 476, 546, *-tana* 2. pl. impv. 426, 441, 454, 472, 478, 505, *-tāt* impv. 418 b, 426, 434, 441, 454, 460, 472, 478, 518, 547, 559 d, *-tai* 523, *-dhi* 2. sing. impv. 418 a, 454, 58, 2 d, *-dhva* 2. pl. mid. 426, *-rata* 3. pl. mid. 425, *-ratām* and *-rām* 3. pl. impv. 454, 490, *-rate* 3. pl. pr. mid. 451, *-ran* 3. pl. impf. and plup. 456, 494, *-ranta* 3. pl. plup. 495, *-ram* 3. pl. plup. 495, root aor. 500, *-rire* 3. pl. pf. mid. 484, 4 α, 485, *-re* 3. pl. mid. pr. 451, 469 a 6, 470, pf. 484, 3, 4, *-hi* 2. sing. impv. 418 a, 454.
Exclamations 659 a.

Foreign words 42, 45 b; 47 B c; 52 b g; 57, 1 β, γ.
Future participles 538.

Genitive: sing. m. formed in two, n. in three ways, in derivative *u*-stems 389.
Gerund: in *-tvī* 590 a; in *-tvā* 590 b; in *-tvāya* 590 c; in *-yā̆* and *-tyā̆* 591.
Gerundive: in *-ya* 578; in *-āyya* 579; in *-enya* 580; in *-tva* 581, in *-tavya* 581 a; in *-anīya* 581 b.
Gradation of vowels 51; in compounds 243, 255; in dissyllabic bases 27 b; in suffixes 27 c.
Guṇa 22; in *i*-stems 380; in *a*-stems 388; in the pr. stem. 421, 451, 457, 469; in the pf. 483; in the root aor. ps. 501; in the *a*-aor. 507 a; in the *s*-aor. 520, 523, 524; in the *iṣ*-aor. 528; in the cs. 553, 557; in the gdv. 578.
Gutturals: interchange with palatals, labials, and *ṣ* 34; with palatals 36 a, 37, 38, 39, 41, b 2, 43 a 4, 43 b 2.

Haplology 64, 499 (p. 367 note 5).
Hiatus 67, 69 a, b, c (duals), 70, 1 b, c (*ā* + *i* or *ṛ*), p. 251[2] (N. sing. f. *ā*-stems), 372 (N. A. n. du. and L. pl. *a*-stems), 374 a, b (N. sing. and L. pl. *ā*-stems).
Hybrid form 348 (N. pl. pf. pt.).

Imperative: endings of the 2. 3. sing. 418.
Infinitive: acc. from roots 586 a, from verbal nouns in *-tu* 586 b; dat. 368, in *-dhyai* from causatives 561 c, from roots 584, from verbal nouns in *-as*, *-i*, *-ti*, *-tu*, *-tavā*, *-tyā*, *-dhyā*, *-man*, *-van* 585; abl. gen., from roots 587 a, from verbal nouns in *-tu* 587 b; loc., from roots 588 a, from stem in *-tar* 588 b, from stems in *-san* 588 c.
Insertion: of *ī* in pr. 450 a 3, 451, 456, in plup. 495, in *s*-aor. 521 a 1, 522, in intv. 546, in reduplicative syllable 545; of *y* between vowels 372; of sibilants 77, 2 a b c; of *t* 77, 2 f.
Instrumental: sing. m. n. formed in two ways in der. *a*-stems 372 (also pl.), f. in der. *ā*-stems 374, m. n. in der. *u*-stems 389, m. f. in der. *i*-stems 381.
Interchange: of vowel and consonant 50 b, 81 e, 469 a 2, 542 b, 573 α; of *r* and *l* 52 a.
Interjections 659; *hiṅ* compounded with √*kṛ*- 653.

Jihvāmūlīya for final *s* 78, 2 c.

Labials 45: *b* often in words of foreign origin 45 b, interchanges with *v* 45 a 3, in place of *m* 45 a 5.
Lengthening of vowels 81, 1 d, 81, 2 f, 82 b, 224 a, 255 b, 313, 315, 318 a 2, 319 a, 329 (N. A. sing. n.), 344 (N. sing.), 354 (N. sing.), 360 (L. sing.), 372 (I. sing.), 513 a (red. aor.), 520 a 2 (*s*-aor.), 554 and 555 (cs.), 563 a, 565 and 566 (den.).
Locative: sing. m. formed in two ways, f. in four ways, in der. *i*-stems 381, m. in two ways, n. in three ways in der. *u*-stems 389; Sandhi of locatives in *-ī* and *-ū* 71, 2 b.
Loss of nasal in pf. 483 a 4;

in *a*-aor. 507; in *s*-aor. 520 a 3; in pp. 574, 2.

Metathesis 50 b, 51 c, 63; in quantity (*āsthas*, *ādat* etc.) 507 a 4.

n- declension: influence on the der. *i*-declension 380 d, on the der. *a*-declension 371.
Nasalization: of vowels 66, 1, 70, 1 b, 70, 2 b, 372 note 5 (p. 256), p. 258 note 3 and note 5; of semivowels 75, of *l* 77, 2 e.
Nominal stems, obsolete, preserved in adverbs 642 d *α*.
Nominative: pl. formed in two ways, in der. *a*-declension 372, in der. *ā*-declension, 374, in der. *i*-declension 381, in der. *u*-declension 389.

Onomatopoetic words 52 f, 659 b; in compounds 251, 5, 650.

Palatals: two series 35; new palatals 36, 37, 38; old palatals 40 (*ch*), 41 (*j*); new palatals revert to gutturals, in pf. 482 d 2, 492, 495, in root aor. 500 note 19 (p. 367), in des. 542 c *α*; *c* becomes *k* 66 b 2; *j* becomes *k* or *ṭ* 66 b 2; *ś* replaces *s* 54 a, becomes *k* before *s* 54 b, 349 b, becomes *ṣ* before *t th* 42 a, 56 a, becomes *ḍ* before *bh* 349 b.
Parallelism, form due to, 327 (p. 206 note 3), 354 c, *náktā* N. A. du. 372.
Particles: three groups 645; *a*-, *sa*-, *dus*-, *su*- as first members of compounds 655—658.
Participial forms compounded with substantives used adverbially 654.
Passive: present system 444—448; aorist 501; past participle formed with -*ta* 572—575, with -*na* 576.
Perfect: irregularities in the root 483 a; subjunctive 487, injunctive 488, optative 489, imperative 490.
Pragṛhya vowels: *ī*, *ū* 69 c, 71, 2; *e* 72, 2, 374 (du. f. of *ā*-stems), *o* 72, 3.
Prakritic words 42 b, 47 B.
Precative 417, 489, 504, 511, 517, 525.
Prepositions: two classes 592; adverbial, not compounded with verbs 593; adnominal, used with cases, 594; accentuation 102, 103, 105, 110 (p. 107).
Pronominal declension: influence on nominal 371.

Reduction of final *ā* to *i* 26, 483 b, 484 a 1, of medial *ā* to *i* 507 a 1, 574, 3, 576 c.
Reduplicated aorist connected with the causative 513.
Reduplication 37 e; aorist 513; rhythmic rule 513 a; intensive 60b, 545; perfect 62, 482, vowel lengthened 482, irregular 482 d, syllable *ān*- 482 c *α*, syllable lost 482 e, rhythmic rule 484 a 4 note 1, note 2.
Rhotacism 51 a, 52 a.

Samprasāraṇa 22, 23, 24, 326 b, 482 b 1, 483 a 1, (cs.) 554; (pp.) 574, 575.
Sandhi 31, 2, 38 c, 46 d *α*, 47 A; duplicate forms 67 b; initial *n* cerebralized 47 A c; 54 a (*ś* for *s*), 57 (*ṣ* for *s*), 58 and 80 b (*h* aspirated), 59 and 74 note 5 (*ḷ* for *ḍ*), 62(*ăv*), 62, 1 (final group of consonants).
Semivowels *y* and *v* pronounced as *iy* and *uv* 48 a, with a syllabic value 48 b, lost 62; *y* inserted between vowels 49 a, interchanges with *v* 49 c; *v* interchanges with *b* and *y* 50 a; final *r* 66, 5, indicated in the Padapāṭha 66 b note 10, becomes *ś* or *s* 79, 2 b, c, lost 62, 4; *l* gradually increases at the cost of *r* 52 a, in foreign words 52 g, *l* for *ḍ* in the later Saṃhitās 52 d, for *d* 52 e, final *l* 66 b 5 note 9.
Shortening of vowels 81, 2 g (*ā*, *ī*), 70, 1 b and p. 259 note 7 (*ā* before *r*), 327 (*ā* in *an*-stems), 352 (-*sāh*-), 360 (du. of -*tar* stems), 362 b (*rāy*-), 369 (radical *ā*), 372 (dual *ā*), 378 (dual *ī*), p. 277 note 4 (*nárī*-), 381 (*ī* of n. pl.).
Sibilant lost: initial and final *ś* and *s* 62, 2, 78 e 2, 3, 81, 2 a—c; *ṣ* and *s* between mutes 62, 3, 355 note 9; *s* before voiced dental 62, 4 b, cerebralized before loss 62, 4 c; palatal spirant (*ź*) before *d*, *dh* 62, 4 d.
Strong forms: in declension 295 d; in conjugation 449, 483, 494, 498, 501, 520, 528.
Subjunctive 414.
Suffixes: primary nominal 113 a (list); secondary nominal 190 (list); adverbial 627—640.
Supplementary stems in declension 315, 326 c, 330 c, 339 b, 343 b, 357, 362 a.
Svarita accent 83, 84; in Sandhi 108.
Syncope 25, 1—3, 324 (-*han*-), 325, 327, 328 b; 483 a 3 (pf.), 513 a 4 (red. aor.), 542 c 2 (des.), 548 a (intv.).

Transfer forms: in declension 313 note 5, 315, 316 (p. 196 note 4), 317 note 7, note 11, 318 a 5, 326 d, 330 d, 334 c, 339 c, 341 b, 343 c, 349 c, 351 c, 354 b, 364 b, 375 a *α*, 378 (p. 275 notes and 276 bottom), 380 c, 381 (f. D. Ab. G. L. sing.), 384 c, 388 d, 389 (G. sing. m., I. du.); in conjugation: 421 a 4, 429 a 3, 4, 457 a 8, 463, 2, 469 a 7, 475 a 4, 495, 499 note 11 (p. 367), 507 a 4 (*a*-aor.).
Transfer stems in compounds 254.

Udātta accent 83, 84.
Unreduplicated perfect forms 482 e, 492 b.
Upādhmānīya for final *s* 78, 1 c

Visarjanīya for final dental *s* 66, 6 *α*, 78, 1 c—e; for final *r* 79, 2 a, d.
Vocative: accentuation 93, 109; formed with -*mas* and -*vas* from -*mant*, -*māṃs* and -*vant* stems 315, 316, 340, with -*vas* from -*van* and -*vāṃs* stems 331, 348, with -*yas* from -*yāṃs* stems 346; final vowel gunated in *i*-stems 381, and *u*-stems 389.
Vowels: *e* for original *as* 15 b 1, 62, 4 b; lost 25, 26 a, 563 c, 564 *α*.
Vṛddhi 22 a, 25 B, 483 (pf.), 501 (ps. aor.), 520 (*s*-aor.), 524, 528, 557 (cs.), 578, 2 (gdv.).

Weak forms for strong 348.

CONTENTS.

INTRODUCTION . . . . page 1—5
General scope of this work 1. — Verbal Authenticity of the Texts 2.

I. PHONOLOGY . . . . page 5—59
Ancient pronunciation 3. — The sounds of the Vedic Language 4. — 1. The simple Vowels 6—14. — 2. The Diphthongs 15—16. — Lengthening of Vowels 17. — Loss of Vowels 18. — Contraction 19. — Hiatus 20. — Vowel Gradation 22—29. — The Consonants 30—47: Doubling of Consonants 30. — Modes of Articulation 31. — Loss of Aspiration 32. — Aspirates in contact with other Mutes 33. — The five Classes of Mutes 34—45: 1. Gutturals 34. — 2. Palatals 35—38. — Irregular Palatalization 39. — Old Palatals 40—41. — 3. Cerebrals 42—43. — 4. Dentals 44. — 5. Labials 45. — Nasals 46. — Cerebral *ṇ* 47. — Semivowels 48—52. — Sibilants 53—57. — The Breathing *h* 58. — Cerebral *ḷ* 59. — Anusvāra and Anunāsika 60. — Voiceless Spirants 61. — Loss of Consonants 62. — Metathesis 63. — Syllable 64.

II. EUPHONIC COMBINATION (SANDHI) page 59—76.
Nature of Vedic Sandhi 65. — Finals in pausā 66. — Rules of Sandhi 67. — Lengthening of Final Vowels 68. — Contraction of Similar Vowels 69. — Contraction of *ă* with Dissimilar Vowels 70. — Final *ĭ* and *ŭ* before Dissimilar Vowels 71. — Final *e* and *o* 72. — The Diphthongs *ai* and *au* 73. — Sandhi of Consonants 74. — Sandhi of Final *m* 75; of Final *t* 76; of Final *n* 77; of Final *s* 78; of Final *r* 79. — Initial Aspiration 80. — Sandhi of Compounds 81. — Extension of External to Internal Sandhi 82.

III. ACCENT . . . . . page 76—107
General Character of the Vedic Accent 83. — Methods of Marking the Accent 84. — Normal Accent, Double Accent, Lack of Accent 85. — 1. Accentuation of Nominal Stems 86. — 2. Accentuation of Compounds 87: of Iteratives 88; of Governing Compounds 89; of Possessives 90; of Determinatives 91; of Copulatives 92. — 3. Accent in Declension 93—94. — 4. Verbal Accent 95—101. — 5. Accent of Nominal Verb forms 102—107. — 6. Accent in Sandhi 108. — 7. Sentence Accent 109—111.

IV. NOMINAL STEM FORMATION page 107—143.
Primary and Secondary Suffixes 112. — 1. Primary Nominal Derivation: Action Nouns and Agent Nouns 113. — 1. Primary Nominal Suffixes 114—189. — 2. Secondary Nominal Derivation: Form and Meaning 190. — Secondary Nominal Suffixes 191—240.

V. COMPOUNDS . . . page 143—178
Form of Compounds 241. — A. First Member of Compounds 242—251. — B. Last Member of Compounds 252—256. — Classification of Compounds 257: 1. Iteratives 258. — 2. Copulatives (Dvandvas) 259—268. — 3. Determinatives 269—284. — 4. Possessives (Bahuvrīhis) 285—291. — 5. Governing Compounds 292. — 6. Syntactical Compounds 293.

VI. DECLENSION . . . page 178—312.
General Character 294. — I. NOUNS 295. — A. Consonant Stems 296—365. — 1. Palatal Stems 297—303. — 2. Cerebral Stems 304. — 3. Dental Stems 305—333: Stems in -*t* 306—308. — Derivate Stems in -*vat*, -*tāt*, -*it*, -*ut* and secondary -*t* 309—310. — Participial Stems in -*at* and -*ant* 311—314. — Stems in -*mant* and -*vant* 315—316. — Stems in Radical -*th* 317. — Stems in -*d* 318—320. — Stems in -*dh* 321—322. — Stems in Radical -*n* 323—324. — Derivative Stems in -*an*, -*man*, -*van* 325—331. — Stems in -*in*, -*min*, -*vin* 332—333. — 4. Labial Stems 334—338. — 5. Stems in Sibilants 339—350: in Radical -*s* and -*ṣ* 339—340, in Derivative -*is* and -*us* 341—342, in Derivative -*as* 343—344, in -*yāṃs* 345—346, in -*vāṃs* 347—348, in Radical -*ś* 349—350. — 6. Stems in Radical *h* 351—352. — 7. Stems in Semivowels 353—365: in Radical -*r* 354—355, in Derivative -*ar* and -*tar* 356—360, in -*y* (-*āy*) and -*v* (-*av* and -*āv*) 361—365. — B. Vowel Stems 366—389. — 1 a. Stems in Radical -*ā* 367—368. — 1 b. Stems in Radical -*a* 369—370. — 2 a. Stems in Derivative -*a* 371—372. — 2 b. Stems in Derivative -*ā* 373—374. — 3 a. Stems in Radical -*ī* 375—376. — 3 b. Stems in Derivative -*ī* 377—378. — 4 a. Stems in Radical -*i* 379. — 4 b. Stems in Derivative -*i* 380—381. — 5 a. Radical -*ū* stems 382—383. — 5 b. Derivative

-*ū* stems 384—385. — 6 a. Radical -*u* stems 386—387. — 6 b. Derivative -*u* stems 388—389.
II. PRONOUNS 390—403: 1. Personal 391. — 2. Demonstrative 392—396. — 3. Interrogative 397. — 4. Relative 398. — 5. Indefinite 399. — 6. Reflexive 400. — 7. Possessive 401. — 8. Pronominal Derivatives and Compounds 402. — 9. Pronominal Adjectives 403.
III. NUMERALS 404—409. — A. Cardinals 405—407. — B. Ordinals 408. — C. Numeral Derivatives 409.
VII. THE VERB . . . page 312—414
General Characteristics 410. — A. THE FINITE VERB 411—570. — Personal Endings 412. — The Augment 413. — Formation of the Moods: Subjunctive 414, Injunctive 415, Optative 416, Precative 417, Imperative 418.
I. THE PRESENT SYSTEM 419—480. — Characteristics 419. — a. First or *a*-Conjugation 420—448: Characteristics 420. — 1. The Radically accented *a*-Class (*bháva-*) 421—428. — 2. The Suffixally accented *á*-Class (*tudá-*) 429—436. — 3. The *ya*-Class 437: A. The Radically accented *ya*-Class 438-443. — B. The Suffixally accented *yá*-Class (Passive) 444—448.
b. The Second or Graded Conjugation 449—480. — α 1. The Root Class 450—456. — α 2. The Reduplicating Class 457—462. — β 1. The Infixing Nasal Class 463—468. — β 2. The *nu*-Class 469—474. — β 3. The *nā*-Class 475—480.
II. THE PERFECT SYSTEM 481—496. — Characteristics 481. — 1. The Reduplicative Syllable 482. — 2. The Root 483. — 3. The Endings 484. — Perfect Indicative 485. — Moods of the Perfect 486—490. — Perfect Participle 491—493. — Pluperfect 494—495. — Periphrastic Perfect 496.
III. THE AORIST SYSTEM 497—536. — Characteristics 497. — 1. Simple Aorist: A. Root Aorist 498—506; B. *a*-Aorist 507—512. — 2. Reduplicated Aorist 513—518. — 3. Sigmatic Aorist 519: A. 1. The *s*-Aorist 520—527. — A. 2. The *iṣ*-Aorist 528—533. — A. 3. The *siṣ*-Aorist 534. — B. The *sa*-Aorist 535—536.
IV. THE FUTURE SYSTEM 537—540. — Formation of the Stem 537. — Subjunctive, Conditional, Participles 538. — Indicative 539. — Periphrastic Future 540.
V. SECONDARY CONJUGATION 541—570. — 1. Desiderative 542—544. — 2. Intensive 545—551. — 3. Causative 552—561. — 4. Denominative 562—570.
B. NOMINAL VERB FORMS 571—591. — Characteristics 571. — a. Past Passive Participles 572—576. — b. Future Passive Participles (Gerundives) 577—581. — c. Infinitive 582—588: 1. Dative Infinitive 583—585. — 2. Accusative Infinitive 586. — 3. Ablative-Genitive Infinitive 587. — 4. Locative Infinitive 588. — d. Gerund 589—591.
VIII. INDECLINABLES . page 414—432.
1. Prepositions 592—625: A. Adverbial Prepositions 593—608. — B. Adnominal Prepositions 609—625.
2. Adverbs 626—644: A. Adverbial Suffixes (in alphabetical order) 627—640. — B. Adverbial Case-forms (in the order of the cases) 641—644.
3. Particles 645—658: emphatic 646, conjunctional 647, negative 648. — a. Adverbial Words in Compounds 649—658.
4. Interjections 659.
ADDENDA AND CORRIGENDA . . page 433
LIST OF ABBREVIATIONS . . . „ 436
SANSKRIT INDEX . . . . . . „ 437
GENERAL INDEX . . . . . . „ 451
TABLE OF CONTENTS . . . . . „ 455

The printing was commenced in May, 1907, and afterwards delayed by the death of the editor Prof. Kielhorn.

Printed by BoD™in Norderstedt, Germany